THE
READER'S
ADVISER

THE READER'S ADVISER

A LAYMAN'S GUIDE TO LITERATURE
12TH EDITION

Volume 1:   The best in American and British fiction, poetry, essays, literary biography, bibliography, and reference

Edited by Sarah L. Prakken

R. R. BOWKER COMPANY
NEW YORK & LONDON, 1974
A XEROX EDUCATION COMPANY

Published by R. R. Bowker Co. (A Xerox Education Company)
1180 Avenue of the Americas, New York, N.Y. 10036
Copyright © 1974 by Xerox Corporation
All rights reserved
International Standard Book Number 0-8352-0781-1
International Standard Serial Number 0094-5943
Library of Congress Catalog Card Number 57-13277
Printed and bound in the United States of America

Contents

Preface

ALTHOUGH THE ELEVENTH EDITION of *The Reader's Adviser* was expanded from one to two volumes to keep up with the ever increasing number of books in print in the United States, now, only five years later, this twelfth edition is again to be enlarged from two volumes to three in order to include the best of the 365,000 volumes listed in *Books in Print* for 1973–1974. There will be expanded bibliographies and additional new topics throughout the new edition, but it is the volume on literature which has outgrown its bounds. This first volume is limited to the chapters on general reference books relating to literature, Essays and Criticism, Literary Biography and Autobiography, and the chapters on British and American literature, exclusive of drama.

For the first time the work of revising each chapter of the first volume of this edition has been entrusted to a single editor who has special expertise in the area of his chapter. These editors have critically examined the text of the eleventh edition, revising and amplifying where they found room for improvement. They have selected the new titles for the bibliographies—both the recent reprints of old books of enduring value and the most recent new publications—and have supplied the annotations for them. Many of the evaluations are still taken from the review media and many are the editors' own comments on books they know well and use. They have selected the new authors to be given main entry listings in the literature sections, and have written the biographical and critical notes on them. Because each chapter was revised by a different person, small individual differences of approach may be detected from chapter to chapter. Nevertheless the spirit of enthusiasm and affection for books which have always been the hallmark of *The Reader's Adviser* have been well maintained, and the continuity of flow from chapter to chapter to which our readers have accustomed themselves has in no way been disrupted. In fact, we are convinced that these minor personal variations will enhance the interest of the book and the pleasure it will afford the reader. "Vive la différence!" Each chapter is signed with the initials of the contributing editor. A list of their full names, arranged alphabetically by initials, is given following this preface.

The chapter on Books about Books was revised by Chandler B. Grannis, well-known bookman and bibliophile who brought to the chapter a long experience and wide knowledge of publishing, publishers, and the book world in general. He has reorganized the arrangement for greater cohesiveness, and enlarged the listings in all sections, particularly in the section on individual publishing houses, in this edition titled "Book Industry Biographies: Persons, Companies, Organizations." The chapter on Bibliography was the labor of love of Jean Peters, Librarian at R. R. Bowker, who also revised the arrangement of material, especially the sections on Types of Bibliographies, and provided much additional information of value. The reader will note considerable revision in the presentation of information again in the chapter on Reference Books—Literature by Mark Piel, Reference Librarian at the Upsala College Library. He has divided the basic indexes into separate groupings according to the subject indexed, and the Bibliographies of Literature and Histories and Dictionaries of Literature sections according to nationality. All of these reorganizations of presentation are intended to assist the user in finding the information he seeks with greater ease and speed. Arline Edelson, Acquisitions Librarian and Adjunct

Professor of English at Westchester Community College has done the careful and thoughtful revision of the chapter on Broad Studies and General Anthologies.

The chapter on British Poetry: Early Period was the concern of Professor Hugh Mclean of the State University of New York at Albany. He has made valuable revisions in the arrangement of the general bibliographies at the beginning of the chapter. This chapter, ranging as it does from Old English to John Keats, covers many disparate periods in the history of English literature. In this edition the general bibliographies have been grouped by period into Old English, Middle English, the Renaissance, the Restoration and the Eighteenth Century, Romantic Poetry, and General Books which covers more than one of these subdivisions. Professor Mclean has added a section on Popular Ballads with introductory comments and bibliographies on books about and anthologies of early English and Scottish ballads and songs, and in addition has introduced several new author listings including Sir Thomas Wyatt and Richard Crashaw. Professor Francis Sypher, also of the State University of New York at Albany, served as editor for the chapter on British Poetry: Middle Period. His special interest in Swinburne and the nineteenth century generally eminently qualify him for the revision of this chapter. The information in the chapter on Modern British Poetry was checked, and the introduction revised by David Shapiro, himself a poet, of Columbia College, Columbia University. Professor James M. Cox of Dartmouth College wrote a new introduction to the chapter on American Poetry: Early Period, and offered new ideas for inclusion in this edition. The Modern American Poetry chapter has been greatly expanded by the addition of many new young poets. The tremendous task of gathering biographical and critical annotations on these contemporary young authors was accomplished by Elizabeth Marraffino who is on the staff of New Directions Books.

The chapter on British Fiction: Early Period was edited by Professor Morris Golden of the University of Massachusetts who provided a new introduction and expanded not only the bibliographies but also many of the biographical-critical commentaries. In the same way, the considerable skill of Professor Fred Kaplan of Queens College, Flushing, New York served us well in the revamping and enlarging of the chapter on British Fiction: Middle Period. Modern British Fiction was revised by Professor Rubin Rabinovitz of Columbia University. Although several authors were dropped from this chapter because of a lack of in-print volumes, listings of new authors—among whom are Colin McInnis, Margaret Drabble, Andrew Sinclair, and David Storey—more than take the places of those dropped. Several new authors have been added to the chapter on American Fiction: Early Period by its editor, Professor William J. Stuckey, of Purdue University. Professor Maurice Beebe of Temple University and editor of the *Modern Literature Journal*, undertook the revision of the chapter on Modern American Fiction, another very large chapter made even larger by the addition of many new author listings and expanded annotations.

The chapter on Essays and Criticism, by Professor Wilbur S. Scott of The New College, Hofstra University, offers a new feature—the general bibliographies for literary criticism and for the informal essay are now in separate groupings. For the last chapter on Literary Biography and Autobiography, our editor was Professor Stanley Weintraub, Director of the Institute for the Arts and Humanistic Studies, Pennsylvania State University, and an eminent biographer in his own right. He has for this edition separated the autobiographers, diarists, and letter-writers from the literary biographers, and provided extensive commentaries on new books and new author listings.

In the acknowledgments above, new introductions and new author listings have only occasionally been mentioned. In fact, the introductions to all but one of the chapters have been completely rewritten. Many of them, of course, use much of the material of the eleventh edition of *The Reader's Adviser*; some are almost completely new. Almost every chapter has been expanded in scope by the addition of new authors. All of the biographical-critical notes have been examined, and many have been enlarged and revised in addition to the necessary updating occasioned by the addition of the latest titles. We acknowledge with gratitude the painstaking and careful work of all the members of our editorial board.

Thanks are also due to our librarian, Jean Peters, and to her assistant, Agatha Derrick, who always cheerfully took the time to help us find the elusive fact, or date, or name. There must have been times when they shuddered at the sight of our walking into their bailiwick, though they never expressed such feelings in word or gesture. Indeed, they sometimes gave us the impression that coming to our aid was their chief delight. And many an item would never have been discovered without their assistance.

In the task of final updating and editing the chapters as they came to us from our editors, we had the assistance of Julia Miele who worked long and hard and—best of all—patiently updating, cutting, pasting, styling, typing and performing all the other chores connected with preparing manuscript for the copy editor under the pressure of a deadline.

The copy editors have been very helpful in catching mistakes of hand and eye that escaped the editor's attention. For meticulous care and observant reading, we salute them.

This twelfth edition of *The Reader's Adviser* has been prepared following new procedures, and with some changes in the arrangement of information. It is nevertheless very much the same *Reader's Adviser* and it is our hope that it will take an honorable place among honored previous editions.

—Sarah L. Prakken

Contributing Editors

A.E.   Arline Edelson, Acquisitions Librarian and Adjunct Professor of English, West-chester Community College

C.B.G.   Chandler B. Grannis, Editor-at-Large, *Publishers Weekly*

D.S.   David Shapiro, Instructor, Columbia College, Columbia University

E.M.   Elizabeth Marraffino, Foreign Rights Editor, New Directions Books

F.K.   Fred Kaplan, Associate Professor, Queens College

F.S.   Francis Sypher, Assistant Professor, State University of New York at Albany

H.M.   Hugh Mclean, Professor, State University of New York at Albany

J.M.C.   James M. Cox, Professor, Dartmouth College

J.R.P.   Jean R. Peters, Librarian, R. R. Bowker Company

M.B.   Maurice Beebe, Professor, Temple University and Editor, *Journal of Modern Literature*

M.G.   Morris Golden, Professor, University of Massachusetts

M.P.   Mark Piel, Reference Librarian, Upsala College Library

R.R.   Rubin Rabinowitz, Professor, Columbia University

S.W.   Stanley Weintraub, Director, Institute for the Arts and Humanistic Studies, Pennsylvania State University

W.J.S.   William J. Stuckey, Associate Professor, Purdue University

W.S.S.   Wilbur S. Scott, Professor, The New College, Hofstra University

Abbreviations

abr.	abridged	*LJ*	*Library Journal*
annot.	annotated	ltd. ed.	limited edition
Am.	American	MLA	Modern Language
app.	appendix		Association
arr.	arranged	Mod.	Modern
assist.	assisted, assistance	mor.	morocco
bibliog.	bibliography	ms., mss.	manuscript(s)
bd.	bound	NYPL	New York Public Library
bdg.	binding		*Branch Library Book*
Bk., Bks.	Book(s)		*News,,* etc.
Booklist	*Booklist and Subscription*	*N.Y. Times*	*New York Times*
	Books Bulletin	orig.	original
c.	circa	o. p.	out of print
Chil.	Children's	pap.	paper
Class.	Classics	PBIP	Paperbound Books in
clo.	cloth		Print
coll.	collected	Perenn.	Perennial
coll. ed.	collected edition	Pock.	Pocket
comp.	compiled, compiler	pref.	preface
d.	died	pseud.	pseudonym
Devot.	Devotional	pt.	part
dist.	distributed	ptg.	printing
ed.	edited, editor, edition	*PW*	*Publishers Weekly*
Eng.	English	*q. v.*	*quod vide* (which see)
enl.	enlarged	rept.	reprint
Enrich.	Enrichment	rev. ed.	revised edition
fl.	flourished	Riv.	Riverside
fwd.	foreword	sel.	selected
gen. eds.	general editors	Ser.	Series
Gt.	Great	*SR*	*Saturday Review*
ill.	illustrated, illustrations	Stand.	Standard
imit. lea.	imitation leather	suppl., suppls.	supplement(s)
in prep.	in preparation	*TLS*, London	*Times Literary*
introd.	introduction		*Supplement*
lea.	leather	trans.	translated, translator,
lg.-type ed.	large-type edition		translation
lib. ed	library edition	Univ.	University, Universal
Lib.	Library, Liberal	Vol., Vols.	Volume(s)
Lit.	Literature		

Notes on Arrangement

Although the coverage of Volume 1 of this twelfth edition of *The Reader's Adviser* is more limited in scope than Volume 1 of the eleventh edition, the order of chapters is again planned so that the background or reference books necessary for the general reader or the bookman precede the main divisions of literature. The background and reference books are to be found in the first four chapters: Books about Books, Bibliography, Reference Books—Literature, and Broad Studies and General Anthologies. The scope of these chapters is not limited to the material covered in Volume 1 alone, but encompasses also the subjects planned for Volume 2 of this edition, Drama in English, and Foreign Literature in Translation. In the first four chapters, covering general reference materials and broad studies, every effort has been made toward logical order and clarity of arrangement by the use of subject groupings under chapter divisions and subdivisions, and even, as in Chapter 3, where the arrangement seemed to require it, subheadings under the subdivisions. All subject divisions and subdivisions are distinguished in the text of the chapters by typographical variations. In addition all chapter divisions, subdivisions, and subheadings are listed in the table of contents, with the page number indicated for the beginning of each section.

In the chapters concerned with genres and periods of literature, the reference books, books of history and criticism, and suggested reading lists which throw light on the general subject of the chapter come at the beginning of that chapter, followed by relevant collections and anthologies. These bibliographies are given in alphabetical sequence by author or editor.

Authors who have main entries are arranged in chronological order. Under their names come first the biographical and critical notes upon that author. These notes include statements on the author's importance in his time and place, his influence upon the development of literature, and the influences affecting him in his own creative growth. They include mention of important works not currently in print which are significant because of their influence, or because they are indicative of the course of development of the author himself; important works not pertinent to the chapter category are mentioned if the author does not have a second listing in another appropriate chapter; and sometimes note is made of useful books edited or translated by him, particularly if they are unlikely to be mentioned elsewhere. The biographical-critical notes are followed by the list of works by the author. Volumes of complete and collected works of the genre with which the chapter is concerned precede selections. In addition, within these groups, we have listed the definitive and variorum editions, if any, ahead of others. Roughly, we have listed other selections and collections by date of publication. This chronological arrangement is indeed very rough. In the first place, volumes with generic titles such as "Complete Short Stories" or "Selected Poems" are given in a single entry alphabetically by publisher, and in the second place, in the case of certain old editions and paperback reprints we were unable to identify the original date and had to be guided by their relative position in the eleventh edition of *The Reader's Adviser*, or the time of entry into the record. The reader should browse through these lists to find items that quicken his interest. After selections, individual works are listed in the order in which they were first published. As in the case of collections and selections, definitive and variorum editions are listed first. Last in the listing come the "self-revelatory" works, which include, in addition to autobiography and correspondence, diaries, journals., notebooks, travel books, and essays of a subjective nature which reveal a personal reaction to any aspect of life and art. Finally, the user will find a selected bibliography of books about the author. These include biographies, critical works, bibliographies, concordances, and the like. They are set off from the list of titles by the author both by a change of type size and by the heading "Books about Dickens [Spenser, Eliot, etc.]." The arrangement here is also chronological by date of publication.

In the general bibliographies at the head of each chapter and in the reading lists about an individual author our editors have been highly selective, choosing only *la crême de la crême*. In the lists of works by an author we have given as complete a representation as possible of in-print titles appropriate to the scope of the chapter. However, in a few instances, particularly in chapters covering nineteenth century fiction, where titles of very widely read novels—frequently used in courses in schools and colleges—are listed in a multiplicity of editions, we have omitted from the detailed listing paperback editions on which we have little or no bibliographic data, and entered them as *see also* references directly beneath, in alphabetical sequence with a notation of the price range.

For all books cited, when the original publisher is not represented among the current available editions, the original publication date is given before any information applying to a publisher listed. If the original publisher is represented, that listing is given first along with the original publication date. Other editions and reprints follow alphabetically by publisher. Paperback imprints, and other special imprints and series are listed along with the publishing house to which they belong, e.g. *Doubleday* Anchor Bks. The same practice is followed for publishers' mergers, etc. where this affects a title page, as *Holt* (Rinehart). Paperback reprints from such houses as Avon or Bantam are frequently available concurrently with the hardcover editions which they reprint. This is also true of those publishers, such as Peter Smith and William Gannon, who put into library bindings original quality paperbacks of other publishers. Wherever we have been able to identify the original counterpart of these reprints and library bound editions, we have listed them together. Although there are many times that we have not been able to verify such a connection, the juxtaposition of original and reprint provides so much more specific information about the nature of the reprint or library binding that it seemed very worth while, even though it may sometimes appear that we have erred in alphabetizing. For all books cited, in addition to the publisher and price, we have endeavored to provide information on dates, bindings, imprints, edition numbers, editors, and series. The number of series identified has been greatly increased since the eleventh edition, although it is still not complete.

The twelfth edition of *The Reader's Adviser* again lists reprints, both in paper and in hardcover, in large numbers. The paperback reprints posed a problem in correct dating, wherever the reprint editions were the only ones available. This information is not often available either in publisher's catalogs, nor in *Books in Print*; although we have tried to track down original dates, we have not always been successful. We have tried to alert the user to this difficulty by careful placement of dates. A date before a publisher is a clear indication of a verified original date; a date following the publisher's name if the house is actively engaged in original publication indicates an original hardcover date; a date following a paperback imprint, as Anchor Bks. or Norton Lib., indicates the date of that particular edition, which may or may not be original; while a date following text ed., lib. bdg., or pap. should be regarded with some misgiving.

There are several helps for locating the innumerable reprints: *Catalog of Reprints in Series* is by Robert M. Orton (Scarecrow Press 21st ed. 1972 $25.00). *Guide to Reprints* (NCR Microcard annually pap. $10.00) is an annual cumulative guide to books, journals and other materials available in reprint, international in coverage, indexing full sized reprinted books published in editions of 200 copies or more. Arrangement is by author, and entries include, in addition to author, publisher, price, and date of original publication. "Paperbound Books in Print" (Bowker 2 cumulative vols. per year in March and November each $18.95) provides an index to paperbound orginal and reprinted editions indexed by author, title, and subject. *Books in Print* (Bowker 2 vols. annually in November $64.50 suppl. annually in Spring $27.95) lists both hardcover and paperback editions. *Forthcoming Books* (Bowker bimonthly $16.95 a year, single copies $3.00) lists in steady cumulation all books due to be published in the following five months.

In addition to hardcover reprints of standard scholarly works, more and more titles are being reproduced in microform editions. These may be on microfilm, microfiche, or microcard. Book distributors are beginning to supply bookstores and other customers their catalogs on microfiche as a book ordering tool. Some of the companies which hold microform collections can supply their titles in book form upon demand, some print selected lists of their titles in book form. There are in this edition of *The Reader's Adviser* a number of titles which publishers are offering in a choice of the conventional book form or in microfiche. *Guide to Microforms in Print* (ed. by A. J. Diaz NCR Microcard cumulative annually pap. $6.00) indexes alphabetically books, journals, and other materials on microforms.

Cross references are provided wherever possible to enhance usefulness. We have again used *(q.v.)* in the continuing text to indicate an author who is treated in detail elsewhere, and a direct *"see also"* reference at the end of an author's main listing if he has a second listing in another chapter of Volume 1. In this edition, however, we have eliminated cross references to future unpublished volumes, because of the risk of setting up cross references which will eventually prove to be blind. Since the information of half of Volume 1 eleventh edition will continue to be valid until Vol. 2 of the twelfth edition is issued, that volume should continue to be of value for its cross references as well as its general information.

This book is intended to be practical for readers, booksellers, and librarians. The editions listed are those currently obtainable in the United States. Although many of these are published abroad and distributed in this country, very few have been listed which have to be ordered abroad. The exception to this is in the reference chapters which do note indispensable reference tools even though they are unavailable in the United States. In general, out of print titles, obtainable in second-hand stores and libraries, have been omitted in the formal bibliographies, but important titles currently unavailable may be mentioned in the biographical notes on authors, or in the introductions to the separate chapters. Again, the reference chapters are an exception, since these chapters discuss the standard basic tools which are requisite to anyone pursuing a literary interest, whether or not he can own them himself. Our book lists are not intended to be exhaustive bibliographies needed by the specialist in a particular subject; they are current in-print volumes readily obtainable, whether the reader has extensive library facilities at his disposal or not.

The information in *The Reader's Adviser* was revised according to the 1972–1973 *Books in Print*, the *Supplement to Books in Print* of March 1973, and the spring issue of *Paperbound Books in Print*. Virtually all material was rechecked against the 1973–1974 *Books in Print*. Some of our editors have added even later material as announcements of very recent publications have appeared. We have made every effort to provide the most recent information possible; but books go in and out of print with astonishing rapidity sometimes, and publishers "reserve the right to change prices without notice"; therefore the reader should consider the prices given here as "relative" and should check from time to time later editions of *Books in Print* and other indexes for desirable titles not mentioned here.

The names of publishers throughout *The Reader's Adviser* have been abbreviated to some extent. We have used certain easily recognized abbreviations as Am., Pub., Int., Univ., for American, Publishing, International, University, and have shortened some of the longer names, such as Harcourt for Harcourt Brace Jovanovich. All of them are readily recognizable and will cause no difficulty or delay in locating titles cited. Other book trade abbreviations are standard and held to a minimum. A list of them is given on the page preceding this section. In general we have supplied only the names of publishers, without addresses or distributor information. This information can be found in the Directory of Publishers in *Books in Print* which is a complete list of all known publishers in the United States. However, when books by associations or organizations which are not primarily publishers are listed, addresses are provided; and, occasionally if some doubt could arise concerning distribution arrangements, this information is given. An example of this is the publications of New American Library, which has its own catalog in the "Publisher's Trade List Annual" and its own ordering address for paperback editions, but its hardcover editions are distributed by, and listed in the Norton catalog. In this instance we have used two codes: *New Am. Lib.* for the paperback editions and *New Am. Lib.* (dist. by Norton) for the hardcovers.

The Reader's Adviser has always been an excellent tool for the person who wants specific information on a particular subject; it has also been a pleasurable hunting-ground for the one who likes "just to browse around." We hope that this expanded revision, and its various reorganizations of presented material will offer a greater usefulness to the searcher and a greater joy to the browser.

THE
READER'S
ADVISER

Chapter 1

Books about Books

"There are more books upon books than upon all other subjects."
—MICHEL DE MONTAIGNE

The world of books has a continuously growing literature of its own, a literature reflecting the fascination which most of those who work in that world feel. The histories, memoirs and biographies of developments, units and people in the book industry are therefore almost always entertaining, often both witty and wise. But they are also instructive. Taken together they provide a survey of the book from the earliest times; and viewed in the light of the present day, they offer an extraordinary store of guidance and experience for the contemporary person whose life is in some way concerned with books. The how-to books about bookselling, bookmaking and other aspects of the industry have, in many cases, equal charm, together with functional value.

For all these reasons, the books named in this chapter are selected for their possible interest on the shelves of a person working in the book world and dedicated—or acquiring a dedication—to it. Along with books about books, a very few basic works about magazines and newspapers are cited.

By no means all the books in print on the subjects covered have been listed; and not all the books listed are in print. But all, in or out of print, are believed to be distinctly useful and interesting; and among the out-of-print volumes, the selection centers upon books of long-term value, likely to be found in many library collections or in the second-hand trade. It will be noticed that the profession of librarianship is not represented; that is a vast field, which deserves and has its own bibliographies, far more pertinent than any brief selection here could be. For the rest, the book person who seeks them out, whether from in-print or antiquarian stocks, will find the search rewarding.

BOOK INDUSTRY HISTORY: GENERAL AND BRITISH

Bennett, H. S. ENGLISH BOOKS & READERS, 1475 TO 1557. *Cambridge* 1952 $14.50 (with the next two vols., as set of 3, $37.50). History of books from Caxton to the incorporation of the Stationers' Company, and an account of society at the opening of the era of printing.

ENGLISH BOOKS & READERS, 1558 TO 1603. *Cambridge* 1965 $14.50. The book trade in the reign of Elizabeth I.

ENGLISH BOOKS & READERS, 1603 TO 1640. *Cambridge* 1970 $14.50. The book trade in the reigns of James I and Charles I.

Curwen, Henry. A HISTORY OF BOOKSELLERS: The Old and the New. 1873. *Gale* 1968 $11.50. Said to be the first history of booksellers. The author undertook the work after reading a statement by Thomas Carlyle: "In these days, ten ordinary histories of kings and courtiers were well exchanged against the tenth part of one good History of Booksellers."

Darton, F. J. Harvey. CHILDREN'S BOOKS IN ENGLAND: Five Centuries of Social Life. *Cambridge* 1932 2nd ed. 1958 $14.50. Illustrated scholarly material on John Newbery, Thomas Day, Peter Parley and others.

Hürlimann, Bettina. THREE CENTURIES OF CHILDREN'S BOOKS IN EUROPE. 1963. Trans. and ed. by Brian W. Alderson. *World Pub.* 1968 o. p. A comprehensive survey; includes American influences.

Kenyon, Frederic G. BOOKS AND READERS IN ANCIENT GREECE AND ROME. 2nd ed. 1951. *Folcroft* $15.00; *Richard West* 1973 $10.00. Bookmaking and early publishing methods from the time of Homer, c. 850 B.C., to 400 A.D., by the late Director and Principal Librarian of the British Museum.

Muir, Percy. ENGLISH CHILDREN'S BOOKS, 1650–1900. A handsomely illustrated chronological history, arranged for the collector as well as the student. *Praeger* 1954 $13.50.

Mumby, Frank A., and Ian Norrie. PUBLISHING AND BOOKSELLING: A History from the Earliest Times to the Present Day. 5th ed. 1974 (Jonathan Cape) *Bowker* $33.50. From Mumby's classic work, 13 chapters, covering book industry history from Roman times to 1870, are reprinted. The remaining 25 chapters, by Ian Norrie, are entirely new, replacing Mumby's later material and updating the story of the British book trade from 1870 to 1970. Roles of 400 publishers and 350 booksellers are shown in recounting developments and trends in historical context.

Rostenberg, Leona. LITERARY, POLITICAL, SCIENTIFIC, RELIGIOUS AND LEGAL PUBLISHING, PRINTING AND BOOKSELLING IN ENGLAND 1551–1700. *Burt Franklin* 1963 2 vols. set $25.00

ENGLISH PUBLISHERS IN THE GRAPHIC ARTS 1599–1700. *Burt Franklin* 1963 $12.50

Taubert, Sigfred, Ed. THE BOOK TRADE OF THE WORLD. *Verlag für Buchmarkt-Forschung* (dist. by Bowker) Vol. I: Europe and International Sections (1972) $18.75 Vol. 2: U.S.A., Canada, Central and South America, Australia and New Zealand (1974) (price to be announced) Vol. 3: Africa, Asia (in prep.). Country-by-country survey of bookselling and publishing today, reported by leading figures in the book industry.

BIBLIOPOLA: Pictures and Texts about the Book Trade. *Bowker* 1966 2 vols. set $65.00. A fascinating and comprehensive history of the book trade throughout the world. Text in English, French, German. Vol. I is history, treated thematically, Vol. 2 an anthology of writings on the subject. More than 500 illustrations, some in color.

Thompson, James Westfall, Trans. and Ed. with introd. THE FRANKFORT BOOK FAIR (1574). By Henry Estienne. *Van Huesden, Amsterdam* (dist. by Abner Schram) 1970 $23.50. Reprint of the Caxton Club's (Chicago) edition of 1911, accompanying Thompson's full and heavily illustrated account of the fair and its meaning in book trade history.

Thwaite, Mary F. FROM PRIMER TO PLEASURE IN READING. *Horn Bk.* 1972 $12.50. History of children's books in England from the invention of printing to 1914, with outline of developments in Australia, North America, Western Europe.

Winship, George Parker. THE CAMBRIDGE PRESS, 1638–1692. 1945. *Bks. for Libraries* 1968 $13.75. A scholarly account of the beginnings of printing and bookmaking in Massachusetts.

Winterich, John T. EARLY AMERICAN BOOKS AND PRINTING. *Gale* 1935 $12.00; *McGrath* 1970 $15.00. Winterich was always painstaking in his scholarship—and irrepressible in his humor and love of the entertaining, illuminating fact.

Woodfield, Denis B. SURREPTITIOUS PRINTING IN ENGLAND 1550–1640. Ill. *Bibliographical Society of America* 1973 $17.50. Unauthorized though not necessarily "underground" publishing of works in English, French, Italian, Spanish, and Dutch.

BOOK INDUSTRY HISTORY: NORTH AMERICAN

Anderson, Charles B., Ed. UNTITLED BOOK TO MARK 75TH ANNIVERSARY OF AMERICAN BOOKSELLERS ASSOCIATION. *Am. Booksellers Assn.* (800 Second Ave., N.Y.C. 10017) 1975 (in prep.). To include essays by Chandler B. Grannis (history of A. B. A.), Sigfred Taubert (developments in bookselling around the world), John Tebbel (history of American bookselling, especially since 1900), Alice Payne Hackett (best seller history).

Bryer, Jackson. THE LITTLE MAGAZINE IN AMERICA AND ENGLAND 1950–1970: An Informal Guide. *Gale* $15.00.

Charvat, William. LITERARY PUBLISHING IN AMERICA: 1790–1850. *Univ. of Pennsylvania Press* 1959 $7.50. Relations between publishers and literary history.

Churchill, Allen. THE LITERARY DECADE. Ill. *Prentice-Hall* 1972 $9.95. A colorful account of the authors, publishers and others who made the 1920s a modern "golden age" in American writing and publishing.

Comparato, Frank E. BOOKS FOR THE MILLIONS: A history of the Men Whose Methods and Machines Packaged the Printed Word. Ill. *Stackpole* 1971 $12.50. A history of book manufacturing, especially of the decisive inventions that made the modern book industry possible.

Darling, Richard L. THE RISE OF CHILDREN'S BOOK REVIEWING IN AMERICA, 1865–1881. *Bowker* 1968 $11.95. A readable survey of an interesting development in our literary history.

Gardiner, C. Harvey. PRESCOTT AND HIS PUBLISHERS. Ill. *Southern Illinois Univ. Press* 1959 $5.95. An account of author-publisher relations in the latter third of the 19th century, involving the eminent historian of the Spanish conquests, William H. Prescott.

Kaser, David, Ed. BOOKS IN AMERICA'S PAST: Essays Honoring Rudolph H. Glelsness. *McGrath* 1966 $14.00. Includes among its 13 essays material on the trade of 18th century and early 19th century booksellers.

Lehmann-Haupt, Hellmut, Lawrence C. Wroth and Rollo G. Silver. THE BOOK IN AMERICA. *Bowker* 1939 rev. ed. 1951 $16.75. Subtitled, "A History of the Making and Selling of Books in the United States"; the most detailed, comprehensive single volume on the subject.

Madison, Charles A. IRVING TO IRVING: AUTHOR-PUBLISHER RELATIONS, 1800–1974. *Bowker* 1974 (in prep.). The love-hate relations between some famous American writers and their publishers—relations through which contracts, copyright and other business arrangements have developed.

BOOK PUBLISHING IN AMERICA. Ill. *McGraw-Hill* 1966 $12.50. The development of American book publishing and some activities of leading companies and personalities from Colonial beginnings to 1965. Considerable anecdotal material.

Mott, Frank Luther. AMERICAN JOURNALISM: A History 1690–1960. 3rd rev. ed. *Macmillan* 1962 $10.95. A comprehensive work; 3rd edition deals with new technology and the electronic media's effects on journalism up to 1960.

A HISTORY OF AMERICAN MAGAZINES. *Harvard Univ. Press* 1930–1968 Belknap Press 5 vols. each $15.00. The successive volumes of this Pulitzer Prize winner cover the years 1741–1930.

Schick, Frank L. THE PAPERBOUND BOOK IN AMERICA. *Bowker* 1958 o.p. A history up to the late 1950s; highly detailed; includes European backgrounds.

Sheehan, Donald. THIS WAS PUBLISHING. *Indiana Univ. Press* 1952 o.p. How American publishing was conducted in "old line" houses 1865–1915.

Stern, Madeleine B. IMPRINTS ON HISTORY: Book Publishers and American Frontiers. *AMS Press* 1956 $20.00. An account of 16 early publishing houses in varied fields; also, condensed histories of 200 other houses that began in the 19th century.

Tebbel, John. THE COMPACT HISTORY OF THE AMERICAN NEWSPAPER. *Hawthorn Bks.* 1963 $7.95. Streamlined but extensive in coverage.

A HISTORY OF BOOK PUBLISHING IN THE UNITED STATES. *Bowker* 3 vols. Vol. I: The Creation of an Industry, 1630–1865 (1972) $29.95 Vol 2: The Expansion of an Industry, 1865–1919 (1974) (in prep.) Vol. 3: Publishing Comes of Age, 1919 to the Present (in prep.). A massive, highly detailed yet continuously readable account of the entire development of American book publishing and its partners in the world of books and book distribution. Each event and development is not merely identified but explained in terms of how and why it came about and to what it led.

BOOK INDUSTRY BIOGRAPHIES: PERSONS, COMPANIES, ORGANIZATIONS

A great many of the biographies of people or units in the book industry are printed in short-run scholarly editions, or in editions for special circulation, or in small trade editions that sell out and do not get reprinted. Hence, many valuable titles are soon out of print. However, we include many of these o.p. titles in this section for the benefit of the history buffs, who, in libraries, personal and company collections, and the second-hand trade, can probably find the volumes they want.

Abingdon Press

Pilkington, James Penn. THE METHODIST PUBLISHING HOUSE: A History. Vol. 1. Ill. *Abingdon* 1968 $7.50. This volume covers the first 100 years (to 1870) of the Methodist publishing enterprises in the U.S.

Bantam Books

Petersen, Clarence. THE BANTAM STORY, TWENTY-FIVE YEARS OF PAPERBACK PUBLISHING. Ill. *Bantam* 1970 pap. (not priced). A narrative that emphasizes Bantam, but places the firm in context; title list.

Sylvia Beach

Beach, Sylvia. SHAKESPEARE AND COMPANY. Ill. 1959 *Harcourt* o.p. The author's American bookshop in Paris was the first publisher of *Ulysses*, and was a center for some of the most famous writers of the 1920s.

R. R. Bowker Co.

Fleming, Edward McClung. R. R. BOWKER: MILITANT LIBERAL. Ill. *Bowker* 1962 $8.00. Life of the versatile journalist, New York political reformer, entrepreneur and publisher who in 1872 helped establish *Publishers' Weekly*, followed by *Library Journal* and associated publications, and who guided the firm until 1933.

Stuart Brent

Brent, Stuart. THE SEVEN STAIRS. 1962. *O'Hara* 1973 pap. $2.95. A Chicago bookseller tells how he started and ran his successful shop, along with a TV show about books, and recounts other adventures.

Cass Canfield

Canfield, Cass. THE PUBLISHING EXPERIENCE. A. S. W. Rosenbach Lectures. *Univ. of Pennsylvania Press* 1969 $5.00

UP AND DOWN AND AROUND: A Publisher Recollects the Time of His Life. *Harper* 1971 $8.95 Colophon Bks. pap. $3.25. The author's career in book publishing, the statesmen and other public figures and writers he knew, the development of publishing in his years of leadership at Harper.

Mathew Carey

Bradsher, Earl L. MATHEW CAREY, EDITOR, AUTHOR AND PUBLISHER. 1912. *AMS Press* $12.00. Basic study of the American book trade pioneer in the early years of the Republic.

Sir Sydney Carlyle Cockerell

Blunt, Wilfrid. COCKERELL. Ill. *Knopf* 1965 o.p. Cockerell (1867–1962), associated with famous literary and artistic figures, worked also with William Morris, Emery Walker and others in the important private presses—Kelmscott, Doves, and Ashendene.

George H. Doran

Doran, George H. CHRONICLES OF BARABBAS, 1884–1934. *Holt* 2nd ed. 1952 $4.50. The well-told story of the pains and pleasures of publishing, full of interesting anecdotes of a brilliant period.

Doubleday & Co.

Doubleday, F. N. THE MEMOIRS OF A PUBLISHER. *Doubleday* 1972 (not priced). Frank Nelson Doubleday's record of his life and work, written in 1926, published as a 75th anniversary volume. Recounts his early years with Scribner's, founding and growth of the Doubleday firm, work with famous people, problems of the book trade; includes a memorial essay, "Effendi," by Christopher Morley.

Victor Gollancz

Gollancz, Victor. REMINISCENCES OF AFFECTION. Fwd. by Livia Gollancz. Ill. Victor Gollancz, Ltd. 1969 *Atheneum* $7.50. Autobiography of a trail-blazing British 20th-century publisher, exuberantly involved in politics of the Left, a successful maverick.

Gotham Book Mart

Rogers, W. G. WISE MEN FISH HERE: The Story of Frances Steloff and the Gotham Book Mart. Ill. *Harcourt* 1965 o.p. Portrait of a remarkable Manhattan bookseller who championed the avant-garde writers and little magazines of the 1920s to the 1960s.

The Grabhorns

Grabhorn, Jane. THE COMPLEAT JANE GRABHORN. *Grabhorn Press* 1968 $25.00. Writings and many reproduced or tipped-in actual specimens of the work of a great woman printer who died in 1973. Foreward by her husband, Robert Grabhorn; Robert, his brother Edwin, and Jane were partners in the historic Grabhorn Press of San Francisco.

Harcourt Brace Jovanovich

Reid, James M. AN ADVENTURE IN TEXTBOOKS. *Bowker* 1969 $10.50. Behind-the-scenes view of business and personalities by a former textbook editor of Harcourt, Brace & Co.

See also Jovanovich in Section on Book Industry and Practices, below.

Harper & Row

Exman, Eugene. THE BROTHERS HARPER, 1817–1853. Ill. *Harper* 1967 $7.95. How the Harpers established their famous house; methods of promotion and sale; relations with U.S. and British writers; printing practices; business ventures and profits.

THE HOUSE OF HARPER: One Hundred and Fifty Years of Publishing. Ill. *Harper* 1967 $8.50. A broad portrait of the firm and its people, candid about failures and foibles, entertainingly written.

See also Cass Canfield, above.

The Hogarth Press

Woolf, Leonard. BEGINNING AGAIN. *Harcourt* 1965 $6.95 pap. $2.75

DOWNHILL ALL THE WAY: An Autobiography, 1919–1939. *Harcourt* 1967 $5.95. The writer describes the private press operated by himself and his wife, the essayist and novelist Virginia Woolf (*q. v.*); their life together, his work as publisher, editor, writer, political worker; and the Woolfs' literary and artistic circle.

Holt, Rinehart & Winston

Madison, Charles A. THE OWL AMONG COLOPHONS: Henry Holt as Publisher and Editor. *Holt* 1966 o.p. A former head of Holt's college department writes a short account that is half history of the firm and half a biography of its strong-minded founder.

Houghton Mifflin Co.

Ballou, Ellen B. The Building of the House: Houghton Mifflin's First Half Century. *Houghton* 1970 $12.50. Achievements and failures of a major publishing firm; includes printing plant and design development, mergers, trade and publishing, the *Atlantic Monthly*—all up to 1921.

Elbert Hubbard

Champney, Freeman. Art and Glory: The Story of Elbert Hubbard. *Crown* 1968 o.p. Life of the turn-of-the-century publisher, populist and arts and crafts proponent.

Alfred A. Knopf

Portrait of a Publisher, 1915–1965. Ed. and with introds. by Paul A. Bennett. Vol. I, Reminiscences and Reflections by Alfred A. Knopf; Vol. 2, Alfred A. Knopf and the Borzoi Imprint: Recollections and Appreciations. *The Typophiles* 1965 o.p.

Knopf, Alfred A. Publishing Then and Now, 1912–1965. *N.Y. Public Lib.* 1965 pap. $1.25. An address given by the publisher in the Richard Rogers Bowker Memorial Lectures Series.

J. B. Lippincott Co.

The Author and His Audience. *Lippincott* 1967 $2.95. Marking the 175th anniversary of the firm, this publication describes the craft of book publishing as the link between author and reader.

McGraw-Hill Publishing Co.

Burlingame, Roger. Endless Frontiers: The Story of McGraw-Hill. Ill. *McGraw-Hill* 1959 o.p. A detailed record of the firm's role in the expansion of scientific and technical book publishing in the U.S.; marks the firm's 50th anniversary.

The Macmillan Co.

Latham, Harold S. My Life in Publishing. *Dutton* 1965 o.p. With Macmillan 1909 to 1951, Mr. Latham became editor-in-chief; he discusses problems of editing and tells of writers he knew.

G. & C. Merriam Co.

Leavitt, Robert K. Noah's Ark: New England Yankees and the Endless Quest. *Merriam* 1947 (not priced). Privately printed. A short history of the original Webster dictionaries and their 100 years with the Merriam Co.

Methodist Publishing House. See Abingdon Press.

Sir Francis Meynell

Meynell, Francis. My Lives. Ill. *Random* 1971 $10.00. Autobiography of a 20th-century renaissance man—poet, journalist, publisher, industrialist, radical, book designer, founder of the Nonesuch Press in London.

James R. Osgood

Weber, Carl J. THE RISE AND FALL OF JAMES RIPLEY OSGOOD. *Colby College Press* 1959 o.p. An important New England publisher in the latter half of the 19th century.

P.E.N.

Chute, Marchette. P.E.N. AMERICAN CENTER: A History of the First Fifty Years. *P.E.N. American Center* (156 Fifth Ave., N.Y.C. 10010). 1972 pap. $2.00. The story of the American branch of the international association of people of letters, showing its growth from the standing of a discreet club to that of a fighter for free expression.

Maxwell E. Perkins

Kuehl, John, and Jackson Bryer, Eds. DEAR SCOTT, DEAR MAX: The Fitzgerald-Perkins Correspondence. *Scribner* 1971 pap. $2.95. Stretching over many years, first of businesslike acquaintance, then of deeply involved friendship, the great Scribner editor's correspondence with F. Scott Fitzgerald provides a portrait of both, and of their work.

Perkins, Maxwell E. EDITOR TO AUTHOR: The Letters of Maxwell E. Perkins. Sel. and ed. with commentary and introd. by John Hall Wheelock. *Scribner* 1950 (not priced). Perkins served Scribner's for the last 20 of his 37 years with the firm (until his death in 1947). Like no other book, this volume of his correspondence with Hemingway, Wolfe, Fitzgerald, Galsworthy and other famous writers shows the essence of author-publisher relations as revealed by a great editor at work.

Paul R. Reynolds

Reynolds, Paul R. THE MIDDLE MAN: The Adventures of a Literary Agent. *Morrow* 1972 $6.95. The dean of American authors' representatives tells of his own experiences and explains the role of the literary agent in the book trade.

Charles Scribner's Sons

Burlingame, Roger. OF MAKING MANY BOOKS: A Hundred Years of Reading, Writing and Publishing. *Scribner* 1946 $10.00. The development of a great family-owned publishing house, told in large part through the publisher's correspondence with authors.

See also Maxwell E. Perkins.

Simon and Schuster

(Smith, Roger H.) SIMON & SCHUSTER: Our First Fifty Years 1924–1974. *Simon & Schuster* 1973 pap. (not priced). A short anniversary review of the firm.

Spiral Press

THE SPIRAL PRESS THROUGH FOUR DECADES: An Exhibition of Books and Ephemera. *Pierpont Morgan Lib.* 1966 pap. o.p. Presents with 60 reproductions of printed items, the work of the distinguished designer, printer and publisher, Joseph Blumenthal, with commentary by him.

Stone & Kimball

Kramer, Sidney. A HISTORY OF STONE & KIMBALL AND HERBERT S. STONE & Co., 1893–1905. *N.W. Forgue* 1940 o.p. Portrait of a young, short-lived firm, important for its new approaches.

Isaiah Thomas

Nichols, Charles Lemuel. ISAIAH THOMAS, PRINTER, WRITER AND COLLECTOR. 1912. *Burt Franklin* 1971 $15.00. Work of the leading American bookman of the revolutionary period and after; includes a bibliography of books he produced. First issued by Boston's Club of Odd Volumes.

Ticknor & Fields

Tryon, Warren S. PARNASSUS CORNER: A Life of James T. Fields, Publisher to the Victorians. *Houghton* 1963 o.p. Account of one of the most outstanding New England publishers in the decades after 1854.

University of North Carolina Press

Univ. of North Carolina Press Staff. A STATESMAN OF THE REPUBLIC OF BOOKS. *Univ. of North Carolina Press* 1970 (not priced). "Statements by and about Lambert Davis . . . upon his retirement as director of the press."

The Unwins

Unwin, Philip. THE PUBLISHING UNWINS. Ill. *Heinmann*, London (dist. by Humanities Press) 1972 $11.00. Saga of the English publishing family and its leading members since early in the 19th century.

Unwin, Sir Stanley. THE TRUTH ABOUT A PUBLISHER. 1960. *Bowker* $4.25. The sprightly English bookman was active until he died at 83. His autobiography gives a lively picture of his youth and his long professional career, the writers and other publishers he encountered, and his battles on behalf of copyright and the book trade.

The Ward Ritchie Press

Ritchie, Ward. THE WARD RITCHIE PRESS AND ANDERSON, RITCHIE & SIMON. *Ward Ritchie* 1961 $17.50. Among the fine printers and publishers for which California is known, one of the most durable is Ritchie's firm, founded in 1932, still flourishing.

Victor Weybright

Weybright, Victor. THE MAKING OF A PUBLISHER: A Life in the 20th Century Book Revolution. *Morrow* (Reynal) 1967 o.p. Mr. Weybright pulls no punches in recounting the beginnings of the New American Library and the preliminaries to founding his own Weybright & Talley in 1966; he also tells of Hull House, Chicago, and of the Office of War Information in wartime London.

John Wiley & Sons

THE FIRST HUNDRED AND FIFTY YEARS: A History of John Wiley and Sons, Incorporated, 1807–1957. *Wiley* 1957 $7.50. The firm's story is told in terms of its leaders and the development of its major subject areas.

H. W. Wilson Co.

Lawler, John Lawrence. H. W. WILSON COMPANY: Half a Century of Bibliographic Publishing. Ed. by Lee Ash. 1950 *Gregg* 1972 $10.00. Ingenious and persistent, Mr. Wilson systematically built a complex of major services for libraries, schools and the book industry.

BOOK INDUSTRY PRACTICES AND PROBLEMS

ABC OF THE BOOK TRADE. *Antiquarian Bookman* (Box 1100, Newark, N.J. 07101) 1966 $3.00. Facts about the retail book trade, especially the conduct of the rare and second-hand book trade.

Anderson, Charles B., Joseph A. Duffy and Jocelyn D. Kahn, Eds. A MANUAL ON BOOK-SELLING. *American Booksellers Assn.* (dist. by Bowker) 1969 $10.50. Chapters on 34 separate aspects of bookstore operation by 28 experts. Free to members of the A.B.A. New edition in preparation under the editorship of Mr. Anderson to be published jointly by A.B.A. and Crown Publishers.

BACKGROUND PAPERS OF THE ONTARIO ROYAL COMMISSION ON BOOK PUBLISHING. *Queen's Printer and Publisher,* Ontario 1972 $5.00.

Bailey, Herbert S., Jr. THE ART AND SCIENCE OF BOOK PUBLISHING. *Harper* 1970 $7.95. A leading university press director's exposition and analysis of management procedure, techniques and computations in both general and scholarly book publishing.

Bernstein, Robert L., and others. BOOK PUBLISHING IN THE USSR. *Harvard Univ. Press* 1971 pap. $4.95. Reports of the delegations of U.S. book publishers visiting the Soviet Union in 1962 and 1970.

Bingley, Clive. THE BUSINESS OF BOOK PUBLISHING. *Pergamon* 1972 $9.50. Written in British terms but valuable as a description of the book publishing business everywhere in the English-speaking world.

Bohne, Harald, and Harald van Ierssel. PUBLISHING: The Creative Business. *Univ. of Toronto Press* 1973 pap. $3.50. The conduct of business procedures in book publishing.

BOWKER LECTURES ON BOOK PUBLISHING. *Bowker* 1957 $8.95. The first 17 in a series presented, 1935–1956, at N. Y. Public Library under Bowker Co. sponsorship in memory of Richard Rogers Bowker. Later lectures o.p. except "Publishing Then and Now" by Alfred A. Knopf (*N.Y. Public Lib.* 1965 pap. $1.25). After a lapse of several years the series was renewed in 1973, in cooperation with Columbia University School of Library Service, with a lecture by Harriet F. Pilpel on "Obscenity and the Law," available upon request from *Bowker.*

Charvat, William. THE PROFESSION OF AUTHORSHIP IN AMERICA. Ed. by Matthew J. Bruccoli. *Ohio State Univ. Press* 1967 $7.00. The published and previously unpublished papers of the late critic William Charvat, relating to his major theme: the working conditions of American authors as paid craftsmen.

Cheney, Orion Howard. ECONOMIC SURVEY OF THE BOOK INDUSTRY, 1930–31. *National Association of Book Publishers* (later American Book Publishers Council) 1932 1949 *Bowker* 1960 3rd printing. o.p. An acerbic diagnosis of the ills of the book trade, with plain-spoken prescriptions for cure; 3rd printing included analytical introd. by Robert W. Frase, with appendixes. Still referred to because much of its critical analysis remains applicable.

Colby, Jean Poindexter. WRITING, ILLUSTRATING AND EDITING CHILDREN'S BOOKS. *Hastings House* 1966 $7.95. Includes material helpful to artists, designers, production people as well as editors.

Dessauer, John P. BOOK PUBLISHING: What It Is, What It Does. *Bowker* 1974 (not priced). The various aspects of book publishing as seen by a financial consultant who has held line jobs and executive posts in the industry.

Emery, Edwin, and others, Eds. INTRODUCTION TO MASS COMMUNICATIONS. 4th ed. *Dodd* 1973 pap. $6.95. The role, backgrounds and current problems of mass communications industries with extensive description of each: newspapers, broadcasting, press associations, photography, film, magazines, books, advertising, public relations, research; also education for these fields.

Escarpit, Robert. THE BOOK REVOLUTION. *UNESCO* 1966 $3.50. Following by 10 years Ronald Barker's excellent, deeply informed "Books for All" (*UNESCO* 1956 o.p.), this is a more personal view of mass market paperback development; provocative, but based in part on observations in one French city.

Grannis, Chandler B., Ed. WHAT HAPPENS IN BOOK PUBLISHING. *Columbia* 1957 rev. ed. 1967 $10.00. Major functions and divisions of book publishing described by experts in the industry.

Gross, Gerald, Ed. EDITORS ON EDITING. *Grosset* Univ. Lib. 1962 $2.65. A selection of highly illuminating articles and essays by, among others: John Farrar, Ken McCormick, Bernard DeVoto, Edward Weeks, M. Lincoln Schuster, Harold Ross, Maxwell Perkins, George Stevens.

PUBLISHERS ON PUBLISHING. 1961. *Grosset* Univ. Lib. $2.95. Daniel Macmillan, Walter Hines Page, Henry Holt, Frank Nelson Doubleday, Sir Geoffrey Faber, J. Henry Harper, John Farrar, Alfred A. Knopf, M. Lincoln Schuster, Charles Scribner, Jr., and Bennett Cerf are some of the illustrious contributors to this fascinating volume.

Gross, Sidney, and Phyllis Steckler, Eds. HOW TO RUN A PAPERBACK BOOKSHOP. *Bowker* 1963 pap. $7.95

Harman, Eleanor T., Ed. PRESS NOTES FROM THE UNIVERSITY OF TORONTO PRESS. *Univ. of Toronto Press.* Vols. available: 1960, 1961, 1965, 1966, 1967, 1968, 1969, 1970 each $5.00. Notes and articles on the problems of scholarly publishing, along with activities of the Univ. of Toronto Press.

Hawes, Gene R. TO ADVANCE KNOWLEDGE: A Handbook on American University Press Publishing. *American Univ. Press Services* (1 Park Ave., N.Y.C. 10016) 1967 $5.00 pap. $1.95. Survey of the history and functioning of university presses, with attention to their day-to-day operation, accomplishment and accelerating expansion.

Henderson, Kathryn. TRENDS IN AMERICAN PUBLISHING. (Allerton Park Institutes No. 14) *Univ. of Illinois School of Library Science* 1968 $4.00

HOW TO PUBLISH, PROMOTE AND SELL YOUR BOOK. rev. ed. *Adams Press* 1971 pap. $2.00. Procedures for self-publication, avoiding entanglements with vanity presses.

Jennison, Peter S., and Robert H. Sheridan, Eds. THE FUTURE OF GENERAL ADULT BOOKS AND READING IN AMERICA. *American Lib. Assn.* 1970 $8.75. Report on a conference sponsored by ALA in 1969 to consider the conflicting pressures of society and the competing demands of many media.

Jovanovich, William. NOW, BARRABAS. 1964. *Harcourt* Harvest Bks. pap. $1.65. Essays on the book industry, the roles of the publisher, editor, author and others, by the head of Harcourt Brace Jovanovich.

Kerr, Chester. THE AMERICAN UNIVERSITY AS PUBLISHER: A Digest of a Report on American University Presses. 1949. *Univ. of Oklahoma Press* pap. $.50

Kujoth, Jean Spealman, Ed. BOOK PUBLISHING: Inside Views. *Scarecrow Press* 1971 $12.50. Anthology of 50 articles published in recent years, showing current concerns about the book industry.

MacCann, Donnarae, and Olga Richard. THE CHILD'S FIRST BOOKS: A Critical Study of Pictures and Texts. Ill. *Wilson* 1973 $10.00. Analysis of young children's picture and picture-story books, their conception and components, their effectiveness, and children's response to them.

MARKETING HANDBOOK FOR SCHOLARLY PUBLISHERS. *American Univ. Press Services* (1 Park Ave., N.Y.C. 10016). 1971–1973 Looseleaf in binder $50.00. Authorities in the university press field contribute detailed chapters covering every step in the marketing of scholarly books.

Minowa, Shigeo, Ed. CONFERENCE OF ASIAN SCHOLARLY PUBLISHERS. *Univ. of Tokyo Press* 1973 (dist. by Assn. of American Univ. Presses, 1 Park Ave., N.Y.C. 10016) sold with *Nickerson* (below) at $5.00. Papers and talks at a Tokyo conference, 1972, on problems of Asian publishers and relations with Western publishers.

Nickerson, Thomas, Ed. TRANS-PACIFIC SCHOLARLY PUBLISHING: A Symposium. *Univ. Press of Hawaii* 1963 pap. $4.50. Proceedings of a key conference among North American, Asian and Pacific scholarly publishers; forerunner of later developments.

Nemeyer, Carol A. SCHOLARLY REPRINT PUBLISHING IN THE UNITED STATES. *Bowker* 1972 $13.50. A thorough description and analysis of a major publishing phenomenon, now past its peak, but still an important segment of the industry.

PLANNING A SCHOOL BOOK FAIR. *Children's Book Council* (175 Fifth Ave., N.Y.C. 10010) pap. $2.00. Step-by-step in organizing and running book fairs in schools.

Reynolds, Paul R. A PROFESSIONAL GUIDE TO MARKETING MANUSCRIPTS. *The Writer* 1968 $6.95. How manuscripts find publishers.

SELLING CHILDREN'S BOOKS. *Children's Book Council* (175 Fifth Ave., N.Y.C. 10010) pap. $.50. Subtitled "Some Facts and Suggestions for New and Part-time Bookstore Personnel."

Smith, Datus C., Jr. A GUIDE TO BOOK-PUBLISHING. *Bowker* 1966 $8.50. A concise, very clearly written "how-it-is-done" book, with emphasis on fundamentals; includes problems of book trade practice in developing countries. Written "with the assistance and on behalf of the worldwide staff of Franklin Book Programs, Inc."

Smith, Roger H., Ed. THE AMERICAN READING PUBLIC: A Symposium. *Bowker* 1964 $9.75. A reprint, with additions, of the winter 1963 edition of *Daedalus*, Journal of the American Academy of Arts and Sciences. A study of the publishing industry and its relationship to the reading public, it includes 19 chapters, 6 not found in the magazine itself. Each is written by a noted publishing executive or representative of a related field.

Unwin, Sir Stanley. THE TRUTH ABOUT PUBLISHING. 1960 *Bowker* 7th ed. $3.25. A complete textbook of sound publishing practice by an outstanding English publisher whose opinions were strongly held and succinctly stated.

Wallick, Clair H. LOOKING FOR IDEAS: A Display Manual for Libraries and Booksellers. *Scarecrow Press* 1970 $5.00

THE WORLD OF TRANSLATION. *P.E.N. American Center* (156 Fifth Ave., N.Y.C. 10010) 1971 $4.00. Papers by 39 translators and writers at a conference on literary translations sponsored in 1970 by American P.E.N. Included are problems of literary translation involving languages other than the major European ones.

Best Sellers

Altick, Richard D. THE ENGLISH COMMON READER, 1800–1900: A Social History of the Mass Reading Public. *Univ. of Chicago Press* 1957 pap. $2.45. The subtitle describes the work.

Hackett, Alice Payne. SEVENTY YEARS OF BEST SELLERS, 1895–1965. *Bowker* 1968 $9.95. First published in 1945 as "Fifty Years of Best Sellers," revised in 1956 as "Sixty Years." The facts and figures about best-selling books in the United States from the beginning of authoritative lists in *The Bookman* down through the annual lists of *Publishers' Weekly*. Supplementary chapters tabulate the sales of 1,000,000 copies and over, and analyze the types of book which sell. There are separate lists of hardbound and paperback best sellers, bibliography of books and articles on best sellers, and other features, with title and author index.

Hart, James D. THE POPULAR BOOK: A History of America's Literary Taste. 1950. *Univ. of California Press* 1961 pap. $1.95

Mott, Frank Luther. GOLDEN MULTITUDES: The Story of Best Sellers in the United States. 1947. *Bowker* 1960 $10.95. A witty, urbane, thought-provoking study of best sellers from "The Bay Psalm Book" through "The Egg and I" (1662 to 1945).

Book Industry References

Here are some of the basic and most widely used reference materials needed by people who work in the industry. Bibliographies, however, are cited in Chapter 2, and books needed in editing, in Chapter 3. Anyone doing a specialized job has to have his or her own favorite guides close at hand; these would of course be too numerous and varied for this listing.

AB BOOKMAN'S YEARBOOK. *Antiquarian Bookman* Annual, $5.00; free with subscription to *AB Bookman's Weekly*. Annual review and forecast for bookmen in the new and out-of-print book trade.

AN ADVERTISER'S GUIDE TO SCHOLARLY PERIODICALS. Annual. *American Univ. Press Services* (1 Park Ave., N.Y.C. 10017) 1973–1974 ed., $35.00. The 1973–1974 edition lists over 1100 journals with full data desired by advertisers.

AMERICAN BOOK TRADE DIRECTORY. *Bowker.* rev. biennially. 21st ed., 1973–1974, ed. by Helaine MacKeigan. 1974 $40.00. Geographical listing, by state and locality, of more than 16,000 U.S. and Canadian book outlets, showing principal stock characteristics and specialties; also listings of book publishers and wholesalers of paperbacks, remainder dealers, other services; also imprints, and former publishing houses.

ANSI Standards Committee Z-39. AMERICAN NATIONAL STANDARD FOR COMPILING BOOK PUBLISHING STATISTICS. *American National Standards Institute* 1968 $2.25. Defines methods of recording and classifying statistics for a wide range of books and pamphlets published in the United States.

ASSOCIATION OF AMERICAN PUBLISHERS INDUSTRY STATISTICS. Comp. by John D. Dessauer. *Association of American Publishers* (not priced). Annual compilation of a great and increasing range of statistics about the income, costs, profits, distribution channels, and other data about all divisions of U.S. book publishing. Free to member houses; others must apply.

BOOK BUYER'S HANDBOOK 1973–1974. 27th ed. *American Booksellers Association.* Free to members, one copy each. Looseleaf, ABA staff-compiled, periodically updated directory of discounts, terms, returns policies, shipping arrangements, etc., of most publishers; also listings of wholesalers and other suppliers. Including list of reference materials, other data for the bookseller. Essential for store operation, valuable as data source.

CHILDREN'S BOOKS: Awards and Prizes. *Children's Book Council* (175 Fifth Ave., N.Y.C. 10010) 1973 pap. $2.95. More than 60 major children's book awards, with a brief history of each award and names of all its winners through 1972.

Henderson, Jeanne J., and Brenda G. Piggins. LITERARY AND LIBRARY PRIZES. *Bowker* 8th ed. 1973 $16.50. Facts on the history, conditions and rules of literary prizes, library awards, fellowships and grants in the U.S., Canada and Great Britain; also internationally important awards; winning authors and titles from establishment of an award to summer of 1973.

INDEX TRANSLATIONUM. *UNIPUB* (UNESCO) Annual, various prices. The international bibliography of translations from and to the principal languages, with breakdowns by nation, region, language, subject and other categories.

Kingman, Lee, Ed. NEWBERY AND CALDECOTT MEDAL BOOKS, 1956–1965. Ill. *Horn Bk.* 1965 $10.00. Acceptance speeches, biographies, descriptions, excerpts.

See also Bertha M. Miller

LITERARY MARKET PLACE WITH NAMES AND NUMBERS. 34th ed. 1974–1975 Annual *Bowker* $19.95. Names, departments, leading personnel of publishing houses, book clubs, wholesalers, manufacturers and suppliers, authors' and artists' agents, organizations; also print and broadcast media, reviewers, prizes, calendar of events, mergers; more than 17,000 of the 25,000 names are selected for an alphabet of addresses and telephone numbers in "Names and Numbers" section.

Miller, Bertha M., and Elinor W. Field, Eds. CALDECOTT MEDAL BOOKS, 1938–1957. Ill. *Horn Bk.* 1957 $10.00. Acceptance speeches, biographies of winners, descriptions of and excerpts from winning books.

NEWBERRY MEDAL BOOKS, 1922–1955. Ill. *Horn Bk.* 1955 $10.00. Acceptance speeches, biographies, descriptions, excerpts.

Peters, Jean R., Ed. A BOOKMAN'S GLOSSARY. *Bowker* 5th ed. 1974 (not priced). A dictionary of book industry terms, extensively revised to reflect recent changes in equipment and practice.

Stevenson, George A. GRAPHIC ARTS ENCYCLOPEDIA. *McGraw-Hill* $16.50. Extensive general reference.

UNESCO STATISTICAL YEARBOOK. *UNIPUB* (UNESCO) Annual, various prices; 1972 ed. $35.00. Prepared with help of national statistical services, National Commissions for UNESCO, U.N. Statistical Office and Population Div. Covers population, education, science, technology, libraries, museums, book title output, newspapers, periodicals, films, radio, television, cultural expenditures.

Trade and Professional Periodicals

Book trade and professional journals have become increasingly vital to the operations of the world of books, and more numerous with its expansion. Here the main ones are described, some general, some specialized.

Not listed are consumer media—the magazines and newspaper supplements that review books upon or after publication. Prepublication reviews are the province of the principal trade media and of several library periodicals. This list does not venture into the vast field of publications for the library world; but a handful of the dominant ones should be mentioned: The Bowker Company's *Library Journal* and *School Library Journal*, the College and Research Libraries' *Choice*, the American Library Association's *Booklist*— each of which reviews several thousand books and gives preview listings; also the H.W. Wilson Company's handsome *Wilson Library Bulletin* and the ALA's *American Libraries*, which, like the others just named, are full of significant professional articles.

Several of the professional and trade groups in the book world publish very informative newsletters and other materials for members and friends. Outstanding are the newsletters of the Association of American Publishers, Authors Guild, P.E.N., Children's Book Council, American Booksellers Association, Franklin Book Programs, Information Industry Association, and regional groups, especially in the West. Finally there are the business newsletters put out by *Knowledge Industry Publications, Inc.*, a private company (Tiffany Towers, P.O. Box 429 White Plains, N.Y. 10602).

AB BOOKMAN'S WEEKLY. *Antiquarian Bookman,* Weekly. $16.00 yr. Dealers' lists of out-of-print and used books wanted and for sale; specialist publishers' and dealers' ads and announcements; news, articles and reviews about the specialist and antiquarian book trade.

THE AMERICAN BOOK COLLECTOR. *American Bk. Collector, Inc.* (11434 S. Yale Ave., Arlington Hts., Ill. 60005). Bi-monthly. $7.50. Articles about collectors and collections, dealers, private presses; reviews of books of interest to collectors; bibliographical notes; sales reports.

BOOK PRODUCTION INDUSTRY. *Market Pubns. Inc.* (125 Elm St., New Canaan, Conn. 06840). Monthly. $10.00 yr. Selective distribution to business and production management people in book publishing design and manufacturing; also in commercial binding and looseleaf production.

BOOKSTORE JOURNAL. Official publication of the *Christian Booksellers Assn.* (2031 W. Cheyenne Rd., Colorado Springs, Colo. 80906). Monthly except Dec. Subscription based on annual sales volume. Articles about bookselling, ads, lists of books and promotions, reviews, best sellers, business news, inspirational pieces, all in the conservative Protestant Christian field.

THE COLLEGE STORE JOURNAL. *National Assn. of College Stores* (528 E. Lorain St. Oberlin, Ohio 44074). Six issues a yr. Members $3.00 per yr.; others $9.00. Covers operations of a college store, especially in bookselling; problems in the college retail field; concerns of the NACS.

KIRKUS REVIEWS. *The Kirkus Service* (60 W. 13 St., N.Y.C. 10011). Bi-monthly. Looseleaf reports. Subscription (apply). Prepublication reviews of adult and children's books, addressed to libraries and the book trade.

THE PUBLISHERS WEEKLY. *Bowker* $20.00 yr. The journal of the book industry since 1872; news, articles, statistics on all aspects of the book world; prepublication reviews of forthcoming books; seasonal lists; Weekly Record of all new U.S. books received.

RELIGIOUS BOOK REVIEW. (Box 296, Williston Park, N.Y. 11596) 5 issues a yr. $5.00. Reviews and previews of religious titles; notes and articles on matters concerning the religious book trade; ads, lists.

SCHOLARLY PUBLISHING: A Journal for Authors and Publishers. *Univ. of Toronto Press* Quarterly $10.00. Articles relating to publishing and authorship, especially university press and other scholarly publishing.

TARTAN BOOK NEWS. *Book News Pub., Inc.* (Box 921, Williamsport, Pa. 17701) (dist. by Bro-Dart, Inc.). Monthly. Free to retailers, literary buyers and others. Detailed annotated listings of forthcoming books arranged in useful categories; order lists, ads.

VISIBLE LANGUAGE. Dr. Merald E. Wrolstad. *Cleveland Museum of Art* (dist. by M.I.T. Press Journals Dept., 28 Charleton St., Cambridge, Mass. 02142). Quarterly. $11.00 to individuals; $16.00 a yr. to companies and institutions. Articles, often technical, on research in the visual media of language expression.

BOOKMAKING, PRINTING, TYPOGRAPHY: HISTORY AND BIOGRAPHY

As one of the titles listed here indicates, the history of the book goes back 5000 years or so; there seems to be no end to the fascination which the subject arouses—hence the length of this list. Letter forms alone stir compulsive interest; the study of manuscript hands and type designs gives rise to book after book. Printing as an art and as a practical necessity, the book as an art form and as a practical object—the two aspects of the study make it rich and endlessly delightful. Moreover, the field of books and printing has always been blessed with strong and colorful personalities, and their stories are among the most readable parts of the literature. It should be noted, too, that books in these categories are among those that especially appeal to collectors—a point to be kept in mind in consulting the sections later on in this chapter, on Book Collecting and Bibliophilia.

ART OF THE PRINTED BOOK 1455–1955: Masterpieces of Typography through Five Centuries from the Collections of the Pierpont Morgan Library New York. Essay by Joseph Blumenthal. Ill. *Pierpont Morgan Library* 1973 trade ed. (dist. by Godine) $20.00 pap. $11.00 from the library. The 9-x-12-inch pages display the 124 specimens generously, one to a page. The essay by the fine printer and typographer who arranged this much-acclaimed show is succinct but highly informative.

Ball, Johnson. WILLIAM CAXTON, 1693–1766. *Roundwood Press*, Kineton, England 1973 (dist. by Abner Schram) $25.00. Detailed, readable account of the great English letter-engraver and typefounder—his family, the forces that influenced his work, analysis of his designs, his effect on the printing arts. Almost 100 plates and figures.

Barker, Nicolas. STANLEY MORISON. *Harvard Univ. Press* 1972 $17.50. Morison (died 1967) was without question the greatest influence in the mid-20th century on type and typography; he was also a man of widely versatile interests. This massive biography has been called "definitive," and it probably is.

Bennett, Paul A. ELMER ADLER IN THE WORLD OF BOOKS. *Grolier Club* (dist. by Univ. Press of Virginia $6.00; Princeton Univ. Library 1964 $5.00). Memoir of the man who founded the fine press, Pynson Printers, conducted a graphic arts center at Princeton, and established today's Casa del Libro in San Juan, Puerto Rico.

POSTSCRIPTS ON DWIGGINS. *The Typophiles* (140 Lincoln Rd., Brooklyn, N. Y. 11225) 1960 2 vols. boxed $12.50. Essays and recollections by 15 friends of the important designer of books and type; specimens of the artist's work; appreciations of his colorful personality; selective checklist of his writings.

Berry, W. Turner, and H. E. Poole. ANNALS OF PRINTING: A CHRONOLOGICAL ENCYCLOPEDIA. *Univ. of Toronto Press* 1967 $16.50

Blades, William. THE LIFE AND TYPOGRAPHY OF WILLIAM CAXTON, ENGLAND'S FIRST PRINTER. 1861–1863. *Burt Franklin* 2 vols. $37.50. Long considered "the standard life."

Boyd, Beverly. CHAUCER AND THE MEDIEVAL BOOK. *The Huntington Library* 1973 $10.00. An introduction to those aspects of Chaucer studies which involve manuscripts and incunabula.

Brady, Elizabeth A. ERIC GILL: Twentieth Century Book Designer. *Scarecrow Press* rev. ed. 1974 $5.00. The English artist died in 1940, but his design output, this analysis shows, is significant for the later as well as the newer technology.

Carter, John, and Percy Muir, Eds. PRINTING AND THE MIND OF MAN. *Cassell*, London. (dist. by Holt) 1967 $27.50. Each of the key books exhibited in the IPEX exposition, London, 1963 is the subject of a critical and historical comment. Introd. by Denys Hay on the significance of printing.

Catich, Edward M. THE ORIGIN OF THE SERIF. Ill. *Catfish Press* (St. Ambrose College, Davenport, Iowa 52803). 1968 $24.00. Specialized, to be sure, but a landmark study. In this handsome book, Father Catich argues from his examinations of Trajan's column in Rome that serifs were born of the brush, not the chisel.

Chappell, Warren. A SHORT HISTORY OF THE PRINTED WORD. Ill. *Knopf* 1970 $12.50. A master illustrator, designer and teacher who is also a lively writer presents the art and process of printing from the earliest formation of letters to the use of 20th-century technology.

Clair, Colin. A CHRONOLOGY OF PRINTING. *Praeger* 1969 $12.50. A year-by-year record of important events, A.D. 105–1967, in printing: inventions, publications, birth dates of people and enterprises.

A HISTORY OF PRINTING IN BRITAIN. Ill. *Oxford* 1966 $10.00. A general history of the subject, strong on technical developments up through the 19th century, with a sketch of 20th-century changes.

THE SPREAD OF PRINTING: A History of Printing Outside Europe in Monographs. *Vangendt & Co.*, Amsterdam (dist. by Abner Schram) 1971–73, 21 monographs each $9.75 (except "South Africa," $18.00). Paperbound historical studies, illustrated from book title pages and other sources. Titles include "Early Printing in Canada" by H. Pearson Gundy; ". . . South Africa" by Anne Smith, $18.00; ". . . the Caribbean Area" by Bradford F. Swan; ". . . Malta" by Colin Clair; ". . . Greenland" by Knud Oldendow; ". . . Indonesia" by H. J. de Graaf; ". . . New Zealand" by Fiona Macmillan; ". . . Mauritius, Madagascar and the Seychelles" by Auguste Tousaint; ". . . India, Pakistan, Burma and Ceylon" by Dennis E. Rhodes; ". . . Australia" by D. H. Borchardt; ". . . Iceland" by Benedikt E. Benediktz. Announced or in preparation: monographs on early printing in the U.S.A. by James M. Wells; Portuguese Overseas Provinces; French Overseas Areas; Spanish Colonial Printing; Missionary Printing in the Far East.

Cobden-Sanderson, Thomas J. JOURNALS: 1879–1922. Together with THE IDEAL BOOK OR THE BOOK BEAUTIFUL: A Tract on Calligraphy, Painting and Illustration and on the Book Beautiful as a Whole. *Burt Franklin* 2 vols. 1901–1926 $35.00. The ideas and work of the printer and binder of the Doves Press, collaborator with Sir Emery Walker.

Dal, Erik. SCANDINAVIAN BOOKMAKING IN THE TWENTIETH CENTURY. Ill. *Univ. of Illinois Press* 1968 $6.50. Scandinavian book design has been less well-known in the U.S. than British and Germanic.

THEODORE LOW DE VINNE. Ill. *The Typophiles* (140 Lincoln Rd., Brooklyn, N. Y. 11225) 1968 2 vols. $20.00. Articles by and about an American printer, scholar and teacher of graphic arts who was important in the 40 years after the Civil War.

Diringer, David. THE ILLUMINATED BOOK: Its History and Production. Ill. *Praeger* rev. ed. 1967 o.p. in the U.S. A monumental work, awesome in its detailed accounting of the known illuminated manuscripts, country by country and era by era, with hundreds of fine halftone illustrations. A scholar in the history of writing, Dr. Diringer analyzes calligraphic development, artists and their schools, and the influences in the evolution of the book.

Fairbank, Alfred. A BOOK OF SCRIPTS. *Penguin* 1949 rev. enl. ed. 1968 pap. $1.95. Showings of the great scripts, classic and modern, with commentary by the distinguished British calligrapher; a book much used by teachers of letter formation.

THE STORY OF HANDWRITING: Origins and Development. Ill. *Watson-Guptill* 1970 $7.95. Concise, instructional review by the top British authority.

Grannis, Chandler B., Ed. HERITAGE OF THE GRAPHIC ARTS. Ill. *Bowker* 1972 $18.75. A selection of 22 of the lectures arranged in New York by Dr. Robert L. Leslie on leaders in the graphic arts and bookmaking. Subjects include Goudy, the Grabhorns, William Morris, Gill, Morison; speakers include Hermann Zapf, John Dreyfus, Paul A. Bennett, Beatrice Warde.

Hunter, Dard. PAPERMAKING: The History and Technique of an Ancient Craft. Ill. *Knopf* 2nd ed. 1947 $20.00. The author studied papermaking throughout the world and founded the Paper Museum at M.I.T.

PAPERMAKING THROUGH EIGHTEEN CENTURIES. Ill. 1930. *Burt Franklin* 1970 $19.50. A standard work by a top American authority, one who was a practitioner of the art of hand papermaking.

Hussein, Mohammed A. ORIGINS OF THE BOOK: From Papyrus to Codex. Ill. *Edition Leipzig* 1970 *N.Y. Graphic Soc.* 1972 $16.50. Broad, extensively illustrated survey of the development of the book and the innovations that determined each stage.

Lehmann-Haupt, Hellmut, Ed. BOOKBINDING IN AMERICA. 1941. *Bowker* rev. ed. 1967 $12.75. Three essays: "Early American Bookbinding" by Hannah Dustin French; "The Rise of American Edition Binding" by Joseph W. Rogers; "On the Rebinding of Old Books" by Hellmut Lehmann-Haupt.

THE GÖTTINGEN MODEL BOOK. Ill. *Univ. of Missouri Press* 1972 $25.00. The eminent historian of the book edits, with translation and commentary, a 15th-century manuscript book giving patterns and models of decorations for use by illuminators; all reproduced in full color.

GUTENBERG AND THE MASTER OF THE PLAYING CARDS. *Yale Univ. Press.* 1967 o.p. A most interesting speculation, with illustrative evidence, about a decorative printing experiment which Gutenberg may have pursued.

Lewis, John. THE TWENTIETH CENTURY: Its Illustration and Design. Ill. *Van Nostrand-Reinhold* 1967 $25.00. The 460-plus illustrations are grouped after the relevant paragraphs of discussion. A basic work.

McLean, Ruari. MODERN BOOK DESIGN. Ill. *Oxford* 1959 $3.40. The range is from William Morris and his work in the late 19th century to design of the late 1950s.

VICTORIAN BOOK DESIGN AND COLOUR PRINTING. Ill. *Univ. of California Press* 2nd ed. 1972 $40.00. The flowering of book illustration in Britain, 1830–1880.

McMurtrie, Douglas C. THE BOOK: The Story of Printing and Bookmaking. *Oxford* 3rd ed. 1943 $17.50. The romantic story of printing and bookmaking from primitive human records to modern methods.

A HISTORY OF PRINTING IN THE UNITED STATES. Vol. 2 (only vol. published) 1936. *Burt Franklin* $25.00. The pioneer period of printing in the Atlantic Coast states, Delaware to Georgia.

Meynell, Francis, and Herbert Simon, Eds. THE FLEURON ANTHOLOGY. *Univ. of Toronto Press* 1973 $45.00. Facsimiles from the journal in book form which the two editors issued from 1923 to 1930, presenting scholarly views of books and graphic arts of that era, the past and the future.

Moran, James. STANLEY MORISON: His Typographic Achievement. Ill. *Hastings House* 1971 $18.50. A leading British historian of printing mixes admiration and sharp criticism in this analysis of Morison's life and work; includes a brilliant capsule history of printing processes: many full-size reproductions of designs and pages.

Morison, Stanley. LETTER FORMS, TYPOGRAPHIC AND SCRIPTORIAL. Introd. by John Dreyfus. Ill. *The Typophiles* (140 Lincoln Rd. Brooklyn, N.Y. 11225) 1968 $10.00. Two essays on classification, history and bibliography of letter forms, with an added biographical essay.

A TALLY OF TYPES: With Additions by Several Hands Edited by Brooke Crutchley. 1953. Introd. rev. and amplified by M. K. Handover. *Cambridge* 1973 $14.95 pap. $5.95. A historical, critical and functional account of the types cut by the Monotype Corporation under Morison's direction of its typographic revival program in the early 1920s and 1930s.

(With Kenneth Day) THE TYPOGRAPHIC BOOK, 1450–1935: A Study of Fine Typography through Five Centuries Exhibited in Upwards of Three Hundred and Fifty Title and Text Pages Drawn from Presses Working in the European Tradition. Ed. by Roger W. Shugg. *Univ. of Chicago Press* 1964 $30.00

Moxon, Joseph. MECHANICK EXERCISES ON THE WHOLE ART OF PRINTING. Ed. by Herbert Davis and Harry Carter. Ill. *Oxford* 2nd ed. 1962 o.p. in the U.S. A modern edition of the first—and very thorough—technical book on printing (1683), with scholarly introduction and notes, and extensive illustrations and specimens.

Nixon, Howard M. SIXTEENTH-CENTURY GOLD-TOOLED BOOKBINDINGS IN THE PIERPONT MORGAN LIBRARY. Ill. with photos of the bindings. *Pierpont Morgan Lib.* 1971 $25.00 pap. $15.00. 72 bindings, with photos.

Ogg, Oscar. THE 26 LETTERS. Ill. *T. Y. Crowell.* 1948 rev. ed. 1971 $6.95. Lavishly and delightfully illustrated by the author with line drawings and letterforms (in a second color), and written with spirit and humor, this handy book by the late art director of the Book-of-the-Month Club relates the origins of calligraphy and lettering, development of the roman alphabet, and the progress of printing.

Oswald, John Clyde. PRINTING IN THE AMERICAS. Ill. 1937. *Hacker Art Books* 1968 $10.00; *Kennikat* $12.50. In 91 chapters, Mr. Oswald recounts the introduction of printing into the countries and states of North, South and Central America and the West Indies.

Rogers, Bruce. A HODGE-PODGE OF THE LETTERS, PAPERS AND ADDRESSES WRITTEN DURING THE LAST SIXTY YEARS. 1953. *Bks. for Libraries* $9.75. Statements, formal and informal, by the graphic artist who led the modern movement for excellence in the design of ordinary as well as "fine" books.

Spell, Lota M. PIONEER PRINTER: Samuel Bangs in Mexico and Texas. *Univ. of Texas Press* 1963 $7.50; pap. $2.25. The activities of the first man known to have operated as a printer in the territory which is now the state of Texas; also a lively picture of Mexico's interior in the 1820s.

Steinberg, S. H. FIVE HUNDRED YEARS OF PRINTING. Ill. 1959. *Penguin* Pelican Bks. pap. $2.50. Covers bookmaking, publishing and the various backgrounds of books with useful illustrations.

Straus, Ralph. JOHN BASKERVILLE. Ill. 1907. *Burt Franklin* $16.50. Long recognized as the basic documented account of the 18th-century English type designer and printer.

Thomas, Isaiah. DIARY OF 1805–1828. 1909. *Johnson Reprint* 2 vols. each $20.00. Source material on the pioneer American publisher and book trade leader.

THE HISTORY OF PRINTING IN AMERICA. Ill. 1810. *Burt Franklin* 2 vols $42.50. The versatile American revolutionary printer-publisher (1749–1831) was also a scholar and bibliographer, and this work is still consulted on the early history of typography in America.

THREE CLASSICS OF ITALIAN CALLIGRAPHY: Arrighi, Tagliente, Palatino. Introd. by Oscar Ogg. 1953. *Dover* pap. $2.75; *Peter Smith* $5.00. Reprint of the writing specimen books of three 16th-century Italian masters who have influenced writing and type design ever since.

Ullman, Berthold Louis. ANCIENT WRITING AND ITS INFLUENCE. 1932. Introd. by Julian Brown. *M.I.T. Press* 1969 pap. $2.45; *Cooper* $3.50. Origins and development of writing and lettering in the Western world.

Updike, Daniel Berkeley. PRINTING TYPES: Their History, Forms and Use—A Study in Survivals. *Harvard Univ. Press* 3rd ed. 1951 2 vols. set $18.00. A monumental and authoritative work on the history and use of types; by the founder and director of the Merrymount Press, Boston.

(With Julian P. Smith). NOTES ON THE MERRYMOUNT PRESS AND ITS WORK. Ill. 1934. *Milford House* $25.00. The work of a leading exponent of excellence in printing in the U.S.A.

Vervliet, Hendrik D. L., Ed. THE BOOK THROUGH FIVE THOUSAND YEARS. Ill. *Phaidon* (dist. by Praeger) 1972 $60.00. Physically too bulky (heavy paper) but handsomely printed, a brilliantly and relevantly illustrated survey by 28 authorities, each on a special aspect of the history; major emphasis on the period before printing.

Warde, Beatrice. THE CRYSTAL GOBLET: Sixteen Essays on Typography. Sel. and ed. by Henry Jacob. *World Pub.* 1956 o.p. Writings by the promotion director of the Monotype Corporation, authority on typography and book design, who preached: "Printing should be invisible."

Warde, Frederic. BRUCE ROGERS, DESIGNER OF BOOKS, and Irving Haas's BRUCE ROGERS, A BIBLIOGRAPHY. 1926 1936 *Kennikat* 1972 $7.00. A reprint of two of the principal works about 20th-century American designers.

White, Jan V. EDITING BY DESIGN. Ill. *Bowker* 1974 $17.50. Subtitled "Word-and-Picture Communication for Editors and Designers," this volume provides a great variety of solutions to graphic problems encountered in all sorts of publications. Flexibility and ingenuity are stressed; lavishly illustrated.

Winship, George Parker. GUTENBERG TO PLANTIN: An Outline of the Early History of Printing. 1926. *Burt Franklin* 1968 $13.50. This overview by a distinguished scholar relates to the period 1450–1600 in Europe.

Winterich, John T. EARLY AMERICAN BOOKS AND PRINTING. 1935. *Gale* $12.00; *McGrath* $15.00. Few writers about books, printing and the book trade will ever match "Wint's" gusto for his subject, his deft grasp of the illuminating fact, his capacity to recount history with brevity and wit.

Wroth, Lawrence C. THE COLONIAL PRINTER. Ill. *Grolier Club* 1931. *Univ. Press of Virginia* 1964 $5.50 pap. $2.75. The beginnings of printing and publishing in America, including accounts of presses, typefounding, ink, paper, binding, employment and economic conditions, content and physical nature of products.

BOOKMAKING, PRINTING, TYPOGRAPHY: PROCEDURES AND PRACTICE

These titles are merely representative of classic works and outstanding current ones that are now in print (and at least one that appears to be out-of-print but shouldn't be). The literature of instructional material for the student and practitioner in the printing industries is too vast, and in scores of instances, too specialized, for this list; but printing school libraries, "Books in Print" and other obvious sources can supply the names.

Bennett, Paul A., Ed. BOOKS AND PRINTING: A Treasury for Typophiles. 1951. *Peter Smith* $4.50. A collection of distinguished discussions on the art and craft of bookmaking.

THE BOOK SHOWCASE CATALOG. Ill. *Children's Book Council.* Annual. 1972–73 $3.95; 1973–74 $4.95. Detailed listings, with specimen pages, of books cited in the Council's annual shows of excellence in children's book graphics and production.

Dair, Carl. DESIGN WITH TYPE. Ill. *Univ. of Toronto Press* 1967 $8.50. One of the finest typographic designers in North America, a man who died at the height of his career, this Canadian presented his working principles in a concise, comprehensive book. Classic taste and craftsmanship are combined with fully contemporary applications.

Goudy, Frederic W. THE ALPHABET and ELEMENTS OF LETTERING. 1918 1922. *Dover* 2 vols. in 1 pap. $2.25; *Peter Smith* $4.75. By the famous typographer and type designer.

Hamilton, Edward A. GRAPHIC DESIGN FOR THE COMPUTER AGE. Ill. *Van Nostrand-Reinhold* 1970 $19.50. Written and designed by a long-time art director (Time-Life Books, etc.), this work presents theory and practice and shows the use of the computer as a tool for graphics.

Lawson, Alexander S. PRINTING TYPES: An Introduction. Ill. *Beacon Press* 1971 $9.95. Derived from the author's course at Rochester Institute of Technology, this is an excellent guide to type recognition and the elements of letters; unusually fine reproduction of specimens; takes into account the new techniques in letter production and composition.

Lee, Marshall. BOOKMAKING: The Illustrated Guide to Design and Production. *Bowker* 1965 $14.00. An easy-to-use American treatment which is really a reference work as well as a textbook.

McLean, Ruari. MAGAZINE DESIGN. Ill. *Oxford* 1969 $22.50. By one of Britain's top graphic designers.

Melcher, Daniel, and Nancy Larrick. PRINTING AND PROMOTION HANDBOOK. *Mc-Graw-Hill* 3rd ed. 1966. $15.95. How to plan, produce and use printing, marketing and direct mail.

Morison, Stanley. FIRST PRINCIPLES OF TYPOGRAPHY. *Cambridge* 1951 pap. $1.75. The basics of classic typography; severely practical, centered upon the criteria of legibility, good proportions and unobtrusive good taste.

Nesbitt, Alexander. DECORATIVE INITIALS AND ALPHABETS. Ill. 1959. *Dover* pap. $2.75; *Peter Smith* $5.00. Sources for designers, by a prominent practitioner and teacher.

THE HISTORY AND TECHNIQUE OF LETTERING. Ill. 1952. *Dover* pap. $2.50; *Peter Smith* $4.50. The original title was "Lettering: The History and Technique of Lettering and Design."

TWO HUNDRED DECORATIVE TITLE PAGES. Ill. 1964. *Dover* pap. $3.50; *Peter Smith* $5.50. Sources and ideas for the designer, assembled by Nesbitt.

THE PENROSE ANNUAL Ed. by Herbert Spencer. Annual. *Hastings House* various prices; no. 66, 1973, $22.50. The international annual survey of the graphic arts is produced by Lund Humphries in Great Britain and presents important summary articles, well illustrated, often with color inserts on latest developments in technology, design and backgrounds in the graphic arts.

Strauss, Victor. THE PRINTING INDUSTRY: An Introduction to Its Many Branches, Processes and Products. *Bowker* (in assoc. with the Printing Industries of America, Inc.) 1967 $29.75. An encyclopedic handbook (800 pages) on composition, full-color reproduction, presswork, paper, ink, binding, art and copy preparation; includes magazine and newspaper production. Each section was reviewed by an expert.

Tschichold, Jan. ASSYMETRIC TYPOGRAPHY. Ill. *Van Nostrand-Reinhold* 1967 $7.50. As a young man, this distinguished German (now Swiss) typographer was a fervent advocate of "modern" typography; this was his statement of the case, recently issued in English.

TREASURY OF ALPHABETS AND LETTERING. Ill. *Van Nostrand-Reinhold* 1966 $17.50. This tall, eminently practical volume is meant as a handbook for all who work with type and letters. It contains precise expositions of what is good and bad lettering, what constitutes good proportions for various purposes, what the different letter forms of the past and present are; 150 complete alphabets.

Williamson, Hugh. METHODS OF BOOK DESIGN: The Practice of an Industrial Craft. *Oxford* 1956 2nd ed. 1966 $12.00. This handsome, extensively detailed volume is a thorough handbook for all who are concerned in any way with the quality of the book.

Wilson, Adrian. THE DESIGN OF BOOKS. *Van Nostrand-Reinhold* 1967 o.p. History, artistic development and current practice are combined by an outstanding designer in a concise, heavily illustrated, handsome book, regretably o.p.

Wooldridge, Dennis, LETTER ASSEMBLY IN PRINTING. *Hastings House* 1974 $17.50. The new technical revolution as it is applied in printing: copy preparation, typesetting, keyboarding, tape control, computer and film systems, page makeup, imposition, planning.

Zapf, Hermann. ABOUT ALPHABETS: Some Marginal Notes on Type Design. Ill. with introd. by Paul Standard. 1960. *M.I.T. Press* 1970 $2.95. Specimens and extensive commentary by the leading contemporary designer of letters.

MANUALE TYPOGRAPHICUM. Ill. *M.I.T. Press* 1954 $18.50 pap. (greatly reduced format) $5.95. 100 typographic pages with quotations on types and printing, in designs by the famous German typographer.

TYPOGRAPHISCHE VARIATIONEN. Ill. *Museum Books* 1963 $35.00. The original German edition of "Typographic Variations Designed by Hermann Zapf on Themes in Contemporary Book Design and Typography" with 78 text and title page designs. In every way identical with the English edition (o.p.) except cover and title page.

Book Illustration

Only the merest sampling of books related to book illustration is possible here. A rich mine of other related books may be found in the literature of the graphic arts, including printmaking and the history of the book; also in the biographies of illustrators and of artists whose work includes book illustration—artists from Dürer to Frederic Remington to Picasso, and from Howard Pyle to Leonard Baskin.

Bland, David. A HISTORY OF BOOK ILLUSTRATION. Ill. *Univ. of California Press* 2nd ed. 1969 $28.75. A thorough account ranging from the illuminated manuscript and early printing to the 20th-century book in North America, Europe and the Orient.

Heller, Jules. PRINTMAKING TODAY. Ill. *Holt* 2nd ed. 1972 $12.95. There is an abundance of current books on prints and printmaking; this is one of the most generally informative and relevant in connection with book illustration.

ILLUSTRATORS OF CHILDREN'S BOOKS. *Horn Bk.* Three books about children's book artists over the past 200-odd years, all extensively illustrated with reproductions, and containing articles by contemporary authorities on techniques, history and role of children's book illustration, with biographies of artists, authors and books on the subject; indexes.

ILLUSTRATORS OF CHILDREN'S BOOKS, 1744–1945. Comp. by Bertha E. Mahony, Louise Payson Latimer and Buelah Folsbee. 1947 $20.00

ILLUSTRATORS OF CHILDREN'S BOOKS, 1946–1956. Comp. by Ruth Hill Viguers, Marcia Dalphin and Bertha Mahony Miller. 1958 $20.00

ILLUSTRATORS OF CHILDREN'S BOOKS, 1957–1966. Comp. by Lee Kingman, Joanna Foster and Ruth Giles Lontoft. 1968 $20.00

Klemin, Diana. THE ILLUSTRATED BOOK: Its Art and Craft. Ill. *Clarkson N. Potter* 1970 $10.00. A survey of the work of 74 book artists, with examples and commentary; 82 illus., eight in full color; by a distinguished designer of books.

THE ART OF ART FOR CHILDREN'S BOOKS. Ill. *Clarkson N. Potter* 1966 $6.95. Picture pages or spreads from more than 60 contemporary books for children are shown, with concise comments on how the artist has illuminated the text.

Kunzle, David. THE EARLY COMIC STRIP. *Univ. of California Press* 1974 $35.00. The subtitle explains this work on popular illustration: "Narrative Strips and Picture Stories in the European Broadsheet from c. 1450 to 1825."

Muir, Percy. VICTORIAN ILLUSTRATED BOOKS. Ill. *Praeger* 1971 $20.00

Reed, Walt, Ed. THE ILLUSTRATOR IN AMERICA, 1900–1960. *Van Nostrand-Reinhold* o.p. 300 brief biographies with one to four examples of the work of each.

Twyman, Michael. LITHOGRAPHY 1800–1850. Ill. *Oxford* 1970 $20.50. Dr. Twyman, a leading English historian of printing, describes (as his subtitle says) "The Techniques of Drawing on Stone in England and France and Their Application to Works of Typography."

Wakeman, Geoffrey. VICTORIAN BOOK ILLUSTRATION. Ill. *Gale* 1973 $12.50. How the development of new printing processes continuously and profoundly changed book illustration throughout the 19th century.

COPYRIGHT

Named here are a few useful books on a complicated subject—a list mainly for general purposes. All sources will undoubtedly be affected by some important possible changes that loom as this edition of *"The Reader's Adviser"* goes to press: changes resulting from recent revisions, for example, in the Universal Copyright Convention; from Soviet copyright policy; from shifting attitudes towards copyright among some developing countries abroad and some members of academic professions in the U.S.A.; from domestic court decisions; and above all from the expected passage of a long-awaited revision of the United States Copyright Law.

Bogsch, Arpad L., Ed. COPYRIGHT LAWS AND TREATIES OF THE WORLD. Comp. by UNESCO and United Int. Bureaux for the Protection of Intellectual Property. *UNESCO* and *Bureau of International Affairs* 1956 2 vols. looseleaf including binders and all supplements $250.00. Suppls. 1–13, 1957–69, available only to purchasers of the basic compilation. Suppl. 14, 1970 $44.00; suppl. 15, 1971 $60.00; suppl. 16, 1972 $50.00. Compilation of domestic and international laws, treaties, etc. UNESCO also issues *Copyright Bulletin*, a quarterly in English, French and Spanish, $3.00. Further information from *UNIPUB, Inc.* (UNESCO Publications Center, Box 433, N.Y.C. 10016).

THE LAW OF COPYRIGHT UNDER THE UNIVERSAL CONVENTION. *Sijthoff,* Leyden, in association with *Bowker* 3rd ed. 1969 $27.50. Complete analysis and commentary on the text of the Universal Copyright Convention; copyright protection in each country; types of works protected; procedures.

Kent, Allen, Ed. COPYRIGHT: Current Viewpoints on History, Laws, Legislation. *Bowker* 1972 $12.75. Articles by 10 leading lawyers and other authorities on aspects of copyright.

Nicholson, Margaret. A MANUAL OF COPYRIGHT PRACTICE FOR WRITERS, PUBLISHERS AND AGENTS. *Oxford* 2nd ed. 1956 $7.50. Standard general work by an authority on rights and permissions.

Patterson, Lyman Ray. COPYRIGHT IN HISTORICAL PERSPECTIVE. *Vanderbilt Univ. Press*
1968 $8.50. The historical background for copyright protection, with landmark stat-
utes and decisions, from its origins 400 years ago.

Pilpel, Harriet F., and Morton D. Goldberg. A COPYRIGHT GUIDE. *Bowker* 4th ed. 1969
pap. $5.50. Answers to 93 "most asked" questions, for practical use by the layman.
Mrs. Pilpel is an attorney noted in the fields of literary property and civil liberties.

Rogers, Joseph W. U.S. NATIONAL BIBLIOGRAPHY AND THE COPYRIGHT LAW: An Historical Study. *Bowker* 1960 $5.25. Background of major U.S. bibliographies, history
of copyright law.

Wincor, Richard. LITERARY PROPERTY. *Clarkson N. Potter* 1967 $5.00. A layman's
guide to business practice in the communications industry.

Wittenberg, Philip. PROTECTION OF LITERARY PROPERTY. *The Writer* 1968 $7.95. By
the author of the widely used "The Law of Literary Property," 1957, 1964.

CENSORSHIP AND THE FREEDOM TO READ

The last word is never said about censorship, nor is the necessity of the freedom to read
ever sufficiently emphasized. The books named here cover the subject in fairly comprehensive, though often detailed terms; more specialized studies may be found in "Subject
Guide to Books in Print."

One thing evident to any reader is that the censorship picture is subject to drastic
change. For example, since the previous edition of *"The Reader's Adviser"* was published, the U.S. Supreme Court has sharply changed, in a 5 to 4 vote, its guidelines on
what is censorable. By introducing the concept that "community standards"—without
definition of "community"—should rule, and by relaxing the test that a work, to be censored, must be "utterly without redeeming social value," the Court has brought new confusions into the situation. New censorship legislation is being presented or adopted in
many states. Defenders of free expression fear that not only publishers, but individual authors, local librarians and booksellers may suffer the brunt of such legislation. Above all,
it is feared that repressive legislation will bring about increasing self-censorship by
writers, publishers, and purveyors of books who cannot bear the costs of defense.

Perhaps, when the next edition of this reference book is published, the freedom to read
will be more firmly assured. But without constant vigilance it will not remain so.

Adams, Michael. CENSORSHIP: THE IRISH EXPERIENCE. *Univ. of Alabama Press* 1968
$6.50. Now greatly mitigated, Irish literary censorship was a scandal to the world of
letters for many years.

American Library Association. FREEDOM OF INQUIRY: Supporting the Library Bill of
Rights. *American Lib. Assn.* 1965 pap. $1.75. The Library Bill of Rights is a major
American statement, and a practical tool in the defense of freedom. Akin to it is "The
Freedom to Read," issued jointly by ALA and the Assn. of American Publishers,
(rev. ed. 1973. A broadside $.10).

Cirino, Robert. DON'T BLAME THE PEOPLE. *Random* 1972 $8.95. The subtitle expresses
the point of view, a challenge to some conventional liberal attitudes: "How the
News Media Use Bias, Distortion and Censorship to Manipulate Public Opinion."

Clor, Harry M. OBSCENITY AND PUBLIC MORALITY. *Univ. of Chicago Press* 1969 $9.50.
An examination of censorship in "a liberal society."

de Grazia, Edward, Ed. CENSORSHIP LANDMARKS. *Bowker* 1969 $22.50. A civil liberties lawyer compiles precedent-setting court decisions and important dissenting opinions.

Downs, Robert B., Ed. THE FIRST FREEDOM: Liberty and Justice in the World of Books. *American Lib. Assn.* 1960 $8.50. Valuable materials assembled in one volume.

Ernst, Morris L., and Alan U. Schwartz. CENSORSHIP. *Macmillan* 1964 $6.95. One of a series of books for the layman on broad aspects of the law, edited by Mr. Ernst, an outstanding civil liberties lawyer of the FDR era and after.

FREEDOM OF THE PRESS. Vol. I, From Zenger to Jefferson, ed. by Leonard W. Levy; Vol. 2, From Hamilton to the Warren Court, ed. by Harold L. Nelson. *Bobbs* 1967 2 vols. each $7.50; pap. $3.75. A comprehensive anthology of primary documents of the freedom-of-the-press concept throughout American history.

Haight, Anne Lyon. BANNED BOOKS. *Bowker* 3rd ed. 1970 $9.75. Facts about the important books in the history of censorship from Homer to the present, and about current trends.

Hughes, Douglas A., Ed. PERSPECTIVES ON PORNOGRAPHY. *St. Martin's* 1970 $5.95. Views quoted from 14 writers—Alberto Moravia, Susan Sontag, Paul Goodman, Kenneth Tynan, Ernest van den Haag among them.

McClellan, Grant S. CENSORSHIP IN THE UNITED STATES. *Wilson* 1967 $3.50. A concise, comprehensive review in the publisher's Reference Shelf Series.

Milton, John AREOPAGETICA. Various eds., e.g. the ed. with commentary by Richard C. Jebb (1918. *AMS Press* 1972 $6.50), or the ed. by George M. Sabine (with "Of Education" *AHM Pub. Corp.* Crofts Class. pap. $.85); *see under Milton in "The Reader's Adviser," Chapter 5, British Poetry: Early to Romantic, for other editions and anthologies*. In 1644, outraged by a licensing law that meant censorship, Milton published this speech addressed to Parliament "for the Liberty of Unlicensed Printing." To this eloquent statement defenders of free expression have turned ever since for the articulation of their principles and supporting arguments.

Moon, Eric, Ed. BOOK SELECTION AND CENSORSHIP IN THE SIXTIES. Introds. by editor and Ervin Gaines. *Bowker* 1969 $12.50. 55 articles from *Library Journal*.

Rembar, Charles. THE END OF OBSCENITY. *Random* 1968 $10.95; *Simon & Schuster* 1970 pap. $3.95. The trials of "Lady Chatterley," "Tropic of Cancer" and "Fanny Hill" by the lawyer who defended them, and who tells the story with style, gusto and legal learning. Introd. by Norman Mailer.

REPORT OF THE COMMISSION ON OBSCENITY AND PORNOGRAPHY. 1970. *Bantam* pap. $1.65. Report (including minority statements) of the National Commission established by Congress to analyze law relating to obscenity and pornography, study methods of distributing alleged obscene material, study its effects on the public including minors, and its relation to crime, and recommend legislation or other action. Majority report rejected by Pres. Nixon without reading it.

THE SUPREME COURT OBSCENITY DECISIONS. *Greenleaf Classics* 1973 $2.25. Complete text of the decisions announced June 21, 1973, which threw the American censorship picture into confusion and led to a national wave of proposed repressive legislation. Included are texts of the dissenting opinions and a rehearing petition. Commentary by Stanley Fleischman, constitutional lawyer.

Widmer, Eleanor, Ed. FREEDOM AND LETTERS: Literary Censorship in the Seventies. *Wadsworth* 1970 pap. $2.95. A Wadsworth Guide to Literary Study.

BOOK COLLECTING AND THE RARE BOOK TRADE

The books mentioned in this section relate to the individual collector, the institutional collector and the dealer. They ease the way not only for personal ownership, but for research scholarship.

All books for, by and about collectors overlap in interest those that are for, by and about bibliophiles. The latter books tend to be much more subjective, the former more tilted to the business side—though the distinction is not always easy to maintain with clarity. Here, an attempt is made to put the more discursive, informal books in the next section, Bibliophilia.

Barrow, W. J. MANUSCRIPTS AND DOCUMENTS: Their Deterioration and Restoration. 1956. *Univ. Press of Virginia* $7.95. In a new introd., Fraser G. Poole points out that Dr. Barrow—librarian, archivist and research scientist—uncovered the fundamental causes of paper deterioration, persuaded papermakers that permanent, durable paper is economically feasible, and showed librarians and archivists the procedures for preserving and restoring deteriorated materials.

Benjamin, Mary A. AUTOGRAPHS: A Key to Collecting. *Walter R. Benjamin Autographs* (790 Madison Ave., N.Y.C. 10021) rev. ed. 1966 $15.00.

Cannon, Carl L. AMERICAN BOOK COLLECTORS AND COLLECTING FROM COLONIAL TIMES TO THE PRESENT. 1940. *Murray* $29.50. The story of great American book collectors from Thomas Prince to Wilberforce Eames, with a description of each collection and an account of its final disposition—usually in a public library.

Carter, John. A B C FOR BOOK COLLECTORS. *Knopf* 1973 $5.95. All the essential terms and topics are given in alphabetical order, with full explanations.

BINDING VARIANTS. 1932. *McGrath Pub. Co.* 1972 $15.00

MORE BINDING VARIANTS. 1938. *McGrath Pub. Co.* $10.00
Both titles above provide technical information for collectors and the book trade.

BOOKS AND BOOK-COLLECTORS. 1957 *Dufour* $5.50. Reprint of this well-known scholar-dealer's essays and studies for the book lover and collector.

(With Graham Pollard). AN ENQUIRY INTO THE NATURE OF CERTAIN 19TH CENTURY PAMPHLETS. 1934. *Haskell* 1971 $15.95. The sensational study that led to the exposure of the book world's most eminent bibliographer as the producer of countless forgeries purporting to be first editions of Victorian authors.

(With Graham Pollard and William B. Todd). THOMAS J. WISE CENTENARY STUDIES. Ed. by W. B. Todd. Ill. *Univ. of Texas Press* 1960 $3.00. Essays on the continuing research into the activities of the master forger.

GROLIER 75. *Grolier Club* (dist. by Univ. Press of Virginia) 1967 boxed $17.00. Biographies of some of the famous members of the club and their achievements in the realms of collecting and bibliography: Folger, Morgan, Widener, Rosenbach, and 71 others.

Hamilton, Charles. COLLECTING AUTOGRAPHS AND MANUSCRIPTS. *Univ. of Oklahoma Press* 1961 2nd ed. 1970 $8.95. A New York dealer has given here a number of ground rules for beginning collectors; a valuable feature is the display of over 800 signatures, real and fake, which might help preliminary identification of important autographs.

Magee, David. INFINITE RICHES: The Adventures of a Rare Book Dealer. *Eriksson* 1973 $8.95. A leading San Francisco bookseller gives a delightful and valuable insight into rare books and the process of getting them into the hands of collectors.

Quayle, Eric. THE COLLECTOR'S BOOK OF BOOKS. Ill. *Clarkson N. Potter* 1971 $8.95. An abundantly illustrated, discursive work ranging over the history of English literature as seen by a book collector; information about books and their authors and points that collectors should know; chapter on bindings; technical glossary; about 150 illustrations, 15 in color.

THE COLLECTOR'S BOOK OF CHILDREN'S BOOKS. Ill. *Clarkson N. Potter* 1972 $8.50. Heavily illustrated with photos of pages and covers by Gabriel Monro. An oversize format; companion to the title above.

Randall, David A. DUKEDOM LARGE ENOUGH: Reminiscences of a Rare Book Dealer. 1929–1956. *Random* 1969 $10.00. The curator of fine books at the Lilly Library gives a spirited account of his years in the book trade, particularly his experiences as manager of the rare book department of the Scribner Book Store.

Ricci, Seymour de. ENGLISH COLLECTORS OF BOOKS AND MANUSCRIPTS, 1530–1930. *Burt Franklin* 1969 $18.50. Shows also the collectors' "marks of ownership."

Rosenbach, A. S. W. BOOK HUNTER'S HOLIDAY: Adventures with Books and Manuscripts. 1936. *Bks. for Libraries* 1968 $12.75. The most famous of American rare book and manuscript dealers talks about collecting, selling, and the items collected. His life story, "Rosenbach: A Biography" by Edwin Wolf, II, and John F. Fleming (*World Pub.* 1960) is reprinted by *AMS Press*, $30.00

EARLY AMERICAN CHILDREN'S BOOKS. Ill. 1933. *Dover* pap. $5.00; *Peter Smith* $7.50

Stewart, Seumas. BOOK COLLECTING: A Beginner's Guide. Fwd. by John F. Fleming. *Dutton* 1972 $8.95. What the budding collector should know about the practices of book collecting, about categories of collected books, about catalogs and dealers, terminology and values.

Weber, Carl J. FORE-EDGE PAINTING: A Historical Survey of a Curious Art in Book Decoration. *Harvey House Pubs.* 1967 $20.00. An updated edition of a 1949 work; the earlier edition, however, contains a finding list of 1001 paintings on the right-hand edges of the books.

Winger, Howard W., and Richard Daniel Smith. DETERIORATION AND PRESERVATION OF LIBRARY MATERIALS. *Univ. of Chicago Press* 1969 $7.95. Papers and discussions among technical advisers, paper and binding makers and users, publishers and librarians, at the 34th annual conference of Chicago's Graduate Library School.

Winterich, John T. THE GROLIER CLUB, 1884–1967: An Informal History. Ill. *Grolier Club* (dist. by Univ. Press of Virginia) boxed $10.00. A 75th anniversary account of the influential group that was founded to study and promote the book arts.

(With David A. Randall). A PRIMER OF BOOK COLLECTING. Ill. *Crown* 3rd ed. 1966 $5.95. Collaboration of a bibliophilic writer and a former dealer, later librarian.

Rare Book Prices

AMERICAN BOOK PRICES CURRENT ANNUAL, 1895–. Early vols. o.p. Vols. 72–76 pub. by *Columbia:* for 1966, Vol. 72, 1969 $32.50; for 1967–70, Vols. 73–76, 1970–73, $40.00 each. Later vols. pub. by *American Book Prices Current.* (121 East 78th St., N.Y.C. 10021 [Bancroft-Parkman]); for 1970–71, Vol. 77 1973 $45.00; for 1971–72, Vol. 78 1974 $45.00. This distinguished series, issued continuously for over 75 years, covers all principal book auction sales in the U.S. and London—and, with the newest volume, covers also some major Continental sales. It was issued originally by *Dodd,* later by *Dutton,* then by *Bowker,* and from 1953 through 1965 by Edward and Ramona J. Lazare with Mr. Lazare, a leading rare book expert, as editor, and Mrs. Lazare as proofreader and publisher. *Columbia* issued it for five years.

AMERICAN BOOK PRICES CURRENT INDEX. 1965–1970 *Columbia* (in prep.). Nine indexes have been issued: 1916–22, 1923–32, 1933–40, 1941–45, 1945–50, 1950–55, 1955–60, 1960–65; all o.p.

BOOK AUCTION RECORDS (ENGLISH) ANNUAL, 1902–. *Int. Pubn. Service.* For 1963–72, Vols. 61–69, $40.00 each. Earlier vols o.p. A priced and annotated annual record of London, Edinburgh and New York book auctions. There have been seven previous general indexes: 1902–12, 1912–23, 1924–33, 1933–43, 1944–48, 1949–58, 1956–60.

BOOK AUCTION RECORDS INDEX. *Int. Pubn. Service.* Index to vols. 61–65 (1963–68) $97.50 Earlier vols. o.p.

Bradley, Van Allen. THE BOOK COLLECTOR'S HAND BOOK OF VALUES. *Putnam* 1972 $17.50. The Chicago book critic, journalist, and one-time bookseller lists (by author) some 15,000 old and contemporary editions desired by collectors, along with approximate prices. Mr. Bradley's popular column about rare books, "Gold in Your Attic," led to a book by that title and a sequel, "New Gold in Your Attic" (*Arc Bks.* 1972 pap. $1.95; *Fleet* 1968 $8.95).

Heard, J. Norman, and Jimmie H. Hoover. BOOKMAN'S GUIDE TO AMERICANA. 6th ed. 1967 *Scarecrow Press* 1971 $10.00. An alphabetical cumulation from about 100 antiquarian booksellers' catalogs in Americana, offering a cross section of market prices.

McGrath Daniel, Ed. THE BOOKMAN'S PRICE INDEX. *Gale.* Published since 1964; vol. 8, 1974; $38.50 per vol. Each volume contains 35,000 to 50,000 entries selected from the catalogs of leading antiquarian and specialist book dealers of the U.S. and Great Britain.

BIBLIOPHILIA

The activity of the bibliophile is hard to define. It obviously merges with that of the collector. The collector, even the director of an institutional collection, is almost certainly a bibliophile, and some bibliophilic books—the Targ anthologies, for instance—could as well be listed in the preceding section as in this one.

Bibliophilia is often said to be akin to mania (*see the item on Richard de Bury, below*); but it is allied to and largely dependent upon sober, scholarly bibliography and the rare book business. Certainly it is one of the *philia*—it involves love and appreciation, focused in this case upon books and their writers—sometimes, too, upon their printers and sellers. But it is not quite the same as reviewing or academic criticism, though reviewers, academics and readers in general can all be infected by it. It lends itself to the writing of delightful essays and of books which are sometimes called parasitic because they are books *about* books.

Included in the listings below are some samples of these appreciative and highly personal writings. More prevalent a few years ago than in the 1970s, a number of them have been brought back into print, some in overpriced library facsimile editions. Listed here also are a few of the many available books about good reading for children, young people and adults.

Altick, Richard D. THE SCHOLAR ADVENTURERS. 1950 *Macmillan* 1966 pap. $2.45. Great episodes in literary detection: the exposure of the Wise forgeries, the uncovering of Boswell's papers at Malahide Castle, the use of codes and ciphers in literature are among the stories told.

Bury, Richard de (Bishop of Durham). LOVE OF BOOKS: Philobiblon of Richard de Bury. 1599 (Latin), first trans. 1834. Trans. by E. C. Thomas; ed. by I. Gollancz. 1926 *Cooper* $4.00. The oldest book about books. Eugene Field said, "Richard de Bury was the king, if not the father, of bibliomaniacs; his immortal work reveals to us that long before the invention of printing, men were tormented and enraptured by those very same desires, envies, jealousies, greeds, enthusiasm and passion which possess and control bibliomaniacs at the present time."

Downs, Robert B. BOOKS THAT CHANGED AMERICA. *Macmillan* 1970 $7.95; *New Am. Lib.* 1971 pap. $1.25

BOOKS THAT CHANGED THE WORLD. *American Lib. Assn.* 1956 $4.95; *New Am. Lib.* 1971 pap. $.95

FAMOUS AMERICAN BOOKS. 1971. *McGraw-Hill* 1973 $8.95 pap. $2.95

FAMOUS BOOKS: Ancient and Medieval. *Barnes & Noble* 1964 $3.95 pap. $1.95. Guides by a leading librarian, former director of the Columbia University Libraries.

Jackson, Holbrook. A BOOKMAN'S HOLIDAY. *Folcroft* 1973 $10.00. Reprint of one of this literary historian's many books about books, authors and bibliophilia.

Morley, Christopher. EX LIBRIS CARISSIMIS. *A. S. Barnes* 1961 pap. $1.25. Reprint of an affectionate memoir by the late novelist, critic and book lover.

THE HAUNTED BOOKSHOP. 1919. *Lippincott* 1955 $4.95

PARNASSUS ON WHEELS. 1917. *Lippincott* 1955 $5.50. The two titles above are novels about bookselling—a literary detective tale and a clever romance—which should form part of every book person's lore.

Newton, A. Edward. THE AMENITIES OF BOOK COLLECTING. Ill. 1918 *Kennikat* 1969 $15.00. A key book by a much admired collector and bibliophilic essayist.

Pearson, Edmund L. BOOKS IN BLACK AND RED. 1923 *Bks. for Libraries* facsimile ed. $13.75. Pearson was an entertaining essayist and literary historian.

Powell, Lawrence Clark. A Passion for Books. 1957. *Greenwood* 1973 $11.25

Books in My Baggage: Adventures in Reading and Collecting. 1960. *Greenwood* 1973 $11.25. Librarian, book collector, lecturer, Dr. Powell is a popular interpreter of the pleasures of books. (*See also Targ.*)

Sayers, Frances C. Summoned by Books. Ed. by Marjeanne J. Blinn. *Viking* 1968 pap. $1.35. A leading librarian and authority on young people's reading conveys her sense of the joy of books.

Starrett, Vincent. Bookman's Holiday. 1942. *Bks. for Libraries* $12.00. Describes "The private satisfactions of an incurable collector."

Born in a Bookshop: Chapters from the Chicago Renascence. Ill. *Univ. of Oklahoma Press* 1965 $8.95. The late critic, journalist and literary historian recalls a spirited period in American letters and publishing.

Targ, William, Ed. Bibliophile in the Nursery: A Bookman's Treasury of Collectors' Lore on Old and Rare Children's Books. Ill. 1957. *Scarecrow Press* 1969 $15.00. Mr. Targ, longtime publisher and collector, supplies introduction and notes and selects articles by 23 fellow bibliophiles.

Bookman's Progress: The Selected Writings of Lawrence Clark Powell. *Ward Ritchie* 1968 $6.75. A publisher-bibliophile selects essays by a librarian-bibliophile.

Bouillabaisse for Bibliophiles. Ill. 1955. *Scarecrow Press* 1968 $12.50. Subtitled "A Treasury of Bookish Lore, Wit & Wisdom, Tales, Poetry & Narratives & Certain Curious Studies of Interest to Bookmen & Collectors." Selections written by 37 collectors and booklovers, from Milton to contemporary times.

Carrousel for Bibliophiles. Ill. 1947 *Scarecrow Press* 1967 $10.00. The first of Mr. Targ's bibliophilic anthologies, an assortment of 45 delightful articles and essays by collectors, designers, bibliophiles, and dealers, and including classic authors.

Viguers, Ruth Hill. Margin for Surprise. *Little* 1964 $4.95. By the former editor of *The Horn Book*, the children's book-reviewing medium.

Walsh, Frances, Ed. That Eager Zest: First Discoveries in the Magic World of Books. *Lippincott* 1961 $3.95. James Thurber, E. E. Cummings, Mary Ellen Chase, H. L. Mencken, Carl Sandburg, Irwin Cobb and Clifton Fadiman give firsthand accounts of their youthful reading experiences.

—C. B. G.

Chapter 2
Bibliography

"Bibliography is an exact science. It has a notation of its own which is almost as intricate as algebra, and the scientific bibliographer requires for his work a technical apparatus almost as complicated as that of the famous detective, Dr. Thorndyke, in Austen Freeman's charming detective stories." —CHRISTOPHER MORLEY

"The end to be attained is that no book or manuscript should be out of reach— that we should be able to know where any book is to be found, and how it may be made accessible as easily as possible. You may think that is a little thing, but in reality it is a great thing." —PROFESSOR H. A. LORENTZ

Bibliography, by the earliest definition, was "the writing or copying of books," the word coming from the Greek, *bibliographia*, book-writing. This meaning was used until the middle of the 18th century, at which time the transition was made from the writing *of* books to the writing *about* books.

In current usage, the word bibliography may be defined as the systematic description and history of books. Its two major divisions are (1) systematic, or enumerative bibliography, which is the listing of books with some recognized relationship to one another; and (2) analytic, or critical bibliography, which is the study of the materials of which books are made, the art of the examination, collation, and description of books. Thus, systematic or enumerative bibliography may be defined as the study of books as a means to convey ideas; and analytic or critical bibliography, as the study of books as material objects.

Although this chapter contains, in the sections on general readings, works on analytic bibliography, and other sections on works in the related areas of cataloging and classification, book trade and library directories and dictionaries of terminology, it is with systematic bibliography that the chapter is largely concerned. This is the most widely practiced form of bibliography, its chief purpose being the mastery over written and published records, or bibliographic control, the effort to bring order out of chaos in the world of books. In our century the production of books has become so voluminous that every day, throughout the world, a flood of books and other bibliographical items are issued. It is the business of the bibliographer to identify this mass of material, to classify, describe and arrange it in a useful way for reference and study. It should be remembered that without bibliography, as Sir Frank C. Francis observed in his article on bibliography in the 15th edition of the *Encyclopaedia Britannica*, "the records of civilization would be an uncharted chaos of miscellaneous contributions to knowledge, unorganized and inapplicable to human needs."

GENERAL READINGS

General Reviews and Summary Articles

Clapp, Verner W. "Bibliography." Article in ENCYCLOPEDIA AMERICANA. 1973 vol. 3 pp. 721–724

Esdaile, Arundell. A STUDENT'S MANUAL OF BIBLIOGRAPHY. Rev. by Roy Stokes. *Barnes & Noble* 1967 $9.95. A comprehensive treatment of bibliography in general, and also a basic source of knowledge in the field of analytic bibliography.

Francis, Frank C. "Bibliography." Article in ENCYCLOPAEDIA BRITANNICA. *Macropaedia* 15th ed. 1974 vol. 2 pp. 978–981

Pollard, A. W. "Bibliography and Bibliology." Article in ENCYCLOPAEDIA BRITANNICA 11th ed. 1910 vol. 3 pp. 908–911

Schneider, Georg. THEORY AND HISTORY OF BIBLIOGRAPHY. Trans. by Ralph R. Shaw. 1934 *Scarecrow Press* 1962 $7.50

Stokes, Roy. THE FUNCTION OF BIBLIOGRAPHY. *Seminar Press* 1971 $5.75

Van Hoesen, Henry B., and Frank K. Walter. BIBLIOGRAPHY: PRACTICAL, ENUMERATIVE, HISTORICAL: An Introductory Manual. 1928 *Burt Franklin* 1971 $22.50

Periodicals

AMERICAN BOOK COLLECTOR. 1950–. *Jason A. Nogee* bimonthly $7.50. Includes as a regular feature, personal bibliographies of collected authors, illustrators or presses.

BIBLIOGRAPHY NEWSLETTER. 1972–. *Terry Belanger* (dist. by School of Library Service, Columbia Univ.) monthly $5.00. Contains listings of new and recently remaindered books in the fields of descriptive and historical bibliography, as well as news of persons, libraries and institutions concerned with the history of books and printing.

BULLETIN OF BIBLIOGRAPHY AND MAGAZINE NOTES. 1897–. *Faxon* quarterly $10.00. Contains in each issue a bibliography of an author, a critical study and bibliographic notes.

THE PAPERS OF THE BIBLIOGRAPHICAL SOCIETY OF AMERICA. 1904–. *Bibliographical Society of America* quarterly $15.00

PROOF: The Yearbook of American Bibliographical and Textual Studies. 1971–. *Univ. of South Carolina Press* annual $14.95

STUDIES IN BIBLIOGRAPHY: Papers of the Bibliographical Society of the University of Virginia. 1948–. Ed. by Fredson Bowers. *Univ. Press of Virginia* annual $15.00

Systematic Bibliography

Besterman, Theodore. THE BEGINNINGS OF SYSTEMATIC BIBLIOGRAPHY. 1935 2nd ed. rev. 1936. *Burt Franklin* 1966 $16.50

Downs, Robert B., and Frances B. Jenkins, Eds. BIBLIOGRAPHY: Current State and Future Trends. *Univ. of Illinois Press* 1967 $8.95

> A collection of 37 articles, originally published as the January and April 1967 issues of *Library Trends*, which seek "to review comprehensively the current status and future outlook of bibliography, general and special, at home and abroad, in every major area." "An authoritative [and] scholarly review"—(*LJ*).

Linder, LeRoy H. THE RISE OF CURRENT COMPLETE NATIONAL BIBLIOGRAPHIES. *Scarecrow Press* 1959 o.p.

Malcles, Louise N. BIBLIOGRAPHY *(La Bibliographie)* 1956. Trans. by Theodore C. Hines. *Scarecrow Press* 1961 repr. 1973 $5.00

Analytic Bibliography

The three books listed here compliment one another, and are the basic guides.

Bowers, Fredson T. PRINCIPLES OF BIBLIOGRAPHICAL DESCRIPTION. 1949 *Russell & Russell* 1962 $19.00. A detailed treatment of analytical bibliography as applied to the description of books.

Gaskell, Philip. A NEW INTRODUCTION TO BIBLIOGRAPHY. *Oxford* 1972 $9.50. Describes methods of book production from 1500 to 1950. Updates and extends the period of coverage of McKerrow (*below*).

McKerrow, Ronald B. AN INTRODUCTION TO BIBLIOGRAPHY FOR LITERARY STUDENTS. *Oxford* 1928 $12.75. Covers all aspects of the making of the printed book up to about 1800, and provides the background of knowledge requisite to bibliographical description.

In addition to the guides and manuals above, there are a number of serial publications devoted to the interests of analytic bibliography.

THE LIBRARY (Formerly "Transactions of the Bibliographical Society") 1889–. *The Bibliographical Society*, London quarterly membership

TYPES OF BIBLIOGRAPHIES

Bibliographies fall into six recognized classes:

General bibliographies (sometimes called *universal*) list books without limitations as to place, time, subject or author, and attempt to be all-inclusive. The "National Union Catalog" is an example.

National or *regional* bibliographies are lists of books published *in* a given country or region and/or lists of works *about* a given country or region.

Trade bibliographies aid the book trade, librarians and others by supplying information as to what books are in print or on sale; when, where and by whom they are published; these usually include the current price of each.

Author bibliographies are lists of the complete works by an author, or lists of works both by and about an author. Bibliographies giving for each volume only its title, publisher and date of publication are often called *checklists* to distinguish them from bibliographies which carry more extensive descriptions.

Subject bibliographies are lists of books about a given subject. They may be a complete bibliography or a selected bibliography of a subject, or a reading list on that subject.

Bio-bibliographies include both the biographies of writers and lists of their writings. An example of a bio-bibliography is "Contemporary Authors" (*Gale Research Company*).

BIBLIOGRAPHIES OF BIBLIOGRAPHIES

Avicenne, Paul. BIBLIOGRAPHICAL SERVICES THROUGHOUT THE WORLD, 1965–69. *UNESCO* (dist. by UNIPUB) 1973 $9.00

Besterman, Theodore. A WORLD BIBLIOGRAPHY OF BIBLIOGRAPHIES AND OF BIBLIOGRAPHICAL CATALOGUES, CALENDARS, ABSTRACTS, DIGESTS, INDEXES AND THE LIKE. Records about 117,000 volumes of bibliography under 16,000 headings. *Rowman* 4th ed. 1963 5 vols. set $200.00

THE BIBLIOGRAPHIC INDEX: A Cumulative Bibliography of Bibliographies. Published three times a year with annual cumulations. *Wilson* Vol. I (1937–42) $45.00 Vol. 2 (1943–46) $25.00 Vol. 3 (1947–50) $25.00 Vol. 4 (1951–55) $22.00 Vols. 5–11 (1956–72) service basis

Collison, Robert L. BIBLIOGRAPHIES, SUBJECT AND NATIONAL: A Guide to Their Contents, Arrangement and Use. 1951 1962. *Hafner* 3rd rev. ed. 1968 $5.75

GENERAL OR UNIVERSAL BIBLIOGRAPHIES

Naturally, there is not, nor will there ever be a truly universal bibliography, complete and unlimited by language, period or subject. Attempts have been made to achieve this ideal, some with valuable results, such as Brunet's *"Manuel du Libraire et de l'Amateur des Livres"* (1860–65), listed in this chapter in the section on bibliographies of early and rare books. In more recent times, it seems reasonable to cite the printed catalogs of the great libraries of the world as approaching nearest to the ideal universal bibliography. In her fine article, "National Bibliographies" in the *AB Bookman's Yearbook*, 1957, Betty Rosenberg comments, " 'National' is, of course, a misnomer for the great national libraries in terms of their contents. Because their contents consist so largely of private libraries, garnered over the centuries by eclectic book lovers, they have an international coverage both in space and time. . . . The Renaissance envisaged a universal man and the culture he understood embraced the culture of the entire world; and the libraries a gentleman collected included the classical languages, the Oriental, Hebrew, French, Spanish, English, Italian, German and Portuguese. Although by the 18th century insularity was well established, a gentleman still took the Grand Tour and philosophy thought in terms of an international, natural man, despite politics, and their libraries reflected the times. By the middle 19th century chaos ensued, and I'll make no more general assumptions; there were men not man, and knowledge had exceeded in diversity the capacities of one man. We miserably became specialists instead of universalists and our book collectors became specialists and our large libraries exceed our comprehension."

American

A CATALOG OF BOOKS REPRESENTED BY LIBRARY OF CONGRESS PRINTED CARDS. Aug. 1898–July 1942. *Rowman* 167 vols. $1650.00. SUPPLEMENT. Aug. 1942–Dec. 1947. 42 vols. $450.00

LIBRARY OF CONGRESS AUTHOR CATALOG, 1948–52. *Rowman* 24 vols. $275.00

NATIONAL UNION CATALOG, A CUMULATIVE AUTHOR LIST, 1953–57. *Rowman* 28 vols. $310.00 Vol. 27 Music and Phonorecords $25.00 Vol. 28 Motion Pictures and Film Strips $25.00

NATIONAL UNION CATALOG, A CUMULATIVE AUTHOR LIST, 1956–67. *Rowman* 120 vols. $2400.00

NATIONAL UNION CATALOG, A CUMULATIVE AUTHOR LIST, 1968–72. *J. W. Edwards* 128 vols. $1390.00. Annual cumulations for these years may be obtained from The Library of Congress, Card Division. Vols. for 1968 and 1969, each $500.00, 1970 $600.00 1971 $675.00 1972 $730.00

NATIONAL UNION CATALOG, PRE-1956 IMPRINTS. A comprehensive retrospective catalog in approximately 610 volumes now being published by *Mansell Information/Publishing Ltd.* (3 Bloomsbury Place, London WC1A 2QA) Vols. 1–240 about $28.00–$31.00 each, depending on payment.

NATIONAL UNION CATALOG, 1972. A cumulative author list representing Library of Congress printed cards and titles reported by other American libraries. *Library of Con-*

gress, Card Div. Nine monthly issues, three quarterly cumulations, and annual cumulation, $730.00. This price also covers the Library of Congress Catalog on Motion Pictures and Filmstrips (three quarterly issues and annual cumulation, $20.00) and the Library of Congress Catalog on Music and Phonorecords (semi-annual issue and annual cumulation $25.00)

LIBRARY OF CONGRESS CATALOG—BOOKS: SUBJECTS, 1950–54. (Orig. "Library of Congress Subject Catalog"). *Rowman* 1955 20 vols. $275.00

LIBRARY OF CONGRESS CATALOG—BOOKS: SUBJECTS, 1955–59. *Rowman* 1960 22 vols. $295.00

LIBRARY OF CONGRESS CATALOG—BOOKS: SUBJECTS, 1960–64. *J. W. Edwards* 1965 25 vols. $325.00

LIBRARY OF CONGRESS CATALOG—BOOKS: SUBJECTS, 1965–69. *J. W. Edwards* 1971 42 vols. $445.00

LIBRARY OF CONGRESS CATALOG—BOOKS: SUBJECTS. *Library of Congress, Card Div.* Cumulation for 1970 $325.00 1971 $375.00 1972 $470.00

British

BRITISH MUSEUM GENERAL CATALOGUE OF PRINTED BOOKS. *Trustees of the British Museum.* 1960–66 263 vols. Annual and ten-year supplements. Previous editions issued as "Catalogue of Printed Books, 1881–1900." *Edwards Brothers* 1946 41 vols. o.p. SUPPLEMENT, 1900–05 10 vols. o.p.

French

CATALOGUE GÉNÉRAL DES LIVRES IMPRIMÉS DE LA BIBLIOTHEQUE NATIONALE: AUTEURS. *Imprimeríe Nationale,* 1897–. in progress

EARLY AND RARE BOOKS

Arrangement is chronological.

Hain, Ludwig, REPERTORIUM BIBLIOGRAPHICUM. 2 vols. in 4. *Cotta,* Stuttgart 1826–38. Repr. *Görlich,* Milan [1948–1962 $50.00. SUPPLEMENT. 2 vols. in 3. *Cotta,* Stuttgart 1895, 1898, 1902. Repr. *Görlich,* Milan] 1950 o. p. Hain's is the first bibliography of incunabula on an international scale, and still a basic list, containing over 16,000 items. A supplement by W. A. Copinger adds nearly 6,000 volumes not listed in Hain.

GESAMTKATALOG DER WIEGENDRUCKE. *Kraus* Vols. 1–7 (1925–58) A-Federicus $385.00. Lists, describes and locates some 40,000 books printed during the 15th century. As far as published, the most comprehensive record of incunabula yet made.

Panzer, Georg Wolfgang Franz. ANNALES TYPOGRAPHICI AB ARTIS INVENTAE ORIGINE AD ANNUM 1500. 1793–97 5 vols.; . . . AB ANNO 1501 AD ANNUM 1586. 1798–1803 6 vols. *Georg Olms Verlag* (32 Hildenshein Am Dammtor, West Germany) 1793–1803 11 vols. $300.000

Brunet, Jacques Charles. MANUEL DU LIBRAIRE ET DE L'AMATEUR DES LIVRES. *Didot*, Paris 1809–10 5th ed. 6 vols. 1860–65. SUPPLEMENT. 2 vols. *Didot*, Paris 1878–80. Repr. *Librairie Dordon-Aine*, Paris. *French & European* 7 vols. set $295.00. A bibliography of over 45,000 rare, valuable or noteworthy books not limited to any one period or language, but particularly strong for French titles before the 19th century. The supplement adds about 12,000 entries.

Grässe, Johann G. T. TRÉSOR DES LIVRES RARES ET PRÉCIEUX. *Kuntze*, Dresden 1859–69 7 vols. Facsimile repr. *Welter*, Paris 1900–01 8 vols.; *Altmann*, Berlin 1922 7 vols.

"Claims 100,000 entries and is particularly strong for German titles, thus supplementing Brunet. . . . Brunet and Grässe between them constitute the main key to noteworthy books published during the first four centuries of European printing"—(A. J. Walford in "Guide to Reference Material," Vol. 3).

Goff, Frederick Richmond. INCUNABULA IN AMERICAN LIBRARIES: A Third Census of Fifteenth Century Books Recorded in North American Collections. Originally published by the *Bibliographical Society of America*, 1964. *Kraus* repr. with substantial annotations by the author in margins to update entries. 1973 $35.00. First Census compiled by the Bibliographical Society, 1919; Second Census compiled by Margaret Bingham Stillwell, 1940.

Stillwell, Margaret Bingham. INCUNABULA AND AMERICANA, 1450–1800: A Key to Bibliographical Study. 1930. *Cooper* 1968 $15.00.

THE BEGINNING OF THE WORLD OF BOOKS, 1450 TO 1470: A Chronological Survey of the Texts Chosen for Printing during the First Twenty Years of the Printing Art. *Bibliographical Society of America* 1972 $10.00.

NATIONAL BIBLIOGRAPHIES

Arrangement is chronological.

American

Evans, Charles. THE AMERICAN BIBLIOGRAPHY: A Chronological Dictionary of all Books, Pamphlets and Periodical Publications Printed in the United States of America from the Genesis of Printing in 1639 down to and including the Year 1800. With bibliographical and biographical notes. Printed for the author, 1903–34, vols. 1–12. Vol. 13, 1799–1800, by Clifford K. Shipton, *American Antiquarian Society*, 1955. *Readex Microprint* incl. Vol. 13 $20.00; *Peter Smith* 1942 12 vols. set $125.00 Vol. 13 $20.00; *Scarecrow Press* 1967 13 vols. in 1 Mini-Print vol. $39.50. Vol. 14, ed. by Roger Pattrell Bristol, is a cumulated author-title index to the whole work. *American Bibliographical Society* 1959. *Peter Smith* 1967 $20.00. The most important general list of early American publications. For each book it supplies the author's name, date of birth and death, full title, date, place, publisher or printer, paging, size, and where possible the name of a library owning a copy. In each volume there is an index by author, subject and publisher or printer. The first volume of this work was published in 1903; the 12th, covering the year 1798–99, was published in 1934, just one year before the bibliographer's death.

Sabin, Joseph. 1821–1881. A DICTIONARY OF BOOKS RELATING TO AMERICA, FROM ITS DISCOVERY TO THE PRESENT TIME, Begun by Joseph Sabin, continued by Wilberforce Eames, and completed by R. W. G. Vail. 29 vols. 1868–1936, may be obtained from *Barnes & Noble* 29 vols. in 15, set $445.00; *Readex Microprint* $35.00; *Scarecrow Press* 1966 29 vols. in 2 Mini-Print vols. set $95.00

Sabin's Dictionary is one of the great bibliographical reference works of the world in that it gives the bibliographical facts (including collations, locations and notes on contents) of more than 100,000 books relating to American history and social life. The Dictionary was begun in the middle of the 19th century by Joseph Sabin, distinguished American antiquarian. After about 15 years of research Sabin published the first part of Vol. 1 in 1868. He continued the work until his death in 1881, by which time he had gone as far as Vol. 14, Part 82. After his death, the great task was continued by one of America's greatest bibliographers, Dr. Wilberforce Eames, who carried the work from Vol. 14, Pt. 83, through Vol. 20, Pt. 116 (page 196, to the entry "Smith, Henry Hollingsworth"). The continuation by Dr. Vail completed the set. The *Scarecrow* edition in "Mini-Print" is said to be readable without aids, but a free bar magnifier is included with each set. It is "the most handy Sabin for bookmen to use"—(*Antiquarian Bookman*).

THE NEW SABIN: Books Described by Joseph Sabin and His Successors, Now Described Again on the Basis of Examination of Originals, and Fully Indexed by Title, Subject, Joint Authors, and Institutions and Agencies. Ed. by Lawrence S. Thompson. *Whitston* in progress. Vol. I, Entries 1–2484, 1973 $25.00 Vol. I, Pt. 2, Author-Subject Index to Entries 1–2484, 1973 $10.00

Shaw, Ralph R., and Richard H. Shoemaker. AMERICAN BIBLIOGRAPHY: A Preliminary Checklist. 1801–1819. *Scarecrow Press* 1958 1961–64 22 vols. (individual prices on request) set $175.50. A preliminary checklist gathered from secondary sources, designed to fill partially the gap in American national bibliography between 1800 where Evans stops, and 1820, where Roorbach begins. Each volume covers one year.

Shoemaker, Richard H. CHECKLIST OF AMERICAN IMPRINTS, 1820– . *Scarecrow Press* 1964– in progress. Already available 13 vols.: 1820 $8.00, 1821 $7.00, 1822 $7.00, 1823 $7.00, 1824 $10.00, 1825 $7.50, 1826 $11.00, 1827 $9.00, 1828 $14.00, 1829 $11.00, Title Index, 1820–29 $15.00, Author Index, Corrections and Sources, 1820–29 $6.00, 1830 $14.00. Designed as a continuation of Shaw's "American Bibliography" to give more complete listings than those in Roorbach (*below*).

Roorbach, Orville Augustus, 1803–1861. BIBLIOTHECA AMERICANA. A Catalogue of American Publications, including Reprints and Original Works, from 1820 [to Jan. 1861]. *The Author,* New York 1852–61; *Peter Smith* 1939 Vol. 1 1820–1852 $13.50; Vols. 2, 3, 4 1852–1861 3 vols. in 1 $12.50 (and Kelly's "American Catalogue") *Scarecrow Press* Mini-Print ed. 1967 $19.50. This is the direct ancestor of the "United States Catalog." Vol. 1 1820–52; Vol. 2 Oct 1852–May 1855; Vol. 3 May 1855–March 1858; Vol. 4 March 1858–Jan. 1861.

Kelly, James. 1829–1907. THE AMERICAN CATALOGUE OF BOOKS (original and reprints). Published in the United States 1861 [to Jan. 1871]. A continuation of Roorbach's "Bibliotheca Americana." Vol. 1 Jan. 1861–Jan. 1866; Vol. 2 Jan. 1866–Jan. 1871. *Peter Smith* 1938 2 vols. each $9.00; (and Roorbach's "Bibliotheca Americana") *Scarecrow Press* Mini-Print ed. 1967 $19.50

Leypoldt, Frederick. 1835–1884. AMERICAN CATALOGUE. 9 vols. in 13 vols. *Peter Smith* 1941. Various prices per vol. $15.00–$20.00. This monumental bibliographical work was published in succeeding volumes in 1876 (2 vols.), 1884 (2 vols.), 1890 (2 vols.), 1895 (2 vols.), 1900 (2 vols.), 1900–05, 1905–07, 1908–10.

British

Pollard, A. W., and G. R. Redgrave. A SHORT-TITLE CATALOGUE OF BOOKS PRINTED IN ENGLAND, SCOTLAND AND IRELAND, AND OF ENGLISH BOOKS PRINTED ABROAD,

1475–1640. This work is now undergoing revision by a committee. *Bibliographical Society*, London 1926. *Oxford* $16.25

Wing, Donald Godard. A SHORT-TITLE CATALOGUE OF BOOKS PRINTED IN ENGLAND, SCOTLAND, IRELAND, WALES AND BRITISH AMERICA AND OF ENGLISH BOOKS PRINTED IN OTHER COUNTRIES, 1641–1700. A continuation of Pollard and Redgrave's "Short-Title Catalogue . . ." *Modern Language Assn. of America* (4 Washington Pl., N.Y.C. 10003) 2nd ed. 1972 $60.00

Lowndes, William Thomas. THE BIBLIOGRAPHER'S MANUAL OF ENGLISH LITERATURE: Containing an Account of Rare, Curious, and Useful Books, Published in or Relating to Great Britain and Ireland, from the Invention of Printing; with Bibliographical and Critical Notices, Collations of the Rarer Articles, and the Prices at Which They Have Been Sold. 1834. Revised, corrected and enlarged by Henry G. Bohn. *Gale* repr. of 1864 ed. 8 vols. 1967 $97.50

Collier, John Payne. A BIBLIOGRAPHICAL AND CRITICAL ACCOUNT OF THE RAREST BOOKS IN THE ENGLISH LANGUAGE. 1866. Compiled by the 19th-century Shakespearean scholar, critic, editor, bibliophile and librarian, this work provides essential information for studies in English literature. Alphabetically arranged. *AMS Press* 4 vols. set $70.00

BRITISH NATIONAL BIBLIOGRAPHY. *Council of the British National Bibliography Ltd.* Annual £22.00 ($49.50). Also issued as cumulative reference service: weekly with interim cumulations and annual volume. Full subscription £55.50 ($125.00) per year. Annual volumes still available: 1970, 1971, 1972 £22.00 ($49.50) each; Cumulated Index: 1955–59, 1960–64, 1965–67 £15.00 ($33.75) each; Cumulated Subject Catalogue: 1951–54, 2 vols. £30.00 ($67.50), 1955–59, 3 vols. £30.00 ($67.50), 1960–64, 3 vols. £30.00 ($67.50), 1965–67, 2 vols. £30.00 ($67.50). An annual reference catalog of the new books published in Great Britain. Based on new books and new editions deposited with the Agent for the Copyright Libraries, with full bibliographical descriptions of every book. Dewey Decimal Classification (with modifications); author, title and subject index. First issued for year 1950.

TRADE BIBLIOGRAPHIES

"Knowledge," said Dr. Johnson, "is of two kinds: we know a subject ourselves, or we know where we can find information upon it." The first kind of knowledge is valuable to a bookman, the second kind is requisite. The following list of trade bibliographies is a basic tool for booksellers, librarians and others seeking current information as to what books are in print or on sale.

American

AMERICAN BOOK PUBLISHING RECORD. 12 issues a year. *Bowker* annual subscription $19.00. Cumulation of the Weekly Record listings from *Publishers Weekly* of over 37,000 books a year, as catalogued by the Library of Congress; arranged by subject under Dewey numbers. Annual Cumulatives 12 vols. 1960–64 4 vols. set $102.00; 1965–69 5 vols. set $125.00; 1970, 1971, 1972, each annual vol. $36.50.

BOOKS IN PRINT. *Bowker* annually in October 1973 2 vols. set $64.50. All the in-print books of some 3,500 American publishers are listed both by title and by author, some 398,000 titles in all. Information provided includes: author, title, edition, Library of

Congress number, series information, language if other than English, whether illustrated, grade range, year of publication, type of binding, price, International Standard Book Number, publisher's order number, imprint and publisher.

BOOKS IN PRINT SUPPLEMENT. *Bowker* annually in Spring 2nd ed. 1973/74 $27.50. Issued six months after the publication of "Books in Print" to update the information that appears there. Includes titles that have had price or other major changes, titles that have gone out of print, and titles that have been published or announced since the publication of the last edition of "Books in Print." Also contains listings of new titles by subject.

CATALOG OF REPRINTS IN SERIES. Ed. by Robert Merritt Orton. *Scarecrow Press* 21st ed. 1972 $25.00

THE CUMULATIVE BOOK INDEX. *Wilson* service basis

> The CBI began publication in 1898. Since 1928, the last single-volume cumulation, it has been an author, title and subject index to current books in the English language published in all countries. Monthly supplements are cumulated quarterly and then annually in bound volumes. Permanent volumes now in print are: 1938–42, 1943–48, 1949–52, 1953–56, 1957–58, 1959–60, 1961–62, 1963–64, 1965–66, 1967–68, 1969, 1970, 1971, 1972. Continually brought up to date.

CUMULATIVE PAPERBACK INDEX, 1939–59. By Robert Reginald and M. R. Burgess. A Comprehensive Bibliographic Guide to 14,000 Mass-Market Paperback Books Issued under 69 Imprints. *Gale* 1973 $24.00

EL-HI TEXTBOOKS IN PRINT. *Bowker* annually in Spring 4th ed. 1974 $19.95 Formerly titled "Textbooks in Print." "Lists about 17,000 textbooks for elementary, junior high and high school levels under 20 broad subject headings, with about 200 sub-categories"—(Publisher's catalog).

FORTHCOMING BOOKS. *Bowker* bimonthly annual subscription $24.00, single copy, $6.00; with "Subject Guide to Forthcoming Books" $32.00 per year. Each issue includes books to be published during the next five months, plus a continuing, cumulative index to books published since the summer. Arranged by author and by title.

GUIDE TO REPRINTS. *Microcard Editions* annual 8th ed. 1974 $12.00. An annual guide to books, journals, and other materials which are available in reprint form.

PAPERBOUND BOOKS IN PRINT. *Bowker* three cumulative vols. per year. Annual subscription $52.50; single vols. $19.50 each.

PAPERBOUND-BOOK GUIDE FOR COLLEGES. *Bowker* annual 1973 rates on request. Lists 10,000 paperbacks in every subject area of interest suitable for use in college or by the serious reader. Free to college professors. Sold in quantity lots at special low prices. Revised annually.

PUBLISHERS' TRADE LIST ANNUAL. *Bowker* annually in September 1973 7 vols. set $37.50. The "PTLA" is a collection of the catalogs of some 2,250 American publishers bound together alphabetically.

PUBLISHERS WEEKLY. *Bowker* weekly annual subscription $20.00; single issues $1.35; all announcement and special numbers $3.25. *PW* is the leading organ of the book trade. In its "Weekly Record of New Publications" this journal lists with Library of Congress cataloging all American book publications.

SUBJECT GUIDE TO BOOKS IN PRINT. *Bowker* annually in October 2 vols. set $44.50. A subject guide to the books listed in "Books in Print"; 290,000 titles arranged under some 63,000 headings with numerous cross-references.

SUBJECT GUIDE TO FORTHCOMING BOOKS. *Bowker* bimonthly annual subscription $11.00; single copy $4.00. A bimonthly subject forecast of books to come.

TITLES IN SERIES. By Eleanor A. Baer. *Scarecrow Press* 2nd ed. 1964 2 vols. set $42.50; SUPPLEMENT 1967 $10.00; 2nd SUPPLEMENT 1971 $15.00

"A work of this kind has been badly needed. . . . It should pay for itself in time saved and books found by dealer and librarian"—(*Antiquarian Bookman*). The Supplement includes new publications since 1963 of series listed in the original volume; new series since January, 1963; series omitted in previous editions—all arranged and numbered to correspond to the 2nd edition. 7,500 new titles have been added. 2nd Supplement includes 9,741 books, bringing the total number of works listed to 55,298.

THE UNITED STATES CATALOG. Books in Print January 1928. *Wilson* o.p. Continued by the "Cumulative Book Index" (*above*).

British

THE BOOKSELLER. *Whitaker*, London. Weekly annual subscription £6.20 ($14.00). The journal of the British book trade. Carries each week the complete list of British books as they are published.

BRITISH BOOKS IN PRINT. *Whitaker*, London (dist. by Bowker). Annual 2 vols. set $47.08. All British books in print at the end of April each year. This is the continuation of "The Reference Catalogue of Current Literature" first published in 1874 and subsequently at four- or five-year intervals. The 1973 edition records over 250,000 in-print titles.

PAPERBACKS IN PRINT. *Whitaker*, London. Semiannually in winter (October) and summer (April). £4.00 ($9.00) each issue. A complete record of all paperbacks in print in the United Kingdom.

WHITAKER'S BOOKS OF THE MONTH AND BOOKS TO COME. *Whitaker*, London. Monthly annual subscription £7.20 ($16.00). Each issue includes a list of books published during the past month, together with those due to be published within the next two months.

WHITAKER'S CUMULATIVE BOOK LIST. *Whitaker*, London. Annually £4.50 ($10.00)

A complete record of British publishing each year, with details as to title, subtitle, author, size, number of pages, price, month of publication, publisher and classification. In two indexes, one in 46 subject classifications; the other alphabetical by author and title, with full details on each entry. Also quarterly cumulative parts, Jan.–Mar., Jan.–June, Jan.–Sept., with Annual Volume, £6.00 ($13.50). 4- and 5–year cumulations, 1939–43 (facsimile repr.) £10 ($24.00); 1944–47 (facsimile repr.) £10 ($24.00); 1953–57 £9 ($21.60); 1963–67 £10 ($24.00).

WHITAKER'S FIVE-YEAR CUMULATIVE BOOK LIST. *Whitaker*, London (dist. by Bowker) 1968–72. $45.00

A complete list of the new books and new editions published in the United Kingdom arranged by author and title, with details as to subtitle, size, number of pages, price, date, classification and publisher. Based on lists printed weekly in *The Bookseller*, monthly in "Current Literature" and quarterly and annually in *Whitaker's Cumulative Book List*.

Canadian

CANADIAN BOOKS IN PRINT: Catalogue des Livres Canadiens en Librairie. Ed. by Harald Bohne. Arranged by author, publisher and title indexes with English and French-Canadian listings interfiled. *Canadian Books in Print Committee* (dist. by Univ. of Toronto Press and Conseil Superieur du Livre) 1970 ed. $25.00; 1971 ed. $25.00; 1972 ed. $25.00

French

BIBLIOGRAPHIE DE LA FRANCE/BIBLIO: Journal Officiel de l'Imprimérie et de la Librairie. *Cercle de la Librairie*, Paris. Weekly with monthly and quarterly supplements. The official journal of the French book trade, established by a decree of Napoleon, Oct. 14, 1811, to meet the need for a complete national bibliography. Records books, pamphlets, official publications, music and prints.

CATALOGUE DE L'EDITION FRANÇAISE (French Books in Print); Une liste exhaustive des ouvrages disponibles publies en français, de par le monde. *Paris Pubns.* 2nd ed. 1973 4 vols. set $120.00 Vol. I Authors, Vol. 2 Titles $85.00; Vols. 3 and 4 Subjects $45.00

LA LIBRAIRIE FRANÇAISE; catalogue général des ouvrages en vente. *French and European* 1946–55 3 vols. set $175.00; 1956–65 4 vols. set $275.00

"Compiled from the annual volumes of the *"Les Livres de l'Année* of the *Bibliographie de la France.* Lists books, periodicals, publications of corporate bodies, and some documents."—(Constance Winchell in "Guide to Reference Books").

LES LIVRES DE L'ANNÉE. *Cercle de la Librairie*, Paris; *French and European* 1967 $55.00, 1968 $57.50, 1969 $61.00, 1970 $75.00, 1971 (published as *"Les Livres de l'Année Biblio"*) $77.50

"Cumulates the listings in the 'Bibliographie de la France,' and is itself cumulated into the 'Librairie Française' . . ."—(Constance Winchell in "Guide to Reference Books").

REPERTOIRE DES LIVRES DISPONIBLES (French Books In Print). *France Expansion* (dist. by Bowker) 1972 2 vols. set $80.00

"This comprehensive work lists nearly 120,000 titles from France, Belgium, Switzerland, Canada, and virtually every other French-speaking country, which are available in France today"—(Publisher's catalog).

German

VERZEICHNIS LIEFERBARER BÜCHER (German Books in Print). *Verlag der Buchhändler-Vereinigung* and *Verlag Dokumentation* (dist. by Bowker) 3rd ed. 1973/74 3 vols. set $99.00. Separate author and title/subject volumes list over 220,000 titles available from 1,839 publishers in West Germany, Austria, and Switzerland.

Spanish

FICHERO BIBLIOGRÁFICO HISPANOAMERICANO. *Bowker* monthly annual subscription $11.00, in Spanish-speaking countries $8.00. Begun in 1962, this bibliography provides information about new books published in Latin America—arranged by subject with an author-title index. Also includes exchange rate conversion table and directory of publishers with addresses.

Libros en Venta. Ed. by Mary C. Turner. *Bowker* 1974 (in prep.). This is a combined "Books in Print—Subject Guide" of Spanish-language books published in the Americas and Spain, consisting of an author, title, and subject index.

Manual de Bibliografía de la Literatura Española. Ed. by José Simón Díaz. *Bowker* 1964 $8.50; Supplement 1, covering 1962–64 $2.50; Supplement 2, covering 1965–70 $6.95. 20,000 selected references to the most important works of Spanish literature, from the earliest times through 1961. Grouped chronologically, with critical references cited. Text in Spanish.

KEYS TO ANONYMOUS BOOKS

The books listed below are either reprints of earlier books, or are now out of print. From 1950 on, authorship of anonymous and pseudonymous works in English and American literature may usually be found in the "British National Bibliography" and in the "National Union Catalog."

Abbatt, William. The Colloquial Who's Who, 1600–1924. 1925. *Gale* 1973 $15.00

Cushing, William. Anonyms: A Dictionary of Revealed Authorship. 1889. *Adler* 1968 $43.75; *Gale* 1973 $26.00

Initials and Pseudonyms: A Dictionary of Literary Disguises. 1885. *Adler* 1969 2 vols. $52.80; *Gale* 1973 $42.00; *Finch Press* (in prep.)

Halkett, Samuel, and John Laing. Dictionary of Anonymous and Pseudonymous English Literature. 1st ed. Edinburgh 1882–88 rev. and enl. 1926–34. *Haskell* 7 vols. set $175.00 Vol. 8 Third Supplement, 1900–1949. By Dennis E. Rhodes and Anna E.C. Simoni. *Barnes & Noble* 1956 o.p. Vol. 9 with addenda and corrigenda 1962 o.p. "The best list for English works."—(Constance Winchell in "Guide to Reference Books").

Stonehill, Charles A., Andrew Block and H. Winthrop Stonehill. Anonyma and Pseudonyma. 1927 *Milford House* 4 vols. in 2 $55.00

Taylor, Archer, and Frederic J. Mosher. The Bibliographical History of Anonyma and Pseudonyma. *Univ. of Chicago Press* for the Newberry Library. 1951. o.p.

TOOLS FOR BOOK SELECTION

"The Reader's Adviser" itself is one of the most widely used book-selection tools in the library and book world.

Haines, Helen E. Living with Books: The Art of Book Selection. The standard compendium. *Columbia* 2nd ed. 1950 $11.00

See also this Chapter: Trade Bibliographies, and Chapter 1, Books about Books: Trade Papers.

General Book Selection Tools

A.L.A. Catalog 1926. Annotated Basic List of 10,000 Books. Ed. by Isabella M. Cooper. *American Lib. Assn.* 1926 o.p.

A.L.A. Catalog 1926–1931. Annotated List of Approximately 3,000 Titles. Ed. by Marion Horton. *American Lib. Assn.* 1933 o.p.

A.L.A. CATALOG 1932–1936. Annotated List of Approximately 4,000 Titles. Ed. by Marion Horton. *American Lib. Assn.* 1938 o.p.

A.L.A. CATALOG 1937–1941. Annotated List of 4,000 Titles. Ed. by Marion Horton. *American Lib. Assn.* 1943 o.p.

A.L.A. CATALOG 1942–49. Annotated List of Approximately 4,500 Titles. Ed. by Florence Boochever. *American Lib. Assn.* 1952 o.p.

The A.L.A. Catalogs are the highest type of evaluated bibliography. Entries are arranged according to the Dewey Decimal Classification. Each entry gives the author, his date years, title, publisher, date of publication (except in fiction in the 1926 Catalog), price, number of pages and a description and evaluation of the contents.

BASIC BOOK LIST OF HARDBOUND BOOKS. *American Booksellers Assn.* 1974. Free to members, extra copies to members $1.75; to nonmembers $2.00. Compiled by a committee representing member stores, this is a list of some 2,000 titles a well-stocked small bookshop should have. Based on actual sales records, the booklist is useful in planning stock of new stores and as an inventory guide for established stores.

BASIC BOOK LIST OF PAPERBOUND BOOKS. *American Booksellers Assn.* 1973. Free to members, extra copies to members $1.75; $2.00 to nonmembers. About 1,100 titles arranged by subject and publisher. The subject classification is in accordance with the 26 standard categories of paperbacks determined by the Joint Associations Book Projects Committee.

BOOK REVIEW DIGEST. *Wilson.* Annually, service basis. Since 1905 this digest of quotations from book reviews has been issued annually. About 6,000 books a year are listed by author with price, publisher and descriptive notes. Published monthly (except February and July) with permanent bound annual cumulations. Every fifth year the annual volume contains a cumulated subject and title index of the previous five years. Reprints of annual volumes, from 1905 through 1959, are available at prices ranging from $7.00 to $22.00; annuals for 1960–72 are sold on the service basis.

THE BOOKLIST. *American Lib. Assn.* twice monthly except once in August annual subscription $15.00; single copy $.85

"An essential aid for selecting and buying currently produced books, 16mm films, 8mm film loops, filmstrips, and non-musical recordings for use in public and school libraries. . . . Books and audiovisual materials for all ages and a broad range of interests are described in concise, objective appraisals that summarize content; note point of view, style of presentation, and special features; and suggest audience or use. Complete ordering and cataloging information is given for each item reviewed"—(Publisher' catalog).

BOOKS FOR COLLEGE LIBRARIES: A Core Collection of 40,000 Titles. *American Lib. Assn.* 2nd ed. 1974. Vol. I, Humanities; Vol. 2, Language and Literature; Vol. 3, History; Vol. 4, Social Sciences; Vol. 5, Science and Technology; Vol. 6, Index; sold by the set only. pap. (in prep.).

Preparation of this new and revised edition of Melvin J. Voight's and Joseph H. Treyz's "Books for College Libraries," 1967, was a project of the Association of College and Research Libraries. The titles selected are considered to be the minimum essential for the four-year undergraduate college. Subject specialists evaluated the titles in the earlier edition as well as titles published between 1964 and 1972. The titles are arranged by Library of Congress classification and are entered in the main catalog only once. Vol. 6 contains author, title, and subject indexes. Each entry is a virtually complete MARC record.

CHOICE. *American Lib. Assn.* with *Assn. of College and Research Libraries* monthly with a combined July–August issue annual subscription $25.00; single copies $2.50

"A current book selection guide for librarians and faculties of undergraduate colleges, universities, junior colleges. . . . Concise, often comparative evaluations of 500–700 new publications each month are written by undergraduate faculty or librarian subject specialists"—(Publisher's catalog).

OPENING DAY COLLECTION. *Choice* (100 Riverview Center, Middletown, Conn.) 1967 3rd ed. 1974 (in prep.). A listing of approximately 1,800 titles considered important for the collection of a new undergraduate library on its opening day. Also contained in four issues of *Choice*: December 1973—Reference; January 1974—Humanities; February 1974—Science; March 1974—Social Sciences. $2.50 each. Order direct from *American Lib. Assn.*

THE FICTION CATALOG: The Standard Catalog Series. *Wilson* 8th ed. 1971 (plus 4 annual pap. supplements) $25.00. Selected by experienced and outstanding librarians, this lists 4,350 works of fiction which have been found most useful in libraries throughout the United States and Canada; the four annual supplements will cover approximately 1,600 additional titles.

KIRKUS REVIEWS. *The Kirkus Service* (60 West 13 St., N.Y.C. 10011) bi-monthly. Subscription price available on request. Prepublication reviews of adult and children's books.

LIBRARY JOURNAL. *Bowker* issued twice a month, except monthly in July and August annual subscription $16.20; single copies $1.35; Spring, Summer, and Fall Announcement issues $3.25 each. Its reviewing service by professional librarians offers objective appraisals of more than 7,000 titles annually. Includes *School Library Journal* which is also available separately, $10.80.

PUBLIC LIBRARY CATALOG (formerly "Standard Catalog for Public Libraries") *Wilson* 6th ed. 1974 (with 4 annual supplements) (in prep.). A classified and annotated list of approximately 8,765 nonfiction titles recommended for small and medium-sized libraries. Pt. 1 is a classified catalog arranged by the Dewey Decimal Classification, with subject headings based on the "Sears List of Subject Headings." Pt. 2 is an author, title, and subject index to Pt. 1, with approximately 15,860 analytical entries for parts of books, Pt. 3 is a directory of publishers.

PUBLISHERS WEEKLY. *Bowker* weekly annual subscription $20.00; single copies $1.35; seasonal announcement issues $3.25. Includes prepublication reviews of forthcoming fiction, nonfiction, paperback and children's books, and provides seasonal indexes of forthcoming books. Includes also the Weekly Record of all new U.S. books received, with full Library of Congress cataloging information.

REVIEWS ON CARDS. *Bowker* annual subscription for the complete file $100.00; for the adult reviews from *Library Journal*, $70.00; for the juvenile reviews from *School Library Journal*, $40.00. This service reproduces on 3 × 5 cards every book review from *Library Journal* and *School Library Journal*. Cards are mailed to subscribers as each issue goes to press.

Many book lists are compiled annually by libraries, wholesalers and various organizations. *See the section "Adult Book Lists & Catalogs" in the "Literary Market Place"* (Bowker, *1973–74 $17.50*).

Reference

Barton, Mary Neill, Comp., with Marion V. Bell. REFERENCE BOOKS: A Brief Guide. *Enoch Pratt Free Library* (Baltimore) 7th ed. 1970 pap. $1.75

Cheney, Frances Neal. FUNDAMENTAL REFERENCE SOURCES. *American Lib. Assn.* 1971 $8.50

Downs, Robert B., and Elizabeth C. Downs. HOW TO DO LIBRARY RESEARCH. *Univ. of Illinois Press* 1966 pap. $1.45. A brief and very helpful guide to research in libraries for both scholars and students. Discussion of American libraries; listing of special collections of "100 Notable American Libraries"; 86 lists of books on particular subjects—"Accounting" to "Writing"—and other features.

Galin, Saul, and Peter Spielberg. REFERENCE BOOKS: How to Select and Use Them. *Random* 1969 $7.95 pap. $1.95

Gates, Jean Key. GUIDE TO THE USE OF BOOKS AND LIBRARIES. *McGraw-Hill* 1962, 2nd ed. 1969 $5.95

GENERAL ENCYCLOPEDIAS IN PRINT: A Comparative Analysis. Comp. by S. Padraig Walsh. *Bowker* 9th ed. 1973 $10.95

"Provides practical guidelines for buying general encyclopedias. This edition includes updated, expanded analyses for more than 32 general encyclopedias currently in print, including excerpts from critical reviews. A merit rating chart further indicates how well encyclopedias meet the needs of their intended audiences. Also includes a directory of publishers and distributors"—(Publisher's catalog).

GENERAL WORLD ATLASES IN PRINT: A Comparative Analysis. Comp. by S. Padraig Walsh. *Bowker* 4th ed. 1973 $12.50

"Provides practical guidelines for selecting atlases for home, school, and public libraries. Charts rank each work on overall merit, age suitability, price, size, and number of index entries. Also includes brief descriptions of 64 inexpensive works"—(Publisher's catalog).

HOME REFERENCE BOOKS IN PRINT: Atlases, English Language Dictionaries, and Subscription Books. Comp. by S. Padraig Walsh. *Bowker* 1969 $10.95

"More than 30 well-known dictionaries published in the U.S., 35 general world atlases and American reference books are described and evaluated in the guide"—(Publisher's catalog).

REFERENCE BOOKS FOR SMALL AND MEDIUM-SIZED PUBLIC LIBRARIES, by the Reference Services Division, American Library Association. Ed. by Richard A. Gray and Judith Z. Cushman. *American Lib. Assn.* 2nd rev. ed. 1973 pap. $5.50

Shores, Louis. BASIC REFERENCE SOURCES: An Introduction to Materials and Methods. With a Chapter on Science Reference Sources by Helen Focke. 1954 *Gregg* 1972 lib. bdg. $13.25. This is the successor to Shores' "Basic Reference Books" (2nd ed. 1939, o. p.); 147 types of sources described; 554 basic reference titles given. The major shortcoming is due to the fact that entries for the book closed in December, 1951.

Taylor, Margaret. BASIC REFERENCE SOURCES: A Self-Study Manual. *Scarecrow Press* preliminary ed. 1971 $7.50

Walford, A. J., Ed. GUIDE TO REFERENCE MATERIAL. Vol. I Science and Technology. *Bowker* 3rd ed. 1973 $17.95; Vol. 2 Social and Historical Sciences, Philosophy and Religion. *American Lib. Assn.* 3rd ed. 1974 (in prep.); Vol. 3 Generalia, Language and Literature, the Arts. *American Lib. Assn.* 3rd ed. 1974 (in prep.). A guide to reference books published by the British Library Association. Although British items are given prominence, much U.S., Russian, French, German and other material is included.

Winchell, Constance M. GUIDE TO REFERENCE BOOKS. *American Lib. Assn.* 8th ed. 1967 $15.00 SUPPLEMENTS, 1965–66 $3.50, 1967–68 $4.00, 1969–70 $4.50, all comp. by Eugene P. Sheehy. One of the superior works, this edition is based on the sixth edition by Isadore Gilbert Mudge and, of course, the Winchell seventh edition and its four supplements, which it entirely supersedes. It now lists and annotates about 7,500 reference works, including scholarly material in English and foreign languages and the works on Russia and Eastern Europe to which special attention was paid in the last edition.

Wynar, Bohdan S. AMERICAN REFERENCE BOOKS ANNUAL. *Libraries Unlimited* 4th ed. 1973 $22.00

Children's Books

The field of children's books has a literature of its own that goes beyond the scope of this chapter. Among the basic book selection tools are:

BASIC BOOK COLLECTION FOR ELEMENTARY GRADES. Comp. by Miriam Snow Mathes. *American Lib. Assn.* 7th ed. 1960 pap. o. p.

BASIC BOOK COLLECTION FOR JUNIOR HIGH SCHOOLS. Ed. by Margaret V. Spengler. *American Lib. Assn.* 3rd ed. 1960 pap. o. p.

BASIC BOOK COLLECTION FOR HIGH SCHOOLS. Comp. by Eileen F. Noonan. *American Lib. Assn.* 7th ed. pap. o. p.

BOOKS FOR SECONDARY SCHOOL LIBRARIES. Comp. by the Library Committee of the National Association of Independent Schools. *Bowker* 4th ed. 1971 $9.95

"Designed to prepare secondary students for the subjects awaiting them at the college level. Helpful lists of library tools and reference materials are included. Fully indexed by author, title and subject, with a special directory of publishers. Material arranged by Dewey Decimal Classification with Library of Congress Subject headings"—(Publisher's catalog).

CHILDREN'S CATALOG. *Wilson* 12th ed. 1971 (includes 4 annual supplements) $25.00. A catalog of children's books found useful in public and elementary school libraries. This edition covers 5,119 books with 13,273 analytical entries. Arranged in three parts: Pt. 1—a classified catalog giving full cataloging information for each book; Pt. 2—an author, title, and subject index with analytical entries; Pt. 3—a directory of publishers and distributors. The four annual supplements, 1972–75, will add about 2,000 titles.

HORN BOOK MAGAZINE. Reviews and news of juvenile books, authors, and illustrators. *Horn Book, Inc.* (585 Boylston St., Boston, Mass. 02116) bimonthly annual subscription $9.50; single copies $1.50. *AMS Press* repr. of vols. 1–44, 1924–68, each vol. $25.00; set $1,100.00

JUNIORPLOTS: A Book Talk Manual for Teachers and Librarians. By John Gillespie and Diana Lembo. *Bowker* 1967 $9.95

"Plot summaries of 80 books for young people, 9 to 16, arranged according to 8 basic behavioral themes that a librarian or educator might want to use in giving a book talk. Thematic analysis, suggested discussion material and a list of other related titles are given for each book described"—(Publisher's catalog).

Larrick, Nancy. A PARENT'S GUIDE TO CHILDREN'S READING. *Doubleday* 3rd ed. 1969 $7.95; *Pocket Bks.* 1969 pap. $1.25

Pellowski, Anne. THE WORLD OF CHILDREN'S LITERATURE. *Bowker* 1968 $22.50. An annotated bibliography on the development of children's literature and children's libraries in 106 countries. Contains 4,500 geographically arranged entries; author-title-subject index.

SCHOOL LIBRARY JOURNAL. *Bowker* monthly Sept. through May annual subscription $10.80. Articles, news, and a comprehensive review service of children's books. Includes approximately 2,200 reviews a year, written by professional librarians.

SENIOR HIGH SCHOOL LIBRARY CATALOG (Formerly "Standard Catalog for High School Libraries"). *Wilson* 10th ed. 1972 (including 5 annual supplements) $35.00; ed. with Catholic supplement $35.00

"Emphasizes materials of value to students in the tenth through twelfth grades . . . provides a list of 4,760 titles, including many adult books to accommodate advanced high school curricula . . . arranged in a classified catalog including complete bibliographic information. With author, title, subject, and analytical index in one alphabet"—(Publisher's catalog).

SUBJECT GUIDE TO CHILDREN'S BOOKS IN PRINT. *Bowker* annually in December 1973 $17.95. A subject listing of 40,000 juvenile titles under more than 8,000 subject headings based on the Sears list. Provides complete ordering information: author, title, publisher, date of publication, price, and, when supplied by the publisher, grade level, binding, and edition.

Many book lists are compiled annually by libraries, wholesalers and various organizations. See the section "Juvenile Book Lists & Catalogs" in "Literary Market Place" (Bowker, *1973–74 $17.50*).

LISTS OF "BEST" BOOKS

The making of lists of "best books" is a form of book selection which is ever popular, both with the makers and with the readers. One of the earliest lists is Sir John Lubbock's famous Hundred Best Books in "The Pleasures of Life" (o.p.), published first in 1887. *For Best Sellers, see that section in Chapter 1, Books about Books.*

Babb, James T., and David Mearns. THE WHITE HOUSE LIBRARY: A Short-Title List. Lists books in the White House Library, a reference and recreational library emphasizing the history and culture of the U.S. *White House Historical Assn.* 1968 pap. ltd. ed. signed by Mrs. Lyndon B. Johnson o.p.

Connolly, Cyril. THE MODERN MOVEMENT: A Discussion of One Hundred Key Books from England, France and America, 1850–1950. *Atheneum* 1966 o.p.

Dickinson, Asa Don. THE WORLD'S BEST BOOKS: Homer to Hemingway. *Wilson* 1953 $8.00

Downs, Robert B. BOOKS THAT CHANGED AMERICA. *Macmillan* 1970 $7.95 *New Am. Lib.* Mentor Bks. pap. $1.25

BOOKS THAT CHANGED THE WORLD. *American Lib. Assn.* 1956 $4.95 *New Am. Lib.* Mentor Bks. pap. $.95

FAMOUS AMERICAN BOOKS. *McGraw-Hill* 1971 $8.95 pap. $2.94

FAMOUS BOOKS, ANCIENT AND MEDIEVAL. *Barnes & Noble* 1964 pap. $1.95

FAMOUS BOOKS SINCE 1492. (Formerly "Molders of the Modern Mind"). *Barnes & Noble* 1961 pap. $2.25

Fadiman, Clifton. THE LIFETIME READING PLAN. *World Pub.* 1960 o.p. A guide to his famous "100 books."

Weber, J. Sherwood, and others. GOOD READING. *New Am. Lib.* Mentor Bks. 1960 1964 pap. o.p. A guide to the world's best books prepared by the Committee on College Reading.

CATALOGING AND CLASSIFICATION OF BOOKS

Library literature contains important articles and reports on cataloging and classification by such well-known authorities as Seymour Lubetzky, Paul Dunkin and Jesse Shera.

A. L. A. RULES FOR FILING CATALOG CARDS. Pauline A. Seely, Chairman of Filing Code Committee. Basic filing rules with alternative rules where the needs of different types of libraries or special collections must be recognized. *American Lib. Assn.* 2nd ed. 1968 $6.75 abr. ed. 1968 $2.00

A. L. A. CATALOGING RULES FOR AUTHOR AND TITLE ENTRIES. Clara Beetle. *American Lib. Assn.* 2nd ed. 1949 o.p.

ANGLO-AMERICAN CATALOGING RULES. Prep. by American Library Assn., Library of Congress, Library Assn., Canadian Library Assn. Ed. by C. Sumner Spalding. *American Lib. Assn.* 1967 $9.50; programmed text by Eric Hunter. *Shoestring* 1972 $6.00

   Supersedes the "A.L.A. Cataloging Rules for Author and Title Entries" (*see above*) and includes a revision of the rules for descriptive cataloging in the Library of Congress.

DEWEY DECIMAL CLASSIFICATION AND RELATIVE INDEX. Devised by Melvil Dewey. Ed. by Library of Congress. *Forest Press* (Lake Placid Club, Essex County, N.Y. 12946) 18th ed. 1971 3 vols. each $15.00; set $45.00. Contents: Vol. 1 Introduction and Tables, Vol. 2 Schedules, Vol. 3 Index. abr. ed. 1971 $12.00

   Since the inception of the Dewey Decimal Classification in 1876, this system of book arrangement has become one of the indispensable tools for the organization of knowledge. Over the years, the problems of cataloging and classification, bibliography and all phases of information retrieval have become more complex. In consequence, great care must now be exercised in applying consistently the rules of the 18,000 heads which have developed from Melvil Dewey's original 10 classes, 100 divisions, and 1,000 sections, if they are to serve their purpose effectively.
   To adhere to the principle of the "integrity of numbers"—the basic meanings assigned to the numbers—and at the same time to meet the conflicting demands involved in keeping pace with the growth of knowledge, calls for consistent yet flexible procedures.

FILING RULES FOR THE DICTIONARY CATALOGS OF THE LIBRARY OF CONGRESS. *Library of Congress, Card Div.* 1956 $2.00

   The present filing system in force at the Library of Congress began with a set of rules drawn up by James K. Boyland for the "Catalog of Books Represented by Library of Congress Printed Cards" (*Edwards Brothers*). Using these rules and committee reports as a basis, the first comprehensive code was compiled by Linn R. Blanchard whose "Filing Manual" was published in looseleaf form in 1945 to be used by the LC staff. The present "Filing Rules" is a revised edition of the Blanchard manual.

Foskett, A. C. THE UNIVERSAL DECIMAL CLASSIFICATION: the History, Present Status and Future Prospects of a Large General Classification Scheme. *Linnet Books* 1973 $9.00

LIBRARY OF CONGRESS CLASSIFICATION SCHEDULES. *Library of Congress, Card Div.* 31 Schedules: A General Works. Polygraphy $5.00; B-BJ Philosophy Psychology $5.25; BL-BX Religion $4.50; C Auxiliary Sciences of History $2.00; D History: General and Old World (Eastern Hemisphere) $4.25; E-F History: America (Western Hemisphere) $3.50; G Geography. Anthropology. Recreation $4.00; H Social Sciences $4.25; J Political Science $4.00; KF Law of the United States $5.00; L Education $2.00; M Music. Books on Music $2.75; N Fine Arts $3.00; P-PA General Philology and Linguistics. Classical Languages and Literatures $3.25; PA Supplement Byzantine and Modern Greek Literature. Medieval and Modern Latin Literature $.75; PB-PH Modern European Languages $2.50; PG Russian Literature $2.00; PJ-PM Languages and Literatures of Asia, Africa, Oceania. American Indian Languages. Artificial Languages $3.25; P-PM Supplement Index to Languages and Dialects $ .90; PN, PR, PS, PZ General Literature. English and American Literature. Fiction in English. Juvenile Literature $3.00; PQ, Pt. 1 French Literature $1.75; PQ, Pt. 2 Italian, Spanish, Portuguese Literatures $2.00; PT, Pt. 1 German Literature $2.35; PT, Pt. 2 Dutch and Scandinavian Literature $1.00; Q Science $9.00; R Medicine $2.00; S Agriculture $1.75; T Technology $3.50; U Military Science $1.50; V Naval Science $1.50; Z Bibliography. Library Science $2.25

LIBRARY OF CONGRESS SUBJECT HEADINGS (formerly "Subject Headings Used in the Dictionary Catalogs of the Library of Congress"). *Library of Congress, Card Div.* 8th ed. 1974 (in prep.) SUPPLEMENTS, beginning January–March 1973, quarterly plus annual cumulation $35.00

Mann, Margaret. INTRODUCTION TO CATALOGING AND THE CLASSIFICATION OF BOOKS. *American Lib. Assn.* 2nd ed. 1943 $4.00

Matthis, Raimond E., and Desmond Taylor. ADOPTING THE LIBRARY OF CONGRESS CLASSIFICATION SYSTEM: A Manual of Methods and Techniques for Application or Conversion. *Bowker* 1971 $14.50

Piercy, Esther J. COMMONSENSE CATALOGING. *Wilson* 1965 2nd ed. rev. by Marion Sanner 1974 $8.00

SEARS LIST OF SUBJECT HEADINGS. Ed. by Barbara Marietta Westby; Suggestions for the Beginner in Subject Heading Work, by Bertha Margaret Frick (1st ed. prep. by Minnie E. Sears). *Wilson* 1972 $10.00

> Sears follows the Library of Congress form of headings, abridged and simplified to meet the needs of smaller libraries. In a few cases there are slight deviations from LC usage—simplification of phrasing, updating of terminology, combining of closely related subjects, omission of Dewey Decimal Classification numbers.

SUBJECT HEADINGS USED IN THE DICTIONARY CATALOGS OF THE LIBRARY OF CONGRESS (1897–June 1964). *Library of Congress, Card Div.* 7th ed. 1966 $15.00 SUPPLEMENTS 1965 $2.50, 1966 $5.00, 1967 $5.00, 1968 $5.00, 1969 $5.00, 1970 $15.00, 1971 $15.00, 1972 $30.00.

Tauber, Maurice F. CATALOGING AND CLASSIFICATION (With Carlyle J. Frarey's "Subject Headings"). *Rutgers Univ. Press* 1960 $8.00. This is vol. I pts. 1 and 2 of "The State of the Library Art" ed. by Ralph R. Shaw.

Wynar, Bohdan S. INTRODUCTION TO CATALOGING AND CLASSIFICATION. *Libraries Unlimited* 4th rev. ed. 1972 $9.50

PERIODICALS

For indexes *to periodicals and pamphlets, see Chapter 3, Reference Books—Literature: General Indexes to Literary Material in Periodicals.*

AYER DIRECTORY OF PUBLICATIONS. Indexes newspapers and magazines in the U.S. and its territories; also includes Canada, Bermuda, Panama and the Philippines. Arranged geographically with classified lists. *N. W. Ayer & Son* annual $45.00

Farber, Evan I. CLASSIFIED LIST OF PERIODICALS FOR THE COLLEGE LIBRARY. *Faxon* 5th rev. ed. 1972 $14.00

IRREGULAR SERIALS AND ANNUALS: An International Directory. Ed. by Emery Koltay. *Bowker* 3rd ed. 1974 $43.50

   This bibliography brings together current data on 19,500 serials, annuals, continuations, proceedings of national and international conferences, and other publications issued irregularly or less frequently than twice a year. Arrangement is by subject, with title and subject indexes. Each entry gives title, subtitle or annotation, date of first issue, frequency (if scheduled), editor, name and address of publisher, price in the currency of the country of publication, and International Standard Serial Number (ISSN).

Katz, William. MAGAZINES FOR LIBRARIES. *Bowker* 2nd ed. 1972 $23.50

NEW SERIAL TITLES, 1950–70 cumulative. *Bowker* 1973 4 vols. set $190.00

   This new edition is a compilation of the new serial titles commencing publication after Dec. 31, 1949. It includes about 260,000 titles, alphabetically arranged. Information includes issuing body, place of publication, date of first issue, and of last issue if publication has ceased, Dewey classification number, country code and International Standard Serial Number. There is a separate list of 20,000 cessations and changes since 1950.

SERIALS SUPPLEMENT, 1974: To Ulrich's International Periodicals Directory, 15th ed. and Irregular Serials and Annuals, 3rd ed. *Bowker* 1974 (in prep.)

Spahn, Theodore J., Janet M. Spahn and Robert H. Muller. FROM RADICAL LEFT TO EXTREME RIGHT: A Bibliography of Current Periodicals of Protest, Controversy, Advocacy or Dissent, with Dispassionate Content-summaries to Guide Librarians and Other Educators. *Scarecrow Press* 2nd ed. rev. and enl. 1972 $12.50

THE STANDARD PERIODICAL DIRECTORY. *Oxbridge Pub. Co.* 4th ed. 1973 $60.00. A guide to more than 62,000 U.S. and Canadian periodicals. Alphabetical subject arrangement with author index and subject guide. Gives name and address of publisher, editorial content and scope, year founded, subscription rate, etc.

ULRICH'S INTERNATIONAL PERIODICALS DIRECTORY. Ed. by Merle Rohinsky. *Bowker* 15th ed. 1973 $46.50. Provides in-depth information for some 55,000 periodicals from all over the world, arranged under 249 subject headings. Special sections listing periodicals which have ceased publication since 1971, indexing and abstracting services, and periodicals launched since 1971 are also included.

WORKING PRESS OF THE NATION. Newspapers, magazines, radio and TV, and feature writer and syndicate directory. *National Research Bureau* annual 4 vols. each $35.00; set $99.50

BOOK TRADE AND LIBRARY TERMINOLOGY

ABC OF THE BOOK TRADE. Ed. by Sol M. Malkin. *AB Bookman's Weekly* (Box 1100, Newark, N.J. 07101) pap. $3.00

A.L.A. GLOSSARY OF LIBRARY TERMS. Elizabeth H. Thompson. *American Lib. Assn.* 1943 $4.00

Carter, John. ABC FOR BOOK-COLLECTORS. *Knopf* 5th ed. rev. 1973 $5.95

Glaister, G. A. ENCYCLOPEDIA OF THE BOOK. *World Pub.* 1960 o.p.

Landau, Thomas. ENCYCLOPEDIA OF LIBRARIANSHIP. Uses British library terms. *Hafner* 1958 3rd ed. 1966 $13.95

Orne, Jerrold. THE LANGUAGE OF THE FOREIGN BOOK TRADE: Abbreviations, Terms and Phrases. 1949. *American Lib. Assn.* 2nd ed. 1962 $6.50

Peters, Jean. THE BOOKMAN'S GLOSSARY. *Bowker* 5th ed. 1974 (in prep.). Covers terminology in all branches of the field of books: antiquarian, printing, publishing, retailing, manufacturing, collecting.

VOCABULARIUM BIBLIOTHECARII. Prep. by Anthony Thompson. 1953 *UNESCO* (Publications Center, N.Y.C.) rev. ed. 1962, 1966 o.p. A multilingual glossary of library terminology which lists more than 3,000 library terms in English with their equivalents in French, German, Spanish and Russian.

DIRECTORIES AND YEARBOOKS

Book Trade

AMERICAN BOOK TRADE DIRECTORY. Ed. by Helaine MacKeigan. *Bowker* 21st ed. 1973 $40.00. Includes lists of publishers, booksellers, book clubs, rental library chains, wholesalers, etc., in the United States and Canada. Also lists major book publishers in Great Britain and Ireland. Revised biennially.

AB BOOKMAN'S YEARBOOK. Ed. by Sol M. Malkin. *AB Bookman's Weekly* (Box 1100, Newark, N.J. 07101) 2 pts. pap. set $5.00, free with *AB* subscription. Issued annually in March, the Yearbook includes book-trade features, "The O. P. Market," "Trade Services Directory," lists of Permanent Book Wants, etc., and a Reference Directory of Antiquarian and Specialist Booksellers.

BOOK BUYER'S HANDBOOK. *American Booksellers Assn.* updated periodically. Free to members of American Booksellers Assn. only. A guide to more than 500 publishers, their discounts, terms, policies and trade features, issued in ring-binder format with correction sheets to be supplied from time to time.

CASSELL'S DIRECTORY OF PUBLISHING. For Great Britain, the Commonwealth, Ireland and South Africa. Covers book publishing and its ancillary services. *Int. Pubns. Service* 7th ed. 1973 $17.50

LA EMPRESA DEL LIBRO EN AMERICA LATINA. Ed. by Mary C. Turner. *Bowker* 1973 $15.95. The key to the book industry in all of Latin America.

INTERNATIONAL LITERARY MARKET PLACE. Ed. by J. A. Neal. A directory to approximately 3,000 active publishers throughout the world. *Bowker* 1974 $18.50. Revised biennially.

LITERARY MARKET PLACE, WITH NAMES AND NUMBERS: The Business Directory of American Publishing. Ed. by J. A. Neal. *Bowker* annually in summer pap. $17.50

O. P. Market: Reference Directory of Antiquarian and Specialist Booksellers. Ed. by
Sol M. Malkin. *AB Bookman's Weekly* (Box 1100, Newark, N.J. 07101) annual
1974 pap. $3.00

Publishers' International Directory *(Internationales Verlagsadressbuch). Verlag
Documentation*, Munich (dist. by Bowker) 1972 $45.00

"The directory gives names and addresses of 20,000 publishers in 152 countries—arranged geographically.... Includes an index listing publishers by subject interests, with 30,000 cross-references; a guide to
publishers' and booksellers' associations in 54 countries; and lists of national and international book trade associations around the globe. Index terms are given in five languages—English, German, French, Spanish and
Italian"—(Publisher's catalog).

Publishers' International Year Book. 3rd ed. Names and addresses of 14,000 book
publishers in 127 countries. *Publishers' International Year Book* (A. P. Wales Organization, 18 Charing Cross Rd., London W.C.2) 6th ed. 1973 £10.50 ($24.00)

The Writers' and Artists' Yearbook. Annual. Directory of British publishers, periodicals, photographers, agents, etc. *A. & C. Black*, London (dist. by The Writer)
$6.95

Library

American Library Directory. Ed. by Helaine MacKeigan. *Bowker* biennially 29th
ed. 1974/75 (in prep.) updating service (6 bimonthly bulletins) $50.00 a year

The "American Library Directory" includes: public libraries, county and regional extension systems, college and university libraries, junior college libraries, special libraries, libraries operated by private organizations, clubs and institutions, government libraries, major research libraries overseas, etc. Arranged geographically by state and city with information as to key personnel, volumes, budget, special departments, branches,
salaries, etc.

Bowker Annual of Library and Book Trade Information. Ed. by Madeline Miele.
Bowker annual 19th ed. 1974 $19.50 Sources of listings, charts, associations and ar-
ticles of interest to the library and book world.

Directory of Special Libraries and Information Centers. *Gale* 3rd ed. 1974
$48.00; Supplement (4 issues per year) $42.00

Subject Collections: A Guide to Special Book Collections and Subject Emphases as
Reported by University, College, Public, Museum, and Special Libraries in the
United States and Canada. Ed. by Lee Ash. *Bowker* 4th ed. 1974 $38.50

"A companion to the "American Library Directory," this volume indexes the book resources of college,
special and public libraries under subjects based upon Library of Congress subject headings, plus innumerable author, place and name collections. Within the subject categories, entries are arranged alphabetically in
geographic order. Typical entries include name and location of library holding the collection, name of curator, whether indexed, book budget, etc."—(Publisher's catalog). 45,000 collections are recorded.

Subject Collections in European Libraries. Ed. by Richard C. Lewanski. *Bowker*
1965 o.p.

Provides such information as name and location of collection, its size and type of material, name of curator,
interlibrary loan and photoreproduction facilities, copyright privileges, number of volumes held, and a bibliographic citation of printed catalogs, guides and other descriptive and historical monographs on the library.

World Guide to Libraries. *Verlag Dokumentation*, Munich (dist. by Bowker) 3rd ed.
1971 4 vols. set $44.50

Lists 36,000 special, university and public libraries from 158 countries in Europe, Africa, America, Asia and Oceania. For each library, the guide provides name and address, subject specialities, year of establishment and number of books. The subject index, subdivided by country, pinpoints all the libraries of any country with particular subject collections.

Many regional and special library groups issue directories covering their particular area, such as the ones listed below.

DIRECTORY OF SPECIAL LIBRARIES IN BOSTON AND VICINITY. *Boston Chapter, Special Libraries Assn.* 7th ed. 1972 (Order from SLA Boston Chapter Publications Office, c/o 77 Allen St., Arlington, Mass. 02174)

SPECIAL LIBRARIES DIRECTORY OF GREATER NEW YORK. *New York Chapter, Special Libraries Assn.* 13th ed. 1974 $15.00 (Order from Sue Palmatier, Federal Reserve Bank of New York, 33 Liberty St., N.Y.C. 10045)

—J. R. P.

Chapter 3

Reference Books—Literature

Reference sources, although sometimes an end in themselves, are usually a step to another work. Listed here are some of the more important and useful tools currently used in literary research. Citations indicate the latest edition at time of editing: if a later edition is available at time of reading ask for it (although it may not necessarily be a more comprehensive treatment for your purpose).

Like other nonfiction, reference works duplicate information among themselves; yet each has its individual competencies and deficiencies. One will know these best through use and comparison; stated purposes in prefaces are not always fulfilled and copyright dates are no proof of up-to-date material. Many reference works are beyond the budget of individuals; however, public and academic libraries should have some titles from each section given below.

See each Chapter for specialized reference books pertaining to the subject.

BASIC INDEXES FOR LITERATURE

Indexes are indispensable for the researcher or the reader wanting to locate a particular short story, poem, article or play.

Bibliography

BIBLIOGRAPHIC INDEX. 1938–. *Wilson* Permanent vols. in print: Vol. I 1937–1942 $45.00; Vol. 2 1943–1946 $25.00; Vol. 3 1947–1950 $25.00; Vol. 4 1951–1955 $22.00. Succeeding volumes sold on a service basis to libraries. Vol. 5 1956–1959; Vol. 6 1960–1962; Vol. 7 1963–1965; Vol. 8 1966–1968; Vol. 9 1969; Vol. 10 1970; Vol. 11 1971; Vol. 12 1972

   This is a subject list of bibliographies, in both English and foreign languages, which contain 40 or more bibliographic citations. Includes bibliographies published separately as books and pamphlets or appearing as parts in these forms. In addition 1900 periodicals are examined for material. Published in paper binding three times a year before annual cumulation.

Biography

BIOGRAPHY INDEX. 1946–. *Wilson* Vol. I Jan. 1946–July 1949; Vol. 2 Aug. 1949–Aug. 1952; Vol. 3 Sept. 1952–Aug. 1955; Vol. 4 Sept. 1955–Aug. 1958; Vol. 5 Sept. 1958–Aug. 1961; Vol. 6 Sept. 1961–Aug. 1964; Vol. 7 Sept. 1964–Aug. 1967; Vol. 8 Sept. 1967–Aug. 1970 each $50.00. Issued quarterly (in November, February, May and August), with annual and permanent three-year cumulations. Annual subscription $25.00

   "Covers biographical material appearing in approximately 1900 periodicals indexed in other Wilson indexes; current books of individual and collective biography in the English language; obituaries, including those of national interest published in the *New York Times*; and incidental biographical material in otherwise non-biographical books. Bibliographies and portraits and other illustrations are noted when they appear in connection with indexed material. *Biography Index* consists of a main or "name" alphabet and an index by professions and occupations"—(Publisher's catalog).

Essays

ESSAY AND GENERAL LITERATURE INDEX. 1900–. *Wilson* Alphabetical by author, subject and (in the case of documents) title. Kept up-to-date by semiannual supplements, with annual cumulations; since 1960 the cumulative period for permanent volumes has been five years. Each vol. $55.00; service basis annual subscription $22.00

> Foundation vol: 1900–1933. Covers 40,000 essays in 2144 vols., 86,698 analytics. Ed. by Minnie Earl Sears and Marian Shaw. 1934. Seven-year vol.: 1934–1940; 23,090 essays and articles in 1241 vols. Ed. by Marian Shaw. 1941. Seven-year vol.: 1941–1947; 32,226 essays and articles in 2023 vols. Ed. by Dorothy Herbert West and Estelle A. Fidell. 1948. Seven-year vol.: 1948–1954; 33,880 essays and articles in 1341 vols. Ed. by Dorothy Herbert West and Estelle A. Fidell. 1955. Five-year vol.: 1955–1959; 20,091 essays in 957 vols. 1960. Five-year vol.: 1960–1964; 21,320 essays in 1088 vols. Ed. by Estelle A. Fidell. 1965. Five-year vol.: 1965–1969.

ESSAY AND GENERAL LITERATURE INDEX: Works Indexed 1900–1969. *Wilson* 1972 $16.00. Cites all 9917 titles that have been analyzed in the seven permanent cumulations.

Fairy Tales and Folk Literature

Eastman, Mary Huse. INDEX TO FAIRY TALES, MYTHS AND LEGENDS. *Faxon* 2nd ed. 1926 $11.00. First Supplement 1937 $11.00; Second Supplement 1952 $11.00

Ireland, Norma Olin. INDEX TO FAIRY TALES, 1949–72, including Folklore, Legends and Myths in Collections. *Faxon* 1973 $14.00. International in scope. Titles arranged alphabetically with references from earliest titles; subjects are cross-referenced. Ireland continues M. H. Eastman's work.

Thompson, Stith. MOTIF-INDEX OF FOLK-LITERATURE. *Indiana Univ. Press* rev. ed. 1955–58 6 vols. Vols. 1–5 each $17.50 Vol. 6 $22.50 set $100.00

Ficton

FICTION CATALOG. *Wilson* 8th ed. 1971 $25.00 1971 Supplement to the 8th edition, 1972; 1972 Supplement to the 8th edition, 1973

> "Primarily a list of works of adult fiction although many titles are suitable for young adult reading (these are designated by a "y"). The staffs of a variety of public library systems have selected 4315 titles for the 8th edition. Out-of-print titles are included. Part 1 is an author alphabet. Bibliographic data and latest known price are listed. Part 2 is a title and subject index to part 1. Part 3 is a directory of publishers and distributors of the books listed"—(Preface). New editions will appear at five-year intervals.

Illustrations

INDEX TO ILLUSTRATIONS. Comp. by Jessie Croft Ellis. *Faxon* 1967 $13.00

> "This is the kind of reference book which almost every library will want despite certain defects. For example, there are some ten references under 'Gauguin, Paul (work of),' but no title identification is given. Except for the paintings, the indexed materials are similar in nature to those found in Vance and Tracey's *"Illustration Index"* [*see below*]. There is only a small amount of overlapping, however, in the books and periodicals indexed. Vance has concentrated on periodicals while Ellis has indexed mainly twenty books and ten years of six periodicals. For both public and school libraries"—(*LJ*).

ILLUSTRATION INDEX. Comp. by Lucile E. Vance and Esther M. Tracey. *Scarecrow Press* 2nd ed. 1966 $12.00 *(See note for Ellis, above.)*

Plays

Chicorel, Marietta, Ed. Chicorel Theater Index to Plays in Anthologies, Period-
ICALS, Discs and Tapes. *Chicorel Library Publishing* Vol. 1 (1970); Vol. 2 (1971);
Vol. 3 (1972); Vol. 4 (1973) indexes recorded media; Vol. 5 (1973) indexes period-
icals; each $45.00

Chicorel Theater Index to Children's Plays in Anthologies, Periodicals,
Discs and Tapes. *Chicorel Library Publishing* 1973 $45.00. Anthologies, period-
icals, editors, plays and authors arranged in one list.

Index to Full-Length Plays 1895–1925. Comp. by Ruth G. Thomson. *Faxon* 1956;
Index to Full-Length Plays 1926–1944. Comp. by Ruth G. Thomson. *Faxon*
1946; Index to Full-Length Plays 1944–1964. Comp. by Norma O. Ireland.
Faxon 1965 each $11.00

Of the latest volume, *Library Journal* reports: "Continuation of important earlier work by Ruth Thomson, . . . the most important feature of this volume is its subject approach to plays found in collections, Broadway plays, and many pamphlet plays. Many new subject headings have been added with cross-references.
Single-alphabet index of authors, subjects, and titles; the main entry is by play title and for each is given the
author, number of characters, number of acts, and whether it is an adaptation."

Index to One-Act Plays: 1900–1924. Comp. by Hannah Logasa and Winifred Ver
Nooy. *Faxon* (1924); Supplement: 1924–1931 (1932); Second Supplement:
1932–1940 (1941); Third Supplement: 1941–1948 (1950); Fourth Supplement:
1948–1957 (1958); Fifth Supplement: 1958–1964 (1966). *Faxon* 1924–1964 5
vols. each $11.00

The first index covers 5000 one-act plays; the first supplement covers 7000. Indexed under title, author,
subject; states the number of characters in each play. The second supplement includes over 500 collections,
many separate plays from pamphlets and periodicals. The fourth and fifth volumes provide information on
characters, setting, background, suitability for school production, etc. The last three supplements are by
Hannah Logasa.

Keller, Dean H. Index to Plays in Periodicals. *Scarecrow Press* 1971 $15.00. Index
to plays published in 103 selected periodicals.

Index To Plays in Periodicals. Supplement. *Scarecrow Press* 1973 $7.50. 37 addi-
tional periodicals are indexed.

Kreider, Barbara. Index to Children's Plays in Collections. *Scarecrow Press* 1972
$5.00. Index of over 500 one-act plays and skits from collections published between
1965 and 1968. Plays are arranged by title, subject, theme and type of play.

Ottemiller's Index to Plays in Collections: An Author and Title Index to Plays Appearing in Collections Published Between 1900 and Mid-1970. 5th ed. rev. and enl.
by John M. and Billie M. Connor. *Scarecrow Press* 1971 $11.00

The first edition (1943) covered 1900–1942. The current edition indexes 3049 different plays by 1644 different authors; 1047 collections are analyzed. Limited to books published in England and the U.S. but includes plays in foreign languages published in anthologies in England and the U.S. Only complete texts are
indexed. Foreign plays translated into English are entered under English titles with references from translated titles.

Patterson, Charlotte A., Comp. Plays in Periodicals: An Index to English Language
Scripts in Twentieth Century Journals. *G. K. Hall* 1970 $17.00. Over 4000 plays
printed in 97 English-language journals published from 1900 through 1968.

PLAY INDEX. *Wilson* 4 vols. Vol. I 1949–1952: An index to 2,616 Plays in 1,138 volumes. Comp. by Dorothy Herbert West and Dorothy Margaret Peake 1953 $8.00; Vol. 2 1953–1960: An index to 4,592 Plays in 1,735 volumes. Comp. by Estelle A. Fidell and D. M. Peake 1963 $11.00; Vol. 3 1961–1967 (1968): An index to 4,793 Plays. Comp. by E. A. Fidell $16.00; Vol. 4 1968–1972: An index to 3,848 Plays (in prep.).

"This volume is in 4 parts: Part 1 lists each play under title and subjects. Requirements for set, dance or music are noted. Part 2, cast analysis, locates plays by number of players or readers needed. Part 3 is a list of collections indexed, including publisher, date and paging. Part 4 is a directory of publishers and distributors"—(Publisher's catalog).

Poetry

Chicorel, Marietta, Ed. CHICOREL INDEX TO POETRY IN COLLECTIONS IN PRINT. *Chicorel Library Publishing* 1973 $49.50

CHICOREL INDEX TO POETRY IN COLLECTIONS OUT OF PRINT. *Chicorel Library Publishing* 1973 $49.50. The main index in both of the above lists title, first line, author, poet, collection title editor and translator in one alphabet.

GRANGER'S INDEX TO POETRY. Ed. by William James Smith. 1904 1918 1940 1945 1962 6th ed. completely rev. and enl. *Columbia* 1973 $80.00. Originally compiled by Edith Granger, this standard work now itemizes more than a quarter of a million individual references to poems by their titles and first lines. 514 volumes are indexed, 121 for the first time in this edition. The Author Index lists some 12,000 poets and translators. The Subject Index has approximately 4500 categories updated to include "Ecology," "Women's Liberation," etc.

INDEX OF AMERICAN PERIODICAL VERSE. By Sander W. Zulauf and Irwin H. Weiser. *Scarecrow Press* 2 vols. Vol. I 1971 (1973) $12.50; Vol. 2 1972 (1974) $15.00. This new work indexes 150 periodicals in the first volume and 160 periodicals in the second. Includes alphabetical directory of the poets with complete bibliographic entries for their poems. If this series continues it will be a valuable reference source for American poetry.

INDEX TO CHILDREN'S POETRY. Comp. by John Edmund Brewton and Sarah W. Brewton. *Wilson* 1942 $16.00. Author, title, subject and first-line entries from 130 collections by 2500 authors; included are more than 15,000 poems for children and youth. FIRST SUPPLEMENT: 1938–1951. Entries from 66 collections; more than 7000 poems by 1300 authors $10.00; SECOND SUPPLEMENT: 1949–1963. Entries from 85 collections; more than 8000 poems by 1400 authors $12.00

INDEX TO POETRY FOR CHILDREN AND YOUNG PEOPLE, 1964–1969. By John E. Brewton, Sarah W. Brewton and G. Meredith Blackburn, III. *Wilson* 1972 $20.00. A title, subject, author and first-line index to poetry in collections for children and young people. Entries from 117 collections.

Short Stories

SHORT STORY INDEX. Comp. by Dorothy E. Cook and Isabel S. Monro. *Wilson* 60,000 stories in 4320 collections published before 1950 (1953) $20.00. FIRST SUPPLEMENT, 1950–1954. Comp. by Dorothy E. Cook and Estelle A. Fidell. An index to 9575 stories in 549 collections (1956) $12.00; SECOND SUPPLEMENT, 1955–1958. Comp. by

E. A. Fidell and Esther V. Flory. 6392 stories in 376 collections (1960) $10.00; Third Supplement, 1959–1963. Comp. by E. A. Fidell. 9068 stories in 582 collections (1965) $15.00; Fourth Supplement, 1964–1968. Comp. by E. A. Fidell. 11,301 stories in 793 collections published in the years 1964–1968 $19.00. "Indexed by author, title, and subject in one alphabet. The author, or main, entry lists the author's full name and dates, the title of each of his stories, and the author (or editor) and title of the collection in which each story appears. A list of the collections indexed includes full bibliographical information." The supplements provide the same kind of information as the original volume, and each includes in addition a directory of publishers and distributors.

Siemon, Frederick. Science Fiction Story Index, 1950–1968. *American Lib. Assn.* 1971 $3.95

Subject and Title Index to Short Stories for Children. *American Lib. Assn.* 1955 $6.50

Songs

Leigh, Robert. Index to Song Books. 1964. *DaCapo* 1973 lib. bdg. $9.50. A title index to over 11,000 copies of almost 6800 songs in 3 song books published between 1933–1962.

Song Index: An Index to More Than 12,000 Songs. 1926. Ed. by Minnie Earl Sears and Phyllis Crawford; with Song Index Supplement: An Index to More than 7,000 Songs. 1934. *Shoe String* 2 vols. in I 1966 $27.50

Speeches

Sutton, Roberta Briggs, Comp. Speech Index: An Index to Collections of World Famous Orations and Speeches for Various Occasions. *Scarecrow Press* 1935 4th ed. 1966 $20.00 Supplement 1966–1970. 1972 $20.00. The Supplement indexes 58 books published between 1966 and 1970.

Translations

Index Translationum. *UNIPUB* (UNESCO). Vol. 19 1966 $36.00; Vol. 20 1967 pap. $40.00; Vol. 21 1968 $40.00; Vol. 22 1971 $42.00; Vol. 23 1970 (1972) $46.00. Arranged by countries and presented under ten major headings of the Universal Decimal Classification system. Entries give name of author, title of translation, name of translation, place, name of publisher, year of publication; price in currency of country where published. Title of original work is given in italics.

BIBLIOGRAPHIES ON ENGLISH AND AMERICAN LITERATURE

The following bibliographies deal with the *total* literatures of Great Britain and America. Bibliographies on particular periods or authors will, of course, add to the research materials given in the titles below.

Modern Language Association International Bibliography of Books and Articles on the Modern Languages and Literatures. 1921–. Modern Language Association of America *New York Univ. Press* 1971 vol. published in 1973 $15.00

An annual listing of books and articles on modern languages and literatures. (The 1971 volume was compiled from 2,300 periodicals and various books.) Four separate volumes are published each year with a cumulative volume published for libraries. Vol. I includes sections on English and American literatures (as well as Medieval, Neo-Latin, and Celtic literatures and folklore). Each section is further divided into century, and authors writing in that century. Authors as subjects appear in heavy type. At the end of each volume is an index containing the name of every author, editor or compiler in the listings. This is the most comprehensive single work giving current research in Great Britain and America.

ANNUAL BIBLIOGRAPHY OF ENGLISH LANGUAGE AND LITERATURE. *Modern Humanities Research Association*, Cambridge 1921–. $16.87. Includes a section on American literature.

THE YEAR'S WORK IN ENGLISH STUDIES. English Association, London, New York *Humanities Press* 192?–. Vol. 52 1971 (1973) $9.75

Annual chapters are: Literary History and Criticism: General Works; English Language; Old English Literature; Middle English, excluding Chaucer; Chaucer; The Earlier Sixteenth Century; Shakespeare; The Later Sixteenth Century, excluding Drama; The Earlier Seventeenth Century, excluding Drama; Milton; The Later Seventeenth Century; The Eighteenth Century; The Nineteenth Century; The Twentieth Century; American Literature to 1900; American Literature: The Twentieth Century; Index. Each chapter is a prose narrative reviewing books and articles of the year.

Bibliographies on American Literature

AMERICAN LITERARY SCHOLARSHIP, AN ANNUAL. Ed. by James L. Woodress. *Duke Univ. Press* 1965–. 1963 (1965) $7.00; 1964 (1966) $7.00; 1965 (1967) $7.00; 1966 (1968) $7.00; 1967 (1969) $7.00; ed. by J. Albert Robbins 1968 (1970) $7.00; 1969 (1971) $8.75; 1970 (1972) $8.75; 1971 (1973) $8.75

Annual review, with annotated chapters on: Emerson, Thoreau, Transcendentalism; Hawthorne, Melville; Whitman, Dickinson; James, Faulkner; Fitzgerald, Hemingway; Literature to 1800; 19th Century Fiction; Poe and 19th Century Poetry; Fiction: 1930 to the Present; Poetry: 1900 to 1930; Poetry 1930 to the Present; Drama; Folklore; Themes, Topics, Criticism.

LITERARY HISTORY OF THE UNITED STATES. Ed. by Robert E. Spiller and others. *Macmillan* 1948 1953 3rd ed. 1963 2 vols. and supplement (1972) Vol. I $17.50; Vol. 2 $16.50; Supp. $14.95

Vol. 2 is a selective bibliography for the general reader divided into four sections: Guide to Resources; Bibliographies: Literature and culture; Bibliographies: Movements and influences; Bibliographies: Individual authors. For the last-named section the 3rd edition has bibliographic essays on 207 American authors, listing primary and secondary works. The sequence of listings here is usually separate and collected works, edited texts and reprints, biography and criticism, primary sources—including location of manuscripts—and bibliographies. Critical comments are given on editions, biographies, etc. This is the essential *retrospective* bibliography of American literature.

Bibliographies on English Literature

THE CAMBRIDGE BIBLIOGRAPHY OF ENGLISH LITERATURE. Ed. by F. W. Bateson. *Cambridge* 1940–57. 5 vols. Vol. I 600–1660; Vol. 2 1600–1800; Vol. 3 1800–1900; Vol. 4 Index; Vol. 5 Supplement 600–1900, ed. by George Watson o.p.

THE CONCISE CAMBRIDGE BIBLIOGRAPHY OF ENGLISH LITERATURE. Ed. by George Watson. *Cambridge* 1958 2nd ed. 1965 $9.95 pap. $4.95. A greatly abridged version of the CBEL which offers the general reader a select list of the best editions by and secondary works on the major English writers.

THE NEW CAMBRIDGE BIBLIOGRAPHY OF ENGLISH LITERATURE. *Cambridge* 1969–.
5 vols. Vol. I 600–1600 (in prep); Vol. 2 1660–1800 (1971) ed. by George Watson
$45.00; Vol. 3 1800–1900 (1969) ed. by George Watson $45.00; Vol. 4 1900–1950
(1972) ed. by I. R. Willison $49.50; Vol. 5 General Index (in prep.)

This work is based on the CBEL published in 1940 and 1957 (the supplement), now out of print. Expanded and brought up-to-date, it retains the systematic arrangement of the earlier work. Possessors of the CBEL are urged to keep their volumes, however, as certain materials have been omitted in the NCBEL: the literatures of Canada, Australia, India and New Zealand and such nonliterary sections as those on science, law, economics, political and social backgrounds.

The scope, as stated by the editor, is nothing less than to "represent the whole of English studies, so far as concern the life of the British Isles, both in primary and secondary materials, 'works by' and 'works about'." A work as large in scope as this is not without errors, which have been pointed to by, for example, Richard Altick, in *Journal of English and German Philology*, Jan., 1971 and by F. W. Bateson, the original editor, in the *Times Literary Supplement*, Dec. 25, 1969. Nevertheless this work is the definitive retrospective coverage of the entire spectrum of English literature.

HISTORIES AND DICTIONARIES OF LITERATURE

A good history or dictionary of literature offers information that is both essential and interesting. Among topics usually covered are the lives, works and evaluations of authors; the aims and techniques of literary movements; the relation of a writer or movement to predecessors or successors; and terms used to describe literature.

Excluded from this chapter are books on a particular period such as Moses Tyler's "Literary History of the American Revolution" or works on a particular author, such as Oscar Campbell and Edward Quinn's superb "The Reader's Encyclopedia of Shakespeare." The reader should consult the bibliographies under the appropriate chapter, or the listings under the individual author for these.

European Literature

Kunitz, Stanley J., and Vineta Colby, Eds. EUROPEAN AUTHORS, 1000–1900: A Biographical Dictionary of European Literature. *Wilson* 1967 $24.00

This "indispensable" work (*LJ*), alphabetically arranged, contains 967 biographies (and 309 portraits) of authors from 31 countries born after 1000 A.D. and dead by 1925. With the general reader in mind, the appended bibliographies stress English translations and studies of works and authors. "These biographies provide quick, satisfactory introductions to a staggering variety of authors and literatures"—(*Choice*). The volume was ten years in preparation.

MODERN ROMANCE LITERATURE. Comp. and ed. by Dorothy Nyren Curley and Arthur Curley. *Ungar* $15.00

Moulton's original 19th-century work has inspired these modern volumes of compilations from criticism in periodicals, newspapers, books, etc., mostly British and American. Alphabetized by author criticized, each excerpt has been chosen to "describe [the author's] qualities, define his status, and show something of his life and personality." Full citations are given for the criticisms, and there is a selective bibliography of each author's work and an index to critics—who are often among the most distinguished of their profession. Many are themselves noted as creative writers.

Priestley, J. B. LITERATURE AND WESTERN MAN. *Harper* 1960 $10.95. A highly readable literary history on a grand scale, from 1450 to 1939.

Saintsbury, George. HISTORY OF CRITICISM AND LITERARY TASTE IN EUROPE, FROM THE EARLIEST TEXTS TO THE PRESENT DAY. 1900–04. *British Book Centre* text ed. $17.50; *Humanities Press* 3 vols. Vol. I Classical and Medieval Criticism; Vol. 2

From the Renaissance to the Decline of 18th Century Orthodoxy; Vol. 3 Nineteenth Century each $7.25

Smith, Horatio Elwin, Ed. COLUMBIA DICTIONARY OF MODERN EUROPEAN LITERATURE. *Columbia* 1947 $17.50. 239 specialists contributed nearly 1200 articles covering the literary activities of 31 continental European countries from about 1870 to the 1940s. Dr. Smith was Professor of French and chairman of the French section of the Department of Romance Languages at Columbia. This is sadly in need of updating.

Thorlby, Anthony, Ed. THE PENGUIN COMPANION TO EUROPEAN LITERATURE. Vol. 2 1969 *McGraw-Hill* $11.95; (with title "Penguin Companion to Literature, Vol. 2 European new ed.") *Penguin* 1973 pap. $4.95. Important European authors, editions and translations of their works, summaries and critical commentaries; guide to entries by language and country.

World Literature

Benet, William Rose, Ed. THE READER'S ENCYCLOPEDIA: An Encyclopedia of World Literature and the Arts. *T. Y. Crowell* 1948 2nd ed. 1965 $10.00 thumb indexed $12.95. Brief descriptions of writers, literary allusions and expressions, literary schools, plots and characters, criticism, etc.

CASSELL'S ENCYCLOPAEDIA OF WORLD LITERATURE. Ed. by Sigfrid Henry Steinberg. *Funk & Wagnalls* 1954 2 vols. text ed. $25.00. Vol. I Histories of literatures of the world. Biographies of various writers up to the 20th century; Vol. 2 Literary forms, schools, genres. Biographies of 20th century authors.

CASSELL'S ENCYCLOPEDIA OF WORLD LITERATURE. Ed. by John Buchanan-Brown. 1954. *Morrow* 1973 3 vols. $47.95. An updating of the work above.

CONTEMPORARY AUTHORS: The International Bio-Bibliographical Guide to Current Authors and Their Works. Ed. by James M. Etheridge. *Gale* 36 vols. 1962–1972. Sold in 4-vol. units, each unit $25.00. This set provides information on 31,000 of today's writers, including minor and first-time authors. Material is provided mainly by the authors themselves. Vols. 1–8 have been revised; the publisher plans periodic updating of the succeeding volumes.

Fleischmann, Wolfgang Bernard, Ed. ENCYCLOPEDIA OF WORLD LITERATURE IN THE 20TH CENTURY. *Ungar* 1967–1971 3 vols. Vol. I A–F $28.50; Vol. 2 G–N $31.50; Vol. 3 O–Z $38.00 3-vol. set $98.00

A translation of the *Lexikon der Weltliteratur im 20. Jahrhundert* revised and updated. "Biographical and bibliographic information about novelists, dramatists, poets, essayists, biographers, and critics throughout the world. The national literature of 55 countries is considered. Special feature articles explain major and minor literary genres and show how modern literature relates to psychological and societal movements—(Publisher's catalog). "A reliable and informative work which will be welcomed by scholars all over the world"—(*Comparative Literature Studies*). The author is Professor of Comparative literature at Montclair State College and former editor of *Books Abroad*.

Grigson, Geoffrey, Ed. THE CONCISE ENCYCLOPEDIA OF MODERN WORLD LITERATURE. *Hawthorn Bks.* 1963 1971 $13.95. Over 300 individual authors treated in readable essays.

Hornstein, Lillian H., and others, Eds. THE READER'S COMPANION TO WORLD LITERATURE. *See Chapter 4, Broad Studies—Reference and Background Materials.*

Ivask, Ivar, and Gero von Wilpert. WORLD LITERATURE SINCE 1945: Critical Surveys of the Contemporary Literatures of Europe and the Americas. *Ungar* 1973 2 vols. $25.00. Twenty-eight articles on major movements and individual literatures, including those lesser known, World War II; bibliographies, lists of English translations. Ivask is editor of *Books Abroad*; von Wilpert is editor of *Lexikon der Weltliteratur.*

Kunitz, Stanley J., and Howard Haycraft, Eds. TWENTIETH CENTURY AUTHORS. *Wilson* 1942 $22.00; First Supplement 1955 $18.00. A revision of Kunitz's "Living Authors" (1931 o.p.) and "Authors Today and Yesterday" (1933 o.p.), with additional material. Contains 1850 biographies. The Supplement brings the original biographies and bibliographies up to 1955, adding some 700 biographies.

Magill, Frank N. MASTERPIECES OF WORLD LITERATURE IN DIGEST FORM. *Harper* 4 vols. Vol. I (1952) $12.95; Vol. 2 (1956) $11.95; Vol. 3 (1960) $11.95; Vol. 4 (1969) $11.95; lib. bdg. each $10.95.

CYCLOPEDIA OF WORLD AUTHORS. *Harper* 1958 $12.95 lib. bdg. $10.69. Fine Collection of 753 biographies and appraisals by authorities; signed articles.

Seymour-Smith, Martin. THE FUNK AND WAGNALLS GUIDE TO MODERN WORLD LITERATURE. *Funk & Wagnalls* 1973 $13.95. Essays on writers from 1900 to the present, chiefly English, French, German, Italian, Russian and Spanish.

American Literature

Blair, Walter, Theodore Hornberger and Randall Stewart. AMERICAN LITERATURE: A Brief History. *Scott, Foresman* 1964 pap. 1973 $4.50. Walter Blair is Emeritus Professor of English, University of Chicago, Hornberger is Professor of English at the University of Pennsylvania; the late Randall Stewart was Professor of English at Vanderbilt University.

Burke, W. J., and Will D. Howe, Eds. AMERICAN AUTHORS AND BOOKS: 1640 to the Present Day. 1943 1962. 3rd rev. ed. by Irving and Anne Weiss. *Crown* 1972 $12.50. An "encyclopedia of American books, authors, personalities, periodicals, awards, organizations and other pertinent information covering all aspects of the literary world." Information is through 1971.

CAMBRIDGE HISTORY OF AMERICAN LITERATURE. Ed. by W. P. Trent, John Erskine, Stuart P. Sherman and Carl Van Doren. 3 vols. in 1. *Macmillan* 1917–21. reissue 1943 1954 $12.50. This work is modeled on the "Cambridge History of English Literature."

Cunliffe, Marcus. THE LITERATURE OF THE UNITED STATES. *Penguin* 1954 1961 rev. ed. 1967 pap. $1.95; *Peter Smith* $4.25. A good short survey from Colonial times to the 1960s. Cunliffe is a Professor of American Studies at the University of Sussex.

Curley, Dorothy Nyren, and Maurice Kramer. MODERN AMERICAN LITERATURE. *Ungar* 4th rev. and enl. ed. 1969 3 vols. $45.00

Duyckinck, Evert Augustus, and George Long Duyckinck. CYCLOPEDIA OF AMERICAN LITERATURE: Embracing Personal and Critical Notices of Authors, and Selections from Their Writings, from the Earliest Period to the Present Day, with Portraits, Autographs, and Other Illustrations. 1856, rev. 1875 by M. Laird Simons. *Gale Research Co.* 1965 2 vols. set $43.00. This older work, cited in bibliographies, is arranged chronologically. Includes survey articles on "The New England Preachers," "Ballad Literature of the Indian," "French and Revolutionary Wars," etc.

Herzberg, Max J., and Staff of Thomas Y. Crowell Co., Eds. THE READER'S ENCYCLOPEDIA OF AMERICAN LITERATURE. Introd. by Van Wyck Brooks. *T. Y. Crowell* 1962 $15.00.

> A quick reference companion volume to Benét's "The Reader's Encyclopedia" (*see World Literature section*) contains 6500 articles dealing with authors, titles and topics; 8 special charts. "A reference tool which no American library, private as well as public, can afford to be without"—(John Barkham, in *SR*).

Howard, Leon. LITERATURE AND THE AMERICAN TRADITION: A Critical History, Particularly of Poetry and Fiction from 1608 to 1950s. 1960 *Gordian* 1972 $10.00. Howard is Professor of English, University of California at Los Angeles.

Kunitz, Stanley J., and Haycraft, Howard, Eds. AMERICAN AUTHORS 1600–1900. *Wilson* 1938 $12.00

THE OXFORD COMPANION TO AMERICAN LITERATURE. Comp. and ed. by James David Hart. *Oxford* 1941 4th ed. 1965 $15.00. The fourth revised, enlarged and entirely reset edition of this large and valuable book contains 223 new entries, ranging from Albee to Tillich. Previous entries have been updated. (The three earlier editions are still valuable for dropped entries.) This work covers American literature from 1608 to the present; biographies and bibliographies of authors, plots of novels, poems and short stories, social and literary background of American writing, etc. An excellent feature is the chronological index, a year-by-year outline, giving in parallel columns literary and social events from 1000 to the present. Hart is Professor of English, University of California, Berkeley.

PENGUIN COMPANION TO USA AND LATIN AMERICAN LITERATURE. Ed. by Malcolm Bradbury, Eric Mottram and Jean Franco. *McGraw-Hill* 1971 $9.95. Colonial days to the 1970s. Bibliographies and summaries.

Spiller, Robert E., and others. LITERARY HISTORY OF THE UNITED STATES. *Macmillan* 1948 1953 1963 4th ed. rev. 1974 2 vols. each $25.00; 3rd Supplement 1972 $14.95. Vol. I, the literary history, contains articles by distinguished contributors, divided according to historical periods; Vol. 2 is the bibliographical supplement and discussion of it will be found in section on Bibliographies on American Literature, this chapter.

WEBSTER'S NEW WORLD COMPANION TO ENGLISH AND AMERICAN LITERATURE. Ed. by Arthur Pollard. *World Pub.* 1973 $15.00

English Literature

Allibone, S. Austin. A CRITICAL DICTIONARY OF ENGLISH LITERATURE AND BRITISH AND AMERICAN AUTHORS, LIVING AND DECEASED: From the Earliest Accounts to the Latter Half of the Nineteenth Century, Containing over 46,000 Articles (authors) with 40 Indexes of Subjects. 1858–71. 3 vols. *Gale* 1965 $84.00; *Gordon Press* $45.00; *Richard West* 1973 $80.00. Supplement by John F. Kirk (37,000 articles, 93,000 titles). 1891. 2 vols. *Gale* $43.00; *Gordon Press* $40.00. A valuable standard work.

ANNALS OF ENGLISH LITERATURE, 1475–1950: The Principal Publications of Each Year together with an Alphabetical Index of Authors with Their Works. *Oxford* 1935 2nd ed. 1961 rev. by R. W. Chapman $10.50

Barnhart, Clarence L., and William D. Halsey. THE NEW CENTURY HANDBOOK OF ENG-
  LISH LITERATURE. *Appleton* 1956 rev. ed. 1967 $15.75

> Some 14,000 entries, alphabetically arranged, with pronunciation. "It is difficult to discover lapses of any
> sort in this [revised] one-volume encyclopedia of British literature and all that bears thereon. The compilers
> intentionally excluded U.S. subject matter, confining the text to Commonwealth and Anglo-American au-
> thors. Plots, themes, and quotations can be found by reference to titles and character names; among the
> 14,000 entries are biographies of authors (through Tolkien, Osborne, and Pinter) and other significant per-
> sons, fables and myths, and literary and rhetorical terms"—(David Glixon, in *SR*).

Baugh, Albert C., and others. A LITERARY HISTORY OF ENGLAND. *Appleton* 4 vols.
  1948 2nd ed. 1967 4 vols. in 1 text ed. $17.85; 4-vol. pap ed. each $6.95. Vol. I The
  Middle Ages, by Kemp Malone and A. C. Baugh; Vol. 2 The Renaissance, by
  Tucker Brooke and Matthias A. Shaaber; Vol. 3 The Restoration and Eighteen
  Century, by G. Sherburn and D. F. Bond; Vol. 4 The Nineteenth Century and After,
  by S. C. Chew and Richard D. Altick.

CAMBRIDGE HISTORY OF ENGLISH LITERATURE. Ed. by A. W. Ward and A. R. Waller.
  Cambridge 1931 cheaper ed. reissue 1949–1953, 1954 15 vols. each $11.95, set
  $165.00

> Every chapter of this monumental work is written by a specialist. The unique feature is the discussion ac-
> cording to type: "Political Literature"; "Ballad Literature"; "Literature of Science"; "The Literature of
> Travel"; "Memoir Writers"; "The Essay," etc. Of special value to bookmen are: "Book Production and
> Distribution" by H. G. Aldis; "The Foundation of Libraries"; "Children's Books" by Harvey Darton;
> "The Introduction of Printing into England and the Early Work of the Press." Originally published in 14
> volumes (1907–17 o. p.), the present edition omits the bibliographies which are now revised and published
> separately as "The Cambridge Bibliography of English Literature," 4 vols. (*see Bibliographies on English
> Literature, this Chapter*). In the original edition each volume was indexed separately, but now Vol. 15 is the
> general index to the entire work.

THE CONCISE CAMBRIDGE HISTORY OF ENGLISH LITERATURE. 1941 1961. rev. 3rd ed.
  Cambridge 1970 $11.95 pap. $5.00. Revised throughout and with additional chapters on the literature of the United States of America and the mid-twentieth century
  literature of the English-speaking world by R. C. Churchill.

THE CONCISE OXFORD DICTIONARY OF ENGLISH LITERATURE. 1939. *Oxford* 2nd ed.
  1970 $8.00 pap. $2.95

> This edition by Dorothy Eagle "contains much new and revised material, especially with reference to the
> literature of the twentieth century. . . . The articles on general literary topics have been revised to take ac-
> count of developments and research during the last thirty years"—(*from the preface*).

Craig, Hardin, Ed. A HISTORY OF ENGLISH LITERATURE. *Oxford* 1950 (o. p.); *Macmillan* Collier Bks. 1962 4 vols. Vol. I Old and Middle English Literature by G. K.
  Anderson; Vol. 2 Literature of the English Renaissance 1485–1660 by Hardin
  Craig; Vol. 3 Literature of the Restoration and Eighteenth Century by L. I. Bredvold; Vol. 4 Literature of the 19th and early 20th centuries by J. W. Beach each
  $.95.

Daiches, David. A CRITICAL HISTORY OF ENGLISH LITERATURE. *Ronald* 1960 2nd ed.
  1970 2 vols. set $15.00

  ENGLISH LITERATURE. *Prentice-Hall* 1964 ref. ed. $7.95

Dobrée, Bonamy, Ed. INTRODUCTIONS TO ENGLISH LITERATURE. *Dover* 1950–1952 4
  vols. Vol. I The Beginnings of English Literature to Skelton, 1509, by W. L. Renwick and H. Orton (1911) rev. ed. 1952; Vol. 2 The English Renaissance, 1510–

1688, by V. De Sola Pinto (1913) rev. ed. 1951–52; Vol. 3 Augustans and Romantics, 1689–1830, by H. V. D. Dyson and J. Butt 2nd. rev. ed. 1951; Vol. 4 The Victorians and After, 1830–1914, by E. C. Batho and B. Dobrée (1918) rev. ed. 1952 each $2.50.

Elton, Oliver. A SURVEY OF ENGLISH LITERATURE, 1730–1880. 1928. 6 vols. (3 sets of 2 vols. each) Set 1, 1730–1780 (o. p.); Set 2, 1780–1830 (o. p.); Set 3, 1830–1880 *St. Martin's* 1963 $16.00. "Written between 1920 and 1928, these six volumes still reveal the indefatigable scholarship of Oliver Elton, professor of English literature at Liverpool, as well as an instinctive taste and individualistic opinions. Covering the 150-year period between the era of Gray, Johnson, Richardson, and Fielding, and that of Meredith, the Rossettis, and Morris, the survey contains data on many minor figures not included in modern literary histories. The notes to each volume are an especially valuable source of bibliographic data." This work is still standard.

Evans, B. Ifor. A SHORT HISTORY OF ENGLISH LITERATURE. *William Gannon* 3rd ed. lib. bdg. $3.50; *Penguin* 1940 1963 pap. $1.25

Ford, Boris, Ed. THE PELICAN GUIDE TO ENGLISH LITERATURE. *Penguin* 7 vols. pap. Vol. I The Age of Chaucer (1965) $1.65; Vol. 2 The Age of Shakespeare (1955) $1.65; Vol. 3 From Donne to Marvell (1956) $1.45; Vol. 4 From Dryden to Johnson (1957) $1.45; Vol. 5 From Blake to Byron (1957) $1.45; Vol. 6 From Dickens to Hardy (1958) $1.65; Vol. 7 The Modern Age (1961) $1.75; *Dufour* 7 Vols. Vols. I, 3, 4, 6, 7 $8.95; Vols. 2 and 5 $7.50; *Gannon* 7 vols. Vols. I, 2, 6 $3.90; Vols. 3, 4, 5 $3.70; Vol. 7 lib. bdg. $4.00. The essays are lively, clear, forceful and provocative.

Kunitz, Stanley J. BRITISH AUTHORS BEFORE 1800. *Wilson* 1952 $10.00. Biographies of 650 writers from the beginnings of English literature to Cowper and Burns.

BRITISH AUTHORS OF THE NINETEENTH CENTURY. *Wilson* 1936 $12.00. Complete in 1 volume with 1000 biographies and 350 portraits.

Legouis, Émile. A SHORT HISTORY OF ENGLISH LITERATURE. Trans. by V. F. Boyson and J. Coulson. *Oxford* 1934 $5.00

HISTORY OF ENGLISH LITERATURE. Trans. by Helen Douglas Irvine rev. ed. *Rowman* 1973 $12.00

The almost classic history of English literature. "A handy and dependable reference (complete in one volume of more than 1,400 pages) for 40 years, the book is still useful for a comprehensive view of English literature and for brief treatments of individual writers. Index"—(*Choice*).

Moody, William Vaughn, and R. M. Lovett. A HISTORY OF ENGLISH LITERATURE. *Scribner* 1902 8th rev. ed. 1964 by F. B. Millett pap. $5.95. The first version of this popular history was written by two young members of the English Department of the new University of Chicago in 1902. Moody died in 1910 having become a well-known poet and dramatist; and Lovett, who died in 1956, had a long and distinguished career as a critic and editor. Since then the revisions have been carried out by Millett, now Emeritus Professor of English at Wesleyan University, and colleagues.

THE OXFORD COMPANION TO ENGLISH LITERATURE. Comp. and ed. by Sir Paul Harvey. *Oxford* 1932 4th ed. rev. by Dorothy Eagle 1967 $15.00. An encyclopedia of authors, characters, plots, mythological references, general topics, etc. A standard.

THE OXFORD HISTORY OF ENGLISH LITERATURE

    Vol. 2, Pt. I. CHAUCER AND THE 15TH CENTURY. By H. S. Bennett. *Oxford* 1947 $11.50

    Vol. 2, Pt. 2. ENGLISH LITERATURE AT THE CLOSE OF THE MIDDLE AGES. By E. K. Chambers. *Oxford* 1945, 1947 $7.25

    Vol. 3. ENGLISH LITERATURE IN THE 16TH CENTURY EXCLUDING DRAMA. By C. S. Lewis. *Oxford* 1954 $11.50

    Vol. 4, Pt. I. THE ENGLISH DRAMA, 1485–1585. By F. P. Wilson. *Oxford* $8.50

    Vol. 5. ENGLISH LITERATURE IN THE EARLIER 17TH CENTURY, 1600–1660. By Douglas Bush. *Oxford* 1945 2nd. rev. ed. 1962 $11.50

    Vol. 6. ENGLISH LITERATURE OF THE LATE SEVENTEENTH CENTURY. By James Sutherland *Oxford* 1969 $12.50

    Vol. 7. ENGLISH LITERATURE IN THE EARLY EIGHTEENTH CENTURY, 1700–1740. By Bonamy Dobrée. *Oxford* 1959 $12.75

    Vol. 9. ENGLISH LITERATURE, 1789–1815. By W. L. Renwick. *Oxford* 1963 $8.00

    Vol. 10. ENGLISH LITERATURE, 1815–1832. By Ian Jack. *Oxford* 1963 $11.00

    Vol. 12. EIGHT MODERN WRITERS. *Oxford* 1963 $11.50

    When completed this will consist of 12 volumes, some of which will be in two parts. Each volume or half-volume will be an independent book, but the whole series will form a continuous history. All the contributors will be acknowledged authorities on their periods and each volume will incorporate in text and bibliography the results of the latest research.

Taine, Hippolyte. HISTORY OF ENGLISH LITERATURE. 1863. Trans. by H. Van Laun 1883 *Ungar* 4 vols. $40.00; *Somerset Pub.* 2 vols. repr. of 1871 ed. $29.50; *Richard West* repr. of 1897 ed. Trans. by H. Van Laun 1871 2 vols. 1973 $19.00; 8 vols. repr. of 1897 ed. $75.00. This 19th-century French critic, philosopher and historian held that literature is the product of deterministic forces: *"La race, le milieu, le moment."* This pioneer work is one of the quintessential expressions of this approach.

Ward, Alfred Charles. ENGLISH LITERATURE: Chaucer to Bernard Shaw. *McKay* (Longmans) 1958 $13.95. A one-volume edition of "Ward's Illustrated History of English Literature" (*Somerset Pubs.* 1953–55 3 vols. $44.50). Including text illustrations but without the plates.

Irish Literature

Hyde, Douglas. A LITERARY HISTORY OF IRELAND: From Earliest Times to the Present Day. 1899. rev. 1903. *Barnes & Noble* 1967 $11.50. New introd. by Brian O'Cun. Sometimes over-enthusiastic but the best comprehensive history by a scholar who was also President of Eire.

O'Connor, Frank. A SHORT HISTORY OF IRISH LITERATURE: A Backward Look. *Putnam* 1967 $6.95 pap. Capricorn Bks. $1.85. By the fine Irish writer of short stories (*q.v.*). Based upon a series of lectures delivered at Trinity College, Dublin. Lively, opinionated.

Canadian Literature

Klinck, Carl F., and others, Eds. LITERARY HISTORY OF CANADA: Canadian Literature in English. *Univ. of Toronto Press* 1965 $20.00. In four parts: New Found Lands; The Transplanting of Traditions; The Emergence of a Tradition; The Realization of a Tradition. Klinck is Senior Professor at University of Western Ontario.

THE OXFORD COMPANION TO CANADIAN HISTORY AND LITERATURE. Comp. and ed. by Norah Story. *Oxford* 1967 $18.50; Supplement 1974 $9.50. The "Companion" has 450 literary and 1500 historical entries; the supplement covers developments from 1967 to the end of 1972.

Literary Characters

Magill, Frank N., Ed. CYCLOPEDIA OF LITERARY CHARACTERS. *Harper* 1963 $11.95 lib. bdg. $10.69. 16,000 characters from 1300 works of all periods and literatures. Includes index of authors and characters.

Walsh, William S. HEROES AND HEROINES OF FICTION. 1914–1915. *Gale* 2 vols. Vol. I Classical, Medieval, Legendary (up to 1500); Vol. 2 Modern Prose and Poetry (since 1500) 2 vols. set $24.00

Literary Terms

Abrams, Meyer Howard. A GLOSSARY OF LITERARY TERMS. 1941. *Holt* (Rinehart) 1957 3rd ed. 1971 pap. $2.00. "Organized as a series of brief essays in which minor terms are discussed under the major terms to which they are related; words that are often employed in conjunction or as contraries (empathy and sympathy, objective and subjective) are discussed together"—(Preface). Index of terms at the end of volume. Abrams is Whiton Professor of English at Cornell University.

Barnet, Sylvan, Morton Berman and William Burto. A DICTIONARY OF LITERARY, DRAMATIC AND CINEMATIC TERMS. *Little* 2nd ed. 1971 pap. $1.95. Fewer terms are discussed than in Holman (*see below*), but Barnet offers some of the fullest and most allusive definitions; bibliographies. Barnet is Professor of English at Tufts University.

Barry, Raymond, and A. J. Wright. LITERARY TERMS: Definitions, Explanations, Examples. *Chandler Pub.* 1966 pap. $2.35

Beckson, Karl, and Arthur Ganz. READER'S GUIDE TO LITERARY TERMS: A Dictionary. *Farrar, Straus* 1960 $6.50 pap. $2.25

Holman, C. Hugh. HANDBOOK TO LITERATURE. *Odyssey Press* 1936 1960 3rd ed. 1972 thumb indexed $10.00 text ed. $6.00 pap. $3.50. The third edition based on the original by William Flint Thrall and Addison Hibbard now contains over 1360 entries, literary terms and movements, English and American literary history, winners of major literary prizes. Holman is Kenan Professor of English at the University of North Carolina.

Shipley, Joseph T. DICTIONARY OF WORLD LITERARY TERMS: Forms, Technique, Criticism. 1943 1953 1970 completely revised and enlarged. *The Writer* $12.95. Originally called "Dictionary of World Literature" (1943 *Finch Press* $14.00). Shipley was on the English faculty at Yeshiva University.

REFERENCE BOOKS ON FICTION

Adelman, Irving, and Rita Dworkin. THE CONTEMPORARY NOVEL: A Checklist of Critical Literature on the British and American Novel Since 1945. *Scarecrow Press* 1972 $15.00. Surveys the critical literature on novels, citing scholarly rather than popular reviews.

Altenbernd, Lynn, and Leslie L. Lewis. HANDBOOK FOR THE STUDY OF FICTION. *Macmillan* 1966 $1.65

Bell, Inglis, and Donald Baird. THE ENGLISH NOVEL, 1578–1956: A Checklist of Twentieth Century Criticism. *Swallow* 1958 (o.p.)

Coan, Otis W., and Richard G. Lillard. AMERICA IN FICTION: An Annotated List of Novels that Interpret Aspects of Life in the United States, Canada and Mexico. *Pacific Bks.* 5th ed. 1967 $6.75

Freeman, William. EVERYMAN'S DICTIONARY OF FICTIONAL CHARACTERS. *Intl. Pubns. Service* 3rd ed. 1973 $10.00

Gerstenberger, Donna, and George Hendrick. THE AMERICAN NOVEL: A Checklist of Twentieth-Century Criticism. *Swallow* 2 vols. Vol. I 1789–1959 (1961) pap. $2.50; Vol. 2 1969–1968 (1970) $12.50

Haydn, Hiram, and Edmund Fuller, Eds. THESAURUS OF BOOK DIGESTS: Digests of the World's Permanent Writings from the Ancient Classics to Current Literature. *Crown* 1949 $5.00 pap. $1.95. Arrangement is by title with indexes to author and character.

Keller, Helen Rex. THE READER'S DIGEST OF BOOKS. 1896 1936. *Macmillan* $9.95. Good for summaries of older, lesser-known works.

McGarry, Daniel D., and Sarah Harriman White. WORLD HISTORICAL FICTION GUIDE: An Annotated Chronological, Geographical and Topical List of Selected Historical Novels. *Scarecrow Press* 1963 2nd ed. 1973 $15.00. 6455 works arranged by geography and chronology to 1900. Author-title index. All works are in English, although some are translations into English. The first edition of 1963 had the title "Historical Fiction Guide."

Magill, Frank N. Ed. MASTERPIECES OF WORLD LITERATURE IN DIGEST FORM. *Harper* 4 vols. Vol. I (1952) $12.95 lib. bdg. $10.69; Vol. 2 (1956) $11.95 lib. bdg. $10.69; Vol. 3 (1960) $11.95 lib. bdg. $10.69; Vol. 4 (1969) $11.95 lib. bdg. $10.69. Many of the works digested are novels.

Palmer, Helen H., and Anne Jane Dyson, Comps. ENGLISH NOVEL EXPLICATION: Criticisms to 1972. *Shoe String* 1973 $12.50. Continues where Bell and Baird (*see above*) left off.

Souvage, Jacques. AN INTRODUCTION TO THE STUDY OF THE NOVEL: With Special Reference to the English Novel. *Hillary House* 1965 $6.50. The second part is a "systematic bibliography for the study of the novel."

Walker, Warren S. TWENTIETH CENTURY SHORT STORY EXPLICATION: Interpretations 1900–1966 Inclusive, of Short Fiction Since 1800. *Shoe String* rev. ed. 1968 $10.00; SUPPLEMENT I TO THE SECOND EDITION, 1967–1969. 1970 $6.00; SUPPLEMENT II TO THE SECOND EDITION, 1970–1972 1973 $7.00

REFERENCE BOOKS ON POETRY

Altenbernd, Lynn, and Leslie L. Lewis. HANDBOOK FOR THE STUDY OF POETRY. *Macmillan* rev. ed. 1966 pap. text ed. $1.65

Cline, Gloria Stark. AN INDEX TO CRITICISM OF BRITISH AND AMERICAN POETRY. Comp. by Cline and Jeffrey A. Baker. *Scarecrow Press* 1974 $9.00. Indexes critical literature published on British and American poetry from 1960 through 1970. Analysis of 30 journals and 34 books.

Deutsch, Babette. POETRY HANDBOOK: A Dictionary of Terms. 1957 1962. *Funk & Wagnalls* 3rd rev. ed. 1969 text ed. $5.59 pap. $2.95

Hamer, Enid. METRES OF ENGLISH POETRY. 4th ed. 1951 *Barnes & Noble* 1966 $6.50 1970 pap. $3.25

Kuntz, Joseph M. POETRY EXPLICATION: A Checklist of Interpretation Since 1925 of British and American Poems Past and Present. *Swallow* rev. ed. 1962 $7.50. Indexes criticism of poems shorter than 500 lines.

Murphy, Rosalie, Ed. CONTEMPORARY POETS OF THE ENGLISH LANGUAGE. *St. Martin's* 1970 $25.00. Bio-bibliographies of 1000 contemporary poets writing in English.

Preminger, Alex, Frank Warnke and O. B. Hardison. ENCYCLOPEDIA OF POETRY AND POETICS. *Princeton Univ. Press* 1965 $25.00 1972 pap. $6.95

"The characteristics of Sanskrit poetry, examples of litotes, the naïve-sentimental relationship to nature, the history of parody, an item on the Pléiade, analysis of every imaginable meter and rhyme, and three columns on inspiration—such is the content of [this] major reference work. There are no studies of individual poems . . . nor biographies of poets, but the history of each of the national bodies of poetry—the section on the American is noteworthy—takes into account the contributions of most of the major poets, and for the foreign literatures examples are quoted in the original as well as in translation"—(David Glixon, in *SR*). Grouped under "four general headings—(I) History of Poetry; (II) Techniques of Poetry; (III) Poetics and Criticism; and (IV) Poetry and its Relationship to Other Fields of Interest—the entries in this encyclopedia are at once generous yet concise, erudite yet lucid, wide-ranging yet germane. It is hard, in fact, to portray the uniform excellence of this volume"—(*Modern Language Journal*). The 200 contributors include Cleanth Brooks, Wallace Fowlie, Louis Untermeyer and William Carlos Williams, among others.

Shapiro, Karl, and Robert Beum. A PROSODY HANDBOOK. *Harper* 1965 $6.00

Spender, Stephen, and Donald Hall. CONCISE ENCYCLOPEDIA OF ENGLISH AND AMERICAN POETS AND POETRY. *Hawthorne* 1963 $17.95

Untermeyer, Louis. LIVES OF THE POETS: The Story of One Thousand Years of English and American Poetry. *Simon & Schuster* 1959 $7.95 pap. $2.95. The lives of 133 poets from Chaucer to Dylan Thomas.

CLASSICAL AND MYTHOLOGICAL DICTIONARIES

A classical dictionary generally offers in addition to accounts of myths and mythological characters, articles on the principal phases of Greek and Roman history, the major historical figures, religion, philosophy, commerce, art, social conditions, and geographical places.

The material in myths has been used by creative writers in all times; mythological dictionaries identify those figures and themes that are continually restated in new forms. In modern times, thanks to Freud and Jung, it has become accepted that myths are not only simplified explanations of creation and natural occurrences, etc.; they also voice experiences and values otherwise unexpressed.

Joseph Campbell, cited below, has uncovered symbolic implications of many myths, and Michael Grant in his "Myths of the Greeks and Romans" shows in masterful detail the influence and source of inspiration myths have given to literature and the arts.

Branston, Brian. GODS OF THE NORTH. *Vanguard.* 1955 $6.00. A somewhat poetic retelling of the sagas of the Verse Edda and the Prose Edda shows their influence on the Anglo-Saxon, Scandinavian and German languages; drawings and reproductions of ancient manuscripts, runes and bronze works enlighten the text.

Brewer, E. Cobham. BREWER'S DICTIONARY OF PHRASE AND FABLE. 1964. rev. by Ivor H. Evans. *Harper* rev. ed. 1972 $10.00. 970 pages of fascinating information.

Bulfinch, Thomas. AGE OF FABLE. 1855. *Airmont* $.60; *Macmillan* Collier 1962 pap. $.95; *Dutton* $3.50 Everyman's $2.25; *Harper* pap. $.75

AGE OF CHIVALRY. 1858. *Airmont* $.75; *Gordon Press* $5.00

LEGENDS OF CHARLEMANGNE. 1963. *Gordon Press* $5.00

BULFINCH'S MYTHOLOGY. 1970 2nd rev. ed. *T. Y. Crowell* $6.95; ed. by Edmund Fuller abr. ed. *Dell* $.95; *Modern Library* Giant $4.95; *New Am. Lib.* 3 vols. pap. Vol. I $.95; Vols. 2 and 3 each $1.25

"Bulfinch's Mythology" as it is generally known, was originally published as three separate books: "The Age of Fable," "The Legends of Charlemagne," and the "Age of Chivalry." The author, a Boston bank clerk, took advantage of the popular interest in mythology awakened by Nathaniel Hawthorne (*q.v.*) in his "Wonder Book" (1851) and "Tanglewood Tales" (1853) to launch his own version of the myths. A selection from the "Age of Fable" has been made for children with illustrations by Helen Sewell: "Book of Myths" (*Macmillan* 1942 1964 $5.50). "Stories of Gods and Heroes" by Sally Benson (*Dial* 1946 $5.95) is another delightful book based on Bulfinch.

Campbell, Joseph. THE MASKS OF GOD. *Viking* 4 vols. 1959–1968 Vol. I Primitive Mythology (1959) $8.95 Compass Bks. pap. $3.25; Vol. 2 Oriental Mythology (1962) $8.95 Compass Bks. pap. $3.75; Vol. 3 Occidental Mythology (1964) $8.95 Compass Bks. pap. $3.75; Vol. 4 Creative Mythology (1968) $12.50 Compass Bks. pap. $4.50 boxed set $32.95

Colum, Padraic. MYTHS OF THE WORLD. 1933. *Grosset* Univ. Lib. 1959 pap. $2.25. Originally entitled "Orpheus: Myths of the World," it includes not only familiar Greek and Roman material but also a large selection from peoples as diverse as the Babylonians and the Indians of the American West.

Croon, J. H. ENCYCLOPEDIA OF THE CLASSICAL WORLD. Trans. from the Dutch. 1965. *Brown Bk.* $5.50 pap. $2.95

"A handy-sized volume useful for anyone interested in the Greek and Roman periods and in classical literature"—(Glixon, in *SR*). 250 pages.

Davidson, H. R. Ellis. GODS AND MYTHS OF NORTHERN EUROPE. *Penguin* Pelican Bks. 1964 pap. $1.45; *Gannon* lib. bdg. $3.70.

A "systematic account" that "can be profitably read straight through" (Glixon, in *SR*), with glossary and index.

Frazer, Sir James Gordon. THE GOLDEN BOUGH: A Study in Magic and Religion. *St. Martin's* 13 vols. Pt. 1 Magic, Art and the Evolution of Kings 2 vols. 3rd ed. (1911) each $12.00; Pt. 2 Taboo and the Perils of the Soul 3rd ed. (1911) $12.00; Pt. 3 Dying God (1911) $12.00; Pt. 4 Adonis, Attis, Osiris: Studies in the History of Oriental Religion 2 vols. 3rd ed. (1914) each $12.00; Pt. 5 Spirits of the Corn and of the Wild 2 vols. 3rd ed. (1912) each $12.00; Pt. 6 Scapegoat 3rd ed. (1913) $12.00; Pt. 7 Balder the Beautiful: Fire-Festivals of Europe and Doctrine of the External Soul 2

vols. (1913) each $12.00; Pt. 8 Bibliography and General Index (1915) $12.00; Pt. 9
Aftermath: Supplement to Golden Bough (1936) $12.00 13 vols. set $125.00

GOLDEN BOUGH. Abr. ed. *Macmillan* $6.95 pap. $3.95; (with title "The New Golden
Bough") abr. ed. by Theodor H. Gaster. 1959 *Phillips* $14.95

"The Golden Bough" was one of the early works to trace the evolution of human behavior from savage to
civilized man. This is a classic study on primitive ritual, myth, magic, taboos, sexual practices and religion.

Gayley, Charles Mills. THE CLASSIC MYTHS IN ENGLISH LITERATURE AND IN ART. 1893
rev. ed. enl. 1911 rev. 1939. *Finch Press* repr. of 1893 ed. $18.00 rev. ed. 1939.
Xerox College Publishing Educational Ctr. $9.00. Based chiefly on Bulfinch, it en-
larges on his idea of "mythology as connected with literature." *See* "Charles Mills
Gayley" by B. P. Kurtz (*Univ. of California Press* 1943 pap. $7.50).

Grant, Michael. MYTHS OF THE GREEKS AND ROMANS. 1962. *New Am. Lib.* Mentor Bks.
1964 pap. $1.75. This "eminent classical scholar refuses to enshrine (or imprison)
the myths of the Greeks and Romans within the concept of legacy but views them as
never-dying themes of human existence."

Graves, Robert. GREEK MYTHS. *Braziller* 1957 $7.50; *Penguin* Pelican Bks. 1955 2 vols.
pap. each $1.45. The *Saturday Review* has called this "a monumental encyclope-
dia."

*See also main entries for Graves in Chapter 7, Modern British Poetry, and Chapter 12,
Modern British Fiction.*

Grimal, Pierre, Ed. LAROUSSE WORLD MYTHOLOGY. 1963. Trans. from the French by
Patricia Beardsworth. *Putnam* 1965 $25.00

"An important publishing event, for it is the most monumental and authoritative volume on mythology
ever published. Ten years of painstaking editorial research were required for this truly sumptuous book, a superb kaleidoscopic panorama of the myths, cults, rites and philosophy-theology of every region in the world,
including Sumer, Babylon, Egypt, Greece, Rome, India, China, Japan, the Slavic and Teutonic countries,
American Indians, Oceania, Eskimos, and African tribes. Solid contributions by 23 outstanding scholars are
presented in lucid, readable English with copious (often unusual) illustrations to complement the text. . . .
Enthusiastically recommended"—(Francis D. Lazenby, in *LJ*).

Hamilton, Edith. MYTHOLOGY. *Grosset* Univ. Lib. pap. $2.50; *Little* 1942 $6.50; *New
Am. Lib.* Mentor Bks. pap. $1.25

The writer is both learned and imaginative, with a lucid, graceful style. After an excellent and stimulating
introduction, she tells the myths briefly in as nearly as possible the words of the classical poet or poets who
told each particular story best. "She has distilled into incidental observations the whole meaning of mythology itself to the modern scholar and man of letters"—(Irwin Edman). There is a supplementary section on
Norse mythology.

Hooke, S. H. MIDDLE EASTERN MYTHOLOGY. The intriguing mythology of the Egyptians, Babylonians, Assyrians, Hittites, Canaanites and Hebrews. *Penguin* Pelican
Bks. 1963 pap. $1.75

Kaster, Joseph. PUTNAM'S CONCISE MYTHOLOGICAL DICTIONARY. Based on Bessie Red-
field's "Gods: A Dictionary of the Deities of All Lands" (1931, o.p.). *Putnam* 1963
Capricorn Bks. pap. $1.45

David Glixon says of this edition (in *SR*): "Deities, heroes, and sacred books of ancient religions compose
most of the 1,100 terms. . . . The essential stories are told succinctly and agreeably, cross-references abound,
and interest is frequently added to the names by their literal meanings."

Kerenyi, Carl. THE GODS OF THE GREEKS. *Vanguard* 1951 $6.00. A compendium by an authority on Greek philosophy and ancient history.

LAROUSSE WORLD MYTHOLOGY. *See Grimal, Pierre, Ed., above.*

Leach, Maria, Ed. STANDARD DICTIONARY OF FOLKLORE, MYTHOLOGY AND LEGEND. *Funk & Wagnalls* 1949–51 1972 1-vol. ed. $17.95. The new edition has minor revisions and a separate index. An excellent work.

Lemprière, John. CLASSICAL DICTIONARY CONTAINING COPIOUS ACCOUNT OF ALL THE PROPER NAMES MENTIONED IN ANCIENT AUTHORS. 1809. *Finch Press* $15.00; *Gale* 1973 $18.00; *Gordon Press* $20.00. One of the oldest classical dictionaries in English now available.

Macpherson, Jay. FOUR AGES OF MAN, THE CLASSIC MYTHS. Ill. with motifs from Greek poetry. *St. Martin's* 1962 text ed. $2.50. This is a most readable guide to all of the myths, which have been organized chronologically in eight sections, the last of which is an interesting account of how the gods passed into medieval life. Among the book's amenities are two family trees, an historical chart, a map, many short quotes from English poetry and a good index.

THE NEW CENTURY HANDBOOK OF GREEK MYTHOLOGY AND LEGEND. Ed. by Catherine B. Avery. *Appleton* 1972 $7.95. A selection from "The New Century Classical Handbook" 1962 (o.p.)

THE OXFORD CLASSICAL DICTIONARY *Oxford* 1949 2nd ed. by N. G. Hammond and H. H. Scullard 1970 $26.00

"A compendium of modern scholarship designed to meet the needs of the general reader and of the specialist in all fields of ancient Greek and Roman civilization"—(*Publisher's catalog*).

Rose, Herbert Jennings. A HANDBOOK OF GREEK MYTHOLOGY. *Dutton* 1928 1959 pap. $1.75. Original in its arrangement, the main facts are in large type, minor details in smaller type, further information at the ends of chapters.

Seyffert, Oskar. DICTIONARY OF CLASSICAL ANTIQUITIES, MYTHOLOGY, RELIGION, LITERATURE, ART. Rev. and ed. by Henry Nettleship and J. E. Sandys. *Peter Smith* $7.00

Smith, William. A SMALLER CLASSICAL DICTIONARY. 1910. Rev. by E. H. Blakeney and John Warrington. *Dutton* 1952 pap. $1.65; (with title "Everyman's Classical Dictionary") new ed. by John Warrington Everyman's Ref. Lib. 1971 $6.95. The author was an English classical and biblical scholar. His Bible dictionary and his classical dictionary have long been standard works of reference. "A Classical Dictionary of Greek and Roman Biography, Mythology and Geography" (1842) is now o.p. "A Smaller Classical Dictionary" includes valuable new material on Greek artists, Greek philosophers, classical architecture, other classical dictionaries, and writers before 1450.

Sykes, Egerton. DICTIONARY OF NON-CLASSICAL MYTHOLOGY. *Dutton* Everyman's Ref. Lib. 1952 rev. ed. $5.00

Tripp, Edward. CROWELL'S HANDBOOK OF CLASSICAL MYTHOLOGY. *T. Y. Crowell* 1970 $10.00

Van Aken, A. R. A. ENCYCLOPEDIA OF CLASSICAL MYTHOLOGY. 150 2-column pages, well cross-referenced. *Prentice-Hall* 1964 Spectrum Bks. pap. $2.45

BOOKS ABOUT WORDS

> *Philologists, who chase*
> *A panting syllable through time and space,*
> *Start it at home, and hunt it in the dark,*
> *To Gaul, to Greece and into Noah's Ark.*
> —WILLIAM COWPER

"Perhaps of all creations of man language is the most astonishing. Those small articulated sounds that seem so simple, so definite, turn out, the more one examines them, to be the receptacles of subtle mystery and the dispensers of unanticipated power," Lytton Strachey (*q.v.*) wrote.

The English language became a world language by 1850; and it has since become *the* international language. Many of the books in this section demonstrate how English and American English have acquired their rich vocabularies. This edition of "The Reader's Adviser" introduces a new section on linguistics, a field of language study which has been called both the most scientific of the humanities and the most humanistic of the sciences. Two reference works that explain linguistic terminology are: Mario Pei's "Glossary of Linguistic Terminology" (*Columbia* 1954 1966 $10.00) and Eric Hamp's "A Glossary of American Technical Linguistic Usage, 1925–1950" (*Int. Pubns. Service* 3rd ed. 1966 $5.25).

Etymology

Asimov, Isaac. WORDS OF SCIENCE AND THE HISTORY BEHIND THEM. *Houghton* 1959 $5.95; *New Am. Lib.* pap. $.95

Funk, Charles E. HEAVENS TO BETSY AND OTHER CURIOUS SAYINGS. 1955 *Harper* $5.95; *Paperback Lib.* 1972 pap. $1.25

A HOG ON ICE AND OTHER CURIOUS EXPRESSIONS. 1948 *Harper* $5.95; *Paperback Lib.* 1972 pap. $1.25

(With Charles Earle Funk, Jr.) HORSEFEATHERS AND OTHER CURIOUS WORDS. 1958 *Harper* $5.95; *Paperback Lib.* 1972 pap. $1.25

THEREBY HANGS A TALE: Stories of Curious Word Origins. 1950 *Harper* $6.95; *Paperback Lib.* 1972 pap. $1.25

The late lexicographer has left a wonderful series of books on the origin and meaning of odd words and phrases. His son completed "Horsefeathers" at his death.

Funk, Wilfred. WORD ORIGINS AND THEIR ROMANTIC STORIES. *Funk & Wagnalls* text ed. $6.95 pap. $1.95. Short word stories behind business, science, religion, sports, art, animal, boudoir, war and other terms. Delightful reading.

Hendrickson, Robert. HUMAN WORDS: The Compleat Unexpurgated, Uncomputerized Word book. *Chilton* 1972 $9.95. Words derived from real or mythical persons.

Klein, Ernest. A COMPREHENSIVE ETYMOLOGICAL DICTIONARY OF THE ENGLISH LANGUAGE: Dealing with the Origin of Words and Their Sense Development, thus Illustrating the History of Civilization and Culture. *Am. Elsevier* Vol. I 1966; Vol. 2 1967 each $32.50; 1-vol. ed. 1971 $29.50. Highly recommended for libraries. Scholarly, up-to-date research.

Lewis, C. S. STUDIES IN WORDS. *Cambridge* 1960 2nd ed. $12.00

Onions, C. T., Ed., with the assist. of G. W. S. Friedrichsen and R. W. Burchfield. THE OXFORD DICTIONARY OF ENGLISH ETYMOLOGY. *Oxford* 1966 $20.00. The most complete and most reliable etymological dictionary of the English language. The superb "Oxford English Dictionary" (*Oxford* 1933 13 vols. $300.00; compact ed. 2 vols. 1971 $75.00) is also an excellent source of etymology of all English words from Chaucer to the present.

Partridge, Eric. ORIGINS: A Short Etymological Dictionary of Modern English. *Macmillan* 1959 $18.00. Intimately cognate groups of words are arranged into single unified treatments (thus, *can, could, con, couth, uncouth, kith, cunning, keen, ken, kenning, know* and *knowledge* are all treated in six numbered paragraphs under *can*, to which the others are cross-referenced).

Skeat, Walter W. AN ETYMOLOGICAL DICTIONARY OF THE ENGLISH LANGUAGE. *Oxford* 1879–82 4th ed. rev. and enl. 1910 $20.50

   A CONCISE ETYMOLOGICAL DICTIONARY OF THE ENGLISH LANGUAGE. *Oxford* 1901 new and corrected impression 1911 $7.00; *Putnam* Capricorn Bks. 1963 pap. $3.45. Skeat's dictionary gives history of selected words of curious or disputed derivation.

Smith, Logan Pearsall. THE ENGLISH LANGUAGE. With an epilogue by R. W. Chapman. *Oxford* 1912 2nd ed. 1952 Paperbacks Univ. Series 1966 pap. $1.75. The author was an American who lived in England and preferred English fashions of speech. His work on English idioms explains the origin of expressions like "hoist with his own petard," "to the manor born," "sour grapes," "curry favor," etc. *See his main entry in Chapter 16, Essays and Criticism.*

Weekley, Ernest. AN ETYMOLOGICAL DICTIONARY OF MODERN ENGLISH. *Dover* 2 vols. pap. each $3.00. An early 20th-century work.

Rhyming Dictionaries

Franklyn, Julian. A DICTIONARY OF RHYMING SLANG. *Fernhill* 1960 2nd ed. $6.25; *Routledge & Kegan Paul* 1969 2nd ed. $5.95

Johnson, Burges. NEW RHYMING DICTIONARY AND POETS' HANDBOOK. *Harper* 1931 rev. ed. 1957 $5.95 lib. bdg. $5.49

Stillman, Frances. THE POET'S MANUAL AND RHYMING DICTIONARY: Based on "The Improved Rhyming Dictionary" by Jane Shaw Whitfield and Frances Stillman. *T.Y. Crowell* 1951 1965 $6.95. The "Manual" is an explanation of verse forms. Short sections cover meter, rhyme, and varieties of form from traditional to modern poetry. Examples illustrate the text. The rhyming dictionary is divided by key vowel sounds. Masculine, feminine, and three-syllable rhymes each have a separate section.

Whitfield, Jane Shaw. UNIVERSITY RHYMING DICTIONARY. *Apollo* pap. $1.95

Wood, Clement. WOOD'S UNABRIDGED RHYMING DICTIONARY. *World Pub.* 1943 $12.50. Wood has one of the longest vocabularies of rhyming dictionaires.

Synonym Dictionaries

Books of synonyms are of two kinds: synonyms discriminated and synonyms undiscriminated—the second kind far outnumbers the first. Since there are not two words in the English language which are at all times of identical meaning, the main purpose of a book of synonyms should be to discriminate: to point out in what senses they are not interchangeable. For instance "still" and "yet" are alike in meaning in the sentence, "I'm hungry still" or "I'm hungry yet." But they are opposite in meaning in two such questions as—"Are you married yet?" and "Are you married still?"—and to confuse them might be most embarrassing. Some dictionaries define "farther" as "further," and "further" as "farther." But a dictionary of discriminated synonyms points out that "further" refers to abstract measurement and "farther" to concrete. "We walked a little farther and discussed the matter further" makes the definition plain. We may also consult a book of synonyms to be reminded of an acceptable substitute so as to avoid ungraceful repetition. All synonym dictionaries help the writer, in addition, to find the *exact* word needed to express what he wants to convey. It can in addition, serve as both a reference aid and vocabulary builder.

Allen, F. Sturges. ALLEN'S SYNONYMS AND ANTONYMS. 1921. Rev. and enl. by T. H. Vail Motter. *Harper* 1938 $6.95 lib. bdg. $5.92 Perenn. Lib. pap. $1.25. This volume, by the general editor of the first edition of "Webster's New International Dictionary," is arranged alphabetically, not classified in categories as in Roget (*q.v.*). In the old edition the synonyms were not discriminated. In the revised edition sense discriminations have been added, as well as many new synonyms and antonyms, slang and colloquialisms, and British equivalents of American words.

Fernald, James Champlin. FUNK & WAGNALLS STANDARD HANDBOOK OF ENGLISH SYNONYMS, ANTONYMS AND PREPOSITIONS. 1896 *Funk & Wagnalls* rev. and enl. 1920 new rev. ed. 1947 $6.95. Over 6000 classified synonyms, with nearly 4000 antonyms, together with examples of the correct use of prepositions.

Hayakawa, S. I., Ed. FUNK & WAGNALLS MODERN GUIDE TO SYNONYMS AND RELATED WORDS. *Funk & Wagnalls* 1967 $8.95. Compares and contrasts more than 6000 synonyms. "There have been more thorough compilations, but few are as conveniently arranged or as pleasant to consult"—(Glixon).

NEW WEBSTER'S DICTIONARY OF SYNONYMS: A Dictionary of Discriminated Synonyms With Antonyms and Analogous and Contrasted Words. *Merriam* 1942 1951 1968 $7.95. The use of the discriminated words is clarified by examples from literature.

ROGET'S INTERNATIONAL THESAURUS: The Complete Book of Synonyms and Antonyms in American and British Usage. *T.Y. Crowell* 1922 1946 rev. ed. Lester V. Berrey 3rd ed. 1962 $5.95 thumb indexed $6.95 thumb indexed boxed, lea. $17.50

A thesaurus is a book of synonyms on a very broad scale. It groups words and phrases which are similar in idea rather than strictly synonymous. Roget (1779–1869) was an English physician and scholar. While practicing medicine, he worked nearly 50 years on his great "Thesaurus." Published first in 1852, it went through 28 editions during his lifetime. In 1879 it was enlarged by his son, John L. Roget, and in 1911 again enlarged by his grandson, Samuel Romilly Roget. The "Thesaurus" was considered somewhat difficult to use until crossword puzzles came and showed many new readers what an easy and indispensable tool it is. To writers it "gives words in exchange for ideas. It is a dictionary reversed. A dictionary gives meanings for words; a thesaurus gives words for meanings." Its greatest feature compared with a book of undiscriminated synonyms is that it gives proverbs, sayings, and parallel expressions. Look up a synonym for "big sounding words" and you will find "macrology," "Johnsonian," "sesquipedalistic," "making little fishes talk like whales." No definition or explantion is offered of these words.

The third edition of "Roget's International Thesaurus," long recognized as the standard thesaurus, is a complete revision, and has been expanded to 240,000 entries. It contains a glossary of foreign words and phrases, and 45,000 additional words especially in the areas of science and technology. Slang and colloquialisms are clearly labeled, and the index expanded and simplified. "Roget's University Thesaurus" (*Apollo* $3.49), edited by C. O. Sylvester Mawson, is based on the first edition of the "International," and contains updated supplements.

Among the many other thesauri from the Roget family are: Peter Mark Roget's "Roget's International Thesaurus (*T.Y. Crowell* 3rd ed. 1962 thumb indexed $6.95, boxed 1 ea. $17.50. pap. $5.95), "Roget's Thesaurus of English Words and Phrases," edited by R. A. Dutch (*St. Martin's* 1965 $7.95 thumb indexed $8.95), "Roget's Thesaurus of Words and Phrases" (*Grosset & Dunlap* $3.95), "New Roget's Thesaurus in Dictionary Form," edited by Norman Lewis (*Berkley* pap. $.95), and "Thesaurus of English Words and Phrases" rev. ed. by John L. and Samuel R. Roget (*Shalom* $12.50 thumb indexed $15.00 *Dutton* Everyman Ref. Lib. pap. $4.95)

Soule, Richard. A DICTIONARY OF ENGLISH SYNONYMS. 1871. Rev. ed. by Alfred Dwight Sheffield *Little* rev. ed. 1938 1959 $7.95

DICTIONARY OF SYNONYMS AND SYNONYMOUS PARALLEL EXPRESSIONS. Rev. by G. Howson. *Shalom* $9.50 thumb indexed $10.50

WEBSTER'S DICTIONARY OF SYNONYMS. *See "New Webster's Dictionary of Synonyms," above.*

THE WRITER'S BOOK OF SYNONYMS AND ANTONYMS. *The Writer* 1960 $2.95

Abbreviations and Acronyms

Crowley, Ellen T., and Robert C. Thomas. ACRONYMS AND INITIALISMS DICTIONARY: A Guide to Alphabetical Designations, Contractions, Acronyms, Initialisms and Similar Condensed Appellations. *Gale* 1960 4th ed. 1973 $27.50

NEW ACRONYMS AND INITIALISMS. Supplements to "Acronyms and Initialisms." *Gale* 2 vols. 1974 and 1975 each $30.00. 1974 Supplement contains 10,000 terms; 1975 Supplement will be ready Feb. 1975.

Guinagh, Kevin. DICTIONARY OF FOREIGN PHRASES AND ABBREVIATIONS. *Wilson* 1972 $10.00 *Berkeley* 1966 pap. $.75

Kleiner, Richard. INDEX OF INITIALS AND ACRONYMS. *Auerbach* 1971 $7.95 pap. $4.95. 7000 terms arranged by subject.

Moser, Reta C. SPACE-AGE ACRONYMS: ABBREVIATIONS AND DESIGNATIONS. *Plenum Pub.* 1969 2nd ed. $17.50. Military and aircraft terms.

Pugh, Eric, A DICTIONARY OF ACRONYMS AND ABBREVIATIONS. *Shoe String* 1970 2nd ed. $15.00. Abbreviations in science and technology. More than 10,000.

Rybicki, Stephen, Ed. ABBREVIATIONS: A Reverse Guide to Standard and Generally Abbreviated Forms. *Pierian Press* 1971 $12.95. 18,000 words and pharases; entries arranged alphabetically with word first, then abbreviation.

Schwartz, Robert J. COMPLETE DICTIONARY OF ABBREVIATIONS. *T.Y. Crowell* 1955 enl. ed. 1959 $7.95

Steen, Edwin B. MEDICAL ABBREVIATIONS. *F. A. Davis* 3rd ed. 1971 $4.50

Development of English

Barnett, Lincoln. THE TREASURE OF OUR TONGUE: The Story of English from Its Beginning to Its Present Eminence as the Most Widely Spoken Language on Earth. *Knopf* 1965 $6.95

"A brilliant and passionate defense of our mother language against those 20th-century encroachers—the jargon speakers, the advertisers and their ilk. Also a fascinating study of the language and how it came into first being and then flower"—*(PW)*.

Baugh, Albert C. HISTORY OF THE ENGLISH LANGUAGE. *Appleton* 2nd ed. 1957 $9.45. Monumental study by a scholar who was for many years Professor of English Language and Literature, University of Pennsylvania.

Jespersen, Otto. GROWTH AND STRUCTURE OF THE ENGLISH LANGUAGE. 1905 *Macmillan* 9th ed. *Free Press* 1968 pap. $1.95. A classic in the field.

Current English Usage

Fowler, Henry W. A DICTIONARY OF MODERN ENGLISH USAGE. 1926 *Oxford* 1937 2nd rev. ed. by Sir Henry Gower 1965 $7.50. Fowler died in 1933, but in the Gower edition his work remains the classic on English style, impeccably British, and in many of its longer entries deliciously opinionated; a volume that is not merely consulted but browsed in and read by those who love the language.

FIND IT IN FOWLER: An Alphabetical Index to the Second Edition (1965) of H. W. Fowler's Modern English Usage by J. Arthur Greenwood. *Wolfhart Book Co.* 1969 o.p.

Freeman, William. A CONCISE DICTIONARY OF ENGLISH IDIOMS. *The Writer* 1951 $3.95

Partridge, Eric. CONCISE USAGE AND ABUSAGE: A Modern Guide to Good English. Shortened and simplified version of "Usage and Abusage." 1954 1965 *Greenwood* $10.50

USAGE AND ABUSAGE: Guide to Good English. *British Book Centre* 6th ed. 1965 $9.00; *Penguin* 5th ed. 1963 $1.60

English Slang

Farmer, John S., and W. E. Henley. SLANG AND ITS ANALOGUES, PAST AND PRESENT. 1890–1904. *Arno* 1970 7 vols. in 1 $17.95 pap. $8.95; *Kraus* 7 vols in 3 set $75.00; *University Books* 1965 2 vols. Vol. I $15.00; Vol. 2 $10.00. Three centuries of slang with synonyms in English, French, German and Italian. Entries are labeled colloquial, provincial, vulgar, etc. In these reprints the supplementary Volume 8, *Vocabula Amatoria*, of the original set has been left out. This was a translation and synthesis by Farmer of several French erotic dictionaries.

Grose, Francis. A CLASSICAL DICTIONARY OF THE VULGAR TONGUE. 1785. Ed. with a Biographical and Critical Sketch and Commentary by Eric Partridge. 1963 *Bks. for Libraries* facsimile ed. $14.50

To this earliest dictionary of English slang Eric Partridge, perhaps the leading authority on slang in English (*see following*), "has contributed illuminating notes" and a biographical sketch of that "antiquarian Falstaff." The early compiler "would be astonished to learn that a few terms he considered vanishing vogue words—'bore' and 'twaddle,' for example—are still very much alive, just as some of us may be astonished to find that certain other terms—such as 'corporation' for belly, 'douse the glim' and 'elbow grease'—date to his time. An incidental asset of the book is the way it brings to sparkling life the mores, the humor and the foibles of the 18th century"—(*N.Y. Times*).

Partridge, Eric. A DICTIONARY OF SLANG AND UNCONVENTIONAL ENGLISH: From the Fifteenth Century to the Present Day. *Macmillan* 4th ed. 1937 5th ed. 1961 6th ed. 1967 7th ed. 1970 $18.50. Here is an immense body of work compressed into one volume by means of abbreviations. It deals not only with slang but with scabrous language as well.

A DICTIONARY OF THE UNDERWORLD, BRITISH AND AMERICAN. *Macmillan* 1950 rev. ed. 1961 $17.50.

Development of American English

Craigie, Sir William, and James R. Hulbert, Eds. A DICTIONARY OF AMERICAN ENGLISH ON HISTORICAL PRINCIPLES. *Univ. of Chicago Press* 1938–44 4 vols. Set $100.00

Krapp, George Phillip. ENGLISH LANGUAGE IN AMERICA *Ungar* 1960 2 vols. $14.00

Mathews, Mitford M. AMERICAN WORDS. *World Pub.* 1959 $4.50

DICTIONARY OF AMERICANISMS ON HISTORICAL PRINCIPLES. *Univ. of Chicago Press* 1951 2 vols. in I 1956 $25.00; (with title "Americanisms" abr. to 1000 entries) $5.95 pap. $1.95

Mencken, Henry Louis. THE AMERICAN LANGUAGE: An Inquiry into the Development of English in the United States. 1919; SUPPLEMENT I 1945; SUPPLEMENT II 1948. 4th ed. corr. enl. and rewritten. *Knopf* 4th ed. 1936 3 vols. each $15.00 set $45.00 abr. with annotations and new material by Raven I. McDavid, Jr. 1963 $12.95 text ed. $9.00.

The author revised the original work in 1921 and again in 1923. This fourth edition is virtually a new work. The book lays special stress on the many divergencies in English and American pronunciations and vocabularies, contending that the variations make for the greater vigor of each language. Supplement I covers the first six chapters of "The American Language," Supplement II the last five. These brilliant and fascinating books digest the material collected since 1936.

See also Mencken's main entry in Chapter 16, Essays and Criticism.

Thornton, Richard H. AN AMERICAN GLOSSARY: Being an Attempt to Illustrate Certain Americanisms upon Historical Principles. Introd. by Margaret M. Bryant. 2 vols. 1912. *Ungar* 1962 3 vols. $30.00. Vol. 3 is added material first published in *Dialect Notes*, Vol. 6, 1928–39.

Current American Usage

THE BARNHART DICTIONARY OF NEW ENGLISH SINCE 1963. Ed. by Clarence L. Barnhart, Sol Steinmetz and Robert K. Barnhart. *Harper* 1973 $12.95. The more than 5000 words and phrases of modern science, technology and culture were collected from the reading of over half a billion running words from United States, Canadian and British sources—newspapers, magazines and books published from 1963 to 1972.

Bryant, Margaret M. CURRENT AMERICAN USAGE: How Americans Say and Write It. *Funk & Wagnalls* 1962 text ed. $5.00

Copperud, Roy H. MODERN AMERICAN USAGE: The Concensus. *Van Nostrand-Reinhold* 1970 $8.95.

Evans, Bergen, with Cornelia Evans. A DICTIONARY OF CONTEMPORARY AMERICAN USAGE. *Random* 1957 $7.95 text ed. $5.55. Their premise is that no one use of language is "correct." An interesting and authoritative volume.

Follett, Wilson. MODERN AMERICAN USAGE, Ed. and completed by Jacques Barzun and others. *Hill & Wang* 1966 $7.50 pap. $1.95.

> "This is an unusual and a valuable . . . intensely personal book, based firmly on and edited consistently in accord with certain of Follett's basic beliefs about language"—(*LJ*). Edward Weeks (*q.v.*) called the author (a distinguished editor, teacher and essayist) "a tart and vigorous defender of the English language . . . with H. W. Fowler one of the two liveliest champions of good English usage in our time." In his introduction the author says of linguists such as those who prepared *Webster's Third New International Dictionary*, "[They] deny that there is any such thing as correctness," but Follett argues "that there is a right way to use words and construct sentences, and many wrong ways." On this basis he proceeds with his own observations and strictures. He died before this book was completed, and a gifted group of editors carried on for him under Barzun's direction: Carlos Baker, F. W. Dupee, Dudley Fitts, James D. Hart, Phyllis McGinley and Lionel Trilling.

Kenyon, John S., and Thomas A. Knott, Eds. A PRONOUNCING DICTIONARY OF AMERICAN ENGLISH. *Merriam* 2nd ed. 1953 $4.75. Cultivated colloquial English pronunciation, using the international phonetic alphabet.

Marckwardt, Albert H. AMERICAN ENGLISH. *Oxford* 1958 $6.50 pap. $2.50

Nicholson, Margaret. A DICTIONARY OF AMERICAN-ENGLISH USAGE. 1957. *New Am. Lib.* pap. $1.25. Starting from Fowler's "Modern English Usage" (*see above*), Ms. Nicholson, who was a Head of the Publishing Department of Oxford University Press, added new words and idioms and included American variations of spelling, pronunciation and usage that "Fowler either ignored or disdained."

Sledd, James H., and Wilma R. Ebbitt, Eds. DICTIONARIES AND THAT DICTIONARY *Scott, Foresman* 1962 $3.95. An excellent anthology discussing the controversial third edition of Webster's.

American Slang

Berrey, Lester V., and Melvin Van den Bark. THE AMERICAN THESAURUS OF SLANG: A Complete Reference Book of Colloquial Speech. *T. Y. Crowell* 1942 1947 2nd ed. rev., reset and enl. 1953 $15.00. Over 100,000 expressions arranged according to dominant idea, occupation, etc.; includes an alphabetical word index.

Claerbaut, David. BLACK JARGON IN WHITE AMERICA. *Eerdmans* 1972 pap. $1.95

A DICTIONARY OF CONTEMPORARY AND COLLOQUIAL USAGE *English Language Institute of America.* 1972 pap. $2.00. Only 32 pages but its 2000 entries update the classic work of Wentworth and Flexner (*below*).

Landy, Eugene E. THE UNDERGROUND DICTIONARY: A Guide to the Language of the American Drug Culture. *Simon & Schuster* 1971 pap. $1.95. Words and phrases as recorded by a clinical psychologist.

Rodgers, Bruce. THE QUEEN'S VERNACULAR: A Gay Lexicon. *Straight Arrow* 1972 pap. $3.50. Male homosexual slang.

Wentworth, Harold, and Stuart Berg Flexner. DICTIONARY OF AMERICAN SLANG. *T. Y. Crowell* 1960 new ed. with supplement by S. B. Flexner 1967 $7.95. Etymologies, quotations and cross-references.

Linguistics

General

Chomsky, Noam. LANGUAGE AND MIND. *Harcourt* 1968. Enl. ed. $6.95 pap. $4.25 text ed. pap. $2.75. In 88 pages the famed linguist presents his principal ideas.

Greenberg, Joseph H. ANTHROPOLOGICAL LINGUISTICS: An Introduction. *Random* 1968 text ed. pap. $3.95. The essentials of linguistics are given in a clear manner.

Moulton, William G. A LINGUISTIC GUIDE TO LANGUAGE LEARNING. *Modern Language Assn.* 1966 2nd ed. 1970 pap. $2.50

Sapir, Edward. LANGUAGE: An Introduction to the Study of Speech. *Harcourt* 1921 pap. $1.45. The relation of language to culture, thought and art. Sapir was one of the first anthropologists to be drawn into the problem of defining language as an aspect of the human being which serves as a point of differentiation from other animal forms.

Philosophy of language

Ayer, Alfred J. LANGUAGE, TRUTH AND LOGIC. 1936 *Dover* pap. $1.50; *Peter Smith* $4.25

Cassirer, Ernest. LANGUAGE AND MYTH. Trans. by Susane K. Langer. *Dover* pap. $1.25; *Peter Smith* $3.25. For Cassirer, the creative activity of the mind accounts for all human experience; to understand man one must understand his language and its symbolic construction.

Whorf, Benjamin L. LANGUAGE: Thought and Reality. Introd. by John B. Carroll. *M.I.T. Press* 1956 $8.00 pap. $2.95. Whorf developed the hypothesis that the structure of one's language influences thinking and understanding.

Culture and Language

Boas, Franz. RACE, LANGUAGE AND CULTURE. 1940. *Free Press* 1966 pap. $3.95. Sixty papers on mythology, art, anthropology, etc., and American Indian language. Boas saw languages as diverse products of diverse histories; each with an individual shape of its own at a given time.

Fishman, Joshua A. SOCIOLINGUISTICS: A Brief Introduction. *Newbury House* 1970 $6.95 pap. $4.50. Elementary introduction that assumes no prior knowledge of sociology, anthropology or linguistics.

Jespersen, Otto. MANKIND, NATION, AND INDIVIDUAL: From a Linguistic Point of View. *Indiana Univ. Press* 1964 pap. $1.95

Pei, Mario. VOICES OF MAN: The Meaning and Function of Language. 1962. *AMS Press* 1972 $10.00. The development and sociopolitical aspects of language.

Pride, John B. THE SOCIAL MEANING OF LANGUAGE. *Oxford* 1971 pap. $3.00. This book, which can be understood by the novice, unites studies in the social sciences and in linguistics.

Psychology of Language

Skinner, B. F. VERBAL BEHAVIOR. *Appleton* 1957. $10.50. Language examined by a behavioral psychologist.

Slobin, Dan I. PSYCHOLINGUISTICS. *Scott, Foresman* 1971 pap. text ed. $2.95. How psychologists are using present linguistic theories.

Translation

Arrowsmith, William, and Roger Shattuck, Eds. THE CRAFT AND CONTEXT OF TRANSLATION. *Univ. of Texas Press* 1961 $7.50

QUOTATIONS

Next to the originator of a sentence is the first quoter of it.
—RALPH WALDO EMERSON

Books of quotations are to be judged principally by their indexes. These are of four kinds: author; straight quotation; concordance; and topical.

The author index is common to all. The straight quotation index gives the first word of the quotation just as it occurs in the text. A concordance index gives the principal word of the quotation, which is usually the noun. For instance, "All that glitters is not gold," in a straight quotation index, will be found in the *a's* under *All.* In a concordance index, it will be found in the *g's*, under *Gold.* A topical index lists under general headings all quotations that bear on that particular subject. In a topical index, the quotation, "All that glitters is not gold" would probably be found under *Appearance.* The purpose of a topical index is to suggest quotations for various topics.

Ungar supplies dictionaries of quotations in foreign languages. An entertaining book with a serious purpose is Paul F. Boller's "Quotemanship: The Use and Abuse of Quotations for Polemical and Other Purposes" (*Southern Methodist Univ. Press* 1967 $7.95). "Mr. Boller, who teaches history at the University of Massachusetts," Eliot Fremont-Smith (in the *N.Y. Times*) "has identified no less than 22 distinct varieties of quotes currently used. . . . The most telling, at least for throwing an opponent off-balance, is the adversary-as-authority quote. . . . The book is not simply a pedant's amusement—though it is certainly that—but an eye-opening analysis of a prevalent method of persuasion. It also illustrates the vulnerability of nearly all public men. . . . 'If you don't want to be misquoted,' Will Rogers once said, 'don't say anything.' " (Or is Will Rogers merely said to have said it?)

Auden, W. H., and Louis Kronenberger, Eds. VIKING BOOK OF APHORISMS: A Personal Selection. *Viking* 1966 pap. $2.95

Bartlett, John. FAMILIAR QUOTATIONS: A Collection of Passages, Phrases and Proverbs, Traced to Their Sources in Ancient and Modern Literature. 1855. *Little* 12th ed. rev. and enl. 1948 13th centennial ed. rev. 1955 14th ed. rev. and enl. 1968 $15.00; Citadel pap $1.95

John Bartlett (1820–1905), a bookseller in Cambridge, Mass., and partner of *Little Brown & Co.*, compiled two famous books of reference: "A Complete Concordance to Shakespeare" (*St. Martin's* 1894 $37.50), and "Familiar Quotations" (1855). Bartlett lived to be 85 and brought out nine editions of his earlier book, enlarging it from 295 pages to 1158. The present edition has 1750 pages of quotations. Some quotations have been dropped; and sayings from non-Western cultures added as well as quotations from persons overlooked before: Chekhov, Brandeis, Flaubert, Freud, Jung, and others. The subject-matter index, prepared with the aid of a computer, now runs to almost 600 pages.

Bohle, Bruce. THE HOME BOOK OF AMERICAN QUOTATIONS. *Dodd* 1967 $10.00; (with title "Apollo Book of American Quotations") *Apollo* 1970 pap. $3.95. Half the 9000 entries are said to be new—not found in Burton Stevenson (*see below*), on which it is modeled.

"We can't confirm this, since the book is arranged by topic and indexed by words, most of the extracts are undated, and there is no index by author. The coverage of standard American speakers and writers and of broad topics is sound and extensive"—(David Glixon, in *SR*).

Browning, David Clayton. EVERYMAN'S DICTIONARY OF QUOTATIONS AND PROVERBS. 1952. *Int. Pubns. Service* 6th ed. 1973 $6.50

EVERYMAN'S DICTIONARY OF SHAKESPEARE QUOTATIONS. *Int. Pubns. Service* 1970 5th ed. $7.50

Cohen, J. M., and M. J. Cohen. THE PENGUIN DICTIONARY OF QUOTATIONS. *Penguin* 1960 pap. $2.95

THE PENGUIN DICTIONARY OF MODERN QUOTATIONS. *Penguin* 1971 pap. $2.25; *Peter Smith* $5.00. Quotations from the 20th century, mostly English, not found in the work above.

Evans, Bergen. DICTIONARY OF QUOTATIONS. *Dell* Delacorte 1968 $15.00

"A lively, up-to-date reference book which keeps the best from the past while utilizing choice items from the present. Thousands of familiar quotations, with the addition of many other new, contemporary, bright sayings chosen for wit as well as wisdom, and about 2000 illuminating and amusing comments (set in italics) by the humorist and word specialist, Bergen Evans. His remarks make this book a gem and a delight for the browser. A very broad and thorough subject index [locates] and cross-indexes each quotation under each of its key words and under [general subjects]. In addition, a topical index suggests related headings under each subject. The book has more than 2100 pages. The [more than 18,000] quotations take up 791 pages, double-column"—(*PW*).

Flesch, Rudolf, Ed. THE NEW BOOK OF UNUSUAL QUOTATIONS. *Harper* 1956 1966 $7.50. 8000 mostly paradoxical or uncommon quotations.

HARVARD CONCORDANCE TO SHAKESPEARE. Comp. by Marvin Spevack. *Harvard Univ. Press* 1974 $40.00 (Orig. pub. by *George Olms Verlag* in Germany). While this section should not legitimately include concordances on one author's writings, we make an exception for the most quoted and quotable of all writers. Both references and cross-references are given for the total of 884,647 words in Shakespeare's vocabulary. This concordance covers the poems and sonnets as well as the 38 plays.

Henry, Lewis C. 5000 QUOTATIONS FOR ALL OCCASIONS. *Doubleday* 1956 $4.95; (abr. as "Best Quotations") *Fawcett* Premier Bks. 1970 pap. $1.25. Arranged alphabetically by subject, with an index of authors, this book of popular quotations includes many from contemporary leaders and statesmen.

Hoyt, Jehiel Keeler. HOYT'S NEW CYCLOPEDIA OF PRACTICAL QUOTATIONS. 1881. *Funk & Wagnalls* new enl. ed. 1896 rev. and enl. 1927 by Kate Louise Roberts 3rd ed. 1927–1940 $8.50 thumb indexed $9.25

A cyclopedia rather than a dictionary. The term "practical" seems to apply to the quotations' usableness and suitability. They are classified under familiar topics. Quotations are from English, Latin and modern foreign authors with names, dates and nationalities of authors, but no Biblical quotations are included. Hoyt's is especially valuable for its three excellent indexes: a complete concordance of quotations, an author index, a subject (topic) index. There are 21,000 quotations from 3000 authors and 115,000 index entries.

Hurd, Charles. A TREASURY OF GREAT AMERICAN QUOTATIONS. 1964. *Doubleday* 1968 $5.95

Hyman, Robin. THE QUOTATION DICTIONARY. Fwd. by the editor. *Macmillan* 1964 $6.95; *Collier* 1967 pap. $2.45

The criterion, says the author, is what *is* familiar, not what ought to be. 1000 proverbs; many quotations from the 20th century and some from foreign sources (original and translation). A good supplement to standard works; a pleasant browsing book. For 515 pages this is excellent value.

Jackson, Percival E. THE WISDOM OF THE SUPREME COURT. 1962. *Greenwood* 1973 $19.75

Compendium of aphorisms and bon mots of the Supreme Court, covering every phase of the human condition. "The book is no mere pompous array of . . . dry-as-dust legal matters, but rather is a pleasing volume into which the literate can dip and make quite as enjoyable discoveries as they can in their Bartlett's."

King, W. Francis H., Ed. CLASSICAL AND FOREIGN QUOTATIONS: A Manual of Historical and Literary Quotations, Proverbs and Popular Sayings. 1887. 3rd ed. 1904. *Ungar* 1958 $9.50

The offset reproduction of the third edition of this useful compilation contains four indexes: I. Authors, Authorities and Editions; 2. English Subject Index; 3. Quotations Index; 4. Greek Quotations Index. There are 3142 quotations with English translations, as well as related sayings and expository comments by the compiler.

Magill, Frank N., Ed. MAGILL'S QUOTATIONS IN CONTEXT. *Harper* First series, 1966 $11.95 lib. bdg. $10.69; Second series, 1969 $11.95

Familiar sayings, important passages from well-esteemed works, and proverbs are given in their original context with commentary. The first series has 2020 entries, the second series, 1500.

Mencken, H. L., Ed. A NEW DICTIONARY OF QUOTATIONS ON HISTORICAL PRINCIPLES FROM ANCIENT AND MODERN SOURCES. *Knopf* 1942 $15.00

Arranged by subject in a single alphabet, this includes some quotations from the 1930s and a few from the 1940s, but they are mainly from the 18th and early 19th centuries. It is of interest as a browsing volume, reflecting as it does the compiler's vigorous individuality. There is no index.

THE OXFORD DICTIONARY OF QUOTATIONS. *Oxford* 1941 2nd ed. 1953 $14.00

Completely reset with more than 1300 new quotations added, this dictionary, in which popularity and not merit is the basis for inclusion, now totals over 40,000 entries. Arranged alphabetically, by author, indexed by key words, it is intended primarily for reference, but provides delightful browsing as well. Exact reference to source is given.

THE CONCISE OXFORD DICTIONARY OF QUOTATIONS. *Oxford* 1964 pap. $1.95

"The length of the quotations is what differentiates this volume (and the parent Oxford Dictionary of Quotations from others of comparable size. The arrangement is alphabetical by author and an explicit subject index occupies nearly half the book's 480 pages"—(David Glixon, in *SR*). Foreign quotations are bilingual.

Seldes, George. THE GREAT QUOTATIONS. Lyle Stuart 1966 $15.00; *Pocket Bks.* 1967 $1.25

Publishers' Weekly commented that, while the hardcover edition was not a great bargain, the paperback is good value. "Definitely not the 'Bartlett's' kind of quotations; Mr. Seldes has chosen some 10,000 of the controversial, the firebrand, left- and right-wing quotations from writers, philosophers and public figures up to the present."

Simpson James B. CONTEMPORARY QUOTATIONS. *T. Y. Crowell* 1964 $6.95. Pertinent quotations, 1950–64. Entries arranged alphabetically by topic, with author and subject indexes. Although limited to quotations made within a short time span, there is a surprising amount of good material here.

Stevenson, Burton Egbert. HOME BOOK OF QUOTATIONS, CLASSICAL AND MODERN. *Dodd* 1934 3rd ed. 1937 9th ed. 1956 10th ed. 1967 $35.00 The third and so-called definitive edition includes 73,000 quotations from 4700 authors. The concordance index was almost doubled, having now 100,000. Like Hoyt and unlike Bartlett, this groups its quotations under subjects, such as Love, Government, Religion, Law, making the index indispensable. The work is particularly strong in American political quotations, campaign slogans, new coinages, and catchlines from popular songs. The ninth revised edition has further quotations and an enlarged index; the tenth adds some 500 additional quotations.

THE HOME BOOK OF SHAKESPEARE QUOTATIONS. 1953. *Scribner* 1966 $22.50. 300 pages of its 2050 are index and concordance.

> Send orders directly to Scribner. 90,000 quotations "arranged topically, each accompanied by its specific location in the play and the name of the speaker"—(Glixon, in *SR*).

Tripp, Rhoda Thomas, Ed. THE INTERNATIONAL THESAURUS OF QUOTATIONS *T. Y. Crowell* 1970 $8.95 thumb-indexed $10.00

> "For persons who have an idea and who are looking for the means to express it . . . (the Thesaurus) is designed for a generation that seldom memorizes literary passages. Its users will very likely turn to it less often to recall a familiar saying than to find fresh words. Quotations are classfied by subject with a profusion of cross-references"—(Publisher's preface).

Van Buren, Maud. QUOTATIONS FOR SPECIAL OCCASIONS. *Wilson* 1938 $5.00. Prose and verse quotations for all national holidays and other celebrations such as Arbor Day, Book Week, Flag Day, Mother's Day, Safety Week, St. Valentine's Day.

Voss, Carl H. QUOTATIONS OF COURAGE AND VISION: A Source Book For Speaking, Writing and Meditation. *Assn. Press* 1972 $9.95

WHAT THEY SAID IN 197–. Comp. and Ed. by Alan F. Pater and Jason R. Pater. *Monitor Book Co.* 1969 to date each $17.50. As of 1974, books from this series are "What They Said in" 1969, 1970, 1971 and 1972. Quotations are documented with date, place and circumstance information.

PROVERBS

Champion, Selwyn Gurney. RACIAL PROVERBS: A Selection of the World's Proverbs Arranged Linguistically with Authoritative Introductions to the Proverbs of 27 Countries and Races. 1938. *Finch Press* $15.00; *Routledge & Kegan Paul* 1966 $26.75

Gluski, Jerzy, Comp. and Ed. PROVERBS: A Comparative Book of English, French, German, Italian, Spanish and Russian Proverbs with a Latin Appendix. *Am. Elsevier* 1971 $8.95

OXFORD DICTIONARY OF ENGLISH PROVERBS. Ed. by William George. *Oxford* 1935; rev. by Sir Paul Harvey 1948; 3rd ed. rev. and enl. by F. P. Wilson 1970 $17.00. An historical dictionary of English proverbs, it is planned on the lines of the "Oxford English Dictionary on Historical Principles," i.e., each proverb is illustrated by dated quotations. Proverbs are arranged alphabetically by the first significant word.

Stevenson, Burton Egbert. THE MACMILLAN BOOK OF PROVERBS, MAXIMS, AND FAMOUS PHRASES. *Macmillan* 1948 5th ed. 1965 $25.00. (Originally titled "Home Book of Proverbs, Maxims and Familiar Phrases.")

Taylor, Archer, and Bartlett Jere Whiting. A DICTIONARY OF AMERICAN PROVERBS AND PROVERBIAL PHRASES 1820–1880. *Harvard Univ. Press* 1958 o.p.

"This superbly edited dictionary is, of course, a book for every student of American language and literature, its comparative reference in, before and after its period being particularly extensive and useful"— (*N. Y. Times*).

Tilley, Morris Palmer, Ed. A DICTIONARY OF THE PROVERBS IN ENGLAND IN THE SIXTEENTH AND SEVENTEENTH CENTURIES: A Collection of the Proverbs Found in English Literature and the Dictionaries of the Period. *Univ. of Michigan Press* 1950 $25.00

Whiting, Bartlett J. and Helen W. Whiting. PROVERBS, SENTENCES, AND PROVERBIAL PHRASES FROM ENGLISH WRITINGS BEFORE 1500. *Harvard* 1968 $25.00

AWARDS

French, Warren G., and Walter E. Kidd, Eds. AMERICAN NOBEL LITERARY PRIZE-WINNERS. *Univ. of Oklahoma Press* 1967 $5.95. An appraisal of the seven Americans who have received the award.

Frenz, Horst, Ed. NOBEL LECTURES IN LITERATURE, 1901–1967. *Am. Elsevier* 1969 $16.50. *See Chapter 4, section on General Works on Writers and Writing, for comment.*

Kingman, Lee, E. NEWBERY AND CALDECOTT MEDAL BOOKS: 1956–1965. *Horn Bk.* 1965 $10.00. Acceptance talks and biographies of winners.

LITERARY AND LIBRARY PRIZES. Jeanne Henderson and Brenda Piggins, Eds. *Bowker* 1935 8th ed. 1973 $16.50. The 1973 edition of this work, first published as "Famous Literary Prizes and Their Winners," gives information on the history, conditions and rules of international, American, Canadian, and British prizes. Hundreds of winning authors and their works are listed up to 1973.

Marble, Annie, NOBEL PRIZE WINNERS IN LITERATURE. 1901–1931. 1932. *Bks. for Libraries* $14.50

Miller, Bertha Mahoney, and Elinor Whitney Field, Eds. CALDECOTT MEDAL BOOKS, 1922–1955. *Horn Bk.* 1957 $10.00. Acceptance talks, biography and appraisal.

NEWBERY MEDAL BOOKS, 1922–1955. *Horn Bk.* 1955 $10.00. The same information as above. The Newbery and Caldecott medals donated by the late Frederic G. Melcher are awarded annually by the Children's Services Division of the American Library Assn.

Stuckey, William J. PULITZER PRIZE NOVELS: A Critical Backward Look. 1966 *Univ. of Oklahoma Press* 1968 $5.95. Stuckey is a Professor of English at Purdue University.

Wasserman, Paul, Ed. AWARDS, HONORS AND PRIZES. *Gale* 1969 2nd ed. 1972 $24.00. Among other fields, literature, librarianship, publishing and journalism awards are cited. Name of organization, terms of eligibility, purpose and form of award are given.

WRITING GUIDES

> *"Although it is possible to think without words and to communicate by signs,*
> *our civilization depends . . . on the written word. Writing is embodied thought,*
> *and the thought is clear or muddy, graspable or fugitive, according to the purity of*
> *the medium. Communication means one thought held in common. What could be*
> *more practical than to try making that thought unmistakable?"*
>
> —JACQUES BARZUN

Selections here have been grouped by emphasis. At one level are guides to good writing which, although they do not espouse the philosophy of grammatical analysis as a study in itself, are nevertheless primarily grammars. Many publishers keep grammars in print for the academic world. Examples are: "The Macmillan Hand-book of English" by John Kierzek and Walter Gibson (*Macmillan* 5th ed. 1965 $5.50); "Prentice-Hall Handbook for Writers" by Glenn Legget and others (*Prentice-Hall* 5th ed. $5.95); Porter G. Perrin's "Writer's Guide and Index to English" (*Scott-Foresman* 1972 5th ed. $7.95 soft bdg. $6.95, also dist. by *Morrow* [Lothrop] 1966 rev. ed. $10.25). The manuals listed below are nonacademic and more informal.

On another level are books on editing, so necessary for assuring uniformity in transforming manuscript into print. There are editing manuals put out by organizations, such as the National Education Association's "NEA Style Manual for Writers and Editors" (1962 1966 $1.00); or the U.S. Government Printing Office's "Style Manual." We list some of the more widely used titles.

Gathering materials, research, can present problems to the beginner; and marketing the finished product is a headache even to the professional. The publisher *The Writer* has many books specifically on writing materials that sell. However, this editor urges the would-be writer to consult books that analyze the masters without consideration of their marketability, such as Wayne C. Booth's "The Rhetoric of Fiction" (*Univ. of Chicago Press* 1961 $7.50 pap. $2.95); Robie Macauley and George Lanning's "Technique in Fiction" (*Harper* 1964 $5.50); or Sean O'Faolain's "The Short Story" (*Devin-Adair* 1951 pap. $3.50).

Guides to Good Writing

Bernstein, Theodore M. WATCH YOUR LANGUAGE. 1958. Pref. by Jacques Barzun. *Atheneum* 1965 $4.50; *Pocket Bks.* pap. $.75

THE CAREFUL WRITER: A Modern Guide to English Usage. *Atheneum* 1965 $10.00

MISS THISTLEBOTTOM'S HOBGOBLINS: The Careful Writer's Guide to the Taboos, Bugbears and Outmoded Rules of English Usage. *Farrar, Straus* 1973 Noonday pap. $2.95. For many editors as well as writers these three well-arranged guides above by a respected *N. Y. Times* editor are daily companions. Usage is made clear by reason and example, often with good humor.

Berry, Thomas Elliot. MOST COMMON MISTAKES IN ENGLISH USAGE. *McGraw-Hill* pap. $1.95

Flesch, Rudolf, and A. H. Lass. THE WAY TO WRITE. 1947. 1949 1955. (with title "A New Guide to Better Writing") *Popular Lib.* 1963 $.75

Gowers, Sir Ernest. PLAIN WORDS. *Knopf* 1954 $4.95; (with title "The Complete Plain Words") *Penguin* Pelican Bks. pap. $1.25.

A good general writing guide "as enjoyable to read as it is worthwhile to consult"—(Glixon, in *SR*).

Morsberger, Robert E. COMMONSENSE GRAMMAR AND STYLE. *T. Y. Crowell* 1972 rev. ed. $8.95 pap. $1.75.

"Like its 1936 predecessor, Janet Aiken's *Commonsense Grammar*, the new book is tolerant and witty, and no more prescriptive than necessary"—(Glixon, in *SR*).

Strunk, William, Jr., and E. B. White. ELEMENTS OF STYLE. 1918. *Macmillan* 1959 2nd ed. 1972 $3.50 pap. $1.25

Concise guide for those who wish to use English style with simplicity and grace. "Distinguished by brevity, clarity, and prickly good sense, it is, unlike most such manuals, a book as well as a tool"—(*New Yorker*).

Vrooman, Alan H. GOOD WRITING: An Informal Manual of Style. *Atheneum* 1967 $4.50 pap. $2.95. 145 pages with index.

It "abounds in excellent examples of good and poor usage"—(Glixon, in *SR*).

Editing

Collins, Frederick Howard, and others. AUTHORS' AND PRINTERS' DICTIONARY: A Guide for Authors, Editors, Printers, Correctors of the Press, Compositors and Typists. *Oxford* 10th ed. rev. 1956 $6.50

Modern Language Association of America. THE MLA STYLE SHEET. *Modern Language Assn.* 1951 2nd ed. 1970 $1.95

NEW YORK TIMES STYLE BOOK FOR WRITERS AND EDITORS. *McGraw-Hill* 1962 $5.50. A leading reference, setting firm standards for journalistic style.

Skillin, Marjorie E., and Robert M. Gay. WORDS INTO TYPE. 1948. rev. ed. *Appleton* 1964 $7.90. Long one of the references most favored by book editors.

Turabian, Kate L. A MANUAL FOR WRITERS OF TERM PAPERS, THESES, AND DISSERTATIONS. 1955 1967 *Univ. of Chicago Press* 4th ed. 1973 $5.00 pap. $1.95. Widely used by college and graduate students.

UNITED STATES GOVERNMENT PRINTING OFFICE STYLE MANUAL. Rev. ed. *Superintendent of Documents, U. S. Govt. Printing Office* 1973 $4.70 pap. $2.95. A thorough work of reference, one of the major ones; of added value for those handling information about government. Order from Superintendant of Documents, Washington, D. C. 20025 by title and catalog number GP 1/4: St 9/973.

University of Chicago Press. A MANUAL OF STYLE. *Univ. of Chicago Press* 1906 12th ed. 1969 $10.00 pap. $1.00. "The first revision since 1949; more than ninety percent of the material is new"—(Publisher's catalog). One of the most helpful and widely consulted authorities, particularly in the book industry.

Research

Altick, Richard D. ART OF LITERARY RESEARCH. *Norton* 1964 text ed. $5.50

Barzun, Jacques, and Henry F. Graff. THE MODERN RESEARCHER. *Harcourt* 1957 rev. ed. $8.50 pap. text ed. $3.95. Combines training in how to use research materials with disciplined understanding of how to organize thoughts and put them down on paper coherently.

Brooks, Phillip C. RESEARCH IN ARCHIVES: The Use of Unpublished Primary Sources. *Univ. of Chicago Press* 1969 $5.75. This guide to using unpublished sources available in American archives is written by the director of the Harry S. Truman Library.

Hook, Lucyle, and Mary Virginia Gaver. THE RESEARCH PAPER: Gathering Library Material, Organizing and Preparing the Manuscript. *Prentice-Hall* 1944 4th ed. 1969 pap. text ed. $2.95

Menzel, Donald H., Howard Mumford Jones and Lyle G. Boyd. WRITING A TECHNICAL PAPER. *McGraw-Hill* 1961 $5.50 pap. $1.95. For writing well in the fields of science and engineering.

Marketing Writing

THE DIRECTORY OF PUBLISHING OPPORTUNITIES, 1973/74: A Comprehensive Guide to Academic, Business, Research, Scientific and Technical Publishing Opportunities. *Academic Media* 2nd ed. 1973 $39.50

LITERARY MARKET PLACE WITH NAMES AND NUMBERS, 1973–1974: The Business Directory of American Book Publishing. Comp. by J. A. Neal. *Bowker* 1940 32nd ed. 1973 pap. $17.50. A practical manual for the publishing and literary trade. Lists authors, agents, editorial services, public relations services, reviewers, wholesalers to book stores, etc.

Reynolds, Paul R. THE NON-FICTION BOOK: How to Write and Sell It. Introd. by John Toland. *Morrow* 1970 $5.00

> Mr. Reynolds is a literary agent of broad experience. "There is no conceivable question, from how to summarize a central idea, do research, fashion an outline, revise the text, and deal with a publisher contractually, that Reynolds does not answer plainly, thoughtfully, and completely"—(S. W. Little in *SR*).

WRITING AND SELLING OF FICTION. *Doubleday* 1965 $4.95

—M.P.

Chapter 4

Broad Studies and
General Anthologies

"Anthologies are, ideally, an essential species of criticism. Nothing expresses and exposes your taste so completely . . . as that vague final treasury of the really best poems that grows in your head all your life. . . ."
—RANDALL JARRELL, *Poetry and the Age*

This chapter has been devised in the attempt to solve the problem of locating books that relate to at least two—sometimes many—chapters of the literature volumes of *"The Reader's Adviser,"* or that reflect overlapping subjects and interests in the field of literature. Thus, the books listed are often more comprehensive in scope than those listed in specific areas; they include, as the chapter title indicates, broad studies and collections rather than detailed studies of a particular era, genre or nationality. (Although some books of more specific coverage are included in the chapter, the intention here is to give emphasis to these works for their background information, or for their particular significance in the study of broad areas of knowledge.) Of course, it often seems that many "general and comprehensive" works belong in several chapters, and where this might occur, we have made cross-references to aid the reader in finding these titles.

It is hoped that a chapter such as this will serve a useful purpose, but it does, of necessity, remain something of a catch-all. The reader looking for a more complete picture may find it convenient to read through the table of contents for the location of material by subject matter, and to consult the index for specific subject needs.

The Oxford English Novels, under the general editorship of James Kinsley, and each volume edited by an authority in the field, is part of an ongoing project planned eventually to reach the present day. Fifty titles have been published to date, mostly of the 18th century. Each volume will contain a critical introduction, a chronological table, a list of biocritical studies, notes on editions and explanatory notes. (*See the introduction to Chapter 13, American Fiction: Early Period,* for the *Modern Language Association's* similar, though not identical, American venture.) *Norton* Critical Editions are works of literature accompanied by textual background and essays by several well-known critics on each work in the series. *Dutton's* Everyman editions and those of the *Modern Library* have long been standbys; Everyman in 1966 celebrated its Diamond Jubilee with the publication of an anthology (*see "Everyman" under General and Comprehensive Anthologies, this chapter*) and of a new revised edition of "The Reader's Guide to Everyman's Library" by A. J. Hoppé (pap. $1.85). The *Viking* Portable Library editions provide paperbound representative samplings of the works of great writers, each treated in a separate volume. Modern poetry series are published by *Yale University Press, Wesleyan University Press, Alan Swallow, City Lights* and others. The *Crowell* Poets is an attractive series of selections from individual major English poets of earlier periods. Critical series are legion; one of the best is that, in paper, of *Oxford* Galaxy Books. Detailed information on books in series is to be found in "Catalog of Reprints in Series" by Orton and "Titles in Series" by Baer, both of which are listed in Chapter 2, Bibliography, under Trade Bibliographies—American.

The 20th-century "little magazines," which nurtured so many budding American writers who have since become famous, are now being reprinted in complete series by

Kraus in quantity (information on request). For those who are interested in the avant-garde writers likely to come to the fore in the future, the Gotham Book Mart (41 West 47 St., New York, N.Y. 10036) can provide guides to present-day little magazines as well as current copies of most of them. A useful guide is *"the* directory of little magazines" (*LJ*), which lists almost 1,000: "Directory of Little Magazines" (3rd ed. 1967 $2.00, order from *Len Fulton*, publisher, Dustbooks, Box 123, El Cerrito, Calif. 94530).

Drama is not included in the present chapter. Histories of poetry and of the novel are dealt with in appropriate sections here, but for comprehensive histories and dictionaries of literature in general, *see Chapter 3, Reference Books—Literature.*

REFERENCE AND BACKGROUND MATERIALS

Altick, Richard D. THE ART OF LITERARY RESEARCH. *Norton* 1964 text ed. $5.50. An excellent and sensible guide to literary research, apprising the reader of the limitations as well as the attributes of various tools of research.

(With Andrew Wright). A SELECTIVE BIBLIOGRAPHY FOR THE STUDY OF ENGLISH AND AMERICAN LITERATURE. *Macmillan* 4th ed. 1971 pap. $3.50 5th ed. (in prep.) A handy guide, with entries sorted by categories. There is a final, excellent list of books everyone interested in literature should read.

ANNALS OF ENGLISH LITERATURE, 1475–1950: The Principal Publications of Each Year together with an Alphabetical Index of Authors and Their Works. Comp. by J. C. Ghosh and E. G. Withycombe; rev. by R. W. Chapman and others. *Oxford* 2nd ed. 1961 $9.00. A useful and reliable book.

Blanck, Jacob. BIBLIOGRAPHY OF AMERICAN LITERATURE. *Yale Univ. Press* 6 vols. 1955–73 Vols. 1–5 each $25.00 Vol. 6 $30.00. This bibliography is in progress. Entries "A" through "Thomas William Parsons" have been completed to date. When completed this will be the standard work.

Bond, Donald F. A REFERENCE GUIDE TO ENGLISH STUDIES. *Univ. of Chicago Press* 1962 2nd ed. 1971 $6.85 Phoenix Bks. pap. $2.45

Brewer, E. Cobham. BREWER'S DICTIONARY OF PHRASE AND FABLE. *Harper* rev. ed. by Ivor H. Evans 1972 $10.00

"Brewer records the chief figures of the world's mythologies, as well as superstitions and customs of ancient and modern times"—(Publisher's note). Originally written in 1870, this is an excellent source, helpful in understanding all manner of references. It will explain d'Artagnan (p. 267) as well as "The fly in the ointment" (p.367).

Curtius, Ernst Robert. EUROPEAN LITERATURE AND THE LATIN MIDDLE AGES. Trans. by Willard Trask. *Princeton Univ. Press* 1953 $15.00 pap. $3.95; *Harper* Torchbks. pap. $3.95. Not armchair reading, but a very useful and important compendium of information on a wide range of topics, such as ancient rhetoric, classicism, mannerism and the like. It is erudite, and should be considered chiefly for reference and "dipping."

Esdaile, Arundell. THE SOURCES OF ENGLISH LITERATURE: A Guide for Students. 1928. *Burt Franklin* $11.00

Grierson, H. J. C. THE BACKGROUND OF ENGLISH LITERATURE AND OTHER COLLECTED ESSAYS AND ADDRESSES. 2nd ed. 1934 1960. *Barnes & Noble* $5.50. Essays on topics here and there. Sir Herbert is consistently intelligent and interesting.

Hadas, Moses. ANCILLA TO CLASSICAL READING. *Columbia* 1954 $1.95

Highet, Gilbert. THE CLASSICAL TRADITION: Greek and Roman Influences on Western Literature. *Oxford* 1949 $14.50 Galaxy Bks. pap. $3.95. Highet brings his discussion up to the present (Camus). He writes well, has a firm grasp of his material and transmits much reliable and illuminating information.

Holman, C. Hugh. A HANDBOOK TO LITERATURE. Based on the original edition of 1936 by William Flint Thrall and Addison Hibbard. *Odyssey* 3rd ed. 1972 $6.00 thumb indexed $10.00 pap. $3.50

"This is one of the standard sources for literary reference .... The handbook remains a remarkable work"—*(Choice).*

Hornstein, Lillian Herlands, Ed., G. P. Percy, Co-ed., Calvin S. Brown, Gen. Ed., and others. THE READER'S COMPANION TO WORLD LITERATURE: A Guide to the Immortal Masterpieces of Writing from the Dawn of Civilization to the Present. 1956. *New Am. Lib.* Mentor Bks. 2nd ed. rev. and updated by Hornstein, Leon Edel and Horst Frenz 1973 pap. $1.95. An invaluable, handy reference book that answers almost any question on authors and books with insight and intelligence.

Thomson, J. A. K. THE CLASSICAL BACKGROUND OF ENGLISH LITERATURE. 1948 1951 *Macmillan* Collier Bks. pap. $.95

GREAT BOOKS

Although John Erskine as early as 1919 sponsored a program of readings of great literature at Columbia College, the impetus for the current interest sprang from the Great Books program of St. John's College, Annapolis, in which the study of approximately 100 books which have most influenced Western civilization replaced conventional courses dealing with specialized subjects. This list is included in Mortimer J. Adler's "How to Read a Book" (*Simon & Schuster* 1940 $6.95 pap. $1.95).

The idea behind the Great Books program was carried into the field of self-education largely through the enthusiastic support of Dr. Robert Maynard Hutchins, formerly president of the University of Chicago. In 1947 the Great Books Foundation was organized with Dr. Hutchins as chairman of the board, with headquarters in Chicago. Its purpose is the self-education of children and adults by training leaders for group discussions of books dealing with the basic issues of mankind. Groups meet in public libraries and other education centers across the country. There are 13,700 such groups, with 148,000 participants. The current program comprises 16 years of reading for the discussion groups. The readings are published by the Foundation in pamphlet form. Harold C. Gardiner has edited an appraisal of the books in "The Great Books: A Christian Appraisal" (*Devin-Adair* 1953 4 vols. each $3.50 set $12.00). Hutchins and Adler are also editors of a yearbook, "Great Ideas Today" (*Encyclopedia Britannica Educational Corp.* 1970 1972 1973 price upon request), relating contemporary developments in the "great ideas" plus additional literary works.

GREAT BOOKS OF THE WESTERN WORLD. Robert M. Hutchins, Ed. in Chief, Mortimer J. Adler, Associate Ed. *Encyclopedia Britannica Educational Corp.* in collaboration with Univ. of Chicago. 1952 56 vols. including a 2-vol. Synopticon index (price upon request). 443 selected works of 74 individual authors spanning 30 centuries. The great ideas of Western civilization reflected in the literary works considered indispensable to a liberal education. The Synopticon is an idea index with 163,000 references on 102 "great ideas."

GATEWAY TO THE GREAT BOOKS. Ed. by Robert M. Hutchins and Mortimer J. Adler. 10 vols. *Encyclopedia Britannica Educational Corp.* (price upon request). 225 selections, 135 authors. Selected literary masterpieces with a synoptical guide to the writings and the 102 "great ideas."

Great Books Foundation. Sets of readings for Great Books Discussion Groups. *Great Books Foundation* (307 North Michigan Ave., Chicago, Ill. 60601) (price upon request)

GENERAL AND COMPREHENSIVE ANTHOLOGIES OF LITERATURE

This section includes anthologies which contain both poetry and prose. In this edition of *"The Reader's Adviser"* we have dropped the subdivision "Useful Popular Anthologies" and combined such collections in the list below. The title itself or the annotation should make clear the nature of the volume. "Popular" collections of poetry will be found in the section "Poetry—Anthologies of Poetry" in this chapter.

Abrams, M. H. THE NORTON ANTHOLOGY OF ENGLISH LITERATURE. *Norton* 1962 rev. ed. 1968 2 vols. each $9.25 pap. each $7.45 shorter 1-vol. major author ed. $11.50 pap. $9.50. A selection of the great and near-great with full bibliographies, biographical and critical commentaries, and documentary excerpts that illuminate the controlling ideas of each major literary period.

Baugh, Albert C., and G. W. McClelland. ENGLISH LITERATURE: A Period Anthology. *Appleton* 1954 2 vols. each $8.95 1-vol. ed. $14.95

Bradley, Sculley, Richmond Croom and E. Hudson Long. THE AMERICAN TRADITION IN LITERATURE. *Norton* 1956 3rd ed. 1967 2 vols. Vol. I Bradford to Lincoln Vol. 2 Whitman to the Present each $8.95 text ed. pap. $6.95 shorter 1-vol. ed. $9.45 pap. $7.75

Brooks, Cleanth, John Thibaut Purser and Robert Penn Warren. AN APPROACH TO LITERATURE. *Appleton* 4th ed. 1964 $9.95. An excellent comprehensive anthology. The choice of selections is outstanding, and the essays and introductory material are interesting and readable. It includes a very helpful glossary, especially for an understanding of poetic terms.

Carlisle, Henry C., Jr. AMERICAN SATIRE IN PROSE AND VERSE. *Random* 1962 $10.00. A fresh and stimulating "selection of satire which is irreverent and comically critical of life . . . in the U.S.A." 110 selections by 70 writers from Benjamin Franklin to the present.

Carmer, Carl. THE TAVERN LAMPS ARE BURNING: Literary Journeys through Six Regions and Four Centuries of New York State. *McKay* 1964 $10.00

> "Mr. Carmer has chosen his literary gems in an effort to persuade those who read this anthology that upstate New York is 'unique and special' "—(*LJ*). Included are excerpts from 98 authors, among them Edith Wharton, Henry James and Francis Parkman.

Curtis, Charles P., Jr., and Ferris Greenslet. THE PRACTICAL COGITATOR, or The Thinker's Anthology. New introd. by John H. Finley, Jr. *Houghton* 1945 1950 3rd ed. 1963 $6.95. Following the pattern established in the first edition, the arrangement includes man reflecting on himself, his past, his fellow men, etc. Here are just the thought-provoking quotations one would jot down while reading. The publisher's note states that the rule for inclusion was "nothing that is not worth re-reading." One realizes with pleasure that this is so.

Davis, Arthur P., and Redding Saunders. CAVALCADE: Negro American Writing from 1760 to the Present. *Houghton* 1971 $11.50. The book covers the years from the pioneer writers to black nationalism and shows the "evolution of this writing as a literary art." The short introductory material is very helpful, and both the format and the print are appealing.

Edwards, S. L. ANTHOLOGY OF ENGLISH PROSE: Bede to Stevenson. *Dutton* Everyman's $3.50

Ellmann, Richard, and Charles Feidelson, Jr. THE MODERN TRADITION: Backgrounds of Modern Literature. *Oxford* 1965 $17.50 text ed. $10.95. Examples from "101 poets, novelists, scientists, artists, and speculative thinkers, whose writings constitute the main documents of 'the modern tradition.'" Edited and selected with great intelligence, it provides a wonderful source for locating the major ideas that have influenced us all.

Emanuel, James A., and Theodore L. Gross. DARK SYMPHONY: Negro Literature in America. *Macmillan* (Free Press) 1968 $8.95 pap. $4.95. The book is divided into four sections: I Early Literature; II The Negro Awakening; III Major Authors; IV Contemporary Literature. This is a very comprehensive anthology. It contains excellent selections with fine background information on the authors chosen. The introductory material is also very helpful to an understanding of the historical framework. Includes bibliography and index.

AN EVERYMAN ANTHOLOGY OF EXCERPTS GRAVE AND GAY. Introd. by J. B. Priestley. *Dutton* Everyman's 1966 $3.50. Over 100 authors are represented in the Diamond Jubilee collection.

Fadiman, Clifton. READING I'VE LIKED. *Simon & Schuster* 1941 1958 pap. $3.50. A personal, discriminating selection, mostly of prose, made when he was the book critic for the *New Yorker*. Especially notable for its witty, autobiographical and critical introduction and brilliant commentary.

CLIFTON FADIMAN'S FIRESIDE READER. *Simon & Schuster* 1961 $5.95

FIFTY YEARS: Being a Retrospective Collection of Novels, Novellas, Tales, Drama, Poetry, and Reportage and Essays (whether Literary, Musical, Contemplative, Historical, Biographical, Argumentative, or Gastronomical) All Drawn from Volumes Issued during the Last Half-Century by Alfred & Blanche Knopf. *Knopf* 1965 $10.00

Fischer, John, and Robert B. Silvers. WRITING IN AMERICA. *Rutgers Univ. Press* 1960 pap. $1.45. An appraisal of our writing—from poetry to TV—and of book reviewing, publishing and creative writing.

Foerster, Norman. AMERICAN POETRY AND PROSE, A Book of Readings, 1607–1916. 1925. Sections on The Colonial Mind; The Romantic Movement; The Realist Movement; from Captain John Smith to Faulkner; excellent critical notes. *Houghton* 5th ed. by Foerster, Norman Grabo, Russel B. Nye, E. Fred Carlisle and Robert

Falk 1970 in 2 pts. and 3 vols. Pts. 1 and 2 each $9.50 3 vols. each $7.50 complete set $13.50

Giamatti, A. Bartlett. WESTERN LITERATURE. *Harcourt* 1971 3 vols. Vol. I The Ancient World ed. by Heinrich Van Staden Vol. 2 The Middle Ages, Renaissance, Enlightenment ed. by Robert Hollander Vol. 3 The Modern World ed. by Peter Brooks each $3.95

Greene, David Herbert. ANTHOLOGY OF IRISH LITERATURE. 1954. *New York Univ. Press* 2 vols. 1971 $12.95 pap. $5.95. Spans more than 12 centuries—from the early Irish lyrics through modern Irish literature in English.

Harris, Stephen. THE HUMANIST TRADITION IN WORLD LITERATURE: An Anthology of Masterpieces from Gilgamesh to the Divine Comedy. *Charles E. Merrill* 1970 $13.95 pap. $8.95. Presents a selection of the best that has been thought and written.

Harrison, George B., Walter J. Bate and others. MAJOR BRITISH WRITERS. *Harcourt* 1954 rev. ed. 1959 2 vols. Vol. 1 Chaucer, Spenser, Shakespeare, Bacon, Donne, Milton, Swift, Pope Vol. 2 Johnson and Boswell, Wordsworth, Keats, Browning, Arnold, Shaw, Yeats, Eliot each $9.95 abr. ed. $6.75. Explanatory notes, excellent introductory essays by various critics.

Hibbard, Addison. WRITERS OF THE WORLD. *Houghton* 2nd ed. by Horst Frenz 1967 $13.95

> "Not the least valuable aspect of Mr. Hibbard's approach is that it lends itself to a consideration of the whole culture of a period, of which literature is one expression"—(General Editor's Note). Includes interesting illustrations, chronological table of authors, a guide to the types of literature, and index of authors, titles, and first lines of poetry.

Hill, Herbert. SOON, ONE MORNING: New Writing by American Negroes, 1940–1962. *Knopf* 1963 $7.95

Irmscher, William F. MAN AND WARFARE: Thematic Readings for Composition. *Little* 1964 pap. $4.70

> " 'Ten different focuses upon man and his thoughts on warfare' in the form of essays by Machiavelli, Thoreau, Ruskin, William James, Orwell, Reinhold Niebuhr, Wylie, Jung, Toynbee, and Bertrand Russell; three 'satires' by C. S. Lewis, Kafka, and Dos Passos; short stories by Stephen Crane, Joseph Conrad, and Edward Loomis, the drama 'Arms and the Man' by Shaw, and Katherine Anne Porter's novelette, 'Pale Horse, Pale Rider' "—(*LJ*).

Kermode, Frank, and John Hollander. THE OXFORD ANTHOLOGY OF ENGLISH LITERATURE. *Oxford* 1973 2 vols. each $9.95 pap. each $7.95 available in 6 vols. pap. each $3.95

> This is a very superior anthology. The two-volume edition is divided into The Middle Ages through the Eighteenth Century, and 1800 to the Present. The paperback editions, dividing the material into six categories, are: Medieval English Literature, ed. by J. B. Trapp; The Literature of Renaissance England, ed. by John Hollander and Frank Kermode; The Restoration and the Eighteenth Century, ed. by Martin Price; Romantic Poetry and Prose, ed. by Harold Bloom and Lionel Trilling; Victorian Prose and Poetry, ed. by Lionel Trilling and Harold Bloom; Modern British Literature, ed. by Frank Kermode and John Hollander.
> "This 4600-page work features a general introduction to each of the six periods; brief biographical and critical essays on major authors; glossaries of literary and historical terms; modernized texts . . . explanatory notes; lists of suggested further readings; indexes; and 192 pages of illustrations"—(*LJ*).

Mack, Maynard, and others. WORLD MASTERPIECES. *Norton* 3rd ed. 1973 2 vols. each $9.95 pap. each $8.25 Continental ed. 1962 $11.95 pap. $9.95 Continental ed. enl. 1966 2 vols. Vol. I $8.45 pap. $6.95 Vol. 2 $8.95 pap. $7.45. A collection of masterpieces of the Western world, ranging from the Bible to Solzhenitsyn. The Continental ed. covers the same span, but excludes American and British material.

Matthiessen, F. O. AMERICAN RENAISSANCE: Art and Expression in the Age of Emerson and Whitman. *Oxford* 1941 4 bks. Bk. 1 From Emerson to Thoreau Bk. 2 Hawthorne Bk. 3 Melville Bk. 4 Whitman $12.50 Galaxy Bks. pap. $3.95

Mercier, Vivian, and D. H. Greene. 1,000 YEARS OF IRISH PROSE: The Literary Revival Anthology. *Grosset* Univ. Lib. pap. $2.45

Miller, Perry, Ed. MAJOR WRITERS OF AMERICA. *Harcourt* 1962 2 vols. each $9.95 shorter ed. 1966 $6.75

O'Connor, Frank. BOOK OF IRELAND. Collection of Irish Literature. *Collins* $4.50

Patterson, Lindsay. AN INTRODUCTION TO BLACK LITERATURE IN AMERICA: From 1746 to the Present. *United Publishing Corp.* 1967 $13.88

> Part of the 10-vol. set, "International Library of Negro Life and History," ed. by Charles H. Wesley under the auspices of the Association for the Study of Negro Life and History, "[This] is an anthology of selections from black writers from the eighteenth century to the present. . . . Selections are arranged chronologically by century. . . . The selection is generally good and quite representative"—*(Booklist)*.

Quiller-Couch, Sir Arthur. THE OXFORD BOOK OF ENGLISH PROSE. *Oxford* 1925 $6.50

Rahv, Philip. LITERATURE IN AMERICA: A Critical Anthology. 1957 *Peter Smith* $5.00. Essays from 1835 to 1956 arranged chronologically with emphasis "on national characteristics and relations to the national experience."

RIVERSIDE POETRY. *Twayne* 1971 No. 2 ed. by Mark Van Doren $2.75 No. 3 ed. by Marianne Moore $3.00 No. 4 ed. by Horace Gregory $3.00

Ross, James B., and Mary M. McLaughlin. THE PORTABLE MEDIEVAL READER. *Viking* $5.50 pap. $3.50

Ross, Ralph, John Berryman and Allen Tate. THE ARTS OF READING. *Apollo* $2.75. A collection of all forms of writing, with critical commentary.

Russell, Diarmuid. THE PORTABLE IRISH READER. *Viking* 1946 $6.50 pap. $3.35

Satin, Joseph. READING LITERATURE: Stories, Plays, and Poems. *Houghton* rev. ed. 1968 pap. $6.95. A good selection, with commentary and interesting notes, of 19 stories, 5 plays, and over 200 poems. Introductory remarks are short, succinct, and helpful. The reader is aided by the listing of dates with the poetry selections.

Scholes, Robert. SOME MODERN WRITERS: Essays and Fiction by Conrad, Dinesen, Lawrence, Orwell, Faulkner and Ellison. *Oxford* 1971 pap. $3.95

> "The selections in this volume have been made so as to afford the opportunity to consider the different ways these six writers approach similar situations and problems . . ."—(Introduction).

Seaver, Richard, Terry Southern and Alexander Trocchi. WRITERS IN REVOLT: An Anthology. *Fell* 1963 $7.50. This book is useful as an introduction to certain writers who reject accepted values and acceptable language. Ranging in time from the Marquis de Sade to the present day, each of the authors is introduced either briefly or by an "adulatory essay by another member of the group." The choice is predominantly contemporary and includes, among others, Henry Miller, Iris Murdoch, Genet, Ionesco and Beckett.

Swados, Harvey. THE AMERICAN WRITER AND THE GREAT DEPRESSION. *Bobbs* 1966
$7.50 pap. $2.75

"Part of the 'American Heritage Series,' this brilliantly edited anthology offers selections from novels, stories, poems and other writings, with photographs, from the Depression years"—(*LJ*).

Trilling, Lionel. THE EXPERIENCE OF LITERATURE: A Reader with Commentaries. *Doubleday* 1967 $12.95; *Holt* text ed. $12.00 abr. ed. 1969 pap. $7.00 3-vol. text ed.
Drama $6.00 Fiction $6.00 Poetry $5.25

"1,316 pages of drama, fiction and poetry, beginning with Sophocles and ending with Allen Ginsberg. . . .
Occasionally . . . there comes along a text so remarkably good and interesting that it can no longer be merely
studied; it demands to be read"—(Robie Macauley, in the *N.Y. Times*). The Holt edition has an instructor's
manual by Charles Kaplan (pap. $1.05) designed for use with either the full or the abridged ed.

Turner, Darwin T. BLACK AMERICAN LITERATURE. *Charles E. Merrill* 1969 in 3 bks.:
Essays, Poetry, Fiction pap. each $1.95 1-vol. ed. with an additional section on
drama 1970 $7.95 pap. $4.95

Wells, Carolyn. A PARODY ANTHOLOGY. 1904. *Dover* pap. $2.50; *Peter Smith* $4.50;
Gale 1967 $6.50

"A very charming period piece," in which "the parodee is not always identified"—(*PW*).

White, E. B., and Katherine S. White. A SUBTREASURY OF AMERICAN HUMOR. *Putnam*
abr. ed. 1962 Capricorn Bks. pap. $2.65. Still a fine collection of the "Algonquin"
humorists.

Woods, Ralph Louis. A TREASURY OF THE FAMILIAR. Fwd. by John Kieran. *Macmillan*
1943–1952 $9.95. Prose and poetry with indexes by title, author and, especially
valuable, by "familiar lines."

A THIRD TREASURY OF THE FAMILIAR. *Macmillan* 1950 $9.95 boxed with "A Trea-
sury of the Familiar" $18.50

*See also this chapter, following, Anthologies of Poetry in English listings, and General
Collections of Fiction.*

POETRY

Histories of Poetry

Bateson, F. W. ENGLISH POETRY AND THE ENGLISH LANGUAGE: An Experiment in Literary History. 1934. Focuses on "diction" from Elizabethan to moderns. Especially
good on the period 1660–1800. *Russell & Russell* 1961 $6.50.

ENGLISH POETRY: A Critical Introduction. 1950. *Barnes & Noble* 2nd ed. 1966 $5.00
An extended general discussion of poetry leads to a series of analyses of English
poems from Chaucer to W. H. Auden, presenting the historical and literary context.
A similar organization, with a very different critical approach, is that of Brooks and
Warren in "Understanding Poetry" (*see under A Reading List on Poetry this chap-
ter*).

Bush, Douglas. ENGLISH POETRY: The Main Currents from Chaucer to the Present.
Written incisively from a broad perspective. *Oxford* 1952 Galaxy Bks. pap. $1.95;
Peter Smith $3.50

SCIENCE AND POETRY: A Historical Sketch, 1590–1950. The Patton Lectures, Indiana Univ., 1949. *Oxford* 1950 $5.50

Courthope, William John. A HISTORY OF ENGLISH POETRY. *Russell & Russell* 1962 6 vols. $100.00. A reprint of the standard work, covering the Medieval to Romantic periods, by the English critic and literary historian, Professor of Poetry at Oxford (1895–1901). 1895–1906.

Fairchild, Hoxie Neale. RELIGIOUS TRENDS IN ENGLISH POETRY. *Columbia* 6 vols. 1939–68 Vol. I Protestantism and the Cult of Sentiment, 1700–1740 (1939) Vol. 2 Religious Sentimentalism in the Age of Johnson, 1740–1780 (1942) Vol. 3 Romantic Faith, 1780–1830 (1949) Vol. 4 Christianity and Romanticism in the Victorian Era, 1830–1880 (1957) Vol. 5 Gods of a Changing Poetry, 1880–1920 (1962) Vol. 6 Valley of Dry Bones, 1920–1965 (1968) each $12.50

Grierson, Sir Herbert, and J. C. Smith, A CRITICAL HISTORY OF ENGLISH POETRY. *Oxford* 1946 $10.00. A scholarly history of 1,200 years of English poetry, from Anglo-Saxon times to 1939, focusing on the greatest poets. Illuminating for the general reader who loves poetry.

Hopkins, Kenneth. ENGLISH POETRY: A Short History. *Lippincott* 1963 $5.95; *Southern Illinois Univ. Press* pap. $4.95

Reeves, James. A SHORT HISTORY OF ENGLISH POETRY, 1340–1940. *Dutton* 1964 $5.95. Intended for the general reader and student (not the specialist) this is a concise but remarkably comprehensive history, "mainly directed toward encouraging first-hand study of the poets" by the use of frequent brief quotations.

Saintsbury, George. HISTORICAL MANUAL OF ENGLISH PROSODY. *Schocken* 1966 $7.00 pap. $2.45

A HISTORY OF ENGLISH PROSODY: From the 12th Century to the Present Day. 1923. *Russell & Russell* 2nd ed. 1961 3 vols. set $40.00

Shapiro, Karl. AMERICAN POETRY. *T. Y. Crowell* 1960 $6.95 pap. $3.95. Bibliography and biographical notes on 54 poets from Anne Bradstreet to Allen Ginsberg; arranged chronologically; list of critical readings.

Spender, Stephen, and Donald Hall. THE CONCISE ENCYCLOPEDIA OF ENGLISH AND AMERICAN POETRY. *Hawthorn Bks.* 1963 $17.95. This valuable reference book surveys English and American poetry from Anglo-Saxon times to our own. The editors achieve "a wonder of poetic criticism and biography." A great advantage is the more than 30 longish essays on such subjects as "American Poetry," "Metaphor," and "Myth and Poetry." "A bibliography for further reading, index of poets quoted, and a general index are added virtues."

Untermeyer, Louis. LIVES OF THE POETS: The Story of One Thousand Years of English and American Poetry. *Simon & Schuster* 1959 $7.95 pap. $2.95. Divided roughly into chronological periods ranging from the time of Beowulf to Dylan Thomas, there are sections of biographical information and critical appraisal with excerpts of verse devoted to the major poets. Linking chapters present a general historical survey and discussion of lesser writers. Mr. Untermeyer writes with ease and perspicacity of 133 poets.

A Reading List on Poetry

Allen, Don Cameron. Four Poets on Poetry. R. P. Blackmur, Ivor Winters, Marianne Moore and Mark Van Doren. *Johns Hopkins Univ. Press* 1959 $9.00

Aristotle. Aristotle's Theory of Poetry and Fine Art. Trans. by Samuel H. Butcher. 1907–1951. *Dover* 1967 pap. $3.00; *Peter Smith* $5.00

   The Butcher translation of the "poetics" faces the Greek text with 300-page comentary. "An intellectual adventure of the most stimulating kind"—(*N.Y. Times*).

Auden, W. H. The Dyer's Hand and Other Essays. *Random* 1962 $10.00 Vintage Bks. pap. $2.45. The poet, wary of critics, says that he has written no criticism himself except in response to a demand by others for a lecture, an introduction or a review. These are his collected prose pieces (some written while he held the chair of Poetry at Oxford). A thoughtful book, witty and precise, this is chiefly on poetry, but contains also his observations on art and life in general.

Brooks, Cleanth, and Robert Penn Warren. Understanding Poetry. *Holt* 1938 rev. ed. 1950 3rd ed. 1960 $10.95 text ed. $7.75. Running commentaries and progressive discussions make this anthology especially valuable for study. In the 1960 revision the editors have reworked their critical contributions to a definitive anthology of over 400 British and American poems.

Ciardi, John. How Does a Poem Mean? A helpful discussion of poetry, with a generous selection of English and American poems from six centuries. *Houghton* 1960 $5.95

Day, Lewis C. Enjoying Poetry. 1947. *Folcroft* lib. bdg. $4.00

   The Lyric Impulse. The Charles Eliot Norton Lectures on Poetry. *Harvard Univ. Press* 1965 $4.25. A rich and delightful discussion of the musical element in English verse.

Drew, Elizabeth. Poetry: A Modern Guide to Its Understanding and Enjoyment. *Dell* Laurel Leaf Eds. pap. $.60; *Norton* 1959–1966 $5.95 lib. bdg. $4.51

Eastman, Max. Enjoyment of Poetry and Anthology for Enjoyment of Poetry. Representative of the whole field of American and English poetry. 2 vols. in I *Scribner* 1951 $7.50

Eliot, T. S. Selected Essays. Profound and influential literary criticism. 1932. *Harcourt* rev. ed 1950 $8.50 (*See also his main entry in Chapter 15, Essays and Criticism.*)

Gross, Harvey. Sound and Form in Modern Poetry: A Study of Prosody from Thomas Hardy to Robert Lowell. *Univ. of Michigan Press* 1964 $8.50 Ann Arbor Bks. pap. $2.65

   "Professor Gross's impressive volume is announced as the first major theoretical and descriptive opus on versification since Saintsbury's three-volume "History of English Prosody" in 1906. . . . Though he approaches thorough coverage only in the sections on Eliot and Pound, insights and courageous value judgments make each poet's treatment vivid"—(*LJ*).

Highet, Gilbert. The Powers of Poetry. *Oxford* 1960 $8.50. 39 excellent articles on poetry and poets. (*See also his main entry in Chapter 15, Essays and Criticism.*)

Hillyer, Robert S. In Pursuit of Poetry. *McGraw-Hill* 1960 $5.50 pap. $2.95

   "A companionable guide to the enjoyment and appreciation of poetry in the English language from Chaucer to the present"—(*Booklist*).

Holmes, John. WRITING POETRY: A Guidebook, Including an Appraisal of Poets and Poetry by Famous Authors and Critics. *The Writer* $8.95

Jarrell, Randall. POETRY AND THE AGE. *Farrar, Straus* Noonday pap. $2.85; *Octagon* 1972 $10.00. A comprensive and detailed study of modern poetry: interesting, witty, very readable.

Johnson, Samuel. LIVES OF THE ENGLISH POETS. *Avon* pap. $.95; *Dutton* Everyman's 2 vols. each $3.50; ed. by G. B. Hill *Octagon* 1967 3 vol. set $45.00; *Oxford* World's class. 2 vols. each $3.75; selections, ed. by Warren L. Fleischauer *Regnery* pap. $.85

Krieger, Murray. NEW APOLOGISTS FOR POETRY. *Univ. of Minn. Press* 1956 $4.00

Leavis, F. R. NEW BEARINGS IN ENGLISH POETRY. Interesting discussions by the English critic. *Univ. of Michigan Press* 1960 $4.40 Ann Arbor Bks. pap. $1.85

MacLeish, Archibald. POETRY AND EXPERIENCE. *Houghton* 1961 $6.95. Based on his Harvard lectures as Boylston Professor, the first four chapters are a good introduction to the appreciation of poetry; the final chapters are devoted to Emily Dickenson, W. B. Yeats, Rimbaud and Keats.

Nemerov, Howard, Ed. POETS ON POETRY. The poet Howard Nemerov asks questions; other poets answer him. *Basic Bks.* 1966–67 $5.95

Reeves, James. UNDERSTANDING POETRY. *Barnes & Noble* 1966 $4.00 pap. $1.50

"An excellent antidote to the semantic orientation of the text [with the same title—*see above*] by Brooks and Warren"—(*LJ*). Reeves emphasizes "the personal character of the English lyric."

Rosenthal, M. L. THE NEW POETS: American and British Poetry Since World War II. *Oxford* 1967 $8.95 Galaxy Bks. pap. $2.50. Excellent discussion with attention to individuals and movements.

Spender, Stephen. THE MAKING OF A POEM. 1955. *Greenwood* 1973 $8.50. He discusses some of the problems of his own art and provides rewarding insights into the nature and meaning of the literary influences of the past, touching on the present predicament of the writer on both sides of the Atlantic.

Stauffer, Donald A. THE NATURE OF POETRY. Its Structure, Texture and Meaning from Spenser to Yeats. 1946 1962. *Peter Smith* $4.00

Vivante, Leone. ENGLISH POETRY AND ITS CONTRIBUTION TO THE KNOWLEDGE OF A CREATIVE PRINCIPLE. Pref. by T. S. Eliot. *Southern Illinois Univ. Press* 1963 $6.00; *Richard West* repr. of 1955 ed., $20.00

Waggoner, Hyatt H. AMERICAN POETS: From the Puritans to the Present. 1968. *Dell* Delta Bks. pap. $2.95

An interesting study "by a critic who finds Emerson all-persuasive as an influence." "A princely view of our poetic experience and history"—(*N.Y. Times*).

Wagner, Jean. BLACK POETS OF THE UNITED STATES: From Paul Laurence Dunbar to Langston Hughes. Trans. by Kenneth Douglas, with fwd. by Robert Bone. *Univ. of Illinois Press* 1973 $15.00 pap. $5.50

". . . full-length study of the major Black poets of the United States from early slavery times to Langston Hughes, now available in English. First published in France in 1963. . ."—(Publisher's note).

Anthologies of Poetry in English

The earliest English anthology was the "Exeter Book," a famous collection of old English poems copied about 975 and given to Exeter Cathedral by Bishop Leofric, who died in 1072. "Tottel's Miscellany," compiled by Richard Tottel 1525–1594 (Ed. by Hyder E. Rollins *Harvard Univ. Press* 2 vols. 1965 $18.00), is the first *printed* anthology of poetry. It contains 271 poems by Surrey, Wyatt, Heywood, Thomas and others and was issued first in 1557. Seven additional editions were called for before the end of the century. "England's Helicon," a collection of pastoral lyrics, is considered the most attractive anthology between "Tottel's Miscellany" (1557) and Palgrave's "Golden Treasury" (1861). (*See Chapter 5, British Poetry: Early to Romantic—Anthologies of Poetry for the "Exeter Book" and "England's Helicon."*) "Reliques of Ancient Poetry" (1765) selected by Bishop Thomas Percy (1729–1811) and mainly of antiquarian interest, is again available (Ed. by H. B. Wheatley *Dover* 1966 3 vols. pap. each $2.75; *Peter Smith* 3 vols. each $5.50).

Palgrave's "Golden Treasury" (1861) is the oldest anthology still popular today and a landmark among anthologies. The early "Oxford Book of English Verse" ed. by Quiller-Couch is now o.p., but it and "The New Oxford Book of English Verse" ed. by Helen Gardner have been and continue to be particularly satisfying and discriminating surveys of the field of English poetry. The excellent selection by Sir Herbert Read and Bonamy Dobrée, "London Book of English Verse," is worthy of a place beside the Oxford Books but does not supersede them. Stevenson's "Home Book of Verse" is a monumental all-inclusive single volume of British and American poetry. Dame Edith Sitwell has emphasized the delight of reading poetry rather than the historic process in her comprehensive "Atlantic Book of British and American Poetry." Louis Untermeyer's "The Book of Living Verse" is also an excellent comprehensive anthology.

Collections of narrower reference will be found in the chapters to which they apply. Since modern British and American poetry are so often treated together and are often the subject of intensive investigation, it has been thought wise to group anthologies and critical works treating both at once in a special listing in Chapter 7, Modern British Poetry, with a clear cross-reference in Chapter 9, Modern American Poetry.

Allen, Gay Wilson, Walter B. Rideout and James K. Robinson. AMERICAN POETRY. *Harper* 1965 $10.95. An excellent, wide-ranging anthology. The editors have further aided the reader by supplying the dates of poets' lives, as well as the dates when the poems were written. Includes bibliographies, succinct commentaries, and many useful notes.

Auden, Wystan Hugh. THE OXFORD BOOK OF LIGHT VERSE. Light-hearted poetry from the time of Chaucer to the present. *Oxford* 1938 $10.00

19TH CENTURY BRITISH MINOR POETS. *Dell* 1966 pap. $.75

"Auden has made his selections from among those British poets who were born between 1770 and 1870 (with poems first between 1800–1900), who neither wrote enough nor variously enough to be judged major. . . . Highly recommended"—(LJ).

(With Norman Holmes Pearson). POETS OF THE ENGLISH LANGUAGE. *Viking* Portable Lib. 1950 5 vols. each $5.95 pap. Vols. 1–3 each $1.85 Vol. 4 $2.95 Vol. 5 $2.25. A distinguished anthology, the cloth edition includes: Vol. 1 Langland to Spenser; Vol. 2 Marlowe to Marvell; Vol. 3 Milton to Goldsmith Vol. 4 Blake to Poe; Vol. 5 Tennyson to Yeats; the paperbound edition with biographical notes includes: Vol. 1 Medieval and Renaissance Poets; Vol. 2 Elizabethan and Jacobean Poets; Vol. 3 Restoration and Augustan Poets; Vol. 4 Romantic Poets; Vol. 5 Victorian and Edwardian Poets.

Baring-Gould, William S. THE LURE OF THE LIMERICK: An Uninhibited History, with Over Five Hundred Examples, British and American. Collected from many sources. *Clarkson N. Potter* (dist. by Crown) 1967 $5.00

Brooks, Cleanth, and Robert Penn Warren. UNDERSTANDING POETRY. *Holt* 1938 rev. ed. 1950 3rd ed. 1960 $10.95 text ed. $7.75. A famous and influential book which presents a series of poems with analytic essays and is especially useful to the reader who feels he "doesn't know how" to read poetry.

Coffin, Charles Monroe. THE MAJOR POETS: English and American. From Chaucer to Lowell. *Harcourt* 1954 2nd ed. rev. by Gerrit H. Roelofs 1969 pap. $4.75. This is an updating of the earlier edition, which included poets from Chaucer to Dylan Thomas.

Cole, William. EIGHT LINES AND UNDER: An Anthology of Short, Short Poems. *Macmillan* 1967 $3.95. Representative of the whole field of American and English Poetry.

EROTIC POETRY: The Lyrics, Ballads, Idyls and Epics of Love—Classical to Contemporary. Fwd. by Stephen Spender. *Random* 1963 $4.50. This is a varied and exciting, unpredictable and nontraditional collection of poems about love. The poems are arranged under categories such as "Of Women," "Incitement and Desire," and "Womanizers and Seducers." In its wide range it does not conflict with Untermeyer's similarly titled volume *(see Untermeyer in list of Anthologies Including World Poetry, this chapter)*.

THE FIRESIDE BOOK OF HUMOROUS POETRY. 450 selections from British and American poets. *Simon & Schuster* 1959 $8.50

Louis Untermeyer, the veteran anthologist *(q.v.)* admits that this "outclasses every other anthology of its kind." The editor's excellent introduction diagnoses the "disease known as 'Anthologist's Quandry,' " and takes an uncompromising stand against sentimental dialect or parody and supports intelligence and wit.

Cook, Roy Jay. ONE HUNDRED AND ONE FAMOUS POEMS. Selected on the ground of their fame and popularity, by English and American authors; ill. with portraits. *Reilly & Lee* 1919 1925 $2.95 pap. $1.50

Creekmore, Hubert. A LITTLE TREASURY OF WORLD POETRY. *Scribner* 1952 $10.00

Daiches, David, and William Charvat. POEMS IN ENGLISH, 1930–1940. Ed. with critical notes and essays. *Ronald* 1950 $6.00

Danziger, Marlies, and Wendell Stacy Johnson. A POETRY ANTHOLOGY. *Random* 1967 pap. text ed. $4.75. Includes: A guide to poetry I. Poems and Poetry; The Anthology II. Techniques of Poetry III. Kinds of Poems. This is a fine anthology, well arranged, with excellent selections and comprehensive coverage of all major poets. Dates are supplied at the beginning of selections. There is an index to poetic genres and to first lines.

De La Mare, Walter. COME HITHER: A Collection of Rhymes and Poems for the Young of All Ages. 1923. Rev. ed. Woodcuts by Alec Buckels. *Knopf* 1926 new ed. 1957 $10.00. The poet's *(q.v.)* introduction is a lasting delight.

Eastman, Arthur M., and others. THE NORTON ANTHOLOGY OF POETRY. *Norton* 1970 text ed. $8.45 pap. $6.95 abr. ed. pap. $3.95. An excellent anthology of poetry with commentary and headnotes similar to those found in other *Norton* anthologies.

Eastman, Max. ENJOYMENT OF POETRY and ANTHOLOGY FOR THE ENJOYMENT OF POETRY. Representative of the whole field of American and English poetry. 1939. *Scribner* 1951 2 vols. in 1 $7.50

Ellmann, Richard, and Robert O'Clair. THE NORTON ANTHOLOGY OF MODERN POETRY. *Norton* 1973 $14.95 pap. $9.95

> "The poets are presented chronologically, with American poets merged with those from Great Britain, Ireland, and the Commonwealth. . . . A chronological table makes it possible to consider each poet . . . within the historical, intellectual, and literary context"—(Publisher's note).

Gannett, Lewis. THE FAMILY BOOK OF VERSE. 300 favorite poems from Britain and America. *Harper* 1961 $6.95

Gardner, Helen. A BOOK OF RELIGIOUS VERSE. *Oxford* 1972 $12.50

> "The result is an admirable selection of poems ranging from 'The Dream of the Rood' to poems by W. H. Auden, Louis Macneice, David Gascoyne, and R. S. Thomas. Traditional, non-surprising and solid . . . as might be expected from the Merton Professor of English Literature at Oxford"—(*Choice*).

THE NEW OXFORD BOOK OF ENGLISH VERSE, 1250–1950. *Oxford* 1972 $10.00

> "The original 'Oxford Book of English Verse' came out in 1900, was revised by its editor, Sir Arthur Quiller-Couch, in 1939 . . . and has kept going to this day. . . . Dame Helen has remade the book for a new public"—(Frank Kermode, in *The Atlantic*).

Hodnett, Edward. POEMS TO READ ALOUD. *Norton* 1957 rev. ed. 1967 $6.95. An attractive collection of 295 English and American poems chosen for "readability, literary excellence, and variety."

Hollander, John, and Harold Bloom. THE WIND AND THE RAIN: An Anthology of Poems. 1967. *Bks. for Libraries* $11.50

> An unhackneyed selection from the whole range of English poetry. It begins with a section called by the book's title; other sections are built around the seasons. "A miracle of freshness and originality. All the poems are chosen with flawless taste, and each is surprising, illuminating, in its aptness"—(Saul Maloff, in the *Nation*).

Hughes, Langston, and Arna Bontemps. THE POETRY OF THE NEGRO, 1746–1970. *Doubleday* 1949 rev. ed. 1970 $8.95. Covers 163 poets and includes a section of white poets throughout American literature, writing on the Negro.

Klemer, D. J., Ed. MODERN LOVE POEMS. *Doubleday* 1961 $3.95. Romantic and idealistic in tone; includes poems by Edna St. Vincent Millay, Louis Untermeyer, Rupert Brooke, Carl Sandburg and others.

Lowry, Howard Foster, and Willard Thorp. THE OXFORD ANTHOLOGY OF ENGLISH POETRY. From medieval lyrics to Housman and Bridges. *Oxford* 1935 2nd ed. with the assistance of Howard C. Horsford 1956 $9.95

THE OXFORD BOOKS OF VERSE (Series).

> The Oxford anthologies are notable for their scope, scholarliness and beauty of manufacture and type.

THE OXFORD BOOKS in English. 19 vols. various prices:

Auden, W. H. THE OXFORD BOOK OF LIGHT VERSE. *Oxford* 1938 $9.00

Cecil, Lord David. THE OXFORD BOOK OF CHRISTIAN VERSE. *Oxford* 1940 $8.50

Chambers, E. K. THE OXFORD BOOK OF SIXTEENTH CENTURY VERSE. *Oxford* 1932 $7.75

Gardner, Helen. THE NEW OXFORD BOOK OF ENGLISH VERSE. *Oxford* 1973 $10.00

Grierson, H. J. C., and G. Bullough. THE OXFORD BOOK OF SEVENTEENTH CENTURY VERSE. *Oxford* 1934 $8.00

Hayward, John. THE OXFORD BOOK OF NINETEENTH CENTURY ENGLISH VERSE. *Oxford* 1964 $10.00

Higham, T. F., and C. M. Bowra. THE OXFORD BOOK OF GREEK VERSE IN TRANSLATION. *Oxford* 1938 $9.75

Kinsley, James. THE OXFORD BOOK OF BALLADS. *Oxford* 1969 $10.00

MacDonagh, D., and L. Robinson. THE OXFORD BOOK OF IRISH VERSE: 17th–20th Century. *Oxford* 1958 $5.75 lea. $8.00

MacQueen, John, and Tom Scott. THE OXFORD BOOK OF SCOTTISH VERSE. *Oxford* 1967 $12.50

"It must be considered the best one-volume anthology of Scottish verse available"—(*LJ*).

Matthiessen, F. O. THE OXFORD BOOK OF AMERICAN VERSE. *Oxford* 1950 $9.50

Milford, Humphrey Sumner. THE OXFORD BOOK OF ENGLISH VERSE OF THE ROMANTIC PERIOD, 1798–1837. *Oxford* 1935 $8.50

Nicholson, D. H. S., and A. H. E. Lee. THE OXFORD BOOK OF ENGLISH MYSTICAL VERSE. *Oxford* 1917 $9.75

Parry, Thomas. THE OXFORD BOOK OF WELSH VERSE. *Oxford* 1962 $9.50

Quiller-Couch, Sir Arthur. THE OXFORD BOOK OF VICTORIAN VERSE. *Oxford* 1913 $10.50

Smith A. J. M. THE OXFORD BOOK OF CANADIAN VERSE. (Bilingual English and French.) *Oxford* 1960 pap. $2.95

Smith, D. N. THE OXFORD BOOK OF EIGHTEENTH CENTURY VERSE. *Oxford* 1926 $9.75

Yeats, W. B. THE OXFORD BOOK OF MODERN VERSE: 1892-1935. *Oxford* 1936 $10.00

THE OXFORD BOOKS in Foreign Languages. 11 vols. various prices. French, German, Greek, Italian, Latin, Medieval Latin, Portuguese, Russian Spanish. (*Consult catalog.*)

Palgrave, Francis Turner. THE GOLDEN TREASURY OF THE BEST SONGS AND LYRICAL POEMS IN THE ENGLISH LANGUAGE. First series 1861 second series 1897. *Collins* New Class $3.00 lea. $5.00; (with additional poems) *Macmillan* 8th ed. 1944 $6.95; rev. by Oscar Williams *New Am. Lib.* Mentor Bks. pap. $1.25; *Oxford* 1931 5th ed. 1964 $7.50

Palgrave's "Golden Treasury" is the most famous anthology in the English language. The first series claimed to be a selection of the best short lyrics, and none but the best, by writers not then living. The second series, 36 years later, was extended to include poets then living. A poet himself, Palgrave was educated at Oxford and was an official in the government education department until he became professor of poetry at Oxford (1885). It was said that his friend Tennyson (*q. v.*) helped him with his selection.

Peacock, William. ENGLISH VERSE. *Oxford* World's Class. 5 vols. Vol. I Early Lyrics to Shakespeare $2.50 Vol. 2 Campion to the Ballads $3.25 Vol. 3 Dryden to Wordsworth $3.75 Vol. 4 Scott to E. B. Browning $3.25 Vol. 5 Longfellow to Rupert Brooke $3.25

Rakow, Edwin. LYRIC VERSE. *Odyssey* 1961 $3.00 pap. $2.00

Reeves, James. THE CASSELL BOOK OF ENGLISH POETRY. *Harper* 1965 $8.95

"With 1002 poems and succinct period introductions, this handy anthology offers an adequate view of the drift of English and American poetry since about 1340"—(*LJ*).

Sitwell, Edith. THE ATLANTIC BOOK OF BRITISH AND AMERICAN POETRY. *Little* 1958 $16.50. In this very important anthology, Dame Edith (*q. v.*) made an interesting and highly personal selection and wrote 34 prefaces on the techniques of the poets she most admired.

Stevenson, Burton Egbert. THE HOME BOOK OF VERSE, American and English. 1912. Covers a tremendous range, from 1580 on. *Holt* 1937 8th ed. 1949 9th ed. 1953 2 vols. $30.00

Untermeyer, Louis. THE BOOK OF LIVING VERSE: English and American Poetry from the Thirteenth Century to the Present Day. *Harcourt* 1932 1939 new ed. 1949 Mod. Class. text ed. $4.25. Limited to the chief poets. One of the very best of anthologies for the newcomer to poetry and for those who love it well.

A TREASURY OF GREAT POEMS, ENGLISH AND AMERICAN: From the Foundations of the English Spirit to the Outstanding Poetry of Our Own Time, with Lives of the Poets and Historical Settings Selected and Integrated. *Simon & Schuster* 1942 rev. and enl. ed. 1955 2 vols. in 1 $12.50 2-vol. ed. pap. Vol. 1 Chaucer to Burns Vol. 2 Wordsworth to Dylan Thomas each $2.95

Williams, Oscar. A LITTLE TREASURY OF GREAT POETRY ENGLISH AND AMERICAN, FROM CHAUCER TO THE PRESENT DAY. *Scribner* 1947 rev. ed. 1955 $7.50

A LITTLE TREASURY OF BRITISH POETRY, The Chief Poets from 1500 to 1950. *Scribner* 1951 rev. ed. 1955 $7.00

IMMORTAL POEMS OF THE ENGLISH LANGUAGE. *Washington Square* pap. $.95

MASTER POEMS OF THE ENGLISH LANGUAGE: Over One Hundred Poems together with Introductions by Leading Poets and Critics of the English-Speaking World. *Simon & Schuster* (Trident Press) 1966 $12.50; *Washington Square* pap. $1.45

"Conceived by the late Oscar Williams, completed after Williams' death by Philip Flayderman of the Trident Press, this handsome anthology begins with Sir Thomas Wyatt and ends with Dylan Thomas, touching most major poets in the time between"—(*LJ*). "An eminently satisfying collection"—(Eliot Fremont-Smith).

For anthologies and critical works treating modern British and American poetry together see special listing in Chapter 7, Modern British Poetry. Anthologies of early English ballads and songs will be found in Chapter 5, English Poetry: Early Period.

Australian, Irish, Scottish and Welsh Anthologies

Cole, William, and Lillian Morrison. POEMS FROM IRELAND. With drawings by William Stobbs. *T. Y. Crowell* 1972 $4.50

Colum, Padraic. ANTHOLOGY OF IRISH VERSE: The Poetry of Ireland from Mythological Times to the Present. 1922 *Liveright* or *Tudor* Black and Gold Lib. rev. enl. by selection of poets, both of Eire and of Northern Ireland, who appeared after 1920. 1948 $7.95

Cooke, John. THE DUBLIN BOOK OF IRISH VERSE, 1728–1909. 1909. *Bks. for Libraries* $24.75

Eyre-Todd, George. EARLY SCOTTISH POETRY: Thomas the Rhymer, John Barbour, Andrew of Wyntown, Henry the Minstrel. 1891. *Greenwood* $9.50

MEDIEVAL SCOTTISH POETRY: King James I, Robert Henryson, William Dunbar, Gavin Douglas. 1892. *Greenwood* 1971 $10.50

SCOTTISH POETRY OF THE SIXTEENTH CENTURY. 1892. *Greenwood* $10.50; *Scholarly Press* $14.50

SCOTTISH POETRY OF THE EIGHTEENTH CENTURY. 1896. *Greenwood* $20.00

MacDonagh, Donagh, and Lennox Robinson. THE OXFORD BOOK OF IRISH VERSE, 17th Century–20th Century. *Oxford* 1958 $10.00

Mackie, Robert Laird. A BOOK OF SCOTTISH VERSE. *Oxford* World's Class. 1934 $3.25

MacQueen, John, and Tom Scott. THE OXFORD BOOK OF SCOTTISH VERSE. *Oxford* 1967 $12.50

"[This] volume, which includes authors from the 13th Century up to those born before 1930, is carefully chosen and edited and presents the most representative selection to date. It must be considered the best one-volume anthology of Scottish verse available"—(*LJ*).

Murphy, Gerard. EARLY IRISH LYRICS. *Oxford* 1956 $10.25

Parry, Thomas. THE OXFORD BOOK OF WELSH VERSE. *Oxford* 1962 $6.50

Taylor, Geoffrey. IRISH POETS OF THE NINETEENTH CENTURY. 1951. *Greenwood* $15.50

Wright, Judith. A BOOK OF AUSTRALIAN VERSE. Sel. with introd. by an Australian poet. *Oxford* 1956 2nd ed. 1968 $8.00 pap. $4.00

NEW LAND, NEW LANGUAGE: An Anthology of Australian Verse. *Oxford* 1957 pap. $2.50

See also other Oxford Books listed under General and Comprehensive Anthologies, this Chapter.

Anthologies Including World Poetry

Burnshaw, Stanley. Assoc. Eds.: Dudley Fitts, Henri Peyre, J. F. Nims. Various translators (bilingual). THE POEM ITSELF. *Schocken* 1967 pap. $2.95

"45 modern poets in a new presentation: more than 150 original French, German, Italian, Portuguese and Spanish poems, with literal renderings and explanatory discussions." Translations are in prose and somewhat broken up by commentary, but the experiment is an interesting one.

Creekmore, Hubert. LITTLE TREASURY OF WORLD POETRY. *Scribner* 1952 $10.00

LYRICS OF THE MIDDLE AGES. 1959. *Greenwood* $12.50. Lyrics from the late Greek through Middle English translated by various hands, many of them notable poets in their own right.

Cromie, Robert, Ed. WHERE STEEL WINDS BLOW. *McKay* 1967 $5.50. An anthology of war poetry, mostly antiwar, ranging over many centuries and many countries.

Drachler, Jacob, and Virginia Terris. MANY WORLDS OF POETRY. *Knopf* 1968 text ed. $4.25

Engelberg, Edward. THE SYMBOLIST POEM: The Development of the English Tradition. *Dutton* pap. $2.45. An anthology to show the influence of French symbolists on poets writing in English from Wordsworth to Stevens.

Engle, Paul, and Joseph Langland. POET'S CHOICE. *Dial* 1962 $7.50

Garrigue, Jean. TRANSLATIONS BY AMERICAN POETS. *Ohio Univ. Press* 1970 $15.00

Lawson, James Gilchrist. WORLD'S BEST LOVED POEMS. *Harper* 1927 $3.95

"The choicest of the world's most helpful short religious and popular poems and brief prose selections. . . . Many of the pieces were selected not from standards of highest literary judgment, but because of their appeal to the human heart"—(Compiler's Introd.).

Pound, Ezra, and Marcella Spann. CONFUCIUS TO CUMMINGS. *New Directions* 1964 $8.50. pap. $3.25. Emphasis on Greek, Latin, Chinese, Troubadour, Renaissance and Elizabethan poets.

Van Doren, Mark. AN ANTHOLOGY OF WORLD POETRY. English translations by Chaucer, Swinburne and others. 1928. *Harcourt* rev. and enl. ed. 1936 $15.00

FICTION

Discussions of the Novel

Allen, Walter. THE ENGLISH NOVEL: A SHORT CRITICAL HISTORY. *Dutton* 1955 $5.95 pap. $1.95. Discerning reappraisals of novelists from Bunyan to Joyce.

Allott, Miriam, Ed. NOVELISTS ON THE NOVEL. *Columbia* 1959 $10.00 pap. $2.45. Statements by the great practitioners of the novel (from Defoe to Gide); of substantial reference and critical value.

Auchincloss, Louis. PIONEERS AND CARETAKERS: A Study of Nine American Women Novelists. Jewett, Wharton, Glasgow, Cather, E. M. Roberts, K. A. Porter, Stafford, McCullers, McCarthy. *Univ. of Minnesota Press* 1965 $5.95

Axthelm, Peter M. THE MODERN CONFESSIONAL NOVEL. *Yale Univ. Press* 1967 $6.50

A "readable and rewarding" work (*LJ*) for serious students of literature, with "provocative comments" on Dostoyevsky, Gide, Sartre, Camus, Golding and Bellow. Includes a comprehensive bibliography.

Baker, Ernest A. A HISTORY OF THE ENGLISH NOVEL. *Barnes & Noble* 11 vols. 1924–29 repr. 1960–67 Vol. 1 Age of Romance Vol. 2 Elizabethan Age Vol. 3 Later Romances and Establishment of Realism Vol. 4 Intellectual Realism from Richardson to Sterne Vol. 5 Novel of Sentiment and the Gothic Romance Vol. 6 Edgeworth, Austen, Scott Vol. 7 The Age of Dickens and Thackeray Vol. 8 From the Brontes to Meredith: Romanticism in the English Novel Vol. 9 The Day before Yesterday (Hardy, George Moore, Henry James) Vol. 10 Yesterday (Conrad, Kipling, Bennett) Vol. 11 by Lionel Stevenson Yesterday and After Vols. 1–10 each $6.50 Vol. 11 $10.00

Burgess, Anthony. THE NOVEL NOW: A Guide to Contemporary Fiction. *Norton* 1967 $5.95; *Pegasus Bks.* pap. $2.25. Relaxed nonacademic study by an important practising novelist (*q.v.*).

Chase, Richard. THE AMERICAN NOVEL AND ITS TRADITION. *Doubleday* Anchor Bks. pap. $1.95

Cowie, Alexander. THE RISE OF THE AMERICAN NOVEL. 1948. *Van Nostrand-Reinhold* 1951 $10.95

Daiches, David. THE NOVEL AND THE MODERN WORLD. 1939. *Univ. of Chicago Press* rev. ed. 1960 $5.95 Phoenix Bks. pap. $1.95

> The author says in his preface: "[The chapters] are all intended to illustrate ... the main problems that have faced the writer of fiction in the present century." A very clearly written, important work on major novelists and the problems of the modern world.

Fiedler, Leslie. LOVE AND DEATH IN THE AMERICAN NOVEL. 1960. *Stein & Day* rev. ed. 1966 $12.50. A complex and penetrating analysis of fiction from 1789 to 1959. Fiedler (*q.v.*) contends that Americans have developed a literature embarrassed by adult sexuality and obsessed with death.

Forster, E. M. ASPECTS OF THE NOVEL. *Harcourt* 1947 $6.50 Harvest Bks. 1956 pap. $1.45. This, together with Percy Lubbock's "The Craft of Fiction" (*below*) has long been a classic in the field.

Grossvogel, David. LIMITS OF THE NOVEL: Evolution of a Form from Chaucer to Robbe-Grillet. *Cornell Univ. Press* 1968 $7.95 pap. $2.45

Howard, David, John Lucas and John Goode. TRADITION AND TOLERANCE IN NINETEENTH CENTURY FICTION: Critical Essays on Some English and American Novels. *Routledge & Kegan Paul* 1966 $7.75. Essays by one or another of the three authors on Cooper, Hawthorne, Mrs. Gaskell, Gissing, Besant, and Henry James.

Kennedy, Margaret. THE OUTLAWS OF PARNASSUS. 1960. *Bks. for Libraries* $10.50

> Orville Prescott in the *N.Y. Times* called this "one of the most urbane, perceptive and readable books about the art of fiction that I have ever read. . . . Novels, she insists quite rightly, are a great art. They can be written with a variety of technical devices, which she brilliantly describes, and they provide guided tours to their authors' visions of life."

Kermode, Frank. THE SENSE OF AN ENDING: Studies in the Theory of Fiction. *Oxford* 1967 Galaxy Bks. pap. $1.75

> Six lectures given at Bryn Mawr in 1965. A "learned and thoughtful work but only for the well-informed reader"—(*LJ*).

Kettle, Arnold. AN INTRODUCTION TO THE ENGLISH NOVEL. *Hillary House* (Hutchinson Univ. Lib.) 2 vols. 1951–53 Vol. 1 Defoe to George Eliot Vol. 2 Henry James to the Present pap. each $1.75. Extremely well written and interesting.

Lubbock, Percy. THE CRAFT OF FICTION. 1921. New fwd. by Mark Schorer. *Viking* 1957 Compass Bks. pap. $1.95. Mr. Lubbock's book, written in a beautiful, calm, lucid prose, is considered "the classic on technique." He sees the reader, as well as the writer, as an active creative artist.

Lukács, Georg. THE HISTORICAL NOVEL. Trans. by Hannah and Stanley Mitchell with pref. by Irving Howe. 1965 *Humanities* $9.00. An outstanding Marxist critic reviews the genre from Sir Walter Scott to the present.

STUDIES IN EUROPEAN REALISM. Introd. by Alfred Kazin. *Grosset* Universal Lib. pap. $1.95

Quinn, Arthur Hobson. AMERICAN FICTION: An Historical and Critical Survey. 1936. *Appleton* 1947 text ed. $11.55

(Ed.) THE LITERATURE OF THE AMERICAN PEOPLE: An Historical and Critical Survey. 1951. *Appleton* $13.65. In 4 pts. Pt. 1 The Colonial and Revolutionary Period by K. B. Murdock; Pt. 2 The Establishment of National Literature by A. H. Quinn; Pt. 3 The Later Nineteenth Century by C. Gohdes; Pt. 4 The Twentieth Century by G. P. Whicher.

Rosenberg, Edgar. FROM SHYLOCK TO SVENGALI: Jewish Stereotypes in English Fiction. *Stanford Univ. Press* 1960 $10.00. Exceedingly interesting critical study.

Rubin, Louis D. THE CURIOUS DEATH OF THE NOVEL. Essays in American Literature. *Louisiana State Univ. Press* 1967 $6.95. Essays, mostly on novelists, from Poe to Flannery O'Connor, by a readable professor who does not think the novel is dead.

Shapiro, Charles, Ed. TWELVE ORIGINAL ESSAYS ON GREAT AMERICAN NOVELS. 1958. *Wayne State Univ. Press* 1959 $7.95 pap. $3.95. On American novels from Cooper's "The Deerslayer" (1841) and Hawthorne's "The Scarlet Letter" (1850) to Hemingway's "The Sun Also Rises" (1926) and Faulkner's "Light in August" (1932); includes essays by Malcolm Cowley, Granville Hicks, Alfred Kazin and others.

Snell, George. THE SHAPERS OF AMERICAN FICTION. 1947. *Cooper* 1961 $6.00. A discussion covering the whole course of American fiction to the present. Mr. Snell discovers four main strains of development, which he traces throughout.

Stevenson, Lionel. THE ENGLISH NOVEL: A PANORAMA. *Houghton* (orig.) 1960 pap. $5.25. A major contribution to the study of the English novel from the beginnings to the present century.

Van Ghent, Dorothy. THE ENGLISH NOVEL: Form and Function. *Harper* Perenn. Lib. 1961 pap. $1.45; *Holt* 1953 text ed. $9.00

Wagenknecht, Edward C. CAVALCADE OF THE AMERICAN NOVEL: From the Birth of the Nation to the Middle of the Twentieth Century. *Holt* 1952 $11.95 text ed. $10.00. A very useful reference survey with long essays on many representative writers; briefer notes on less important ones.

CAVALCADE OF THE ENGLISH NOVEL. From Elizabeth to George VI. *Holt* 1943 new ed. with supplementary bibliography 1954 $11.95 text ed. $10.00. Excellent and imaginative survey of the great novelists from Defoe to the recent past.

See also the lists for Chapters 10–12 on British Fiction; for Chapters 13–14 on American Fiction; and Chapter 3, Reference Books—Literature: Reference Books on Fiction.

General Collections of Fiction

It should be noted that these are collections covering a longer period than any single chapter, or a wider geographical area. For other collections see all Chapters on Fiction.

Angus, Douglas and Sylvia. GREAT MODERN EUROPEAN SHORT STORIES. *Fawcett* Premier Bks. (orig.) 1967 pap. $.95. By Camus, Chekhov, Conrad, Dinesen, Huber, Joyce, Kafka, Landolfi, Lawrence, Mann, Maugham, Pirandello, Sillitoe and others.

Bowen, James K., and Richard Vanderbeets. CLASSIC SHORT FICTION: An International Collection. *Bobbs* 1972 $3.75. 25 short stories, 5 novellas, readings and criticism.

Cowley, Malcolm, and Howard E. Hugo. LESSON OF THE MASTERS. *Scribner* 1971 $10.00. An anthology of the novel from Cervantes to Hemingway. Contains text and commentary.

Davis, Robert G. TEN MODERN MASTERS. *Harcourt* 3rd ed. 1972 $5.25. Three stories each by Borges, Chekhov, Faulkner, Joyce, Lawrence, Malamud, Mann, O'Connor, and Welty, and two longer stories by Conrad. Also includes nine stories by other modern writers and a selection of writings by the ten authors on their art.

Gordon, Caroline, and Allen Tate. HOUSE OF FICTION. *Scribner* 2nd ed. 1960 $4.95. 23 stories by both masters and contemporaries.

Hall, J. B. THE REALM OF FICTION. *McGraw-Hill* 2nd ed. 1970 $6.95 pap. $4.95. Short stories.

Herr, Dan, and Joel Wells. MOMENTS OF TRUTH. *Doubleday* Image Bks. pap. $.95

An interesting group of British and American short stories "selected for their pinpointing of the moment of truth or crisis in human experience"—(*LJ*).

Howe, Irving. CLASSICS OF MODERN FICTION: Ten Short Novels. *Harcourt* 2nd ed. 1973 $5.95. Includes Dostoyevsky, Tolstoy, James, Forster, Conrad, Mann, Kafka, Flannery O'Connor, Bellow, Solzhenitsyn. With a critical introduction to each author.

Ludwig, Richard M., and Marvin Perry. NINE SHORT NOVELS. *Heath* 2nd ed. 1964 $5.95

Marcus, Steven. THE WORLD OF MODERN FICTION. Vol. 1 American, Vol. 2 European. *Simon & Schuster* 1966 2 vols. boxed $17.50. An excellent and significant collection of postwar fiction—from Bellow, Flannery O'Connor, and Sartre to Doris Lessing, Camus, Singer and Mailer: 16 Americans and 20 Europeans; 1,035 pages of stories and short novels.

Neider, Charles. GREAT SHORT STORIES FROM THE WORLD'S LITERATURE. *Holt* 1950 $7.25

SHORT NOVELS OF THE MASTERS. *Holt* 1948 enl. ed. 1972 $5.95. Includes Melville's "Benito Cereno," Dostoyevsky's "Notes from the Underground," Flaubert's "A Simple Heart," Tolstoy's "The Death of Ivan Ilyich," James's "The Aspern Papers," Chekhov's "Ward No. 6," Mann's "Death in Venice," Joyce's "The Dead," Kafka's "The Metamorphosis." Lawrence's "The Fox," and others.

Stern, Richard. HONEY AND WAX: The Pleasures and Powers of Narrative. *Univ. of Chicago Press* 1966 $7.95 Phoenix Bks. pap. $3.95. A comprehensive international story collection chosen to illuminate the function of narrative in widely disparate works.

GENERAL WORKS ON WRITERS AND WRITING

For biographical reference works confined to authors, see Chapter 3, Reference Books—Literature: Histories and Dictionaries of Literature.

Allen, Walter, Comp. and ed. WRITERS ON WRITING. 1948. *Dutton* 1959 pap. $1.45; *The Writer* 1959 $6.00. Poets and novelists themselves define, defend, explain, and question their own theories and practices in this collection of pieces about the writing of poetry and the novel.

Bader, A. L., Ed. TO THE YOUNG WRITER. Hopwood Lectures, 2nd Series. *Univ. of Michigan Press* 1965 lib. bdg. $4.40 pap. $1.95

   A compilation of the lectures given annually on the presentation of the Hopwood Awards in creative writing at the University of Michigan. This series was delivered (1953–64) by Saul Bellow, John Ciardi, Malcolm Cowley, John Gassner, Alfred Kazin, Archibald MacLeish, Arthur Miller, Howard Nemerov, Philip Rahv, Theodore Roethke, Mark Schorer and Stephen Spender. "Brief, informative, worthwhile statements on many aspects of the craft and mystery of authorship" (*LJ*), aimed at the young writer.

Booth, Wayne. THE RHETORIC OF FICTION. *Univ. of Chicago Press* 1961 $7.50 Phoenix Bks. pap. $2.95

   "My goal is not to set everyone straight about my favorite novelists, but rather to free both readers and novelists from the constraints of abstract rules about what novelists must do, by reminding them in a systematic way of what good novelists have in fact done"—(Author's preface). Includes an excellent annotated bibliography.

Brooks, Van Wyck. *For his "Makers and Finders" series and other works, see his main entry in Chapter 15, Essays and Criticism.*

Burke, W. J., and Will D. Howe, Eds.; augmented and rev. by Irving Weiss. AMERICAN AUTHORS AND BOOKS: 1640 to the Present Day. 1943. *Crown* 1962 3rd ed. 1972 $12.50. The biographies of American authors and the titles of their best known books, without critical evaluation (*see Chapter 3, Reference Books—Literature: Histories and Dictionaries of Literature: American for further comment*).

Dahlberg, Edward. CAN THESE BONES LIVE? 1941. *New Directions* rev. ed. 1960 $4.75; *Univ. of Michigan Press* 1967 Ann Arbor Bks. pap. $2.25. Interpretations of Shakespeare, Cervantes, Dostoyevsky, Thoreau, Melville, Whitman and others.

Frenz, Horst, Ed. NOBEL LECTURES IN LITERATURE, 1901–1967. *American Elsevier* 1969 $16.50. This volume, part of the complete series of Nobel lectures, including physics, chemistry, physiology and medicine, is a very welcome addition for the reader interested in major literary statements. Many of these lectures have become classics; e.g., those of Faulkner, Camus, and Hemingway. Although Solzhenitsyn's (written) speech was too recent to be included, it can be found as a separately published work (*see Solzhenitsyn listing, below*).

Gibson, Walker. TOUGH, SWEET AND STUFFY: An Essay on Modern Prose Styles. *Indiana Univ. Press* 1966 $5.95 Midland Bks. pap. $1.95. Professor Gibson of New York University regards modern prose styles as falling into these three categories, or mixtures thereof. A useful detailed analysis both for the writer and for the reader who wishes to understand modern writing.

(Ed.) THE LIMITS OF LANGUAGE. *Hill and Wang* 1962 American Century pap. $1.95. A wonderful compilation of essays expressing the concern of scientists and artists that we must make sense of the universe and must express it all in words.

Hahn, Emily. ROMANTIC REBELS: An Informal History of Bohemianism in America. *Houghton* 1967 $5.95

From the mid-19th century to the recent past. Miss Hahn "follows the ups and downs of these restless spirits, writing about them with grace and humor and a certain amount of respect"—(*New Yorker*).

Hersey, John, Ed. THE WRITER'S CRAFT. *Knopf* 1974 $10.00

Selections from writers on all aspects of the writer's art by James, Forster, Robbe-Grillet, Burroughs, Lubbock, Fowles, Flaubert and others. "I envy them [Mr. Hersey's students] their time to study the book in relative leisure . . . . I envy them their chance to read slowly and carefully such classic works as Leo Tolstoy's 'What Is Art?', Elizabeth Bowen's 'Notes on Writing a Novel,' Gertrude Stein's 'Poetry and Grammar,' and Edgar Allan Poe's 'The Philosophy of Composition' "—(Christopher Lehmann-Haupt, in the *N.Y. Times*).

James, Henry. LITERARY REVIEWS OF AMERICAN, ENGLISH AND FRENCH LITERATURE. Ed. by A. Mordell. 1957. *AMS Press* $17.50; *College & Univ. Press* 1962 pap. $3.95

McCormack, Thomas, Ed. AFTERWORDS: Novelists on Their Novels. *Harper* 1974 $5.95

Essays by Truman Capote, Mary Renault, Louis Auchincloss, Anthony Burgess, Norman Mailer and others. "A practical, fascinating guide to writing culled from the expert knowledge of the world's most noted novelists"—(*Booklist*).

Paris Review. WRITERS AT WORK: The Paris Review Interviews. An outstanding series pub. by *Viking*:

FIRST SERIES. Ed. by Malcolm Cowley. 1958 $7.95 Compass Bks. pap. $1.65. Mauriac, Forster, Cary, Dorothy Parker, Thurber, Wilder, Faulkner, Simenon, Frank O'Connor, Robert Penn Warren, Moravia, Algren, Angus Wilson, Styron, Capote, Sagan.

SECOND SERIES. Introd. by Van Wyck Brooks. 1963 $7.95 Compass Bks. pap. $2.25. Pasternak, Eliot, Hemingway, Marianne Moore, Ellison, Frost, Perelman, Lawrence Durrell, Mary McCarthy, Aldous Huxley, Pound, Henry Miller, Robert Lowell, Katherine Anne Porter.

THIRD SERIES. Introd. by Alfred Kazin. 1967. $7.95 Compass Bks. pap. $2.45. Albee, Burroughs, Céline, Cendrars, Cocteau, Ginsberg, Hellman, James Jones, Mailer, Arthur Miller, Pinter, Evelyn Waugh, William Carlos Williams.

Parry, Albert. GARRETS AND PRETENDERS: A History of Bohemianism in America. *Dover* rev. ed. 1960 pap. $2.50; *Peter Smith* $4.50

From Whitman to Ginsberg. "Thoroughly fascinating"—(*N.Y. Times*).

Powys, Llewelyn. THIRTEEN WORTHIES. Pref. by Van Wyck Brooks. 1923. *Bks. for Libraries* $7.75; *Richard West* $7.50. Discussion of Chaucer, Montaigne, Marlowe, Coryat, Urquhart, Walton, Bunyan, Culpeper, Beau Nash, Woolman, Bewick, Barnes, Hardy.

Solzhenitsyn, Alexander I. THE NOBEL LECTURE ON LITERATURE. Bilingual ed. trans. by F. D. Reeve *Farrar, Straus* 1972 $4.00 pap. $1.00; trans. by Thomas P. Whitney *Harper* 1972 $3.50

Both translations are excellent and eloquently convey Solzhenitsyn's message of the importance of literature. F. D. Reeve is a poet as well as a Russian scholar. "Portions of [this lecture] have been widely reprinted in newspapers around the country "the present [Whitney] translation appeared in slightly different form in the *New York Times* on Sept. 30 and Oct. 7, 1972"—(*LJ*). "Solzhenitsyn has written an extraordinarily moving testament to the power of art and literature as a uniting force in the modern world"—(M. S. Cosgrave).

Wilson, Edmund. *See his main entry in Chapter 15, Essays and Criticism, for collections of his lively and perceptive essays on American and foreign writers.*

Woolf, Virginia. COLLECTED ESSAYS. *Harcourt* 1967 4 vols. Vols. 1–2 each $6.50 Vols. 3–4 each $5.95

See also her main entry in Chapter 15, Essays and Criticism.

See also Chapter 15, Essays and Criticism, and Chapter 3, Reference Books—Literature.

BROAD STUDIES OF LITERATURE, GENERAL WORKS OF CRITICISM

Atkins, J. W. H. LITERARY CRITICISM IN ANTIQUITY. *Peter Smith* 2 vols. Vol. 1 Greek $4.00 Vol. 2 Graeco-Roman $6.00

Auden, W. H. THE ENCHAFED FLOOD: Three Critical Essays on the Romantic Spirit. *Random* Vintage Bks. $1.65

"An attempt to understand the nature of Romanticism through an examination of its treatment . . . the sea." "A small critical masterpiece"—(*N.Y. Times*).

FOREWORDS AND AFTERWORDS. *Random* $12.50. Auden's wonderfully astute and interesting observations.

Auerbach, Erich. MIMESIS: The Representation of Reality in Western Literature. Trans. by Willard Trask. *Princeton Univ. Press* 1953 $13.50 pap. $3.45. Brilliant, profound, scholarly, but never pedantic, this is one of the dozen or so key books of 20th-century criticism. Ranging from Homer to Virginia Woolf, it is always illuminating.

SCENES FROM THE DRAMA OF EUROPEAN LITERATURE. Essays, translated by various hands. 1959. *Peter Smith* $5.00

Bate, Walter Jackson, Ed. CRITICISM: THE MAJOR TEXTS. *Harcourt* 1952 enl. ed. 1970 $11.50. Selections compiled by a distinguished Harvard scholar. The first ed. ranged from Aristotle to Edmund Wilson. The enlarged ed. contains selections from Northrop Frye to the section on "The Modern Period" and a new final section, "Further Modern Developments."

Brophy, Brigid, Michael Levey and Charles Osborne. FIFTY WORKS OF ENGLISH LITERATURE WE COULD DO WITHOUT. *Stein & Day* pap. $1.95. Iconoclastic and not necessarily true, but stimulating, entertaining and controversial.

Columbia University. LECTURES ON LITERATURE. 1911. *Bks. for Libraries* 1967 $11.75. Lectures by members of the Columbia faculty on Oriental, Classical and European literature; on various literary epochs and related topics.

Coveney, Peter. THE IMAGE OF CHILDHOOD: The Individual and Society. Introd. by F. R. Leavis. 1957. *Gannon* lib. bdg. $5.20; (with title "Poor Monkey") *Dufour* $8.50

"Poor Monkey: The Child in Literature from Rousseau's *Emile* to the Freudian Novelists" was the original title of this book. "This original and interesting book" starts from "a brilliant initial perception—the recognition that the whole of the romantic movement can be freshly charted in terms of the treatment of the child in literature. And although he has kept scrupulously to his apparently limited and limiting theme, what Mr. Coveney has achieved is a new and illuminating study of the main tradition of English literature since Wordsworth"—(Philip Toynbee, in the *Observer*, London).

Emerson, Everett H., Ed. MAJOR WRITERS OF EARLY AMERICAN LITERATURE. *Univ. of Wisconsin Press.* 1972 $12.50

"An outstanding collection of original critical essays by distinguished specialists . . . this book is both a chronological survey of nearly 200 years of American Literature and an exciting reappraisal of the major figures of that period. . . . Especially noteworthy are the studies of Bradstreet, Taylor, Mather . . . Franklin . . . and Brown . . ."—*(Choice)*.

Foerster, Norman. AMERICAN CRITICISM: A Study in Literary Theory from Poe to the Present. 1928 1956. *Russell & Russell* reissue 1962 $12.00

In the 19th century the American national spirit, according to the author, "aspired to the creation of a national culture comparable with that of each of the great countries of Europe. This passion gave impetus to the literature of the century of Cooper, Poe, Emerson, Hawthorne, Thoreau, Longfellow, Whitman, Mark Twain, and Howells." This book is a study of American literary theory in Poe, Emerson, Lowell and Whitman with a concluding chapter on the twentieth century.

Gordon, Ian A. THE MOVEMENT OF ENGLISH PROSE. *Indiana Univ. Press* 1967 $5.75. A most enlightening brief, readable survey of the changes in English prose from Anglo-Saxon times onward, supported by end-of-chapter source footnotes—which do not intrude on the fascinating subject matter. It does not *look* like·a textbook and one comes on a short group of exercises at the end of its 167 pages with surprise.

Howard, Leon. LITERATURE AND THE AMERICAN TRADITION. 1960 *Gordian* $10.00. An entertaining examination of the formation of our literary individuality.

Jones, Edmund David. ENGLISH CRITICAL ESSAY, 16th–18th CENTURIES. 1922. *Oxford* World's Class. 1930 $1.95

ENGLISH CRITICAL ESSAYS OF THE 19TH CENTURY. *Oxford* 1922 pap. 1971 $2.75

Jones, Howard Mumford. THE THEORY OF AMERICAN LITERATURE. 1948. *Cornell Univ. Press* rev. ed. 1967 $7.50 pap. $1.95

"Brief, trenchant, authoritative, [this] pioneer study of American literary histography . . . well deserves a new lease on life"—*(TLS,* London).

BELIEF AND DISBELIEF IN AMERICAN LITERATURE. *Univ. of Chicago Press* 1967 $5.00 Phoenix Bks. pap. $1.95.

A brief discussion of the religion or skepticism of key American writers and their writings from the 18th to 20th centuries.

See also Jones' main entry in Chapter 15, Essays and Criticism.

Kaplan, Charles, Ed. CRITICISM: TWENTY MAJOR STATEMENTS. *Chandler Pub.* 1964 pap. $5.75. A fine selection of what certainly are major statements, presented in a readable and appealing format. Includes: Plato, Aristotle, Longinus, Horace, Sir Philip Sidney, Dryden, Pope, Edward Young, Samuel Johnson, Wordsworth, Coleridge, Charles Lamb, Keats, Shelley, Poe, Matthew Arnold, Walter Pater, Henry James, Leo Tolstoy, and T. S. Eliot. A final short section of "Questions for Discussion" will probably not annoy the reader and may even prove stimulating.

Kostelanetz, Richard, Ed. ON CONTEMPORARY LITERATURE. *Avon Bks.* 1964 pap. $1.95; *Bks. for Libraries* $20.00. Sixteen essays cover such topics as American Fiction, American Theater, British Writing, British Poetry, British Theater, Canadian Writing, French Fiction, etc. Thirty-six other essays treat individual writers, mostly American, British and French (plus Nabokov, Pasternak, Moravia). Contributors include Kazin, Fiedler, Rexroth, Kermode, Jarrell, Walter Allen, Hyman, Howe, Eric Bentley and others of equal standing.

Kwiat, Joseph J., and Mary C. Turpie, Eds. STUDIES IN AMERICAN CULTURE: Dominant Ideas and Images. 1960. *Johnson Reprint* lib. bdg. $10.00. Thoughtful discussions with helpful notes by 16 specialists.

Levin, Harry. REFRACTIONS: Essays in Comparative Literature. *Oxford* 1966 $8.00 Galaxy Bks. pap. $2.50. Includes a caustic analysis of the major histories of English literature.

Lewis, R. W. B. THE AMERICAN ADAM. *Univ. of Chicago Press* 1955 $6.00 pap. $1.75. Mr. Lewis expresses his stimulating point of view on American life and letters.

TRIALS OF THE WORD. Essays in American Literature and the Humanistic Tradition. *Yale Univ. Press* 1965 $6.50

Nine extended literary essays that "cannot fail to delight anyone remotely or professionally involved with literature"—(*LJ*).

A LIBRARY OF LITERARY CRITICISM. *See Chapter 15, Essays and Criticism—Literary Criticism: Books, Essays and Collections.*

Poirier, Richard. A WORLD ELSEWHERE: The Place of Style in American Literature. *Oxford* 1966 $6.50

Professor Poirier discusses "the creation of those works that allow their characters 'unhampered freedom of consciousness' "—and the stylistic problems the (mainly 19th-century) authors working in this manner encountered. "Close reasoning" and a "wealth of literary illustration"—(*N.Y. Times*).

Rowse, A. L. THE ENGLISH SPIRIT: Essays in Literature and History. *Funk & Wagnalls* 1967 $5.95 pap. $2.95

Simms, William Gilmore. VIEWS AND REVIEWS OF AMERICAN LITERATURE, HISTORY AND FICTION. 1846. Ed. by C. Hugh Holman. First Series. *Harvard Univ. Press* 1962 pap. $1.95. These 11 essays were originally published in Southern literary journals in the 1840s. Simms was a prolific writer of novels, poetry, biography, Southern history, and editor of several Southern literary journals. Many of his books are currently available in reprint. The *Univ. of South Carolina Press* has published vol. 1 and 3 of "The Centennial Edition of the Works of William Gilmore Simms" (Vol. 1 Voltmeier [1968] Vol. 2 As Good as a Comedy and Paddy Mcgann [1972] each $25.00) and five volumes of "Letters" (ed. by Mary C. Simms Oliphant 1952–56 each $25.00).

Spiller, Robert E. THE CYCLE OF AMERICAN LITERATURE: An Essay in Historical Criticism. *Macmillan* 1955 $5.95 (Free Press) pap. $1.95. An impressive and perceptive study of our literary history. Spiller is one of the editors of "Literary History of the United States."

THE THIRD DIMENSION: Studies in Literary History. Essays 1929–63. *Macmillan* 1965 $5.95

Symons, Arthur. THE SYMBOLIST MOVEMENT IN LITERATURE. 1908. Ed. by Richard Ellmann *Dutton* pap. $1.35; *Haskell* repr. of 1908 ed. lib. bdg. $15.95

Tate, Allen. ESSAYS OF FOUR DECADES. *Swallow* 1969 $10.00; *Apollo* 1970 pap. $4.95. Forty-two essays and six prefaces by Mr. Tate covering many aspects of literature. A fine collection; a delight to read.

See also his main entry in Chapter 15, Essays and Criticism.

THE TIMES LITERARY SUPPLEMENT (London). *See Chapter 15, Essays and Criticism— Literary Criticism: Books, Essays and Collections.*

Wellek, René, and Austin Warren, Eds. THE THEORY OF LITERATURE. *Harcourt* rev. ed. Harvest Bks. pap. $2.45. Contains an excellent bibliography.

Wimsatt, William K., and Cleanth Brooks. LITERARY CRITICISM: A Short History. *Knopf* 1957 $9.75; *Random* Vintage Bks. 1967 $3.45. From Plato's "Ion" to the moderns. The standard, excellent work.

See also Chapter 15, Essays and Criticism, and Chapter 3, Reference Books—Literature.

—A.E.

Chapter 5

British Poetry: Early to Romantic

". . . if you demand on the one hand,
the raw material of poetry in
all its rawness and
that which is on the other hand
genuine, then you are interested in poetry."
—MARIANNE MOORE

This Chapter covers the finest flowering of English literature—the period from "Beowulf" (c. 750 A.D.) to the death of Keats (1821). That "period" in fact encompasses five literary periods: Old English poetry, which (as a written literature) began in the 7th century; the Middle English period (14th–15th centuries), dominated by Chaucer's art; the Elizabethan and Jacobean Renaissance, with its wealth of gifted poets, headed by Spenser, Donne, and Milton (not forgetting Shakespeare); the period of the Restoration and the 18th century, when the achievements of Dryden and Pope looked on to those of such "pre-Romantic" poets as Gray and Cowper; finally, the revolutionary Romantics themselves, including figures so various as the mystic William Blake, the aristocratic and sexually precocious Lord Byron, the restless nonconformist Shelley, and the doomed genius Keats, cut down by disease at 25.

While the appeal of this great body of poetry is in some degree timeless and universal, there is no doubt that it speaks with particular force to readers who know something of the cultural backgrounds of each period. In this regard (for example), Dorothy Whitelock's "The Beginnings of English Society" (*Penguin* 1952 pap. $1.65) will help readers of "Beowulf"; for the Middle English period, D. M. Stenton's "English Society in the Early Middle Ages" (*Penguin* 1952 pap. $1.75) or Eileen Power's "Medieval People" (*Barnes & Noble* rev. ed. 1963 $4.50 pap. $2.50) are valuable. Among books on Elizabethan England, one might single out A. L. Rowse's "The England of Elizabeth" (*Macmillan* 1950 pap. $2.95) or "Shakespeare's England: An Account of the Life and Manners of His Age," ed. by W. Raleigh and others, 2 vols. (*Oxford* 1916 $22.00). For later periods, the books by Basil Willey, Martin Price, James Sutherland, and Carl Woodring (included in the Selected Bibliography) are similarly instructive.

Each period, in a general sense, has its own character and tone: the cool rationalism of much 18th-century verse contrasts sharply with the emotional turbulence of romantic poetry; again, 17th-century poetry is apt to be relatively thoughtful, melancholy, analytic, in contrast to the somewhat more passionate, even more confident note often struck in Elizabethan literature, which can mirror "a spirit of joy and gaiety, of innocence and lightheartedness, that future ages were to look back on as 'merry England'," (Hallett Smith). But it is also true that a sense of continuing tradition echoes through the larger period covered by this Chapter. Classical literature and thought, Christian belief (rooted in Holy Scripture), and Renaissance Italian literature are perhaps the dominant elements in this regard. So Chaucer recalls and reveres "olde bokes" written in Latin, while he imitates and improves upon literary models provided by Dante and Boccaccio. As Spenser acknowledges the influence of Vergil and Chaucer, so his own Christian humanism anticipates that of Milton's poetry. Keats adopts the Spenserian stanza for "The Eve of St. Agnes"; Wordsworth, in trying times, longs for Milton's "cheerful godliness"; the Hellenism of Byron and Shelley combines revolutionary fervor with a deep concern for ancient

Greek culture. Nor is the force of literary tradition transmitted in an exclusively chronological fashion; Old English poetry was scarcely known before the early 19th century, and
the popular ballads had virtually no written existence before the middle of the 18th century. Each kind of poetry therefore entered the stream of English literary tradition centuries after its composition; and this very tardiness enhanced and brightened the distinctly
original character of ancient themes and poems.

Tradition and originality, then, combine and fuse in the varied and wonderful poetry of
these centuries, delightfully illustrating Jonathan Miller's view of "the function of art
throughout the ages—a constant act of sacking the past in order to repossess it."

Selected Bibliography

Old English Poetry

Bessinger, J. B. A SHORT HISTORY OF ANGLO-SAXON POETRY. *Toronto Univ. Press* 1960
    pap. $4.50. A handy and valuable reference book.

Creed, R. P., Ed. OLD ENGLISH POETRY: Fifteen Essays. *Brown Univ. Press* 1967 $10.00.
    Contains studies of Beowolf and other poems, as well as essays on Old English po-
    etry and the harp.

Greenfield, Stanley. A CRITICAL HISTORY OF OLD ENGLISH LITERATURE. *New York
    Univ. Press* 1965 $8.95 pap. $2.95. Probably the most useful recent study of the field.

Wrenn, C. L. A STUDY OF OLD ENGLISH LITERATURE. *Norton.* 1968 pap. $3.45. Writ-
    ten by the Oxford Professor of Anglo-Saxon; covers literature from Caedmon to
    the Norman Conquest.

The Middle English Period

Chambers, Sir Edmund Kerchever. ENGLISH LITERATURE AT THE CLOSE OF THE MIDDLE
    AGES. Vol. 2 Pt. 2 of Oxford History of English Literature. Contains Medieval
    Drama; The Carol and the Fifteenth-Century Lyric; Popular Narrative Poetry and
    the Ballad; Malory. *Oxford* 1945 $7.25

Kane, George. MIDDLE ENGLISH LITERATURE: A Critical Study of the Romances, the Re-
    ligious Lyrics, Piers Plowman. 1951. *Barnes & Noble* 1970 $8.50

Lewis, C. S. THE ALLEGORY OF LOVE: A Study in Medieval Tradition. *Oxford* 1936
    $7.50 Galaxy Bks. pap. $2.50. A classic on the tradition of courtly romance which af-
    fected Spenser and other English poets.

Moorman, Charles. A KNYGHT THERE WAS. *Univ. of Kentucky Press* 1967 $6.00. A
    study of the medieval literature of knighthood "that is good reading as well as being
    scholarly"—(*L J*).

Oliver, R. POEMS WITHOUT NAMES: The English Lyric, 1200–1500. *Univ. of Califor-
    nia Press* 1970 $6.50

Speirs, John. MEDIAEVAL ENGLISH POETRY: The Non-Chaucerian Tradition. 1958.
    Hillary House $8.50. A badly needed book, enthusiastically written; for laymen and
    scholars.

Tuve, Rosemond. ALLEGORICAL IMAGERY: Some Medieval Books and Their Posterity.
    Princeton Univ. Press 1966 $15.00

Vasta, Edward. MIDDLE ENGLISH SURVEY: Critical Essays. *Univ. of Notre Dame Press* 1965 $6.95 pap. $3.00

"These 15 essays by various hands offer the student and the informed layman a very effective introduction to Middle English literature (exclusive of Chaucer)"—(*LJ*).

Woolf, Rosemary. THE ENGLISH LYRIC IN THE MIDDLE AGES. *Oxford* 1968 $17.00

The Renaissance: The Sixteenth Century

Alpers, Paul J., Ed. ELIZABETHAN POETRY: Modern Essays in Criticism. Includes essays by T. S. Eliot, C. S. Lewis, G. Wilson Knight, I. A. Richards, and others. *Oxford* Galaxy Bks. 1967 $2.95

Bush, Douglas. MYTHOLOGY AND THE RENAISSANCE TRADITION IN ENGLISH POETRY. 1932. *Gordon Press* $11.25; *Norton* Norton Lib. rev. ed. 1963 pap. $2.45

PREFACES TO RENAISSANCE LITERATURE. 1965. *Norton* Norton Lib. pap. $1.45. Five important essays on backgrounds of Renaissance poetry.

John, L. ELIZABETHAN SONNET SEQUENCES. 1938. *Russell & Russell* $11.00

Lever, J. W. THE ELIZABETHAN LOVE SONNET. 1956. *Barnes & Noble* 1966 $5.75

Lewis, C. S. ENGLISH LITERATURE IN THE SIXTEENTH CENTURY, EXCLUDING DRAMA. *Oxford* 1954 $11.50

Peterson, Douglas. THE ENGLISH LYRIC FROM WYATT TO DONNE: A History of the Plain and Eloquent Styles. *Princeton Univ. Press* 1967 $11.00. Learned and readable.

Smith, Hallett. ELIZABETHAN POETRY: A Study in Convention, Meaning, and Expression. *Harvard Univ. Press* 1952 $9.50; *Michigan Univ. Press* Ann Arbor Bks. 1968 pap. $2.45. Probably the best general survey.

Tuve, Rosemond. ELIZABETHAN AND METAPHYSICAL IMAGERY: Renaissance Poetic and Twentieth Century Critics. *Univ. of Chicago Press* 1947 $7.50 Phoenix Bks. pap. $3.45

Wilson, Frank Percy. ELIZABETHAN AND JACOBEAN. *Oxford* 1945 $5.00. Provocative essays on the literature of this period and its cultural background.

The Renaissance: The Early Seventeenth Century

Bennett, Joan. FIVE METAPHYSICAL POETS. *Cambridge* 3rd ed. 1965 $6.95 pap. $1.95. An English critic's study of the poetry of Donne, Herbert, Vaughan, Crashaw, and Marvell.

Bradbury, Malcolm, and David Palmer. METAPHYSICAL POETRY. *St. Martin's* Stratford-on-Avon Studies 1970 $8.75; *Indiana Univ. Press* pap. 1971 $2.75

Bush, Douglas. ENGLISH LITERATURE IN THE EARLIER SEVENTEENTH CENTURY, 1600–1660. Vol. 5 of Oxford History of English Literature. *Oxford* 1945 2nd ed. rev. 1962 $11.50. A "learned and gracious" analysis.

Cruttwell, Patrick. THE SHAKESPEARIAN MOMENT AND ITS PLACE IN THE POETRY OF THE SEVENTEENTH CENTURY. *Columbia* 1954 $7.50

Jones, Richard F., and others. THE SEVENTEENTH CENTURY: Studies in the History of English Thought and Literature from Bacon to Pope. *Stanford Univ. Press* 1969 $10.00 pap. $2.95

Keast, William R., Ed. SEVENTEENTH CENTURY ENGLISH POETRY: Modern Essays in Criticism. *Oxford* rev. ed. 1971 Galaxy Bks. pap. $3.95. Twenty-nine essays discussing 17th-century poetry generally, and the major poets of the era themselves, exclusive of Milton.

Kermode, Frank, Ed. THE METAPHYSICAL POETS. *Fawcett* Premier Bks. 1969 pap. $1.25. Collection of key essays on metaphysical poets, with introduction and commentary.

Martz, Louis L. THE POETRY OF MEDITATION: A Study of English Religious Literature of the Seventeenth Century. *Yale Univ. Press* 1954 $10.00 pap. $2.95

Mazzaro, Jerome. TRANSFORMATIONS IN THE RENAISSANCE ENGLISH LYRIC. *Cornell Univ. Press* 1970 $6.75

Miner, Earl. THE CAVALIER MODE FROM JONSON TO COTTON. *Princeton Univ. Press* 1971 $9.00

THE METAPHYSICAL MODE FROM DONNE TO COWLEY. *Princeton Univ. Press* 1969 $9.00

Summers, Joseph. THE HEIRS OF DONNE AND JONSON. *Oxford Univ. Press* 1970 $6.00. Elegant and interesting studies of eight 17th-century poets.

Wedgwood, C. V. POETRY AND POLITICS UNDER THE STUARTS. *Cambridge* 1960 $6.95; *Univ. of Michigan* Ann Arbor Bks. 1964 pap. $1.50

White, Helen C. METAPHYSICAL POETS: A Study in Religious Experience. 1936. *Macmillan* Collier Bks. pap. $1.50

Willey, Basil. THE SEVENTEENTH CENTURY BACKGROUND: Studies in the Thought of the Age in Relation to Poetry and Religion. *Columbia* 1942 $9.00; *Doubleday* Anchor Bks. 1953 pap. $1.95

Williamson, George. SIX METAPHYSICAL POETS: A Reader's Guide. *Farrar, Straus* Noonday 1967 o.p.

"A sensible synthesis of criticism and an excellent *explication de texte* of the more popular works of Donne, Herbert, Crashaw, Cowley, Vaughan, and Marvell. . . . The text should be a vade mecum for initiates into the seventeenth century and a refresher for others"—(*LJ*).

The Restoration and the Eighteenth Century

Beers, Henry A. A HISTORY OF ENGLISH ROMANTICISM IN THE EIGHTEENTH CENTURY. 1899 1910. *Dover* repr. of 1899 ed. pap. $3.50; *Peter Smith* $5.00; *Gordian* repr. of 1910 ed. 1966 $7.50

Clifford, James L., Ed. EIGHTEENTH-CENTURY ENGLISH LITERATURE: Modern Essays in Criticism. *Oxford* 1959 pap. $2.95

Dobrée, Bonamy. ENGLISH LITERATURE IN THE EARLY EIGHTEENTH CENTURY, 1700–1740. *Oxford* 1959 $12.75. The best general survey of the period.

Hagstrum, Jean H. THE SISTER ARTS: The Tradition of Literary Pictorialism and English Poetry from Dryden to Gray. *Univ. of Chicago Press* 1958 $8.50. A precise and significant assessment.

Jack, Ian. AUGUSTAN SATIRE: Intention and Idiom in English Poetry, 1660–1750. *Oxford* 1952 $6.00 pap. $1.50

Price, Martin. TO THE PALACE OF WISDOM: Studies in Order and Energy from Dryden to Blake. *Southern Illinois Univ. Press* lib. bdg. $7.00 pap. $2.95

    "An almost formidably imposing and rich analysis of 'the way in which movements of ideas interact with literary form in Restoration and 18th-century England' "—(*LJ*).

Spacks, Patricia Meyer. THE POETRY OF VISION: Five Eighteenth-Century Poets. *Harvard Univ. Press* 1967 $6.50

    "An illuminating study of . . . the poetry of Thomson, Collins, Gray, Smart, and Cowper"—(*LJ*).

Sutherland, James. A PREFACE TO EIGHTEENTH-CENTURY POETRY. *Oxford* 1948 $7.75 pap. $1.85. An invaluable introduction.

Trickett, Rachel. THE HONEST MUSE: A Study in Augustan Verse. *Oxford* 1967 $12.00. An interesting investigation into the "underlying ethos" of the poetry of the period with emphasis on Dryden, Pope, and Johnson.

Willey, Basil. EIGHTEENTH CENTURY BACKGROUND: Studies on the Idea of Nature in the Thought of the Period. *Columbia* 1941 $9.00; *Beacon* 1961 pap. $1.95

Romantic Poetry

Abrams, Meyer Howard, Ed. THE ENGLISH ROMANTIC POETS: Essays in Criticism. *Oxford* Galaxy Bks. 1960 pap. $2.95

    THE MIRROR AND THE LAMP: Romantic Theory and the Critical Tradition. *Oxford* 1953 $9.50 Galaxy Bks. pap. $2.75

Bloom, Harold, Ed. ROMANTICISM AND CONSCIOUSNESS: Essays in Criticism. *Norton* 1970 pap. $3.25. Valuable essays on the English Romantic poets.

    THE VISIONARY COMPANY: A Reading of English Poetry. 1961. *Cornell Univ. Press* 3rd ed. 1971 pap. $3.95. Interprets Blake, Wordsworth, Coleridge, Byron, Shelley, and Keats.

Bowra, Sir Cecil Maurice. THE ROMANTIC IMAGINATION. *Oxford* Galaxy Bks. 1961 pap. $1.95. A study of major English Romantic poets.

Brinton, Crane. THE POLITICAL IDEAS OF THE ENGLISH ROMANTICS. 1926. *Russell & Russell* $7.00; *Univ. of Michigan Press* Ann Arbor Bks. 1966 pap. $1.95

    "One of the most thorough and thoughtful essays in literary criticism that has appeared for some time"—(*TLS*, London).

Bush, Douglas. MYTHOLOGY AND THE ROMANTIC TRADITION IN ENGLISH POETRY. 1937. *Harvard Univ. Press* rev. ed. 1969 $10.00; *Norton* Norton Lib. 1963 pap. $3.95

Gleckner, Robert F., and Gerald E. Enscoe, Eds. ROMANTICISM: Points of View. *Prentice-Hall* 1970 $7.50 pap. $4.25

Green, David B., and Edwin G. Wilson, Eds. KEATS, SHELLEY, BYRON, HUNT, AND THEIR CIRCLES: A Bibliography, July 1, 1950–June 30, 1962. *Univ. of Nebraska Press* 1964 $7.60

Hilles, F. W., and Harold Bloom. FROM SENSIBILITY TO ROMANTICISM: Essays Presented to Frederick A. Pottle. *Oxford* 1965 $12.50 pap. 1970 $2.95

Hough, Graham G. THE ROMANTIC POETS. 2nd ed. 1957. *Norton* Norton Lib. 1964 pap. $1.65

Jack, Ian. ENGLISH LITERATURE, 1815–1832. *Oxford* 1963 $11.00

Jordon, Frank Jr., Ed. THE ENGLISH ROMANTIC POETS: A Review of Research and Criticism. *Modern Language Assn.* 3rd ed. 1972 $9.00 pap. $4.00

Knight, G. Wilson. THE STARLIT DOME: On the Poetry of Wordsworth, Coleridge, Shelley, and Keats. *Barnes & Noble* 1960 $6.95; *Oxford* pap. $3.25

Kroeber, Karl. ROMANTIC NARRATIVE ART. *Univ. of Wisconsin Press* 1960 pap. $2.95

Kumar, Shiv K., Ed. BRITISH ROMANTIC POETS: Recent Revaluations. *New York Univ. Press* 1966 $8.95 pap. $2.75

> This "useful sampling of recent criticism of Romantic literature . . . offers some articles that should delight anyone even slightly familiar with the field. . . . All 19 essays are responsible, well researched and consistently in touch with their texts"—(*LJ*).

Perkins, David. THE QUEST FOR PERMANENCE: The Symbolism of Wordsworth, Shelley and Keats. *Harvard Univ. Press* 1959 $8.50. This study shows their influence upon such moderns as Arnold and Eliot.

Renwick, William L. ENGLISH LITERATURE, 1789–1815. *Oxford* 1963 $8.00

Robinson, H. C. HENRY CRABB ROBINSON ON BOOKS AND THEIR WRITERS. Ed. by E. J. Morley. 1938. *AMS Press.* 3 vols. set $42.50. An informal but authoritative contemporary testimony from 1811 to after 1860.

Thorpe, Clarence, and others. THE MAJOR ENGLISH ROMANTIC POETS: A Symposium in Reappraisal. Excludes Blake. *Southern Illinois Univ. Press* 1957 pap. $2.45

Willey, Basil. NINETEENTH CENTURY STUDIES: Coleridge to Matthew Arnold. *Columbia* 1941 $9.00; *Harper* Torchbks. pap. $1.95

Woodring, Carl. POLITICS IN ENGLISH ROMANTIC POETRY. *Harvard Univ. Press* 1970 $10.00. The best book on the subject.

General Books on Early British Poetry

Brooks, Cleanth. THE WELL WROUGHT URN: Studies in the Structure of Poetry. *Harcourt* Harvest Bks. 1947 1956 pap. $1.85. Discussions of Donne, Milton, Wordsworth, etc.

Fairchild, Hoxie Neal. RELIGIOUS TRENDS IN ENGLISH POETRY. *Columbia* 6 vols. 1939–68. Vol. I 1700–1740 (1939) Vol. 2 1740–1780 (1942) Vol. 3 1780–1830, Romantic Faith (1949) Vol. 4 1830–1880, Christianity and Romanticism in the Victorian Era (1957) Vol. 5 1880–1920, Gods of a Changing Poetry (1962) Vol. 6 Valley of Dry Bones: 1920–1965 (1968) each $12.50

Johnson, Samuel. Lives of the English Poets. 1779–81. *Adler's* repr. of 1905 ed. by George B. Hill. 3 vols. $84.00; *Dutton* Everyman's 2 vols. each $3.50; ed. by G. B. Hill *Octagon* 3 vols. $45.00; *Oxford* World's Class. 2 vols. Vol. I $2.50 Vol. 2 $3.75; ed. by W. L. Fleischauer *Regnery* Gateway Eds. pap. $.85

Johnson's often sharp and unorthodox opinions of some 50 poets—well known and less so—including Milton, Dryden, Addison, Congreve, Gay, Swift, Pope, Collins, Young, and Gray. Taken in small doses, these are entertaining and enlightening, particularly for the informed reader.

Tillyard, Eustace M. W. The English Epic and Its Background. *Oxford* Galaxy Bks. 1954 1966 pap. $3.95. A discussion of English epics from the 14th to the 19th century, with emphasis on the Greek, Latin and Italian sources.

Anthologies of Poetry

Old English Poetry

Gordon, R. K., Trans. Anglo-Saxon Poetry 650–1000. *Dutton* Everyman's $3.50

Kennedy, Charles W. An Anthology of Old English Poetry. Trans. into alliterative verse. *Oxford* 1960 $5.75 pap. $2.50

Early English Christian Poetry. With a general introduction to the historical background, manuscript sources, content and meter of medieval poetry. *Oxford* Galaxy Bks. 1953 pap. $2.50

Malone, Kemp, Trans. and Ed. Ten Old English Poems Put into Modern English Alliterative Verse. 1941. *Somerset Pubs.* $6.00

Pope, John C., Ed. Seven Old English Poems. *Bobbs* 1966 $7.50 pap. $3.25

Thorpe, Benjamin, Trans. and Ed. Exeter Book: Codex Exoniensis. A Collection of Anglo-Saxon Poetry from a Manuscript in the Library of the Dean and Chapter of Exeter, with an English translation, notes, and indexes. 1841. *AMS Press* $27.50

Wyatt, Alfred J., Ed. Exeter Book: Old English Riddles. 1912. *AMS Press* $10.00; *Folcroft* $10.00

The Middle English Period

Brown, Carleton F. English Lyrics of the XIIIth Century. With introd., notes, glossary, and indexes. *Oxford* 1932 $8.00

Religious Lyrics of the XIVth Century. 1924 2nd ed. rev. by G. V. Smithers *Oxford* 1952 $8.00

Religious Lyrics of the XVth Century. With introd., notes, glossary, index. *Oxford* 1939 $8.50

Davies, Reginald T., Trans. and Ed. Medieval English Lyrics: A Critical Anthology. *Northwestern Univ. Press* 1964 pap. $2.95. Contains 187 of the most interesting and best shorter poems, each with translation.

Gibbs, A. C. Middle English Romances. York Medieval Texts. *Northwestern Univ. Press* 1966 $5.50 pap. $2.50. Extracts from nine romances in a brief, attractive volume, with critical notes and glossary. The York Medieval Texts are designed to make important Middle English writings accessible to the modern reader or beginning student.

Loomis, Roger S., and Rudolph Willard. MEDIEVAL ENGLISH VERSE AND PROSE. *Appleton* 1948 $9.45

Robertson, Durant Waite, Jr. THE LITERATURE OF MEDIAEVAL ENGLAND. *McGraw-Hill* 1970 $10.95. Copious selections of poetry and prose.

The Renaissance: The Sixteenth Century

Auden, Wystan Hugh, and Chester Kallman. ELIZABETHAN SONG BOOK: Lute Songs, Madrigals, and Rounds. Music ed. by Noah Greenberg. 1944 1956. *Hillary House* pap. $2.50

Ault, Norman. ELIZABETHAN LYRICS. From the original texts. 1949. *Putnam* Capricorn Bks. 1960 pap. $2.50; *Somerset Pubs.* repr. of 1949 ed. $23.50. "Authentic, scholarly, selective, and practically flawless."

Bender, Robert M. FIVE COURTIER POETS OF THE ENGLISH RENAISSANCE. *Washington Square* 1967 pap. $1.45. The major works of Sir Thomas Wyatt; Henry Howard, Earl of Surrey; Sir Philip Sidney; Fulke Greville, Lord Brooke; Sir Walter Raleigh.

Bullett, Gerald William. SILVER POETS OF THE 16TH CENTURY. *Dutton* Everyman's 1948 $3.50 pap. $2.25. Sir Thomas Wyatt; Henry Howard, Earl of Surrey; Sir Philip Sidney; Sir Walter Raleigh; Sir John Davies. Good biographical information in the introduction.

Chambers, Sir Edmund. OXFORD BOOK OF SIXTEENTH CENTURY VERSE. *Oxford* 1932 $7.75

Doughtie, Edward. LYRICS FROM ENGLISH AIRS, 1596–1622. *Harvard Univ. Press* 1970 $12.50. Carefully edited texts, with variants, explanatory notes, glossary, and a good prefatory essay.

Hebel, J. William, and Hoyt H. Hudson. POETRY OF THE ENGLISH RENAISSANCE 1509–1660. 1929 1938. *Appleton* $10.95

Inglis, Fred. ENGLISH POETRY: 1550–1660. *Barnes & Noble* 1966 $4.00

"Helpfully but unobtrusively annotated, the collection should appeal more to the informed layman than to the scholar. Brief bibliographical notes and an index of first lines commend the beautifully printed volume for public and academic collections"—(*LJ*).

Kermode, Frank. ENGLISH PASTORAL POETRY. 1952. *Bks. for Libraries* $7.50; *Norton* Norton Lib. 1972 pap. $2.95. A selection of pastorals from the beginnings to Andrew Marvell.

Macdonald, Hugh. ENGLAND'S HELICON. Ed. from the edition of 1600 with additional poems from the edition of 1614. *Harvard Univ. Press* Muses Library 1950 pap. $3.50

The scholarly edition of this collection of pastoral lyrics is that edited by Hyder E. Rollins—"England's Helicon, 1600–1614," Vol. I Text, Vol. 2 Introduction, Notes and Indexes (1935 2 vols. *Somerset Pubs.* $29.50).

The Renaissance: The Early Seventeenth Century

THE ANCHOR ANTHOLOGY OF SEVENTEENTH CENTURY VERSE. 2 vols. 1969. Vol. I (with
title "Seventeenth Century Verse: An Anthology") ed. by Louis L. Martz. *Norton*
Norton Lib. pap. $4.95; Vol. 2 ed. by Richard Sylvester. *Doubleday* Anchor Bks.
pap. $4.95

> Volume I is a full collection of metaphysical verse, a revised and enlarged edition of Martz's "The Medi-
> tative Poem" (*see below*). Volume 2 is a full collection of Jonsonian and Cavalier verse.

Dalgleish, Jack. EIGHT METAPHYSICAL POETS. *Barnes & Noble* 1961 $2.50

> This contains a selection of the best and best-known poems of Donne, Herbert, Carew, Crashaw,
> Vaughan, King, Marvell, and Cowley; with "admirable concise, informative and interesting commentary
> and notes on the life and work of each poet."

Gardner, Helen. THE METAPHYSICAL POETS. *Oxford* 2nd ed. 1967. $7.50; *Penguin* 1957
pap. $1.45. Over 200 poems by some 40 poets, among them Donne, Herbert, Cra-
shaw, Vaughan; provides explanatory and biographical notes.

Grierson, H. J. C., and Geoffrey Bullough. OXFORD BOOK OF SEVENTEENTH CENTURY
VERSE. *Oxford* 1934 $7.75

Howarth, Robert Guy. MINOR POETS OF THE SEVENTEENTH CENTURY. *Dutton* Everyman's 1953 $3.50 pap. $1.95

Kenner, Hugh. SEVENTEENTH CENTURY POETRY: The Schools of Donne and Jonson.
Holt (Rinehart) 1964 pap. $4.00

Lewalski, Barbara, and A. J. Sabol. MAJOR POETS OF THE EARLIER SEVENTEENTH CEN-
TURY. *Bobbs* 1973 $25.00 pap. $7.50. Copious selections from Donne, Herbert,
Vaughan, Crashaw, Jonson, Herrick, Marvell.

Martz, Louis L. THE MEDITATIVE POEM. *New York Univ. Press* Stuart Eds. 1963
$10.00. A full collection of 17th-century metaphysical verse.

Skelton, Robin. THE CAVALIER POETS. *Oxford* 1970 $7.50. An interestingly varied collec-
tion, including many minor poets.

Starkman, Miriam K. SEVENTEENTH CENTURY ENGLISH POETRY. 1966. *Knopf* 1967
2 vols. text ed. pap. Vol. I $4.25 Vol. 2 $3.95; *Peter Smith* 2 vols. each $3.95

White, Helen C., and others. SEVENTEENTH-CENTURY VERSE AND PROSE. *Macmillan*
Vol. I 1600–1660 (1951) Vol. 2 1660–1700 (1952) each $9.95

The Restoration and the Eighteenth Century

Bredvold, Louis I., A. D. McKillop and L. Whitney. EIGHTEENTH CENTURY POETRY
AND PROSE. 1939. 3rd ed. prepared by J. M. Bullitt *Ronald* 1973 $11.50

Middendorf, John H. ENGLISH WRITERS OF THE EIGHTEENTH CENTURY. *Columbia*
1971 $10.00

Pinto, Vivian de Sola. POETRY OF THE RESTORATION, 1653–1700. With introd., notes,
and commentary. *Barnes & Noble* 1966 $2.50

Smith, David Nichol. THE OXFORD BOOK OF EIGHTEENTH CENTURY VERSE. *Oxford*
1926 $9.75

Tillotson, Geoffrey, Paul Fussell, and Marshall Waingrow, with the assistance of Brewster Rogerson. EIGHTEENTH-CENTURY ENGLISH LITERATURE. *Harcourt* 1969 $11.95

"Presents authoritative texts, based on contemporary editions, of poetry, prose, and drama from the Restoration to the beginning of the 19th century. With extensive footnotes, a biographical headnote and bibliography for each author, a headnote for each selection, a general introduction, and a general bibliography on the whole period"—(Publisher's catalog).

Romantic Poetry

Bloom, Harold. ENGLISH ROMANTIC POETRY: An Anthology. *Doubleday* 1961 $5.95 Anchor Bks. pap. $2.45. A substantial and carefully chosen collection of works by the Romantics, from Collins to Thomas Wade.

Campbell, Oscar James, J. F. A. Pyre and Bennett Weaver. POETRY AND CRITICISM OF THE ROMANTIC MOVEMENT. *Appleton* 1932 $10.95

Miles, Alfred Henry, and others. THE POETS AND POETRY OF THE NINETEENTH CENTURY. 1905–07. Vols. I–3 *AMS Press* each $25.00

Milford, Sir Humphrey Sumner. THE OXFORD BOOK OF ENGLISH VERSE OF THE ROMANTIC PERIOD, 1798–1837. (previous title: "The Oxford Book of Regency Verse" *Oxford* 1928) *Oxford* 1935 $8.50

Perkins, David. ENGLISH ROMANTIC WRITERS. *Harcourt* 1967 $11.95. An anthology of both poetry and prose, concentrating on 20 major authors. Includes bio-critical information and a bibliography for each.

Other collections

Baring-Gould, William, and Ceil Baring-Gould. THE ANNOTATED MOTHER GOOSE. Nursery Rhymes Old and New Explained. *Clarkson N. Potter* 1962 $10.00; *World Pub.* Meridian Bks. pap. $3.95

Intended for adults, this is a history and anthology of the all-purpose nursery rhyme. The 18 chapters, each preceded by informative and delightful commentaries, contain 757 thoroughly annotated verses arranged roughly by genre, such as riddle, proverb, lullaby, charm, or seasonal song. The notes are themselves rich with historical and bibliographical information.

BEOWULF. 750 A.D.

The oldest English epic, written in strongly accentual alliterative verse, celebrates in two parts the feats of the hero Beowulf in Denmark and Sweden. It contains both pagan and Christian elements and is evidently older than the one extant manuscript, in the British Museum, written by two scribes about 1000 A.D. (*see first entry above*). This copy was owned by a 16th-century English collector, Sir Robert Bruce Cotton, whose descendants turned his library over to the government in 1700. Much of the collection was destroyed by fire in 1731. An Icelandic scholar, Grimur Jonsson Thorkelin, came to London looking for historical data and copied Beowulf without realizing its literary significance. His transcripts, in the Great Royal Library of Denmark, survived the British bombardment of Copenhagen in 1807 and are part of an ambitious plan to preserve valuable Anglo-Saxon manuscripts (*See* "Thorkelin Transcripts of Beowulf" *below*).

BEOWULF: Reproduced in Facsimile from the Unique MS. British Museum MS. Vitelius A. Cotton. Trans. with notes Julius Zupitza. 2nd ed. containing a new reproduction of the MS. with an introductory note by Norman Davis. *Oxford* 1959 $18.00

THE THORKELIN TRANSCRIPTS OF BEOWULF. Ed. by Kemp Malone. *Johns Hopkins Press* 1951 subscription pap. $58.00 half lea. $78.25 nonsubscription pap. $72.50 half lea. $98.00

This is the first volume in a series of rare Anglo-Saxon manuscripts to be photographed and photostated by the Danish firm of Rosenkilde & Bagger and distributed by Allen & Unwin in England and by Johns Hopkins Press in America. Eighteen volumes in the series have now been published, 1952–72. Consult catalog for titles and prices.

BEOWULF and THE FIGHT AT FINNSBURG. Ed. by Friedrich Klaeber. 1904. *Heath* 1922 1936 3rd ed. 1941 with 1st and 2nd supplements 1950 $9.95. With bibliography, notes and glossary. Considered the best edition.

BEOWULF, with THE FINNSBURG FRAGMENT. Ed. by Alfred J. Wyatt. Rev. with notes by R. W. Chambers. *Cambridge* 1914 $9.50

BEOWULF. Ed. by C. L. Wrenn. Rev. by W. F. Bolton. *St. Martin's* 1973 $7.95

BEOWULF and JUDITH. Ed. by Elliott van Kirk Dobbie. *Columbia* 1973 $10.00

BEOWULF and JUDITH. Ed. by F. P. Magoun, Jr., done in normalized orthography, *Harvard Univ. Press* 1959 pap. $2.00

BEOWULF. In Anglo-Saxon, with an English translation by Benjamin Thorpe. *Barron's* $5.00 pap. $2.25

Translations into Modern English. *For Anglo-Saxon texts with translation, see above.*

BEOWULF. Trans. by Charles L. Brown. *Academy Press.* Campbell, Calif. 1972 $9.45; (and "The Finnsburg Fragment") trans. into English prose by John R. Hall, with notes by C. L. Wrenn. 1950. *Barnes & Noble* $5.50; trans. by Kevin Crossley-Holland *Farrar, Straus* 1968 $5.95 Noonday pap. $1.95; trans. by Lucien D. Pearson, with introd. and notes by R. L. Collins *Indiana Univ. Press* $5.00 pap. $1.75; trans. by Burton Raffel *New Am. Lib.* Mentor Bks. pap. $.75 durabind $1.75; trans. by E. Talbot Donaldson *Norton* 1966 pap. $.95; (and Other English Poems) trans. by Constance B. Hieatt *Odyssey* 1967 pap. $1.25; (with title "Beowulf, the Oldest Epic") trans. into alliterative verse with a critical introd. by Charles W. Kennedy *Oxford* 1940 $3.50; trans. by David Wright *Penguin* pap. $.95 trans. by Michael Alexander Classics Series 1973 pap. $1.05; (and "Sir Gawain and the Green Knight") trans. and ed. by G. H. Gerould *Ronald* 1935 1953 $3.50; trans. by William Ellery Leonard 1923 *Richard West* 1973 $7.45; trans. into modern English verse by Edwin Morgan *Peter Smith* $3.50; trans. by E. Morgan. *Univ. of California Press* 1962 pap. $.95; trans. by Burton Raffel with ills. by Leonard Baskin *Univ. of Massachusetts Press* $10.00

Books about Beowulf

Beowulf: An Introduction. By R. W. Chambers. 2nd ed. 1932 3rd ed. rev. by C. L. Wrenn. The authoritative indispensable critical work. *Cambridge* 1959 $23.50
Beowulf and Epic Tradition. By William W. Lawrence. 1930. *Hafner* 1963 $5.75
An Anthology of Beowulf Criticism. Ed. by Lewis E. Nicholson. Major articles from British and American scholarly journals. *Univ. of Notre Dame Press* 1963 pap. $3.95; *Bks. for Libraries* $14.00
The Art of Beowulf. By Arthur Brodeur. 1959. Library Reprint Series. *Univ. of California Press* 1969 $10.50. Combines general criticism with specialized discussion.
The Beowulf Poet: A Collection of Critical Essays. Ed. by Donald Fry. Twentieth Century Views Series. *Prentice-Hall* 1968 $5.95 pap. $1.95
An Introduction to Beowulf. By Edward Irving, Jr. *Prentice-Hall* 1969 $5.95

LANGLAND, WILLIAM. 1330?–1400?

Little is known of the life of this early English poet, a contemporary of Chaucer (*q. v.*) Langland represents the close of the period of Old English alliterative verse. His "Vision of Piers Plowman," an allegorical and satirical poem, survives in many manuscripts, representing three separate versions known as the A, B and C texts. The poem contains vivid pictures of contemporary life and is in two parts: "*Visio*—primarily an examination of the right use of the world's goods in man's search for truth, with Piers and his helpers representing Christian society; and the *Vita*—the search for Dowel, Dobet and Dobest (the good, better and best ways of life)—an allegorical handling of the problems of the individual in his search for self-knowledge and perfection." The authoritative Old English version is that edited by W. W. Skeat (10th rev. ed. 1924 *Oxford* $2.95, parallel texts A, B, C 1886 2 vols. $20.50). There are two editions of the A Version: "Piers the Plowman: A Critical Edition of the A-Version" (ed. with introd. notes and glossary by T. A. Knott and D. C. Fowler *Johns Hopkins Univ. Press* 1952 $6.00) and "The Vision of William concerning Piers Plowman together with Vita of Dowel, Dobet, et Dobest secundum Wit et Resoun." Ed. from the "Vernon" MS., collated with MS. R.3.14 in the Library of Trinity College, Cambridge, MSS. Harl 875 and 6041, the MS. in University College, Oxford, MS. Douce 323 etc. by Walter W. Skeat (*Oxford* 1867 $7.00). For the C-text, see E. Talbot Donaldson's "Piers Plowman: The C-Text and Its Poet" (1949 *Shoe String Press* 1966 $7.00).

THE VISION OF PIERS PLOWMAN. Trans. into metrical English with introd. and notes by Walter W. Skeat. 1900. *Cooper Square* $4.00; trans. by Henry W. Wells 1959. *Greenwood* $13.00; trans. into modern English by Donald and Rachel Attwater *Dutton* Everyman's 1931 $3.50; trans. into modern English by Nevill Coghill *Oxford* 1950 $3.50; trans. by J. F. Goodridge *Penguin* 1959 pap. $1.45; trans. by Margaret Williams *Random* 1971 $10.00

Books about Langland

Piers the Plowman: Literary Relations of the A and B Texts. By David C. Fowler. *Univ. of Washington Press* 1952 $5.75

Piers Plowman as a Fourteenth-Century Apocalypse. By Morton W. Bloomfield. *Rutgers Univ. Press* 1962 $10.00

Piers Plowman: An Essay in Criticism. By John Lawlor. *Barnes & Noble* 1962 $10.00

Piers Plowman: An Introduction. By Elizabeth Salter. *Harvard Univ. Press* 1962 $3.75

Style and Symbolism in Piers Plowman: A Modern Critical Anthology. *Univ. of Tennessee Press* 1969 $7.50 pap. $3.25

THE PEARL-POET. c. 1390.

"The Pearl" is a poet's lament, depicting an allegorical vision seen at the grave of his little daughter. It is one of four anonymous alliterative poems all in the same handwriting in an illustrated British Museum manuscript. The other three are "Cleanness," "Patience," and "Gawaine and the Green Knight." It is not known if the four poems were written by the same poet.

THE PEARL-POET: His Complete Works. Trans. with introd. by Margaret Williams, R.S.C.J. *Random* 1967 $15.00 Vintage Bks. pap. $2.95

THE COMPLETE WORKS OF THE GAWAIN POET. Trans. into modern English by John Gardner; woodcuts by Fritz Kredel. *Univ. of Chicago Press* $10.00; *Southern Illinoise Univ. Press* pap. $2.85. An edition "that could hardly be improved"—(*LJ*).

PEARL, CLEANNESS, PATIENCE AND SIR GAWAIN. Reproduced in facsimile from the unique MS. Cotton Nero A.x. in the British Museum,. with introd. by Israel Gollancz. *Oxford* 1923 $40.00

THE PEARL. c. 1390. In Middle English, ed. with a modern translation on facing pages by Sara de Ford and others. *AHM Pub. Corp.* Crofts Classic. pap. $.85; trans. into modern verse by Stanley P. Chase 1932. *Branden* $2.95; ed., with a modern rendering, together with Boccaccio's "Olympia" in Latin and an English rendering by Israel Gollancz 1926. *Cooper Square* 1966 $5.00; (and "Sir Gawain and the Green

Knight") ed. by A. C. Cawley *Dutton* Everyman's reissue 1962 $3.60; ed. by Eric V. Gordon *Oxford* 1953 $4.25; the medieval text ed. with a literal translation and an interpretation by Sister Mary Vincent Hillmann *Univ. of Notre Dame Press* 1968 pap. $1.95

SIR GAWAIN AND THE GREEN KNIGHT. Retold in modern prose by Jessie L. Weston. 1898. *AMS Press* $10.00; *Folcroft* 1973 $9.95; *Richard West* 1973 $9.95; trans. by Theodore H. Banks, Jr. *Appleton* 1957 pap. $1.75; trans. by Gwyn Jones *Golden Cockerel* $30.00 deluxe ed. $80.00; trans. by James L. Rosenberg, ed. by James R. Kreuzer *Holt* (Rinehart) 1959 text ed. pap. $2.00; introd. by Burton Raffel *New Am. Lib.* Mentor Bks. 1970 pap. $1.25; ed. by R. A. Waldron *Northwestern Univ. Press* 1967 $5.00 pap. $2.50; trans. into verse by Marie Borroff *Norton* 1967 pap. $.95; ed. by Israel Gollancz *Oxford* 1940 $3.00; ed. by J. R. R. Tolkien and Eric V. Gordon *Oxford* 2nd ed. 1967 $7.00 pap. $3.50; trans. by Brian Stone *Penguin* pap. $2.50

Books about the Pearl-Poet

Art and Tradition in Sir Gawain and the Green Knight. By Larry Benson. *Rutgers Univ. Press* 1965 $12.50

Sir Gawain and Pearl: Critical Essays. Ed. by Robert J. Blanch. *Indiana Univ. Press* 1966 Midland Bks. pap. $2.95

A Reading of Sir Gawain and the Green Knight. By John Burrow. *Barnes & Noble* 1966 $6.50. Analyzes the poem section by section, using many allusions to other literature, and many quotations.

The Pearl: An Interpretation. By P. M. Kean. *Barnes & Noble* 1967 $8.00

Twentieth Century Interpretations of Sir Gawain and the Green Knight. Ed. by Denton Fox. *Prentice-Hall* 1968 $4.95

Critical Studies of Sir Gawain and the Green Knight. Ed. by Donald Howard and Christian Zacher. *Univ. of Notre Dame Press* 1969 $7.95 pap. $2.95. A collection of critical essays written since 1960.

The Middle English Pearl: Critical Essays. Ed. by John Conley. *Univ. of Notre Dame Press* 1970 $9.95. A collection representative of 20th-century criticism.

The Gawain-Poet. By A. C. Spearing. *Cambridge* 1971 $8.50. A discussion of "Pearl," "Cleanness," "Patience," and "Sir Gawain," beginning with a general study of the whole group, followed by an analysis of each one individually.

CHAUCER, GEOFFREY. 1340–1400.

Chaucer laid the foundation of our present English tongue by adapting a vocabulary that was a happy fusion of both Norman-French and Saxon speech. His poems are usually printed today with a glossary, as a key to his Middle English, but it will be found that his language does not vary from our own nearly so much in vocabulary as in spelling. "Chaucer is 'the Prince of story-tellers' and the 'Canterbury Tales' is a story-book than which the world does not posses a better"—(Alexander Smith). Many of the tales are borrowed from the "Decameron" of Boccaccio (*q.v.*); few, if any, are of Chaucer's own invention. The 24 stories are supposed to be told by pilgrims journeying on horseback from the Tabard Inn, Southwark, to the shrine of St. Thomas à Becket in Canterbury Cathedral.

Of the "Canterbury Tales," any list of the best and most popular would include "The Pardoner's Tale," "The Wife of Bath's Prologue and Tale," "The Merchant's Tale," "The Clerk's Tale" (of Patient Griselda), and "The Nun's Priest's Tale" (of Chanticleer and the Fox). "Troilus and Cressida," a separate narrative of well-ordered plot, shows the influence of Italian literature. "The House of Fame," borrowed from Ovid's "Metamorphoses" (*q.v.*) and "The Legend of Good Women"—among whom he numbers Cleopatra, Medea, and Ariadne—are his other important works.

Chaucer created and used two metrical forms: the seven-line stanza, which was later called "rime royal," because James I of Scotland used it in "The King's Quair"; and the rhyming or "heroic" couplet. Chaucer's later and best work was done in such couplets, the form of "The Knight's Tale," "The Nun's Priest's Tale," and "The Legend of Good Women." John Masefield (*q.v.*) later revived this metrical form to great advantage in his long narrative poems.

Son of a London wine merchant, Chaucer married a lady-in-waiting to Edward III's queen, Philippa, and had two sons. He served as a page to Elizabeth, Countess of Ulster; a soldier in Edward's army in France; a diplomat, and a government official in various capacities. He is buried in Westminster Abbey, which eventually established a "Poets' Corner" for the interment of such great literary figures. An important work of recent scholarship, mainly in Latin—the language of official records in Chaucer's time—is the 600-page

"Chaucer Life-Records," begun in 1927 and edited by Martin M. Crow and Clair C. Olson from materials compiled by John M. Manly and Edith Rickert with the assistance of Lilian J. Redstone and others (*Univ. of Texas Press* 1966 $15.00).

COMPLETE WORKS (poetry and prose). "The Oxford Chaucer." Ed. by Walter W. Skeat *Oxford* 1894–97. 7 vols. Vols. 1–5 2nd ed. 1899–1900. Vol. 6 1894 imprint of 1926 Vol. 7 1897 repr. of 1935 set $95.00 1-vol. ed. Stand. Authors 1933 $6.00

THE WORKS OF GEOFFREY CHAUCER AND OTHERS. Being a reproduction in facsimile of the first collected edition, 1532, from the copy in the British Museum. Introd. by Walter W. Skeat. 1905. *Burt Franklin* $97.50; with suppl. material from the eds. of 1542, 1561, 1598, and 1602 *Scholarly Press* 1971 $39.50

WORKS. Ed. by Alfred W. Pollard. The Globe ed. 1898. *Bks. for Libraries* 1972 $27.75. Pollard's collaborators for this edition were H. F. Heath, M. H. Liddell and Sir W. S. McCormick.

WORKS. Ed. by Fred Norris Robinson. *Houghton* 1957 $10.95

THE POETICAL WORKS. Ed. by Sir Harris Nicolas. The Aldine ed. 6 vols. 1845. *AMS Press* each $10.00 set $60.00

THE MODERN READER'S CHAUCER: His Complete Poetical Works. Trans. into modern English by J. S. P. Tatlock and Percy MacKaye. *Macmillan* 1912, 1938 reissue 1943, 1951, 1967 $7.95

THE PORTABLE CHAUCER. Sel., trans., and ed. by Theodore Morrison. *Viking* 1949 $5.95 pap. $2.75

SELECTED POEMS. Ed. by Louis O. Coxe. *Dell* Laurel Eds. pap. $.75

CHAUCER'S POETRY: An Anthology for the Modern Reader. Ed. by E. Talbot Donaldson. *Ronald* 1958 $8.50. All of the "Canterbury Tales" and a selection of other works.

CHAUCER'S MAJOR POETRY. Ed. by Albert C. Baugh. *Appleton* 1963 $10.50

GEOFFREY CHAUCER: A SELECTION OF HIS WORKS. Ed. by Kenneth Kee. *Odyssey* 1966 pap. $1.65

THE COMPLETE TALES OF CANTERBURY, AND SELECTED SHORT POEMS. Ed. by Robert A. Pratt. *Houghton* 1973 $9.95

THE CANTERBURY TALES. c. 1475. The Text of the Canterbury Tales. Ed. by John M. Manly and Edith Rickert. *Univ. of Chicago Press* 9 vols. 1940 Vol. I Descriptions of the Manuscripts Vol. 2 Classification of the Manuscripts Vols. 3–4 Text and Critical Notes Vols. 5–9 Corpus of Variants set $80.00

THE CANTERBURY TALES: To Which Are Added an Essay upon His Language and Versification, an Introductory Discourse and Notes and Glossary. Ed. by Thomas Tyrwhitt. 5 vols. 1775–78. *AMS Press* each $15.00 set $75.00

THE CANTERBURY TALES. Ed. with introd. and notes by John Halverson. *Bobbs* 1971 $8.50 pap. $3.75; trans. into modern English by J. U. Nicolson with ills. by Rockwell Kent *Doubleday* 1936 $7.95; trans. by Robert M. Lumiansky *Holt* 1954 $2.25; ed. by Thomas Wright 3 vols. 1847–51 *Johnson Reprint* each $17.25; ed. by Walter W. Skeat *Oxford* World's Class. $2.95; trans. by Nevill Coghill *Penguin* Class. 1952 pap. $1.75; trans. by David Wright *Random* 1965 $10.00 Vintage Bks. pap. $1.95; trans. by H. L. Hitchens *Transatlantic* $4.50; trans. by Robert M. Lumiansky *Washington Square* pap. $.90

Selections and Single Titles from "Canterbury Tales." The following volumes include choices from "The Canterbury Tales" only. For more inclusive titles consult the "Works" and selections at the head of this list.

THE CANTERBURY TALES. Ed. by Robert D. French. *AHM Pub. Corp.* Crofts Classics pap. $.85; selections with interlinear trans. ed. by Vincent F. Hopper *Barron's* 1948 1960 $5.00 pap. $2.25; sel. and ed. by Daniel Cook *Doubleday* Anchor Bks. 1961 pap. $1.95; 17 tales out of 24 ed. by A. C. Cawley *Dutton* Everyman's $3.50; (with title "A Taste of Chaucer") ed. by Anne Malcolmson *Harcourt* 1964 $3.95; sel. and ed. by Donald Howard and James Dean *New Am. Lib.* Signet 1969 pap. $1.25; ed. by Carl Fischer *Pflaum-Standard* pap. $.60; *Pyramid* pap. $.35

THE PROLOGUE, THE KNIGHT'S TALE, THE NONNE PREESTES TALE. Ed. with introd., notes, and glossary by Frank Jewett Mather. 1907. *AMS Press* $8.00; ed. by Richard Morris, with collations and additional notes by Walter W. Skeat *Oxford* 1907 $2.25

GENERAL PROLOGUE TO THE CANTERBURY TALES. Ed. by James Winny. *Cambridge* 1965 $2.95

THE KNIGHT'S TALE. Ed. by A. C. Spearing. *Cambridge* 1966 $2.95

THE MILLER'S PROLOGUE AND TALE. Ed. by James Winny. *Cambridge* 1970 $2.95; ed. by Constance B. Hieatt *Odyssey* 1970 pap. $1.25

THE CANON'S YEOMAN'S TALE. Ed. by Maurice Hussey, A. C. Spearing and James Winny. *Cambridge* 1965 $2.95

THE NUN'S PRIEST'S PROLOGUE AND TALE. Ed. by Maurice Hussey. *Cambridge* 1966 $2.95

THE MERCHANT'S PROLOGUE AND TALE. Ed. by Maurice Hussey. *Cambridge* 1966 $2.95

THE CLERK'S PROLOGUE AND TALE. Ed. by James Winny. *Cambridge* 1966 $2.95

THE FRANKLIN'S PROLOGUE AND TALE. Ed. by A. C. Spearing. *Cambridge* 1966 $2.95

THE WIFE OF BATH'S PROLOGUE AND TALE. Ed. by James Winny. *Cambridge* 1966 $2.95

THE PARDONER'S PROLOGUE AND TALE. Ed. by A. C. Spearing. *Cambridge* 1966 $2.95; ed. by Carleton Brown *Oxford* 1935 $1.80

TROILUS AND CRISEYDE. Ed. by John Warrington. *Dutton* Everyman's $3.50

TROILUS AND. CRESSEYDE. Trans. by Margaret Stanley-Wrench *British Bk. Centre* 1973 $8.50; trans. by Margaret Stanley-Wrench *Branden* 1967 $7.50; trans. by Nevill Coghill *Penguin* 1971 pap. $1.85; (with title "Troilus and Cressida") trans. by George Philip Krapp *Random* Vintage Bks. pap. $1.95; trans. by Margaret Stanley-Wrench *Saifer* $7.00

Books about Chaucer

Chaucer: A Bibliographical Manual. By Eleanor Prescott Hammond. 1908. *Peter Smith* 1933 $6.75

Geoffrey Chaucer. By Émile Legouis. 1913. Trans. by L. Lailavoix. 1928 *Russell & Russell* repr. of 1928 ed. 1961 $9.00

Chaucer and His Poetry. By George Lyman Kittredge. *Harvard Univ. Press* 1915 $6.50 pap. $2.45

The Poetry of Chaucer: A Guide to Its Study and Appreciation. By Robert K. Root. Rev. ed. 1922. *Peter Smith* 1950 $5.00

Five Hundred Years of Chaucer Criticism and Allusion: 1357–1900. By Caroline F. E. Spurgeon. Facsimiles of original Chaucer mss, and related matter. 1925. *Russell & Russell* 1960, 3 vols. set $45.00

Geoffrey Chaucer. By John Livingston Lowes. *Oxford* 1934 new ed. 1949 $5.00

On Re-reading Chaucer. By Howard R. Patch. *Harvard Univ. Press* 1939 $7.50

Geoffrey Chaucer of England. By Marchette Chute. *Dutton* 1946 1951 $7.50 pap. $1.75

Chaucer and the Fifteenth Century. By Henry S. Bennett. *Oxford* 1947 $11.50. The volume covering this period of the "Oxford History of English Literature." Includes material on Lydgate, Hoccleve, and Caxton.

A Chaucer Handbook. By Robert D. French. *Appleton* 2nd ed. 1947 $8.40

Chaucer's World. Comp. by Edith Rickert ed. by C. C. Olson and M. M. Crow. *Columbia* 1948 1962 pap. $2.95 Distinctive and valuable collection of hundreds of documents and passages describing all known phases of life in Chaucer's London.

The Poet Chaucer. By Nevill Coghill. 1949 *Oxford* 2nd ed. Galaxy Bk. pap. $1.95

Chaucer and His England. By G. G. Coulton. *Dutton* reprint 1950 $5.00; *Barnes & Noble* 1963 $6.00 pap. $3.50

Chapters on Chaucer. By Kemp Malone. *Johns Hopkins Univ. Press* 1951 $7.50

Bibliography of Chaucer, 1908–1953. By Dudley D. Griffith. *Univ. of Washington Press* rev. ed. 1955. $7.00 This replaces the 1908–1924 edition of 1926 now o. p. (*See also the 1967 supplement by William R. Crawford, listed below.*)

Of Sondry Folke: The Dramatic Principle in the Canterbury Tales. By Robert M. Lumiansky. *Univ. of Texas Press* 1955 $7.50

Chaucer and the French Tradition: A Study in Style and Meaning. By Charles Muscatine. *Univ. of California Press* 1957 pap. $2.45

Chaucer. By Derek S. Brewer. 2nd ed. 1960 *Barnes & Noble* 1965 $4.00; *Longman, Inc.* 3rd ed. 1973 $12.50 pap. $6.00

Chaucer Criticism: The Canterbury Tales. Ed. by Jerome Taylor and Richard Schoeck. *Univ. of Notre Dame Press* 1960 pap. $2.75

Chaucer Criticism: Troilus and Criseyde and the Minor Poems. Ed. by Richard Schoeck and Jerome Taylor. *Univ. of Notre Dame Press* 1961 $2.75

Chaucer's Verse. By Paull Franklin Baum. *Duke Univ. Press* 1961 $7.25

Chaucer: Modern Essays in Criticism. By Edward C. Wagenknecht. *Oxford* 1959 Galaxy Bk. pap. $3.50

Chaucer: Poet of Mirth and Morality. By Helen Storm Corsa. *Univ. of Notre Dame Press* 1964 $3.25. "A thorough and lucid presentation of an essential aspect of Chaucer's vision of the world's comic way and serious destination" (*America*), but "her reader should know his Chaucer thoroughly"—(*TLS*, London).

A Reader's Guide to Geoffrey Chaucer. By Muriel A. Bowden. *Farrar, Straus* 1964 Noonday pap. $2.25; *Octagon* 1971 $9.00

A Reading of the Canterbury Tales. By Bernard E. Huppé. "Fresh, suggestive and provocative rather than exhaustive or ponderous in documentation"—(*LJ*). *State Univ. of N.Y. Press* 1964 pap. $2.45

An Introduction to Chaucer. By Maurice Hussey, A. C. Spearing, and James Winny. *Cambridge* 1965 $9.50 pap. $3.95. This is the introductory volume of the Cambridge series "Selected Tales from Chaucer." The second volume of the series, also introductory, is "Chaucer's World: A Pictorial Companion" ed. by M. Hussey (*Cambridge* 1967 $12.50 pap. $3.95). The individual tales in print are listed in the bibliography above.

A New View of Chaucer. By George Williams. *Duke Univ. Press* 1965 $6.75. "Of special interest to the Chaucerian, the book's absorbing thesis, sound scholarship, and engaging style commend it to any teacher or student of English literature"—(*LJ*).

Bibliography of Chaucer, 1954–63. By William R. Crawford. A supplement to the 1955 Bibliography, listed above, by Dudley D. Griffith. *Univ. of Washington Press* 1967 $5.95

A Companion to Chaucer Studies. Ed. by Beryl Rowland. *Oxford* 1968 pap. $2.95. A most useful collection of essays on various aspects of Chaucer's art.

A Preface to Chaucer: Studies in Medieval Perspectives. By Durant W. Robertson. *Princeton Univ. Press* 1969 $17.50 pap. $4.95

Chaucer and the English Tradition. By Ian Robinson. *Cambridge* 1972 $16.50

POPULAR BALLADS

The English ballads (anonymous narrative songs preserved by oral transmission) were probably composed over a period of some 500 years, from 1200 to 1700; but very few were printed before the 18th century, when Bishop Thomas Percy (1729–1811) discovered a 17th-century manuscript containing a number of ballads and other poems. He published these under the title "Reliques of Ancient English Poetry" in 1765; this volume stimulated an interest in the subject on the part of other writers, notably Sir Walter Scott. Ballads are typically simple in form (normally combining tetrameter quatrains with a repeated refrain), spare and dramatically tragic in content. The ballads crossed the Atlantic with Scottish and Irish immigrants to America, and thrived in various regions of the United States. A good collection is "English Folk Songs from the Southern Appalachians," ed. by C. J. Sharp and Maud Kerpeles, 2 vols. (*Oxford* 1932 $15.00). See also "The Ballad Tree: A Study of British and American Ballads," by Evelyn K. Wells (*Ronald* 1950 $6.00).

ENGLISH AND SCOTTISH POPULAR BALLADS. Ed. by F. J. Child. 5 vols. 1882–1898. *Dover* 1965 5 vols. each $5.00 set $25.00; *Peter Smith* 5 vols. set $35.00

ENGLISH AND SCOTTISH POPULAR BALLADS. Ed. by George Lyman Kittredge and Helen Child Sargent. A 1-vol. abridgement of Child's collection. *Houghton* 1904 Cambridge Eds. $9.50; *Gordon Press* $13.95; *Richard West* 1973 $20.00

OLD ENGLISH BALLADS. Ed. by Francis B. Gummere. 1894. *Russell & Russell* 1967 $11.00; *Richard West* $10.95

BALLAD LITERATURE AND POPULAR MUSIC OF THE OLDEN TIME. Ed. by William Chappell. 2 vols. 1855–59. *Dover* pap. each $3.00; *Peter Smith* set $9.50

THE OXFORD BOOK OF BALLADS. Ed. by Sir Arthur Quiller-Couch. *Oxford* 1911 1955 rev. ed. by James Kinsley 1969 $12.00; *Somerset Pub.* repr. of 1955 ed. 2 vols. $35.50

THE COMMON MUSE: An Anthology of Popular British Ballad Poetry, 15th to 20th Century. Ed. by Vivan de Sola Pinto and Allan E. Rodway. 1957. *Scholarly Press* $19.50

ENGLISH AND SCOTTISH BALLADS. Ed. by Robert Graves. 1957. *Barnes & Noble* 1969 pap. $2.00

Books about Popular Ballads

The Popular Ballad. By Francis B. Gummere. 1907. *Gordon Press* $11.00; *Peter Smith* $4.50
European Balladry. By William J. Entwistle. *Oxford* 1939 corrected repr. 1951 $12.00
The Ballads. By Matthew J. Hodgart. *Norton* 1966 pap. $1.65

SKELTON, JOHN. 1460–1529.

As royal tutor, parson, orator, poet-satirist and courtier, Skelton has been called "the most considerable figure in poetry between Chaucer and Spenser, a lonely star shooting his fiery and erratic spears into the twilight dawn before the risen sun of the Elizabethans." His "Colyn Cloute" furnished suggestions for some of Spenser's poems.

"A Ballade of the Scottysshe Kynge" celebrates the victory of the English forces of Henry VIII under the earl of Surrey over the army of James IV at the battle of Flodden. "Magnificence" is an allegory in which the generous prince Magnificence is first destroyed by his own ill-advised generosity, then restored by Goodhope, Perseverance, etc.

He was awarded the degree of laureate by the Universities of Oxford and Cambridge, was honored by the University of Louvain and was chosen as tutor to the young Prince Henry, who became Henry VIII. When Erasmus visited England, he called Skelton "the one light and glory of British letters," mainly because of his translations of the classics and his Latin verses. His translation of the 1st-century Greek historian, Diodorus Siculus,' "Bibliotheca Historica," Vol. I Text, edited by F. M. Salter and H. L. R. Edwards, has been published by *Oxford* (Early Eng. Text. Soc. 1956–57 2 vols. Vol. I $16.75 Vol. 2 $6.25).

Skelton directed his satire against the clergy, particularly Cardinal Wolsey. After a lifelong hatred of Henry's Chancellor, Skelton was finally forced to take sanctuary at Westminster in 1523 for writing "Why Came Ye Not to Court." He died before Wolsey met his downfall.

THE POETICAL WORKS. Ed. by Alexander Dyce. 1843. *AMS Press* 2 vols. set $55.00

THE COMPLETE POEMS OF JOHN SKELTON, LAUREATE. Ed. by Philip Henderson. Modernized in spelling, based on the Dyce ed. of 1843. 1931. *Dutton* $7.00

THE POEMS. Sel. and ed. by Robert S. Kinsman. The Clarendon Medieval and Tudor Texts Series. *Oxford* 1969 $7.25 pap. $4.25

A BALLADE OF THE SCOTTYSSHE KYNGE. 1513 1882. *Gale* 1969 $4.75

MAGNIFICENCE. (Magnyfycence, A Goodly Interlude and a Mery) written c. 1515 first printed c. 1530. A moral play. 1910. *AMS Press* $15.00

Books about Skelton

John Skelton, Laureate. By William Nelson. 1939. *Russell & Russell* 1964 $8.50
Skelton and Satire. By Arthur Ray Heiserman. *Univ. of Chicago Press* 1961 $9.50
John Skelton's Poetry. By Stanley Eugene Fish. This "major reassessment of the early Tudor poet . . . proves to be a brilliant explication of the Skelton canon"—(*LJ*). *Yale Univ. Press* Studies in English 1965 $7.50

WYATT (OR WIAT), SIR THOMAS THE ELDER. 1503–1542.

Born in Kent and educated at St. John's College, Cambridge, Wyatt served King Henry VIII as a diplomat and ambassador to Spain and to the Emperor Charles V. His poetry reflects the influence of French and Italian literature (notably the Italian sonneteer Petrarch), and also the troubled course of his career as a courtier: he was twice arrested and imprisoned (1536, 1541) by Henry VIII.

Wyatt introduced the Italian sonnet into English verse, for the most part translating and paraphrasing Petrarchan originals, and employing rhyme-schemes derived from other Italian poets. His poetry also includes epigrams, satires, and devotional poems, as well as many lyrics that look to Chaucerian precedent in form and outlook. Patricia Thomson calls him "a Chaucerian student of the relation between experience and conventional behavior or doctrine." He and Henry Howard, Earl of Surrey (1517–1547), who established the "English" sonnet form (3 quatrains and a couplet, rhyming *abab, cdcd, efef, gg*), were described by a contemporary critic as "the first reformers of our English metre and style." Surrey's poems have been most recently edited by Emrys Jones (*Oxford* 1964 $5.50 pap. $3.50).

Although Wyatt's poems circulated in manuscript during his lifetime, and a few appeared in print before 1540, the bulk of his work was first published after his death in the poetical collection known as "Tottel's Miscellany: Songs and Sonnets written by the Right Honorable Lord Henry Howard Late Earl of Surrey and Others" in 1557, ed. by Hyder Rollins (*Harvard Univ. Press* 2nd ed. 2 vols. 1965 set $18.00). Ninety-seven of the 271 poems in this anthology are attributed to Wyatt, 40 to Surrey.

A complete and definitive edition of the "Collected Poems," ed. by Kenneth Muir and Patricia Thomson, has recently been published (*Liverpool Univ. Press* 1969). Unfortunately it is not yet available from American distributors.

THE WORKS OF HENRY HOWARD AND OF SIR THOMAS WYATT THE ELDER. Ed. by George Frederick Nott. 2 vols. 1815–16. *AMS Press* each $38.00 set $75.00

THE POEMS. Ed. by Agnes K. Foxwell. 2 vols. 1913. *Russell & Russell* 1964 set $20.00

COLLECTED POEMS. Ed. by Kenneth Muir. *Harvard Univ. Press* Muses' Lib. 1950 $6.00 pap. $2.25

THE POETRY: A Selection and a Study. By E. M. W. Tillyard. Elizabethan Gallery Series. 1929. *Somerset Pub.* $7.50

Books about Wyatt

A Study of Sir Thomas Wyatt's Poems. By Agnes K. Foxwell. 1911. *Russell & Russell* 1964 $7.50
Sir Thomas Wyatt and His Background. By Edmund Kerchever Chambers. 1933. *Russell & Russell* 1965 $8.00
Sir Thomas Wyatt, and Some Collected Studies. By Patricia Thomson. *Stanford Univ. Press* 1964 $8.50

SPENSER, EDMUND. 1552–1599.

Spenser was born in London; he attended the Merchant's Taylors' School there, proceeding to Cambridge University in 1569. About 1579 he came to know Sir Philip Sidney; his first significant work, "The Shepheardes Calender," published under a pseudonym in 1580, and consisting of 12 "eclogues," one for each month of the year, was dedicated to Sidney. Spenser hoped for advancement at the court of Queen Elizabeth; but in August, 1580, he took a minor position in Ireland, where he spent the rest of his life, save for two visits to England. In 1594 he married Elizabeth Boyle, in Cork; the sonnet sequence "Amoretti" bears on his courtship, and the great marriage hymn, "Epithalamion," celebrates the wedding.

The first three books of Spenser's allegorical epic-romance "The Faerie Queene" appeared in 1590; three more in 1596. A fragment, the "Cantos of Mutabilitie," which may or may not have been intended to form part of the great poem, appeared in 1609, after Spenser's death. Spenser appended a "Letter" to his friend Sir Walter Raleigh to the edition of 1590, explaining "the general intention and meaning" of "The Faerie Queene," and giving some account of his sources and allegorical method. Although Spenser planned to write twelve books in all, only six, and the two "Cantos of Mutabilitie," survive. The rest may possibly have been destroyed by Irish rebels when, in 1598, they sacked Spenser's Irish residence at Kilcolman; but it is equally possible that the poet never managed to bring his massively planned work to completion.

C. S. Lewis's "The Allegory of Love: A Study in Medieval Tradition" (*Oxford* 1936 $7.50 Galaxy Bks. pap. $2.95) relates Spenser to the tradition of the earlier courtly romances. *Russell & Russell* has reprinted several older studies of Spenser that remain valuable, notably those by Cory, B. E. C. Davis, Isabel Rathborne, and Janet Spens.

Works: A Variorum Edition. Ed. by Edwin Greenlaw, Charles Grosvenor Osgood, Frederick Morgan Padelford and Ray Heffner. *Johns Hopkins Univ. Press* 11 vols. Vols. 1–6 The Faerie Queene (1932–38) each $17.50 Vols. 7 and 8 The Minor Poems (1943 1947) each $17.50 Vol 9 Index to the Poetry (1957) $10.00 Vol. 10 The Prose Works (1949) $17.50 Vol. 11 The Life of Edmund Spenser by Alexander Corbin Judson (1945) $10.00. This exhaustive and massive edition follows in the main the edition of 1596, all other important editions and their variants being noted.

Works. Ed. by John Hughes. 6 vols. 1715. *AMS Press* each $13.75 set $82.50; ed. by H. J. Todd. With the principal illustrations of the various commentators. 1805. *AMS Press* 8 vols. each $14.50 set $115.00

The Complete Poetical Works. Ed. by R. E. N. Dodge. *Houghton* Cambridge Eds. 1908 $10.00

The Poetical Works. Ed. by James Cruickshanks Smith and Ernest de Selincourt. *Oxford* Stand. Authors 1924 $7.00 pap. $4.95

Edmund Spenser's Poetry. Ed. by Hugh Maclean. *Norton* Critical Eds. 1968 $8.50 pap. $3.25

Minor Poems. Ed. by Ernest de Selincourt. *Oxford* 1910 $11.50

Selections. Ed. by S. K. Heninger, Jr. *Houghton* Riv. Eds. pap. $5.15; ed. by Ian C. Sowton 1967 *Odyssey* 1968 pap. $1.80; (with essays by Hazlitt, Coleridge, and Leigh Hunt) ed. by W. Renwick *Oxford* 1923 $2.50

Selected Poetry. Ed. by A. Kent Hieatt and Constance B. Hieatt. 1969. *AHM Pub. Corp.* Crofts Classics pap. $.85; ed. by A. C. Hamilton *New Am. Lib.* Signet pap. $1.25

Selections from the Minor Poems and The Faerie Queene. Ed. by Frank Kermode. *Oxford* 1965 $2.50

Faerie Queene, Bks. 1 and 2, The Mutability Cantos and Representative Minor Poems. Ed. by Robert L. Kellogg and Oliver L. Steele. *Odyssey* 1965 pap. $1.95

SHEPHEARDES CALENDER. [Shepherd's Calendar] 1580. (And Other Poems) ed. with
   introd. by Philip Henderson *Dutton* Everyman's $3.50; facsimile of 1579 ed. with
   introd. by H. Oscar Sommer. Spenser Society Publications 1890. *Burt Franklin*
   $25.00

THE FAERIE QUEENE. 1590. Ed. by Richard Morris *Dutton* Everyman's 2 vols. each
   $3.50; ed. by Edwin Greenlaw and others (included in "Works" above) *Johns Hop-
   kins Univ. Press* 6 vols. each $17.50; Bks. 1 and 2 (and The Mutability Cantos and
   Representative Minor Poems) ed. by Robert Kellogg and Oliver L. Steele *Odyssey*
   1965 pap. $1.95; ed. by J. C. Smith *Oxford* 1909 2 vols. set $29.00 Bks. 1 and 2 ed.
   by P. C. Bayley Bk. 1 (1966) $2.50 Bk. 2 (1965) $2.75

COMPLAINTS, CONTAINING SUNDRIE-SMALL POEMES OF THE WORLDS VANITIE. 1591
   1594. The English Experience Series. facsimile of 1594 ed. *Da Capo* $18.00; repr. of
   1928 ed. by W. L. Renwick *Scholarly Press* 1970 $14.50

DAPHNAÏDA. 1591. (And Other Poems) ed. by W. L. Renwick 1929 *Somerset Pub.*
   $11.50

AMORETTI AND EPITHALAMION. 1595. The English Experience Series. facsimile ed. *Da
   Capo* $10.00

COLIN CLOUTS COME HOME AGAINE. 1595. The English Experience Series. facsimile
   ed. *Da Capo* $8.00

FOWRE HYMNES. From the 1596 ed. of Daphnaïda, with Fowre Hymnes. The English
   Experience Series. facsimile ed. *Da Capo* $8.00

Books about Spenser

Spenser. By Richard W. Church. 1879. Ed. by John Morley. 1887. *AMS Press* repr. of 1887 1968 $7.80;
   Folcroft repr. of 1887 ed. $7.50; *Gale* repr. of 1906 ed. 1968 $7.80; *Richard West* repr. of 1887 ed.
   $7.75
Edmund Spenser: An Essay in Renaissance Poetry. By William L. Renwick. 1925. *Folcroft* lib. bdg.
   $4.50; *St. Martin's* $4.50
Classical Mythology in the Poetry of Edmund Spenser. By Henry G. Lotspeich. Princeton Studies in Eng-
   lish. 1932. *Folcroft* $4.50; *Gordian* $5.00; *Octagon* $5.00. Lists of Spenser's classical allusions with a
   valuable introductory essay.
Life of Edmund Spenser. By Alexander C. Judson. Vol. 11 of the variorum ed. of the "Works" listed
   above. *Johns Hopkins Univ. Press* 1945 $10.00
A Spenser Handbook. By Harry S. V. Jones. *Appleton* 1950 $7.30
Spenser's Images of Love. By Clive Staples Lewis. Ed. by Alastair Fowler. *Cambridge* 1967 $6.50
The Allegorical Temper: Vision and Reality in Book II of Spenser's Faerie Queene. By Harry Berger.
   Yale Studies in English. 1957. *Shoe String* 1967 $6.50. Written with unusual clarity, vigor, and wit.
Short Time's Endless Monument: The Symbolism of Numbers in Edmund Spenser's Epithalamion. By
   A. Kent Hieatt. 1960 *Kennikat* 1971 $7.00
Form and Convention in the Poetry of Edmund Spenser. Selected papers from the English Institute,
   1959–1960. Ed. by William Nelson. *Columbia* 1961 $7.00. These well-written critiques add much to
   the modern understanding of the poet.
The Structure of Allegory in The Faerie Queene. By Albert Charles Hamilton. *Oxford* 1961 $8.50
Spenser's 'Shepheardes Calender': A Study in Elizabethan Allegory. By Paul E. McLane. *Univ. of Notre
   Dame Press* 1961 $6.95 pap. $2.95
The Poetry of Edmund Spenser: A Study. By William Nelson. *Columbia* 1963 $10.00 pap. $2.95
Spenser's Image of Nature: Wild Man and Shepherd in The Faerie Queene. By Donald Cheney. Yale
   Studies in English. *Yale Univ. Press* 1966 $7.50
   An "impressively contemporary study [which considers] generally Spenser's use of pastoral and of chi-
   valric narrative allegory [and explores] 'specific problems of interpretation' within areas of the
   text . . . least often studied"—(*LJ*).

Spenser: A Collection of Critical Essays. Ed. by Harry Berger, Jr. Twentieth Century Views Series. *Prentice-Hall* 1968 $5.95 pap. $1.95

Prince of Poets: Essays on Edmund Spenser. Ed. by John R. Elliott. *New York Univ. Press* 1968 $8.95 pap. $2.45

The Veil of Allegory. By Michael J. Murrin. *Univ. of Chicago Press* 1969 $8.75. Stimulating discussion of allegory with special reference to Spenser.

Spenser, Marvell, and Renaissance Pastoral. By Patrick Cullen. *Harvard Univ. Press* 1970 $7.00

Edmund Spenser. Ed. by Paul J. Alpers. *Penguin* Critical Anthologies. 1970. *Peter Smith* $4.50

Spenser's Anatomy of Heroism: A Commentary on the Faerie Queene. By Maurice Evans. *Cambridge* 1970 $9.50

The Faerie Queene: A Companion for Readers. By Rosemary Freeman. *Univ. of California Press* 1970 $7.50

Spenser and Literary Pictorialism. By John B. Bender. *Princeton Univ. Press* 1972 $8.50

Three useful bibliographical volumes are:

A Reference Guide to Edmund Spenser. By Frederic I. Carpenter. 1923. *Peter Smith* 1950 $5.00

Edmund Spenser: A Bibliographic Supplement. By Dorothy Atkinson. 1937. *Haskell House* 1969 $11.95

An Annotated Bibliography of Edmund Spenser, 1937–60. By Waldo F. McNeir and Foster Provost. 1962. *AMS Press* $32.50

SIDNEY, SIR PHILIP. 1554–1586.

Regarded by his contemporaries as epitomizing the attributes of character they admired, Sidney (the nephew of Robert Dudley, Earl of Leicester, the favorite of Queen Elizabeth), served the Queen as courtier and ambassador before his death in battle in the Low Countries. Elizabethans thought highly of his pastoral prose romance "Arcadia," 1590 (English Reprint Series *Kent State Univ. Press* 1971 $8.00), and of his influential critical treatise "A Defence of Poesie," 1595 (editions available from *Barnes & Noble, Bobbs, Oxford,* and *California State Univ.* Renaissance Editions). His sonnet sequence "Astrophil and Stella" ("Star-lover and Star" 1951 o.p. in separate volumes) is the first and in some ways the finest of the great Elizabethan sonnet cycles. Although it contains hints of a liaison between Sidney and Penelope Devereux, Lady Rich, what gives the sequence its special appeal is Sidney's ability to bring fresh vigor to poetical conventions and to dramatize the entire sequence of 108 sonnets.

An edition of Sidney's "Complete Prose Works" ed. by A. Feuillerat in 4 volumes is available from *Cambridge Univ. Press,* 1912–26 $14.50–$19.50.

The Complete Poems. Ed. by Alexander B. Grosart. 3 vols. 1877. *Bks. for Libraries* set $32.50

The Poems. Ed. by William Ringler. *Oxford* 1962. $16.00. The definitive edition.

The Psalms of Sir Philip Sidney and the Countess of Pembroke. Ed. by J. C. A. Rathmell. *New York Univ. Press* 1963 $10.00. A verse translation, first published in 1843, of which 43 are by Sidney, the rest by his sister.

Selected Prose and Poetry. Ed. by Robert Kimbrough. *Holt* 1970 pap. $3.50

Books about Sidney

Three Studies in the Renaissance: Sidney, Jonson, Milton. By Richard B. Young and others. 1958 *Shoe String* 1969 $8.00

Symmetry and Sense: The Poetry of Sir Philip Sidney. By Robert L. Montgomery, Jr. 1961. *Greenwood* $8.50

Sidney's Poetry: Contexts and Interpretations. By David M. Kalstone. *Harvard Univ. Press* 1965 $5.50; *Norton* Norton Lib. 1970 pap. $1.85. The best general study of Sidney's art.

Heroic Love: Studies in Sidney and Spenser. By Mark Rose. *Harvard Univ. Press* 1968 $4.75

CAMPION, THOMAS. 1567–1620.

A practicing physician throughout his life, Campion wrote poetry, songs, masques, and a treatise on music and on poetry. In his introduction to the collected works (*below*) Walter Davis says, "Campion's pursuit of the movements of sound is recorded in that strange but subtle treatise, 'Observations in the Art of English Poesie' [1602 *Da Capo* The English Experience Series $5.00], and its fruits are preserved in his songbooks. He is a poet—perhaps *the* poet—of the auditory rather than the visual imagination. . . . He offers us experiences that strike the ear."

WORKS. Ed. by A. H. Bullen. 1889 *Folcroft* 1973 $35.00; ("Songs, Masques, and Treatises, with a Selection of Latin Verse") ed. with introd. by Walter R. Davis 1967 *Norton* Norton Lib. pap. $2.95; ed. by Percival Vivian 1909 *Oxford* 1966 $8.00

SELECTED SONGS. Ed. by W. H. Auden. *Godine* 1973 $15.00 deluxe ed. $40.00

SONGS AND MASQUES, with OBSERVATIONS IN THE ART OF ENGLISH POESIE. Ed. by A. H. Bullen 1903. *Folcroft* 1973 $20.00

Books about Campion

England's Musical Poet, Thomas Campion. By Miles M. Kastendieck. 1938. *Russell & Russell* 1963 $7.00
Thomas Campion: Poet, Composer, Physician. By Edward Lowbury and others. *Barnes & Noble* 1970 $7.50

DONNE, JOHN. 1573–1631.

The Dean of St. Paul's, the foremost preacher of his day, has had an influence on English literature that is singularly wide and deep. The great revival of Donne in the 20th century is reflected in the poetry of a number of poets, including T. S. Eliot (*q. v.*). Donne was educated at Oxford and Cambridge. His early career was ruined by his secret marriage to the niece of his employer, the Lord Keeper Sir Thomas Egerton. His early poetry—sensual love lyrics and satires on society—was cynical and realistic. After 1601, when he began his satirical "Progresse of the Soule," it became more serious in tone. The greatest of the "metaphysical" poets, whose intense passion is interwoven with reasoning and religion, he was an exquisite shaper of ideas in compact form and made use of "conceits" and inversions to produce verse of great subtlety and power. He became Dean of St. Paul's in 1619, and his prose "Sermons" and satires are his most important contribution to literature after some of the lyrics and elegies. His earnest and vigorous mind, expressed in flashes of wit and beauty, and his daring phrases—coupled with a certain roughness of form—have made him attractive to modern readers. Izaak Walton (*q. v.*), his intimate and adoring friend, has written the famous contemporary biography in his "Lives," first published in 1640.

COMPLETE POETRY AND SELECTED PROSE. Ed. with introd. by Charles M. Coffin. *Modern Library* 1952 $2.95

POETRY AND PROSE. Ed. by Frank J. Warnke. *Modern Library* 1967 pap. $1.65; (with Izaak Walton's life, appreciations by Ben Jonson, Dryden, Coleridge, and others) introd. and notes by H. W. Garrod. Clarendon English Series *Oxford* 1946 $2.10

SELECTIONS. Ed. by Andrews Wanning. *Dell* Laurel Leaf Lib. pap. $.40; *Pyramid* pap. $.50

Poetry:

COMPLETE POETRY. Ed. by Hugh l'Anson Fausset. *Dutton* Everyman's 1936 $3.50; ed. by Roger Bennett *Hendricks House* 1958 $3.50 pap. $1.95; (with the "Complete Poetry of William Blake") *Modern Library* $4.95; ed. with introd. notes and variants by John T. Shawcross *New York Univ. Press* 1967 $12.50; *Doubleday* Anchor Bks. 1967 pap. $4.50

POEMS. Ed. by H. J. C. Grierson from the old editions and numerous manuscripts. Oxford English Texts. *Oxford* 2 vols. 1912 $19.25 Stand. Authors 1933 $6.00 pap. $2.95

COMPLETE ENGLISH POEMS. Ed. by A. J. Smith. *Penguin* 1971 pap. $3.75

JOHN DONNE'S POETRY. Sel. and ed. by Arthur L. Clements. *Norton* Critical Lib. 1966 pap. $1.75

SELECTED POEMS. Ed. by M. A. Shaaber. Crofts Classics Series. *AHM Pub. Corp.* pap. $.85; ed. by James Reeves *Barnes & Noble* 1952 $1.75; ed. by Marius Bewley *New Am. Lib.* Signet pap. $1.75; ed. by John Hayward *Penguin* pap. $1.25

DIVINE POEMS. Ed. by Helen L. Gardner. *Oxford* 1952 $8.00

THE ELEGIES AND THE SONGS AND SONNETS. Ed. by Helen L. Gardner. *Oxford* 1965 $11.25

THE SONGS AND SONETS OF JOHN DONNE. An *editio minor* with introd. and explanatory notes by Theodore Redpath. *Barnes & Noble* 1957 $5.25 pap. $3.00. Because of its notes, "Redpath's is the reader's edition."

SATIRES, EPIGRAMS, AND VERSE LETTERS. Ed. by W. Milgate. *Oxford* 1967 $13.00

THE ANNIVERSARIES. 1611. (First published with the title "An Anatomy of the World.") Ed. with introd. by Frank Manley. *Johns Hopkins Press* 1963 $7.50

Prose:

SELECTED PROSE. Ed. by Evelyn Simpson, Helen L. Gardner and Timothy Healy. Includes Paradoxes and Problems; Biathanatos; Pseudo-Martyr; Essays in Divinity; Devotions upon Emergent Occasions; Letters; Sermons. *Oxford* 1967 $9.75

THE SERMONS. Ed. with introds. and critical apparatus by George R. Potter and Evelyn M. Simpson. *Univ. of California Press* 1953–1962 10 vols. set $172.50

  The publication of the 160 extant sermons is completed, and this may be considered the standard edition. Vol. I contains essays on the bibliography of the printed sermons, a study of manuscripts, textual problems, literary value, and an introduction on background and content. The sermons are presented in exact transcriptions with introductions on their contents and circumstances of delivery, and with textual notes. Vol. 10 contains "appendixes on Donne's sources (a study of high scholarship), notes on the printed folios of 1640, 1649 and 1661, an index of Biblical texts, addenda and corrigenda, and a general index."

SERMONS: Selected Passages. With an essay by Logan Pearsall Smith. *Oxford* 1919 1952 $7.00

SERMONS ON THE PSALMS AND GOSPELS: With a Selection of Prayers and Meditations. Ed. with introd. by Evelyn M. Simpson. Contains 10 sermons and a few prayers and meditations with explanatory footnotes; a good introduction to Donne's prose. *Univ. of California Press* 1963 $7.00 pap. $1.95

DONNE'S PREBEND SERMONS. Ed. by Janel Mueller. *Harvard Univ. Press* 1971 $10.00

PRAYERS. Ed. by Herbert H. Umbach. *College & Univ. Press* 1962 pap. $1.25

ESSAYS IN DIVINITY. Ed. by Evelyn M. Simpson. *Oxford* 1952 $7.75

DEVOTIONS, with DEATH'S DUEL and Selections from Walton's Life of Donne. *Univ. of Michigan Press* 1959 $4.40 pap. $1.95

IGNATIUS HIS CONCLAVE. 1611. English and Latin text ed. by T. S. Healy. *Oxford* 1969 $10.25. Donne's commentary on the Jesuits, and religious controversy in general.

DEVOTIONS UPON EMERGENT OCCASIONS. 1624. *Folcroft* 1973 lib. bdg. $25.00

DEATHS DUELL. 1632. Ed. by Geoffrey Keynes. *Godine* 1972 $12.00 deluxe ed. $40.00

IVVENILIA, or CERTAINE PARADOXES, AND PROBLEMES. 1633. The English Experience Series. facsimile ed. *Da Capo* $7.00

Books about Donne

Lives of John Donne, Sir Henry Wotton, Richard Hooker, George Herbert, and Robert Sanderson. By Izaak Walton. With introd. by George Saintsbury. *Oxford* World's Class. $2.50

The Life and Letters of John Donne. By Edmund Gosse. 1899. *Somerset Pub.* 2 vols. set $29.50
"It is extremely unreliable. All students of Donne need to be on their guard against . . . Gosse's habitual inaccuracy and constitutional inability to distinguish between fact and surmise"—(*Encyclopaedia Britannica*).

John Donne: A Study in Discord. By Hugh l'Anson Fausset. 1924 *Russell & Russell* 1967 $10.00; *Somerset Pub.* $15.00

Donne, the Craftsman: An Essay upon the Structure of the Songs and Sonnets. By Pierre Legouis. 1928 *Russell & Russell* 1962 $8.00

The Donne Tradition. By George Williamson. 1930. *Octagon* 1973 lib bdg. $10.50

A Garland for John Donne, 1631–1931. Ed. by Theodore Spencer. 1931. *Peter Smith* $4.50. Valuable essays by T. S. Eliot and others.

Donne's Imagery: A Study in Creative Sources. By Milton Rugoff. 1939. *Russell & Russell* 1961 $7.50

John Donne: His Flight from Mediaevalism. By Michael F. Moloney. 1944 *Russell & Russell* 1965 $7.50; *Folcroft* 1973 $17.50

A Study of the Prose Works of John Donne. By Evelyn M. Simpson. *Oxford* 2nd ed. 1948 $7.50

Donne's Poetry and Modern Criticism. By Leonard Unger. 1950. *Russell & Russell* 1962 $8.50

The Monarch of Wit. By James B. Leishman. *Hutchinson Univ. Lib.* (dist. by Hillary House) 1951 1962 $5.00 pap. $2.50

Donne's Poetry: Essays in Literary Analysis. By Clay Hunt. 1954. *Shoe String* 1970 $8.00

Contrary Music: The Prose Style of John Donne. By Joan Webber. *Univ. of Wisconsin Press* 1963 $7.50. The best book on this subject.

John Donne's Lyrics: The Eloquence of Action. By Arnold Stein. *Univ. of Minnesota Press* 1962 $5.75

John Donne: A Collection of Critical Essays. Ed. by Helen L. Gardner. *Prentice-Hall* 1963 $5.95 Spectrum Bks. pap. $1.95

John Donne, Petrarchist: Italian Conceits and Love Theory in the Songs and Sonnets. By Donald Guss. *Wayne State Univ. Press* 1966 $8.95

The Progress of the Soul: The Interior Career of John Donne. By Richard Hughes. *Morrow* 1968 $7.95; *Apollo* 1969 pap. $2.50

John Donne: A Life. By Robert C. Bald. Ed. by Wesley Milgate. *Oxford* 1970 $15.00. The definitive biography.

John Donne's Poetry. By Wilbur Sanders. *Cambridge* 1971 $8.50

JONSON, BEN. 1572–1637.

A great comic dramatist and an influential critic, Jonson was also the author of many lyrics, epigrams, verse-letters, satires, and odes in various meters. reflecting his interest in classical literature and his command of its various modes of poetry. His poems in turn influenced the taste and style of his contemporaries and successors, especially the group known as the "Tribe of Ben," which included Herrick (*q. v.*), Thomas Carew, and others. The "Cavalier Poets" (Lovelace, Suckling, and many lesser figures) looked chiefly to Jonson's verse for their model.

COMPLETE WORKS. Ed. by Charles Harold Herford and others. *Oxford* 11 vols. 1925–52 Vols. I–8 each $12.00 vols 9–11 each $13.75. Jonson's poems appear in Vol. 8 of this definitive edition; notes on the poems are in Vol. 11.

COMPLETE POETRY. Ed. by William B. Hunter, Jr. *New York Univ. Press* 1963 Stuart Eds. $2.50; *Norton* Norton Lib. 1968 pap. $3.50

POEMS. Ed. by George B. Johnston. *Harvard* Muses' Lib. 1954 $6.00 pap. $1.95

JONSON AND THE CAVALIERS. Ed. by Maurice Hussey. *Barnes & Noble* 1966 pap. $1.00

Books about Jonson

> Martial and English Epigram from Sir Thomas Wyatt to Ben Jonson. By Thomas K. Whipple. 1925. *Phaeton Press* 1970 $6.00
>
> Ben Johnson and Elizabeth Music. By Willa M. Evans. 1929. With a new preface by the author. *Da Capo* 1965 $5.95
>
> Classical Influences on the Tribe of Ben. By Kathryn McEuen. 1939. *Folcroft* $8.95; *Octagon* 1968 $10.50
>
> Ben Jonson: Poet. By George B. Johnston. 1945. *Octagon* 1970 $8.50
>
> Ben Jonson's Poems: A Study of the Plain Style. By Wesley Trimpi. *Stanford Univ. Press* 1962 $8.50
>
> The Poetry of Ben Jonson. By John G. Nichols. *Routledge & Kegan Paul* 1969 $9.25

HERRICK, ROBERT. 1591–1674.

Swinburne (*q. v.*) called Herrick "the greatest song writer ever born of the English race." He left some 1,200 short lyrical poems. All that he thought worthy of preservation he published in 1648 in "Hesperides and Noble Numbers," his only book. His verse is intensely musical. Edmund Gosse said, "There is not a sunnier book in the world than the 'Hesperides'." However, his verse is by no means trivial, reflecting as it does classical and Anglican ceremony, English folklore and timeless myth. Herrick took Holy Orders and lived a secluded life in Dean Prior, a Devonshire vicarage, never marrying, and in his long life saw England ruled by Elizabeth I, James II, Charles I, Oliver Cromwell, and Charles II.

THE COMPLETE POETRY. Ed. by J. Max Patrick. *New York Univ. Press* 1963 $12.50; *Norton* Norton Lib. 1968 pap. $2.95

POETICAL WORKS. Ed. by L. C. Martin. *Oxford* Eng. Texts 1956 $14.50

POEMS. Ed. by Winfield T. Scott. *T. Y. Crowell* Poets Series 1967 $3.50; Ed. by L. C. Martin. *Oxford* Stand. Authors $8.00 World's Class. $1.75

Books about Herrick

> Robert Herrick: A Biographical and Critical Study. By Frederic Moorman. The best life and an outstanding scholarly work. 1910. *Russell & Russell* 1962 $12.00
>
> The Universe of Robert Herrick. By Sidney Musgrove. 1950. *Folcroft* $5.50. An important pioneer study.
>
> Two Gentle Men: The Lives of George Herbert and Robert Herrick. By Marchette Chute. The two poets, both ministers of the church, are contrasted but shown as representative of their time. *Dutton* 1959 $6.95
>
> Robert Herrick. By Roger B. Rollin. English Authors Series. *Twayne* 1966 $5.00

HERBERT, GEORGE. 1593–1633.

The religious poetry of George Herbert, one of the leading metaphysical poets, has the unusual distinction of being poetic as well as religious. In his early life he served as Public Orator at Cambridge, writing all the letters that passed between the university and royalty or persons of high estate. If "Donne may be described as the poet of religious doubt, of strain, of anxiety, Herbert is the poet of religious faith, of submission, of acceptance"—(R. M. Adams). As Rector of Bemerton, he wrote "The Country Parson" (1956, o. p.), observations on the life he led there, as well as poems expressive of his new contentment. He died after being Rector for three years. His fame owes much to Izaak Walton's (*q. v.*) discussion in the "Lives" (*Oxford* World's Class. $2.75). Herbert's poetry is interestingly discussed by Joan Bennett, Helen White, and George Williamson in their studies of metaphysical poetry. (*See "Selected Bibliography" at opening of this Chapter*).

WORKS. Ed. with a commentary by F. E. Hutchinson. *Oxford* 1941 $16.00

THE POEMS. Introd. by Helen L. Gardner. *Oxford* World's Class. 2nd ed. 1961 pap. $3.00

SELECTED POETRY. Ed. by Gareth Reeves *Barnes & Noble* 1971 $5.00; Ed. by Joseph H. Summers *New Am. Lib.* Signet 1967 pap. $1.25; (with the title "Herbert") ed. by W. H. Auden *Penguin* 1972 pap. $1.75

THE LATIN POETRY OF GEORGE HERBERT: A Bilingual Edition. Trans. by John Mark McCloskey and Paul R. Murphy. *Ohio Univ. Press* 1964 $5.50

THE TEMPLE: Sacred Poems and Private Ejaculations. 1633. *Bks. for Libraries* 1876, reissued with an essay by J. H. Shorthouse 1882 $10.75; (with "A Priest to the Temple") 1671. Ed. by Francis Meynell. 1927. *Somerset Pub.* $15.50

Books about Herbert

George Herbert, His Religion and Art. By Joseph H. Summers. *Harvard Univ. Press* 1954 $7.00

Two Gentle Men: The Lives of George Herbert and Robert Herrick. By Marchette Chute. *Dutton* 1959 $6.95. Authoritative and written in a simple, direct, and entertaining style.

George Herbert. By T. S. Eliot. *British Bk. Centre* 1962 $2.38 pap. $1.20

A Reading of George Herbert. By Rosemond Tuve. *Chicago Univ. Press* 1962 $6.75

George Herbert's Lyrics. By Arnold Stein. *Johns Hopkins Univ. Press* 1968 $7.95

CRASHAW, RICHARD. 1613–1649.

Crashaw differs from the other English "metaphysical" poets chiefly by virtue of his intense attachment to Roman Catholicism and to the spirit of the Counter-Reformation. The son of a Puritan clergyman, he attended Peterhouse College, Cambridge, and took Anglican orders in 1638; but during the Civil Wars he was converted to the Church of Rome, and (in 1646) went to Italy, where he was made a canon at Lorete shortly before his death at that place. His poetry is strongly influenced by Spanish and Italian models, notably the work of Giambattista Marino, whose poetry is marked by extravagantly sensuous conceits. Crashaw obsessively employs the imagery of wounds, kisses, nests, breasts, milk and blood: his poetry is not to every critic's taste. "Each poem of Crashaw's is a great *performance*; T. S. Eliot has suggested an analogy with the interior of St. Peter's at Rome"—(Hugh Kenner).

POEMS, ENGLISH, LATIN, AND GREEK. Ed. by Leonard C. Martin. *Oxford* 2nd ed. 1957 $11.25

COMPLETE POETRY. Ed. by George W. Williams. *Doubleday* 1968 Anchor Bks. 1970 pap. $3.50

Books about Crashaw

Richard Crashaw: A Study in Baroque Sensibility. By Austin Warren. 1957. *Somerset Pub.* $11.50; *Univ. of Michigan Press* Ann Arbor Bks. pap. $1.35

Rhyme and Meaning in Crashaw's Poetry. By Mary Ellen Rickey. 1957. *Haskell House* 1972 $8.95

Image and Symbol in the Sacred Poetry of Richard Crashaw. By George W. Williams. *Univ. of South Carolina Press* 1963 $7.95

The Art of Ecstasy: Teresa, Bernini and Crashaw. By Robert Torsten Petersson. *Athenaeum* 1970 $8.95

MILTON, JOHN. 1608–1674.

Milton's tremendous poetic gift showed itself early: in the two companion pieces written in 1633, "*L'Allegro*" (the mirthful man) and "*Il Penseroso*" (the contemplative man); "Comus, A Masque," which was acted in 1634, a work which "rose into a poem to the glory of temperance and under its allegory attacked the court"; and "Lycidas," 1637, a pastoral elegy mourning the death of the poet's college friend, Edward King, who was drowned in crossing the Irish Channel.

Milton's prose belongs to his middle life, when he turned away from poetry for a time, to help bring about "the establishment of real liberty" (as he wrote in 1654); from 1640 to 1660 he actively supported the Puritan cause, serving Cromwell as Latin Secretary from 1649 to 1655. His greatest prose work, the "Areopagitica" or "Speech for the Liberty of Unlicensed Printing," took its name from the Areopagus, the hill of Ares, on the site of the Acropolis in Athens, where a judicial court met. (*See Chapter 1, Books about Books, Section on Censorship.*)

"Paradise Lost" was published in 1667, in ten books; the 2nd edition of 1674 contains 12 books, of which Books 1, 2, 4, and 9 are most admired. Milton had been destined for the Church, but while in Cambridge gave up his intention of taking orders. Theology continued throughout his life to occupy his thoughts, particularly in the great epic poem of the Fall of Man, "Paradise Lost." "Paradise Regained" is its sequel.

For the last 22 years of his life Milton was blind. His three daughters, children of his first wife, Mary Powell, read aloud to him in Greek and Latin and Hebrew, and the youngest took down all of "Paradise Lost" in dictation. Mary Powell died in 1652; Milton married Katherine Woodcock in 1656, and, after her death in 1658, married Elizabeth Minshull in 1663. These later marriages seem to have alienated his children from him. Something of Milton's unhappy experiences in marriage certainly echoes in his last great poem, "Samson Agonistes" (Samson the Athlete or Wrestler). This is written in the style of a Greek tragedy, the story founded on the biblical account of Samson's blindness and his deception at the hands of Delilah.

Milton's sonnets are few in number but are unsurpassed; "On His Blindness" is perhaps the most famous. He was a great Latin scholar, who wrote poetry in Latin which has been widely admired by classicists. *Russell & Russell* has reprinted early studies of Milton by R. D. Havens, I. Langdon, E. M. Pope, Denis Saurat, and E. N. S. Thompson.

WORKS. Ed. by Frank Allen Patterson and others. *Columbia* 1931–38 18 vols in 21 bks. index 1940 2 vols. Vols. I–2 in 4 pts. each $10.00 set $40.00 Vols. 3–18, index o.p.; *Somerset Pub.* repr. ed. 21 bks. in 23 vols. each $24.50 set $495.00. The first complete and definitive edition contains all the poetry considered to be genuine, all the variant readings of other editors, together with translations of such works as were not originally written in English.

THE PORTABLE MILTON. Ed. with introd. by Douglas Bush. *Viking* 1949 lib. bdg. $5.50 pap. $2.95. Includes Paradise Lost, Paradise Regained, Samson Agonistes, complete; early poems and sonnets, selections from prose works, including Areopagitica complete.

COMPLETE POETRY AND SELECTED PROSE. Ed. by Cleanth Brooks. *Modern Library* 1942 $2.95 pap. $1.45; (with English metrical translations of the Latin, Greek and Italian Poems) ed. by E. H. Visiak *Random* 1942 $12.50

THE STUDENT'S MILTON. Rev. by Frank A. Patterson. *Appleton* 1933 $10.50. Complete poetical works, with the greater part of his prose works added.

JOHN MILTON: Complete Poems and Major Prose. Ed. by Merritt Y. Hughes. *Odyssey* 1958 $8.75

Poetry:

COMPLETE POETICAL WORKS: Illinois Facsimile Edition. Ed. by Harris Francis Fletcher. *Univ. of Illinois Press* 4 vols. 1943–48 Vol. I The Minor Poems (1943) o. p. Vol. 2 Paradise Lost, 1st ed., 1667–1669 (1945) o. p. Vol. 3 Paradise Lost, 2nd ed., 1674 (1948) Vol. 4 Paradise Regained and Samson Agonistes, 1671 ed. (1948) each $20.00

POETICAL WORKS. Ed. by Helen Darbishire. Oxford English Texts. *Oxford* 2 vols. 1952–55 Vol. I Paradise Lost (1952) Vol. 2 Paradise Regain'd, Samson Agonistes, and Poems upon Several Occasions, both English and Latin (1955) each $8.00. This may be a final text from the scholar's point of view. Helen Darbishire was formerly Principal of Somerville College, Oxford.

COMPLETE POETICAL WORKS. Ed. by Frank Allen Patterson. *Appleton* 1930 (with new trans. of Italian, Latin, and Greek poems) rev. ed. 1933 $6.00; ed. by Douglas Bush *Houghton* 1941 Cambridge Eds. 1965 $8.75; ed. by James Holly Hanford *Ronald* 2nd ed. 1953 $5.50

COMPLETE POETRY. Ed. by John T. Shawcross. *New York Univ. Press* 1963 $12.50; *Doubleday* Anchor Bks. pap. $4.95

POEMS. Ed. by Helen Darbishire. *Oxford* 1961 $6.00

THE POEMS OF JOHN MILTON. Ed. by John Carey and Alastair Fowler. Longman/Norton Annotated English Poets Series. *Norton* 1972 $13.95

POEMS: The 1645 Edition, with Essays in Analysis. Ed. by Cleanth Brooks and John E. Hardy. 1952. *Gordian* 1968 $9.50

POEMS. *Dutton* Everyman's $3.50

COMPLETE ENGLISH POETRY. Ed. by John D. Jump. *Washington Square* 1964 pap. $.90

THE ENGLISH POEMS. Comp. by Walter W. Skeat; introd. by Charles Williams with a reader's guide to Milton. *Oxford* World's Class. $2.75

POEMS IN ENGLISH. With ills. by William Blake. 2 vols. 1926–27 *Scholarly Press* Vol. I Paradise Lost Vol. 2 Miscellaneous Poems, Paradise Regained, Samson Agonistes set $34.50

SHORTER POEMS. Ed. by Dennis H. Burden. *Barnes & Noble* 1970 $2.75

THE SONNETS. Ed. by John S. Smart. *Oxford* 1966 pap. $4.00

THE LATIN POEMS. Ed. with introd., English translations and notes by Walter McKellar. 1930 *Somerset Pub.* $15.50

ON THE MORNING OF CHRIST'S NATIVITY. Milton's hymn with ill. by William Blake. Ed. by Geoffrey Keynes. 1923. *Folcroft* $10.00

A MASKE: The Earlier Versons (Performed 1634) Ed. by S. E. Sprott. *Univ. of Toronto Press* 1973 $25.00

COMUS (1637) AND OTHER POEMS. Ed. by F. T. Prince. *Oxford* 1968 $1.85

PARADISE LOST. 1667. Ed. by Richard Bentley. 1732. *AMS Press* $16.00; ed. by B. Rajan *Asia Pub. House* bks. 1 and 2 $3.50; ed. by A. W. Verity *Cambridge* 2 vols. Vol. I Books 1 and 2 Vol. 2 Books 9 and 10 each $2.45; ed. by David Masson 1877. *Folcroft* $30.00 ed. by A. W. Verity 1921 $35.00; ed. by William G. Masden *Modern Library* 1969 pap. $1.25; (and Other Poems) introd. by Edward Le Comte *New Am. Lib.* Mentor Bks. pap. $.95; ed. by Merritt Y. Hughes *Odyssey* 1935 new ed. 1962 $3.00 pap. $1.45; ed. by Helen Darbishire (Vol. I of "Poetical Works" *above*) *Oxford* 1952 $8.00 ed. by F. T. Prince Bks. 1 and 2 1962 $1.80 ed. by R. E. C. Houghton Bks. 9 and 10 1969 $2.50

PARADISE REGAINED. 1671. (And the Minor Poems, Samson Agonistes) ed. by Merritt Y. Hughes. *Odyssey* 1935 $3.50

PARADISE LOST and PARADISE REGAINED. *Assoc. Booksellers* Airmont Bks. pap. $.95; ed. by Christopher Ricks *New Am. Lib.* Signet 1968 pap. $1.95

PARADISE LOST AND SELECTED POETRY AND PROSE. Ed. with introd. by Northrop Frye. *Holt* (Rinehart) 1951 pap. $3.00

PARADISE LOST; PARADISE REGAINED; SAMSON AGONISTES. With new introd. by Harold Bloom. *Macmillan* Collier Bks. 1962 pap. $.95

SAMSON AGONISTES. 1671. (And Shorter Poems) ed. by A. E. Barker. Crofts Classics Series. *AHM Pub. Corp.* pap. $.85; ed. by F. T. Prince *Oxford* 1957 $1.90

For other editions of "Paradise Lost," "Paradise Regained," or "Samson Agonistes" in various combinations, consult the general collections and selections, and the collections and selections of poetry above.

Prose:

THE COMPLETE PROSE WORKS. *Yale Univ. Press* 1953–. Vol. 1 1624–1642 ed. by Don M. Wolfe (1953) $20.00; Vol. 2 1643–1648 ed. by Ernest Sirluck (1959) $17.50; Vol. 3 1648–1649 ed. with introd. by Merritt Y. Hughes (1959) $15.00; Vol. 4 1650–1655 ed. by Don M. Wolfe (1966) 2 pts. set $20.00; Vol. 5 The History of Britain and the Miltonic State Papers ed. by French Fogle and J. Max Patrick (1970) 2 pts. set $20.00; Vol. 6 Christian Doctrine ed. by Maurice Kelley trans. by John Carey (1972) 2 pts. set $25.00

The prose works will be published complete and in chronological order in eight volumes in this thoroughly reedited edition, with full notes, facsimile title pages, new translations from the Latin and new appraisals of the works; the definitive scholarly edition.

PROSE WORKS. Sel. and ed. from the original texts with introd., notes, trans., and accounts of all his major prose writings by J. Max Patrick. *New York Univ. Press* 1967 $12.50; sel. and ed. by J. Max Patrick *Doubleday* Anchor Bks. 1967 pap. $3.95

PROSE SELECTIONS. Ed. by Merritt Y. Hughes. *Odyssey* 1947 $3.50

PROSE WRITINGS. *Dutton* 1955 Everyman's $3.50 pap. $1.95

AN APOLOGY AGAINST A PAMPHLET CALLED A MODEST CONFUTATION OF THE ANIMADVERSIONS UPON THE REMONSTRANT AGAINST SMECTYMNUS. 1642. Pamphlet. Ed. by Milford C. Jochums. Facsimile; crit. ed. *Univ. of Illinois Press* 1950 $5.00

OF EDUCATION. 1644. (and "Areopagitica") ed. by George H. Sabine *AHM Pub. Corp.* Crofts Class. pap. $.85; (with supplementary extracts from other writings) ed. by Oliver M. Ainsworth 1928 *Scholarly Press* 1971 $19.50

AREOPAGITICA. 1644. Ed. by Richard C. Jebb. 1918 *AMS Press* $6.50; (and "Of Education") ed. by George H. Sabine *AHM Pub. Corp.* Crofts Class. pap. $.85; ed. by Edward Arber 1868 *Saifer* 1972 $6.00; *Richard West* repr. of 1644 ed. $5.95

A COMMON-PLACE BOOK OF JOHN MILTON AND A LATIN ESSAY AND LATIN VERSE PRESUMED TO BE BY MILTON. 1876. Rev. ed. by A. J. Harwood. *Johnson Reprint* 1965 $14.50

MILTON ON HIMSELF: His Utterances upon Himself and His Work. Ed. by J. S. Diekhoff. *Humanities Press* 1965 $7.50

Books about Milton

Milton. By Walter A. Raleigh. 1900. *Blom* 1967 $8.75; *Richard West* 1973 $8.50

Milton's Prosody: With a Chapter on Accentual Verse, and Notes. By Robert Bridges. 1921. *Folcroft* $6.00; *Oxford* rev. ed. $7.00

Milton. By E. M. W. Tillyard. 1930 3rd imp. 1947. *Barnes & Noble* 1965 $7.25; *Macmillan* Collier Bks. pap. $2.45

Early Lives of Milton. Ed. by Helen Darbishire. 1932. *Scholarly Press* 1971 $19.50

Milton's Debt to Greek Tragedy in Samson Agonistes. By William R. Parker. 1937. *Barnes & Noble* 1969 $4.00

The Miltonic Setting, Past and Present. By E. M. W. Tillyard. 1938. *Barnes & Noble* 1963 $3.50

A Milton Handbook. By James Holly Hanford. *Appleton* 1939 5th ed. by J. H. Hanford and James G. Taaffe 1970 $9.95

A Preface to Paradise Lost. By C. S. Lewis. *Oxford* 1941 rev. and enl. 1942 $5.00 pap. $1.50. An interpretation of Milton's purpose in writing the epic.

Milton and the Puritan Dilemma. By Arthur E. Barker. *Univ. of Toronto Press* 1942 $12.50

Paradise Lost and Its Critics. By A. J. A. Waldock. 1947. *Cambridge* 1961 pap. $1.75; *Peter Smith* 1959 $3.75

Paradise Lost and the Seventeenth Century Reader. By Balachandra Rajan. 1947. *Barnes & Noble* $3.50; *Univ. of Michigan Press* Ann Arbor Bks. 1967 pap. $1.95

John Milton, Englishman. By James Holly Hanford. 1949. *Crown* pap. $1.45

Milton's Samson and the Christian Tradition. By F. Michael Krouse. 1949. *AMS Press* $8.25; *Octagon* $9.00

Life Records of John Milton. Ed. by Joseph Milton French. 5 vols. 1949-58. *Gordian* 5 vols. each $15.00 set $75.00

Milton Criticism: Selections from Four Centuries. Ed. by James Ernest Thorpe. 1950. *Octagon* 1966 $12.50

Milton and Science. By Kester Svendsen. 1956. *Greenwood* $11.50

Milton. By David Daiches. 1957. *Hutchinson Univ. Lib.* (dist. by Hillary House) 1961 $6.23; *Norton* Norton Lib. 1966 pap. $2.45

Paradise Lost as Myth. By Isabel G. MacCaffrey. *Harvard Univ. Press* 1959 $6.00

The Living Milton: Essays by Various Hands. Ed. by Frank Kermode. *Routledge & Kegan Paul* 1960 $5.95 pap. $2.25

Milton's God. By William Empson. *New Directions* 1961 $10.00. A controversial discussion of the religion of "Paradise Lost" by the British critic.

John Milton: A Reader's Guide to His Poetry. By Marjorie Nicolson. 1963. *British Bk. Centre* $10.00; *Farrar, Straus* Noonday pap. $3.50; *Octagon* 1971 $12.00

John Milton: A Sketch of His Life and Writings. By Douglas Bush. *Macmillan* 1964 Collier Bks. pap. $1.95

"Mr. Bush presents the orthodox understanding, defended both by learning and devotion"—(*TLS*, London).

Milton: Modern Essays in Criticism. Ed. by Arthur E. Barker. *Oxford* 1965 Galaxy Bks. pap. $3.95

The Return of Eden: Five Essays on Milton's Epics. By Northrop Frye. *Univ. of Toronto Press* 1965 $4.95

Plato and Milton. By Irene Samuel. *Cornell Univ. Press* 1965 pap. $1.45

The Lyric and Dramatic Milton: Selected Papers from the English Institute. Ed. by Joseph H. Summers. *Columbia* 1965 $8.00

A Reading of Paradise Lost: The Alexander Lecture in the University of Toronto, 1962. By Helen L. Gardner. *Oxford* 1965 $7.00 pap. $2.50

A work with "lucidity, moderation, downrightness in places where it is needed and an absence of inconsequential learning. . . . Miss Gardner lacks the calm certainty of the extremist but her perceptions are for that reason more likely to guide the typical reader into the truth of the poem"—(*TLS*, London).

Milton: A Collection of Critical Essays. Ed. with introd. by Louis L. Martz. *Prentice-Hall* 1966 $5.95 Spectrum Bks. pap. $1.95

This focuses "chiefly on *Paradise Lost.* Included are 11 solid pieces by English and American authorities like T. S. Eliot, C. S. Lewis, and Douglas Bush"—(*LJ*).

John Milton, Poet and Humanist. By James H. Hanford. *Press of Case Western Reserve* 1966 $6.00

Milton and the Modern Critics. By Robert M. Adams. *Cornell Univ. Press* 1966 pap. $1.95

Milton's Brief Epic: The Genre, Meaning, and Art of Paradise Regained. By Barbara K. Lewalski. *Brown Univ. Press* 1966 $8.50

"Mrs. Lewalski's book is not an investigation of the genre alone. It is also a valuable account of the structure of a poem which many have found inaccessible. . . . For some time to come anything said on *Paradise Regained* will need to be placed within the framework she has given us"—(*TLS*, London).

Milton and the Christian Tradition. By C. A. Patrides. *Oxford* 1966 $9.50

Language and Style in Milton: A Symposium in Honor of the Tercentenary of *Paradise Lost.* Ed. by Ronald D. Emma and John T. Shawcross. *Ungar* 1967 $11.50

Milton: The Modern Phase; A Survey of Twentieth Century Criticism. By Patrick Murray. *Barnes & Noble* 1967 $5.00

Milton and the Masque Tradition: The Early Poems, Arcades, Comus. By John Demaray. *Harvard Univ. Press* 1968 $6.00

A Masque at Ludlow: Essays on Milton's Comus. Ed. by John Diekhoff. *Press of Case Western Reserve* 1968 $8.95

Milton: A Biography. By William R. Parker. *Oxford* 2 vols. 1968 $51.00. The most useful life since David Masson's "Life of John Milton: Narrated in Connection with the Political, Literary, and Ecclesiastical History of His Time" 7 vols. 1859-94 (*Peter Smith* $73.50).

The Muse's Method: An Introduction to Paradise Lost. By Joseph H. Summers. *Harvard Univ. Press* 1970 $6.00

Paradise Lost: A Tercentenary Tribute. Ed. by B. Rajan. *Univ. of Toronto Press* 1969 $6.50. Papers given at the Conference on the Tercentenary of "Paradise Lost." Very useful essays.

The Harmonious Vision: Studies in Milton's Poetry. Ed. by Don C. Allen. *Johns Hopkins Univ. Press* enl. ed. 1970 $6.50

The Heavenly Muse: A Preface to Milton. By A. S. P. Woodhouse. Ed. by Hugh MacCallum. *Univ. of Toronto Press* 1972 $20.00

Two indispensable bibliographical works are:

John Milton: An Annotated Bibliography, 1929–68. rev. ed. by Calvin Huckabay. *Duquesne Univ. Press* 1970 $17.50

A Reference Guide to Milton from 1800 to the Present Day. By David Stevens. 1930. *Russell & Russell* 1967 $10.00

MARVELL, ANDREW. 1621–1678.

This enchanting poet was at once a Puritan and sympathetic to the Cavaliers. A partisan of Charles I, he became tutor to Cromwell's ward, friend of Milton (*q. v.*) and assistant Latin Secretary in the Cromwell government; he was later a member of the Restoration Parliament, surviving very well in the shifting political climate of his age. Close to the Metaphysical poets in method and diction, Marvell is usually secular in approach; he is fascinated by the charm and also the rude power of nature, with which his poetry is centrally concerned. His best-known poem, "To His Coy Mistress," rings witty changes on the theme of *carpe diem* ("seize the day"). For general works including Marvell among others, see the studies by Joan Bennett and George Williamson in the "Selected Bibliography" above, this Chapter.

COMPLETE WORKS IN VERSE AND PROSE. Ed. by Alexander B. Grosart. 4 vols. 1872–75. *AMS Press* each $29.50 set $115.00

POEMS AND LETTERS. Ed. by H. M. Margoliouth. *Oxford* 1927 1952 3rd ed. rev. by Pierre Legouis Oxford English Texts 2 vols. 1972 Vol. I Poems Vol. 2 Letters set $44.25. Contains the complete poems and letters.

COMPLETE POETRY. Ed. by George D. Lord. *Random* 1968 $10.00; *Modern Library* 1968 pap. $1.65

COMPLETE POEMS. Ed. by Elizabeth Story Donno. *Penguin* 1973 $3.95

POEMS. Printed from the copy in the British Museum, with some other poems by him. Ed. by Hugh Macdonald. *Harvard Univ. Press* Muses' Lib. 1952 $3.00 pap. $1.45

POEMS. Ed. by James Reeves and Martin Seymour-Smith. Poetry Bkshelf Series. *Barnes & Noble* 1956 $3.00

SELECTED POETRY. Ed. with introd. by Frank Kermode. *New Am. Lib.* Signet 1967 pap. $.95

THE REHEARSAL TRANSPOS'D (1672) and THE REHEARSAL TRANSPOS'D, SECOND PART (1673). Ed. by D. I. B. Smith. *Oxford* 1971 $18.75. "Elaborate and successful essay in satiric controversy"—(*Concise Cambridge History of English Literature*).

Books about Marvell

Andrew Marvell, 1621–1678. Ed. by William H. Bagguley. 1922. *Russell & Russell* 1965 $7.00. Tercentenary tributes, with an official record of the tercentenary celebrations at Kingston-upon-Hull and in London.

Andrew Marvell: Poet, Puritan, Patriot. By Pierre Legouis. 1929. *Oxford* 1965 2nd ed. 1968 $7.25; (with title "André Marvell: Poète, Puritan, Patriote, 1621–1678") *Russell & Russell* the original French text 1965 $16.50

Andrew Marvell. By Lawrence W. Hyman. English Authors Series *Twayne* 1964 $5.50

Marvell's Ironic Vision. By Harold E. Toliver. *Yale Univ. Press* 1965 $8.50

The Art of Marvell's Poetry. By James B. Leishman. *Funk & Wagnalls* 1966 $4.95 Minerva Bks. 1968 pap. $2.50

Andrew Marvell: A Collection of Critical Essays. Ed. by George D. Lord. Twentieth Century Views Series. *Prentice-Hall* 1968 $5.95 Spectrum Bks. pap. $1.95

My Echoing Song: Andrew Marvell's Poetry of Criticism. By Rosalie Colie. *Princeton Univ. Press* 1969 $14.50

Spenser, Marvell, and Renaissance Pastoral. By Patrick Cullen. *Harvard Univ. Press* 1970 $7.00

Marvell's Pastoral Art. By Donald M. Friedman. *Univ. of California Press* 1970 $7.95

VAUGHAN, HENRY. 1622–1695.

Henry Vaughan was born in South Wales. He studied at Oxford with his twin brother Thomas; Thomas became an alchemist and dealer in magic, and studied the hermetic philosophy which is also reflected in Henry's poems. Henry left Oxford for London, and, after serving as a Royalist soldier during the Civil War, retired to Wales, where he served as a physician for the last 20 years of his life. His early work was secular, but he is best remembered for his religious verse in "Silex Scintillans." The best of his work shines with a childlike innocence and clarity of vision. He wrote about nature as a reflection of God; "All things that be, praise him . . . Stones are deep in admiration." Vaughan's views on nature and childhood are believed to have influenced Wordsworth (*q. v.*). Vaughan's poetry is discussed in the studies of metaphysical poetry by Joan Bennett, Helen White, and George Williamson. See the "Selected Bibliography" above, this Chapter.

WORKS. Ed. by Leonard C. Martin. *Oxford* 2nd ed. 1957 2 vols. set $19.25

POETRY AND SELECTED PROSE. Ed. with introd. by Leonard C. Martin. *Oxford* 1963 $8.00

THE COMPLETE POETRY. Ed. by French Fogle. *New York Univ. Press* 1965 $12.50; *Norton* Norton Lib. 1969 pap. $2.95

Books about Vaughan

Henry Vaughan and the Hermetic Philosophy. By Elizabeth Holmes. 1932. *Haskell House* 1970 pap. $3.95; *Russell & Russell* 1967 $5.00

Henry Vaughan: A Life and Interpretation. By Francis E. Hutchinson. *Oxford* 1947 $13.75

A Comprehensive Bibliography of Henry Vaughan. Comp. by Esmond L. Marilla. *Univ. of Alabama Press* 1948 pap. $1.25; *Haskell House* lib. bdg. $5.95

Henry Vaughan: Experience and the Tradition. By Ross Garner. *Univ. of Chicago Press* 1959 $5.00

On the Mystical Poetry of Henry Vaughan. By R. A. Durr. *Harvard Univ. Press* 1962 $6.00

Henry Vaughan: A Bibliographical Supplement. Comp. by Esmond L. Marilla and James D. Simmonds. *Univ. of Alabama Press* 1963 pap. $1.25

The Paradise Within: Studies in Vaughan, Traherne, and Milton. By Louis L. Martz. *Yale Univ. Press* 1964 pap. $1.45

Masques of God: Form and Theme in the Poetry of Henry Vaughan. By James D. Simmonds. *Univ. of Pittsburgh Press* 1972 $9.95

DRYDEN, JOHN. 1631–1700.

Dryden was the third Poet Laureate of England (1670–1688) and the only Laureate dismissed from the post. When he refused to take the oath of allegiance to William and Mary after the Revolution of 1688, the laureateship was given to his enemy, Thomas Shadwell.

Dryden's range was very wide. His poetical works include dramas, satires, translations, lyrics. He excelled, too, in "that other harmony," prose, and his "Prefaces" are famous examples of fine English style. George Saintsbury writes in his life of Dryden: "He is not our greatest poet; far from it. But there is one point in which the superlative may safely be applied to him. . . . He must be pronounced, without exception, the greatest craftsman in English letters." Lowell called the satire for which Dryden is famous "polished banter. There is no malice in it."

Dryden's English version of Virgil (*q. v.*) in rhyming couplets was a translation, said Elizabeth Browning, "not only into English but into Dryden." It was "the matter of the original, tolerably unadulterated, and dressed up in splendid diction and nervous verse." His Juvenal (*q. v.*) is the standard verse translation of the great Roman satirist, and its prefatory essay on satire is worthy of study.

The "Fables" of 1699 was Dryden's last work—some think his greatest. This volume contained poetical paraphrases of five pieces from Chaucer (*q. v.*), three from Boccaccio (*q. v.*) and Dryden's great ode for St. Cecilia's day.

Works. To be published in 21 vols. *Univ. of California Press* 1956–. Vol. I Poems, 1649–1680 ed. by Edward N. Hooker and H. T. Swedenberg, Jr. (1956) $17.50 Vol. 2 Poems, 1681–1684 ed. by H. T. Swedenberg, Jr. (1973) $20.00 Vol. 3 Poems, 1685–1692 ed. by Earl Miner and Vinton A. Dearing (1970) $17.50 Vol. 8 Plays: The Wild Gallant, The Rival Ladies, The Indian Queen ed. by John Harrington Smith and Dougald Macmillan (1962) $20.00 Vol. 9 Plays: The Indian Emperour, Secret Love, Sir Martin Mar-All ed. by John Loftis and Vinton A. Dearing (1966) $20.00 Vol. 10 Plays: The Tempest, Tyrannick Love, An Evening's Love ed. by Maximillian E. Novak and George R. Guffey (1970) $20.00 Vol. 17 Prose, 1668–1691: An Essay of Dramatick Poesie and Shorter Works ed. by Samuel H. Monk and A. E. Wallace Maurer (1971) $20.00

Poetry, Prose and Plays. Ed. by Douglas Grant. *Harvard Univ. Press* Reynard Lib. 1952 $12.50

Poetry and Prose. With essays by Congreve, Johnson, Scott, and others. Ed. by D. Nichol Smith. Clarendon Eng. Ser. *Oxford* 1925 $2.25

The Best of Dryden. Ed. by Louis I. Bredvold. *Ronald* 1933 $4.50

Selections. (With title "Selected Works") ed. by William Frost *Holt* (Rinehart) 1953 pap. $2.25; (with title "Selected Poetry and Prose") ed. by Earl Miner *Modern Library* 1969 pap. $1.95

Poetry:

Complete Poetical Works. Ed. by George R. Noyes. *Houghton* Cambridge Eds. rev. and enl. 1950 $10.95

Poems. Ed. by James Kinsley *Oxford* 1958 4 vols. set $51.25

Selected Poems. Ed. by Roger Sharrock. *Barnes & Noble* 1963 $1.75; (with title "Poems") ed. with introd. by Bonamy Dobrée *Dutton* Everyman's 1934 1954 $3.50; ed. by James Kinsley *Oxford* 1963 $2.50

Poems and Fables. Ed. by James Kinsley. *Oxford* Stand. Authors 1962 $8.00 pap. $4.50

Songs and Poems. *Golden Cockerell* (dist. by A. S. Barnes) white art canvas $45.00 mor. $80.00

Songs. Ed. by Cyrus L. Day. 1932. *Russell & Russell* 1967 $8.00

Prose:

Essays. Sel. and ed. by William P. Ker. 1900. *Russell & Russell* 2 vols. set $22.50

An Essay of Dramatic Poesy. 1668. (And Other Critical Writings) ed. by John L. Mahoney *Bobbs* Lib. Arts 1965 pap. $1.25; (and Other Critical Essays) ed. with introd. by George Watson *Dutton* Everyman's 1962 2 vols. each $3.50; (with title "Of Dramatick Poesie") preceded by a dialogue on poetic drama by T. S. Eliot 1928 *Folcroft* lib. bdg. $9.50; *Haskell House* repr. of 1928 ed. lib. bdg. $9.95; (with Sir Robert Howard's Preface, and Dryden's "Defence of An Essay") ed. by James T. Boulton *Oxford* 1964 $1.85

CRITICAL OPINIONS. Ed. by John M. Aden *Vanderbilt Univ. Press* 1963 $10.00. A compendium arranged in self-indexed dictionary form.

LITERARY CRITICISM. Ed. with introd. by Arthur C. Kirsch. Regents Critics Series. *Univ. of Nebraska Press* 1966 $5.95 Bison Bks. pap. $2.25

SELECTED CRITICISM. Ed. by James Kinsley and G. A. Parfitt. *Oxford* 1970 pap. $2.75

Books about Dryden

Dryden. By George Saintsbury. English Men of Letters Series. 1881. *Gale Research Co.* $7.80; ed. by John Morley. 1888. *AMS Press* lib. bdg. $7.80; *Richard West* repr. of 1888 ed. 1973 $7.75

The Poetry of John Dryden. By Mark Van Doren. 1920. *Haskell House* lib. bdg. $13.95; (with title "John Dryden: A Study of his Poetry") *Indiana Univ. Press* Midland Bks. 1960 pap. $1.95; *Peter Smith* $4.50

Dryden and His Poetry. By Allardyce Nicoll. With pref. by William Henry Hudson. 1923. *Folcroft* lib. bdg. $5.50; *Russell & Russell* 1967 $6.50

The Intellectual Milieu of John Dryden: Studies in Some Aspects of Seventeenth-Century Thought. By Louis I. Bredvold. *Univ. of Michigan Press* 1956 $4.40 Ann Arbor Bks. pap. $1.75

Concordance to the Poetical Works of John Dryden. Comp. by Guy Montgomery with pref. by Josephine Miles. 1957 *Russell & Russell* 1967 $30.00

The Life of John Dryden. By Charles E. Ward. *Univ. of North Carolina Press* 1961 $8.50

This life is "in effect, a microcosm of 17th century England. Recounting as it does in an exceedingly detailed and authoritative fashion Dryden's career . . . it is a substantial and important contribution to the study of English literature"—(*LJ*).

The Life of Dryden. By Sir Walter Scott. Ed. with introd. by Bernard Kreissman. *Univ. of Nebraska Press* 1963 $5.00 Bison Bks. pap. $1.70

John Dryden's Imagery. By Arthur Hoffman. *Univ. of Florida Press* 1962 $6.00

Dryden: A Collection of Critical Essays. Ed. by Bernard Schilling. *Prentice-Hall* 1963 $5.95 Spectrum Bks. pap. $1.95

Dryden's Poetry. By Earl Miner. *Indiana Univ. Press* 1967 $12.50 Midland Bks. pap. $2.95

"A welcome and valuable addition to the criticism of Dryden's poetry"—(Eugene M. Waith, in the *Yale Review*).

Dryden: The Critical Heritage. Ed. by James and Helen Kinsley. *Barnes & Noble* 1971 $15.00. Contains some critical work by Dryden himself as well as criticism by Samuel Johnson, Sir Walter Scott, and other contemporaries and near-contemporaries of Dryden.

Dryden's Political Poetry: The Typology of King and Nation. By Steven N. Zwicker. *Brown Univ. Press* 1972 $8.00

"A historical and critical approach to seventeenth-century typological symbolism, and Dryden's use of it to interpret English political life"—(Publisher's note).

POPE, ALEXANDER. 1688–1744.

Pope's "Essay on Criticism," written in verse when he was 21, contains the literary maxims which governed his life. Brilliance and wit he valued above all else; he excelled in the terse, pointed epigram. All his verse is written in heroic couplets, each rhyming pair of lines being more or less separate and detached. These read like independent precepts; they are eminently quotable, but the uniformity of his verse is occasionally monotonous. "The Rape of the Lock," written on the loss of a lock of hair by a lady of fashion, mocks the romance of heroism most attractively.

As a satirist Pope could be malignant and scurrilous. His "Dunciad" is, according to Andrew Lang, "a satire on minor men of letters, in which he shows wit and ill-nature enough . . . but the dirt and personalities are now rather amazing than agreeable." The "Moral Essays" appeared 1731–35 and consisted of letters or "epistles" to men and women on such matters as "Taste," "Riches," "The Character of Men," and "The Character of Women," the last reflecting considerable misogyny. Pope's "Epistle to Dr. Arbuthnot," 1734, is a full account of "that long disease, his [Pope's] life." The "Essay on Man" is a "philosophical" poem only in a very pragmatic and quotable 18th-century sense.

WORKS. Collected in part by John Wilson Croker, with introd. and notes by Whitwell Elwin and William John Courthope. 10 vols. 1871–86. Vols. I–5 Poetry Vols. 6–10 Correspondence and Prose Works. *Gordian* 1967 set $125.00

COMPLETE POETICAL WORKS. Ed. by H. W. Boynton. *Houghton* Cambridge Eds. 1903 1967 $8.95

POEMS. The Twickenham ed. *Yale Univ. Press* 1951–70 11 vols. of text and an index: The Rape of the Lock ed. by Geoffrey Tillotson 2nd ed. rev. (1954) $12.50; An Essay on Man ed. by Maynard Mack (1951) $7.50; Epistles to Several Persons [Moral Essays] ed. by F. W. Bateson (1951) $7.50; Imitations of Horace ed. by John Butt 2nd ed. (1954) $12.50; The Dunciad ed. by James Sutherland rev. ed. (1953) $15.00; Minor Poems ed. by Norman Ault and completed by John Butt (1954) $15.00; Pastoral Poetry and An Essay on Criticism ed. by E. Audra and Aubrey Williams (1961) $15.00; The Iliad of Homer ed. by Maynard Mack (1967) 2 vols. set $37.50; The Odyssey of Homer ed. by Maynard Mack 2 vols. (1967) set $37.50; Index ed. by Maynard Mack (1970) $10.00

COLLECTED POEMS. Ed. by Bonamy Dobrée. *Dutton* Everyman's 1956 $3.50

POETICAL WORKS. Ed. by Herbert Davis. *Oxford* Stand. Authors 1967 $8.00

THE BEST OF POPE. Ed. by George Sherburn. 1929. *Ronald* rev. ed. 1940 $4.50; *Scholarly Press* repr. of 1929 ed. $24.50

SELECTED WORKS. Ed. by Louis Kronenberger. *Modern Library* 1947 $1.95 pap. $1.15

POETRY AND PROSE. Ed. by H. V. D. Dyson (with essays by Johnson, Coleridge, Hazlitt and others). *Oxford* 1933 $2.50

SELECTED POETRY AND PROSE. Ed. with introd. by William K. Wimsatt, Jr. *Holt* (Rinehart) 1951 2nd ed. 1971 pap. $1.95; (with title "Poetry and Prose") ed. by Aubrey Williams *Houghton* Riverside Eds. 1969 $2.95

SELECTED POEMS. (with title "The Poetry of Pope: A Selection") ed. by M. H. Abrams *AHM Pub. Corp.* Crofts Classics pap. $.85; ed. by J. Heath-Stubbs *Barnes & Noble* 1966 $1.75; ed. by Douglas Grant *Oxford* 1965 $2.25

HORATIAN SATIRES AND EPISTLES. Ed. by H. H. Erskine-Hill. *Oxford* 1964 $2.50

EPISTLES TO SEVERAL PERSONS (Moral Essays). Introd. by James E. Wellington. *Univ. of Miami Press* 1963 pap. $2.00

THE RAPE OF THE LOCK. 1714. Embroidered with 9 drawings by Aubrey Beardsley. 1896. *Dover* pap. $1.75; ed. by John D. Hunt Casebook Series. *Aurora Pubs.* pap. $2.50; ed. by J. S. Cunningham *Oxford* 1966 pap. $1.80; ed. by Bernard Groom *St. Martin's* 1929 $.75

POPE'S OWN MISCELLANY: Being a Reprint of Poems on Several Occasions (1717) Containing New Poems by Alexander Pope and Others. Ed. by Norman Ault. 1935. *Folcroft* 1973 lib. bdg. $25.00

AN ESSAY ON MAN. 1733–34. Ed. by Frank Brady. *Bobbs* Lib. Arts Lib. 1965 pap. $.50

PROSE WORKS. Ed. by Norman Ault. 1936. *Barnes & Noble* 1961 Vol. I The Earlier Works, 1711–1720 $11.50

THE ART OF SINKING IN POETRY: Martinus Scriblerus' *Peri Bathous*. Ed. by Edna Steeves and others. 1952. *Russell & Russell* 1968 $10.00

(With others) MEMOIRS OF THE EXTRAORDINARY LIFE, WORKS AND DISCOVERIES OF MARTINUS SCRIBLERUS, Written in Collaboration by the Members of the Scriblerus Club. Ed. by C. Kerby-Miller. 1950. *Russell & Russell* 1966 $16.00

CORRESPONDENCE. Ed. by George Sherburn. *Oxford* 1956 5 vols. set $64.00

Books about Pope

A Concordance to the Poetry of Alexander Pope. Ed. by Emmett G. Bedford and Robert J. Dilligan. *Holt* 3 vols. 1972 set $75.00

Alexander Pope as Critic and Humanist. By Austin Warren. 1929. *Peter Smith* $5.00

Alexander Pope. By Edith Sitwell. 1930. *Bks. for Libraries* 1972 $16.00

The Early Career of Alexander Pope. By George Sherburn. *Oxford* 1934 $9.00; *Russell & Russell* $11.00

On the Poetry of Pope. By Geoffrey Tillotson. *Oxford* 1938 2nd ed. 1950 $5.00

New Light on Pope, with Some Additions to His Poetry. By Norman Ault. 1949. *Shoe String* 1967 $10.00 "Important miscellaneous contributions to Pope's biography"—(Samuel Monk).

Pope and Human Nature. By Geoffrey Tillotson. *Oxford* 1958 $4.50

Alexander Pope: The Poetry of Allusion. By Reuben A. Brower. *Oxford* 1959 pap. 1968 $2.25

The Character-Sketches in Pope's Poems. By Benjamin Boyce. *Duke Univ. Press* 1962 $6.00. The first major study of the schemes and traditions of Pope's verbal paintings.

Alexander Pope. By Bonamy Dobrée. 1951. *Greenwood* $7.00; *Oxford* pap. 1963 $1.75

Alexander Pope. By Donald B. Clark. English Authors Series. *Twayne* 1966 $5.50

The Poetic Workmanship of Alexander Pope. By Rebecca Price Parkin. *Octagon* 1968 $9.00. A very readable analysis of Pope's work from the point of view of "irony," "humor," "metaphor," "the approach to correctible evil," "Pope's poetic world," and so on.

The World of Pope's Satires: An Introduction to the Epistles and Imitations of Horace. By Peter Dixon. 1968 *Barnes & Noble* $5.95

Essential Articles for the Study of Alexander Pope. Ed. by Maynard Mack. 1964. *Shoe String* rev. and enl. ed. 1968 $12.00

Pope's Dunciad, A Study of Its Meaning. By Aubrey Williams. 1955. *Shoe String* 1968 $5.50

The Garden and the City: Retirement and Politics in the Later Poetry of Pope. By Maynard Mack. *Univ. of Toronto Press* 1969 $12.50

Alexander Pope: The Education of Genius, 1688–1728. By Peter Quennell. *Stein & Day* 1969 $7.95 pap. 1970 $2.95

An Argument of Images: The Poetry of Alexander Pope. By Patricia Spacks. *Harvard Univ. Press* 1971 $10.00

Alexander Pope, a Bibliography. By Reginald Griffith. 2 vols. 1922. *AMS Press* each $18.00 set $35.00; *Dufour* set $32.50

THOMSON, JAMES. 1700–1748.

Thomson, the son of a Scottish clergyman, was educated for the ministry, but went instead to London, where he joined Pope's (*q. v.*) literary circle. His early works were nature poems, collected as "The Seasons" (1730). "Although Thomson sometimes wrote like a complacent country parson, his benevolent and often unctuous view of nature is sharpened by an imagery which is both sensuous and exact"—(Louis Untermeyer). "The Castle of Indolence" is a long allegorical poem. Patricia Spacks discusses Thomson's poetry in "The Poetry of Vision" (*see the "Selected Bibliography," opening of this Chapter*).

Another James Thomson (1834–1882), not to be confused with this one, was the Scottish poet who wrote "The City of Dreadful Night."

COMPLETE POETICAL WORKS. Ed. by J. L. Robertson. *Oxford* Stand. Authors 1908 $7.00

THE SEASONS. 1730 (with title "Thomson's Seasons") critical ed. being a reproduction of the original texts with all the variant readings of the later editions, historically arranged, by Otto Zippel. 1908. *Folcroft* lib. bdg. $18.50; *Johnson Reprint* $19.00 pap. $17.00; (and "The Castle of Indolence" [1748]) ed. by James Sambrook *Oxford* 1972 pap. $4.50

Books about Thomson

The Art of Discrimination: Thomson's "The Seasons" and the language of Criticism. By Ralph Cohen. *Univ. of California Press* 1963 $11.50

GRAY, THOMAS. 1716–1761.

Gray is the most important figure in English poetry between Pope (*q. v.*) and Wordsworth (*q. v.*). Though he produced little, his works are unique in the 18th century in providing a kind of transition from Classicism to Romanticism. His "Elegy Written in a Country Church-yard" (1751) admirably illustrates the change; its humble subject and simplicity of treatment herald the new order, but there remains a distinct trace of restrained and scholarly Classicism in the style. His Pindaric odes, as well as "The Progress of Poesy" and "The Bard," greatly influenced the poetry of Coleridge (*q. v.*) and Shelley (*q. v.*). In his later life Gray became enthusiastic about the ancient poetry of Iceland and produced many poems based upon the "Edda." "The living Gray," finally, "is to be sought in his correspondence, where his genial humor, shy affection, and wide intellectual interests are revealed"—(Samuel Monk).

WORKS IN VERSE AND PROSE. 1844. Ed. by Edmund Gosse. *AMS Press* 4 vols. each $19.00 set $70.00

COMPLETE POEMS. English, Latin and Greek. Ed. by H. W. Starr and J. R. Hendrickson. *Oxford* 1966 $15.25

POETRY AND PROSE. With Essays by Johnson, Goldsmith and others. Ed. by J. Crofts. *Oxford* 1926 $2.10

ENGLISH POEMS. Original and translated from the Norse and Welsh. Ed. by Duncan Crookes Tovey. 1898 1922. *Scholarly Press* 1971 $17.50

POEMS. (with Poems by William Collins) Ed. by A. L. Poole. *Oxford* Stand. Authors 3rd ed. 1937 $4.50

POEMS: With a Selection of Letters and Essays. Introd. by John Drinkwater and biographical notes by Lewis Gibbs. *Dutton* Everyman's 1955 $3.50

THE CORRESPONDENCE OF THOMAS GRAY. Ed. by Paget Toynbee and Leonard Whibley. *Oxford* 1935 repr., with corrections and additions by Herbert W. Starr 1971 $48.00

HORACE WALPOLE'S CORRESPONDENCE WITH THOMAS GRAY, RICHARD WEST AND THOMAS ASHTON. Ed. by W. S. Lewis. Vols. 13–14 of "Horace Walpole's Correspondence." New, illuminating and entertaining information appears in the commentary. *Yale Univ. Press* 1948 2 vols. in I $35.00

LETTERS. Sel. with introd. by John Beresford. 1925 1951 *Somerset Pub.* $15.50

Books about Gray

Concordance to the English Poems of Thomas Gray. By Albert S. Cook. 1908. *Folcroft* lib. bdg. $10.00; *Peter Smith* $5.50

Thomas Gray, Scholar: The True Tragedy of an 18th Century Gentleman, with Two Youthful Notebooks from the Original Manuscripts in the Morgan Library, New York City. By William Powell Jones. 1937. *Russell & Russell* 1965 $7.50

Thomas Gray: A Biography. By Robert W. Ketton-Cremer. *Cambridge* 1955 $12.50

Thomas Gray. By Morris Golden. English Authors Series. *Twayne* 1964 $5.50

Twentieth Century Interpretations of Gray's Elegy. Ed. by Herbert W. Starr. *Prentice-Hall* 1968 $4.95 Spectrum Bks. pap. $1.25

A Bibliography of Thomas Gray, 1917–1951, with Material Supplementary to C. S. Northup's Bibliography of Thomas Gray. By Herbert W. Starr. 1953. *Kraus* 1969 $9.00

SMART, CHRISTOPHER. 1722–1771.

Smart spent his early years as a journalist and writer of unexceptional verse; he contributed pseudonymously to the publications of John Newbery—remembered for his children's books—and married the printer's stepdaughter, Anna Maria Carnan. Subject to religious mania and an "overexcited mind," Smart suffered a breakdown and spent seven years in mental asylums. During his confinement, deprived of paper and pen, he scratched with a key on the wainscot of his room his masterpiece, "A Song to David" (1763). "Much of it is taken at secondhand from the Bible and it abounds in repetition and verbiage; but . . . the old romance-six or rime couee once more acquires soar and rush, so that the whole crowd of emotional thought and picturesque image sweeps through the page with irresistible force"—(*Concise Cambridge History of English Literature*). In 1771, in debt and drunkenness, Smart was confined to King's Bench Prison, where he died.

In his greatest poetry, Smart wrote rationally but ecstatically, shedding the narrow poetic shackles of his time, and anticipating the poetry of Blake, especially in "*Jubilate Agno*" ("Rejoice in the Lamb"), also from Smart's "mad" period, in which the poet glorifies all the creatures of God; there is a charming section on his cat Jeoffry. Benjamin Britten has set "Rejoice in the Lamb" to music.

COLLECTED POEMS. Ed. by N. Callan. *Harvard Univ. Press* Muses' Lib. o. p.

JUBILATE AGNO. Ed. by W. H. Bond. 1954. *Greenwood* $8.50

Books about Smart

Christopher Smart as a Poet of His Time. By Sophia Blaydes. *Humanities Press* 1966 $9.00
Christopher Smart, Scholar of the University. By Arthur Sherbo. *Michigan State Univ. Press* 1967 $8.50
The Poetry of Christopher Smart. By Moira Dearnley. *Barnes & Noble* 1969 $8.00

COWPER, WILLIAM. 1731–1800.

Cowper suffered from intermittent attacks of insanity and melancholia throughout his life. His engaging personality won him devoted friends, however, among them a Mr. and Mrs. Unwin who took him into their home, where he spent his life in charity and good works. Cowper was the son of a minister and his poetry is always didactic, preaching the beauty of religion—but religion of a very stern and puritanical variety. Although his subjects are sometimes forbidding, his style is always easy, straightforward and conversational. Cowper is best known for his humorous narrative poem about John Gilpin, for his poetic meditation, "The Task," and for his delightful letters. Robert Southey said that Cowper was the best letter writer in the English language.

WORKS. Ed. by Robert Southey. 15 vols. 1837. *AMS Press* each $11.00 set $162.00

COMPLETE POETICAL WORKS. Ed. by Humphrey Sumner Milford. *Oxford* Stand. Authors 4th ed. 1934 $7.00

POEMS. *Dutton* Everyman's $3.50

SELECTED POEMS AND LETTERS. Ed. by A. Norman Jeffares. *Oxford* 1963 $1.85

VERSE AND LETTERS. Ed. by Brian Spiller. *Harvard Univ. Press* Reynard Lib. 1968 $12.00

THE CORRESPONDENCE OF WILLIAM COWPER. Ed. by Thomas Wright. 4 vols. 1904. *AMS Press* 1968 set $30.00; *Haskell House* 1969 lib. bdg. set $34.95; *Scholarly Press* 1970 set $48.00

THE LETTERS OF WILLIAM COWPER. Ed. by James G. Frazer. 1912. *Bks. for Libraries* facsimile ed. $34.50

UNPUBLISHED AND UNCOLLECTED LETTERS OF WILLIAM COWPER. Ed. by Thomas Wright. 1925. *Somerset Pub.* $6.00

Books about Cowper

Concordance to the Poetical Works of William Cowper. By John Neve. 1887. *Burt Franklin* $15.00
William Cowper. By Hugh Fausset. 1928 *Russell & Russell* 1968 $9.00
William Cowper and the 18th Century. By Gilbert Thomas. 1947 rev. ed. 1948 *Hillary House* $3.50
The Stricken Deer, or, The Life of Cowper. By Lord David Cecil. 1947. *Somerset Pub.* $15.50
William Cowper: A Critical Life. By Maurice Quinlan. 1953. *Greenwood* $10.75
William Cowper of the Inner Temple. By Charles Ryskamp. *Cambridge* 1959 $7.50. Concentrates on the
poet's early life.
In Search of Stability: Poetry of William Cowper. By Morris Golden. 1960. *College & Univ. Press* pap.
$1.95
A Bibliography of William Cowper to 1837. By Norma Russell. *Oxford* 1963 $13.75

CRABBE, GEORGE. 1754–1832.

Crabbe was a parson as well as a poet. He was as ordinary a parson as he was an extraordinary poet—the
extraordinariness lying in his power to put mussels, eels, colds, weeds, teapots, etc., and also whole villages of
sympathetically observed characters into couplets that are undeniably poetry. Benjamin Britten's opera, "Peter Grimes," is based upon a section of Crabbe's poem "The Borough" (1810, o. p.)

THE POETICAL WORKS OF GEORGE CRABBE. Ed. by A. J. and R. M. Carlyle. 1914
1932 *Scholarly Press* repr. of 1932 ed. 1971 $29.50

SELECTED POEMS. Ed. by C. Day Lewis. *Penguin* 1973 pap. $1.65

TALES, 1812 AND OTHER SELECTED POEMS. Ed. with introd. by Howard Mills. *Cambridge* 1967 $13.50 pap. $5.95

Books about Crabbe

The Life of George Crabbe. By George Crabbe, his son. 1834. Introd. by Edmund Blunden. 1933. *Dufour*
1949 $4.95
The Poetry of Crabbe. By Lilian Haddakin. 1955. *Fernhill* $3.50
George Crabbe. By Robert L. Chamberlain. English Authors Series. *Twayne* 1964 $5.50
Crabbe: The Critical Heritage. Ed. by Arthur Pollard. *Routledge & Kegan Paul* 1972 $21.75

BLAKE, WILLIAM. 1757–1827.

Blake, an engraver by training, is unique in English literature as a man who was a great artist as well as a
great poet. He printed and published all his own works. Every page was hand-lettered and had to be cut in
reverse, mirror fashion, on copper before being printed. It was then ornamented and illustrated and painted
over in water colors by the poet-engraver and his wife. Every copy was in a sense a first edition because every
copy differs from every other copy. Blake's illustrations for the Book of Job, reproduced in "Blake's Job"
(*Brown Univ. Press* 1966 $7.50; *Dutton* pap. $1.75) and for Blair's "Grave," published as "Blake's Grave:
A Prophetic Book" (*Brown Univ. Press* 1963 $8.00) are his masterpieces. He also illustrated Dante, Thomas
Gray, "The Canterbury Pilgrims," and "Paradise Lost." "Blake's Illustrations to the Divine Comedy," by
Albert Sutherland Roe, is published by the *Princeton Univ. Press* (1953 $30.00).
Blake was a visionary whose social criticism was much ahead of his day. He worked as an illustrator and
engraver against financial odds and in poor health—for clients whom his independence often displeased—assisted by his acquiescent and childless wife and encouraged by a few believing friends. He was quite isolated
from other poets of his time and was usually considered slightly mad when noticed at all in the literary world.
But the short poems of the "Innocence" and "Experience" volumes—such as "The Tyger"—have come to
be recognized as some of the finest and most enduring in the English language. The long and difficult "Prophetic Books" develop an elaborate religious mythology which Blake said he derived from his "visions." He
was a Christian with a difference, despising the hypocrisy he found in religious institutions and preaching a
sort of natural Christianity in which human beings were free to develop—and to love each other—without artificial restraints. His genius has been fully appreciated only in the 20th century.

THE COMPLETE WORKS. Variorum Edition. Ed. by Geoffrey Keynes. *Random* 1957
$15.00

"Sir Geoffrey Keynes, supreme among editors of Blake, has now been able to rectify any shortcomings,
great or small, of his two earlier editions. . . . It is likely to supersede Sloss and Wallis's text (1925), for it
contains every variant reading and deletion that is ever likely to be deciphered"—(*TLS*, London).

THE COMPLETE WRITINGS WITH VARIANT READINGS. Ed. by Geoffrey Keynes. *Oxford* Stand. Authors 1966 $10.00 pap. $4.75

WORKS: Poetic, Symbolic and Critical. Ed. with lithographs of the illustrated "Prophetic Books" and a memoir and interpretation by John Edwin Ellis and William Butler Yeats. 1893. *AMS Press* 3 vols. each $35.00 set $100.00

POETICAL WORKS. Ed. with a prefatory memoir by William M. Rossetti. 1914. *AMS Press* $15.00

POEMS AND PROSE. Ed. by David V. Erdman with commentary by Harold Bloom. *Doubleday* 1965 Anchor Bks. pap. $6.95

POEMS. Ed. by William Butler Yeats. 1905. *Harvard Univ. Press* 1969 $3.25; ed. by W. H. Stevenson, with text by David V. Erdman. Longman's/Norton Annotated English Poets *Norton* 1972 $14.95

SELECTED POETRY AND PROSE. Ed. by R. Gleckner *AHM Pub. Corp.* Crofts Classics pap. $.85; (and "Jerusalem") ed. by Hazard Adams *Holt* (Rinehart) 1970 pap. $2.50; ed. by Northrop Frye *Modern Library* 1953 pap. $1.25; ed. by J. Bronowski *Penguin* pap. $1.25

THE PORTABLE BLAKE. Ed. by Alfred Kazin. *Viking* 1946 lib. bdg. $5.50 pap. $3.25

SELECTED POEMS. Ed. by F. W. Bateson *Barnes & Noble* 1957 $2.00; (with title "Poems") sel. and ed. by Amelia H. Munson *T. Y. Crowell* 1964 $3.50; ed. by Richard Wilbur and Ruthven Todd *Dell* pap. $.40; ed. by Stanley Gardner 1964 *Dufour* $3.75; ed. by Denis Saurat 1947 *Folcroft* 1973 $10.00

THE PROPHETIC WRITINGS. Ed. by D. J. Sloss and J. P. R. Wallis *Oxford* 1926 2 vols. set $21.00

POEMS AND PROPHECIES. Ed. with introd. by Max Plowman. *Dutton* Everyman's 1954 1959 $3.50 pap. $1.95

TIRIEL. 1789. Ed. by Gerald E. Bentley, Jr. *Oxford* facsimile and transcript 1967 $13.75. A reproduction of the drawings and a commentary on the poem.

THE BOOK OF THEL. 1789. A facsimile and a critical text. Ed. by Nancy Bogen with fwd. by David V. Erdman. *N.Y. Public Lib.* and *Brown Univ. Press* 1971 $10.00. A reproduction in full color of the copy in the Berg Collection of the New York Public Library. The textual annotations are based on all the extant original copies. A new interpretation is given in the foreword.

SONGS OF INNOCENCE. 1789. *Dover* color facsimile 1971 $3.50 pap. $2.00

THE MARRIAGE OF HEAVEN AND HELL. 1790. Introd. by Clark Emery. *Univ. of Miami Press* 1963 pap. $2.00

SONGS OF INNOCENCE AND EXPERIENCE. 1794. Ed. by Margaret Bottrall. Casebook Series. *Aurora Pubs.* 1970 pap. $2.50; *Avon* Bard Bks. pap. $.60; ed. by Ruthven Todd *Folcroft* $5.00; ed. with introd. and notes by Sir Geoffrey Keynes, with 54 color plates *Grossman* Orion Press facsimile ed. 1970 $7.95

THE BOOK OF URIZEN. 1794. Introd. by Clark Emery. *Univ. of Miami Press* 1966 pap. $3.00

JERUSALEM. 1804. Simplified ed. by William R. Hughes *Barnes & Noble* 1965 $5.00; (and "Selected Poems and Prose") ed. by Hazard Adams *Holt* (Rinehart) 1970 pap. $2.50

MILTON. 1804. Ed. by A. Russell and E. Maclagan. 1907. *Folcroft* lib. bdg. $6.50

THE NOTEBOOK OF WILLIAM BLAKE, Called the Rosetti Manuscript. Ed. by Sir Geoffrey Keynes. 1935. *Cooper Square* 1971 lib. bdg. $10.00. The sketchbook and commonplace book kept by Blake 1793–1818.

LETTERS. Ed. by Sir Geoffrey Keynes. *Harvard* 2nd ed. rev. 1969 $8.00

LETTERS FROM WILLIAM BLAKE TO THOMAS BUTTS. *Folcroft* repr. 1973 lib. bdg. $10.00

Books about Blake

The Life of William Blake. By Alexander Gilchrist. 1863 1880. *Rowman* repr. of 1880 ed. $16.50; (with Selections from Poems and Other Writings) *Phaeton* repr. of 1880 ed. 2 vols. 1969 set $32.50; ed. by W. Graham Robertson. 1907. *Richard West* 1973 $32.00

William Blake: A Critical Essay. By Algernon Charles Swinburne. 1868. *Blom* $12.50; ed., with introd. and notes by Hugh J. Luke *Univ. of Nebraska Press* 1970 pap. $2.50; *Richard West* repr. of 1868 ed. $12.45

William Blake. By John Middleton Murry. 1933. *Haskell* 1971 lib. bdg. $14.95; *Richard West* $13.75

William Blake and the Age of Revolution. A biography. By Jacob Bronowski. 1944. *Harper* 1965 Colophon Bks. pap. $1.95

William Blake: A Man without a Mask. By Jacob Bronowski. 1944 *Haskell* 1969 lib. bdg. $10.95

William Blake. By Mark Schorer. 1946 rev. ed. 1959 *Peter Smith* $4.50. An interpretation of the moral and intellectual structure of Blake's "visionary" art.

Fearful Symmetry: A Study of William Blake. By Northrop Frye. 1947 *Princeton Univ. Press* 1969 $14.50 pap. $3.45

William Blake: His Philosophy and Symbols. By S. Foster Damon. 1947. *Peter Smith* $12.50

English Blake. By Bernard Blackstone. 1949. With a new fwd. by the author. *Shoe String* Archon Bks. 1966 $11.00

   An attractively written study, handsomely printed, whose main argument is still valid, by a British scholar. "In [this] book, Blake emerges as a comprehensible and comprehending giant, a noble figure in his history of thought"—(*New Republic*).

Blake's Marriage of Heaven and Hell: A Critical Study. By Martin K. Nurmi. 1957 *Haskell* $7.95

The Piper and the Bard: A Study of William Blake. By Robert Gleckner. *Wayne State Univ. Press* 1959 $9.95

The Valley of Vision: Blake as Prophet and Revolutionary. By Peter Fisher; ed. by Northrop Frye. *Univ. of Toronto Press* 1961 $10.00

Blake's Apocalypse. By Harold Bloom. 1963. *Cornell Univ. Press* 1970 $12.50 pap. $2.95

William Blake: A Reading of the Shorter Poems. By Hazard Adams. *Univ. of Washington Press* 1963 o.p. available on microfiche $8.00

   "In this superb study Adams introduces the serious student to Blake"—(*Virginia Quarterly Review*).

Innocence and Experience: An Introduction to Blake. By E. D. Hirsch, Jr. *Yale Univ. Press* 1964 $7.50

A Blake Dictionary: The Ideas and Symbols of William Blake. By S. Foster Damon. *Brown Univ. Press* 1965 $20.00 *Dutton* 1971 pap. $4.45

   "An encyclopedic guide that Sir Geoffrey Keynes has called 'a mine of information for generations to come' "—(Publisher's note).

Vision and Verse in William Blake. By Alicia Ostriker. *Univ. of Wisconsin Press* 1965 $10.00. The book's "appeal is not limited to its careful analysis of Blake's verse, but extends to readers generally interested in poetry"—(*LJ*).

Blake: A Collection of Critical Essays. Ed. by Northrop Frye. *Prentice-Hall* 1966 $5.95 Spectrum Bks. pap. $1.95. "Articles by some of the most qualified Blake scholars"—(*LJ*).

Blake's Contrary States: The Songs of Innocence and Experience as Dramatic Poems. By D. G. Gillham. *Cambridge* 1966 $11.50. "Dr. Gillham demonstrates that the poems can be understood without esoteric scholarship"—(*LJ*).

A Concordance to the Writings of William Blake. Ed. by David Erdman. *Cornell Univ. Press* 1967 2 vols. set $35.00

The New Apocalypse: The Radical Christian Vision of William Blake. By Thomas J. J. Altizer. *Michigan State Univ. Press* 1967 $8.50

Blake and Tradition. By Kathleen Raine. A. W. Mellon Lectures in the Fine Arts, no. 11. *Princeton Univ. Press* 2 vols. 1969 $22.50

Blake in the Nineteenth Century. His Reputation as a Poet from Gilchrist to Yeats. By Deborah Dorfman. *Yale Univ. Press* 1969 $8.75.

BURNS, ROBERT. 1759–1796.

Robert Burns, Scotland's greatest poet and one beloved in English literature for his lusty yet sensitive humanity, called himself "a bard from the plough." "The flavor of the soil can be tasted in everything he wrote," said one critic. Burns' rollicking verses in the hitherto despised Scots vernacular—about people and animals and country doings, country love affairs—convey with wry humor his great vitality and universality which has kept them vigorously alive. His first collection, "Poems Chiefly in the Scottish Dialect," (*AMS Press* $12.50) was published at Kilmarnock in 1786. This is the famous "Kilmarnock Burns," a rare prize for book collectors, and it made his reputation overnight. His two most ambitious poems are "Tam o' Shanter," a humorous narrative written to order in a few hours, and "The Cotter's Saturday Night," a description of his father's daily devotions. Burns had to struggle all his life against his penchant for love affairs and extravagant living which contributed to his early death.

COMPLETE POETICAL WORKS. Ed. by William E. Henley. *Houghton* Cambridge Eds. 1904 $7.00

POETRY. Ed. by William E. Henley and Thomas F. Henderson. 4 vols. 1896–97. *AMS Press* each $20.00 set $75.00

POEMS AND SONGS. Ed. by James Kinsley *Dutton* Everyman's 1958 $3.50; ed. by James Kinsley *Oxford* Oxford English Texts 3 vols. 1968 set $51.00 Stand. Authors 1969 $10.00 pap. $3.75

In the Oxford English Texts edition "all of Burns' surviving poems and songs are included . . . along with the airs for the songs in their 18th century form. The first 2 volumes contain the text and the third volume is a literary and textual commentary"—(Publisher's note).

SONGS. With "Notes on Scottish Songs" by Robert Burns, (1908) ed. by James C. Dick, and "Annotations of Scottish Songs" (1922) by Davidson Cook. 1962 *Gale Research Co.* 3 vols. in 1 $12.50. Contains both words and music of all 361 songs with James Dick's notes; includes bibliography and indexes of first lines and tunes.

SONGS. With the melodies for which they were written. Ed. with bibliography, notes, and glossary by James C. Dick. 1903. *AMS Press* $18.00

SELECTIONS. Ed. by John C. Weston. *Bobbs* 1967 $7.50 pap. $2.95

POEMS. Sel. by Lloyd Frankenberg with ills. by Joseph Low. *T. Y. Crowell* 1967 $3.50 lib. bdg. $4.25

SELECTED POEMS. Ed. by G. S. Fraser. *Barnes & Noble* 1960 $2.00. Good introd. and notes.

POEMS AND SONGS. Ed. with introd. by James Barke. *Collins* New Class. 1955 $3.00 lea. $5.00

SONGS AND POEMS. Comp. with introd. by Ralph Knight; musical arrangements by Paul Nordoff. *Twayne* 1959 $10.00

HAND IN HAND WE'LL GO: Poems. *T. Y. Crowell* 1965 $3.75 lib. bdg. $4.50

THE MERRY MUSES OF CALEDONIA. c. 1800. Ed. by James Barke and Sidney G. Smith. *Putnam* 1964 Capricorn Bks. pap. $1.25

THE JOLLY BEGGARS: A Cantata. Ed. by John C. Weston. *Univ. of Massachusetts Press* 1967 $7.50

ROBERT BURNS' COMMONPLACE BOOK, 1783–1785. Introd. by Raymond Brown. *British Bk. Centre* repr. of 1872 ed. 1973 $6.50; ed. by David Daiches *Southern Illinois Univ. Press* facsimile ed. 1966. $19.50

LETTERS. Ed. by J. De Lancey Ferguson. 1931. *Scholarly Press* 2 vols. in 1 1971 $39.50

POEMS AND LETTERS IN THE HANDWRITING OF ROBERT BURNS. From the collections of William K. Bixby and Frederick W. Lehmann. Ed. with introd. and notes by Walter B. Stevens. 1908. *AMS Press* $5.50

Books about Burns

A Complete Word and Phrase Concordance to the Poems and Songs of Robert Burns, Comp. and ed. by J. B. Reid. 1889. *Burt Franklin* $23.50; *Russell & Russell* $25.00. This includes a glossary of Scotch words, with notes, index, and appendix of readings.

The Life of Robert Burns. By Franklin B. Snyder. 1932. *Shoe String* 1968 $14.00

Pride and Passion: Robert Burns, 1759–1796. By J. De Lancey Ferguson. 1939. *Russell & Russell* 1964 $15.00

Robert Burns. By David Daiches. 1950. *Macmillan* rev. ed. 1967 $8.95. A delightful, frank and erudite study, more critical than biographical.

Robert Burns. By David Daiches. Writers and Their Work Series. *British Bk. Centre* $2.38 pap. $1.20

Burns: A Study of the Poems and Songs. By Thomas Crawford. *Stanford Univ. Press* 1960 $10.00 pap. $2.95. Traces Burns' sources and his use of them.

Robert Burns: The Man and the Poet. By Robert T. Fitzhugh. *Houghton* 1970 $10.00. Makes copious use of quotations from Burns and from his contemporaries.

WORDSWORTH, WILLIAM. 1770–1850.

Wordsworth and Coleridge (*q. v.*) are the chief English "Lake Poets"—friends who lived for a long period exiled from city life in the Lake District of England and who became equally famous. Wordsworth's first important book was the "Lyrical Ballads" of 1798, written in collaboration with Coleridge and containing Coleridge's great contribution, "The Ancient Mariner." Its preface, by Wordsworth, enunciated a new poetic creed and a new freedom—which signaled the onset of the great Romantic Period of English poetry. The volume was received with a shout of derision. Wordsworth's celebration of things simple and pastoral, his "impassioned contemplation" of nature, and his poetic narratives of lowly life were ridiculed as subjects too insignificant for poetry. The second volume of "Lyrical Ballads" in 1800 was more kindly treated by the critics. Wordsworth's long autobiographical poem "The Prelude," the history of his mind's growth, was published in 1814 as an introduction to his longer philosophical poem "The Excursion," the latter a fragment of great significance in his development. Many of the shorter poems of this period have endured, but it is the philosophy developed in the longer poems—the sense of the wholeness of human and natural life—that has chiefly interested modern critics. "Tintern Abbey" and "Ode on the Intimations of Immortality" are his other great works of this genre.

Walter Pater said: "Of all poets equally great he would gain most by a skillfully made anthology." Matthew Arnold (*q.v.*) accomplished this (1879, o.p.). His collection included his famous essay on the poet. Quite late in life (1843), Wordsworth succeeded Robert Southey as Poet Laureate.

His sister Dorothy's prose "Journals" today seem almost equally interesting with his own nature poetry. She was closely associated with him through most of his life and her diary is a fascinating one. Professor George McLean Harper discovered in July, 1917 in the British Museum some letters of Dorothy Wordsworth in which she alluded to her brother's daughter Caroline. This daughter was born of an illegitimate union with Annette Vallon, a Frenchwoman and a royalist. The story of this discovery and the full documentation of the facts are given in Professor Harper's "Wordsworth's French Daughter: The Story of Her Birth, with the Certificates of Her Baptism and Marriage" (1921, *Folcroft* lib. bdg. $4.50; *Russell & Russell* 1967 $5.00; *Richard West* 1973 $4.95).

POETICAL WORKS. Ed. from the manuscripts with textual and critical notes by Ernest de Selincourt and Helen Darbishire. *Oxford* English Texts 5 vols. 1940–49. Vol. 1, poems written in youth, poems referring to childhood, (1940) $12.00; Vol. 2, poems founded on the affections, etc., (1944) 2nd ed. 1952 $16.00; Vol. 3, miscellaneous poems, (1946) 2nd ed. 1954 $13.75; Vol. 4, miscellaneous poems, (1947) $13.75; Vol 5, The Excursion, The Recluse, pt. 1, bk. 1, (1949) $19.25

COMPLETE POETICAL WORKS. Ed. by A. J. George Houghton *Houghton* Cambridge Eds. $10.00; ed. with introd. and notes by Thomas Hutchinson. 1895. rev. by Ernest de Selincourt *Oxford* Stand. Authors 1936 $8.00 pap. $2.25

A WORDSWORTH ANTHOLOGY. Comp. by H. Davies. *Collins* 1965 imit. lea. $1.75

POEMS. *Collins* New Class. $3.00 lea. $5.00; comp. by Elinor Parker *T. Y. Crowell* 1964 $3.50 lib. bdg. $4.25; ed. with introd. by Philip Wayne *Dutton* Everyman's 1955 3 vols. each $3.50

SELECTED POEMS AND PREFACES. Ed. by J. Stillinger. *Houghton* Riv. Eds. pap. $2.60

SELECTED POETRY. Ed. with introd. by Mark Van Doren. *Modern Library* 1950 pap. $1.45

SELECTED POEMS. Ed. by George W. Meyer *AHM Pub. Corp.* Crofts Classics pap. $.85; ed. by Roger Sharrock *Barnes & Noble* 1958 $1.75; ed. by Richard Wilbur and David Ferry *Dell* Laurel Eds. pap. $.40; *Oxford* World's Class. $2.75

POETRY AND PROSE. Sel. by W. M. Merchant. *Harvard Univ. Press* Reynard Lib. 1955 $12.00 pap. $4.50

LYRICAL BALLADS. 1798 1800. Text of 1798 with the additional poems of 1800 and the prefaces, ed. by R. L. Brett and A. R. Jones. *Barnes & Noble* 1963 $7.25 pap. $5.00

THE PRELUDE. 1799–1805. Ed. from the manuscripts with introd. and notes by Ernest de Selincourt. 1926. Rev. ed. by Helen Darbishire *Oxford* English Texts 1959 $17.75 text of 1805 ed. by E. de Selincourt Stand. Authors 1933 new impr. 1960 $4.50 rev. ed. corrected by Stephen Gill 1970 pap. $2.95; ed. by J. C. Maxwell *Penguin* 1971 pap. $3.75; ed. by P. M. Yarker Routledge English Texts *Routledge & Kegan Paul* 1968 $3.25 pap. $1.75

THE PRELUDE. With a selection from the shorter poems and the sonnets, and the 1800 preface to "Lyrical Ballads." Ed. by Carlos Baker. *Holt* (Rinehart) 1948 rev. ed. 1954 pap. $2.50

LUCY GRAY, or Solitude. c. 1799. ill. by Gilbert Riswald. *Prentice-Hall* 1964 $3.95

PROSE WORKS. For the first time collected, with additions from unpublished manuscripts. Ed. by Alexander B. Grosart 3 vols. 1876. *AMS Press* each $24.50 set $70.00; ed. by W. J. Owen and Jane W. Smyser *Oxford* 3 vols. 1973 set $64.00

LITERARY CRITICISM. Ed. by Paul M. Zall. *Univ. of Nebraska Press* 1966 Bison Bks. pap. $2.25

(With Samuel Tayler Coleridge) SELECTED CRITICAL ESSAYS. Ed. by Thomas Raysor. *AHM Pub. Corp.* Crofts Classics pap. $.85

WORDSWORTH'S POCKET NOTEBOOK. Ed. by George Harris Healey. 1942. *Kennikat* 1971 $7.50

THE LETTERS OF WILLIAM AND DOROTHY WORDSWORTH. Arr. and ed. by Ernest de Selincourt *Oxford* 6 vols. 1933–39 o.p. 2nd ed. in progress, 1967—. Vol. 1 The Early

Years, 1787–1805 rev. by Chester L. Shaver (1967) $17.00 Vol. 2 The Middle
Years, pt. 1, 1806–1811 rev. by Mary Moorman (1969) $14.50 Vol. 3 The Middle
Years, pt. 2, 1812–1820 rev. by Mary Moorman and Alan G. Hill (1970) $21.00

LETTERS OF THE WORDSWORTH FAMILY FROM 1787 TO 1855. Ed. by William Knight.
1907. *Haskell* 3 vols. $48.95; *Scholarly Press* 1971 3 vols. $49.50

Books about Wordsworth

Memoirs of William Wordsworth, Poet-Laureate. By Christopher Wordsworth, the poet's nephew. 1851.
Ed. by Henry Reed. *AMS Press* 2 vols. each $20.00 set $37.50

The Early Life of William Wordsworth, 1770–1798: A Study of "The Prelude." By Émile Legouis. 1896.
Trans. by J. W. Matthews. 1897. 2nd ed. with pref. by Leslie Stevens. 1921. *Russell & Russell* 1965
$10.00

Wordsworth. By Sir Walter Alexander Raleigh. 1903. *Scholarly Press* 1970 $13.50; *Richard West* 1973
$12.50

A Concordance to the Poems of William Wordsworth. Ed. for the Concordance Society by Lane Cooper.
1911. *Russell & Russell* 1965 $35.00

William Wordsworth: His Life, Works and Influence. By George McLean Harper. 1916 rev. ed. 1929.
Russell & Russell repr. of 1929 ed. 1960 2 vols. in 1 $20.00. For many years this biography was stand-
ard. Among more recent biographical studies, those by Mary Moorman, Edith Batho, and H. M. Margoliouth (*see below*) are of particular interest.

Wordsworth: Lectures and Essays. By Heathcote W. Garrod. *Oxford* 1923 2nd ed. rev. 1927 $4.25

Presiding Ideas in Wordsworth's Poetry. By Melvin M. Rader. 1931. *Folcroft* lib. bdg. $4.50; *Gordian*
1968 $5.00

Wordsworth and Coleridge: Studies in Honor of George McLean Harper. Ed. by Earl Leslie Griggs.
1939. *Russell & Russell* 1962 $12.00 A standard reference.

The Mind of a Poet. By Raymond D. Havens. *Johns Hopkins Univ. Press* 2 vols. 1941 Vol. 1 A Study of
Wordsworth's Thought Vol. 2 The Prelude: A Commentary each $7.50

Wordsworth. By Herbert Read. 1949. *Hillary House* pap. $1.75

The Poet Wordsworth. By Helen Darbishire. *Oxford* 1950 $4.25 pap. $1.75. A study concentrating on
the decade 1798–1808.

Wordsworth and Coleridge, 1795–1834. By Herschel M. Margoliouth. 1953. *Shoe String* 1966 $6.00

William Wordsworth. By Mary Moorman. *Oxford* 2 vols. Vol. 1 The Early Years: 1770–1803 (1957)
$12.75 pap. $3.95 Vol. 2 The Later Years: 1803–1850 (1965) $15.25 pap. $3.95

The Quest for Permanence: The Symbolism of Wordsworth, Shelley, and Keats. By David Perkins. *Harvard Univ. Press* 1959 $8.50

The Limits of Mortality: An Essay on Wordsworth's Major Poems. By David Ferry. *Wesleyan Univ.
Press* 1959 $10.00

Wordsworthian Criticism: A Guide and Bibliography. By James Venable Logan. *Ohio State Univ. Press*
1961 $6.00

DeQuincey to Wordsworth: A Biography of Relationship, with the Letters of Thomas DeQuincey to the
Wordsworth Family. By John E. Jordan. *Univ. of California Press* 1962 $12.00

On Wordsworth's Prelude. By Herbert S. Lindenberger. *Princeton Univ. Press* 1963 $9.50

Wordsworth and the Poetry of Sincerity. By David Perkins. *Harvard Univ. Press* Belknap 1964 $7.50

Wordsworth's Poetry, 1787–1814. By Geoffrey H. Hartman. *Yale Univ. Press* 1965 rev. ed. 1972 $12.50
pap. $3.95

Wordsworth. By Carl R. Woodring. 1965 *Harvard Univ. Press* 1968 $6.00
This "excellent introduction to Wordsworth . . . concentrates on the major poems and also has solid
sections on Wordsworth's prose"—(*Choice*).

Wordsworthian Criticism, 1945–1964: An Annotated Bibliography. By Elton Henley and David H.
Stam. *N.Y. Public Lib.* 1965 $6.50 pap. $5.00 supplementary vol. Wordsworthian Criticism, 1964–
1971. By David H. Stam.

Rebels and Conservatives: Dorothy and William Wordsworth and Their Circle. By Amanda M. Ellis. *Indiana Univ. Press* 1967 $10.00
"A biographical introduction to a remarkable set of remarkable people"—(*SR*).

Wordsworth: A Collection of Critical Essays. Ed. by Meyer H. Abrams. Twentieth Century Views Series.
Prentice-Hall 1972 $5.95 Spectrum Bks. pap. $1.95

The Art of the Lyrical Ballads. By Stephen M. Parrish. *Harvard Univ. Press* 1973 $12.00

The Making of Wordsworth's Poetry, 1785–1798. By Paul D. Sheats. *Harvard Univ. Press* 1973 $9.00

Biographies of Dorothy Wordsworth throw much light on the life of her brother. *See* "Dorothy Wordsworth: A Biography" by Ernest de Selincourt (*Oxford* 1933 $13.00) and her "Journals," ed. by Mary
Moorman with introd. by Helen Darbishire (*Oxford* 1971 pap. $2.95) or the 2-vol. set edited by Ernest
de Selincourt (1959 *Shoe String* 1970 $30.00).

COLERIDGE, SAMUEL TAYLOR. 1772–1834

Coleridge was one of the "Lake Poets"—a name given in contempt by the *Edinburgh Review* to Wordsworth (*q. v.*), Southey and Coleridge, who lived near each other in the English Lake District. "Poems on Various Subjects," 1796, was his first book; it also contained three sonnets by Charles Lamb (*q. v.*). In 1798 Wordsworth and Coleridge published anonymously the "Lyrical Ballads," to which the latter contributed the opening poem, "The Rime of the Ancient Mariner." "Christabel" and "Kubla Khan" were not published until 1816, although they were written 18 years before.

Coleridge's important prose works consist of "Biographia Literaria," a miscellaneous collection of notes, and "Notes and Lectures upon Shakespeare and Some of the Old Poets and Dramatists," which laid the foundations of modern Shakespearean criticism. The poet's conversation is almost as great a literary tradition as that of Dr. Johnson (*q. v.*). The publication of the "Collected Letters" (*see below*) reveals still further his great originality. The publication of the first two double volumes of his 67 personal "Notebooks" (*see below*) is of the greatest literary importance.

Swinburne (*q. v.*) said of Coleridge: "His good work is the scantiest ever done by a man so famous in so long a life"; and Stopford Brooke said: "All that he did excellently might be bound up in twenty pages, but it should be bound in pure gold." Coleridge was a poet of "magnificent beginnings"; he rarely completed anything, but his fragments have survived better than the tomes of many other writers. "Kubla Khan," "an ecstasy of sound," was left unfinished. Coleridge had fallen asleep while reading about the Oriental monarch. He had a dream about him so vivid that, on the poet's awakening, the poem sprang to life—and Coleridge wrote it feverishly until interrupted "by a person on business from Porlock" (according to Coleridge himself)—an innocent, no doubt, but forever damned for cutting short one of the greatest of poems in English. "Christabel," "a splendid fragment," stops short in the second part. Donald A. Stauffer considers the poet's enduring subject "relationship," and his life a ceaseless search "for unity in a phantasmal cosmos," whether he was occupied with science, religion, art, ethics or politics.

His personal life was erratic and unhappy. Brilliant and studious, he was nevertheless often supported financially by his friends and came more and more to depend on opium, which in association with constant ill health eventually brought about his death. Though married and a father he nurtured for some years a hopeless passion for Wordsworth's sister-in-law Sara Hutchinson.

THE COLLECTED WORKS. General ed., Kathleen Coburn and Bart Winer. *Princeton Univ. Press* Bollingen Ser. 1970–. vols. published to date: Vol. I Lectures, 1795, on Politics and Religion ed. by Lewis Patton and Peter Mann (1970) $15.00 Vol. 2 The Watchman ed. by Lewis Patton (1970) $12.50 Vol. 4 The Friend ed. by Barbara Rooke 2 pts. (1969) $20.00 Vol. 6 Lay Sermons ed. by Reginald James White (1972) $12.50. This multivolume series, when complete, will become the definitive edition of Coleridge's works.

THE PORTABLE COLERIDGE. Ed. with introd. by I. A. Richards. Includes The Ancient Mariner (1898), Christabel (1816), Kubla Khan (1816) and most of the shorter poems; ample representation of the Biographia Literaria (1817); and other selections. *Viking* 1950 $5.25 1961 pap. $3.25

POETRY AND PROSE. With essays by Hazlitt, Jeffrey, DeQuincey, Carlyle and others. Introd. and notes by H. W. Garrod. *Oxford* 1925 $2.50

SELECTED POETRY AND PROSE. Ed. by Elisabeth Schneider *Holt* (Rinehart) 1951 2nd ed. 1971 pap. $2.95; ed. by Donald Stauffer *Modern Library* 1951 pap. $1.45; ed. by Stephen Potter *Random* $12.50

THE LITERARY REMAINS OF SAMUEL TAYLOR COLERIDGE. Ed. by Henry Nelson Coleridge. 1836–39. *AMS Press* 4 vols. each $20.00 set $75.00

Poetry:

COMPLETE POETICAL WORKS. Ed. with textual and bibliographical notes by Ernest Hartley Coleridge. *Oxford* English Texts 2 vols. 1912 Vol. I Poems Vol. 2 Dramatic Works and Appendices set $19.25

POEMS. Including poems and versions of poems published for the first time, ed. with textual and bibliographical notes by Ernest Hartley Coleridge. *Oxford* 1912 Stand. Authors 1945 $6.00 pap. 1961 $3.95 World's Class. 1930 $2.50

POEMS. Ed. by Babette Deutsch *T. Y. Crowell* 1967 $3.50 lib. bdg. $4.25; ed. by John Beer *Dutton* Everyman's 1962 $3.50 pap. $1.95

COLERIDGE'S VERSE: A SELECTION. Ed. by William Empson and David Pirie. *Schocken* 1973 $10.00

COLERIDGE'S POEMS: A Facsimile Reproduction of the Proofs and Manuscripts of Some of the Poems. Ed. by James D. Campbell. 1899. *Folcroft* lib. bdg. $17.50

SELECTED POEMS. Ed. by R. C. Bald *AHM Pub. Corp.* Crofts Classics pap. $.85; ed. by James Reeves *Barnes & Noble* 1959 $2.50; ed. by Harold Bloom *New Am. Lib.* pap. $1.25

THE RIME OF THE ANCIENT MARINER. 1798. Ed. by Walter Hallenborg *Avon* Bard Bks. pap. $.60; *Coward* 1971 $5.95 lib. bdg. $4.97; with 42 ills. by Gustave Doré 1878, with new introd. by Millicent Rose *Dover* 1970 pap. $2.50; *Hawthorn* 1966 $3.95; ill. by Charles Mosely *Franklin Watts* lib. bdg. $3.95

THE ANNOTATED ANCIENT MARINER. Ed. by Martin Gardner. *Clarkson N. Potter* 1966 $7.50; *World Pub.* Meridian Bks. pap. $3.95

Prose:

BIOGRAPHIA LITERARIA, or Biographical Sketches of My Literary Life and Opinions. 1817. Ed. with introd. by George Watson. *Dutton* Everyman's new ed. 1956 $3.50

BIOGRAPHIA LITERARIA and AESTHETICAL ESSAYS. Ed. by John Shawcross. *Oxford* 1907 2 vols. set $10.25

CONFESSIONS OF AN INQUIRING SPIRIT. 1840. Ed. by H. St. J. Hart. *Stanford Univ. Press* 1957 pap. $1.85

SEVEN LECTURES ON SHAKESPEARE AND MILTON. Ed. by J. Payne Collier. 1856. *AMS Press* $12.50; *Burt Franklin* 1967 $18.00

COLERIDGE ON SHAKESPEARE: The texts of the Lectures of 1811–12. Ed. by R. A. Foakes. Folger Monographs on Tudor and Stuart Civilization. *Univ. Press of Virginia* 1971 $5.75. Based on previously unpublished transcripts of J. P. Collier's notes, now in the Folger Shakespeare Library.

LECTURES AND NOTES ON SHAKESPEARE AND OTHER ENGLISH POETS. Comp. and ed. by T. Ashe. 1884. *Bks. for Libraries* 1970 $17.00

SHAKESPEAREAN CRITICISM. Ed. by Thomas Middleton Raysor. *Dutton* Everyman's 1930 rev. ed. 1960 2 vols. each $3.50

CRITICAL ANNOTATIONS. Ed. by William F. Taylor. 1889. *Folcroft* lib. bdg. $10.00. Marginal notes inscribed in volumes formerly in the possession of Samuel Taylor Coleridge.

COLERIDGE'S LITERARY CRITICISM. Mostly marginalia. Ed. by J. W. Mackail. 1908. *Folcroft* lib. bdg. $15.00

COLERIDGE'S MISCELLANEOUS CRITICISM. Ed. by Thomas Middleton Raysor. 1936. *Folcroft* lib. bdg. $20.00. Contains lectures of 1818, manuscripts, reports of lectures and marginalia on the same subjects, miscellaneous marginalia, early reviews, table talk, conversations on Henry Crabb Robinson.

THE NOTEBOOKS OF SAMUEL TAYLOR COLERIDGE. Ed. by Kathleen Coburn. *Princeton Univ. Press* Bollingen Series 3 vols. Vol. I 1794–1804 (1957) $27.50 Vol. 2 1804–1808 (1961) $27.50 Vol. 3 1808–1819 (1973) $37.50

The first 3 double volumes in the publication of the 67 personal notebooks which will total at least a dozen separate volumes. Vol. I offers "an incredible gathering of notes, thoughts, lists, accounts, and references" annotated, "analyzed and explained by Miss Coburn with a devoted scholarship." The second double volume gives details of his "voyage from England to the Mediterranean, his government service in Malta, and his travels in Sicily and Italy, his metrical experiments, studies of the Italian language and Italian poetry, attempts at writing in cipher, his love for Sara Hutchinson and his addiction to opium."

COLLECTED LETTERS. Ed. by Earl Leslie Griggs. *Oxford* 6 vols. Vols. I and 2 (1956) $24.00 Vols. 3 and 4 (1959) $24.00 Vols. 5 and 6 (1971) $35.25

This is an important and complete collection drawn mainly from original manuscripts. "After decades of patient search during which he traced holographs dispersed in 150 collections from Scotland to New Zealand, Professor Griggs has brought together all the known letters of the man who, besides being the author of 'The Ancient Mariner,' had perhaps the most inquiring and seminal mind of the early nineteenth century"—(*SR*).

Books about Coleridge

The Road to Xanadu. By John Livingston Lowes. *Houghton* 1927 $7.95 Sentry Eds. pap. $2.85. Excellent literary history, by a Harvard professor who devoted much of his career to the study of Coleridge.
Coleridge on Imagination. By I. A. Richards. 1934. 2nd ed. 1950. *Univ. of Indiana Press* 1960 pap. $1.95; *Peter Smith* $4.25
Coleridge and S. T. C.: A Study of Coleridge's Dual Nature. By Stephen Potter. 1935. *Russell & Russell* 1965 $8.50. A serious work by the expert on "gamesmanship" (*q.v.*).
Samuel Taylor Coleridge. By E. K. Chambers. *Oxford* 1938 $12.00
The Life of Samuel T. Coleridge: The Early Years. By Lawrence Hanson. 1939. *Russell & Russell* $12.50. One of the standard biographies.
Wordsworth and Coleridge: Studies in Honor of George McLean Harper. Ed. by Earl Leslie Griggs. 1939. *Russell & Russell* 1962 $12.00
Wordsworth and Coleridge, 1795–1834. By Herschel Maurice Margoliouth. Ed. by Earl Leslie Griggs. *Shoe String* 1966 $6.00
Coleridge and Sara Hutchinson and the Asra Poems. By George Whalley. *Univ. of Toronto Press* 1955 $6.00
Coleridge: Critic of Society. By John Colmer. *Oxford* 1959 $6.00
The Dark Night of Samuel Coleridge. By Marshall Edward Suther. *Columbia* 1960 $7.50. Examines Coleridge's preoccupation with philosophy and theology and attempts to explain the poet's emotional life.
Visions of Xanadu. By Marshall E. Suther. *Columbia* 1965 $9.00.
"Suther uses the whole of Coleridge's poetry and prose and the insights of recent scholarship to demonstrate that 'Kubla Khan' is not only symbolically meaningful but important for understanding the entire Romantic Movement—(*LJ*).
Samuel Taylor Coleridge. By Virginia L. Radley. English Authors Series. *Twayne* 1966 $5.50
Coleridge: A Collection of Critical Essays. Ed. by Kathleen Coburn. Twentieth Century Views Series. *Prentice-Hall* 1967 $5.95 Spectrum Bks. pap. $1.95
Coleridge and the Abyssinian Maid. By Geoffrey Yarlott. *Barnes & Noble* 1967 $8.75 pap. $3.00.
"In this admirably thorough and scholarly work on the critical years 1795–1804 . . . the author discusses at length the poet's relationships with his friends and with the women in his life, . . . offers detailed interpretation of the major poems, and analyses his critical ideas. It is a highly intelligent . . . always lucidly written work of scholarship"—(*Books and Bookmen*).
A Concordance to the Poetry of Samuel Taylor Coleridge. Ed. by Eugenia Logan. *Peter Smith* $20.00
Coleridge. By Walter Jackson Bate. *Macmillan* 1968 $5.95 Collier Bks. pap. $2.95. An excellent short biography.
Twentieth Century Interpretations of the Rime of the Ancient Mariner. Ed. by James D. Boulger. *Prentice-Hall* 1969 $4.95 Spectrum Bks. pap. $1.25

Coleridge: The Critical Heritage. Ed. by James R. Jackson. *Barnes & Noble* 1970 $13.50
Coleridge, the Damaged Archangel. By Norman Fruman. *Braziller* 1971 $12.50. Studies Coleridge's debt
to other authors.

BYRON, GEORGE GORDON NOËL, 6th Baron Byron. 1788–1824.

Lord Byron left an immense body of work. "Shakespeare excepted, his versatility is without parallel among English poets"—(Churton Collins), but he is probably the important English Romantic least read today. His great satire "English Bards and Scotch Reviewers" was written when he was 21. It is as abusive and as denunciatory as Pope's "Dunciad" (*q.v.*). Byron in later life pronounced it to be the best of his works.

"The Pilgrimage of Childe Harold" appeared in 1812, and Byron, as he said, "awoke to find himself famous." He completed the poem later in four cantos and 186 Spenserian stanzas. The scene of "Childe Harold" is laid in Spain, Portugal, Greece and Italy. Its immense popularity in its day has been explained on the ground of its subject matter. "The desultory wanderings of Childe Harold traversed ground every mile of which was memorable to men who had watched the struggle which had been going on in Europe, with scarcely a pause for twenty years. Descriptive journalism was then unknown, and the poem by its descriptiveness . . . made the same kind of success that vividly written special correspondence would today." Byron's masterpiece, "Don Juan," is a long work in 16 cantos, founded on the old Spanish saga, familiar to us in the works of Molière (*q.v.*), Shadwell, Mozart, Dumas (*q.v.*) and others. In his day the poet with the club foot— handsome, aristocratic, unconventional and self-assured—became a legend, and his work influenced that of many writers abroad. Prototype of the "Byronic hero"—the cynical genius breaking hearts all around him— he nevertheless died in the service of the liberation of Greece. In May, 1968, Lord Byron received at last the honor denied him at the time of his burial—a plaque in the Poets' Corner of Westminster Abbey.

Russell & Russell has recently reprinted two early-20th-century studies of Byron by Samuel C. Chew, one by W. J. Calvert, one by Fuess and one, slightly revised, by Marjarum.

WORKS. Ed. by E. H. Coleridge and R. E. Prothero. *Octagon* 1966 13 vols. set $160.00

COMPLETE POETICAL WORKS. Ed. by Paul E. More. *Houghton* Cambridge Eds. $12.50

POETICAL WORKS. Ed. by Frederick Page. *Oxford* reset ed. 1945 $8.00 new ed. corrected by John Jump Stand. Authors pap. 1972 $4.95

POETICAL WORKS. Ed. by E. H. Coleridge. 1905. *Hillary House* 1972 $15.00

POEMS. Ed. by Horace Gregory. *T. Y. Crowell* 1969 $3.50. lib. bdg. $4.25

POEMS AND PROSE. *Collins* New Class. $3.00 lea. $5.00

POEMS AND DRAMATIC WORKS. *Dutton* Everyman's rev. ed. 1948 3 vols. each $3.50

SELECTED POETRY, CAIN AND LETTERS. Ed. by Edward Bostetter. *Holt* (Rinehart) 1951 2nd ed. 1971 pap. $2.50

SELECTED POEMS AND LETTERS. Ed. by William H. Marshall. *Houghton* Rev. Eds. 1968 pap. $2.35

SELECTIONS FROM POETRY, LETTERS AND JOURNAL. Ed. by Peter Quennell. *Random* $12.50

SELECTED POEMS. Ed. by Robin Skelton *Barnes & Noble* 1966 $2.00; ed. by George Creeger *Dell* 1963 pap. $.35; *Oxford* World's Class. $3.00

SELECTED POETRY. Ed. by Leslie A. Marchand *Modern Library* $2.95 pap. $1.45; ed. by W. H. Auden *New Am. Lib.* Signet 1966 pap. $.95

FUGITIVE PIECES. 1806. With biographical note by Marcel Kessel. 1933 *Haskell* facsimile ed. 1972 lib. bdg. $5.95

CHILDE HAROLD'S PILGRIMAGE (1812–1818) and OTHER ROMANTIC POEMS. Ed. by Samuel C. Chew. *Odyssey* 1936 $3.50

DON JUAN. 1819–1824. A variorum ed. by Truman Guy Steffan and Willis W. Pratt. *Univ. of Texas Press* 1957 2nd ed. 1972 4 vols. set $50.00

DON JUAN. Ed. by L. A. Marchand *Houghton* Riv. Eds. 1959 pap. $2.10; ed. by Truman Guy and E. Steffan *Penguin* 1972 pap. $5.95

CAIN. 1821. Twelve Essays and a Text with Variants and Annotations ed. by Truman Guy Steffan. *Univ. of Texas Press* 1969 $15.00

LIFE, LETTERS AND JOURNALS. 1901. *Scholarly Press* $39.50

LORD BYRON IN HIS LETTERS. Ed. by V. H. Collins. 1927. *Haskell* lib. bdg. $11.95; *Richard West* $11.75

THE LETTERS OF GEORGE GORDON, SIXTH LORD BYRON. Sel. by R. G. Howarth. 300 letters from 1799–1824 with introd. by André Maurois. *Dutton* Everyman's 1933–1936 rev. ed. 1961 $3.50

BYRON: A SELF PORTRAIT. Letters and Diaries, 1798 to 1824. Ed. by Peter Quennell. *Humanities Press* 1950 2 vols. set $15.00. An excellent selection from a huge correspondence, arranged in six sections to tell a continuous story.

Books about Byron

Conversations of Lord Byron. By Thomas Medwin. 1824. Rev. ed. by E. J. Lovell, Jr. *Princeton Univ. Press* 1966 $12.50

"Although [Medwin] claimed that his verbatim conversations were drawn from his diary, he could never produce that documentary proof. He must have relied on memory embellished with imagination. . . . If Medwin's facts are unreliable, his style is remarkably vivacious, and frequently rings with Byron's racy and bluff informality"—(*SR*).

Lord Byron and Some of His Contemporaries. 1828. by Leigh Hunt. *AMS Press* $25.00

Byron. By Ethel C. Mayne. 1924. *Barnes & Noble* 1969 $12.50; *Bks. for Libraries* $14.50; *Scholarly Press* $19.50; *Richard West* $14.45

Byron and the Need of Fatality. By Charles DuBos; trans. by Ethel C. Mayne. 1932. *Folcroft* lib. bdg. $10.00; *Haskell* 1970 $11.95; *Scholarly Press* $14.50

Byron: Romantic Paradox. By William J. Calvert. 1935. *Russell & Russell* 1962 $10.00

Byron: The Years of Fame. By Peter Quennell. 1935. *Shoe String* rev. ed. 1967 $7.50

Byron in Italy. By Peter Quennell. 1941. *Bks. for Libraries* $14.00

Byron's Don Juan: A Critical Study. By Elizabeth F. Boyd. *Humanities Press* 1945 $7.50

The Flowering of Byron's Genius: Studies in Byron's Don Juan. By Paul G. Trueblood. 1945. *Russell & Russell* 1962 $9.00

Byron: The Record of a Quest: Studies in a Poet's Concept and Treatment of Nature. By E. J. Lovell. 1949. *Shoe String* 1966 $6.50

Lord Byron: Christian Virtues. By George Wilson Knight. 1952. *Routledge & Kegal Paul* $9.25

Byron and Goethe. By E. M. Butler. 1956. *Hillary House* $7.25

Lord Byron's Marriage. By George Wilson Knight. 1957. *Routledge & Kegan Paul* $9.25

Byron: A Biography. By Leslie A. Marchand. *Knopf* 1957 3 vols. boxed $25.00. A monumental and authoritative study incorporating the results of recent Byron scholarship.

Byron. By André Maurois; trans. by Miles Hamish. *Ungar* pap. $2.75

The Style of Don Juan. By George M. Ridenour. 1960. *Shoe String* 1969 $5.50

Byron: A Critical Study. By Andrew Rutherford. *Stanford Univ. Press* 1961 $7.50 pap. $2.95

The Structure of Byron's Major Poems. By William H. Marshall. *Univ. of Pennsylvania Press* 1962 $7.50

Lord Byron's Wife. By Malcolm Elwin. *Harcourt* 1963 $8.75

Byron's Poetry. By Leslie A. Marchand. 1963. *Harvard Univ. Press* $7.50

"Within a year or two, this excellent handbook will appear on all reserve reading lists for courses in the Romantic movement, and many teachers of such courses will be describing it as 'indispensable' "—(*Choice*).

Byron: A Collection of Critical Essays. Ed. by Paul West. *Prentice-Hall* 1963 Spectrum Bks. pap. $1.95

Byron and Shakespeare. By G. Wilson Knight. *Barnes & Noble* 1966 $7.00

"The overall conviction that 'Byron lived Shakespeare' . . . may be in some measure a *tour de force*, but it works translucently to make this an exciting study of Byron—of the whole Byron, man and poet and diarist, as seen almost from within"—(*TLS*, London).

Byron and the Ruins of Paradise. By Robert F. Gleckner. *Johns Hopkins Univ. Press* 1967 $11.00
"An important and scholarly book that should be in all the smallest literature collections"—(*LJ*).
The title refers to Byron's feeling that modern man had corrupted an idyllic past.

Byron: The Critical Heritage. Ed. by Andrew Rutherford. *Barnes & Noble* 1970 $15.00

SHELLEY, PERCY BYSSHE. 1792-1822.

Matthew Arnold (*q.v.*) described Shelley as "a beautiful and ineffectual angel beating in the void his luminous wings in vain." Time has not confirmed the "in vain": Shelley's daring in his tragically short life before his drowning has proved as fascinating as his verse.

Shelley wrote two great dramatic works: "Prometheus Unbound" (1820), a lyrical drama in four acts, which has many long passages of polemic "in favor of suffering and oppressed humanity" but also has lovely lyrics; and "The Cenci" (1820), a tragedy in five acts founded on the life story of the beautiful Italian, Beatrice Cenci. His elegiac poem "Adonais" was written on the death of Keats (*q.v.*), whom he had known only slightly. Shelley's shorter poems, such as "To a Skylark," have proved most enduring.

THE COMPLETE WORKS. Ed. by Roger Ingpen and Walter E. Peck. 10 vols. 1926–30. *Gordian* 1965 Vols. 1–4 Poems Vols. 5–7 Prose Vols. 8–10 Letters set $125.00. The standard collection.

THE COMPLETE POETICAL WORKS. Ed. by G. E. Woodberry *Houghton* Cambridge Eds. 1901 $8.00; ed. by Neville Rogers *Oxford* English Texts 2 vols. Vol. I 1802–1813 (1972) $16.00 Vol. 2 1814–1817 (1974) $24.00 ed. by Thomas Hutchinson 1934 1961 new ed. corrected by G. M. Matthews 1971 $8.00

POEMS. Ed. by Tobias Smollett. *Collins* New Class. $3.00 lea. $5.00; ed. by Leo Gurko *T. Y. Crowell* 1968 $3.50 lib. bdg. $4.25

POETRY AND PROSE. Ed. by A. M. D. Hughes (with essays on Shelley by Browning, Bagehot, Swinburne, Hogg, Peacock, and Trelawny). *Oxford* 1931 $2.50

SELECTED POETRY, PROSE AND LETTERS. Ed. by A. S. B. Glover. *Random* $12.50

SELECTED POETRY AND PROSE. Ed. by Kenneth N. Cameron *Holt* (Rinehart) 1951 pap. $2.50; ed. by Carlos Baker *Modern Library* 1951 $2.95 pap. $1.25; ed. by G. M. Matthews *Oxford* 1964 $2.50

SELECTED POETRY. Ed. by Neville Rogers *Houghton* Riv. Eds. pap. $2.35; ed. by Harold Bloom *New Am. Lib.* pap. $1.25

SELECTED POEMS. Ed. by Frederick L. Jones *AHM Pub. Corp.* Crofts Class. pap. $.85; ed. by John Holloway *Barnes & Noble* 1965 $1.75; *Oxford* World's Class. $2.50

THE ESDAILE NOTEBOOK. A volume of early poems. Ed. by Kenneth N. Cameron *Knopf* 1964 $7.95; (with title "The Esdaile Poems") ed. by Neville Rogers *Oxford* 1966 $6.50

ZASTROZZI: A Romance. 1810. *Golden Cockerel Press* 1/4 mor. $20.00 mor. with gold decorations $45.00

PROMETHEUS UNBOUND. 1820. A poetic drama. Variorum ed. by Lawrence John Zillman. *Univ. of Washington Press* 1959 $15.00

THE CENCI. 1820. Introd. by Alfred and H. Buxton Forman. Shelley Society Publications. 1886. *Phaeton* (dist. by Gordian) 1970 $6.00; ed. by Roland A. Duerksen *Bobbs* Lib. Arts 1970 pap. $1.75

HELLAS: A Lyrical Drama. 1822. Ed. by Thomas J. Wise. 1886. *Phaeton* (dist. by Gordian) 1970 $6.00

A DEFENSE OF POETRY. 1840. (And "The Political Writings") ed. by Roland A. Duerksen *AHM Pub. Corp.* Crofts Class. 1970 pap. $1.25; (and Peacock's "Four Ages of Poetry") ed. by John E. Jordan *Bobbs* Lib. Arts 1965 pap. $.95; (and "A Letter to Lord Ellenborough") 1948 *Folcroft* lib. bdg. $5.50 (and Blunden's "Lectures on the Defence") lib. bdg. $5.50

LETTERS. Ed. by Frederick L. Jones. *Oxford* 1964 2 vols. Vol. 1 Shelley in England Vol. 2 Shelley in Italy set $29.00

LETTERS AND ESSAYS. Ed. by Ernest Rhys. 1886. *Bks. for Libraries* facsimile ed. $13.75

THE NOTE BOOKS. Ed. by H. Buxton Forman. 1911. *Phaeton* (dist. by Gordian) 1967 3 vols. $25.00

Books about Shelley

The standard collection of Shelley's writings is "The Complete Works" in 10 vols. ed. by Roger Ingpen and Walter E. Peck (see above). Among earlier studies of the poet which have been recently reprinted, those by W. E. Peck, Burt Franklin, O. W. Campbell, Haskell and Russell & Russell, and Solve, Russell & Russell are of particular interest.

The Life of Percy Bysshe Shelley. By Edward Dowden. 1886. *Barnes & Noble* 1966 $5.00; *Folcroft* lib. bdg. $8.00

Ariel: The Life of Shelley. By André Maurois; trans. by Ella D'Arcy. 1923. *Ungar* 1958 $7.50 pap. $1.75. A sympathetic and sentimental interpretive life.

A Newton among Poets: Shelley's Use of Science in Prometheus Unbound. By Carl Grabo. 1930. *Cooper Square* 1968 $5.50; *Gordian* 1968 $5.50

The Unextinguished Hearth: Shelley and his Contemporary Critics. By Newman Ivey White. 1938. *Octagon* 1966 $12.00

Shelley. By Newman Ivey White. 2 vols. 1940. *Octagon* 1972 $65.00. The definitive biography.

Portrait of Shelley. By Newman Ivey White. *Knopf* 1945 $6.95. A scholarly and sympathetic condensation of the 2-volume definitive life (*see above*).

Shelley: A Life Story. By Edmund Blunden. 1946. *Oxford* 1965 $2.95

Shelley's Major Poetry: The Fabric of a Vision. By Carlos H. Baker. 1948. *Princeton Univ. Press* 1966 pap. $3.45; *Russell & Russell* 1961 $13.50

The Imagery of Keats and Shelley: A Comparative Study. By Richard H. Fogle. 1949. *Univ. of North Carolina Press* 1969 $6.95 pap. $2.95

Young Shelley: The Genesis of a Radical. By Kenneth N. Cameron. 1950. *Octagon* 1973 $15.00

Deep Truth: A Study of Shelley's Scepticism. By C. E. Pulos. 1954. *Univ. of Nebraska Press* 1962 Bison Bks. pap. $1.65

Shelley at Work: A Critical Inquiry. By Neville Rogers. *Oxford* 1956 rev. ed. 1967 $12.75
The author discusses "a wealth of material bearing on Shelley's reading, the origin and development of his leading ideas and symbols, and his habits of composition"—(*SR*).

The Subtler Language: Critical Readings of Neo-classic and Romantic Poems. By Earl Wasserman. 1959. *Johns Hopkins Univ. Press* pap. 1968 $3.45

Shelley: His Thought and Work. By Desmond King-Hele. 1960. *Bucknell Univ. Press* 2nd ed. $10.00; *Fairleigh Dickinson Univ. Press* 2nd ed. 1971 $10.00

Apocalyptic Vision in the Poetry of Shelley. By Ross Woodman. *Univ. of Toronto Press* 1964 $7.50

Shelley and His Circle, 1773–1822. The Carl H. Pforzheimer Library. *Harvard Univ. Press* 8 vols. to be published Vols. 1–2 ed. by Kenneth Neill Cameron (1961) boxed set $30.00 Vols. 3–4 ed. by K. N. Cameron (1970) boxed set $40.00 Vols. 5–6 ed. by Donald Reiman (1972) boxed set $60.00
"Mr. Cameron and his contributing editors have rescued the material from felonious footnotery primarily by enclosing it in a continuous narrative that contains detailed introductions to each of the characters of the circle, and a general background of their relationship and of the times. Urbanely written and seemingly omniscient within its area"—(*SR*).

Shelley. By Stephen Spender. *British Bk. Centre* $2.38 pap. $1.20

Toward the Understanding of Shelley. By Bennett Weaver. *Octagon* 1966 $9.50

The Mutiny Within: The Heresies of Percy Bysshe Shelley. By James Rieger. *Braziller* 1967 $6.50 pap. $2.95. An "intellectual biography" that is at once scholarly, lively and controversial. It attempts to shed new light on the poet's drowning.
Shelley's Mythmaking. By Harold Bloom. *Cornell Univ. Press* 1969 pap. $1.95
Shelley: A Collection of Critical Essays. Ed. by George M. Ridenour. *Prentice-Hall* 1967 $5.95

See also Chapter 11, British Fiction: Middle Period, for Mary Wollstonecraft Shelley, Shelley's second wife.

KEATS, JOHN. 1795–1821.

Keats, one of England's greatest poets, was a pagan in spirit, "a true Greek," although he knew nothing of the Greek language. Some of his best-known poems are concerned with Greek subjects: "Hyperion," about the war of the Titans and the Olympians; the "Ode on a Grecian Urn"; "Endymion"; and "Ode to Psyche." His matchless sonnet on Chapman's Homer was also of Greek inspiration. The great Keats scholar, Sir Sidney Colvin, found Keats' poetic treatment "as far from being a Greek or 'classical' manner as possible. . . .but in his own rich and decorated English way he writes with a sure insight into the vital meaning of Greek ideas." His warm and affectionate personality, which permeates his magnificent lyrics, made him many close friends: *see* Hyder Rollins, "The Keats Circle," *in Books about Keats below.*

Keats trained for medicine, forsook it for poetry and died of tuberculosis after a tragically brief career. He revealed himself so completely and charmingly in the letters he wrote during his short life that there are many volumes combining his poetry and letters. The letters are perhaps now read as much as the poetry for their high literary value. Hyder Rollins' edition is definitive.

Sir Sidney Colvin wrote a brief life of Keats in the English Men of Letters Series (*see Books about Keats below*) and another in a volume of Keats' Letters to His Family and Friends, which he edited in 1887 (1891 5th ed. 1921, o.p.). These two formed the foundation for his great biography, "John Keats: His Life and Poetry, His Friends, Critics and After-Fame" (*see Books about Keats below*). Colvin, who had devoted most of his life to Keats, wrote this in his 73rd year. Amy Lowell's "John Keats" (1925, *see Books about Keats below*) contributed much new material from her own collection of manuscripts and included a forceful defense of Fanny Brawne, with whom Keats was passionately in love and whom he never married because of his failing health. "The Life and Letters of John Keats," by Richard Monckton Milnes (*see Books about Keats below*) containing the earliest life of Keats, and published in 1848, was written during the lifetime of Fanny Brawne, but does not even mention her name. "All earlier biographies have now been replaced, however, by W. J. Bate's notable study of the poet's life, writings, and place in the English poetic tradition."—(M. H. Abrams). *For comment see Books about Keats below.*

The "Selected Prose of John Hamilton Reynolds," edited by Leonidas M. Jones (*Harvard Univ. Press* 1966 $14.00) is the work of one of Keats' intimate friends and is "not only a study of Keats and his circle but a Pepysian view of life, literature and the theater in the early 1800's. . . .Recommended"—(*LJ*). Of similar interest are "The Letters of Charles Armitage Brown" (ed. by Jack Stillinger, *Harvard Univ. Press* 1966 $12.00), Keats' close friend during the two most important years of his life, and "Lord Elgin and His Marbles" by William St. Clair (*Oxford* 1967 $7.75), about a matter in which Keats was deeply interested.

COMPLETE WORKS. Ed. by H. Buxton Forman. 5 vols. 1900. *AMS Press* 1970 each $17.50 set $85.00; rev. ed. by Maurice Buxton Forman, with introd. by John Masefield. 8 vols. 1938. *Phaeton* (dist. by Gordian) 1970 set $100.00

COMPLETE POETICAL WORKS. Ed. by Horace E. Scudder. *Houghton* Cambridge Eds. $7.00

COMPLETE POETICAL WORKS OF KEATS AND SHELLEY. *Modern Library* Giants 1932 $4.95

COMPLETE POETRY AND SELECTED PROSE. Ed. with introd. by Harold Edgar Briggs. *Modern Library* 1951 $2.95 pap. $1.25

COMPLETE POEMS AND SELECTED LETTERS. Ed. by Clarence Dewitt Thorpe. *Odyssey* 1935 $3.50

POETICAL WORKS. Ed. by Heathcote W. Garrod. *Oxford* Oxford English Texts 1939 2nd ed. 1958 $17.75 ed. by H. W. Garrod Stand. Authors 1956 $7.00 pap. $3.00 World's Class. $2.50

POEMS. Ed. by Edmund Blunden *Collins* New Class. $3.00 lea. $5.00; comp. by Stanley Kunitz *T. Y. Crowell* 1964 $3.50 lib. bdg. $4.25; ed. by Gerald Bullett *Dutton* Everyman's new ed. $3.50 pap $1.55; *Nelson* Poets $1.72; ed. by Miriam Allott. Annotated English Poets Series. *Norton* 1972 $9.95

SELECTED POEMS. Ed. by George H. Ford. 1950. *AHM Pub. Corp.* Crofts Class. pap. $.85

SELECTED POETRY AND LETTERS. Ed. by Robert Gittings *Barnes & Noble* 1966 $1.75; ed. with introd. by Richard Harter Fogle *Holt* (Rinehart) 1951 pap. $2.50; ed. by Douglas Bush *Houghton* Riv. Eds. $2.25; ed. by Roger Sharrock *Oxford* 1964 $2.50; ed. by Carlos Baker *Scribner* 1970 pap. $4.50

THE ANATOMICAL AND PHYSIOLOGICAL NOTEBOOK. Ed. by Maurice Buxton Forman. 1934. *Haskell* 1972 $7.95

THE LETTERS OF JOHN KEATS, 1814–1821. Ed. by Hyder Edward Rollins. *Harvard Univ. Press* 2 vols. 1958 boxed set $25.00. The "most nearly complete edition of Keats' correspondence."

LETTERS, PAPERS AND OTHER RELICS. Ed. by Maurice Buxton Forman. 1931. *Folcroft* 1973 lib. bdg. $65.00

LETTERS. Ed. by Robert Gittings. *Oxford* 1970 pap. $3.75

See also "Life and Letters of John Keats" by Lord Houghton, below.

Books about Keats

Earlier studies of interest, not listed below, which have been recently reprinted, include those by C. D. Thorpe and M. R. Ridley (Russell & Russell), Fausset (Shoe String) and Zilman (Octagon).

The Life and Letters of John Keats. By Richard Monckton Milnes, Lord Houghton. 1848. *Dutton* Everyman's $3.50 pap. $1.75 *(for comment see bio-critical notes above)*.

Keats. By Sir Sidney Colvin. English Men of Letters Series. 1887. *St. Martin's* 1957 $4.25 pap. $1.75; ed. by John Morley. 1889. *AMS Press* lib. bdg. $12.50 *(for comment see bio-critical notes above)*.

John Keats: His Life and Poetry, His Friends, Critics and After-Fame. By Sir Sidney Colvin. 1917 rev. ed. 1925. *Octagon* 1970 $20.00; *Richard West* 1973 $18.45 *(for comment see bio-critical notes above)*.

Keats and Shakespeare: A Study of Keats' Poetic Life from 1821–1895. By John Middleton Murry. *Oxford* 1924 $10.25

John Keats. By Amy Lowell. 2 vols. 1925. *Shoe String* 1969 $25.00 *(for comment see bio-critical notes above)*.

Keats: A Critical Essay. By H. W. Garrod. 1926. *Oxford* 2nd ed. 1939 $4.00

Keats' Shakespeare. By Caroline F. Spurgeon. 1928. *Oxford* 1967 $6.50. A fascinating study based on Keats' marginalia in his copy of Shakespeare's works.

The Stylistic Development of Keats. By Walter J. Bate. 1945. *Humanities Press* $7.50

The Imagery of Keats and Shelley: A Comparative Study. By Richard H. Fogle. 1949. *Univ. of North Carolina Press* 1969 $6.95 pap. $2.95

Keats. By John Middleton Murry. The 1949 (3rd) edition was entitled "The Mystery of Keats." *Funk & Wagnalls* Minerva Bks. pap. $2.95

Keats: A Bibliography and Reference Guide, 1816–1946, with an Essay on Keats' Reputation. Ed. by J. R. MacGillivray. *Univ. of Toronto Press* 1949 $9.50

The Finer Tone: Keats' Major Poems. By Earl J. Wasserman. *Johns Hopkins Univ. Press* 1953 $8.00 pap. $3.45

The Keats Circle: Letters and Papers and More Letters and Poems of the Keats Circle. Ed. by Hyder Edward Rollins *Harvard Univ. Press* 1955 2nd ed. 1965 2 vols. boxed $25.00

John Keats: The Growth of a Genius. By Walter Jackson Bate. *Harvard Univ. Press* 1963 $15.00; *Oxford* Galaxy Bks. pap. $4.95

Twenty years in preparation, this is the first critical biography in a generation. With much new material, Professor Bate provides an equally thorough reinterpretation of Keats' work, the nature of its development, and its meaning for today's readers. Professor Bate is Abbott Lawrence Lowell Professor of the Humanities and Chairman of the Department of English, Harvard University. For this book he received in 1964 the Pulitzer Prize, the Harvard Faculty Prize and the Christian Gauss Award of Phi Beta Kappa. It "is the most definitive and most perceptive biography of Keats to have been written"— (Stephen Spender). In "the consideration of the elements of Keats's style and the development of his philosophy of poetry [Bate] is probably as knowledgeable as any man alive"—(*SR*).

John Keats: The Making of a Poet. By Aileen Ward. The relation between his greatness as a poet and his development as a man. Winner of the National Book Award, 1964. *Viking* 1963 $8.95 Compass Bks. pap. $1.85

Aesthetic and Myth in the Poetry of Keats. By Walter H. Evert. "A highly perceptive and original study"—(*PBIP*). *Princeton Univ. Press* 1964 $11.50 1966 pap. $2.95

Keats: A Collection of Critical Essays. Ed. by Walter Jackson Bate. *Prentice-Hall* 1964 $5.95 Spectrum Bks. pap. $1.95

A "discriminating collection of illuminating present-day critical studies. . . .Such distinguished scholar-critics as T.S. Eliot, Richard Harter Fogle, Douglas Bush and David Bloom are among the contributors"—(*LJ*).

The Keats Inheritance. By Robert Gittings. *Barnes & Noble* 1965 $3.50

John Keats: His Life and Writings. By Douglas Bush. *Macmillan* 1966 $4.95 Collier Bks. pap. $1.95

"The general reader will enjoy the simplicity and clarity of its presentation while the more serious student of poetry will benefit by Bush's insights and scholarship"—(*LJ*).

Keats and the Mirror of Art. By Ian Jack. *Oxford* 1967 $12.00

John Keats. By Robert Gittings. *Little-Atlantic* 1968 $10.00

"Following close on the heels of two fine American biographies . . . by Aileen Ward and W. J. Bate (both 1963) comes a third comprehensive life, this time by an Englishman. . . . It is the one to read if you have not read a life of the poet before. It combines, in the most authoritative way, the facts of his life, the states of the poet's mind, the occasion and genesis of the work"—(Eliot Fremont-Smith). "A splendid work, impressive and deeply moving"—(Lionel Trilling).

Keats: The Critical Heritage. Ed. by G. M. Matthews. *Barnes & Noble* 1972 $17.50

—H.M.

Chapter 6

British Poetry: Middle Period

"I found in dreams a place of wind and flowers."
—Swinburne

The writers named in this section are often called "Victorian" after the name of the Queen who reigned from 1837 to 1901. But it is worth recalling that Tennyson, the most essentially Victorian of the Victorian poets, was writing poems in the regency period, and published his first important volumes in the days of good King William. At the other end of the period one looks well beyond the First World War even to the eve of the second (Kipling and Housman died in 1936). The "Victorians," then, are not exclusively Victorian. And even the period of Victoria's reign is by no means as homogeneous as the happy accident of her continuous presence on the throne would lead one to suspect.

Three main subdivisions can be discerned in the long history of Victorian poetry. The first includes the twilight of the great romantics, and the brief efflourescence of minor figures like Hood, Aytoun, or Bailey, beside the growing fame of Tennyson and Browning (*q.v.*), whose ascent culminated in "In Memoriam" and "Idylls of the King"; "Men and Women," and "The Ring and the Book." But a second generation of poets soon began to make their distinctive voices heard in such revolutionary volumes as Morris's "Defence of Guenevere" (*q.v.*), Swinburne's "Poems and Ballads" (*q.v.*), and Rossetti's "Poems" (*q.v.*). Their attention was turned not to the political, religious, and moral issues that had preoccupied thoughtful writers of the thirties, forties, and fifties, but to the inner life of the individual, for whom, in Walter Pater's much-quoted and much-misunderstood phrase, "not the fruit of experience, but experience itself" was the end. By the end of the century, the members of movements known as "aesthetic" or "decadent" had rejected all hope of working out the mystery of that one far-off divine event towards which the whole creation moves, and instead revelled in the sensations of beauty, and the excitement of art. Out of the work of the Victorians then came forth a new poetry in the very different writing of Pound, Eliot, and Yeats, each of whom had grown up in the worship of the old gods, but now set off to make his own way.

The Victorian poets wrote in an era of revolutionary change in which the most bewildering feature was the rapidity with which the changes took place: in politics, manufactures, and population, and in religion, science, and the arts. Good general introductions to the background of the period are: Sir Llewellyn Woodward, "The Age of Reform 1815–1870" (*Oxford* 2nd ed. 1962 $10.50); R. C. K. Ensor's "England 1870–1914" (*Oxford* 1936). G. M. Young's classic study "Victorian England: Portrait of an Age" (*Oxford* 2nd ed. 1964 Galaxy Books pap. $1.95) is invaluable, but highly allusive. Walter Houghton, in "The Victorian Frame of Mind, 1830–1870" (*Yale Univ. Press* 1957 $12.50 pap. $3.75), gives a lucid, admirably well-informed discussion of Victorian attitudes, emotional, intellectual, and moral. See also Jerome Hamilton Buckley's "The Victorian Temper" (*Harvard Univ. Press* 1951 1969 $7.50; *Random* Vintage Bks. pap. $2.20).

HISTORY AND CRITICISM

Beach, Joseph W. The Concept of Nature in Nineteenth Century English Poetry. 1933 1936 1956 *Russell & Russell* $12.50

Benziger, James. IMAGES OF ETERNITY: Studies in the Poetry of Religious Vision, From Wordsworth to T. S. Eliot. Includes the great Victorian poets. *Southern Illinois Univ. Press* 1962 pap. $2.25

Chesterton, G. K. THE VICTORIAN AGE IN LITERATURE. 1913. *Oxford* Galaxy Bk. 1946 pap. $1.50; *Univ. of Notre Dame Press* 1963 pap. $1.75

Drinkwater, John. VICTORIAN POETRY. 1924. *Richard West* $10.00

Fairchild, Hoxie Neale. RELIGIOUS TRENDS IN ENGLISH POETRY. Vol. 4: 1830–1880, Christianity and Romanticism in the Victorian Era. *Columbia* $12.50

> Victorian poets were "simply obsessed by the religious problems. . . . They cannot be studied without close attention to this aspect of their thought." Detailed chapters are devoted to major poets, and minor poets are considered in some detail. *For other volumes in this study see Chapter 4, Broad Studies and General Anthologies.*

Faverty, Frederic Everett, Ed. VICTORIAN POETS: A Guide to Research. By Paul Franklin Baum and others. *Harvard Univ. Press* 1956 2nd ed. 1968. $12.00

Gaunt, William. THE PRE-RAPHAELITE DREAM. *Schocken* 1966 pap. $2.95

> Originally published here in 1942 as "The Pre-Raphaelite Tragedy," this work on the "Pre-Raphaelite phenomenon in painting and poetry is "scholarly, but . . . makes delightful reading"—(*LJ*).

Hough, Graham. THE LAST ROMANTICS. 1961. *Barnes & Noble* pap. $2.50. A perceptive discussion of the Pre-Raphaelite and Aesthetic Movements.

Johnson, E. D. H. THE ALIEN VISION OF VICTORIAN POETRY. 1952. *Shoe String* 1963 $6.00. Valuable interpretations of the work of Tennyson, Browning, and Arnold.

Langbaum, Robert. THE POETRY OF EXPERIENCE: The Dramatic Monologue in Modern Literary Tradition. *Norton* 1963 pap. $1.75

Lucas, Frank. TEN VICTORIAN POETS. 1948 *Shoe String* 1966 $6.00

Martin, Robert B. VICTORIAN POETRY. *Random* 1963 $9.95

Stedman, Edmund C. VICTORIAN POETS. 1875. rev. ed. 1903. *AMS Press* repr. of 1903 ed. $15.00; *Folcroft* 1973 lib. bdg. $14.50; *Scholarly Press* repr. of 1900 ed. $24.00. Old-fashioned, but still of interest for the author's critical comments.

Stevenson, Lionel. DARWIN AMONG THE POETS: His Influence on Alfred Tennyson, Robert Browning, George Meredith and Thomas Hardy. 1932. *Russell & Russell* 1963 $10.00

THE PRE-RAPHAELITE POETS. *Univ. of North Carolina Press* 1972 $10.95. Treats the interrelationships among members of the Pre-Raphaelite Brotherhood, and the influence of Browning and Tennyson upon them.

Warren, A. H. ENGLISH POETIC THEORY, 1825–65. *Octagon* 1966 $8.50

Willey, Basil. NINETEENTH CENTURY STUDIES: Coleridge to Matthew Arnold. *Columbia* 1949 $9.00; *Harper* Torchbks. pap. $1.95

See also Chapter 4, Broad Studies and General Anthologies.

COLLECTIONS

Auden, W. H. 19TH CENTURY BRITISH MINOR POETS. *Dell* Laurel Eds. 1966 pap. $.75

Includes "a sampling of satire, burlesque and (deliberate) nonsense. . . . All in all a stimulating, unhackneyed collection"—(*Observer*, London). Biographical notes.

(With N. H. Pearson). TENNYSON TO YEATS. Vol. 5 of "Poets of the English Language." *Viking* Portable Lib. 1950 $5.95 (with title "Victorian and Edwardian Poets") 1950 pap. $3.25

Bowyer, John W., George Bond, Irma H. Herron and John Lee Brooks. THE VICTORIAN AGE: Prose, Poetry and Drama. 1938. *Appleton* 2nd ed. 1954 $11.45

Brown, Edward K., and J. O. Bailey. VICTORIAN POETRY. *Ronald* 2nd ed. 1962 $8.75

Buckley, Jerome H., and George Benjamin Woods. POETRY OF THE VICTORIAN PERIOD. Sel. and ed. with critical and explanatory notes, brief biographies and bibliographies. *Scott, Foresman* 1955 3rd ed. 1965 $13.95. The fullest and best-annotated anthology of Victorian poetry.

Carr, Arthur J. VICTORIAN POETRY: Clough to Kipling. *Holt* (Rinehart) 1958 2nd ed. 1972 pap. $2.50

Day, Lewis Cecil. ENGLISH LYRIC POEMS 1500–1900. *Appleton* 1961 pap. $4.15

Hayward, John. OXFORD BOOK OF NINETEENTH CENTURY ENGLISH VERSE. *Oxford* 1964 $12.00

Houghton, Walter E., and G. Robert Strange. VICTORIAN POETRY AND POETICS. *Houghton* 1959 2nd ed. 1968 $12.95

Johnson, E. D. H. THE WORLD OF THE VICTORIANS: An Anthology of Poetry and Prose. *Scribner* pap. $3.95. The editor also compiled that fine anthology of nature literature, "The Poetry of Earth."

MacBeth, George. THE PENGUIN BOOK OF VICTORIAN VERSE: A Critical Anthology. *Penguin* 1969 pap. $1.45

Marshall, William H. THE MAJOR VICTORIAN POETS. Poems of Tennyson, Browning, Arnold, D. G. Rossetti and Swinburne, with biographical and critical information. *Washington Square* 1966 pap. $1.45

Miles, Alfred Henry, and others. THE POETS AND POETRY OF THE NINETEENTH CENTURY. London 1905–07. *AMS Press* 12 vols. each $25.00 set $280.00. A "representative selection with a biographical and critical notice of each poet represented."

Munro, John M. ENGLISH POETRY IN TRANSITION, 1880–1920. *Pegasus* 1967 $11.95 pap. $3.95. 38 poets are included. Contains "short biographies of about 20 lines and short but valuable up-to-date bibliographies of works by and about the poets represented"—(*LJ*).

Quiller-Couch, Sir Arthur. THE OXFORD BOOK OF VICTORIAN VERSE. *Oxford* 1913 $10.50

See also Chapter 4, Broad Studies and General Anthologies, for General and Comprehensive Anthologies of English Poetry.

BROWNING, ELIZABETH BARRETT. 1806–1861.

So great was Mrs. Browning's popularity and her fame that on the death of Wordsworth (*q.v.*) it was urged from many sides that the vacant post of Poet Laureate be offered to her—a woman laureate would be a graceful tribute to England's young Queen. Robert Browning's (*q.v.*) fame at that time was so far behind that of his wife that his name was not mentioned for the position.

The "Sonnets from the Portuguese" were called by her husband "the finest sonnets written in any language since Shakespeare's." The story of their writing and publication is told in Fannie Ratchford's introduction to the Centennial Variorum Edition. None of the sequence of 44 sonnets is dated, but it is believed that they were written in retrospect after Elizabeth had accepted Robert's insistence upon marriage 16 months after their first meeting. When she had agreed to an elopement from the home of her domineering father, where she had lived as an "invalid" for many years, she wrote in a note of July 22, 1846, "You shall see some day at Pisa what I will not show you now." But because Robert "happened early to say something against putting one's loves into verse," it was not until three years later at Bagni di Lucca after the birth of their son and after Browning's saying something on the other side that "next morning she said hesitatingly, 'Do you know I once wrote some poems about you? . . . There they are, if you care to see them.' " He insisted upon their inclusion in the 1850 revision of her "Poems," which first appeared in 1844. Because of their personal nature they were disguised as a translation.

Browning had called his wife his "little Portuguese": she was of dark complexion and had translated "Catarina to Camoëns," a love poem addressed to Portugal's greatest poet (*q.v.*). *Chapman and Hall's* new 1850 edition of the "Poems" carried "Sonnets from the Portuguese" as the final title of Volume 2. The "Poems" was twice revised and reprinted, in 1853 and 1856, before her death; and in 1897 Sir Frederick Kenyon made further revisions "apparently on the authority of Elizabeth herself." The first separate edition of "The Sonnets" was issued by the American firm of *Ticknor and Co.* of Boston c. 1886.

Two important collections of letters are now o. p.: "The Letters of Robert and Elizabeth Barrett Browning" (ed. by F. C. Kenyon 1899 new ed. 1930) and "Elizabeth Barrett to Mr. Boyd" (ed. by Barbara P. McCarthy, 1955). *For biographical information on E. B. Browning, see also the biographies under Robert Browning.*

COMPLETE WORKS. Ed. by Charlotte Porter and Helen A. Clarke. 1900. *AMS Press* 6 vols. each $14.50 set $85.00. The best collected edition, and the only complete one with extensive annotations.

COMPLETE POETICAL WORKS. Ed. by Harriet Waters Preston. *Houghton* Cambridge Eds. $7.00; *Scholarly Press* repr. of 1900 ed. $24.50

SONNETS FROM THE PORTUGUESE AND OTHER LOVE POEMS. Ill. in full color by Adolph Hallman. *Doubleday* 1954 $3.95

SONNETS FROM THE PORTUGUESE AND OTHER POEMS. Includes Catarina to Camoëns, Insufficiency, A Denial. *Funk & Wagnalls* 1967 pap. $.95

SONNETS FROM THE PORTUGUESE. *Avon Bks.* pap. $.60; *Harper* 1932 $2.95

LETTERS TO MRS. DAVID OGILVY. Ed. by Peter N. Heydon and Philip Kelley. *Quadrangle* 1973 $7.95

TWENTY-TWO UNPUBLISHED LETTERS OF ELIZABETH BARRETT BROWNING AND ROBERT BROWNING ADDRESSED TO HENRIETTA AND ARABELLA MOULTON-BARRETT. 1935. *Folcroft* $10.00; *Haskell* $9.95

LETTERS OF THE BROWNINGS TO GEORGE BARRETT. Ed. by Paul Landis with Ronald E. Freeman. *Univ. of Illinois Press* 1958 $7.95

" 'The most complete and continuous record of Browning-Barrett relations,' covering 51 years from 1838 to Robert Browning's death in 1889. . . . George Barrett, a lawyer, was 'the one useful brother' of Elizabeth's eight. . . . The 58 letters from 'Ba' (Mrs. Browning) and 30 from Robert given here, fully annotated, are from a collection acquired by the University of Illinois in 1950. Vivacious, affectionate, and often filled with literary and political gossip, Elizabeth's letters both before and after her marriage dispel any notion that she was a morbid, malingering invalid"—(*LJ*).

DIARY OF E. B. B.: The Unpublished Diary of Elizabeth Barrett Browning, 1831–1832. Ed. by Philip Kelley and Ronald Hudson. *Ohio Univ. Press* 1969 $15.00

Books about Elizabeth B. Browning

The Barretts of Wimpole Street: A Comedy in Five Acts. By Rudolf Besier. *Little* 1930 $5.95. The play in which Katharine Cornell and Brian Aherne starred for so long on Broadway.

Flush: A Biography [of Mrs. Browning's cocker spaniel]. By Virginia Woolf. *Harcourt* 1933 $5.95

Immortal Lovers: Elizabeth Barrett and Robert Browning. By Frances Winwar. *Harper* 1950 $7.95. A fictionalized biography that is sympathetic and readable, not scholarly or definitive, with many quotations from the work of both poets.

Elizabeth Barrett Browning. By Dorothy Hewlett. 1952. *Octogon* lib. bdg. 1972 $14.50. The emphasis is on the life rather than the poetry; much of the material is drawn from correspondence.

The Life of Elizabeth Barrett Browning. By Gardner B. Taplin. 1957. *Shoe String* 1970 $14.00. A scholarly account.

Elizabeth Barrett Browning. By Alethea Hayter. Pamphlet. *British Bk. Centre* 1965 pap. $1.20

TENNYSON, ALFRED, 1st Baron. 1809–1892.

On the death of Wordsworth (*q.v.*) in 1850, the post of Poet Laureate was offered to Samuel Rogers, 87, who declined it on the ground of age. It was then offered to Tennyson, because of the Prince Consort's admiration of "In Memoriam." This poem, written at intervals since 1833, had been published anonymously that very year, but its authorship was at once recognized. It is a lament, in "short swallow-flights of song," for Arthur Hallam, his brilliant college friend.

Tennyson's masterpiece is "Idylls of the King," a work which covered a period of 20 years. His version of the cycle of Arthurian legends is based on that of Sir Thomas Malory (*q.v.*) who wrote *"Le Morte d'Arthur"* in 1485. He also wrote several verse plays. "Becket" (1884) was successful in its time. Tennyson "enjoyed the greatest popularity ever accorded to an English poet during his lifetime."

WORKS. Ed. by Hallam Tennyson. 9 vols. 1907–08. *Greenwood* $135.00. The standard text, with Tennyson's final revisions, and with comments and notes by him.

POEMS. Ed. by Christopher Ricks. Annotated English Poets Series *Norton* 1972 $17.50. This is by far the most complete and best-annotated edition of Tennyson's poems. It contains many works never before published or collected.

COMPLETE POETICAL WORKS. Ed. by W. J. Rolfe. *Houghton* Cambridge Eds. 1947 $8.00 new ed. 1974 $12.50

A COLLECTION OF POEMS BY ALFRED TENNYSON. Comp. with introd. by Christopher Ricks. *Doubleday* 1973 $7.95

POEMS AND PLAYS. Ed. by T. Herbert Warren; rev. by Frederick Page. *Oxford* 1953 Stand. Authors $6.00 pap. $4.00

POEMS. Ed. by Charles Tennyson *Collins* $3.00 lea. $5.00; comp. by Ruth G. Rausen *T. Y. Crowell* 1964 $3.50 lib. bdg. $4.25; ed. by J. H. Buckley *Houghton* Riv. Eds. pap. $2.25; ed. by Robert W. Hill, Jr. *Norton* Critical Eds. 1972 $10.00; ed. by Clyde de L. Ryals *Univ. of Pennsylvania Press* 1966 $7.50 pap. $2.45

SELECTED POETRY. Ed. with introd. by Herbert Marshall McLuhan *Holt* (Rinehart) 1956 pap. $2.00; ed. with introd. by Douglas Bush *Modern Library* 1956 pap. $1.25

SELECTED POEMS. Ed. by W. C. DeVane *Appleton* text ed. $8.95 pap. $.85; ed. by Edmund Blunden *Barnes & Noble* 1960 $1.75; sel. with introd. by Stephen Gwynn *Oxford* World's Class. new ed. 1950 $2.50; ed. by Michael Millgate *Oxford* 1963 $2.50

POETRY AND PROSE. Introd. and notes by F. L. Lucas. With criticisms by the *Quarterly Review*, Fitzgerald, Matthew Arnold, Sir Leslie Stephen, Harold Nicolson. *Oxford* 1947 $2.50

UNPUBLISHED EARLY POEMS. Ed. by Charles Tennyson. 1932. *Folcroft* $10.00; *Bern Porter* 1973 $12.50

POEMS OF 1842. Ed. by Christopher Ricks. *British Bk. Centre* $4.50; *Collins* pap. $2.95

IDYLLS OF THE KING. 1859–85. A variorum ed. by John Pfordresher. *Columbia* 1973 $25.00

IDYLLS OF THE KING. *Assoc. Bksellers* Airmont Bks. pap. $.75; ed. by Stephen J. Rusnak *Bantam* pap. $.60; (with Alan Jay Lerner's "Camelot") selections ed. by Allan Knee *Dell* pap. $.50; *St. Martin's* $2.95; Reader's Enrich. Ser. *Washington Square* pap. $.95

IDYLLS OF THE KING AND A SELECTION OF POEMS. *New Am. Lib.* Signet pap. $.75

Books about Tennyson

Alfred Lord Tennyson: A Memoir by His Son. By Hallam Tennyson. 1899. 4 vols. *AMS Press* $34.50; *Greenwood* $43.00; *Scholarly Press* $35.00; *Richard West* $34.95. A source of primary importance for the life of the poet; it contains many poems and letters published here for the first time.

A Concordance to the Poetical and Dramatic Works of Alfred, Lord Tennyson: Including the Poems Contained in the "Life of Alfred, Lord Tennyson," and the "Suppressed Poems," 1830–1868. By Arthur E. Baker. 1914. An exhaustive volume. *Barnes & Noble* 1966 $25.00

The Life and Times of Tennyson (1809 to 1850). By Thomas Raynesford Lounsbury. 1915. *Russell & Russell* 1962 $13.50

Alfred Tennyson. By Charles Tennyson. 1949. *Shoe String* 1968 $10.00. The definitive biography, written by the poet's grandson with understanding candor and keen literary appreciation.

Tennyson and the Reviewers: A Study of His Literary Reputation and of the Influence of the Critics upon His Poetry, 1827–1851. By Edgar F. Shannon. 1952. *Shoe String* 1967 $7.00

Tennyson. By F. L. Lucas. Writers and Their Works Ser. *British Bk. Centre* 1957 $2.38 pap. $1.20

Tennyson and "The Princess": Reflections of an Age. By John Killham. 1958. *Humanities* (Athlone Press) $11.75

Critical Essays on the Poetry of Tennyson. Ed. by John Killham. *Routledge & Kegan Paul* 1960 $7.75 pap. $2.75; *Barnes & Noble* pap. 1967 $2.50

Tennyson: The Growth of a Poet. By Jerome Hamilton Buckley. *Harvard Univ. Press* 1960 $8.50; *Houghton* Riv. Lib. 1965 pap. $4.00
Of interest to the general reader as well as to the serious student, this is the "first thoroughgoing study of Tennyson's life and work in many years." "Within a biographical framework [the author] follows Tennyson's lifelong quest for the enduring. He has been able to draw upon Sir Charles Tennyson's . . . biography and upon the recently acquired unpublished Tennyson Papers in the Harvard University Library"—(*SR*).

The Tennyson Collection Presented to the University of Virginia in Honor of Edgar Finley Shannon, Jr. Can be obtained from the Acquisitions Dept. of the Alderman Library, University of Virginia, Charlottesville, Va. 22903, $2.50

Tennyson, Laureate. By Valerie Pitt. *Univ. of Toronto Press* 1962 $9.50 pap. $3.50

Alfred Tennyson: An Annotated Bibliography. Ed. by Sir Charles Tennyson and Christine Fall. *Univ. of Georgia Press* 1967 $7.50. The poet's grandson and Professor Fall of Baylor University here provide a listing of all worthy books and articles written in English, with a note for each one.

From the Great Deep: Essays on Idylls of the King. By Clyde de L. Ryals. *Ohio Univ. Press* 1967 $8.00.
"Mr. Ryals writes smoothly, uses memoirs and criticisms of Tennyson's contemporaries, and makes his point with quotations from the *Idylls*"—(*LJ*).

Tennyson. By Christopher Ricks. Masters of the World Literature Ser. *Macmillian* 1972 $8.95 Collier Bks. 1972 pap. $3.95. The best critical study to date: well-informed, and rich in sensitive and original comment on the poems.

BROWNING, ROBERT. 1812–1889.

Much of Browning's early work was cast in stage form or intended as closet drama: "Paracelsus," "Strafford," "Pippa Passes," and "Luria, a Soul's Tragedy." His best work began with his married life in 1846. To this period belong his "Bells and Pomegranates"; his 50 poems, "Men and Women"; and His "Dramatis Personae," in which he perfected the dramatic monologue.

After the death of Mrs. Browning (*q.v.*) in 1861, Browning spent six years writing "The Ring and the Book." This work, which he always referred to as his "murder poem," is a kind of detective story. G. K. Chesterton (*q.v.*) in his "Life of Browning" says, "Its difference from the ordinary detective story is that it seeks to establish not the center of criminal guilt, but the center of spiritual guilt." The source of the plot was an old yellow volume which Browning bought at a bookstall in Florence. This old Latin record of the criminal case of Guido Franceschini, tried for the murder of his wife Pompilia in 1698, became the ground plan for the poem. Louis Untermeyer says (in "Lives of the Poets") that "it expresses the complete man who was one of the greatest exemplars of sheer energy in literature."

Several volumes of letters are now o.p., including the "Letters of Robert and Elizabeth Barrett Browning" (ed. by F. C. Kenyon, 1899, new ed. 1930 2 vols.). The carefully edited "New Letters" is a collection of about 400, hitherto unpublished, covering the years 1835 to 1889 (ed. by W. C. DeVane and K. L. Knickerbocker 1950, o.p.) "Dearest Isa: Robert Browning's Letters to Isabella Blagdon" contains 154 letters written over an 11-year period after Mrs. Browning's death in 1861. Browning had gone to England to educate their son, hoping to return to Italy and to his friend "Dearest Isa." He had asked her to write him once a month on the 12th, he promising to answer on the 19th. These entertaining letters, edited with skill and scholarship, are the best source of biographical material on Browning during the period 1861–72.

COMPLETE WORKS. Ed. by Roma A. King, Jr. *Ohio Univ. Press* 1967–72 4 vols. each $20.00. An ambitious attempt at recording all textual variants, and at exhaustive annotation of the poems.

WORKS. Introd. by F. G. Kenyon. A repr. of the 1912 Centenary Edition. *AMS Press* 1967 10 vols. each $12.00 set $100.00

COMPLETE POETICAL AND DRAMATIC WORKS. Ed. by Horace E. Scudder. *Houghton* Cambridge Eds. new ed. 1947 $10.00

POEMS AND PLAYS. Vols. I and 2 1833–64, introd. by John Bryson; Vols. 3 and 4 1871–90, ed. with introd. by Mildred Bozman. *Dutton* Everyman's 4 vols each $3.50

POETRY AND PROSE. Comp. and ed. by Simon Nowell-Smith *Harvard Univ. Press* Reynard Lib. 1951–1967 $12.00 pap. $4.50; ed. with introd. and notes by Sir Humphrey Sumner Milford, with appreciations by Landor, Bagehot, Swinburne, Henry James, Saintsbury and F. L. Lucas *Oxford* 1941 $2.50

POEMS. Ed. by Rosemary Sprague. *T. Y. Crowell* 1964 $3.50 lib. bdg. $4.25; ed. by D. Smalley *Houghton* Riv. Eds. pap. $1.60

POEMS, 1835–1889. Ed. by Sir Humphrey Milford. *Oxford* World's Class. 1949–1954 $3.75

POETICAL WORKS. Complete from 1833 to 1864. 1940. Ed. by Ian Jack. *Oxford* Stand. Authors 1970 $8.50

SHORTER POEMS. Ed. by William C. DeVane. *Appleton* 1934 $6.25

SELECTED POEMS. Ed. by William C. DeVane *AHM Pub. Corp.* Crofts Classics pap. $.85; ed. by James Reeves *Barnes & Noble* 1955 1966 $1.75; ed. by Kenneth Allott *Oxford* 1967 $2.40; ed. by W. E. Williams *Penguin* pap. $1.25

SELECTED POETRY. Ed. by Horace Gregory *Holt* (Rinehart) 1956 pap. $2.00; ed. by K. L. Knickerbocker *Modern Library* pap. $1.25; ed. by George Ridenour *New Am. Lib.* Signet pap. $.95

POETRY. Ed. by Jacob Korg. *Bobbs* Literature Lib. 1971 $9.50 pap. $3.95

PIPPA PASSES (1841) AND SHORTER POEMS. Ed. by J. E. Baker. *Odyssey* 1947 $3.50

THE PIED PIPER OF HAMELIN. 1842. *Coward* 1971 $5.95 lib. bdg. $4.97; *Scholastic Bk. Services* 1972 pap. $.60; ill. by Kate Greenaway *Warne* 1947 lib. bdg. $5.95

MEN AND WOMEN. Poems. 1855. Ed. by Paul Turner. *Oxford* 1972 pap. $3.50

DRAMATIS PERSONAE.1864. *Collins* pap. $2.75

THE RING AND THE BOOK. 1868–69. Ed. by Theodore Ehrsam *Barron's* 1972 pap. $.95; introd. by John Bryson *Dutton* Everyman's $3.50 pap. $2.45; introd. by Wylie Sypher *Norton* 1961 pap. $2.95; ed. by Richard Altick *Penguin* pap. $4.25

BROWNING'S ESSAY ON CHATTERTON. Ed. and ill. by Donald Smalley. 1945 *Greenwood* 1948 $10.75

LETTERS OF THE BROWNINGS TO GEORGE BARRETT. Ed. by Paul Landis with Ronald E. Freeman. *Univ. of Illinois Press* 1958 $7.95. To Elizabeth's brother; *see comment under E. B. Browning.*

DEAREST ISA; Robert Browning's Letters to Isabella Blagden. Ed. by Edward C. McAleer. 1951 *Greenwood* $14.75

LEARNED LADY: Letters From Robert Browning to Mrs. Thomas FitzGerald. *Harvard Univ. Press* 1966 $7.00

Written to a good friend after the death of Elizabeth Barrett Browning, they "give us an almost complete picture of the life of Robert Browning, his son and his sister"—(*LJ*).

Books about Browning

There is no really satisfactory biography. The standard one is by W. Hall Griffin (see below). Betty Miller's (see below) is also valuable. Works on Browning of the early 20th century by Curry, Hood and Lounsbury have recently been reprinted by Haskell; those of Cook, Duckworth, and Pottle by Shoe String; that of Brooke by AMS Press; and that of Brockington by Russell & Russell and Folcroft.

Browning Cyclopedia. By Edward Berdoe. 1897 2nd ed. 1916. *Barnes & Noble* 2nd ed. 1964 $9.50; *Folcroft* lib. bdg. $20.00; *Scholarly Press* 2 vols. set $29.50

A Handbook to the Works of Robert Browning. By Alexandra Orr. 6th ed. 1902. *Kraus* 1969 $17.50. Still valuable for its first-hand information.

Browning. By G. K. Chesterton. 1904. *Richard West* $10.00

Concordance to the Works of Robert Browning. By L. N. Broughton and B. F. Stelter. 1925. *Haskell* 4 vols. set $175.00

A Browning Handbook. By William Clyde DeVane. *Appleton* 1935 2nd ed. 1955 $9.45

The Life of Robert Browning: With Notice of His Writings, His Family, and His Friends. By W. Hall Griffin. Ed. by H. C. Minchin. 1938. *Shoe String* 1972 $9.50

Immortal Lovers; Elizabeth and Robert Browning: A Biography. By Frances Winwar. *See comment under E. B. Browning. Harper* 1950 $7.95

Browning and America. By Louise Greer. 1952. *Greenwood* 1973 $15.00

Robert Browning: A Portrait. By Betty Miller. *Hillary House* 1952; *Scribner* 1973 $7.95; *Richard West* 1974 $4.95

"A critically challenging and skillfully written biography by . . . an English novelist"—(*SR*). Its strongly Freudian interpretation is not, however, universally accepted. With this proviso, it is one of the best biographies to have appeared.

Robert Browning. By J. M. Cohen. 1952. *Barnes & Noble* $4.00

Robert Browning: A Bibliography, 1830–1950. Comp. by Leslie Nathan Broughton and others. *Burt Franklin* 1953 $22.50. The most complete record in existence of the works of Robert Browning, of his correspondence, and of writings about him; it supersedes all earlier ones; indispensable to advanced students of Browning and Victorian literature.

Browning's Characters: A Study in Poetic Technique. By Park Honan. *Shoe String* 1967 $10.00

The Poetry of Experience. By Robert Langbaum. *Norton* 1963 Norton Lib. pap. $1.75

"The best book on Browning"—(*N.Y. Review of Books*).

The Infinite Moment and Other Essays on Robert Browning. By William O. Raymond. *Univ. of Toronto Press* 2nd ed. 1965 Canadian Univ. Paperbacks pap. $2.50. An important collection of essays, which discuss Browning's intellectual milieu as well as his art.

Robert Browning: A Collection of Critical Essays. By Philip Drew. *Houghton* 1966 pap. $3.50

Robert Browning: A Study of his Poetry. By Thomas Blackburn. 1967. *Rowman* $8.50. An interesting study by the British poet and scholar, who is a discriminating Browning admirer.

Robert Browning and His World. By Maisie Ward. *Holt* 2 vols. 1967–69 Vol. I The Private Face, 1812–1861 Vol. 2 Two Robert Brownings? 1861–1889 each $8.50. A sane, popular biography.

Browning's Roman Murder Story: A Reading of the Ring and the Book. By Richard D. Altick and James F. Loucks. *Univ. of Chicago Press* 1968 $8.00. A careful study of Browning's purpose, and of the design of the poem.

The Poetry of Browning: A Critical Introduction. By Philip Drew. *Barnes & Noble* 1970 text ed. $14.50. Lively, original comments on Browning's poems.

The Variance and the Unity: A Study of Robert Browning's Complementary Poems. By William E. Harrod. *Ohio Univ. Press* (in prep.)

ARNOLD, MATTHEW. 1822–1888.

Arnold's career as a poet was practically over (by about 1855, except for a few later poems including "Thyrsis") before his prose career began. His collected poems first appeared in 1869, four years after his prose work, "Essays in Criticism." "As a poet and as a prose writer Matthew Arnold addressed two different generations"; the poems expressed the hopes and despairs of youth. Arnold's most famous poem in its day was the elegy "Thyrsis" (1864), a monody on the death of the poet Arthur Hugh Clough, who had been his friend at Oxford. In 1857 Arnold became Professor of Poetry at Oxford, and it was there he wrote his two fine essays "On Translating Homer," in 1861 and 1862. By 1867, when he was devoting himself entirely to prose, he resigned his chair. Of Arnold's longer narrative poems, "Sohrab and Rustum" (1853) is based on a tale in the Persian epic. "Shah Namah" and "Tristram and Iseult" (1852) is his rendering of one of the late Arthurian legends.

WORKS. 1903. 15 vols. *AMS Press* each $12.00 set $180.00; *Scholarly Press* 1970 each $14.50 set $220.00

POETICAL WORKS. Ed. by Chauncey B. Tinker and H. F. Lowry. *Oxford* Stand. Authors new ed. 1950 $5.00. Contains all the known poetical works.

POEMS. Ed. by Kenneth Allott. 1965. *Dutton* Everyman's new ed. 1945 $3.50 pap. $2.75; ed. by Kenneth Allott Annotated Poets Ser. *Norton* 1972 $9.95

SELECTED POEMS. Ed. by E. K. Brown. *AHM Pub. Corp.* pap. $.85

PROSE AND POETRY. Ed. by John Bryson. *Harvard Univ. Press* 1954 $12.00 pap. $4.50

POETRY AND PROSE. With William Watson's Poem, and Essays by Lionel Johnson and H. W. Garod. Ed. by E. K. Chambers. *Oxford* 1939 $2.25

POETRY AND CRITICISM. Ed. by A. Dwight Culler. *Houghton* Riverside Eds. pap. $2.65

SELECTED POEMS AND PROSE. Ed. by Denys Thompson. Poetry Bkshelf Ser. *Barnes & Noble* 1971 $4.00

THE PORTABLE MATTHEW ARNOLD. Ed. by Lionel Trilling. *Viking* Portable Lib. 1949 $5.50 pap. $3.35. Includes poems, critical and political essays, "Culture and Anarchy" (abr.) letters to A. H. Clough and others.

Books About Arnold

A Bibliography of Matthew Arnold. By Thomas B. Smart. 1892. *Burt Franklin* $12.50; *Bern Porter* $10.00

Matthew Arnold. By George E. Saintsbury. 1899. *Folcroft* 1973 $7.00; *Russell & Russell* $7.50

Matthew Arnold: A Study in Conflict. By Edward K. Brown. 1948 *Shoe String* 1966 $6.00

Matthew Arnold. By Kenneth Allott. Writers and Their Works Ser. *British Bk. Centre* 1955 $2.38 pap. $1.20

Touchstones of Matthew Arnold. By John Shepard Eells. 1955. *AMS Press* $10.00; *College and Univ. Press* 1963 pap. $2.95

A Concordance to the Poems of Matthew Arnold. By Stephen M. Parrish. *Cornell Univ. Press* 1959 $15.00

Matthew Arnold and the Decline of English Romanticism. By David Gwilym James. *Oxford* 1961 $5.99

Imaginative Reason: The Poetry of Matthew Arnold. By A. Dwight Culler. *Yale Univ. Press* 1966 $7.50 The Professor of English at Yale has written a study that is "soundly reasoned, carefully researched, and . . . interestingly written"—(*LJ*).

Matthew Arnold: The Poet as Humanist. By G. Stange. *Princeton Univ. Press* 1967 $11.50

Matthew Arnold: A Study of the Aesthetic Temperament in Victorian England. By William A. Madden. Humanities Ser. *Indiana Univ. Press* 1967 $6.00. A discussion of the relation of Arnold's aesthetics to Victorian religious and moral issues.

The Time-Spirit of Matthew Arnold. By R. H. Super. *Univ. of Michigan Press* 1970 $6.95. Three lectures; in the first, the author discusses "Empedocles on Etna."

Matthew Arnold. By Douglas Bush. Masters of World Literature Ser. *Macmillan* 1971 $6.95 Collier Bks. pap. $2.95. A masterly survey of Arnold's work.

Matthew Arnold: A Collection of Critical Essays. Ed. by David J. DeLaura. Twentieth Century Views Ser. *Prentice-Hall* 1973 $5.95 Spectrum Bks. pap. $1.95

See also Chapter 15, Essays and Criticism.

MEREDITH, GEORGE. 1828–1909. *See Chapter 11, British Fiction: Middle Period.*

ROSSETTI, DANTE GABRIEL. 1828–1882.

Rossetti's first publication was his most characteristic poem, "The Blessed Damozel," written when he was only 18. It appeared in 1850 in *The Germ*, a short-lived magazine, the literary organ of the Pre-Raphaelite Brotherhood, as his circle of writers and artists called itself. In 1877 he painted "The Blessed Damozel," which, like the poem, became enormously popular. Pre-Raphaelite design has recently enjoyed a fashionable revival. In 1861 Rossetti published his inspired translations of Italian poets before Dante (*q.v.*). He was a pioneer in the field, Longfellow's (*q.v.*) translations of Dante following in 1865.

On the death of his wife in 1862 Rossetti buried in the coffin with her the manuscript of his entire poetic work up to that time. Five years later, failing eyesight caused him to turn from painting to literature again, and the manuscript was disinterred and published in 1870. His last volume of verse was his "Ballads and Sonnets" published in 1881. Rossetti's prose work, "Hand and Soul," an allegorical prose poem, voices many of his artistic beliefs. *See also William Morris, following.*

COLLECTED WORKS. 2 vols. 1890 *Scholarly Press* set $24.50

WORKS. Ed. by William M. Rossetti. 1911. *Adler's* 1972 $36.50. Standard edition, with notes by the poet's brother.

ROSSETTI'S POEMS. Ed. with introd. and notes by Oswald Doughty. *Dutton* Everyman's 1961 1968 $3.50. The most convenient recent edition.

POEMS AND TRANSLATIONS. 1850–70. With the prose story "Hand and Soul." *Oxford* Stand. Authors 1913 $6.00; *Dutton* Everyman's $3.50

JAN VAN HUNKS. Ed. by John R. Wahl from the original manuscript. *N. Y. Public Lib.* 1952 $7.50

THE ROSSETTI-MACMILLAN LETTERS: Some 133 Unpublished Letters Written to Alexander Macmillan, F. S. Ellis, and Others by Dante Gabriel, Christina, and William Michael Rossetti, 1861–1889. Ed. by Lona Mosk Packer. *Univ. of California Press* 1963 $6.75

"Not really exciting . . . the sort of thing that would today be telephoned"—(*LJ*). Of interest, however, to students of the period.

LETTERS. Ed. by Oswald Doughty and John Robert Wahl. 4 vols. Vol. 1 1835–1860 Vol. 2 1861–1870 Vol. 3 1871–1876 Vol. 4 1877–1882 *Oxford* 1965–1967 vols. 1–2 set $41.00 vols. 3–4 set $34.00. The largest collection to date, but incomplete nevertheless; for a detailed evaluation, see the review by W. E. Fredeman in *Victorian Studies*, 12 (1968) 104–108.

DANTE GABRIEL ROSSETTI: His Family Letters. With a memoir by William M. Rossetti. 1895 *AMS Press* 2 vols. set $27.50

Books about Rossetti

Dante Gabriel Rossetti: A Record and a Study. By William Sharp. 1882. *AMS Press* $12.50; *Folcroft* lib. bdg. $12.50; *Richard West* $12.45
Dante Gabriel Rossetti: An Analytical List of Manuscripts in the Duke University Library with Hitherto Unpublished Verse and Prose. Ed. by Paul F. Baum. 1931. *AMS Press* 1966 $9.00. Includes some facsimile pages of Rossetti's drawings and poemscripts.
A Victorian Romantic: Dante Gabriel Rossetti. By Oswald Doughty. *Oxford* 1949 2nd ed. 1960 $13.75. The definitive biography.

Portrait of Rossetti. By Rosalie G. Gryllis. 1965 *Southern Illinois Univ. Press* 1970 pap. $2.45. A useful counterpart to Doughty's biography.

No Peacocks Allowed: Gabriel Rossetti and His Circle. By Gale Pedrick. 1966. *Southern Illinois Univ. Press* 1970 pap. $2.45

This "delightful memoir . . . is an interesting supplement to Doughty's [*see above*] definitive, full-length biography"—(*LJ*). The author is the great-nephew of Henry Treffry Dunn, Rossetti's companion and secretary. The original 1966 title was "Life with Rossetti: No Peacocks Allowed."

Lost on Both Sides: Dante Gabriel Rossetti, Critic and Poet. By Robert M. Cooper. *Ohio Univ. Press* 1970 $8.50

The Dark Glass: Vision and Technique in the Poetry of Dante Gabriel Rossetti. By Ronnalie Howard. *Ohio Univ. Press* 1972 $8.50

ROSSETTI, CHRISTINA G. 1830–1894.

Christina was the sister of Dante Gabriel Rossetti (*q.v.*). She was a devout member of the Anglican church and her life was conditioned by her strong religious bent as well as by her delicate health. Virginia Woolf (*q.v.*), in an essay about her, noted that a firm hand pruned her lines, a sharp ear tested their music and nothing soft, otiose or irrelevant cumbered her pages except for very rare lapses. Marya Zaturenska (*q.v.*), herself a poet, calls Christina's "Monna Innominata," "this songbook of unhappy love," one of the great sonnet sequences. Miss Zaturenska's "Christina Rossetti: A Portrait with Background" (1949 *Kraus* $12.00) makes liberal use of the poems for a study of Christina Rossetti's technique. The shy Christina in her simple Quakerlike dress stands in relief against the rich and intricately patterned Pre-Raphaelite tapestry which was her brother's background.

POETICAL WORKS. Ed. by William M. Rossetti. 1906. *Adler's* 1971 $33.75. The standard work.

SELECTED POEMS. Ed. by Marya Zaturenska. *Macmillan* 1970 $5.95

POEMS. *Random* Stanyan Bks. 1973 $3.00

DOVES AND POMEGRANATES. Ed. by David Powell. *Macmillan* 1971 $3.95

GOBLIN MARKET. Adapted and ill. by Ellen Raskin. *Dutton* 1970 $4.95 lib. bdg. $4.95; *Franklin Watts* 1970 lib. bdg. $3.95

SING-SONG: A Nursery Rhyme Book. 1872. *Dover* 1969 pap. $1.25; *Macmillan* 1952 $3.50

WHAT IS PINK? *Macmillan* 1971 $4.95

FAMILY LETTERS OF CHRISTINA GEORGINA ROSSETTI. With some supplementary letters and appendices. Ed. by William M. Rossetti 1908. *Folcroft* $12.75; *Haskell* 1969 lib. bdg. $12.95

Books about Christina Rossetti

Christina Rossetti: A Biographical and Critical Study. By Mackenzie Bell. 1898. *AMS Press* $12.50; *Haskell* 1971 $14.95; *Richard West* 1973 $14.75. Contains interesting information on the literary life of the time, and on the whole Rossetti family.

Christina Rossetti: By Lona Mosk Packer. *Univ. of California Press* 1963 $12.50. A valuable biography.

MORRIS, WILLIAM. 1834–1896.

Morris was an artist, a poet, and a socialist thinker. He worked at architecture and painting and helped found a decorating firm which greatly influenced Victorian taste. He organized The Socialist League and edited *The Commonweal*, its journal; his fantasy of a socialist commonwealth in England is described in "News from Nowhere" (ed. by James Redmond *Routledge & Kegan Paul* 1970 $5.25 pap. $2.25) and "A Dream of John Ball' (*Oriole Eds.* 1971 pap. $1.25). George Bernard Shaw, and many critics today, have admired his initiative and versatility in trying to make all of life pleasant and attractive for all men.

Morris, in his first volume of poems, "The Defense of Guenevere" (1858), revived medieval diction and meter in such a way as to set a new (Pre-Raphaelite) style for English verse. His early poems strongly influenced Swinburne (*q.v.*). He turned to narrative verse in "The Earthly Paradise" (1868–70) and "The Life and Death of Jason" (1867). He later translated or retold the "Aeneid," the "Odyssey," the "Volsunga Saga," and "The Story of Sigurd the Volsung and The Fall of the Nibelungs." Toward the end of his career he published a series of highly fanciful prose romances: "The Wood beyond the World" (1894. facsimile of the Kelmscott Press edition. *Dover* 1972 pap. $3.50; *Peter Smith* $6.00), "The Well at the World's End" (1896. *Ballantine Bks.* 2 vols. 1970 each $1.25), and "The Water of the Wondrous Isles" (1897. *Ballantine Bks.* 1971 pap. $1.25).

In 1891 Morris started the Kelmscott Press, where he printed many books, including several of his own, in typography he himself designed. "Three Works by William Morris" (News from Nowhere; A Dream of John Ball; Pilgrims of Hope—all prose) was published early in 1968 by *International Pubs.* (pap. $1.95). Morris's "Letters to His Family and Friends," edited with introduction and notes by Philip Henderson (1950, o.p.) contains a representative selection, mostly from his later correspondence.

COLLECTED WORKS. 1910–15. Ed. with introd. and bibliographical material by May Morris. *Russell & Russell* 1966 24 vols. set $250.00

WORKS. Ed. by R. C. Briggs. 1962. *Folcroft* $10.00; *Richard West* $10.00

SELECTED WRITINGS. Ed. by G. D. H. Cole. *Random* $10.00

WILLIAM MORRIS: Selected Writings and Designs. Ed. by Asa Briggs. *Penguin* Pelican Bks. 1962 pap. $1.65; *Peter Smith* $4.00

POLITICAL WRITINGS. Ed. by A. L. Morton. *Int. Pubns. Service* 1973 pap. $1.95

ORNAMENTATION AND ILLUSTRATIONS FROM THE KELMSCOTT CHAUCER. *Dover.* 1973 pap. $2.50

Books about Morris

The Books of William Morris Described, with Some Account of his Doings in Literature and the Applied Arts. By Henry Buxton Forman. 1897. A bibliography. *Burt Franklin* 1967 $19.50

The Life of William Morris. By John W. Mackail. 2 vols. 1899. *Blom* 2 vols in 1 1968 $12.50; *Folcroft* 2 vols. in 1 $12.50 repr. of 1902 ed. $4.50 repr. of 1910 ed. $4.50; *Haskell* repr. of 1900 ed. 1970 $9.95; *Richard West* repr. of 1900 ed. $11.95. This is a classic biography. But Mackail was reticent on certain aspects of Morris's private life; his book must be supplemented by Oswald Doughty's "Dante Gabriel Rossetti: A Victorian Romantic" (1948, o.p.).

William Morris and His Poetry. By B. Ifor Evans. 1925. *AMS Press* $7.25; *Folcroft* lib. bdg. $7.50

William Morris. By R.D. MacLeod. 1956. *Folcroft* lib. bdg. $4.50

The Work of William Morris. By Paul Thompson. *Viking* 1967 $10.00. With illustrations, some in color. "Scholarly and readable"—(*LJ*).

William Morris as Designer. By R. Watkinson. A discussion of Morris's stained glass, pattern designs, printing and esthetic theories, with a brief account of his life; excellent illustrations, some in color. *Reinhold* 1967 $16.50

SWINBURNE, ALGERNON CHARLES. 1837–1909.

That the young Swinburne enjoyed the companionship and encouragement of the leading literary figures of his period is shown in his "Letters." He modeled for some of Rossetti's (*q.v.*) paintings and had the painter's personal direction in his writings. "Further," writes Louis Untermeyer, "his affiliation with the Pre-Raphaelite movement drew attention to his work, which early struck his contemporaries as clever, audacious and erudite. From 'Atalanta in Calydon' and 'Chasteland,' published in 1865, Swinburne's place in public awareness was important, and remained so for about fifteen years."

His poetical works are usually divided into dramatic poems and lyrical poems. Of his classical dramas, "Atalanta in Calydon" is noted for the beauty of its occasional lyrics, of which "The Hounds of Spring" is one. "Erechtheus" was his second classic drama modeled on the Greek choral plays. All his dramas are tragedies, and few were intended for stage production.

A number of Swinburne's volumes of literary criticism have recently been reprinted, including "William Blake, a Critical Essay" (1868. *Blom* $12.50; ed. by Hugh J. Luke *Univ. of Nebraska Press* Bison Bks. 1970 pap. $2.50), "A Study of Shakespeare" (1880. *AMS Press* $10.00) and "A Study of Ben Jonson" (1889. *Haskell* 1969 $9.95; ed by Howard B. Norlad *Univ. of Nebraska Press* Bison Bks. pap. $2.25; *Peter Smith* $4.25).

A Swinburne novel, "Love's Cross-Currents" (o.p.), was serialized in 1877 as "A Year's Letters" and published in book form in 1905. The manuscript of another, "Lesbia Brandon"—a novel written about 1864 and considered then too daring for publication—was dispersed for many years. It was finally reassembled and lodged in the British Museum. Two missing papers were found in 1967 by John S. Mayfield of Syracuse University and offered through Syracuse as a gift to the Museum.

Swinburne was in the Victorian age, but not of it. As a rebel against priests and kings, the Victorians rejected him. Tennyson (q.v.) called his verse "poisonous honey," and Swinburne retorted by speaking of the Laureate's verse as "treacle." Edmund Gosse in Ward's "English Poets" says that "the gift by which Swinburne first won his way to the hearts of a multitude of readers was unquestionably the melody of his verse."

COMPLETE WORKS. Ed. by Sir Edmund Gosse and Thomas J. Wise. 1925–27. *Russell & Russell* 1965 20 vols. set $225.00. This edition is useful, but it must be used with caution, since it omits several important essays and some poems which were published by Swinburne himself. The editors' presentation of unpublished material is extremely selective.

POEMS. 1904. *AMS Press* 2 vols. each $16.00 set $95.00. The most accurate edition of the poems prepared for the press by the poet.

NEW WRITINGS BY SWINBURNE, OR MISCELLANEA NOVA ET CURIOSA: Being a Medley of Poems, Critical Essays, Hoaxes and Burlesques. Ed. by Cecil Y. Lang. Previously unpublished: 10 poems, 5 essays and 5 burlesques. Some of the material is in French. *Syracuse Univ. Press* 1965 $6.50

SELECTED POETRY AND PROSE. Ed. with introd. by John D. Rosenberg. *Modern Library* (dist. by Random) $2.95

POEMS AND BALLADS AND ATALANTA IN CALYDON. Ed. by Morse Peckham. Lib. of Literature Ser. *Bobbs* 1970 $8.50 pap. $2.95

BALLADS OF THE ENGLISH BORDER. Ed. with introd. and notes by William A. MacInnes. 1925. *Gale Research Co.* $15.00

"Fifty-four ballads of the English border, rewritten or composed by Swinburne. In the first part are ballads that the poet reconstructed from extant variants; in the second are original ballads in imitation of border themes and style; in the third are unique, refined ballads showing the influence of the Pre-Raphaelites"— (Publisher's note). This collection is valuable, but its text cannot always be relied upon; unfortunately no adequate collection exists of poems not published by Swinburne himself.

POSTHUMOUS POEMS. Ed. by Edmund Gosse and Thomas James. 1917. *Bks. for Libraries* 1972 $9.75

ATALANTA IN CALYDON. 1865. *Scholarly Press* repr. of 1923 ed. $9.00

SWINBURNE REPLIES: Notes on "Poems and Reviews," "Under the Microscope," "Dedicatory Epistle." Ed. by C. K. Hyder. *Syracuse Univ. Press* 1966 $5.25

THE SWINBURNE LETTERS. Ed. by Cecil Y. Lang. 6 vols. Vol. 1 1854–1869 Vol. 2 1869–1875 Vol. 3 1875–1877 Vol. 4 1877–1882 Vol. 5 1883–1890 Vol. 6 1890–1909 *Yale Univ. Press* 1959–1962 each $12.50

This superbly edited definitive collection, of interest to the general reader as well as to the scholar, is "a model of accuracy, learning and tact." The editor, formerly at Yale and now at Syracuse University, "presents also among its more than two thousand letters, a good deal of unpublished material and includes, besides Swinburne's own letters, many others from his family and friends, and from writers such as Browning and Matthew Arnold, Victor Hugo and Baudelaire, with whom he exchanged books and compliments. The correspondence has been supplemented by extracts from obscure memoirs which record impressions of Swinburne at various times in his life"—(*New Yorker*). Volume 6 contains additions and corrections to the first four volumes and very useful indexes.

Books about Swinburne

A Study of Swinburne. By T. Earle Welby. 1926. *Barnes & Noble* 1969 $5.00; *Folcroft* lib. bdg. $10.00; *Kennikat* 1968 $10.00, *Richard West* 1973 $7.25. Contains much intelligent criticism of Swinburne's poetry.

Swinburne. By Samuel C. Chew. 1929. *Shoe String* 1966 $8.00. This is the most balanced general study of
the poet's whole work.

Swinburne: A Nineteenth Century Hellene. By William R. Rutland. 1931. *Folcroft* lib. bdg. $20.00;
Scholarly Press $19.50. The best study of Greek influences in Swinburne.

Swinburne. By H. J. C. Grierson. Writers and Their Works Ser. *British Bk. Centre* 1953 $2.38 pap. $1.20

The Crowns of Apollo, Swinburne's Principles of Literature and Art: A Study in Victorian Criticism
and Aesthetics. By Robert L. Peters. *Wayne State Univ. Press* 1965 $9.95
"An original and intelligent discussion of Swinburne's aesthetic theories which reveals a thorough
familiarity with the poet's writings and with past scholarship"—(*Choice*).

Swinburne's Theory of Poetry. By Thomas E. Connolly. *State Univ. of New York* 1965 $6.50
"Connolly has performed a valuable service for all students of Swinburne by mining his prose, ex-
tracting a solid core of aesthetic principles, and demonstrating that Swinburne steadfastly based his
criticism upon them, contrary to the common belief that his writings lack coherence. . . . An indispensable work"—(*Choice*).

At the Pines: Swinburne and Watts-Dunton in Putney. By Mollie Panter-Downes. *Gambit* 1971 $6.95
A sympathetic portrait of Swinburne in his later years.

HARDY, THOMAS. 1840–1928.

Hardy was a remarkable Victorian novelist and a remarkable Georgian poet. It was in 1895, when he was
approaching his 60s, that he abandoned prose for poetry, and he was prouder of his poetry than his novels.
His poetic masterpiece, "The Dynasts, an Epic-Drama of the War with Napoleon," in 3 parts, 19 acts, and
130 scenes, Hardy described as a dramatic monster intended for mental performance only. Louis Untermeyer
speaks of the "sense of nobility that illumines Hardy's poetry . . . stark, gnarled and natural as an apple
tree. . . . His three richest books of verse appeared after he was eighty; he continued to write his character-
istically knotted, delicately acrid, and clean-stripped verse until he was almost ninety."

COLLECTED POEMS. *Macmillan* 1926 1953 $10.00

SELECTED POEMS. Ed. by John Crowe Ransom *Macmillan* 1961 pap. $2.45; ed. by
G. M. Young *St. Martin's* $2.95

SELECTED SHORTER POEMS. Ed. by John Wain. *St. Martin's* 1966 (orig.) pap. $2.75

LETTERS. Ed. by Carl J. Weber. 1954. *Kraus* $8.00

Books about Hardy

Thomas Hardy, Poet and Novelist. By Samuel C. Chew. 1921 *Russell & Russell* 1964 $8.00. A compre-
hensive study by an authoritative scholar.

The Poetry of Thomas Hardy, with a New Preface. By James Southworth. 1947. *Russell & Russell* 1966
$8.50

Thomas Hardy and the Cosmic Mind: A New Reading of The Dynasts. By James Osler Bailey. *Univ. of
North Carolina Press* 1956 $6.00

The Pattern of Hardy's Poetry. By Samuel Lynn Hynes. *Univ. of North Carolina Press* 1961 $5.00

The Shaping of The Dynasts: A Study in Thomas Hardy. By Walter F. Wright. *Univ. of Nebraska Press*
1967 $7.95

The Poems of Thomas Hardy: A Critical Introduction. By Kenneth Marsden. *Humanities* (Athlone
Press) $7.75. A general discussion of Hardy's verse and voice.

Thomas Hardy and British Poetry. By Donald Davie. *Oxford* 1972 $6.95

See also Chapter 11, British Fiction: Middle Period.

HOPKINS, GERARD MANLEY. 1844–1889.

Hopkins, of an Anglican family, scholar, esthete and ascetic, was received into the Roman Catholic Church
while still an undergraduate at Oxford, where his friends included Walter Pater, who was one of his tutors,
Ruskin, Williams Morris, and Robert Bridges, later England's Poet Laureate and Hopkins's posthumous editor. The great classicist Jowett considered Hopkins the star of Balliol, and one of the finest of its Greek
scholars.

In 1868 Hopkins entered a Jesuit Novitiate and burned all his early poems, "resolved to write no more till
he should, by ecclesiastical authority, be enjoined to do so. After seven years (a round, symbolic number), the
silence was lifted by a superior's suggestion that some member of the community should elegize the five Fran-
ciscan nuns who perished in the wreck of the *Deutschland*"—("Gerard Manley Hopkins" by the Kenyon
Critis 1946 o.p.).

It was not until 1918 that his poems were first collected and published by Bridges. His experiments and inventiveness, his "perception of images and words, his appetite for detail, in nature and in architecture, his joy in the unique configuration of the sensuously transient which he called 'inscape,' " were directed toward creating an English and Catholic convention of poetry and poetic language. His religious fervor permeates his verse. He was never successful by ordinary professional standards as parish priest, teacher or classical lecturer, but the 20th century found him a marvelous poet. The conflict between his desire to be a saint and his desire to be an artist was necessary to his great poetic achievement, but produced the "nervous prostration" from which he did not recover.

POEMS. Ed. by Robert Bridges. 1918. With additional poems and critical introd. by Charles Williams *Oxford* 2nd ed. 1937; with additional poems and a biographical introd. by W. H. Gardner 3rd ed. 1948; with latest versions of all extant poems and verse fragments ed. by W. H. Gardner and N. H. MacKenzie 4th ed. 1967 $8.50 Galaxy Bks. pap. $2.95

A HOPKINS READER. Ed. by John Pick. *Oxford* 1953 $6.75

SELECTED POEMS AND PROSE. Ed. by W. H. Gardner. 1953. *Penguin* pap. $1.45

SELECTED POEMS. Ed. by J. Reeves. *Barnes & Noble* 1953 $1.50

SELECTIONS. Ed. by Graham Storey. *Oxford* 1967 $2.50

THE WRECK OF THE DEUTSCHLAND. 1874. *Godine* 1971 $6.00 special ed. $8.00

SERMONS AND DEVOTIONAL WRITINGS. Ed. by Christopher Devlin. *Oxford* 1959 $12.00

THE LETTERS OF GERARD MANLEY HOPKINS TO ROBERT BRIDGES; THE CORRESPONDENCE OF GERARD HOPKINS AND RICHARD WATSON DIXON. Ed. with notes and introd. by Claude Colleer Abbott. *Oxford* 1935 2nd rev. ed. 1955 2 vols. set $18.75

FURTHER LETTERS OF GERARD MANLEY HOPKINS. Ed. by C. C. Abbott. *Oxford* 1938 1956 $18.75

JOURNALS AND PAPERS. Ed. by Humphrey House; completed by Graham Storey. *Oxford* 1959 $17.00

"A scholarly and distinguished elaboration of the poet's life and development. . . . This enlarged edition of Hopkins's notebooks and papers contains much new and important material discovered since the appearance of the 1937 edition which has long been out of print. The two 'Early Diaries' (1862–66) are given virtually complete, including about 500 lines of verse printed for the first time. Five more undergraduate 'Essays' have been added to the three originally reproduced from the Oxford notebooks, and, most important, the 'Journal' (1886–75) has been completed by the publication of three exercise books, found in 1947, which cover the period of the poet's conversion. A series of 'Lecture Notes' on rhetoric and a number of appendixes . . . further increase the value of this work, which is well indexed and annotated"—(*LJ*).

Books about Hopkins

Gerard Manley Hopkins: A Study of Poetic Idiosyncracy in Relation to Poetic Tradition. By William H. Gardner. *Oxford* 2 vols. 2nd ed. 1948 $17.00 A definitive study of Hopkins's innovations and use of tradition.

The Shaping Vision of Gerard Manley Hopkins. By Alan Heuser. 1958. *Shoe String* 1968 $4.50

Gerard Manley Hopkins: A Study of his Ignatian Spirit. By David A. Downes. A scholarly study of the influence of St. Ignatius Loyola on the poet. *Twayne* 1959 $4.50

Metaphor in Hopkins. By Robert Boyle, S.J. *Univ. of North Carolina Press* 1961 $7.50

Hopkins: A Collection of Critical Essays. Ed. with introd. by Geoffrey Hartman. Twentieth Century Views Ser. *Prentice-Hall* Spectrum Bks. 1966 $5.95 pap. $1.95. An excellent selection of 12 essays by modern writers and scholars. Selected bibliography, chronology, notes.

The Unmediated Vision. By Geoffrey H. Hartman. *Harcourt* 1966 Harbinger Bks. pap. $1.85

Gerard Manley Hopkins. By Todd K. Bender. *Johns Hopkins Univ. Press* 1966 $7.00

Gerard Manley Hopkins. By Francis N. Lees. Pamphlet. *Columbia* Essays on Modern Writers 1966 pap. $1.00

Gerard Manley Hopkins: The Poet as Victorian. By Wendell S. Johnson. *Cornell Univ. Press* 1968 $7.50. Hopkins's work discussed in its post-Romantic context.

Commentary on the Complete Poems of Gerard Manley Hopkins. By Paul L. Marianai. *Cornell Univ. Press* 1970 $12.50

STEVENSON, ROBERT LOUIS. 1850–1894. *See Chapter 11, British Fiction: Middle Period, and Chapter 15, Essays and Criticism.*

WILDE, OSCAR. 1845–1900.

Oscar Wilde was educated at Trinity College Dublin, and Magdalen College Oxford, where he became known as the founder of the Art-for-Art's Sake movement, caricatured in Gilbert and Sullivan's comic opera "Patience." His first poem, the prizewinning "Ravenna," was published in 1878. "The Ballad of Reading Gaol" is Wilde's best-known poem; it was written in France and published more than a year after he had been released from prison. It appeared first over the signature "C. 3. 3," the number of his cell in Reading Prison, and recorded a hanging which took place while he was confined there for homosexuality, the scandal that ruined his life. His famous symbols were "a peacock feather, sunflowers, dados, blue china, long hair and velveteen breeches. . . . He was lampooned in cartoons, in novels, and even in comic opera; but he remained for years the center of attention, the lion of the hour, the most sought after of many famous talkers. . . . Many of the unsavory aspects of Wilde's personal life have been forgotten, but his witty paradoxes remain alive, especially in the plays."

WORKS. Ed. by Robert Ross. 15 vols. 1909–1922. First collected edition. *Barnes & Noble* 1969 15 vols. $175.00; *AMS Press* 15 vols. each $12.00 set $175.00

PLAYS, PROSE WRITINGS AND POEMS. Introd. by Hesketh Pearson. *Dutton* Everyman's 1955 $3.50 pap. $1.95

THE PORTABLE OSCAR WILDE. Sel. and ed. by Richard Aldington. *Viking* 1946 $6.50 pap. $3.25

POEMS AND FAIRY TALES. *Modern Library* $1.95

SELECTED WRITINGS. Ed. by Richard Ellmann. *Oxford* World's Class. $2.75; ed. by Russell A. Fraser *Houghton* Riv. Eds. pap. $1.75

BALLAD OF READING GAOL. 1898. *Dufour* $1.75

THOMPSON, FRANCIS. 1859–1907.

Thompson was born and brought up in the Catholic faith and his poems are those of a religious mystic. Arthur Symons says of "The Hound of Heaven": "It is full of fine and significant symbolism, it is an elaborate pageant of his own life, with all its miseries, heights, relapses, and flight after some eternity; but, as he writes it, it turns intellectual and the voice is like that of one declaiming his confession." Louis Untermeyer says that the poet "saw man as the mortal quarry, the frightened creature running to hide in nature, and God as the divine hunter, pursuer and rescuer." In his poetry, Thompson "allowed himself a prodigality of conceits as wild as any fashioned by seventeenth-century metaphysicians; he scattered baroque images and fancy neologisms with wayward extravagance." Thompson, addicted to opium and in dire poverty, was befriended by Mr. and Mrs. Wilfred Meynell, who took him into their home and arranged for the publication of his first volume, "Poems," which appeared when he was 34.

During the last decade of his life Thompson (at least partially cured of his drug addiction) wrote many book reviews and critical essays. In the excellent "Francis Thompson and Wilfred Meynell: A Memoir" by Viola Meynell (1953, o. p.) "the intimate details of the famous friendship between the gifted poet . . . and Meynell, journalist and editor, are vividly reflected from these personal recollections and family papers."

WORKS. Ed. by Wilfred Meynell. 1918. *AMS Press* 3 vols. each $15.00 set $42.00

FRANCIS THOMPSON. Ed. by Wilfred Meynell. 1947. *Bks. for Libraries* 3 vols. in 1 $22.50

POEMS. Ed. by Wilfred Meynell. In this definitive edition the author's own instructions were followed by his literary executor. *Oxford* Stand. Authors 1937 $6.50

POEMS. Ed. by the Rev. Terence L. Connolly. The complete poems annotated from a Catholic point of view. *Appleton* 1932 rev. ed. 1941 $9.45

THE HOUND OF HEAVEN AND OTHER POEMS. *Branden* pap. $.85

THE HOUND OF HEAVEN. 1890. Ill. by Valenti Angelo. *Morehouse* pap. $.85

Books about Thompson

> The Life of Francis Thompson. By Everard Meynell. 1913. *Scholarly Press* 1971 $19.50; *Richard West* $19.45. The standard life of the poet.
> A Critical Bibliography of Works by and about Francis Thompson. By Myrtle P. Pope. *N.Y. Public Lib.* 1959 pap. $1.50
> Francis Thompson: A Critical Biography. By Paul Van K. Thomson. 1961. *Gordian* 1972 $8.50. A careful, well-informed study of Thompson.
> Francis Thompson. By Peter Butter. Writers and Their Works Ser. *British Bk. Centre* 1962 $2.38 pap. $1.20

HOUSMAN, A(LFRED) E(DWARD). 1859–1936.

"Of all the poets of modern times, none has won so great a reputation from such a small body of work"—three small volumes and some posthumous lines from manuscript. Most of Housman's verses consist of but a few quatrains. "His themes are few—personal loss, cosmic betrayal, cruelty, waste, war, death"—(Louis Untermeyer). Housman was not a native of Shropshire. "The hilly Shropshire country was merely a background in his youth; it became a symbolic setting against which he placed his fantasies." The poet was Kennedy Professor of Latin in the University of Cambridge from 1892 until his death. His classical studies were the serious interest of his life. He thought his first book of poems was so slight and unimportant that he did not copyright it in the United States; it has had, in consequence, many publishers. For over 25 years Housman kept an eager public—much of it a youthful one—waiting for a second collection of his poignant lyrics. "Last Poems" is in the same vein of romantic pessimism as "A Shropshire Lad," with its magical evocation of the English countryside. "More Poems" (1936) was a posthumous collection.

The "Introductory Lecture, 1892" (*Cambridge* 1937 $1.95), was given at University College, London, to the united faculties at the opening of the academic year. Housman, who had just become Professor of Latin there, spoke about the "value of learning for its own sake." "The Name and Nature of Poetry" (1933 o. p.) was the Leslie Stephen lecture delivered at Cambridge in 1933—of great interest as a discussion of his own creative view. In it Housman defines the function of poetry as the transfusing of emotion, not the transmitting of thought. A volume of his "Selected Prose" has been published (ed. by John Carter. *Cambridge* 1961 $5.50 pap. $1.45).

Maude M. Hawkins' "tactful, slightly rhapsodic biography," "A. E. Housman: Man Behind a Mask" (1958, o. p.) is based on letters, notebooks and conversations with Housman's family and friends. She concentrates on his personality and attempts to solve certain riddles of Housman's life. Edmund Wilson (*q.v.*) has a most interesting essay on Housman as man and classical scholar in "The Triple Thinkers."

COLLECTED POEMS. Centennial Edition. Ed. with introd. by Basil Davenport; history of the text by Tom Burns Haber. *Holt* 1959 rev. ed. 1965 $6.95 pap. $2.45

In the 1959 edition "A Shropshire Lad" and "Last Poems" stood almost as they were in 1940; "More Poems" and "Additional Poems" showed 30 changes, mostly of punctuation, but there were two added stanzas, several different wordings and four changed lines. Haber's changes were careful ones and his textual history is useful. The 1965 revision contains very few changes from editions of the 1940s, according to *Choice*. The Chronology of the Poems is no longer included.

MANUSCRIPT POEMS. Ed. by Tom Burns Haber. Some 800 lines of hitherto unpublished poetry from the Housman notebooks in the Library of Congress; also variants from manuscript copies of "A Shropshire Lad" and "Last Poems." *Univ. of Minnesota Press* 1955 $4.50

THE MAKING OF A SHROPSHIRE LAD. 1896. A Manuscript Variorum. Ed. by Tom B. Haber. *Univ. of Washington Press* 1966 $10.00

"Each poem in the book receives three treatments: (1) the established version; (2) a page explaining the bibliographical and critical problems of the manuscript; and (3) the drafts themselves (from Housman's notebooks in the Library of Congress)"—(*Choice*)

A SHROPSHIRE LAD. 1896. *Avon* pap. $.60; introd. by J. Mersand *Branden* pap. $.95; ed. by Humphrey House *Dufour* 1965 $1.95

LAST POEMS. 1922. *Dufour* $1.95

LETTERS. Ed. by Henry Maas *Harvard Univ. Press* 1970 $11.50

Books about Housman

> A. E. Housman; A sketch together with a list of his writings and indexes to his classical papers. By A. S. F. Gow. 1936. *Haskell* lib. bdg. $8.95
>
> My Brother: A. E. Housman. By Laurence Housman. Personal recollections together with 30 hitherto unpublished poems. 1938. *Kennikat* 1969 $9.50
>
> A Concordance to the Poems of A. E. Housman. By Clyde K. Hyder. 1940. *Peter Smith* $7.50
>
> A. E. Housman. By Ian Scott-Kilvert. Writers and Their Work Ser. *British Bk. Centre* $2.38 pap. $1.20
>
> A. E. Housman. By Tom Burns Haber. English Authors Ser. *Twayne* 1967 $5.50

KIPLING, RUDYARD. 1865–1936. (Nobel Prize 1907)

The definitive edition of Kipling's "full-bodied and active" verse is a final evidence of his career as a poet. Many of his early poems, on the same general themes of empire and India that inspired his prose, had a lilt and swing and narrative interest—a concentration on "people at work" against difficulties—that made them enormously popular. "Gunga Din," "Danny-Deever," "If" and the like were still known to every school-child in the 1930s. "Kipling is greater as a prose writer than as a poet, but he has a very considerable place in English poetry, although rhetoric has played a greater part than poetry in his verse equipment"—(Clement Shorter). T. S. Eliot (*q.v.*) before his death showed himself an (unlikely!) admirer of certain facets of Kipling's verse. He pointed out that Kipling wrote transparently, "so that our attention is directed to the object and not the medium. [He was economic] of words, had an unsurpassed ability with ballads, and was in 'Recessional' a great hymn writer."

COLLECTED WORKS. The Burwash ed. 28 vols. 1941. *AMS Press* set $745.00. This and the Sussex ed. (1937–39) are the only ones containing all acknowledged and authorized works. The two editions are identical in content.

RUDYARD KIPLING'S VERSE. Definitive Edition. 1885–1936. The final edition containing every poem he ever wrote, including 13 never before in book form. *Doubleday* new ed. 1940 reissue 1949 $10.00

KIPLING: A Selection of His Stories and Poems. Ed. by John Beecroft; ill. by Richard M. Powers. Includes 86 pages of representative verse. *Doubleday* 1956 2 vols. set $10.95

IF. 1910. The celebrated poem. *Doubleday* Dolphin Bks. pap. $1.00; (and Other Poems) Pyramid pap. $.35

Book about Kipling

> The Art of Rudyard Kipling. By J. M. S. Tompkins. *Barnes & Noble* 2nd ed. 1965 $4.00; *Peter Smith* $4.00; *Univ. of Nebraska Press* 1966 Bison Bks. pap. $1.90

See also Chapter 11, British Fiction: Middle Period.

—F.S.

Chapter 7

Modern British Poetry

"First, then, the point of view that modern poetry expresses toward life in general is that of a Romantic aestheticism. The Self seeks to discover itself. . . . Secondly, our poetry of political and cultural criticism centers on the individual as the victim. . . . Thirdly—an extension from the previous point—the private life of the poet himself, especially under stress of psychological crises, becomes a major theme. Often it is felt at the same time as a symbolic embodiment of national and cultural crisis."
—M. L. ROSENTHAL ("The New Poets")

In the foreword to her "Poetry: A Modern Guide to its Understanding and Enjoyment," Elizabeth Drew writes: "The aim of any critic who is a lover of poetry must be to make the reading of it an exploration, which constantly reveals new insights to the reader about himself as well as about the writers and writing of poems. It must be an invitation to look, to listen, to linger in the presence of poetry and to feel its spell." She compares and contrasts the new and the old with interpretations of the greatest value. Several British poets have written critical works on poetry, notably A. E. Housman, C. Day Lewis, T. S. Eliot (*see Chapter 15, Essays*), Stephen Spender and Lawrence Durrell. The ambiguity of much modern verse has meant an increase in the number of handbooks for the understanding of it which are included in the following reading list.

"Poetry in Our Time," by the American poet Babette Deutsch, is an excellent and perceptive introduction to 20th-century poetry. In her chapter on Wars and Rumors of Wars, she comments: "The difference between the poems of World War I and those of World War II . . . might be said to lie in this fact: the soldier poets of the later generation were all haunted. Their pages are haunted by the performance of their literary forbears . . . the ghostly presence of Pound's precise imagery, of Eliot's subterranean music, of the concentration transmitted through these poets from the French masters, of Yeats' high talk, of Hopkins' intensity of apprehension and immediacy of language. . . . But the starry-eyed romanticism that had fashioned some dreams of the future was killed even before the explosion of the atom bomb."

The Second World War seems to have effected a radical change in the vitality of English poetry—a change that has no parallel in America. Auden came to live in America and became an American citizen; Eliot turned his genius to drama; Dylan Thomas died; Graves moved to Majorca. Many of the younger poets, too, have since come to America. "For the postwar English generation, America has dominated the scene. . . . There is, since 1945, a new sense of the American superiority being taken for granted: it is the complete reversal of the time when Americans took European superiority for granted, because of the European rootedness in tradition. In England, it is felt, especially by the young, that tradition and class and the literary community provide a barrier between the life that they should be concerned with; but it is a kind of life which those who live it—the industrial workers and the shopkeepers—do not want to read about"—(Stephen Spender). James Reeves writes in "A Short History of English Poetry": "The history of English poetry seems to have come to rest, at any rate for the time being, in a paradox: an immense amount is being written . . . and the criticism of poetry is a thriving academic industry— yet never did the status of poetry and the general esteem in which it is held seem more in question."

The causes for the poetic confusion following World War II are many. First came the overwhelming influence of Auden, Eliot, Empson and Graves. "With this notable body of work pressing on him [the poet], it must often be a real question to him what he can add to it"—(G. S. Fraser in *The London Magazine*). Publishers' costs of printing are high and British poets lack, according to Roy Fuller, a "persistent little magazine to get them together and present them to the public." They lack, too, the American paperback originals and reprints. "There are few poets today who are not harried and bothered both by the need to make a living and the compulsion to write," Elizabeth Jennings has commented. M. L. Rosenthal's analysis at the head of this chapter applies equally to British and American poets of the 60's, but, he says, "An American reader of British poetry is still on more alien ground than he may at first realize. He is likely to be repelled by what looks like a morass of petty cleverness . . . that seems quite dead at the center. . . . A tolerance for facile mediocrity, [it appears], at times pervades every level of poetic activity. An American needs the experience of much re-reading and, indeed, of getting used to contemporary British speech in general to correct this over-all impression to a significant degree. . . . [British] education encourages greater articulateness than the American, but not necessarily greater originality." For the moment, then, British and American poetry are, in general, dissimilar in approach if not in theme, and the Americans seem to have the edge in popular interest and in presenting a broad spectrum of diverse and lively poetic activity.

Possibly the greatest difficulty British poetry has had in reasserting itself, in the postwar decade, has been its unwillingness to come to grips with any French surrealist or Spanish surrealist influence. While American poets, such as John Ashbery, Frank O'Hara, Kenneth Koch, James Schuyler and others were busy synthesizing a new and fertile formlessness from such poets as Apollinaire, Eluard, and St-John Perse, the British poets consistently rejected French forms for something less ecstatically disjunct, seemingly nonsensical, and dream-logical. Only David Gascoygne and F. T. Prince succeeded in enucleating and developing the French resource. As for the rhapsodical strength of a Lorca, who so reinvigorated American poets such as Robert Bly and James Wright, the British poets such as Larkin and Macbeth were hardly involved.

In the last five years, there have been signs of change in English poetry, notably in Cambridge. Jeremy Prynne, Nick Totton, and others have begun a British poetry that borrows the palette of Charles Olson and John Ashbery and yet revivifies within Anglican idiosyncracies. Frank O'Hara's personalist strain, and that of Allen Ginsberg, has lightened the almost depersonalized modality of the academic verse of England. A new sense of "occasional" verse, along the lines of "pop" art and the so-called New York School, has revitalized the contemporary English poets. Just as British artists took their first look at a big DeKooning exhibit only five years ago, so British poets are beginning to have available the fine neglected American poets of the 50s. For, if one admits, no matter how chauvinistically it may sound, that English poetry, dessicated and eroded, depended for much vitality upon American poetry, it is even sadder to admit that the English poet was not generally able to discover the most significant American poets, buried under the sustained voluminousness of the Beat poets, so much lauded and decried in the press. Thus, it is now, in the 70s, that a hopeful sense of British poetry arrives, as the young poets give a sustained and vigorous reading to the masterworks of Ashbery and O'Hara and Olson, with the inevitable corollary of an increased attentiveness to the Parisian center of the 20s and 30s. As a sign of this concentrated alertness to the Dadaist and surrealist heritage, one thinks of Mr. Trevor Winkfield's magazine *Julliard*, which throughout the late 60s and early 70s published side by side American, English, and French poets, with a richness unparalleled in the decade by any other British periodical or quarterly.   —D.S.

See also Chapter 4, Broad Studies and General Anthologies and Chapter 3, Reference Books—Literature for the often extensive Poetry sections in both.

HISTORY AND CRITICISM OF MODERN BRITISH POETRY

Daiches, David. THE PRESENT AGE IN BRITISH LITERATURE. *Indiana Univ. Press* 1958 $8.50 Midland Bks. pap. $2.65. A survey of trends since 1914, this includes a commentary on poetry with an extensive bibliography and critical notes.

Durrell, Lawrence. A KEY TO MODERN BRITISH POETRY. *Univ. of Oklahoma Press* 1952 $5.95 pap. $2.50

Fairchild, Hoxie Neale. RELIGIOUS TRENDS IN ENGLISH POETRY: Vol. 5, 1880–1920: Gods of the Changing Poetry. *Columbia* 1962 $12.50. Written "with lucidity, understanding and wit," Volume 5 of this monumental study covers that "peculiarly crucial and generally glossed over" period during which Victorian poetry came to be "modern." (*See Chapter 5, British Poetry: Early to Romantic, for the earlier volumes.*)

Johnston, John H. ENGLISH POETRY OF THE FIRST WORLD WAR: A Study in the Evolution of Lyric and Narrative Form. *Princeton Univ. Press* 1964 $12.50. An enlightening analysis of the work of Brooke, Grenfell, Nichols, Sorley, Blunden, Owen, Resenberg, Read and Jones.

Leavis, F. R. NEW BEARINGS ON ENGLISH POETRY: A Study of the Contemporary Situation. 1932. *Univ. of Michigan Press* $4.40 Ann Arbor Bks. pap. $1.85

Loftus, Richard J. NATIONALISM IN MODERN ANGLO-IRISH POETRY. *Univ. of Wisconsin Press* $10.00

"A broad perspective of Irish history, politics, folklore and literary squabbles against which the achievements of a host of poets from Yeats and A. E. to Austin Clarke may be viewed. Carefully written and abundantly documented, this important contribution to literary history and criticism illuminates brilliantly a complex, misunderstood, but exciting aspect of modern poetry"—(*LJ*).

Pinto, Vivian de Sola. CRISIS IN ENGLISH POETRY, 1880–1940. 1957. *Hillary House* Hutchinson Univ. Lib. $6.00 pap. $2.25

Press, John. THE CHEQUER'D SHADE: Reflections on Obscurity in Poetry. "A balanced, clear, and never boring analysis of some of the elements which have gone to produce this common sense of the obscurity of twentieth-century poetry." *Oxford* 1958 pap. 1963 $1.75

Ross, Robert H. THE GEORGIAN REVOLT 1910–1922: Rise and Fall of a Poetic Ideal. *Southern Illinois Univ. Press* 1965 $6.50 pap. $3.00

"By careful placement of the Georgians in a milieu that vibrated with manifestos, anthologies, little magazines, attacks and counterattacks, Imagists, Vorticists, Futurists and strident Yankees, Professor Ross has defined very precisely the accomplishments of Rupert Brooke, Edmund Blunden, John Drinkwater, Lascelles Abercrombie, D. H. Lawrence, Wilfrid Gibson, and other luminaries of the Georgian blaze and eclipse. . . . This excellent study should be available to informed laymen and to literary scholars"—(*LJ*).

Schmidt, Michael, and Grevel Lindop. BRITISH POETRY SINCE 1960. 1973 *Dufour* $14.00

Sisson, C. H. ENGLISH POETRY, 1900–1950: An Assessment. *St. Martin's* 1970 $8.95

Tindall, William York. FORCES IN MODERN BRITISH LITERATURE, 1885–1946. 1947. *Bks. for Libraries* $15.50. This witty, suggestive and informative evaluation includes the modern poets.

THE LITERARY SYMBOL. Symbolism as one of the most profound and pervasive forces in modern poetry and fiction. 1955. *Indiana Univ. Press* pap. $1.95; *Peter Smith* $4.00

MODERN POETRY IN ENGLISH

Anthologies and Criticism of British and American Poetry

Alvarez, A. STEWARDS OF EXCELLENCE: Studies in Modern English and American Poets. 1958. *Gordian* $7.50

> "Shrewd and persuasive," this English critic compares the Englishmen Yeats, Auden, Empson and Lawrence with the Americans Eliot, Pound, Hart Crane and Wallace Stevens, with some extended remarks on Frost, Eberhart and Robert Lowell. The author considers that "modernism" in poetry has been "a predominantly American concern" and has hardly affected English poets. This is "an enjoyable book, informed by . . . 'relish and vitality.' "

Brinnin, John Malcolm, and Bill Read. THE MODERN POETS: An American-British Anthology. With photographs by Rollie McKenna. *McGraw-Hill* 1963 2nd ed. 1970 $6.50

> "Our aim has been to pick, from the works of the finest living poets, poems of representative substance and power that can travel freely in any English-speaking country without an interpreter. Having found these in abundance, we present them in confidence that they will move, delight, and beguile even those readers who encounter them for the first time. Instead of the usual notes, we have informal commentaries and brief biographies"—(Preface).

Cane, Melville. MAKING A POEM: An Inquiry Into the Creative Process. *Harcourt* 1953 $2.95 Harvest Bks. pap. $1.85

Cecil, Lord David, and Allen Tate, Eds. MODERN VERSE IN ENGLISH, 1900–1950. *Macmillan* 1958 $8.50. An anthology with critical introds. of 45 British and 61 American poets; biographical notes included.

Drew, Elizabeth. POETRY: A MODERN GUIDE TO ITS UNDERSTANDING AND ENJOYMENT. *Norton* 1959 $5.95; *Dell* pap. $.60. Includes an excellent comment on T. S. Eliot.

Engle, Paul, and Joseph Langland, Eds. POET'S CHOICE. *Dial* 1962 $7.50. An anthology presenting 103 contemporary poets, each of whom was asked "to select a favorite or crucial poem from his own work and comment on it." Among the Americans are Elizabeth Bishop, Allen Tate and Richard Eberhart.

Friar, Kimon, and John Malcolm Brinnin, Eds. MODERN POETRY: AMERICAN AND BRITISH. *Appleton* 1951 $10.50. An anthology that emphasizes "writers of the metaphysical, surrealist and symbolist kind."

Gross, Harvey. SOUND AND FORM IN MODERN POETRY: A Study of Prosody from Thomas Hardy to Robert Lowell. *Univ. of Michigan Press* 1964 $8.50 Ann Arbor Bks. pap. $2.65. This "impressive volume [is a] major theoretical and descriptive opus on versification"—(*LJ*).

Hall, Donald, Robert Pack, and Louis Simpson. NEW POETS OF ENGLAND AND AMERICA. Introd. by Robert Frost. *World Pub.* Meridian Bks. 1957 pap. $4.95. An excellent collection of poets born between 1917 and 1935.

Hall, Donald, and Robert Pack. New Poets of England and America: Second Selection. *World Pub.* Meridian Bks. 1962 pap. $3.95. A valuable compendium of the younger writers; the English poets were chosen by Hall, the Americans by Pack. As before (*see above*), no poets born before 1922 are included. This section includes 62 poets (10 more than previously) of whom 35 are new.

Harrison, John R. The Reactionaries, Yeats—Wyndham Lewis—Pound—Eliot—Lawrence: A Study of the Anti-Democratic Intelligentsia. *Schocken* 1967 $6.00 pap. $2.25. The author "digs into these men's political notions with skill, objectivity and understanding, substantiating his points with references to pertinent works"—(*PW*).

Hollander, John. Poems of our Moment: Contemporary Poets of the English Language. *Pegasus* 1967 $7.50 pap. $2.45. An anthology that includes James Dickey, Allen Ginsberg, W. S. Merwin, Philip Larkin, James Merrill, Anthony Hecht and A. D. Hope among others.

"In this anthology the oldest poet represented is 60 years old, and the youngest, 20; all were first published after 1950"—(*LJ*). It includes Americans, Australians, Canadians, English.

Modern Poetry: Essays in Criticism. *Oxford* 1968 Galaxy Bks. pap. $3.95

Kuntz, Joseph M. Poetry Explication: A Checklist of Interpretation since 1925 of British and American Poems, Past and Present. *Swallow* rev. ed. 1962 $7.50

This listing of critical articles on poets and their poetry is very helpful for the interpretation of difficult poems, especially modern ones. The first edition (with George Warren Arms, 1950) covered publications appearing between 1925 and 1949. This second revised edition, "not so much a supplement to or a revision of the earlier work (though some errors and omissions have been rectified) but an extension . . . presents a comprehensive index of poetry explications printed during the period 1925–1959 inclusive."

Miller, James Edwin and others. Start with the Sun: Studies in the Whitman Tradition. *Univ. of Nebraska Press* 1960 Bison Bks. pap. $1.50

James E. Miller, Jr., Karl Shapiro and Bernice Slote contribute to a nonorthodox study of the Romantic tradition in the 20th century by analyzing Walt Whitman's influence on such writers as Hart Crane, D. H. Lawrence, Dylan Thomas, William Carlos Williams and Henry Miller. Expansive cosmic poetry "full of pagan joy and wonder" in the Whitman tradition is examined as it occurs in, or influences, some of his successors.

Miller, Joseph Hillis. Poets of Reality: Six Twentieth Century Writers. *Harvard Univ. Press* 1965 $9.00; *Atheneum* pap. $3.25

Discusses Yeats, Eliot, Dylan Thomas, Wallace Stevens and William Carlos Williams. The book begins with a chapter on Conrad who "led readers to explore the innermost limits of late 19th century nihilism and began to blaze a path out of that wilderness"—(*LJ*).

Moore, Marianne. Predilections. *Viking* 1955 $2.75. Among the poets included in these brief critical essays are her favorite fellow poets, Stevens, Eliot, Pound, Cummings and Auden.

Nemerov, Howard, Ed. Poets on Poetry. *Basic Bks.* 1966 $5.95. "These biographical [and autobiographical] essays provide fascinating insights into what the poets want readers to know about them"—(*N.Y. Times*).

O'Connor, William Van. Sense and Sensibility in Modern Poetry. 1948. *Gordian* $9.00. This covers "meter, metaphor, obscurity, the Symbolist School, the Imagist School, the alienation between artist and society" to explain modern obscurities.

Paris Review. WRITERS AT WORK: The *Paris Review* Interviews. *See Chapter 4, Broad Studies: General Works on Writers and Writing.*

Press, John. MAP OF MODERN ENGLISH VERSE. *Oxford* 1969 $7.50 Galaxy Bks. pap. $3.95. A survey which uses poems, critical extracts and commentaries on individuals.

Rosenthal, M. L. THE MODERN POETS: A Critical Introduction. *Oxford* $6.95 Galaxy Bks. pap. $2.50. A comment on the understanding, or lack of it, between contemporary poets and their general readers; on the continuity of poetry past and present; and on the distinctly "modern" sensibility of such writers as Yeats, Eliot, Muir, MacDiarmid and other, younger poets.

THE NEW MODERN POETRY: British and American Poetry Since World War II. *Macmillan* 1967 $7.95

An excellent and comprehensive selection of the "representative and important" work of 104 poets. "Short notes on the poets, their background, and something about their works, an index of authors and titles, and an index of first lines make this collection useful"—(*L J*).

THE NEW POETS: American and British Poetry Since World War II. *Oxford* 1967 $8.95 Galaxy Bks. pap. $2.95. An incisive critical interpretation with many poems interspersed.

Sanders, Gerald De Witt, and John H. Nelson. CHIEF MODERN POETS OF ENGLAND AND AMERICA. Anthology. *Macmillan* 1929 rev. ed. 1936 3rd ed. 1943 rev. ed. 1948 rev. ed. 1962 5th ed. 1970 2 vols. in 1 $9.25

SCRUTINY. *Cambridge* 1963 each $12.50 set $195.00. The quarterly journal of criticism, issued from 1932 to 1953 under the direction of F. R. Leavis, reprinted as a set of 20 vols. (19 vols. of original text and a new volume containing a "Retrospect" by Leavis and a complete index).

Shapiro, Karl, Ed. PROSE KEYS TO MODERN POETRY. *Harper* 1962 pap. $6.00

Stallman, Robert Wooster, Ed. CRITIQUES AND ESSAYS IN CRITICISM, 1920–1948: Representing the Achievement of Modern British and American Critics. With fwd. by Cleanth Brooks. *Ronald* 1949 $8.50. Among the contributors: Stephen Spender, J. C. Ransom, Allen Tate, Cleanth Brooks, R. P. Warren, Yvor Winters, Delmore Schwartz, T. S. Eliot, Edmund Wilson.

Stevenson, Burton Egbert. THE HOME BOOK OF MODERN VERSE: An Extension of the Home Book of Verse: being a Selection from American and English Poetry of the Twentieth Century. *Holt* 1925 rev. ed. 1950 2nd ed. 1953 $10.95

Townsend, John R., Ed. MODERN POETRY. *Lippincott* 1974 $5.95

Untermeyer, Louis. LIVES OF THE POETS: The Story of One Thousand Years of English and American Poetry. *Simon & Schuster* 1959 $7.95 pap. $3.95. A good historical and critical survey; about the last 100 pages are devoted to the 20th century.

MODERN AMERICAN POETRY: MODERN BRITISH POETRY. Anthology. *Harcourt* rev. 1950 rev. ed. 1962 $10.95. Combined edition complete with critical and biographical notes.

NEW MODERN AMERICAN AND BRITISH POETRY. *Harcourt* Mid-Century Ed. 1950 rev. ed. 1962 $11.25 abr. ed. $8.25. A collection of 61 American and 54 British poets.

(With Karl Shapiro and Richard Wilbur) THE NEW MODERN AMERICAN AND MODERN BRITISH POETRY. *Harcourt* 1955 $7.95. Revised shorter edition with 700 poems by 62 poets.

Wheelwright, Philip. METAPHOR AND REALITY. *Indiana Univ. Press* 1962 Midland Bks. pap. $2.45. A "remarkably lucid and convincing exposition of the philosophic and semantic makeup of metaphor, symbol, and myth, liberally illustrated by vivid examples."

Williams, Oscar. A LITTLE TREASURY OF MODERN POETRY: English and American. *Scribner* 1946 1949 rev. and enl. 1955 $8.95 text ed. $4.95

   THE POCKET BOOK OF MODERN VERSE. Anthology. 1954. *Washington Square* pap. $1.25

Wilson, Edmund. AXEL'S CASTLE: A STUDY IN THE IMAGINATIVE LITERATURE OF 1870–1930. *Scribner* 1931 1939 1942 $6.95 pap. $2.95. On both poetry and prose, with a chapter on symbolism.

Yeats, William Butler. THE OXFORD BOOK OF MODERN VERSE, 1892–1935. *Oxford* 1936 $7.50. British, Irish and American Verse.

ANTHOLOGIES OF MODERN BRITISH POETRY

Coblentz, Stanton A., Ed. MODERN BRITISH LYRICS: An Anthology. 1925. *Bks. for Libraries* $10.00

Garrity, Devin. NEW IRISH POETS: Representative Selections from the Work of 37 Contemporaries. With woodcuts by Harry Kernoff. *Devin-Adair* 1948 $6.50

Horowitz, Michael, Ed. CHILDREN OF ALBION: Poetry of the Underground in Britain. *Penguin* 1970 pap. $2.25

Larkin, Philip, Ed. THE OXFORD BOOK OF TWENTIETH CENTURY ENGLISH VERSE. *Oxford* 1973 $12.50

Lucie-Smith, Edward. BRITISH POETRY SINCE 1945. *Penguin* 1970 pap. $1.95; *Peter Smith* $4.00

   (With Philip Hobsbaum, Eds.) GROUP ANTHOLOGY. *Oxford* 1963 $4.00. 61 poems read and discussed at meetings of "The Group," chosen from 3000 poems read and discussed at these meetings.

Parsons, I. M. MEN WHO MARCH AWAY: Poems of the First World War. *Viking* 1965 Compass Bks. pap. $1.65

   Poems by 34 poets that "convey the experience of an awful war with immediacy and power. Parsons's introduction is a distinguished essay"—(*LJ*).

PENGUIN MODERN POETS: Jack Clemo, Edward Lucie-Smith, George Macbeth. *Penguin* (orig.) 1968 pap. $.95

PENGUIN MODERN POETS: Brownjohn, Hamburger, Tomlinson. *Penguin* 1969 pap. $1.95

Robeson, Jeremy, Ed. THE YOUNG BRITISH POETS. *St. Martin's* 1972 $8.95

SCOTTISH POETRY: One, Two, Three, Four, Five and Six. Ed. by Maurice Lindsay and others. 1966–70. *Aldine* (Edinburgh Univ. Press) each $4.95. Anthologies of Contemporary Scottish verse.

Smith, A. J. M. MODERN CANADIAN VERSE IN ENGLISH AND FRENCH: An Anthology. *Oxford* 1967 $6.95. The best of Canada's poetry written within the last 40 years.

Untermeyer, Louis. MODERN BRITISH POETRY. 1920. *Harcourt* 6th rev. ed. Mid-Century Ed. rev. and enl. ed. 1962 text ed. $8.25. The new revised and enlarged 1962 edition (from Thomas Hardy to Charles Tomlinson), with its excellent updated critical and biographical material, maintains its authoritative place. There is also a new combined edition, "Modern American Poetry and Modern British Poetry" (*Harcourt* rev. and enl. ed. 1962 $11.25).

For anthologies of general English, Irish, Welsh and Scottish verse, see Chapter 4, Broad Studies.

YEATS, WILLIAM BUTLER. 1865–1939. (Nobel Prize 1923)

T. S. Eliot (*q.v.*) gave a memorial lecture on Yeats in Dublin in 1940 and said: "There are some poets whose poetry can be considered more or less in isolation, for experience or delight. There are others whose poetry, though giving equally experience and delight, has a large historical importance. Yeats was one of the latter: he was one of those few whose history is the history of their own time: who are part of the consciousness of an age which cannot be understood without them." This opinion is still generally held. Critical and biographical works on Yeats are increasing. He is unlike most modern poets in his insistence on the value of aristocracy and in the fact that he was a national poet. His "poetry does have a consciously dramatic character which comes from his sense that all life is conflict and that poetry is the expression of that conflict. It gives his poetry an atmosphere of excitement and grandeur and a magnificence which is rare in contemporary poets"—(Elizabeth Drew).

Yeats founded the Gaelic League in 1893 to rescue Irish folklore and legend from oblivion. He himself began to write poems in Gaelic, but so fine were they that the public demanded their translation into English. The poet compromised by using English, stating that his purpose was "to write always out of the common thought of the people." His collection of "Irish Fairy and Folk Tales" is now o.p. *Grosset* publishes "Irish Folk Stories and Fairy Tales" (1957 pap. $2.25). His early, purely romantic idea of Ireland as a Celtic Utopia broadened, later, to a belief in a society that drew its strength from the soil but had as leaders aristocrats and artists. Issued in London in 1959, "Essays and Introductions" (*Macmillan* 1961 Collier Bks. pap. $3.50) reprints two volumes of critical essays—"Ideas of Good and Evil" and "The Cutting of an Agate"—with ten additional essays and introductions from separate works. "Yeats writes a strong, clean, yet figurative and musical prose. These essays, blending Celticism, oriental mysticism, and a keen perception and craftsmanship furnish a valuable insight into his aesthetic philosophy and his theories of poetry and the drama"—(*LJ*); "Explorations," selected by Mrs. W. B. Yeats, is a similar collection, long out of print, including one short play (*Macmillan* 1963 $5.95).

After winning the Nobel Prize in 1923, Yeats was generally recognized as one of the greatest British poets. He is extraordinary in that all his finest poetry was written after he was 50. He never ceased to struggle to develop his personality, to learn and to discipline himself and to grow. Toward the end of his life he turned his attention to revising and rewriting his poems. In the "Collected Poems" will be found the altered version of his earlier work. While "good plays are never written, they are rewritten," good poems are not. The changes have set a premium upon the original editions. His voluminous work divides into poetry, plays, essays, stories and autobiographies.

COLLECTED POEMS. *Macmillan* 1933 2nd ed. with later poems added, 1951 definitive ed. with the author's final revisions 1956 $7.95

THE VARIORUM EDITION OF THE POEMS OF WILLIAM BUTLER YEATS. Ed. by Peter Allt and Russell K. Alspach. *Macmillan* 1957 $12.95

SELECTED POEMS. Ed. by Macha L. Rosenthal. *Macmillan* 1962 pap. $1.95

RUNNING TO PARADISE: Poems. Ed. by Kevin Crossley-Holland. *Macmillan* 1968 $4.50. A selection of 47 poems for children exemplifying the various themes prevalent in Yeats's poetry.

THE CELTIC TWILIGHT [short stories, 1893] AND A SELECTION OF EARLY POEMS. *New Am. Lib.* Signet 1962 pap. $.60

THE GREEN HELMET AND OTHER POEMS. 1910. *Irish Univ. Press* (Cuala Press) 1971 $14.25

POEMS WRITTEN IN DISCOURAGEMENT. 1913. *Irish Univ. Press* (Cuala Press) 1971 $10.50

THE HOURGLASS. 1914. *Irish Univ. Press* (Cuala Press) $14.25

A SELECTION FROM THE LOVE POETRY. 1913. *Irish Univ. Press* (Cuala Press) 1971 $14.25

SEVEN POEMS AND A FRAGMENT. 1922. *Irish Univ. Press* (Cuala Press) $14.25

THE CAT AND THE MOON AND CERTAIN POEMS. 1924. *Irish Univ. Press* (Cuala Press) 1971 $14.25

NEW POEMS. 1938. *Irish Univ. Press* (Cuala Press) 1971 $14.25

LAST POEMS AND TWO PLAYS. 1939. *Irish Univ. Press* (Cuala Press) 1971 $14.25. Includes "The Death of Cuchulain" and "Purgatory."

IF I WERE FOUR AND TWENTY. 1940. *Irish Univ. Press* (Cuala Press) $14.25

POEMS. Read by William Yeats, Siobhan McKenna and Michael MacLiammoir. *Spoken Arts* 753 (H-C) $5.95

LETTERS ON POETRY FROM W. B. YEATS TO DOROTHY WELLESLEY. *Oxford* 1964 pap. $2.25

LETTERS TO THE NEW ISLAND. 1934. Ed. by Horace Reynolds. *Harvard Univ. Press* 1970 $5.00

MEMOIRS. *Macmillan* 1973 $7.95

AUTOBIOGRAPHY. 1953. *Macmillan* $6.95 Collier Bks. pap. $1.95

Books about Yeats

Yeats: The Man and the Masks. By Richard Ellmann. 1948. *Dutton* pap. $1.95. An excellent critical biography tracing the poet's intellectual and literary development.

W. B. Yeats: Man and Poet. By Alexander N. Jeffares. 1949. *Barnes & Noble* 1966 pap. $2.50

The Permanence of Yeats. Ed. by James Hall and Martin Steinman. 1950. *Macmillan* Collier Bks. pap. $1.50; *Peter Smith* $4.00

Lonely Tower. By Thomas R. Henn. 1950. *Barnes & Noble* 2nd rev. ed. 1965 $6.95 pap. $4.00

The Identity of Yeats. By Richard Ellmann. *Oxford* 1954 rev. ed. 1964 $10.00 Galaxy Bks. pap. $2.45. A critical work essential to the understanding of Yeats as a symbolist, who kept the same poetic identity all his life.

A Reader's Guide to William Butler Yeats. By John Unterecker. *Farrar, Straus* Noonday 1959 pap. $1.95; *Octagon* 1971 $10.00. A valuable book, it explains the symbols, the mythology, the links between poems and other things necessary for the understanding of the individual poems.

W. B. Yeats: His Poetry and Thought. By A. G. Stock. *Cambridge* 1961 $9.50 pap. $3.45

W. B. Yeats: Images of a Poet. Ed. by D. J. Gordon and others. *Barnes & Noble* 1961 $7.75

W. B. Yeats: The Poems. By A. Norman Jeffares. *Barron's* 1962 pap. $1.00

Yeats. Ed. by John Unterecker. *Prentice-Hall* 1963 $5.95 Spectrum Bks. pap. $1.95. A symposium of modern appraisals by T. S. Eliot, Blackmur, Tate, Alex Zwerdling and Richard Ellmann.

W. B. Yeats. By George S. Fraser. Writers and Their Work Series. *British Bk.* Centre $2.38 pap. $1.20

W. B. Yeats. By B. Rajan. *Hillary House* Hutchinson Univ. Lib. $5.00 pap. $2.50

William Butler Yeats. By William York Tindall. Essays on Modern Writers Series. *Columbia* pap. $1.00. An excellent critical pamphlet.

William Butler Yeats. By Oliver St. J. Gogarty. *Dufour* 1963 $2.75

A Concordance to the Poems of W. B. Yeats. Ed. by Stephen M. Parrish and J. A. Painter. *Cornell Univ. Press* 1963 $20.00

Rilke, Valéry and Yeats: The Dominion of Self. By Priscilla Shaw. *Rutgers Univ. Press* 1963 $6.00. A close reading of specific texts and a theoretical elaboration of the questions to which they give rise.

Between the Lines: Yeats' Poetry in the Making. By Jon Stallworthy. *Oxford* 1963 $8.50

W. B. Yeats: The Later Poetry. By Thomas Parkinson. *Univ. of California Press* 1964 $5.00

"This work plumbs the rich mystery of Yeats's poetic imagination and craft. . . . Most highly recommended"—(*LJ*).

Swan and Shadow: Yeats's Dialogue With History. By Thomas R. Whitaker. *Univ. of North Carolina Press* 1964 $7.50.

"An impressively complex and erudite presentation sown with allusions and cross-references to historical, philosophical and literary sources of Yeats's inspiration"—(*LJ*).

Yeats at Work. By Curtis Bradford. *Southern Illinois Univ. Press* 1964 $12.50

Barbarous Knowledge: Myth in the Poetry of Yeats, Graves and Muir. By Daniel Hoffman. *Oxford* 1967 $6.00. An intelligent critical study treating each poet in turn.

Eminent Domain: Yeats among Wilde, Joyce, Pound, Eliot and Auden. By Richard Ellman. *Oxford* 1967 $5.50 Galaxy Bks. pap. $1.75.

"Richard Ellman's study, a series of short essays contrived around Yeats as center, describes a wide and graceful arc that encompasses many of the major developments in English poetry during a full half-century"—(*SR*). "The book is lucid, perceptive, urbane, in itself a graceful occasion"—(*N.Y. Times*).

A Commentary on the Collected Works of W. B. Yeats. By A. Norman Jeffares. *Stanford Univ. Press* 1968 $15.00

Yeats's Autobiography: Life as Symbolic Pattern. *Harvard Univ. Press* 1968 $5.00

Yeats. By Harold Bloom. *Oxford* 1970 $12.00 Galaxy Bks. pap. $3.50. A detailed analysis of Yeats's precise relations with the Romantic movement.

William Butler Yeats. By Denis Donaghue. Modern Master Series. *Viking* 1971 $4.95 pap. $1.65

DE LA MARE, WALTER. 1873–1956.

"With the sudden going of Walter de la Mare a poet unrivaled in his own field passes from the scene. He was not only a gentle, wise and hospitable being possessed of immense charm and fun, but no poet in his native England, or indeed in the world, had his gift of fantasy, his intense hunger for the land just across the border of reality, that land of light and shadow made memorable in both his poetry and his stories"—(Laura Benét, in *SR*). Louis Untermeyer described him as "distinctively in the world and yet not wholly of it." Not since Blake and Stevenson had a poet written verse for children of such haunting charm. Auden speaks of his "metrical fingering," his masterly variety in the use of poetic forms. In a poem honoring de la Mare on his 75th birthday, T. S. Eliot points out his peculiar talent for rendering the familiar scene "suddenly strange . . ."

As de la Mare grew older, he lost none of his poetic magic and it is to be regretted that so many volumes are now o.p. In his later years he attained the honors and recognition he so richly deserved. In 1948 he was named Companion of Honour by the late George VI. Four universities had made him a Doctor of Letters. He was an honorary Fellow of Keble College, Oxford and an honorary Fellow of the American Academy of Arts and Letters. He received the Carnegie Medal in 1949 for his "Collected Stories for Children."

He was one of the great masters of the supernatural story: "The Collected Tales" (1950) and "Ghost Stories" (1956) are now o.p. Two unusual stories for children are still in print: "The Three Mulla-Mulgars" (1919 new ed. 1925), republished as "The Three Royal Monkeys" (*Knopf* new ed. 1948 $3.50 lib. bdg. $4.79) and "Mr. Bumps and his Monkey" (ill. by Dorothy P. Lathrop *Holt* [Winston] 1942 lib. bdg. $3.59). A new edition of "Told Again" was published as "Tales Told Again" (*Knopf* 1927 new ed. 1959 $3.00 lib. bdg. $4.79). His "Stories from the Bible" (1929. *Knopf* 1961 lib. bdg. $5.79) contains 34 stories. But that haunting story, "The Memoirs of a Midget" (1922), considered by several critics the greatest British novel of the 20th century, is now o.p. He edited several anthologies with delightful notes and comment and proved that the anthology could be a genuine artistic genre. "Come Hither" (1923 *Knopf* 1926 3rd ed. 1957 $10.00) and his collection of poetry chosen and annotated for children, "Tom Tiddler's Ground" (*Knopf* 1962 $3.50 lib. bdg. $5.19) are still available.

COMPLETE POEMS. *Knopf* 1970 $17.50

SONGS OF CHILDHOOD. 1902. *Dover* pap. $1.25; *Peter Smith* $3.75

PEACOCK PIE: A Book of Rhymes. 1913. *Knopf* 1961 $3.00 lib. bdg. $4.59

RHYMES AND VERSES: Collected Poems for Children; with drawings by Elinore Blaisdell. *Holt* 1947 $6.95

Walter de la Mare, Speaking and Reading. *Caedmon* TC 1046 $5.95. A recording of a conversation and twelve poems.

Books about de la Mare

Walter de la Mare and "The Traveller." By V. Sackville-West. *Oxford* 1953 pap. $.85
Walter de la Mare. By Kenneth Hopkins. Writers and Their Works. *British Bk. Centre* $2.38 pap. $1.20
Walter de la Mare. By Doris Ross McCrosson. In the English Authors Series. *Twayne* 1966 $5.50

MASEFIELD, JOHN. 1878–1967.

Masefield has been called the most protean of poets, for, like Proteus, a sea-god, he would assume many shapes. Above all he is a storyteller in verse. His long narrative peoms in a colloquial vein revived an almost forgotten form and remain his greatest literary contribution. But he is also known as a prose dramatist, verse dramatist, romantic novelist, historian of the sea, literary critic and writer for children. Of his 15 novels (he wrote 70 books in all), the following are available: "Mainsail Haul" (1905. *Fernhill* $4.25), "The Bird of Dawning" (*Macmillan* 1933 $4.95), "Victorious Troy, or The Hurrying Angel" (1935. *Macmillan* 1967 $5.95), "The Taking of the *Gry*" (1934. *Macmillan* 1967 $4.95) and "Sard Harker" (1924. *Scholarly Press* $19.50). A work of criticism is "William Shakespeare" (1964. *Barnes & Noble* $3.50). He has written memoirs of Synge, "John M. Synge: A Few Personal Recollections" (1915. *Irish Univ. Press* [Cuala Press] 1971 $11.75) and W. B. Yeats, "Some Memories of W. B. Yeats" (1940. *Irish Univ. Press* [Cuala Press] 1971 $11.75).

He was born in Ledbury, Herefordshire. Both parents died while he was still young and he went, with the other Masefield children, to live with an aunt. At 14 he went to sea; this is vividly described in the autobiographical "New Chum" (1945, o.p.). At 17 he came to America and worked in New York in a bakery, livery stable, saloon, and carpet factory. During this period he began to buy new books and have time for reading. He once wrote: "I did not begin to read poetry with passion and system until 1896. I was living then in Yonkers, New York. . . . Chaucer was the poet, and the 'Parliament of Fowls' the poem of my conversion." He eventually returned to England to begin his varied literary career, which culminated in his appointment to the Poet Laureateship in 1930. Though at first criticized, "his salty language, the homeliness of his images and his sea locales came to be accepted. According to J. Donald Adams, it was Masefield, 'more than any other man at the time [who] brought poetry out of the doldrums into which it had declined. He made poetry a vital literary topic . . . and rescued it from the inertia into which the Tennysonian tradition had descended.' [And] although critics declined to praise the royal odes ('dead as mutton,' said Edith Sitwell of one of them), Masefield's earlier poetry was widely acclaimed and became part of the British tradition"—(*N.Y. Times*). He received the Order of Merit from King George V in 1935. In 1952 he was the recipient of the Hanseatic Shakespeare Prize, awarded by Hamburg University.

Most of the earlier separate volumes of plays and verse are now o.p. But in 1961 he won the William Foyle Poetry Prize for "The Bluebells and Other Verse." In reviewing it for the *N. Y. Times*, Robert Hillyer wrote: "Age has renewed Masefield's laurels more richly than ever. Here is the delight in fine stanza forms—the couplet, the rime royal, the Spenserian stanza and several of his own invention. . . . Let the anthologists who have ignored him for years take note that John Masefield is still a very important poet." Of "Old Raiger and Other Verse" *Library Journal* said: "His métier is the verse tale; in it he continues unsurpassed." Of "In Glad Thanksgiving" the same journal wrote: "There is much in this last collection of Masefield to make the reader recall the early 'Salt-Water Ballads' and be thankful for this quality of poetry in an age when serenity is not always near."

Poems. *Macmillan* 1953 $10.50. The second edition of "Collected Poems" contains all the poems Masefield wished preserved.

Salt-Water Poems and Ballads. 1902. Ill. by Charles Pears. *Macmillan* new ed. 1953 $4.95 pap. $1.25

The Bluebells and Other Verse. *Macmillan* 1961 $4.95 pap. $1.25

Old Raiger and Other Verse. *Macmillan* 1965 $3.95

In Glad Thanksgiving. *Macmillan* 1967 $3.95

John Masefield Reading Sea Fever and Other Poems. A recording. *Caedmon* TC 1147 $5.95

GRACE BEFORE PLOUGHING: Fragments of Autobiography. *Macmillan* 1966 $3.95

28 "slight" fragments "typical of his best prose" form a "poetic recall of his earliest life"—(*LJ*).

Books about Masefield

A Bibliography of John Masefield. By Charles H. Simmons. 1930. *AMS Press* $9.00
John Masefield. By L. A. G. Strong. *British Bk. Centre* $2.38 pap. $1.20
Remembering John Masefield. By Corliss Lamont. *Fairleigh Dickenson* $6.00
John Masefield's England: A Study of the National Themes in His Work. By Fraser Drew. *Fairleigh Dickenson* 1972 $15.00

COLUM, PADRAIC. 1881–1972.

Padraic Colum was one of the major writers of the Irish Literary Renaissance. He "has been recognized as the best of the poets of the Irish countryside, and as a playwright with a list of Abbey successes to his credit." In 1952 he received the award of the American Academy of Poets and, in 1953, the Gregory Medal of the Irish Academy of Letters. "Carricknabauna," some of his poetry dramatized, played in New York in 1967. He wrote and edited many books for children (*Macmillan*), many of them charming retellings of the stories of mythology—Classical, Scandinavian, Irish, and others. His "Story Telling New and Old" (*Macmillan* 1961 lib. bdg. $1.95) is available. With his wife, Mary Colum, he wrote "Our Friend James Joyce" (1958. *Peter Smith* $4.25). He has edited an "Anthology of Irish Verse" (1922. *Liveright* Black & Gold Lib. rev. ed. 1948 $7.95 pap. $3.45) and "A Treasury of Irish Folklore" (1954. *Crown* $3.95).

Mr. Colum and his wife early dedicated themselves (and supported their writing by lecturing on the subject) to making better known, particularly in America, the rich heritage of Irish literature. Endowed with unquenchable energy and a contagious vitality and charm tempered by high standards of scholarship, they traveled, spoke and wrote indefatigably in this cause.

COLLECTED POEMS. *Devin-Adair* 1953 $7.50

IMAGES OF DEPARTURE: Poetry. *Dufour* $6.95

ROOFS OF GOLD: Poems to Read Aloud. *Macmillan* 1964 lib. bdg. $3.94

STONE VICTORY AND OTHER POEMS. *McGraw* 1966 $3.95 lib. bdg. $3.83

IRISH ELEGIES. 1966. *Dufour* $2.75

Books about Colum

Life and the Dream: Autobiography. By Mary Colum. *Dufour* rev. ed. 1964 $8.95
Padraic Colum: A Biographical-Critical Introduction. By Zack Brown. *Southern Illinois Univ. Press* 1970 $4.95

MILNE, A(LAN) A(LEXANDER). 1882–1956.

These classics of childhood have been best sellers from their first appearance, the English sales always topping the American by some thousands. The population increase in the last few years has been enormously helpful, a spokesman for *Dutton* reported in 1963—"It's rather fashionable to raise your child on 'Pooh.' Sales of all the books are now counted in the millions in both countries. In 1967 the Soviet Union, which had made no bones about translating "Pooh" into Russian without permission, had its pirated version pirated back by *Dutton*. In addition to Russian, there are translations of Pooh stories available in Esperanto, French, Spanish, German and Latin.

Milne also wrote several light, whimsical comedies, available from *French* and *Baker*. Of his novels and short stories, "The Red House Mystery" (*Dutton* 1936 $3.95) is still available. His "good natured spoof of all fairy tales" for sophisticated children and unsophisticated adults has recently been reprinted: "Once On a Time" (1917. *Avon Bks.* 1966 pap. $.60; *N.Y. Graphic Society* 1962 $3.95). His chief fame, of course, rests on the four juveniles and he himself wrote rather wryly in an autobiographical sketch for the *N.Y. Herald Tribune:* "When I wrote them, little thinking/ All my years of pen-and-inking/ Would be almost lost among/ Those four trifles for the young."

THE WORLD OF CHRISTOPHER ROBIN: The Complete WHEN WE WERE VERY YOUNG and NOW WE ARE SIX. With decorations and new illustrations in full color by E. H. Shepard. *Dutton* 1958 $6.95; boxed with The World of Pooh $12.50

THE CHRISTOPHER ROBIN BOOK OF VERSE. Ill. by Ernest Shepard. *Dutton* 1967 $3.95 lib. bdg. $3.91

THE WORLD OF POOH: The Complete WINNIE-THE-POOH and THE HOUSE AT POOH CORNER. Ill. by E. H. Shepard. *Dutton* $6.95 boxed with the World of Christopher Robin. $12.95

POOH'S LIBRARY: WHEN WE WERE VERY YOUNG, NOW WE ARE SIX, WINNIE THE POOH, THE HOUSE AT POOH CORNER. *Dutton* $12.50

POOH'S BIRTHDAY BOOK. *Dutton* 1963 $3.95

WHEN WE WERE VERY YOUNG. 1924. Poems. *Dutton* 1950 rev. ed. 1961 $3.50 lib. bdg. $3.46

NOW WE ARE SIX. 1927. Poems. *Dutton* 1950 rev. 1961 $3.50 lib. bdg. $3.46

WINNIE-THE-POOH. Prose. 1926. *Dutton* 1950 rev. 1961 $3.50 lib. bdg. $3.46

WINNIE ILLE PU. Trans. into Latin by Alexander Lenard. *Dutton* 1960 $4.50

VINNI-PUKH I VSE, VSE, VSE: A Russian Edition of Winnie-the-Pooh and House at Pooh Corner. Trans. into Russian by Boris Zakhoder; ill. by B. Diodorov and G. Kalinovskiy. *Dutton* 1967 $4.95

THE HOUSE AT POOH CORNER. 1928. Prose. *Dutton* 1950 rev. 1961 $3.50 lib. bdg. $3.46 pap. $1.25

PRINCE RABBIT AND THE PRINCESS WHO COULD NOT LAUGH. Prose. *Dutton* 1966 $4.50 lib. bdg. $3.91

Books about Milne

The Pooh Perplex: A Freshman Casebook. By Frederick C. Crews. *Dutton* 1963 $3.50 pap. $1.25
In an amusing collection of parody-essays based upon an imaginary study (supposedly representing serious schools of academic criticism), the "author" of each essay examines the "hidden meaning" of the Milne books and finds exactly what his school of criticism (Marxist, Freudian, New Critical) wishes to find. The book reaches a climax when no one is able to agree on the ultimate meaning of Winnie-the-Pooh.

LAWRENCE, D(AVID) H(ERBERT). 1885–1930. *See Chapter 12, Modern British Fiction.*

BROOKE, RUPERT. 1887–1915.

Among the poets who died in World War I Brooke had great promise and became the idol of his generation, though recent critical opinion puts the more disillusioned Wilfred Owen well ahead of him in quality. "The title of [his] posthumous book, '1914,' signifies that moment of English history which is reflected in his work. He is the symbol of that year in a double sense"—(Mary C. Sturgeon). "Rupert Brooke: A Memoir" by Edward Howard Marsh (1918, o.p.) tells the story of his short life. Educated at Cambridge, he wrote attractive romantic poetry about Cambridge and the English countryside, young love and the sacrifices of war.

POEMS. *Dodd* 1930 $3.95; *Apollo* pap. $1.75

RUPERT BROOKE: A REAPPRAISAL AND A SELECTION. *Barnes & Noble* 1971 $7.00

LETTERS. Ed. by Geoffrey Keynes. *Harcourt* 1969 $12.50.

MUIR, EDWIN. 1887–1959.

A distinguished Scottish poet and scholar, Edwin Muir in his "Autobiography," a book of "singular beauty and enchantment," draws an evocative picture of the creative mind, mirroring the events of his crowded life and the people who came into it from his childhood in the Orkney Islands to his postwar travels in Europe. As in the similar works of Yeats and Coleridge, it tells the "story of the inner man." The "narration of outer events is accompanied by a sensitive self-interpretation, particularly rare in our day, which reveals a mind and temperament continually open to the findings of the spirit"—(*New Yorker*). In his poems the writer shows a directness and meditative power so profound and moving that Horace Gregory said of him, "Since the death of W. B. Yeats, no mature poet of Celtic origins has made so impressive a contribution to modern literature."

With his wife, Willa, he translated many of the stories and novels of Kafka (*q.v.*). Muir lived in Dalkeith, Scotland, where he was Warden of Newbattle Abbey College, 1950–55. He was Charles Eliot Norton Professor of Poetry at Harvard, 1955–56. "The Estate of Poetry" (fwd. by Archibald MacLeish *Harvard Univ. Press* 1962 $3.00) contains the Charles Eliot Norton Lectures, 1955–56. "These amiable statements are valuable for the light they shed on poetry and for their revelations of the belief of an important poet."

COLLECTED POEMS. *Oxford* 1960 1965 $7.50

AUTOBIOGRAPHY. 1940. Ed. by P. T. Butterfield. *Seabury* 1968 pap. $2.45

Books about Muir

Edwin Muir. By J. G. Hall. In Writers and Their Works Series. *British Bk. Centre* $2.38 pap. $1.20
Barbarous Knowledge: Myth in the Poetry of Yeats, Graves and Muir. By Daniel Hoffman. *Oxford* Galaxy Bks. pap. $2.25
The Poetry of Edwin Muir: The Field of Good and Ill. By Elizabeth L. Huberman. *Oxford* 1971 $7.95

SITWELL, DAME EDITH. 1887–1964.

In October, 1962, the *N.Y. Times* reported that 3000 admirers had packed Royal Festival Hall, London, for the concert by the English Chamber Orchestra in formal celebration of Dame Edith Sitwell's 75th birthday. "Dressed in a flowing gown of red velvet, offset by a great gold necklace, her head crowned with a huge gold hat, Dame Edith sat in a wheelchair and read her poems for half an hour. The only concession to modernity in her Tudor ensemble were shellrimmed reading glasses and a microphone round her neck."

Dame Edith was "the nearest thing to a major poet that the British Isles have produced since Hardy, Lawrence and Yeats. With the possible exception of Hugh MacDiarmid she is now the only British poet who possesses that special accent of both individuality and scope which makes a writer a member of world literature. Possibly this is because, like the others mentioned above, she is both intensely national, even local, and yet aware in a living way of the literature of the whole civilized community, its problems, its ambitions, its disasters"—(Kenneth Rexroth, in the *N.Y. Times*). She was the elder sister of Sir Osbert (*q.v.*) and Sacheverell Sitwell (*q.v.*), all literary, cultured and famous for their deliberate eccentricity. At first she was considered somewhat artificial and absurd as a poet, but always an original and brilliant technician with a marvelous sense of the possibilities of language. Her poetry sequence "Façade," set to music by William Walton, and delightful by today's standards, had in 1923 somewhat the same effect in poetry as Gertrude Stein produced in fiction. "The critical reaction in London after the first performance bordered on the savage"—(*N.Y. Times*).

When she edited "The Atlantic Book of British and American Poetry" (*Little* 1958 $16.50) David Daiches said in the *N.Y. Times*: "This is a generous, exciting, disorganized, unequal and sometimes acutely exasperating anthology . . . a selection made by a poet of highly individual views. The whole book is stamped with Dame Edith's personality, with her prejudices and preferences and her patches of brilliant knowledge and odd ignorance." From 1916 to 1921 she edited "Wheels," an annual anthology of modern verse. She has written biography, fiction and history as well as acute and perceptive criticism. Her "English Eccentrics" (1933. *Vanguard* new ed. 1957 $5.75) is still available, as is "I Live under a Black Cloud: A Novel" (1938. *Greenwood* $13.25) and "Aspects of Modern Poetry" (1934. *Bks. for Libraries* $8.75; *Scholarly Press* 1972 $8.50).

She received many honors, including three doctorates (Leeds 1948, Durham 1948, Oxford 1951). She was awarded the medal of the Royal Society of Literature for her poetry in 1933 and the William Foyle Poetry Prize in 1958 for her "Collected Poems." She was elected to the American Institute of Arts and Letters. In June 1954 she was named Dame Grand Cross of the Order of the British Empire by Elizabeth II, the first poet to be so honored.

Timothy Green wrote an article about her for *Life* in 1963 in which he quoted from her preface of "The Outcasts": "It is as unseeing to ask what is the *use* of poetry as it would be to ask what is the use of religion. . . . Poetry is the deification of reality, and one of its purposes, amongst others, is to show that the dimensions of man are, as Sir Arthur Eddington said, 'half way between those of an atom and a star.' "

THE COLLECTED POEMS OF EDITH SITWELL. Poems from Green Song; The Song of the Cold; The Canticle of the Rose; Gardeners and Astronomers; and some early poems. *Vanguard* 1954 $10.00

THE SONG OF THE COLD. Poems. *Vanguard* 1948 $3.00. Not identical with the English book of the same title published in 1945.

A POET'S NOTEBOOK. 1950 *Greenwood* $12.00

GARDENERS AND ASTRONOMERS. New Poems. *Vanguard* 1953 $2.75

MUSIC AND CEREMONIES. *Vanguard* 1963 $3.50. Her first volume of new poetry after the "Collected Poems." None of these poems has appeared in book form in America, and three never before in book form anywhere.

SELECTED LETTERS, 1919–1964. *Vanguard* 1970 $8.50

TAKEN CARE OF: The Autobiography of Edith Sitwell. *Atheneum* 1965 $5.95. In this memoir completed just before her death, Dame Edith writes—sometimes tartly, but always entertainingly—of many literary friends and enemies—the latter justly "taken care of."

Books about Sitwell

A Bibliography of Edith, Osbert and Sacheverell Sitwell. By Richard Fifoot. 1963. *Shoe String* 1971 $15.00

Edith Sitwell. By John Lehmann. In the Writers and Their Work Series. *British Bk. Centre* $2.38 pap. $1.20

Edith Sitwell: The Symbolist Order. By James Brophy. Pref. by Harry T. Moore. *Southern Illinois Univ. Press* 1968 $4.95

A Nest of Tigers: The Sitwells in Their Times. By John Lehmann. *Little-Atlantic* 1969 $7.50

ELIOT, T(HOMAS) S(TEARNS). 1888–1965. (Nobel Prize 1948)

T. S. Eliot, the giant of pre-World War II poetry, influential literary critic and successful playwright, was awarded the Nobel Prize for Literature in 1948. He was "one of the first to formulate in English poetry the reactions of a keen sensibility to an age of scientific mastery and moral anarchy"—(Babette Deutsch). He was the first to use the symbolist method extensively in English. His far reaching influence on the language of poetry, as a "force both of discipline and of liberation," did not so much "create a poetic diction as make it possible for other poets to create theirs." He used that vast reservoir of language of the educated modern, drawn from every possible source—slang, journalism, literature English and foreign. "The Waste Land" is notable for "its manifold echoes of poems, prayers, popular songs, the voices of the sages and of the public house, sounding together in a symphony that presents the machine age in all its desiccation and despair."

When the *Dial* Prize went to this long poetic vision of a modern Hell and disintegration in 1922, a storm of protest arose as to its merit, which has since been vindicated—by 1968 he had even become somewhat old-fashioned, as recent idols will. He was born in St. Louis, Mo., graduated from Harvard and studied at the Sorbonne, the University of Marburg and Merton, Oxford. He is of the same Eliot family as Charles W. Eliot of Harvard. He lived abroad after 1914 and in 1927 became a naturalized British subject. He declared himself "Anglo-Catholic in religion, royalist in politics, and classicist in literature." He was a director of the London publishing house of *Faber & Faber*.

His first books were published in England. His poems are in an unusual rhyming free verse and consist of narrative psychological portraits of blasé, jaded and disillusioned persons—who appear somewhat mild today in the era of "black" disillusion. He liked to use lines from other writers in his poems, acknowledging them in the notes. His first more hopeful volume of religious poems was entitled "Ash Wednesday" (1930, o.p.). "Four Quartets," in which his genius is almost lyrical and suffused with religious faith, yet cool and measured and sad, showed again his remarkable mastery of language—so often weakly imitated by other poets in his heyday. After his second marriage he mellowed, but the meticulous stringency of his verse never lost its power and it seems likely that he will last as one of the few great poets of his era.

COLLECTED POEMS, 1909–1962. *Harcourt* 1963 $7.95

Published on his 75th birthday, this volume holds "all of his poetry through 1962 that he wishes to preserve," from "Prufrock" to "Four Quartets." "The main begetter of the poetic sensibility of his own age, Eliot has undertaken not only to appraise its ailments but to 'redeem the time.' And that progression may be followed from the landmark symbol 'The Waste Land' through the suggestive metrical hesitancies and acute lyric beauty of the pivotal 'Ash Wednesday' to his later more discursive and public speech, in this new presentation of the most influential poetry of our century to date"—(*LJ*). This volume includes several new and previously unpublished poems.

COMPLETE POEMS AND PLAYS 1909–1950. *Harcourt* 1952 $9.75

SELECTED POEMS. *Harcourt* Harbrace Mod. Class. 1967 $.95. An excellent selection including "The Waste Land" entire.

POEMS WRITTEN IN EARLY YOUTH. Ed. by John Hayward; pref. by Valerie Eliot. *Farrar, Straus* 1967 $3.95; Noonday Bks. pap. $1.95

"A handful of juvenilia (1904–10), carefully and authoritatively edited. . . . The poems written for official occasions are fittingly dull"—(*New Yorker*).

THE WASTE LAND (1922) AND OTHER POEMS. *Harcourt* Harvest Bks. 1955 pap. $1.25

THE WASTE LAND. Ed. by Valerie Eliot. *Harcourt* 1971 $22.50 limited ed. $50.00. A facsimile and transcript of the original drafts, including the annotations of Ezra Pound.

THE CAEDMON TREASURY OF MODERN POETS READING THEIR OWN POETRY. *Caedmon* TC 2006 HC set $11.90. T. S. Eliot reading "The Waste Land" occupies the entire side of one of two records.

OLD POSSUM'S BOOK OF PRACTICAL CATS. Poems. *Harcourt* 1939 $3.95 pap. $.75

FOUR QUARTETS. *Harcourt* 1943 $3.95 Harvest Bks. pap. $1.25. Includes "Burnt Norton" (1941), "East Coker" (1940), "The Dry Salvages" (1941), "Little Gidding" (1942). Four long poems in a new form described by the poet as "quartets."

THE CULTIVATION OF CHRISTMAS TREES. *Farrar, Straus* 1956 $2.00

T. S. ELIOT READING POEMS AND CHORUSES. A recording. *Caedmon* TC 1045 $5.95

Books about Eliot

The Achievement of T. S. Eliot: An Essay on the Nature of Poetry. By F. O. Matthiessen. *Oxford* 1939 2nd ed. rev. and enl. 1947 3rd ed. 1958 with a chapter on Eliot's later works by C. L. Barber. 1959 $6.50 Galaxy Bks. pap. $2.75. Probably the best single introduction to Eliot's poetry and critical writing.

T. S. Eliot: The Design of His Poetry. By Elizabeth A. Drew. 1949. *Scribner* 1961 $3.50 pap. $2.95. A most useful and detailed chronological survey of all the poems.

The Art of T. S. Eliot. By Helen Louise Gardner. *Dutton* 1950 1959 pap. $1.25. A detailed interpretation of "Four Quartets" with some sympathetic analysis of the earlier poems and plays.

The Poetry of T. S. Eliot. By Desmond E. S. Maxwell. *Humanities Press* 1952 $6.00 pap. $1.95

A Reader's Guide to T. S. Eliot: A Poem-by-Poem Analysis. By George Williamson. *Farrar, Straus* 1955 $6.50 Noonday pap. $2.45. The Noonday edition has an epilogue entitled "T. S. Eliot, 1888–1965."

T. S. Eliot's Poetry and Plays: A Study in Sources and Meaning. By Grover Cleveland Smith. *Univ. of Chicago Press* 1956 $6.95 Phoenix Bks. pap. $3.45

T. S. Eliot and the Idea of Tradition. By Sean Lucy. *Routledge & Kegan Paul* 1960 $6.50

T. S. Eliot. By Leonard Unger. Pamphlets on American Writers. *Univ. of Minnesota Press* 1961 pap. $1.25

T. S. Eliot: Esthetics and History. By Lewis Freed. *Open Court* 1961 $5.95 pap. $1.95. Associate Professor of English at Purdue University, Freed has made a study of Eliot's theory of poetry.

The Still Point: Recurrent Thought Patterns in the Writings of T. S. Eliot, Coleridge, Yeats, Henry James, Virginia Woolf and D. H. Lawrence. By Ethel F. Cornwell. *Rutgers Univ. Press* 1962 $7.50

T. S. Eliot: The Metaphysical Perspective. By Eric Thompson. *Southern Illinois Univ. Press* 1963 $4.95. "A brief, occasionally illuminating book with much to say about a difficult yet seminal figure."

T. S. Eliot. By A. C. George. *Asia Pub. House* 1963 $9.00

T. S. Eliot: Moments and Patterns. By Leonard Unger. *Univ. of Minnesota Press* 1966 $5.75 pap. $1.95 "For the average reader much of the poetry and many plays of T. S. Eliot remain unexplained mysteries, but in these eight critical essays written over the last 30 years, Mr. Unger is admirably successful in dispelling some of the mystery. . . . He thoroughly enjoys the poetry and plays and [uses] a clear and precise English prose style to explore this difficult subject"—(*LJ*).

T. S. Eliot: The Man and His Work, A Critical Evaluation by 26 Distinguished Writers. Ed. by Allen Tate. *Delacorte* 1967 $6.50

"Allen Tate has done the job very well indeed and there is hardly any dross in this collection of tributes to the man and studies of his work. . . . The portrait which emerges is the expected one, more or less, but with unexpected touches here and there"—(Philip Toynbee, in the London *Observer*).

Word Unheard: A Guide Through Eliot's Four Quartets. By Harry Blamires. *Barnes & Noble* 1969 $5.00 pap. $2.50

T. S. Eliot: Poems in the Making By Gertrude Patterson *Barnes & Noble* 1971 $8.00

Eliot and His Age. By Russell Kirk. *Random* 1972 $12.50

MacDIARMID, HUGH (pseud. of Christopher Murray Grieve). 1892–

Louis Simpson, writing in the *N.Y. Times*, called Hugh MacDiarmid "the most important poet now alive in Britain." This energetic Marxist author, journalist, broadcaster and lecturer was one of the founders of the Scottish Nationalist party, the founder of the Scottish Centre of the P.E.N. and is the editor of the quarterly magazine, *The Voice of Scotland*. "Since the publication of his first volume of Scots lyrics, 'Sangschaw,' in 1925, MacDiarmid has been the whip of the very active Scottish literary movement, and has lashed his compatriots—and his enemies south of the border—into smarting knowledge of the native vigor of the Scots tongue and cultural heritage. . . . Like Burns . . . MacDiarmid writes both in eclectic Scots of his own contriving and in the language of his enemies. The lyrics from his first two volumes, 'Sangschaw' and 'Pennywheep' (1926) are the finest poems in Scots since the death of Burns. Their subjects—love, death, the stars—are handled with Burns' earthy vigor but without his sentimentalism"—(Charles G. Osgood). Mr. MacDiarmid has edited "The Golden Treasury of Scottish Poetry" (1940, o.p.). "The Company I've Kept" (*Univ. of California Press* 1967 $7.50) is a collection of essays about his many intellectual friends, who include O'Casey and Pound, as well as others, less famous, whom he considers remarkable. His critical works include "At the Sign of the Thistle" (1934. *Scholarly Press* 1971 $14.50; *Somerset Pub.* $11.50) and "Contemporary Scottish Studies" (1926. *Scholarly Press* 1971 $15.50; *Somerset Pub.* $15.50). His autobiography, "Lucky Poet," expresses his strong Anglophobia and passionate desire for Scottish independence, as well as his desire to establish "Workers Republics" in Scotland, Ireland, Wales and Cornwall.

THE HUGH MacDIARMID ANTHOLOGY: Poems in Scots and English. Ed. by Michael Grieve and L. Alexander. *Routledge & Kegan Paul* 1972 (unpriced)

MORE COLLECTED POEMS. *Swallow* 1970 $6.00

A DRUNK MAN LOOKS AT THE THISTLE. Poems. 1926. Ed. by John C. Weston. *Univ. of Massachusetts Press* $7.50 pap. $2.95

LUCKY POET: A Self Study in Literature and Political Ideas Being the Autobiography of Hugh MacDiarmid. *Univ. of California Press* 1972 $12.95

OWEN, WILFRED. 1893–1918.

"Wilfred Owen grew from a minor poet to a major voice in the nightmare of World War I. In a brief period of 13 months before he was killed in action, Owen produced a corps of great war poetry which ranks him among England's foremost poets. He is the fervent spokesman of the horrors of war, 'the bell of the church of the broken body,' as Dylan Thomas put it"—(*LJ*). Owen was born in Oswestry and educated at London University before enlisting. Wounded and hospitalized, he met Siegfried Sassoon (*q.v.*), a fellow patient, who encouraged him to write poetry. It was Sassoon who, after Owen's death at the age of 25, published his poems posthumously in 1920. Sassoon said of him: "He never wrote his poems (as so many war poets did) to make the effect of a personal gesture. He pitied others; he did not pity himself." In 1933 Edmund Blunden prepared a more comprehensive edition of Owen's work, now superseded by that of C. Day Lewis. Blunden called Owen "an unwearied worker in the laboratory of word, rhythm, and music of language." He discovered the para-rhyme (as "rumbles" with "brambles"), says Kenneth Allott, and used it in his war poems "to create 'remoteness, darkness, emptiness, shock.' "

Rupert Brooke (*q.v.*), who also died in World War I, was the poet who in his time became the symbol of the spirit of those years in which such a tremendous proportion of Britain's finest young men were slaughtered; Brooke wrote in a mood of exalted patriotism. Since World War II, however, Wilfred Owen's bitter mood has come to seem closer to the fact. In a preface found among his papers after his death he had written the now famous lines (to which Sassoon was probably referring above): "Above all I am not concerned with Poetry. My subject is War, and the pity of War. The Poetry is in the pity." There has been a recent revival of interest in Owen's work, particularly since Benjamin Britten set 12 of his poems to music as the "War Requiem"—among them two of the most remarkable, "Strange Meeting" and "Anthem for Doomed Youth."

COLLECTED POEMS. Ed. with introd. by C. Day Lewis; memoir by Edmund Blunden. *New Directions* (dist. by Lippincott) rev. ed. 1959 $6.50 pap. $1.95

This new edition "is most certainly the definitive text." It includes facsimiles of "Anthem for Doomed Youth" and "a useful 20-page introduction"—(*LJ*).

COLLECTED LETTERS. Ed. by Harold Owen, his brother, and John Bell. *Oxford* 1967 $17.75. Of the 673 letters, 550 were written to his mother.

Books about Owen

Wilfred Owen: A Critical Study. By D. S. R. Welland. 1960. *Fernhill* $3.75
   "Useful but too brief"—(Kenneth Allott, in "The Penguin Book of Contemporary Verse").
Journey from Obscurity: Memoirs of the Owen Family: Wilfred Owen 1893–1918. By Harold Owen, the poet's brother. *Oxford* 1963–65 Vol. 1 Childhood Vol. 2 Youth Vol. 3 War set $10.25.
   "Thanks to the warm and charitable heart of Harold Owen, who was so responsive to the potential richness of his brother's nature that he forgave the narrow coldness of much that he actually said and did, we have a full and sympathetic portrait of this dedicated youth, who in so many ways reminds us of the young Milton"—(John Wain, in the London *Observer*).
Wilfred Owen. By Gertrude M. White. In the English Authors Series. *Twayne* $5.50

READ, SIR HERBERT (EDWARD). 1893–1968. *See Chapter 15, Essays and Criticism.*

JONES, DAVID (MICHAEL). 1895–

Welsh by birth, Celtic in his verbal clarity, the poet-painter David Jones is best known in England today for his sensitive water colors. His output of published poetry has been limited: it has, however, received critical acclaim from the first. "In Parenthesis" was published in 1937 and won the Hawthornden Prize the following year. T. S. Eliot called it "a work of genius . . . a work of literary art which uses language in a new way." Autobiographical and experimental in form, it is prose-poetry or a poetic novel; its very uniqueness eludes categorizing. The experiment is successful to such a degree that John Simon wrote in the *New Republic*: "Jones' work fulfills the basic requirement for a work of art: the perfect fusion of idea and expression, the oneness of content and form." "In Parenthesis" re-creates the poet's experiences as a rifleman of the Welsh Fusiliers in the trenches during World War I. Modern soldiers are identified with traditional Welsh heroes and with the Christian knights of the Arthurian legends. W. H. Auden described "The Anathemata" as "very probably the finest long poem written in English in this century." It is a mingling of prose and verse that has been compared to the work of Joyce and Pound.

Although very little of Jones' writing has appeared in American magazines, he has been given two awards by *Poetry* and was presented with the Russell Loines Award of the National Institute of Arts and Letters in 1954.

IN PARENTHESIS. Introd. by T. S. Eliot. 1937. *Chilmark Press* (dist. by Random) 1962 $5.75; *Viking* Compass Bks. 1963 pap. $2.45

THE ANATHEMATA. 1952. *Chilmark Press* (dist. by Random) 1963 $5.75; *Viking* Compass Bks. 1965 pap. $1.45

GRAVES, ROBERT. 1895–

Robert Graves has been writing poetry since the summer of 1914 and considers himself, in spite of his "brillant, if eccentric historical novels" and important critical works, a poet above all. He has called his prose "my show dog" and claims he writes it so that he can maintain his cat, poetry. He has recently concentrated on love poems, "the only thing that interests me at the moment." His "work has passed through several cycles of change, but has never lost its mark of the poet's individuality." "His poems are small, meticulous and jewel-like, with lines that scan and rhymes that rhyme. For years it was held against him that in the midst of world depressions, hot wars, cold wars and political upheaval, he sought his subject-matter within the circle of his personal life. He writes of marriage, of dreams, insomnia, winter, hope and, above all, love. . . . He rewrites his peoms as often as 35 times and his prose at least five times. The expenditure of energy required to achieve his lifetime average of 500 words per day seems incredible"—(*N.Y. Times*). *Library Journal* has called him "one of the finest poets of our day" (Professor Robert Regan, Univ. of Virginia). Bill Katz (Assoc. Prof. of Library Science, Univ. of Kentucky) has said (also in *LJ*): "Few poets in England are as well known and as respected as Graves. The reputation is deserved. Nothing demonstrates this better than ["Collected Poems 1966"]. Anyone who thinks winter begins at 70 had best turn to this lover of life. Thank the gods for Graves! We are all richer for his voice."

"Goodbye to All That" is an autobiography as well as a commentary on the post-war disillusionment of his generation. He is the author of a number of books of poetic criticism. "The White Goddess" (1948. *Farrar, Straus* rev. ed. 1966 $5.95 Noonday pap. $3.45) is considered the most important. Others currently available are: "On Poetry: Collected Talks and Essays" (*Doubleday* $10.00), "Poetic Unreason and Other Studies" (1925. *Biblo & Tannen* $10.00; *Scholarly Press* $1.50), "Contemporary Techniques of Poetry" (1949. *Folcroft* lib. bdg. $7.50) and "The Common Asphodel" (1949. *Folcroft* 1973 lib. bdg. $13.50; *Haskell* lib. bdg. $14.95; *Richard West* 1973 $13.75). With these and other essays and novels he has incurred the wrath of many scholars, who deplore his unorthodox views and interpretations. Graves has said: "I am not a scholar. A scholar is someone who obeys the rules of a school. I know the rules but am always ready to break them." In 1961 he was elected to the poetry chair at Oxford University; he held it until 1966. With the help of Omar Ali-Shah, a Sufi poet, he has made a new translation of the "The Original Rubaiyat of Omar Khayaam" (*Doubleday* 1968 $5.00 signed ltd. ed. $15.00). The famous Edward FitzGerald version was translated from a 15th-century Persian text; Graves claims to have gone back to a 12th-century manuscript. The Graves translation is notable for the use of blank verse; the poet feels that FitzGerald's "basic mistake" was his "unvaried sequence of iambics [which] tires the alerted ear." Some critics have found that Mr. Graves has not improved upon FitzGerald; certain scholars have questioned that his manuscript was as authentic and definitive as he has said. He has obviously, in any case, had a great time at his task. Exuberance and strength of feeling are two characteristics which keep him young and as happily in love (with his second wife, mother of his younger children) as any 20-year-old—and still the happy iconoclast.

COLLECTED POEMS 1955. Earlier collections and selections appeared in 1926, 1938, 1947 and 1955. *Doubleday* 1961 $5.95 Anchor Bks. pap. $2.50

POEMS, 1938–1945. *Farrar, Straus* 1967 $4.95

LOVE RESPELT. *Doubleday* 1966 $3.95.

A "small volume incorporating section 18 of the [English] *Collected Poems* 1965 plus 7 more poems—40 in all. . . . Highly recommended"—(*LJ*).

LOVE RESPELT AGAIN. *Doubleday* 1969 signed ltd. ed. $15.00. Facsimile of handwritten copy of the author's love poems, with illuminations by Aemilia Laracuen.

ROBERT GRAVE'S POEMS ABOUT LOVE. *Doubleday* 1969 $5.00. Chosen from more than 20 of the author's books.

POEMS, 1965–1968. *Doubleday* 1969 $4.95. Includes more than 90 new poems.

POEMS ABRIDGED FOR DOLLS AND PRINCES. *Doubleday* 1972 ltd ed $15.00

POEMS, 1968–1970. *Doubleday* 1971 $5.95. Includes 75 new poems.

POEMS, 1970–1972. *Doubleday* 1973 $5.95

GOODBYE TO ALL THAT. 1929. *Doubleday* Anchor Bks. pap. $2.50

Books about Graves

Swifter than Reason: The Poetry and Criticism of Robert Graves. By Douglas Day. *Univ. of North Carolina Press* 1963 pap. $2.45
This is the "first full-length study of the four periods in the work of a unique English poet and critic . . . who—although pigeonholed until recently by most critics as 'primarily a poet of the Twentieth'—is now increasingly rated as England's greatest living poet. . . . Succinct and selective rather than a poem-by-poem set of explications . . . this book is important as the best extant introduction to 'a grizzled and tough old poet who . . . asks only . . . to write careful, honest, and tightly disciplined poems which make sense; good sense; penetrating, often heart-rending sense' "—(*LJ*).
Robert Graves. By M. Seymour Smith. *British Bk. Centre* $2.38 pap. $1.20
Robert Graves. By George Stade. *Columbia* Essays on Modern Writers pap. $1.00. A pamphlet concentrating on the poetry which also considers his criticism, his fiction and his use of myth, history and religion.
Barbarous Knowledge: Myth in the Poetry of Yeats, Graves, and Muir. By Daniel Hoffman. *Oxford* 1967 $6.75 Galaxy Bks. 1970 pap. $2.25
A Bibliography of the Works of Robert Graves. By Fred Higginson. *Shoe String Press* 1966 $15.00
The Poetry of Robert Graves. By Michael Kirkham. *Oxford* 1969 $6.75

See also Chapter 12, Modern British Fiction.

BLUNDEN, EDMUND (CHARLES). 1896–

Poet, critic, teacher and editor, Blunden condemned war. He served as a lieutenant with the Royal Sussex Regiment in France and Belgium, was gassed and received the Military Cross in World War I. A volume of poems "The Shepherd and Other Poems of Peace and War" (1922, o.p.) won the Hawthornden Prize in 1922. From 1924 to 1927 he was Professor of English Literature at Tokyo University and taught at Oxford as a Fellow and Tutor in English Literature at Merton College. He has been Head of the Department of English, University of Hong Kong, a position he attained in 1953. Nature and war are the chief themes of this Georgian poet, who continues to write with "old-fashioned grace and courtly humor." He often depends upon unusual and obsolescent words for his effects, but he expresses simple emotion and a tenderness for rural people and their countryside. "After the Bombing," written during World War II, is a quiet, meditative book of which the *Spectator* said: "Wild flowers, fern and shrub still adorn the bombed areas of London and other cities. Many writers have been tempted to moralize on those gay displays of nature that hide moments of horror and destruction. But [he] avoids an obvious conclusion, and imagination is stirred all the more effectively by his reticence." He received the Queen's Gold Medal for Poetry in 1956. His critical and editorial work is sensitive and distinguished. Defeating the American, Robert Lowell, Mr. Blunden was elected by undergraduates to be Professor of Poetry at Oxford in 1966.

AFTER THE BOMBING AND OTHER SHORT POEMS. 1949. *Bks. for Libraries* facsimile ed. $6.50

Books about Blunden

Edmund Blunden. By Alec M. Hardie. In the Writers and Their Work Series. *British Bk. Centre* $2.38 pap. $1.20

CLARKE, AUSTIN. 1896–

M. L. Rosenthal (in "The New Poets") calls Austin Clarke "the dean of active Irish poets. . . . Though Clarke began his career under the influence of the Celtic renaissance, he always combined romanticism with harsh wit and realism. His major books between the *Collected Poems* of 1935, now long out of print, and *Mnemosyne Lay in Dust* are, like the latter, the work of his old age. *Later Poems* (1961) and *Flight to Africa* (1963) contain a good deal of satire of an unusual sort. It is the self-flagellant satire of a man of strong and compassionate feeling, and this is the root of Clarke's late confessional tendency. His identification with Ireland is as complete and unselfconscious as with his own family, [and] the lyrical assimilation of national preoccupations and problems is striking."

Born in Dublin, Clarke studied and later lectured at University College there. A period in London followed. In 1932, the same year he became a founding member of Eire's Academy of Letters, he was awarded his country's first national poetry prize. Working as a free-lance writer and broadcaster, he has been constantly active in the theater and closely associated with the Irish Lyric Theater Company in the production of verse plays. Clarke's own early drama in verse, "The Son of Learning" (1927. *Dufour* 1964 $2.50), and his "Collected Plays" (*Dufour* 1964 $7.95) are available. He has also edited "The Plays of George Fitzmaurice, Volume I: Dramatic Fantasies" (*Dufour* 1967 $7.50). "The Bright Temptation" (*Dufour* $5.95) was his first novel. He wrote "Mnemosyne Lay in Dust," a narrative poem, autobiographical in tone, on the occasion of his 70th birthday in 1966. Of "Old-Fashioned Pilgrimage and Other Poems," consisting of "travel verse, poems in honor of poets, and poems expressing Mr. Clarke's attitudes about issues as different as the napalm bomb and sex," *Library Journal* said: "Mr. Clarke writes conventional poems, but he writes them always with skill."

FLIGHT TO AFRICA. *Dufour* 1963 $5.75; *Humanities* $3.75. A recommendation of the (British) Poetry Book Society.

POEMS BY AUSTIN CLARKE, TONY CONNOR AND CHARLES TOMLINSON. *Oxford* 1964 pap. $1.75

MNEMOSYNE LAY IN DUST. Ill. by Jack Coughlin. *Dufour* 1966 ltd. ed. $11.50

OLD-FASHIONED PILGRIMAGE AND OTHER POEMS. *Dufour* 1967 $4.50; *Humanities* pap. $2.75 The Spring 1967 choice of the Poetry Book Society.

ECHO AT COOLE AND OTHER POEMS. *Dufour* 1968 $5.50

Two Interludes. *Dufour* 1968 $3.50; *Humanities* pap. $2.00

Impuritans. *Humanities* 1972 pap. $6.00

Books about Clarke

Tribute to Austin Clarke on his Seventieth Birthday. Ed. by John Montague and Liam Miller. *Dufour* 1966 $4.50; *Humanities* pap. $2.25. Padraic Colum, Denis Donoghue, Serge Fauchereau, Ted Hughes, Anthony Kerrigan, Thomas Kinsella, Hugh MacDiarmid, Christopher Ricks, Charles Tomlinson and Richard Weber are among the contributors. A checklist of Clarke's publications is included.

DAY LEWIS, C(ECIL). 1904–

An Irish poet, educated at Oxford with Auden and Spender, Day Lewis was regarded at the time as "the most articulate spokesman of the group." "A Hope for Poetry" (1936, 5th ed. 1942, o.p.) is an excellent analysis of the poetry of his circle. In the essay "Revolution in Writing" he stated the dilemma that confronted his generation of writers—whether to serve Marx and the revolutionary masses or Freud and man's individual unconscious. His other essays on poetry include: "The Poetic Image" (*Oxford* 1947 $2.90), "Enjoying Poetry" (1947. *Folcroft* 1973 lib. bdg. $4.00) and "The Poet's Way to Knowledge" (1959, o.p.). He has edited several poetry anthologies and translated Vergil's "Aeneid."

He once considered himself a political and poetic revolutionary. His "Poems, 1943–1947" (1948, o.p.) seems to show a change from his early point of view. The London *Times* comments: "He has taken a quieter, even at times a duller, path [than Spender, Auden or MacNeice], and it has led him more and more from a poetry of ideas to one of feelings—in the contemporary case, so often an improvement. His progress has been from iron to feathers, and it is curious that a movement in the other direction should ever have been thought progressive." Of his "Selected Poems" *Library Journal* said: "One must admire Day Lewis. For 40 years he has written poetry that is clearly out of tune with the times. He is not afraid of the pathetic fallacy, personification, and the hero. . . . Reading these poems one is aware of a voice that remains true to its own ear. There are no straining for effects, no tensions, no profundity. Instead there are, to quote [the poet]: 'admiration for the heroic, a sense of life's transience, the riddle of eternity.' After reading these poems, one is not terribly excited, but one respects the voice behind the lines; its integrity, its dedication to certain values may keep these poems viable when other more touted and demon-ridden poets are remembered as literary curiosities." "The tone of his memoir, 'The Buried Day' (1960, o.p.), is quietly introspective. It hauntingly evokes life in a succession of rectories, first in Ireland and then in England. The various schools in which the author studied or taught are faithfully and sometimes amusingly depicted. The sensitivity to nature grows gradually sharper and more subtle. . . . The double thread that seems to run through the book is the quest for personal identity and the determination to be a poet. The two things are closely linked"—(*N.Y. Herald Tribune*).

Apart from his poetry and two novels (o.p.), Day Lewis has continued to write detective thrillers—among the best of their kind—under the pseudonym of Nicholas Blake. During World War II, he was editor of books and pamphlets for the Ministry of Information. In 1946 he became Clark Lecturer, Trinity College, Cambridge and during 1951–56 he was professor of poetry at Oxford University. In 1958 he was elected vice-president of the Royal Society of Literature. He is a director of *Chatto & Windus Ltd.*, the London publishers. In the 1964–65 academic year, he came to the United States as the Charles Eliot Norton Professor of Poetry at Harvard; his lectures delivered there have been collected as "The Lyric Impulse" (*Harvard Univ. Press* 1965 $4.25). In January, 1968, he succeeded the late John Masefield (*q.v.*) as Britain's Poet Laureate amid controversy as to whether the post should not be abolished. Mr. Day Lewis commented: "I think the man himself can give the post some meaning and one must not assume that it is an entirely antiquated thing." His first official poem exhorted Britons to work harder. One section began, "Do you remember those mornings after the blitzes . . ." and ended "Be as you were then, tough and gentle islanders"—(*N.Y. Times*). He clearly brings an attractive quality to his task.

Selected Poems. *Harper* 1967 $5.00

"A severely pruned selection from forty years' work"—(*New Republic*).

Whispering Roots and Other Poems. *Harper* 1970 $5.00

Books about Day Lewis

Cecil Day Lewis. By Clifford Dyment. *British Bk. Centre* $2.38 pap. $1.20
MacNeice, Spender, Day-Lewis: The Pylon Poets. By Derek Stanford. *Eerdmans* 1969 $.95
C. Day Lewis. By Joseph N. Riddel. In the English Authors Series. *Twayne* $5.50

EMPSON, WILLIAM. 1906–   *See Chapter 15, Essays and Criticism.*

BETJEMAN, JOHN. 1906–

John Betjeman's poetry offers a commentary on the contemporary scene with perception and wit. In reviewing his autobiography in blank verse, "Summoned by Bells" (1960, o. p.), which pictures a boy's growth to manhood, the *N.Y. Times* said: "Thousands of readers who normally do not read a line of verse from one year's end to another will revel in it. Betjeman is a wit and an eccentric whose poetry and behavior alike have delighted a small circle for many years." He has since proved that he has wide mass appeal as well; he is the first poet in years to become a runaway best seller in Britain. "Not since Longfellow and Tennyson has a poet managed to produce a kind of verse which appeals to ordinary people as well as the literary Establishment," says the *N.Y. Times*. "The obvious explanation of Betjeman's popularity is that his poems, while sophisticated, are simple and direct; the rhythms, with their prose-like qualities, easy to follow. His themes are the familiar experiences: love, lust, joy, childhood, death, doubt and melancholy. But 'Betj' offers another answer. 'It's appearing on telly that's done it,' he says." Edmund Wilson at one time found him one of the "two most considerable English poets writing today." Louise Bogan has written: "His verse forms, elaborately varied, reproduce an entire set of neglected Victorian techniques, which he manipulates with the utmost dexterity and taste. His diction and his observation are delightfully fresh and original. And it is a pleasure to . . . recognize sentiment so delicately shaded, so sincerely felt, that it becomes immediately acceptable to our modern sensibilities"—(*New Yorker*). W. H. Auden calls him "a satirist with a delicate lyrical gift."

Betjeman received the Heinemann award in 1949 for his "Selected Poems" (o. p.), and in 1956, the Russell Loines Memorial Award of the National Institute of Arts and Letters. His "Collected Poems" was awarded the Duff Cooper Memorial Prize for 1958 and the William Foyle Poetry Prize in 1959. In 1960 he was given the Queen's Gold Medal for poetry. He was educated at Marlborough and Oxford, was British Press Attaché in Dublin and has held a post with the British Admiralty. He has been book critic on various newspapers including the *Daily Telegraph*, and has appeared often, as he says, on British television. Next to poetry he loves architecture, on which he has written a number of books, such as the attractive and comprehensive "American's Guide to English Parish Churches: Including the Isle of Man" (*Astor-Honor* 1959 $7.95).

COLLECTED POEMS. Comp. with introd. by the Earl of Birkenhead. *Houghton* 1959 $6.00 2nd ed. 1971 $7.50. Selected poems from 7 earlier volumes and with a group of 16 poems written since 1954 which have not previously appeared in book form.

HIGH AND LOW. *Houghton* 1967 $3.95

"In this newest, small collection, the sly fun remains attractive"—(*New Yorker*).

FIRST AND LAST LOVES. *Transatlantic* pap. $2.50

Books about Betjeman

John Betjeman. By Jocelyn Brooke. In the Writers and Their Work Series. *British Bk. Centre* 1962 $2.38 pap. $1.20

WATKINS, VERNON (PHILLIPS). 1906–1967.

Vernon Watkins was an official of Lloyd's Bank; he was born in Wales and lived there most of his life. Educated at Repton and Magdalene College, Cambridge, he served with the RAF, 1941–46. He draws to some extent upon Welsh legend but is essentially of the English traditional school. "The central experience of [his volume of poetry, "The Death Bell," 1954, o. p.]," says the London *Times*, "is a sustained wonder at the glories of the created world, told in twin and merging moods of the rhapsodic acceptance and grave meditation." "Vernon Watkins is very consciously a Romantic, in a decade in which younger poets have, on the whole, turned against Romanticism. . . . He is a poet who has created his own recognizable world; and who, in an age in love with ambiguity and hedging, can declare with obvious dignity, 'Truth is simple' "—(*TLS*, London). His fine, easily understood verse has appeared in the *New Yorker* and other American periodicals. The University of Swansea, Wales (Swansea was his home, as it was Dylan Thomas'), created during his lifetime a Poetry Chair in his honor. Watkins was awarded the Levinson prize in 1953 by *Poetry* magazine (Chicago). He has translated the poems of Heinrich Heine in "North Sea" (1951, o. p.). A close friend of Dylan Thomas (*q. v.*), Watkins edited "Dylan Thomas' Letters to Vernon Watkins" (*New Directions* 1957 $3.75). Thomas said of him: "I think him to be the most profound and greatly accomplished Welshman writing poems in English."

SELECTED POEMS. *Old Oregon* 1948 $4.00. Selections from two books published in England but not available separately here: "The Ballad of the Mari Lwyd and Other Poems" (1941 new ed. 1948) and "The Lamp and the Veil" (1945).

SELECTED POEMS [another collection]. Watkins' choice from 5 earlier volumes, 1930–60. *New Directions* 1967 pap. $2.25

UNCOLLECTED POEMS. *Enitharmon Press* 1969 ltd. ed. $15.00

FIDELITIES. *New Directions* 1967 $5.00

AUDEN, W(YSTAN) H(UGH). 1907–1973.

Auden was educated at Christ Church, Oxford, where he was considered even then as one of the leaders of the young poets of his generation.

His body of work is "so diverse and extensive that it hardly seems possible one writer in our terse age could have done it all. Long poems, short poems, verse drama, light verse, occasional verse, songs, opera libretti, political odes and epistles have poured from his pen. And in between poems, he has turned out literally hundreds of magisterial, pithy essays and articles on subjects ranging from music in Shakespeare to detective novels. With learned friends, he has edited collections of Elizabethan songs, aphorisms and, in one peerless anthology ["Poets of the English Language," *see below*], the full span of English poetry"—(*Newsweek*). With the assistance of translators he has rendered into English a number of poems by the Russian Andrei Voznesensky. "His work, from the political satires and exhortations of the nineteen-thirties to his most recent meditative, often mannered odes, has been unfailingly responsive to the moral and ideological pressures of the time.... The crises of war and uprootedness have burned their silhouette into his writing." "The brilliant mixture of the wildly colloquial and the obscurely learned, the interest in puzzles, riddles, games, and mock strategies, the devoted craftsman's attitude toward meter and verse form, the acute sense of stylistic openness and of the need for a whole array of formal and rhetorical modes for different themes and occasions that have become so familiar in his work all got their start in [his] early years.... His more recent poetry has become, like his discourse, more personal, even to the point of homeliness, as exemplified by a suite of poems, each one devoted to establishing the myth of a different room in the modern dwelling, that gives its title to his last book, *About the House*"—(John Hollander, in the *Atlantic*). Louis Untermeyer has said: "Auden has become not only the most eloquent and influential but the most impressive poet of his generation."

"The Age of Anxiety," (a title which became a common description for the 1950's) received the Pulitzer Prize for Poetry in 1948. For "The Shield of Achilles" he won the National Book Award in 1956. Karl Shapiro commented in the *N.Y. Times:* "The romantic agonizing is almost gone from Auden's poetry. In its place we find a disarming first-person-singular Auden.... This friendly, witty, serious tutorial Auden chats comfortably of literary manners and the psychological phases of the mind."

Auden traveled for a time in Germany, Spain, Iceland and China. In 1937 he received the King's Gold Medal for Poetry, the second to be awarded. After 1939 he made his home in New York and became an American citizen. He spent summers in Austria and received the Austrian State Prize for European Literature. He was elected Professor of Poetry at Oxford University in 1956, "mainly by the demand of the undergraduates," says V. S. Pritchett. Auden's inaugural lecture, delivered in June, 1956, was "Making, Knowing and Judging" (1956, o. p.). In addition to the Pulitzer Prize and the National Book Award, he has received the Award of Merit Medal from the American Academy of Arts and Sciences (1945), the Bollingen Prize in Poetry (1954), the Alexander Droutzkoy Memorial Award (1959), the ASCAP Special Award (1966), the gold medal of the National Institute of Arts and Letters (1968) and the National Medal for Literature (1967). The citation for this highest American award was for "poetry that has illuminated our lives and times with grace, wit and vitality. His work, branded by the moral and ideological fires of our age, breathes with eloquence, perception and intellectual power."

"The Enchaf̀ed Flood: The Romantic Iconography of the Sea" (1950, with subtitle "Three Critical Essays on the Romantic Spirit" *Random* Vintage Bks. 1967 pap. $1.65) comprises three penetrating essays about the sea as a theme in the work of Romantic writers; the *N.Y. Times* described it as a "small critical masterpiece." "The Dyer's Hand and Other Essays" (*Random* 1962 $10.00 Vintage Bks. pap. $2.45) also contains critical pieces (a number written while he held the Chair of Poetry at Oxford). His witty and thoughtful observations are chiefly on poetry, but some are on art and life in general. He has compiled four notable anthologies: "The Oxford Book of Light Verse" (*Oxford* 1938 $10.00 pap. $4.95); "19th Century British Minor Poets" (*Dell* 1966 pap. $.75); with N. H. Pearson, "Poets of the English Language" *Viking* 1950 5 vols. each $5.95 pap. Vols. 1-3 each $1.85 Vol. 4 $2.95 Vol. 5 $3.25); and, with Louis Kronenberger, "The Viking Book of Aphorisms: A Personal Selection" (*Viking* 1962 Compass Bks. 1966 pap. $2.95). In addition to all his other accomplishments, "he has become, in collaboration with Chester Kallman, the most distinguished librettist for grand opera since Hofmannsthal"—(John Hollander). The libretto for Stravinsky's "The Rake's Progress" is his outstanding work in this field.

COLLECTED POETRY. *Random* 1945 $8.95

COLLECTED SHORTER POEMS, 1927–1957. *Random* 1967 $8.95

In preparing this selection of 300, Auden has "thrown out" certain poems "because they were dishonest, or bad-mannered, or boring." "These three categories account, alas, for some of his best work"—(A. Alvarez, in the *Observer*, London).

COLLECTED LONGER POEMS. *Random* 1969 $7.50

SELECTED POETRY. *Modern Library* 1959 $2.95; *Random* Vintage Bks. 1971 pap. $1.95

THE ORATORS: An English Study. 1932. Pref. by the author. *Random* rev. ed. 1967 $5.95; *Scholarly Press* repr. of 1932 ed. $8.50

An important early work on the subject of hero worship, this seems less shocking than on first publication, when it was "a slashing, often bitter attack on everything and everyone the English considered to be untouchable"—(*LJ*). John Hollander calls it "that glittering and perplexing book of prose, verse, schoolboy games, and private jokes written when he was twenty-five."

THE AGE OF ANXIETY: A Baroque Eclogue. *Random* 1947 $5.95. A long poem with three characters speaking in alliterative verse.

NONES. *Random* 1951 $5.95. Poems written in the four preceding years, some previously unpublished.

THE SHIELD OF ACHILLES. Poems. *Random* 1955 $5.95

HOMAGE TO CLIO. *Random* 1960 $5.95

ABOUT THE HOUSE. *Random* 1966 $4.95

CITY WITHOUT WALLS AND OTHER POEMS. *Random* 1969 $4.50

ACADEMIC GRAFFITI. *Random* 1972 $5.00. 61 clerihews about famous people, some reprinted from "Homage to Clio" each with a drawing by Filippo Sanjust.

EPISTLE OF A GODSON AND OTHER POEMS. *Random* 1972 $5.00

A CERTAIN WORLD: A Commonplace Book. *Viking* 1970 $10.00

(With Louis MacNeice) LETTERS FROM ICELAND. 1937. *Random* 1969 $7.50

(With Christopher Isherwood) JOURNEY TO A WAR. 1939. *Octagon* 1972 lib. bdg. $12.50. A travel book of China.

Books about Auden

W. H. Auden. By Richard Hoggart. In the Writers and Their Works Series. *British Bk. Centre* $2.38 pap. $1.20
Auden: An Introductory Essay. By Richard Hoggart. *Hillary House* 1956 $4.00
The Making of the Auden Canon: Revisions and Eliminations in the Collected Poetry of W. H. Auden. By Joseph Warren Beach. 1957. *Russell & Russell* $15.00
The Poetry of W. H. Auden: The Disenchanted Island. By Monroe K. Spears. *Oxford* 1963 $8.00
"The best book by anybody about a living poet. The immense versatility of this great poet has met its match in the scholarship and intellectual power of his critic"—(Allen Tate).
Auden: A Collection of Critical Essays. Ed. by Monroe K. Spears. *Prentice-Hall* 1964 $5.95 Spectrum Bks. pap. $1.95
The Poetic Art of W. H. Auden. By John G. Blair. *Princeton Univ. Press* 1965 $9.50
Quest for the Necessary: W. H. Auden and the Dilemma of Divided Consciousness. By Herbert Greenberg. *Harvard Univ. Press* 1968 $5.95
W. H. Auden. by James D. Brophy. In the Essays in Modern Writers Series. *Columbia* 1970 pap. $1.00
A Reader's Guide to W. H. Auden. By John Fuller. *Farrar, Straus* 1970 $6.50 Noonday pap. $2.25

MacNEICE, LOUIS. 1907–1963.

"MacNeice remained distinctly his own man, keeping his Anglo-Irish wit intact and never forsaking his early role of 'an anarchic and mocking seeker after the deep springs of action and faith.' Wonderfully at home in the most exigent verse forms, he repeatedly proved his narrative skill and the ability not only to record but to interpret his experience in the time of the great slump and up to and beyond the beginning of the war—in Oxford, London, Ireland, and revolutionary Barcelona"—(*New Yorker*).

An Irish poet, but for many years a Londoner, MacNeice was also a teacher of the classics, a critic and a radio dramatist. He was the "junior member of the Auden-Isherwood-Spender literary axis of the 30's." In 1940, he lectured in English at Cornell University, returning to England for military service in World War II. He has written all kinds of poetry—lyric, didactic, narrative—and excellent parodies.

Some felt that his later poems, as in "Holes in the Sky" (1947, 1949, o. p.) had become uncertain and increasingly hortatory. But "Ten Burnt Offerings" (1953, o. p.), ten long poems written during a year the poet lived in Greece, is "one of the rare rewards—a book for readers to delight in and for poets to fall in love with"—(*Nation*). "Visitations" was called "not obscure but richly textured with ingenious figures, literary allusions, and with lines of great beauty and intense meaning."

"The Burning Perch" is a collection of poems, sometimes lyrical, sometimes in the language of everyday life; here he treats the themes of death and life in the grim shadow of nuclear warfare. In the (1967) "Collected Poems," "the reader can follow the development of a lyric talent which displayed itself at first in dazzling fireworks, then in a flickering but always interesting middle period, and finally in great classic calm"—(*N.Y. Times*). Babette Deutsch says of him: "Apparently casual, his work has the restraint, the light touch, of the Latin lyricists he knows so well. The result is exceptionally candid verse about his lack of illusions, his uncertainties, and his unease, which are also ours." "The Strings are False" consists of an unfinished and possibly forgotten manuscript left with his friend E. R. Dodds during World War II and another autobiographical fragment. "For the existence of this impressive though fragmentary prose record of his childhood and youth (up to 1941) we must be grateful to Professor Dodds. . . . An accent of sincerity comes through in this account because of the fact of its never being rigidly planned or severely worked over, and we are often sent back to the poems—always a pleasure"—(*New Yorker*).

COLLECTED POEMS. Ed. by E. R. Dodds. *Oxford* 1967 $10.95

His poetry, 1925–63, "as he himself would have wanted it presented"—(*N.Y. Times*).

LAST DITCH. 1940. *Irish Univ. Press* (Cuala Press) 1971 $11.75

Books about MacNeice

Louis MacNeice. By John Press. In Writers and Their Works Series. *British Bk. Centre* 1965 $2.38 pap. $1.20
MacNeice, Spender, Day Lewis: The Pylon Poets. by Derek Stanford. *Eerdmans* pap. $.95
Louis MacNeice. By Elton E. Smith. In the English Authors Series. *Twayne* $5.50

SPENDER, STEPHEN. 1909–

Spender was one of the radical Oxford group of poets with Auden, MacNeice and Day Lewis. During World War II he edited the magazine *Horizon* with Cyril Connolly. Spender has been a resident of the United States for some years and has written an honest and moving autobiography: "World Within World," which describes his experiences in "love; poetry; politics; the life of literature; childhood; travel; and the development of certain attitudes towards moral problems." In 1953 he became co-editor of *Encounter*, an international monthly magazine sponsored by the Congress for Cultural Freedom. He resigned the editorship in May, 1967, when he found that U.S. Central Intelligence Agency funds had been subsidizing the Congress (and *Encounter*) for ten years. A selection from the magazine which he helped choose is still available—"Encounters" (ed. by Stephen Spender, Melvin J. Lasky and Irving Kristol *Simon & Schuster* 1965 pap. $2.45). He held the Elliston Chair of Poetry, University of Cincinnati in 1953, became Beckman Professor at the University of California in 1959, and lectured at Northwestern University in 1963. In 1965 he became a Consultant in Poetry in English for the U.S. Library of Congress.

Mr. Spender has written more prose than poetry, and the prose has none of the ambiguity of the poetry. His studies of modern writers include James Yeats, D. H. Lawrence, and Auden. He has translated Federico García Lorca, Rilke and Toller. Two short novels are included in "Engaged in Writing" (*Saifer* $4.00). "The Making of a Poem" (1955 *Greenwood* 1973 $8.50) is a collection of essays, some of which describe the works and writers that have influenced him. In "The Struggle for the Modern" (*Univ. of California Press* 1963 pap. $1.75), he discusses the place of the writer in our society. An early critical work is "The Destructive Element" (1936. *Folcroft* $5.00; *Saifer* pap. $3.00). With Donald Hall he has edited the "Concise Encyclopedia of English and American Poets and Poetry" (*Hawthorn Bks.* 1963 $17.95).

COLLECTED POEMS, 1928–1953. *Random* 1955 $6.50

Louise Bogan, in the *New Yorker*, said of Spender's "Collected Poems": "It is a virtue in Spender that he has moved steadily toward a controlled expression of the romantic spirit and has continued to find subjects . . . entirely suited to his gifts. His feeling of pity, excessively apparent in his early poems, has taken on balance and direction. He has persevered in becoming emotionally centered and artistically responsible."

SELECTED POEMS. His own choice, a representation of his life work. *Random* 1964 $6.95 pap. $1.95

In a review of his "Selected Poems," *Library Journal* wrote: "Mr. Spender is a major spokesman for the Romantic movement in contemporary poetry, and has been characterized often as an eloquent singer of glowing sentiment. Though most critics sadly view his work of later years, it remains a poetry of human dimensions: a combination of unexaggerated emotion and delicate, extraordinary writing. For this he is a major poet."

GENEROUS DAYS. Poems. *Random* 1971 $5.00 pap. $1.95

STEPHEN SPENDER READING HIS POETRY. A recording. *Caedmon* TC 1084 HC $5.95

WORLD WITHIN WORLD: The Autobiography of Stephen Spender, 1951. *Univ. of California Press* 1951 pap. $1.75

Books about Spender

MacNeice, Spender, Day Lewis: The Pylon Poets. By Derek Stanford. Contemporary Writers in Christian Perspective Series. *Eerdmans* pap. $.95
Stephen Spender: Poet in Crisis. By H. B. Kulkarni. *Utah State Univ. Press* 1970 $4.00

FULLER, ROY (BROADBENT). 1912–

Roy Fuller first gained fame as one of Britain's wartime poets. He served with the Royal Navy 1941–46 and his volume of poetry, "The Middle of the War" (1942, o. p.) was well reviewed. The Navy sent him to East Africa to train as a radar mechanic; he finally served as Lieutenant at the Admiralty, as Technical Assistant to the Director of Naval Air Radio. He has always practiced as a lawyer and has been Solicitor to Woolwich Equitable Building Society since 1958. His wartime African poems were collected in "A Lost Season" (1944, o. p.). He was influenced by Auden and Spender and other writers of the 30s. "I feel," he has written, "that the lessons I learnt in the thirties are still valid—that verse in our time must try to comprise the experience of the majority, despite working in minority terms—although the poet and his public may only be able to find each other in times of common crisis or suffering." Robert Conquest has written of him in the *Spectator:* "Even when young, Mr. Fuller was setting his chisel to harder stone. He never fails to try to illuminate all the segments and fragments of experience before putting them back into synthesis. And I am far from implying that he is lacking in a sense of humour or a sense of proportion when I say that he seems to me to be the only truly serious poet of his generation, as well as one of the finest." Mr. Fuller has also written several novels, none of which are available at present in the U.S.

COLLECTED POEMS, 1936–1961. *Dufour* 1962 $8.50

BUFF. Poems. *Dufour* 1965 $4.50

NEW POEMS. *Dufour* 1968 $4.95

DURRELL, LAWRENCE. 1912–

"Although Lawrence Durrell is now known to a wide public as a novelist, his *Collected Poems* come as a convenient reminder that he was an established poet long before his Alexandria novels made him a fashionable literary figure. . . . He is essentially a lyrical poet, sometimes poignant, sometimes witty, who relies on an unsurpassed sense of style to capture the most evanescent experiences. He constantly returns to Mediterranean subjects, not as a mere landscape painter but because the Mediterranean ethos is essential to his poetic temperament"—(*Guardian*, Manchester, England). In "The Ikons" "the poems are often splendid representations of Greek scenes and classical iconography, and the suggestions and associations are comparable to a rich, heady, powerful, thick wine, immediately intoxicating and sustained"—(*LJ*). "He is a very subjective writer, witty, romantic, sophisticated, but not at all worldly. He can bring a landscape to life more beautifully and economically than any living English (or American) poet"—(*TLS*, London). Durrell has also ventured successfully into writing (in verse) for the stage. "Acte" is "a compelling drama of romantic love and power politics during the reign of Emperor Nero. . . . It would be an exciting evening in the theater to see and hear this play performed"—(*LJ*). "A Key to Modern British Poetry" (*Univ. of Oklahoma Press* 1952 $5.95 pap. $2.50) is based on lectures he gave in Argentina in 1948. The general thesis is that "the dissolution by recent physicists of previous concepts of space, time and matter ('the outer universe'), together with the psychoanalysts' 'vitalist' conclusions on the nature of the self ('the world within'), has radically altered the face of literature, of poetry especially"—(*SR*).

COLLECTED POEMS. *Dutton* 1960 $5.75. More than 150 poems, from four books which appeared between 1943 and 1955.

POETRY. *Dutton* pap. $1.45

ACTE. *Dutton* 1966 $3.75. A play in free verse; revised from the 1961 version first performed in Germany.

THE IKONS AND OTHER POEMS. *Dutton* 1967 $3.95. 32 poems, many previously published in periodicals.

RED LIMBO LINGO: A Poetry Notebook. *Dutton* 1971 $12.95 signed ed. $30.00

LOVE POEMS. A recording of Mr. Durrell reading. *Spoken Arts* 818 (C) $5.95

See also Chapter 12, Modern British Fiction.

THOMAS, DYLAN. 1914–1953.

Dylan Thomas first appeared in print when he was 16 or 17, and his first volume of "Eighteen Poems" (London 1934) was published when he was only 19. A "wild Welshman," he loved the landscape of that wild country and put much of his childhood and youth there into his work—as in the stories entitled "Portrait of the Artist as a Young Dog." In his 20's, Thomas worked as a newspaper reporter and hack journalist and was for a while employed by the BBC. A number of his later years were spent lecturing in the U.S.A., and it was on one of these tours that he died in New York City. "Under Milk Wood" (*New Directions* 1954 1959 pap. $1.50) is a "gaily gruesome" play peopled with eccentric, outrageous and charming Welsh villagers. Originally written for radio, it was presented in New York in 1967. His prose is available in three volumes: "Dylan Thomas: Early Prose Writings" (ed. by Walford Davies *New Directions* 1972 $8.95), "Collected Prose: Adventures in the Skin Trade, Portrait of the Artist as a Young Dog, and Quite Early One Morning" (*New Directions* 1969 pap. $4.90), and "Adventures in the Skin Trade and Other Stories" (*New Am. Lib.* pap. $.95). These few pieces of fiction indicate his great potential as a writer of novels. "A Child's Christmas in Wales" (*New Directions* 1954 1959 $5.00 limited ed. $200.00 pap. $1.50) has become a classic. It is the snowswept ecstasy of a small boy in a Welsh village who escapes a somnolent collection of uncles and aunts after Christmas dinner for wintry adventures with his young friends and then returns gratefully to the warm family fold. To capture full flavor it should be heard as read in Thomas's marvelous voice on a recording. "A Child's Christmas" is included in "Quite Early One Morning," which Edward Weeks (in the *Atlantic*) found a delightful and moving book—"the closest we will come to the autobiography of one of the finest lyric poets of our time."

Thomas at his death had apparently left no major work unpublished, but there have since appeared a number of lesser ones to round out the record. "The Beach at Falesa" (1963, o. p.), a film script, was written in 1948. "Dylan Thomas's Choice" (ed. by Ralph Maud and A. T. Davis *New Directions* 1964 boxed $6.50) is a collection of some of his favorite works by other poets which he gave as readings. "The Doctors and the Devils and Other Scripts" (*New Directions* 1966 $5.00 pap. $1.95) "show Thomas as a highly professional writer and one of considerable range"—(*LJ*). "Rebecca's Daughter" (1946, o. p.), a screenplay, "is a romantic melodrama which reads smoothly and is written so vividly that one can clearly see the intended film. [But] neither in style nor in subject matter is it easy to recognize Dylan Thomas as the author"—(*LJ*). "The Notebooks of Dylan Thomas" are manuscripts of poems and drafts of poems written from his 15th to his 19th years, which he sold for $140 at the age of 27 when he was hard up. They went to Thomas B. Lockwood, patron of the Lockwood Library of the University of Buffalo, who deposited them there. They are chiefly of interest to scholars and critics. "There is much to think about in this edition of Mr. Maud's, and we must be grateful to him for helping us reconsider [many] issues. . . . Some of the writing is merely adolescent, some has the kick of Thomas's great power without quite making it, and some will seem to many to warrant a birth certificate"—(M. L. Rosenthal, in *SR*).

Soon after the poet's death, the publication of the John Malcolm Brinnin journal (*see list below*) and Mrs. Thomas's "Leftover Life to Kill" (1957, o. p.) brought into harsh daylight Thomas's profligate last years, when drink, adulation and despair at his inability to cope with ordinary life sent him finally out of control. "Dylan," the play by Sidney Michaels, brought that period to the Broadway stage with Alec Guinness in the title role in 1963–64 (one of the "ten best" plays of the season). Since then Constantine FitzGibbon's excellent and affectionate biography (by far the best to date) has set Thomas's life in perspective.

Vivid and violent, passionate and intense, Thomas became a poet, he says, because "I had fallen in love with words," and the sense of the richness and variety and flexibility of the English language, as well as the glory of nature and even of human nature as he knew it in rural Wales, is everywhere apparent in his work. His poetry now seems less obscure than it did in his lifetime; in it he conveys unmistakably his feeling that "it is my aim as an artist . . . to prove beyond doubt to myself that the flesh that covers me is the flesh that covers the sun, that the blood in my lungs is the blood that goes up and down in a tree." He said, "I am in the path of Blake [of the "Songs of Innocence,' and of] Donne." The cycle of birth and flowering, love and death suffuse his writing, and he may have written one of the great poems of the English language in the poignant valedictory to his dying father, "Do Not Go Gentle into That Good Night" ("Rage, rage against the dying of the light"). Another poem on death lifts the awesome fact of our small dying into the immense rhythm of the universe—the fine "And Death Shall Have No Dominion." But mostly he celebrated life, in the seas and fields and hills and towns of his native Wales. One need not agree entirely with the "claustrophobia" judgment of Horace Gregory (reviewing the "Notebooks" in the *N.Y. Times*)—the two poems cited above are surely exceptions, and there are more—to feel that Mr. Gregory has assessed Thomas as well as is yet possible when he says: "But what of all the Thomas poems? Do they place him with John Keats, with Donne? Not quite. Despite their power, despite their findings in a world of marvels, they close in upon one, they create the feelings of claustrophobia, whereas the minute particulars of Keats and Donne open outward into a greater universe. It was the eccentric, self-speculative character of Thomas's intensely personal language that caused his poems to move inward from the world of nature out of which they drew their imagery. Yet Thomas's accomplishment was a marvel in itself—and that was why a tragic sense of loss attended the news of his early death. And a likely immortality may be found in his re-creations of a pastoral childhood at Fern Hill, a childhood to be rediscovered by young readers of poetry in many future generations."

COLLECTED POEMS: 1934–1953. *New Directions* 1953 $4.25 pap. $2.75

Contains all the poetry written up to that time "that I wish to preserve. . . . I read somewhere of a shepherd who when asked why he made, from within fairy rings, ritual observances to the moon to protect his flocks, replied, 'I'd be a damn' fool if I didn't!' These poems, with all their crudities, doubts, and confusions, are written for the love of Man and in praise of God, and I'd be a damn' fool if they weren't"—(Author's note).

DYLAN THOMAS READING HIS COMPLETE RECORDED POETRY. *Caedmon* TC 2014 2 records set $11.90. Thomas must be one of the most superb readers in the history of English poetry, as the popularity of his recordings shows.

DYLAN THOMAS READING. *Caedmon* TC 1002, TC 1018, TC 1043, TC 1061, TC 1132 5 records each $5.95. Thomas reads his own poems and stories, talks about himself and reads from the poetry of others. TC 1002 includes "A Child's Christmas in Wales."

AN EVENING WITH DYLAN THOMAS READING HIS OWN AND OTHER POEMS. *Caedmon* TC 1157 $5.95. A recording that includes "On Reading Poetry Aloud," a BBC talk by Thomas.

THE NOTEBOOKS. Ed. with introd. by Ralph Maud. *New Directions* $8.50. Four manuscript notebooks, 1930–34, containing 200 poems.

A PORTRAIT OF THE ARTIST AS A YOUNG DOG. *New Directions* 1940 1956 pap. $1.35. Semiautobiographical short stories.

QUITE EARLY ONE MORNING. *New Directions* 1954 pap. 1960 $1.60. Shorter prose pieces—autobiographical and critical; includes "A Child's Christmas in Wales" and "A Visit to America."

LETTERS TO VERNON WATKINS. Ed. by Vernon Watkins. *New Directions* 1957 $3.75. These letters to Watkins (*q. v.*) reveal the younger poet's remarkable personality, his zest for living and superb wit. Thomas had a great respect for Watkins' poetic judgment and consulted him freely.

SELECTED LETTERS. Ed. with commentary by Constantine FitzGibbon. *New Directions* 1967 $8.50

"In 'Selected Letters of Dylan Thomas,' brilliantly edited by Mr. FitzGibbon, the tensions and dynamics of Thomas's creative life, his life behind the scenes, are made clear. Though the roaring boy does not wholly vanish—he is painfully coy, tail-between-the legs and blubbering in his apologies and begging letters—we are drawn much closer to the glorious, often hilarious, writer of short stories as well as to the maker of some of the best poems written in our century. FitzGibbon's great find here is the letters written to Pamela Hansford Johnson when Thomas was under 21, she a year or two older, and they thought themselves in love with one another"—(Horace Gregory, in the *N.Y. Times*). "An extraordinary collection of letters . . . 231 of them and not a cliché in the lot. Certain to rank among the most original letters of any literary man of this century, they may indeed equal the best of all times. . . . There's something for everyone: comedy, philosophy, politics, misbehavior, models for thank-you letters and asking-for-money letters, literary criticism, literary gossip, and hundreds of superb literary puns"—(*SR*).

Books about Thomas

The Poetry of Dylan Thomas. By Elder Olson. *Univ. of Chicago Press* 1954 Phoenix Bks. 1961 pap. $1.75. A balanced and helpful evaluation with a valuable bibliography by William H. Huff.

Dylan Thomas in America: An Intimate Journal. By John Malcolm Brinnin. 1955. *Little* pap. $2.45. The first of the "reminiscences" to appear, this is "sharp, candid" and "illuminating," but merciless in its detailed depiction of Thomas's decline on the U.S. lecture circuit just before his death here.

A Reader's Guide to Dylan Thomas. By William York Tindall. *Farrar, Straus* 1962 Noonday pap. $3.45; *Octagon* 1973 $11.00

The World of Dylan Thomas. By Clark Emery. *Univ. of Miami Press* 1962 $6.50

"Confirmed Dylanists and baffled neophytes alike will find rich pasturing in the deft explications and sympathetic but nonsycophantic critiques provided for each of the 90 titles in Thomas's 'Collected Poems.' . . . This is no pedantic variorum or synthesis; each poem is tackled with gusto and insight"—(*LJ*). Tindall's and Emery's explications are complementary; each was written without reference to the other.

Concordance to the Collected Poems of Dylan Thomas. By Robert C. Williams. *Univ. of Nebraska Press* $13.95

Dylan Thomas. By George S. Fraser. In the Writers and Their Works Series. *British Bk. Centre* pap. $2.38 pap. $1.20

The Life of Dylan Thomas. By Constantine FitzGibbon. *Little-Atlantic* 1965 pap. $2.65

FitzGibbon, a friend of Thomas's, was chosen by the trustees of the Thomas estate to write this, "the authorized biography. . . . FitzGibbon has a novelists's eye for the relevant. He sees the dark and bright side of the moon of Thomas's character and we accept his view, since his objectivity is clear, almost heroic. . . . Not since Philip Horton's perfect biography of Hart Crane has the material of a 20th-century poet's life been in such competent hands. One feels Thomas himself would approve"—(*New Republic*).

The Days of Dylan Thomas. By Bill Read. Photographs by Rollie McKenna and others. *McGraw-Hill* 1965 pap. $1.95

"Concentrating primarily on Thomas's early life and career before he came to America, Read . . . has written an interesting and informative biography [that] captures Thomas's life, work and surroundings in a lucid, captivating manner which will have wide appeal"—(*LJ*).

Dylan Thomas: A Collection of Critical Essays. Ed. with introd. by C. B. Cox. In the Twentieth Century Views Series. *Prentice-Hall* 1966 $5.95 pap. $1.95. 13 essays by British, Canadian and American university professors.

The Craft and Art of Dylan Thomas. By William T. Moynihan. *Cornell Univ. Press* 1966 pap. $1.95

"A careful, extremely thorough, and imaginative explication of Dylan Thomas's poetry"—(*LJ*).

Sound and Sense in Dylan Thomas's Poetry. By Louise B. Murdy. *Humanities Press* 1966 $10.50

Dylan Thomas: The Code of Night. By David Holbrook. *Univ. of Alabama Press* 1972 $10.50

LEE, LAURIE. 1914?–

Born into a large and impoverished family in the Cotswolds, Laurie Lee was educated "a little by the country school, a lot by the life around him." He has written of his early circumstances in "The Edge of Day: A Boyhood in the West of England" (*Morrow* 1959 $4.50; with title "Cider with Rosie" *Curtis Bks.* pap. $.75). He says he wrote it in "celebration: to praise the life I'd had and so preserve it, and to live again both the good and the bad." At the age of 20, he left home to seek his fortune, travelling to Spain where he lived by playing the violin in streets and cafés. During the Spanish Civil War he was a member of the International Brigade. He has published several books of poems, plays, and a travel book on Spain, "A Rose for Winter: Travels in Andalusia" (1956, o.p.). "The Firstborn" (1964, o.p.) describes in text and photographs what Mr. Lee describes as the "miracle" of his firstborn child. His first volume of poetry, published in 1944, was acclaimed for its "brilliant and novel imagery." Mr. Lee is not sure exactly when he was born, but believes it was close to the beginning of World War I.

My Many-Coated Man. 1955. 15 poems. *Morrow* 1961 $3.00

The Sun My Monument. In the Phoenix Living Poets Series. *Wesleyan Univ. Press* $4.00

Edge of Day: Boyhood in the West of England. *Morrow* 1960 $4.50. The first of two volumes of autobiography.

As I Walked Out One Midsummer Morning. *Atheneum* 1969 $5.95. The second autobiographical volume. Tells of his life as a London laborer and as a travelling fiddler in Spain before the Spanish Civil War.

CONQUEST, ROBERT. 1917–

"Whether he is writing of Nantucket, Catullus, the United Nations, space travel, Paul Klee, extrasensory perception, love, nature, war or death . . . he writes with clarity, authority and cunning," wrote Selden Rodman of Mr. Conquest's first volume of poetry. Such a listing indicates the range of this writer's intelligence. He brings an unusually well-informed concern to bear on "apparent inconsistencies between poetic awareness of what appear to be absolute realities and recent scientific discoveries."

He now varies free-lance writing with university appointments in England and the United States. In addition to his poetry, he has had several works on Soviet Russia published by *Macmillan*, *Harper* and *Praeger*, and an analysis, with important documents of Soviet actions in "The Pasternak Affair: Courage of Genius" (*Lippincott* 1962 $3.95). He has written some science fiction, and, with Kingsley Amis (*q. v.*) edited "Spectrum: A Science Fiction Anthology" (*Harcourt* 5 vols. 1962–67 Vols. 1–3, o. p. Vols. 4–5 each $4.75). As editor, Mr. Conquest brought a number of talented writers, among them Larkin, Gunn, Amis, John Wain and Elizabeth Jennings, to the eye of the English public in his anthology "New Lines" (1956).

Arias from a Love Opera and Other Poems. *Macmillan* 1970 $4.95

HEATH-STUBBS, JOHN. 1918–

Poetic skill, deftness and elegance in the true Greek spirit are emphasized in the work of John Heath-Stubbs. Several of the poems are translations or adaptations of Greek and Latin verses and many others are written in classical forms. The poems "remind one of the sophisticated intelligence and delicate balance of the Latin wits, and of the deliberate craftsmanship of the medieval lyricists. . . . It is the ability to fuse the satiric with the philosophic, the trivial with the profound, and the urbane with the passionate that gives these poems their highly individual appeal"—(*Manchester Guardian*). Some of the shorter poems were inspired by Alexandria, where the author has taught. He was born in London, educated at private schools and by tutors because of poor eyesight. He took a "First" in English Language and Literature at Queen's College, Oxford and stayed for an additional year of research. In 1952 he was appointed Gregory Fellow in Poetry (Poet in Residence) at the University of Leeds. His critical works include "Charles Williams" (Writers and their Works Series *British Bk. Centre* $2.38 pap. $1.20), and "The Verse Satire," "The Pastoral" and "The Ode" (*Oxford* 1969 pap. each $1.70).

Selected Poems. *Oxford* 1965 pap. $4.50

LARKIN, PHILIP. 1922–

"The wan, underpaid, overtaxed hopelessness that has smothered the country since the War . . . is Mr. Larkin's theme," wrote the London *Times Literary Supplement* of "The Less Deceived" (1955, o.p.). That he succeeds so "perfectly" is due partly to his wit, partly to his high level of technical accomplishment, his "meticulous control." He has created a tone of voice of which Robert Lowell writes: "No post-war poetry has so caught the moment. . . . This is something new and imperishable."

Of "The Whitsun Weddings," Professor Robert Regan wrote in *Library Journal*: "Philip Larkin never claims that the men we meet in his poems are like—or lamentably unlike—Prince Hamlet or Odysseus; his characters are typical, not archetypal. In this respect and in many others he resembles Auden. Both treat the particular as particular; both confront experience with the austere objectivity which is rightly called classical. Succinctly, Larkin evokes scenes and suggests stories which speak of a destitution not even the blare of television and the hum of electric labor-savers can cover; yet his poems are informed by a view of life which asserts, half in faith, half in hope, that 'What will survive of us is love.' Deeply moving and masterfully controlled, the poems in this, Larkin's third and best volume, merit a place in every library."

Born in Coventry, Warwickshire, Larkin was educated at King Henry School and St. John's College, Oxford. A librarian by vocation, he has written fiction as well as verse. Originally he had hoped to become a famous novelist "like Somerset Maugham," but after two early novels failed in Britain, he decided that he was better suited to poetry. "It's like moving to a much smaller house after finding you cannot afford to keep up the mansion of your dreams," he confessed. But with his "poet's reverence for the small detail that shapes a scene or character," he has made for himself an impressive reputation.

THE WHITSUN WEDDINGS. *Random* 1964 pap. $6.00

ALL WHAT JAZZ: A Record Diary, 1961–1968. *St. Martin's* 1970 $6.95. Articles originally published in the *Daily Telegraph* about jazz music.

AMIS, KINGSLEY. 1922–   *See Chapter 12, Modern British Fiction.*

JENNINGS, ELIZABETH. 1926–

"A Way of Looking" (1956, o.p.) was this young British poet's first collection to appear in America. Her talent is delicate, but pure. "It is not easy to grasp Miss Jennings' work at a first reading," Louise Bogan (*q. v.*) wrote in the *New Yorker*, "because of her compression and simplicity—qualities we are not used to. A second reading helps to bring out her musical quality—everywhere present—as well as her meaning." Italy, to which the poet was able to go after winning the Somerset Maugham. Award of 1956 for her second volume, "no doubt strengthened her predilection for monochromes." She has also won an Arts Council prize and had one of her books selected by the (British) Poetry Book Society. " 'Shadow' is the key word of this poet: again and again it appears. And on every page, pallid but entire, lies the finely cut shadow of poetic thought"—(*N.Y. Herald Tribune*). Miss Jennings has said: "Prose has always seemed to me an attempt to find words for something which I already know, whereas my best poems manage to say in a strict inevitable form something that I did not know before."

Born in Boston, England, she was educated in private schools and at Oxford University. A free-lance writer, she lives in Oxford but spends as much time as she can in Rome. "Every Changing Shape" (*Dufour* 1962 $7.50) is a volume of literary essays on religion and poetry. "Poetry Today" is a discussion of contemporary poetry.

COLLECTED POEMS. *Dufour* 1967 $9.50

SECRET BROTHER AND OTHER POEMS. *Dufour* 1967 $3.95. A group of poems for young readers.

ANIMALS ARRIVAL. *Dufour* 1969 $4.95

TOMLINSON, CHARLES. 1927–

"How the mind and eye cooperate to build a world," "what the poet sees in light and space"—these elements of visual perception form the vocabulary of this poet's work. For its "kinetic imagination," Richard Wilbur (*q. v.*) has called Tomlinson's "Seeing Is Believing" "the freshest, most exhilarating [work] . . . to come out of England in years." "Tomlinson's two more recent volumes, *A Peopled Landscape* (1963) and *American Scenes* (1966), reflect a continuing relationship with the formal discoveries of American poetry and also with literal American experience. Since the appearance of *Seeing Is Believing*, he has taught at the University of New Mexico for a year and made other American visits. . . . Without surrendering either his British consciousness or the special characteristics of his earlier style—the restraint, precision, fine 'sculptural' eye, and feeling for the literal realities of place and atmosphere—he has come rather strongly under the influence of Williams and of the Black Mountain poets"—(M. L. Rosenthal, in "The New Poets").

Born in Staffordshire, the poet attended Queen's College, Cambridge. He has published widely in the United States and has been awarded several prizes including the Hokin (1956), the Blumenthal (1960) and the Union League (1961).

THE NECKLACE. 1955. *Oxford* 1966 $2.25

SEEING IS BELIEVING. *Astor-Honor* $4.00

A PEOPLED LANDSCAPE: Poems. *Oxford* 1963 pap. $3.00

AMERICAN SCENES AND OTHER POEMS. *Oxford* 1966 $3.50

WAY OF A WORLD. *Oxford* 1969 $3.75. A continuation of "American Scenes and Other Poems."

WRITTEN ON WATER. *Oxford* 1972 $4.00

"Grappling with the difficulty of seizing visual appearances, the poet moves between the surfaces and depths of things and the world of necessity"—(Publisher's catalog).

GUNN, THOM. 1929–

"Britain's most promising export since Auden," Thom Gunn grew up in London and graduated from Cambridge. He has been an Assistant Professor of English at the University of California, Berkeley, and still lives in California. His verse has been called "lean, sinewed and tawny, expertly though casually crafted." His themes are, for the most part, philosophical: he writes of "questions which have troubled poets and thinkers in all ages." His second book of verse "The Sense of Movement" (1959, o.p.) won the Somerset Maugham Award for 1959. "Positives" is a "chronicle of life" that begins at birth and ends with old age and the approach of death. "The poems are short, not difficult and not sentimental. 'Positives,' a title that applies nicely both to the prints and the attitude of the poet, is a modest book. Yet after looking at the illustrations you are likely to return again to the verses. They are the work of an honest mind that responds sympathetically to human beings and to the life that bubbles up in the most untoward places"—(*N.Y Times*). *Library Journal* calls it "a perfect liaison of word and picture."

MY SAD CAPTAINS AND OTHER POEMS. *Univ. of Chicago Press* 1961 $2.50 Phoenix Bks. pap. $1.50

POSITIVES. Verse by Thom Gunn and photographs by his brother, Ander. *Univ. of Chicago Press* 1966 $7.00

HUGHES, TED. 1930–

"The most striking single figure to emerge among the British poets since the last war is undoubtedly Ted Hughes. [He possesses an] exuberantly horrid imagination. An ultimate terror and fascination at the gross brutality of nature, and of man in his more unreflective animal aspect and in the savagery of his wars, makes itself felt in this poet as it did in the writing of his wife, Sylvia Plath"—(M. L. Rosenthal, in "The New Poets"). Poems about animals, in which the poet actually "becomes the animal," fill most of Mr. Hughes' first two volumes—"The Hawk in the Rain," which won him the First Publication Award of the Poetry Center in 1957, and "Lupercal" (1960). Yet "there was, as someone once remarked, a problem: what would Hughes do when he ran out of animals? 'Wodwo' provides the beginnings of an answer.... Like its title, then, the book is a halfway stage between the animal world and the human. [Hughes] now seems to be after something more elusive and abstract than ever appeared in his earlier poems. [He] is no longer describing a world of creatures but a supernatural world of demons. [Here he is] a master of concentrated language who controls every detail for his own subtle ends. The best poems in 'Wodwo' may be as sardonic and hard as the bleak northern country to which they continually return, but the tension in them is that of an extraordinary poetic intelligence, always driving on a little further"—(A. Alvarez, in the London *Observer*).

Ted Hughes was born in Yorkshire. After serving in World War II, he went to Cambridge, where he met his wife, the poet Sylvia Plath (*q. v.*). She committed suicide when their two sons were still very young. Mr. Hughes contributes poems and stories to many British and American periodicals.

SELECTED POEMS. *Harper* 1973 $6.95

WODWO. *Harper* 1967 $4.95

The title comes from the Old English *wuduwasa*, meaning wood-dweller and later "troll of the forest." 60 poems, 5 short stories and a play written for the BBC, about which Ted Hughes has said: "The stories and the play in this book may be read as notes, appendix, and unversified episodes of the events behind the poems, or as chapters of a single adventure to which the poems are commentary and amplification. Either way, the verse and the prose are intended to be read together as parts of a single work."

THE IRON GIANT: A Story in Five Nights. *Harper* 1968 $3.95 lib. bdg. $3.79. Stories for children.

CROW: From the Life and Songs of the Crow. *Harper* 1971 $5.95 pap. $2.95

MACBETH, GEORGE (MANN). 1932–

George Macbeth was born in a mining village in Scotland and educated at New College, Oxford. His work is enjoyable for its "romping wit and vitality". His "Collected Poems" are from five earlier volumes, including "The Colour of Blood" and "Night of Stones." Of "The Colour of Blood" which is his first volume published in this country, D. M. Thomas said: "[The poems] move in the post-Einstein world where Time and Ego are fluid." "Night of Stones" was not as well received by the critics as his first American publication, but it seems generally agreed that he is a young poet who will increase in growth and stature.

He has been editor of *Poet's Voice* from 1958–65, of *New Comment* from 1959–64, and of *Poetry Now* from 1965 on. He is also the author of the juveniles "Noah's Journey" (*Viking* 1966 $3.50 lib. bdg. $3.37) and "Jonah and the Lord" (*Holt* 1970 lib. bdg. $3.59).

COLLECTED POEMS, 1958–1970. *Atheneum* 1972 $7.50

THE COLOUR OF BLOOD. *Atheneum* 1967 pap. $1.95

NIGHT OF STONES. 1968 *Atheneum* 1969 pap. $2.45

(Ed.) THE PENGUIN BOOK OF SICK VERSE. *Penguin* 1963 pap. $.95

(Ed.) THE PENGUIN BOOK OF VICTORIAN VERSE. *Penguin* 1969 pap. $1.45

Chapter 8

American Poetry: Early Period

"Of Life immense in passion, pulse, and power,
Cheerful—for freest action form'd, under the laws divine,
The Modern Man I sing."

—WHITMAN

The task facing the American poet from the beginning has been to make a national poetry without benefit of a native language. Even before the Declaration of Independence, the Puritan poets Anne Bradstreet (*q. v.*) and Edward Taylor (*q. v.*) felt the pressure of the wild, savage country and showed a marked tendency to reach through their English form and language toward the rude, homely experience of a new land. Though such groping roughened their meter and almost breached sentence structure, they both occasionally achieved a power which still seems immediate and striking.

Beside them, Philip Freneau (1752–1832) and Joel Barlow (1754–1812), though much more literary, seem less original. Unlike Barlow who lost himself in a grandiose attempt to cast his American epic vision—*The Columbiad*—in heroic couplets, Freneau mastered eighteenth-century satiric and elegiac forms, and, in such a poem as "The Indian Burying Ground," he beautifully enclosed an American subject in traditional English form. But it is William Cullen Bryant (*q. v.*) who emerges as the first sure handed poet in America. Writing after Coleridge and Wordsworth, Bryant achieved a form which invaded post-romantic vision with pre-romantic diction. His blank verse, in such a poem as "Thanatopsis," echoes the stateliness and sententiousness of James Thompson and Edward Young at the same time that it clearly reflects Wordsworth's abiding trust in nature.

Bryant's successful work sets the stage for the genteel American poetry which followed. Henry Wadsworth Longfellow (*q. v.*), John Greenleaf Whittier (*q. v.*), James Russell Lowell (*q. v.*), and Oliver Wendell Holmes (*q. v.*) combined to write a poetry which showed that there were American poets who could hold their own on the terms which English poetry had established for them. Every one of these poets cultivated the English tradition in a new country. That is why there is always an element of competitive imitation in their work. They are trying to be new yet are always a bit old fashioned. The old eighteenth-century didacticism thus stands alongside their nineteenth-century awareness of issues and attitudes. For a relatively young nation which had retained the language of its parent, these poets provided models of excellence—a proof that Americans would at once accommodate themselves to English forms and at the same time establish American letters as a cultural reality. It is small wonder that they came to be known as the School-room Poets, for their success both here and in England was a promise that this nation could, with education and effort, emulate the literature of its language. Longfellow perhaps more than any of the others, embodied the possibilities of such a poetic identity. Marvelously proficient in European languages, he was at once remarkably popular and extraordinarily urbane.

Yet accomplished though these poets were, their conventionality outweighs their originality. Though they were able to set American subjects to English meters, they were unable to discover new forms for their new subjects. That was the true task—the burden and the glory—of the American poetic imagination. Fortunately for American literature there were poets who took the risk. First, there was Edgar Allan Poe, (*q. v.*). Scorning the didactic element in poetry, Poe sought to separate beauty from morality. At his best, he achieved an intensification of sound sufficient to threaten the common sense of the poetic line and release a buried, even a morbid, sense which, clinging to his redoubled rhyme, would be spellbound in the sonic pitch of the poem. Defining poetry as "the rhythmic creation of beauty," Poe not only sought the dream buried beneath the poetic vision— Coleridge had done that—but abandoned the moral rationale which gave the buried dream symbolic meaning. The dream, or nightmare, was thus released to sound itself as the very rationale of verse.

If Poe threatened sense with sound, Ralph Waldo Emerson (*q. v.*) threatened sound with sense. Insisting that poetry was "a meter making argument," Emerson sought a meter which would be equal to the rude strokes of nature he feared were being lost to the civilizing process of gentility. He realized that blank verse, which was both the natural and the royal line of English poetry, would have to be naturalized and democratized if it was ever to be true to the America he meant to find in the West. For the most part, he eschewed blank verse altogether, seeking four, three, and even two foot lines to sound the primordial sense of nature he tried so hard to hear. More than any other American writer, he called American literature into being. Like the true prophet that he was, he did not so much predict the future as he made the future happen. It is no wonder that Ezra Pound (*q. v.*), looking back upon him, would say that he broke the back of blank verse.

The poet which Emerson prophesied was Walt Whitman (*q. v.*). Whereas Poe had threatened poetic sense with sound and Emerson had threatened poetic sound with sense, Walt Whitman threatened poetry itself. Releasing himself from the uniformly measured line, Whitman all but broke down the distinction between poetry and prose. He wanted a freedom of verse equal to the freedom of his vision; he wanted the poet to be equal to the reader, and was able to imagine the two figures as being identical. He thus envisioned himself as dying into his words and being reborn as the reader's voice. Realizing that in the English pronominal system, the pronoun *you* retains its form whether singular or plural, Whitman made that linguistic fact the heart of his poetic program. Thus in any one of his poems the *you* always refers to the simple separate reader as well as to the mass of readers Whitman dreamed of as an audience. His poetry is thus at once incredibly public and incredibly intimate, just as his vision is at once extraordinarily general and extraordinarily concrete. In going forward into his free democratic vision, Whitman actually went back behind both English and classical meters to a Biblical past. His poetry is more like the psalms than anything else, which is as it should be, since Whitman imagines himself as a god incarnating the word which will in turn embody his readers.

After Whitman, there is Emily Dickinson (*q. v.*) who, instead of expanding broadly and horizontally over the landscape as Whitman had done, contracts and concentrates into riddling quatrains. Drawing heavily on Protestant hymns, she so slants her rhymes, buckles sentence patterns, and transports herself into metaphor that each of her poems is overcharged with meaning and spirit. If Whitman had played God in order to incarnate himself into all readers, Emily Dickinson played the Devil and democratically voted herself into heaven, thus claiming a divine election which would have startled and staggered her Calvinistic ancestors.

There were other poets of course. There were the vernacular poets John Hay (1838–1905), Bret Harte (1836–1902), and James Whitcomb Riley (*q. v.*), but their dialect poems tended to be performances—poems to be memorized and recited rather than remembered. And there were Southern poets like Henry Timrod and Sidney Lanier (*q. v.*), but in one way or another they followed the genteel poets. Above all, there were the strong minor poets, Jones Very (1813–1880) and Frederick Goddard Tuckerman (1821–1873), who found themselves in mastering a single form—the sonnet. Though unknown to many readers of American poetry, both these poets are unforgettable the moment their work is once seen.

Yet it was Poe, Emerson, Whitman, and Dickinson who truly sounded an American poetry. After them an American poetry was not only possible; it was inevitable. Moreover, poetry in English would never quite be the same.

HISTORY AND CRITICISM

Arms, George. THE FIELDS WERE GREEN: A New View of Bryant, Whittier, Holmes, Lowell and Longfellow with a Selection of their Poems. *Stanford Univ. Press* 1953 $8.00

Burke, W. J., and Will D. Howe, Eds. Augmented and rev. by Irving Weiss. AMERICAN AUTHORS AND BOOKS: 1640 to the Present Day. 1943. *Crown* 3rd ed. 1972 $12.50. The biographies of American poets and the titles of their best known books, without critical evaluation, are included. Short articles on "Little Magazines" and the "Beat Generation" and a list of "Pulitzer Prizes" are valuable. (*For additional note, see Chapter 3, Reference Books—Literature: Histories and Dictionaries of Literature.*)

Gittleman, Edwin. JONES VERY: THE EFFECTIVE YEARS, 1833–1840. *Columbia* 1967 $12.50. A study of the New England scholar, teacher, poet and essayist whose spiritual convictions influenced the thought of Emerson, Hawthorne and others.

Hoffman, Daniel G., Ed. AMERICAN POETRY AND POETICS: Poems and critical documents from the Puritans to Robert Frost. *Doubleday* Anchor Bks. (orig.) 1962 pap. $1.45

Pearce, Roy Harvey. THE CONTINUITY OF AMERICAN POETRY. *Princeton Univ. Press* 1961 $11.50. Covers poetry from the 17th century to the present.

Shapiro, Karl. AMERICAN POETRY. *T. Y. Crowell* 1960 $6.95 pap. $3.50. Bibliography and biographical notes on 54 poets from Anne Bradstreet to Allen Ginsberg; arranged chronologically; list of selected critical readings.

Untermeyer, Louis. LIVES OF THE POETS: The Story of One Thousand Years of English and American Poetry. *Simon & Schuster* 1959 $7.95 pap. $3.95. Many Americans are included among the 133 poets in this far-reaching history.

Waggoner, Hyatt Howe, AMERICAN POETS. 1968. *Dell* Delta 1970 pap. $2.95

Wegelin, Oscar. BIBLIOGRAPHY OF AMERICAN POETRY 1650–1820. 2 vols. in one. *Peter Smith* 1930 $10.00

See also Chapter 3, Reference Books—Literature, and Chapter 4, Broad Studies and General Anthologies, which includes A Reading List on Poetry.

COLLECTIONS

General and Comprehensive

Allen, Gay Wilson, Walter B. Rideout and James K. Robinson, Eds. AMERICAN POETRY. *Harper & Row* 1966 $9.00

> An "impressive volume" of nearly 700 poems from Colonial times to the present day, including the much neglected poets Jones Very and Frederick Tuckerman. "All has been sown with a full and generous hand, so the variety and the striking originality of the period's poetry . . . are brilliantly displayed"—(*New Yorker*).

Gelpi, Albert. THE POET IN AMERICA, 1650 to the Present. *Heath* 1973 text ed. $9.95

Matthiessen, Francis Otto. THE OXFORD BOOK OF AMERICAN VERSE. *Oxford* new ed. 1950 $9.50. 51 poets are arranged in this excellent anthology. The earlier "Oxford Book of American Verse" was compiled by Bliss Carman in 1927.

Rodman, Selden. ONE HUNDRED AMERICAN POEMS. *New Am. Lib.* (orig.) 1949 pap. $.95

Untermeyer, Louis. AN ANTHOLOGY OF THE NEW ENGLAND POETS FROM COLONIAL TIMES TO THE PRESENT DAY. *Random* 1948 $10.00. 33 poets from Anne Bradstreet to Robert Lowell, with valuable biographical and critical comments—liberal representation of Longfellow.

Van Nostrand, Albert D. and Charles H. Watts III, Eds. THE CONSCIOUS VOICE: An Anthology of American Poetry from the Seventeenth Century to the Present. *Bobbs* 1959 pap. $3.75; facsimile ed. *Bks. for Libraries* $11.00

Whicher, George F. POETRY OF THE NEW ENGLAND RENAISSANCE, 1790–1890. *Holt* (Rinehart) 1950 pap. $2.00; *Peter Smith* $4.00

Whicher, Stephen E., and Lars Ahnebrink, Eds. TWELVE AMERICAN POETS. *Oxford* 1961 pap. $1.95. A discriminating selection of poems by Longfellow, Poe, Whitman, Dickinson, Robinson, Frost, Stevens, Williams, Pound, Jeffers, Cummings and Lowell, with substantial commentary.

Williams, Oscar. A LITTLE TREASURY OF AMERICAN POETRY. *Scribner* 1948 rev. ed. 1955 $10.00

NEW POCKET ANTHOLOGY OF AMERICAN VERSE. *Washington Square* 1961 pap. $1.25

(With Edwin Honig), Eds. THE MENTOR BOOK OF MAJOR AMERICAN POETS. *New Am. Lib.* Mentor Bks. (orig.) 1962 pap. $1.50

See also Chapter 4, Broad Studies and General Anthologies.

American Indian and American Negro

Bontemps, Arna, Ed. AMERICAN NEGRO POETRY. *Hill & Wang* 1963 $4.95 rev. ed. 1973 (in prep.) Am. Century 1964 pap. $1.95. Selections from more than 55 poets, including Le Roi Jones, Richard Wright and Langston Hughes; biographical notes.

Barksdale, Richard, and Kenneth Kinnamon. BLACK WRITERS OF AMERICA: A Comprehensive Anthology. *Macmillan* 1972 text ed. $11.95. An excellent anthology of Black writing in America containing a generous selection of poetry.

Cronyn, George. THE PATH ON THE RAINBOW. 1918. (With title "American Indian Poetry: An Anthology of Songs and Chants"). *Liveright* 1934 new ed. 1970 $7.95 pap. $2.95; *Ballantine Bks.* pap. $1.65

Hughes, Langston, and Arna Bontemps. THE POETRY OF THE NEGRO, 1746–1949. *Doubleday* 1949 $8.95 Anchor Bks. pap. $4.95. The works of 147 Negro poets from pre-Revolutionary to modern times.

Johnson, James Weldon. THE BOOK OF AMERICAN NEGRO POETRY. 1922 *Harcourt* rev. ed. 1931 pap. $1.45. 40 writers with biographical and critical sketches.

Turner, Frederick W., Ed. THE PORTABLE NORTH AMERICAN INDIAN READER. *Viking* 1974 $7.95 pap. $3.25. Contains an impressive and discriminating selection of Indian poetry.

ANTHOLOGY OF NEGRO POETS IN THE USA—200 YEARS. Record. (Recorded by Arna
   Bontemps.) *Folkways* FL 9792 (FP91/2) $5.79. Includes Lucy Terry, Laurence
   Dunbar, J. W. Johnson, Countee Cullen, and others.

BRADSTREET, ANNE. 1612–1672.

Anne Bradstreet, daughter of an early Governor of the Massachusetts colony (Thomas Dudley) and wife of
another (Simon Bradstreet), came to this country from England just ten years after the Pilgrims, in 1630. A
Puritan matron who eventually had eight children, she was a bookworm from childhood, though a careful
housekeeper in the wilderness and a loving wife and mother to a happy family not without its share of illness
and sorrow. She and Edward Taylor (*q. v.*) were the only two American poets of consequence in the 17th century, and her poetry only found its way to print through the agency of her brother-in-law, who carried it to
England without her knowledge. There it was first published in 1650, as "The Tenth Muse, Lately Sprung
Up in America."

Much of her early work was competent but conventional: "The Four Seasons," "The Four Monarchies,"
"Dialogue Between Old England and New" and the like. Her religious poems of spiritual struggle often read
like something from an old hymnbook. It is in her love poems to her husband, particularly those expressing
her longing for him when he had to travel away, and in her poems about family affairs that she shines. Anne
Bradstreet felt the oddness of being a writing woman when others might think she should be sewing; she
asked for a wreath of household parsley or thyme rather than bay. Her gentle, accepting spirit was warm and
feminine but endowed with strength and a self-assertiveness that broke through the Puritan mold. Admirably
she was never ashamed to be human. The poet John Berryman (*q. v.*) had discovered her by 1956, when he
published his long poem "Homage to Mistress Bradstreet" (*Farrar, Straus* $4.95) with illustrations by
Ben Shahn.

Library Journal called the *Harvard* "Works" "a brilliant and probably definitive edition of . . . America's
first genuine poet. It supersedes all previous editions in thoroughness and scholarship."

THE WORKS OF ANNE BRADSTREET. Ed. by Jeannine Hensley; fwd by Adrienne Rich.
   Harvard Univ. Press Belknap Press 1967 $9.00

WORKS IN PROSE AND VERSE. 1867. Ed. by J. H. Ellis. *Peter Smith* $7.50

THE POETRY OF ANNE BRADSTREET. Ed. by Robert Hutchinson. *Dover* 1970 pap.
   $2.00

Books about Bradstreet

Anne Bradstreet. By Josephine K. Piercy. *Twayne* 1964 $5.50; *College & Univ. Press* 1964 pap. $2.45
Anne Bradstreet: The Tenth Muse. By Elizabeth Wade White. *Oxford* 1971 $12.50. Concerned with her
   personal life in England and America, her literary background and her development as an artist.

TAYLOR, EDWARD. c. 1642–1729.

A Congregational minister engaged in the task of establishing a spiritual code in a new country, Taylor
wrote in the metaphysical tradition of Herbert (*q. v.*), Donne (*q. v.*) and Crashaw (*q. v.*). Born in England,
he was a graduate of Harvard (1671). He went to Westfield, Mass., and stayed there the rest of his life, acting
as clergyman and physician. At his own request, he remained virtually unpublished until 1939, when "The
Poetical Works of Edward Taylor" was edited by Thomas H. Johnson.

His "Poems," (the first edition of the bulk of Taylor's poetry) "will stand at the fore of American belles let-
tres. . . . Stanford's careful 'Introduction' discusses in turn Taylor's life, deeply experienced Calvinist faith,
the extant manuscripts, the publication record, and the establishment of the present text"—(*LJ*).

POETICAL WORKS. 1939. Ed. by Thomas H. Johnson. *Princeton Univ. Press* 1966 pap.
   $2.95

POEMS. Ed. with introd. by Donald E. Stanford; fwd. by Louis L. Martz. *Yale Univ.
   Press* abridged ed. 1960 $15.00

EDWARD TAYLOR'S TREATISE CONCERNING THE LORD'S SUPPER. Ed. by Norman S.
   Grabo. *Michigan State Univ. Press* 1966 $7.50

Books about Taylor

Edward Taylor. By Norman S. Grabo. *Twayne* 1962 $5.50; *College & Univ. Press* 1962 pap. $2.45

Edward Taylor. By Donald E. Stanford. Pamphlets on American Writers. *Univ. of Minnesota Press* 1965 pap. $1.25

Edward Taylor: An Annotated Bibliography, 1668–1970. Ed. by Constance J. Gefvert. *Kent State Univ. Press* 1971 $4.75

BRYANT, WILLIAM CULLEN. 1794–1878.

Bryant's simple nature poetry is unmistakably American. His most famous poem in his day was "Thanatopsis," the title being a compound of two Greek words meaning "a meditation on death." Written when he was 17 or 18, it was first published in the *North American Review* in 1817. Always solemn and stately, his verse seemed cold to Lowell (*q. v.*) who spoke of Bryant's "iceolation." Bryant was editor-in-chief of the New York *Evening Post* from the year 1829 until his death. When he was nearly 80, he translated Homer's "Iliad" (1870, o. p.) and "Odyssey" (1871–72, o. p.) into English blank verse.

POETICAL WORKS. Ed. by Parke Godwin. 1883. *Russell & Russell* 1967 2 vols. set $17.50; *AMS Press* repr. of 1903 ed. 1969 $15.00

PROSE WRITINGS. Ed. by Parke Godwin. 1884. *Russell & Russell* 1964 2 vols. set $27.50

Books about Bryant

William Cullen Bryant. By Andrew J. Symington. 1880. *Folcroft* $15.00

A Biography of William Cullen Bryant: With Extracts from His Private Correspondence. By Parke Godwin. 1883. *Russell & Russell* 1967 2 vols. set $20.00. A detailed but highly readable account.

William Cullen Bryant. By John Bigelow. 1890. *Arno* $12.50; *Folcroft* $20.00

Chronologies of the Life and Writings of William Cullen Bryant. By Henry C. Sturgis. 1903. *Burt Franklin* $16.00

Gotham Yankee. A Biography of William Cullen Bryant. By Harry H. Peckham. 1950. *Russell & Russell* 1971 $12.50

William Cullen Bryant and Isaac Henderson: New Evidence on a Strange Partnership. By Theodore Hornberger. 1950. *Haskell* 1972 $6.95

William Cullen Bryant. By Albert F. McLean, Jr. U.S. Authors Ser. *Twayne* 1964 $5.50; *College & Univ. Press* 1964 pap. $2.45

Bryant. By Charles H. Brown. *Scribner* 1971 $12.50

"Thoroughly researched and straightforward in manner and style"—(*Choice*).

William Cullen Bryant. By William Aspenwall Bradley. *Folcroft* 1973 lib. bdg. $15.00

EMERSON, RALPH WALDO. 1803–1882.

Emerson regarded himself as "more of a poet than anything else." He wrote his verse for himself without regard for an audience, and his poetry has a more spontaneous quality than most of his prose. W. C. Brownell in "American Prose Masters" speaks of the poems as "a kind of intimate reverberation" of the essays. "They are largely Emerson's communion with himself, as the Essays are his communication with the world." His poems are nearly always short, lyrical and meditative. He was a rebel in poetry as well as prose. Robert E. Spiller (in "The Cycle of American Literature") writes: " 'Poetry was all written before time was,' [Emerson] tells us in his essay on 'The Poet,' 'and whenever we are so finely organized that we can penetrate into that region where the air is music, we hear those primal warblings and attempt to write them down.' The poet has his special function in the order of nature; he is 'the sayer, the namer, and represents beauty.' ... 'The experience of each new age requires a new confession, and the world seems always waiting for its poet.' In stating so clearly his case for an organic view of art [says Spiller] Emerson was describing not only his own method but the instinctive approach of most really great American writers."

THE PORTABLE EMERSON. Sel. and arr. with introd. and notes by Mark Van Doren. *Viking* 1946 lib. bdg. $5.50 pap. $3.35

SELECTED PROSE AND POETRY. Ed. with introd. by Reginald L. Cook. *Holt* (Rinehart) 1950 2nd ed. 1969 college ed. pap. $2.50

SELECTED WRITINGS. Ed. by Brooks Atkinson with fwd. by Tremaine McDowell. *Modern Library* $2.95 College ed. pap. $1.35; ed. by William H. Gilman *New Am. Lib.* Signet pap. $1.50

SELECTIONS. Ed. by Stephen E. Whicher. *Houghton* Riv. Eds. pap. $1.75

BASIC SELECTIONS. Ed. by Eduard C. Lindeman. *New Am. Lib.* Mentor Bks. pap. $1.25

POEMS. Ed. by J. D. Adams. *T. Y. Crowell* 1965 $3.50 lib. bdg. $4.25; *Apollo* pap. $1.45

See also Chapter 15, Essays and Criticism.

LONGFELLOW, HENRY WADSWORTH. 1807–1882.

"Modern criticism represents Longfellow as an adolescent balladist and romancer," John Reeve wrote. "Yet his popularity in his lifetime was as great as that of Tennyson. Longfellow is the classic case of a poet who would have been better had he found it more difficult to express himself in verse. Unfortunately his mechanical facility spoils almost all his work, and it is difficult to find more than a few poems that are readable today." However, his experimentation with classical meters influenced many of the poets who followed him. His three most popular narrative poems are thoroughly rooted in American soil: "Evangeline," "the flower of American idylls"; "Hiawatha," "the first genuinely native epic in American poetry"; and "The Courtship of Miles Standish," a Puritan romance of Longfellow's own ancestors, John Alden and Priscilla. "Paul Revere," the best known of the "Tales of a Wayside Inn," is also intensely national.

Longfellow's home in the heart of the business district of Portland, Maine, has long been maintained as a shrine. In 1955 his birthplace near the waterfront was torn down. The poet traveled abroad, then lived in Maine, where he taught at Bowdoin, until an appointment to Harvard brought him (eventually) to the beautiful Craigie House, still standing as a Longfellow landmark in Cambridge, Mass. Here he enjoyed the fame and affluence of his later life in a manner somewhat more luxurious than was approved by the literary men and women of Concord. (Emerson commented on this wryly.) He outlived two beloved wives. The early letters (Vols. 1 and 2), says Louis Untermeyer (in *SR*), "fail to move us because, although a courteous correspondent, he hated to write them." He was "not an impassioned, provocative or even interesting letter-writer." His translation of Dante, much admired in its day, is now o. p.

WORKS. 1886–1891. *AMS Press* 14 vols. each $18.00 set $250.00

COMPLETE POETICAL WORKS. Ed. by H. E. Scudder. *Houghton* Cambridge Eds. 1948 text ed. $7.25

POETICAL WORKS. *Oxford* 1904 Stand. Authors $6.00

POEMS. *Dutton* Everyman's 1950 $3.50 pap. $2.25; *Modern Library* $2.95

POEMS. Ed. by Edmund Fuller. *T. Y. Crowell* 1967 $3.50 lib. bdg. $4.25

SELECTED POEMS. Ed. by Richard Wilbur and Howard Nemerov. *Dell* pap. $.35

FAVORITE POEMS. Introd. by Henry Seidel Canby. *Doubleday* 1967 $4.95

ESSENTIAL LONGFELLOW. Ed. by Lewis Leary. *Collier* 1963 pap. $.95

REPRESENTATIVE SELECTIONS. Ed. by Odell Shepard. *American Bk.* 1934 $5.00

EVANGELINE. 1847. (And Other Poems) *Assoc. Booksellers* Airmont Bks. pap. $.60; ed. by Stephen J. Rusnak *Bantam* pap. $.45; ed. by M. Lewiton *Hawthorn* 1966 $3.95; *Houghton* Riv. Lib. $1.20 pap. $.65; *McKay* Pocket Class. $2.25; *Meredith* 1966 $3.95; (and Selected Tales and Poems) *New Am. Lib.* Signet pap. $.75; *Scholastic Bk. Service* 1972 pap. $.60; *Washington Square* Reader's Enrich. Ser. pap. $.60

SONG OF HIAWATHA. 1855. *Crown* 1969 $2.98; *Dutton* 1959 $4.50; *Hawthorn* 1966 $3.95

TALES OF A WAYSIDE INN. 1863. *McKay* Pocket Class. $2.25

PAUL REVERE'S RIDE. *T. Y. Crowell* 1963 $4.50 lib. bdg. $5.25; *Windmill Bks.* 1973 lib. bdg. $5.88

CONTINENTAL TALES. *A. S. Barnes* pap. $1.25

KAVANAGH: A Tale. 1849. Ed. by J. Downey. *College & Univ. Press* 1965 $5.00 pap. $1.95

THE LETTERS OF HENRY WADSWORTH LONGFELLOW. 4 vols. 1966–1972. Vol. I 1814–1836 Vol. 2 1837–1843 Vol. 3 1844–1856 Vol. 4 1857–1865. Ed. by Andrew Hilen. *Harvard Univ. Press* Balknap Press vols. 1–2 set $37.50; vols. 3–4 $40.00

> Longfellow's letters—805 of them—many in print for the first time, give an account of the poet's life from age 7 to 36 with little reference to his ambitions as a poet. "Meticulously edited"—(*SR*).

Books about Longfellow

> Professor Longfellow of Harvard. By Carl L. Johnson. *Univ. of Oregon Press* 1944 pap. $1.00
> Diary: A European Tour with Longfellow, 1835–1836. By Clara Crowninshield; ed. by A. Hilen. *Univ. of Washington Press* 1956 $6.50
> Longfellow: His Life and Work. By Newton Arvin. *Little Brown* 1963 $6.75 pap. $2.45. "A good study but a poor biography"—(*LJ*).
> Henry Wadsworth Longfellow. By Edward L. Hirsh. Pamphlets on American Writers *Univ. of Minnesota Press* 1964 pap. $.95
> Henry Wadsworth Longfellow. By Cecil B. Williams. U.S. Authors Ser. *Twayne* 1964 $4.95; *College & Univ. Press* 1964 pap. $2.45
> Henry Wadsworth Longfellow: Portrait of an American Humanist. By Edward Wagenknecht. *Oxford* 1966 $6.50
> The Young Longfellow, 1807–1843. By Lawrance Thompson. *Octagon* 1963 $13.00

WHITTIER, JOHN GREENLEAF. 1807–1892.

> Whittier, the Quaker poet, was the "man of peace and the poet militant." He himself said that he "set a higher value on his name as appended to the Anti-Slavery Declaration in 1833 than on the title page of any book." His "Voices of Freedom," sung in the cause of Abolition, was second only to "Uncle Tom's Cabin" in influencing the public against slavery. Regarding his poetic achievement Whittier wrote, "My vehicles have been of the humbler sort—merely the farm wagon and buckboard of verse. . . . I am not one of the master singers and don't wish to pose as one."
> Whittier's "Snow-Bound, a Winter Idyll" contains fine descriptions of New England and was immensely popular in its day. The portraits are firelight sketches of the members of his home circle drawn from memory after most of his family were dead. His uncollected criticism, "On Writers and Writings," is edited by E. H. Cady and H. H. Clark (1950. *Bks. for Librariesx* $9.75).
> "Whittier's Unknown Romance" (with Elizabeth Lloyd) by Marie V. Denervand (1922, o. p.) contained a few of the Lloyd-Whittier letters which are now a part of the Pickard-Whittier papers at Harvard and were edited by T. Franklin Currier as "Elizabeth Lloyd and the Whittiers: A Budget of Letters" (1937, o. p). "John Greenleaf Whittier, Friend of Man" by John Albert Pollard (1949. *Shoe String* 1969 $15.00) is a long, scholarly, meticulously documented biography of Whittier as Abolitionist, poet, philosopher and political leader—with chapters of criticism of his work.

WRITINGS. Ed. by Horace E. Scudder. 1894. *AMS Press* 7 vols. set $138.50

COMPLETE POETICAL WORKS. Ed. by Horace E. Scudder. 1894. *Houghton* Cambridge Eds. $7.00. text ed. $6.75

SELECTED POEMS. Ed. by D. Hall. *Dell* pap. $.40

LEGENDS OF NEW ENGLAND. 1831. *Scholars' Facsimiles* 1965 $7.50

NATIONAL LYRICS. 1865. *Bks. for Libraries* facsimile ed. $8.50

ANTI-SLAVERY POEMS. 1888. *Arno* 1969 $13.50

BARBARA FRIETCHIE. *T. Y. Crowell* 1965 $3.75 lib. bdg. $4.50

Books about Whittier

> John Greenleaf Whittier. By Lewis Leary. *Twayne* 1961 $5.50, *College and Univ. Press* 1962 pap. $2.45
> John Greenleaf Whittier: A Portrait in Paradox. By Edward Wagenknecht. *Oxford* 1967 $6.50. A "compact, meaty introduction to the mind, personality and writings" (*N.Y. Times*) of the popular and successful poet in his time.
> John Greenleaf Whittier's Poetry: An Appraisal and a Selection. By Robert Penn Warren. *Univ. of Minnesota Press* 1971 $8.95 pap. $2.95. 36 selections.

HOLMES, OLIVER WENDELL. 1809–1894.

Many of Holmes' best poems appeared first in his "Breakfast Table" series. "The Deacon's Masterpiece, or The Wonderful One-Hoss Shay," "The Chambered Nautilus" and "The Living Temple" may all be found in "The Autocrat of the Breakfast Table" (1858). (*See Chapter 15, Essays and Criticism*). So many events are commemorated in his verses—nearly half are of this nature—that a social history of the times may be read in his complete poems. His work has preserved the distinctive idiom of New England speech.

THE COMPLETE WORKS OF OLIVER WENDELL HOLMES. 1892. *Scholarly Press* 13 vols. each $19.50 set $250.00

COMPLETE POETICAL WORKS. Ed. by H. E. Scudder. 1895. *Houghton* Cambridge Eds. $6.50

See Chapter 15, Essays and Criticism for biocritical comment and bibliography.

POE, EDGAR ALLAN. 1809–1849.

Poe's life is the battleground of modern biographers but his poetry is the meeting ground of poets. "No other American poet has been so unanimously accepted by all the poets of the world," said John Macy. The quantity of Poe's verse is small, but because he wrote so little, people who read him read all of him. He is known more thoroughly than most poets. His poems are melancholy, mysterious, but, above all, melodious. Sound is to him more than sense. Death is his favorite subject. Stedman says: "He was not a single-poem poet, but the poet of a single mood." Edmund Wilson (*q. v.*) has said that there was in Poe "a dash of the actor who delights in elaborating a part." He was a "precocious and imaginative youth whose first poems appeared when he was 18. Some of his work achieved popularity during his short life, and after his death . . . his reputation for romantic decadence increased, especially in France. . . . He played no small part in the formation of the mind and character of the French poet Baudelaire, another and more gifted decadent. . . . Poe's poetry as a whole is a mixture of the tawdry and the inspired, and was ruined both by the increasing toll taken on him by his dissipation and by his obsession with the idea of poetry as a kind of magical incantation"— (James Reeves). Two biographies of Poe, important in their day, are now o. p.: "Israfel" by H. Allen (1926 rev. ed. 1934) and "The Life of Poe" by Thomas Holley Chivers (1952).

WORKS. Ed. by Edmund C. Stedman and George E. Woodberry. 1895. *Bks. for Libraries* 10 vols. set $165.00

COMPLETE WORKS. Ed. by James A. Harrison. 1902 *AMS Press* 17 vols. set $200.00

COMPLETE TALES AND POEMS. *Modern Library* Giants $4.95

COMPLETE POEMS AND STORIES OF EDGAR ALLAN POE. Ed. by Arthur Hobson Quinn and Edward H. O'Neill. *Knopf* 1946 2 vols. boxed $17.50; *Doubleday* $6.95

COMPLETE POEMS AND SELECTED CRITICISM. Ed. by Allen Tate. *New Am. Lib.* Signet pap. $1.25

COLLECTED WORKS. Ed. by Thomas O. Mabbott. Vol. I. *Harvard Univ. Press* 1969 $15.00. Poems.

COMPLETE POEMS. Ed. by Richard Wilbur. *Dell* pap. $.40

THE POEMS OF EDGAR ALLAN POE. 1917 *Russell & Russell* 1963 $14.00

POEMS. (And Essays) *Dutton* Everyman's $3.25 pap. $1.95

POEMS. Ed. by Dwight Macdonald. *T. Y. Crowell* 1965 $3.50 lib. bdg. $4.25; ed. by Floyd Stovall. *Univ. Press of Virginia* 1965 $1.00; *Apollo* pap. $1.95

THREE POEMS. *McGraw-Hill* $2.95 lib. ed. $2.96

EDGAR ALLAN POE: REPRESENTATIVE SELECTIONS. Ed. with introd., bibliography and notes by Margaret Alterton and Hardin Craig. 1935. *Hill & Wang.* Am. Century rev. ed. 1962 pap. $2.25; *Peter Smith* 1962 $5.00

SELECTED WRITINGS. Ed. by E. H. Davidson. *Houghton* Riv. Eds. pap. $2.50; ed. by David Galloway *Penguin* 1968 pap. $1.45

THE PORTABLE POE. Ed. Introd. and notes by Philip Van Doren Stern. *Viking* 1945 lib. bdg. $5.50 pap. $3.25. Includes stories, poems, articles, letters, opinions.

SELECTED POETRY AND PROSE. Ed. by T. O. Mabbott. *Modern Library* $2.95 pap. $1.15

SELECTED PROSE AND POETRY. Ed. with introd. by W. H. Auden. *Holt* (Rinehart) 1950 rev. ed. 1956 pap. $2.50

SELECTIONS. Ed. by Margaret Alterton and Hardin Craig. *Hill & Wang* Am. Century 1961 pap. $2.25

SELECTED STORIES AND POEMS. *Assoc. Booksellers* Airmont Bks. 1964 pap. $.60; ed. by Floyd Zulli *Franklin Watts* 1967 lg.-type ed. Keith Jennison Bks. $8.95

GREAT SHORT WORKS. Ed. by J. R. Thompson. *Harper* 1970 pap. $1.50

GREAT TALES AND POEMS. *Pocket Bks.* pap. $.75

TALES, POEMS AND ESSAYS. *Collins* New Class. $3.00 lea. $5.00

LETTERS. Ed. by John Ward Ostrom. 1948. *Gordian* 1967 2 vols. set $20.00

Books about Poe

The Mind and Art of Poe's Poetry. By John Phelps Fruit. 1899. *AMS Press* $9.00; *Folcroft* lib. bdg. $15.00. An interesting early study.

Edgar Allan Poe: A Study in Genius. By Joseph Wood Krutch. 1926. *Russell & Russell* 1965 $7.50
In "The Shores of Light" Edmund Wilson (*q. v.*) called this "the ablest and most important of recent American books on Poe."

The Mind of Poe, and Other Studies. By Killis Campbell. 1933. *Russell & Russell* 1962 $10.00. The title essay of this important book is an invaluable summary.

Edgar Allan Poe: A Critical Biography. 1941. By Arthur H. Quinn. *Cooper* 1970 lib. bdg. $17.50

On Poe: Critical Papers. By Charles Pierre Baudelaire. Trans. and ed. by Lois and Francis E. Hyslop, Jr. *Bald Eagle Press* 273 Woodland Drive, State College, Pa. 1952 $4.00

Poe: A Critical Study. By Edward Hutchins Davidson. *Harvard Univ. Press* Belknap Press 1957 $8.00. Sound and readable inquiry into the mind and writings.

The Power of Blackness: Hawthorne, Poe, Melville. By Harry Levin. *Knopf* 1958 $5.95; *Random* Vintage Bks. pap. $1.45

Haunted Palace: A Life of Edgar Allan Poe. By Frances Winwar. *Harper* 1959 $7.95. Written from a romantic and readable viewpoint for the general reader.

Edgar Allan Poe. By Vincent Buranelli. U.S. Authors Ser. *Twayne* $5.50; *College & Univ. Press* 1962 pap. $2.45

Poe: A Biography. By William Bittner. *Little* 1962 pap. $2.75. A carefully documented work.

Edgar Allan Poe: The Man Behind the Legend. By Edward Wagenknecht. *Oxford* 1963 $7.50
"This volume tersely and impartially debunks and defends Poe. . . . An indispensable addition to the shelves of all libraries."—(*LJ*).

The Recognition of Edgar Allan Poe: Selected Criticism Since 1829. Ed. by Eric W. Carlson. *Univ. of Michigan Press* 1966 $7.50 Ann Arbor Bks. pap. $2.90

"A most valuable selection of historical criticism, which dramatically illustrates the varied and conflicting attitudes that have been taken towards Poe from his own time to the present"—(*LJ*).

Poe: A Collection of Critical Essays. Ed. by Robert Regan. *Prentice-Hall* 1967 $5.95 Spectrum Bks. pap. $1.95

"Here was an author, curiously able to see the reality of terror and the demonic, yet often paradoxically decking it out in obvious stage trappings. An interesting collection, for much-maligned Poe can neither be swallowed whole nor completely rejected"—(*LJ*).

Poe the Detective: The Curious Circumstances behind the Mystery of Marie Roget. By John Walsh; introd. by Thomas Ollive Mabbott. *Rutgers Univ. Press* 1967 $7.50. A detective story about a detective story.

Poe Poe Poe Poe Poe Poe Poe. By Daniel G. Hoffman. *Doubleday* 1973 $7.95 Anchor Bks. pap. $2.50. A sound interpretation.

Poe's Fiction: Romantic Irony in the Gothic Tales. By G. R. Thompson. *Univ. of Wisconsin Press* 1973 $12.50

For his prose works see Chapter 13, American Fiction: Early Period.

LOWELL, JAMES RUSSELL. 1819–1891.

"The Vision of Sir Launfal" was once regarded as a "high mark of American poetry." Today his reputation as a poet and essayist has diminished considerably, but his versatility as a lifelong leader of the Cambridge group of 19-century literary New Englanders has never been denied. "He was at various times, and sometimes concurrently, a poet, a radical political writer, a conservative political writer, a satirist, an editor, a critic, a diplomat, and a teacher; and in all of these efforts he won the praise of his contemporaries." Lowell was particularly successful in his public poetry. His "Concord Ode," "Centennial Ode," and "Commemoration Ode" are poems of occasion that have shown enduring quality. "A Fable for Critics" (1848), a long literary comment in verse, helped establish his national reputation. It is interesting to remember that Lowell and Longfellow (*q. v.*) are two American authors who have been given monuments in Westminster Abbey.

COMPLETE WRITINGS. Ed. by Charles Eliot Norton. 1904. *AMS Press* 1967 16 vols. set $290.00

THE COMPLETE POETICAL WORKS OF LOWELL. Ed. by Horace E. Scudder. *Houghton* Cambridge 1952 $7.00

LETTERS OF JAMES R. LOWELL. Ed. by Charles Eliot Norton. 1894. *AMS Press* 2 vols. set $35.00 each $18.50; *Richard West* 1973 2 vols. set $34.95

See also Chapter 15, Essays and Criticism.

WHITMAN, WALT. 1819–1892.

The publication of the first two of a projected 14 volumes of "The Collected Writings of Walt Whitman" in 1961 was a publishing event of the year. (The next four volumes appeared in 1963 and 1964.) During 1961 and 1962 a citizens' and writers' group was formed and called on public officials to preserve the Brooklyn building where Walt Whitman helped to set type and print the first edition of the "Leaves of Grass" in 1855. Among those on the committee were Carl Sandburg, Robert Frost, Marianne Moore, Archibald MacLeish, Arthur Miller, Aaron Copland and Malcolm Cowley. The Interior Department has approved of the existing preservation of his birthplace home in Huntington, L. I., by New York State.

Whitman's stature as a poet is constantly advancing. "After his death [his] influence on literature was ever-enlarging. It broke down borderlines between prose and verse; its spirit impelled new themes for the novel, its idiom caused a revolution in poetry." Whitman used a verse form which was at first a stumbling block to many readers. The gains made by his literary descendants, the writers of *vers libre*, are gains in which he has shared. The nearest parallel to the verse form of "Leaves of Grass" is found in the poetry of the English Bible, where the structure is based on a symmetry of clauses called parallelism. While Whitman's is not a conventional poetic form, it is far from lawless. Its cadence and rhythm are carefully wrought. Occasionally he used rhyme, as in "O Captain, My Captain."

"Yet, in spite of Whitman's perplexing mannerisms, the poems justify their boundless contradictions. They shake themselves free from rant and bombastic audacities and rise into the clear air of major poetry. Such poetry is not large but self-assured; it knows, as Whitman asserted, the amplitude of time and laughs at dissolution. It contains continents; it unfolds the new heaven and new earth of the Western world"—(Louis Untermeyer).

A small volume recently published contains two unique Whitman items: a facsimile reproduction of a "remembrance copy" of "Memoranda during the War" and Whitman's reading copy of his lecture, "Death of Abraham Lincoln": "Walt Whitman's Memoranda during the War and Death of Abraham Lincoln," reproduced in facsimile, edited by Roy P. Basler (1962. *Greenwood* $9.00). The early 20th-century studies by Weirick and Carpenter have recently been reprinted by *Biblo & Tannen* and *Gale Research Co.*, respectively.

COMPLETE WRITINGS: Prose and Poems. Ed. by R. M. Bucke and Others. 1902. *Scholarly Press* 10 vols. each $14.50 Vols. 1–3 set $39.50 Vols. 4–10 set $100.00 complete set $125.00

THE COLLECTED WRITINGS OF WALT WHITMAN. Gay Wilson Allen and Sculley Bradley, Gen. Eds. Consists to date of two series (Correspondence and Works) and unnumbered volumes; 14 vols. projected. Correspondence (ed. by Edwin Haviland Miller): Vol. 1 1842–1867 (1961); Vol. 2 1868–1875 (1961); Vol. 3 1876–1885 (1964). Prose Works 1892 (ed. by Floyd Stovall): Vol. I Specimen Days (1963); Vol. 2 Collect and Other Prose (1964). Unnumbered volumes: The Early Poems and the Fiction, ed. by Thomas L. Brasher (1963). Leaves of Grass: Comprehensive Reader's Edition, ed. by Harold W. Blodgett and Sculley Bradley (1965. $12.50). *New York Univ. Press* 1961 6 vols. each $15.00 except where noted.

These are the first six volumes of the long awaited Whitman "variorum," which enlists the work of the major Whitman scholars. With "an increase of about 60 per cent to the hitherto published letters, we have [in two volumes of "Correspondence"] all the known and available letters, post cards, and notes arranged in chronological sequence without abridgement. Miller has corrected dates or has suggested reasonable dates, he has identified recipients, he has supplied impressive editorial explanation of references and historical background, and he has set up a very useful system of cross reference. . . . A completely admirable job of editing, printing and binding, these letters (and no doubt the volumes to follow) are indispensable for the serious student of American literature"—(*LJ*). "Floyd Stovall . . . has given us a complete and meticulously edited text of *Specimen Days* and *Collect*—the rambling prose reminiscences and comments which remain, as Stovall points out, perhaps the best single commentary upon the *Leaves*"—(*LJ*).

WORKS. Vol. 1 The Collected Poetry; Vol. 2 The Collected Prose. *Funk & Wagnalls* Minerva Press pap. each $7.95

WALT WHITMAN. Sel. with notes by Mark Van Doren. *Viking* Portable Lib. 1945 lib. bdg. $5.50 pap. $2.95

COMPLETE POETRY, SELECTED PROSE AND LETTERS. Ed. by Emory Holloway. *Random* Nonesuch Lib. $15.00

COMPLETE POETRY AND SELECTED PROSE. Ed. by James E. Miller, Jr. *Houghton* Riv. Eds. 1960 $3.00 pap. $2.00

WALT WHITMAN: Representative Selections. Ed. by Floyd Stovall. *Peter Smith* rev. ed. 1962 $4.50

WALT WHITMAN: Poet of American Democracy. Ed. by Samuel Sillen. Selections from his poetry and prose. *International Pubs.* 1955 $2.50

THE TENDEREST LOVER: Walt Whitman's Love Poems. Ed. by Walter Lowenfels. 1970. *Dell* Delta Bks. pap. $2.45

SELECT POEMS AND PROSE. Ed. by A. Norman Jeffares. *Oxford* 1966 $5.00

WALT WHITMAN'S POEMS: Selections with Critical Aids. Ed. by Gay Wilson Allen and Charles T. Davies. *New York Univ. Press* 1955 $9.75 pap. $3.50

POEMS. Comp. by Lawrence C. Powell. *Crowell* 1964 $3.50 lib. bdg. $4.25; *Apollo* pap. $1.95

WHITMAN READER. Ed. by Maxwell Geismar. *Pocket Bks.* 1955 pap. $.50

LEAVES OF GRASS. 1855. Inclusive ed. by Emory Holloway. *Doubleday* 1924 1954 $5.95. The standard one-volume edition based on the 1902 text. Contains Whitman's prefaces of 1855, 1872, 1876 and 1888, and the variorum readings by O. L. Triggs. Rejected poems are included.

WALT WHITMAN'S LEAVES OF GRASS: His Original Edition. Introd. by Malcolm Cowley. *Viking* 1959 $5.00 Compass Bks. 1961 pap. $1.45

"The first edition of 'Leaves of Grass' (1855) contained an introduction and 12 untitled poems, the longest and most remarkable being the poem later known as 'Song of Myself.' Many additions and revisions were made in later editions; mannerisms and new attitudes were introduced. . . . The present reprint is the first aimed at a wide audience."—(*LJ*).

WALT WHITMAN'S BLUE BOOK: The 1860–61 Leaves of Grass Containing His Manuscript Additions and Revisions. Vol. I Facsimile of the Unique Copy in the Oscar Lion Collection; Vol. 2 Textual Analysis by Arthur Golden. *N.Y. Public Lib.* 1968 2 vols. set boxed $30.00

LEAVES OF GRASS. Ed. by Harold W. Blodgett and Sculley Bradley. *New York Univ. Press* variorum ed. 1973 4 vols. set $97.50 comprehensive reader's ed. 1965 $15.00; *Norton* comprehensive reader's ed. pap. $3.95

LEAVES OF GRASS. Facsimile edition of the 1860 text, with an introd. and an index of titles by Roy Harvey Pearce. *Cornell Univ. Press* 1961 pap. $2.95

LEAVES OF GRASS. *Adler's* 1969 $12.50; introd. by Francis Gemme *Assoc. Booksellers* Airmont Bks. pap. $.75; *Avon* 1969 pap. $.60; *Chandler Pub.* 1968 pap. $1.95; ed. by Emory Holloway *Dutton* Everyman's 1947 $3.50; *Eakins* facsimile of 1855 ed. $17.50; (with title "Illustrated Leaves of Grass") ed. by Howard Chapnick *Grosset* 1971 $9.95; introd. by Oscar Cargill *Harper* Mod. Class. $2.00; *Modern Library* Giants $4.95; *New Am. Lib.* Signet pap. $.75; ed. by Sculley Bradley and Harold W. Blodgett *Norton* Critical Eds. 1973 $17.50 pap. $3.45

WHITMAN'S MANUSCRIPTS: LEAVES OF GRASS (1860). Ed. by Fredson Bowers. Parallel printing of the original draft of "Leaves of Grass" and the final 1860 edition; traces successive stages of composition with new material from the Clifton Waller Barrett Collection of Whitman Manuscripts; received Walt Whitman Award 1957. *Univ. of Chicago Press* 1955 $12.50

I HEAR AMERICA SINGING. *Delacorte* Seymour Laurence Bks. 1973 $4.95 lib. bdg. $4.58

CALAMUS: A Series of Letters Written during the Years 1868–1880 to a Young Friend. 1898. *Folcroft* lib. bdg. $20.00; *Porter, Bern* 1972 $32.50; *Richard West* 1973 $32.45

SPECIMEN DAYS. Ed. by Alfred Kazin. *Godine* 1971 $25.00 deluxe ed. $35.00 pap. $10.00

WALT WHITMAN'S CIVIL WAR. Comp. and ed. from published and unpublished sources by Walter Lowenfels, with the assistance of Nan Braymer. *Knopf* 1960 $5.00. A "realistic, personal and deeply touching account," this is a collection of notes, letters and poems written during the Civil War. "Winslow Homer's on-the-spot illustrations give additional strength to a powerful and moving book."

WALT WHITMAN AND THE CIVIL WAR. Ed. by Charles I. Glicksberg. *A. S. Barnes* 1962 pap. $1.95

WALT WHITMAN'S NEW YORK: FROM MANHATTAN TO MONTAUK. Ed. by Henry M. Christman. *Macmillan* 1963 $4.50. In 1861, Whitman began a series of unsigned articles about his observations and reminiscences of life in Brooklyn and Manhattan. Entitled "Brooklyniana" by the Brooklyn *Standard*, in which they first appeared, they are collected here for the first time.

I SIT AND LOOK OUT: Editorials from the Brooklyn *Daily Times*, 1932. Ed. by Emory Holloway and Vernolian Schwartz. *AMS Press* $14.00

WALT WHITMAN'S WORKSHOP: A Collection of Unpublished Manuscripts. 1928. Ed. with introd. and notes by Clifton J. Furness. *Russell & Russell* 1964 $12.00

FAINT CLEWS AND INDIRECTIONS: Manuscripts of Walt Whitman and His Family. 1949. Ed. by C. Gohdes and Rollo G. Silver. *AMS Press* $9.00

LEAVES OF GRASS AND SELECTED PROSE. Ed. by John Kouwenhoven. *Modern Library* pap. $1.35; ed. by Sculley Bradley *Holt* (Rinehart) 1949 pap. $3.00

THE CORRESPONDENCE OF WALT WHITMAN. Ed. by Edwin H. Miller. *New York Univ. Press* 5 vols. Vol. I 1842–1867 Vol. 2 1868–1875 Vol. 3 1876–1885 Vol. 4 1886–1889 Vol. 5 1890–1892 each $15.00

WHITMAN AND ROLLESTON: A Correspondence. 1951. *Kraus* $6.00

LETTERS OF WALT WHITMAN AND ANNE GILCHRIST. Ed. by Thomas B. Harned. 1918. *Folcroft* 1973 lib. bdg. $25.00; *Haskell* 1972 lib. bdg. $10.95; *Richard West* $10.75

Books about Whitman

A Leaf of Grass from Shady Hill, with a Review of Walt Whitman's Leaves of Grass. By Charles E. Norton. 1928. *Folcroft* 1973 $15.00

Walt Whitman Handbook. By Gay Wilson Allen. *Hendricks House* 1946 1957 1962 $6.50. Discusses all aspects of Whitman studies.

The Times of Melville and Whitman. (Vol. 3 of "Makers and Finders".) By Van Wyck Brooks. *Dutton* 1947 Everyman's Am. ed. 1953 $3.50

A Concordance of Walt Whitman's "Leaves of Grass" and Selected Prose Writings. By Edwin Harold Eby. *Greenwood* 1950–55. Complete in I vol. 1955 $25.00. Originally printed in 5 pts. now o. p. separately.

Walt Whitman. By Frederik Schyberg. Trans. from the Danish by Evie Allison Allen. 1951. *AMS Press* $15.00.

An interesting evaluation of the poet and the man by the late Danish critic. "An excellent translation [and] an important addition to Whitman scholarship and appreciation"—(*SR*).

Whitman in Camden, April 8–Sept. 14, 1889. By Horace Traubel. Ed. by Gertrude Traubel. (Vol. 5 of the Horace Traubel Papers.) *Southern Illinois Univ. Press* 1963 $12.50; *Rowman* 3 vols. boxed set $30.00

Walt Whitman Reconsidered. By Richard Chase 1955. *Apollo* pap. $1.65

"Impressive and extremely readable bio-critical work"—(*LJ*).

Walt Whitman. By Richard Chase. *Univ. of Minnesota Press* Pamphlets on American Writers 1961 pap. $1.25

Start with the Sun: Studies in the Whitman Tradition. By James Edwin Miller, Jr., and others. *Univ. of Nebraska Press* 1960 Bison Bks. 1963 pap. $1.50

Three authors, including Karl Shapiro and Bernice Slote, contribute separate essays on the influence of Whitman's romantic tradition on such 20th-century writers as Hart Crane, D. H. Lawrence and Dylan Thomas. Mrs. Slote's essay "manages the most effectual criticism that has been made of 'The Bridge' "—(*SR*).

The Evolution of Walt Whitman. By Roger Asselineau. Vol. I The Creation of a Personality (1960). Trans. by Richard P. Adams and the author; Vol. 2 The Creation of a Book (1962). *Harvard Univ. Press* 1960–1962 2 vols. each $11.00

The Presence of Walt Whitman: Selected Papers from the English Institute Essays, 1961. Ed. with a fwd. by R. W. B. Lewis. *Columbia* 1962 $5.50. 7 scholar-critics have "probed deeply the theory and practice of our greatest and most puzzling poet."

Whitman: A Collection of Critical Essays. Ed. by Roy Harvey Pearce. *Prentice-Hall* 1962 $5.95

Whitman, the Poet: Materials for Study. Ed. by John C. Broderick. *Wadsworth* 1962 pap. $2.95

Walt Whitman. By James E. Miller, Jr. U.S. Authors Ser. *Twayne* 1962 $5.50; *College & Univ. Press* 1963 pap. $2.45. A critical and biographical study of the life and works of Whitman against the background of his time.

Whitman's "Song of Myself": Origin, Growth, Meaning. Ed. by James E. Miller, Jr. Original text (1885) and revised edition (1892) of the poem appear on facing pages. *Dodd* 1964 pap. $4.95. Includes essays by Malcolm Cowley, Roy Harvey Pearce, Randall Jarrell, Richard Chase and the editor.

Whitman: Explorations in Form. By Howard J. Waskow. *Univ. of Chicago Press* 1966 $6.95
"[A] penetrating and original work of [which] contributes more to an understanding of the form and structure of Whitman's poetry than any other work written within the last decade"—(*LJ*).

Walt Whitman's Poetry: A Psychological Journey. By Edwin H. Miller. *Houghton* Riv. Lit. 1968 pap. $4.00; *New York Univ. Press* 1969 $8.95

Walt Whitman: A Study in the Evolution of Personality. By Jan C. Smuts. Ed. with introd. by Alan L. McLeod. *Wayne State Univ. Press* 1973 $10.95

Whitman at Auction. By Gloria A. Francis. *Gale Research Co.* 1973 $25.00

DICKINSON, EMILY. 1830–1886.

Emily Dickinson is considered a very great American poet. "Wholly underivative, her poetry was unique; her influence, negligible at first, is now incalculable"—(Louis Untermeyer). Her verses are all short, but her output was large—a total of 1,775 in Johnson's definitive edition. Except for a few poems in magazines, all her work was published after her death, augmented in 1945 by the 650 poems in "Bolts of Melody." These had remained locked in a camphor wood box since 1896, when Mabel Loomis Todd abruptly ended her painstaking editorial work after the publication of "Poems, Third Series." Mrs. Todd, wife of the Professor of Astronomy at Amherst, edited the first edition of Poems in 1890 with Colonel Thomas Wentworth Higginson, a close friend of the Dickinson family, from the manuscripts she had received for the purpose from William Austin and Lavinia, the poet's brother and sister, shortly after Emily's death. Millicent Todd Bingham carried on the work after her mother died.

In 1956 Mrs. Bingham gave to Amherst College one of the largest collections of American literary material ever received by an educational institution—some 900 manuscript poems, as well as letters and notes of Emily Dickinson, correspondence of other members of the Dickinson family, Mrs. Bingham's material relating to the work on the poet, first editions of the original volumes and other Dickinson material.

Readers and critics were quick to appreciate the fine and unusual quality of the first three series of "poems" when they were first published (1890, 1891, 1896), but public taste changed and the poet's audience grew very slowly for the next 40 years. In 1924, Martha Dickinson Bianchi's "Life and Letters of Emily Dickinson" was published. It was reissued as a centennial edition in 1930. In the same year, the first "Collected Poems" and the first British "Selected Poems," with a penetrating foreword by Conrad Aiken appeared. The literary excitement revived at that time and, by further publications during 1930, the centenary year, has never abated. Now we at last have the definitive variorum edition of the "Poems" and the "Letters." "The six volumes, considered as a unit, contain every word, including prose fragments, that Emily Dickinson is known to have written"—(*N.Y. Times*).

Emily's mysterious seclusion and the confused controversial problems of her life and her family have been the subject of speculation by many of the admirers of her poetry. Her letters as well as her poems reveal her true world, "enriched by her books and a captivating intimacy with nature." Nature, Love and Death were her great themes. Her poems are as "varied, as baffling as was she" and illustrate her love of words, "her insurgent imagination, her unconventional use of rhyme, her audacious experimentation with form and assonance"—(Josephine Pollitt). Most of her poems are short, most lyrical, with the intellectual precision (in Emily's case, rhymed and metered) of the modern Marianne Moore (*q. v.*). Her birthplace in Amherst was named a National Historic Landmark in 1964.

Two dramatic portrayals of Emily Dickinson were presented on the New York stage in the winter of 1966. In the one-woman show "Past Midnight! Past the Morning Star!" Julia Beals played Emily as a "repressed and slightly stiff spinster whose poems were a safety valve for emotions she was otherwise powerless to express."—(*N.Y. Times*). Kim Hunter, in "Come Slowly, Eden," revealed a vigorous, vibrant Emily—"She was the Emily that Emily should have been"—(*N.Y. Times*). The next year Archibald MacLeish (*q. v.*) published (in *SR*, Oct. 28, 1967) "Magic Prison," a "dialogue for music" commissioned by André Kostelanetz and first performed by him with the New York Philharmonic at Lincoln Center in 1967. In introducing it, MacLeish wrote: "The two speakers are Emily Dickinson, as she was in her thirties in the 1860s, and her friend and correspondent, Col. Thomas Wentworth Higginson. Higginson, a cousin of the founder of the Boston Symphony Orchestra, was a Cambridge-born Unitarian minister, abolitionist, soldier, and magazine contributor well known for his generosity to the young. The text is drawn from Emily's poems and from an essay of Higginson's in *The Atlantic Monthly* in 1891." Higginson provided one of the few opportunities for guesswork about a possible romance in Emily's outwardly narrow life at Amherst.

THE POEMS OF EMILY DICKINSON: Including Variant Readings Critically Compared with All Known Manuscripts. Ed. by Thomas H. Johnson. *Harvard Univ. Press.* Belknap Press 1955 3 vols. $30.00

This is the definitive edition. "It is not only a major work of scholarship; it is a monument in American literature"—(*N.Y. Times*). "Nearly seventy years after her death, we finally know what Emily Dickinson really wrote, and how she wrote it. In this noble edition, every recoverable word of her poetry is set down precisely as she left it; the unique genius who shares with Whitman the primacy among our nineteenth-century poets is revealed in the full stature"—(*N.Y. Herald Tribune*).

THE COMPLETE POEMS OF EMILY DICKINSON. Ed. by Thomas H. Johnson. *Little* 1960 $15.00

This is the first single-volume collection of all 1775 poems in chronological arrangement. It should become the basic and definitive reading text. The editor of the three-volume critical variorum edition (*see above*) has selected but one form of each poem, omitting the variant readings. The poems are now as Emily wrote them, "with corrections going only so far as misspellings, and misplaced apostrophes"—"the breathless punctuation and unorthodox scattering of capitals are retained." It has been said that this "volume becomes more than just a collection; it is at the same time a poetic biography of the thoughts and feelings of a woman whose beauty was deep and lasting."

FINAL HARVEST: EMILY DICKINSON'S POEMS. Sel. and with introd. by Thomas H. Johnson. *Little* 1962 $6.95 pap. $2.45. This selection of 575 poems by the editor of the two definitive editions above may now be regarded as the preferred one-volume edition. Without the variant readings and notes which were in the three volume work, this text and punctuation must now be accepted as standard: the poems appear as she wrote them.

THE POEMS OF EMILY DICKINSON. Ed. by Martha Dickinson Bianchi and Alfred Leete Hampson. *Little* 1930 new ed. 1937 $7.50. A collected edition including the 131 poems in the "Unpublished Poems" (o. p.) and earlier separate edition 1890–1937.

POEMS, 1890–1896. *Scholar's Facsimiles* 1967 3 vols in 1 $20.00. A reproduction of the original volumes issued in 1890, 1891, 1896, with an introduction by George Monteiro.

BOLTS OF MELODY: New Poems. Ed. by Mabel Loomis Todd and Millicent Todd Bingham. *Harper* 1945 $6.50; *Dover* pap. $3.00. Over 650 new poems, published here for the first time, composed largely of the poet's mature work; excellent editing with sympathetic understanding; facsimile pages.

SELECTED POEMS. Ed. by James Reeves *Barnes & Noble* 1966 $2.00; ed. by Richard Wilbur and John Brinnin *Dell* pap. $.40; introd. by Conrad Aiken. *Modern Library* 1948 $2.95

FOURTEEN BY EMILY DICKINSON: With Selected Criticism. Ed. by Thomas M. Davis. *Scott, Foresman* 1964 pap. $3.50

POEMS. Comp. by Helen Plotz; ill. by Robert Kipniss. *Crowell* 1964 $3.50 lib. bdg. $4.25

POEMS FOR YOUTH. Ed. by Alfred Leete Hampson. *Little* 1934 $4.50

SELECTED POEMS AND LETTERS. Ed. by Robert N. Linscott. *Doubleday* Anchor Bks. 1959 pap. $2.50

AMAZING SENSE: Selected Poems and Letters. Ed. by J. R. Vitelli. 1966 *Verry* $2.50

A LETTER TO THE WORLD. Ed. by Rumer Godden 1969 *Macmillan* $3.95

LAST FACE: Emily Dickinson's Manuscripts. Ed. by Edith Wylder. *Univ. of New Mexico Press* 1971 $6.00

SELECTED LETTERS. Ed. By Thomas H. Johnson *Harvard Univ. Press* 1970 $10.00

THE LETTERS OF EMILY DICKINSON. Ed. by Thomas H. Johnson; Theodora Ward, Associate Ed. *Harvard Univ. Press* 1958 3 vols. boxed $30.00. 1049 letters, addressed to some hundred-odd recipients, arranged chronologically to cover her life from age 11.

EMILY DICKINSON FACE TO FACE: The Unpublished Letters, with Reminiscences and Notes by Her Niece. Ed. by Martha Dickinson Bianchi. 1932. *Shoe String* 1970 $10.00

THE LIFE AND LETTERS OF EMILY DICKINSON. By Martha Dickinson Bianchi. 1924 1930. *Biblo & Tannen* $12.50

Books about Dickinson

Ancestors' Brocades: The Literary Discovery of Emily Dickinson, the Editing and Publication of Her Letters and Poems. By Millicent Todd Bingham. 1945. *Dover* 1967 pap. $3.50; *Peter Smith* $5.00. The major source of information about the emergence of Emily Dickinson as a poet. Documented with poems, letters, reviews and personal recollections.

Emily Dickinson. By Richard Chase. 1951. *Greenwood* $13.50

Emily Dickinson's Home: The Early Years, As Revealed in Family Correspondence and Reminiscences. By Millicent Todd Bingham. 1955. *Dover* 1967 pap. $3.50; *Peter Smith* $5.00. This study aids in dispelling the many myths about Emily Dickinson.

Emily Dickinson: An Interpretive Biography. By Thomas H. Johnson. *Harvard Univ. Press* Belknap Press 1955 $7.50; *Atheneum* 1967 pap. $3.45. Mr. Johnson, editor of the three-volume variorum edition of the poems, has expanded his preface for this "reliable, scholarly—and fascinating" biography.

Emily Dickinson's Poetry: Stairway of Surprise. By Charles Roberts Anderson. *Holt* 1960 $6.95. "The first sustained book-length study of Emily Dickinson's poetry that seems wholly adequate" is penetrating and discriminating. Anderson selects 25 poems as "great ones" for line-by-line analysis.

The Years and Hours of Emily Dickinson. By Jay Leyda. 1960. *Shoe String* 1970 2 vols. set $27.50. This documentary biography, a compilation of relevant materials without editorial comment is an "extraordinary, interesting and original approach" to the poet.

The Capsule of the Mind: Chapters in the Life of Emily Dickinson. By Theodora Ward. *Harvard Univ. Press* 1961 $6.00. Six essays, of which the first three deal with the poet's emotional life, and the last three discuss her friendships. "Of the many attempts to write a life," this one by the editor associated with T. H. Johnson "has the richest sources and the best authority."

Emily Dickinson: A Collection of Critical Essays. Ed. by Richard B. Sewall. *Prentice-Hall* 1963 $5.95 Spectrum Bks. pap. $1.95

The Recognition of Emily Dickinson. Ed. by Caesar R. Blake and Carlton F. Wells. *Univ. of Michigan Press* 1964 $7.50 Ann Arbor Bks. pap. $2.45

   A selection of critical essays spanning the past 70 years by American and British writers. "The editors . . . serve as guides not only to the evolution of her reputation but to a better understanding of her poetry"—(*LJ*). Among those included are Thomas Wentworth Higginson, Conrad Aiken, Sir Herbert Read and Thomas Johnson.

Emily Dickinson: The Mind of the Poet. By Albert Gelpi. *Harvard Univ. Press* 1965 $5.75; *Norton* 1971 pap. $1.85 "Mr. Gelpi performs well in considering the poet in the overall context of American literature. . . . His chapter entitled 'The Flower, the Bee, and the Spider: The Aesthetics of Consciousnes' is a brilliant statement in itself of what constitutes poetry"—(*LJ*).

A Concordance to the Poems of Emily Dickinson. Ed. by Stanford P. Rosenbaum. *Cornell Univ. Press* 1965 $13.50

The Lyman Letters: New Light on Emily Dickinson and Her Family. By Richard B. Sewall. *Univ. of Massachusetts Press* 1966 $5.00

The Art of Emily Dickinson's Early Poetry. By David T. Porter. *Harvard Univ. Press* 1966 $6.00

   "Mr. Porter's scholarship is admirable and makes refreshing use of some of the poet's less frequently cited poems. . . . Excellent bibliography"—(*LJ*).

Emily Dickinson's Reading: 1836–1886. By Jack L. Capps. *Harvard Univ. Press* 1966 $6.50
  A close examination of the reading matter (books, periodicals, newspapers and early school texts) available to Emily Dickinson "to further the understanding of [the poet] and her poetry"—(Jack L. Capps). "Well documented, with interesting appendixes."—(*LJ*)
Circumference and Circumstance: Stages in the Mind and Art of Emily Dickinson. By William Robert Sherwood. *Columbia* 1967 $10.00
Portrait of Emily Dickinson: The Poet and Her Prose. By David Higgins. *Rutgers Univ. Press* 1967 $7.50
  "A solid work of scholarship, carefully documented, that is based in large part on the letters of Emily Dickinson and those of her family and friends"—(*LJ*).
The Editing of Emily Dickinson: A Reconsideration. By R. W. Franklin. *Univ. of Wisconsin Press* 1967 $10.00. A technical study of the 19th- and 20th-century editions of Emily Dickinson's poems, describing certain inaccuracies. The author discusses the problems involved in editing Dickinson manuscripts.
After Great Pain: The Inner Life of Emily Dickinson. By John Cody. *Harvard Univ. Press* 1971 $14.95

LANIER, SIDNEY. 1842–1881.

Lanier is the foremost poet of the South. He volunteered for the Confederate Army, served and was taken prisoner. He was made lecturer on English in Johns Hopkins University in 1879. He died at an early age and left a slender volume of verse. His great poem, "The Marshes of Glynn," "a symphony without musical score," won him the title of "the poet of the marshes." "He had a profound knowledge of the analogies between poetry and music and applied musical theory to his own verse. He left behind him no really finished work; he is a poet of magnificent fragments. He was too excited, too impetuous to finish anything." Lanier wrote works of criticism on English literature and edited "The Boy's Froissart" in 1879, and in the following year the best selling "The Boy's King Arthur" (ill. by N. C. Wyeth *Scribner* Ill. Class $6.00 pap. $3.95). His first publication was a novel, "Tiger Lilies" (1867. *Univ. of North Carolina Press* 1969 pap. $2.95). His lectures of 1879 at the Johns Hopkins University were published as "The Science of English Verse" (1880. *Folcroft* 1973 lib. bdg. $25.00); in it he maintained that the artistic laws governing music and poetry were the same. Some of his later lectures at Johns Hopkins were published as "The English Novel" (1883, o. p.) and "Shakespeare and His Forerunners" (1902 1908. *AMS Press* 2 vols set $18.00; *Somerset Pub.* repr. of 1908 ed. 2 vols. in 1 $19.50; *Richard West* repr. of 1902 2 vols. set $24.95 repr. of 1908 ed. 2 vols in 1 $19.45).

THE CENTENNIAL EDITION OF THE WORKS OF SIDNEY LANIER. Under the general editorship of Charles R. Anderson. *Johns Hopkins Univ. Press* 1945 10 vols. Vol. I Poems and Poem Outlines Vol. 2 The Science of English Verse and Essays on Music ed. by Paull F. Baum Vol. 3 Shakespeare and His Forerunners ed. by Kemp Malone Vol. 4 The English Novel and Essays on Literature ed. by Clarence Gohdes and Kemp Malone Vol. 5 Tiger Lilies and Southern Prose ed. by Garland Greever and Cecil Abernethy Vol. 6 Florida and Miscellaneous Prose ed. by Philip Graham Vols. 7–10 Letters ed. by Charles R. Anderson and Aubrey H. Starke each $12.00

POEMS. Ed. by Mary Lanier. 1884. *Univ. of Georgia Press* 1944 $5.00

POEMS AND LETTERS. Ed. by Charles R. Anderson. *Johns Hopkins Univ. Press* 1970 $8.00 pap. $2.95

Books about Lanier

Sidney Lanier. By Edwin Mims. 1905. *Gordon Press* $11.25; *Kennikat* $11.00
Sidney Lanier: A Biographical and Critical Study. By Aubrey H. Starke. 1933. *Russell & Russell* 1964 $11.50
Concordance to the Poems of Sidney Lanier, including the Poem Outlines and Some Uncollected Items. By Philip Graham and Joseph Jones. 1939. *Johnson Reprint* 1969 lib. bdg. $25.00
Sidney Lanier, the Man the Poet and the Critic. By Edd W. Parks. *Univ. of Georgia Press* 1968 $4.00
Sidney Lanier. By Jack DeBellis. U.S. Authors Ser. *Twayne* $5.50

RILEY, JAMES WHITCOMB. 1849–1916.

Poet, lecturer and journalist, Riley gained popularity with his series of poems in the Hoosier dialect written under the pseudonym "Benjamin F. Johnson of Boone." These originally appeared in the Indianapolis *Journal*, where he worked from 1877 to 1885; in 1883 they were published as " 'The Old Swimmin'-Hole' and ' 'Leven More Poems.' " Riley went on numerous lecture tours, entertaining as an actor and humorist. Although best known for his dialect poetry—"comforting, familiar platitudes restated in verse" (Richard Crowder)—he also wrote humorous sketches and other poems.

COMPLETE WORKS. Ed. by Edmund Henry Eitel. 6 vols. 1913. *AMS Press* 6 vols. each
$25.00 set $145.00. The Works are arranged in the order in which they were written, with photographs, bibliographical notes and a sketch of Riley's life.

COMPLETE POETICAL WORKS. Pref. by Donald Culross Peattie. *Grosset* 1950 $6.95

BEST LOVED POEMS. *Grosset* 1932 1953 $2.95

JOYFUL POEMS FOR CHILDREN. Ill. by Sally Tate. *Bobbs* 1946 $3.75

A CHILD-WORLD. 1896. *Bks. for Libraries* $9.50

RILEY CHILD-RHYMES. 1899. *Bks. for Libraries* $7.75

BOOK OF JOYOUS CHILDREN. 1902 *Bks. for Libraries* $8.50

LETTERS OF JAMES WHITCOMB RILEY. Ed. by William Lyon Phelps. 1930. *AMS Press*
$15.00

LOVE LETTERS OF A BACHELOR POET, James Whitcomb Riley to Miss Elizabeth
Kahle. 1922. *Gordon Press* $11.00

Books about Riley

Bibliography of James Whitcomb Riley. By Anthony and Dorothy Russo. 1944. *Haskell* 1972 lib. bdg.
$15.95
James Whitcomb Riley. By Peter Revell. U.S. Authors Ser. *Twayne* $5.50

FIELD, EUGENE. 1850–1895.

Eugene Field was born in Missouri, and there served his apprenticeship as a journalist. In 1882 he joined
the staff of the Denver *Tribune* as a columnist, and in 1883 he began the column "Sharps and Flats" for the
Chicago *Daily News*. His poems are simple dialect sketches (sometimes the dialect is an imaginary one), fairy
tales, fables and pictures of home life. He is now best known as a children's poet. "Wynken, Blynken and
Nod" and "Little Blue Boy" were set to music by Reginald DeKoven and Ethelbert Nevin. "Wynken, Blynken, and Nod" and "The Gingham Dog and the Calico Cat" are still perennial favorites. Many of his publi-
cations are collections of his newspaper contributions: "The Complete Tribune Primer" (*Dillon Press*
1967 $4.95), "A Little Book of Profitable Tales" (1889. *Bks. for Libraries* $8.75), "With Trumpet and
Drum" (1892. *Bks. for Libraries* $6.50), "Holy Cross and Other Tales" (1893. *Bks. for Libraries* $8.75) and
"The Love Affairs of a Bibliomaniac" (1896. *Richard West* $10.00). The latter reflected his devotion to
McClurg's rare book department, which he named "The Saints and Sinners Corner."

THE EUGENE FIELD BOOK. Ed. by Mary E. Burt and Mary B. Cable. 1898. *Bks. for
Libraries* $6.50

LOVE SONGS OF CHILDHOOD. 1894. *Bks. for Libraries* $6.00

POEMS OF CHILDHOOD. Ill. by Maxfield Parrish. *Scribner* 1904 Ill. Class. $6.00; *Assoc.
Booksellers* Airmont Bks. pap. $.60

THE GINGHAM DOG AND THE CALICO CAT. Ill. by Helen Page. *Follett* 1945 $1.00

WYNKEN, BLYNKEN AND NOD. Ill. by Helen Page. *Follett* 1945 $1.00; *Hale* 1956 lib.
bdg. $2.97; *Hastings* 1970 lib. bdg. $4.25

Books about Field

Eugene Field's Creative Years. by Charles H. Dennis. 1924. *Scholarly Press* $19.50

—J.M.C.

Chapter 9

Modern American Poetry

"Every generation accumulates a store of verbal fat—the euphemisms of hypocrisy, the clichés of servility and status-seeking, the imprecisions of lazy thinking—which serves to clog the arteries of feeling like cholesterol and dims the mind trying to observe and understand. Poets burn away the corruptions of fat thinking and feeling with exact phrases and fresh metaphors that may strike the reader, at first, as strange and even obscure. In reality they serve an important public function in maintaining the vitality of the language and the morality of the state."
—STEPHEN STEPANCHEV
"To write badly is an offense to the state since the government can never be more than the government of words. If the language is distorted crime flourishes."
—WILLIAM CARLOS WILLIAMS

During the past 60 years two movements have dominated American poetry. Traditionalism, the search for a primarily literary mainstream on which to launch the vessel of American poetry, as found in the works of T. S. Eliot and the New Critics; and Experimentalism, with its quest for a truly American culture and poetic language, as in the works of Ezra Pound and particularly William Carlos Williams. While Eliot, the New Critics, and to a lesser extent Ezra Pound provided the main impetus to the increasingly obscure academic poetry which developed during the forties and fifties, becoming the crux of American poetry courses in the universities, Williams and Pound became the forefathers of the current upsurge of a new, primarily oral, tradition.

So much has been written about both movements that we shall only discuss those elements of the latter as they relate to current trends. Should the reader wish to pursue the study of poetry in this century, numerous books are listed in the History and Criticism section of this chapter which give introductory and in depth treatment of the subject.

Since the last edition of *"The Reader's Adviser,"* poetry continues to flourish in the midst of general economic decline in the publishing industry. The real poetry boom exists these days in the underground. The most creative poetry surfaces primarily in inexpensive, often beautifully produced small press books and little magazines, printed and published very often by the poets themselves. The plethora of styles and poetic schools existing together, sometimes within the covers of the same anthology, is astounding: it points dramatically to the current vitality of the American poetry "industry."

The single most pervasive influence on this underground poetry has been the work of William Carlos Williams. Williams' intense struggle with the language of poetry, which characterized his entire career, resulted in a medium richer in both oral and aural possibilities. Williams himself was not primarily an "oral" poet. It was only toward the end of his lifetime that America became obsessed with poetry readings, with the figure of the poet not as a hidden, secretive scribe, but as a kind of preacher, teacher or entertainer. Dylan Thomas was the single *raison d'etre* for the sudden revival of interest in the oral presentation of poetry. But it was Williams' lifelong simplification of poetic language that made such oral presentation endemic to American poetry. Rhetoric in poetry does not appeal to the American public, unused to the more flamboyant and studied idiom of even modern English verse. An American audience, in love with the romantic/tragic figure of Dylan Thomas, needed to understand and sympathize with the poetry it heard in order to continue to support it.

In 1960 the anthology which was to become a literary landmark in post-World War II poetry made its appearance. "The New American Poetry," edited by Donald Allen, presented for the first time a selection of poets, from diverse movements or schools, who held one thing in common: they spoke less obscurely and in a more familiar language than the academicians bred by the New Criticism, then dominant in the poetry world. Allen's anthology included seminal statements on poetics, not by critics, but by the contributors— this in itself being against the predominating trends. It was a lively and protean assemblage. From the Black Mountain School were found Charles Olson, Paul Blackburn, Robert Creeley, Edward Dorn, Denise Levertov. From the New York School Allen chose Frank O'Hara, Kenneth Koch, James Schuyler. The Beats and the closely allied San Francisco poets, including Lawrence Ferlinghetti, Allen Ginsberg, Brother Antoninus (William Everson), LeRoi Jones, Lew Welch, Gregory Corso, Gary Snyder, and others, were best represented.

As Allen pointed out in his introduction to this work, the poets selected all owed literary debts to Pound and Williams. Yet since the anthology's appearance in 1960, the Pound-influenced poetry in some of the same poets' work has dwindled. Olson's "The King-fishers" is more obscure, in spite of its projective verse, than any poetry in the most contemporary tradition. The poets who in practice, not in theory, were to become some of the leading spokesmen of the next generation were the Beats. The Beats, alienated from society, spoke brazenly and boldly about the discrepencies between American ideals and American realities. Drawing from Whitman's idealism they saw themselves as American visionaries and priests. They dared attack the sacred cows that poets and public had ignored, or bowed down to, since the McCarthyism of the early fifties. They also spoke with a zest for life that was immediately communicable to cheering audiences. Their mood and their lifestyle, their poetry, was like their music, the "bop" of Charlie Parker and his contemporaries. Racing back and forth across the country, by car, by railroad and by thumb, they gathered in New York or San Francisco, sharing their work with all in readings not dissimilar in tone to a jam session.

During the sixties, the movement toward a more oral poetry retracted a bit to the underground as the Beats were temporarily forgotten. Yet in the poetry of Robert Bly and the Deep Image School, disparate elements of Pound, Williams, Olson and Beat poetics melded. This meld in turn was wedded to the European Surrealist tradition from which Bly and his followers published numerous translations in his *Fifties, Sixties* and now *Seventies* magazine. Neruda, Vallejo, Machado, Desnos, Prevert, Reverdy, Quasimodo and Serini, all major figures in European literature, began to dominate American poetry. The work of the Deep Image School, though in part a continuance of the academic poetic tradition of the fifties, is actually quite dissimilar. Robert Bly popularized the school, mostly through his intense belief in the vatic tradition. He became one of the leading antiwar spokesmen, and his readings, as those of W. S. Merwin and James Wright, communicated the irregular pulse of the times to a broad American public.

During the sixties another force was at work feeding the movement toward a more oral verse. The folk music revival beginning in the late fifties, brought to the attention of a sizeable audience, including younger poets, the work of Woody Guthrie and Bob Dylan. The Dust Bowl ballads of the former opened the road to a more socially conscious yet natively American political poetry. Dylan's song/poems have spoken to whole generations of Americans about the life within and outside of them, in some of the most immediate poetry of the century. (*See* "The Writings and Drawings of Bob Dylan," *Knopf* 1973 $6.95.)

The first artists of the new minstrelsy among poets were the younger black writers, soon followed by their already established black elders like Gwendolyn Brooks and LeRoi Jones. With their determination to find a purely black literary idiom the poets turned toward the popular music and street culture of their own people. Street poetry is not a new phenomenon, and its emergence into the mainstream of literature may mean the recognition of some hitherto unknown major underground figures. Chief among these is Charles Bukowski, whose poetry, dating from the mid-fifties, is a paradigm of street "poetics": nonliterary, spontaneous, primarily oral in nature, free-formed, open to any subject perceivable to the poet.

Now that the century is nearly midway into its seventh decade, it becomes increasingly clear which two forces have contested to dominate an emerging American poetic. The traditionalism of the twenties, thirties, forties and fifties is, at least temporarily, fading away. The seventies have eagerly embraced the poetics of the moment; there is a sense of immediacy in the times and in the poetry. Truth must be accessible to the reader/listener of poetry and this truth is exchanged in a direct relationship between poet and audience. The current poetry movement reflects the times and often seems fevered and hyperactive. Poetry readings are no longer limited to the campus circuit but occur in economically and culturally deprived areas, small town public schools, prisons, Indian reservations and urban ghettos. In New York City alone numerous experiments designed to bring the poet to the public are taking place: there have been poetry readings in Battery Park during lunch hour, videotaped memorial readings for the anniversary of the Brooklyn Bridge, and poetry workshops in public libraries for children throughout the city.

Poetry has become a gift again—a way for the minstrel to win his bread. Something once again like a freely given folk song or tale, pertinent to the listeners because they know the story already, because it has happened in their town or world. The poet in the midst of this protean involvement must himself evolve a protean aesthetic, if he is to remain accessible to the people of his time. There are great dangers involved: the cheapening of the form as a result of its becoming a commodity in our commodity-oriented culture, and the possibility of success being determined by how the poet speaks rather than by the truth he struggles to utter. It is very difficult for a poet to speak the truth and at the same time speak it in the language of common, imprecise, everyday untruthful perceptions. Yet if one can judge by some of the younger poets represented here, many are trying desperately to be free of form, tradition and habit, to speak what they feel is true, and to speak it more clearly. There is an immediacy and life in the work of most young poets that resists categorization, the only one being, perhaps, their constant search for truth. Sometimes this search has taken the writers in the direction of primitive cultures. Jerome Rothenberg has indicated to vast audiences at his readings and chantings how the poet must seek in some sense the primitive and ritualistic, must become the spokesman for his own tribe. Sometimes this search leads to the shoals of politics where only the most talented and astute self-critics can hope to speak out for the poor and oppressed of all times, without resort to imitative and garbled rhetoric. Sometimes this search leads to new forms, expressing more fully the poet's experience of truth. Thus throughout the century the long poem or epic has undergone constant transformation and renewal, moving from the grandiose intellectual beauty of the Cantos to the newer lyricism of Harrison's or Kinnell's or Levendosky's recent book-length works.

Whatever direction this search for an accessible poetic medium may take, the fact that the poet desires to speak to his fellow man more universally is one of the most optimistic trends in all American literature. No longer is the comprehension of beauty to be limited to an intellectual elite. At last there is a seed in American poetry, which if valued and tended, is capable of growth toward the betterment of our whole culture.

This chapter in no way pretends to be a complete listing of all the poets who have or are contributing to the body of American poetry. Many writers have had to be omitted who probably would have been included had the space and scope of this volume permitted. We have tried to reflect a broad range of trends and styles in the new additions to this chapter, often putting aside poets whose work might have been included for those who seem to typify a particular phase of poetry. Lastly this guide is intended to encourage the poetry-lover, student, bookstore, or librarian to begin the study and collection of an art capable of bringing deep and lasting rewards.

HISTORY AND CRITICISM

There are a number of anthologies which contain biographical material and extensive commentary. For these, see the list of Collections following this one.

Allen, Don Cameron, Ed. THE MOMENT OF POETRY. (The 1961 Percy Graeme Turnbull Memorial Lectures on Poetry.) *Johns Hopkins Univ. Press* 1962 $7.50. Five distinguished poet-professors (May Sarton, Richard Eberhart, Richard Wilbur, Randall Jarrell and John Holmes) speak here about the craft to which they have devoted their lives.

Allen, Donald M. and Warren Tallman, Eds. THE POETICS OF THE NEW AMERICAN POETRY. A definitive collection of statements by 25 major poets. 1960 *Grove* 1973 $10.00 pap. $3.95

Bigsby, C. W. E. THE BLACK AMERICAN WRITER. Vol. 2 Poetry and Drama. 1969 *Everett Edwards* $20.00; *Penguin* Pelican Bks. 1971 $1.45. Short essays by various writers grouped into poets and dramatists. Langston Hughes and Gwendolyn Brooks are among the poets discussed.

Bogan, Louise. ACHIEVEMENT IN AMERICAN POETRY, 1900–1950. *Regnery* Twentieth-Century Lit. in America 1951 1956 pap. $1.25

Bontemps, Arna, Ed. THE HARLEM RENAISSANCE REMEMBERED: Essays Edited with a Memoir. *Dodd* 1972 $6.95. Essays are by George Kent, Hiroko Sato, Patricia E. Taylor, Ronald Primeau and others. The Harlem Renaissance and its major writers are discussed in depth. A necessary book for those interested in black studies and black poetry as well as in the history of American poetry. Notes and bibliographies are included.

Burden, Jean. JOURNEY TOWARD POETRY. *October House* 1966 $5.95 pap. $2.95

Cambon, Glauco. THE INCLUSIVE FLAME: Studies in American Poetry. *Indiana Univ. Press* 1964 Midland Bks. pap. $2.45; *Peter Smith* $5.00

   "An exceedingly interesting and provocative study of American poetry written by an Italian scholar"—(*LJ*).

Carroll, Paul. THE POEM IN ITS SKIN. A Big Table Book *Follett* $5.95 pap. $3.95. Critical essays on the important poets who came to prominence in the sixties: Ashbery, Creeley, Dickey, Isabella Gardner, Ginsberg, Logan, Merwin, Frank O'Hara, W. D. Snodgrass and James Wright.

Charters, Samuel. SOME POEMS AND SOME POETS: Studies in American Underground Poetry Since 1945. Ill. with photographs. *Oyez* 1971 $5.95 pap. $2.95. A readable and perceptive group of essays on Jack Spicer, Robert Duncan, Brother Antoninus (William Everson) Larry Eigner, Allen Ginsberg, Lawrence Ferlinghetti, Lew Welch, Charles Olson, Robert Creeley and Gary Snyder.

The Chicago Review. ANTHOLOGY OF CONCRETISM. Ed. by Eugene Wildman. *Swallow* 1967 $7.50 pap. $2.50. An international movement now in vogue in the United States, "concretism" presents poetry in graphic design. "The medium is the message."

Cook, Bruce. THE BEAT GENERATION: The Tumultuous '50's Movement and Its Impact on Today. *Scribner* 1971 Lyceum Eds. pap. $2.45

An illuminating study of the "beatnik" poets and writers, which links that movement with the more recent hippie revolution. "A first-rate piece of literary journalism. . ."—(*Look*)

Cowan, Louise. THE FUGITIVE GROUP: A Literary History. *Louisiana State Univ. Press* 1959 $7.50 pap. text ed. $2.45. An examination of the poets who published in *The Fugitive* in Nashville in the early 1920s: Ransom, Donald Davidson, Allen Tate and Robert Penn Warren. The appendix lists the contents of *The Fugitive.*

Cowley, Malcolm. EXILE'S RETURN: A Literary Odyssey of the 1930's. 1934. *Viking* Compass Bks. 1956 pap. $2.25

"Far and away the best book about this generation by a participant. . ."—(Arthur Mizener). An excellent reminiscence and study of Pound, Crane, Cummings and others.

Day, A. Grove. THE SKY CLEARS: Poetry of the American Indians. 1951 *Univ. of Nebraska Press* 1964 Bison Bks. pap. $1.75. A discussion for the general reader of the best translations of American Indian poetry. Generous quotes from poems. Bibliography.

Dembo, L. S. CONCEPTIONS OF REALITY IN MODERN AMERICAN POETRY. *Univ. of California Press* 1968 $8.50

Dickey, James. BABEL TO BYZANTIUM: Poets and Poetry Now. *Farrar, Straus* 1968 $6.95 *Grosset* Univ. Lib. 1971 pap. $2.95; *Octagon* 1973 $10.95

A successor to Mr. Dickey's "The Suspect in Poetry" (1964, o.p.), this presents a series of his essays (many previously published in magazines) on some 60 contemporary poets and the poet-critic's appraisal of his own life and work. "James Dickey is remarkable among critics for his consuming, and even cauterizing, love of the art of poetry. What makes him more than remarkable—what makes him unique—is the fact that his conception of poetry allows for an art other than his own"—(Richard Howard). The book is stringent but has unity and shows a clear mind at work.

Duberman, Martin B. BLACK MOUNTAIN: An Experiment in Community. *Dutton* 1972 $12.95; *Doubleday* Anchor Bks. 1973 $4.95. This history of the 23-year existence of the experimental artistic community in North Carolina is an essential work for students of the literature, and all the other arts, of this century. Particularly pertinent to the study of Olson and the other poets involved in and influenced by Black Mountain College.

Frohock, W. M. STRANGERS TO THIS GROUND: Cultural Diversity in Contemporary American Writing. *Southern Methodist Univ. Press* 1961 $4.95. A native New Englander and, since 1956, a member of the Department of Romance Languages at Harvard, the critic presents here a fresh evaluation, which aims at proving there is still considerable cultural diversity in the United States. Among the authors examined are Emily Dickinson, Edna St. Vincent Millay and Ezra Pound. Original concepts and a witty, vigorous style recommend this to the intelligent general reader.

Fussell, Edwin. LUCIFER IN HARNESS: American Meter, Metaphor and Diction. *Princeton Univ. Press* 1973 $9.50. A surprisingly clearly written book pivotal to the understanding of the forms and apparent "formlessness" of American poetics in this century. The discussion centers around Williams, Pound, Crane, and Eliot and their relentless pursuit of a truly American, as opposed to English, diction and speech in the language of their poetry.

Gayle, Addison. Jr. THE BLACK AESTHETIC. *Doubleday* Anchor Bk. pap. $2.50

"... some of the best writing there is on some of the most explosive ideas black people have had ..."— (*N.Y. Times*). Essays contributed by Langston Hughes, LeRoi Jones and Ishmael Reed among others. Bibliography included. Covers other arts: music, drama and fiction.

Gibson, Donald B. MODERN BLACK POETS: A Collection of Critical Essays. Twentieth Century Views Ser. *Prentice-Hall* 1973 $5.95 Spectrum Bks. pap. $1.95

These critical essays are an example of the excellent Twentieth Century Views series. "[This is an] anthology of criticism tracing the growing unity of black poetry as a distinct body of American Literature. . . . From the Harlem Renaissance of the 1920's to the black rage of the 1970's . . ."—(*Booklist*).

Holmes, John. WRITING POETRY. *The Writer* 1960 $8.95

Howard, Richard. ALONE WITH AMERICA: Essays on the Art of Poetry in the United States since 1950. *Atheneum* 1969 $12.95 pap. 1971 $4.95. This excellent collection is of immense value to all librarians and students of contemporary poetry since in most cases it provides the only readily available critical guidance and approach to a whole generation of poets including A.R. Ammons, James Wright, James Dickey, John Logan, Mark Strand, Anne Sexton and 35 others.

Hungerford, Edward B., Ed. POETS IN PROGRESS: Critical Prefaces to Ten Contemporary Americans. *Northwestern Univ. Press* 1962 pap. $3.50. Comments by ten critics, who quote, then note, so that poem and judgment come to the reader together. Ten critical essays from the *TriQuarterly* at Northwestern on Roethke, Lowell, Kunitz, Wilbur, Eberhart, Snodgrass, Nemerov, Cunningham, Jarrell and Merwin.

Jones, Howard Mumford, and Richard M. Ludwig. GUIDE TO AMERICAN LITERATURE AND ITS BACKGROUNDS SINCE 1890. *Harvard Univ. Press* 1964 4th ed. rev. and enl. 1972 $10.00 pap. $2.95. A selected bibliography and outline of American literature since 1890 in its intellectual, social and cultural context. Useful to any student of this century's literature.

Kherdian, David. SIX POETS OF THE SAN FRANCISCO RENAISSANCE: Portraits and Checklists. Introd. by William Saroyan. *The Giligia Press* (4524 E. Illinois Ave., Fresno, Calif. 93702) 1967 $17.50 pap. $1.95

Lawrence Ferlinghetti, Gary Snyder, David Meltzer, Phillip Whalen, Michael McClure and Brother Antoninus; for each there is a thorough bibliography and "well-written description delightfully styled to the individual poet"—(*LJ*).

Lee, Don L. DYNAMITE VOICES: Black Poets of the 1960's. *Broadside Press* 1971 pap. $2.75. One of the major black poets discusses the direction and aim of the black literature critic and then comments on the work of 14 young poets, including Nikki Giovanni, Sonia Sanchez, Etheridge Knight, David Henderson and Carolyn Rodgers. A seminal book in the contemporary black poetry movement.

Mills, Ralph J., Jr. CONTEMPORARY AMERICAN POETRY. 1958. *Random* 1965 pap. $2.95

"Ralph Mills boldly enters the perilous, unmarked area of writings by living poets, who haven't yet been safely judged or evaluated. What he so subtly says about them is fresh, knowledgeable, persuasive, the result of familiarity with modern poets in several languages. An excellent guide to twelve poets born between 1904 and 1928"—(Richard Ellmann).

Moore, Marianne. PREDILECTIONS. *Viking* 1955 $3.50. Among the poets included in these brief critical essays are her favorite fellow poets, Stevens, Eliot, Pound, Cummings and Auden.

Nemerov, Howard. POETS ON POETRY. *Basic Bks.* 1966 $5.95. Nineteen poets, including Conrad Aiken, Marianne Moore, Richard Eberhart, J. V. Cunningham, John Berryman, Vassar Miller, Robert Duncan, Gregory Corso and James Dickey, answer questions posed by Nemerov about the nature of modern poetry and their personal views on it. A fascinating book which is an asset to the library of every writer and poetry lover.

O'Connor, W. V. SENSE AND SENSIBILITY IN MODERN POETRY. 1948. *Gordian* 1972 $9.00

Ossman, David. THE SULLEN ART: Interviews with Modern American Poets: Kenneth Rexroth, Paul Carroll, Paul Blackburn, Jerome Rothenberg, Robert Kelly, Robert Bly, John Logan, Gilbert Sorrentino, Robert Creeley, W. S. Merwin, Denise Levertov, LeRoi Jones, Edward Dorn, Allen Ginsberg. *Corinth Bks.* (dist. by The Book Organization) 1962 pap. $1.45

Ostroff, Anthony, Ed. THE CONTEMPORARY POET AS ARTIST AND CRITIC: Eight Symposia. *Little* 1964 pap. $4.95

"The structure of this selection of verse and commentary is both simple and instructive: for each of eight contemporary poems (most of them previously unpublished) the editor invited three other poets to write critical judgments and the author to tell as much as he could about his intention." Poems by John Crowe Ransom, Richard Wilbur, Theodore Roethke, Stanley Kunitz, Robert Lowell, Richard Eberhart, W. H. Auden and Karl Shapiro are treated. "To study this collection thoughtfully is to gain new insights into the development of poetry and criticism. . . . For the informed layman as well as the literary scholar"—(*LJ*).

Paris Review: Writers at Work. See Chapter 4, Broad Studies and General Anthologies: General Works on Writers and Writing.

Parkinson, Thomas F. A CASEBOOK ON THE BEAT. *T. Y. Crowell* 1961 pap. text ed. $3.95. This book presents, together with a selection of 39 pieces of "beat" writing, prose and poetry, a singular collection of critical comment pro and con on the beat movement. Original writings by Ferlinghetti, Snyder, Corso, Ginsberg, Kerouac and others; critical writings by Kenneth Rexroth, Henry Miller and many others. Bibliography.

Pearce, Roy Harvey. THE CONTINUITY OF AMERICAN POETRY. *Princeton Univ. Press* 1961 $11.50. A valuable study of the history of American poetry from the 17th century to the age of Eliot.

Quinn, Sister Bernetta. METAMORPHIC TRADITION IN MODERN POETRY: Essays on the Work of Ezra Pound and Other Poets. 1955. *Gordian* 1966 $8.00. Perhaps one of the best and most lucid studies of modern poetry, particularly of the contemporary epic poem (e.g. "The Cantos," "The Wasteland," "Paterson," and "The Bridge").

Rago, Henry, Ed. POETRY: The Golden Anniversary Issue. 1962. *Univ. of Chicago Press* 1967 Phoenix Poets pap. $1.95. Reissue of the popular number of this periodical.

Rexroth, Kenneth. AMERICAN POETRY IN THE TWENTIETH CENTURY. *McGraw* 1971 $5.95; *Seabury Press* 1973 $2.95. This book is very readable, eccentric, and idiosyncratic but provides an intelligent and solid picture of American poetry. Of value especially because it discusses some little-known authors and some famed ones with fresh new perceptions.

Stepanchev, Stephen. AMERICAN POETRY SINCE 1945: A Critical Survey. *Harper* 1965
    $6.95 Colophon Bks. $1.95

> "Written with verve, insight, and a merciful clarity, this excellent volume should be in high school, college,
> and any but the smallest public library"—(*LJ*).

Stewart, John L. THE BURDEN OF TIME: The Fugitives and Agrarians. *Princeton Univ.
    Press* 1965 $17.50

> The Nashville Groups of the 1920s and 1930s, and the writing of John Crowe Ransom, Allen Tate, and
> Robert Penn Warren. This book, "highly informed, based on important sources from many areas, and . . .
> written in an incisive style . . . is likely to remain a standard reference for some time to come"—(*LJ*).

Sutton, Walter. AMERICAN FREE VERSE: The Modern Revolution in Poetry. *New Direc-
    tions* 1973 $10.00 pap. $3.95. By a professor of the humanities at Syracuse Univer-
    sity, this book gives special attention to the work of Williams and Pound, as well as
    Cummings, Moore, Olson, Creeley and the Beats. A fine guide for the general reader
    as well as the student through the labyrinth of the whys and wherefores of the
    contemporary poetic medium.

Unger, Leonard, Ed. SEVEN MODERN AMERICAN POETS: An Introduction. *Univ. of Min-
    nesota Press* 1967 $8.50

> This "well-written and documented" volume comprises "seven numbers from the excellent University of
> Minnesota Pamphlets on American Writers" (Robert Frost, Wallace Stevens, William Carlos Williams,
> Ezra Pound, John Crowe Ransom, T. S. Eliot and Allen Tate). Mr. Unger "has written a fine introduction
> on modern American poetry"—(*LJ*).

UNIVERSITY OF MINNESOTA PAMPHLETS ON AMERICAN WRITERS. Ed. by William Van
    O'Connor, Allen Tate, Leonard Unger and Robert Penn Warren. 103 titles in print,
    more in prep. *Univ. of Minnesota Press* 1959—each $.95. Poets include: Frost, Wal-
    lace Stevens, Robinson, John Crowe Ransom, Ezra Pound, William Carlos Wil-
    liams, Conrad Aiken, Roethke, Tate, Robert Penn Warren, Crane, Marianne
    Moore, Eberhart.

Wagner, Jean. BLACK POETS OF THE UNITED STATES: From Paul Laurence Dunbar to
    Langston Hughes. 1963. Trans. by Kenneth Douglas. *Univ. of Illinois Press* 1973
    $15.00 pap. $5.50

Weatherhead, A. Kingsley. THE EDGE OF THE IMAGE: Marianne Moore, William Carlos
    Williams, and Some Other Poets. The others are Charles Olson, Denise Levertov
    and Robert Duncan. Modern poetry in the context of our age. *Univ. of Washington
    Press* 1967 $6.95

Whittemore, Reed. LITTLE MAGAZINES. *Univ. of Minnesota Press* 1963 pap. $.95. This is
    a general historical survey of the little poetry magazines of the early 20th century un-
    til date of this pamphlet's publication. Discusses the *Poetry* circle and Harriet Mon-
    roe as well as the Fugitive Group. A good general outline.

Wilentz, Elias, Ed. THE BEAT SCENE. Photographs by Fred McDarrah. *Corinth Bks.*
    (dist. by The Book Organization) 1960 pap. $3.50. "Without presuming to be all-in-
    clusive," the editor writes, "the attempt here is to show the new young literary world
    of New York's Greenwich Village—its writers, its parties, its readings, its *scene*. . . .
    The selection of contributions attempts to illustrate the chief currents presently evi-
    dent among these writers." Included are previously unpublished poems by Jack Ke-
    rouac, Allen Ginsberg and others.

See also lists in Chapter 7, Modern British Poetry, Chapter 4, Broad Studies and General Anthologies, and Chapter 3, Reference Books—Literature.

COLLECTIONS

Adoff, Arnold. I AM THE DARKER BROTHER: An Anthology of Modern Poems by Negro Americans. Ill. by Benny Andrews. *Macmillan* 1968 $4.95 text ed. pap. $1.88 Collier Bks. pap. $1.25

THE POETRY OF BLACK AMERICA: Anthology of the 20th Century. *Harper* 1973 $12.50. An excellent anthology—comprehensive, broad, good selections from W. E. DuBois and James Weldon Johnson through Richard Wright, Sun Ra, Imamu Amiri Baraka (LeRoi Jones) to Nikki Giovanni and Victor Hernandez Cruz.

Aíkèn, Conrad. TWENTIETH-CENTURY AMERICAN POETRY. An enlarged edition of the earlier "Modern American Poets" (1927, o.p.). *Modern Library* 1944 $2.95

Allen, Donald M. THE NEW AMERICAN POETRY, 1945-1960. *Grove* Evergreen Bks. (orig.) pap. $2.95; *Peter Smith* $5.50. An important collection of 215 poems of 44 poets, arranged to illuminate some of their differences and similarities. The preface by Mr. Allen makes one of the strongest claims yet voiced on behalf of American poetry. Included are biographies, bibliographies and statements on poetics by the poets themselves.

Anania, Michael. NEW POETRY ANTHOLOGY I. *Swallow* 1969 $6.50 pap. $2.50. Work of Dennis Schmitz, William Moebius, Peter Michelson, James McMichael, Richard Lourie, Barbara Harr, Charles Doria, and the editor.

Astrov, Margot. AMERICAN INDIAN POETRY AND PROSE: An Anthology. 1946. *John Day* 1972 $7.95; *Putnam* 1962 Capricorn Bks. pap. $2.45; *Peter Smith* $5.00; (with title "The Winged Serpent") *Fawcett* Premier 1973 pap. $.95. This reissue of the famed "Winged Serpent" anthology provides a good introduction to Indian thought and mythology.

Berg, Stephen, and S. J. Marks. ABOUT WOMEN: An Anthology of Contemporary Fiction, Poetry, and Essays. *Fawcett* Premier 1973 pap. $.95. A unique collection in that at least one of the editors is a man. Selections from Gary Snyder, Philip Levine, Louis Simpson and Stephen Berg as well as from Sylvia Plath, Muriel Rukeyser, Diane Wakoski and others.

(With Robert Mezey). NAKED POETRY: Recent American Poetry in Open Forms. *Bobbs* 1969 $8.50 pap. $2.95. An anthology of the work of 19 major poets with brief biographical sketches and photos of the poets. Includes Levertov, Creeley, Rexroth, Roethke, Patchen, Berryman and Snyder.

Bierhorst, John. IN THE TRAIL OF THE WIND: American Indian Poems and Ritual Orations. 1971. *Farrar, Straus* Noonday Bk. 1972 pap. $2.75. The introduction describes the history and origins of American Indians. Poems from many tribes are included: Zuni, Creek, Tewa, Navajo, Aztec, Arapaho and Sioux.

Bly, Robert. FORTY POEMS TOUCHING ON RECENT AMERICAN HISTORY. 1970. *Beacon* $5.95 pap. $2.45

Brandon, William. THE MAGIC WORLD: American Indian Songs and Poems. *Morrow* $6.00 pap. $2.50. A scholarly rather than general collection which seems to be well-researched. There is a discussion of themes and atmosphere and a postface giving sources.

Brooks, Gwendolyn. A BROADSIDE TREASURY, 1965–1970. *Broadside* $6.00 pap. $4.00. Poems by 50 black poets from the *Broadside Press* series. Includes work by Gwendolyn Brooks, LeRoi Jones, Nikki Giovanni, Lance Jeffers, Don L. Lee, and Sonia Sanchez among others. One of the more timely black poetry collections with good strong selection from the major young and contemporary poets.

JUMP BAD: A New Chicago Anthology, 1971. *Broadside Press* 1971 $6.00 pap. $4.00. The work of 12 black poets, essayists and fiction writers, though the emphasis is on poetry. Gwendolyn Brooks introduces this volume which includes Don L. Lee, Carol Clark, Linyatta, Mike Cook and James Cunningham among others. An interesting cross section of black writers, generally political and militant but always articulate and original.

THE CAEDMON TREASURY OF MODERN POETS READING THEIR OWN POETRY. *Caedmon* TC 2006 1967–68 $11.90. These two records include Aiken, Bishop, Cummings, Eberhart, Frost, Moore, Williams and others.

Carruth, Hayden. THE VOICE THAT IS GREAT WITHIN US: American Poetry of the Twentieth Century. *Bantam* 1970 $1.95

This is certainly the best and most important century-wide anthology in recent years. Carruth gives a fine and unique selection of the various poets, and only a few notables are absent, with many hitherto neglected writers generously represented. "Not only the best of its period, I think, but is even perhaps safe from the competition of rivals"—(Robert Lowell).

Charters, Samuel B. THE POETRY OF THE BLUES. *Oak* (dist. by Quick Fox) 1963 $2.95. An essay, with photographs by Ann Charters, and collection of poems of the Blues, which is of great interest and use to students of contemporary poetry, especially of the Beat and black movements.

Chester, Laura, and Sharon Barba. RISING TIDES: 20th Century American Women Poets. Introd. by Anais Nin. *Washington Square* 1973 pap. $1.95. A book which presents "the beginning of a poetic renaissance for women." Perhaps the best and most carefully selected of the numerous feminist anthologies currently available, this book presents many diverse voices: Nikki Giovanni and H. D., Marianne Moore and Erica Jong, and many others.

Ciardi, John. MID-CENTURY AMERICAN POETS. *Twayne* 1950 $6.00. A book of verse with explanatory prose by 15 modern poets, and a fwd. giving an excellent evaluation.

Cronyn, George W. AMERICAN INDIAN POETRY: An Anthology of Songs and Chants. (Orig. title "Path on the Rainbow"). *Liveright* 1970 $7.95 pap. $2.95; *Ballantine* pap. $1.65. Good introduction to the poetry of the American Indian with a broad selection of ceremonial rites and chants.

DeLoach, Allen. THE EAST SIDE SCENE: American Poetry 1960–1965. *Doubleday* Anchor Bks. 1972 pap. $2.50. Collects the work of poets who were dominant forces of American avant-garde poetry in the early sixties. All the poets lived for a time on Manhattan's Lower East Side and read at Le Metro and the 10th Street Coffee

House. Besides Wakoski, Blackburn, Ginsberg and Joel Oppenheimer, there is a wonderful representation of poets whose work is only now becoming recognized, including Susan Sherman, Carol Berge, Allen Planz and Robert Kelly.

Drew, Elizabeth, and G. Connor. DISCOVERING MODERN POETRY. *Holt* 1961 pap. text ed. $6.25

Elliott, George Paul. FIFTEEN MODERN AMERICAN POETS. *Holt* (Rinehart) 1956 pap. $2.25; *Peter Smith* $4.25. Includes Elizabeth Bishop, Randall Jarrell, Robert Penn Warren, Delmore Schwartz and others.

Eshleman, Clayton. A CATERPILLAR ANTHOLOGY: A Selection of Poetry and Prose from *Caterpillar* Magazine. *Doubleday* 1971 Anchor Bks. $2.50. An interesting assemblage of material from the first through the twelfth issue of the magazine, including the poetry of Diane Wakoski, Paul Blackburn, David Antin, David Bromige and Jack Spicer.

FUGITIVE: A Magazine of Verse. 1922–25. *Peter Smith* 4 vols. in I $10.00. The first publication of the group that became known as the New Critics (*see introduction to Chapter 15, Essays and Criticism*).

Gross, Ronald, George Quasha, Emmett Williams, John Robert Colombo and Walter Lowenfels. OPEN POETRY; Four Anthologies of Expanded Poems. *Simon & Schuster* 1973 $14.95. This volume is divided in to four sections, Metropoetry, Language Happenings, Found Poetry, and The Poetry of Survival, each of which treats of a different possible direction in modern poetry, from an expansion of "the domain of the sayable," through concrete and multimedia poetry, found poetry (related to Bauhaus) and finally a poetry of survival reflecting mainly black poets, but all other poets as well who are interested in oral communication. A giant-size book including a great many poets, from Helen Adam to Mary Ellen Solt, from Jerome Rotherberg to Sonia Sanchez and other writers, some well-known, some relatively obscure.

Hall, Donald. CONTEMPORARY AMERICAN POETRY. *Penguin* (orig.) 1963 pap. $1.50

Hewitt, Geof. QUICKLY AGING HERE: Some Poets of the 1970's. *Doubleday* 1969 Anchor Bks. pap. $2.50. An interesting and carefully selected anthology representing a wide variety of styles in the work of the 35 young poets including Rochelle Ratner, Philip Dow, Gregory Orr and Shirley Kaufman.

Hughes, Langston. NEW NEGRO POETS, U.S.A. Fwd. by Gwendolyn Brooks. *Indiana Univ. Press* 1964 $5.95 pap. $1.95. A collection of lyrical, personal and protest poems by 37 Negro poets.

Jones, LeRoi. FOUR YOUNG LADY POETS. *Corinth Bks.* (dist. by The Book Organization) 1962 pap. $1.50. A most interesting collection in that three of the poets have become well-known since the publication of this book. Good picture of presently unobtainable early work of Diane Wakoski and Rochelle Owens.

Kessler, Jascha. AMERICAN POEMS: A CONTEMPORARY COLLECTION. *Southern Illinois Univ. Press* 1964 $4.95

Leary, Paris, and others. A CONTROVERSY OF POETS: An Anthology of Contemporary American Poetry. *Doubleday* Anchor Bks. 1965 pap. $2.95. An excellent collection of poems by poets of all schools.

A LITTLE TREASURY OF 20TH CENTURY AMERICAN POETRY. *Colpix* PS 1000 and PS 1001 1964 each $5.98. A recording, the poems read by their authors. Includes Jeffers, Cummings, MacLeish, Moore, Nash, Robert Penn Warren and others.

Lowenfels, Walter. FROM THE BELLY OF THE SHARK: Poems by Chicanos, Eskimos, Hawaiians, Indians and Puerto Ricans in the United States, with Related Poems by Others. *Random* Vintage Bks. 1973 pap. $1.95

WHERE IS VIETNAM? AMERICAN POETS RESPOND: An Anthology of Contemporary Poems. *Doubleday* Anchor Bks. (orig.) 1967 pap. $1.45

> The collection includes Lowell's "Fall 1961," Eberhart's "World War," Nemerov's "August 1945" as well as poems by Denise Levertov, Ginsberg, Bly, Dickey, Ferlinghetti and Kunitz. "Among our best contemporary voices"—(*LJ*).

IN A TIME OF REVOLUTION: Poems from Our Third World. *Random* Vintage Bks. 1969 $1.95

POETS OF TODAY: A New American Anthology. *International Pubs.* 1964 pap. $1.95. Unusual collection of poets, including many not anthologized widely, such as Bob Dylan, Allen Planz and George Hitchcock.

Martz, William J. DISTINCTIVE VOICE: Twentieth Century American Poetry. *Scott, Foresman* 1966 soft bdg. $5.75

Meltzer, David. SAN FRANCISCO POETS. *Ballantine* 1971 pap. $1.65. Good and lively interviews with Kenneth Rexroth, William Everson, Lawrence Ferlinghetti, Lew Welch, Michael McClure and Richard Brautigan. A scanty collection of the poems of each poet but a useful chronology of the life of poetry in the Bay Area over a 25 year period, with bibliography of each poet interviewed.

Monaco, Richard. NEW AMERICAN POETRY. *McGraw-Hill* 1973 pap. $3.95.

> "This is how an anthology of poetry should look; if it were two or three times as big, it would be the best collection of post-World War II American poets we have. . .—(*Choice*).

Murphy, Beatrice M. TODAY'S NEGRO VOICES: An Anthology of Young Negro Poets. *Messner* 1970 $3.95. A solid and strong selection of poets and poems including work by Nikki Giovanni, Carolyn M. Rodgers and 32 other poets ranging in age from 14 to 30 years at time of publication.

Myers, John Bernard. THE POETS OF THE NEW YORK SCHOOL. *Gotham Book Mart* (Univ. of Penna. Graduate School of Fine Arts) 1969 $9.50. This finely produced book gathers together the chief figures of the New York School, John Ashbery, Kenneth Koch, Frank O'Hara and others, and their work as well as a number of the painters associated with it.

Padgett, Ron, and David Shapiro. ANTHOLOGY OF NEW YORK POETS. *Random* 1970 $12.95 Vintage Bks. pap. $3.95. Important for the student of "The New York School" of poets with sizeable selections from the work of James Schuyler, Clark Coolidge, Kenward Elmslie and Ted Berrigan among others.

Pearson, Norman Holmes. DECADE: A Collection of Poems from the First Ten Years of the Wesleyan Poetry Program. *Wesleyan Univ. Press* $2.95. This book gathers together the work of 33 poets published by *Wesleyan* up to 1968, including John Ashbery, Robert Bly, Donald Davie, James Dickey, Harvey Shapiro, Jon Silkin and James Wright. Includes notes and introduction.

Perrine, Laurence, and James M. Reid. 100 AMERICAN POEMS OF THE TWENTIETH CEN-
TURY. *Harcourt* 1966 $5.95. Includes work by such poets as Robinson, Frost, Ste-
vens and Williams. Commentaries accompany the poems.

Pratt, William. THE IMAGIST POEM: Poetry in Miniature. *Dutton* 1963 pap. $1.25. 122
poems by 18 poets representative of the Imagist movement—from T. E. Holme to
Marianne Moore.

Rago, Henry. POETRY: The Golden Anniversary Issue. *Univ. of Chicago Press* 1967
Phoenix Bks. pap. $1.95

Robinson, James K., and Walter B. Rideout. COLLEGE BOOK OF MODERN VERSE. *Harper* 1958 $9.00; *Bks. for Libraries* repr. of 1953 ed. $14.75

Rothenberg, Jerome. SHAKING THE PUMPKIN: Traditional Poetry of the Indian North
Americas. *Doubleday* 1972 $8.95 Anchor Bks. pap. $4.50. Rothenberg gathers here
translations by numerous poets including W. S. Merwin and Gary Snyder, of Indian
poetry of the Sioux, Seneca, Eskimo, Fox and others. His preface, commentaries and
"Breakdown of Tribe and Region" are extremely helpful to those who are new to the
field.

Sanders, Thomas E., and Walter W. Peek. LITERATURE OF THE AMERICAN INDIAN. *Macmillan* (Glencoe) 1973 text ed. $10.95. The one anthology, at least at time of this
writing, which includes contemporary young Indian poets like James Welch. Gathered together by Indians, this is an excellent collection of poems, some of which voice
the current problems and protest of Indians in the United States.

Schreiber, Ron. 31 NEW AMERICAN POETS. Fwd. by Denise Levertov. *Hill & Wang* 1969
$5.95 Am. Century pap. $2.45. A truly representative cross-section of various
"schools of American poetry" by young, little-known writers, most of whom to date
appear only in little magazines and virtually no anthologies. Work of Jack Anderson, Besmilr Brigham, Victor Contoski, Gene Fowler, John Gill, Phyllis Harris,
Dick Lourie and Jay Wright.

Segnitz, Barbara, and Carol Rainey. PSYCHE: The Feminine Poetic Consciousness. *Dial*
1973 $10.00; *Dell* Laurel Eds. pap. $1.50. This book dips a bit into the nineteenth
century with Emily Dickenson, and includes one Canadian poet, Margaret Atwood,
but essentially is compiled from living American women writers. 20 poets among
whom are Marianne Moore, Gwendolyn Brooks, Adrienne Rich, Rochelle Owens,
Lyn Lifshin and Erica Jong.

Simpson, Louis A. M., Comp. INTRODUCTION TO POETRY. *St. Martin's* 1967 2nd ed.
1972 pap. $3.95

Skelton, Robin. FIVE POETS OF THE PACIFIC NORTHWEST: Kenneth O. Hanson, Richard
Hugo, Carolyn Kizer, William Stafford and David Wagoner. *Univ. of Washington
Press* 1968 pap. $2.95

Smith, Chard Powers. POETS OF THE TWENTIES: 100 Great Poems. Fwd. by Peter Viereck. *Brown Bk.* 1967 $6.95 pap. $3.95. Chard Powers Smith has written an extensive introduction to this collection, which includes Frost, Amy Lowell, Millay, Cummings and others.

Strand, Mark. CONTEMPORARY AMERICAN POETS. (Orig. title: "Modern American Poetry"). *New Am. Lib.* 1969 $9.95 Mentor Bks. 1971 pap. $1.50; *World Pub.* Meri-

dian Bks. 1969 pap. $1.50. Selections from 92 poets published since the 1940s. Gives a good cross-section of various movements and individuals from Ginsberg to James Wright.

Stryk, Lucien. HEARTLAND: Poets of the Midwest. *Northern Illinois Univ. Press* 1967 $6.50 pap. $3.00

Talisman Editors. A WESTERN SAMPLER: Nine Contemporary Poets. *Talisman Press* 1962 $5.00 pap. $3.00

Tedlock, Dennis, Trans. FINDING THE CENTER: Narrative Poetry of the Zuni Indians (From "Performances in the Zuni" by Andrew Peynetsa and Walter Sanchez). With an Appreciation by Jerome Rothenberg. *Dial* 1972 $8.50 pap. $2.95. Nine narrative poems, with a guide to reading aloud, are translated here from oral presentation. Each poem is exquisitely beautiful. A fine and intelligent collection recommended for all who are interested in Indian poetry, and perhaps all who are interested in just beautiful poetry.

Turner, Darwin T. BLACK AMERICAN LITERTURE: Poetry. *Charles E. Merrill* 1969 pap. $1.95. One of a set of 3 volumes covering black American literature. (*See Chapter 4, Broad Studies—General and Comprehensive Anthologies.*)

Untermeyer, Louis. MODERN AMERICAN POETRY. 1919 *Harcourt,* 7th rev. ed. 1950 rev. and enl. ed. 1962 text ed. $8.25. An excellent critical anthology enlarged to include 772 poems by 76 poets, ranging from Whitman to Anne Sexton.

Waldman, Anne. WORLD ANTHOLOGY: Poems from the St. Marks Poetry Project. *Bobbs* 1969 $7.50 pap. $3.95. Poems drawn from the Lower East Side literary magazine of the Poetry Project of St. Marks Church In-The-Bowery.

ANOTHER WORLD: A Second Anthology of Works from the St. Marks Poetry Project. *Bobbs* 1971 $6.95 pap. $2.95. Includes some of same contributors as to the first "World Anthology."

Walsh, Chad. TODAY'S POETS. *Scribner* 1964 pap. $4.95

Weishaus, Joel. ON THE MESA: An Anthology of Bolinas Writing. *City Lights* 1971 pap. $3.00. Poems by David Meltzer, Jeanne Kyger, Bill Berkson, Lew Walsh, Tom Clark, and others.

Welentz, Ted, and Tom Weatherly. NATURAL PROCESS: An Anthology of New Black Poetry. *Hill & Wang* 1970 $5.95 pap. $1.95. A good selection of poems with short biographies and statements on poetics included. Poems by Sam Cornis, Nikki Giovanni, Michael S. Harper, William J. Harris, David Henderson, Andre Lourde, N. H. Pritchard, Sonia Sanchez and Al Young.

SERIES OF CONTEMPORARY POETRY

Besides the series listed below, the "little magazines," as mentioned earlier, have, with the small presses, provided the single most prolific outlet for new poetry. Since the last edition of *"The Reader's Adviser,"* the number of good new little magazines has increased tremendously. Not even a partial listing can be made here, but the reader is referred to the *Dust Books* (of El Cerrito, California) publication, "Directory of Little Magazines and Small Presses" (annually $4.00) which provides a handy reference source to this medium.

Among the larger "littles," with better formats than most, are *Antaeus* and *The New*

York Quarterly, the former devoted mainly to poetry with some prose and interviews with writers, and the latter chiefly a poetry magazine with articles by poets, and interviews with them, primarily concerned with aspects of poetic craft. Robert Bly's *The Seventies* (previously *The Sixties, The Fifties*) continues to provide a vehicle for the deep image poets and translations of European writers. A variation on the little poetry magazine came with Stephen Berg and Stephen Parker's *American Poetry Review*, a tabloid published every two months with dynamic articles, debates, and presentation of new poetry. *Choice*, edited by John Logan, recently reappeared after a long absence from the magazine stands with its usually high standards of poetry and photography. Other noteworthy major magazines include *The Minnesota Review, The Mediterraen Review, Expatriate Review* and *Poetry Northwest*.

The Summer 1973 issue of *Salmagundi* was devoted to a study of Contemporary Poetry in America and should be obtained by anyone interested in this field.

ALAN SWALLOW NEW POETRY SERIES. *AMS Press* 35 vols. each $7.00 set $245.00; ed. by Michael Anania *Swallow Press* 7 vols. in print each $2.75. Established in 1949, this series publishes first volumes of poetry. *Swallow* specializes in poetry; in addition to the series, it prints the work of more than two dozen established poets including Yvor Winters, Allen Tate, J. V. Cunningham and others. Michael Anania, now editor of *Swallow Press*, has gathered together a strong group of young poets in his series, including Albert Cook, Donald F. Drummond, Barbara Harr, James McMichael, Linda Pastan and Alan Stephens.

ATHENEUM POETRY SERIES. *Atheneum* various prices. This series is published irregularly at the rate of 3–6 per year. Poets already represented include Anthony Hecht, John Hollander and W. S. Merwin.

CHICAGO POETRY VOLUMES. *Univ. of Chicago Press* 18 vols. various prices (some titles also in their Phoenix ed.)

CONTEMPORARY POETRY SERIES. *Univ. of North Carolina Press* $3.50–$7.50; some vols. available in pap. $1.65–$1.85. Significant poetry by living poets.

THE FOLLETT SERIES: Big Table Books. *Follett* various prices. This series of books by and about young American poets is devoted to promoting their publication. It takes its name from the magazine *Big Table*, Chicago, 1959–61.

INDIANA UNIVERSITY POETRY SERIES. *Indiana Univ. Press* 20 vols. in print various prices. Twenty-three titles printed since 1952 in this series of collections of work by established poets. Among them are Conrad Aiken, Kenneth Fearing, Josephine Miles, Theodore Roethke.

THE PITT POETRY SERIES. *Univ. of Pittsburg Press* 31 vols. in print various prices. The first Pitt book was published in 1967. The series features first books, selected via a contest, of young poets as well as various other books, sometimes by the same poets or randomly selected. Some of the poets included are Shirley Kaufman, Michael S. Harper, Norman Dubie and Jon Anderson.

THE WESLEYAN POETRY PROGRAM. *Wesleyan Univ. Press.* 63 vols. in print each $4.25 pap. $2.45. This important series was begun in 1959 to make widely available from one source the work of talented poets writing today. Four volumes are published each year. Poets include John Ashbery, Robert Bly, Barbara Howes, Vassar Miller, Donald Justice, James Dickey, Louis Simpson.

YALE SERIES OF RECORDED POETS. 12 recordings. *Carillon Records* various prices. These recordings make up an anthology of over 200 American and British poems. The album covers contain introductory essays. Among the poets who read their own poems and often comment on them are: Frost (YP 320); Robert Penn Warren (YP 313); Marianne Moore (YP 312); Conrad Aiken (YP 307); R. P. Blackmur (YP 311) and Richard Eberhart (YP 314).

THE POCKET POETS SERIES. *City Lights Books* 24 vols. pap. $1.00–$2.00. Lawrence Ferlinghetti, poet and owner of the famous San Francisco bookshop, publishes contemporary poets. Allen Ginsberg's "Howl and Other Poems" is one of the notable volumes of this series, which also includes books by Corso, Patchen, Williams, Lowry, Rexroth and Ferlinghetti himself.

POETS OF TODAY SERIES. *Scribner* 8 vols. in print various prices. Since 1953, Poets of Today Series has issued annually three books by three poets in one volume, with critical introductions by John Hall Wheelock, editor and poet. Poets include May Swenson, James Dickey, Norma Farber, Albert Herzing, John M. Ridland and David R. Slavitt.

THE YALE SERIES OF YOUNGER POETS. Ed. by Dudley Fitts. *Yale Univ. Press* 9 vols. in print in both cloth and paper hardbound $3.75–$5.00 pap. $1.25–$1.95. Oldest and most important of the series, the Yale Series has provided since 1919 a publishing medium for 67 first volumes of promising American poets. Recent poets include Margaret Walker, James Tate, Helen Chasin, Judith Johnson Sherwin, Hugh Seidman, Peter Klappert, Michael Casey.

MASTERS, EDGAR LEE. 1869–1950.

The Kansas-born poet of "Spoon River" was a man of many books who continues to be known for only one, so great was the extraordinary success of that performance. The character of the verses—short post-mortem monologues in a cemetery in epitaph form—is borrowed from the old "Greek Anthology." "With every new attack (and its frankness continued to make fresh enemies) its readers increased. It was imitated, parodied, reviled as a 'piece of yellow' journalism; it was hailed as an 'American Comédie Humaine.' Finally, after the storm of controversy, it has taken its place as a landmark in American literature"—(Louis Untermeyer). "The New Spoon River," a sequel (1924), has now been reissued. "Sangamon" (*Holt*, Rinehart ed. 1942 $4.00) is in the Rivers of America Series. "Unanimously acclaimed" by the critics, an excellent dramatization of "Spoon River" appeared briefly on Broadway in the late fall of 1963. Masters' "Mark Twain" (1938) is again available (*Biblo & Tannen* $8.50) as is also "Vachel Lindsay" (1935 *Biblo & Tannen* $15.00).

A BOOK OF VERSES. 1898. *Gregg* 1970 $9.50

SPOON RIVER ANTHOLOGY. With additional poems, ill. by Oliver Herford. *Macmillan* 1916 new ed. 1925 $4.95 ill. with woodcuts by J. and C. R. Ross. Collectors' Ed. 1963 $7.95 Collier pap. $1.25

NEW SPOON RIVER ANTHOLOGY. 1924. Introd. by Willis Barnston with short biography of Masters. *Macmillan* 1968 $5.95 Collier Bks. pap. $1.25. A continuation of the "Spoon River Anthology."

ACROSS SPOON RIVER. 1936. *Octagon* 1967 $13.00. An autobiography.

Books about Masters

Spoon River Legacy. By Harry L. Blout. *RSVP Pub. & Dist.* 1969 $4.65

ROBINSON, EDWIN ARLINGTON. 1869–1935.

Amy Lowell spoke of Robinson's "difficult and beautiful poetry" and considered him "one of the most intellectual poets in America." He was a slow writer and waited long for recognition. His gift is for the delineation of character, the portrayal of human types. His is the poet's interpretation of character rather than the novelist's development of character. His study of Shakespeare in the volume "The Man Against the Sky" (1916) won much praise in its time.

Robinson won the Pulitzer Prize in 1922, 1925 and 1928. The third Pulitzer was for one of his most intricate works, "Tristram," (1927 o.p.) a single poem of over 40,000 words. It was a best seller and with the later works established the poet in popular favor. The Poetry Center at the 92nd Street YMHA (New York City) presented "Tristram" in 1962 with a cast of six. By the 1960s, for the time being at least, Robinson was somewhat in eclipse.

COLLECTED POEMS. *Macmillan* 1927 new ed. 1937 $12.50. The first "Collected Poems" was published by *Macmillan* in 1927 in five volumes, containing: The Children of the Night (1897); Captain Craig (1902); The Man Against the Sky (1916); The Town Down the River (1910); The Man Who Died Twice (1924); Merlin (1917); Lancelot (1920); Tristram (1927); Three Taverns (1920); Dionysius in Doubt (1925); Roman Bartholow (1923); Avon's Harvest (1921). A number of shorter poems and long narrative poems, not previously included, appear in the new edition of 1937. The narrative poems are: The Glory of the Nightingales (1930); Nicodemus (1932); Talifer; Amaranth (1934); Matthais at the Door (1931); and King Jasper.

TILBURY TOWN. Selected Poems. Ed. by Lawrance Thompson. *Macmillan* 1953 text ed. $4.50. 65 dramatic portraits, lyrics and narratives integrated through common setting and theme.

SELECTED POEMS OF EDWIN ARLINGTON ROBINSON. Ed. by Morton D. Zabel. *Macmillan* 1963 (orig.) 1965 $5.00 Collier Bks. pap. $1.95

SELECTED EARLY POEMS AND LETTERS. Ed. by Charles Davis. *Holt* (Rinehart) 1960 pap. $1.25

THE CHILDREN OF THE NIGHT. 1897. *Gordon Press* $12.50

UNTRIANGULATED STARS: Letters of Edwin Arlington Robinson to Harry de Forest Smith, 1890–1905. Ed. by Denham Sutcliffe. 1947. *Greenwood* $14.25

LETTERS TO EDITH BROWER. Ed. by Richard Cary. *Harvard Univ. Press* 1968 $8.75. A fascinating correspondence between the poet and a sympathetic admirer to whom he openly speaks his mind and heart during the period 1897–1930.

Books about Robinson

The Poetry of Edwin Arlington Robinson: An Essay in Appreciation. By Lloyd Morris; bibliography by W. Van R. Whitall. 1923. *Bks for Libraries* $9.75; *Haskell* 1969 lib. bdg. $7.95; *Kennikat* 1969 $5.00; *Richard West* 1973 $4.95. As interesting essay on Robinson written during his lifetime.

Edwin Arlington Robinson. By Laura Elizabeth Richards. 1936. *Russell & Russell* 1967 $5.00

A Bibliography of the Writings and Criticisms of Edwin Arlington Robinson. By Lillian Lippincott. *Faxon* 1937 $2.25

New Poetry of New England: Frost and Robinson. By Robert P. Tristram Coffin. 1938. *Russell & Russell* $10.00

Edwin Arlington Robinson: A Critical Study. By Ellsworth Barnard. 1939 *Octagon* 1969 $11.00. A good scholarly introduction to Robinson with an index to Robinson's works and characters.

Philosophy in the Poetry of Edwin Arlington Robinson. By Estelle Kaplan. 1940. *AMS Press* $9.50; *Richard West* $9.25

Edwin Arlington Robinson. By Yvor Winters. 1947. *New Directions* rev. ed. 1971 $7.95 pap. $3.45. A study of Edwin Arlington Robinson's technique by a major critic readable enough for the general reader. Careful analysis of the poems with a chapter devoted to Robinson's life. Bibliography included.

Edwin Arlington Robinson. by Emery Neff. 1948. *Russell & Russell* 1968 $10.00. A biographical critical work.

Edwin Arlington Robinson. By Louis Coxe. *Univ. of Minnesota Press* Pamphlets on American Writers 1961 pap. $1.25

Where the Light Falls: A Portrait of Edwin Arlington Robinson. By Chard Powers Smith. *Macmillan* 1965 $7.50

"Mr. Smith presents a vivid and sympathetic portrait of the quotidian Robinson, in his folly as well as in his wisdom. And certainly one of the most entertaining aspects of Robinson exhibited in the book is the poet's humor"—(*Christian Science Monitor*). "This is the best book on Robinson we have, and I recommend it with enthusiasm" —(Granville Hicks, in *SR*).

Edwin Arlington Robinson: A Critical Introduction. By Wallace L. Anderson. *Harvard Univ. Press* 1967 $6.00; *Houghton* pap. $4.00

Edwin Arlington Robinson. By Hoyt C. Franchère. United States Authors Ser. *Twayne* 1968 $5.50

Edwin Arlington Robinson: Centenary Essays. *Univ. of Georgia Press* 1969 $6.50 Collected on the hundredth anniversary of Robinson's birth by Ellsworth Barnard.

Edwin Arlington Robinson: A Collection of Critical Essays. Ed. by Francis Murphey. Twentieth Century Views. *Prentice-Hall* 1970 $5.95 Spectrum Bks. pap. $1.95. A useful and excellent source for a range of critical responses to Robinson. Essays are by Yvor Winters, Conrad Aiken, Robert Froms, Louis Coxe, James Dickey, Josephine Miles among others.

JOHNSON, JAMES WELDON. 1871–1938.

Johnson was the first incumbent of the Spence Chair of Creative Literature in Fisk University. He was an educator, poet, author and composer and one of the great leaders of his people. "God's Trombones" is considered his richest book of poems. His books are classics of black literature. "The Autobiography of an Ex-Colored Man" (*Knopf* 1927 $5.85; *Hill & Wang* Am. Century 1960 pap. $1.95), is a useful source book on the life of the black man in America. He edited "American Negro Poetry: An Anthology" (*Harcourt* new rev. ed. 1931 $5.95 pap. $1.45) and, with his brother J. Rosamond Johnson, "Lift Every Voice and Sing" (*Hawthorn* 1970 $13.00), a collection of Negro spirituals.

God's Trombones: Seven Sermons in Verse. *Viking* 1927 $3.95 Compact Bks. pap. $1.35

Along This Way. *DaCapo* 1973 $5.00; *Viking* $7.95 Compass Bks. pap. $2.95. His autobiography.

DUNBAR, PAUL LAURENCE. 1872–1906.

The first important black poet in America was born in Ohio of parents who had been slaves. He did newspaper work, served on the staff of the Library of Congress, and died of tuberculosis at 34. His collected poems include four earlier volumes of his poetry, one of them the "Lyrics of Lowly Life," with the original preface by William Dean Howells (*q.v.*). His poems for young people, "Little Brown Baby," were edited by Bertha Rodgers (*Dodd* 1940 $3.00).

Life and Works: Containing His Complete Poetical Works, His Best Short Stories, Numerous Anecdotes and a Complete Biography. 1911. *Kraus* $19.50

Complete Poems. *Dodd* 1913 1940 $4.95 Apollo Eds. pap. $1.95. Includes "Lyrics of Lowly Life," "Lyrics of the Hearthside," "Lyrics of Love and Laughter" "Lyrics of Sunshine and Shadow."

Majors and Minors: Poems. 1896. *Bks. for Libraries* $7.50

Lyrics of the Lowly Life. 1896 1899. *Arno* 1969 $7.00 *Bks. for Libraries* $6.95; *Gregg* $6.50

Lyrics of the Hearthside. 1899. *AMS Press* $10.50; *Bks. for Libraries* $8.50

Poems of Cabin and Field. 1899. *AMS Press* $5.00; *Bks. for Libraries* $7.50

Lyrics of Sunshine and Shadow. 1905. *AMS Press* $5.00

Books about Dunbar

Paul Laurence Dunbar, Poet of His People. By Benjamin Brawley. 1936. *Kennikat* $7.50. Has a bibliography, index and appendix which contains some interesting poems in praise of Dunbar written by other black poets. This biography is not scholarly but is of interest to the general reader. Criticism of Dunbar's poetry is sketchy.

Paul Laurence Dunbar Critically Examined. By V. Lawson. 1941. *Gordon Press* $12.95. A general evaluation of Dunbar's poetry with a chapter devoted to his prose. Useful bibliography included.

Paul Laurence Dunbar and His Song. By Virginia Cunningham. 1947. *Biblio & Tannen* 1969 $10.00. Illustrated with photographs. An easy-to-read biography general in nature rather than scholarly or critical. Point of view is dated and the work is of interest only in that it gives a retrospective picture of the approach to "black studies" less than 20 years ago.

Oak and Ivy: A Biography of Paul L. Dunbar. By Addison Gayle, Jr. *Doubleday* 1971 $4.50 pap $1.95

LOWELL, AMY. 1874–1925.

Amy Lowell did not look like a poet—she was of ample build and enjoyed smoking cigars. But she wrote delicate and lovely verse, revolutionary for its time. "It is almost impossible to separate the legendary and the real Amy Lowell," writes Louis Untermeyer in his introduction to "The Complete Poetical Works." "She was to a great extent the victim of her fabulous quest for novelty, and the legend of her inexhaustibility—a myth which she herself accepted—was probably responsible for her death." The dynamic leader of the Imagist School in America, she waged a continuous war for the New Poetry. After her first book in conventional meter and rhyme, her second "heralded the era's growing dissatisfaction with traditional measures and the determination to try new verse forms, strange cadences, and unfamiliar responses to standard sentiments." "Her final place in the history of American literature has not yet been determined, [but] the importance of her influence remains unquestioned. Underneath her preoccupation with the need for novelty, the disruption of traditional patterns, and other theoretical departures, she was a dynamic force. She was not only a disturber but an awakener. Her exhilarating differences invigorated the old forms while affecting the new techniques. Her pioneering energy cleared the field of flabby accumulations and helped establish the fresh and free-searching poetry of our day." "What's O'Clock," published posthumously, was awarded the 1926 Pulitzer Poetry Prize.

Of her several volumes of prose, "Poetry and Poets: Essays" (*Biblo & Tannen* 1930 $7.50), "Tendencies in American Poetry" (*Haskell* 1921 $10.95) "Tendencies in Modern Poetry" (*Haskell* 1969 $10.95; *Octagon* 1967 $11.00) and "Six French Poets" (1915. *Bks. for Libraries* $13.75), essays on Emile Verhaeren, Albert Semain, Remy de Gowmont, Henri de Regnier, Francis Jammes Fort are available. Miss Lowell wrote a monumental biography of Keats (2 vols. 1925. *Shoe String* $25.00), in which she was one of the first to defend Fanny Brawne, Keats' fiancée, against the detraction to which she had been subject up to that time.

The Complete Poetical Works of Amy Lowell. Introd. by Louis Untermeyer. *Houghton* 1955 Cambridge Eds. $10.00. A Dome of Many-Coloured Glass (1912); Sword Blades and Poppy Seed (1914); Men, Women and Ghosts (1916); Can Grande's Castle (1918); Pictures of the Floating World (1919); Legends (1921); Fir-Flower Tablets (1921); A Critical Fable (1922); What's O'Clock (1925); East Wind (1926); Ballads for Sale (1927); and six previously uncollected poems, some 650 poems in all, make up this comprehensive collection; index of first lines and index of titles.

Selected Poems. 1928. *Scholarly Press* 1971 $14.50

Shard of Silence: Selected Poems. Ed. with introd. by G. R. Ruihaley. *Twayne* 1957 $5.00

Can Grande's Castle. 1918. *Scholarly Press* $14.50

Books about Lowell

Amy Lowell: A Chronicle. By Foster S. Damon. Ill. 1935. *Shoe String* 1966 $15.00. A complete definitive biography of Amy Lowell using numerous excerpts from letters. Index.

Amy Lowell: A Mosaic. By George H. Sargent. 1926. *Folcroft* $10.00. A pleasant appreciation and review of Amy Lowell's monumental biography of John Keats (*q.v.*).

Amy Lowell: A Critical Study. By Clement Wood. 1926. *Folcroft* $15.00. This very readable but nevertheless critical appraisal of Amy Lowell and her works is a good introduction to the poetry.

Amy Lowell. By Cudworth F. Flint. Pamphlets on American Writers *Univ. of Minnesota Press* 1969 pap. $1.25. A useful general introduction to Amy Lowell and her work, not of much help to a serious student. Selected bibliography gives not just her primary works but also biographies and bibliographical and critical sources.

FROST, ROBERT. 1874–1963.

Robert Frost was, in a sense, our national "Poet Laureate." Indeed, he was made the state of Vermont's official poet laureate by a joint House and Senate Resolution, and during the Eisenhower administration he received a special Congressional medal. At the Inauguration of President John F. Kennedy in January, 1961, Frost was invited to recite "The Gift Outright," a poem from more than 20 years before. He had also written, especially for this occasion, a longer poem expressing gratification that the arts and sciences were being recognized in the ceremony. The glare of the sunshine prevented his reading it. Both poems are reprinted in "In the Clearing." In August, 1962, he went to Russia to recite his poems as part of an exchange in which Russian poet Alexander Tvardovsky came to the United States. Frost was greeted by Yevgeni Yevtushenko and other Russian poets.

Frost won the Pulitzer Poetry Prize in 1924, 1931, 1937 and 1943. The years brought him a succession of honors, including honorary degrees from 17 colleges. Among his many other awards was the 1962 Edward MacDonald Medal from the Academy of American Poets. But American recognition had been slow in coming to Robert Frost.

Of old New England stock, he was born and lived ten years in San Francisco. On his father's death the family returned to "North of Boston." He studied at Dartmouth and at Harvard, then gave up college for teaching. From 1912 to 1915 he lived in England. After his return to America he taught at Amherst College in 1917; in 1920 he was instrumental in founding the Bread Loaf School in Middlebury, Vt.; in 1921 he accepted a fellowship in creative art at the University of Michigan, and then again returned to Amherst for three months each year. When asked his philosophy of life on one occasion, the poet replied wryly, "It goes on."

Both "A Boy's Will" and "North of Boston" were published first in England, where the author was hailed by Edward Garnett as 'a fresh creative force, an original voice in literature." It is as a delineator of pastoral life that Frost's "native touch" shows to best advantage. His verse has a "strange, soil-flavored quality" not favorably received at first by American editors. As a poet, "Frost loves what he loves with a fierce attachment, a tenderness fixed beyond a more easily transferred regard. His devotion to the intimacies of earth is, even more than Wordsworth's rich, almost inordinate in its fidelity; what his emotion (or his poetry) may lack in windy range, is trebly compensated for by its untroubled depths"—(Louis Untermeyer).

The late President Kennedy and the poet Archibald MacLeish spoke on Oct. 26, 1963, at a special Amherst convocation held in conjunction with the dedication of the $3.5 million library in honor of the poet. President Kennedy "issued an appeal to the nation . . . to recognize the contributions of men of spirit and insight as well as those of action." He praised Frost, "a personal friend in the closing years of the poet's life, as 'one of the granite figures of our time in America' "—(*N.Y. Times*). His "Selected Prose," ed. by H. Cox and E. C. Lathem, has been published by (1966 *Macmillan* Collier Bks. pap. $1.95).

"Robert Frost Speaks" by Daniel Smythe (*Twayne* 1964 $5.00) is a record of the conversations between the author, who is himself a poet and professor, and Frost during the years 1939–62. "It is a journalistic piece, and Mr. Smythe has the good eye and avid ear of the journalist. . . . Frost's usual mixture of warmth and crustiness is in high evidence"—(*LJ*). "Interviews With Robert Frost" (ed. by Edward Connery Lathem *Holt* 1966 $7.50), compiled by the associate librarian of Dartmouth, includes about 60 selections arranged chronologically from 1915–62. *Library Journal* said of the book: "Frost's remarkable ability to be consistent without becoming a bore is well illustrated, although the journalistic format throughout forces a kind of aphoristic quality on the poet, and there are often varying degrees of trustworthiness as to what Frost may actually have said. An interview with marginal comments by the poet himself is reproduced in facsimile."

ROBERT FROST: HIS POETRY AND PROSE. Ed. by Edward C. Lathem and Lawrance Thompson. *Holt* 1972 $7.95. Lines of poems are numbered. Title and first line indexes.

THE POETRY OF ROBERT FROST. *Holt* 1969 $10.95

THE ROAD NOT TAKEN. An introduction to Robert Frost. Ill. by John O'Hara Cosgrave II. *Holt* 1951 $5.95. A selection of his poems with a biographical preface and running commentary by Louis Untermeyer.

COME IN AND OTHER POEMS. 1943. *Franklin Watts* lg.-type ed. Keith Jennison Bks. 1967 $8.95. Contains 80 poems selected from seven previous volumes. This volume is an enlargement with over 50 poems added.

SELECTED POEMS. Ed. by Robert Graves. *Holt* (Rinehart) 1963 pap. $2.75

NEW ENLARGED ANTHOLOGY OF ROBERT FROST'S POEMS. Ed. by Louis Untermeyer. *Washington Square* rev. ed. pap. $.95

YOU COME TOO: Favorite Poems for Young Readers. With wood engravings by Thomas W. Nason. *Holt* 1959 $3.50 lib. bdg. $3.27

A MASQUE OF MERCY: Companion piece to "A Masque of Reason." *Holt* 1947 $2.50

IN THE CLEARING. *Holt* 1962 $4.95 pap. $1.95. The first collection of new poems since 1947; includes a reprinting of "The Gift Outright," which Frost recited at the Inauguration of President John F. Kennedy (Jan. 20, 1961), as well as the special dedication which the poet wrote but could not read on that occasion because of the glaring sunlight.

ROBERT FROST: Farm-Poultry Man. Ed. by Edward C. Lathem and Lawrance Thompson. *Univ. Press of New England* 1963 $5.00

ROBERT FROST READS HIS POETRY. A recording. *Caedmon* TC 1060 $5.95

THE SELECTED LETTERS OF ROBERT FROST. Comp. by Lawrance Thompson, Frost's official biographer. *Holt* 1964 $10.00

Books about Frost

Robert Frost: A Study in Sensibility and Good Sense. By Gorham B. Munson. 1927. *Haskell* 1967 $5.95; *Kennikat* 1968 $6.00

New Poetry of New England: Frost and Robinson. By Robert P. T. Coffin. 1938. *Russell & Russell* 1964 $10.00

Fire and Ice: The Art and Thought of Robert Frost. By Lawrance Thompson. 1942. *Russell & Russell* 1961 $10.00

Swinger of Birches: A Portrait of Robert Frost. By Sidney Cox. Introd. by Robert Frost. *New York Univ. Press* 1957 $6.95; *Macmillan* Collier Bks. pap. $.95

Robert Frost. By Lawrance Thompson. Pamphlets on American Writers *Univ. of Minnesota Press* 1959 rev. ed. 1964 pap. $1.25. Critical appraisal with biographical notes and bibliography. This book is a general brief introduction to Frost's poetry. Lawrance Thompson's consistent scholarship makes it also of interest to the serious student of Frost's work. Selected bibliography is useful.

The Pastoral Art of Robert Frost. By John F. Lynen. *Yale Univ. Press* 1960 $7.50 pap. $1.45. A major contribution to the art of criticism.

Robert Frost: The Trial by Existence. By Elizabeth Shepley Sergeant. *Holt* 1960 $6.50. This was authorized by Frost in the 1940s and was many years underway. Part biography, part criticism and part interpretation based on long personal acquaintance.

Robert Frost: An Introduction. Ed. by Robert A. Greenberg and James G. Hepburn. *Holt* 1961 (orig.) pap. $2.65

A Collection of Crtical Essays. Ed. by James M. Cox. *Prentice-Hall* $5.95 Spectrum Bks. $1.95

An Introduction to Robert Frost. By Elizabeth Isaacs. 1962. *Haskell* 1972 $8.95. A valuable analytical study.

The Poetry of Robert Frost. By John R. Doyle, Jr. *Hafner* 1962 $8.95

The Major Themes of Robert Frost. By Radcliffe Squires. *Univ. of Michigan Press* 1963 $3.95 Ann Arbor Bks. pap. $1.95

The Poetry of Robert Frost: Constellations of Intention. By Reuben A. Brower. *Oxford* 1963 $7.50 Galaxy Bks. pap. $2.50. This thorough appraisal is by a professor of English at Harvard.

Robert Frost: The Aim Was Song. By Jean Gould. *Dodd* 1963 $6.95. A biography including material the author gathered from Frost himself in his Vermont cottage.

Robert Frost: Life and Talks–Walking. By Louis Mertins. *Univ. of Oklahoma Press* 1965 $8.50
"It is [the] recorded talk . . . which makes Mr. Mertin's book so fascinating and so valuable. In fact, he has come within an ace of creating Frost's autobiography"—(*N.Y. Times*).

Robert Frost and His Reputation. By Douglas Grant. *Sidney Univ. Press* (dist. by Intl. Scholastic Bk. Services) pap. $1.05

Frost: The Poet and His Poetry. By David A. Sohn and R. Tyre. *Holt* 1967 pap. $2.60 text ed. $1.95; *Bantam* pap. $.75

Robert Frost. By Philip L. Gerber. United States Authors Ser. *Twayne* 1966 $5.50; *College & Univ. Press* 1967 $2.45

Robert Frost: The Early Years, 1874–1915. By Lawrance Thompson. *Holt* 1966 $12.50
Dr. Thompson received the Melville Cane Award for this definitive early biography. "To see the man close yet not to be one with him, to be broadly sympathetic and understanding, but to extenuate nothing nor make the ill appear good, to present the poet, warts and all, is a job that requires unrelenting honesty and literary skill—all of which Mr. Thompson has in abundance. The result is a life that has the pulse of good fiction, with a central hero who never leaves the stage, who is presented in all his complexities, with his truculence, his moodiness, his brooding and his sometimes violent temperament"— (*N.Y. Times*).

New Hampshire's Child: Derry Journals of Lesley Frost. By Lesley Frost. Supplementary notes by Lawrance Thompson and Arnold Grade. *State Univ. of New York Press* 1968 $9.25 microfiche $14.00. A handsome facsimile edition of Frost's daughter's journals. The reader catches a fascinating glimpse of Frost's personality "backstage."

Robert Frost: The Years of Triumph 1915–1938. By Lawrance Thompson. *Holt* 1970 $15.00 This second volume of the projected three-volume biography of Robert Frost evinces the same depth and perceptiveness as the award-winning "The Early Years" (*see above*). The period dating from Frost's return from Europe in 1915 to death of his wife in 1938 is treated in this fine book, necessary to any collection of Frost materials.

Time to Talk: Conversations and Indiscretions Recorded by Robert Francis. By Robert Francis. *Univ. of Massachusetts Press* 1972 $7.50. These conversations and reminiscences are drawn from the author's journals during the 1930s and 1950s. A fascinating sort of book sure to be of interest to Frost students and also to the reader of biographies. Francis was one of the young poets to receive encouragement from Frost over the years.

SANDBURG, CARL. 1878–1967.

At Sandburg's death eulogies were given by Mark Van Doren, Archibald MacLeish and President Johnson. In the President's tribute he said, "Carl Sandburg was more than the voice of America, more than the poet of its strength and genius. He was America. We knew and cherished him as the bard of democracy, the echo of the people, our conscience and chronicler of truth and beauty and purpose. Carl Sandburg needs no epitaph. It is written for all time in the fields, the cities, the face and the heart of the land he loved and the people he celebrated and inspired. . . . He gave us the truest and most enduring vision of our own greatness."

"Poet, newspaper man, historian, wandering minstrel, collector of folk songs, spinner of tales for children, his place in American letters is not easily categorized. But it is a niche that he has made uniquely his own"— (*N.Y. Times*). Carl Sandburg was the labor laureate of America. He sang the feelings of the working classes. Hardly an industry but is celebrated in his pages. His is the poetry of commonplace livelihoods.

Sandburg received the Pulitzer Prize for Poetry in 1951 for his "Complete Poems." (One of his most famous—and briefest—poems, "Fog," was written in the anteroom of a juvenile court as he was waiting to interview a judge.) The last four volumes of his life of Lincoln had brought him the Pulitzer Prize for History in 1940. Sixteen years in the writing, it was lengthier than the Bible or all the known works of Shakespeare. "Always the Young Strangers," "a long nostalgic autobiographical memoir," gives the background of his boyhood in a typical small town located in the heart of the Lincoln country. His Swedish immigrant parents had settled and he was born in Galesburg, Ill., where there were people who had known Lincoln. "Prairie Town Boy" (*Harcourt* 1955 $3.75) contains selections of interest to young people. The little Galesburg cottage in which he was born was dedicated in 1946 as a literary shrine. In 1956 the University of Illinois acquired his manuscripts, books and papers, held in a special collection.

In addition to the Lincoln volumes, his prose works include "Rootabaga Stories" for children (*Harcourt* 1936 $5.45); an omnibus volume which combines "Rootabaga Stories" (1922) and "Rootabaga Pigeons" (1923); and a very long, not wholly successful, historical novel "Remembrance Rock" (*Harcourt* 1948 $12.00; *Pop. Lib.* pap. $1.50). He compiled "The American Songbag" 280 songs, ballads and ditties sung by men in the making of America (1927 *Harcourt* 1936 $7.95 *Harvest Bks.* pap. $4.95) and edited "The New American Songbag" (1950, o. p.).

He received honorary degrees from colleges and universities both here and abroad. Among his many awards were the 1952 Gold Medal for History and Biography from the American Academy of Arts and Letters; the 1953 Poetry Society of America's gold medal for distinguished achievement; and the 1955 Boston Arts Festival Award in recognition of "continuous meritorious contribution to the art of American poetry." In 1959 he was asked to address a Joint Session of Congress on the 150th anniversary of Abraham Lincoln's birth. Later that year he traveled under State Department auspices to the United States Trade Fair in Moscow, to Stockholm, Paris and London. In 1960 he received from the Chamber of Commerce of the United States a citation as a Great Living American "for the significant and lasting contribution which he has made to American literature."

COMPLETE POEMS. *Harcourt* 1950 rev. ed. 1970 $12.50. All the poems in his six previously published volumes, with 74 poems not hitherto collected.

SELECTED POEMS. Ed. by Rebecca West. *Harcourt* 1926 $6.50

HARVEST POEMS: 1910–1960. Introd. by Mark Van Doren. *Harcourt* Harvest Bks. 1960 pap. $1.45. Representative selection including 13 poems never before in book form.

WIND SONG. Ill. by Willaim A. Smith. *Harcourt* 1960 $3.75 pap. $.45. The poet's choice of 79 of his poems particularly suitable for children, with 16 new poems.

THE SANDBURG TREASURY: Prose and Poetry for Young People. Introd. by Paula Sandburg. *Harcourt* 1970 $8.50. Includes "Rootabaga Stories," "Early Moon," "Wind Song," "Prairie Town Boy" and "Abe Lincoln Grows Up."

EARLY MOON. 1930. *Harcourt* $4.70. A selection of Sandburg's poetry for young people.

THE PEOPLE, YES. *Harcourt* 1936 $7.50

THE PEOPLE, YES. A record of Sandburg reading. *Caedmon* TC 2023 $11.90

HONEY AND SALT. New verse, 1958–62; the poet's "intensely lyrical and human volume" published on his 85th birthday. *Harcourt* 1963 $5.50 pap. $.50

CARL SANDBURG READING HIS POETRY. A recording. *Caedmon* TC 1150 $5.95

ALWAYS THE YOUNG STRANGERS. Autobiography. *Harcourt* 1953 $8.75

CARL SANDBURG READS FROM HIS AUTOBIOGRAPHY, ALWAYS THE YOUNG STRANGERS. *Caedmon* TC 1209 $5.95

LETTERS. Ed. by Herbert Mitgang. Over 600 letters covering 64 years. *Harcourt* 1968 $12.50

Books about Sandburg

Carl Sandburg. By Richard Crowder in the United States Authors Ser. *Twayne* 1963 $5.50; *College & Univ. Press* 1964 pap. $2.45

The America of Carl Sandburg. By Hazel Durnell. *Univ. Press of Washington D.C.* $4.00 lib. bdg. $6.00

Sandburg: Photographers View Carl Sandburg. Ed. by Edward Steichen. *Harcourt* 1966 $10.75
   These photographs "picture a man of love, warmth, and integrity. Picture-biographies are not always successful, but this one creates . . . the life of a man integrated with his environment and proud of his heritage"—(*LJ*).

Carl Sandburg. By Gay Wilson Allen. Pamphlets on American Writers *Univ. of Minnesota Press* 1972 pap. $1.25. A good introduction to the poetry of Sandburg, with a selected bibliography. Background of the poetry is given, the general mood of America at the time. Useful to the beginning student.

Carl Sandburg: Poet and Historian. By Lucas Longo. Ed. by Steve Rahmas. *SamHar Press* 1973 $1.98 pap. $.98

Carl Sandburg, Lincoln of Our Literature: A Biography. By North Callahan. *New York Univ. Press* 1970 $6.95. Illustrated with photographs of Carl Sandburg and his family. Index and notes. A well-written biography with emphasis on life of the poet, not his works.

LINDSAY, (NICHOLAS) VACHEL. 1879–1931.

The appeal of Lindsay's poetry is first and foremost one of sound. Many of the poems are meant to be chanted aloud, intoned and sung. The poet was a new phenomenon in his day and became famous for his recitation of his own poems. He made two famous walking trips on which he carried only his pamphlet "Rhymes to Be Traded for Bread"; the story of these trips appears in "Adventures While Preaching the Gospel of Beauty" (1914 1921, *Finch Press* $12.00) and "A Handy Guide for Beggars" (1916, o. p.). He preached a "gospel of beauty" expressed in almost primitive cadences; "The Congo" was a poem that became enormously popular. His early art studies under Robert Henri gave him the ability to illustrate his own poems. "Going-to-the-Sun" (1923, o. p.) and "Every Soul Is a Circus" (1928, o. p.) contain some of his curious and original conceptions. "Where a Lad Is," an appealing memoir of Lindsay's early life, family associations and close ties with Springfield, Ill., was written by Ralph L. Schroeder (1962, o. p.). The author drew upon Lindsay's own writings, excerpts from his diaries and letters and other material.

COLLECTED POEMS. 1923. *Macmillan* rev. ed. ill. by the author. 1925 $7.95

SELECTED POEMS. Ed. with introd. by Mark Harris. *Macmillan* 1963 $5.95 Collier Bks. pap. $1.95

JOHNNY APPLESEED AND OTHER POEMS. *Macmillan* 1928 $4.50. A selection made chiefly with boys and girls in mind.

SPRINGFIELD TOWN IS BUTTERFLY TOWN (1922) AND OTHER POEMS FOR CHILDREN. Ed. by Pierre Dussert. *Kent State Univ. Press* 1969 $3.95

ADVENTURES, RHYMES AND DESIGNS: Early Writings. Introd. by Robert F. Sayre. *Eakins* 1968 $8.95 pap. $3.95

VACHEL LINDSAY READING THE CONGO, THE CHINESE NIGHTINGALE, AND OTHER POEMS. A recording. *Caedmon* TC 1041 $5.95

Books about Lindsay

Some Modern Poets and Other Critical Essays. By Edward Davison. Facs. ed. 1928 *Bks. for Libraries* 1968 $9.75. Though this book of criticism ranging from Robert Burns through William Butler Yeats is more a collection of general poetry critiques, it treats of Vachel Lindsay in a separate chapter. The essay on Lindsay is a good perceptive discussion of interest to Lindsay scholars.

Vachel Lindsay: A Poet in America. By Edgar L. Masters. 1935. *Biblo & Tannen* 1969 $15.00. A sensitively written and informative biography more personal than critical.

Vachel Lindsay: Field Worker for the American Dream. By Ann Massa. *Indiana Univ. Press* 1970 $10.00. The axis of this book is the delineation of Lindsay's American ideology. Gives a perspective on American culture of interest to the general reader as well as to the critic of Lindsay's poetry. The illustrations include Lindsay's cartoons, his American hieroglyphics and drawings for children's poems. Indexes, bibliography and notes.

STEVENS, WALLACE. 1879–1955.

"Wallace Stevens was so fine and rare a poet, such a dazzling virtuoso on the keyboard of language, that he became one with his instrument. . . . In the natural universe he found his lights and colors, things in themselves, an infinite store of metaphors. . . . His formality, his air of imperturbable urbanity, his coolness, his assiduous cultivation of the role of burgher and connoisseur, of 'spiritual epicure,' [perhaps] masked a fundamental insecurity [which flawed the man, not his art. Today he stands] as one of the unchallenged masters of modern poetry"—(Stanley Kunitz, in the *New Republic*).

After attending Harvard and New York Law School, Stevens was admitted to the bar in 1904, was associated with the Hartford Accident and Indemnity Company after 1916, was made a vice president in 1934 and was also vice president of the Hartford Livestock Insurance Company. He believed that "it gives a man character as a poet to have this daily contact with a job." He did not gain general recognition until Harriet Monroe included four of his poems in a war number of *Poetry* in 1914. In 1915 *Poetry* awarded him a prize for his "Three Travelers Watch a Sunrise," a one-act play in free verse. He received the Bollingen Prize in Poetry in 1949 and the National Book Award for Poetry in 1950 for "The Auroras of Autumn" (1950, o. p.). In 1955 he received the National Book Award for the second time for "The Collected Poems," "because he is a great poet," and the same year the Pulitzer Prize. "The Necessary Angel: Essays on Reality and the Imagination" (1951, *Random* Vintage Bks. pap. $1.45) stands as his poetic credo.

COLLECTED POEMS. Contains all but three of previously published works and 25 later poems. Its publication celebrated his 75th birthday. *Knopf* 1954. $10.00

OPUS POSTHUMOUS. Poems, plays, prose. Ed. with introd. by Samuel French Morse. *Knopf* 1957 $8.95

THE PALM AT THE END OF THE MIND: Selected Poems and a Play. Ed. by Holly Stevens. *Knopf* 1971 $10.00; *Random* Vintage Bks. pap. $2.45

WALLACE STEVENS READING HIS POEMS. A recording. *Caedmon* TC 1068 $5.95

LETTERS OF WALLACE STEVENS. Ed. by Holly Stevens. *Knopf* 1966 $17.50

This collection of over 800 letters is selected by Mr. Stevens' daughter, who has, in addition, supplied extracts from his unpublished private journal and letters to him from his father. "A rich unforgettable mailbag. . . . Few poets in their letters have talked so freely about their art and their intentions and scruples. . . . The result is a treasury . . . a harvest . . . a delight, . . . as close to a true biography as we are likely to get or need. . . . His letters are the notes through which he created not only his poems but himself"—(Norman Holmes Pearson, in the *N.Y. Times*).

Books about Stevens

Shaping Spirit: A Study of Wallace Stevens. By William V. O'Connor. 1950. *Russell & Russell* 1964 $8.00

Wallace Stevens Checklist and Bibliography of Stevens Criticism. By Samuel French Morse. *Swallow* 1954 rev. ed. 1963 $3.50

Wallace Stevens: An Approach to His Poetry and Thought. By Robert Pack. 1958 *Gordian* $7.00

The Achievement of Wallace Stevens. By Ashley Brown and Robert S. Haller. 1962. *Gordian* 1973 $9.00

The Comic Spirit of Wallace Stevens. By Daniel Fuchs. *Duke Univ. Press* 1963 $7.25

Wallace Stevens: A Collection of Critical Essays. Ed. by Marie Boroff. *Prentice-Hall* 1963 Spectrum Bks. pap. $1.95

Wallace Stevens: Images and Judgements. By John J. Enck. *Southern Illinois Univ. Press* 1964 $4.95

Acts of the Mind: Essays on the Poetry of Wallace Stevens. Ed. by R. H. Pearce and J. H. Miller. *Johns Hopkins Univ. Press* 1965 $8.00

Clairvoyant Eye: The Poetry and Poetics of Wallace Stevens. By Joseph N. Riddel. *Louisiana State Univ. Press* 1964 $7.50 pap. $2.25

Treats Stevens' poems as "individual and complete 'acts of mind' " and comments on Wallace Stevens' theory of poetry and aesthetic generalizations. A good solid study of his poetry considered one of "the best books we have had"—(Norman Holmes Pearson).

Wallace Stevens: An Anatomy of Figuration. By Eugene P. Nassar. *Univ. of Pennsylvania Press* 1965 $8.00

Stevens' Poetry of Thought. By Frank Doggett. *Johns Hopkins Univ. Press* 1966 $8.50 pap. $2.25 "An Important study"—(*LJ*).

Wallace Stevens: Art of Uncertainty. By Herbert J. Stern. *Univ. of Michigan Press* 1966 $5.95

Wallace Stevens: Musing the Obscure—An Interpretation and a Guide to the Collected Poetry. By Ronald Sukenick, with introd. *New York Univ. Press* 1967 $8.95 pap. $2.75

Stevens' "philosophical, theoretical textures become less formidable [with this] relentless, well-annotated examination of individual poems. . . . Useful for both serious student and frustrated layman"—(*LJ*). These are line-by-line readings of several poems.

Wallace Stevens: The Making of *Harmonium*. By Robert Buttel. *Princeton Univ. Press* 1967 $10.00

A critical study tracing Stevens' poetic development from his Harvard days through his first published work. One "seldom encounters such an interesting, valuable and unlabored presentation utilizing many unpublished sources"—(*LJ*).

The Dome and the Rock: Structure in the Poetry of Wallace Stevens. By James Baird. *Johns Hopkins Univ. Press* 1968 $12.00. This book is a well-documented volume useful to the serious reader of Wallace Stevens. Baird explores Stevens' concept of the essential poem and the idea of Stevens' separate lyrics interrelating into one final organic poem. Interesting discussion of architectural concepts as they relate to Stevens' work.

Wallace Stevens. By William Burney. United States Authors Ser. *Twayne* 1968 $5.50; *College and Univ. Press* pap. $2.45. This is the first book to deal with a complete paraphrase of Stevens' "Collected Poems." Major themes are treated as they arise chronologically in the book. A good introductory work.

On Extended Wings: Wallace Stevens Longer Poems. By Helen H. Vendler. *Harvard Univ. Press* 1969 $9.50 pap. $2.45. This in depth study of the longer poems was awarded the James Russell Lowell prize and the Explicator prize and certainly deserves all the critical acclaim given it. Examines the style/form of each of the poems as well as subject matter. An illuminating work which is the definitive study on the subject.

Wallace Stevens: His Life as Poetry. By Samuel French Morse. Ed. by John Mulder. 1950. *Pegasus* 1970 $6.95

Wallace Stevens, Whole Harmonium. By Richard A. Blessing. *Syracuse Univ. Press* 1970 $7.50. A close textual analysis of the poems, letters and critical works of Wallace Stevens. Blessing deals with the idea of the "grand poems." Use of explication rather than biography as a critical approach makes this a particularly informative book.

Wallace Stevens: The Poem as Act. By Merle E. Brown. *Wayne State Univ. Press* 1971 $8.50. A difficult book dealing with approaches to the criticism of Stevens' poems as well as proving the author's theory that "the poem itself is the translating of feeling into vision and both feeling and vision are included within the act of translating and have their only existence as part of that action." Of interest only to the scholar or serious student.

Images of Wallace Stevens. By Edward Kessler. *Rutgers Univ. Press* 1972 $10.00. A discussion of the general patterns of Stevens' major imagery. Kessler treats the influence of the French symbolists on Stevens, though not as thoroughly as Benamou (*see below*). He analyzes the repeating specific image patterns which inform Stevens' poems from the earliest to the final one. A good scholarly introduction to Stevens' work.

Introspective Voyager: The Poetic Development of Wallace Stevens. By Walton A. Litz. *Oxford* 1972 $7.50. A discussion primarily of the early poems, this book seeks to illuminate the complex stages of Stevens' poetic development. Using a chronological approach to the poems, Litz does treat in less detail the later works. This is a solid scholarly work of interest to Stevens students. A good critical book complete with various appendixes and separate indexes of works and general items.

Wallace Stevens and the Symbolist Imagination. By Michel Benamou. *Princeton Univ. Press* 1972 $7.50. Part of the Princeton Essays in European and Comparative Literature, this book is a scholarly study of Stevens' relationship to the symbolists of the French poetic tradition. Stevens' affinities with and differences from Baudelaire, Laforgue, Mallarmé, the Impressionists, and the Cubists are considered. Appendix gives suggested further readings and a note on Stevens' personal art collection. A thorough and first-rate consideration necessary to the reader and student of Stevens' poetry.

Wallace Stevens: A Descriptive Bibliography. By J. M. Edelstein *Univ. of Pittsburgh Press* 1973 $24.00

BYNNER, WITTER. 1881–1968.

After his graduation from Harvard, where he was on the staff of the *Advocate*, Bynner became assistant editor of *McClure's Magazine*. He began writing and publishing poetry in New Hampshire after the success of his first book of poems, "Young Harvard" (1907, o. p.). A year of teaching a course in verse-writing at the University of California was followed by extensive travels in the Orient, particularly in China. Chinese poetry became the great literary influence in his life. His melodious lyric style changed with the translation of "The Jade Mountain: A Chinese Anthology" (*Knopf* 1929 $4.95), the first volume of Chinese verse to be translated in full by an American poet. The love of epigram and concentrated simplicity within conventional verse forms marked his work. His translation of the Chinese poet-philosopher Laotzu (*q. v.*), "The Way of Life According to Laotzu" (trans. with introd. by Witter Bynner *Putnam* Capricorn Bks. 1962 pap. $.95) is unique in its poetic vision and serenity.

BOOK OF LYRICS. *Knopf* 1955 1958 $4.50

NEW POEMS, 1960. *Knopf* 1960 $4.50

Books about Bynner

The Spectra Hoax. By William Jay Smith. *Wesleyan Univ. Press* 1961 $6.00
" 'Spectra' was a volume of 'experimental' poems by Emanuel Morgan and Anne Knish, published in 1916. It was taken seriously by the critical pundits as establishing a new school of poetry. For almost two years the identity of its perpetrators and that it was a hoax, were not known to the public. . . . It was thought up by a young poet, Witter Bynner . . . and worked out with his friend, Arthur Davison Ficke. . . . To spoof the current furore over free verse they wrote freer verse to prove that anyone can toss words together, no matter how nonsensically and have the result accepted as serious experimental poetry"—(*Chicago Sunday Tribune*).

WILLIAMS, WILLIAM CARLOS. 1883–1963.

Poet, artist and formerly a practicing physician of Rutherford, N.J., Dr. Williams wrote poetry experimental in form, ranging from imagism to objectivism with great originality of idiom and human vitality. He has been credited with changing and directing American poetry toward a new metric and language, cut off from British tradition, more than any poet since Whitman (*q. v.*). Dr. Williams developed in the idiom of the United States with ever-increasing strength. "Although his lines rarely descend to slang, they are full of the conversational speech of the country; they express the brusque nervous tension, the vigor and rhetoric of American life"—(Louis Untermeyer). "Paterson," about the New Jersey city of that name, was his epic, his magnum opus. The British critic Philip Toynbee views it dispassionately in the *Observer* (London): "Like Pound's Cantos, 'Paterson' is partly an assault on modern America and the financial vices of the capitalist system. . . . Beyond the mistakes, the affectations, the mannerisms of his age, one can't help hearing a real poet struggling to get out. 'Paterson' may not quite succeed in its immensely ambitious aim—which was both to celebrate and excoriate the whole of modern America by describing one man's life in one small town—but it is a poem which leaves image after image in the mind. . . . I cannot end without saying that Williams knew—as all good poets have known—that his proper function was to glorify the world; and every passage of disgust in 'Paterson' is a contribution to that end."

National recognition did not come early, but eventually he received many honors: a vice-presidency of the National Academy of Arts and Letters in 1952; the 1953 Bollingen Award; the $5,000 Fellowship of the Academy of American Poets; the Loines Award of the National Institute of Arts and Letters and the Brandeis

Award (1957). Book II of "Paterson" received the first National Book Award for Poetry in 1949. Dr. Williams was named consultant in Poetry in English to the Library of Congress for 1952–53.

John Ciardi (q. v.) wrote in the *Saturday Review*: "His death leaves the feeling of an age ending. First Wallace Stevens. Then Robert Frost. Now William Carlos Williams. But if that age closes, it yet leaves us a golden record of American poetry. The fifty years of Dr. Williams' great productivity were the years in which American poetry threw off its last colonial dependence on England and came securely to rest in the American language. In that literary revolution, of which Eliot and Pound are now the only surviving leaders, Dr. Williams played a powerful part as the maker not only of his own poems, but of the heritage of American poetry." Raymond Rosenthal has recently said in the *New Leader*: "Williams' ability to see all of the banal, stupid, violent, upthrusting and acquiescent aspects of the life around him from that special historical and poetic perspective explains a great deal about his tone and essential outlook. His was a proud stance, full of professional briskness and dignity, yet also dependent on a hard-eyed optimism that has gone completely out of our poetry. That is why he is the last of a great line." And another critic: "As modern poetry consolidates its academic position and ceases to challenge the young and adventurous, the singularity of Williams' contribution is being discovered, rediscovered, and put to uses that presage the most striking development in American poetry"—(J. M. Brinnin).

His prose works in print include: "Voyage to Pagany" (1928. *Folcroft* 1973 lib. bdg. $22.50; ed. by Harry Leven *New Directions* 1970 $2.95), an autobiographical novel about a small-town American doctor in Europe; "The Great American Novel" (1923. *Folcroft* lib. bdg. $10.00), a group of impressionistic essays; "In the American Grain," a series of essays on America and American historical figures (1929. introd. by Horace Gregory *New Directions* 1939 $5.00 pap. $1.95); the novel "The Build-up" (1952. *New Directions* $4.95 pap. $2.35); the three novels of the trilogy about a businessman, Joe Stecher—"White Mule" (1937. *New Directions* 1967 $4.95 pap. $2.45), "In the Money" (1940. *New Directions* 1967 $4.95 pap. $2.75) and "The Build-up" (1952. *New Directions* 1968 $4.95 pap. $2.35); a selection of critical and evaluative essays representing more than 30 years of defense and promotion of the best modern literature, "Selected Essays" (1954. *New Directions* $7.00 pap. $2.45); "Many Loves and Other Plays" (*New Directions* 1961 $6.50 pap. $2.95); and "Yes, Mrs. Williams: A Personal Record of My Mother" (*Astor-Honor* 1959 $4.95). In "The Farmers' Daughters: The Collected Stories of William Carlos Williams" (introd. by Van Wyck Brooks *New Directions* 1961 $7.00 pap. $3.25), 52 stories from earlier books long out of print are gathered. Written in a "terse, pithy, impressionistic style," Williams "captured the pathos and heroism in the lives of the unsuccessful."

WILLIAM CARLOS WILLIAMS READER. Ed. with introd. by M. L. Rosenthal. *New Directions* 1966 pap. $3.45

"Mr. Rosenthal gives us a very persuasive and intelligent introduction, followed by 100 pages of verse, 30 pages of assorted prose-poetry and nearly 300 pages of assorted prose"—(*Observer*, London).

COLLECTED EARLIER POEMS. *New Directions* 1951 $10.00

COLLECTED LATER POEMS. *New Directions* 1950 rev. ed. 1962 $6.50. Poetry written in the 1940s. In addition to "The Wedge" and "The Clouds," a large number of poems not previously published, notably the sequences entitled "The Pink Church" and "Two Pendants: for the Ears."

SELECTED POEMS. With introd. by Randall Jarrell. *New Directions* 1949 1963 pap. $1.75

PATERSON: A Long Poem. Consists of Books I–V. *New Directions* 1946–58 1-vol. ed. 1968 $6.00 pap. 1963 $1.95

KORA IN HELL: Improvisations. Pocket Poet Ser. *City Lights Books* 1957 pap. $1.50

PICTURES FROM BRUEGHEL. *New Directions* 1967 $5.00 1955 pap. $1.75. New poems and the complete texts of "The Desert Music" (1954) "Journey to Love" (1955).

SELECTED LETTERS. Ed. by John C. Thirwell. 1937 *Astor-Honor* $6.95

AUTOBIOGRAPHY. *New Directions* $6.50 pap. $3.25

DESCENT, THE YELLOW FLOWER, THE HOST, SEAFARER, WORK IN PROGRESS AND OTHER POEMS. A recording. *Caedmon* TC 1047 $5.95

Books about Williams

I Wanted to Write a Poem. Reported and ed. by Edith Heal. *Beacon* 1958 pap. $1.95. Dr. Williams tells how various poems came into being.

William Carlos Williams. By John Malcolm Brinnin. Pamphlets on American Writers. *Univ. of Minnesota Press* 1963 pap. $1.25

The Poems of William Carlos Williams: A Critical Study. By Linda W. Wagner. *Wesleyan Univ. Press* 1964 $6.50

A textual study in which the poet and his widow assisted. "Mrs. Wagner's tough, thorough study supplants Vivienne Koch's 'William Carlos Williams' as the definitive extended statement about a major contemporary poet"—(*LJ*).

Williams' Poetry Talked About. By Eli Siegel and W. C. Williams. 1964 (with title Williams-Siegel "Documentary"). *Definitions* 1970 $5.95

The Poetic World of William Carlos Williams. By Alan Ostrom. *Southern Illinois Univ. Press* 1966 $4.95

William Carlos Williams: A Collection of Critical Essays. By J. Hillis Miller. *Prentice-Hall* 1966 $5.95

Approach to Paterson. By Walter S. Peterson. *Yale Univ. Press* 1967 $6.00

Bibliography of William Carlos Williams. By Emily M. Wallace. *Wesleyan Univ. Press* 1968 $20.00. A magnificent piece of scholarship. The essential reference tool for a Williams collection. As important to the study of Williams as Gallup's "Bibliography" (*q.v.*) is to the study of Pound.

The Music of Survival: A Biography of a Poem by William Carlos Williams. By Paul Sherman. *Univ. of Illinois Press* $5.95. A study and explication of "The Desert Music" from "A Desert Music and Other Poems" by William Carlos Williams, which was written by the poet after a nearly fatal stroke. Contains the full text of the 12-page poem. The book is clearly written with index and notes.

William Carlos Williams. By Thomas R. Whitaker. United States Authors Ser. *Twayne* 1968 $5.50

The Art of William Carlos Williams: A Discovery and Possession of America. By James Guimond. *Univ. of Illinois* 1968 $6.95 pap. $2.45

"This book is a valuable contribution not only to students of the *oeuvre* of a poet of tremendous influence on American poetry, but to those who would like to begin their reading of Williams with an exceptionally good critical introduction to his work"—(*PW*)

Hieroglyphics of a New Speech: Cubism, Stieglitz and the Early Poetry of William Carlos Williams. By Bram Dijkstra. *Princeton Univ. Press* 1969 $10.00. A brilliant study of the influence of Cubisim and the photographer Alfred Stieglitz on the verse of Williams. Illustrated, this book is easy to read and gives general feeling and mood of the period. Index and selected bibliography.

Prose of William Carlos Williams. By Linda Wagner. *Wesleyan Univ. Press* 1970 $8.00. To date the definitive study of William Carlos Williams prose, using worksheets and manuscript notes of the author. Interrelates the prose and poetry with discussions of "Many Loves," "The Stecher Trilogy," and "Kora in Hell' among other prose writings. A piece of excellent scholarship complete with scholarly apparatus (notes, selective biography, index).

William Carlos Williams: An American Artist. By James E. Breslin. *Oxford* 1970 $6.95. A critical study which discusses not only his poetry, but also his experiments with the historical essay, short story, novel, and "epic." It is informative with an unusual subject and thesis.

William Carlos Williams' Paterson: Language and Landscape. By Joel Conarroe. *Univ. of Pennsylvania Press* 1970 $6.95

A Companion to William Carlos Williams' Paterson. By Benjamin Sankey. *Univ. of California Press* 1971 $8.50. A book-length study of Williams' epic using manuscript material to elucidate the poems. Traces the part this work played in the poetic development of Williams. A line-by-line guide to the poem which helps the reader approach the work and study it.

William Carlos Williams: The American Background. By Mike Weaver. *Cambridge* 1971 $9.50. The author stresses the American viewpoint and attitudes which shaped William Carlos Williams' work. The poems are explored in terms of American cultural experience, particularly that with which Williams had personal contact. An excellent study of the early part of this century as well as an insightful interrelating of the poet's familial and personal background to the times and his work. Appendix A contains selections from Thomas Ward's "Passaic" and B contains notes to "Paterson."

TEASDALE, SARA. 1884–1933.

When her early work appeared in the first two decades of this century, critics were warm in their praise of her poems, agreeing that the brevity, the simplicity, the rare musical quality and the technical perfection of her work placed it among the finest American lyric poetry. Many of her poems have been set to music and many have been translated into foreign languages, notably Japanese. She was the editor of "The Answering Voice: Love Lyrics by Women" (1928. *Bks. for Libraries* $9.50). Margaret Haley Carpenter's biography (1960) has recently gone out of print.

COLLECTED POEMS. 1937. Ed. with a long biographical introd. by Marya Zaturenska. *Macmillan* 1967 $5.95 Collier Bks. pap. $1.95

STARS TO-NIGHT. *Macmillan* 1930 $3.50

WYLIE, ELINOR (HOYT). 1885–1928.

Elinor Wylie wrote four exquisite novels and four slim books of poetry. Her "Collected Prose" (1933, o.p.) contains: "Jennifer Lorn" (1923) and "The Venetian Glass Nephew" (1925), both laid in the 18th century; "The Orphan Angel" (1926, o.p.), a story about the poet Shelley, who in it does not drown but comes to America; and "Mr. Hodge and Mr. Hazard" (1928).

It is as a poet that Elinor Wylie will be remembered. "Whether she spins a web of words to catch an elusive whimsicality, or satirizes herself, or plunges from the fragmentary to the profound, every line bears her authentic stamp. The intellectual versatility is eventually reinforced by spiritual strength, insuring permanence to work which 'preserves a shape utterly its own' "—(Louis Untermeyer).

Two volumes of interest are o.p.: "Elinor Wylie" by Nancy Hoyt, her sister, which contains a number of previously unpublished poems (1935), and "Last Poems," transcribed by Jane D. Wise, with other poems hitherto unpublished in book form, with a foreword by William Rose Benét and a tribute by Edith Oliver (1943).

COLLECTED POEMS. Ed. with fwd. by her husband, William Rose Benét. Nets to Catch the Wind (1921); Black Armour (1923); Trivial Breath (1928); Angels and Earthly Creatures (1929). *Knopf* 1932 $8.95

Books about Wylie

Eleanor Wylie. By William Rose Benét. *Bern Porter* 1971 $7.50

POUND, EZRA. 1885–1972.

"Pound's letters to James Joyce, written from December 1913, to December 1939 . . . reveal Pound as Joyce's link with the English literary world during Joyce's years of exile. . . . The volume contains all of Pound's surviving letters to Joyce, some 62 of them, most of which are published for the first time, and articles on Joyce which have never before been reprinted"—(*LJ*). "Read points out how fruitful the relationship was for both men and in what a good-humored and generous light it shows Pound. Read's editing is careful and thoughtful; his interspersed notes are graceful and informative"—(*PW*).

With T. S. Eliot, Ezra Pound was one of the two main influences on British and American poetry between the two World Wars. Hayden Carruth wrote in the *Saturday Review* in 1966: "Pound alone in our time has created Style. . . . Pound's best poetry attracts every literate sensibility without reference to temperament or sympathy; it transcends taste." The collection of the 384 "Letters, 1907–1941" revealed the great erudition of this most controversial expatriate poet. Pound was born in Idaho. He was graduated from the University of Pennsylvania and went abroad to live in 1908. His first book, a small collection of poems, "A Lume Spento," was published in Venice in 1908. With the publication of "Personae" in London in 1909, he became the leader of the imagists abroad. Later he withdrew from the movement, "but the critical concepts he propounded during his imagist period probably had more to do with the development of modern poetry in England and America than any other single influence"—(*Reader's Encyclopedia of American Literature*).

His writings have been subject to many foreign influences. First he imitated the troubadours, using five of their forms; then he came under the influence of the Chinese and Japanese poets. "The Cantos," his major work, which he added to over many years, is a mixture of modern colloquial language and classical quotation. "The Pisan Cantos," written during his imprisonment in Italy, is more autobiographical.

Pound's prose as well as his poetry has been influential. "The Spirit of Romance" is a revision of his studies of little-known Romance writers (1910. *New Directions* 1952 pap. $2.45). "A B C of Reading" (1934. *New Directions* New Classics Series 1951 1960 pap. $1.75) is a characteristic exposition of a critical method. Critical writings are "Literary Essays of Ezra Pound," with an introduction by T. S. Eliot (*New Directions* 1953 pap. $3.25); "Instigations" (1920. *Bks. for Libraries* $12.00), "Polite Essays" (1937. *Bks. for Libraries* 1967 $9.00), "Antheil and the Treatise on Harmony" (1924. *DaCapo* $7.50) and "Patria Mia and The Treatise on Harmony" (*Hillary House* 1950 rept. 1962 $7.25). His "Guide to Kulchur" (1938. *New Directions* 1952 pap. $2.95) contains short, dynamic and stimulating chapters on the world's "kulchur" from the Chinese philosophers to the modern poets.

Mr. Pound was a linguist, and T. S. Eliot (*q.v.*) has called him "the inventor of Chinese poetry for our time." His greatest translating achievements from Japanese, Chinese, Anglo-Saxon, Italian, Provençal and French are collected in "The Translations of Ezra Pound" (*New Directions* 1953, with 40 pages of additional uncollected translations 1963 rev. ed. pap. $2.95). Among his other writings are: "Make it New: Essays" (1935. *Scholarly Press* 1971 $22.00), "Jefferson and/or Mussolini" (*Liveright* 1970 $6.95 pap. $1.95), a discussion of American democracy and capitalism and fascism, and "The Classic Noh Theatre of Japan" with Ernest Fernollosa (*New Directions* 1953 pap. $2.25).

Living in Italy, Pound felt that some of the practices of Mussolini were in accord with the doctrines of "social credit," in which he had become interested in the 1920s and 1930s, and he espoused some of the general applications of Fascism. During World War II he broadcast, on the Italian radio, a series of programs addressed to the Allied troops. He was indicted for treason and brought to the United States to stand trial in 1946. He was adjudged mentally incompetent to prepare a defense and was committed to St. Elizabeth's Hospital in Washington, D.C. After a concerted appeal to the federal government by American poets, led by Robert Frost, Pound was at last released in 1958 and returned to Italy.

PERSONAE: COLLECTED POEMS. 1926. All the early work he cares to preserve. *New Directions* new and enl. ed. 1949 $7.50.

SELECTED POEMS. *New Directions* New Class. 1949 rev. ed. 1957 pap. $1.50

SELECTED PROSE. 1909–1965. Ed. by William Cookson. *New Directions* 1973 $15.00. Gathers previously uncollected prose pieces of Pound's, including pieces on religion, Confucius, America (including the famed "What I feel about Walt Whitman") economics and history, poetry, and his contemporaries. The whole of *"Patria Mia"* is also reprinted in this valuable and well-edited volume. Necessary to any Pound collection.

A LUME SPENTO AND OTHER EARLY POEMS. Pound's first two volumes of poetry (1908) and other unpublished pieces. *New Directions* $7.50

A QUINZAINE FOR THIS YULE. 1908. *Gordon Press* $8.95

EXULTATIONS. 1909. *Haskell* 1973 $7.95

THE CANTOS. (Cantos 1–117). 1911–1969. Rev. ed. incorporating "Thrones," "Drafts and Fragments" and "Canto 120". *New Directions* 1963 rev. ed. 1972 $12.50

DRAFTS AND FRAGMENTS, CANTOS 110–117. *New Directions* 1969 $3.95

SELECTED CANTOS. *New Directions* 1970 pap. $1.95. Pound's own selection from the monumental Cantos. Of use to the general poetry reader and beginning Pound student.

LUSTRA. 1916. *Haskell* 1973 $8.95

EZRA POUND IN ITALY: From the Pisan Cantos. *Wittenborn* 1971 $24.00

PAVANNES AND DIVAGATIONS. Collection of lighter pieces, both prose and poetry. *New Directions* 1958 $5.75

EZRA POUND READING HIS POETRY. A recording. *Caedmon* TC 1122 $5.95

GAUDIER-BRZESKA: A Memoir. 1916. This remarkable French sculptor was killed in World War I at the age of 24. *New Directions* rev. ed. 1960 $7.50

POUND/JOYCE: THE LETTERS OF EZRA POUND TO JAMES JOYCE, with POUND'S ESSAYS ON JOYCE. Ed. with commentary by Forrest Read. *New Directions* (dist. by Lippincott) 1967 $10.00 pap. $2.75

Books about Pound

The Poetry of Ezra Pound. By Alice S. Amdur. 1936. *Russell & Russell* $8.00
An Examination of Ezra Pound: A Collection of Essays. Ed. by Peter Russell. 1950. *Gordian* 1971 $10.00; *Haskell* lib. bdg. $9.95. This early collection of Pound criticism was gathered for the poet's sixty-fifth birthday. Although the essays are now old and some have been superceded by more recent Pound scholarship, the contributions are still interesting. Particularly notable are pieces by Hemingway, Eliot, Edith Sitwell, Marshall McLuhan and Wyndham Lewis.
The Poetry of Ezra Pound. By Hugh Kenner. 1941 *Kraus* 1968 $14.00. Once again available, this classic of Pound scholarship is, as the author points out, intended for "the reader who does not need to be persuaded about contemporary writing in general . . . but whom thickets of misunderstanding have kept at a distance from the poetry of Ezra Pound."

New Bearings in English Poetry. By Frank R. Leavis. *Univ. of Michigan Press* 1960 $4.40 Ann Arbor Bks. pap. $1.85. A selective critical book on what is most significant in modern poetry in general, this work has one chapter devoted to Ezra Pound. A very good book which has been called "The best book of sheer criticism" (Geoffrey Grigson), this would be of interest to anyone in the Pound and modern poetry fields.

Ezra Pound. By George S. Fraser. 1961. *Barnes & Noble* 1965 $2.25

Motive and Method in the Cantos of Ezra Pound. Ed. by Lewis Leary. *Columbia* 1961 $7.50 pap. $1.50. A collection of essays by Guy Davenport, Hugh Kenner and others.

Ezra Pound. Ed. by Walter Sutton. *Prentice-Hall* 1963 $5.95. A collection of critical essays.

Ezra Pound. By William Van O'Connor. Pamphlets on American Writers *Univ. of Minnesota Press* 1963 pap. $1.25

Sailing after Knowledge: The Cantos of Ezra Pound. By George Dekker. 1963. *Routledge & Kegan Paul* $8.25

Ezra Pound: The Poet as a Sculptor. By Donald Davie. *Oxford* 1964 $6.50

Bibliography of Ezra Pound. By Donald Gallup. *Oxford* 1964 $20.00
"A model of modern bibliographic style"—(*LJ*).

Ezra Pound and Sextus Propertius: A Study in Creative Translation. By J. P. Sullivan. *Univ. of Texas Press* 1964 $7.50. An examination and defense of Pound's methods of translation, this book includes a detailed study of "The Homage" as a model for verse translation. The text of the Latin poem is included with the complete Pound translation.

Influence of Ezra Pound. By K. L. Goodwin. *Oxford* 1966 $8.25. This book of general criticism discusses Pound's interests and friends chronologically. Then it goes on to discuss the major influences: Pound and Yeats, Pound and Eliot and finally Pound and Williams and Pound and MacLeish.

Reading the Cantos: The Study of Meaning in Ezra Pound. By Noel Stock. *Funk & Wagnalls* 1967 Minerva Bks. pap. $1.95
"In this short, penetrating volume he is mainly worried by a suspicion that many recent critics of The Cantos, especially Hugh Kenner, Donald Davie, and George Dekker have tended to take, in their examination of this longest and most ambitious poem of our century, intention . . . for achievement. He thinks that there is a general belief that the Cantos are far more of a unity, more intricately interlinked, more easy to understand in design and in detail, than a scrupulously close scholarly examination proves them to be. . . . Mr. Stock is not writing polemically. . . . His study demonstrates that . . . Pound has in fact written much grand poetry, if not a complete or coherent major poem—(*TLS*, London).

Ezra Pound: A Close-Up. By Michael Reck. *McGraw-Hill* 1967 $5.95 pap. $2.95
The author, a young poet, was a frequent visitor at St. Elizabeth's during Pound's confinement. "Michael Reck enters a forceful plea for Pound, the man and artist. . . . Pound's madness (if it was that) and his tragedy become on these pages both understandable and moving. Not intended to be a scholarly work, this is an intriguing personal document"—(*PW*).

The Caged Panther: Ezra Pound at St. Elizabeth's. By Harry Meacham. The author worked for Pound's release from the hospital. *Twayne* 1968 $5.00

Early Poetry of Ezra Pound. By Thomas H. Jackson. *Harvard Univ. Press* 1969 $8.25. This book concentrates on "*A Lume Spento*," the original "Personae" and "Exultations" and the "*Canzoni*." Jackson studies the formatory poetics of the young Pound and discusses the influence of Browning on Pound as well as that of the pre-Raphaelites and the decadent poets of the nineties.

The Barb of Time: On the Unity of Ezra Pound's Cantos. By Daniel D. Pearlman. *Oxford* 1969 $8.50. Pearlman tackles the problem of "major form" in "The Cantos" and proves the unity of the work by a discussion of Pound's development of a theory of time. The book treats the analogy between the structure of "The Divine Comedy" and "The Cantos." It is exceptionally readable for such an abstruse subject and seems to be a valuable contribution to Pound scholarship.

Ezra Pound: The Image and the Real. By Herbert N. Schneidau. *Louisiana State Univ. Press* 1969 $5.95. This work is an examination of the poetic interaction and relationships between Pound and Joyce, Eliot, Ernest Fenollosa, Ford Madox Ford, T. E. Hulme and others. Studies Pound's relationship to imagism in depth. This is an excellent study of Pound's poetry.

New Approaches to Ezra Pound: A Coordinated Investigation of Pound's Poetry and Ideas. Ed. and introd. by Eva Hesse. *Univ. of California Press* 1969 $9.50. Eva Hesse, who writes the introduction to this collections of critical essays, is one of the foremost Pound scholars in the world and has translated his works into German. These seminal writings on Pound are by Richard Ellmann, Forrest Read, Christine Brooke-Rose, Hugh Kenner, Leslie Fiedler and other Pound luminaries. Index, chronology and contributors' notes are included.

The Poetry of Ezra Pound: Forms and Renewal 1908–1920. By Hugh Wittemeyer. *Univ. of California Press* 1969 $6.50. A critical study of Ezra Pound's poetry from "*A Lume Spento*" (1908) to "Hugh Selwyn Mauberley" (1920), this book covers the period up to when Pound devoted himself mainly to "The Cantos." Wittemeyer examines Pound's unpublished prose and from this record illuminates the verse. An unusual first-rate critical book called by Hugh Kenner "an indispensible contribution to Pound studies." There is an appendix which includes Richard Aldington's humorous parodies of satires in Ezra Pound's "Lustra."

Vision Fugitive: Ezra Pound and Economics. By Earle Davis. *Univ. Press of Kansas* 1969 $6.95. As necessary to a study of Pound's poetry as a discussion of Provençal troubadours, this book speaks of Pound's "vision" and his economic perspective of history. An elightening guidebook for a controversial subject which becomes essential to an approach to "The Cantos." Index and notes.

Ideas into Action: A Study of Pound's Cantos. By Clark Emery. *Univ. of Miami Press* 1970 $5.95. A work that tries to demonstrate that Pound's Cantos have a method and intelligible form behind them. Not for the general reader, this is a good book for a student with its broad overview of Pound's philosophy and history theories. According to one reviewer it "organizes aspects of Pound's thought as Pound himself has never done"—(*Sewanee Review*).

Life of Ezra Pound. By Noel Stock. *Pantheon* 1970 $10.00. This large and well-documented biography, replete with literary, historical and period detail, is probably the best and most level-headed biography on Pound written so far.

Rose in the Steel Dust: An Examination of the Cantos of Ezra Pound. By Walter Baumann. *Univ. of Miami Press* 1970 $5.95. Approaches "The Cantos" by focusing on two Cantos, Canto IV and Canto LXXXII. A well-documented and scholarly book, this work gives almost a line-by-line interpretation of the two Cantos to support the author's thesis of Pound's form and content.

The Pound Era. By Hugh Kenner. *Univ. of California Press* 1973 pap. $5.95. This detailed account of Pound and the age which seems to surround him, its chief characters (Eliot, Joyce, Lewis) and the chief works, is one of the most fascinating accounts of any period in 20th-century literature. This is a scholarly book sure to interest other readers besides academicians and students, written by one of the eminent Pound authorities. The illustrations are primarily of artworks and artifacts which seem to turn up in the texts of Pound's poems.

A ZBC of Ezra Pound. By Christine Brooke-Rose. *Univ. of California Press* 1971 $7.95. As the author notes this work is primarily a book for "newcomers" to the work of Ezra Pound; it is a good easy-to-read yet scholarly book.

Concordance to the Poems of Ezra Pound. By Gary Lane. *Haskell* 1972 lib. bdg. $17.95. A useful reference book, particularly for a poet of Pound's diversity and difficulty.

Ezra Pound: The Critical Heritage. Ed. by Eric Homberger. *Routledge & Kegan Paul* 1972 $19.50. These writings, essays, reviews and pamphlets on Ezra Pound and his work trace the developing pattern of Pound's reputation during his lifetime. The introduction by the editor gives a general survey of Pound's life and works which discusses in some detail T. S. Eliot as a critic of Pound. The selections are divided in the text into sections dealing with Pound personally (essays by William Carlos Williams, T. S. Eliot and others) and then with the individual books chronologically. An excellent collection.

Ezra Pound and the Troubadour Tradition. By Stuart Y. McDougal. *Princeton Univ. Press* 1973 $8.00. A discussion of Pound's fascination with the troubadours of medieval Provence—Bertran du Born, Arnaud de Mareuil and Peire Bremon, lo Tord and how this fascination led to his development of themes and technique in the early poems. Surprisingly readable in a field where most of the criticism is nearly impenetrable, this book gives background of the medieval period along with important insights to Pound's method of Provençal translations.

Ezra Pound: An Introduction to the Poetry. By Sister Bernetta Quinn. *Columbia* 1973 $8.95. A well and clearly written book essential to a beginning Pound student because of its concise general picture of Pound's life and influences. Chapters are devoted to Pound's early lyrics, his translations and "The Cantos." Written for a nonspecialist, but still founded on solid scholarship, Sr. Bernetta Quinn's book seems to be the best introductory work.

WHEELOCK, JOHN HALL. 1886–

"The past had overtaken him," John Hall Wheelock writes in a presumably autobiographical poem. Perhaps, indeed, the special quality of his verse, noble in sentiment and language, traditional in form and meter, lies in the fact that "the poet . . . has been most deeply influenced by the writers of the last century." His upbringing and education followed a traditional mode—summers on the South Shore (of Long Island), Harvard, postgraduate study at German universities. In 1905 his first volume of verse appeared. Others followed, developing his lifelong themes of "the mystery, the beauty, the sadness and the unity of life." But if committed to the past, Wheelock has not "been taken prisoner." "Neither time nor fashion can dull" his true romanticism, said Louise Bogan of his "Collected Poems." Babette Deutsch (*q.v.*) extolled his durable value: "Deep feeling, set to grave music, stamps the mature work with a timeless quality." "Dear Men and Women" are "elegiac sonnets, celebrations, [and] reflections [which] glimmer with fully ruminated and comprehended experience"—(Peter Davison, in *Atlantic*).

As a senior editor of *Charles Scribner's Sons*, Wheelock has championed the new and unknown in poetry. In his important series, "Poets of Today" he introduced some two dozen American poets previously unpublished, among them Robert Pack, May Swenson and James Dickey. He holds several poetry awards, is a Chancellor of the Academy of American Poets and a member of the National Institute of Arts and Letters. His "What is Poetry?" (1963, o.p.) is an "unabashed defense of poetry, [which] takes a *via media* through poetry's rich varied growth, for Wheelock is slavish neither to tradition nor to mere fashion. His genuine concern is the genuine."

The Gardener and Other Poems. *Scribner* 1961 $3.00

Dear Men and Women: New Poems. *Scribner* 1966 $3.50

By Daylight and in Dream: New and Collected Poems. *Scribner* 1970 $6.95 pap. $2.45

In Love and Song. *Scribner* 1971 lib. bdg. $4.95

H. D. (Hilda Doolittle) 1886–1961.

"H. D.—Imagist," as the poet signed herself, is, in the opinion of Louis Untermeyer, the most perfect of the Imagists, in fact the only true Imagist. Nearly all her poems are on Greek subjects. The "Collected Poems" (1924, new ed. 1940, o.p.) contains all of H. D.'s early works except what appears in the anthology, "Some Imagist Poets" (1915–17, o.p.). Horace Gregory wrote of "Helen in Egypt" (1961, o.p.), "Her critics are well in advance of most of the 'newest' poetry being written today. . . . The latest accomplishments of her lyric style are flawless, the diction clear and pure." "Trilogy" is three long poems written under the impact of World War II.

Born in Bethlehem, Pa., she was educated at a private school and Bryn Mawr. In 1911, after a visit abroad, she helped to organize the Imagists with Ezra Pound and married Richard Aldington, the English poet and novelist, whom she later divorced. Written in poetic prose, her poignant and subtle "Tribute to Freud: With Unpublished Letters by Freud to the Author" (1956. *Godine* 1974 $10.00) is a record of her memories of her analytical experiences 1933–34, a memoir of Freud in London in 1938–39 and a description of the impact of his unique personality. In "Palimpsest" she explored the difficulties a woman finds living sensitively (trying to cultivate both love and art) in a world that is ugly, vulgar and violent. Her novel, "Bid Me to Live, A Madrigal," (1960, o.p.) about a woman's loneliness and self-discoveries during World War I, is a poetic stream-of-consciousness study. She had lived in London since 1911, through the bombings of two world wars and during the latter years in Zurich, Switzerland, coming to New York only on brief visits. In 1959 she was awarded the Brandeis University Creative Arts Award, and in 1960 the Award of Merit Medal for Poetry from the American Academy of Arts and Letters—the first time the latter was awarded to a woman.

Selected Poems of H. D. *Grove* 1957 Evergreen Bks. pap. $2.45. Collected here are 46 poems including excerpts from each of the three long poems in "Trilogy."

Palimpsest. 1926. Ed. by Matthew J. Bruccoli. *Southern Illinois Univ. Press* 1968 $7.95. (A palimpsest is a parchment from which one writing has been erased to make room for another.)

Hermetic Definition. *New Directions* 1972 $8.75 pap. $3.25. Poems.

Trilogy: The Walls Do Not Fall, Tribute to the Angels, The Flowering of the Red. *New Directions* 1973 $6.95 pap. $2.25

Books about H. D. (Hilda Doolittle)

The Classical World of H. D. By Thomas Burnett Swann. *Univ. of Nebraska Press* 1962 $4.75
H. D. By Vincent Quinn. United States Authors Ser. *Twayne* 1967 $5.50; *College & Univ. Press* pap. $2.45

JEFFERS, ROBINSON. 1887–1962.

Here was a poet who after years of traveling settled on a wild, sea-beaten cliff at Carmel, Calif., in what was virtually a literary hermitage, and there set down the tragic folktales of Northern California in ironic epic verse. Jeffers was a poet concerned with cruelty and horror, whose dramatic narratives are filled with scenes of blood and lust, and whose verse shows vigorous beauty and great originality. "Not Man Apart" (ed. by David R. Brower, *Sierra Club* $25.00 *Ballentine* pap. $3.95) is a book of remarkable nature photographs accompanied by descriptive lines from Jeffers' poetry.

He was best known for his free adaptation of Euripides' "Medea" (*French* 1948 $1.75) which was given a notable performance by Judith Anderson in 1947–48. In 1955 it was presented, again with Judith Anderson, in Paris as part of the cultural exchange program. Jeffers won the 1960 Shelley Memorial Award.

SELECTED POETRY. 125 poems arranged chronologically; selected by the poet and his wife. *Random* 1938 $10.00, (with title "Selected Poems") Vintage Bks. pap. $1.65

THE BEGINNING AND THE END. *Random* 1963 $5.95

CAWDOR and MEDEA. *New Directions* 1970 pap. $2.45. Long poem and verse version of Greek classic.

CALIFORNIANS. *Cayucos Bks.* 1971 lib. bdg. $20.00

THE ALPINE CHRIST AND OTHER POEMS. *Cayucos Bks.* 1973 $10.00

SELECTED LETTERS: 1897–1962. Ed. by Ann N. Ridgway. Fwd. by Mark Van Doren. "The strangely impersonal letters of a dignified and modest poet"—(*PW*). *Johns Hopkins Press* 1968 $10.95

Books about Jeffers

A Bibliography of the Works of Robinson Jeffers. By Sydney S. Alberts. 1933. *Burt Franklin* $18.50. A detailed bibliography complete through the date of first publication, with an introduction by Robinson Jeffers.

Robinson Jeffers: The Man and His Work. By Lawrence Clark Powell. 1934 rev. ed. 1940. *Haskell* $11.95

Robinson Jeffers and the Sea. By Melba Berry Bennett. 1936. *Folcroft* 1971 lib. bdg. $12.50

Shine, Perishing Republic: Robinson Jeffers and the Tragic Sense in Modern Poetry. By Rudolph Gilbert. 1936. *Haskell* $9.95

The Loyalties of Robinson Jeffers. By Radcliffe Squires. *Univ. of Michigan Press* 1956 Ann Arbor Bks. 1963 pap. $1.85

Robinson Jeffers. By Frederic I. Carpenter. United States Authors Ser. *Twayne* 1962 $5.00; *College & Univ. Press* 1963 pap. $2.45

The Stone Mason of Tor House: The Life and Work of Robinson Jeffers. By Melba Berry Bennett. Fwd. by Lawrence Clark Powell. *Ward Ritchie* (dist. by Lane) 1966 $10.00
The somewhat "gossipy" life authorized by Jeffers, whom the author knew well. "Mrs. Bennett's perceptive biography affords new insights into the poet and his work. Jeffers comes through as a heroic, uncompromising, taciturn man who cherished his privacy and solitude. . . . The love story of Una and Robin reads like some 19th-Century romance. . . . The most valuable parts of the book are Jeffers' comments in letters on his own work and his theory of poetry and some of his hard-to-obtain public lectures"—(*LJ*).

Robinson Jeffers: Fragments of an Older Fury. By William Everson (Brother Antoninus) *Oyez* 1968 $7.50

Robinson Jeffers: Poet of Inhumanism. By Arthur B. Coffin. *Univ. of Wisconsin Press* 1971 $12.50. A scholarly work arguing that Jeffers was more influenced by Nietzsche and the cyclical view of history than by Schopenhauer.

Critical Reputation of Robinson Jeffers: A Bibliographical Study. By Alex A. Vardamis. *Shoe String* 1972 $12.50. A brief but comprehensive discussion of the work and life of Jeffers with a thorough bibliography.

Robinson Jeffers: Myth, Ritual and Symbol in His Narrative Poems. By Robert J. Brophy. *Press of Case Western Reserve* 1973 $7.95

MOORE, MARIANNE. 1887–1972.

Three major American poetry prizes were given to Marianne Moore in the single year 1952—the Bollingen, the National Book Award and the Pulitzer Prize. T. S. Eliot wrote, in introducing "Selected Poems" in 1935: "My conviction has remained unchanged for the last fourteen years: that Miss Moore's poems form part of the small body of durable poetry written in our time . . . in which an original sensibility and alert intelligence and deep feeling have been engaged in maintaining the life of the English language." In preparation for eight years, her translation of all 241 of La Fontaine's "Fables" (*Viking* 1954 Compass Bks. pap. $1.65) into the modern English idiom displays her "gifts of serious, yet witty precision." It was hailed as "an event in American poetry." In "Tell Me, Tell Me: Granite, Steel, and Other Topics," Thomas Lask (in the *N.Y. Times*) finds "her qualities . . . as scintillating as ever." Muriel Rukeyser says of the book (in *SR*): "The objects appear to face each other; forms that had seemed crystals, twin crystals, take on a further growth. The polarity is clearer and greater than one had guessed." Miss Moore's "probity, scrupulousness," "personal bravery" (*SR*) and wit are observable in her "Collected Poems"—all the poetry she wishes to preserve. Her style is unique—her work is exquisite, convoluted prose-poetry which takes its point of exploration from an insect, perhaps, or something else in nature, or from a city object, or a newspaper clipping. "A sense of the moral and intellectual order of the creation," Edwin Muir has said, "an endless interest in the curious forms in which it is manifested, and a courtesy toward all things: these explain the special delight which her poetry gives." And W. H. Auden has commented, "Miss Moore is one of the very few poets whom I can read on any day in any mood." "Predilections" (*Viking* 1955 $3.50), a collection of essays assembled over 30 years, is an original and perceptive book on poetry and language written with her own "crystalline perfection."

Born in St. Louis, the "first lady of American poetry" was graduated from Bryn Mawr in 1909. A few of her friends "pirated" her work in 1921 and "Poems" was published without her cooperation by *The Egoist Press*. Her profile appeared in the *New Yorker* of Feb. 16, 1957. On her 75th birthday, Nov. 15, 1962, she was honored by the National Institute of Arts and Letters and, in a special interview for the *N.Y. Times*, spoke of her definite prejudices against the maltreatment of poetry. "I'm very doubtful about scholasticizing poetry," she said, "I feel very strongly that poetry should not be an assignment but a joy." On her 80th birthday she went for a quiet celebration with Glenway Wescott and her brother and sister-in-law and said: "I wonder that I can bear myself to be in a world where they don't outlaw war." In 1967 Miss Moore received both the MacDowell Medal and a Gold Medal. Mayor Lindsay of New York hailed her as "truly the poet laureate of New York City," and Robert Lowell said, "She is the best woman poet in English." A baseball fan all her life, Miss Moore in 1968, at 81, threw the first ball to open the season at Yankee Stadium and received a warm kiss from Frank Fernandez, Yankee catcher. She read poetry with Mayor Lindsay to a gathering at Bryant Park in 1968. Her death in 1972 came as a great blow to those who had known and loved this "difficult" but charming poet in the George Washington tricorner hat. The famed Rosenback Museum in Philadelphia has a collection devoted to her work, and a detailed replica of a room in her Brooklyn home. "The Achievement of Marianne Moore: A Bibliography 1907–1957," compiled by Eugene Paul Sheehy and K. A. Lohf (1958. *Folcroft* $6.00) is once again in print.

COMPLETE POEMS. *Viking-Macmillan* (dist. by Viking) 1967 $10.00. Includes the Collected Poems" (1951); "Like a Bulwark" (1956); "O to Be a Dragon" (1959); "Tell Me, Tell Me" (1966) and a selection of "The Fables of La Fontaine."

COLLECTED POEMS. *Macmillan* 1951 $4.95. Contains "Selected Poems" (with introd. by T. S. Eliot 1935, o.p.); "What Are Years" (1941, o.p.); "Nevertheless" (1944); and "Hitherto Uncollected."

A MARIANNE MOORE READER. *Viking* 1961 $6.95 Compass Bks. 1965 pap. $1.95. Contains a generous selection from the "Collected Poems"; "Like a Bulwark" and "O To Be a Dragon" complete; some previously uncollected poems; selections from "The Fables of La Fontaine" and from her prose "Predilections"; and other essays not before collected.

LIKE A BULWARK. *Viking* 1956 $2.50

O TO BE A DRAGON: Poems. *Viking* 1959 $2.75

TELL ME, TELL ME: Granite, Steel, and Other Topics. *Viking* 1966 $3.95

MARIANNE MOORE READING HER POEMS AND FABLES FROM LA FONTAINE. A recording. *Caedmon* TC 1025 $5.95

Books about Moore

Marianne Moore. By Bernard F. Engel. *Twayne* 1963 $5.50; *College & Univ. Press* 1964 pap. $2.45
This addition to the Twayne series is especially interesting because of the contemporaneity of the subject and because it is the first book-length study of Miss Moore's work. . . . [It] would be most useful for undergraduates"—(*Choice*).
Marianne Moore. By Jean Garrigue. Pamphlets on American Writers *Univ. of Minnesota Press* 1965 pap. $1.25
Marianne Moore. By Sister Mary Therese. Contemporary Writers in Christian Perspective Ser. *Eerdmans* $.95
The Edge of the Image: Marianne Moore, William Carlos Williams and Some Other Poets. By A. Kingsley Weatherhead. *Univ. of Washington Press* 1967 $6.95
Marianne Moore: A Collection of Critical Essays. Ed. by Charles Tomlinson. *Prentice-Hall* 1969 $5.95 Spectrum Bks. pap. $1.95. This is a collection of 20 critical essays on the work of Moore by distin-

guished critics, among them Ezra Pound, T. S. Eliot, W. C. Williams, R. P. Blackmur, Hugh Kenner
and Wallace Stevens. The editor has included an introduction, letters from Marianne Moore to Ezra
Pound, a bibliography, and notes on the contributors.

Marianne Moore: An Introduction to the Poetry. By George W. Nitchie. *Columbia* 1969 $10.00. A thor-
oughly researched critical appraisal with many quotations from Moore and other writers. An introduction by John Unterecker. ". . . the book offers many piercing glances into the poems . . . often
clarifying what had previously been obscure . . ."—(*American Literary Scholarship*).

Marianne Moore: The Cage and the Animal. By Donald Hall. *Pegasus* 1970 $6.95. This is a readable
survey of Marianne Moore's life and work with a book-by-book examination of her poetry. Bibliography included.

RANSOM, JOHN CROWE. 1888–

A Rhodes scholar who went to Oxford from Vanderbilt University, Mr. Ransom taught at Vanderbilt
from 1914 to 1937. Professor of poetry at Kenyon College, Ohio, from 1937 to 1958, Mr. Ransom founded
The Kenyon Review in 1939. He was also one of the seven residents of Nashville, Tenn., who founded and
edited *The Fugitive* (1922–25) and according to Louis Untermeyer, "he, more than any of the others, was responsible for the new awakening of poetry in the South." He won the 1962 Academy of American Poets
$5000 Fellowship Prize for his "distinguished poetic achievement." He has also won the Bollingen Prize for
Poetry and the Russell Loines Memorial Fund Prize. Although at times his poetry is somewhat tortuous and
involved, "he has been at pains to salt his rhymes and pepper his diction with fresh, realistic words; he has
wrenched his cadences to fit his wayward thought; he has written with an original and almost acid gaiety"—
(Mark Van Doren).

Among Mr. Ransom's critical works are "God Without Thunder: An Unorthodox Defense of Orthodoxy"
(1930, *Shoe String* 1965 $9.00); "The World's Body" (1938, *Louisiana State Univ. Press* 1968 $2.95);
"Beating the Bushes: Selected Essays, 1941–1970" (*New Directions* 1972 $7.95 pap. $3.45); "Poetic Sense:
A Study of Problems in Defining Poetry by Content" (*Humanities* 1971 in prep).

SELECTED POEMS. *Knopf* 1945. 1963 3rd ed. 1969 $5.95. Selections from "Chills and
Fever" (1924) and "Two Gentlemen in Bonds" (1927), with five later poems that
appeared only in periodicals. This won the 1964 National Book Award for poetry.

Books about Ransom

The Fugitive Group: A Literary History. By Louise S. Cowan. *Louisiana State Univ. Press* 1959 $7.50
pap $2.45

John Crowe Ransom. By John L. Stewart. Pamphlets on American Writers *Univ of Minnesota Press*
1962 pap. $1.25. Brief critical introduction to Ransom's poetry with an original approach.

The Burden of Time: The Fugitives and Agrarians—the Nashville Groups of the 1920's and 1930's and
the Writings of John Crowe Ransom, Allen Tate, and Robert Penn Warren. By John L. Stewart.
Princton Univ. Press 1965 $17.50

"Urbane in tone, refined in method, strict in criticism, 'The Burden of Time' is one of those undertakings
that does credit to American literary scholarship. . . . Mr. Stewart grasps the ways in which the
Agrarian effort to create a myth or 'fictive version' of the South . . . gave Ransom and Tate a vantage-
point of powerful criticism of American society"—(Irving Howe, in the *N.Y. Times*).

Equilibrist: A Study of John Crowe Ransom's Poems 1916–1963. By Robert Buffington. *Vanderbilt
Univ. Press* 1967 $5.95

John Crowe Ransom, Critical Essays and a Bibliography. Ed. by Thomas D. Young. *Louisiana State
Univ. Press* 1968 $8.50. This is a distinguished collection of criticism geared toward the serious stu-
dent. Included are essays by Robert Penn Warren, Delmore Schwartz, Cleanthe Brooks, Randall Jarell, F. O. Matthiessen, and a selected bibliography by Mildred Brooks Peters.

John Crowe Ransom. By Thornton H. Parsons. *Twayne* 1969. This general discussion uses formal analysis and evaluation to examine the work of Ransom not only as poet, but also as teacher, editor and
critic.

The Poetry of John Crowe Ransom. By Miller Williams. *Rutgers Univ. Press* 1972 $7.50. Ransom's
poems are discussed individually with attention paid to the poet's use of irony and symbolism.

ELIOT, T(HOMAS) S(TEARNS). 1888–1965. *See Chapter 7, Modern British Poetry, and Chapter 15, Essays and Criticism.*

AIKEN, CONRAD. 1889–

This Georgia-born poet, a Harvard graduate, lived at South Yarmouth, Mass., until 1921, when he moved
his family to England. After a brief return to America in 1928, he alternated between England and America
and finally settled in Massachusetts in a labyrinthine house at Brewster called "Forty Doors," where he

writes and his wife paints. Mr. Aiken (then 40) was much admired by the 19-year-old Malcolm Lowry (*q.v.*), and in 1929 the young Lowry "arrived on Aiken's doorstep with a battered suitcase containing . . . notes for Lowry's *Ultramarine.*" Throughout that summer Lowry stayed in the Aiken house and the two remained friends. The story—and that of Aiken's influence on Lowry—is told by R. H. Costa in the *Nation* of June 26, 1967.

Allen Tate (*q. v.*) says that Aiken "represents the perfection of a vanishing American type: the complete man of letters." "I would put Mr. Aiken's poetry first," Tate continues, "but had he not written it, his novels, his short stories, his plays and his criticism would place him among the half-dozen most important writers in English of this century." The reader is referred to Louis Untermeyer's article, "Conrad Aiken: Our Best Known Unread Poet," in the *Saturday Review* of Nov. 25, 1967. Mr. Untermeyer says, "I believe that the future will treat Aiken better than the present," and Costa, "It is possible . . . that a major Aiken revival is underway. It may be, too, that literary history will show Aiken as a major literary force, the discoverer of, and catalyst for, other talents." Aiken's criticism from 1916 to the present appears in "Collected Criticism" (formerly "A Reviewer's ABC," 1958, introd. by Rufus A. Blanshard, pref. by I. A. Richards *Oxford* 1968 Galaxy Bks. pap. $3.50). His "Scepticisms: Notes on Contemporary Poetry" 1919. *Bks. for Libraries* $9.75; *Johnson Reprint* 1969 $9.00; *Bern Porter* 1972 $10.00; *Richard West* $8.50) includes essays on Amy Lowell, Edgar Lee Masters, William Carlos Williams, war poetry, as well as poetry in general. His "Short Stories" (1950) have been reprinted (*Bks. for Libraries* $13.75).

All of Aiken's work shows a mature and craftsmanlike skill, a quiet subtlety. "His deep and persistent preoccupation with the psychological, philosophical, and scientific issues of our time here becomes manifest; as does his ability to carry poetry into the disturbed world of the twentieth century—the world, as he puts it, 'of the fractured atom on the one hand and the fragmented ego on the other.' His poetry has attempted, perhaps, the most complete world-view of our time." "Thee," a long poem, is Aiken's examination of man's relationship to God and the unknown.

He received the 1930 Pulitzer Prize, the Shelley Memorial Award, the National Book Award for Poetry in 1954, the Bollingen Prize in 1956, the Gold Medal for Poetry of the National Institute of Arts and Letters in 1958, the Huntington Hartford Foundation Award in 1960 and the Brandeis University Medal of Achievement in 1967. He was Consultant in Poetry at the Library of Congress from 1950 to 1952.

COLLECTED POEMS. *Oxford* 1953 2nd ed. 1970 $15.00

SELECTED POEMS. *Oxford* 1961 $7.50 Galaxy Bks. pap. $1.95. Representative of his most important work since 1917.

THE JIG OF FORSLIN. 1916. *Branden* 1964 pap. $.95

TURNS AND MOVIES AND OTHER TALES IN VERSE. 1916. *Richard West* 1973 $8.50

CHARNEL ROSE, SENLIN: A Biography, and Other Poems. 1918. *Haskell* 1972 $8.95

THE MORNING SONG OF LORD ZERO: Poems Old and New. *Oxford* 1963 $5.00. Twenty-three new poems make up the first two sections of this collection. The third, fourth and fifth sections of the book are drawn respectively from "A Letter from Li Po," "Skylight One" and "Sheepfold Hill."

BROWNSTONE ECLOGUES AND OTHER POEMS. 1942. *Indiana Univ. Press* 1962 pap. $1.75

DIVINE PILGRIM. Poems. *Univ. of Georgia Press* 1949 $6.50

PRELUDES: PRELUDES FOR MEMNON (1931) and TIME IN THE ROCK (1936). *Oxford* Galaxy Bks. 1966 pap. $1.95; *Peter Smith* $3.75

"His fertility and energy of imagination, his natural gift of poetic eloquence is the mark of a great poet. . . . Aiken's several series of poems . . . together make up what may be seen as a single epic whose 'I' is not the poet's subjectivity, but the one life in all lives"—(*TLS*, London).

A SEIZURE OF LIMERICKS. *Holt* 1964 $2.95

THEE. A single long poem, ill. by Leonard Baskin. *Braziller* 1967 $5.00

USHANT: An Essay. Autobiographical. 1952. *Oxford* 1971 $9.50

Conrad Aiken Reading. A recording of "A Letter from Li Po," "The Blues of Ruby Matrix" and two poems from "Time in the Rock." *Caedmon* TC 1039 $5.95

Books about Aiken

Conrad Aiken. By Frederick J. Hoffman. *Twayne* 1962 $5.50; *College & Univ. Press* 1963 pap. $2.45
Conrad Aiken: A Life of His Art. By Jay Martin. *Princeton Univ. Press* 1962 $10.00 "In me," commented Aiken in a letter to Malcolm Cowley, "you behold an almost unique phenomenon, a poet who has acquired a Reputation . . . without ever having been caught in the act." In this book, Aiken's work receives its long-overdue critical attention.
Conrad Aiken. By Reuel Denney. Pamphlets on American Writers *Univ of Minnesota Press* 1964 pap. $1.25

MILLAY, EDNA ST. VINCENT. 1892–1950.

Edna St. Vincent Millay was born in Maine and was graduated from Vassar College. She joined the Provincetown Players, acting many leading roles including those of her own plays. Her earliest poem, "Renascence," was written when she was 19. It appeared first in "The Lyric Year" (*Kennerley* 1912), an anthology of competitive poems. Its mature philosophy marked it as one of the most thoughtful poems in the collection. Although other poems took the prizes, it attracted the greatest attention. The Pulitzer Poetry Prize was awarded to "The Ballad of the Harp Weaver" in 1923. "The King's Henchman" (1927, o.p.) was set to music by Deems Taylor and was enthusiastically received when it was performed at the Metropolitan Opera House, New York, in February, 1927. As the Bohemian spokesman of early 20th-century youth, she won further fame with her poetry of love and gaiety and longing and death, especially her sonnets. She translated, with George Dillon, Baudelaire's "Flowers of Evil" (1936, *Harper* $6.00).

Her great charm for her public lay in the versatility and freshness of her lyrics. In commenting on romantic women poets in his opening address at the first National Poetry Festival in Washington (October, 1962), Randall Jarrell called Edna St. Vincent Millay "the most powerful and most popular. . . . One thinks with awe and longing of this real and extraordinary popularity of hers: if only there were *some* poet—Frost, Stevens, Eliot—whom people still read in canoes!"

She was found dead of a heart attack at the foot of the stairs in her isolated home in Dutchess County, New York. She had lived alone since the death of her husband, Eugen Jan Boissevain, in 1949. Her "Letters," a true self-portrait, show her as "one of the few who are able to appreciate that ineffable treasure, the present; [these] letters are radiant with immediacy"—(Robert Hillyer). Quotations from her letters and verse were adapted by Dorothy Stickney for dramatic presentation as "A Lovely Light" in 1960. Royce Smith of the Yale Co-op Bookstore remarked of Edna St. Vincent Millay in 1968: "Still sells like a house afire!"

Collected Poems. Ed. by Norma Millay. *Harper* 1956 $10.00. The collected works without dramatic pieces.

Collected Lyrics. *Harper* 1943 $10.00 pap. $.95. Miss Millay's own selection.

Collected Sonnets. *Harper* 1941 $7.50 pap. $.95. 175 selected sonnets.

Renascence and Other Poems. 1917. *Bks. for Libraries* 1972 $7.50

Poems Selected for Young People. *Harper* 1929 $3.50 lib. bdg. $3.79

The Letters of Edna St. Vincent Millay. Ed. by Allan Ross McDougall. 1952 *Greenwood* $15.25

Poetry of Edna St. Vincent Millay. A recording by Judith Anderson. *Caedmon* TC 1024 $5.95

Books about Millay

Edna St. Vincent Millay and Her Times. By Elizabeth Atkins. 1936. *Russell & Russell* $9.00
Bibliography of the Works of Edna St. Vincent Millay. By Karl Yost. 1937. *Burt Franklin* $16.50
Edna St. Vincent Millay. By Norma A. Bittin. United States Authors Ser. *Twayne* $5.50; *College & Univ. Press* pap. $2.45
Edna St. Vincent Millay. By James Gray. Pamphlets on American Writers *Univ. of Minnesota Press* 1967 pap. $1.25
The Poet and Her Book: A Biography of Edna St. Vincent Millay. By Jean Gould. *Dodd* 1969 $6.50 *Apollo* pap. $2.50. Biographical profile of the poet with some criticism on her work, with photographs.

MacLEISH, ARCHIBALD. 1892–

MacLeish is a poet who has passed through several successive styles and manners. His early poems show the influence of Eliot and Pound. His theme is tragic in "The Pot of Earth" and introspective in "The Hamlet of A. MacLeish." "Conquistador," a book-length poem, is a stirring narrative of the conquest of Mexico. "Poems, 1924–1933" (1933, o. p.) included "Conquistador," "You, Andrew Marvell," "American Letter" and many other memorable favorites, but it omitted many favorites of his public which Mr. MacLeish himself does not like. His later verse is increasingly social in import. The long poem, "Actfive," portentous in its disillusionment, is the latest included in "Collected Poems: 1917–1952." He is known for his "high level of craftsmanship and humaneness of spirit." "Few poets have so fully and sensitively reflected the wide-sweeping social and intellectual currents of the modern age."

"Poetry and Experience" (*Houghton* 1961 $6.95 is based on his Harvard lectures as Boylston Professor. "Although the book retains the lucidity and fervor of the best public address, it is a serious and provocative contribution to the theory of poetry"—(*N.Y. Times*). "A Continuing Journey: Essays and Addresses" (*Houghton* 1967 $5.95), which was warmly received, is Mr. MacLeish's reflections on his life as a poet and philosopher. Other nonfiction includes "Remarks at the Dedication of the Wallace Library" (pref. by E. Greenaway *St. Onge* 1967 $4.50) and "A Time to Act: Selected Addresses" (1951. *Bks for Libraries* $8.75).

Mr. MacLeish was Librarian of Congress, 1939–1944, and during World War II he was Director of O.F.F. (the first U.S. "Ministry of Information"), Assistant Director of O.W.I. and later, Assistant Secretary of State, 1944–45. In November, 1945, he went to London as Chairman of the U.S. Delegation to the first General Conference of UNESCO in Paris, 1946, and resigned in 1947. Throughout his life Mr. MacLeish has managed to play a public role as well as a private one, and has been fearless in battles against censorship and intimidation, and in defense of civil liberties. He has been Boylston Professor at Harvard since 1949. "J.B.: A Play in Verse," the story of Job transferred to contemporary life, won the 1958 Pulitzer Drama Prize, MacLeish having won two previous Pulitzer Prizes in 1932 and 1953. In 1953 also he was awarded the Bollingen Prize in Poetry and the National Book Award. John Wain, in the *New Republic*, found MacLeish's "Herakles" "deftly constructed as one large-scale metaphor: of man's achievement resulting in a sharpened confrontation with what is tragic in his destiny. [The play] presents two great achievers: powerful, driving males, flanked by their ministering, suffering and disbelieving females." Writing in the *Virginia Quarterly Review*, Richard Eberhart says: "MacLeish has given us great quickenings of poetic imagery, flashes of profound insight set forth with staccato force, a vehicle of language so pliable and sharp as to catch the Greek spirit of lightness and truth . . . splendid, swift, passionate." MacLeish's short television play, "An Evening's Journey to Conway," (*Grossman* 1967 $15.00) was written to celebrate the bicentennial of his home in Massachusetts. Its theme was the need for identity in an age of uncertainty, and if it was not altogether successful as drama it demonstrated MacLeish's continuing concern for the best in America's past—and present. The theme of "Scratch" was suggested by Stephen Vincent Benét's story "The Devil and Daniel Webster."

In connection with a discussion of "J.B." in 1958, MacLeish said: "[There are those who would claim that] the modern god of the scientific age does not control events—not, at least, events in the world of here and now. . . . To me, a man committed to no creed, and more uncertain than I should be of certain ultimate beliefs, the God of J.B. seems closer to this generation than he has to any other in centuries." Speaking at the ceremonies opening the 1967 Lincoln Center Festival, Mr. MacLeish attacked political leaders all over the world for their failures of understanding in sensitive human areas like the arts. "Without those last quartets of Beethoven," he said, "without Oedipus the King, without a Hamlet or a Lear, or Michelangelo's ceiling, or the odes of Keats, the electronic age could be a nightmare—a brighter, louder, more disastrous nightmare than any that has gone before. With the arts, instructed by the arts, it could become a great, perhaps the greatest, age."

COLLECTED POEMS 1917–1952. *Houghton* 1952 Sentry Eds. 1963 pap. $3.75. Includes many short poems as well as the longer works: "The Pot of Earth" (1925); "The Hamlet of A. MacLeish" (1928); "Einstein" (1929); "Conquistador" (1932); "Elpenor" (1933); "America Was Promises" (1939); "Colloquy for the States" (1943) and "Actfive" (1948).

HUMAN SEASON: Selected Poems. 1926–1972. *Houghton* 1972 $6.00 limited ed. $15.00. About 120 poems are collected here with a foreword by MacLeish.

AIR RAID. Radio verse play. 1938. *Dramatists* acting ed. $1.25

J.B.: A Play in Verse. *Houghton* 1958 $4.95 Sentry Eds. 1961 pap. $1.75

HERAKLES: A Play in Verse. *Houghton* 1967 $4.00

WILD OLD WICKED MAN AND OTHER POEMS. *Houghton* 1968 $4.00

SCRATCH: A Play. *Houghton* 1971 $4.95

ARCHIBALD MACLEISH READS HIS POETRY. A recording. *Caedmon* TC 1009 $5.95

THE DIALOGUES OF ARCHIBALD MACLEISH AND MARK VAN DOREN. Ed. by Warren
V. Bush. *Dutton* 1964 $6.95

"On the whole the book is charming. . . . The two men talk of poetry, nature, politics, and say many
sensible and interesting things. . . . Civilized talk, often stimulating, always pleasant"—*(SR)*.

Books about MacLeish

Archibald MacLeish. By Signi L. Falk. *Twayne* 1965 $5.95; *College & Univ. Press* 1965 pap. $2.45
"More a review of MacLeish's accomplishments than a critical interpretation . . . consisting, for the
most part, of short mechanical statements of fact snapped one to the other. . . . Miss Falk's treatment is
somewhat superficial. Although her study cannot be considered 'definitive,' it will prove valuable to the
undergraduate as well as the graduate student desiring an introduction to MacLeish and his works"—
(Choice).

Archibald MacLeish. By Grover Smith. Pamphlets on American Authors. *Univ. of Minnesota Press* 1971
pap. $1.25. A brief introduction to the work of MacLeish in the context of the contemporary American
scene.

CUMMINGS, E. E. 1894–1962.

E. E. Cummings' experiments with language (he styled himself e. e. cummings) led him to employ various
unorthodox typographical and punctuation devices—a radical break with tradition in his day. But he used
them to give his poetry a maximum of communication and excitement; "his verse is meant to strike the ear
and not the eye." He was concerned to say things oddly and originally, and the themes of desire and death are
much present in his generally lyrical and often humorous poetry. John Ciardi has said in the *Nation*: "What
is most fascinating to me about Cummings, aside from the presence of a talent that takes and stays, is the way
he can be both silly and profound, sometimes both at once." His novel "The Enormous Room" (1922, *Modern Library* 1934 $2.95; *Liveright* $5.95 pap. $2.95) was written as the result of his three months' experi-
ence in a detention camp during the first World War. It is now a classic. Cummings' otherwise unpublished
prose is included in "E. E. Cummings: A Miscellany Revised" (fwd. by the poet, ed. with introd. by George
J. Firmage. *October House* 1965 $7.50 pap. $2.95). Four stories written for his young daughter are collected
in "Fairy Tales" (*Harcourt* 1966 $4.50).

Cummings, a Harvard graduate, lived in Greenwich Village and spent his summers on a farm in New
Hampshire. Many honors came to him, including the 1958 Bollingen Prize.

"Full of originality, high spirits, and aphoristic dicta, they express a credo of intense individualism," the
Atlantic said of his "I. Six Nonlectures" (*Harvard Univ. Press* 1953 $4.50 pap. $1.95). These were his unconventional lectures given while at Harvard in 1952. He wrote the delightful commentaries for the 50 photographs in "Adventures in Value" (*Harcourt* 1962 $10.75) by his wife, Marion Morehouse, a fine and sensi-
tive photographer. "These multum-in-parvo bits of prose, ranging from one word to small essays, are good
Cummings and sometimes Cummings at his best:

"a wave . . . beginning—e-x-p-a-n-d-i-n-g—UpReArInG—to:"
His own art—sketches and watercolors of the 1920s and 1930s—was exhibited in 1968 at the Gotham Book
Mart in New York City.

COMPLETE POEMS, 1913–1962. *Harcourt* 1972 $12.50. This includes the contents of 12
individual volumes as well as other unpublished works, editorially supervised by
Cummings' bibliographer, George James Firmage.

POEMS, 1923–1954. 604 poems from all collections. *Harcourt* 1954 $10.50

"This volume brings together for the first time all the poems from all the collections of verse Cummings has
published to date, presenting in one definitive volume the contents of ten books. . . . It includes 114 poems
which were omitted from 'Collected Poems' when it was originally issued in 1938, as well as 175 poems written since that date"—(Publisher's note).

COLLECTED POEMS. *Harcourt* 1938 $7.95. "Collected Poems" includes his previously
published volumes: "Tulips and Chimneys" (1923); "&" ("Ampersand," 1925);
"XLI Poems" (1925); "Is V" (1926); "Christmas Tree" (1928); and "1/20
Poems" (1937).

100 Selected Poems. *Grove* 1959 Evergreen Bks. pap. $1.95

A Selection of Poems. Introd. by Horace Gregory. *Harcourt* Harvest Bks., 1965 pap. $1.95

Him. A play. *Liveright* 1927 1946 new ed. 1970 $4.95 pap. $2.25

50 Poems. 1940 rep. 1946 *Grosset* 1960 Univ. Lib. pap. $1.25

One Times One. Poems. *Harcourt* 1944 1954 $4.95 pap. $1.15

95 Poems. *Harcourt* 1958 $6.75 pap. $1.25

73 Poems by e. e. cummings. Poems written after 1958. *Harcourt* 1963 $5.75 pap. $1.25

Is Five. *Liveright* new ed. 1970 $6.00 pap. $1.75

Viva. *Liveright* new ed. 1970 $6.00 pap. $1.95

Three Plays and a Ballet. Ed. with introd. by George J. Firmage. All of Cummings' dramatic work. *October House* 1966 $7.50 pap. $2.95

E. E. Cummings Reads His Poetry. A recording. *Caedmon* TC 1017 $5.95

Selected Letters. Ed. by F. W. Dupee and George Stade. *Harcourt* 1969 $8.95

Books about Cummings

> E. E. Cummings: The Magic-Maker (originally "The Magic-Maker: E. E. Cummings"). By Charles Norman. 1958. *Bobbs* $10.00; *Little* pap. 1973 $3.45
> "The author was long a personal friend of the poet, and his appraisal is very frankly admiring . . . a lively biography, filled with intimate details. The poet himself gave to Mr. Norman many of his private and family papers and letters"—(*PW*).
> E. E. Cummings: A Bibliography. By George J. Firmage. *Wesleyan Univ. Press* 1960 $10.00
> E. E. Cummings: The Art of his Poetry. By Norman Friedman. A very useful analysis. *Johns Hopkins Press* 1960 $6.50 pap. $2.25
> EΣTI : e e c : E. E. Cummings and the Critics. Ed. with introd. by S. V. Baum. *Michigan State Univ. Press* 1961 $7.50 Appearing so soon after his untimely death, this anthology of critical essays is a fitting tribute to one of America's most important and controversial poets. Gathered together in chronological sequence are 35 cogent and often sharply divergent pieces written by such well-known authors and critics as Harriet Monroe, Marianne Moore (*q. v.*), F. O. Matthiessen and Randall Jarrell (*q. v.*); valuable indexes and bibliographies.
> E. E. Cummings: The Growth of a Writer. By Norman Friedman. Pref. by Harry T. Moore. *Southern Illinois Univ. Press* 1964 $4.95. Mr. Friedman summarizes the poet's ontology, examines the works chronologically, and classifies them as satires, comedies, transcendental poems, etc. "I admire the efficiency and thoroughness of this book. Almost all of the factual conclusions and informative observations are indisputable"—(R. E. Wegner, in *American Literature*).
> E. E. Cummings. By Barry A. Marks. United States Authors Ser. *Twayne* 1963 $5.50 *College & Univ. Press* 1964 pap. $2.45
> The Poetry and Prose of E. E. Cummings. By Robert E. Wegner. *Harcourt* 1965 $4.95.
> "Wegner pays homage to Cummings in a respectful and careful analysis of philosophy, themes and style"—(*LJ*). "Competent in discussing the technical side of the poems, he prefers to dwell on their interpretation. His examination of themes, images and ideas is patient, bland and superficial"—(*N.Y. Times*).
> E. E. Cummings: A Collection of Critical Essays. By Norman Friedman. Twentieth Century Views 1972 *Prentice-Hall* $5.95 Spectrum Bks. pap. $1.95. This is a collection of 14 essays on the work of Cummings by distinguished critics, among them R. P. Blackmur, Allan Tate, W. C. Williams, Robert Graves, and the editor of this volume. Also included are a bibliography and biography of Cummings, a chronology of dates, and notes on the contributors.

REZNIKOFF, CHARLES. 1894–

A native New Yorker, born in Brooklyn, Charles Reznikoff worked as a lawyer and legal editor, a profession reflected in his "Testimony: The United States 1885–1890" (*New Directions* $3.75 pap. $1.95) which portrays lives of various people in criminal law cases. If in this book he is reminiscent of an urban Edgar Lee Masters, he is also strongly allied with the Objectivist group of poets of the 1930s. His verse as a result is clean, centered and sparse. Emotion is controlled and bursts forth at moments like a flame from shadow, as when he speaks of the Jews in America, one of his best subjects: "They will take away/ our cakes and delicacies,/ the cheerful greetings, the hours of pleasant speech, the smiles/ and give us back/ the sight of our eyes and our silent thoughts;/ they will take away our groans and signs/ and give us—/ merely breath."—(from "I Will Go into the Ghetto").

"Clear, mystical, sometimes bitter or disconsolate, his poems evoking the Hebrew tradition and the life of Jewish emigrants in America are especially noteworthy"—(Hayden Carruth).

One critic has likened his objectivist style to the paintings of Edward Hopper ". . . and of cubist . . . heightening certain effects to the entire exclusion of others. . . . Reznikoff must have sacrificed a vast array of powers in order to risk all with the objectivist treatment of the experience of urban alienation. Often one feels a straining toward a savage mysticism . . ."—(David Ray). Reznikoff has only recently begun to get wider recognition, chiefly because his realistic and human perception of the city strikes a true chord in the hearts of younger poets and audiences today.

The author of several novels, including "The Lionhearted" (o.p.) and "Family Chronicle" (*Universe Books* 1971 $5.95), Reznikoff is represented in anthologies of Jewish poetry and recently in "On City Streets" (*Evans* 1968).

BY THE WATERS OF MANHATTAN. Introd. by C. P. Snow. *New Directions* 1962 pap. $1.75. This selection of poems includes works from "Five Groups of Verse" (1927), "Editing and Glosses" (1929), "Jerusalem the Golden" (1934), "In Memoriam: 1933" (1934). "Separate Way" (1936), "Going to and fro and Walking up and down" (1941) and "Inscriptions: 1944–1956" (1959).

BY THE WELL OF LIVING AND SEEING: Selected Poems. Ed by Seamus Cooney. *Black Sparrow* 1973 signed ed. $15.00 pap. $4.00

TESTIMONY: The United States, 1885–1890, Recitative. *New Directions* 1965 $3.75 pap. $1.95. Poems drawn from criminal court cases.

VAN DOREN, MARK. 1894–1972.

Poet, critic and scholar, Mark Van Doren's poems chronicled the American scene with a quiet fidelity to fact, but with a delicate awareness of some of life's intangibles. His plain poetic statements have "a warmth, maturity, and intellectual integrity." "A Winter Diary" (1935) is considered by Louis Untermeyer to be Van Doren's richest volume "even though the book represents an alternation of tradition and technical experiment." "Collected Poems: 1922–1938" was awarded the Pulitzer Prize. Mr. Van Doren won the Golden Rose Trophy in 1960. In 1962 he was selected by the Huntington Hartford Foundation as the recipient of its "annual creativity award," which consists of a cash prize of $1,000 and an invitation to the winner and his wife to live at the Foundation Estate for six months. In 1967 he received the Fellowship of the Academy of American Poets. His verse play "The Last Days of Lincoln" (1959, o.p.) is a moving appreciation in dramatic form. He attended the Florida performance in the fall of 1961.

As a critic he has always had something provocative to offer. "Introduction to Poetry: Commentaries on 30 Poems" (1951. *Hill & Wang* 1961 $3.95 pap. $1.95) is a widely used text. "The Noble Voice" (1936) has been reprinted as "Mark Van Doren on Ten Great Poems" (*Macmillan* Collier Bks. pap. $.95). "The Happy Critic and Other Essays" (*Hill & Wang* 1961 $1.45) contains "some carefully considered wisdom on the nature of poetry and its importance in the survival of civilization." He edited several excellent collections of poetry including "An Anthology of World Poetry" (1928. *Harcourt* rev. and enl. 1936 $15.00); with G. M. Lapolla, "The World's Best Poems" (1945–1946); and, with Marianne Moore and Richard Eberhardt, "Riverside Poetry 2" (*Twayne* $2.75). His "Autobiography" (1958. *Greenwood* 1968 $17.25) is also available. He retired from Columbia University in 1959, after nearly 40 years as a professor in the English Department. He was still active as a critic and anthologist until his death in 1972.

COLLECTED AND NEW POEMS, 1924–1963. *Hill & Wang* 1963 Am. Century pap. $3.65

The definitive one-volume collection contains 800 poems selected by the poet, nearly 100 of which have never before appeared in print. It "contains some of the best and most enduring poetry of this century"—(Allen Tate).

MARK VAN DOREN: 100 POEMS, Selected by the author. *Hill & Wang*, 1967 Am. Century pap. $1.50

THE DIALOGUES OF ARCHIBALD MACLEISH AND MARK VAN DOREN. Ed. by Warren
V. Bush. *Dutton* $6.95. A record of the "unrehearsed, uninhibited"—(*LJ*) conver-
sation held for CBS-TV in 1962 at MacLeish's Uphill Farm in Massachusetts.

See also Chapter 15, Essays and Criticism, for his prose works.

HUMPHRIES, ROLFE. 1894–1969.

Rolfe Humphries, one of the best of the "genuine lyric craftsmen in America," was also a gifted translator.
W. H. Auden has called Humphries' verse translation of Virgil's "Aeneid" (*q.v.*) the best in the English language. He made verse translations of Ovid's "Metamorphoses" and "The Art of Love," of Juvenal's "Satires," and of García Lorca. Marius Bewley in the *N.Y. Review of Books* said of his "Collected Poems,"
"[Rolfe Humphries] is clearly an important writer. The trouble is—and I suspect this may be why Humphries has not been more 'taken up'—there is often a slightly old-fashioned lyrical quality to his verse. A representative poem like 'A Landscape, and a Lady' is a case in point, presenting us with a blend of the modern
and the Victorian. . . . But Humphries's late Romantic imagery is usually qualified from lushness by the clarity and precision with which he outlines action, episode and motive. 'The King of the Grove,' based on the
opening pages of Frazer's *The Golden Bough* is a genuinely distinguished poem, and it perfectly exemplifies
these qualities." And *Choice* commented: "An impressive collected edition, one which belongs in every representative library of modern American literature. Although [the poet's] surpassing skill and artistry will be no
surprise, the broad variety of poetical topics is. . . . [They] include observations on city life, baseball, radio,
the Spanish Civil War, love and sex, the cult of the 'private eye.' . . . Humphries displays also a bawdy irreverent wit which is extremely amusing without being indelicate or in poor taste. . . . As a poet Humphries encompasses a range of forms and techniques which illustrate the breadth of the conservative, more traditional
side of modern American verse." "Coat on a Stick: Late Poems," published posthumously, received the Melville Cain Award in 1970.

COLLECTED POEMS. *Indiana Univ. Press* 1965 $6.95

COAT ON A STICK: Late Poems. *Indiana Univ. Press* 1969 $4.50

DEUTSCH, BABETTE. 1895–

Miss Deutsch is a poet, critic and teacher whose verse is notable for its lucidness and sense of color, perfection of technique, balance and compassion. She has translated poems of Villon, Baudelaire, Rilke and Pasternak. George Garrett wrote of her "Collected Poems" (1963, o.p.) in the *Virginia Quarterly Review:*
"This book is the harvest of half a century of continuous creativity, and it is one which dazzles the reader with
its virtuosity and at the same time defies him to remark any lessening of the essential vigor and energy of the
artist. This is the voice not just of a poet, but of an artist in exactly the same sense that Picasso is an artist or
Stravinsky." She is a native New Yorker whose first published work appeared while she was still an undergraduate at Barnard. Her prose works include "This Modern Poetry" (1935 *Kraus* 1969 $11.50) in which
she discusses the trends and backgrounds of modern poetry, concentrating on H. D., William Carlos Williams and other American poets at the beginning of the century, and "Poetry Handbook: A Dictionary of
Terms" (*Funk & Wagnalls* 1957 rev. ed. 1962 $5.95 Minerva Bks. pap. $2.95; *Grosset* 1962 Univ. Lib. pap.
$1.50), the revised edition covering "beat poetry" and other recent developments with excerpts from the
works of 150 poets. She is married to Avrahm Yarmolinsky.

COMING OF AGE: New and Selected Poems. *Indiana Univ. Press* 1959 Poetry Paperbacks 1963 pap. $1.75

BOGAN, LOUISE. 1897–1970.

Richard Eberhart (in the *N.Y. Times*) said of Miss Bogan's "Collected Poems": "The feeling is of somber
strength, of a strong nature controlling powerful emotions by a highly conscious art. There is marked skill in
her restraint. Her best poems read as if time would not be likely to break them down." She was co-winner
with Léonie Adams of the 1954 Bollingen Prize in poetry for this volume. She won the Academy of American
Poets Fellowship in 1959 and the 1961 Brandeis Prize for poetry. Her "Achievement in American Poetry,
1900–1950" (*Regnery* 1951 pap. $1.25) is a distinguished and spirited book of criticism. Miss Bogan was for
many years the *New Yorker's* poetry critic.

BLUE ESTUARIES: Poems. 1923–1968. *Farrar Straus* 1968 Noonday pap. $1.95. The
collected poems.

POET'S ALPHABET. *McGraw-Hill* 1970 $12.95

WHAT THE WOMAN LIVED: Selected Letters of Louise Bogan, 1920–1970. Ed. by Ruth Limmer. *Harcourt* 1973 $14.50

LOWENFELS, WALTER. 1897–

Born in New York City in 1897, Lowenfels is noted for his prolific editing of anthologies, including "Poets of Today" (*International Pubs.* 1964 pap. $1.95), "Where is Vietnam" (*Doubleday* 1967 Anchor Bks. pap. $1.45; *Peter Smith* $4.00) "The Writing on the Wall, 108 Poems of Protest" (*Doubleday* 1969 $4.95 pap. $1.95) and "In a Time of Revolution" (*Random* Vintage Bks. 1969 pap. $1.95). Lowenfels is the recipient of the Richard Aldington Award for American Poets, Mainstream Award and the Longville Foundation Award. When he was one of the expatriate writers in Paris in the twenties Henry Miller called him "probably the poet of the age." "The Revolution Is to Be Human" is the author's personal manifesto on poetry and life. He has been a contributor to various literary magazines and has been called by Kenneth Rexroth "one of the most significant poets of my generation."

THE PORTABLE WALTER: From the Prose and Poetry of Walter Lowenfels. Ed. by Robert Gover. *International Pubs.* 1968 $5.95 pap. $1.95

FOUND POEMS AND OTHERS. *Barlenmir* 1972 $4.95

THE REVOLUTION IS TO BE HUMAN. *International Pubs.* 1973 pap. $1.50

GREGORY, HORACE. 1898–

Allen Tate has said that Gregory "writes some of the best poetry of his time. Always he has looked for the permanent or, as he calls them, the *mythical* values in contemporary life. To be of his own age and surroundings is with him a passion." Reviewing "Medusa in Gramercy Park," *Library Journal* said: "United by their tone of muted or impending tragedy, the 'Dramatic Episodes and Lyrics' which make up most of the volume . . . present a modern crisis-tempered commentary in classical and Renaissance stage settings." Mr. Gregory won the Academy of American Poets Fellowship in 1961. His "Collected Poems" won the Bollingen Prize in 1965. Theodore Weiss wrote of this volume in *Poetry:* "Few poets have been as successfully occupied with our day's Medusa-like powers. . . . Why then has this work not taken the time's appetite more? It is the very mastery, its imperturbability, and its indifference to itself for total involvement in its world. It is Mr. Gregory's ability to turn a beggar, say, into something mythical by the fundamental, terrible power—a power by his merely being—housed in him and shining through. It is his ability to treat modern material with classical containment, classical material with an immediate modern awareness and application. . . . Much more than skill, his work is a generous air, brooding over hallucinated, nightmared multitudes, an air listening, absorbing, and singing it all forth, transformed, somehow fulfilled in its very failures." And M. L. Rosenthal said (in the *Reporter*): "A fine, sensitive, original voice, a spirit at once generous and fastidious, sophisticated and energetic, has long been among us, and . . . we now have the opportunity to read in a single volume one of the most interesting bodies of poems to be made available to us in some years."

Poet, critic, editor and translator, he has also been an outstanding teacher and lecturer for many years, principally at Sarah Lawrence College. He resigned in 1961 because of ill health. He was born in Wisconsin, and lives in New York with his wife the poet Marya Zaturenska (*see below*). Together they have had the hardihood to evaluate their contemporaries in "A History of American Poetry 1900–1940," (*Gordian* 1969 $12.50), to write for younger readers "The Crystal Cabinet: An Invitation to Poetry" (*Holt* 1962 lib. bdg. $3.27; *Macmillan* Collier pap. $1.50), and to edit "The Silver Swan: Poems of Romance and Mystery" (*Holt* 1966 $3.95 lib. bdg. $3.59). He has rendered into the American idiom Catullus's "Poems," Ovid's "Metamorphoses" and "Love Poems of Ovid." His biographies include "D. H. Lawrence: Pilgrim of the Apocalypse" (*Grove* Evergreen Bks. 1957 pap. $1.95; *Bks. for Libraries* $8.50) and "The World of James McNeill Whistler" (1959. *Bks. for Libraries* $12.50). His collected essays, "The Spirit of Time and Place" have been published (*Norton* 1973 $8.95). Earlier collections of essays have also been reprinted: "The Shield of Achilles: Essays on Beliefs in Poetry" (1944. *Greenwood* $10.00), "The Dying Gladiators and Other Essays" (1961. *Greenwood* 1968 $9.75) and "Dorothy Richardson: An Adventure in Self-Discovery" (*Holt* 1967 $4.95).

His wife, MARYA ZATURENSKA (1902–   ), won the 1938 Pulitzer Prize for Poetry with her second volume "Cold Morning Sky" (1937, *Greenwood* $7.50). She was born in Kiev, came to the United States when she was eight and had to leave school to find work when she was thirteen. She attended night high school and the University of Wisconsin and began writing in her teens. Her work is restrained but highly imaginative, with fresh and unusual images. She is a poet who has been "true to her special gift, which is meditative lyricism." Now available is "The Collected Poems of Marya Zaturenska" (*Viking* 1965 $6.00), which includes some previously unpublished. Barbara Guest wrote in the *N.Y. Times:* "What is so fine about these poems is that the control implicit in them does not lead to sterility or to false emotion. . . . The poems of the 1960's continue with their imagery of 'bright passions fever-high.' . . . They are really bravely sad poems and strike to tears. Craft, design, obligatory polishing, and then what a sensibility is exposed to us in these 'Collected

Poems'—and not a single faltering or nerveless rhyme." "Terraces of Light," another collection of poems, has recently been reissued (1960 *Greenwood* 1972 $7.00).

COLLECTED POEMS. *Holt* 1964 $5.00

MEDUSA IN GRAMERCY PARK. *Macmillan* 1961 pap. $2.45

BENÉT, STEPHEN VINCENT. 1898–1943.

"John Brown's Body," which won the Pulitzer Prize for Poetry in 1929, and brought the poet instant popularity, is a history of the Civil War in rhyme and blank verse—a history told from the point of view of ordinary people, a rank-and-file history, of the North and of the South equally. This narrative of "the rich man's war and the poor man's fight" is a remarkable epic of America. Benét was a 17-year-old schoolboy when he published his first small book containing six remarkable dramatic portraits, "Five Men and Pompey" (1915, o.p.).

His short stories have been published in several collections, of which "The Devil and Daniel Webster" (*Holt* 1937 $3.95) and "The Devil and Daniel Webster and Other Stories" (*Pocket Bks.* pap. $.60) are still in print. The title story has been dramatized as a one-act folk comedy (*Dramatists* 1939 $.50). "Thirteen O'Clock, Stories of Several Worlds" has recently been reissued (1937. *Bks. for Libraries* $11.00).

Before Benét's untimely death, he had planned an epic poem based on the western migration of the pioneers who founded what he called this "outsize country." "Western Star," (1943, o.p.) the only section completed, tells of the beginnings of the colonies at Jamestown and Plymouth. It received the Pulitzer Poetry Award in 1944. Younger brother of William Rose Benét, he went to Yale, then on to the Sorbonne. As a writer of poetry and fiction he made effective use in verse and prose of the fascinating body of American folklore.

SELECTED WORKS: Poetry and Prose. 1942. *Holt* 1959 $8.50. Contains the complete text of "John Brown's Body" and an early novel "Spanish Bayonet," with poems and stories from all his books and four stories and two poems not included in other books.

SELECTED POETRY AND PROSE. Ed. by Basil Davenport. *Holt* 1960 pap. $1.25

BALLAD OF WILLIAM SYCAMORE. 1923. *Little* 1972 $4.95. One of Benét's major ballads.

(with Rosemary Benét) A BOOK OF AMERICANS. *Holt* (Rinehart) 1933 rev. ed. 1952 $3.95 lib. bdg. $3.59

JAMES SHORE'S DAUGHTER. 1934 *Scholarly Press* $14.50

AMERICA. *Holt* (Rinehart) 1944 $4.50

THE LAST CIRLCE. 1946. *Bks. for Libraries* 1973 $12.50. Last poem.

STEPHEN VINCENT BENÉT ON WRITING. Ed. and with comment by George Abbe. *Stephen Greene Press* 1963 $3.95. Letters of advice to a beginning author.

Books about Benét

Stephen Vincent Benét. By Parry Stroud. United States Authors Ser. *Twayne* 1962 $5.50; *College & Univ. Press* 1963 pap. $2.45

CRANE, (HAROLD) HART. 1899–1932.

Hart Crane is a poet with much appeal for the student generation of the 1960s. His tortured, rootless life with its moments of mystic vision and inspired writing is revealed in his letters. He shared with Whitman the feeling of the grandeur and expanse of America and had a passion for the sea, "his chosen symbol for mystic union and one which had a curious significance in his personal history. . . . When he was writing 'Voyages' he was living in Brooklyn, overlooking the East River. Ultimately he committed suicide by drowning"—(Babette Deutsch).

Robert Martin Adams has written of him in the *N.Y. Times*: "A Dionysian ecstatic from Cleveland, drunk on metaphysics and cheap red wine, a self-educated, self-tortured, self-destroyed homosexual visionary with a lavish gift of words strangled by a profusion of inchoate thought, Hart Crane was evidently the stuff of which legends are made. . . . [He was] an ambitious and important poet, if we understand that the importance of Crane derives as much from his myth as from his achievement. His poetry could never have satisfied his dream, and sometimes it bears most eloquent witness to the glory of that dream by straining to the limit and yet falling short. But the arc of his vision can be projected from the fragments he left behind, and it is dazzling indeed. As we become more conscious of the depth and complexity of our commitment to romanticism, it will appear less likely that any effort to understand one of its major spokesmen can really be excessive.'' Most of Crane's poems are to be found in the three brief collections published in his lifetime: "White Buildings," "The Bridge," his major collection, and "Key West" (o.p.) in a separate edition included in the "Complete Poems." In 1966 a moving series of interviews with Crane's friends together with readings of the poetry, "In Search of Crane," appeared on U.S. educational television.

THE COMPLETE POEMS AND SELECTED LETTERS AND PROSE OF HART CRANE. Ed. by Brom Weber. *Doubleday* Anchor Bks. 1967 pap. $2.50; *Liveright* Black & Gold Lib. $7.95.

WHITE BUILDINGS. 1926. *Liveright* 1970 pap. $1.95

THE BRIDGE. 1930. *Liveright* 1970 pap. $1.95

TEN UNPUBLISHED POEMS. *Gotham Bookmart* 1972 $8.50

THE LETTERS OF HART CRANE: 1916–1932. Ed. by Brom Weber. *Univ. of California Press* 1952 pap. $2.25

ROBBER ROCKS: Letters and Memories of Hart Crane, 1923–1932. Ed. by Susan J. Brown. *Wesleyan Univ. Press* 1969 $5.95. A well-edited scholarly edition which gives a glimpse into the day-to-day life of this poet.

Books about Crane

Hart Crane, a Biographical and Critical Study. By Brom Weber. 1948. *Russell & Russell* corrected ed. 1970 $18.00

Hart Crane. By Vincent Quinn. United States Authors Ser. *Twayne* 1963 $5.50; *College & Univ. Press* 1964 pap. $2.45

The Literary Manuscripts of Hart Crane. Comp. by K. A. Lohf. *Ohio State Univ. Press* 1967 $6.50. Bibliographic description of Crane's 278 literary manuscripts held in public and private collections, as well as of 805 of his letters and 455 letters written to him.

Hart Crane. By Monroe K. Spears. Pamphlets on American Writers *Univ. of Minnesota Press* 1965 pap. $1.25

The Poetry of Hart Crane: A Critical Study. By R. W. B. Lewis. *Princeton Univ. Press* 1967 $14.50
"His book is by all odds the most ambitious critical effort yet made in Crane's behalf. It is sympathetic, resourceful, free of pretension and jargon . . . it uses copiously the biography, the manuscripts and early drafts, as well as the influences from Crane's reading"—(Robert Martin Adams in the *N.Y. Times*).

Hart Crane: An Introduction to the Poetry. By Herbert A. Leibowitz. *Columbia* 1968 $10.00 pap. $2.95
"Leibowitz in his analysis of Hart Crane and his poetry tries to provide some balance for the 'New and Moral Criticism's' thumbs-down judgments of this poet. Leibowitz maintains that Crane's poetry has been 'vilified and misconstrued' by people like R. P. Blackmur, Allen Tate, Yvor Winters. . . . Leibowitz . . . makes a clear and convincing case for a reassessment of the New Critics' earlier decision about Crane—and in the process provides an excellent study of a very interesting romantic American poet"—(PW).

Voyager: A Life of Hart Crane. By John Unterecker. *Farrar Straus* 1969 $15.00. This complete and readable biography includes letters and interviews with Crane's contemporaries who knew him. It seeks to illuminate the nature of the poet.

Hart Crane: An Annotated Critical Bibliography. By Joseph Schwartz. *David Lewis* 1970 $15.00. Also contains a chronology.

Broken Arc: A Study of Hart Crane. By R. W. Butterfield. 1969. *Fernhill* 1972 $10.00. This book is divided into ten chapters which treat the major works chronologically. Three chapters are on "The Bridge." A good book of criticism which includes a selected bibliography of names and periodicals, an index of poems, and four appendixes.

Concordance to the Poems of Hart Crane. By Gary Lane. *Haskell* 1972 $14.95. A new concordance to the works of Crane.

A Concordance to the Poems of Hart Crane. By Elaine and Hilton Landry; rev. by Robert DeMott. *Scarecrow Press* 1973 $12.50

TATE, ALLEN. 1899–

Allen Tate, poet, essayist, novelist, biographer, critic and Professor Emeritus of English at the University of Minnesota, was one of the founders, with other Southern poets, in 1922, of *The Fugitive,* fleeing "social optimism" and modern materialism. His best-known poem, "Ode to the Confederate Dead," ten years in the writing, is typical of his work in its irony and intellectualism. He is at his best as a critic of poetry. He has edited many anthologies, among them "Princeton Verse between Two Wars" (1942. *Bks. for Libraries* $7.00), "The Language of Poetry" (*Russell & Russell* 1960 $8.00), "Six American Poets from Emily Dickinson to the Present: An Introduction" (*Univ. of Minnesota Press* 1971 $8.50), and, with Lord David Cecil, "Modern Verse in English: 1900–1950" (1950. *Macmillan* $8.50). His novel "The Fathers" (1938. *Swallow* 1968 pap. $2.95) is now back in print, as is "Stonewall Jackson: The Good Soldier" (1928. *Univ. of Michigan Press* Ann Arbor Bks. 1957 pap. $2.25).

He was elected to the National Institute of Arts and Letters in 1949, and in 1956 won the Bollingen Prize for Poetry. He received the 1963 Award of the Academy of American Poets. The Autumn 1959 issue of the *Sewanee Review* was devoted to "Homage to Allen Tate—Essays, Notes and Verses in Honor of his Sixtieth Birthday," by 19 English and American writers.

POEMS. *Swallow* 1961 $2.50

SWIMMERS AND OTHER SELECTED POEMS. *Scribner* 1971 pap. $2.95. Contains all the poems in "Poems" (1960, o.p.) which were selected over a 50-year period. Also 17 poems are included which have been long out of print or never published in book form.

MR. POPE AND OTHER POEMS. 1928. *Bks. for Libraries* $5.50

Books about Tate

The Fugitive Group: A Literary History. By Louise S. Cowan. *Louisiana State Univ. Press* 1959 $7.50 pap. $2.45

Last Alternatives: Allen Tate. By Roger Miners. 1963. *Haskell* 1972 $10.95. An examination of Tate's critical ideas, his novel "The Fathers" as well as the poems, this book is a useful study for students of American literature and criticism. The appendix includes the entire text of "Seasons of the Soul."

Allen Tate. By George Hemphill. Pamphlets on American Writers *Univ. of Minnesota Press* 1964 pap. $1.25

The Burden of Time: The Fugitives and Agrarians. By John L. Stewart. *Princeton Univ. Press* 1965 $17.50. *See entry on John Crowe Ransom for comment.*

Allen Tate. By Ferman Bishop. United States Authors Ser. *Twayne* 1967 $5.50; *College & Univ. Press* pap. $2.45

Allen Tate: A Bibliography. By Marshall Fallwell, Jr. (with Marcha Cook and Francis Immler). Fugitive Bibliographies Ser. *David Lewis* 1969 $10.00. This bibliography includes a whole section on Tate's poems.

Allen Tate: A Literary Biography. By Radcliffe Squires. American Authors Ser. *Pegasus* 1971 $6.95

Allen Tate and His Works: Critical Evaluations. Ed. by Radcliffe Squires. *Univ. of Minnesota Press* 1972 $10.75. This book gathers together critical essays on Tate the man, the essayist and finally the poet, by numerous scholars, including John Crowe Ransom, Mark Van Doren, Robert Lowell, Herbert Read, Richard Howard, Frank Kermode and Cleanth Brooks.

See also his main entry in Chapter 15, Essays and Criticism.

RIDING, LAURA. (Laura [Riding] Jackson). 1901–

Laura Riding is surely one of the most mysterious and neglected poets of the century. She is unknown to most casual readers of poetry, and Kenneth Rexroth has said of her, "Laura Riding is the greatest lost poet in American literature."

She was born in New York City and educated at Cornell University. During the twenties her work appeared in numerous small literary magazines, including *The Fugitive.* In 1925 she went to Europe, where she and Robert Graves ran the Seizin Press in Majorca. In 1939 she returned to the United States, renounced poetry, and since then has lived in Florida writing studies on the nature of language with her husband, Schuyler.

Though poets of the younger generation have read and revered her, Riding is largely unknown because, except for the publication of her "Collected Poems" in 1938 (now o.p.), her work was unavailable until 1970. She refused to let her poetry be anthologized. She only permitted the reprinting of a small selection of poetry in 1970 ("Selected Poems") on the condition that it contain the following statement on her work: "My cause is something poetry fails to be—belying its promisory advertisement of itself. May the poems of this selection excite some sense of wherein the failure of poetry lies, and some fore-sense of what that failure might be."

Her other writings include various works of fiction: "A Progress of Stories," short stories (1935. *Bks. for Libraries* \$12.00), "A Trojan Ending," a historical novel (1937 o.p.), and "Lives of Wives," historical stories (1939 o.p.). Her recent book, "The Telling" (1972 o.p.), is prose work concerned with the nature of language. "Contemporaries and Snobs" is a critical work currently available (1928. *Scholarly Press* 1971 \$14.50). With Robert Graves she has written an excellent critical work, "Survey of Modernist Poetry" (1927. *Folcroft* lib. bdg. \$11.75; *Haskell* 1969 lib. bdg. \$11.95; *Scholarly Press* 1971 \$14.50; *Richard West* 1973 \$17.50), and, also with Robert Graves, "A Pamphlet against Anthologies" (1928. *AMS Press* 1970 \$9.00).

"Laura Riding has meant more to me than any other American poet, and in the years since her retirement she has been a woman much missed. I think the history of the last thirty years of American poetry would have been different had she been around"—(Kenneth Rexroth).

SELECTED POEMS: In Five Sets. *Norton* 1973 \$6.95 pap. \$1.95. All the poems Laura Riding wishes to be preserved are included in this volume.

VOLTAIRE, a Biographical Fantasy. 1927. *Folcroft* lib. bdg. \$5.00. Poetry.

FEARING, KENNETH. 1902–1961.

Born in Chicago and resident most of his adult life in New York, Kenneth Fearing spoke with the voice of the big city. Of himself he wrote: "I was brought up and educated in the public schools of Oak Park, and graduated from the University of Wisconsin in 1924. In Chicago I did newspaper work as a reporter, have been a salesman, mill-hand, clerk, etc. Since 1924 I have lived almost continuously in New York City [working as] a free-lance writer. Much of that [has been] purely commercial."

His attitude toward the "purely commercial" imbued all of his writing with a tone of sardonic disenchantment. He chose his literary tools from the catch phrases of advertisements and journalese jargon, and used the tools to dissect their source. His chief concern was for content, character and caricature; his purpose that of social critique. With diction of the street and his subject matter that of the tabloid news sheets, Fearing created a poetry taut with excitement.

The novels carry on the excitement and the semisociological aim of exposé. "The Crozart Story" (1960, o.p.) was last; his earliest was "The Hospital" and his most famous "The Big Clock." He had written seven novels and seven volumes of verse (most now o.p.) before his death.

NEW AND SELECTED POEMS. *Indiana Univ. Press* 1956 \$5.95

HUGHES, LANGSTON. 1902–1967.

Langston Hughes "was most widely known as the chronicler of Harlem, where he lived for many years. Unlike the generation of Negro writers that came after him, Mr. Hughes' approach to racial matters was more wry than angry, sly than militant"—(*PW*). But he helped set the mood for the present firmness on the part of his people. "If conditions are better today, surely he deserves part of the credit"—(*N.Y. Times*). Hughes was born in Missouri and educated in the Middle West. He was discovered, while working as a busboy in Washington, by Vachel Lindsay (*q. v.*). He is in no sense a traditional poet, but takes his poetic forms and material from folk sources, a great deal of his work expressing in words the spirit of the musical "blues." With Countee Cullen he was outstanding in the Harlem literary renaissance of the twenties.

After 1926 he devoted his time to writing and lecturing. In prose he carried his protagonist Jessie B. Semple, or "Simple"—the humorous Harlem dweller who nevertheless "spoke his mind" sharply on matters of racial injustice—through many newspaper columns, stories and three collections. The basis of Simple's humor is expressed in the title of one of Mr. Hughes' short-story collections, "Laughing to Keep from Crying"; "White folks," said Simple, "is the cause of a lot of inconvenience in my life." Among Hughes's prose works in print are: "Not Without Laughter" (*Knopf* 1930 \$6.95; *Macmillan* Collier Bks. pap. \$1.50), a novel; "Simple's Uncle Sam" (*Hill & Wang* 1965 \$3.95 Am. Century pap. \$1.75; *Franklin Watts* large type ed. \$7.99); "Famous American Negroes;" a juvenile, (*Dodd* 1954 \$3.50; *Apollo* pap. \$1.75); "The Best of Simple" (*Hill & Wang* 1961 \$4.50 Am. Century pap. \$.95); "The Ways of the White Folks" (*Knopf* 1934 \$4.95; *Random* Vintage Bks. pap. \$1.95) and "Five Plays by Langston Hughes" (ed. by Webster Smalley *Indiana Univ. Press* 1963 \$6.95 Midland Bks. pap. \$2.65). He edited "The Book of Negro Humor" (1945. *Dodd* 1965 \$5.00; *Apollo* pap. \$1.95); "An African Treasury: Articles, Essays, Stories and Poems by Black Africans" (1960. *Crown* \$4.00; *Pyramid* pap. \$.95); with Arna Bontemps, "The Poetry of the Negro, 1746–1949" (*Doubleday* 1949 \$8.95 Anchor Bks. pap. \$4.95); "The Book of Negro Folklore" (*Dodd* 1958 \$7.50; *Apollo* pap. \$3.45); "Poems from Black Africa" (*Indiana Univ. Press* 1963 \$5.95 pap. \$1.75); with Milton Meltzer, "A Pictorial History of the Negro in America" (*Crown* 1956 3rd. ed. 1968 \$6.95 pap. \$3.95) and "Black Magic: A Pictorial History of the Negro in American Entertainment" (*Prentice-Hall* 1967 \$14.95).

Langston Hughes took an active part in the promotion of new African writers and in 1962 was a founder of the Mbari Artists and Writers Club to foster and publish African writers in Ibadan, Nigeria. His "Something in Common and Other Stories" (*Hill & Wang* 1963 $4.50 Am. Century pap. $2.25) contains 37 stories selected by the author and includes 9 which have never appeared in book form before. "Fight for Freedom: The Story of the NAACP" (fwd. by Arthur Spingarn *Norton* 1962 $4.95) is a detailed and valuable account of the history of the Negro struggle for equality of opportunity in the U.S. By liberal use of anecdote and personal narratives, he has made this history read like the adventure story that it is. He has edited "New Negro Poets: U.S.A.," a collection of the younger writers (*Indiana Univ. Press* 1964 $5.95 pap. $1.95).

THE LANGSTON HUGHES READER. Comprehensive edition of poems, songs, plays and prose. *Braziller* 1958 $5.95

SELECTED POEMS OF LANGSTON HUGHES. Spanning his career from 1926 to 1958. *Knopf* 1959 $6.95

THE NEGRO MOTHER. 1931. *Bks. for Libraries* $7.50

DREAM KEEPER. 1932. *Knopf* $2.75 lib. bdg. $4.19. Poems for young people.

ASK YOUR MAMA: 12 Moods for Jazz. *Knopf* 1961 $4.95

These 12 short related poems in anger at the Negro condition resemble "beat" material. "The best sections concern daily life in Southern shacks and Northern slums; they have a rhythmic drive and intensity well fitting them to be read aloud in front of jazz bands"—(*LJ*).

THE PANTHER AND THE LASH. *Knopf* 1967 $4.50 pap. $2.50. Includes 44 new poems and 26 from previous books.

BLACK MISERY. 1967. *Eriksson* 2nd ptg. 1969 $2.95

DON'T YOU TURN BACK. (Originally "I Bring You My Songs"). Ed. by Lee B. Hopkins. *Knopf* 1969 $3.95 lib. bdg. $4.79

LANGSTON HUGHES AND STERLING BROWN. A recording to go with "Simple Speaks His Mind." *Folkways* FL 9790 $5.79

THE BIG SEA. First volume of a projected 3-volume autobiography. 1963–65. *Hill & Wang* 1963 $4.95 Am. Century pap. $2.75

I WONDER AS I WANDER. Autobiography. *Hill & Wang* 1964 Am. Century pap. $2.45

TAMBOURINES TO GLORY. *Hill & Wang* 1970 $4.95 Am. Century pap. $1.95. Play.

FAMOUS NEGRO MUSIC MAKERS. *Dodd* 1955 $3.50. Historical survey.

FAMOUS NEGRO HEROES OF AMERICA. *Dodd* 1958 $3.50. Historical survey.

Books about Hughes

Langston Hughes. By James A. Emanuel. United States Authors Ser. *Twayne* 1967 $5.50; *College & Univ. Press* pap. $2.45
"This is the first full length study of Hughes [and] Mr. Emanuel has done a workmanlike job in providing readers with a scholarly account of Hughes's life and a relatively sound assessment of some of Hughes's works. A chronology and useful bibliographies are appended"—(*LJ*).
A Bio-bibliography of Langston Hughes, 1902–1967. By Donald C. Dickinson. Introd. by Arna Bontemps. *Shoe String* 1967 $12.50
"The biographical section gives an excellent summary of Langston Hughes's career, and the bibliographical listing of his publications provides an extremely useful guide which will be welcomed by students and scholars"—(Donald Gallup).

NASH, OGDEN. 1902–1971.

Ogden Nash's "versus" are written in outrageous rhyming schemes, satirizing the life of our times. He takes every liberty with the sound and spelling of the King's English and with the rhyming dictionary. Typical of his parallel but incorrect spelling for some of his rhymes:—"Kitchens" and "obstetritchens," "King Midas" and "tonsilidas." His witty inventiveness is unique. When reviewing "Everyone But Thee and Me" for the *N.Y. Times*, Morris Bishop called Nash "the only American except Walt Whitman who has created a new poetic form and imposed it on the world. . . . One may well say (may not one?): "Free from flashiness, free from trashiness/ Is the essence of ogdenashiness./ Rich, original, rash and rational/ Stands the monument ogdenational!"

He entered Harvard but left after one year (his own idea and not the dean's, he says); spent a year teaching in St. George's School; went to New York as a bond salesman (in two years, sold one bond—"to my godmother"); "doubledayed" in the advertising department of *Doubleday, Page* for several years; joined the editorial staff of the *New Yorker*; and was a member of the National Institute of Arts and Letters. Before his death in 1971, however, he began devoting his entire time to writing. About "Marriage Lines" he said, "It has occurred to me that my notes jotted down through the years might help other student husbands. . . . Most of them are the result of long and earnest observation of the endearing but baffling feminine charm of one wife in particular and the equally baffling non-masculine peculiarities of many wives in general." "Santa Go Home," Nash said, is an "exposé of the childhood of Santa Claus and the bizarre psychological quirk which impels him, even in his old age, to continue giving things away." "The Cruise of the Aardvark" is about an animal of that variety who saves Noah's ark.

MANY LONG YEARS AGO. *Little* 1945 $4.95. Poems from five early volumes.

VERSES FROM 1929 ON. *Little* 1959. $6.95; *Modern Library* $2.95. One-volume collection of his finest verse.

THE POCKET BOOK OF OGDEN NASH. (Former title, "Ogden Nash Pocket Book") 1944–45 *Pocket Bks.* 1962 pap. $.75

FAMILY REUNION. *Little* 1950 $4.50. Verse.

PARENTS KEEP OUT: Elderly Poems for Youngerly Readers. *Little* 1951 $3.95

YOU CAN'T GET THERE FROM HERE. *Little* 1957 $4.95. New Poems.

A BOY IS A BOY. *Franklin Watts* 1960 $2.95

CUSTARD THE DRAGON AND THE WICKED KNIGHT. *Little* 1961 $3.95

GIRLS ARE SILLY. *Franklin Watts* 1962 $2.95

EVERYONE BUT THEE AND ME. Ill. by John Alcorn. *Little* 1962 $4.95

THE MOON IS SHINING BRIGHT AS DAY. *Lippincott* 1963. $3.95

THE ANIMAL GARDEN. *M. Evans* 1965 $3.95

THE CRUISE OF THE AADVARK. *M. Evans* 1967 $3.95

THE MYSTERIOUS OUPHE. *Hale* 1967 lib. bdg. $2.79

THERE'S ALWAYS ANOTHER WINDMILL. *Little* 1968 $4.95

BEDRIDDANCE: A Posy for the Indisposed. *Little* 1970 $4.95

OLD DOG BARKS BACKWARDS. *Little* 1972 $5.95. This posthumous collection includes 77 poems never before published, with drawings by Robert Binks.

OGDEN NASH READS OGDEN NASH. A recording. *Caedmon* TC 1015 $5.95

Books about Nash

An Index to the Poems of Ogden Nash. By Lavonne Axford. *Scarecrow Press* 1972 $7.50

CULLEN, COUNTEE. 1903–1946.

Born on May 30, 1903 in New York City, Cullen was separated from his mother in early childhood and subsequently raised by a Mrs. Porter and after her death by the Reverend Frederick Cullen, a Methodist minister. In high school Cullen already was praised for his poetry. The poem "Life's Rendezvous," was published in a high school literary magazine and won first prize in a city-wide contest. Educated at New York University and Harvard, Cullen worked as an assistant editor on the Urban League's *Opportunity: A Journal of Negro Life*, writing a monthly literary column. His many awards for poetry included the first Harmon prize for distinguished achievement in literature by a black writer, and a Guggenheim Fellowship. He taught junior high school in New York until his death.

Cullen's work is a far cry from the black poetry of today. He writes in rhymed stanza form and has been criticized for his failure to be a more positive spokesman for Afro-Americans. However, he "eloquently evoked sympathy and admiration for them, extolled the African heritage, and protested against the American chauvinism which today is shown as white racism"—(Darwin T. Turner).

His children's books, "The Lost Zoo" and "My Lives and How I Lost Them" are still well-known.

ON THESE I STAND: An Anthology of the Best Poems of Countee Cullen Selected by Himself and Including Six New Poems Never Before Published. 1947. *Harper* $5.95.

COLOR 1925. American Negro: His History and Literature Ser. no. 3. *Arno* $4.50. Written while Cullen was concerned primarily with Afro-American themes, this collection includes love poems and poems eliciting sympathy for the outcast.

THE LOST ZOO: A Rhyme For the Young But Not Too Young. 1940. *Follett* 1969 $4.98

MY LIVES AND HOW I LOST THEM. 1942. *Follett* 1971 $4.95 lib. bdg. $4.99 pap. $.95

Books about Cullen

Countee Cullen and the Negro Renaissance. By Blanche E. Ferguson. Dodd 1966 $5.00. This is a good readable biography of Cullen within the context of his environment, with a discussion of his relationship with Langston Hughes and others then in the Harlem Renaissance. Illustrated with photographs of Cullen and New York City, and some drawings of Cullen.

RAKOSI, CARL (CALLMAN RAWLEY). 1903–

Like the other objectivists Charles Reznikoff and George Oppen, Rakosi is enjoying a well-deserved return to fashion. Rakosi was born in Berlin, Germany, of Hungarian parentage. He was educated at the Universities of Wisconsin and Pennyslvania, where he received a degree in social work, his profession for which he gave up writing poetry for a long period.

Rakosi's social concerns are evident in his work, and his poetry is "humane, attentive to the ordinary, until the ordinary ceases to be so"—(Jim Harrison). Another critic seconds Harrison on Rakosi's ability to transform the mundane into something on the level of pure perfection and sensibility: "What Rakosi has, delightfully, is an ability to translate emotion into objects, tastes and smells . . . and the reader is almost surprised to find himself moving from a homely, apparently naive, sometimes even domestic landscape, into a mind that is neither naive nor domestic. . ."—(Stanley Cooperman).

AMULET. *New Directions* 1967 $4.50 pap. $1.50

ERE-VOICE. *New Directions* 1971 $6.50 pap. $2.45

EBERHART, RICHARD. 1904–

In "Contemporary American Poetry" Ralph J. Mills, Jr., in an excellent analysis, stresses the religious quality of Richard Eberhart's verse and his effort to come to terms with the large questions of life: "The Groundhog," for example, his musings on a dead animal, expands to encompass all death and change and passing away. "With Walt Whitman . . . and other American writers he shares a distrust of writing that refuses to submit itself to near-domination by the experience it renders. . . . At his peak he acquires an intensity of focus on his material that is matched by only a few of his contemporaries. . . . The poet turns a naked gaze on his experience and writes unreservedly from such perception. The surrender of himself to a luminous instant of vision and the momentous effort to seize it in words imbue Eberhart's poetry with its amazing power. [His responses to the questions raised by experience] frequently border on religious vision, partake of it, or further probe spiritual torment. [His] forcefulness . . . depends upon his fidelity to the inwardness of his moods, inspirations and perceptions; but he rejects the idea of systematizing them lest their essential truth be warped or lost."

"No other contemporary poet has been so unabashedly unafraid of universal questions, none has acknowledged the pleasure of a personal mysticism with such lyric gusto. His poems, by definition of their nature, run the constant danger of toppling, headlong, from the highwire of cosmic assertion on which they are balanced; but perhaps because he continues to practice his art with no safety net, such performances as "The Fury of Aerial Bombardment" are completely breathtaking"—(from a *Christian Science Monitor* review of "The Collected Poems"). In "Thirty-One Sonnets" (1967, o.p.)—written 35 years before their publication, in reaction to an unhappy youthful love affair—he "is always impassioned, at times tender, vindictive, philosophical. Like Shakespeare, the young Eberhart sees love in many aspects, by no means all splendid; he is aware most poignantly of time and change, of the shortness of life and the overwhelming forces of indifferent nature"—(*LJ*). Kenneth Rexroth has praised him for his "perfect clarity of vision, perfect clarity of utterance, perfect control of the material means," visible, too, in "Shifts of Being," which reflect recent travel to Europe, Mexico and Africa. Eberhart frequently expresses his opposition to warfare; he has, with Seldon Rodman, edited the anthology, "War and the Poet."

His poems, said Dame Edith Sitwell, "have strong intellectual sinews, are poems of ideas, but have a warmth of humanity as strong as their intellect." Mr. Eberhart was born in Austin, Minn., and educated at Dartmouth, Cambridge on a Rhodes scholarship, and Harvard. He was a training officer in aerial free gunnery for the Navy during World War II, tutored the son of King Prajhadipok of Siam and taught English at St. Mark's. Now Professor of English and Poet in Residence at Dartmouth, he has been poet in residence, professor, or resident fellow at the University of Washington, the University of Connecticut, Wheaton College and Princeton. In 1959–61 he served as Consultant in Poetry to the Library of Congress and from 1963–66 as its Honorary Consultant in American Letters. He has received many prizes, including the 1952 Shelley Memorial Award, the 1955 Harriet Monroe Poetry Award, the 1962 Bollingen Prize and the 1966 Pulitzer Prize for Poetry. He is a member of the National Institute of Arts and Letters.

COLLECTED POEMS, 1930–1960. *Oxford* 1960 $6.50. Selections from eight of the author's volumes of poems, with a group of 51 poems not previously published in book form.

SELECTED POEMS, 1930–1965. *New Directions* 1966 pap. $1.75

QUARRY: New Poems. *Oxford* 1964 $5.25

SHIFTS OF BEING. *Oxford* 1968 $3.95

FIELDS OF GRACE. *Oxford* 1972 $5.95. The first collection of new poems in four years.

RICHARD EBERHART, READING HIS POETRY. A recording. *Caedmon* TC 1243 1967–68 $5.95

Books about Eberhart

Richard Eberhart. By Ralph J. Mills, Jr. Pamphlets on American Writers *Univ. of Minnesota Press* 1966 pap. $1.25
Richard Eberhart: The Progress of an American Poet. By Joel H. Roach. *Oxford* 1971 $8.50. A biography of the poet illustrated with biographical photographs. Has bibliography, notes and index.
Richard Eberhart. By Bernard F. Engel. United States Authors Ser. *Twayne* $5.50. Engle has written a general informative study of Eberhart and his works. The approach of this book is scholarly but aimed at the new student.

ZUKOFSKY, LOUIS. 1904–

"Zukofsky, over the years, has appealed to poets without becoming known outside the community of poetry. Yet Zukofsky's work belongs in the front rank of American poetry, alongside that of William Carlos Williams. Difficult and complex because of the manner in which they have been pared down to fundamental images, rhythms, and sounds, the poems in 'All: The Collected Short Poems, 1956–1964' . . . have a lyric power not easily surpassed in modern writing"—(Robert D. Spector, in *SR*).

" 'A' 1–12," is part of Mr. Zukofsky's continuing "poem of life," this section of it written between 1928 and 1951 as he responded to the Depression, to World War II and to social injustice. In his words, "In a sense the poem is an autobiography: the words are my life." *Library Journal* found it "often difficult, but valuable reading." It was nominated for the 1968 National Book Award and was chosen as the third volume in the *Paris Review* Editions.

His "Bottom: On Shakespeare" (1963, o.p.) is written in prose, but he considers it a long poem. Guy Davenport wrote of Volume 1 in the *National Review*: "The momentum that carries the reader fascinated through this poet's notebook of perceptions is generated in the introduction. . . . What emerges is a kind of dance of imagery and words which Zukofsky, with pure delight, has set in motion. . . . One feat Zukofsky has performed without saying a word: he has wrested Shakespeare from two centuries of embattled siege by the English professors. . . . [This] is a book that belongs to that scarce genre which we can only call a *book*, like Boswell's 'Johnson,' Burton's incredible 'Anatomy,' Walton's 'Compleat Angler.' Zukofsky gives us a lover's insight into the way he reads Shakespeare; he makes lines that we have read all our lives turn to gold before our eyes. . . . The two volumes are physically handsome, designed by Kim Taylor, with fetching drawings by Cyril Satorsky." Volume 2, by Celia Zukofsky, is Shakespeare's "Pericles" set to music.

"A-24" is a modern masque which combines words and music. The music is by George Friedrich Händel, the words come from essays, dramas, stories and poems by the author. The autobiography is written in prose and poetry, with music scores by Celia Zukofsky.

Louis Zukofsky first achieved a reputation in the literary world during the twenties when he was published by Ezra Pound in *Exile*. Later he became editor of *Poetry*, in which, in 1931, he actively promoted the as yet relatively unknown William Carlos Williams and Kenneth Rexroth, among others. Mr. Zukofsky was born in New York City on the Lower East Side. He received both an A.B. and an M.A. from Columbia and taught for two years at the Brooklyn Polytechnic Institute.

He has written a book of short stories, "Ferdinand and It Was" (*Grossman* 1968 pap. $1.95), and a novel, "Little" (*Grossman* 1970 $5.95), about a child who was a musical genius. Zukofsky himself is father to a violin virtuoso. He and his wife Celia have translated Catullus with parallel English and Latin texts (*Grossman* 1969 $9.50 pap. $4.50).

In the spring of 1973 performances of Zukofsky's music and poetry were given, with the poet and his wife present, at New York's experimental Cubiculo Theater.

ALL: The Collected Short Poems, 1923–58. *Norton* 1965 $6.00 pap. $2.45

ALL: The Collected Short Poems, 1956–1964. *Norton* 1966 $4.50

A TEST OF POETRY. 1948. *Corinth Bks.* 1964 pap. $2.95

A-24. *Grossman* 1972 $12.95

AUTOBIOGRAPHY. *Grossman* 1970 $5.95. In prose and poetry, with music scores by Celia Zukofsky.

KUNITZ, STANLEY (JASSPON). 1905–

"I admire Mr. Kunitz's savage, symbolic drive. He has been one of the masters for years," said Robert Lowell on the publication of "Selected Poems" in 1958. Richard Wilbur said of the volume: "One of the best poetry manuscripts of the century. . . . Kunitz has every technical virtue. What's more, he can put his perfected and rather lapidary style at the service of the most fundamental themes and passions." And Henry Rago, editor of *Poetry*: "This volume of his new and selected poems is long overdue. Stanley Kunitz seems to me one of the very best poets of his generation, and he is now at the height of his powers. He has two qualities that stand out for me. One is in his language: an extraordinary combination of toughness and polish; a classical strength. The other is his vision which goes beyond the easier uses of irony and achieves the genuinely tragic." "Selected Poems" received the Pulitzer Prize for Poetry in 1959; he had won the Harriet Monroe Poetry Prize in 1958; later he received a Ford Foundation Grant and an award from the National Institute of Arts and Letters. He has been elected to the Literature Department of the National Institute of Arts and Letters.

Mr. Kunitz was born in Worcester, Mass., the posthumous son of a Russian-Jewish father who resolved by suicide a business partner's misappropriation of funds. He attended public school in Worcester and Harvard, where he graduated *summa cum laude* and received the Garrison Medal for Poetry. He entered the Army as a private during World War II and rose to staff sergeant before his discharge in 1945. He has taught at Bennington College and at many literary seminars. His early volumes of poetry, "Intellectual Things" (1930) and "Passport to the War" (1944), are now o.p. With Howard Haycraft, he has edited "Twentieth Century Authors" and other reference works. Also with Haycraft he has translated Akhmatova's "Poems" (*Little* Atlantic 1973 $7.95 pap. $3.95) (*see Chapter 3, Reference Books—Literature: Histories and Dictionaries of Literature*). In recent years Mr. Kunitz has translated many poems of the Russians Yevtushenko and Voznesensky and has often appeared on the platform with them in their American public readings. He was honored in 1968 with the $5,000 Fellowship of the Academy of American Poets.

SELECTED POEMS, 1928–1958. *Little-Atlantic* 1958 pap. $1.95

TESTING-TREE: Poem. *Little* Atlantic 1971 $4.95 pap. $1.95. 30 new poems including the 4-page title-poem.

WARREN, ROBERT PENN. 1905–

A Kentucky-born poet, editor, scholar and novelist, Warren spent some of his boyhood in Tennessee. His education included a Rhodes Scholarship at Oxford. He became one of the managing editors with Cleanth Brooks, Jr., of the *Southern Review*, forum of the New Criticism (*see introduction to Chapter 15, Essays and Criticism*) and, after its demise in 1942, became associated with the *Kenyon Review* as advisory editor. Extraordinarily active and versatile, he has taught fiction, poetry and playwriting and produced work in all forms of literature. His poetry is intellectual, rich in the powerful images of the true creative imagination and has its roots in the pre-Civil War South. He is "at his best in a kind of rough balladry" and has an "unusual ability to join the narrative and the lyric." James Dickey has written of him: "When he is good, and often even when he is bad, you had as soon read Warren as live. He gives you the sense of poetry as a thing of final importance to life: as a way or *form* of life. In his practice it is a tortured, painful, sometimes rhetorical means of exploring man's fate, often nearer to tragic melodrama than to tragedy, but never anything less than fully engaged in its problems, never inconsequential"—(in "Babel to Byzantium").

" 'Understanding Poetry' [*Holt* 3rd ed. 1960 $10.95 text ed. $7.75], the college textbook that he and Cleanth Brooks wrote in 1938, made the New Criticism, whose advocates believe that *how* a poem is put together matters more than *who* put it together, a dominant force in the English departments of most American universities"—(*N.Y. Times*), With Cleanth Brooks, Jr., he has also edited "Understanding Fiction" (*Appleton* 2nd ed. 1959 $8.50) and with Robert B. Heilman, "Understanding Drama" (*Holt* 1948 $10.50). Also with Cleanth Brooks, Jr., "Fundamentals of Good Writing" (*Harcourt* $10.75) and "Modern Rhetoric" (*Harcourt* 1958 3rd ed. 1970 $8.95 pap. abr. $5.95), among other works. He has edited, with Albert Erskine, "Six Centuries of Great Poetry" (*Dell* pap. $.95). In 1958 Mr. Warren won both the Pulitzer Prize for Poetry and the National Book Award for "Promises." He received the 1967 Bollingen Prize for his "Selected Poems," which were cited as demonstrating "the full range of an extraordinarily gifted writer's poetic accomplishment." He has won many other awards. Of his "Selected Essays" (*Random* 1958 $4.95 Vintage Bks. pap. $1.95) L. L. Martz wrote in the *Yale Review* of March, 1961: "Warren's achievement in ['Brother to Dragons,' 'Promises' and 'You, Emperors, and Others'] leads one to say what might have seemed impossible ten years ago: that Warren may come to be remembered as a poet who also wrote novels." Since 1950 he has taught at Yale. He is married to the writer Eleanor Clark.

BROTHER TO DRAGONS: A Tale in Verse and Voices. *Random* 1953 $7.95

PROMISES: Poems 1954–1956. *Random* 1957 $3.50

YOU, EMPERORS, AND OTHERS: Poems 1957–60. *Random* 1960 $3.50

INCARNATIONS: Poems 1966–68. *Random* 1968 $5.95 limited ed. $10.00. Thirty-four new poems never before in book form with photographs of the author.

AUDUBON: A Vision. *Random* 1969 $4.00. A beautifully produced series of poems suggested to the poet by episodes from the life and reading of John James Audubon.

Books about Warren

Robert Penn Warren and History: The Big Myth We Live. By Hugh L. Moore. *Humanities* 1970 text ed. $12.00

See also Chapter 14, Modern American Fiction.

McGINLEY, PHYLLIS, 1905–

A wise and witty writer of "light" verse, a difficult poetic genre whose masters have been few, Phyllis McGinley "has achieved a magical sense of communication and intimacy between herself and the reader, and in so doing has not compromised by so much as a syllable her own standard of integrity"—(*N.Y. Times*). She was born in Ontario, Oreg., lives in Larchmont, N.Y., and has written several books for children published by *Lippincott* and *Franklin Watts*. "The Province of the Heart" (*Viking* 1959 $3.50) contains 18 pieces on husbands, children, gardens, that touch modern life at many points. "Sixpence in Her Shoe" (*Macmillan* 1964 $4.95), a collection of 22 essays, is a "partial autobiography, combined with household hints and homilies. Its first-person emerges warm, wistful and snug in her nest"—(*N.Y. Times*).

The Pulitzer Prize for Poetry in 1961 went to "Times Three," which carried an appreciative foreword by W. H. Auden, "who, like Miss McGinley, has helped break down the once rigid line between light verse and serious poetry." Her "subject matter, like her style, is larger than is apparent at first glance; it is compact with ironic sidelights and sharp appraisals"—(Louis Untermeyer).

TIMES THREE: Selected Verse from Three Decades. Introd. by W. H. Auden. *Viking* 1960 $5.50 Compass Bks. pap. $1.65

A POCKETFUL OF WRY. 1940. *Grosset* 1960 Univ. Lib. $1.25. Poems on her favorite themes.

LOVE LETTERS OF PHYLLIS MCGINLEY: Humorous Verse. *Viking* 1954 $5.95 Compass Bks. 1956 pap. $1.35

A WREATH OF CHRISTMAS LEGENDS. Ill. by Leonard Weisgard. *Macmillan* 1967 $4.95

"Poems that have appeared in Christmas issues of various magazines are collected here in a small but beguiling book"—(*LJ*).

Books about McGinley

Phyllis McGinley. By Linda W. Wagner. *Twayne* 1971 $5.50. Criticism of McGinley's work by a foremost William Carlos Williams scholar. This book is particularly useful as an introductory study.

REXROTH, KENNETH. 1905–

Mr. Rexroth was born in South Bend, Ind., and lived in various places in the Midwest. He worked, he says, at "every imaginable sort of job, mucker, harvest hand, forest patrolman, packer, factory hand, fruit packer, insane asylum attendant." He took various courses and is "self-educated." One of the first abstract painters, he now lives in San Francisco, where he has conducted a column for the *Examiner* and where he co-founded the San Francisco Poetry Center. His first poems were eccentric, heavily influenced by surrealism and experimental forms. His mature work is characterized by "firm control, the brilliant wit, the quick ear, and the deep humanistic passion"—(Dudley Fitts). In "The Collected Shorter Poems," nominated for the 1968 National Book Award, "one moves through imagist lyrics, Chinese and Japanese forms, surreal constructions, poems intended to be read against the improvisations of jazz combos, other poems intended to be sung to the tune of folk ballads, poems influenced by Apollinaire and poems that influenced, one assumes, Ferlinghetti, Ginsberg and Corso"—(*N.Y. Times*). He won the 1957 Eunice Tietjens Memorial Prize, the 1958 Shelley Memorial Award, the 1959 Amy Lowell Travelling Fellowship and the 1964 National Institute of Arts and Letters Literature Award. He has translated "100 Poems from the Japanese" (*New Directions* 1955 $5.00 1963 pap. $1.75), "100 Poems from the Chinese" (*New Directions* 1956 $5.50 pap. $1.75), "Love and the Turning Year: 100 More Chinese Poems (*New Directions* 1970 $5.50 pap. $1.95), "Thirty Spanish Poems of Love and Exile" (1956. *City Lights Books* pap. $1.00) and "Poems from the Greek Anthology" (*Univ. of Michigan Press* Ann Arbor Bks. 1962 pap. $1.75).

He is a lively and entertaining critic. In his collection, "Bird in the Bush: Obvious Essays" (*New Directions* 1959 $2.50; *Bks. for Libraries* $11.50), he ranges from jazz to D. H. Lawrence and in "Assays" (*New Directions* 1961 $4.50 pap. $2.25) he explains Kabbalism and deals extensively with literature including novelists, historians and poets.

"An Autobiographical Novel" is "a chronicle of Rexroth's spiritual-temporal odyssey . . . [his] sojourns throughout the length and breadth of America and briefly abroad, mainly in the company of Bohemians"—(*LJ*). Although he never completed high school, Mr. Rexroth's erudition, readability and freshness of approach are particularly evident in his frequent *Saturday Review* page, "The Classics Revisted," which appeared intermittently for many years. The collection is now available in book form from *Quadrangle* 1968 $7.50, and *Avon* pap. $1.25.

THE COLLECTED SHORTER POEMS. *New Directions* 1967 $7.50 pap. $2.95

COLLECTED LONGER POEMS. *New Directions* 1968 $7.50 pap. $2.95

THE PHOENIX AND THE TORTOISE. *New Directions* 1944 1959 $4.50. Poem and adaptations of classic epigrams.

WITH EYE AND EAR. *McGraw-Hill* (Herder & Herder) 1970 $6.95

SKY SEA BIRDS TREES EARTH. *Unicorn Press* 2nd ed. 1972 $5.00 pap. $2.00

LATTIMORE, RICHMOND (ALEXANDER). 1906–

A distinguished scholar and translator, Lattimore considers himself primarily a poet. He was graduated from Dartmouth, studied under Rhodes and Fulbright Scholarships at Oxford, Rome and Greece. "Sestina for a Far-Off Summer" (1962, o.p.) is a volume of "sedate, elegant, reasonable poetry," concerned primarily "with unredeemable time." His own poetic gift has contributed to the richness of his many translations. In 1962 he shared the Bollingen Prize of $2500 for the best translation of poetry into English with Robert Lowell. Mr. Lattimore was selected for his translation of "The Frogs" by Aristophanes (*Univ. of Michigan Press* 1962 $4.95). He calls his translation of "The Revelation of John" 1962, o.p. a "literary experiment." His 1967 "Odyssey" of Homer was called "the best Odyssey in modern English" by Gilbert Highet. In 1964 he taught at Oxford on a Fulbright and lectured at other English universities.

POEMS FROM THREE DECADES. *Scribner* 1972 $7.95. Includes some translations from the French and Greek.

OPPEN, GEORGE. 1908–

"Oppen's goal in poetry has been clarity"—(Geof Hewitt). It is certain that he has achieved this, with very simply and prosaically written poetry. He emerged as one of the outstanding representatives of the Objectivist group, which was centered around Louis Zukofsky (*q.v.*) in New York in the thirties. Oppen "tries to control words in such a way that full energy, of sensation and concept, can be extracted from each, and that a complex range of relations may be set up within the space of the poem as a field of action. . ."—(Thomas Clark). The following excerpt from a short poem demonstrates Oppen's simple and unique style: "And indeed a poet's room/ Is a boy's room/ and I suppose that women know it./ Perhaps the unbeautiful banker/ Is exciting to a woman, a man/ Not a boy, gasping/ For breath over a girl's body."—(from "A Boy's Room").

Born in New Rochelle, N.Y., Oppen has travelled widely and had an assortment of vocations. He served in the U.S. Army during the Second World War, worked as a tool and die maker, a cabinet maker, and owned and managed a shop in Mexico City where he built and designed furniture. In 1969 he received the Pulitzer Prize.

Oppen's work appears in the anthologies "American Literary Anthology, 3" (ed. by George Plimpton and Peter Ardery *Viking* 1970 $7.95 Compass Bks. $2.95) and "Inside Outer Space" (1970, o.p.).

MATERIALS. *New Directions* 1963 pap. $1.25

THIS IS WHICH. *New Directions* 1965 $3.50 pap. $1.95

OF BEING NUMEROUS. *New Directions* 1968 $5.25 pap. $1.45

SEASCAPE: Needle's Eye. *Sumac Press* 1972 $7.50 pap. $2.45

ROETHKE, THEODORE. 1908–1963.

The "well-made, humane and wise lyrics" of "The Waking" (1953, o. p.) make up a verse autobiography beginning with the nonsense language of his childhood, and ending with the love poems of his maturity. It "gives the impression of a poet gradually wakening to himself or discovering his own 'identity.' " "The Waking" brought Theodore Roethke the Pulitzer Prize for Poetry in 1954. In 1959, "Words for the Wind" won for him the National Book Award for Poetry, the Bollingen Prize, the Millay Memorial Award and the Borestone Mountain Poetry Award. He won the Poetry Society of America Annual Award and the Shelley Award in 1962. He spent his childhood in Saginaw, Mich., was educated at the University of Michigan and at Harvard, and was Professor of English at the University of Washington at the time of his death. A Theodore Roethke Memorial Foundation to aid American poets has since been established in his honor. "On the Poet and His Craft: Selected Prose of Theodore Roethke" (ed. by Ralph J. Mills, Jr. *Univ. of Washington Press* 1965 $4.95 1966 pap. $2.45) contains Roethke's analyses of some of his own work as well as essays on Dylan Thomas and Louise Bogan. "Roethke's most interesting single essay is 'Open Letter,' an account of his poems 'The Lost Son' and 'Praise to the End' containing valuable indications of his method, which lead to revelations of the psychic chaos behind them"—(M. L. Rosenthal, in the *N.Y. Times*). The new volume of "Letters" throws rewarding light on the struggles of the poet with the circumstances of his life and on his poetic creation.

COLLECTED POEMS. *Doubleday* 1966 $7.95

"A most important volume of American poetry. . . . Mr. Roethke wrote from the center of his violent calm with a total control of his own range of symbols and rhythms and a total commitment to humane values"—(*LJ*).

THE ACHIEVEMENT OF THEODORE ROETHKE. Ed. by William J. Martz. *Scott, Foresman* 1966 pap. $2.65. A comprehensive selection.

THE FAR FIELD. *Doubleday* 1964 $4.50 Anchor Bks. pap. $1.95

"The verses sing triumphantly of an unabashed delight, where banality never enters, in nature, children, animals and love. For discriminating readers of poetry"—(*LJ*).

STRAW FROM THE FIRE: From the notebooks of Theodore Roethke, 1943–1963. Ed. by David Wagoner. Doubleday $7.95 limited ed. $25.00. An excellent selection from the notebooks of Roethke, including poems and fragments with reproductions of manuscript pages and illustrations.

SELECTED LETTERS. Ed. by Ralph J. Mills, Jr. *Univ. of Washington Press* 1968 $6.95. Includes Roethke's correspondence with William Carlos Williams, Marianne Moore, Katherine Anne Porter, Dylan Thomas, Louise Bogan, Stanley Kunitz, Rolfe Humphries and Kenneth Burke.

Books about Roethke

Theodore Roethke. By Ralph J. Mills, Jr. Pamphlets on American Writers. *Univ. of Minnesota Press* 1963 pap. $1.25
Theodore Roethke. Ed. by Arnold Stein. *Univ. of Washington Press* 1965 (o. p.) available in microfiche $6.00
"This is a splendidly rewarding book. . . . Most of the writers of the essays know Roethke personally"—(H. H. Waggoner, in *American Literature*). The essayists are Stephen Spender, John Wain, Roy Harvey Pearce, Louis L. Martz, William Meredith, W. O. Snodgrass, Frederick J. Hoffman, Ralph J. Mills, Jr., and Dennis Donoghue.
An Introduction to the Poetry. By Karl Malkoff. *Columbia* 1966 $10.00 pap. $2.95
A "thorough and scrupulous examination of the structural elements, the philosophical, spiritual and technical coherences of Roethke's poetry"—(*N. Y. Times*).
Theodore Roethke: A Manuscript Checklist. Ed. by James A. McLeod. *Kent State Univ. Press* $7.50
A Concordance to the Poems of Theodore Roethke. By Gary Lane. *Scarecrow Press* 1972 $15.00

OLSON, CHARLES. 1910–1970.

The elder statesman of the Black Mountain school of poets, "Charles Olson is central to any description of literary climate dated 1961," wrote Robert Creeley, poet and editor, in *The Big Table*. Through Mr. Olson's writing classes at Black Mountain College, he directly impinged on the work of fellow-teachers Robert Duncan (*q.v.*) and Robert Creeley (*q.v.*) as well as students including John Wieners, Jonathan Williams, Joel Oppenheimer and Edward Dorn. His catalytic theory of poetry, expounded in the essay "Projective Verse," was published by *Totem Press* in 1959 and was reprinted in part in William Carlos Williams' "Autobiography" and in Donald M. Allen's "The New American Poetry 1945–1960" (*Grove* Evergreen Bks. 1960 pap. $2.95; *Peter Smith* $5.50). "Olson's prose style . . . proceeds by a bulletlike series of assertions. . . . The writing is full of energy, but also knotty and gnarled"—(Thomas Lask, in the *N.Y. Times*). "All of Olson's poems are written in 'breath-conditioned' lines, in accordance with his theories, and their themes are on such matters as the rise and fall of civilizations (Olson was an archaeologist and student of ancient history), the health of the good society threatened by 'pejorocracy,' and the value of good writing as an index to the life and moral condition of a people"—(Stephen Stepanchev, in "American Poetry Since 1945"). Olson's poetry and prose have been printed chiefly by *Black Mountain Review* and *Origen* magazines, and by small presses such as *Divers* and *Jargon*. In "Selected Writings" Olson's emphasis is "how to restore man to his 'dynamic.' There is too much concern, he feels, with end and not enough with instant. It's not things that are important, but what happens between them. . . . He thinks of poetry as transfers of energy and he reminds us that dance is kinesis, not mimesis. Life, too, should possess the qualities of art"—(Lask). *Grove* produced his "Call Me Ishmael: Herman Melville, Moby Dick and America" (*City Lights* $2.00). "Human Universe and Other Essays" (*Grove* 1967 Evergreen Bks. pap. $1.95) are pieces on subjects ranging from Homer to Yeats. "Olson reveals an interesting bias in these essays, away from the Graeco-Roman roots to the pre-classical societies. He is fascinated by the ancient cultures of the Middle East"—(Lask). "Proprioception" (*Four Seasons Foundation* 1963 pap. $1.00) is one of Olson's seminal essays on verse and the poet's awareness, written, or rather typed, in his rambling idiosyncratic style. Geography, poetry, and primitivism all blend into one brilliant formulation of American poetical aesthetics. "A Special View of History" (ed. by Ann Charters. *Oyez* 1970 $5.00 pap. $2.50) is notes from the Black Mountain Lecture Series. "Poetry and Truth: Beloit Lectures and Poems" (ed. by George Butterick with pref. by Chad Walsh *Four Seasons Foundation* 1971 $5.00 pap. $2.50) is a very lively series of lectures given in 1968 and edited by his bibliographer. "Letters for Origin, 1950–1956 (ed. by Albert Glover. *Grossman* (Cape Goliard) 1969 $8.95 pap. $3.95) contains "comments, analyses, muses."

The poet was born in Worcester, Mass., and attended Wesleyan, Harvard and Yale. He taught at Clark, Harvard and Black Mountain colleges. He received two Guggenheim fellowships and a grant from the Wenner-Gren Foundation to study Mayan hieroglyphs in Yucatan. His involvement with primitive Indian cultures stimulated his interest in mysticism and the drug culture. He died of cancer in 1970.

SELECTED WRITINGS. Ed. with introd. by Robert Creeley. *New Directions* 1967 $7.95 pap. $2.45. Poetry and criticism, including selections from "The Maximus Poems"; "Projective Verse"; "Human Universe"; "Quality in Verse"; "Shakespeare's Late Plays"; "Appolonius of Tyana"; "Mayan Letters."

MAXIMUS POEMS, 1, 2, 3. *Corinth Bks.* 1960 $10.00 pap. $3.00; *Grossman* 1974 $12.95 pap. $6.95

DISTANCES. *Grove* 1971 pap. $1.75

ARCHAEOLOGIST OF MORNING. *Grossman* (Cape Goliard) $12.95 pap. $3.95. All the poems authorized for publication except the "Maximus" sequence.

MAYAN LETTERS. Ed. by Robert Creeley. 1953. *Grossman* Cape Eds. 1968 $3.50. The famed letters from Olson to Creeley while the former was in the Yucatan.

BISHOP, ELIZABETH. 1911–

In his *N.Y. Times* column, the late Harvey Breit applauded the awarding of the Pulitzer Prize for 1956 to "the peripatetic Massachusetts-born poet, Elizabeth Bishop, Vassar '34, traveler through Europe and Africa, ex-resident of Key West and Mexico, and present dweller in Brazil. We applaud because (1) she is a handsome woman, (2) a friend of Marianne Moore, and (3) she once said she was opposed 'to making poetry monstrous or boring and proceeding to talk the very life out of it.'" The *N.Y. Herald Tribune* said of her "Poems": "In the sum of Miss Bishop's poetry to the present there is a small group of poems which can be expected to become a permanent part of the poetry of our time." About "Questions of Travel" Philip Booth has said, "No poet now writing achieves more naturally right notes or greater flexibility in formally structured poems. . . . Miss Bishop's skill is lyrically demonstrated by the 47 quatrains of 'The Burglar of Babylon,' and by the marvelous ease of 'Sestina,' which may well be the best American poem yet written in that intricate French form. . . . Miss Bishop is not only our most valuable export to Brazil, she is one of the true poets of this, or any, hemisphere"—(*Christian Science Monitor*). The "Complete Poems" won the National Book Award for poetry in 1970. It includes "North and South," "A Cold Spring," "Questions of Travel," "Translations from the Portuguese," and new and uncollected work. It is a fine volume. She has also written the nonfiction "Brazil!" (*Silver Burdett* 1962 $5.70) and with Emanuel Brasil has edited "An Anthology of Twentieth Century Brazilian Poetry" (trans. by Paul Blackburn and others *Wesleyan Univ. Press* 1972 $12.50 pap. $3.45). "The Caedmon Treasury of Modern Poets Reading Their Own Poetry" (*Caedmon* TC 2006 $11.90) includes a selection by Miss Bishop entitled "Manuelzinho."

COMPLETE POEMS. *Farrar, Straus* 1969 $7.50 pap. $2.95. Includes: "North and South," "A Cold Spring," "Questions of Travel," "Elsewhere," "Translations from the Portuguese," and new and uncollected work.

QUESTIONS OF TRAVEL. *Farrar, Straus* 1965 $4.95 Noonday pap. $1.95. Nineteen poems grouped under "Brazil" and "Elsewhere," plus a story, "In the Village."

BALLAD OF THE BURGLAR OF BABYLON. *Farrar, Straus* 1968 $4.50

Books about Bishop

Elizabeth Bishop. By Anne Stevenson. United States Authors Ser. *Twayne* 1966 $5.50; *College & Univ. Press* 1967 pap. $2.45
"This first full-length study of her work offers a perceptive and enthusiastic introduction to her craftsmanship and thought"—(*LJ*).

MILES, JOSEPHINE. 1911–

The Chicago-born Josephine Miles is a poet who "exalts 'the American idiom' into the standard language of poetry."—(David Ray). Educated at the University of California (Los Angeles and Berkeley) Miss Miles still teaches at Berkeley. She is noted for her critical work in English and American literature including "Wordsworth and the Vocabulary of Emotion" (1942. *Octagon* 1965 $7.50), "The Continuity of Poetic Language: Studies in English Poetry from the 1540's to the 1940's" (1951. *Octagon* 1965 $16.50), "The Pathetic Fallacy in the Nineteenth Century" (1942. *Octagon* 1965 $7.50), "Ralph Waldo Emerson" (Pamphlets on American Writers *Univ. of Minnesota Press* 1964 pap. $1.25) and "The Ways of the Poem" (*Prentice-Hall* rev. ed. 1972 pap. $5.95).

Her poetry is characterized by a gentleness and compassion in presenting the details of the American landscape and life with a precise clear language. In the tradition of William Carlos Williams (*q.v.*) her poems seem to arise out of her sense of the connectedness of people. About her own work she has said her interest is "in the poetry of spoken thought . . . of literally making sense of ideas. Main themes, human doubt and amazement."

POEMS, 1930–1960. Poetry Ser. *Indiana Univ. Press* 1960 $4.95

FIELDS OF LEARNING. *Oyez* 1966 pap. $1.00

CIVIL POEMS. *Oyez* 1966 pap. $1.00

KINDS OF AFFECTIONS. Poetry Program Ser. *Wesleyan Univ. Press* 1967 $4.75 pap. $2.45

PATCHEN, KENNETH. 1911–1972.

"One of America's most unusual and powerful contemporary poets," said the *San Francisco Chronicle* of this versatile West Coast poet, writer and painter. Born in Niles, Ohio, Patchen worked in a steel mill in his youth and as a migratory worker doing all sorts of jobs in the United States and Canada before settling in California. In 1957 he pioneered in the "public birth of Poetry-Jazz" by reading his poems to the accompaniment of the well-known Chamber Jazz Sextet in nightclubs and concert halls on the West Coast, breaking attendance records in San Francisco and Los Angeles. In 1954 he received the Shelley Memorial Award. Patchen died in 1972 after a prolonged illness, during which he continued his prolific writing projects.

In "The Journal of Albion Moonlight" "Kenneth Patchen sets off on an allegorical journey of his own in which the far boundaries of love and murder, madness and sex are sensually explored. His is the tale of a disordered pilgrimage to H. Roivas (Heavenly Savior) in which the deranged responses of individuals point up the outer madness from which they derive in a more imaginative way than social protest generally allows. A chronicle of violent fury and compassion, written two decades ago when Surrealism was still vigorous and doing battle with psychotic 'reality,' "The Journal of Albion Moonlight" is the American monument to *engagement*. Like Camus, Kenneth Patchen is anti-cool, anti-hip, anti-beat. He is involved with Man's tormented soul . . . and with the abusive and destructive purposes to which it succumbs. Possessed by a wild, mordant humor and an agonized pity, he protests the war-mad years of the Forties and, unluckily, his work has gained rather than lost its timeliness"—(Publisher's note). Henry Miller has said of it " 'The Journal of Albion Moonlight' is a work of unmistakable genius. Nothing like it has been written . . . in all English literature it stands alone. . . . I know of no other American writer capable of giving us such a . . . truthful, fearless, and harrowing account. . . . Albion Moonlight is the most naked figure of a man I have encountered in all literature."

Of his "picture poems," "Hallelujah Anyway," *Library Journal* said: "The anti-war, pantheistic, tough-minded Patchen is still here, and this collection . . . will please Patchen fans." In 1967 "Now You See It," a play called "a comedy of annihilation" by its author, opened off-Broadway. "It is a fable about seven persons attending a party who suddenly find themselves—after the lights have gone out à la 'Black Comedy'—standing on the ceiling instead of on the floor. Even more disconcerting, they find themselves trapped inside a huge, invisible whirlpool of silence, which threatens to choke their cocktail babble forever. Unfortunately, nothing that happens in the play is as strong as this first image. . . . Perhaps the simplicity and cleanness-of-heart that make Mr. Patchen such a wonderful lyric poet [worked] against him here as a dramatist"—(*N.Y. Times*). "Memoirs of a Shy Pornographer" (1945 *New Directions* 1965 pap. $1.95) is a novel, often reprinted. It is the picaresque sage of Alfred Budd, of Bivalve, N.J. "The 'Memoirs of a Shy Pornographer' reveals an American humorist more daring than Perelman and as original as Thurber"—(Selden Rodman). Another novel, "Sleepers Awake" (1946. *New Directions* 1969 pap. $3.45) is again available.

COLLECTED POEMS. *New Directions* 1968 $12.50 pap. $3.95

The poet's own choice. "The range and dexterity of technique are sufficiently expressive; the scope of ideas represents an even rarer attainment"—(PW).

SELECTED POEMS. *New Directions* 1946 rev. 1958 pap. $1.50. 139 poems chosen from 10 volumes published over the last 20 years.

BECAUSE IT IS. *New Directions* 1960 pap. $1.50. Poems and drawings in a humorous vein.

LOVE POEMS. *City Lights Books* 1960 pap. $1.00

POEMS OF HUMOR AND PROTEST. *City Lights Books* pap. $1.00

DOUBLEHEADER. *New Directions* 1966 $1.50. Includes "Hurrah for Anything," "Poemscapes," and "A Letter to God."

HALLELUJAH ANYWAY. *New Directions* 1967 $7.50 pap. $1.25. "Picture poems" inspired by the "illuminated printing" of William Blake.

CLOTH OF THE TEMPEST. 1943. *Assoc. Booksellers* $3.00

THE JOURNAL OF ALBION MOONLIGHT. *Assoc. Booksellers $3.00; New Directions* 1961 pap. $2.25. Written in the 1940s.

BUT EVEN SO. *New Directions* 1968 $4.50 pap. $1.25

OUT OF THE WORLD OF KENNETH PATCHEN. 4 vols. Vol. I Because It Is, Vol. 2 But Even So, Vol. 3 Doubleheader, Vol. 4 Hallelujah Anyway. *New Directions* 1970 pap. boxed set $5.50

THREE PROSE CLASSICS. 3 vols. *New Directions* 1971 pap. set $6.85. Includes "The Journal of Albion Moonlight," "Sleepers Awake," and "Memoirs of a Shy Pornographer."

WONDERINGS. *New Directions* 1971 $5.95 pap. $1.75. Poems and drawings.

IN QUEST OF CANDLELIGHTER. *New Directions* 1972 $6.95 pap. $1.95

SELECTED POEMS OF KENNETH PATCHEN. A recording. *Folkways* $5.95

EVERSON, WILLIAM (Brother Antoninus). 1912–

William Everson (Brother Antoninus) was born in Sacramento, California in 1912. Though he was raised as a Christian Scientist, he became an agnostic in his early teens. During World War II he was a conscientious objector and spent several years in prison, during which time he and several others published a small literary magazine. His third book, "The Residual Years," (1948. *New Directions* 1968 $6.50 pap. $2.25) details this experience and others leading to his conversion to Catholicism. In 1949, Everson entered the Dominican Order as a lay brother, changing his name to Brother Antoninus. After a ten-year silence he published under his new name the poetic record of his personal spiritual development in "The Crooked Lines of God," and at this time came to be associated with the San Francisco "beat" poets, the best of whom have never been nihilistic but inclined to forms of religion such as Zen Buddhism.

He published five more books of poetry under the name of Brother Antoninus, concerning himself with the wrestlings of spirit between natural instincts and religious concerns. In 1969, after 20 years, he left the order, married and once again became William Everson.

THE ACHIEVEMENT OF BROTHER ANTONINUS. Ed. by William E. Stafford. *Scott, Foresman* 1967 (orig.) pap. $2.65. Poems with critical commentary.

THE CROOKED LINES OF GOD. 1959. *Univ. of Detroit Press* 1962 $4.25

THE HAZARDS OF HOLINESS. 1962 *Serendipity* pap. $3.50

WHO IS SHE THAT LOOKETH FORTH AS THE MORNING? 1970 *Capra Press* pap. $4.50; *Serendipity* signed limited ed. $30.00

EARTH POETRY. *Oyez* 1971 pap. $3.50

TENDRIL IN THE MESH. *Cayucos Bks.* 1973 $35.00

MAN-FATE: The Swan Song of Brother Antoninus. *New Directions* 1974 $6.95 pap. $2.75. Poems mainly since Everson (Brother Antoninus) left the monastic life.

SARTON, MAY. 1912–

"May Sarton's sure technique and effortless word-mastery coupled with pungent metaphysical insights make ['Cloud, Stone, Sun, Vine'] an exquisite residuum of 20 years of assiduous craftsmanship and inner vision"—(*LJ*). Her poems, mainly lyrics, are written with "admirable simplicity." Raymond Holden in the *N.Y. Times* speaks of her "extraordinary gift, her ability to make the actualness of physical existence and motion serve as the imaginative metaphor pointing to a metaphysical reality." James Dickey says: "The only regret Miss Sarton raises is that she is not likely to become much of an 'influence.' What good effects her practice may have on others will have to take place like the working of a charm or a secret spell: they must be felt in the loving skill with which her poems are built, rather than in the quiet, true, unspectacular sound of her voice"—(in "Babel to Byzantium"). "I Knew A Phoenix" [1958 *Norton* $5.00] was the earlier volume of her autobiography. Now in "Plant Dreaming Deep" she shows a growing creative genius and an easy style as she analyzes herself and her 'intangibles'—her life and thought as an author, her fears, and her decisions—her 'demons'—and her rewards"—(*LJ*). She begins the book with the house she bought in 1958 in a New Hampshire village—her "dream house," as it has proved to be.

Born in Belgium, May Sarton came with her distinguished parents as refugees to Cambridge, Massachusetts, during World War I. After her school days she spent some years in repertory theater work before becoming wholly concerned with writing. Her prose, which has frequently appeared in the *New Yorker*, includes a number of novels, including "Shower of Summer Days" (*Norton* 1970 $5.95), "The Fur Person" (*New Am. Lib.* Signet 1970 pap. $.75), and "Faithful Are the Wounds" (*Norton* 1972 $6.95).

CLOUD, STONE, SUN, VINE: Poems, Selected and New. *Norton* 1961 $4.00. 76 of her verses.

JOURNAL OF A SOLITUDE, 1970–1971. *Norton* 1973. $6.95. Journal.

I KNEW A PHOENIX. 1958. *Norton* 1969 $5.00

A PRIVATE MYTHOLOGY. *Norton* 1966 $4.00. About her travels in Japan, India and Greece and her return home.

PLANT DREAMING DEEP. *Norton* 1968 $5.00. Autobiography.

GRAIN OF MUSTARD SEED. *Norton* 1971 $6.00 pap. $1.95

A DURABLE FIRE: New Poems. *Norton* 1972 $6.00 pap. $1.95

Books about Sarton

May Sarton. By Agnes Sibley. United States Authors Ser. *Twayne* 1972 $5.50. This is the first study of Sarton's work in book form to appear. Illuminating and detailed, it includes a bibliography, index and chronology.

SHAPIRO, KARL (JAY). 1913–

Karl Shapiro's poetry is vigorous, yet tender, his subjects taken from the day-to-day world, either of the Army or civilian life. The Pulitzer Prize was awarded to him in 1945 for "V-Letter and Other Poems" (1944, o.p.), every poem but one of which was written while on active duty with the Army Medical Corps in the Southwest Pacific. Born in Baltimore, this poet, critic and editor attended the University of Virginia and Johns Hopkins. After his service in the Army, he was appointed Consultant in Poetry at the Library of Congress in 1946, and joined the faculty of Johns Hopkins, where he taught writing courses until he resigned in 1950 to become editor, for a period, of *Poetry*. He is now professor of English at the University of California. In "The Bourgeois Poet" Shapiro "breaks with accepted metrical patterns to attempt a poetry of direct speech. . . . 'The Bourgeois Poet' definitely has about it the air of a new imaginative release. Irony and social criticism are still there, but autobiography, invective, heavy doses of sexuality, often dominated by an atmosphere of the dream and of irrationality, and an occasional prophetic note are now blended together"— (Ralph J. Mills, Jr., in "Contemporary American Poetry"). He continues to use grotesque images to convey the vulgarities of urban life. "In Defense of Ignorance" (1960, o.p.), his first collection of essays, which roused a storm of controversy, is an attack on the intellectualized poetry of the first half of this century. Other discussions of poetry are "An Essay on Rime" (*Random* 1945 $5.95) and "English Prosody and Modern Poetry (*Folcroft* 1973 lib. bdg. $5.00). He has published a novel, "Edsel" (*Bernard Geis* 1971 $6.95; *New Am. Lib.*

Signet pap. $1.25). "American Poetry" (*T. Y. Crowell* 1960 $6.95 pap. $3.95) is his selection of poets from Anne Bradstreet to Allen Ginsberg. He has edited "Prose Keys to Modern Poetry" (*Harper* 1962 pap. $6.00) and with Robert Beum has written "A Prosody Handbook" (*Harper* 1965 $6.00).

POEMS: 1940–1953. *Random* 1953 $6.50. The poet's choice of the contents of 3 previous books with 18 unpublished poems.

SELECTED POEMS. *Random* 1968 $7.95 *Vintage Bks.* pap. $2.45. Critical of bourgeois values, Shapiro in his later poems shows a gradual lessening of tension, says Thomas Lask.

POEMS OF A JEW. *Random* 1958 $5.95

THE BOURGEOIS POET. *Random* 1964 $5.95

WHITE-HAIRED LOVER. *Random* 1968 $6.00. A cycle of 39 love poems.

RUKEYSER, MURIEL. 1913–

Richard Eberhart in his *N. Y. Times* review of "Waterlily Fire" (1962, o.p.) said, "Muriel Rukeyser is a strong, direct-speaking, richly evocative poet . . . never a cultist, never given to this fad or that, or labeled with the mark of only one decade . . . expressing through her vigorous images and feelings a sense of life and the world." The poet was born in New York City and is living there. She attended Vassar and Columbia. Later, as a newspaper reporter, she was arrested during the second Scottsboro trial in Alabama. In the 1930's she worked for the Government Medical Bureau in Spain and witnessed the Civil War from the Loyalist vantage point.

As a poet, she has "progressed from a precocious debut in the Auden-Spender vein (in 1935), through periods of social protest (the Spanish Civil War, miners in West Virginia) and earthy lyricism to an almost mystical poetic and political affirmation"—(*LJ*). She has been honored by a Guggenheim fellowship, a National Academy Grant and the Harriet Monroe prize. She has written "The Life of Poetry: On the Meaning and Significance of Poetry in the Modern World" (1949, *Kraus* $10.00). She is a fellow of the American Council of Learned Societies and of the National Institute of Arts and Letters. Among her biographies are "One Life" (*Simon & Schuster* 1957 $5.00), dealing with Wendell Wilkie, "Traces of Thomas Hariot" (*Random* 1971 $10.00), the life of the explorer and friend of Sir Walter Raleigh. She has translated the poetry of Octavio Paz and Gunnar Ekelof (with Leif Sjoberg). For the latter she received the Award of the Swedish Academy for translation in 1967.

THEORY OF FLIGHT. Fwd. by Stephen Vincent Benét. 1935. *AMS Press* $8.50

THE SPEED OF DARKNESS. *Random* 1968 $6.95 Vintage Bks. pap. $1.95. Poems.

SCHWARTZ, DELMORE. 1913–1966.

Born in Brooklyn, N. Y., Delmore Schwartz was educated at Columbia, the University of Wisconsin and New York University. He taught at Harvard 1940–47 and lectured at various schools and universities. He was associated with *Partisan Revew* from 1943–55 and he served as literary consultant for *New Directions*. From 1955–57 he was poetry editor of the *New Republic*. Allen Tate has described Schwartz's poetic style as "the only genuine innovation since Pound and Eliot came upon the scene twenty-five years ago." His first volume, "In Dreams Begin Responsibilities" (1938, o.p.) caused a sensation and received praise from many critics. He received the Bollingen Prize, as well as the Shelley Memorial Prize and two other poetry awards, after the publication of "Summer Knowledge: New and Selected Poems, 1938–1958," now reprinted by *New Directions* as "Selected Poems," in 1959—the youngest winner of the Bollingen Prize since its establishment. He had been awarded a Guggenheim Fellowship in his 26th year.

"The World is a Wedding" (*New Directions* 1948 $4.00) contains short stories and two novelettes. "Successful Love and Other Stories" (1961, o.p.) consists of two unpublished short novels and six short stories, which treat of modern love in all its varieties of sophistication and subtlety. His stories are "marvelously well written and engrossing." Until a year before his death from a heart attack he had been teaching at Syracuse University.

SUMMER KNOWLEDGE: Selected Poems. 1959. *New Directions* 1967 pap. $1.75

BERRYMAN, JOHN. 1914–1972.

John Berryman's poetry has a depth and obscurity that in turn discourage readers and entice critics. His major work, "The Dream Songs," forms a poetic notebook, capturing the ephemera of mood and attitude of this most mecurial of poets. The poems in "The Dream Songs" range quickly from the humorous to the blackly dispairing. Each dream song is 18 lines long. Primarily the group derives its plot and somewhat fictional continuity from the daily routine, during a 10-year period, of Henry, who functions as Berryman's alter ego. Like Robert Lowell, who in many respects Berryman resembles, Berryman is primarily a confessional poet. His technical dexterity lends his verse a classical eloquence and beauty. Coupled with this is a rough, almost deranged diction. The following passage from "Homage to Mistress Bradstreet" shows the power and haunting, metaphysical landscape of his poetry: "The winters close, Springs open, no child stirs/ under my withering heart, O seasoned heart/ God grudged his aid./ All things else soil like a shirt./ Simon is much away. My executive stales./ The town came through for the cartway by the pales,/ but my patience is short,/ I revolt from, I am like, these savage foresters./"

John Berryman was born John Smith in McAlester, Okla., and educated at Columbia and at Clare College, Cambridge. He taught at Wayne University, Princeton, Harvard and the University of Minnesota. He received the 1948 Shelley Memorial Award, the 1957 Harriet Monroe Award, the 1964 Loines Award for Poetry from the National Institute of Arts and Letters and the 1966 Fellowship of the Academy of American Poets. In 1964 he won the Pulitzer Prize in Poetry for "77 Dream Songs." His short story "The Imaginary Jew" received the Kenyon-Doubleday Award and was listed in "Best American Short Stories, 1946." He also wrote "Stephen Crane" (*Peter Smith* 1950 $5.00). He is the author of a novel, "Recovery" (*Farrar, Straus* 1973 $6.95). In 1972, Berryman committed suicide.

HOMAGE TO MISTRESS BRADSTREET. *Farrar, Straus* 1956 $4.95 Noonday pap. $1.95

77 DREAM SONGS. *Farrar, Straus* 1964 $4.95 Noonday pap. $1.95

BERRYMAN'S SONNETS. *Farrar, Straus* 1967 $5.50 Noonday pap. $2.25

SHORT POEMS. *Farrar, Straus* 1967 $4.95. A collection of 64 poems including "The Dispossessed" (1948, o.p.) and "Formal Elegy," written in 1963 commemorating John F. Kennedy's death.

THE DREAM SONGS. *Farrar, Straus* 1969 $10.00 Sunburst Bks. 1971 pap. $3.95

LOVE AND FAME. *Farrar, Straus* 1970 $6.50 limited ed. signed and numbered $25.00 rev. ed. Noonday pap. $2.25. Scholia to Second Edition by Berryman was added in 1971 explaining the deletion of some poems and voicing thoughts on the poems in general.

DELUSIONS, ETC. *Farrar, Straus* 1972 $6.95 Noonday pap. $2.65. Posthumous book.

Books about Berryman

John Berryman. By William J. Martz. Pamphlets on American Writers *Univ. of Minnesota Press* 1969 pap. $.95. An introduction to Berryman's poetry.

John Berryman: A Checklist. By Richard Kelly. Fwd. by William Merridith: introd. by Michael Berryhill. *Scarecrow Press* 1972 $5.00. Bibliographical reference tool.

GARRIGUE, JEAN. 1914–1972.

Jean Garrigue was born in Evansville, Indiana and received her education at the University of Chicago and the University of Iowa. She served as instructor in English literature at Iowa, Bard College, Queens College (in New York), the New School for Social Research, University of Connecticut at Storrs, and Smith College. Among the numerous awards she received were a Rockefeller Grant in Creative Writing (1954), a Guggenheim Fellowship in 1960–61, a National Institute of Arts and Letters Grant, 1962, and The Melville Cane Award in 1968.

Her poetry is characterized by a "complex richness in rhythm and diction"—(Theodore Roethke) and she has been called "a rare perfectionist of attitudes, a poet habituated to verbal elegance"—(Richard Eberhardt).

In her lifetime a very productive poet, Miss Garrigue was a kind of individualist whose work was always in her own direction, uninfluenced by the shifting trends and experiments of American poetry in the last three decades. *Saturday Review* called her "undeniably original and individual as an artist, and a craftsman in complete control of her medium." She has been called a "romantic lyricist"—(Lucien Stryk) and her verse exhibits an elegance rare for modern American poetry and somewhat out of fashion. There is a formality in her work which may or may not outlast the more experimental and flatter-languaged verse typical of the second half of this century.

THE EGO AND THE CENTAUR. 1947. *Greenwood* 1972 $8.50

ANIMAL HOTEL. *Eakins Press* 1966 $5.95

NEW AND SELECTED POEMS. *Macmillan* 1967 $5.95

CHARTRES AND PROSE POEMS. *Eakins Press* 1971 $4.95 pap. $2.95

STUDIES FOR AN ACTRESS AND OTHER POEMS. *Macmillan* 1973 $6.95 pap. $1.95. New poems.

IGNATOW, DAVID. 1914–

Describing his own poetry, Ignatow has written: "I search for *now,* using the method of introspection and dream in tandem with objective events or things." His early work was realistic and objective after William Carlos Williams, with whom, Ignatow writes, "I maintained a personal, informal relationship." He became interested in surrealism after his second book. His style is flat and free-formed with ". . . no obvious brilliance of language . . . words are merely a vehicle for recounting what happened: what happens . . . the incident, the judgement is what you remember: . . . an inspired and brilliantly successful metaphysical reportage . . . "— (James Dickey).

Ignatow served as an instructor at the New School for Social Research (1964–65) and as lecturer at the Universities of Kentucky, Kansas, and Vassar College. He was Poet-in-Residence at York College of the City University of New York in 1969, and has been a member of the faculty at Columbia University since 1969. He is the recipient of the National Institute of Arts and Letters Award (1964), a Guggenheim Fellowship (1965–66), a Shelley Memorial Prize (1966), and a Rockefeller Grant (1968–69).

"Never a participant in the momentary fads and fancies of the literary life, David Ignatow has quietly and persistently developed his art over the past two decades and now emerges as one of the very best poets of his generation"—(Ralph J. Mills, Jr.).

POEMS, 1934–1969. *Wesleyan Univ. Press* 1970 $9.95. The collected poems to date including: "Poems" (1948), "The Gentle Weight Lifter" (1955), "Say Pardon" (1961), "Figures of the Human" (1964) and "Rescue the Dead" (1968).

SAY PARDON. Poetry Program Ser. *Wesleyan Univ. Press* 1961 $4.75 pap. $2.45

FIGURES OF THE HUMAN. Poetry Program Ser. *Wesleyan Univ. Press* 1964 $4.74 pap. $2.45

RESCUE THE DEAD. Poetry Program Ser. *Wesleyan Univ. Press* 1968 $4.75

NOTEBOOKS. *Swallow Press* 1974 $9.95

STAFFORD, WILLIAM (EDGAR). 1914–

Although a prolific writer and frequent contributor to magazines, William Stafford did not publish a volume of verse until 1960, when *Talisman Press* brought out his "West of Your City" (now o.p.). With his second poetry collection, "Travelling through the Dark," Stafford became the 1962 National Book Award winner in Poetry. He won the Shelley Memorial Award of the Poetry Society of America in 1964 and received a Guggenheim Foundation Award for 1966–67. In "The Rescued Year" he demonstrates a "remarkable ability to charge a poem level by level with integrity and loving kindness and veils of half-apprehended hope."— (*Cleveland Plain Dealer*). This collection contains "repeated references to the barren, slow-paced and sage-like life of the Western United States"—(*LJ*). "Allegiances" contains many poems previously published in periodicals. He deals with landscapes—Kansas, Montana, Oregon. "Someday, Maybe" is a new collection which includes Stafford's American Indian group of poems.

Born in Kansas, the poet was educated in the Midwest and has taught at Lewis and Clark College in Oregon. He is a consciously "Western" poet, a word-painter of Western landscapes. Roderick Nordell of the *Christian Science Monitor* has commented on the "frontier tang of William Stafford's poems of nature and humanity." Writing about a poem of his own, the poet recognizes "an appearance of moral commitment mixed with a deliberate—even flaunted—nonsophistication; an organized form cavalierly treated; a trace of narrative for company amid too many feelings. . . . And the *things* here—plains, farm, home, winter, lavished all over the page—these command my allegiance in a way that is beyond my power to analyze at the moment."

TRAVELLING THROUGH THE DARK. *Harper* 1962 $5.95

THE RESCUED YEAR. *Harper* 1966 pap. $2.45

ALLEGIANCES. *Harper* 1970 $4.95 pap. $2.45

DOWN IN MY HEART. *Brethren Press* 1971 pap. $2.50

SOMEDAY, MAYBE. *Harper* 1973 $5.95

JARRELL, RANDALL. 1914–1965.

"The Woman at the Washington Zoo" won the 1961 National Book Award for Poetry and it was said that "each poem . . . has his usual expert technical skill in use of rhyme or assonance, meter and imagery." Poet, critic, novelist and teacher, Randall Jarrell was born in Nashville, Tenn. He graduated from Vanderbilt University, received his M.A. from Vanderbilt in 1938, and taught at the University of Texas, Sarah Lawrence and the Woman's College of the University of North Carolina. In 1947 he won a Guggenheim Fellowship and in 1951 he was awarded a grant from the National Institute of Arts and Letters. From 1956 to 1958 he served as Poetry Consultant at the Library of Congress; later he became literary editor of *The Nation* and poetry critic for the *Partisan Review* and the *Yale Review*.

He is a poet of great originality and power. The "Selected Poems" shows his achievements as "a poetic observer of life, both in war and in peace." In many of his poems his childhood and Army experiences are recurring themes. "Jarrell's imagination and wit pounce upon Army routines, armor, strategies, and engagements and make them yield symbolic experience. His war poems have a powerful urgency and clarity"—(Stephen Stepanchev, in "American Poetry Since 1945"). "The 22 poems of 'The Lost World' would seem few were they not so full. Most of them are long by contemporary standards, yet none is padded; each explores its meanings with such a quiet flexibility that even the careful rhymes of the title poem seem natural. Within such technical brilliance . . . the final value of Jarrell's new poetry lies in its seemingly casual wisdom"— (Philip Booth, in the *Christian Science Monitor*).

His book of criticism, "Poetry and the Age," (1953. *Farrar, Straus* 1972 Noonday pap. $2.85; *Octagon* 1972 $10.00) is "effervescent and catalytic," and his "Third Book of Criticism" (*Farrar, Straus* 1971 $7.50 Noonday pap. $3.45), a collection of essays on American fiction, poetry and translations, merited the same high praise when Jarrell was called "the most exhilarating critic America has produced"—(Kirkus). His fictional comedy, "Pictures from an Institution" (1954. *Farrar, Straus* $5.95 Noonday pap. $2.25), is a brilliant comment on college faculty capers. "A Sad Heart at the Supermarket: Essays and Fables" (*Atheneum* 1962 $5.00) contains his ironic and devastating observations on the decline in taste, learning and culture in the United States. He was also the author of a number of children's books. Jarrell gave the witty opening address at the first National Poetry Festival held in Washington in October, 1962. He was hit by a car in Chapel Hill, N.C., in October, 1965, and injured fatally, apparently a suicide. His poetry has gained many readers since his death.

COMPLETE POEMS. *Farrar, Straus* 1969 $12.95 Sunburst pap. $4.95. Includes poems from "Selected Poems (1955–64), "The Woman at the Washington Zoo" (1960), "The Lost World" (1965), "New Poems," "The Rage for the Lost Penny" (1940), "Blood for a Stranger" (1942), "Little Friend, Little Friend" (1945), "Losses" (1948), "The Seven-League Crutches" (1951), "Uncollected Poems" (1924–65), "Unpublished Poems" (1935–65) and some translations from the German.

SELECTED POEMS, including The Woman at the Washington Zoo. 1955. *Atheneum* 1964 pap. $2.75

THE LOST WORLD. *Macmillan* 1965 $3.95 pap. 1966 $1.50

JEROME: The Biography of a Poem. With three etchings by Albrecht Dürer and 50 facsimiles of Jarrell's worksheets. *Grossman* 1971 $10.00. A truly beautiful book with introductory "Reflections" on "Jerome" by Jarrell's wife Mary. Published for the 500th anniversary of Dürer's birth.

Books about Jarrell

Randall Jarrell. By Karl Shapiro. This booklet contains Shapiro's memorial lecture for Jarrell plus a bibliography of 169 items by Jarrell in the Library of Congress. *Library of Congress Information and Publications Office* 1967 pap. $.25

Randall Jarrell, 1914–1965. Ed. by Robert Lowell, Peter Taylor and Robert Penn Warren. *Farrar, Straus* 1967 $6.50 Noonday pap. $2.45

Most contributors to this collection of essays and poems "knew Jarrell well and speak as insiders"—
(*SR*). They are Hannah Arendt, John Berryman, Alfred Kazin, John Crowe Ransom, Elizabeth
Bishop, Cleanth Brooks, James Dickey, Leslie Fiedler, Robert Lowell, Marianne Moore, Karl Shapiro and Mrs. Randall Jarrell. "The essays . . . are far more distinguished than most collections made
in a spirit of piety"—(Stephen Spender, in the *N.Y. Review of Books*). "Here is a credible version of a
richly complicated man, and his work is weighed up judiciously. . . . In this admiring book about Jarrell at least six distinguished writers, firm stylists all, have composed—unconsciously—sentences, passages, whole paragraphs that are unmistakably possessed by the style and voice of Randall Jarrell. The
impersonation is unthinking and uncanny and recurrent. Praise indeed!"—(Erik Wensberg, in the
N.Y. Times).

Poetry of Randall Jarrell. By Suzanne Ferguson. *Louisiana State Univ. Press* 1971 $8.95. This is the first
major critical study on Randall Jarell. Ms. Ferguson surveys the poetry chronologically, bringing biographical reference in to illuminate the poetry. A detailed and well-thought-out book, it includes a selected bibliography and index.

Randall Jarrell, 1914–1965. By M. L. Rosenthal. Pamphlets on American Writers. *Univ. of Minnesota
Press* 1972 pap. $.95. A brief general introduction to the poetry of Jarrell.

CIARDI, JOHN. 1916–

Teacher, editor, translator and critic, John Ciardi was born in Boston, went first to Bates College in Lew-
iston, Maine, then graduated from Tufts. After teaching and serving in the Air Corps, he went to Harvard as
Briggs-Copeland Instructor in English 1946–47 and as Briggs-Copeland Assistant Professor 1947–53. In
1949 he became editor and later executive director of *Twayne Publishers*. He was on the faculty of Rutgers
University as lecturer in creative writing (1953–1961) and served as poetry editor of the *Saturday Review*
from 1956 to 1971. "Dialogue with an Audience" (*Lippincott* 1963 $5.95) is a record of Ciardi's first seven
years there—"seven years of insight, controversy, and liveliness" his publisher calls them. The book collects
the articles that *Saturday Review* readers have answered with "blasts and bravos." The reviews include the
now-celebrated one of Anne Morrow Lindbergh's book of verse, "The Unicorn and Other Poems," and the
almost equally famous article on Edna St. Vincent Millay. There are three articles on Robert Frost. "Manner of Speaking" was his weekly feature in the *Saturday Review* from 1961 to 1969—informal discussions of
poets, poetry and related topics. Since 1972 he has been a contributing editor to the *World* magazine, and
now, *Saturday Review/World*.

David Daiches calls him "a poet of genuine if unequal gifts, whose best poetry has wit, perception and humanity." Reviewing "In the Stoneworks," *Library Journal* said that Ciardi writes a "robust, witty, virile poetry notable for its concern with and sympathy for the condition of man." He received the Avery Hopwood
Award in Poetry in 1939 and has received three awards from *Poetry*: the Blumenthal Prize (1944), the Eunice Tietjens Prize (1945) and the Levinson Prize. He has translated (in verse) Dante's "Inferno" (*Rutgers
Univ. Press* 1954 $6.00), the "Purgatorio" (*New Am. Lib.* Mentor pap. $1.25) and "Paradiso" (*New Am.
Lib.* Mentor 1970 pap. $1.25). His excellent translations of the three books of "The Divine Comedy" are
currently in preparation in one volume by *World*. He has edited "Mid-Century Poets" (*Twayne* $6.00).

Ciardi's "Person to Person" has "the wit and sharp images and tough language we have come to expect,
the observant talk about contemporary civilization. . . . There is a strong effort here to be quiet in a noisy life,
to be more 'with' the birds, animals, vegetation, seasons and elements"—(*N.Y. Times*). *Library Journal* calls
"An Alphabestiary" a "zestful excursion"—it is a beautifully produced book with 15 lithographs by Milton
Hebald to illustrate 26 allegorical poems on animal themes from Ants to Zoology. Some of the poems in
"This Strangest Everything" were originally published in *The New Yorker* and the *Atlantic*. One is written
in mourning—but more in admiration—for Theodore Roethke. "Throughout the book runs concern . . . for
Man and for men"—(*SR*). "Mr. Ciardi's sound is ironic, mildly sophisticated, and learned"—(*LJ*). "A
Genesis" (*Touchstone Publishers Ltd.* 1967) contains 15 poems by Ciardi and 15 color etchings by Gabor
Peterdi. (Information on this volume is available from the Borgenicht Art Gallery, 1018 Madison Ave., New
York, N.Y.)

"You Read to Me, I'll Read to You," written and spoken by John Ciardi and family, was an unusual collaboration between a publisher, *Lippincott*, and a recording firm, *Spoken Arts*, in the fall of 1962. The book
presents nonsense verse and easy-to-read poems for children. On the disk Ciardi reads to his own three children, with their active cooperation and frequent comments. (The package of book and record $8.90—the
book $3.95 lib. bdg. $3.93, the recording $5.95). His "How Does a Poem Mean?" (*Houghton* 1960 $5.95)
was originally published as one section, Part 3, of "Introduction to Literature" by Herbert Barrows and others (1959–1960, o.p.).

As If: Poems New and Selected. *Rutgers Univ. Press* 1955 $3.75

As If: A recording. *Folkways* $5.95

I Marry You: A Sheaf of Love Poems. *Rutgers Univ. Press* 1958 $3.50. A diary in po-
etry of a happy marriage.

39 POEMS. *Rutgers Univ. Press* 1959 $3.00

IN THE STONEWORKS. *Rutgers Univ. Press* 1961 $5.00. Poems.

IN FACT. *Rutgers Univ. Press* 1962 $3.50. Poems.

PERSON TO PERSON. *Rutgers Univ. Press* 1964 $3.50

THIS STRANGEST EVERYTHING. *Rutgers Univ. Press* 1966 $3.75

THIS STRANGEST EVERYTHING. *Spoken Arts* H-C 956 (Vol. 1), 957 (Vol. 2) $5.95 each. A recording in which the poet reads.

AN ALPHABESTIARY. Ill. by Milton Hebald. *Lippincott* 1967 $5.95

LIVES OF X. *Rutgers Univ. Press* 1971 $5.95

MANNER OF SPEAKING. *Rutgers Univ. Press* 1972 $10.00

VIERECK, PETER (ROBERT EDWIN). 1916–

"Terror and Decorum: Poems, 1940–1948," this poet's first collected volume, won the Pulitzer Prize for Poetry in 1949. In the *Saturday Review* Selden Rodman wrote: "His book as a whole is so rich in experimental vigor, so full of new poetic attitudes toward civilization and its discontents, so fresh and earthy in its reanimation of the American spirit, that it seems to offer endless possibilities of development—both for Viereck himself, and for other young poets who are certain to take the cue." Of his "New and Selected Poems" Karl Shapiro says, "A reader can comb this volume with admiration," and James Dickey comments, "What has always been best about him: a sense of youthful, high-spirited intellectual excitement and a delightful gift for seizing on bold, unorthodox and sometimes hilarious ways of dramatizing ideas. . . . Viereck is a good lyric poet who seems to need, in order to write lyrically, to be also a kind of vaudeville poet, whose colored juggling balls are the principal contributing ideas of modern culture and world crisis. He sees a surprising lot of contemporary life, and sees behind it with wit and precision; there is brio, verve and intelligence in his work and, above all, he cares." His verse play "God and the Basket Cases," "written out of human indignation," about Vietnam amputees returning to America, was read in part at St. Mark's Church in the Bowery (New York City). A number of the lines are from "New and Selected Poems." Lucifer is one of the characters; there are other elements of fantasy and shock. Thomas Lask said, "Many of these stanzas are amusing and pointed, and we can always feel the indignation that provoked them. But in the abbreviated reading, Mr. Viereck's true compassion hardly gets a chance to show"—(*N.Y. Times*).

His political work, "Conservatism Revisited: The Revolt against Revolt" (1949, *Macmillan* (Free Press) 1965 pap. $1.95) attracted widespread attention both here and in England. Other political works are "The Unadjusted Man" (1965. *Greenwood* 1973 $14.50), "Inner Liberty" (*Pendle Hill* 1957 pap. $.45), "Metapolitics: The Roots of the Nazi Mind" (*Putnam* Capricorn Bks. 1961 pap. $2.85) and "Shame and Glory of the Intellectuals" (*Putnam* Capricorn Bks. 1965 pap. $1.95). His other prose includes: "Dream and Responsibility: Four Test Cases of the Tension between Poetry and Social Ethics" (*Univ. Press of Washington, D.C.* 1953 $3.00) and "Conservatism: From John Adams to Churchill" (*Van Nostrand* Anvil Bks. 1956 pap. $1.45).

Peter Viereck was born in New York City, took his degrees at Harvard and Oxford, was in the African Italian campaigns, World War II, was an instructor at Smith and is now Professor of Modern History at Mount Holyoke. In 1955 he occupied the newly-found Chair in American Poetry and Civilization at the University of Florence, on a Fulbright grant.

TERROR AND DECORUM: Poems, 1940–1948. *Greenwood* $7.75

STRIKE THROUGH THE MASK: New Lyrical Poems. 1950. *Greenwood* $7.25

THE FIRST MORNING: New Poems. 1952. *Greenwood* $7.75

TREE WITCH: A Poem and Play (First of All a Play). 1961. *Greenwood* $8.50

NEW AND SELECTED POEMS, 1932–1967. *Bobbs* 1967 $6.00

Books about Viereck

Peter Viereck. By Marie Henault. United States Authors Ser. *Twayne* 1968 $4.95; *College & Univ. Press* pap. $2.45

BROOKS, GWENDOLYN. 1917–

The *Nation* carried a "critical reassessment" of Miss Brooks in 1962, which said in part: "Gwendolyn Brooks has never denied her engagement in the contemporary situation or been over-obsessed by it. . . . Like all good writers she acknowledges Now by vivifying it, accepts herself and the distinguished background that is part of her distinction. But she refuses to let Negroness limit her humanity. . . . Compared . . . to the best of modern poets, she ranks high."

Gwendolyn Brooks was born in Topeka, Kansas, and had her first poem published at the age of 13 in a children's magazine. After the publication of her first book of poetry, "A Street In Bronzeville" (1945, o. p.), she was chosen as one of the Ten Women of the Year by *Mademoiselle* magazine. In 1946 she received an award for creative writing from the American Academy of Arts and Letters and a Guggenheim Fellowship. Early in 1968 she was appointed the state's "poet laureate" by Governor Otto Kerner of Illinois, to succeed the late Carl Sandburg. Her second book of poems, "Annie Allen" (1949, *Greenwood* $6.95), won the 1950 Pulitzer Prize. The *Nation* said of this volume: "Her strength consists of boldness, invention, a daring to experiment, a naturalness that does not scorn literature but absorbs it, exploits it, and through this absorption and exploitation comes out with the remark made in an entirely original way, not offhand so much as forthright."

In 1960 Miss Brooks published her third book of poems, "The Bean Eaters" (o. p.). Of "Selected Poems," the *N.Y. Times* said, "Her ability to distinguish between what is sad and what is silly is unfailing, and she deals with race, love, war and other matters with uncommon common sense and a mellow humor that is as much a rarity as it is a relief." Her subjects are her own people and their concerns, often treated cheerfully but sometimes sharply with bitterness, as in "The Chicago Defender Sends a Man to Little Rock," which ends: "I saw a bleeding brownish boy. . . ./The lariat lynch-wish I deplored./The loveliest lynchee was our Lord." "Riot" is one long poem written after the assassination of Martin Luther King in 1968, and the subsequent disturbances in Chicago. Only one section of the work had appeared in print before this publication. She has written tributes to Robert Frost and to Langston Hughes. Miss Brooks is also the author of the novel "Maud Martha" (1953, o. p.), concerning a black girl in Chicago.

See also section on Collections, this Chapter.

SELECTED POEMS. *Harper* 1963 $4.95 pap. $1.65. This volume includes some not previously published in book form.

IN THE MECCA. *Harper* 1968. $4.95

RIOT. 1969. *Broadside* 1970 $5.00 pap. $1.00 tape $5.00

FAMILY PICTURES. *Broadside* 1971 $4.50 pap. $1.00 tape $5.00

WORLD OF GWENDOLYN BROOKS. *Harper* 1971 $8.50

ALONENESS. *Broadside* 1972 pap. $3.00. Blue, handwritten with drawings.

REPORT FROM PART ONE: An autobiography. *Broadside* rev. ed. 1972 $4.95

PORTION OF THAT FIELD: The Centennial of the Burial of Lincoln (1967). *Univ. of Illinois Press* $3.00. Commemorative selections by Gwendolyn Brooks, Otto Kerner, Allan Nevins, Paul M. Angle, Mark Van Doren, Paul H. Douglas, Bruce Catton and Adlai Stevenson.

LOWELL, ROBERT. 1917–

Born in Boston, Robert Lowell, great-grandnephew of James Russell Lowell and distant cousin of Amy Lowell, is the latest brilliant (but rebellious) member of this distinguished family. He received his B.A. in 1940 from Kenyon College, where he had studied under John Crowe Ransom and come to know Allen Tate. In 1940 he also became a convert to Catholicism. During World War II he tried twice to enlist, but by the time he was called he had become a conscientious objector because of his strong feeling against the bombing of civilians. He is married to Elizabeth Hardwick, distinguished as a drama critic and as editor of the *N.Y. Review of Books*. They live in New York. His subject matter includes New England and its traditions, colored—in the early poems—by an intellectualized religious symbolism and savage satire against the materialism of modern American life.

Mr. Lowell won the 1947 Pulitzer Prize for Poetry for "Lord Weary's Castle," in which religion was beginning to fade as a source of symbolism. In "Life Studies," which won the National Book Award for Poetry in 1960, his remarkable poetic powers become clearly evident. Much of it is portraiture of his New England relatives, through whom he studies himself and his origins. It was with the fresh approach and vision of this volume that critics began to speak of him as a "confessional" poet. "For the Union Dead," another collection, continued the exploration of his own and America's past and present. The three verse plays of "Old Glory" are based on two short stories by Hawthorne and one ("Benito Cereno") by Melville, and mark a return to more broadly social concerns, such as the effect upon innocent people of a corrupt society or group. Not all the critics thought that Lowell's venture into drama was successful ("Benito Cereno," the adaptation of the Melville story of a mutiny at sea, was considered the strongest), but the *Christian Science Monitor* wrote: "Taken together, 'The Old Glory' is an immense and impressive feat of imaginative assimilation and imaginative projection. No one concerned with American letters—and America—can overlook these plays; they are the first successful American poetic drama, and a tragic reading of our destiny pronounced with the measured ferocity of a moral concern as deep as it is dark." "The Old Glory," as produced off-Broadway without "Endecott and the Red Cross" in the 1964–65 season, won its author a Tony and a Vernon Rice Award. "Endecott," starring Kenneth Haigh, received separate production off-Broadway in 1968. Reviewing it as part of "The Old Glory," Clive Barnes said (in the *N.Y. Times*): "All three plays have as a kind of unifying architectonic device a flag, but their deeper unity is to be found in Lowell's poetic view of the entire North American experience and sensibility. His plays are about the past, but are to be comprehended only from the viewpoint of the present. [The theme of "Endecott" is that of Puritan vs. libertine in the American psyche, but] the play is more than merely a confrontation between the dual and restive spirits of America's schizophrenia. It is also an attempt to dissect and analyze the violence and nonconformity at the heart of America, which are as American as apple pie, racial riots and draft-card burning."

"Near the Ocean," a collection of poems, received mixed reviews weighted toward the favorable, but with some strictures about the illustrations by Sidney Nolan accompanying the text. Webster Schott wrote in *Life*: " 'Near the Ocean' may not advance Lowell's literary position. But it consolidates it. His energized language leaps across opacity and illusion. His visual gifts lift the poems through beauty above despair. His Nestor cries from ancient Rome into our time, 'Why have I lived? What crime have I committed?' Lowell's poems, perhaps without his sensing it, respond." And Philip Toynbee (in the *Observer*, London) said: "Of the seven original poems in this volume—the others are translations of Horace, Juvenal, Date, Quevedo and Gongora—it seems to me that five are brilliantly successful. . . . Since the [two unsuccessful] poems are short and all the others are longer, the proportion of success is remarkable." Robert Lowell's adaptation of Aeschylus's "Prometheus Bound" was produced at the Yale Drama School in 1967, with Kenneth Haigh and Irene Worth in the leading roles. Walter Kerr of the *N.Y. Times* was ecstatic over the acting and production—and, indeed, the play itself: "The lungs fill, the heart lifts, the head shakes itself clear of months of accumulated debris. [Mr. Lowell] has worked freely, using as many of his own nerve-wracked, eye-straining insights as those of Aeschylus, and he has cast the whole attempt to pierce the smog of centuries in what he calls prose, but is in fact poetry, from trumpeted overture to sober curtain call. Other critics found the play too static for successful Broadway showing—it is a torrent of words—but as university theater it was superb, lifting the beholder into the regions where even human life manipulated by the gods is more significant than we have recently been told, and the human ability to transcend circumstance magnificent." "Voyage and Other Versions of Poems by Baudelaire" is a fine gift edition, not so much translated as expressed by Lowell. The poems are charged with the aesthetic electricity of the meeting of the two poetic masters, the younger of whom, Lowell, seems to expand and widen the horizons of the other genius.

Among Robert Lowell's prizes have been the Harriet Monroe Memorial Prize for poetry in 1961 and a sharing of the 1962 Bollingen Prize of $2,500 with Richmond Lattimore for "Imitations."

Mr. Lowell has also been showing that a fine poet can concern himself actively with the quality of American life. Bitterly opposed to the Vietnam war, he caused a sensation in 1965 when he rejected a White House invitation to appear there at a festival of the arts. In his letter to President Johnson he wrote: "Every serious artist knows that he cannot enjoy public celebration without making subtle public commitments." Mr. Lowell has been active in introducing Russian poets to American audiences. On one such occasion, at New York's YMHA Poetry Center, he remarked with considerable charm of delivery that both Andrei Voznesensky (the subject of his introduction) and himself had in common "really terrible governments." He has demonstrated (notably with Norman Mailer and a vast gathering at the Pentagon in 1967) and spoken repeatedly in favor of peace and accompanied Senator Eugene McCarthy in the early phases of the latter's campaign for the 1968 Presidential nomination. Robert Lowell's thoughtful and visionary genius is clearly at once a response and challenge to his times. If New England provided the finest flowering of a brash New World perhaps it is fitting that a Lowell now so powerfully calls America to account.

THE ACHIEVEMENT OF ROBERT LOWELL. Ed. by William J. Martz. *Scott, Foresman* 1966 soft bdg. $2.65. A comprehensive selection of his poems, with a critical introduction.

LORD WEARY'S CASTLE and THE MILLS OF THE KAVANAUGHS. 1946. *Harcourt* Harvest Bks. pap. $1.45

THE MILLS OF THE KAVANAUGHS AND OTHER POEMS. *Harcourt* 1951 $4.95

LIFE STUDIES. *Farrar, Straus* 1959 $4.95. New poems and a prose autobiographical fragment.

IMITATIONS. *Farrar, Straus* 1961 $5.50 Noonday 1962 pap. $2.25. English versions, not translations, of 66 poems ranging from a passage of Homer to Pasternak.

FOR THE UNION DEAD: Thirty-five New Poems. *Farrar, Straus* 1964 $4.95

THE OLD GLORY. Three Plays: "Benito Cereno," "My Kinsman Major Molineux," and "Endecott and the Red Cross." Introd. by Robert Brustein. *Farrar, Straus* 1965 $6.50 Noonday pap. $2.25

NEAR THE OCEAN: Poems. Ill. by Sidney Nolan. *Farrar, Straus* 1967 $6.95 Noonday pap. $1.95

PROMETHEUS BOUND. *Farrar, Straus* 1967 $5.95 Noonday pap. $1.95. A free adaptation from Aeschylus.

LIFE STUDIES and FOR THE UNION DEAD. *Farrar, Straus* Noonday 1967 pap. $2.25

VOYAGE AND OTHER VERSIONS OF POEMS BY BAUDELAIRE. Ill. by Sidney Nolan. *Farrar, Straus* 1968 $15.00

NOTEBOOK. 1969. *Farrar, Straus* rev. expanded ed. 1970 $7.50 Noonday pap. $2.45. The new expanded edition of the original "Notebook" includes changes in the original poems, 90 new poems throughout.

THE DOLPHIN. *Farrar, Straus* 1973 $6.95. Thirty-two page poem sequence, including the title-poem.

HISTORY. *Farrar, Straus* $7.95. About 400 poems in this volume, 80 of which have not been in book form before this, the remainder of which appeared in "Notebook," 1967–68.

FOR LIZZIE AND HARRIET. *Farrar, Straus* 1973 $6.95. Poems in complete form which were earlier published in "Notebook," 1967–68.

Books about Lowell

The Poetic Themes of Robert Lowell. by Jerome Mazzaro. *Univ. of Michigan Press* 1965 $4.50

Lowell: A Collection of Critical Essays. Ed. by T. Parkinson. *Prentice-Hall* 1968 $5.95 Spectrum Bks. pap. $1.95. Nineteen critical essays by Tate, Blackmur, Eberhart, Jarrell, William Carlos Williams and others, including an essay on himself by Robert Lowell. The introduction gives a brief critique of Lowell by the editor. A solid selection.

The Autobiographical Myth of Robert Lowell. By Philip Cooper. *Univ. of North Carolina Press* 1970 $7.50. A study of Lowell's work through "Notebook 1967–68" which attempts to prove the inter-relationship of the entire body of Lowell's poetry. Cooper deals primarily with the autobiographical "confessional" element in Lowell's work. Bibliography and index.

Everything to be Endured; An Essay on Robert Lowell and Modern Poetry. By Roger Meiners. Literary Frontiers Ser. *Univ. of Missouri Press* 1970 pap. $2.00

Robert Lowell. By Jay Martin. Pamphlets on American Authors *Univ. of Minnesota Press* $1.25. A readable nonscholarly introduction to Lowell's poetry. With selected bibliography on plays, prose and critical studies of Lowell.

Robert Lowell: A Portrait of the Artist in His Time. Ed. by Michael London and Robert Boyars. With Checklist of materials on Robert Lowell 1939–1968 by Jerome Mazzaro. *David Lewis Pub.* 1970 $15.00. A distinguished, excellent and beautifully produced selection of essays on Robert Lowell by Allen Tate, R. P. Blackmur, Leslie Fiedler, Randall Jarrell, M. L. Rosenthal, Robert Bly, Hayden Carruth, Norman Mailer and others.

Robert Lowell. By R. J. Fein. United States Authors Ser. *Twayne* 1971 $4.95. Fein discusses the development of Lowell's poetry from the early work to the early seventies. In striving for an overall view of Lowell's poetry and a definition of his position in the century's American literature, the author provides a good and thorough introduction to the work of this sometimes difficult poet. Chronology, selected bibliography and notes.

The Public Poetry of Robert Lowell. By Patrick Cosgrave. *Taplinger* 1972 $7.95. Cosgrave has written a scholarly and serious book tracing what the author calls "the line of gravity"—a tradition in English poetry—which runs from Shakespeare through Pope, Johnson and Yeats to Lowell. This is a somewhat controversial work with its linkage of Lowell to Yeats, and thus the implication of Lowell's affiliation with the more "English" than "American" literary tradition. Separate chapters on the major works. A fine and readable work of criticism.

Robert Lowell: A Checklist. Ed. by J. M. Edelstein. Modern Authors Checklist Ser. *Gale* 1972 $8.50

The Poetic Art of Robert Lowell. By Marjorie G. Perloff. *Cornell Univ. Press* 1973 $9.50. Ms. Perloff studies the poetry of Lowell, its images, genre, syntax and tone and finally examines his poetry against the background of contemporary American poetry movements.

FERLINGHETTI, LAWRENCE. 1919?–

San Francisco has become the center of an interesting movement in poetry; it was there that the reading of poems with jazz accompaniment was introduced. A central figure in the "Beat" poetic movement, Ferlinghetti owns the City Lights Bookshop, where such readings are held and from which he also publishes volumes of modern verse in paperback. Williams, Ginsberg, Patchen, Rexroth, Artaud and many newer poets have appeared under his imprint.

Like Allen Ginsberg a poet of genuine merit, he has particular appeal for the generation of disaffected young people, and his "Coney Island of the Mind" (written "out of love," said its television director; "he loves this country for its bigness, its naiveté, its crassness") has met the mood of that generation and become a best seller. It was dramatized under the direction of Steven Kyle Kent, a 23-year-old, on television in 1967 by 20 members of the University of Southern California's School of Performing Arts, emerging as "sort of a revue with poetic material, a unique combination of singing, choral speaking, mime"—(John E. Blankenchip). "Secret Meaning of Things" is six long poems including "Moscow in the Wilderness, Segovia in the Snow." "Mexican Journal" is a "poem journal" decorated with the author's drawings. "Back Roads to Far Places" are poems after Basho in linked verse form. "Love Is No Stone on the Moon" is a single 16-page poem subtitled "automatic poem"; those pages of the book on which are printed geology text notes are printed upside down. Though a dissenter, Mr. Ferlinghetti claims commitment: "Only the dead are disengaged. And the waggy nihilism of the Beat hipster, if carried to its natural conclusion, means the death of the creative artist himself." He says that one of his methods of creation is to give a "little twist" to the hackneyed phrases of slogans and advertising. "Starting from San Francisco," says its publisher, is his "halfway house toward his hope for a higher form of poetry in the direction of the Dharma." He has written "Unfair Arguments with Existence: Seven Plays for a New Theatre" (*New Directions* 1963 pap. $1.00). "Routines" (*New Directions* 1964 pap. $1.00) is another collection of unorthodox plays. Ferlinghetti has also written "Her" (*New Directions* 1960 pap. $1.50), a novel, and a long political prose statement printed in his own hand: "Tyrannus Nix"? (*New Directions* 1969 $1.25), a satire on President Nixon. He has edited the *City Lights Journal* (*City Lights Books* o.p. except Vol. 3 $3.00). Mr. Ferlinghetti holds the *Doctorat* of the University of Paris and an M.A. from Columbia.

A CONEY ISLAND OF THE MIND. *New Directions* 1958 boxed $5.50 pap. $1.00

PICTURES OF THE GONE WORLD. *City Lights Books* pap. $1.00

STARTING FROM SAN FRANCISCO. *New Directions* 1961 rev. ed. 1967 pap. $1.00

SECRET MEANING OF THINGS. *New Directions* 1969 $3.95 signed limited ed. $25.00 pap. $1.00

MEXICAN NIGHT: Travel Journal. *New Directions* 1970 pap. $1.50

BACK ROADS TO FAR PLACES. *New Directions* 1971 pap. $1.50. Poems after Basho, in linked verse form.

LOVE IS NO STONE ON THE MOON. 1971. *Arif Press* (dist. by Book People) pap. $1.00. This is a single 16-page poem which is subtitled "automatic poem." Written in the poet's own hand with his own illustrations the pages of this book on which are printed geology text notes are upside down.

OPEN EYE, OPEN HEART. *New Directions* 1973 $7.50 pap. $1.75. A new large collection of poems.

DUNCAN, ROBERT (EDWARD). 1919–

A leading poet of the San Francisco Renaissance, Robert Duncan is "easily recognizable as a member of the international *avant garde*." Born in Oakland, Calif., he has been an editor, a teacher at Black Mountain College, and assistant director of The Poetry Center at San Francisco Sate College. Highly regarded by fellow nonacademic poets, Duncan's poetry is at once learned and spontaneous. Its form seems innate rather than wrought, complex, and wonderfully musical. "Duncan has the old or pagan sense of the poem as a divine form of speech which works intimately with the animism of nature, of the renewals that believed-in ceremonials can be, and of the sacramental in experience"—(James Dickey). "Roots and Branches" "ranges from lyrics of a few stanzas to a verse play of over twenty pages. There are sonnets, hymns, variations on classical poems, poems interwoven with prose"—(Publisher's note).

His prose, drama and prosody published by small or private presses is listed in Donald M. Allen's "The New American Poetry 1945–1960" (*Grove* Evergreen Bks. 1960 $2.95; *Peter Smith* $5.50), and many of his nonpoetry titles are available from *Oyez*. In the Allen work, too—p. 400—can be found the poet's "Pages from a Notebook," a statement on poetics, and—on p. 432—his brief autobiography. M. L. Rosenthal has written a rewarding study of his verse in "The New Poets": "The most interesting of his pieces have been collected in two books, 'The Opening of the Field' (1960) and 'Roots and Branches' (1964). Though it seems clear now that Duncan's art is to some degree self-defeating, one has only to leaf through these books to find poems and passages that mark him as a modern romantic whose best work is instantly engaging by the standards of the purest lyrical traditions." The marring factor, says Rosenthal, are Duncan's "intrusions"—the purposeful introduction of private, jarring or baffling elements that are "employed at times arbitrarily, to break his own spell, as it were." He received the Harriet Monroe Memorial Prize in 1960, a Guggenheim Memorial Award in 1963; the Levinson Poetry Prize in 1964; a National Endowment for the Arts Grant in 1967; and the Eunice Tietjens Memorial Prize in 1967.

THE OPENING OF THE FIELD. 1960. *New Directions* 1973 pap. $2.75

ROOTS AND BRANCHES. *Scribner* 1964 pap. $1.75

BENDING THE BOW. *New Directions* 1968 $5.00 pap. $2.25

THE YEARS AS CATCHES: First Poems. 1966 *Oyez* pap. $2.50. Duncan's first poems (1939–46) with a retrospective introduction by the poet.

CAESAR'S GATE. 1955. *Sand Dollar* 1972 $8.50 pap. $3.50

THE TRUTH AND LIFE OF MYTH: An Essay in Essential Autobiography. *Sumac* 1968 $2.45

SWENSON, MAY. 1919–

May Swenson was born in Utah and educated at Utah State University, Logan. A former editor at *New Directions* publishing corporation, she has been a Poet-in-Residence at Purdue University in Indiana. She has taught poetry seminars at the University of North Carolina, Greensboro, 1968–69. Twice a recipient of a Rockefeller Fellowship (1955–1967) May Swenson has also been awarded a Guggenheim Fellowship, 1959; a National Institute of Arts and Letters Award, 1969; a Ford Foundation Grant, 1964; a Lucy Martin Donnelly Fellowship from Bryn Mawr College, 1968 and a Shelley Memorial Award in the same year. She presently resides in New York State. Her work has appeared in the *New Yorker, Hudson Review, Atlantic* and *Harper's*.

Besides her poetry Ms. Swenson has also written the introduction to the 1962 edition of Edgar Lee Masters (*q.v.*) "Spoon River Anthology" (*Macmillan* Collier Bks. pap. $1.25) and is the author of "The Contemporary Poet as Artist and Critic" (o.p.). With Lief Sjöberg she has translated "Windows and States: Selected Poems of Tomas Tranströmer," (Pitt Poetry Ser. *Univ. of Pittsburgh Press* 1972 $5.95 pap. $2.95).

"May Swenson is extremely deft and inventive with sounds and shapes in language . . . she is reckless, an attempter at oddities"—(William Stafford). Her poetry is at once imagistic and precise. There is a crispness coupled with sensuousness which intrigues the reader of her work, akin to the metaphysicals at times.

Ms. Swenson also is an observer of nature (even in the heart of the city) in a truly American way. Rocks, trees, landscape are so clearly viewed it seems a magic impossibility that the poet becomes so singular and united with it. Her aim seems to be "to get out of herself and into those larger warmer energies of earth, and to do so by integral means"—(Stephen Stepanchev).

For May Swenson the experience of poetry is "based on a craving to get through the curtains of things as they *appear* to things as they *are*, and there into the larger wilder space of things as they *are becoming*."

She has recorded for "Today's Poets: Their Poems, Their Voices" Vol. 2, Scholastic Records, 1968; and for The Library of Congress, Spoken Arts Records, Folkway Records, and others. Her poems have been set to music by Otto Leuning among others.

To Mix with Time: New and Selected Poems. *Scribner* 1963 pap. $1.45

Poems to Solve. *Scribner* 1969 $3.50 text ed. pap. $2.00. A selection of poems for young readers.

Iconographs. *Scribner* 1970 $4.95

More Poems to Solve. *Scribner* 1970 lib. bdg. $4.50

BUKOWSKI, CHARLES. 1920–

Bukowski began writing poetry at the age of 35 after years of writing prose fiction. He is the most famed of a breed called "street poets"—ones who are destined to have poetry published by small presses that remain unknown; ones who not only produce writings derived from "street life," but whose own life is also in some sense of the street. On and off, Bukowski has worked as a dishwasher, truck driver, mailman, elevator operator, in a dog biscuit factory and a slaughterhouse, and has hung posters in a New York subway.

His writing is typified by a rough, large, prophetic style. It has been called a "crude dishevelled kind of poetry." Though in some strains Whitmanesque, and reminiscent of Ginsberg, his work is earthier and more immediate than even theirs. His vision of America is first-hand and has a strong surrealistic bend to it: "I get on the train on the way to the track it's down near Dago/and this gives some space and rolling and/ I have my pint/ and I walk to the barcar for a couple of/ beers/ and I weave upon the floor—/ THACK THACK THACKA THACK THACK THACKA THACK—/ and some of it comes back/ a little of it comes back/ like some green in a leaf after a long/ dryness"—(from "On the Train to Del Mar").

These poems ramble and twist leaving the reader physically and emotionally enervated, and yet comforted. There is a ferocity and directness about his work that a more "academically" trained poet would find hard to muster up.

Bukowski was born in Germany, and has lived in the United States since he was two years old. He lives in Los Angeles and has written a weekly column for *Open City* in Los Angeles, called "Notes of a Dirty Old Man." Two volumes of stories, "South of North: Stories of the Buried Life" (*Black Sparrow* 1973 $4.00), and "Erections, Ejaculations, and Other Tales of Ordinary Madness," ed. by Gail Chiarrello (*City Lights Books* 1972 pap. $3.95) have recently been published. He was awarded the Discovery Award of the National Endowment for the Arts in 1973.

Crucifix in a Death-Hand: New Poems 1963–1965. Ill. with etchings by Noel Rocknoe. *Lyle Stuart* signed ed. $7.50

Days Run away Like Wild Horses over the Hills. 1970. *Black Sparrow* 1973 pap. $4.00

Burning in Water, Drowning in Flame. *Black Sparrow* 1974 $15.00 pap. $4.00

NEMEROV, HOWARD. 1920–

Howard Nemerov, one of the most vital and interesting of the younger poets, has become known for his wit, intelligence and good taste. Marius Bewley compares Nemerov to Thoreau: "Poems after poem . . . has sent me back to "Walden,' and everywhere I have been impressed by a similarity that is not, certainly, parallelism, but which exists in a serenity of temperament, a water-clear and air-cool vision of reality that both writers share"—(in *Partisan Review*). "The Blue Swallows" received mixed reviews but won him the first Roethke Memorial Prize. Thomas Lask said, "The poet's earlier irony, hard-hitting satire and wit have been changed into feelings of loathing and contempt for man and his works. His primary target is the Great Society, but his bitterness infects all he sees"—(*N.Y. Times*). Peter Davison wrote in the *Atlantic*, "These poems have a calm surface, whether they be witty glosses on the Great Society or somber riddles about man and nature and history. The surpassing virtue of Nemerov's poetry has always been clarity rather than passion."

In 1958 he received the Oscar Blumenthal Prize, in 1959 the Harriet Monroe Memorial Prize, in 1961 the National Institute and American Academy Award in Literature, in 1962 the Golden Rose Trophy and in 1971 the Frank O'Hara Prize. A lively and uncompromising critic, he has selected for his "Poetry and Fiction: Essays" (*Rutgers Univ. Press* 1963 $7.50) his most important essays of the past decade, emphasizing 20th-century literature and the contemporary stance of the critic. Nemerov's most recent book of essays, "Reflexions on Poetry and Poetics" (*Rutgers Univ. Press* 1972 $10.00) again explores contemporary poetry. "Journal of the Fictive Life" (*Rutgers Univ. Press* 1965 $6.00) is Nemerov's somewhat grim introspective search for the conditions that make a writer most creative. "Poets on Poetry," ed. by Nemerov and others, (*Basic Bks.* 1965 $5.95) presents poems by leading poets, essays on trends in modern poetry and additional essays by Aiken, Wilber, Eberhart, Marianne Moore and others. Mr. Nemerov taught at Bennington College 1948–66. Since then he has been Professor of English at George Washington University in St. Louis.

NEW AND SELECTED POEMS. *Univ. of Chicago Press* 1960 $3.95 Phoenix Bks. 1963 pap. $1.95. Part 1 includes 15 new poems not heretofore collected; Part 2, poems selected from "The Salt Garden" (1955) and "Mirrors and Windows" (1958); Part 3, selected from "The Image and the Law" (1947) and "Guide to the Ruins" (1950), represents his early work.

THE BLUE SWALLOWS. Poems. *Univ. of Chicago Press* 1967 $4.50 Phoenix Bks. pap. $1.95

THE NEXT ROOM OF THE DREAM AND TWO PLAYS. *Univ. of Chicago Press* 1963 $5.00 Phoenix Bks. pap. $2.45. Poems and two poetic dramas: "Endor," and "Cain."

GNOMES AND OCCASIONS. *Univ. of Chicago Press* 1973 $5.95. Contains poetry which Allen Tate has called "subtle and profound."

Books about Nemerov

Howard Nemerov. Peter Mienke. *Univ. of Minnesota Press* 1968 pap. $1.25. The author gives a general critical outline on Nemerov and his works along with a selected bibliography of Nemerov's poetry, fiction, critical articles and reviews. A good beginning to a study of this poet.

The Shield of Perseus: The Vision and Imagination of Howard Nemerov. By Julia A. Bartholomay. *Univ. of Florida Press* 1971 $6.00

Critical Receptions of Howard Nemerov: A Selection of Essays and a Bibliography. Ed. by Bowie Duncan. *Scarecrow Press* 1971 $6.00. Duncan has collected essays by Julia Randall and Peter Meinke, and book reviews by Vivienne Koch, Robert Hillyer, Randall Jarrell, Joel Cannaroe and others. There is a bibliography by Duncan and an introduction by Reed Whittemore.

CARRUTH, HAYDEN. 1921–

Perhaps one of the most neglected of contemporary masters of poetry, Hayden Carruth is a solitary figure in American letters. He is unfortunately better known as an editor and critic than as a master of the modern poetic idiom. His technical prowess and highly attuned sensitivity to the fluctuation give his verse a kind of excitement and intensity in spite of its apparent calm and control. ". . . Carruth blends his tremendous and sensitive vocabulary (surely the largest and most extensive since Hart Crane's) with a mixture of cold steady fury and nightmarish passion in the presence of which I can do little more than record my amazement and gratitude"—(James Dickey). His work "represents an indispensible and—happily—increasingly honored achievement in American poetry"—(Lucien Stryk). His imagery derives from the rural landscape around him, and his pictures of winter and man among the shifting seasons are notable for their physicality as well as their feeling. "Where two boots labored yesterday across the snowdrifted pasture/ today each boothole is an offertory of bright seeds/ bittersweet yellowbirch hemlock pine thistle burning unconsumed."—(from "North Winter").

Carruth was born in Waterbury, Conn., and has received degrees from the Universities of North Carolina and Chicago. He has been editor of *Poetry* Magazine, associate editor for the *Univ. of Chicago Press*, and the project administrator for *International Publications*. He is a free lance editor, and has published many reviews in *Poetry, The Nation, Hudson Review*, and *The New Republic*. He is presently a resident of Vermont, and has recently edited "The Voice That Is Great within Us" (*see Anthologies of Poetry, this Chapter*).

He has been awarded numerous grants and poetry prizes, among them the Bess Hokin Prize, 1954, the Levinson Prize, 1958, the Harriet Monroe Poetry Prize with Yvor Winters, 1960–61, the Eunice Tietjens Memorial Prize, 1964, and the Morton Dauwen Zabel Prize, 1968.

BIRD POEM BOOK. *Saturday Review Press* 1970 $5.00

FOR YOU. *New Directions* 1970 $5.95 pap. $2.25

FROM SNOW AND ROCK, FROM CHAOS. *New Directions* 1973 $5.95 pap. $2.25

WILBUR, RICHARD. 1921–

"By general agreement Richard Wilbur is one of the most versatile and brilliant American poets to make his debut since World War II. His intelligence, imaginative agility, command of language, and flexibility of technique are awesome and frequently breathtaking. . . . [He] is a poet of ceaseless celebrations [and] he is deeply concerned with an experience of life and of the universe as sacramental"—(Ralph J. Mills, Jr.).

When Richard Wilbur's "Things of This World," which won the 1957 Pulitzer Prize, was chosen for the National Book Award the same year, the *N.Y. Times* commented editorially: "A seemingly effortless craftsman, Mr. Wilbur reveals a fine lyrical gift, a searching wit and, in his translations, a sympathetic kinship to the works of others." "Opposites," poems for children of all ages illustrated with numerous pictures, won him his second Pulitzer Prize in 1974. He was born in New York City, educated at Amherst and Harvard, and was on the English faculty at Harvard and Wellesley College.

Library Journal said that in "Advice to a Prophet" (1961, o.p.) there is "manifested the rare gift of making much from little and the power of transforming past, present, and future into a timelessness which is the essence of all real poetry." With this volume, he became the first (1961) holder of the Melville Cain Award, established in 1960. He is a member of the American Academy of Arts and Sciences and the National Institute of Arts and Letters. With Lillian Hellman he wrote the libretto for the opera "Candide." He has translated Molière's "Tartuffe" and "Misanthrope" and was a co-recipient of the Bollinger Translation prize in 1963. He has also translated many poems of Andrei Voznesensky and others from the Russian.

POEMS. *Harcourt* Harvest Bks. 1957 pap. $2.25

THINGS OF THIS WORLD. *Harcourt* 1956 $4.75. A selection from his poems.

OPPOSITES. *Harcourt* 1973 $3.75

WALKING TO SLEEP. *Harcourt* 1969 $4.95 Harvest Bks. pap. $1.45. New poems and translations. The translations include the works of Borges, Akhmatova, Villion, D'Orleans and Voznesensky.

THE POEMS OF RICHARD WILBUR. A recording read by the poet. *Spoken Arts* HC 747 $5.95

Books about Wilbur

Richard Wilbur. By Donald Hill. United States Authors Ser. *Twayne* 1967 $4.95 *College & Univ. Press* pap. $2.45
Richard Wilbur: A Bibliographic Checklist. By John P. Field. *Kent State Univ. Press* 1971 $4.50

MOSS, HOWARD. 1922–

Poetry Editor of the *New Yorker* magazine since 1948, Howard Moss has been described as "a sophisticated poet of many parts and writing styles; . . . it is pleasurable to read clean, clear, compact lines about ordinary events. . ."—(Harry Roskolenko).

Born in New York City, Moss was educated at the University of Michigan, Harvard University, the University of Wisconsin and Columbia University. Recipient of the Janet Sewall Davis Award from *Poetry Chicago* (1944), the National Institute of Arts and Letters Award in creative writing, 1968, and the National Book Award for Poetry for "Selected Poems," 1972; he is also lauded for his critical works, such as "The Magic Lantern of Marcel Proust" (1962. *Grosset* Univ. Lib. pap. $1.95); he edited "The Poet's Story" (*Macmillan* 1973 $9.95), "The Selected Poems of John Keats" (*Dell* Laurel Leaf Lib. 1952 $.40) and "Writing against Time: Critical Essays and Reviews" (*Morrow* 1969 $5.00; *Apollo* 1969 pap. $1.95).

"Howard Moss is . . . the pioneer and respected possessor of a lucid compressed poetic style that expresses a dynamic sensitivity to his world"—(Carol Bergé).

SECOND NATURE. *Atheneum* 1968 $4.50 pap. $1.95

SELECTED POEMS. *Atheneum* 1971 $6.95

DICKEY, JAMES. 1923–

James Dickey is a colorful personality and one of the strongest voices in poetry America has recently produced. An exponent of free verse and not an "easy" poet, he is apparently not too difficult for a host of poetry lovers. By May, 1967, *Wesleyan Univ. Press* had sold 20,566 copies of his volumes of verse.

Born in Atlanta, Ga., Mr. Dickey was a pilot in World War II and the Korean War. He spent six years in advertising, which he gave up in 1961. He was educated at Vanderbilt University and has taught at Rice Institute and the University of Florida. He has been poet-in-residence at Reed and at San Fernando State colleges, writer-in-residence at the University of Wisconsin and Consultant in Poetry in English to the Library of Congress from 1966 to 1968. *Library Journal* said of "Helmets": "The helmet is the protector of the warrior, implement of multiple uses, collector of thoughts, marker of graves, common emblem of position, as well as other things. Dickey changes helmets often and deftly. His subjects, like the steel hat, are rugged, simple, and noble. . . . He follows the single object to its ultimate relation: he sees the farm through the fence surrounding it, the horror of war through an abandoned helmet. The bite of his poems is sudden and sure; he seeks not to lift the reader to the plateau of ultimate meaning but to confront him with the significance of experience and the silent dramas performing in stilled objects. His images are often grotesque and fantastic. . . . These are tough poems that insist on the attention of the reader long after the book has been put away." "Buckdancer's Choice" won both the Melville Cane Award and the National Book Award in 1966, the latter "for the clarity, subtlety and passion with which he has used the imagination and the craft of the poet to explore a diverse vision of contemporary experience and extend the resources of poetry."

"Poems 1957–1967" contains verse from his previous collections, including the entire "Buckdancer's Choice," "here augmented by enough new poems for another whole volume. The new poems are stronger and darker in mood than the earlier ones, but some of the same themes—animals in the wild, snakes and snakebite, the father-and-son tie, the perceptive sense of the blind—reappear in different form. The title poem of the newest section, 'Falling,' is a transfixing picture of a woman hurtling thousands of feet through air from a plane when the door accidentally opened. (This poem, based on an actual happening—the woman was an airline stewardess—appeared recently in the New Yorker). The collection will facilitate critics' comparison of James Dickey's styles and help them to trace his preoccupations and to perceive his use of the deep southern countryside as an important source of his images"—(PW). Louis Untermeyer notes that "the impact of an event, personally experienced or experienced through others, acts upon Dickey like a welcome blow. He has an immediate response to violence as if he were glad to be challenged to equal vehemence, as if he believed that men were living more and more lifelessly, dependent on mechanical things to do their work, their entertaining, and what is left of their thinking." Mr. Dickey is the author of four collections of critical essays, "The Suspect in Poetry" (1964, o.p.), "Babel to Byzantium: Poets and Poetry Now" (Farrar, Straus 1968 $6.95; Grosset 1971 pap. $2.95; Octagon 1973 $10.50) which discusses some 80 contemporary British and American poets, "The Self as Agent" (1970, o.p.) and "Sorties: Journals and New Essays" (Doubleday 1971 $6.95). Mr. Dickey's opinions on poets and poetry are clear and definite. Describing the Beat poets to a N.Y. Times interviewer, he called them "hopelessly bad"; Theodore Roethke is his great admiration among recent American poets. "Writing is a continuous act with me," he said "[I write] late at night, early in the morning, at home, on streetcars or buses." His Library of Congress post has recently taken him to Australia and other parts of the world as an American cultural ambassador. He lives in Virginia with his wife and two sons. James Dickey's first novel, "Deliverance" (Houghton 1970 $5.95; Dell pap. $1.25) is now a major motion picture starring Burt Reynolds and featuring an appearance by Dickey himself as a backwoods sheriff.

DROWNING WITH OTHERS. Wesleyan Univ. Press 1962 $4.75 pap. $2.45

HELMETS. Wesleyan Univ. Press 1964 $4.75 pap. $2.45

BUCKDANCER'S CHOICE. Wesleyan Univ. Press 1965 $4.75 pap. $2.45

POEMS 1957–1967. Wesleyan Univ. Press $9.95; Macmillan Collier bks. pap. $1.95

EYE-BEATERS, BLOOD, VICTORY, MADNESS, BUCKHEAD, AND MERCY. Doubleday 1970 $4.95 signed limited ed. $25.00 pap. $2.45

SELF-INTERVIEWS. Ed. by Barbara and James Reiss. Doubleday 1970 $5.95; Dell Delta Bks. 1972 pap. $2.25. The poet's criticism of his own work and his opinions on the work of others.

Books about Dickey

James Dickey: A Checklist. By Franklin Ashley. Gale 1973 $11.00. A bibliographic work.

DUGAN, ALAN. 1923–

The Saturday Review said of this first volume, "Poems," by a young native New Yorker: "His poetry is a special way of looking at things. . . . Through personal experience of war he shapes universal messages, while he takes history, religion, and mythology and gives them an intimate meaning." This book won the National Book Award and the Pulitzer Prize in 1962, and in the same year the poet won a Fellowship in Literature at the American Academy in Rome. The N.Y. Times found that in "Poems 2" (1963, o.p.) Dugan reveals "a sharp eye for the sights and sounds of New York." In "Poems 3" Dugan "writes with an anger at society that moves from artless outcry to black resignation in the face of the world's evils, and back again"—(SR). Of this volume Peter Davison wrote in the Atlantic: "Alan Dugan is one of the most consistent poets of his generation—consistent even in his inconsistencies. He writes in personas, each an extension of himself, the most powerful and productive of which is still that of the army veteran, the conscript, the shanghaied, the scapegoat: 'tradition is for the rich/ to love, the clerks/ to ape, the poor/ to suffer. . : .' Though his subjects and situations vary widely, the outcome and the moral are mostly the same. He is a closed-end poet who starts his verses with striking titles and finishes them off with the air of having temporarily delayed an avalanche. His language is strong, his style pungent, and he does what he sets out to do. I mean this as praise. In 'Poems 3' . . . he continues to mine the veins of style and subject he struck in his first two books, and there is no reason to expect or require that he turn in a different direction in future." "The Collected Poems" gathers the poetry of "Poems" 1, 2 and 3 into one volume.

COLLECTED POEMS. *Yale Univ. Press* 1969 pap. $2.95. Poems from three earlier books: "Poems," "Poems 2," "Poems 3."

POEMS. Fwd. by Dudley Fitts. *AMS Press* $8.50

POEMS 3. *Yale Univ. Press* 1967 $5.00 pap. $1.45

HECHT, ANTHONY. 1923–

Anthony Hecht was born in New York, educated at Bard College and Columbia, and published his first book of poems, "A Summoning of Stones" (o.p.), in 1954. The poet Richard Wilbur said of this work, "His characteristic performance is an extended and ornate essay-poem, full of ingeniously linked materials from art, literature and travel; the form is commonly intricate; the execution is excellent"—(*N.Y. Times*). The composer Leo Smits set a number of these poems to music as "A Choir of Starlings." Mr. Hecht's second book, "The Hard Hours," won the 1968 Pulitzer Prize for Poetry. "These poems are ornate, brocaded, stately, and beautiful, but they also have the capacity to strike on the nerve: 'What the intelligence/ Works out in pure delight/ The body must learn in pain' "—(*Atlantic*). This volume marked a transition in his manner; as Ted Hughes, the English poet, has said, "This most fastidious and elegant of poets shed every artifice and began to write with absolutely raw simplicity and directness. Only a poet with an immense burden of something to say ever dreams of taking this course and only an inspired artist can bring it off. The result here has been some of the most powerful and unforgettable poems at present being written in America." Allen Tate wrote: "I can only say that whoever else may be at the top, Hecht is there too; for there is nobody better."

With the poet John Hollander, Mr. Hecht has edited a collection of limericks, "Jiggery-Pokery: A Compendium of Double Dactyls" (*Atheneum* 1967 $3.95). He has received the Brandeis University Creative Arts Award and the 1968 Loines Award for poetry from the American Academy of Arts and Letters.

THE HARD HOURS. *Atheneum* 1967 pap. $3.95. Includes a number of poems from his first volume, "A Summoning of Stones," and seven woodcuts by Leonard Baskin.

AESOPIC. *Grossman* (Gehenna Press) 1968 limited ed. $25.00. Twenty-four couplets to accompany the Thomas Bewick Wood engravings for "Select Fables" with an afterword on the blocks by Philip Hofer. A beautiful book. Short poems.

LEVERTOV, DENISE. 1923–

Born in Essex, England, Denise Levertov became an American after her marriage to Mitchell Goodman (the writer indicted, for his antiwar activities, with Dr. Spock and the Rev. William Sloane Coffin). She came to New York to live in 1948. She has written of herself, "My mother was descended from the Welsh tailor and mystic Angel Jones of Mold, my father from the noted Hasid Schneour Zalman (d. 1831), 'the Rav of Northern White Russia.' My father had experienced conversion to Christianity as a student. . . . He was a priest of the Anglican church. . . . I did lessons at home and never attended any school or college, except for some years at a ballet school."

She acknowledges as influential to her writing the poets Wallace Stevens, William Carlos Williams, Charles Olson, Robert Duncan, the religious philosopher Martin Buber and certain painters. She is one of a group of poets who "aim at an expression of the most personal kind of experience, an authentic statement about themselves, what they see and know, suffer and love; their responses to things, relationships, and heightened instants of their lives. [Miss Levertov is] one whose art, fresh and compelling, convinces us of her genuine rapport with the reality she presents at its core. Her poetry is frequently a tour through the familiar and the mundane until their unfamiliarity and otherworldliness suddenly strike us. Her imaginative gaze feasts on the small objects we usually treat as insignificant appendages to our lives, or pauses with affectionate interest on the seemingly trivial activities in which we spend so much of those lives"—(Ralph J. Mills, Jr.). She herself says, "I long for poems of an inner harmony in utter contrast to the chaos in which they exist." Her theme in "The Sorrow Dance" is the problem of coming to terms with life's tragedy, waste and grief. The first section is written in memory of her sister, the second expresses her troubled reactions to the Vietnamese War. Many of the poems in "O Taste and See" are "intimate perceptions of things about her; most striking is her ability to mingle sensitivity and beauty"—(*LJ*). "Relearning the Alphabet" is her first major collection after "The Sorrow Dance." It reflects the poet's growing public political consciousness. "To Stay

Alive" contains some poems from "Relearning the Alphabet," and some from "The Sorrow Dance." It primarily reflects the author's experience in the sixties and early seventies in the resistance movement with which she has become increasingly involved. "The Poet in the World" (*New Directions* 1973 $6.95 pap. $2.45) is essays gathered from various magazines and anthologies on the nature of poetry and its creation. With Edward C. Dimock she has edited "In Praise of Krishna: Songs from the Bengali" (*Doubleday* 1972 Anchor Bks. pap. $1.25).

After her first book, "The Double Image" (o.p.), was published in England in 1946, Miss Levertov did not produce a volume until 1957, when *City Lights* brought out "Here and Now" (o.p.). Much published in little magazines, Miss Levertov has steadily accumulated an audience for her poetry. In 1961 she was Poetry Editor for the *Nation*, and in 1965 she received the Grant in Literature from the National Institute of Arts and Letters. She has read her poems at the poetry centers of New York and San Francisco as well as at many colleges. In 1966–67 she was Visiting Lecturer in English at Vassar College.

WITH EYES IN THE BACK OF OUR HEADS. *New Directions* 1960 pap. $1.50

THE JACOB'S LADDER. *New Directions* 1961 pap. $1.55

O TASTE AND SEE. *New Directions* 1964 $1.75 pap. $1.50

THE SORROW DANCE. *New Directions* 1967 pap. $1.75

RELEARNING THE ALPHABET. *New Directions* 1970 $4.75 pap. $1.75

TO STAY ALIVE. *New Directions* 1971 $6.50 pap. $1.95

FOOTPRINTS: Poems. *New Directions* 1972 $5.00 pap. $1.75. A book of reflective poems written concurrently with "Relearning the Alphabet" and "To Stay Alive."

Books about Levertov

Denise Levertov. By Linda Welshimer Wagner. United States Authors Ser. *Twayne* 1967 $4.95; *College & Univ. Press* pap. $2.45

A Bibliography of Denise Levertov. Comp. by Robert Wilson. The Phoenix Bibliographers. *The Phoenix Book Shop* (18 Cornelia St., New York, N.Y.) 1972 $3.00

LOGAN, JOHN. 1923–

John Logan's poetry "evinces a remarkable quality of tenderness, of genuine love of creation"—(Robert Boyars). Perhaps the most outstanding spokesman for "poetry of the heart," Logan is one of the most wrongly neglected poets and influences of his generation.

Born in Red Oak, Iowa, educated at Coe College, the University of Iowa (Iowa City) and Georgetown University, Logan found inspiration for his early poetical works in his conversion to Catholicism. Influenced primarily by Rainer Maria Rilke, his poetry has moved from a religious formalistic style to a freedom of line and voice achieved by few other modern poets. He is a skilled technician with a clear and precise ear and a penchant for wit and puns both auditory and conceptual. Most renowned as a teacher, John Logan's students already number some of the most outstanding poets of the younger generation including Bill Knott (St. Geraud) (*q.v.*), Naomi Lazard, Barbara Harr, Bill Hunt, Phil Dow and Nathan Whiting, (*q.v.*).

The spiritual and artistic life of others (Keats, Heine, Rimbaud) as well as the current state of his own heart combine to form his subject matter. His poem "The Search" reveals his quest for love and communion with others, particularly his anonymous readers, in moments of extreme tenderness and delicacy: "When I was young I thought/ I wanted (yearned for) older age./ Now I think I hunt with so much rage/ that I will risk or lose/ family or friends for the ghost of my youth." And he says of his own work: "I think of poetry as a reaching, an anonymous loving which becomes personal when there are those present who care to listen."

Editor of *Choice* a major magazine of poetry and photography, Logan has received an Indiana School of Letters Fellowship (1965, 1969); the Miles Modern Poetry Award (1967); and a Rockefeller Grant (1968). He presently resides in Buffalo, N.Y., where he teaches at the State University. He is active on the poetry reading circuit and has read at The Poetry Center of the YMHA in New York City, and has taught poetry workshops there from time to time.

GHOSTS OF THE HEART. *Univ. of Chicago Press* 1960 $3.50 Phoenix Bks. pap. $1.50

ZIG-ZAG WALK: Poems, 1963–1968. *Dutton* 1969 pap. $2.95

THE ANONYMOUS LOVER. *Liveright* 1973 $5.95 pap. $2.95

SIMPSON, LOUIS. 1923–

Born in the British West Indies in 1923, Simpson became an American citizen while serving in the U.S. Army for which he had volunteered in 1943. Considered "one of the principal poets now writing"—(Richard Ellmann and Robert O'Clair) he draws his material from the daily events of his own life. Several of his best-known poems are "war" poems dealing with the hardness, brutality, and "the other side of glory," as he expressed it. There are strains of imagism and surrealism in his basically realistic verse, and as one critic noted, he "appears to stand between the New World and the Old, the present and the past, the mythical and the real . . . to radiate ironies"—(John Woods). The fact that he is a naturalized citizen contributes to the objective clarity with which he views America in his work. His poetry is typified above all by an innate musicality and sensitivity to the American idiom, evident in his earlier rhymed verses. Educated at Munro College in Jamaica and at Columbia, Simpson has been an editor at *Bobbs-Merrill* and taught at Columbia, Berkeley, and Stony Brook. His awards include a Hudson Review fellowship, 1957; the Millay Award, 1960; a Guggenheim Fellowship, 1962 and 1970; and the Pulitzer Prize for Poetry, for "At the End of the Open Road," 1964.

He co-edited with Robert Pack and Donald Hall "New Poets of England and America," (*World Pub.* Meridian Bks. 2 vols. First Selection pap. $3.95; Second Selection 1962 pap. $4.95) first published in 1957, and is well-known for his "An Introduction to Poetry" (1968. *St. Martin's* 2nd ed. 1972 text ed. pap. $3.95).

SELECTED POEMS. *Harcourt* 1965 $4.95 Harvest Bks. pap. $1.45. Includes poems from "The Arrivistes" (1949, o.p.) "Good News of Death" (1955, o.p.) "A Dream of Governors," "At the End of the Open Road" and new poems.

A DREAM OF GOVERNORS. Poetry Program Ser. *Wesleyan Univ. Press* 1959 $4.75 pap. $2.45

AT THE END OF THE OPEN ROAD. Poetry Program Ser. *Wesleyan Univ. Press* 1963 $4.75 pap. $2.45

ADVENTURE OF THE LETTER I. *Harper* 1972 pap. $2.25

NORTH OF JAMAICA: Autobiographical memoirs. *Harper* 1972 $6.95

Books about Simpson

Louis Simpson. By Ronald Moran. *Twayne* 1972 $5.50. This first book-length study of Louis Simpson analyses the poems in the light of their American and historical context and the early influence of Jamaica. A chronology and bibliography are included.

WHALEN, PHILIP. 1923–

A classmate of Gary Snyder's at Reed College in Oregon, Philip Whalen is closely associated in style and subject matter with the poets of the San Francisco Renaissance. He has often been compared to Gary Snyder, but their work actually differs markedly. While Snyder writes calmly, with a singleness of purpose, Whalen concentrates on an open form made visually distinctive with the use of capitals and odd arrangements of phrases and words. The freshness of new experience is conveyed, and a sense of immediacy and clarity pervades. At times his work borders on the surreal, and yet never loses its concrete, tangible reality.

"A hummy-bird attacks the redwood trees
              CLOUDS!   look
How dark it is, it will rain it is so dark
Something must happen
Earthquake, volcanic manifestations"—(from "How Beautiful").

Whalen was born in Portland, Oreg., and after serving in the Air Force (1943–46), got his degree in 1951. He has taught intermittently and lived for some time in Kyoto, Japan. He is the recipient of a Poets Foundation Award (1967), American Academy of Arts and Letters Grant-in-Aid (1965), and Committee on Poetry Grant-in-Aid (1968).

ON BEAR'S HEAD: Poems 1950–1967. *Harcourt* 1969 $17.50. Harvest Bks. pap. $3.95. Includes "Like I Say," "Memoirs of an Interglacial Age," "Braincandy," "Every Day," "Vanilla," "The Winter."

EVERY DAY: Poems. 1965. *Serendipity* pap. $1.75

SCENES OF LIFE AT THE CAPITAL. *Grey Fox Press* 1971 $5.00 pap. $2.50

CORMAN, CID. 1924–

Cid Corman was born in Boston and educated at Tufts College, the Universities of Michigan and North Carolina, and at the Sorbonne in Paris. He has taught in Europe and Japan, where he now lives, and his travels are reflected in the French, Italian, and Japanese echoes heard in his poetry. Best known as the editor of *Origin* magazine ("No poetry magazine has been better edited"—[Kenneth Rexroth]), which carried on when *Black Mountain Review* ceased publication, Corman provided the proving ground for the major poets of a whole generation: Charles Olson, Robert Duncan, Robert Creeley, Denise Levertov and Louis Zukofsky. Corman has received the Hapgood Award in poetry, University of Michigan 1946–47, and the Chapelbrook Foundation Grant, 1967–69.

The Japanese influence is reflected in the clear concise quality of Corman's poetry, like the haiku, and in the quiet nonintellectual ambience of the spirit of Zen. And as a disciple of William Carlos Williams, Corman's work arises out of the presence of things which hold in themselves the ultimate secrets of their own reality. At times his poems are filled with whimsy and humor: "Call it a louse—I'm/ not so fussy about/ the nomenclature/ of small insects. This one,/ crushed, at any rate,/ between pages, looks/ more like a period/ than a former creature—/ but its pause has legs." Corman is a prolific poet, writing short poems with short lines, and an essayist whose work has appeared in various magazines. He has translated, with Kaamia e Susuna, from the Japanese "Frogs and Others" by Kusano Shimpei (A Mushinsha Bk. *Grossman* 1969 $8.95) and the famed "Roads to Far Towns" by Basho (A Mushinsha Bk. *Grossman* 1971 $8.50 pap. $3.95) as well as the French poet René Char's "Leaves of Hypnos" (A Mushinsha Bk. *Grossman* 1973 $20.00 pap. $5.95).

NONCE. *Elizabeth Press* 1965 pap. $6.00

STEAD. *Elizabeth Press* 1966 pap. $6.00

FOR GRANTED. *Elizabeth Press* 1967 pap. $4.00

& WITHOUT END. *Elizabeth Press* 1968 $4.00

NO LESS. *Elizabeth Press* 1968 pap. $4.00

NO MORE. *Elizabeth Press* 1969 pap. $4.00

LIVINGDYING. *New Directions* 1970 $5.00 signed limited ed. $25.00 pap. $1.75

NIGH. *Elizabeth Press* 1970 pap. $4.00

PLIGHT. *Elizabeth Press* 1970 $5.00

SUN ROCK MAN. *New Directions* 1970 pap. $1.75

WORDS FOR EACH OTHER. 1967. *Transatlantic* 1971 pap. $2.95

BE QUEST. *Elizabeth Press* 1972 signed ed. $7.00 pap. $5.00

OUT AND OUT. *Elizabeth Press* 1972 $16.00 pap. $8.00

SO FAR. *Elizabeth Press* 1973 signed ed. $8.00 pap. $6.00

KAUFMAN, BOB. 1925–

In France Bob Kaufman has been called the "Black American Rimbaud." His reputation abroad, like several of the Beats, is greater than in his native United States.

Born in New Orleans, Kaufman came from an unusual family, his father an orthodox German Jew and his mother a Martinique Negress of the Catholic faith. At 13 he left home to go to sea and sailed for 20 years with the Merchant Marine. During those years the older crewmen imparted to him a taste for literature. He fell in with the Beats in the fifties in Los Angeles and became part of the California "renaissance." He gave frequent poetry readings during that period and edited the now historical beat magazine *Beatitude*.

Kaufman's poetry is textured with the rhythms and music of the jazz and blues idioms. His use of repetitive and precise physically concrete images and pictures from his life makes for a primarily oral, strangely biblical poetry.

"Solitudes Crowded with Loneliness" and "Golden Sardine" "are amongst the best products of the Beat Generation"—(Kenneth Rexroth.)

SOLITUDES CROWDED WITH LONELINESS. *New Directions* 1965 $1.95

GOLDEN SARDINE. *City Lights Books* 1967 pap. $1.50

KOCH, KENNETH. 1925–

Born in Cincinnati, Ohio, Kenneth Koch began writing at the age of 5, and became serious about it at the age of 17. After serving in the Army he received his B.A. from Harvard, and later, his Ph.D. at Columbia where he now teaches. He is best known for his work with children. He has taught creative writing to children, and using works of his own pupils as examples, has written several books on the subject, notably "Wishes, Lies and Dreams: Teaching Children to Write Poetry" (*Random* [Chelsea House] 1970 $7.95 Vintage Bks. pap. $1.95), and the most recent "Rose, Where Do You Get That Red"? (*Random* 1973 $7.95). Koch is the recipient of a Fullbright Fellowship (1950–51), a Guggenheim Fellowship (1961), and an Ingram-Merrill Foundation Fellowship (1969).

He is associated with the New York School of Poets. Much of his early work was obscure, influenced largely by Jacques Prévert among others, but since then his poetry has taken on a simpler and more realistic style. It is "remarkably inventive and accurate . . . fixed in his poems is a depth of metaphysical concern that gives them the drive and intensity of genuinely serious experiments"—(Hayden Carruth).

Like other New York poets, Koch has been actively interested in theater, and many of his plays, including "Little Red Riding Hood," "The Election," and "Perides" have been performed by off-Broadway groups. "Bertha and Other Plays" was published by *Grove Press* in 1966 (o.p.).

THANK YOU AND OTHER POEMS. *Grove* 1962. Evergreen Bks. pap. $1.95

KO, OR A SEASON ON EARTH. *Grove* 1969. Evergreen Books pap. $1.95. A comic poem of epic length and spirit.

THE PLEASURES OF PEACE AND OTHER POEMS. *Grove* 1969. Evergreen Bks. pap. $1.95

MERRILL, JAMES. 1925–

James Merrill was born in New York and attended Amherst College, where he later spent a year teaching English. An extensive traveler, he has lived in Italy, and now divides his time between Stonington, Conn., and Greece. In "First Poems" (1951, o. p.), "Merrill's images derive from both Symbolist and metaphysical sources—substances such as glass, crystal, and flint are linked with apparatuses of one kind or another (compasses, barometers, spectrums, and hourglasses)—and he speaks of 'the machinery of light' and 'the machinery of decay' "—(Louise Bogan, in the *New Yorker*). Miss Bogan found them "impeccably written [but] frigid and dry as diagrams." Rolfe Humphries said in the *Nation:* "Mr. Merrill is a young poet who writes very proficiently indeed; he has a wealth of vocabulary and illusion, yet does not verbalize, does not gush, is not sentimental." William Meredith said of "The Country of a Thousand Years of Peace and Other Poems." (*Atheneum* new ed. 1970 pap. $2.95), "It is clear that from behind a mask of wit and urbanity speaks a serious philosopher, perhaps even a moralist." *Poetry* found the poems in "Water Street" "slow, thoughtful confrontations of the self, which have the solemnity of a man addressing his own awareness rather than a less formidable audience of imagined others." "Nights and Days" won Mr. Merrill a 1967 National Book Award for "his scrupulous and uncompromising cultivation of the poetic art, evidenced in his refusal to settle for an easy and profitable stance; for insistence on taking the tough poetic chances which make the difference between esthetic failure or success." Of this volume, the *N.Y. Times* wrote: "He can be self-deprecatory, impressionistic, and surreal. And he can describe both the breakup of a home and an eagle's seizure of a lamb with utmost technical ease."

Mr. Merrill's play, "The Immortal Husband," has been performed off-Broadway. He has written two novels, "The Seraglio" (1957, o. p.), about an aging businessman, and "The (Diblos) Notebook" (*Atheneum* 1965 $4.50; *Popular Lib.* pap. $.60), which was a runner-up for the 1966 National Book Award in fiction. Set in Greece, it concerns a young man "who believes that the materials of his life and family provide him with the essentials of a novel if faithfully recorded and remembered and revised in a notebook. [He] finds that at the end of his stay on Diblos, a tiny, primitive Greek island, he has achieved in sorrow and inner searching that rare thing, a work of worth. [The book] deserves to be read because it is skillful and beautiful, and these qualities are rare"—(*Choice*).

WATER STREET. *Atheneum* 1962 pap. $1.65

NIGHTS AND DAYS. *Atheneum* 1966 $2.45

FIRE SCREEN. *Atheneum* 1969 pap $3.95

BRAVING THE ELEMENTS. *Atheneum* 1972 $5.95. A collection of 24 poems.

AMMONS, A. R. 1926–

Considered to be an "American Romantic in the tradition of Emerson and Whitman"—(Daniel Hoffman), A. R. Ammons easily communicates to men of science as well as men of letters. After attending Wake Forest College he studied at the University of California (Berkeley) and later became an executive in the biological glass industry. Since 1964 he has taught at Cornell and his "Collected Poems 1951–1971" won a National Book Award for poetry in 1973.

His work synthesizes the scientific and literary sides of experience; his first book was entitled "Ommateum" (1955, o.p.) meaning the eye of an insect.

His use of images of nature to impart his perception of human ambiguity is similar to Robert Frost's. He types his poems rather than handwrites them; his "Tape for the Turn of The Year" was typed on a roll of adding machine tape and is an experimental book-length piece. Its "combination . . . of memory, introspection, and observation, rendered in an everchanging musical phrasing is impressive"—(Daniel Hoffman).

The brief metaphysical fable is a characteristic poem style or genre which leads to interesting interplays on the connectedness between nature and man. "So it came time/ for me to cede myself/ and I chose/ the wind/ to be delivered to . . ."—(from "Mansion"). His poems of the sea and the immediate land environs are unusually rich in the feeling of man and sea and marsh and inlet as one web of life and spirit.

Collected Poems, 1951–1971. *Norton* 1972 $12.50. Winner of the National Book Award in 1973.

SELECTED POEMS. *Cornell Univ. Press* 1968 $6.95 pap. $2.95

EXPRESSIONS OF SEA LEVEL. *Ohio State Univ. Press* 1964 $4.00

CORSON'S INLET. *Cornell Univ. Press* 1965 $4.95

TAPE FOR THE TURN OF THE YEAR. *Cornell Univ. Press* 1965 $5.95; *Norton* 1972 pap. $2.25

NORTHFIELD POEMS. *Cornell Univ. Press* 1966 $4.95

BRIEFINGS. *Norton* 1970 $6.00 pap. $1.95

UPLANDS: New Poems. *Norton* 1970 pap. $1.95

BLACKBURN, PAUL. 1926–1971

Considered one of the "best practitioners" of the Black Mountain School of poetry, Paul Blackburn might even be considered the master of ordinary common speech usage in poetry during the last decade. His innate musicality and rhythmic sense give a depth and beauty to the kind of verse that in poets with a lesser ear falls into monotonous flatness. His language is precise and at times prosaic but suddenly will turn poetic with an unexpected pleasant use of rhyme. Although Blackburn was born in St. Albans, Vt., he was really a city poet. His poems bustle with the landscape of park benches, lampposts and especially people: crowds, children, subway riders.

Blackburn was educated at New York University and the University of Wisconsin. In 1954 he travelled to France on a Fullbright Fellowship and studied in Toulouse, later serving there as *lecteur américain*. He traveled and lived in Spain and Morocco, and after his return to New York City he was grouped with the East Side poets in the sixties. In New York he taught at City College.

A brilliant translator he has published an excellent rendition of *The Cid.* Presently in print are his translations of Julie Cortazar and other Latin American poets. Blackburn died of cancer in 1971.

THE CITIES. *Grove* Evergreen Bks. 1967 pap. $2.95. An impressive collection of poems.

IN, ON OR ABOUT THE PREMISES. Cape Goliard Poetry Ser. *Grossman* 1968 $4.50 pap. $2.95. A collection of poems originally intended for British publication, so duplicates to some degree "The Cities."

EARLY SELECTED Y MAS: Collected Poems, 1949–1961. *Black Sparrow* 1972 signed ed. $15.00 pap. $4.00

BLY, ROBERT. 1926–

Robert Bly was born in Minnesota and has lived on a farm there; he now lives in Madison, Minn., where he edits *The Seventies* magazine, which he founded as *The Fifties* and in the next decade called *The Sixties*. In 1966, with David Ray, he organized the American Writers against the Vietnam War. "A pungent critic, an undaunted moralist, a hackled dissenter, he is a sworn enemy of worldliness in the conduct of life and in the conduct of poetry"—(*Atlantic*). "He is a poet of Western space, solitude, and silence. He writes poems about driving a car through Ohio, hunting pheasants, watering a horse, getting up early in the morning, and watching Minnesota cornfields, lakes, and woods under the siege of rain, snow, and sun. His distinction in treating these subjects lies in the freshness of his 'deep images,' which invest the scene he describes with an intense subjectivity and a feeling of the irremediable loneliness of man, who can never make contact with the things of the world"—(Stephen Stepanchev). In "Silence in the Snowy Fields," he conveys "the inhumanly cold atmosphere of the Minnesota winter, say: a sparse landscape, the isolation of human beings in the countryside, the importance (and treacherousness) of one's automobile and the roads that will get one to the post office in the village and back again"—(M. L. Rosenthal). "The Light around the Body," which won the National Book Award in 1968, "is strongly critical of the war in Vietnam, of the callousness of American foreign policy in other areas and of the general tenor of American life"—(*N.Y. Times*).

Mr. Bly is a translator of Scandinavian literature, his most recent translation being "Twenty Poems of Tomas Transtromer" (*Seventies Press* [dist. by Book People] $3.00 pap. $2.00). Through the *Sixties Press* and currently the *Seventies Press* he has introduced little-known European and South American poets to American readers. *The Sixties,* now *The Seventies*, has been the center of a poetic movement involving the poets Donald Hall, Louis Simpson, James Wright and James Dickey (as well as Mr. Bly)—*see introduction to this Chapter*.

SILENCE IN THE SNOWY FIELDS. *Wesleyan Univ. Press* 1962 $4.75 pap $2.45

THE LIGHT AROUND THE BODY. *Harper* 1967 $3.95 pap. $2.25

MORNING GLORY: Prose Poems. 1969. *Kayok* 1970 pap. $1.50. Twelve prose poems with drawings by Tomi de Paola.

TEETH-MOTHER NAKED AT LAST. 1970 *City Lights Books* pap. $1.00

JUMPING OUT OF BED. *Barre Pub.* 1972 $7.95 pap. $3.95

SLEEPERS JOINING HANDS (originally "Shadow-Mothers"). 1970. *Harper* 1972 $5.95 pap. $2.95

OLD MAN RUBBING HIS EYES. *Unicorn Press* 1973 $6.00 pap. $3.00. Twenty new poems with twenty drawings by Franz Richter.

(And others) MCGRATH. *Stone-Marrow* 1972 pap. $2.00. Selected critical studies of the book "Letter to an Imaginary Friend."

THE SEA AND THE HONEYCOMB. *Beacon* 1971 $5.95 pap. $2.45. A book of tiny poems. Poems by Quasimodo, D. H. Lawrence, Machado, Issa with originals of foreign language poems at back of volume.

FORTY POEMS TOUCHING ON AMERICAN HISTORY. *Beacon Press* $5.95 pap. $2.45

CREELEY, ROBERT. 1926–

Robert Creeley, who has a large readership, is one of the poets known as the "Black Mountain group," who came to know each other while teaching or studying at Black Mountain College. He is a former editor of the *Black Mountain Review*. "Of all the poets associated with Charles Olson in the projective-verse movement [*see introduction to this Chapter*], Robert Creeley is the most laconic, bare, and tangential in phrasing, the least interested in rendering, dramatizing, and persuading. . . . His major subject is love, or, rather, the transformations of love that occur as a man moves from courtship to marriage, responsibility, habit, and fatherhood. His poems describe the transports, disenchantments, crises of trust, hopes, and despairs of the love relationship, which is often made to bear a greater weight than it is capable of bearing"—(Stephen Stepanchev, in "American Poetry Since 1945"). "Words," said *Book Week*, "shows a growing seriousness of tone, a willingness also to experiment with longer lines and multi-part poems," but Peter Davison (in the *At-*

lantic) and Thomas Lask (in the *N.Y. Times*) felt that Creeley's elliptical and flat approach was narrowing him into a corner. "A battle against glibness has been won but at a terrible price: almost all the organs of language have been removed," said Davison. And M. L. Rosenthal has said "It all seems too confined to settle for just yet."

Mr. Creeley was born in Massachusetts, attended Harvard, and has lived abroad in France, Spain and Guatemala, and, during World War II, in India and Burma where he served in the American Field Service. In 1960 he won the Levinson Prize. He has written a novel, "The Island" (*Scribner* 1963 pap. $2.45) concerning the shifting marital moods of an American husband and wife in Mallorca, where Mr. Creeley himself once ran *Divers Press*, and a collection of short stories, "Gold Diggers" (*Scribner* 1965 pap. $2.45). He has taught English at the University of New Mexico in Albuquerque and at the State University of New York at Buffalo.

FOR LOVE. *Scribner* 1962 pap. $1.95

WORDS. *Scribner* 1967 pap. $2.95

CHARM: Early and Uncollected Poems. *Four Seasons Foundation* 1968 pap. $2.50. Preface by Creeley. Seventy-five poems.

PIECES: Poems by Robert Creeley. *Scribner* 1969 $4.50 pap. $1.95. Poems which form one long poem.

(With Arthur Okamura) 1234567890. *Shambola Pubns.* 1971 $12.50 pap. $2.95. An elegant book profusely illustrated by Arthur Okamura; One long poem by Creeley.

ST. MARTIN'S. *Black Sparrow* 1971 pap. $3.00. Fifteen poems.

A DAY BOOK. *Scribner* 1972 $6.95 pap. $3.95. Part one is prose, part two poems, all drawn in somewhat fragmented journal form from the author's daily life.

GINSBERG, ALLEN. 1926–

"I saw the best minds of my generation destroyed by madness . . . ." So begin the prophetic intonations of "Howl," Allen Ginsberg's strong indictment of his society, which he here experiences at the level of its "dregs." "Howl," now acclaimed as "The Waste Land" of our age," was published in 1956 with an introduction by William Carlos Williams and created an immediate sensation. The first edition, printed in England for Lawrence Ferlinghetti's *City Lights Books*, was seized by Customs and impounded until cleared of obscenity charges by a San Francisco court. This publishing event, coupled with the appearance of Jack Kerouac's novel "On the Road," brought into focus a new movement in the literary world—"Beat Writing."

Allen Ginsberg describes himself as "the son of Naomi Ginsberg, Russian emigré, and Louis Ginsberg, lyric poet and school teacher." In 1968 father and son gave a joint poetry reading at the Brooklyn Academy of Music, about which Thomas Lask commented (in the *N.Y. Times*): "Listening to a poetry reading by Louis and Allen Ginsberg is very much like going to a recital concert by Brigit Nilsson and Lena Horne—each has her own distinctive qualities but you don't think of them together." The younger Ginsberg was born in Paterson, N.J., and attended school there and at Columbia College. Since then his travels read like a Kerouac version of the Odyssey: "merchant marine, Texas and Denver, copyboy, Time Square . . . Mexico City . . . Satori in Harlem, Yucatan and Chiapas . . . Arctic Sea Trip and then Tangier, Venice, Amsterdam, Paris, London . . . New York . . . SF . . . awhile in the Orient." In 1966 he participated with William Burroughs (*q. v.*) and others in the movie "Chappaqua." Two years later he was once again cleared of charges of obscenity—this time in Italy where he had been accused of reading a poem that violated public decency at the Spoleto Culture Festival. He has suffered other, similar adversities at home and abroad but usually comes up smiling.

It was to Naomi Ginsberg that his second long poem "Kaddish" was addressed. Quieter, less angry than "Howl," it carries the same tone of anguish, the same search for meaning in the life of one person—or, in "Kaddish," the painful death of one person. "Here we have the story of Naomi Ginsberg's paranoia, degeneration, and death told in humiliating detail [by] the single writer of the 'Beat' poets who has shown outstanding imagination and feeling for a strong poetic line"—(M. L. Rosenthal, in "The New Poets").

His later poetry remains concerned with "the same basic subjects," according to Thomas Parkinson (in *The Reader's Encyclopedia of American Literature*): "Focused on life and death [with] a tone of great sadness . . . Ginsberg's work displays many of the interests of the Beats: drugs, hallucinogenic and addictive; sexual disorder; voluntary poverty; rejection of the society; quest for illumination; jazz rhythms and hip language; rootless wandering."

In the spring of 1968 Mr. Ginsberg showed alarming signs of becoming enmeshed in the Establishment he so despises. Beneath the beard and strange garb there is a winning if outrageous human being who is totally honest (and depraved, by Establishment standards). In a television program that reminded one of the Impossible Interviews of Miguel Covarrubias in the old *Vanity Fair*, he took on William Buckley and appeared to get the better of the match, restricting his language dutifully to the rules of the medium. He sang, in the original East Indian tongue, the ancient *mantra* "Hare Krishna" to music of his own accompaniment and read a (clean) poem on Wales—and a very fine one—which had recently reached the pages of the *New Yorker*. His own contribution to "Who's Who" has been considerably censored. But Mr. Ginsberg is a serious poet with a serious message, and a phenomenon we'd best try to understand.

REALITY SANDWICHES: Poems 1953–1960. *City Lights Books* 1963 pap. $1.50

HOWL AND OTHER POEMS. *City Lights Books* 1956 pap. $1.00

KADDISH AND OTHER POEMS. 1958–1960. *City Lights books* 1960 pap. $1.50

THE EMPTY MIRROR: Early Poems. *Corinth Bks.* (dist. by The Book Organization) 1961 pap. $2.50

(With William Burroughs) THE YAGE LETTERS. Written in 1953 when Burroughs was in South America. *City Lights Books* 1963 pap. $1.50

PLANET NEWS. 1968. *City Lights Books* 1970 signed ed. $15.00 pap. $2.00. Forty poems on the United States, Indian religions and cosmology.

AIRPLANE DREAMS. 1969. *City Lights Books* pap. $1.75. From journals kept 1948–1968.

INDIAN JOURNALS: March 1962–May 1963. *City Lights Books* 1970 $6.50 pap. $3.00. With drawings and photos of India by Allen Ginsberg, this book is a multimedia journal of Ginsberg's trip through northern India.

THE FALL OF AMERICA: Poems of These States, 1965–1971. Pocket Poets Ser. *City Lights Books* 1972 pap. $2.50. Continuation of "Planet News" with After Words by Allen Ginsberg. Winner of the National Book Award 1974.

BIKBY CANYON OCEAN PATH WORD BREEZE. *Gotham Bookmart* 1972 pap. $3.00. Poetry.

Books about Ginsberg

Allen Ginsberg. By Thomas F. Merrill. United States Authors Ser. *Twayne* 1969 $4.95. Merrill gives a fair and objective critical analysis of Ginsberg's poems. There is a good general discussion on the Beat movement and Ginsberg's role in it, as well as a thorough discussion of the major works of Ginsberg.
Allen Ginsberg in America. By Jean Kramer *Random* 1970 pap. Vintage Bk. $1.95. An interesting chatty book about Ginsberg, not scholarly or critical.
Scenes along the Road: Photographs of the Desolation Angels, 1944–1960. Collected by Ann Charters, with three poems and comments by Allen Ginsberg. *Gotham Bookmart* 1970 $3.00. A photographic essay on the Beats: Ginsberg, Kerouac, Burroughs, Cassidy, Corso and others. A pleasurable and vivid documentary of the movement, with poems and commentary by Ginsberg.
A Bibliography of the Works of Allen Ginsberg. Ed. by George Dowden and Laurence McGilvery. Illus. *City Lights Books* 1971 $17.50. The chronology and index are by McGilvery with a foreword by Ginsberg. Works covered are from October 1943–July 1, 1967.

O'HARA, FRANK. 1926–1966.

O'Hara was born in Baltimore, Md., and raised in Worcester, Mass. After serving in the Navy during the Second World War, he received his degree from Harvard where he met Kenneth Koch and John Ashbery, and helped found the Poet's Theatre. He later studied at the University of Michigan. In 1951 he moved to New York City and became involved with the art scene that was burgeoning at that time. He was an art critic, worked for *Art News*, and later became associate curator for exhibitions of paintings and sculpture. In the early sixties he became the center of the group to be known as the New York School of Poets, in which John Ashbery and Kenneth Koch were also involved. O'Hara was a man generous with his time and interest, helping all the younger poets who came to him.

O'Hara's poetry has dreamlike, irrational sequences of images, possibly inspired by surrealist painting and film. The dominant quality of his work is its strength of visual imagery, influenced to some degree by the leading painters of the decade: Pollock, Kline and de Kooning. His "personal spur-of-the-moment spontaneity"—(Ellman and O'Claire) may be what O'Hara himself was referring to when he said that he "could use the telephone instead of writing the poems." His work is akin to the pop art culture manifested in movies, advertising and billboards. At times however, there is an almost classic simplicity in his work. "To the Harbormaster" is a good example, beginning simply: "I wanted to be sure to reach you,/ though my ship was on the way/ it got caught/ in some moorings. . . ."

O'Hara died tragically when a dune buggy ran over him on Fire Island, and after his death, the National Book Award was awarded him for his "Collected Poems" (o.p.) in 1972.

SELECTED POEMS. Ed. by Donald Allen. *Knopf* 1974 $7.95; *Random* Vintage Bks. pap. $2.45

MEDITATIONS IN AN EMERGENCY. *Grove* 1957 Evergreen Bks. pap. $1.45

SECOND AVENUE. Poems. *Corinth Bks.* (dist. by Book Organization) 1960 pap. $1.25

LUNCH POEMS. *City Lights Books* 1964 $1.25

SNODGRASS, W(ILLIAM) D(EWITT). 1926–

In "Heart's Needle" W. D. Snodgrass "spoke in a distinctive voice. It was one that was jaunty and assertive on the surface . . . but somber and hurt beneath. His work had a colloquial ease but was traditional in form. It was one of the few books that successfully bridged the directness of contemporary free verse with the demands of the academy. His poetry was appealing in that the poet stood in front of the work—there was no need to hunt for the man in the lines. [Now, in "After Experience"] he comes as close as anyone in capturing the mood, and attitude, the characteristic disposition of the decade we have lived through"—(Thomas Lask, in the *N.Y. Times*). His poetry, which has appeared in many magazines, was collected in his "Heart's Needle," which won the 1960 Pulitzer Prize. He had previously been awarded a grant of $1,500 by the National Institute of Arts and Letters.

HEART'S NEEDLE. *Knopf* 1959 $4.50

ASHBERY, JOHN. 1927–

A contemporary and fellow classmate at Harvard of Kenneth Koch, Ashbery is considered one of the most obscure of the New York School of Poets. He is noted for his mixtures of diction and elegant wit, and when the meaning in his poetry comes across to the reader, he is obviously a master musician of words: "She is slightly taller than he, and looks quietly/ down into his sincere eyes./ She is wearing white. The breeze ruffles her long/ fine black hair against her olive cheek./ Obviously she is in love. . . ."—(from "The Instruction Manual")

Ashbery's influences include early Auden, Laura Riding and Wallace Stevens; "to be tough, incisive, and melliflouous were perhaps the lesson he derived from these three writers"—(Ellman and O'Claire).

Born in Rochester, N.Y., Ashbery grew up near Lake Ontario. He studied, after graduation from Harvard, at Columbia University where he obtained his M.A. He was awarded a Fullbright Scholarship to study in France in 1955 and while in Paris he wrote art criticism for the *New York Herald Tribune*, Paris edition. Like others in the New York School, Ashbery was closely associated with art and artists and eventually wrote for *Art News* in New York. His first book won the Yale Younger Series of Poets award in 1956 and was prefaced by W. H. Auden.

Ashbery's plays, "The Heroes" and "The Compromise or Queen of the Caribou" have both been produced, the former by The Living Theatre and the latter at The Poet's Theatre in Cambridge, Mass., in 1956.

SOME TREES. 1956. *Corinth Bks.* 1970 $6.50 pap. $3.00

THE TENNIS COURT OATH. Poetry Program Ser. *Wesleyan Univ. Press* 1962 $4.75 pap. $2.45

RIVERS AND MOUNTAINS: Poems. *Holt* 1966 pap. $2.95

DOUBLE DREAM OF SPRING. *Dutton* 1970 $4.95

THREE POEMS. *Viking* 1972 $5.95 Compass Bks. pap. $2.25. Three long prose poems.

KINNELL, GALWAY. 1927–

A New Englander by birth, Kinnell is a poet who eludes those who would put him into any school. His poetry at its heights speaks of city as well as country, and indeed his "The Avenue Bearing the Initial of Christ into the New World" is a kind of literary landmark for New York's Lower East Side and was praised as "the most exciting and by far the most readable poem of a bleak decade . . ."—(Selden Rodman). At his best in long poems—his most recent book, "The Book of Nightmares" is one 75-page poem—Gallway Kinnell is most famed (to date) for his masterpiece "The Bear" in which a hunter unites with the hunted, the poet unites with the prey and the predator. A great empathy and understanding of nature, not in a romantic sense but in a deep real ecological sense typifies this poem as well as most of Kinnell's "nature poems." "What distinguishes . . . [Kinnell's] visions from anything else on the contemporary scene is its continuation of the titanism of the last century—whatever flowed from Goethe's "Faust," through Melville, Nietzsche, Rimbaud, to Rilke, Yeats, Jeffers"—(Charles G. Bell). The largeness of his vision is coupled with an intense ability to weave a detailed tapestry out of American life and experience. There is a universality in his work lacking in most of his contemporaries' canons.

Kinnell has also written a novel, "Black Light" (*Houghton* 1966 $3.95), set in the Middle East. He has travelled extensively in Europe and in the Middle East and taught in Grenoble, France. Educated at Princeton and the University of Rochester, Kinnell was the winner of a Fullbright Fellowship to study in Paris. His awards include a Guggenheim Fellowship for 1961–62, a National Institutes of Arts and Letters Grant in 1961 and a Rockefeller Grant (1967–68). He gives extensive reading tours and has read for The Academy of American Poets in New York's Donnell Library. Among his translations are Villon's poems, "The Lackawanna Elegy" by Yvan Goll (*Sumac Press* 1970 $7.50 pap. $2.45) and "On the Motion and Immobility of Douve" by Yves Bonnefoy. (In French and English. *Ohio Univ. Press* 1968 $6.00).

WHAT A KINGDOM IT WAS. *Houghton* 1960 $3.95

BODY RAGS. *Houghton* 1968 $4.00 pap. $2.95

THE BOOK OF NIGHTMARES. *Houghton* 1971 $4.50 pap. $2.95. Book-length poem.

MERWIN, W(ILLIAM) S(TANLEY). 1927–

Born in New York City, educated at Princeton, W. S. Merwin has in a short space of time lived in Boston, Spain, France and England, published four volumes of verse and three of translations. His first book of poetry, "A Mask for Janus" was sponsored by the Yale Series of Younger Poets; his second, "The Dancing Bears" (1954, o. p.), won the Kenyon Review Fellowship; and his third, "Green With Beasts" (1960, o.p.), won a British Poetry Book Society award.

"W. S. Merwin in his early work wrote . . . with a verse technique as dazzling as that of any poet of his generation"—(Peter Davison, in the *Atlantic*). "His dramatic change of style in the 1960's, from close metrical structures to open form, should not obscure the fact that he has always been preoccupied with cycles of birth, death, and rebirth. He describes archetypal voyages, journeys, floods, and returns of the prodigal son"—(Stephen Stepanchev, in "American Poetry Since 1945"). This change was first visible in "The Drunk in the Furnace." The two collections "The Moving Target" and "The Lice" "explore the elusiveness of our perceptions, . . . express the vagueness of our intimations of ourselves, . . . expose the uncertainty of anything but the search for veracity, . . . and achieve all this in a groping syntax that re-enacts the movements of the mind. Merwin has invaded dangerous and uneasy areas of consciousness, and if his new poetic style sometimes seems forbidding and opaque, it may be the resistance of the reader's perceptions that makes it so"—(Davison). He has made a number of translations from the Spanish.

A MASK FOR JANUS. 1952 *AMS Press* $8.50

THE DRUNK IN THE FURNACE. *Macmillan* 1960 pap. $1.25

THE MOVING TARGET. *Atheneum* 1963 pap. $3.95

THE LICE. *Atheneum* 1967 $4.50 pap. $3.95

PRODUCTS OF THE PERFECTED CIVILIZATION. *Macmillan* 1969 $7.50

CARRIER OF LADDERS. *Atheneum* 1970 pap. $3.95

WRITINGS TO AN UNFINISHED ACCOMPANIMENT. *Atheneum* 1973 pap. $3.95

MINER'S PALE CHILDREN. *Atheneum* 1970 $6.50. A book of prose.

WRIGHT, JAMES. 1927–

Time will probably prove James Wright to be the greatest of the "deep image" poets, and certainly one of the major writers of his generation. His work is typified by a gentle humanitarian tenderness, compassion, a keen sense of man's alienation and loneliness. He has written of his own work: "I have written about the things I am deeply concerned with—crickets outside my window, cold and hungry old men . . . a feeling of desolation in the fall, some cities I have known." His work presents an unusual vision of Middle America: the decayed and at times beautiful landscapes of train yards, bars, whore districts in Minneapolis. As Richard Ellman and Robert O'Clair have pointed out, "Men and women 'apart' provide Wright with his most characteristic . . . subjects." Stylistically Wright has moved from a traditional rhymned and metered verse, drawing heavily on the dramatic and descriptive techniques of the now classic modernists—Robinson, Masters, Frost and even Thomas Hardy—to experimentalism in form and image. At the same time his work has shifted from an "outward to an inward concern"—(Norman Friedman). His more recent poems exhibit an almost oriental delicacy yet retain the peculiar vision of the native American idiom: "She is black and white,/ Her mane falls wild on her forehead,/ And is delicate as the skin over a girl's wrist./ Suddenly I realize/That if I stepped out of my body I would break/ Into blossom."—(from "A Blessing").

Born in Martin's Ferry, Ohio, Wright attended Kenyon College. After serving in the armed forces he studied at the University of Washington. Recipient of a Fullbright scholarship to study in Vienna, he has also been awarded a National Institute of Arts and Letters Grant, a Guggenheim Grant, the Oscar Blumenthal Award, and a Pulitzer Prize for his, "Collected Poems" in 1972.

SAINT JUDAS. Poetry Program Ser. *Wesleyan Univ. Press* 1959 $4.75 pap. $2.45. Poems collected from the following volumes: "The Green Wall" (1957), "St. Judas" (1959), "The Branch Will Not Break" (1963), "Shall We Gather at the River?" (1968), translation and new poems.

COLLECTED POEMS. *Wesleyan Univ. Press* 1971 $9.95 pap. $3.45

THE BRANCH WILL NOT BREAK. Poetry Program Ser. *Wesleyan Univ. Press* 1963 $4.75 pap. $2.45

SHALL WE GATHER AT THE RIVER? Poetry Program Ser. *Wesleyan Univ. Press* 1968 $4.75 pap. $2.45

TWO CITIZENS. *Farrar, Straus* 1973 $5.95 pap.

HALL, DONALD. 1928–

Donald Hall was born in New Haven, Conn., and attended Harvard and Oxford. The poem "Exile" from his first collection, "Exiles and Marriages" (1955, o. p.), won the Newdigate Prize in England. In "The Dark Houses," his second volume, "the author's power to show us convincing suburban and small-town reality is backed by an interesting attitude composed both of love for the 'residential streets' and distaste. Furthermore the technique is icily witty and beautiful"—(*Canadian Forum*). In "A Roof of Tiger Lilies" (1964, o. p.), "A sure feeling for context is his great strength; details are not allowed to usurp more than their fair share of attention, and the best of the poems have a fulness of momentum, describing an arc"—(*New Statesman*). Many of Mr. Hall's poems have been published in the *New Yorker*.

Mr. Hall has been poetry editor for the *Paris Review*. He has edited "Contemporary American Poetry" (*Penguin* 1963 pap. $1.50) and (with others) the two volumes of "New Poets of England and America" (*World Pub.* 1962 rev. ed. 1972 Meridian Bks. $3.95). He is also the editor of several anthologies including "Modern Stylists: Writers on the Art of Writing" (*Free Press* [dist. by Macmillan] 1968 $4.50 pap. $2.50), "Poetry Sampler" (*Franklin Watts* 1962 $7.95 large type ed. $8.95), and "Pleasures of Poetry" (with a recording of selections read by the compiler. *Harper* 1971 $6.95 pap. $4.50 record $6.50—record is by *Spoken Arts* HS 1100 and may be obtained from them as well as from *Harper*). He is also the author of "Henry Moore: The Life and Work of a Great Sculptor" (*Harper* 1966 $7.50) and a member of the English faculty at the University of Michigan.

ALLIGATOR BRIDE: Poems New and Selected. *Harper* 1970 $4.95 pap. $2.25. A selection of Hall's earlier work, long unavailable, as well as 25 new poems.

YELLOW ROOM: Love Poems. *Harper* 1971 $4.95 pap. $2.45. Fifty poems, some of which appeared in "Alligator Bride" but which are revised here.

WRITING WELL. *Little* 1973 $5.95

String Too Short to be Saved. *Viking* 1961 $5.00. About his childhood on his grandfather's farm; in prose.

SEXTON, ANNE. 1928–

Anne Sexton's painful personal experiences form the subject matter of most of her poetry. Her first collection, "To Bedlam and Part Way Back," focuses on her mental illness and subsequent hospitalization. "Live or Die" also "palpates human suffering, personal, physical, psychic"—(*LJ*). The poems, says Ralph J. Mills, are "undisguised revelation and examination—of her parents, her lovers, her friends; of the unbelievable torment of both mental and physical illness as she had to endure them; of her struggles with a religious belief that eludes her but doesn't leave her; of the face of death as she has frequently seen it [(her mother's death from cancer, her father's shortly after, and her brother's in World War II). Her poetry generally is] built upon an attitude of stoic pessimism that occasionally lapses into morbidity" yet infrequently, he continues, she does achieve images of compassion and tenderness. There is, however, a recent trend in her verse disturbing to her admirers. Ian Hamilton, writing in the *Observer* (London) has put his finger on it (he too was an admirer of her "remarkable first book"). He quotes her poem to Sylvia Plath (*q.v.*), which ends, "O tiny mother / you too! / O funny duchess! / O blonde thing!" and says: "This effortful exclamatory brightness runs throughout the book and casts none of the triumphal glow it seems to aim for," he finds the lines quoted "flatly vulgar." Such retreats into coyness seem unworthy of this fine, strong talent.

Mrs. Sexton was born in Newton, Mass., and attended public and private schools. She won the Robert Frost Fellowship in Poetry for 1959, became a scholar at the Radcliffe Institute from 1961 to 1963, received a traveling fellowship from the American Academy of Arts and Letters for 1963–64, and was awarded a Ford Foundation Grant in 1965. In 1965 she also won the first literary magazine travel grant from The Congress for Cultural Freedom and was elected a Fellow of The Royal Society of Literature in London. In 1967 she received the Shelley Award for the excellence of her total work and the Pulitzer Prize for "Live or Die." Mrs. Sexton lives in Weston, Mass., with her husband and two daughters.

To Bedlam and Part Way Back. *Houghton* 1960 pap. $2.95

All My Pretty Ones. *Houghton* 1962 pap. $2.95

Live or Die. *Houghton* 1966 $4.00 pap. $2.95

Love Poems. *Houghton* 1969 $4.00 pap. $2.95. Twenty-five poems.

Transformations. *Houghton* 1972 $5.00. Poem/stories derived from Grimm's fairy tales, with a preface by Kurt Vonnegut, Jr.

Book of Folly. *Houghton* 1973 $5.95 deluxe ed. $15.00

"This book is wonderfully mad and madly wonderful"—(John Untermeyer).

DORN, EDWARD. 1929–

One of the younger "Black Mountain Poets," Ed Dorn was a student of Robert Creeley and Charles Olson. His work is not so much influenced by the Black Mountain school as it is integral to it. A deep sense of the necessities of speech patterns transmitted by projective verse and of geography, myth and prehistoric times puts Dorn particularly close to the work and thought of Charles Olson. In fact Olson compiled his "Bibliography for Ed Dorn" to reflect this interest in the latter three subjects. Like Olson, Dorn finds his greatest challenge and accomplishment in the long poem. For Olson's death Dorn composed the lengthy "From Glocester Out"; and his "Gunslinger" series of books—a continuing epic of the American West seen in an ostensibly satiric-comic mode but actually a deep expression of the poet's concern with the idea of hero and "free ego"—is already a landmark in this decade's contribution to American letters.

Dorn is also a master of the shorter lyric, such as: "Thus days go by / and I stand knowing her hair / in my mind as a dark cloud, its presence / straying over the rim of a volcano / of desire, and I take something / as closed as a book / into the world where she is."—(From "The Song").

Ed Dorn is a midwesterner by birth, though he writes mainly of the American West. He was educated at the University of Illinois in Urbana and then at Black Mountain College. He has been a Visiting Professor of American Literature at the University of Essex (1965–68) under a Fullbright grant and taught at the University of Kansas. He has also published "some of the best criticism to have come so far from the Black Mountain Poets"—(Hayden Carruth). A bibliography of Ed Dorn's works is currently being prepared by The Phoenix Bibliographers, and will soon be available from *The Phoenix Book Shop* (18 Cornelia St., New York, N.Y.).

Dorn has also translated, with Gordon Brotherston "Our Word: Guerilla Poems from Latin America" Cape Goliard *Grossman* 1968 bilingual English and Spanish ed. 1968 $4.50 pap. $2.95.

HANDS UP. 1964 *Corinth Bks.* pap. $1.50

GEOGRAPHY. 1965. *Horizon Press* $4.50. Poems.

SONGS, SET TWO: A Short Count. *Frontier Press, Calif.* 1970 pap. $1.00

BY THE SOUND. *Frontier Press, Calif.* 1971 pap. $3.50

THE CYCLE. *Frontier Press, Calif.* 1971 pap. $2.00

SOME BUSINESS RECENTLY TRANSACTED IN THE WHITE WORLD. *Frontier Press, Calif.*
   1971 pap. $2.00. Stories.

HOWARD, RICHARD. 1929–

Richard Howard was born in Cleveland and educated at Columbia University and the Sorbonne. Noted
for his translations of French literature, including the works of Robbe-Grillet and the memoirs of Charles de
Gaulle, he is also the author of one of the more important books on contemporary American poetry: "Alone
with America" (*Atheneum* 1969 $12.95 pap. $4.95). He also is a reviewer and critic for *Poetry* magazine,
and was a Guggenheim Fellow for poetry in 1966–67.

Howard's most notable poetic achievement is his fine adaptation of Browning's dramatic monologues, first
compiled in "Untitled Subjects" (1969). Howard Bloom writes of them: "Richard Howard's dramatic monologues with their intricate blendings of our emergent sensibility and the anguish and splendor of the great
Victorians, represent one of the handful of surprising and refreshing inventions in American poetry of the
Sixties."

QUANTITIES. Poetry Program Ser. *Wesleyan Univ. Press* 1962 $4.75 pap. $2.45

THE DAMAGES. Poetry Program Ser. *Wesleyan Univ. Press* 1967 $4.75 pap. $2.45

FINDINGS: A Book of Poems. *Atheneum* 1971 pap. $3.95

RICH, ADRIENNE. 1929–

On her graduation from Radcliffe in 1951, Adrienne Rich's first book of poems, "A Change of World,"
was chosen by W. H. Auden for the Yale Younger Poets Series. Both Auden and her father, who had encouraged her writing throughout her childhood, served as strong influences on her early writing. Her poetry was
traditional, largely in emulation of Auden's, and when "The Diamond Cutters" (1955, o. p.) came out, she
was married, had three children, and struggled with being a woman and a poet in the American environment
of that time. Her poetry started to change remarkably in the 1960s, and with "Snapshots of a Daughter-in-
Law" she not only started writing directly as a woman rather than in the tradition of the men before her, but
also her political dissatisfaction had reached a synthesis: "I think I began at this point to feel that politics was
not something 'out there' but something 'in here' and of the essence of my condition." She moved to New
York and became involved in antiwar activities, taught in the SEEK program, and now, after several published books, her poetry has an integrity born of the earlier struggles and incompatibilities. Her poems manifest a merging between highly personal experience and social themes, in which, she says, "at last the woman
in the poem and the woman writing the poem become the same person."

In the late 1950s, Ms. Rich lived in Holland and translated poetry from the Dutch. She has received a
Guggenheim Fellowship, taught at Swarthmore and Columbia, and is currently teaching at Brandeis.

A CHANGE OF WORLD. Fwd. by W. H. Auden. 1951. *AMS Press* $8.50

NECESSITIES OF LIFE. *Norton* 1966 $4.50 pap. $1.95. A reissue of the author's first
   book which won the Yale Younger Poets Series award in 1951.

SNAPSHOTS OF A DAUGHTER-IN-LAW: Poems 1954–62. 1963. *Norton* 1967 $4.50 pap.
   $1.95

LEAFLETS: Poems 1965–68. *Norton* 1969 $4.95 pap. $1.95

THE WILL TO CHANGE: Poems 1968–70. *Norton* 1971 pap. $1.95. Includes some ex-
   periments in the ghazal form.

DIVING INTO THE WRECK: Poems 1971–72. *Norton* 1973 $5.95 pap. $1.95. New poems with an intense personal and feminist slant. Winner of the National Book Award, 1974.

SORRENTINO, GILBERT. 1929–

Born in Brooklyn and educated at Brooklyn College, Sorrentino is a frequent contributor to *American Review* and a 1973–74 Guggenheim fellow.

His work combines a straightforward plain-talking American speech idiom with a high, almost archaic diction. In his most recent book, the long prose-poem "Splendide-Hôtel," he is inspired by Rimbaud and his work is "built in the chaos of ice and of polar night," yet echoes the verbal cadences of William Carlos Williams.

Sorrentino's novels include "The Sky Changes" (1966, o.p.), "Steelwork" (*Pantheon* 1970 $5.95) and "Imaginative Quality of Actual Things" (*Pantheon* 1971 $6.95).

BLACK AND WHITE. Ed. by LeRoi Jones. *Corinth Bks.* 1961 pap. $1.50. Poems.

PERFECT FICTION. *Norton* 1968 $4.95 pap. $1.95. Poems.

CORROSIVE SUBLIMATE. *Black Sparrow* 1971 signed limited ed. $15.00 pap. $4.00. Poetry.

SPLENDIDE-Hôtel. *New Directions* 1973 signed limited ed. $20.00 pap. $3.25. Long prose-poem after Rimbaud.

FLAWLESS PLAY RESTORED. *Black Sparrow* 1974 signed limited ed. $15.00 pap. $3.00

CORSO, GREGORY. 1930–

In 1957 Allen Ginsberg wrote of Gregory Corso, "He's probably the greatest poet in America, and he's starving in Europe." Today, Corso has emerged as one of the major Beat poets, whose work, with Ginsberg's and Snyder's, will probably be read by posterity. A "more introverted poet than Ginsberg—(Derek Parker), Corso combines in his work an unlikely mixture of street language and slang with lofty poetic rhetoric. It is always rhythmic and musical even when Corso's technique gives way to wild Dionysian impulse. Rexroth describes Corso as "a genuine *naif*. A real wildman with all the charm of a hoodlum . . . a wholesome Antonin Artaud, or a 'sincere' Tristan Tzara." Corso's main themes are death and beauty, always in American terms. There is great humor and irony in his verse, coupled with accurate perception. Though he taught himself to write poetry in prison his poems never speak of prison life. Corso comments on this fact: "If one must climb a ladder to reach a height and from that height see, then it were best to write about what you see and not about how you climbed. Prison to me was such a ladder."

Virtually an orphan, Corso was born on Bleecker Street in New York's Greenwich Village, spending his childhood and youth in and out of foster homes. During his numerous prison terms he was introduced to literature by a fellow convict, and upon his release he met Allen Ginsberg who immediately recognized his talent and helped him. Corso presently lives in New York.

A BIBLIOGRAPHY OF WORKS BY GREGORY CORSO. Comp. by Robert Wilson. By The Phoenix Bibliographers. *The Phoenix Book Shop* (18 Cornelia Street, New York, N.Y.) 1966 $1.50

VESTAL LADY ON BRATTLE. *City Lights Books* 1955 $1.00

GASOLINE. Introd. by Allen Ginsberg. *City Lights Books* 1958 pap. $1.00

THE HAPPY BIRTHDAY OF DEATH. *New Directions* 1960 pap. $1.95

LONG LIVE MAN. *New Directions* 1962 pap. $1.75

ELEGIAC FEELINGS AMERICAN. *New Directions* 1970 pap. $2.25

OPPENHEIMER, JOEL. 1930–

One of the true Black Mountain poets, Oppenheimer was born in Yonkers, New York, and educated at Cornell and at the University of Chicago, as well as at Black Mountain College in North Carolina. He has been project director at the Poetry-Project at St. Marks Church in-the-Bowery, poet-in-residence at the City College of New York, and poetry consultant to *Bobbs-Merrill, Inc.* He is presently working as a typographer in New York.

Oppenheimer's poetry maintains a certain dignity in the midst of simple events described skillfully in simple, direct speech. A real literary descendent of Charles Olson, with whom he studied for a time, his work is, as he describes it himself, "good poems about sex, love, and life." The following excerpt from "An Undefined Tenderness" demonstrates the clear beauty of his poetry: "finally, i think, we could face to it: / there is no love possible beyond / those first moments of fire and / trembling passion. this makes more / sense than a roomful of roses / . . . ."

Oppenheimer has been represented in several major anthologies, including "A Controversy of Poets" (*Doubleday* Anchor Bks. 1965 $2.95).

IN TIME: Poems 1962–1968. *Bobbs* 1969 $5.95

ON OCCASION: Some Births, Deaths, Weddings, Birthdays, Holidays and Other Events. *Bobbs* 1973 $6.95 pap. $4.95. Oppenheimer's versions of "occasional" poems.

THE WRONG SEASON. *Bobbs* 1973 $6.95. Prose work on the New York Mets' 1972 season.

SNYDER, GARY. 1930–

Gary Snyder was born in San Francisco and received a B.A. in Anthropology at Reed College. He attended Indiana University and pursued the study of oriental languages at the University of California at Berkeley. When he was 18 he shipped out of New York as a seaman, worked later as a logger and forest look-out in Oregon, Washington and California. He is one of the four most famous "Beat" poets (the others being Allen Ginsberg, Gregory Corso and Lawrence Ferlinghetti). Prior to moving to Japan to study in a Zen monastery under a Bollingen Foundation Grant, Snyder worked on an American tanker in the Persian Gulf and South Pacific Islands, then spent four months in India (1961–62) at various temples and ashrams. He has taught at the University of California at Berkeley and presently resides in California with his Japanese-born wife and two children.

Gary Snyder is perhaps the most controlled and concise of the Beat poets. Certainly his work is more structured and careful than that of any of his fellow "Beats." His adventurous life has given his verse a unique range of subject and feeling. Snyder, always close to nature since childhood, is the most widely known poet of the ecology movement. Often his poems have a Zen-like stillness and sharpness of perception—which serves to sensitively define the great connective web between man and the natural universe. There is a grace and ease in Snyder's expression of this connection: "In this burning, muddy, lying / blood-drenched world / that quiet meeting in the mountains / cool and gentle as the muzzles of / three elk, helps keep me sane . . . ." Though his work is personal and always derived from his immediate experiences, he differs from confessional poets in his great objectivity. The experiences are presented as they were, with little interpretation or added image or aura.

Snyder, like Jerome Rothenberg (*q.v.*) is deeply interested in the American Indian and the idea of tribe as an alternative to modern culture, or at least as an example for modern culture. He spent a year in the Southwest under a Guggenheim Fellowship studying various tribal customs and languages. Besides receiving the first Zen Institute of America Award in 1956, and the above-mentioned grants, Snyder is also the recipient of an American Academy of Arts and Sciences poetry prize in 1966.

His essays, "Earth House Hold" (*New Directions* 1969 pap. $10.95)—also composed of journal notes and diary excerpts—have become a classic in the "underground" ecology movement.

MYTHS AND TEXTS. *Corinth Bks.* 1960 pap. $1.75

RIPRAP AND COLD MOUNTAIN: Poems. *Four Seasons Foundation* 1965 pap. $1.50

BACK COUNTRY. *New Directions* 1968 $4.25 pap. $1.75

REGARDING WAVE. *New Directions* 1970 $4.75 pap. $1.75

SIX SECTIONS FROM MOUNTAINS AND RIVERS WITHOUT END PLUS ONE. *Four Seasons Foundation* 1970 pap. $2.25. Contains the newest section of this continuing series.

FUDO TRILOGY. *Shaman Drum Press* 1972 pap. $2.00. Three poems, including "Smokey the Bear Sutra."

Books about Snyder

Some Notes to Gary Snyder's Myths and Texts. By Howard McCord. *Sand Dollar* 1971 $1.00. Identification of allusions in poems.

ROTHENBERG, JEROME. 1931–

Born in New York City in 1931, Jerome Rothenberg is an anomaly in American poetry. His interests, if reduced to three elements, are of the European tradition, the American tradition, particularly the American Jew's roots in Europe (as in "Poland/1933" to be published 1974 by *New Directions*) and then the tradition of the American Indian, with its concommittant idea of America as having a tribal or primitive origin. As editor of *Alcheringa*, the first magazine to present "ethnopoetics," and of anthologies of primitive and Indian rituals and poetry, Rothenberg has become a leader in the new efforts to preserve and learn from ancient and extant primitive cultures. Among the anthologies he has edited are "Ritual: A Book of Primitive Rites and Events" (1966, o.p.) and "Technicians of the Sacred" (*Doubleday* 1968 $3.95). Rothenberg's latest anthology, edited with George Quasha, "America a Prophecy: A New Reading of American Poetry from Pre-Columbian Times to the Present" (*Random* 1973 $12.95 Vintage Bks. pap. $3.95) is a monumental work gathering poems from ancient times to the present.

He says of his own work, "I look for new forms and possibilities, but also for ways of presenting in our own language the oldest possibilities of poetry going back to the primitive and archaic cultures that have been opened to us over the last 100 years." In some of his recent work he has tried to provide the reader with a guide to the auditory value of the written line by introducing empty spaces around the lines of poetry, with directives as to how long a pause they represent. He strongly believes in the primary oral quality of poetry and as a frequent reader on poetry circuits he includes ritual chanting and sometimes the singing of traditional whaling songs.

Rothenberg is represented in many anthologies, among which are "East Side Scene" (ed. by A. DeLoach. *See section on Collections above*) and "Where Is Vietnam?" (*Doubleday*, 1967 $1.45).

Poems for the Game of Silence, 1960–1970. *Dial* 1971 pap. $2.45

Esther K. Comes to America. *Unicorn Press* 1973 $7.00 pap. $3.00

Between. *Horizon Press* $4.50

(and Dennis Tedlock, Eds.) Alcheringa: Ethnopoetics 1970–. *Alcheringa* nos. 2–5. No. 2 pap. $2.00 Nos. 3–5 pap. each $2.50

McCLURE, MICHAEL. 1932–

A native Midwesterner, McClure is more associated with the San Francisco Renaissance of the mid-fifties than with the "Heartland" poetry of James Wright, Robert Bly, or Bill Knott. His work, in the tradition of Blake and Artaud, is prophetic in tone and usually quite experimental on the printed page. The typographical effects seem to echo the shouts and whispers of his soul:

And
we
move
on
the
same
mattress
DISCOVERING
WE ARE GODS
and finally human—and mammals.
What a lovely foot!—(From "Finally")

And yet it has been pointed out that, despite the unconventional form taken by his work, as in the poetry in "Dark Brown," or in his play, "The Beard," his "language is more classical than innovatory, more musical than bestial"—(Carol Bergé). There is often a simplicity, hidden at times beneath the visual rhetoric of his lines, reminiscent of e.e. cummings, or sometimes even of a medieval love lyric.

He is also the author of an essay on the famed Hell's Angel, Free Wheelin' Frank (1967, o.p.), which is actually Free Wheelin' Frank's self-portrait as told to McClure. His plays, "The Beard" and "The Tooth of Crime," are underground theater classics presently showing in the New York's Soho at the Performing Garage. He is part of the "poet's-theater" movement which is now reviving itself on the San Francisco scene.

New Book: A Book of Torture. *Grove* Evergreen Bks. 1961 pap. $1.95

MEAT SCIENCE ESSAYS. *City Lights Books* 1963 pap. $1.95

GHOST TANTRAS. *Four Seasons Foundation* 1969 pap. $2.25

THE STAR. *Grove.* Evergreen Bks. 1970 pap. $2.45

RARE ANGEL. *Black Sparrow* 1973 $15.00 pap. $3.00

SEPTEMBER BLACKBERRIES. *New Directions* 1974 $6.95 pap. $3.25

Books about McClure

A Catalog of Works by Michael McClure 1956–1965. Comp. by Marshall Clements. The Phoenix Bibliographers. *The Phoenix Book Shop* (18 Cornelia St., New York, N.Y.) 1965 $1.50

PLATH, SYLVIA. 1932–1963.

Sylvia Plath's best poetry was produced, tragically, as she pondered—in her poems as well as her life—
self-destruction, and her suicide left her two young sons behind her. She had an extraordinary impact on British as well as American poetry in the few years before her death. She is a "confessional" poet, influenced by
the approach of Robert Lowell, Anne Sexton and others of this trend. An excellent discussion of her is to be
found in M. L. Rosenthal's "The New Poets."

Born in Boston, a graduate of Smith College, she attended Newnham College, Cambridge, on a Fulbright
Fellowship and married the British poet Ted Hughes (*q.v.*) in England. Of her first collection, "The Colossus
and Other Poems," the *Times Literary Supplement* (London) remarked, "Miss Plath writes from phrase to
phrase as well as with an eye on the larger architecture of the poem; each line, each sentence is put together
with a good deal of care for the springy rhythm, the arresting image and—most of all, perhaps—the unusual
word." George Steiner, who devotes an essay to her in "Languages and Silence," notes, in "Colossus," the
theme of the "the infirm or rent body, and the imperfect, painful resurrection of the psyche, pulled back, un-
willingly, to the hypocrisies of health."

Her second book of poetry, "Ariel," written in 1962 in a last fever of passionate creative activity, was published posthumously. It displays a "new frankness of women about the specific hurts and tangles of their ner-
vous-physiological makeup"—(Steiner). But it is also the world's hurt killing a woman: "Sometimes . . . she
could not distinguish between herself and the facts of, say, Auschwitz and Hiroshima. She was victim, killer,
and the place and process of horror all at once"—(M. L. Rosenthal). Robert Lowell found the poet of
"Ariel" "feminine, rather than female, though almost everything we customarily think of as feminine is
turned on its head." And she is not all grim; the poignancy of her despair is constantly intensified by sharp
images of loveliness. Writing of the poem "Ariel," M. L. Rosenthal says, "In a single leap of feeling, it identifies sexual elation (in the full sense of the richest kind of encompassment of life) with its opposite, death's
nothingness." "And I," she wrote, "Am the arrow,/ The dew that flies/ Suidical, at one with the drive/ Into
the red/ Eye, the cauldron of morning." A revealing study of the doomed personality that Sylvia Plath was is
her one novel, "The Bell Jar," (*Harper* 1971 $6.95; *Bantam* pap. $1.50) about a neurotic college girl's first
experience in New York and its destructive effect on her. It was first published under a pseudonym in 1963
and under her own name (in England) in 1966.

THE COLOSSUS AND OTHER POEMS. *Knopf* 1962 $4.50; *Random* Vintage Bks. 1968
pap. $1.65

ARIEL. *Harper* 1966 $4.95 pap. $1.95

"One of the most marvelous volumes of poetry published for a very long time"—(*TLS*, London).

CROSSING THE WATER. *Harper* 1971 $5.95. Poems written between "The Colossus"
(1960) and "Ariel" (1965).

WINTER TREE. *Harper* 1972 $5.95. These poems, written in the last months of the
poet's life in 1962, were put together posthumously.

Books about Plath

The Art of Sylvia Plath. Ed. by Charles Newman. Ill. *Indiana Univ. Press* 1971 pap. $2.95. Newman has
compiled criticism by A. Alvarez, M. L. Rosenthal, Richard Howard, John Frederick Nims and reminiscences by Anne Sexton and Ted Hughes. There is a complete bibliography, a checklist of criticism
and an appendix of uncollected and yet unpublished work. The checklist of criticism and bibliography
was compiled by Mary Kenzie.

A Closer Look at Ariel: A Memory of Sylvia Plath. By Nancy H. Steiner. Ill. *Harper* 1973 $5.00. Critical introduction by George Stade gives a biographical survey. A biographical description and character analysis of the poet.

BERRY, WENDELL. 1934–

Wendell Berry is a native Kentuckian and presently lives and teaches at the University of Kentucky. His work has appeared in numerous little magazines, and as well as his poetry, he has written the novels "Nathan Coulter" (1960 *Houghton*), and "A Place on Earth" (1967 *Harcourt*). He is the recipient of a Guggenheim Fellowship, 1961–62, and a Rockefeller Foundation Grant, 1965–66. His work is found in various anthologies, including "The Voice That Is Great Within Us" (*q.v.*). He is a renowned essayist and a collection of his essays, "The Long-Legged House," on conservation, morals, and Vietnam, was published in 1969 (*Harcourt* 1969 $5.95; *Ballentine Bks.* 1971. pap. $1.25).

The title of Wendell Berry's recent poetry collection, "Farming: A Handbook" aptly describes his relationship to the earth: he is a farmer in the most genuine sense; one who loves the land, and recognizes his dependence on it. It is not surprising, then, to see his work ranking with that of the better-known Gary Snyder (*q.v.*) as an important contribution to the present consciousness of ecology and return to nature. His poetry seems to reach the heart of things, and one feels his "journey" is also of the soul, finding expression in a realized unity of man and nature. "When I rise up,/ let me rise up joyful/ like a bird./ When I fall/ let me fall without regret/ like a leaf./ . . . Sowing the seed,/ my hand is one with the earth."—(from "Prayers and Sayings of the Mad Farmer").

"The quality in his work that comes first to mind is a certain *nobility* of spirit and sentiment—a beautiful dignity. . . . The second quality is his sanctity . . . which springs . . . from his deliberate choice of an old and fundamental way of life, his apparently firm-rooted attachment to his original and right place on earth"—(Edward Abby).

He is the author of a number of collections of essays: "The Hidden Wound" (*Houghton* 1970 $4.95; *Ballantine Bks.* 1971 pap. $1.25), (with Gene Meatyard) "The Unforeseen Wilderness" (*Univ. Press of Kentucky* 1971 $6.95; *Ballantine Bks.* pap. $3.95) and "A Continuous Harmony" (*Harcourt* 1972 $5.95).

NOVEMBER 26, 1963. *Braziller* 1964 $5.00 signed limited ed. $15.00. Calligraphy and drawings by Ben Shahn.

OPENINGS. *Harcourt* 1968 $4.50

FARMING: A Handbook. *Harcourt* 1970 $4.95 Harvest Bks. pap. $2.65

THE COUNTRY OF MARRIAGE. *Harcourt* 1973 $4.95

JONES, LeROI (Imamu Amiri Baraka). 1934–

LeRoi Jones had proved himself so powerful, accomplished and versatile in many literary fields that he had made himself a name in literature before he became a militant against the oppression of black by white Americans. "His technique" in poetry, says Stephen Stepanchev, "derives from projective verse [*see introduction to this Chapter*]; he stresses speech rhythm; and his diction is that of the hipster. In putting his poems together, he is not afraid of discontinuities—they represent reality to him—or prosaic statement if it serves his purpose; but he has more imagery than most hip poets, and he enjoys projecting a wild, comic, sexual fantasy to contrast with the boredom of urban life."

His early poems were often personal and uncommitted; he showed in these a strong lyric talent. M. L. Rosenthal, "The New Poets," says that as a poet he has a "natural gift for quick, vivid imagery and spontaneous humor, and his poems are filled with sensuous or slangily knowledgeable passages." Rosenthal finds some diffuseness in the earlier verses. 'The Dead Lecturer' . . . still suffers from difficulty in focusing on its controlling insights except in the pieces that fall back on the politics of racial enmity, often in obvious sexual disguise. On the other hand [certain poems] show not only Jones's art of rhapsodic inwardness in full growth . . . but also his capacity to keep aloof from easy political self-identification." Mr. Jones has not been trying to keep "aloof" of late, either in his plays or in life, and he was recently sentenced in connection with the Newark, N.J., riots of 1967. An editorial in *Publishers' Weekly* was among the many protests against a courtroom reading by the prosecution of a poem of his to prove that he was counseling violence. Before serving his possible term of imprisonment, however, he and other black militants were instrumental in helping maintain order in Newark at the time of Martin Luther King's assassination in 1968. Since then, he has become ever more active in the black nationalist movement, and was a major force in the election of Kenneth Gibson as Newark's first black mayor.

BLACK MAGIC POETRY: Collected Poetry 1961–67. 1969. *Bobbs* 1970 $5.95 pap. $3.95. Poetry written from 1961–1967 includes the following volumes: "Sabotage," "Target Study," "Black Art."

Preface to a Twenty Volume Suicide Note. *Corinth Bks.* 1961 pap. $1.50

The Dead Lecturer. *Grove* 1964 pap. $1.45

The Baptism and The Toilet. *Grove* Evergreen 1967 pap. $1.45

(With Billy Abernathy) In Our Terribleness: Pictures of the Hip World. *Bobbs* 1969 $7.95. Photographs illustrate this work of short prose poems.

(Writing as Imamu Amiri Baraka) Raise Race Rays Raze. *Random* 1972 $5.95 Vintage Bks. pap. $1.95

STRAND, MARK. 1934–

Although not associated with any one school of poetry, Mark Strand's work seems to possess qualities of the European and Latin American Surrealists. As Strand is a translator of Paz, Borges, Guillen, Quasimodo and Serini, this surrealist quality is not surprising. His poetry, often uttered matter-of-factly, seems singularly removed from the here and now, filled with the impossibilities of the restless world lying between dream and wakefulness. "Ink runs from the corners of my mouth./ There is no happiness like mine./ I have been eating poetry./ The librarian does not believe what she sees./ Her eyes are sad/ and she walks with her hands in her dress."—(from "Eating Poetry").

As one critic put it, Strand "by frequent restatement of his themes, . . . develops a tonal consistency that is a great part of his growing strength and persuasion. Here is an imagination vitally concerned with man in the world today; or is there a world today, and is man in it?"(Holly Stevens).

This Canadian-born American poet received his degree from Antioch College, and studied at Yale. He studied literature in Florence on a Fulbright Grant (1960–61) and later studied at the University of Iowa, where he also taught. He was a Fulbright Lecturer 1965–66 and during 1966–67 he held an Ingram Merrill Fellowship and taught at Mount Holyoke College. He has been a visiting porfessor at the University of Washington and his prizes include an award from the National Council on the Arts (1967–68) and a Rockefeller Fellowship (1968–69). He is presently a lecturer at Yale and has taught at Columbia's School of the Arts. Besides his poetic works, he has edited "The Contemporary American Poets: American Poetry Since 1940" (*q.v.*) and "New Poetry of Mexico" (*Dutton* 1970 $10.00 pap. $4.95). He has also translated "The Owl's Insomnia" by Rafael Alberti (*Atheneum* 1973 $4.95).

Reasons for Moving. *Atheneum* 1968 $4.95 pap. $2.95

Darker. *Atheneum* 1970 pap. $2.95

The Sargeantville Notebook. A Burning Deck Bk. Wittenborn 1973 pap. $2.50. Poems and prose jottings.

The Story of Our Lives. *Atheneum* 1973 pap. $2.95. New poems.

BENEDIKT, MICHAEL. 1937–

Born in New York in 1937, Michael Benedikt was educated at New York and Columbia Universities. He has been an associate editor with *Horizon Press* (1959–61), New York correspondent for *Art International* (1965–67), and associate editor of *Art News*. He has taught at Bennington College, and holds the Chair in Poetry at Sarah Lawrence. One of his former students is Erica Jong (*q.v.*). He received a Guggenheim Fellowship in Poetry in 1969.

His poetry ranges from surrealist fables to direct statement. He has a talent for assuming different voices in his poetry. In "The Cities," the voice shifts from a chemist's to his assistant's. A kind of dramatic situation arises, wherein the characters are deftly sketched in a few lines or stanzas. His poetry is often flat statement, the shock of which provides poetic weight. "Nothing can be fitted into the/ past once it is over. No/ future act can be committed/ then or inserted."—(from "Psalm II").

His art criticism has appeared in "Minimal Art" (*Dutton* 1968 $3.95), his film criticism in "Jean-Luc Goddard" (*Dutton* 1968 $2.45) and his Rock criticism in "The New Music" (*Dutton* 1970 $3.45). He also produced a happening based on his book of poetry, "The Body" at the loft of Robert Rauschenberg, and in Central Park. His happening "Box" was also produced at the Cubiculo Theatre in New York.

The Body. Poetry Program Ser. *Wesleyan Univ. Press* 1968 $4.75 pap. $2.45

Sky. Poetry Program Ser. *Wesleyan Univ. Press* 1970 $4.75

Mole Notes. *Wesleyan Univ. Press* 1971 $10.00 pap. $3.45

HARRISON, JIM. 1937–

Born in Grayling, Mich., Jim Harrison seems to be among the most promising young poets of his generation. After receiving his B.A. from Michigan State, he continued his education there and earned an M.A. degree in Comparative Literature. Harrison has lived since then in San Francisco, Boston and New York and taught for a time at the State University of New York at Stony Brook. He has moved back to Michigan where he presently lives on a farm.

Harrison's poetry is written in plain language, and he is one of the masters of the long poem—particularly in its linked-stanza form. In "Outlyer and Ghazals" he turned to a more complex verse technique, that of the Indian Ghazal. His work however is generally rural in tone, but without any echos of Frost. He exhibits a tendency toward surrealist image and horror: "This other speaks of bones, blood wet/ and limber, the rock in bodies. He takes/ me to the slaughter house, where lying/ sprawled, as a giant coil of rope,/ the bowels of cattle. . . ."—(from "fair/boy Christain Takes a Break").

Harrison is the recipient of a Guggenheim Fellowship and a grant from The National Endowment for the Arts.

PLAIN SONG. *Norton* 1965 $4.50

LOCATIONS. *Norton* 1968 $4.95 pap. $2.45

OUTLYER AND GHAZALS. *Simon & Schuster* 1971 $4.95 pap. $1.95

LETTERS TO YESENIN. *Sumac Press* 1973 $7.50 pap. $2.45

WAKOSKI, DIANE. 1937–

Diane Wakoski is perhaps the best-known poet of her generation. Her work is confessional and surreal, but belongs to no specific school. She seems more related in language to the native American idiom of William Carlos Williams than to the French Surrealists/Imagists like Prevert or Reverdy. Wakoski has admitted a poetic kinship with Allen Ginsberg, yet hers is truly as unique and perhaps strong a voice as his in American poetry. Contrasted with Ginsberg or some of the other Beats, Ms. Wakoski's subject matter almost always is personal, not political or public, and like Ginsberg's work finds expression in long, rambling musical poems. Recently her work has become more didactic—a direction which she considers her "main concern" in poetry. She shows a great sense of whimsey and humorous imagination even when writing of difficult emotional subjects, as may be seen in "The Betrayer." "You chopped down my trees—/ they were my legs—/ and unlike George Washington you did tell/ many lies./ You are my betrayer/ you woodsman,/ the man who stamps into the heart of this/ forest."

A particularly strong and gifted reader, Diane Wakoski is very active teaching workshops at the New School of Social Research in New York and at universities throughout the country. She gives frequent extensive reading tours. Recipient of a National Council on the Arts Prize and a Robert Frost Fellowship to the Bread Loaf Conference in Vermont, Ms. Wakoski makes her home mainly in New York, on the Lower East Side.

INSIDE THE BLOOD FACTORY. *Doubleday* 1968 pap. $1.95

THE MOTORCYCLE BETRAYAL POEMS. *Simon & Schuster* 1971 $6.95 Touchstone Bks. pap. $1.95

SMUDGING. *Black Sparrow* 1972 pap. $4.00

DANCING ON THE GRAVE OF A SON OF A BITCH. *Black Sparrow* 1973 signed ed. $15.00 pap. $4.00

GREED. *Black Sparrow* Pts. 5–7 1973 pap. $3.00 Pts. 8, 9, 11 1973 signed ed. $15.00 pap. $3.00

MAGELLANIC CLOUDS. *Black Sparrow* 1973 pap. $4.00

YOUNG, AL. 1939–

During the late fifties and early sixties, Al Young sang professionally and worked as a free lance musician playing guitar and flute. He was a disc-jockey for a California radio station, then taught creative writing at the San Francisco Museum of Art, later at the Berkeley Neighborhood Youth Corps, and is now a lecturer in creative writing at Stanford. Young is the recipient of the Wallace E. Stegner Fellowship in Creative Writing (1966–1967), the Joseph Henry Jackson Award (1969) of the San Francisco Foundation for his first book,

"Dancing," and a National Endowment for the Arts Grant for poetry (1969–70).

A novelist as well as poet, Young has received critical acclaim for "Snakes" (*Holt*, 1970 $4.95; *Dell* 1972 pap. $.75), which he describes as the story of "the emerging consciousness of a black teenager out of the urban Midwest." His poetry reflects his musical background and is written in the free easy speech idiom of the new "Black Renaissance."

DANCING: Poems. *Corinth Bks.* 1969 pap. $2.50

THE SONG TURNING BACK INTO ITSELF. *Holt* 1971 $5.95 pap. $2.95

KNOTT, BILL (St. Giraud, pseud.) 1940–

Bill Knott (who is alive and presumably resides in New York City) is the sort of artist whose life and attitudes are inseparable from his art. Paul Carroll describes hearing Knott's work for the first time at a university poetry reading, and he speaks of the power and magic of the unkempt soft-spoken poet, doing in American poetry what no one had really done before. His poems and surrealist imagist style derive largely from French, Spanish and other European surrealists like Desnos. His first book of poems, "The Naomi Poems, Book I: Corpse and Beans" (1968, o.p.) became an underground campus bestseller—the short, cryptic, sometimes exquisitely beautiful poems are the quintessence of a romantic tradition in American literature transformed by his contact with the European surrealists: "GOODBYE/ If you are still alive when you read this,/ close your eyes. I am/ under their lids, growing black." Knott's major themes are love, beautiful women, poems, and America. His poems are direct expressions of a lonely existence and the valuable connective fibres established when relationships intrude or visit.

Knott was born in 1940 in Gratiot County, Mich., and worked as a hospital orderly after serving in the Army as a private. He is active on the poetry reading circuit and his work is widely anthologized, appearing in "The Young American Poets" ed. by Paul Carroll, among other anthologies.

His "death" was announced via a letter from a friend to *Epoch* magazine, saying that at 26 Knott had committed suicide in his room in a North Clark Street tenement in Chicago. His existence, Knott states, has been posthumous thereafter.

AUTO-NECROPHILIA. *Big Table* pap. $2.95

NIGHTS OF NAOMI. *Barn Dream* 1971 signed ed. $15.00 with an inscription by the poet $25.00 pap. $3.00

LOVE POEMS TO MYSELF. *Barn Dream* 1973 signed ed. $20.00 pap. $3.00

JONG, ERICA. 1942–

Erica Jong is one of the young feminist poets who have become dramatically well-known in the past few years. Born Erica Mann in New York City, she was educated at Barnard and Columbia, and lived in Heidelberg, Germany for three years. Her first book, "Fruits and Vegetables" received wide critical acclaim. Since then she has published a novel, "Fear of Flying" (*Holt*, 1973, $6.95), and a second book of poetry entitled "Half-Lives." She teaches a poetry workshop at the YMHA Poetry Center in New York, and has read in women's prisons and at a Feminist Arts Festival in Buffalo. She is the recipient of *Poetry*'s Bess Hokins Prize and a grant from the New York State Council on the Arts (1971). Jong writes with a simplicity of diction derived from daily speech, and yet is witty and often epigramatic. Her peoms are concerned mainly with women, their new self-awareness and their liberation from the traditional roles in this society. "Already I hear stirrings of dissent./ He says he could have been a movie star/ He says he needs a full-time maid./ He says he never *meant*/ to marry God."—(from "Back to Africa").

FRUITS AND VEGETABLES. *Holt* 1971 pap. $2.95. The poet's first book.

HALF-LIVES. *Holt* 1973 $6.95 pap. $3.95. Jong's second book of poems.

GIOVANNI, NIKKI. 1943–

Born in Knoxville, Tenn., Giovanni grew up in Lincoln Heights, Ohio, and is rapidly becoming the most widely known contemporary black poet in America. She went to Fisk University when she was 16 and worked in the Writers' Workshop there, studied briefly at the University of Pennsylvania, and in Cincinnati she organized the city's first Black Arts Festival. Through her appearances on late-night television talk shows and at a gala reading at Philharmonic Hall at New York's Lincoln Center, she has popularized the poetic medium, particularly as it finds expression in the new vibrant black idiom. Presently teaching black literature at Rutgers University in New Brunswick, Giovanni has received grants from the Harlem Cultural Council, the Ford Foundation, and the National Council of the Arts. She has been working with Nina Simone on Simone's autobiography, and has also written poetry for children: "Spin a Soft Black Song: Poems for Children" (*Hill & Wang* 1971 $5.50) and "Ego Tripping and Other Poems for Young Readers" (*Lawrence Hill* 1973 $5.95 pap. $2.95). The power in her work stems directly from the experience of the black American woman, and yet amid the pain and anger there is often a great sense of humor and a joy and tenderness.

The following excerpt is taken from "Nikki-Rosa:" "and I really hope no white person ever has cause to write/ about me/ because they never understand Black love is Black wealth and/ they'll/ probably talk about my hard childhood and never understand that all the while I was quite happy. . . ."

BLACK JUDGEMENT. *Broadside* 1968 pap. $1.50

BLACK FEELING, BLACK TALK. *Broadside* 3rd ed. 1970 pap. $1.00

BLACK FEELING, BLACK TALK, BLACK JUDGEMENT. *Morrow* 1970 pap. $1.75

RE: Creation. *Broadside* 1971 $4.50 pap. $1.50 tape $5.00

GEMINI: An Extended Autobiographical Statement on My First Twenty-five Years of Being a Black Poet. *Bobbs* $5.95; *Viking* Compass Bks. 1973 pap. $1.95

MY HOUSE. *Morrow* 1972 $5.95 pap. $1.95. Poems.

TATE, JAMES. 1943–

Tate was born in Kansas City, Mo. and was educated at the University of Missouri and Kansas State College. He received his M.F.A. in the Creative Writing Program at the University of Iowa, Iowa City. One of the editors of the *Barn Dream Press*, a small Boston press devoted to the publication of younger poets, Tate has been a lecturer at the University of Iowa's Writer's Workshop, 1965–67, at the University of California in Berkeley, and presently is an assistant professor at Columbia University where he teaches in the School of the Arts. Of all the poets of the younger generation Tate is already the most widely anthologized, his poems appearing in *McGraw-Hill*'s "Modern Poets" (1963), "Heartland" (1967), Paul Caroll's "Young American Poets" (1968), Mark Strand's "Contemporary American Poets" (1969) and in the new big "Norton Anthology of Modern Poetry" (Ellman and O'Clair, 1973). His first book, "The Lost Pilot" was the winner of the Yale Series of Younger Poets prize in 1966.

James Tate says of himself and his work that it is "in the tradition of . . . Whitman, Williams and Neruda." He is at times allied with the Bly/Wright deep image/surrealist movement: "Unconsumable material is everywhere;/ red machinery washes out the gutter./ And the grim musicians/ are seen stalking themselves with rare/ cacti in their saxophones./ Mosquitoes linger in the air/ like snowy egrets."—(from "The Square at Dawn").

But there is often a more Williamesque quality to his work, as in "The Blue Bobby," which simply presents the subject—a bird native to the Galapagos—letting the poem and its images arise from the "thing" as it is. Tate has been called "an ironical, original, self-absorbed poet who glances with amusement at love, humanity, himself"—(Julian Symons). His work according to some critics is reminiscent of Robert Lowell and Sylvia Plath, but his "low-keyed, off-hand style is his own and counterpoints forcefully with the feelings of estrangement, anger, and self-abasing humor to be found in a good many of the poems"—(H. Jaffe). A prolific poet, Tate has published well over a dozen books of poetry—mainly with small presses—since the appearance of "The Lost Pilot."

THE LOST PILOT. Series of Younger Poets. *Yale Univ. Press* 1967 $4.50 pap. $1.65

THE OBLIVION HA-HA. *Little-Atlantic* 1970 pap. $1.95

HINTS TO PILGRIMS. *Halty Ferguson* 1971 $40.00 pap. $4.50

TORCHE. *Unicorn Press* 2nd ed. rev. & enl. 1971 $5.95

ABSENCES. *Little-Atlantic* 1972 $5.95 pap. $1.95

WHITING, NATHAN. 1946–

Nathan Whiting, born in Illinois in 1946, has already become a popular and recognized figure in today's poetry underground. Although a Midwesterner who spent some time at the Universities of Oklahoma and Iowa (in the famed creative writing program in the latter school), Whiting has become one of the major voices speaking for the New York urban culture. His second book, "Buffalo Poem," is a book-length exploration of an isolated man, against a vividly and empathetically described background of Buffalo, N.Y., where the poet himself worked for a year as a cook in a mental institution.

Nathan Whiting's poetry seems to be a relentless search for freedom: spiritual, psychological and above all poetical. Intensely concerned with the liberation of form, even of the now-habitual free form most young writers have made their medium, he brings to his poetry an enviable control of line and plain, honest language nearly unparalleled in this youngest generation of poets: "I try to carve the smoke/ As it sneaks from the fire/ onto a row of hams/ In this gray walled smoke house./ I see myself on the wall/ advertised for sale/ I would rest here,/ Pounding nails/ to hold this place together,/ But to escape, I must be owned"—(from "Poems of an Ownerless Slave").

Associated earlier in his career with Bill Knott and James Tate, and more recently with Hugh Seidman, Michael Heller and Charles Levendosky—the latter three associated with a movement toward incorporation of science and technology into their poetry—Whiting seems to belong to no existing school of poetry. Perhpas through his originality he will prove to be the nucleus of a movement yet to evidence itself. He is currently active giving poetry readings, teaching workshops in the New York Public Libraries, and participating in various city-oriented poetry projects sponsored by The Academy of American Poets.

WHILE COURTING THE SERGEANT'S DAUGHTER. *Pym Randall* 1969 $2.00. First book of poems.

BUFFALO POEM. *Pym Randall* 1970 $2.00. A book-length poem.

TRANSITIONS: Positions and Directions Undefined. *Seven Woods Press* 1972 pap. $2.75. A book-length poem.

SHAPIRO, DAVID. 1947–

Not only has he published several books of poems, but David Shapiro also has been an art critic for *Art News* and *Craft Horizons*, and a professional violinist. Since 1964 he has been a teacher and has studied writing done by children. He has taught at the Academy of American Poets, the Bedford-Stuyvesant Children's Museum, Lincoln Center, and Teachers and Writers Cooperative, and with Kenneth Koch, collected an anthology of writing by the children from some of these programs. In 1970 *Random House* published "An Anthology of New York Poets" edited by Shapiro and Ron Padgett.

Shapiro's poetry has been published in many magazines, among them *Poetry* and *The Paris Review*. His first book of poems, "January," was brought out in 1965 by *Holt, Rinehart and Winston*. He has received the Book-of-the-Month Club Award, the Robert Frost Fellowship of Bread Loaf, and a Merrill Foundation grant. He was also offered a Kellett Fellowship to Clare College, Cambridge, where he took a degree, and is now living in New York while a doctoral candidate at Columbia.

POEMS FROM DEAL. *Dutton* 1969 $4.50 pap. $2.45

MAN HOLDING AN ACOUSTIC PANEL AND OTHER POEMS. *Dutton* 1971 $6.95

THE PAGE-TURNER. *Liveright* 1973 $4.95 pap. $2.50

(with Ron Padgett) ANTHOLOGY OF NEW YORK POETS. *Random* 1970 $12.95 Vintage Bks. pap. $3.95

—E.M.

Chapter 10

British Fiction: Early Period

"These books are written chiefly to the young, the ignorant, and the idle, to whom they serve as lectures of conduct, and introductions into life."
—SAMUEL JOHNSON, *Rambler No. 4.*
Novel: "A small tale, generally of love."   —JOHNSON'S DICTIONARY.

Whatever the English novel is—whether essentially an exciting story, a conflict between individuals, a "realistic" portrayal of the outer details of life or of psychological complexities, a social analysis, an allegory of human fate, or, as E. M. Forster has most generally defined it, a narrative prose fiction at least fifty thousand words long—critics agree that it came to its first maturity in the 18th century in the masterpieces of Richardson, Fielding, and their contemporaries. Its name comes from the French *nouvelle*, or short story, and from the Italian *novella*, a story of a kind popular in the Renaissance, both stemming from the Latin *novella*—"new things, news"—and its characteristics derive from a great variety of sources across the centuries. Keeping in mind that a novelist has available all of cultural history and his own complex experience—that he or she may have grown up with more feeling for Homer or Shakespeare than for any prose fiction, and that a scene may be shaped more by family breakfast than by a recollection of Cervantes—we may usefully glance at the narrative prose fiction available to the early English novelist.

Historical surveys of imaginative prose usually start with the Joseph story in the Bible, not as a source but as an example of the antiquity of the form (sophisticated western narrative *verse* goes back at least to the Homeric epics). The Greek romances of the second and third centuries A.D., widely read in modern times, already show the two main directions that the novel still takes and often tries to unite—the marvelous beyond the control of time and space, and the tumults of human life realistically and even satirically portrayed. The former is most conveniently demonstrated in such stories as Longus's "Daphnis and Chloe," Xenophon's "An Ephesian Tale," and Dio Chrysostom's "The Hunters of Euboea" collected in Moses Hadas's, "Three Greek Romances" (*Bobbs* 1964 $6.00 pap. $1.45); the latter, in the "Satyricon" of Petronius (*q.v.*) and "The Golden Ass" of Apuleius (*q.v.*).

The next major contributions to the storehouse of narrative prose, in the middle ages, include saints' lives, fables, sermons with illustrative examples, and romances, which after verse successes like those of the French Chrétien de Troyes (*q.v.*) proliferated in prose in the 14th and 15th centuries and culminated artistically in Malory's (*q.v.*) "*Morte d'Arthur.*" The short Italian novelles, beginning about the 13th century, were often collected, sometimes with frames to tie them together. Of these the most famous was Boccaccio's (*q.v.*) "Decameron" of the 14th century, in which ten young people, fleeing the plague of 1348, stay ten days at a country estate, each telling a story every day. These were often translated into other languages, including English, and imitated.

With the printing press in the late 15th century came a new era of mass reading, which meant a mass audience educated as far as narrative prose. In the 16th century, the great humanist Thomas More wrote his "Utopia" in Latin, but the popular English translation made the combination of satiric condemnation of the real with a fanciful elaboration of the ideal available as an important influence. His younger contemporary François Rabelais provides a focus on comic invention, the humorous miscellany strung on a weird series of events and combining the very earthy with the immensely imaginative, consciously in the comic tradition of Aristophanes and Lucian. From the Spanish, particularly "*Lazarillo de Tormes*" (1554), comes the powerful picaresque element (*picaro*, rogue), the strung-out adventures of a rogue outsider wandering through society, preying on it, and satirically exposing its hypocrisy. In Gascoigne's "Adventures of F. J." (1573; available in "Complete Works" ed. by John W. Cunliffe 2 vols. 1907 *Scholarly Press* $44.50), the startling Italian manner is effectively domesticated by an English setting. Toward the end of the century the traditions of the realistic and the fanciful appear separately in two of the most notable prose fictions, Thomas Nashe's "Unfortunate Traveler" (1594; available in vol. 2 of "Works" ed. by R. B. McKerrow 5 vols. 1904. *Barnes & Noble* 1966 set $60.00; available separately ed. by J. B. Steane *Penguin* pap. $2.95) and Sir Philip Sidney's pastoral "Arcadia" (ed. by Carl Dennis *Kent State Univ. Press* 1970 $8.00 pap. $4.75). Shorter prose narratives continued to appear not only in translation and imitation of the *novelle* but also in the inserted narratives in Sidney's "Arcadia" and in such popular pieces as Thomas Deloney's "Novels" (ed. by Merritt E. Lawlis 1961 o.p.), Thomas Dekker's (*q.v.*) "Non-Dramatic Works" (ed. by Alexander B. Grosart. 5 vols. 1884 *Russell & Russell* 1964 $60.00), and Robert Green's pamphlets printed by Bodley Head (1923–24, o.p.) on London tradespeople and rogues, and cheap little pamphlets (chapbooks) on celebrities like the German conjurer Johannes Faustus.

The 17th century opened with the single most lasting and massive influence on the later English novel, Cervantes' (*q.v.*) quickly translated "Don Quixote." It provided the model of a continued narrative arising from the fundamental human paradoxes in its two singular and yet representative main characters—Quixote the obsessed idealist and Sancho the spontaneous pragmatist, both facing a world in its modern danger of disintegration—and of unifying point of view, concentrated in the rational, aristocratic, and humane narrator, Cide Hamete Benengeli, who can plausibly test the oddities of the main characters and himself be tested by Cervantes and ourselves. Later in the century came the influences of the Theophrastan "character" a sketch of a type, as in Samuel Butler's (*q.v.*) collection "Characters" (ed. by Charles W. Daves *Press of Case Western Reserve* 1970 $10.50), as of "a politician" or "an author"; the religious allegory in prose, often spurred by the Puritan spiritual autobiography, as best shown in Bunyan's (*q.v.*) "Pilgrim's Progress'; French courtly romances, as in Mme. de la Fayette's (*q.v.*) "Princesse de Cleves," and the social-psychological elaborations of Scudery; English romances, wonder tales and love intrigues, as in Congreve's (*q.v.*) "Incognita" or Aphra Behn's pieces, notably "Oroonoko" the superb story of the African prince brought as a slave to the West Indies; travel accounts and biographies in the heyday of exploration.

In the 18th century, these elements came together with the rise to dominance of bourgeoisie, a social class less attuned than its predecessor to the classical niceties of poetry and drama. The novel as it developed taught manners as well as morals, useful characteristics in an age of social change. It had the practical value of exhibiting people like ourselves facing the problems we also face. For practical people concerned with understanding human society and acting in it, Defoe, Richardson, and Fielding claimed to provide models of conduct even more useful than those in histories, biographies, or the periodical essays of Addison and Steele.

Capitalizing on the problems of making prose fiction artistically respectable, satisfying its readers' wishes for social and ethical guidance as well as escape, and fashioning some sort of order in a world where the old rules were apparently breaking down, the great masters of the 18th century and their lesser contemporaries left a rich legacy to their successors. In the process, they incorporated a diversity of new materials, notably the journalistic description of real or imagined places (particularly by Swift, Defoe, and Smollett); the essay (by Fielding and Goldsmith); the eastern tale, developed after the translation of the "Arabian Nights" into French in 1700, in famous short stories by Addison, Goldsmith, and Johnson, in Johnson's (*q.v.*) short novel "Rasselas," and William Beckford's "Vathek"; the rogue biography as in Defoe's (*q.v.*) "Moll Flanders" and Fielding's (*q.v.*) "Jonathan Wild," the dramatic scene, especially by Richardson and Fielding; the miscellany, as in Swift's (*q.v.*) "Tale of a Tub" and Sterne's (*q.v.*) "Tristram Shandy."

In technique, the 18th-century novelists explored varieties of points of view, particularly in the nature of the first-person narrator. Their fictional spokesmen range from the apparently simple autobiographers of Defoe through the participants in Richardson's epistolary experiments (in "Sir Charles Grandison," he even hides a stenographer in a closet to give the illusion of authenticity to a reported conference) to the complexities of Swift's, Goldsmith's, Burney's and Sterne's narrators, who arouse in us subtler feelings than straightforward sympathy. Structurally, Fielding achieves in "Tom Jones" the Aristotelian ideal of unity, showing that plot, theme, characters, scenes, all can be brought together coherently around one main action—Tom's movement from chaos to prudence and harmony. After this achievement of a unified vision in a narrative prose fiction not only of the English world of 1745 but of universal human character, any subsequent looseness in a novel indicates either deliberate subversion, as in Sterne, or a lesser degree of artistic commitment, as in the remaining novelists of the 18th century until Jane Austen.

As another technical legacy, the novelists provided their successors with various forms of realism, from Defoe's literalness of surface, where we know exactly how many bolts of cloth Moll stole, what they were worth, who testified, and the judge's manner; through Richardson's rendition of psychological details and their way in people's faces, words, and gestures; through Fielding's unearthing the local versions of eternally real human qualities; through Stern's pursuit of eccentric psychology into what we would call the neurotic, which he persuades us is our mental makeup as well as his. What unites them in this respect is interest in the way people's minds work in recognizable situations. Even Defoe's details are mainly effective in showing the practical motivations of his adventurers, and Swift's "Gulliver's Travels" gains life as we discover that the speaker wants what we want. Goldsmith's sense of the day-to-day life of a country parson's family, Fanny Burney's sympathy for a 17-year-old girl with aristocratic expectations and vulgar relatives (a great base for Jane Austen), and Smollett's exaggeration of the filth of London milk or the noise at Bath all persuade us of other people's existence through their responses to the details of life.

In the latter part of the 18th century a pervasive concern with psychology, particularly with the contents of the mind at the moment, tends to assume in lesser hands than Richardson's and Sterne's the alternatives of sentimentality and melodramatic thrill-seeking. Among the more notable sentimental novels—where domestic problems of love, trust, marriage, education, friendship, sibling relationships, etc., are likely to be explored in a tearful bourgeois milieu—are Sarah Fielding's "David Simple" (for which her famous brother wrote a foreword), Henry Mackenzie's "Man of Feeling" and "Man of Sentiment," and Thomas Day's "History of Sandford and Merton." The corresponding tendency toward romance developed in what came to be called the gothic novel, which comes to prominence with Walpole's "Castle of Otranto" and rides a course through such oddities as Ann Radcliffe's "Mysteries of Udolpho," M. G. Lewis's "The Monk," and Beckford's (*q.v.*) eccentrically fascinating "Vathek."

These last are chiefly notable for what they led to: Jane Austen's achievements with domestic situations, problem novels like Godwin's "Caleb Williams" or the social explorations of the Victorians, Scott's historical romances, and the incorporation of the eerie into the larger concerns of Poe, Emily Bronte, and Hawthorne. But the final achievement of the 18th century novel, its chief legacy to us, is its small group of actual masterpieces, possibly "Moll Flanders," "Joseph Andrews," "The Vicar of Wakefield," "Rasselas," "Humphry Clinker," and certainly "Gulliver's Travels," "Clarissa," "Tom Jones," and "Tristram Shandy."

ANTHOLOGIES, HISTORY AND CRITICISM

Allen, Walter. THE ENGLISH NOVEL. *Dutton* 1955 $6.95 pap. $1.95

Ashley, R., and E. M. Moseley, Eds. ELIZABETHAN FICTION. *Holt* (Rinehart) 1953 pap. $3.00; *Peter Smith* $5.00. A substantial collection.

Baker, Ernest A. A HISTORY OF THE ENGLISH NOVEL. *Barnes & Noble* 11 vols. 1924–1939 Vol. I The Age of Romance Vol. 2 The Elizabethan Age and After Vol. 3 Later Romances and the Establishment of Realism Vol. 4 Intellectual Realism from Richardson to Sterne Vol. 5 The Novel of Sentiment and the Gothic Romance. vols. 1-5 each $6.50. *For a full listing see Chapter 4, Broad Studies and General Anthologies: Discussions of the Novel.*

Baugh, Albert C., and others, Eds. A LITERARY HISTORY OF ENGLAND. *Appleton* 1949. 2nd ed. 4 vols. in 1 1967 $17.85 4 vols. pap. each $6.25 Literary chronicle, scholarly and readable. Vol. I The Middle Ages Vol. 2 The Renaissance Vol. 3 The Restoration and Eighteenth Century. *For comment see Chapter 3, Reference Books—Literature: Histories and Dictionaries.*

Booth, Wayne C. THE RHETORIC OF FICTION. *Univ. of Chicago Press* 1961 $7.50 Phoenix Bks. pap. $2.75. One of the most influential studies of the last scholarly generation, largely on the nature of the fictional narrator.

Brissenden, R. F., Ed. STUDIES IN THE EIGHTEENTH CENTURY. *Univ. of Toronto Press* 2 vols. Vol. I (1968) Vol 2 (1973) each $15.00

Clifford, James L., Ed. EIGHTEENTH CENTURY ENGLISH LITERATURE. *Oxford* Galaxy Bk. 1959 pap. $2.95. Reprints a number of essays valuable to understanding the ideas and literature of the time.

MAN VERSUS SOCIETY IN EIGHTEENTH CENTURY BRITAIN. *Cambridge* 1968 $9.00; *Norton* Norton Lib. 1972 pap. $2.25. A number of original essays by distinguished scholars on such matters as the condition of the musician or painter of the time.

Collier, J. Payne, Ed. ILLUSTRATIONS OF EARLY ENGLISH POPULAR LITERATURE. 1863 *Blom* 2 vols. 1966 $37.50

Coulton, G. G. MEDIEVAL PANORAMA: The English Scene from Conquest to Reformation. 1938 1944 1955. *Norton* Norton Lib. 1974 pap. $4.95; *Richard West* repr. of 1944 ed. $20.00. A well-written and informative survey.

Davis, Walter R. IDEAL AND ACT IN ELIZABETHAN FICTION. *Princeton Univ. Press* 1969 $11.50

Day, Robert Adam. TOLD IN LETTERS: Epistolary Fiction before Richardson. *Univ. of Michigan Press* 1966 $7.50. A valuable analysis of plots and themes from which Richardson's work derived.

Elliott, Robert C. THE POWER OF SATIRE: Magic, Ritual, Art. *Princeton Univ. Press* 1960 pap. $3.45. A fine analysis of Swift, stimulating background for the other satiric novelists.

ENGLISH LITERATURE, 1660–1800: A Bibliography of Modern Studies. *Princeton Univ. Press* 6 vols. 1950–72. vols. I–2 ed. by L. A. Landa Vol. I 1926–1938 (1950) $12.50 Vol. 2 1939–1950 (1952) o.p. Vols. 3–4 ed. by G. J. Kolb and C. A. Zimansky Vol. 3 1951–1957 (1962) $12.50 Vol. 4 1957–1960 (1962) o.p. Vol. 5 1961–1966 (1972) ed. by G. S. Alleman and others Vol. 6 (1966–1970) with index to vols. 5–6 (1972) ed. by C. A. Zimansky each $15.00. Present-day criticism on literature of the period 1600–1800.

George, M. Dorothy. LONDON LIFE IN THE EIGHTEENTH CENTURY. *Putnam* Capricorn Bks. 1965 pap. $2.95; *Peter Smith* $5.00. An authoritative historical description based on the materials available 40 years ago and not yet superseded.

Golden, Morris. THE SELF OBSERVED: Swift, Johnson, Wordsworth. *Johns Hopkins Univ. Press* 1972 $8.00. An attempt to relate the writings, the authors' views of themselves, and the attitudes of the times. Some pertinent materials on the prose fictions of Swift and Johnson.

Grierson, Herbert J. CROSS CURRENTS IN ENGLISH LITERATURE OF THE SEVENTEENTH CENTURY. 1959. *Peter Smith* $5.00. Lectures given at Cornell (1926–27) focusing on the "conflict between Renaissance humanism and the English Puritanism of the Reformation"—(*PW*).

Harrison, G. B., Ed. THE ELIZABETHAN JOURNALS: Being a Record of Those Things Most Talked of during the Years. *Peter Smith* 2 vols. Vol. I 1591–1597 Vol. 2 1598–1603 each $10.00. An abridgement of the original three-volume edition (1928–33).

"These delightful gossip books comprise what is virtually a day-by-day account of the things, serious and frivolous, which most Englishmen were talking about during the last 12 years of Elizabeth's reign"—(*LJ*).

Henderson, Philip, Ed. SHORTER NOVELS: Seventeenth Century. Contains Emanuel Ford, "Ornatus and Artesia" (1634); Aphra Behn, "Oroonoko" (1688); Henry Neville, "The Isle of Pines" (1668); William Congreve, "Incognita" (1692). *Dutton* Everyman's 1960 1967 $3.50 pap. $1.50

Huizinga, Johan. THE WANING OF THE MIDDLE AGES: A Study of the Forms of Life, Thought and Art in France and the Netherlands in the 14th and 15th Centuries. 1924. *St. Martin's* $9.50; *Doubleday* Anchor Bks. pap. $2.50. The authoritative, influential study of the late medieval background.

Jones, Richard F., Ed. THE SEVENTEENTH CENTURY: Studies in the History of English Thought and Literature from Bacon to Pope. *Stanford Univ. Press* 1951 $10.00 pap. $2.95. This volume reprints a number of essays by noted scholars. It focuses largely on the intellectual context of the works discussed.

Kane, George. MIDDLE ENGLISH LITERATURE: A Critical Study of the Romances, the Religious Lyrics, Piers Plowman. 1951. *Barnes & Noble* 1970 $8.50

Kettle, Arnold. AN INTRODUCTION TO THE ENGLISH NOVEL. 2 vols. Vol. I Up to George Eliot. *Harper* Perenn. Lib. 2 vols. in 1 pap. $1.75; *Hillary House* 2 vols. each $5.50. An excellent, readable discussion of authors and works covered in this chapter.

Kuhn, Albert J., Ed. THREE SENTIMENTAL NOVELS. Sterne's "A Sentimental Journey," Mackenzie's "The Man of Feeling" and Day's "The History of Sandford and Merton." *Holt* (Rinehart) 1970 pap. $2.25

Kunitz, Stanley J., and Howard Haycraft, Eds. BRITISH AUTHORS BEFORE 1800: A Biographical Dictionary. Complete in I vol. with 650 biographies and 220 portraits. *Wilson* 1952 $10.00

Lewis, C. S. ENGLISH LITERATURE IN THE SIXTEEN CENTURY EXCLUDING DRAMA. *Oxford* 1954 $11.50. On the medieval literature of Scotland and the works of Sidney, Spenser and Hooker.

Lovejoy, Arthur O. ESSAYS IN THE HISTORY OF IDEAS. *Johns Hopkins Univ. Press* 1948 $11.00. Reprints a number of the author's studies in the history of ideas, some of them (like the "Parallel between Classicism and Deism") fundamental to knowing the early 18th century.

THE GREAT CHAIN OF BEING. *Harvard Univ. Press* 1936. $9.00 pap. $2.75. A seminal and still standard study of an idea fundamental to western thought from Plato to Pope.

McKillop, Alan Dugald. EARLY MASTERS OF ENGLISH FICTION. *Univ. of Kansas Press* 1956 $7.00 pap. 1968 $2.95. A penetrating account of the originality and vigor of the essential contributions to the novel form made by Defoe, Richardson, Fielding, Smollett and Sterne.

Miller, Edwin Haviland. THE PROFESSIONAL WRITER IN ELIZABETHAN ENGLAND: A Study of Nondramatic Literature. *Harvard Univ. Press* 1959 $8.00

A scholarly examination which "documents and analyzes the many social, political, and aesthetic tensions which attended the development of a new English creature—the would-be professional writer"—(*L J*).

Mish, Charles C. ENGLISH PROSE FICTION, 1600–1700: A Chronological Check List. *Univ. Press of Virginia* 2nd ed. 1967 $7.50

RESTORATION PROSE FICTION, 1666–1700: An Anthology of Representative Pieces. *Univ. of Nebraska Press* 1970 $8.95

Nugent, Elizabeth M., Ed. THOUGHT AND CULTURE OF THE ENGLISH RENAISSANCE: An Anthology of Early Tudor Prose, 1481–1555. *Humanities* 1954 pap. 1969 2 vols. set $8.25

O'Dell, Sterg. CHRONOLOGICAL LIST OF PROSE FICTION IN ENGLISH PRINTED IN ENGLAND AND OTHER COUNTRIES, 1475–1640. 1954 *Kraus* $9.50

Paulson, Ronald. THE FICTIONS OF SATIRE. *Johns Hopkins Univ. Press* 1967 $7.00. Valuable both for theoretical positions and for analysis of specific works in this period.

SATIRE AND THE NOVEL IN EIGHTEENTH-CENTURY ENGLAND. *Yale Univ. Press* 1967 $8.50

"Comprehensive, balanced, and authoritative. . . . Will surely be required reading for all students of the novel"—(*L J*).

Richetti, John J. THE POPULAR FICTION BEFORE RICHARDSON: Narrative Patterns, 1700–1739. *Oxford* 1969 $11.00 An authoritative study of the context of the novel's birth.

Rose, Mark. HEROIC LOVE: Studies in Sidney and Spenser. *Harvard Univ. Press* 1968 $4.75. Useful here for its discussion of "Arcadia."

Röstvig, Maren-Sofie. THE HAPPY MAN: Studies in the Metamorphoses of a Classical Ideal. 2 vols. 1958 *Humanities Press* Vol. I 1600–1700 2nd ed. (1962) $7.75 Vol. 2 1700–1760 2nd ed. (1971) $10.75

Schilling, Bernard N., Ed. ESSENTIAL ARTICLES FOR THE STUDY OF ENGLISH AUGUSTAN BACKGROUNDS. *Shoe String* 1961 $8.50. Reprints a large number of valuable essays on the literature and ideas of the 17th and 18th centuries.

Sherbo, Arthur. STUDIES IN THE EIGHTEENTH CENTURY ENGLISH NOVEL. *Michigan State Univ. Press* 1969 $6.00. A hardheaded, sometimes amusing attack on the excesses of contemporary criticism of the 18th-century novel.

Spector, Robert Donald, Ed. ESSAYS ON THE EIGHTEENTH-CENTURY NOVEL. On Defoe, Richardson, Fielding, Smollett and Sterne. *Peter Smith* $4.00

Tave, Stuart M. THE AMIABLE HUMORIST. *Univ. of Chicago Press* 1960 $7.50. A thoughtful and informative study of a character type in 18th-century literature.

Tompkins, J. M. S. THE POPULAR NOVEL IN ENGLAND, 1770–1800. 1932. 1961. *Peter Smith* $4.00

Van Ghent, Dorothy. THE ENGLISH NOVEL: Form and Function. *Holt* (Rinehart) 1953 text ed. $9.00; *Harper* 1961 Perenn. Lib. pap. $1.45. 18 superb essays on the major classics from Richardson to Lawrence.

Wagenknecht, Edward Charles. CAVALCADE OF THE ENGLISH NOVEL. From Elizabeth to George VI. *Holt* 1943 new ed. with supplementary bibliography 1954 $11.95 text ed. $10.00. Survey of the great novelists from Defoe to the recent past.

Wasserman, Earl R., Ed. ASPECTS OF THE EIGHTEENTH CENTURY. *Johns Hopkins Univ. Press* 1965 $10.00. Reprints several major essays on the ideas of the 18th century.

Watkins, W. B. C. PERILOUS BALANCE: The Tragic Genius of Swift, Johnson, and Sterne. 1939 *Somerset Pub.* $7.50. Perceptive study of how the sensitivities of the writers affected what they saw and how they described it.

Watt, Ian. THE RISE OF THE NOVEL: Studies in Defoe, Richardson and Fielding. *Univ. of California Press* 1957 $7.00 1959 pap $2.50. The single best book in the field: brilliant, learned, and immensely stimulating.

Williams, Kathleen., Ed. BACKGROUNDS TO EIGHTEENTH-CENTURY LITERATURE. *Chandler Pub.* 1971 pap. $5.50. Reprints a number of valuable essays largely on the intellectual context.

MALORY, SIR THOMAS. fl. 1470.

Sir Thomas Malory's works (consisting of the legends of Sir Lancelot, Sir Gareth, Sir Tristram and the Holy Grail as well as the stories of Arthur's coming to the throne, his wars with the Emperor Lucius and his death) are the most influential expression of Arthurian material in English. The author's sources are principally French romances, but his own contributions are substantial and the result is a vigorous and resonant prose. "Le Morte d'Arthur," finished between March 1469 and March 1470, was first printed in 1485 by William Caxton, the earliest English printer.

Historically, Malory is identified with a member of an old Warwickshire family, a knight who came into his father's estates about 1433 and spent 20 years of his later life in jail, accused of various crimes. The discovery of a manuscript version of "Le Morte d'Arthur" in 1934 in the library of Winchester College supported the identification of Malory the author with Malory the traitor, burglar and rapist, and showed that many of the inconsistencies in the text were traceable to the printing house rather than to the author. The most reliable modern version, therefore, is one like Eugène Vinaver's (*Oxford*) which is based on the Winchester manuscript.

WORKS. Ed. by Eugène Vinaver. *Oxford* 1947 2nd ed. 1967 3 vols. $80.00 Stand. Auth. $9.00

LE MORTE D'ARTHUR. Ed. by Oskar H. Sommers. 1889–91. *AMS Press* 3 vols in 2 set $85.00; ed. by C. R. Sanders and C. E. Ward *Appleton* pap. $2.05; *Dutton* Everyman's 2 vols. each $3.50; *Folcroft* repr. of 1903 ed. 1973 3 vols. $100.00 3 vols. in 1 lib. bdg. $19.50; trans. by Keith Baines *New Am. Lib.* Mentor pap. $1.25; ed. by D. S. Brewer *Northwestern Univ. Press* $5.00 pap. $2.50; ed. by Janet Cowen *Penguin* 2 vols. pap. each $2.45; *Clarkson N. Potter* $6.00; *St. Martin's* 1972 $50.00; *Scholarly Press* repr. of 1903 ed. $19.50; *University Books* 2 vols. in 1 $15.00

KING ARTHUR AND HIS KNIGHTS. Sel. and ed. by R. T. Davies *Barnes & Noble* 1967 $5.50; ed. by Sidney Lanier *Grosset* Ill. Jr. Lib. $2.95 special ed. $3.95 deluxe ed. $4.95 lib. bdg. $3.79

THE BOOK OF MARVELLOUS ADVENTURES AND OTHER BOOKS OF MORTE D'ARTHUR. *Folcroft* 1973 lib. bdg. $12.50

THE TALE OF THE DEATH OF KING ARTHUR. Ed. by Eugène Vinaver. *Oxford* 1955 $3.75

Books about Malory

Sir Thomas Malory, His Turbulent Career: A Biography. By Edward Hicks. 1928. *Octagon* 1970 $7.50
Malory. By Eugène Vinaver. 1929. *Oxford* $7.75. Malory's foremost modern editor.
Malory's Originality: A Critical Study of "Le Morte d'Arthur." Ed. by R. M. Lumiansky. *Johns Hopkins Univ. Press* 1964 $9.00
    This critique by six scholars undertakes to prove that "Malory's purpose was to reveal the tragic destruction over-taking the society of the Round Table"—(*LJ*).
The Ill-framed Knight: A Skeptical Inquiry into the Identity of Sir Thomas Malory. By William Matthews. *Univ. of California Press* 1966 $7.50
Sir Thomas Malory. By Edmund Reiss. English Authors Ser. *Twayne* 1966 $5.50. With chronology and selected bibliography.

MORE, SIR THOMAS, ST. 1478–1535.

More is probably best known for his "Utopia" which was first written in Latin (then the language of literary and intellectual Europe) and printed in Louvain, where the author was living as envoy, in 1516; it was translated into English in 1551. As the first part of this small masterpiece indicates, More was then weighing an offer to be an adviser to Henry VIII. He was well aware of the compromises, bitterness, frustration, and dirty work that such an office involved in a feudal world breaking up into nations and ravaged by greedy, warring princes unconcerned for the multitudes of uprooted and oppressed (a world well described in Huizinga's "Waning of the Middle Ages"). In the second part, More develops his famous *utopia*—a Greek word punning on the meanings "a good place" and "no place"—a religious communistic society where the common ownership of goods, obligatory work for everyone, and the regular life of all before the eyes of all ensures that man's baser nature will remain thoroughly under control. Inspired by Plato's "Republic," More's "Utopia" became in turn the urbane legacy of the humanistic movement (in which More's friends were most notably Erasmus, Colet and Grocyn) to succeeding ages. More's career decision, as everyone knows, was to accept Henry's employment, which led to an agonizing test of political loyalty and personal integrity, to martyrdom, and to eventual sainthood.

THE COMPLETE WORKS OF ST. THOMAS MORE. Projected in 16 vols. 7 vols. now available. *Yale Univ. Press* 1963–72 The History of King Richard III ed. by Richard S.

Sylvester (1963) $12.50 Utopia ed. by Edward Surtz, S. J., and J. H. Hexter (1965)
$17.50 *Responsio ad Lutherum* ed. by John Headley 2 vols. (1969) $30.00 Confutation of Tyndale's Answer ed. by Louis A. Schuster, 3 vols. (1972) $60.00

It is generally accepted that More's "Richard III" initiates modern historical writing. This scholarly edition offers this work complete, with parallel English (1557) and Latin (1565) texts, major variant readings, a
collation of all extant manuscript versions and, for the first time in full, the important early draft of the Latin
text, Manuscript Arundel 43 in the College of Arms. The first scholarly treatment of More's "Utopia" incorporates the advances made in Renaissance studies in the 20th century and thus places the work within the
context of its times. The definitive Latin text is based on the edition of March 1518, the last to be corrected by
More himself. There is a complete list of variant readings from the editions of 1516, 1517 and November
1518, with a parallel English text, a revision of the G. C. Richards translation.

SELECTED WORKS OF ST. THOMAS MORE. Projected in 7 vols. 2 vols. now available.
Yale Univ. Press 1961—. Selected letters ed. by Elizabeth Frances Rogers with fwd.
by L. L. Martz and R. S. Sylvester (1961) $7.50 pap. $1.95 Utopia ed. by Edward
Surtz, S. J. (1964) $7.00 pap. $1.95

The "Selected Letters" is the first volume in the *Yale* edition. Although the scholarly series will generally
precede the modernized versions, the "Selected Letters" is an exception. Dr. Roger's standard edition of the
"Correspondence" will appear as two volumes of "The Complete Works." The letters reveal the great humanist and scholar at his best and make it easy to see why he had so many friends. They are arranged in chronological order and are excellently annotated. This edition of "Utopia" is based on the volume of "The Complete Works" (*see above*). Included are an introduction by the editor, summarizing the import of "Utopia"
for the general reader, and notes which provide explanatory comment on the text.

THOMAE MORI OPERA OMNIA LATINA. (All the Latin Works of Thomas More.) 1565.
Johnson Reprint 1963 $58.35

UTOPIA. 1516. Ed. by H. V. Ogden *AHM Press* Croft's Classics pap. $.85; *British Bk.*
Centre repr. of 1556 ed. $13.00; (with title "Fruteful and Pleasant Worke of the
Beste State of a Publique Weale and of the New Yle Called Utopia") *Da Capo* repr.
of 1551 ed. $15.00; *Dutton* pap. 1973 $2.45; ed. by J. C. Collins *Oxford* 1904 $2.25;
trans. by Paul Turner *Penguin* pap. $.95; ed. by H. B. Cotterill *St. Martin's* 1908
$2.50; (in "Three Renaussance Classics" with Machiavelli's "The Prince" and
Castiglione's "The Courtier") ed. by B. A. Milligan *Scribner* $3.95; trans. by P.
Marshall *Washington Square* pap. $.75

APOLOGYE OF SYR THOMAS MORE, KNYGHT. 1533. *De Capo* facsimile ed. $30.00; ed.
by A. I. Taft *Kraus* repr. of 1930 ed. $14.50

THE SUPPLYCACYON OF SOULYS: Against the Supplication of Beggars. *Da Capo* facsimile ed. repr. $10.00

A DIALOGUE OF COMFORT AGAINST TRIBULATION. 1534. *Christian Classics* $6.00;
(and "Utopia") trans. by Ralph Robinson *Dutton* Everyman's rev. ed. with modernized spelling 1951 $3.50; ed. by Leland Miles *Indiana Univ. Press* 1965 pap. $2.65;
Peter Smith $5.00

CORRESPONDENCE. Ed. by Elizabeth Frances Rogers. 1947. *Bks. for Libraries* $19.50

THOMAS MORE'S PRAYER BOOK. Transcribed and trans. with introd. by Louis L.
Martz and Richard S. Sylvester *Yale Univ. Press* 1969 $12.50. A facsimile repro-
duction of the annotated pages, with the English translation. Published for the Elizabethan Club, it is intended as a companion volume to "The Complete Works of
Thomas More" (*see above*).

Books about More

  The Life and Death of Sir Thomas More. By Nicholas Harpsfield. Ed. from mss. by E. V. Hitchcock.
    1932. *Somerset Pub.* $19.50; *Richard West* 1973 $19.45
  The Life and Illustrious Martyrdom of Saint Thomas More. 1588 1689. Trans. by Philip E. Hallett.
    1928. Ed. and annot. by E. E. Reynolds *Fordham Univ. Press* 1967 $7.50. The edition of 1588 was pt.
    3 of *"Tres Thomae"* [St. Thomas, Thomas à Becket and More]. The 1689 ed., published in Frankfurt,
    was titled *"Vita Thomae Mori."* The life is based on Roper's (d. 1578) notes, incorporating the mem-
    oirs of members of More's household. Roper was the son-in-law of Sir Thomas More.
  The Mirror of Vertue, or The Life of Sir Thomas More. By William Roper. 1625. (And George Cav-
    endish, "The Life and Death of Cardinal Wolsey" in "Two Early Tudor Lives") ed. by Richard S.
    Sylvester and Davis P. Harding *Yale Univ. Press* 1962 $7.50 pap. $2.45
  Sir Thomas More and His Friends, 1477–1535. By Enid M. G. Routh. 1934. *Russell & Russell* 1963
    $8.75; *Richard West* 1973 $8.50
  Thomas More. By Raymond W. Chambers. *Univ. of Michigan Press* Ann Arbor Bks. 1958 pap. $2.65
  The Praise of Pleasure: Philosophy, Education, and Communism in More's Utopia. By Edward Louis
    Surtz, S. J. *Harvard Univ. Press* 1957 $7.00
    An intense and scholarly study which endeavors to reconcile its communist and Epicurean principles
    with More's Catholicism. "The clearest elucidation so far given of the meaning of More's enigmatic
    book"—(*TLS*, London).
  A Man for All Seasons. By Robert Bolt. *Random* 1962 $5.50 Vintage Bks. pap. $1.65. The thoughtful
    and immensely successful play and movie.
  Born for Friendship: The Spirit of Sir Thomas More. By Bernard Basset. *Sheed & Ward* 1965 $4.50
    "Thomas More's genius for friendship and family life is the special province of a brief, discerning biog-
    raphy that indirectly reveals the harmonious unity of [his] activities"—(*Booklist*).
  Thomas More and Erasmus. By Ernest Edwin Reynolds. *Fordham Univ. Press* 1966 $8.00. A study of the
    relations between two outstanding contemporaries.
  Twentieth Century Interpretations of Utopia. Ed. by William Nelson. *Prentice-Hall* 1968 $4.95 Spec-
    trum Bks. pap. $1.25
  Thomas More and Tudor Polemics. By Rainer Pineas. *Indiana Univ. Press* 1968 $9.50

Some of the more famous Utopias:

Bacon, Francis. THE NEW ATLANTIS. 1627. (and "The Advancement of Learning" and
  Other Pieces) ed. by R. F. Jones *Odyssey* $3.50; (and "The Advancement of Learn-
  ing") *Oxford* World's Class. 1938 $1.95; (in "Francis Bacon") ed. by A. Johnston
  Schocken pap. $1.95 (*See also Chapter 15, Essays and Criticism, for Bacon.*)

Bellamy, Edward. LOOKING BACKWARD, 1888. Ed. by John L. Thomas *Harvard Univ.
  Press* Belknap Press 1967 $7.50; ed. by Frederic R. White *Hendricks House* 1946
  $3.50 pap. $1.95; ed. by Robert C. Elliott *Houghton* pap. $1.30; *Modern Library*
  pap. $1.05; *New Am. Lib.* Signet pap. $.95 (*See also Chapter 13, American Fiction:
  Early Period, for Bellamy.*)

Butler, Samuel. EREWHON. 1872. *Assoc. Booksellers* Airmont Bks. pap. $.60; (and
  "Erewhon Revisited") *Dutton* Everyman's $3.50; (with title "Erewhon, or Over the
  Range") *Fernhill* 1965 $5.25; *New Am. Lib.* Signet pap. $.95; ed. by Peter Mudford
  Penguin 1970 pap. $1.25

  EREWHON REVISITED. 1901. (and "Erewhon") *Dutton* Everyman's $3.50; *Fernhill*
  1964 $3.50 (*See Chapter 11, British Fiction: Middle Period, for Butler.*)

Harrington, James. THE COMMONWEALTH OF OCEANA. 1656. (and Other Works) ed. by
  John Toland *International Pubs.* repr. of 1771 ed. $55.00; *Burt Franklin* repr. of
  1737 ed. $30.00; *McGrath Pub. Co.* repr. of 1656 ed. 1972 $23.00

Huxley, Aldous. BRAVE NEW WORLD. *Harper* 1932 $5.95 lib. bdg. $4.43 pap. $.95 (and
  "Brave New World Revisited") *Colophon Bks.* pap. $2.75

  BRAVE NEW WORLD REVISITED. *Harper* 1958 $5.95 Perenn. Lib. pap. $.65 (*See
  Chapter 12, Modern British Fiction, for Huxley.*)

Plato. THE REPUBLIC. Trans. by H. Spens. 1763. *AMS Press* $23.50; trans. by Benjamin Jowett *Assoc. Booksellers* Airmont Bks. 1968 pap. $.95; trans. by Allen Bloom *Basic Bks.* 1968 $12.50 pap. $4.95; (and Other Works) trans. by Benjamin Jowett *Doubleday* Anchor $2.50; trans. by A. D. Lindsay *Dutton* pap. $1.95; *Harvard Univ. Press* Loeb Lib. 2 vols each $5.00; *Modern Library* $2.95; trans. by Francis M. Cornford *Oxford* 1945 pap. $1.50; trans. by H. D. Lee *Penguin* pap. $1.45; trans. by Benjamin Jowett *Random* Vintage Bks. pap. $1.95; trans. by D. F. Pears 1866 *St. Martin's* $6.50

Skinner, B. F. WALDEN II. *Macmillan* 1948 pap. 1960 $2.25

Swift, Jonathan. GULLIVER'S TRAVELS. 1726. Ed. by Martin Price *Bobbs* 1964 pap. $1.45; *Collins* Class. $3.00 lea. $5.00; *Dodd* Gt. Ill. Class. $5.00; *Dutton* Children's Ill. Class. 1952 $3.95 Everyman's $3.50 pap. 1972 $1.50; *Grosset* $2.95 special ed. $3.95 deluxe ed. $4.95; *Harper* Mod. Class. 1950 $2.28; ed. by John F. Ross *Holt* (Rinehart) pap. $2.00; ed. by Louis A. Landa *Houghton* Riv. Eds. pap. $2.00 (and Other Writings) Riv. Eds. pap. $2.40; *Macmillan* 1962 $4.24; (and Other Writings) ed. by Ricardo Quintana *Modern Library* $2.95 pap. $1.15 ed. by Robert Heilman 2nd ed. pap. $1.15; ed. by Robert A. Greenberg *Norton* Critical Eds. 1970 pap. $1.95; ed. by P. Pinkus *Odyssey* 1968 pap. $1.25; ed. by Paul Turner *Oxford* 1971 pap. $2.50 World's Class. pap. $2.00; ed. by Peter Dixon and J. Chalker *Penguin* 1967 pap. $1.25; *Franklin Watts* 1969 $4.50 (*See below for Swift.*)

Other paperback editions of "Gulliver's Travels" are available from Amsco School Pubns., Assoc. Booksellers Airmont Bks., Bantam, Dell, New Am. Lib. Signet, Washington Square, $.60–$.95

Books about Utopias:

THE HISTORY OF UTOPIAN THOUGHT. By Joyce O. Hertzler. Analyzes the origin, selection and strength of social ideas and ideals conceived by exceptional men. 1923. *Cooper* 1965 $6.50

THE STORY OF UTOPIAS. By Lewis Mumford. 1924. *Peter Smith* $4.50; *Viking* Compass Bks. 1962 pap. $1.95

IDEOLOGY AND UTOPIA: An Introduction to the Sociology of Knowledge. By Karl Mannheim. 1929. Trans. from the German by Louis Wirth and Edward Shils. *Harcourt* Harvest Bks. 1955 pap. $1.95. Charles A. Beard said that this is "one of the three of four books which must be read by everyone who wants to discuss public affairs intelligently."

AMERICAN DREAMS: A Study of American Utopias. By Vernon L. Parrington, Jr. 1947. *Russell & Russell* 2nd ed. enlarged with postscript 1964 $10.00

UTOPIAS AND UTOPIAN THOUGHT. Ed. with introd. by Frank E. Manuel. *Beacon* pap. $2.95; *Houghton* 1966 $6.50. This volume of scholarly essays, all but three reprinted from the magazine *Daedalus*, includes opinions on utopias and utopian thinking by Crane Brinton, Paul Tillich, Lewis Mumford, Northrop Frye and others.

BUNYAN, JOHN. 1628–1688.

Imprisoned most of 1660–1672 for preaching Puritan doctrine in an England barely recovering from a civil war fought over religion, the tinker John Bunyan created the most intense prose allegories in English. In his first, autobiographical work, "Grace Abounding" (1666), he found his subject, spiritual conversion, which he treated most magnificently in his "Pilgrim's Progress." Again imprisoned in 1675 for six months, he wrote this famous allegory of Christian, the ordinary man who makes the painful journey from the City of Destruction to the Heavenly Gates through dangers set up by others (notably those in Vanity Fair) and by his own mind (as in the Slough of Despond). His theme is universal, as witness almost at random Dante's "Divine Comedy," Defoe's "Moll Flanders," Dostoevski's "Crime and Punishment," Bellow's "Henderson the Rain King"; he brought to it intense conviction, brilliant economy and vigor of statement, and the ability to evoke living characters in the guise of allegorical figures. While "Mr. Badman" (1680), "The Holy War" (1682), and "Pilgrim's Progress Part II" (1684) are not quite up to the masterpiece, they constitute an impressive expansion of his range of prose fiction. Novelists like Defoe owed him much, and so did moral prose writers of another sort like G. B. Shaw; "Pilgrim's Progress" was one of the very few books that the American pioneer carried with him along with the Bible; and now with the return to favor of allegory and symbolism, we can expect a resurgence of interest in Bunyan.

WORKS: With an Introduction to Each Treatise, Notes and a Sketch of His Life, Times and Contemporaries. Ed. by George Offor. 3 vols. 1856. *AMS Press* each $49.50 set $145.00

COMPLETE WORKS. Ed. with original introductions, notes and memoir of the author by Henry Stebbing. 4 vols. 1859? *Adler's* $165.00; *Johnson Reprint* 1970 set $120.00

GOD'S KNOTTY LOG: Selected Writing of John Bunyan. Ed. with introd. by Henry A. Talon. *Peter Smith* 1961 $3.75. A good practical edition of two related works: "The Heavenly Footman" is important for the better understanding of "The Pilgrim's Progress," of which the first part is reprinted almost completely, and all the best of the second part. Bunyan's biblical references are retained; brief clear notes.

GRACE ABOUNDING TO THE CHIEF OF SINNERS. 1666. Bunyan's spiritual autobiography. (and "The Life and Death of Mr. Badman") *Dutton* Everyman's 1953 $3.50 pap. 1972 $1.75; ed. by James Thorpe *Houghton* Riv. Eds. pap. $1.65; *Moody Press* pap. $.50; ed. by Roger Sharrock *Oxford* English Texts 1962 $9.50 (and "The Pilgrim's Progress from This World to That Which is to Come") Stand. Authors 1966 $7.00

THE PILGRIM'S PROGRESS FROM THIS WORLD TO THAT WHICH IS TO COME. 1678, 1679, 1684. Ed. by James B. Wharey *Oxford* English Texts 1929 rev. by Roger Sharrock 2nd ed. 1960 $14.50 World's Class. pap. $2.25

The edition by J. B. Wharey is a collation of the 11 editions published during Bunyan's lifetime and the first really authentic text, with bibliographical analysis. For the new edition of 1960, the late Professor Wharey's 2nd edition of 1929 has been thoroughly revised by Roger I. Sharrock. The most important change is a return to the text of Bunyan's first edition, supplemented by Bunyan's afterthoughts and additions taken from the earliest edition in which each appears. He has added a full commentary in two new sections and revised the "Introduction."

THE PILGRIM'S PROGRESS. Facsimile reprint of the 1678 edition. *British Bk. Centre* $11.00

PILGRIM'S PROGRESS. *Collins* New Class. $3.00 lea. $5.00; *Dodd* Gt. Ill. Class. 1967 $5.50; introd. and notes by G. B. Harrison *Dutton* $4.50 Everyman's $3.50 pap. 1972 $1.75; *Holt* pap. 1949 $2.00; *Lippincott* abr. ed. 1939 $5.50; (and "Grace Abounding to the Chief of Sinners") ed. by R. Sharrock *Oxford* Stand. Authors 1966 $7.00

Other paperback editions are available from Assoc. Booksellers Airmont Bks., Christian Literature Crusade, Keats, Moody Press, New Am. Lib. Signet, Penguin, Pyramid, Revell, Washington Square, and Zondervan, $.50–$1.75

THE HOLY WAR. 1682. *New York Univ. Press* 1968 $8.75; *Reiner* $2.00

Books about Bunyan

Bunyan. By James A. Froude. Ed. by John Morley. 1888. *AMS Press* $12.50; *Richard West* repr. of
  1895 ed. $12.00
John Bunyan, His Life, Times and Work, 1628–1688. By John Brown; ed. by Frank M. Harrison. 1928.
  Scholarly Press 1971 $13.75; *Shoe String* 1969 $14.00. The standard biography.
John Bunyan: A Study in Personality. By G. B. Harrison. 1928. *Shoe String* 1967 $6.00; *Folcroft* 1973
  $5.50
A Bibliography of the Works of John Bunyan. By Frank M. Harrison. 1932. *Folcroft* $12.50; *Bern Por-
  ter* 1972 $15.00
John Bunyan, Mechanick Preacher. By William York Tindall. 1934. *Russell & Russell* 1964 $13.50
John Bunyan, The Man and His Works. By Henri Antonine Talon, trans. by Barbara Wall. 1951 *British
  Bk. Centre* 1955 $2.38 pap. $1.20; *Somerset Pub.* $15.50; *Richard West* 1971 $15.45
Journey into Self. By M. Esther Harding. *McKay* (Longmans) 1956 $5.00. Dr Harding, a student of Dr.
  C. G. Jung (*q.v.*) sees in "The Pilgrim's Progress" a record of man's spiritual experience. She stresses
  the universal nature of Christian's journey—the journey to find Self.
God, Man and Satan: Patterns of Christian Thought and Life in Paradise Lost. By Roland Mushat Frye.
  Kennikat 1971 $9.00
John Bunyan in America. By David E. Smith. *Indiana Univ. Press* 1966 pap. $3.00
John Bunyan. By Richard L. Greaves. *Eerdmans* 1970 $5.50
Ethel Barrett's Holy War, with Apologies to John Bunyan. By Ethel Barrett. An adaptation of Bunyan's
  "Holy War." *Regal Bks.* 1970 $5.95 pap. $1.95

DEFOE, DANIEL. 1661–1731.

Although "Robinson Crusoe," based on the actual experience of Alexander Selkirk, alone on an island for
years, will no doubt continue to be Defoe's most popular book for young readers, his masterpiece is now
thought to be "Moll Flanders," the brilliantly persuasive recollections of a long lifetime in the underworld attributed to an early-18th-century criminal. In it, the heroine moves from her birth in prison through early re-
spectability to seduction, polygamy, theft, prostitution, incest, arrest, religious salvation, reform, trans-
portation to America, and wealth. Since Defoe was a notable ironist (witness his "The Shortest Way with
Dissenters" [1702, o. p.], which advocated killing dissenters from the established church for everyone's good),
critics have recently differed over the seriousness of Moll's claims to religious conversion while in jail awaiting execution.

His unsurpassed realism of detail, fostered by a lifetime of journalism, political activity (including espionage), and business ventures that involved careful analysis of people and circumstances, and his compassionate sense of individual courage in the face of jungle society, have been his most important legacies to
later novelists as well as his most vivid gifts to his readers. Among his many works—usually anonymous so
that there may never be a reliable list of them—"Roxana," the unfinished story of a late-17th-century courte-
san, has been highly praised by Virginia Woolf; "Captain Singleton" and "Colonel Jack" are lively and at
times earthy narratives of adventure in exotic parts of the world; and "A Journal of the Plague Year" (the
year 1665, when Defoe was a little boy) so well simulates any eyewitness account that Albert Camus (*q.v.*)
could use it as a source of his graphic power in his "The Plague."

The Facsimile Text Society's "Defoe's Reviews," with an introduction and bibliography by Arthur
Wellesley Secord, is published by *AMS Press* (9 vols. bd. in 22 pts. $380.00). "The Best of Defoe's Reviews"
is an anthology compiled and edited by William Lytton Payne (1951. *Bks. for Libraries* $13.50), who also
compiled the "Index to Defoe's Review" (1948, o.p.). Defoe's "Vindication of the Press," with an introduction by Otho Clinton Williams (1951, o.p.) was published in 1718.

Southern Illinois Univ. Press has undertaken the publication of the most extensive collection of Defoe's
writings to date. The nearest to a full listing of such writings is "A Checklist of the Writings of Daniel Defoe"
by Robert Moore (1960. *Shoe String* 1971 $10.00).

NOVELS AND MISCELLANEOUS WORKS. With biographical memoir, notes, literary prefaces and all contained in the edition attributed to the late Sir Walter Scott. 20 vols.
1840–41. *AMS Press* each $18.50 set $370.00

THE EARLIER LIFE AND CHIEF EARLIER WORKS OF DANIEL DEFOE. 1889. Ed. by
Henry Morley. *Burt Franklin* 1968; *Richard West* 1973 $20.00

ROMANCES AND NARRATIVES. Ed. by George Aitken. With an etched portrait and 48
rotogravure illus. by J. B. Yeats and 50 illus. by J. Ayton Symington. 16 vols. 1895–
99. *AMS Press* each $11.00 set $175.00

NOVELS AND SELECTED WRITINGS. The Shakespeare Head edition. 1927. *Somerset Pub.* 14 vols. each $21.50 set $280.00

SELECTED POETRY AND PROSE. Ed. by Michael F. Shugrue. *Holt* (Rinehart) pap. 1968 $1.25

DANIEL DEFOE. Ed. by J. T. Boulton. *Schocken* 1965 pap. $1.95

Selections "admirably chosen to display the range and styles of the author"—(*LJ*).

THE CONSOLIDATOR. Memoirs of Sundry Transactions from the World in the Moon, Translated from the Lunar Language. 1705. *McGrath Pub. Co.* 1972 $28.00

ACCOUNTS OF THE APPARITION OF MRS. VEAL. Daniel Defoe and others. *Augustan* 1965–66 price on request. Defoe's account dates from 1706 and was called "A True Relation of the Apparition of One Mrs. Veal," who allegedly appeared after death, on Sept. 8, 1705, to a Mrs. Bargrave of Canterbury.

A BRIEF HISTORY OF THE POOR PALATINE REFUGEES. 1709. *Augustan* 1963–64 price on request

ROBINSON CRUSOE. (The Life and Strange Surprizing Adventures of Robinson Crusoe, of York, Mariner). 1719 1720. *Collins* New Class. pts. 1–2 $3.00; *Dutton* Every-man's $3.50 pap. $1.95; *Grosset* Companion Lib. $1.25 Ill. Jr. Lib. $2.95 special ed. $3.95 deluxe ed. $4.95; *Macmillan* 1962 $3.95; ed. by Frank L. Beals *Naylor* $3.95; ed. by Donald J. Crowley *Oxford* 1972 $8.50 World's Class. $2.25; ed. by Angus Ross *Penguin* pap. 1965 $1.30; ill. by N. C. Wyeth *Scribner* Ill. Class. $10.00; *Franklin Watts* lg.-type ed. Keith Jennison Bks. $7.95

Other paperback editions are available from Amsco School Pubns., Assoc. Booksellers Airmont Bks., Dell, Fearon, Moody, New Am. Lib. Signet and Washington Square, $.50–$.95

CAPTAIN SINGLETON. (The Life, Adventures and Piracies of the Famous Captain Sin-gleton). 1720. *Dutton* Everyman's 1963 $3.50; ed. by Shir K. Kumar *Oxford* 1969 $7.25 pap. 1973 $3.25

MOLL FLANDERS. (The Fortunes and Misfortunes of the Famous Moll Flanders). 1722. Ed. by J. Paul Hunter *T. Y. Crowell* 1970 pap. $2.95; *Dutton* pap. 1972 $1.50 Ev-eryman's $3.50; *Harcourt* 1963 deluxe ill. ed. $5.75; ed. by Godfrey Davies *Holt* (Rinehart) 1949 pap. $2.25; ed. by J. R. Sutherland *Houghton* Riv. Eds. pap. $1.85; ed. by Edward Kelly *Norton* Critical Eds. 1973 $10.00 pap. (in prep.); ed. by G. A. Starr *Oxford* $8.50

Other paperback editions are available from Assoc. Booksellers Airmont Bks., Modern Library, New Am. Lib. Signet and Washington Square, $.50–$1.05

A JOURNAL OF THE PLAGUE YEAR 1722. Introd. by G. A. Aitken *Dutton* Everyman's $3.50 pap. 1972 $1.75; *New Am. Lib.* Signet pap. $.95; ed. by Louis Landa *Oxford* 1969 $7.25; ed. by Anthony Burgess *Penguin* $1.25; *Peter Smith* $3.25

COLONEL JACK. 1722. Ed. with introd. by S. H. Monk. *Oxford* 1965 $5.50 pap. $2.50

ROXANA, OR THE FORTUNATE MISTRESS. 1724. Ed. by J. Jack. *Oxford* 1964 $6.25 pap. $2.50

CONJUGAL LEWDNESS, OR MATRIMONIAL WHOREDOM. 1727. *Scholars' Facsimiles* 1967 $15.00

A Tour through the Whole Island of Great Britain. 1724–27. *Dutton* Everyman's 1928 2 vols. each $3.50; *Kelley* 1927 2 vols. $35.00; ed. by P. Rogers *Penguin* pap. 1972 $3.75

A General History of the Robberies and Murders of the Most Nortorious Pyrates. 1724. Ed. by Manuel Schonhorn. *Univ. of South Carolina Press* 1972 $25.00

The Complete English Tradesman. 1726. Reprinted with notes; together with "An Humble Proposal to the People of England for the Increase of Their Trade and Encouragement of Their Manufactures." 1889. *Burt Franklin* 3 vols. in 1 1970 $29.50; *Kelley* 2 vols. with supplement repr. of 1727 ed. $37.50

The Complete English Gentleman. Ed. by Karl Bülbring. Written between 1726 and 1731, but first published in 1890. *Folcroft* lib. bdg. $30.00

A Tour through London About the Year 1725. 1727. Ed. by Mayson M. Beeton and E. Beresford Chancellor. 1929. *Blom* $18.75

Letters. Ed. by George Harris Healey. *Oxford* 1955 $13.75. This is the first single volume of all of Defoe's 235 known letters, almost all based on manuscript sources, and all clearly and fully annotated. They give "an extremely vivid impression of the bankrupt merchant, convicted libeler and hack journalist who achieved fame as a literary artist when he was nearly 60."

Books about Defoe

Defoe. By James Sutherland. 2nd ed. 1950 *Barnes & Noble* 1971 $11.00; *British Bk. Centre* $2.38 pap. $1.20. The best and most readable biography.
Daniel Defoe: Citizen of the Modern World. By John R. Moore. A sympathetic, detailed and scholarly biography. *Univ. of Chicago Press* 1958 $8.50
Defoe and the Nature of Man. By Maximillian E. Novak. Examines the moral and philosophical basis of Defoe's fiction. *Oxford* 1963 $7.00
Defoe and Spiritual Autobiography. By G. A. Starr. *Gordian* 1965 $8.50
"Starr begins with a long chapter analyzing the thematic patterns in . . . 17th century English spiritual biographies. He then persuasively shows how these patterns . . . form the basis of 'Robinson Crusoe,' 'Moll Flanders,' and 'Roxana' "—(*Choice*).
The Reluctant Pilgrim: Defoe's Emblematic Method and Quest for Form in Robinson Crusoe. By J. Paul Hunter. *Johns Hopkins Univ. Press* 1966 $8.50
"A well-done study. . . . [The author] provides new insight into 'Robinson Crusoe' in particular and into the early English novel in general"—(*LJ*).
Daniel Defoe: A Critical Study. By James Sutherland. *Harvard Univ. Press* 1971 $8.75; Riverside Studies in Literature Ser. *Houghton* 1971 pap. $4.00. An examination of Defoe as journalist, poet, and novelist, by the most distinguished Defoe scholar.

SWIFT, JOHNATHAN. 1667–1745.

Apparently doomed to an obscure Anglican parsonage in Laracor, Ireland, even after he had written his anonymous masterpiece "A Tale of a Tub," Swift turned a political mission to England from the Irish Protestant clergy into an avenue toward prominence as the chief propagandist for the Tory government. His exhilaration at achieving importance in his forties appears engagingly in his "Journal to Stella," addressed to Esther Johnson, a young protege for whom Swift felt more warmth than for anyone else in his long life. At the death of Queen Anne and the fall of the Tories in 1714, Swift became Dean of St. Patrick's Cathedral, Dublin. In Ireland, which he considered exile from a life of power and intellectual activity in London, Swift found time to defend his oppressed countrymen, sometimes in contraband essays like his "Drapier Letters" (1724, o.p.), and sometimes in short mordant pieces like the famous "Modest Proposal"; and he wrote there the greatest work of his time, "Gulliver's Travels."

Using his chracteristic device of the persona (a developed and sometimes satirized narrator like the anonymous hack writer of "A Tale of a Tub" or the Isaac Bickerstaff in "Predictions for the Ensuing Year" [1708 o.p.], who exposes an astrologer), Swift provides in his hero a figure who stands in the first instance for the bluff, decent, average Englishman, then for man generally, and most powerfully for us, the readers. Gulliver is a full and powerful vision of man always in a world where violent passions, intellectual pride, and external chaos can degrade him—to animalism, in Swift's most horrifying images—but where man has scope to act, guided by the classical–Christian tradition. "Gulliver's Travels" has been an immensely successful children's book (though Swift didn't much care for children), so widely popular through the world for its imagination, wit, fun, freshness, vigor, and narrative skill that its hero is in many languages a common noun. Perhaps as a consequence, its meaning has been the subject of continuing dispute, and its author has been called everything from sentimental to mad.

"The Poems of Jonathan Swift," edited by Harold Williams, is published by *Oxford* (1937 2nd ed. 1958 set $29.00) and, edited by Padraic Colum, by *Macmillian* Collier Bks. (1962 pap. $.95); "Poetical Works," edited by Herbert Davis (*Oxford* 1967 Stand. Authors $8.00), "Selected Poems," edited by James Reeves (*Barnes & Noble* 1967 $2.50) and "Selected Poetry" ed. by Martin Price (*New Am. Lib.* Signet 1970 pap. $1.25) are also available.

THE PROSE WORKS. Ed. by Temple Scott with a biographical introd. by W. E. H. Lecky. 12 vols. 1898–1909. *AMS Press* 12 vols. $145.00

THE PROSE WORKS. Ed. by Herbert Davis. The Shakespeare Head ed. 13 vols. 1939. repr. 1964–1968 with index (Vol. 14 1968) *Barnes & Noble* 14 vols. $115.00 index alone $8.50. The index was compiled by William J. Kunz, Steven Hollander and Susan Staves under the supervision of Irvin Ehrenpreis. Addenda, errata, corrigenda were edited by Herbert Davis and Irvin Ehrenpreis.

THE PORTABLE SWIFT: Gulliver's Travels, Satires, Poems, Letters, Journals. Ed. by Carl Van Doren. *Viking* 1948 lib. bdg. $4.95 pap. $1.95

JONATHAN SWIFT: A SELECTION OF HIS WORKS. Ed. by P. Pinkus. *Odyssey* 1965 pap. $1.85

WRITINGS OF JONATHAN SWIFT. Ed. by Robert A. Greenberg and William B. Piper. *Norton* Critical Eds. 1972 $15.00 pap. $3.95

GULLIVER'S TRAVELS AND OTHER WRITINGS. Introd. and commentaries by Ricardo Quintana. *Modern Library* $2.95 pap. $1.15. Includes Gulliver's Travels; A Tale of a Tub; The Battle of the Books; A Discourse Concerning the Mechanical Operation of the Spirit; A Meditation upon a Broom-Stick; selected prose from the Journal to Stella, the Partridge-Bickerstaff Papers and other writings; selected letters; and selected verse 1709–1733.

GULLIVER'S TRAVELS AND OTHER WRITINGS. (and "The Battle of the Books," "A Tale of a Tub" and "A Modest Proposal") ed. by Miriam Starkman *Bantam* pap. $.95; ed. by Louis A. Landa *Houghton* Riv. Eds. 1960 $3.00 pap. $2.40

SELECTED PROSE AND POETRY. Ed. with introd. by Edward Rosenheim. *Holt* (Rinehart) 1959 pap. $2.25. Eight stories, poems and selected letters.

A DISCOURSE OF THE CONTESTS AND DISSENTIONS BETWEEN THE NOBLES AND THE COMMONS IN ATHENS AND ROME WITH THE CONSEQUENCES THEY HAD UPON BOTH THOSE STATES. 1701. Ed. by Frank H. Ellis *Oxford* 1967 $11.00. Swift's first satire and first published work—an allegory of English history.

A TALE OF A TUB: Written for the Universal Improvement of Mankind. 1704. Ed. by Edward Hodnett. 1930. *AMS Press* $15.00; (and "The Battle of the Books") *Dutton* Everyman's $3.50 pap. 1972 $1.95; (and "The Battle of the Books" and "The Mechanical Operation of the Spirit") ed. by A. C. Guthkelch and David N. Smith *Oxford* 2nd ed. 1958 $12.00

GULLIVER'S TRAVELS. Ed. by Robert A. Greenberg. Text of 1735 Dublin ed.; includes critical essays on Swift and extracts from his correspondence. *Norton* Critical Eds. 1967 pap. $1.95

GULLIVER'S TRAVELS. 1726. Ed. by Martin Price *Bobbs* 1964 pap. $1.45; *Collins* Class. $3.00 lea. $5.00; *Dodd* Gt. Ill. Class. $5.00; *Dutton* Children's Ill. Class. 1952 $3.95 Everyman's $3.50 pap. 1972 $1.50; *Grosset* $2.95 special ed. $3.95 deluxe ed. $4.95; *Harper* Mod. Class. 1950 $2.28; ed. by John F. Ross *Holt* (Rinehart) pap. $2.00; ed. by Louis A. Landa *Houghton* Riv. Eds. pap. $2.00 (and Other Writings) Riv. Eds. pap. $2.40; *Macmillan* 1962 $4.24; (and Other Writings) ed. by Ricardo Quintana *Modern Library* $2.95 pap. $1.15 ed. by Robert Heilman 2nd ed. pap. $1.15; ed. by Robert A. Greenberg *Norton* Critical Eds. 1970 pap. $1.95; ed. by P. Pinkus *Odyssey* 1968 pap. $1.25; ed. by Paul Turner *Oxford* 1971 pap. $2.50 World's Class. pap. $2.00; ed. by Peter Dixon and J. Chalker *Penguin* 1967 pap. $1.25; *Franklin Watts* 1969 $4.50

Other paperback editions of "Gulliver's Travels" are available from Amsco School Pubns., Assoc. Booksellers Airmont Bks., Bantam, Dell, New Am. Lib. Signet, Washington Square, $.60–$.95

A MODEST PROPOSAL [for Preventing the Children of Poor People from being a Burthen to Their Parents or the Country; and for Making Them Beneficial to the Publick]—by making them food for the rich. 1729 1730. (in "Gulliver's Travels and Other Writings,") ed. by Miriam Starkman *Bantam* pap. $.95; *Grossman* 1970 $13.95; ed. by Charles Beaumont *Charles E. Merrill* pap. $1.75

SATIRES AND PERSONAL WRITINGS. Ed. by W. A. Eddy. *Oxford* Stand. Authors 1932 $5.25

POLITE CONVERSATIONS. Originally published as "A Complete Collection of Genteel and Ingenious Conversations according to the Most Polite Mode and Method Now Used in Court and in the Best Companies of England." 1738. Annotated by Eric Partridge. 1963 *Seminar Press* $5.95

AN ENQUIRY INTO THE BEHAVIOR OF THE QUEEN'S LAST MINISTRY. First published in 1765 in Vol. 8 of J. Hawkesworth's 4th ed. of the "Works." Ed. by I. Ehrenpreis. 1956. *Kraus* pap. $6.00

CORRESPONDENCE. Ed. by Harold Williams. *Oxford* 1963 5 vols. Vols. 1–3 (1965) set $43.50 Vols. 4–5 set $34.00. Vol. 1, 1690–1713 Vol. 2, 1714–23 Vol. 3, 1724–31 Vol. 4, 1732 Vol. 5, 1737–45. "Meticulously annotated" collection of Swift's correspondence, the largest to date. Included are letters from Pope, Addison, Steele, and others.

"Swift's letters follow the shifts of his fortune and reveal his clarity of mind, the strength of his style, and his command of language"—(*LJ*).

Books about Swift

The Sin of Wit: Jonathan Swift as a poet. By Maurice Johnson. 1950. *Gordian* 1966 $6.00. The best study of Swift's poetry so far.

Swift's Satire on Learning in A Tale of a Tub. By Miriam Kosh Starkman. 1950. *Octagon* 1968 $8.50. A valuable study of the victims of Swift's satire and of 17th-century controversies.

The Masks of Jonathan Swift. By William Bragg Ewald, Jr 1954. *Russell & Russell* repr. 1967 $10.00. A very useful examination of Swift's preferred device of speaking through an invented character.

Swift and the Church of Ireland. By Louis A. Landa. *Oxford* 1954 $7.75. The authoritative study of Swift's career as a churchman.

Swift: An Introduction. By Ricardo Quintana. *Oxford* 1955 repr. 1962 pap. $2.00. Its author calls it "substantially a résumé of modern scholarship and criticism."

Jonathan Swift and the Age of Compromise. By Kathleen Williams. *Univ. Press of Kansas* 1959 $5.00 pap. $2.95. Clear and persuasive discussions of the works, particularly "Gulliver's Travels," in relation to Swift's intellectual milieu.

Theme and Structure in Swift's Tale of Tale of a Tub. By Ronald Paulson. 1960. *Shoe String* repr. 1972 $9.50. The best volume on Swift's early masterpiece.

A Casebook on Gulliver among the Houyhnhnms. Ed. by Milton P. Foster. *T. Y. Crowell* 1961 pap. $3.95. Reprints a number of interpretive essays.

Swift and Anglican Rationalism: The Religious Background of A Tale of a Tub. By Philip Harth. *Univ. of Chicago Press* 1961 $6.00. A learned discussion of the theological milieu of the book.

Discussions of Jonathan Swift. Ed. by John Traugott. *Heath* 1962 pap. $2.25. Reprints a number of interpretive essays.

Swift: The Man, His Works, and the Age. By Irvin Ehrenpreis. The first 2 of a projected 3 vols. *Harvard Univ. Press* Vol. 1 Mr. Swift and His Contemporaries (1962) $8.50 Vol. 2 Dr. Swift (1967) $20.00. The most authoritative biography so far, particularly useful on Swift's Irish background. Learned and perceptive critical analyses of Swift's writings.

Swift: A Collection of Critical Essays. Ed. by Ernest Tuveson. *Prentice-Hall* 1964 $5.95 Spectrum Bks. pap. $1.95. Reprints a number of interpretive essays.

Rage or Raillery: The Swift Manuscripts at the Huntington Library. By George P. Mayhew. *Huntington Library* 1967 $6.50. An attractive reminder of Swift's play with language.

The World of Jonathan Swift: Essays for the Tercentenary. Ed. by Brian Vickers. *Harvard Univ. Press* 1968 $7.25. A collection of interpretive essays.

The Self Observed: Swift, Johnson, Wordsworth. By Morris Golden. *Johns Hopkins Univ. Press* 1972 $8.00. On Swift's projection of certain views of himself into the vision of man in his writings.

RICHARDSON, SAMUEL. 1689–1761.

A printer and bookseller who as an apprentice wrote love letters for servant girls, studied nights to improve himself, and married the boss's daughter, Samuel Richardson undertook at 50 to write a book of sample courtesy notes, marriage proposals, job applications, and business letters for young people. While imagining situations for this book, he recalled an old scandal and developed it into "Pamela: or, Virtue Rewarded," a novel about a servant girl whose firmness, vitality, literacy, and superior intelligence turn her master's lust into a decorous love that leads to their marriage. All of "Pamela's" virtues of fresh characterization, immediacy (what Richardson called "writing to the moment" of the character's consciousness), and the involvement of the reader in the character's intense and fluctuating fantasies, together with a much more focused seriousness, a more varied and differentiated cast of letter writers, and a more fundamental examination of moral and social issues, make of his second novel, "Clarissa," one of the great masterpieces of the form. Though anyone who reads this huge novel for its plot may hang himself (as Richardson's friend Samuel Johnson said), readers have been fascinated by the immensely complex conflict between Clarissa Harlowe and Robert Lovelace, two of the most fully realized characters, psychologically and socially, in all literature. Like such great successors as Rousseau (an acknowledged follower), Dostoevski, and Lawrence, Richardson understands and shows us (in Diderot's appreciative image) the black recesses of the cave of the mind.

Although Richardson's last novel, "Sir Charles Grandison," (1753–54, o.p. in separate ed.), like "Pamela Part II," mainly undertakes comic delineation of manners, it examines the serious issue of love between a Protestant and a Catholic and it experiments technically with flashbacks, with stenographic reports, and most assertively with a pure hero, a male Clarissa of irresistible social class, charm, and power. In his work at its best Richardson fuses the epistolary technique, the use of dramatic scenes, the traditions of religious biography, and the elements of current romantic fiction to achieve precise analysis, an air of total verisimilitude, and a vision of a world of primal psychological forces in conflict.

The Novels. Complete and unabridged, with a life of the author and introductions by William Lyon Phelps. 19 vols. 1901–02. *AMS Press* repr. 1970 each $12.50 set $225.00; *Scholarly Press* repr. 1971 each $21.50 set $390.00

Pamela, or Virtue Rewarded. 1740. Introd. by George Saintsbury *Dutton* Everyman's 2 vols. each $3.50; ed. by T. C. Duncan Eaves and B. D. Kimpel *Houghton* Riv. Eds. 1971 pap. $3.95; *Norton* Norton Lib. 1958 pap. $1.45

Clarissa Harlowe, or The History of a Young Lady. 1747–48. *Dutton* Everyman's 4 vols. 1932 each $3.50; abr. and ed. by Philip Stevick *Holt* (Rinehart) 1971 $3.00; ed. by George Sherburn *Houghton* Riv. Eds. 1962 pap. $2.75

The Correspondence of Samuel Richardson. 1804. Ed. by Anna Laetitia Barbauld. *AMS Press* 6 vols. each $17.75 set $100.00

SELECTED LETTERS OF SAMUEL RICHARDSON. Ed. by John Carroll. *Oxford* 1964 $9.75

Books about Richardson

Richardson. By Brian W. Downs. 1928. *Barnes & Noble* 1969 $5.00. A penetrating, concise, smoothly written critical study.

Samuel Richardson, Master Printer. By William M. Sale. *Cornell Univ. Press* 1950 $14.50

Samuel Richardson. By R. F. Brissenden. *British Book Centre* $2.38 pap. $1.20. Critical and biographical material; bibliography of the works.

Richardson's Characters. By Morris Golden. *Univ. of Michigan Press* 1963 $5.00. An occasionally amusing examination of the sexual, psychological, and social qualities of Richardson's characters.

Samuel Richardson: A Collection of Critical Essays. Ed. by John Carroll. *Prentice-Hall* 1969 $5.95 Spectrum Bks. pap. $1.95. Reprints some major approaches to the novels.

Twentieth Century Interpretations of Pamela. Ed. by Rosemary Cowler. *Prentice-Hall* 1969 $4.95 Spectrum Bks. pap. $1.25. Reprints valuable essays on the novel.

Samuel Richardson: A Biography. By T. C. Duncan Eaves and Ben D. Kimpel. *Oxford* 1971 $22.00. The only extensive and authoritative modern biography of the novelist.

Samuel Richardson and the Eighteenth Century Puritan Character. By Cynthia G. Wolff. *Shoe String* 2nd ed. 1972 $9.25. A thoughtful examination of the novels, especially "Clarissa,"—in the light of psychological and sociological theories.

FIELDING, HENRY. 1707–1754.

A successful playwright in his twenties, Fielding turned to the study of law and then to journalism, fiction, and a judgeship after his "Historical Register" (1737. With "Eurydice Hissed" ed. by William W. Appleton. *Univ. of Nebraska Press* 1968 $4.75 Bison Bks. pap. $1.00), a political satire on the Walpole government, contributed to the censorship of plays that put him out of business. As an impoverished member of the upper classes, he knew the country squires and the town nobility; as a successful young playwright, the London "jet set"; and as a judge at the center of London, the city's thieves, swindlers, petty officials, shopkeepers, and vagabonds.

When Fielding undertook prose fiction to ridicule the simple morality of Richardson's "Pamela," he first produced the hilarious burlesque "Shamela." Shortly, however, he found himself considering all the forces working on man, and in "Joseph Andrews" (centering on his invented brother of Pamela) he played with the patterns of Homer, the Bible, and Cervantes to create what he called "a comic epic poem in prose." His preface, in which he describes this new art form, is one of the major documents in literary criticism of the novel. "Jonathan Wild," a fictional rogue biography of a year later, plays heavily with ironic techniques that leave unsettled Fielding's great and recurring theme: the difficulty of uniting goodness (an outflowing love of others) with prudence in a world where corrupted institutions support divisive pride rather than harmony and self-fulfillment.

In his masterpiece, "Tom Jones," Fielding not only faces this issue persuasively, but shows for the first time the possibility of bringing a whole world into an artistic unity, as his model Homer had done in verse. Not only does Fielding develop a coherent and centered sequence of events—something Congreve (*q.v.*) had done casually on a small scale in "*Incognita*" 60 years before—but he relates the plot organically to character and theme, giving us all of 18th-century England (if not indeed, as he wished, all humanity) in a vision of the archetypal good man (Tom) on a journey toward understanding, with every act by every character both reflecting the special and typical psychology of that character and incurring the proper moral response.

If in "Tom Jones" Fielding affirms the existence of an order under the surface of chaos, in his last novel, "Amelia," which realistically examines the hell of London, he can find nothing reliable except the prudent good heart, and that only if its possessor escapes into the country. Himself ill, saddened by the deaths of his intensely beloved first wife and his daughter, depressed by a London magistrate's endless toil against corruption, he saw little hope for goodness in that novel or in his informal "Journal of a Voyage to Lisbon." Shortly after reaching that city in his search for health, he died at 47, having proved to his contemporaries and successors that the novel was capable of the richest achievements of art.

WORKS. Ed. by George Saintsbury. 12 vols. 1893–99. *AMS Press* each $12.50 set $145.00

THE COMPLETE WORKS OF HENRY FIELDING. Ed. by William E. Henley. 1902–03. *Barnes & Noble* reprint 1967 16 vols. $125.00

APOLOGY FOR THE LIFE OF MRS. SHAMELA ANDREWS. 1741. Ed. by Brian Downs *Folcroft* 1973 lib. bdg. $10.00; ed. by Brimley Johnson *Folcroft* 1973 lib. bdg. $10.00; (and "Joseph Andrews") ed. by Martin C. Battestin with extensive bibliographic and historical introd. *Houghton* Riv. Eds. 1961 pap. $2.00; ed. by Douglas Brooks *Oxford* 1970 $7.25 pap. $3.75. His famous parody of Richardson's "Pamela."

JOSEPH ANDREWS (The History of the Adventures of Joseph Andrews). 1742. *Dutton* pap. $1.75 Everyman's $3.50; *Harper* pap. $.75; *Holt* (Rinehart) 1949 pap. $2.25; ed. by Martin C. Battestin *Houghton* Riv. Eds. pap. $1.15; *Modern Library* pap. $.95; *New Am. Lib.* Signet pap. $.75; introd. by Mary Ellen Chase *Norton* pap. 1958 $.95; *Oxford* World's Class. $3.00; ed. by Maynard Mack *Washington Square* pap. $.95; ed. by Martin C. Battestin, the Wesleyan edition of the "Works." *Wesleyan Univ. Press* 1966 $15.00

JONATHAN WILD. (The History of the Life of the Late Mr. Jonathan Wild, the Great). 1743. (and "The Journal of a Voyage to Lisbon") *Dutton* Everyman's $3.50; *New Am. Lib.* Signet 1961 pap. $.95

MISCELLANIES. 1743. Ed. by Henry K. Miller, textual introd. by Fredson Bowers. Vol. 2 of the Wesleyan edition of the "Works." *Wesleyan Univ. Press* Vol. 1 1972 $15.00

TOM JONES: The History of a Foundling. 1749. *Assoc. Booksellers* Airmont Bks. pap. $.95; *Collins* New Class. $3.00; *Dodd* Gt. Ill. Class. $5.95; introd. by George Saintsbury *Dutton* Everyman's 2 vols. each $3.50; introd. by George Sherburn *Modern Library* pap. $1.60; *New Am. Lib.* Signet pap. $1.25; ed. by Sheridan Baker *Norton* Critical Eds. 1973. $17.50 pap. $3.45; *Penguin* pap. $1.95; *Random* Vintage Bks. pap. $1.95; *Washington Square* 1963 pap. $.90

AMELIA. 1751 *Dutton* Everyman's 2 vols. each $3.50

THE JOURNAL OF A VOYAGE TO LISBON. 1755. (and "Jonathan Wild") *Dutton* Everyman's $3.50

Books about Fielding

The Lives of Henry Fielding and Samuel Johnson, together with Essays from the Gray's-Inn Journal (1752–92). Reprinted from the "Works" of Arthur Murphy (1786), the "Works" of Fielding (1762) and "Works" of Samuel Johnson (1792), with an introd. by Matthew Grace. *Scholar's Facsimiles* 1968 $15.00. The Fielding "Life" is a superb essay by his friend, which accompanied the first collected edition of his works.

The History of Henry Fielding. By Wilbur L. Cross. 1918. *Russell & Russell* 1964 3 vols. $30.00. The basic biography which has not been superseded by the more recent scholarly, detailed and admirable study, "Henry Fielding: His Life, Works and Times" by Frederick Homes Dudden (*see below*).

Henry Fielding: His Life, Works and Times. By Frederick Homes Dudden 1952. *Shoe String* 2 vols. 1966 $27.50

Henry Fielding's Theory of the Comic Prose Epic. By Ethel Thornbury. 1931. *Folcroft* $6.50

The Moral Basis of Fielding's Art: A Study of Joseph Andrews. By Martin Battestin. *Wesleyan Univ. Press* 1959 $7.50. A basic study of Fielding's ideas on the novel.

Essays on Fielding's Miscellanies: A Commentary on Volume One. By Henry Knight Miller. *Princeton Univ. Press* 1961 $17.50. The best study of Fielding's thought, essential for understanding his novels.

Fielding's Art of Fiction: 11 Essays on Shamela, Joseph Andrews, Tom Jones, and Amelia. By Maurice Johnson. *Univ. of Pennsylvania Press* 1961 $7.50. Thoughtful, stimulating approach to the art of the novel as well as to Fielding.

Fielding: A Collection of Critical Essays. Ed. by Ronald Paulson. *Prentice-Hall* 1962 $5.95

Henry Fielding: Mask and Feast. By Andrew H. Wright. *Univ. of California Press* 1965 pap. $1.50 A close study of "Joseph Andrews," "Tom Jones," and "Amelia" in which "Wright brilliantly interprets Fielding's conception of art as a rehearsal of civilization"—(*Choice*).

Fielding's Moral Psychology. By Morris Golden. *Univ. of Massachusetts Press* 1966 $7.00. Sees Fielding's novels as reflections and exemplifications of his conception of human nature.

Henry Fielding and the Language of Irony. By Glenn W. Hatfield. *Univ. of Chicago Press* 1968 $7.50. Fielding's rhetorical approaches in his novels.

Twentieth Century Interpretations of Tom Jones. Ed. by Martin C. Battestin. *Prentice-Hall* 1968 $4.95

Henry Fielding: The Critical Heritage. Ed. by Ronald Paulson and Thomas Lockwood. *Barnes & Noble* 1969 $9.00. A useful collection of essays ranging back to the mid-18th century.

STERNE, LAURENCE. 1713–1768.

If Fielding showed that the novel (like the traditional epic or drama) could make the chaos of life coherent in art, Sterne only a few years later in "The Life and Opinions of Tristram Shandy, Gentlemen," of which the best edition is James A. Work's, laughed away the notion of order; in his world, everyone is sealed off in his own mind so that only in unpredictable moments of spontaneous feeling can we have the sense of another human being. Reviewers attacked the obscenity of Tristram's imagined autobiography as it appeared (two volumes each in 1759, early 1761, late 1761, 1765, and one in 1767), particularly when the author revealed himself as a clergyman, but the presses teemed with imitations of this great literary hit of the 1760s.

Ostensibly working through casual associations in the mind of the eccentric hero, Sterne was tapping the archetypes of conception, birth, childhood, education, and the contemplation of maturity and death, so that Tristram's concerns touched his contemporaries and are still important to us now. The hero isn't born until the end of Volume 3, but since we are always listening to his learned and witty mind we know all about him and about two of the most engaging characters ever to join the tradition of Cervantes, his theory-spinning father Walter and his earthbound, loving Uncle Toby. Since "Tristram Shandy" is patently a great and lasting comic work that yet seems, as E. M. Forster said, ruled by the Great God Muddle, much recent criticism has centered on the question of its unity or lack of it; and its manipulation of time and of mental processes has been considered particularly relevant to the problems of fiction in our day.

Sterne's "Sentimental Journey," the best edition of which is Gardner D. Stout, Jr.'s, has been immensely admired by some critics for its superb tonal balance of irony and sentiment. His "Sermons of Mr. Yorick" catch the spirit of their time in dramatically preaching benevolence and sympathy as superior to doctrine. Whether as Tristram or as Yorick, his is the most memorably personal voice of 18th-century fiction.

WORKS. Ed. by George Saintsbury. 1894. *AMS Press* 6 vols. each $10.00 set $60.00

THE COMPLETE WORKS AND LIFE OF LAURENCE STERNE. Ed. by Wilbur L. Cross, with a life by Percy Fitzgerald. The Yorick ed. 1904. *AMS Press* 12 vols in 6. each $27.50 set $160.00

TRISTRAM SHANDY. (The Life and Opinions of Tristram Shandy, Gent.). 1760–67. Sterne's masterpiece. *Assoc. Booksellers* Airmont pap. $.75; *Dutton* Everyman's $3.50 pap. $1.95; introd. by H. S. Monk *Holt* (Rinehart) 1950 pap. $2.50; ed. Ian Watt *Houghton* pap. $2.10; *Modern Library* pap. $1.15; *New Am. Lib.* Signet pap. $.95; ed. by James A. Work *Odyssey* 1955 $3.50 pap. $1.95; *Oxford* World's Class. $3.75; ed. by Graham Petrie *Penguin* 1967 $1.75

A SENTIMENTAL JOURNEY THROUGH FRANCE AND ITALY BY MR. YORICK, 1768. 1768. (and "The Journal and Letters to Eliza") *Dutton* Everyman's $3.50 pap. $1.75; (and "Journal to Eliza" and "A Political Romance") ed. with introd. by Ian Jack *Oxford* 1968 $6.60 pap. $3.25; introd. by Virginia Woolf *Oxford* World's Class. pap. $2.00; ed. by Graham Petrie, introd. by A. Alvarez *Penguin* Eng. Lib. 1967 pap. $1.10; ed. with introd. by Gardner D. Stout, Jr. *Univ. of California Press* 1967 $10.00

THE JOURNAL AND LETTERS TO ELIZA (1775). (and "A Sentimental Journey") introd. by Daniel George *Dutton* Everyman's $3.50

MEMOIRS: THE LIFE AND OPINIONS OF TRISTRAM SHANDY; A SENTIMENTAL JOURNEY; SELECTED SERMONS AND LETTERS. Ed. by Douglas Grant. *Harvard Univ. Press* 1950 1970 $12.00 pap. $4.95

THE SERMONS OF MR. YORICK. 1760–69. Ed. by Lansing V. D. Hammond. Yale Studies in English Ser. 1948. *Shoe String* 1970 $6.00

THE LETTERS OF LAURENCE STERNE. Ed. by Lewis Perry Curtis. *Oxford* 1935 $10.25

Books about Sterne

The Life and Times of Laurence Sterne. By Wilbur L. Cross. The standard biography. 1920 1925 3rd ed. with alterations and additions 1929. *Russell & Russell* 1967 $15.00

Tristram Shandy's World: Sterne's Philosophical Rhetoric. By John Traugott. 1954. *Russell & Russell*
1970 $9.00. Still the best study of Sterne's thought in the novels.
Laurence Sterne: From Tristram to Yorick: An Interpretation of Tristram Shandy. By Henri Fluchere,
trans. from the French by Barbara Bray. *Oxford* 1965 $14.50. An extensive study of the life and ideas
of the author as they appear in the novels.
Laurence Sterne. By William B. Piper. In the English Authors Series, with chronology and selected bibliography. *Twayne* 1965 $5.50
Laurence Sterne: An Essay and a Bibliography of Sternean Studies, 1900–1965. By Lodwick Hartley.
Univ. of North Carolina Press 1966 $6.00 pap. $2.45. A repr. of his "This is Lorence," a clear and
useful biographical study.
Sterne's Comedy of Moral Sentiments. By Arthur H. Cash. *Duquesne Univ. Press* 1966 $6.50. A valuable
analysis of Sterne's ideas, particularly in his "Sentimental Journey."
The Comic Art of Laurence Sterne: Convention and Innovation in Tristram Shandy and A Sentimental
Journey. By John M. Stedmond. *Univ. of Toronto Press* 1967 $6.50. Well-considered essays on
Sterne's ideas and techniques.
Laurence Sterne: A Collection of Critical Essays. Ed. by John Traugott. *Prentice-Hall* 1968 $5.95 Spec-
trum Bks. pap. $1.95
Image and Immortality: A Study of Tristram Shandy. By William V. Holtz. *Brown Univ. Press* 1971
$7.00. An admirable discussion of Sterne's use of the visual arts.

WALPOLE, HORACE (or Horatio), 4th Earl of Orford. 1717–1797. *See Chapter 16, Literary Biography and Autobiography.*

SMOLLETT, TOBIAS GEORGE. 1721–1771.

Smollett, the only major 18th-century English novelist who can seriously be called picaresque, came to
novel writing with a strong sense of Scottish national pride (an alienating element in the London of the 1750s
and 1760s), a Tory feeling for a lost order, horrifying experiences as a physician, and a fierce determination
to make his way in the literary world. Prolific in a variety of forms, he was particularly successful as popular
historian, magazine editor, translator of Cervantes, and author of novels about adventurous, unscrupulous,
poor young men of family fighting their ways—in echoes of "Lazarillo de Tormes" and "Gil Blas"—
through a hypocritical society. His work is marked by vigorous journalistic descriptions of contemporary horrors like shipboard amputations or the filthy curative waters of Bath; by a flair for racy narrative often built
on violence and sentiment and a comedy often relying on practical jokes and puns; and by a great gift for
creating comic caricatures like Commodore Trunnion in "Peregrine Pickle" or Captain Lismahago in
"Humphry Clinker." His peppery "Travels Through France and Italy" was something of a spur to Sterne's
(*q.v.*) "Sentimental Journey," where Smollett is referred to as Dr. Smelfungus who "set out with the spleen
and jaundice, and every object he passed by was discolored or distorted—He wrote an account of them, but
'twas nothing but the account of his miserable feelings."
Smollett's most notable novels were "Roderick Random," "Peregrine Pickle," "Ferdinand Count Fathom," "Sir Launcelot Greaves" (1762, o.p.), which set a precedent by first being serialized in his *British
Magazine*, Jan. 1760–Dec. 1761, and especially "The Expedition of Humphry Clinker," a relatively mellow
work that follows the travels of Matthew Bramble, an excitable Welshman, from his home through chaotic
England to idyllic Loch Lomond and back, in the company of his sister, his niece, and the sister's maid, all of
whom find husbands on the way. He himself finds what Smollett had irrecoverably lost, his health, as well as
a son from his youth. Smollett died in 1771, the year of the novel's appearance, in Leghorn, Italy.

NOVELS. The Shakespeare Head ed. 1925. *Scholarly Press* 11 vols. each $24.50 set
$250.00

RODERICK RANDOM. 1748. *Dutton* Everyman's $3.50 pap. $2.50; *New Am. Lib.* Signet
1964 pap. $1.25

PEREGRINE PICKLE. 1731. *Dutton* Everyman's 2 vols. each $3.50; ed. with introd. by
James L. Clifford *Oxford* 1964 $7.00 pap. $3.95

THE ADVENTURES OF FERDINAND, COUNT FATHOM. 1753. Ed. by Damian Grant. *Oxford* 1971 $9.00

THE EXPEDITION OF HUMPHRY CLINKER. 1771. *Collins* New Class. $3.00; *Dutton* Ev-
eryman's $3.50 pap. $1.95; ed. by R. G. Davis *Holt* (Rinehart) 1950 pap. $2.50;
New Am. Lib. pap. $.95; ed. with an introd. by Lewis M. Knapp *Oxford* 1966 $6.95
pap. $3.95; ed. by Angus Ross *Penguin* 1967 pap. $1.25

TRAVELS THROUGH FRANCE AND ITALY. 1766. Ed. by James Morris. *Praeger* 1970
$22.50

LETTERS. Ed. by Edward S. Noyes. 1926. *Bks. for Libraries* $14.50; ed. by Lewis M.
Knapp *Oxford* 1970 $9.75

Books about Smollett

The Later Career of Tobias Smollett. By Louis L. Martz. 1942. *Shoe String* 1967 $6.00. A study of his
creative work after 1753.
Tobias George Smollett, Doctor of Men and Manners. By Lewis M. Knapp. 1949. *Russell & Russell*
1963 $10.00. The "first trustworthy full-scale picture of the man and writer and the most authoritative
study."
Tobias Smollett: Bicentennial Essays Presented to Lewis M. Knapp. Ed. by G. S. Rousseau and P. G.
Bouce. *Oxford* 1971. $9.50. Current scholarly interpretations of Smollett and his works.
Tobias Smollett. By Robert D. Spector. English Authors Ser. *Twayne* 1969. $5.50. An excellent bio-
graphical and critical study.
Tobias Smollett: Traveler-Novelist. By George Kahri. *Octagon* 1967 $8.50

GOLDSMITH, OLIVER. 1728–1774.

As Samuel Johnson said in his famous epitaph on his friend, Goldsmith ornamented whatever he touched
with his pen. A professional writer who died in his prime, Goldsmith wrote the best comedy of his day, "She
Stoops to Conquer"; one of its finest poems, "The Deserted Village"; its most engaging essays, particularly
in his newspaper column of Chinese Letters, which were reprinted as "The Citizen of the World"; histories
of Rome, Greece, and England that remained in use in schools for a century; a "History of the Earth and Animated Nature" that at times, as Johnson predicted, is as amusing as a Persian tale; biographies and even
book reviews that still give pleasure in their wit and sympathy; and "The Vicar of Wakefield," which despite
major plot inconsistencies and the intrusion of poems, essays, tales, and lectures apparently foreign to its central concerns remains one of the most engaging fictional works in the language. One reason for its appeal is
the character of the narrator, Dr. Primrose, who is at once a slightly absurd pedant, an impatient traditional
father of teenagers, a Job-like figure heroically facing life's blows, and an alertly curious, helpful, loving person. Another reason is Goldsmith's own mixture of delight and amused condescension (analogous to, though
not identical with, Sterne's (*q.v.*) in "Tristram Shandy" and Johnson's (*q.v.*) in "Rasselas," both contempo-
raneous) as he looks at the Vicar and his domestic group, fit representatives of a ludicrous but workable
world.

COLLECTED WORKS OF OLIVER GOLDSMITH. Ed. by Arthur Friedman. *Oxford* 1966
5 vols. $68.00. The standard edition of his original writings.

SELECTED WORKS. Chosen by Richard Garnett. *Harvard Univ. Press* Reynard Lib.
1951 $12.00 pap. $4.50

THE VICAR OF WAKEFIELD; SHE STOOPS TO CONQUER (play); THE DESERTED VIL-
LAGE and OTHER POEMS. *Collins* New Class. $3.00

THE VICAR OF WAKEFIELD. 1766. *Assoc. Booksellers* Airmont Bks. 1964 pap. $.60;
Dutton Everyman's $3.25 pap. 1972 $1.50; *Macmillan* Collier Bks. pap. $1.50;
New Am. Lib. Signet pap. $.60; *Oxford* World's Class. $2.75; *Washington Square*
1961 pap. $.50 *Collateral Class.* pap. $.50

COLLECTED LETTERS. Ed. by Katharine C. Balderston. 1928. *Folcroft* lib. bdg. $15.00;
(and K. Balderston's "The History and Sources of Percy's Memoir of Goldsmith")
1928. *Kraus* $15.00

Books about Goldsmith

Oliver Goldsmith: A Georgian Study. By Ricardo Quintana. *Macmillan* 1967 $4.95
Oliver Goldsmith. By Ralph Wardle. 1957. *Shoe String* 1969 $9.00. Useful for the facts of Goldsmith's
life.

BURNEY, FANNY (MME. [FRANCES] D'ARBLAY). 1752–1840.

Although lovers of Jane Austen may think of Fanny Burney as merely an essential precursor, at least the first of her novels, "Evelina," has deserved its devotees. Consisting largely of the letters of the heroine, a young marriageable girl visiting London and registering freshly the responses to the metropolis and its people that had been featured in the novels of Defoe, Richardson, Fielding, Smollett, and a multitude of their inferiors, it shows sharp observation, a precise sense of the shifting feelings of the girl and the men who are interested in her, and a delight in and fear of the grotesque middle-class and foreign relatives she meets. After Fanny Burney was revealed as the author of the widely admired novel, she left the intellectually exciting household of her father Charles Burney, the leading musicologist of his time and a friend of Dr. Samuel Johnson, for the onerous boredom of being a lady in waiting to Queen Charlotte. She married late, wrote "Cecilia" (1782, o.p.). "Camilla" (1796), and "Wanderer" (1802, o.p.), and lived with apparent contentment to a very old age.

EVELINA, or A Young Lady's Entrance in the World. 1778. *Dutton* Everyman's $3.50; *Norton* 1965 pap. $2.25; ed. by Edward A. Bloom *Oxford* 1968 $6.50 pap. $3.00

CAMILLA. 1796. Ed. by Edward A. and Lillian D. Bloom. A reproduction of the original text of 1796. *Oxford* 1972 $22.00

THE DIARY OF FANNY BURNEY. Published first in 7 vols. 1842–46. Sel. and ed. by Lewis Gibbs. *Dutton* Everyman's $3.50. A vivacious picture of life at George III's court.

EARLY DIARY OF FRANCES BURNEY, 1768–78. Ed. by Annie R. Ellis 1899. *Bks. for Libraries* 2 vols. set $29.50; *AMS Press* 2 vols. each $20.50 set $40.00

DIARY AND LETTERS OF MME. D'ARBLAY, 1778–1840. Ed. by Charlotte Barrett with pref. and notes by Austin Dobson. 6 vols. 1904–05. *AMS Press* each $36.50 set $215.00. The volumes are profusely illustrated, and a bibliography is included. Charlotte Barrett was Fanny Burney's niece.

JOURNALS AND LETTERS OF FANNY BURNEY. Ed. by Joyce Hemlow and others. *Oxford* 4 vols. Vol. I 1791–1792. Letters 1–39. Ed by Joyce Hemlow, Curtis D. Cecil and Althea Douglas (1972) $11.00 Vol 2 Courtship and Marriage 1793. Letters 40–121. Ed. by J. Hemlow and A. Douglas (1972) $11.00 Vol. 3. Great Bookham 1793–1797. Letters 122–250. Ed. by J. Hemlow and others. (1973) text ed. $16.00 Vol. 4 West Humble. Letters 251–422. Ed. by J. Hemlow (1973) text ed. $24.00

Books about Burney

Memoirs of Dr. Burney. Arranged from his own manuscripts, from family papers and from personal recollections, by his daughter. 1832. *AMS Press* 3 vols. each $20.50 set $60.00
The History of Fanny Burney. By Joyce Hemlow. *Oxford* 1958 $11.00. Based largely on unprinted parts of her journal-letters, notebooks, unpublished works and voluminous correspondence, and on other unpublished sections of other Burney papers. "Her search is original, accurate, and exhaustive, and this will be for years to come the standard reference book."

Note: In general, only volumes applying to British Fiction: Early Period or closely related subjects are listed in this Chapter. For complete histories of English literature, etc., covering this period, see Chapter 3, Reference Books—Literature. See also Chapter 4, Broad Studies and General Anthologies: Fiction.

—M.G.

Chapter 11

British Fiction: Middle Period

"The whole secret of fiction and the drama—in the constructional part—lies in the adjustment of things unusual to things eternal and universal. The novelist who knows exactly how exceptional, and how non-exceptional, his events should be made, possesses the key to the art." —THOMAS HARDY

British fiction exploded into sustained greatness in the middle period which begins in the first 20 years of the 19th century with the panoramic historical romances of Scott and the carefully crafted character explorations of Jane Austen. Scott's combinations of romantic medievalism and contemporary sentiment were widely popular; Austen's careful and restrained illuminations of the relationship between character, environment, and moral choice were hardly read. But the modern judgment is that she is the most impressive literary artist working in the novel between the final publications of the major 18th-century novelists and the first novel of Charles Dickens in 1836.

The years between pass with interesting but secondary figures like Ann Radcliffe and Mary Shelley, who popularize Gothic fiction, Maria Edgeworth, who creates the regional novel, and Thomas Love Peacock, whose novels emphasize intellectual wit and literary humor. Such special subject areas anticipate in the mid-century the sea-adventure novels of Marryat, the historical novels of Bulwer-Lytton and Ainsworth, the political novels of Disraeli, the Christian-socialist novels of Kingsley, the labor novels of Gaskell, the utopian novels of Butler, the proletarian novels of Gissing, the novels of international adventure and moral testing of Conrad, the novels of colonial empire of Kipling, and so on. Each represents a popular type of fiction whose many practitioners contributed to a form of communication and entertainment that dominates the Victorian age.

Interestingly, the novelist most acclaimed during the high years of Victorian culture, Charles Dickens, has returned from comparative neglect to a position of the highest esteem, valued for the depth and precision of his psychological insight, the brilliance of his metaphoric style, and his capacity to sustain complex structures in which purposeful artifice, accurately realized satire, and poetic invention are integrated successfully. Dickens contains within himself all the strands that his contemporaries and followers, extraordinary in their own right, weave separately. Thackeray becomes the master of satire, George Eliot of psychological realism, Trollope of behavioral norms, Collins of detective sensationalism, Hardy of the landscape of pessimistic despair.

No period in the history of the English novel reflects so dramatically the movement from the past to the present, from pastoral containment to urban chaos, from aristocratic forbearance to democratic emotionalism, from belief in firm opinions and a settled faith to uncertainty and relativism. But, at the same time, no literature since the Renaissance in England has communicated quite the fullness and variety of life, the sense of sustained exploration of the relationship between man and himself and man and society, as the fiction of the middle period.

HISTORY AND CRITICISM

Altick, Richard D. THE ENGLISH COMMON READER: A Social History of the Mass Reading Public, 1800–1900. *Univ. of Chicago Press* 1957 Phoenix Bks. 1963 pap. $2.45

Ausubel, Herman. THE LATE VICTORIANS: A Short History. *Van Nostrand-Rheinhold* Anvil Bks. pap. $1.75; *Peter Smith* $3.25

Baker, Ernest Albert. A HISTORY OF THE ENGLISH NOVEL. Complete in 10 vols. (with added Vol. 11: *see below*) Vol. 5 The Novel of Sentiment and the Gothic Romance Vol. 8 From the Brontës to Meredith, Romanticism in the English Novel Vol. 9 The Day Before Yesterday (Hardy, George Moore, Henry James) Vol. 10 Yesterday (Conrad, Kipling, Bennett) *Barnes & Noble* 1929–1939 each $6.50

   A HISTORY OF THE ENGLISH NOVEL. Vol. 11 Yesterday and After. By Lionel Stevenson. An addition to the previous work by another author to bring it up to date. *Barnes & Noble* 1967 $10.00

Birkhead, Edith. THE TALE OF TERROR: A Study of the Gothic Romance. 1921. *Russell & Russell* 1963 $10.00

Bleiler, Everett F., Ed. THE CASTLE OF OTRANTO, Horace Walpole; VATHEK, William Beckford; THE VAMPIRE, John Polidori, with a Fragment by Lord Byron; Three Gothic Novels. 1967 *Peter Smith* $4.50

Block, Andrew. THE ENGLISH NOVEL, 1740–1850: A Catalogue including Prose Romances, Short Stories and Translations of Foreign Fiction. 1939. *Oceana* new ed. 1962 $28.00. A valuable reference source.

Cecil, David. VICTORIAN NOVELISTS. *Univ. of Chicago Press* 1958 $7.00 Phoenix Bks. pap. $2.25

Chesterton, G. K. THE VICTORIAN AGE IN LITERATURE. 1913. *Oxford* 1946 2nd ed. 1966 pap. $1.50; *Univ. of Notre Dame Press* 1963 pap. $1.75

Colby, Robert A. FICTION WITH A PURPOSE: Major and Minor Nineteenth-Century Novels. *Indiana Univ. Press* 1967 $10.00. One novel of each of the following writers is discussed with reference to its contemporary environment: Scott, Austen, Dickens, Thackeray, Charlotte Brontë and George Eliot. Each chapter contains a list of other novels of the period (most now unknown) which had better reviews than the one discussed, when first published.

Cunliffe, John W. LEADERS OF THE VICTORIAN REVOLUTION. 1934. *Kennikat* $10.00; *Russell & Russell* 1963 $9.50

Donovan, Robert Alan. THE SHAPING VISION: Imagination in the English Novel from Defoe to Dickens. *Cornell Univ. Press* 1967 $8.75

Drew, Elizabeth. THE NOVEL: A Modern Guide to Fifteen English Masterpieces. *Norton* 1963 $5.95; *Dell* pap. $.60

Ellmann, Richard, Ed. EDWARDIANS AND LATE VICTORIANS: English Institute Essays, 1959. *Columbia* 1960 $7.00. The essays are drawn from conferences on "The Last Victorians" and "The Edwardians."

Elwin, Malcolm. VICTORIAN WALLFLOWERS: A Panoramic Survey of the Popular Victorian Literature. 1934. *Richard West* $10.95

Fairchild, Hoxie N. THE NOBLE SAVAGE: A Study in Romantic Naturalism. 1928. *Russell & Russell* 1961 $15.00

Fleishman, Avrom. THE ENGLISH HISTORICAL NOVEL: Walter Scott to Virginia Woolf. *Johns Hopkins Univ. Press* 2nd ed. 1972 $10.00 pap. $2.95

Ford, Boris, Ed. A GUIDE TO ENGLISH LITERATURE. 7 vols. Vol. 6 From Dickens to Hardy: A Survey of the Literature of the Age in Its Social and Intellectual Context *Dufour* $8.95; (with title "A Pelican Guide to English Literature") *Penguin* pap. $1.65; *Walter Gannon* $3.90

Harvey, John R. VICTORIAN NOVELISTS AND THEIR ILLUSTRATORS. *New York Univ. Press.* 1971 $13.50

Hearn, Lafcadio. SOME STRANGE ENGLISH LITERARY FIGURES OF THE EIGHTEENTH AND NINETEENTH CENTURIES. Ed. by R. Tanabé. *Bks. for Libraries* $8.75

Holloway, John. THE VICTORIAN SAGE: Studies in Argument. 1953. *Norton* 1965 pap. $1.95; *Shoe String* 1968 $7.00

Houghton, Walter E., Ed. THE WELLESLEY INDEX TO VICTORIAN PERIODICALS. *Univ. of Toronto Press* 2 vols. Vol. I 1824–1900 (1967) $95.00 Vol. 2 (1972) $125.00 set $195.00

> "It is no exaggeration to say that such a work might eventually produce a revolution in nineteenth-century studies"—(*Victorian Studies*). "Highly recommended for the research library and the special collection"—(*LJ*).

THE VICTORIAN FRAME OF MIND, 1830–1870. *Yale Univ. Press* 1857 $12.50 pap. $3.75

Howard, David, John Lucas and John Goode. TRADITION AND TOLERANCE IN NINETEENTH-CENTURY FICTION. *Routledge & Kegan Paul* 1966 $7.75

> Six essays deal with Dickens, James, Cooper, Hawthorne, Elizabeth Gaskell, Walter Besant and Disraeli. They show "how the attitudes, feelings and intellectual limitations of an author infect the very life of a novel: its structure, characters, language and resolution"—(*N.Y. Times*).

Hoyt, Charles Alva, Ed. MINOR BRITISH NOVELISTS. Pref. by Harry T. Moore. *Southern Illinois Univ. Press* 1967 $4.95. Essays by various hands on Fanny Burney, Maria Edgeworth, Peacock, Surtees, Disraeli, Mrs. Gaskell, Arthur Machen, Charles Williams and Rose Macauley.

Karl, Frederick R. AN AGE OF FICTION: The Nineteenth-Century British Novel. *Farrar, Straus* 1965 $7.50 Noonday pap. $2.25

> "Karl's informed and balanced survy critique ... will challenge serious students, and yet not repel neophytes"—(*LJ*).

Knoepflmacher, U. C. LAUGHTER AND DESPAIR: Readings in Ten Novels of the Victorian Era. *Univ. of California Press* 1971 $10.00 pap. $2.95

Kroeber, Karl. STYLES IN FICTIONAL STRUCTURE: The Art of Jane Austen, Charlotte Brontë, George Eliot. *Princeton Univ. Press* 1971. $11.00

Kunitz, Stanley J., and Howard Haycraft. BRITISH AUTHORS OF THE NINETEENTH CENTURY. *Wilson* 1936. 1955 $12.00. Complete in I vol. with 1000 biographies and 350 portraits.

Leavis, F. R. THE GREAT TRADITION: George Eliot, Henry James, Joseph Conrad. 1948. *New York Univ. Press* 1963 $8.95 pap. $2.45. Important study of the novel.

Lerner, Lawrence. TRUTH TELLERS: Jane Austen, George Eliot, D. H. Lawrence. *Schocken* 1967 $7.50

Miller, J. Hillis. THE DISAPPEARANCE OF GOD: Five Nineteenth Century Writers. *Harvard Univ. Press* 1963 $9.00

THE FORM OF VICTORIAN FICTION. Ward Phillips Lecture Ser. *Univ. of Notre Dame Press* 1969 $3.95

Phillips, Walter C. DICKENS, READE AND COLLINS: Sensation Novelists. 1919. *Russell & Russell* 1962 $7.50. A study of the conditions and theories of novel writing in Victorian England.

Praz, Mario. THE HERO IN ECLIPSE IN VICTORIAN FICTION. Trans. from the Italian by Angus Davidson. *Oxford* 1956 pap. 1969 $3.75

"Deals with the relationships between genre painting and the novel, shows how Romanticism 'turned bourgeois' in the Victorian age, and considers the diminishing stature of the hero in Dickens and others"— (Publisher's catalog).

Russell, Frances T. SATIRE ON THE VICTORIAN NOVEL. 1920. *Russell & Russell* 1964 $12.50

Stang, Richard. THE THEORY OF THE NOVEL IN ENGLAND 1850–1870. *Columbia* 1959 $9.00. Mr. Stang demonstrates that "mid-Victorian criticism of fiction has been very much underrated, that it should be considered as an important part of the history of English criticism as a whole, and that it must further be considered in any study of the mutations of the English novel."

Stevenson, Lionel, Ed. VICTORIAN FICTION: A Guide to Research. *Harvard Univ. Press* 1964 $10.00

"The difficult problem of conveying solid bibliographical information in essay form has been generally well mastered, with occasional flashes of humour and, usually, a proper harshness"—(*TLS*, London).

Tillotson, Kathleen. NOVELS OF THE EIGHTEEN-FORTIES. *Oxford* 1954 $10.25 pap. 1961 $2.25. Discusses these novels in the context of their relationship to each other, their time, and their first readers.

Van Ghent, Dorothy. THE ENGLISH NOVEL: Form and Function. *Holt* 1953 $9.00; *Harper* Perenn. Lib. pap. $1.45

Varma, Devendra P. THE GOTHIC FLAME: Being a History of the Gothic Novel in England: Its Origins, Efflorescence, Disintegration, and Residuary Influences. 1957. *Russell & Russell* 1966 $8.50

"Both historically and analytically thorough, besides being entertaining, [it] is wide embracing and scholarly; a vast amount of reading has gone into it"—(*TLS*, London).

Watt, Ian, Ed. THE VICTORIAN NOVEL: Essays in Criticism. *Oxford* Galaxy Bks. pap. $3.95

Whistler, James McNeill. THE GENTLE ART OF MAKING ENEMIES. Introd. by Alfred Werner. *Dover* 1967 pap. $3.00 *Peter Smith* $4.25. Fascinating background on the period. The artist's account of his battles with Ruskin, Wilde, Swinburne and others.

Wilson, F. P. and Bonamy Dobrée, Gen. Eds. OXFORD HISTORY OF ENGLISH LITERATURE. *Oxford* 1945 Vol. 9 English Literature 1789–1815 by W. L. Renwick (1963) $8.00; Vol. 10 English Literature 1815–1832 by Ian Jack (1963) $11.00

RADCLIFFE, ANN (WARD). 1764–1823.

Ann Radcliffe originated the romantic mystery novel known as "Gothic." It is characterized by vivid scenic descriptions and by seemingly supernatural elements which are later explained by natural causes. Her novels—the best-known is "The Mysteries of Udolpho"—influenced Scott (*q. v.*) in his development of narrative method, and Byron (*q. v.*) in his conception of the "Byronic hero." "Udolpho" was one of the literary inspirations of Keats' "Eve of St. Agnes."

POETICAL WORKS. 1834. *AMS Press* 2 vols. each $18.50 set $36.00

A SICILIAN ROMANCE. 1790. *Arno Press* repr. of 1821 ed. $35.00; *Johnson Reprint* repr. of 1792 ed. 2 vols. $25.00

THE ROMANCE OF THE FOREST. First published anonymously in 1791. 1792 *Johnson Reprint* 3 vols. 1971 $50.00

THE MYSTERIES OF UDOLPHO. 1794. *Dutton* Everyman's 2 vols. each $3.50; ed. by Michael Eenhoorn *Juniper Press* 1960 $4.50 pap. $1.95; ed. by B. Dobrée *Oxford* 1966 $8.50 pap. $4.50

THE MYSTERIES OF UDOLPHO (abr.). (and Austen's "Northanger Abbey" and Walpole's "Castle of Otranto.") Ed. by A. Wright. *Peter Smith* $4.75; *Holt* (Rinehart) 1963 pap. $3.00

THE CASTLES OF ATHLIN AND DUNBAYNE: A Highland Story. 1796. *Arno Press* repr. of 1821 ed. $35.00; *Johnson Reprint* repr. of 1796 ed. $15.00

THE ITALIAN, or The Confessional of the Black Penitents. 1797. Ed. by Frederick Garber *Oxford* 1968 $7.25 pap. $2.75

GASTON DE BLONDEVILLE, or The Court of Henry III Keeping Festival in Ardenne. 1826. *Arno Press* 1972 4 vols. in 2 $35.00. A metrical tale with some poetical pieces, published posthumously, with a memoir of the author.

Books about Radcliffe

Ann Radcliffe in Relation to Her Time. By C. F. McIntyre. 1920. *Shoe String* 1970 $4.50
Ann Radcliffe. By Gene Murray. English Authors Ser. *Twayne* $5.50

EDGEWORTH, MARIA. 1767–1849.

Following Fanny Burney (*q. v.*), Maria Edgeworth wrote in the tradition of the novel of manners. Her stated purpose was to diminish the frivolity of the times. She was one of the 21 children of Richard Lowell Edgeworth, an educator of landed Irish descent, who influenced her novels. When she was 15, the family moved to her father's Irish estate, and she became his agent. "Castle Rackrent" and "The Absentee," usually considered her best novels, were both based on her observation of the tenant system there, and portrayed the degeneration of Irish estates. These local-color stories for adults were a permanent contribution to literature, and Scott (*q. v.*) declared in the first edition of "Waverley" that his aim was "in some distant degree to emulate the admirable Irish portraits of Miss Edgeworth." As the sympathetic interpreter of national characteristics, she contributed to the Celtic revival and was one of the first to introduce the "lower classes" into fiction.

WORKS. 1893. *Adler's* 10 vols. set $160.00

TALES AND NOVELS. 1893. *AMS Press* 1967 10 vols. set $100.00

CASTLE RACKRENT. 1800. *Norton* 1965 pap. $.95; ed. by G. Watson *Oxford* 1964 $3.50 pap. $1.75; *Univ. of Miami Press* 1964 pap. $2.00

CASTLE RACKRENT and THE ABSENTEE (1812). *Dutton* Everyman's $3.50

LETTERS OF MARIA EDGEWORTH AND ANNA LETITIA BARBAULD. *A. S. Barnes* (Golden Cockerel) $15.00 cloth of gold brocade $30.00

THE LIFE AND LETTERS OF MARIA EDGEWORTH. Ed. by Augustus J. Hare. 1894. *Bks. for Libraries.* $25.00

LETTERS FROM ENGLAND, 1813–1844. Ed. by Christina Colvin. *Oxford* 1971 $24.00

Books about Edgeworth

Doubt and Dogma in Maria Edgeworth. By Mark D. Hawthorne. *Univ. of Florida Press* 1967 pap. $2.00
Maria Edgeworth and the Public Scene. By Michael Hurst. *Univ. of Miami Press* 1969 $7.95

SCOTT, SIR WALTER. 1771–1832.

Scott began his literary career by writing metrical tales. "The Lay of the Last Minstrel" (1805), "Marmion" (1808) and "The Lady of the Lake" (1810) made him the most popular poet of his day. 6,500 copies of "The Lay of the Last Minstrel" were sold in the first three years, a record such as poetry had never made before. His later romances in verse, "The Vision of Don Roderick," "Rokeby," (both o. p.) "The Lord of the Isles," met with waning interest, owing to the rivalry of Lord Byron (*q.v.*), whose more passionate poetic romances superseded Scott's in the public favor.

Scott then abandoned poetry for prose. In 1814 he published anonymously "Waverley, or Sixty Years Since," the first of his series known as the Waverley novels. He continued to write anonymously for 13 years. Twenty-five of the Waverley novels had been completed before he acknowledged his authorship. It is said that the snatches of verse which he used in his chapter headings finally betrayed him, for it was noted that he quoted from every known poet except the best known, Sir Walter Scott. He brought to perfection of form the historical novel, a genre of literature which Jane Porter claimed to have originated in her "Thaddeus of Warsaw" in 1803 (*AMS Press* $17.50) and in her "Scottish Chiefs" in 1809 (*Scribner* Ill. Class. $6.00). Scott's novels are often spoken of as semihistorical, because they are historical in background rather than in characters. Historical characters are never the protagonists in Scott's novels. It is always a fictitious person that holds the foreground. While the Waverley novels show trifling anachronisms, they are on the whole accurate. In their historical sequence, they range in setting from the year 1090 at the time of the First Crusade down to 1700, the period covered in "St. Ronan's Well," (o.p.) set in a Scottish watering place. Starting with the 11th century, Scott wrote novels covering every period of European history excepting the 13th century. Six of his 26 books were laid in the 17th century and eight were in the 18th century.

WORKS. *Dutton* Everyman's 10 vols. each $3.50 pap. each $1.50–$2.50 *Nelson* Class. 6 vols. each $1.95 *Modern Library* Giants $3.95

THE MOST POPULAR NOVELS: Quentin Durward; Ivanhoe; Kennilworth. *Modern Library* Giants $3.95

The Waverley Novels were issued as follows:

WAVERLEY. 1814. *Dutton* Everyman's $3.50; *New Am. Lib.* Signet pap. $.75; ed. by Andrew Hook *Penguin* pap. $2.45

GUY MANNERING. 1815. *Dutton* Everyman's $3.50 pap. $1.95

THE ANTIQUARY. 1816. *Dutton* Everyman's $3.50 pap. $1.95

OLD MORTALITY. 1817. *Collins* New Class. $3.00; *Dutton* Everyman's $3.50 pap. $1.95

THE HEART OF MIDLOTHIAN. 1818. *Collins* New Class. $3.00; *Dutton* Everyman's $3.50 pap. $1.95; ed. by David Daiches *Holt* (Rinehart) 1948 pap. $2.50; ed. by J. H. Raleigh *Houghton* Riv. Eds. pap. $1.95

ROB ROY. 1818. *Dutton* Everyman's $3.50 pap. $1.95; *Houghton* Riv. Eds. pap. $1.25; *Nelson* Class. $1.75

THE BRIDE OF LAMMERMOOR. 1819. *Dutton* Everyman's $3.50 pap. $1.95

IVANHOE. 1820. *Collins* New Class. $3.00 lea. $5.00; *Dodd* Gt. Ill. Class. $5.50; *Dutton* Everyman's $3.50; *Harper* Class. pap. $.85; *Macmillan* Collier Bks. pap. $.95; *Nelson* Class. $1.75; *Franklin Watts* 1967 lg.-type ed. Keith Jennison Bks. $7.95

Other paperback editions are available from Assoc. Booksellers, Dell, New Am. Lib.

KENNILWORTH. 1821. *Assoc. Booksellers* Airmont Bks. pap. $.75; *Collins* New Class. $3.00 lea. $5.00; *Dutton* Everyman's $3.50 pap. $2.25

THE FORTUNES OF NIGEL. 1822. *Dutton* Everyman's $3.50 pap. $2.25; *Peter Smith* $4.00 *Univ. of Nebraska Press* 1965 Bison Bks. pap. $1.95

QUENTIN DURWARD. 1823. *Assoc. Booksellers* Airmont Bks. pap. $.95; *Collins* New Class. $1.95; *Dodd* Gt. Ill. Class. $3.95; *Dutton* Everyman's $3.50 pap. $1.95; *New Am. Lib.* Signet pap. $.75; ill. by C. B. Chambers *Scribner* Ill. Class. 1923 $5.00

REDGAUNTLET. 1824. *Dutton* Everyman's $3.50 pap. $2.25

THE TALISMAN. 1825. *Dodd* Gt. Ill. Class $3.95; *Dutton* Everyman's $3.50 pap. $1.50

WOODSTOCK. 1826. *Dutton* Everyman's $3.50

THE MONASTERY. 1826. *Dutton* Everyman's $3.50

THE FAIR MAID OF PERTH. 1828. *Dutton* Everyman's $3.50

THE JOURNAL OF SIR WALTER SCOTT. From the original manuscript at Abbotsford. 1890. *Burt Franklin* 2 vols. 1970 $35.00

LETTERS. Ed. by Herbert Grierson and others. 1932–37. *AMS Press* 12 vols. $265.00

"Established wherever possible after original manuscripts and including many letters hitherto entirely unpublished, or printed in a abridged or garbled form. The centenary edition"—(Publisher's catalog).

LETTERS ON DEMONOLOGY AND WITCHCRAFT. 1830. *Gordon Press* $15.50; *Ace Books* pap. $.75

Other prose:

(Ed.) THE BANNATYNE MISCELLANY. 3 vols. 1827–1855. Vol. 1 (1827) by Scott Vols. 2–3 ed. by David Laing. *AMS Press* $70.00

The Bannatyne Club, of which Scott was the first president, was founded in 1823 for the purpose of publishing old Scottish documents chiefly concerned with the history and literature of that country. It was disbanded in 1861.

LIFE OF DRYDEN. 1808. Ed. by Bernard Kreissman. *Univ. of Nebraska Press* 1963 $5.00 Bison Bks. pap. $1.70

Poetry:

COMPLETE POETICAL WORKS. *Houghton* $8.95

POETICAL WORKS. Ed. by J. L. Robertson. *Oxford* Stand. Authors 1904 $9.00

(Ed.) MINSTRELSY OF THE SCOTTISH BORDER. 1802. Ed. by T. F. Henderson 1902. *Gale Research Co.* 4 vols. $64.50; *Richard West* $64.00

THE LADY OF THE LAKE. 1810. (and Other Poems) *Assoc. Booksellers* Airmont Bks. pap. $.75; (and Other Poems) *New Am. Lib.* Signet 1962 pap. $.75

THE LORD OF THE ISLES. 1815. 1914 *Scholarly Press* 1971 $14.50

Books about Scott

Reminiscences: Sir Walter Scott in Italy. By William Gell. 1832. *Hillary House* 1957 $3.00

Memoirs of Sir Walter Scott. By John Gibson Lockhart. 7 vols. 1837–38 *AMS Press* repr. of 1902 ed. 10 vols. each $15.00 set $150.00. The standard authorized biography by Scott's son-in-law. It is regarded as one of the great literary biographies.

The Life of Sir Walter Scott. By John Gibson Lockhart. Introd. by W. M. Parker. 1848. *Dutton* Everyman's $3.50. An abridgement of the "Memoirs" above.

The Waverley Dictionary: An Alphabetical Arrangement of All the Characters in Sir Walter Scott's Waverley Novels With a Descriptive Analysis of Each Character, and Illustrative Selections from the Text. By May Rogers. 1,500 entries. 2nd ed. 1885. *Gale Research Co.* $16.00

Sir Walter Scott as a Critic of Literature. By Margaret Ball. 1907. A standard work now back in print. *Kennikat* $7.50

Sir Walter Scott. By John Buchan. 1932. *Kennikat* $10.00

Sir Walter Scott, Bard. By Sir Herbert Grierson. 1938. *Folcroft* $15.00; *Haskell* 1969 lib. bdg. $13.95. Of the older biographies, this and Dame Una Pope-Hennessey's "Sir Walter Scott" (*see below*) are standard. For the definitive modern biography, *see* Edgar Johnson's "Sir Walter Scott: The Great Unknown" *below.*

Bibliography of Sir Walter Scott. By J. C. Corson. 1943. *Burt Franklin* $25.00

Sir Walter Scott. By Dame Una Pope-Hennessey. 1949. *AMS Press* $15.50; *Kraus* $7.00

Sir Walter Scott Lectures 1940–1948. By Herbert Grierson and others. *Aldine* 1950 $2.95

Sir Walter Scott, His Life and Personality. By Hesketh Pearson. *Harper* 1955 $6.95
An "absorbing and beautifully comprehensive book"—(Edward Weeks).

Sir Walter Scott. By Ian Jack. *British Bk. Centre* 1958 $2.38 pap. $1.20

A Dictionary of Characters in the Waverley Novels of Scott. By M. F. A. Husband. *Humanities Press* 1962 $8.50

The Author of Waverley: A Study in the Personality of Sir Walter Scott. By Christina Keith. *Roy Pubs.* 1966 $5.95
"Eminently readable and helpful"—(*LJ*).

Sir Walter Scott. By John Lauber. English Authors Ser. *Twayne* 1966 $4.95

The Waverley Novels and Their Critics. By J. T. Hillhouse. A "mine of useful information." *Octagon* 1967 $10.00

The Hero of the Waverley Novels. By Alexander Walsh. *Atheneum* 1968 pap. $2.45

The Achievement of Walter Scott. By A. O. J. Cockshut. *New York Univ. Press* 1969 $7.95 pap. $2.25. The book is divided into two parts. Pt. 1 discusses Scott's use of the historical novel, and his relation with other 18th-century writers. Pt. 2 discusses "Waverley," "Old Mortality," "Rob Roy," "The Heart of Midlothian" and "Redgauntlet," which the author considers the core of Scott's achievement.

Scott's Mind and Art. Ed. by A. Norman Jeffares. Vol. 6 in the Essays Old and New Ser. *Barnes & Noble* 1970 $7.75. Essays by Thomas Crawford, David Daiches and others.

Sir Walter Scott: The Great Unknown. By Edgar Johnson. *Macmillan* 2 vols. 1970 $25.00. An exhaustive and definitive modern biography, awarded the American Heritage Biography Prize.

Sir Walter Scott and His World. By David Daiches. *Viking* Studio Bks. 1971 $8.95. A pictorial biography.

AUSTEN, JANE. 1775–1817.

Jane Austen's novels were largely neglected during her own lifetime and in the decades of high Victorian commitment to seriousness and social issues. But the subtleties of her art and of her moral vision, particularly as embodied in her masterpiece, "Emma," have attracted high praise from modern readers. Her fiction reveals the strong influence of 18th-century classicism in its concentration on the nuances of character and in its purposefully nonrealistic depiction of a limited and controlled environment. Like Henry Fielding (*q.v.*), though with a great deal more restraint, her subject is human nature. She pursues through the dramatization of the daily activities of a small group of typological inhabitants of a specialized community the moral and social significance of basic relationships. Her style is spare, direct, her narrative rapidly paced and made effective by the skillful use of dialogue. Ultimately the dominant tone of her fiction is irony, the dramatization and revelation of pretension, falsity, ambition, selfishness, and, worst of all, bad judgment. Underlying her fiction is a vision of the partial perfectability of the moral sensibility which can, despite pervasive obstacles, create a balance of interests and an almost pastoral resolution of tensions. Two volumes of table talk, "Speaking of Jane Austen" (1944) and "More about Jane Austen" (1949), by Sheila Kaye-Smith and G. B. Stern, are now o.p.

OXFORD ILLUSTRATED JANE AUSTEN. Ed. by R. W. Chapman; the text based on collations of the early eds. *Oxford* 6 vols. Vol. 1 Sense and Sensibility (1933) Vol. 2 Pride and Prejudice (1932) Vol. 3 Mansfield Park (1934) Vol. 4 Emma (1933) Vol. 5 Northanger Abbey and Persuasion (1933) Vol. 6 Minor Works (1954) Juvenilia 1790–93 (Vols. 1, 2, 3), Lady Susan, Fragments of Novels: The Watsons and Sanditon, The Plan of a Novel, Opinions of Mansfield Park and Emma, Verses, Prose; with ills. from contemporary sources each $8.00

WORKS. *Collins* 5 vols. set $15.00 lea. $25.00; ed. by R. W. Chapman 6 vols. (*see above*) *Oxford* World's Class. pap. each $2.75

THE WATSONS. c. 1805. Continued and completed by John Coates. 1958. *Greenwood* 1973 $13.00. "The Watsons" was an unfinished fragment, written c. 1805, first published posthumously in 1871, along with two other fragments, "Lady Susan" (c. 1805) and "Sanditon" (1817), in J. E. Austen-Leigh's "A Memoir of Jane Austen". "Lady Susan" and "Sanditon" are both o.p. in separate editions.

SENSE AND SENSIBILITY. 1811. *Collins* New Class. $3.00 lea. $5.00; *Dodd* Gt. Ill. Class. $5.50; ill. by Brock *Dutton* 1950 Everyman's $3.50 pap. $1.75; *Harcourt* 1962 $3.95; introd. by Edward Wagenknecht *Harper* Mod. Class. $2.00; *Macmillan* Collier Bks. pap. $.65; (and "Pride and Prejudice") *Modern Library* 1949 $2.45 pap. $1.25; ed. by Claire Lamont, textual notes and bibliography by James Kinsley *Oxford* 1970 $6.00 World's Class. $2.25; ed. by Tony Tanner *Penguin* 1970 pap. $1.45; *Franklin Watts* ultratype ed. $4.50

Other paperback editions are available from Amsco School Pubns., Assoc. Booksellers Airmont Bks., Dell, Lancer, New Am. Lib. Signet, Washington Square, $.60–$1.15

PRIDE AND PREJUDICE. 1813. *Collins* New Class. $3.00 lea. $5.00; *Dodd* Gt. Ill. Class. $5.50; ill. by Brock *Dutton* $3.95 Everyman's $3.50; *Harcourt* 1962 $3.95 ed. by Bradford A. Booth: text, backgrounds, criticism pap. $3.50; *Harper* Mod. Class. $2.28; ed. by Robert Daniel *Hold* (Rinehart) 1949 $2.25; ed. by M. Schorer *Houghton* $3.00 Riv. Eds. pap. $1.00; *Macmillan* 1962 $3.95 lib. bdg. $4.24 Collier Bks. pap. $.95; (and "Sense and Sensibility") *Modern Library* 1949 $2.45 pap. $1.25; ed. by Donald Gray *Norton* 1966 pap. $1.95; ed. by W. Bradbrook *Oxford* 1970 $5.75 World's Class. $2.50; ed. by Tony Tanner *Penguin* pap. $1.45; *Franklin Watts* 1966 lg.-type ed. Keith Jennison Bks. $8.95 ultratype ed. $4.95

Other paperback editions are available from Amsco School Pubns., Assoc. Booksellers Airmont Bks., Dell, Lancer, New Am. Lib. Signet, Scholastic Bk. Services, Washington Square, $.60–$1.15

MANSFIELD PARK. 1814. *Collins* New Class. $3.00 lea. $5.00; introd. by R. Brimley Johnson *Dutton* Everyman's $3.50 pap. $1.75; *Harcourt* 1962 $3.95; ed. by John Lucas, textual notes and bibliography by James Kinsley· *Oxford* 1970 $7.25 ed. by R. W. Chapman 1929 World's Class. $3.50; ed. by Tony Tanner *Penguin* pap. $1.45; *Franklin Watts* 1971 $4.50

Other paperback editions are available from Assoc. Booksellers Airmont Bks., Dell, Lancer, New Am. Lib. Signet, Washington Square, $.50–$.75

EMMA. 1816. *Collins* New Class. $3.00 lea. $5.00; *Dodd* Gt. Ill. Class. 1961 $5.50; introd. by R. Brimley Johnson *Dutton* $3.95 Everyman's $3.50 pap. $1.95; *Harcourt* 1962 $3.95; ed. by Lionel Trilling *Houghton* $3.00 Riv. Eds. pap. $1.35; ed. by Stephen Parrish *Norton* Critical Eds. 1972 $12.95 pap. $2.25; ed. by David Lodge, textual notes and bibliography by James Kinsley *Oxford* 1971 $7.75 ed. by E. V. Lucas 1907 World's Class. $2.25; ed. by Ronald Blythe *Penguin* pap. $1.25; *Franklin Watts* 1971 $4.50

Other paperback editions are available from Assoc. Booksellers Airmont Bks., Aurora, Dell, New Am. Lib. Signet, Washington Square, $75–$2.50

Northanger Abbey. 1818. (And "Persuasion") *Collins* New Class. $3.00 lea. $5.00; (and "Persuasion") introd. by R. Brimley Johnson *Dutton* $4.50 Everyman's $3.50 pap. $1.95; (and Walpole's "Castle of Utranto" and Radcliffe's "Mysteries of Udolpho") (abr.) ed. by A. Wright *Holt* (Rinehart) 1963 pap. $3.00; *Peter Smith* $4.25; (and "Persuasion") ed. by John Davie *Oxford* 1971 $8.00 World's Class. $2.75; ed. by Anne Ehrenpreis *Penguin* 1972 pap. $1.25; *Franklin Watts* ultratype ed. 1971 $4.50

Other paperback editions are available from Dell, Lancer, New Am. Lib. Signet, Paperback Lib., $.50–$.75

Persuasion. 1818. (And "Northanger Abbey") *Collins* New Class. $3.00 lea. $5.00; (and "Northanger Abbey) introd. by R. Brimley Johnson. *Dutton* $4.50 Everyman's $3.50 pap. $1.95; text based on the early eds. of R. W. Chapman, introd. by David Daiches *Norton* 1958 pap. $.95; ed. by F. Reid *Oxford* World's Class. 1930 $2.50; (and "A Memoir of Jane Austen") ed. by D. W. Harding *Penguin* pap. $1.25; *Franklin Watts* ultratype ed. $4.50

Other paperback editions are available from Assoc. Booksellers Airmont Bks., Lancer, New Am. Lib. Signet, each $.60

Letters to Her Sister Cassandra and Others. Coll. and ed. by R. W. Chapman. 1932 *Oxford* 2nd ed. 1952 $18.00

Letters, 1796–1817. Sel. and ed. by R. W. Chapman. *Oxford* 2nd ed. 1952 $18.00 World's Class. $2.75

Books about Austen

The Life of Jane Austen. By Goldwin Smith. 1890. *Folcroft* 1972 $9.00

Jane Austen: Her Life and Letters; A Family Record. By William and Richard Arthur Austen-Leigh. 1913. *Russell & Russell* 2nd ed. 1965 $10.00

Memoir of Jane Austen. By. J. E. Austen-Leigh. Ed. by Robert W. Chapman. 1926. Written by her nephew. *Oxford* $7.75

Jane Austen Dictionary. By George L. Apperson. 1932. *Folcroft* lib. bdg. $5.50; *Haskell* 1969 $8.95
    "A citation, in a single alphabet, of every person, place, book, and author mentioned in Miss Austen's works, plus the names of her family and friends, and the names of all her works, together with the writing and publishing history of each one"—(Publisher's catalog).

Jane Austen and Some Contemporaries. By Mona Wilson. 1938. *Folcroft* 1973 lib. bdg. $25.00; *Haskell* lib. bdg. $11.95

Jane Austen and Her Art. By Mary Lascelles. 1939. *Oxford* $5.75 pap. $1.95
    "Not only a masterly study of one of the finest artists in English literature but also an outstanding contribution to the criticism of the craft of fiction"—(*TLS*, London).

Jane Austen: Facts and Problems. By. R. W. Chapman. *Oxford* 1948 $5.75. Biographical and critical problems with bibliography, chronology, iconography, etc.

Jane Austen. By Elizabeth Jenkins. 1949. *Funk & Wagnalls* Minerva Bks. pap. $2.95

Jane Austen's Art of Allusion. By Kenneth L. Moler. *Univ. of Nebraska Press* 1968 $7.25

Jane Austen: Irony as Defense and Discovery. By Marvin Mudrick. *Univ. of California Press* 1968 pap. $2.25

The Language of Jane Austen. By Norman Page. *Barnes & Noble* 1972 $9.50. Discusses the linguistic aspects, "key words," syntax, dialogue, and the role of letter writing in the novels.

The Improvement of the Estate: A Study of Jane Austen's Novels. By Alistair M. Duckworth. *Johns Hopkins Univ. Press* 1972 $9.00. The author treats Jane Austen's "estate" as a symbol of the whole society, and her characters as representing the means to improve social attitudes.

The Novels of Jane Austen: An Interpretation. By Darrel Mansell. *Barnes & Noble* 1973 $13.00

PEACOCK, THOMAS LOVE. 1785–1866.

Thomas Love Peacock was a poet, novelist and critic, as well as a conservative businessman employed by the East India Company for several years. He was a close friend of Shelley and other Romantics, but his writing differed from theirs in its wit and detachment. He was essentially a classicist in temperament and was self-taught and well read in Latin and Greek. Peacock satirized radicalism, medievalism and transcendentalism as well as individual romanticists like Wordsworth (*q.v.*), Coleridge (*q.v.*), Byron (*q.v.*) and Shelley (*q.v.*). "Crotchet Castle," appealing for its wit, humor and clever irony, has remained the most popular of his novels. His two early novels, "Headlong Hall" and "Nightmare Abbey," are both short and both "remarkable for high-spirited satire in 'romantic' settings." "Gryll Grange" (1860) is now out of print.

WORKS. Ed. by H. F. B. Brett-Smith and C. E. Jones. 1924–1934. The Standard or "Halliford" Edition. *AMS Press* 10 vols. set $195.00

HEADLONG HALL (1816) and NIGHTMARE ABBEY (1818). Introd. by P. M. Yarker. *Dutton.* Everyman's $3.50

NIGHTMARE ABBEY. 1818. (and "Crotchet Castle" [1831] and "The Misfortunes of Elphin" [1829]) *Holt* (Rinehart) 1971 pap. $2.95; *Norton* 1964 pap. $1.25; (and "Crotchet Castle") ed. by Raymond Wright *Penguin* 1969 pap. $1.45

FOUR AGES OF POETRY. 1820. (and Shelley's "Defense of Poetry") Ed. by J. E. Jordan *Bobbs* Lib. Arts 1965 pap. $.95

SONGS FROM THE NOVELS OF THOMAS LOVE PEACOCK. *Folcroft.* 1972 $12.50

LETTERS TO EDWARD HOOKHAM AND PERCY B. SHELLEY WITH FRAGMENTS OF UNPUBLISHED MSS. Ed. by R. Garnett. 1910. *Folcroft* lib. bdg. $17.50

Books about Peacock

The Life of Thomas Love Peacock. By Carl Van Doren. 1911. *Russell & Russell* 1966 $8.50

George Meredith and Thomas Love Peacock: A Study in Literary Influence. By Augustus Able. 1933. *Folcroft* lib. bdg. $6.00; *Phaeton* (dist. by Gordian) $6.50

Thomas Love Peacock. By Olwen W. Campbell. 1953. *Bks. for Libraries* 1973 $7.50

His Fine Wit: A Study of Thomas Love Peacock. By Carl Dawson. *Univ. of California Press* 1970 $7.50

Peacock, His Circle and His Age. By Howard W. Mills. *Cambridge.* 1969 $11.00

MARRYAT, CAPTAIN FREDERICK. 1792–1848.

Marryat is a master of the sea tale. All his novels deal with life in the English Navy, in which he himself served. His stories were written for children but read by old and young alike. "Masterman Ready" at one time stood next to "Robinson Crusoe" in popularity with boy readers. "Peter Simple" (1834, o.p.) is the most autobiographical of the novels, "Mr. Midshipman Easy" the most humorous. "Percival Keene" (1842, o.p.), the least estimable of his heroes, is a very melodramatic story. "The Little Savage" (1848, o.p.) is a "horror tale" of remarkable power, strong in plot and in character development. Marryat's novels are all very didactic, but his moral lessons never intrude or offend. The details of his adventurous life, so far as they are known, are well described in Oliver Warner's "Captain Marryat: A Rediscovery" (1953, o.p.).

"A Diary in America" appeared first in 1839. The recognition now given to Marryat as a source for social history is fully deserved, since his opinionated account of his journey gives us an invaluable view of American life at the time when Jacksonian democracy was in full development in the new nation."—(*LJ*)

MR. MIDSHIPMAN EASY. 1836. Introd. by Oliver Warner *Dutton* Everyman's $3.50 pap. $2.25

MASTERMAN READY. 1841. *Dutton* Everyman's $3.50

NARRATIVES OF THE TRAVELS AND ADVENTURES OF MONSIEUR VIOLET. 1843. *Gregg* 1970 3 vols. in 1 $40.00

THE CHILDREN OF THE NEW FOREST. 1847 *Collins* New Class. $3.00

THE SETTLERS IN CANADA. 1844. *Dutton* Everyman's $3.50

THE MISSION, or Scenes in Africa. Introd. by Tony Harrison. 1845. *Holmes & Meier* 1970 $15.00

A DIARY IN AMERICA. 1839. Ed. by Jules Zanger *Indiana Univ. Press* 1960 $6.95

SHELLEY, MARY WOLLSTONECRAFT (nee Godwin). 1797–1851.

Mary Shelley was the daughter of William Godwin, the English philosopher and writer, and Mary Woll-stonecraft (*q.v.*), author of the "Vindication of the Rights of Women" (1792). She fell in love with the poet Shelley (*q.v.*), went to the Continent with him in 1814 and married him after the death of his first wife in 1816. She is best known for her novel of horror, "Frankenstein," which she wrote when Byron proposed that he and each of his companions write a tale of the supernatural. It was an immediate sensation. After Shelley's death she edited his writings and wrote biographies, articles and fiction to educate her surviving son. Because of her association with Byron (*q.v.*), Trelawny, and Leigh Hunt (*q.v.*), her "Letters" (1946, o.p.) and "Journal" are excellent sources of literary material on the period. "My Best Mary" reveals in detail Shelley's life and loves as well as his wife's feelings and flirtations. Elizabeth Nitchie's "Mary Shelley: Author of Frankenstein" (1953 *Greenwood* $10.75) presents her as a woman and writer and as a liberal thinker in 19th-century society, by using her own and contemporary writings.

FRANKENSTEIN, or The Modern Prometheus. 1818. *Assoc. Booksellers* Airmont Bks. pap. $.60; ed. by Robert Spector *Bantam* pap. $.75; ed. by James H. Rieger *Bobbs* Lib. Arts $7.50 pap. $3.25; *Dell* Laurel Leaf Lib. pap. $.60; *Dutton* Everyman's $3.50 pap. $1.35; *Macmillan* Collier Bks. 1966 pap. $.65; *New Am. Lib.* Signet pap. $.60; ed. by M. K. Joseph *Oxford* 1969 $5.00

THE LAST MAN. 1826. Ed. by H. J. Luke, Jr. *Univ. of Nebraska Press* 1965 $5.00 pap. $1.95

THE CHOICE: A Poem on Shelley's Death. 1876. *Folcroft* $5.00

JOURNAL. Ed. by Frederick L. Jones. *Univ. of Oklahoma Press* 1947 $8.50

MY BEST MARY: The Selected Letters of Mary Wollstonecraft Shelley. Ed. by Muriel Spark and Derek Stanford. 1953. *Folcroft* lib. bdg. $15.00

BULWER-LYTTON (Edward George Earle Bulwer, afterwards 1st Baron Lytton of Knebworth). 1803–1873.

Immensely popular in his own lifetime, Bulwer-Lytton introduced the "silver spoon" novel with "Pelham" and initiated a series of historical romances with "Falkland," the most notable of which are "The Last Days of Pompeii," "Rienzi," and "Harold, the Last of the Saxons" (1848, o.p.). Lytton's versatility was equalled only by his eccentricity. He wrote essays, travel volumes, drama, poetry, heroicized romance, fiction-alized fact and factualized fiction, domestic fiction ("The Caxtons"), mystery tales, and, as a deeply committed adept of magic and the occult, novels of the supernatural, the most readable of which is "Zanoni: A Rosicrucian Tale." The standard life is "The Life, Letters, and Literary Remains," edited by his son (1883, 2 vols. o.p.). Robert L. Wolff's "Strange Stories: An Examination of Victorian Literature" (*Gambit* 1971 $8.95) contains a long section on Bulwer-Lytton's fascination with the occult.

FALKLAND. 1827. Ed. by Herbert Van Thal. *Dufour* 1964 $4.50 pap. $1.50

PELHAM, or The Adventures of a Gentleman. 1828. Ed. by Jerome J. McGann. *Univ. of Nebraska Press* 1972. $15.00

THE LAST DAYS OF POMPEII. 1834. *Dodd* Gt. Ill. Class. $5.50; *Dutton* Everyman's $3.50.

RIENZI: The Last of the Roman Tribunes. 1835. *Scholarly Press* repr. of 1882 ed. $19.50

ZANONI: A Rosicrucian Tale. 1842. *Multimedia/Biograph* (Rudolf Steiner) 1971. pap. $2.45

THE CAXTONS: A Family Picture. 1849. *Scholarly Press* 1971 repr. of 1898 ed. $24.50

A STRANGE STORY. 1862. *Shambala Publications* 1973 pap. $3.95

VRIL: The Power of the Coming Race. (Originally "The Coming Race") 1871. Introd. by Paul M. Allen. *Multimedia/Biograph* (Rudolf Steiner) 1972 pap. $1.95

ENGLAND AND THE ENGLISH. 1833. *Barnes & Noble* 2 vols. repr. of 1883 2nd ed. 1972 $26.50; ed. by Standish Meacham *Univ. of Chicago Press* 1970 $13.00 Phoenix Bks. 1972 pap. $3.45

LETTERS OF THE LATE EDWARD BULWER, LORD LYTTON, TO HIS WIFE. With extracts from her manuscript "Autobiography" and other documents, published in vindication of her memory, by Louisa Devey. 1889. *AMS Press* $18.00; *Richard West* $17.95

Books about Bulwer-Lytton

Edward Bulwer. By T. H. Escott. 1910. *Kennikat* 1970 $11.00

DISRAELI, BENJAMIN, 1st Earl of Beaconsfield. 1804–1881.

Disraeli, a great master of the political novel, may be said to have originated the genre. Trollope (*q.v.*) in his Parliamentary Novels is his closest rival. Disraeli's early books were all *romans à clef*, novels in which he introduced real personages easily recognizable beneath fictitious names. With "Coningsby," "Sybil" and "Tancred" Disraeli produced his best work, all political novels and more or less of a trilogy, as the same characters appear and reappear. He then gave up writing temporarily, "gradually rose to be three times Chancellor of the Exchequer, and finally, Prime Minister from 1867–68 and again from 1874–80. During his second term of office, when he was knighted, he took a name from his first novel and became the first Earl of Beaconsfield. In his later years he resumed his writing and became an intimate friend of Queen Victoria," who referred to his death as "a national calamity."

"The Life of Benjamin Disraeli, Earl of Beaconsfield," (2 vols. rev. ed. 1929 *Russell & Russell* 4 vols. 1968 $85.00, originally published in 6 volumes 1910–20) was written by William Flavelle Monypenny (1866–1912), who completed only two volumes before his death, and George Earl Buckle (1854–1935) who finished the work. In spite of an impatient public, Buckle delayed the publication of the last two volumes purposely until after the decease of the sisters, Lady Chesterfield and Lady Bradford, to each of whom Disraeli had proposed after the death of Lady Beaconsfield. The biography by Hesketh Pearson is now o.p.

WORKS. With a critical introd. by Edmund Gosse, and a biographical pref. by Robert Arnot. The Empire ed. 1905. *AMS Press* 20 vols. each $16.50 set $325.00

VIVIAN GREY. 1826. Ed. by Herbert Van Thal. *Dufour* 1969 $5.95 pap. $3.95

THE VOYAGE OF CAPTAIN POPANILLA. 1828. (with title "Popanilla and Other Tales") 1934. *Bks. for Libraries* $10.75; *McGrath Pub. Co.* 1972 $21.00

CONINGSBY. 1844. *Dutton* Everyman's $3.50; *Putnam* Capricorn Bks. pap. 1961 $1.75; *Scholarly Press* repr. of 1933 ed. $19.50

SYBIL, or The Two Nations. 1845. *Oxford* World's Class. $3.00

TANCRED, or The New Crusade. 1847. *Greenwood* repr. of 1877 ed. $15.00; *Scholarly Press* $15.00

LOTHAIR. 1870. *Greenwood* repr. of 1906 ed. $15.50; *Scholarly Press* repr. of 1933 ed. 1971 $24.50

Books about Disraeli

Lord Beaconsfield, By George Brandes. 1966. *Apollo* 1968 pap. $1.95; *Peter Smith* $4.25

Disraeli. By Robert Blake. *Oxford* pap. $2.50; *St. Martin's* $12.50

"[Blake] has portrayed, with delicacy and penetration, the most exciting and, in a curious way, the most modern of all Victorian statesmen. A great book"—(Harold Macmillan). "Blake's biography is a triumph . . . in Mr. Blake [Disraeli] has found a biographer to do his complex personality justice."—(*LJ*).

GASKELL, MRS. ELIZABETH (CLEGHORN STEVENSON). 1810–1865.

Mrs. Gaskell's novels deal with the social problems of the poor working class of her day. Humor and pathos abound in her stories. Because her father and her husband were both ministers, she came in close contact with the poor, and her books won great sympathy for them. Mrs. Gaskell knew the Brontë family personally and is particularly remembered for her "Life of Charlotte Brontë" (1857 *Dutton* Everyman's $3.50; World's Class. $3.00)

WORKS. Ed. by A. W. Ward. 1906. *AMS Press* 8 vols. each $24.00 set $185.00

MARY BARTON. 1848. *Dutton* Everyman's $3.50 pap. $1.95; *Norton* 1958 pap. $2.25; ed. by Stephen Gill *Penguin* 1970 pap. $2.45

CRANFORD. 1851–53. (and Other Tales) *Bks. for Libraries* repr. of 1886 ed. $14.50; *Collins* New Class. $3.00; introd. by Frank Swinnerton *Dutton* Everyman's $3.50; (and "The Cage at Cranford" and "The Moorland Cottage") ed. by Elizabeth P. Watson *Oxford* 1972 $7.00 World's Class. $2.50

RUTH. 1853. *Dutton* Everyman's $3.25

LIZZIE LEIGHT AND OTHER STORIES. 1854. *Bks. for Libraries* repr. of 1865 ed. $9.75

NORTH AND SOUTH. 1855. *Dutton* Everyman's $3.25; ed. by Dorothy Collins *Penguin* 1970 pap. $2.45; *Scholarly Press.* repr. of 1914 ed. 1971 $24.50

SYLVIA'S LOVERS. 1863. *Dutton* Everyman's $3.50

THE GREY WOMAN AND OTHER TALES. 1865. *Bks. for Libraries* $10.50

WIVES AND DAUGHTERS. 1866. *Dutton* Everyman's $3.50

THE LETTERS OF MRS. GASKELL. Ed. by J. A. V. Chapple and Arthur Pollard. *Harvard Univ. Press* 1967 $27.50

Letters dating from her marriage to her death, 1832–1864. A collection of all her letters extant. "Their value lies less in revealing [her] daily cares and preoccupations . . . than in the light they throw on . . . Dickens, Florence Nightingale, Harriet Beecher Stowe, Carlyle, Ruskin, Thackeray—and on the vulgar commercial vitality of her home city of Manchester in its first flush of industrial wealth"—(*N.Y. Times*).

Books about Mrs. Gaskell

Elizabeth Gaskell. By Gerald DeWitt Sanders. 1929. *Russell & Russell* 1971 $13.00; *Scholarly Press* 1971 $12.00

Mrs. Gaskell and Her Friends. By Elizabeth Haldane. 1931. *AMS Press* $13.50

Elizabeth Gaskell: Her Life and Work. By A. B. Hopkins. 1952. *Octagon* 1970 $13.00

Mrs. Gaskell: Novelist and Biographer. By Arthur Pollard. *Harvard Univ. Press* 1965 $7.50

Elizabeth Gaskell. By John McVeagh. *Humanities* 1968 $3.00

Mrs. Gaskell: The Basis for Reassessment. By Edgar Wright. *Oxford* 1965 $6.75

"Probably the best study available on Mrs. Gaskell"—(*Choice*).

Elizabeth Gaskell. By Margaret Ganz. English Authors Ser. *Twayne* 1969 $6.00

See also Chapter 16, on Literary Biography, for further comment on her "Life of Charlotte Brontë."

THACKERAY, WILLIAM MAKEPEACE. 1811–1863.

Generally considered the most effective satirist and humorist of the mid-19th century, Thackeray moved from humorous journalism to successful fiction with a facility that was partially the result of a genial fictional *persona* and a graceful, relaxed style. At his best, he held up a mirror to Victorian manners and morals, gently satirizing, with a tone of sophisticated acceptance, the inevitable failures of the individual and of society. He took up the popular fictional situation of the young person of talent who must make his way in the world and dramatized it with satiric directness in "The Luck of Barry Lyndon," with the highest fictional skill and appreciation of complexities inherent within the satiric vision in his masterpiece, "Vanity Fair," and with a great subtlety of point of view and background in his one historical novel, "Henry Esmond." "Vanity Fair," a complex interweaving in a vast historical panorama of a large number of characters, derives its title from Bunyan's (*q.v.*) "Pilgrim's Progress," and attempts to invert for satirical purposes the traditional Christian image of the City of God. "Vanity Fair," the corrupt City of Man, remains Thackeray's most appreciated and widely read novel. Constantly attuned to the demands of incidental journalism and his sense of professionalism in his relationship with his public, Thackeray wrote entertaining sketches and children's stories, and published his humorous lectures on 18th-century life and literature. His own fiction shows the influence of his dedication to 18th-century models such as Henry Fielding (*q.v.*), particularly in his satire which accepts human nature rather than condemns it and takes quite seriously the applicability of the true English gentleman as a model for moral behaviour.

Thackeray requested that no authorized biography of him should ever be written. Members of his family did write about him, but of these accounts only the article by Sir Leslie Stephen, his son-in-law, in the *Dictionary of National Biography* (1898. *Oxford*) is in print. Now o.p. are "Thackeray and His Daughters" (1924), by Hester Thackeray Ritchie; and "The Letters and Private Papers of William Makepeace Thackeray," collected and edited for Mrs. Richard Thackeray Fuller—the novelist's granddaughter—by Gordon N. Ray (1945–46).

CENTENARY BIOGRAPHICAL EDITION OF THE WORKS OF THACKERAY. With an introd. by Ann Thackeray Ritchie and a memoir by Leslie Stephens. 1910–11. *AMS Press* 26 vols. each $16.50 set $425.00

THE LUCK OF BARRY LYNDON. 1844. Ed. by Herbert Van Thal *Dufour* 1967 $4.25 pap. $2.25; ed. by Martin J. Anison *New York Univ. Press* critical ed. 1970 $10.00 pap. 1972 $3.50; (with title "The Memoirs of Barry Lyndon") ed. by Robert L. Morris *Univ. of Nebraska Press* 1962 Bison Bk. pap. $1.75. Written for *Fraser's Magazine* under the pseudonym of George Savage Fitz-Boodle.

VANITY FAIR. 1847. *Amsco School Pubns.* text ed. pap. $2.10; *Assoc. Booksellers* Airmont Bks. pap. $.95; *Collins* New Class. $3.00 lea. $5.00; (abr.) *Dell* Laurel Leaf Lib. pap. $.50; *Dodd* Gt. Ill. Class. $5.95; introd. by M. R. Ridley *Dutton* Everyman's $3.25 pap. $2.50; *Harper* Mod. Class. $2.96; ed. by John W. Dodds *Holt* (Rinehart) 1955 pap. $2.25; ed. by G. and K. Tillotson *Houghton* Riv. Eds. pap. $2.95; introd. by J. W. Beach *Modern Library* pap. $1.35; *New Am. Lib.* Signet 1962 pap. $1.25; ed. by F. E. Priestley *Odyssey* 1969 pap. $2.65; ed. by J. M. Stewart *Penguin* 1969 pap. $2.35; *Washington Square* Readers Enrich. Ser. $1.25 Collateral Class pap. $.50

VANITY FAIR. Dramatized by Jevan Brandon-Thomas. *French* $1.75

PENDENNIS. 1850. Introd. by M. R. Ridley *Dutton* Everyman's 2 vols. each $3.50; ed. by D. Hawes Penguin 1972 pap. $3.95

A SHABBY GENTEEL STORY. 1852 *New York Univ. Press* 1971 $6.50. First published in *Fraser's Magazine* in 1840. A sequel, "The Adventures of Philip," which appeared in *Cornhill Magazine* in 1861, is o.p.

HENRY ESMOND (The History of Henry Esmond, Esquire). 1852. *Collins* New Class. $3.00 lea. $5.00; *Dodd* Gt. Ill. Class. $5.50; *Dutton* pap. $2.25; ed. by G. Robert

Stange *Holt* (Rinehart) pap. $1.25; *Modern Library* pap. $1.25; ed. by John Sutherland and Michael Greenfield *Penguin* 1970 pap. $2.65; *Washington Square* Collateral Class. pap. $50

THE NEWCOMES. 1853. Introd. by M. R. Ridley *Dutton* Everyman's 2 vols. each $3.25; pap. each $2.75

THE ROSE AND THE RING. 1854. *Pierpont Morgan Library* facsimile ed. 1947 boxed $35.00

THE ROSE AND THE RING, or The History of Prince Giglio and Prince Bulbo. 1854. (and Dickens' "The Magic Fishbone") ill. by Thackeray and others *Dutton* Chil. Ill. Class. $3.95

THE VIRGINIANS. 1859. Introd. by M. R. Ridley *Dutton* Everyman's 2 vols. each $3.50

THE ENGLISH HUMORIST (1851) and THE FOUR GEORGES (1855). Lectures in England and America. *Dutton* Everyman's $3.50

THE HITHERTO UNPUBLISHED CONTRIBUTIONS OF W. M. THACKERAY TO PUNCH. With a complete and authoritative bibliography, 1843–48. By M. H. Spielmann, with numerous illustrations and explanatory notes. 1899. *AMS Press* $14.00; *Haskell* lib. bdg. $14.50

STRAY PAPERS. Stories, reviews, verses, sketches. Ed. by Lewis Melville (pseud. of Lewis Saul Benjamin). 1901 *Kraus* $16.00

CONTRIBUTIONS TO THE MORNING CHRONICLE. Ed. by Gordon N. Ray. *Univ. of Illinois Press* 1955 pap. $1.45

A COLLECTION OF LETTERS OF W. M. THACKERAY, 1847–55. With Portraits and reproductions of letters and drawings. 1887. *Haskell* 1970 $16.95

Books about Thackeray

Thackeray the Humorist and the Man of Letters. By Theodore Taylor. 1864. *Haskell* 1971 $10.95. Writing shortly after the death of Thackeray, the author was able to obtain much information from source material and from his friends, while memories of him were still sharp.
A Thackeray Library. By Henry S. Van Duzer. 1919 *Burt Franklin* 1971 lib. bdg. $13.50; *Kennikat* $12.50
Thackeray: A Personality. By Malcolm Elwin. 1932. *Folcroft* $10.95; *Russell & Russell* 1966 $11.00
Thackeray: A Critical Portrait. By John W. Dodds. 1941. *Russell & Russell* 1963 $8.50
The Showman of Vanity Fair: The Life of William Makepeace Thackeray. By Lionel Stevenson. 1947. *Russell & Russell* 1968 $15.00
The Buried Life: A Study of the Relation between Thackeray's Fiction and His Personal History. By Gordon N. Ray. 1952. *Folcroft* $12.50
Thackeray. By Gordon N. Ray. 2 vols. Vol. I The Uses of Adversity, 1811–1846 (1955) Vol. 2 The Age of Wisdom, 1847–1866 (1958) Octagon 1972 $45.00
A Thackeray Dictionary. By I. G. Mudge and M. E. Sears. *Humanities Press* 1962 $10.00
Thackeray and the Form of Fiction. By John Loofbourow. 1964 *Gordian* $10.00
Thackeray's Critics: An Annotated Bibliography of British and American Criticism, 1836–1901. By Dudley Flamm. *Univ. of Carolina Press* 1967 $6.00. An interesting introduction describes Thackeray's critical fortunes in his own century. Over 700 entries.
Thackeray: The Critical Heritage. Ed. by Geoffrey Tillotson and Donald Hawes. *Barnes & Noble* 1968 $8.00. First edition reviews from Thackeray's time.
Thackeray: A Collection of Critical Essays. By Alexander Welsh. Twentieth Century Views Ser. *Prentice-Hall* 1968 $5.95 pap. $1.95. Essays on various aspects of Thackeray's life and art by G. K. Chesterton, P. Lubbock, J. W. Dodds, J. Y. T. Greig, M. Praz, J. Sutton, K. Tillotson, G. A. Craig, J. Loofbourow, G. Lukács, J. E. Tilford, Jr., G. N. Ray and J. E. Baker.
Patterns in Thackeray's Fiction. By James M. Wheatley. *M.I.T. Press* 1969 $7.50 pap. $1.95
Thackeray: The Major Novels. By Juliet McMaster. *Univ. of Toronto Press* 1972 $7.50

The Exposure of Luxury: Radical Themes in Thackeray. By Barbara Hardy. *Univ. of Pittsburgh Press* 1972 $7.50. Ms. Hardy discusses Thackeray as moralist and social critic in a study of four major novels: "Vanity Fair," "Pendennis," "The Newcomes," and "Henry Esmond."

DICKENS, CHARLES. 1812–1870.

With a reputation that now places him among the half dozen most significant and formidable literary artists in English literature, Charles Dickens dominates modern critical opinion of the Victorian novel to the same extent that he dominated his contemporaries in his own day. Dickens was richly educated in the trials of a bankrupt household, in the difficulties of earning his own way from a young age on, and in the pressures of modern urban life. London becomes in his fiction the symbol of the condition of modern man; the pressures of economic survival become the illuminator of character and environment; and the experiences of childhood are transformed into a threatening landscape of exploitation.

Dickens' first success, "Sketches by Boz," a series of vignettes on London life and character, was followed by the immensely popular "Pickwick Papers" which like all of Dickens' novels was published in serial form. His reputation was firmly established by a succession of novels between 1837 and 1848 in which the dominant tone of ironic satire, outraged liberalism, comic extravagance, and imaginative fancy dramatized his concern with the themes of power, ambition, exploitation, self-destruction, and dehumanization. He drew on traditions of fairy tale and fantasy, developed immense skill with narrative and characterization, and revealed a brilliant flair for metaphor, psychological realism, and symbolic action. After "David Copperfield," his "favorite" but flawed child, Dickens' novels became dark with a kind of visionary pessimism. His earlier liberalism and optimism were replaced in "Bleak House," "Little Dorrit," and "Our Mutual Friend" with an increasing sense of the corruption and imperfectability of man and society in general, though he maintained his belief in the capability of special individuals to live productive and even happy lives. Dickens' fiction, in its richness and variety, its fascination with people and society, its embrace of man and acceptance of the withdrawal of God, its emphasis on urban life, economic pressures, and psychological realism both embodies and transcends Victorian culture.

A definitive edition of the letters in 12 volumes, "The Pilgrim Edition of the Letters of Charles Dickens," two volumes of which have been published, and a definitive edition of the novels, "The Clarendon Dickens," three volumes of which have been published, are in progress (see below). For the time being, The *Nonesuch Press* (1938 o. p.) edition of the letters is the fullest.

NOVELS. *Collins* 16 vols. set $48.00 1ea. $80.00

NEW OXFORD ILLUSTRATED DICKENS. *Oxford* 21 vols. each $7.00 set $145.00 écrasé set $250.00 (Consult listings below for individual titles)

CHRISTMAS BOOKS: A Christmas Carol, The Chimes, The Cricket on the Hearth, The Battle of Life, The Haunted Man. *Oxford* New Ill. Dickens $7.00

CHRISTMAS TALES. Introd. by May Lamberton Becker *Dodd.* Gt. Ill. Class. $5.50

THE CHRISTMAS STORIES: A Christmas Carol, The Chimes, The Cricket on the Hearth. Ill. by G. Dalziel and others *Oxford* New Ill. Dickens $7.00

THE COMIC WORLD OF DICKENS. Introd. by B. N. Shilling. *Peter Smith* $5.00

The order of publication of his principal works:

SKETCHES BY BOZ. 1836. *Dutton* Everyman's $3.50; *Oxford* 1957 $9.00 écrasé $12.50; *St. Martin's* $4.25

THE PICKWICK PAPERS (The Posthumous Papers of the Pickwick Club). 1836–37. *Collins* New Class. $3.00 lea. $5.00; introd. by G. K. Chesterton *Dutton* Everyman's $3.50 pap. $2.25; (with title "Posthumous Papers of the Pickwick Club") ill. by Seymour and Phiz *Oxford* $7.00; ed. by Robert Patten *Penguin* pap. $3.95

Other paperback editions are available from Assoc. Booksellers Airmont Bks., Dell, Modern Library (dist. by Random), New Am. Lib. Signet, Washington Square, $.60–$1.25

OLIVER TWIST (The Adventures of Oliver Twist) 1837–39. *Collins* New Class. $3.00 lea. $5.00; *Dodd* Gt. Ill. Class. $5.50; *Dutton* Everyman's $3.50 pap. $1.95; ed. by

J. Hillis Miller *Holt* (Rinehart) 1962 pap. $2.25; ill. by George Cruikshank *Oxford* New Ill. Dickens 1949 $7.00 boxed $12.50 World's Class. $2.50 ed. by Kathleen Tillotson Clarendon Dickens 1966 $13.75; ed. by Angus Wilson *Penguin* pap. $1.45

Other paperback editions are available from Assoc. Booksellers, Amsco School Pubns., Dell, New Am. Lib., Scholastic Bk. Services, Washington Square, $.45–$1.25

NICHOLAS NICKLEBY (The Life and Adventures of Nicholas Nickleby). 1838–39. *Collins* New Class. $3.00 lea. $5.00; *Dutton* Everyman's $3.50; ill. by Phiz *Oxford* New Ill. Dickens 1950 $7.00

THE OLD CURIOSITY SHOP. 1840–41. *Collins* New Class. $3.00 lea. $5.00; introd. by G. K. Chesterton *Dutton* Everyman's *$3.50; ill. by Phiz *Oxford* New Ill. Dickens $7.00; ed. by A. Easson *Penguin* 1972 pap. $3.75

MASTER HUMPHREY'S CLOCK. 1841. (And "Edwin Drood") *Dutton* Everyman's $3.50; (and "A Child's History of England," 1853) ill. by George Cattermole and others *Oxford* 1958 New Ill. Dickens $7.00

BARNABY RUDGE: A Tale of the Riots of Eighty. 1841. *Collins* New Class. $3.00 lea. $5.00; *Dodd.* Gt. Ill. Class. $5.95; *Dutton* Everyman's $3.50 pap. $2.25; (and "The Mystery of Edwin Drood") ill. by George Cattermole and others *Oxford* New Ill. Dickens $7.00

AMERICAN NOTES. 1842. Ed. by Arnold Goodman and John Whitley *Penguin* 1972 pap. $2.85; *Peter Smith* $5.00

A CHRISTMAS CAROL. 1843. *Assoc. Booksellers* Airmont Bks. pap. $.50; *Atheneum* $4.95 lib. bdg. $4.43; *Doubleday* $4.95; (and "The Cricket on the Hearth") *Dutton* ill. by Brock Chil. Ill. Class. $4.50 Everyman's $3.50 pap. $2.25; (and "The Chimes") *Harper* Class. pap. $.75; ill. by Arthur Rackham *Lippincott* $5.00; *Macmillan* 1963 $3.95 lib. bdg. $3.24; *N.Y. Public Lib.* the public reading version 1971 $15.00; ill. by Ruth McCrea *Peter Pauper* $2.95 vest pocket ed. $1.00; *Scholastic Bk. Services* pap. $.60; *Franklin Watts* lg.-type ed. Keith Jennison Bks. $7.95

A CHRISTMAS CAROL. Facsimile of the ms. in the Pierpont Morgan Library. Introd. by Monica Dickens with a pref. by Frederick B. Adams and ill. by John Leech. Transcript from the first ed. *James H. Heineman, Inc.* 1967 $12.50; *Dover* pap. $3.00; *Peter Smith* $6.00

MARTIN CHUZZLEWIT. (The Life and Adventures of Martin Chuzzlewit) 1843–48. *Collins* New Class. $3.00 lea. $5.00; *Dutton* Everyman's $3.50; *New Am. Lib.* Signet pap. $1.25; ill. by Phiz *Oxford* New Ill. Dickens 1950 $7.00

THE CHIMES. 1844. *See collections of Christmas stories, above, and "A Christmas Carol."*

THE CRICKET ON THE HEARTH. 1845. *Wake-Brook* $5.00; *Warne* rev. ed. $4.95

DOMBEY AND SON (Dealings with the Firm of Dombey and Son, Wholesale, Retail, and for Exportation). 1846–48. *Collins* New Class. $3.00 lea. $5.00 *Dutton* Everyman's $3.50; *New Am. Lib.* Signet pap. $.95; ill. by Phiz *Oxford* New Ill. Dickens 1950 $7.00 Clarendon Dickens ed. by Alan Horsmang 1973 $38.50

DAVID COPPERFIELD (The Personal History of David Copperfield). 1849–50. *AMS Press* repr. of 1850 ed. 20 nos. in 1 vol. $45.00; introd. by N. Collins *Collins* New

Class. $3.00 lea. $5.00; *Dodd* Gt. Ill. Class. $5.95; introd. by G. K. Chesterton *Dutton* Everyman's $3.50; ed. by G. H. Ford *Houghton* Riv. Eds. $2.00; *Macmillan* Class. $5.95 lib. bdg. $4.94; ill. by Phiz *Oxford* New Ill. Dickens 1947 $7.00 écrasé boxed $12.50; ed. by Trevor Blount *Penguin* pap. $2.45; *St. Martin's* $4.25; *Franklin Watts* 2 vols. each $5.50

Other paperback editions are available from Assoc. Booksellers Airmont Bks. (abr.), Dell, Modern Library (dist. by Random), New Am. Lib. Signet, Scholastic Bk. Services, Washington Square, $.50–$1.45

BLEAK HOUSE. 1852–53. Ed. by A. E. Dyson *Aurora* pap. $2.50; *Collins* New Class. $3.00 lea. $5.00; ed. by Duane DeVries *T. Y. Crowell* pap. $4.95; introd. by G. K. Chesterton *Dutton* Everyman's $3.50; *Holt* (Rinehart) pap. $3.00; ed. by Morton D. Zabel *Houghton* Riv. Eds. $3.00 pap. $2.10; *New Am. Lib.* Signet 1964 $1.25; *Oxford* New Ill. Dickens 1948 $7.00 écrasé boxed $12.50; ed. by Norman Page *Penguin* 1971 pap. $3.95

A CHILD'S HISTORY OF ENGLAND. 1853. *Dutton* Everyman's $3.50; (and "Master Humphrey's Clock") ill. by George Cattermole and others *Oxford* New Ill. Dickens 1958 $7.00

HARD TIMES (Hard Times for These Times) 1854. *Collins* New Class. $3.00 lea. $5.00; introd. by G. K. Chesterton *Dutton* Everyman's $3.50 pap. $1.55; *Fawcett* Premier Bks. pap. $.95; introd. by Monica Dickens with ill. by Richard Scollins *Imprint Soc.* 1972 $35.00; *Harper* Class. pap. $.75; ed. by William Watt *Holt* (Rinehart) 1958 pap. $2.00; *New Am. Lib.* Signet pap. $.95; ed. by G. H. Ford and S. Monod *Norton* Critical Eds. 1966 $5.50 pap. $1.95; ill. by F. Walker and M. Greiffenhagen *Oxford* New Ill. Dickens 1955 $7.00; ed. by David Craig *Penguin* 1969 pap. $1.35

LITTLE DORRIT. 1855–57. *Collins* New Class. $3.00 lea. $5.00; introd. by G. K. Chesterton *Dutton* Everyman's $3.50 pap. $2.50; ed. by R. D. McMaster *Odessey* pap. $2.95; ill. by Phiz *Oxford* New Ill. Dickens $7.00; ed. by John Holloway *Penguin* 1967 pap. $2.55

A TALE OF TWO CITIES. 1859. *Collins* New Class. $3.00 lea. $5.00; *Dodd* Gt. Ill. Class. $5.50; introd. by G. K. Chesterton *Dutton* Everyman's $3.50 pap. $1.95; *Grosset* special ed. $3.95 deluxe ed. $4.95; *Harper* Class. pap. $.75; *Macmillan* $4.95 Collier Bks. pap. $.95; introd. by E. Wagenknecht *Modern Library* pap. $.95; (and Steinbeck's "The Moon is Down") ed. by Edgar M. Schuster *Noble & Noble*; *Oxford* World's Class. $2.50 ill. by Phiz New Ill. Dickens 1949 $7.00; ed. by George Woodcock *Penguin* pap. $1.65; *Franklin Watts* lg.-type ed. Keith Jennison Bks. $8.95 ultratype ed. $4.50

Other paperback editions are available from Amsco School Pubns., Assoc. Booksellers Airmont Bks., Cambridge Bk. Co., Dell Laurel Leaf Lib., New Am. Lib. Signet, Scholastic Bk. Services, Washington Square, $.60–$2.05

THE UNCOMMERCIAL TRAVELLER. 1860. *Dutton* $3.50; (and "Reprinted Pieces") ill. by G. J. Pinwell, F. Walker, and "W. M." *Oxford* New Ill. Dickens 1958 $7.00

REPRINTED PIECES. 1860. *Dutton* Everyman's $3.50; (and "The Uncommercial Traveller") ill. by G. J. Pinwell, F. Walder and "W. M." *Oxford* New Ill. Dickens 1958 $7.00

GREAT EXPECTATIONS. 1861. Ed. by Louis Crompton *Bobbs* 1963 pap. $1.45; *Collins* New Class. $3.00 lea. $5.00; *Dodd* Gt. Ill. Class $5.95; introd. by G. K. Chesterton *Dutton* Everyman's $3.50; *Harper* Class. pap. $.85; ed. by Earle Davis *Holt* (Rinehart) 1949 pap. $2.50; introd. by F. Chapman *Macmillan* Collier Bks. pap. $.95; ed. by R. D. McMaster *Odyssey* (dist. by Bobbs) 1965 pap. $1.75; *Oxford* World's Class. $2.95 ill. by F. W. Pailthrope with introd. by Frederick Page New Ill. Dickens $7.00 écrasé boxed $12.50; ed. by Angus Calder *Penguin* pap. $1.45; ed. by Ernest H. Winter *St. Martin's* pap. $2.00; *Franklin Watts* lg.-type ed. Keith Jennison Bks. $9.95 ultratype ed. $4.50

Other paperback editions are available from Assoc. Booksellers Airmont Bks., Lancer, New Am. Lib. Signet, Scholastic Bk. Services, Washington Square, $.75–$1.75

OUR MUTUAL FRIEND. 1864–66. *Collins* New Class. $3.00 lea. $5.00; *Dutton* Everyman's $3.50; ill. by Marcus Stone with introd. by E. S. Davies *Oxford* New Ill. Dickens 1956 $7.00; ed. by Stephen Gill *Penguin* 1971 pap. $3.95

THE MYSTERY OF EDWIN DROOD. 1870. *Asoc. Booksellers* Airmont Bks. pap. $.60; *Collins* New Class. $3.00 lea. $5.00; (and "Master Humphrey's Clock") *Dutton* Everyman's $3.50; *New Am. Lib.* Signet pap. $.95; *Oxford* ed. by Margaret Cardwell the Clarendon Dickens 1972 $15.25 ill. by Luke Fildes and Charles Collins with introd. by S. C. Roberts New Ill. Dickens $7.00

THE MAGIC FISHBONE. (and Thackeray's "The Rose and the Ring") *Dutton* $3.95; *Harvey House Pubs.* $4.50 lib. bdg. $4.39; *Transatlantic* 1972 $4.25; ill. by Louis Slobodkin *Vanguard* 1953 $4.50; *Warne* $3.95

UNCOLLECTED WRITINGS FROM HOUSEHOLD WORDS, 1850–1859. Ed. by Harry Stone *Indiana Univ. Press* 2 vols. 1969 $25.00

LETTERS. Ed. by Madeline House and Graham Storey. To be completed in about 12 vols., arranged chronologically. *Oxford* Pilgrim ed. 1965–. Vol. I 1820–1839 (1965) Vol. 2 1840–1841 (1969) each $34.00

LETTERS TO WILKIE COLLINS. Ed. by Georgina Hogarth. 1892 *Kraus* $10.00

CHARLES DICKENS AS EDITOR: Being Letters Written by Him to William Henry Wills, His Sub-editor. Ed. by R. C. Lehmann 1912. *Haskell* $13.95; *Kraus* $13.00; *Richard West* $12.95

THE UNPUBLISHED LETTERS OF CHARLES DICKENS TO MARK LEMON. Ed. by W. Dexter. 1927. *Haskell* $9.95. Mark Lemon was the first editor of *Punch*, and shared with Dickens an interest in the stage. Many of the letters are concerned with this mutual interest, and the book is illustrated with copies of playbills from shows with which one or the other was involved.

MR. AND MRS. DICKENS: His Letters to Her. Ed. by Walter Dexter, with fwd. by Dickens's daughter, Kate Perugini. 1935. *Haskell* $12.95; *Richard West* $11.75

THE LOVE ROMANCE OF CHARLES DICKENS. Told in his letters to Maria Beadnell (Mrs. Winter). Introd. and notes by Walter Dexter. 1936. *Kraus* $5.00

SPEECHES OF CHARLES DICKENS. Ed. by K. J. Fielding. *Oxford* 1960 $14.50. A definitive edition.

Books about Dickens

The Life of Charles Dickens. By John Forster. 1872–74 *Dutton* Everyman's 2 vols. each $3.50. Written by Dickens' most intimate friend, a "professional" biographer.

Dickens Dictionary. By Gilbert A. Pierce. 1878. *Haskell* lib. bdg. $19.95; rev. ed. with additions by W. A. Wheeler 1914 *Kraus* $20.00

The Minor Writings of Charles Dickens: A Bibliography and a Sketch. By Frederic G. Kitton. 1899. *AMS Press* $11.00

Dickens and His Illustrators: Cruikshank, Seymour, Buss, Phiz, Cattermole, Leech, Doyle, Stanfield, Maclise, Frank Stone, Tenniel, Landseer, Palmer, Topham, Marcus Stone, and Luke Fildes. By Frederic G. Kitton. 1899. *AMS Press* $16.50; *Abner Schram* $42.50. Contains 22 portraits and 70 facsimiles of original drawings.

Charles Dickens. By G. K. Chesterton. 1906. *Schocken* 1965 pap. $1.95

Appreciations and Criticisms of the Works of Charles Dickens. By G. K. Chesterton. 1911. *Haskell* lib. bdg. $10.95. Originally published as prefaces to the separate works of Dickens.

The Dickens Circle. By J. W. T. Ley. 1919. *Haskell* 1972 lib. bdg. $15.95. An intimate portrait of Dickens, his family, and his friends.

Critical Studies of the Works of Charles Dickens. By George Gissing. Ed. with a bibliography of Gissing by Temple Scott. 1924. *Haskell* lib. bdg. $9.95. A critical handbook to which have been added nine papers which Gissing originally wrote as introductions to Dickens' novels.

Dickens Encyclopedia. By Arthur L. Hayward. 1924. *Shoe String* 1969 $8.50. An alphabetical dictionary of reference to every character and place mentioned in the works of fiction, with explanatory notes on obscure allusions and phrases.

Dickens. By André Maurois. 1934. Trans. by Hamish Miles. *Ungar* 1967 $4.50 pap. $1.45. Lectures delivered in French in 1927.

London for Dickens Lovers. By William C. Kent. 1935. *Haskell* 1972 $10.95. The London backgrounds of Dickens' life and work.

Charles Dickens: Progress of a Radical. By Thomas Jackson. 1937. *Haskell* 1971 $11.95. An evaluation from the point of view of the class conflict philosophy prevalent in the thirties.

The Dickens World. By Humphrey House. 1942. *Oxford* 2nd ed. pap. $2.25

Charles Dickens, 1812–1879. By Dame Una Pope-Hennessy. 1945. *Hillary* 1968 $6.50. Based on the 8000 collected letters published by *Nonesuch Press* in 1938.

Dickens, Dali and Others: Studies in Popular Culture. By George Orwell. *Harcourt* 1946 $5.95 pap. $2.45

Charles Dickens: A Biographical and Critical Study. By J. Lindsay. 1950 *Kraus* $18.00

Dickens and Ellen Ternan. By Ada Blanche Nisbet. *Univ. of California Press* 1952 $4.75. About Dickens' association with the actress during the last 12 years of his life.

Charles Dickens: His Tragedy and Triumph. By Edgar Johnson. 1952. *Little* 1965 2 vols. $20.00 The definitive biography.

Dickens at Work. By John Butt and Kathleen Tillotson. *Oxford* 1957 $5.50

Charles Dickens: The World of His Novels. By J. Hillis Miller. *Indiana Univ. Press* 1958 Midland Bks. pap. $2.95

Charles Dickens: A Critical Introduction. By K. J. Fielding. 1958. *Houghton* Riv. Eds. pap. $4.00. A study of his career as a novelist, arranged as a biography.

The Maturity of Dickens. By Monroe Engel. *Harvard Univ. Press* 1959 $6.00. Treats the novels in chronological order to show the developing maturity of Dickens' art.

Dickens and the Structure of the Novel. By E. A. Horsman. 1959. *Folcroft* lib. bdg. $4.50

Dickens on Education. By John Manning. *Univ. of Toronto Press* 1959 $8.50

The Love-Lives of Charles Dickens. By Charles G. DuCann. 1961 *Greenwood* 1972 $12.75

Discussions of Charles Dickens. Ed. by William R. Clark. Discussions of Literature Ser. *Heath* 1961 pap. $2.25

The Dickens Critics. Ed. by George H. Ford and Lauriat Lane, Jr. *Cornell Univ. Press* 1961 pap. $2.45; *Greenwood* $15.50

Dickens and Crime. By Philip Collins. *St. Martin's* 1962 2nd ed. 1964 pap. 1968 $2.95

The Imagination of Charles Dickens. By A. O. Cockshut. *New York Univ. Press* 1962 $6.95 pap. $1.95. "A pungent and controversial" volume.

Charles Dickens: A Pictorial Biography. By J. B. Priestley. *Viking* 1962 Studio Bks. $6.95

Dickens and the Twentieth Century. Ed. by John Gross and Gabriel Pearson. *Univ. of Toronto Press* 1962 pap. $2.95

The Flint and the Flame: The Artistry of Charles Dickens. By Earle Davis. *Univ. of Missouri Press* 1963 $6.95

Dickens: From Pickwick to Dombey. By Steven Marcus. *Basic Bks.* 1965 $8.95

Dickens: The Dreamer's Stance. By Taylor Stoehr. *Cornell Univ. Press* 1965 $8.50

Dickens and the Scandalmongers: Essays in Criticism. By Edward C. Wagenknecht. *Univ. of Oklahoma Press* 1965 $4.95

The Dickens Theater: A Reassessment of the Novels. By Robert Garis. *Oxford* 1965 $7.75.

Circle of Fire: Dickens's Vision and Style and the Popular Victorian Theater. By William F. Axton. *Univ. Press of Kentucky* 1966 $7.25

The Charles Dickens Companion. By Michael and Mollie Harwick. *Holt* 1966 $5.50; *Dutton* pap. 1968 $1.65

The Man Charles Dickens. By Christopher Hibbert. *Harper* 1967 $5.95. Good popular biography, with bibliography.

Dickens: A Collection of Critical Essays. Ed. with introd. by Martin Price. *Prentice-Hall* 1967 $5.95 Spectrum Bks. pap. $1.95. An excellent collection by Auden, Trilling, et al.

Dickens the Novelist. By Sylvère Monod. *Univ. of Oklahoma Press* 1968 $8.95. The author's own translation and revision of *"Dickens Romancier"* originally published in 1953. "David Copperfield" receives heavy emphasis.

Dickens, Money and Society. By Grahame Smith. *Univ. of California Press* 1968 $7.95

Charles Dickens: An Introduction to the Reading of His Novels. By E. D. H. Johnson. *Random* pap. 1969 $1.95

The Inimitable Dickens: A Reading of the Novels. By A. E. Dyson. *St. Martin's* 1970 $8.95. Devotes 12 separate chapters to a discussion of each of the major novels from "The Old Curiosity Shop" to "Edwin Drood."

Dickens and the Art of Analogy. By H. M. Daleski. *Schocken* 1970 $9.50. Traces the development of Dickens' art through analyses of representative examples from his early, middle and later novels.

Dickens Nineteen Seventy. Ed. by Michael Slater. *Stein & Day* 1970 $7.95. Centenary essays by Walter Allen, J. Holloway, R. Williams, M. Slater, C. P. Snow, M. Lane, P. H. Johnson, and Angus Wilson.

The Moral Art of Dickens: Essays. By Barbara Hardy. *Oxford* 1970 $6.00. Seven essays, collected, with introductions by the author and some revisions.

The Narrative Art of Charles Dickens: The Rhetoric of Sympathy and Irony in His Novels. By Harvey P. Sucksmith *Oxford* 1970 $10.25

Melancholy Man: A Study of Dickens' Novels. By John Lucas. *Barnes & Noble* 1970 $9.50 pap. $4.50

The World of Charles Dickens. By Angus Wilson. *Viking* Studio Bks. 1970 $14.95. Shows how Dickens' private and public life fed the creative imagination of the novelist. 200 black and white illustrations, 40 color plates.

The Language of Dickens. By George L. Brook. 1970. *Seminar Press* $7.50

Dickens as Satirist. By Sylvia Manning. Yale Studies in English Ser. *Yale Univ. Press* 1971 $9.50 $9.50

Dickens: The Critical Heritage. Ed. by Philip Collins. *Barnes & Noble* 1971 $15.00. A collection of contemporary criticisms, grouped for each work, and arranged chronologically.

Stature of Dickens: A Centenary Bibliography. Comp. by Joseph Gold. *Univ. of Toronto Presss* 1971 $14.50

Dickens and the Rhetoric of Laughter. By James R. Kincaid. *Oxford* 1971 $9.50

Dickens Centennial Essays. Ed. by Ada Nisbet and Blake Nevius. *Univ. of California Press* 1972 $7.00. Eight of the nine essays originally appeared in the special Dickens issue of *Nineteenth Century Fiction*.

Noah's Arkitecture: A Study of Dickens' Mythology. By Bert G. Hornback. *Ohio Univ. Press* 1972 $8.50. A study of the novelist's use of the myths of "the Creation, the Flood, Noah's Ark, and the tower of Babel."

Charles Dickens: Radical Moralist. By Joseph Gold. *Univ. of Minnesota Press* 1972 $9.50
"A critical discussion, making use of contemporary psychoanalytical method, of the moral or ethical aspects of Dickens' novels"—(Publisher's catalog).

Here Comes Dickens: The Imagination of a Novelist (British title "The Violent Effigy"). By John Carey. *Schocken* 1974 $9.00

READE, CHARLES. 1814–1884.

Reade wrote the didactic novel, the novel with a lesson. Dickens (*q.v.*) is thought to have influenced Reade greatly. His one historical romance, his masterpiece, "The Cloister and the Hearth," is a picture of life in Germany and Italy at the close of the Middle Ages, the hero being the father of Erasmus (*q.v.*). Reade's novels were compiled rather than written. He went to endless historical research and investigation for the facts they contain. For his historical novel he is said to have read "not only volumes but bookshelves and libraries."

WORKS. 1895. *AMS Press* 17 vols. each $19.75 set $325.00

THE CLOISTER AND THE HEARTH. 1861. Introd. by Algernon Charles Swinburne *Dutton* Everyman's $3.50

Books about Reade

Dickens, Reade and Collins: Sensational Novelists. By Walter C. Phillips. 1919. *Russell & Russell* 1962 $7.50

Charles Reade. By Malcolm Elwin. 1931. *Russell & Russell* 1969 $10.50

TROLLOPE, ANTHONY. 1815–1882.

Trollope's works number a hundred or more volumes, including novels, tales, history, travel and biography. Forty-odd novels are divided into three series: "The Chronicles of Barsetshire, or The Cathedral Stories"; "The Parliamentary Novels" and "The Manor House Novels." In each series the same characters appear repeatedly, but each volume is complete in itself. The Barsetshire novels, the most popular of the group, are all laid in the imaginary town of Barchester (based on Winchester, according to Trollope), and the characters are mainly clergy of various ranks, and their families.

The autobiography, published posthumously in 1883, has been blamed for the eclipse of Trollope's fame right after his death. In it he confesses his custom of writing with his watch before him, requiring of himself 250 words every quarter of an hour. He did this at 5:30 every morning without fail and prided himself on living a full, varied life the rest of the day—he was employed until afternoon in the Post Office until 1867. But Trollope's novels are by no means such mechanical performances as he would have us believe. "His pleasant tales have considerable value as sociological insights into a mellow and tranquil age now forever past." Their tranquility provides an attractive escape from turbulent times: interest in Trollope revived during both World Wars. Trollope's Letters are now o.p.

The Chronicles of Barsetshire

The Warden. 1855. *Dutton* Everyman's $3.50 pap. $1.95; *Harcourt* 1962 $3.95; *New Am. Lib.* Signet pap. $.50; *Oxford* World's Class. $2.00; *Washington Square* 1962 pap. $.45; *Wehman* $2.75

Barchester Towers. 1857. *Collins* New Class. $3.00 lea. $5.00; *Dutton* Everyman's $3.50; ed. by Bradford A. Booth *Holt* (Rinehart) 1949 pap. $1.25; *New Am. Lib.* Signet pap. $.95; ed. by Michael Sadleir *Oxford* World's Class. $3.00; *Washington Square* 1963 pap. $.45

The Warden and Barchester Towers. *Modern Library* pap. $1.60

Dr. Thorne. 1858. *Dutton* Everyman's $3.50; *Harcourt* 1962 $3.95; ed. by Elizabeth Bowen *Houghton* Riv. Eds. 1960 pap. $1.15; *Oxford* World's Class. $3.25

Framley Parsonage. 1861. *Dutton* pap. $2.25; *Harcourt* 1962 $3.95; *Oxford* World's Class. $3.00

The Small House at Allington. 1864. *Dutton* Everyman's $3.50 pap. $2.25; *Harcourt* 1962 $3.95; *Oxford* World's Class. $4.00

The Last Chronicle of Barset. 1867. *Dutton* Everyman's $3.50; ed. by Arthur Mizener *Houghton* Riv. Eds. pap. $2.50; *Norton* 1964 pap. $2.25; *Oxford* World's Class. $3.75

The Parliamentrary Novels

Can you Forgive Her? 1864. Pref. by Edward Marsh with ills. by Lynton Lamb *Oxford* 1948 1973 $12.50 pap. $2.95 World's Class. $5.75

Phineas Finn. 1869. Pref. by Sir Shane Leslie *Oxford* 1973 $12.50 pap. $2.95 World's Class. $4.00

The Eustace Diamonds. 1873. Pref. by Michael Sadleir with ills. by B. Hughes-Stanton *Oxford* 1973 $12.50 pap. $2.95 World's Class. $3.75; ed. by Stephen Gill *Penguin* pap. $1.95

Phineas Redux. 1874. Pref. by R. W. Chapman with ills. by L. T. B. Huskinson *Oxford* 1973 $12.50 pap. $2.95 World's Class. $5.50

The Prime Minister. 1876. Pref. by L. S. Amery with ills. by Hector Whistler *Oxford* 1973 $12.50 pap. $2.95 World's Class. $4.75

THE DUKE'S CHILDREN 1880. Pref. by Chauncey B. Tinker with ills. by Charles Mozley *Oxford* 1954 1973 $12.50 pap. $2.95 World's Class. $4.00

THE MANOR HOUSE NOVELS

ORLEY FARM. 1862. *Oxford* World's Class. $4.00

IS HE POPENJOY? 1878 *Oxford* World's Class. $4.50

THE BELTON ESTATE. 1866. *Oxford* World's Class. $3.00

THE WAY WE LIVE NOW. 1875. Ed. by Robert Tracy *Bobbs* $12.00 pap. $4.75; *Oxford* World's Class $4.00

OTHER NOVELS IN PRINT:

THE CLAVERINGS. 1867. *Oxford* World's Class. $2.50

HE KNEW HE WAS RIGHT. 1869. *Oxford* World's Class. $3.75

THE VICAR OF BULLHAMPTON. 1870. *Oxford* World's Class. $2.50

DR. WHORTLE'S SCHOOL. 1881. *Oxford* World's Class. $2.00

AYALA'S ANGEL. 1881. *Oxford* World's Class. $2.50

THE FIXED PERIOD. 1882. *McGrath Pub. Co.* 2 vols. $42.00

TRAVEL BOOKS AND AUTOBIOGRAPHY

THE WEST INDIES AND THE SPANISH MAIN. 1859. *Int. Scholarly Bk. Services.* $12.50

NORTH AMERICA. 1862. Ed. by Robert Mason *Penguin* pap. $1.25; *William Gannon* lib. bdg. $3.50; *Kelley* repr. of 1862 ed. 2 vols. $32.50

AUSTRALIA. 1873. *Humanities Press* $19.50

THE NEW ZEALANDER. 1873. Ed. by John N. Hall *Oxford* 1972 $10.25

"This hitherto unpublished work of non-fiction provides an intimate, knowledgeable and comprehensive picture of Victorian England"—(Publisher's catalog).

SOUTH AFRICA. 1878. *Humanities* 2 vols. 1968 $27.00

AN AUTOBIOGRAPHY. 1883. Ed. by Michael Sadleir *Oxford* World's Class. $2.50

Books about Trollope

Domestic Manners of the Americans. By Frances Trollope. 1832 1927. Introd. by James Mooney *Imprint Soc.* repr. of 1832 ed. 1970 $35.00; *Random* Vintage Bks. 1949 pap. $1.95; ed. by Donald Smalley *Peter Smith* $4.00. Observations by the author's mother.

Trollope: A Commentary. By Michael Sadleir. 1927. *Oxford* 1961 pap. $2.50

The Trollopes: The Chronicles of a Writing Family. By Lucy and Richard Stebbins. 1945. *AMS Press* $14.00; *Richard West* $13.95. Based on family journals and other writings; includes Frances and her two sons, the historian Thomas Adolphus and the novelist Anthony.

A Guide to Trollope. By Winifred Gregory Gerould and James T. Gerould. 1948. *Greenwood* $11.00. Encyclopedic listing of characters, synopses of plots, place locations; annotated bibliography; maps.

Anthony Trollope: A Critical Study. By A. O. Cockshut. 1968. Gotham Library *New York Univ. Press* $7.95 pap. $2.25

The Changing World of Anthony Trollope. By Robert M. Polhemus. *Univ. of California Press* 1968 $7.00

Trollope: The Critical Heritage. Ed. by Donald Smalley. *Barnes & Noble* 1969 $10.00. A collection of contemporary criticisms.

The Moral Trollope. By Ruth Ap Roberts. *Ohio Univ. Press.* 1971 $8.50

Anthony Trollope. By James Pope-Hennessy. *Little* 1972 $10.00. A critical biography which includes 25 illustrations from the original editions of the novels.

THE BRONTË SISTERS.

With the Brontë sisters we come for the first time to the novel of few characters and narrow range. The sisters lived most of their lives at the parsonage in Haworth where their father, the Reverend Patrick Brontë, had been appointed perpetual curate. The mother had died soon after they moved there, leaving six small children, who were cared for by Elizabeth Branwell, their mother's oldest sister. The two older girls died of tuberculosis within the next five years. Left very much to their own devices, the three remaining sisters and their brother, Branwell, entertained themselves with creative writings recorded in tiny volumes. When Charlotte went away to school, Emily and Anne started an imaginative saga of their own called "Gondal." When Charlotte returned, she attempted to revive their earlier work and expand it into a realm named Angria, but without success. From that time on Charlotte and Branwell played and wrote about Angria, Emily and Anne about Gondal. These experiments in writing led to a joint volume of verse printed at their own expense (1846), "Poems by Currer, Ellis and Action Bell," of which only two copies were sold.

THE LIFE AND WORKS OF THE SISTERS BRONTË (Original title "The Life and Works of Charlotte Brontë and Her Sisters") 7 vols. 1899–1903. *AMS Press* each $25.00 set $175.00. The "Life" is Elizabeth Gaskell's biography of Charlotte, with annotations of Clement K. Shorter. The prefaces to the works are by Mrs. Humphrey Ward. The Haworth edition.

NOVELS AND POEMS. *Collins* 6 vols. $12.00 lea. $25.00

THE LETTERS OF THE BRONTËS. Sel. and with an introd. by Muriel Spark. *Univ. of Oklahoma Press* 1954 $3.75

"This is better than any biography; it is the human material from which biographies are made"—(*N.Y. Times*). The 130 letters are arranged to tell the story of the adult lives of Emily, Anne, Charlotte and Branwell Brontë. Almost all of them were written by Charlotte.

Books about the Brontës

The Brontës: Life and Letters. By Clement K. Shorter. 1908. *Haskell* 2 vols. 1969 $34.95
The Brontës and Their Circle. By Clement K. Shorter. 1917. *Kraus* $18.00. Includes some early letters, as does Ernest Dimnet's "The Brontë Sisters" (1928, o.p.).
The Brontës' Web of Childhood. By Fannie E. Ratchford. 1941. *Russell & Russell* 1964 $15.00
The Brontë Sisters. By Phyllis Bentley. 1947. *British Bk. Centre* 1950 $2.38 pap. $1.20
The Four Brontës: The Lives and Works of Charlotte, Branwell, Emily, and Anne Brontë. By Lawrence and Elizabeth Hanson. 1949. *Shoe String* Archon Bks. 1967 $12.00 A new edition, only minimally revised, with a new preface by the author. The first comprehensive life after the discovery of the juvenilia, "Gondal Poems" and the complete letters.
The Brontë Sisters. Ed. by Ruth H. Blackburn. Selected Source Materials for College Research Papers Ser. *Heath* 1964 pap. $2.25
Their Proper Sphere: A Study of the Brontë Sisters as Early Victorian Female Novelists. By Inga-Stina Ewbank. *Harvard Univ. Press* 1966 $5.95
The Brontës and Their World. By Phyllis Bentley. *Viking* Studio Bks. 1969 $8.95. A pictorial biography, with 140 monochrome plates.
Haworth Harvest: The Story of the Brontës. By N. Brysson Morrison. *Vanguard* 1969 $6.95
Charlotte and Emily Brontë. By Norman Sherry. *Arco* 1970 $3.95 pap. $1.95

BRONTË, CHARLOTTE ("Currer Bell," pseud.). 1816–1855.

Charlotte (Mrs. Arthur Bell Nichols) outlived her sisters, and of all her family attained the greatest fame. Her books were transcriptions of her somber surroundings and the tragic events of her life. "The Professor" was a short early sketch which Charlotte enlarged in "Villette." In "Jane Eyre" she introduced the first ugly heroine in fiction, and immediately achieved success. The heroine of "Shirley" is modeled on her sister Emily, and the story describes the misery that followed the introduction of machinery into Yorkshire. "Villette" is laid in Brussels, where the author once taught school. The original ending was so painful to her readers that Charlotte changed it in later editions.

The first biography of Charlotte was the famous one by Mrs. Gaskell (*q.v.*), which appeared two years after Charlotte's death. The discovery of Charlotte's Lost Letters to Constantin Heger (the original of "The Professor"), the Juvenilia and other later letters and data has led to several new interpretations. Of these Margaret Lane's "The Brontë Story" is an excellent sequel to Mrs. Gaskell. Miss Lane says in her foreword: "This book, in fact, is offered as a sort of footnote to Mrs. Gaskell, bringing the reader back at every point to her incomparable text, and at the same time putting him in possession of everything of importance that has come to light in the century since she wrote. Provided with this footnote as well as her 'Life,' he will, I hope, have in his hands the whole of the Brontë story."

FIVE NOVELETTES. Transcribed from the original manuscripts and ed. by Winifred
Gérin. Contains "Passing Events," "Julia," "Mina Laury," "Captain Henry Hastings," and "Caroline Vernon." *Rowman & Littlefield* 1971 $18.75

JANE EYRE. 1847. *Collins* New Class. $3.00 lea. $5.00; *Dodd* Gt. Ill. Class. $5.50;
Dutton Everyman's $3.50 pap. $1.95; *Harcourt* 1962 $3.95; ed. by J. L. Davis *Holt*
(Rinehart) pap. $1.25; ed. by Mark Schorer *Houghton* Riv. Eds. pap. $.95; *Macmil-
lan* 1964 $4.95 Collier Bks. pap. $.95; *Modern Library* $2.95 pap. $1.15; ed. by
Richard J. Dunn *Norton* Critical Eds. 1971 $8.50 pap. $2.25; ed. by Jane Jack and
Margaret Smith *Oxford* 1969 $15.25 World's Class. 1954 $2.75; ed. by Q. D.
Leavis *Penguin* pap. $1.40; *Franklin Watts* lg.-type ed. Keith Jennison Bks. $7.95
ultratype ed. $5.50

*Other paperback editions are available from Amsco School Pubns., Assoc. Booksellers,
Dell, Scholastic Book Services, Washington Square*

SHIRLEY. 1849. *Collins* New Class. $3.00 lea. $5.00; introd. by Margaret Lane *Dutton*
Everyman's $3.50 pap. $2.50; *Oxford* World's Class. $3.00; *Popular Lib.* pap.
$1.25

VILLETTE. 1853. *Collins* New Class $3.00 lea. $5.00; *Dutton* Everyman's $3.50 pap.
$2.25; *Harper* Colophon Bks. pap. $3.45; ed. by Geoffrey Tillotson and Donald
Hawes *Houghton* Riv. Eds. 1971 pap. $4.10 *Oxford* World's Class. 1954 $4.25

THE PROFESSOR. 1857. *Dutton* Everyman's $3.50 pap. $1.95; *Oxford* World's Class.
$2.50

THE SPELL: An Extravaganza. Ed. by George E. MacLean. 1931 *Folcroft* lib. bdg.
$15.00

Works of Poetry by Charlotte Brontë

COMPLETE POEMS. Ed. by Clement K. Shorter and C. W. Hatfield. 1924 *Scholarly
Press* 1972 $12.00

LEGENDS OF ANGRIA. Ed. by Fannie E. Ratchford and William C. DeVane. Compiled
from the early writings. 1933. *Kennikat* 1973 $14.50

Books about Charlotte Brontë

The Life of Charlotte Brontë. By Mrs. Elizabeth Cleghorn Gaskell. 1857. *Dutton* Everyman's $3.50
   "A great reckless biography . . . the very manner seems touched by the Brontean fire—(*N.Y. Times*).
The Bronte Story. By Margaret Lane. 1953. *Greenwood* 1971 $14.00
Accents of Persuasion: Charlotte Brontë's Novels. By Robert B. Martin. *Norton* 1966 pap. $1.85
Charlotte Bronte: The Evolution of Genius. By Winifred Gérin. *Oxford* Clarendon Press 1967 $15.00
   Galaxy Bks. pap. $2.95. An excellent definitive recent biography.

BRONTË, EMILY JANE ("Ellis Bell," pseud.). 1818–1848.

Emily Brontë wrote one novel, "Wuthering Heights." Drawing upon the Gothic horror tradition and the
Romantic obsession with Byronic intensity and wildness of feeling, "Wuthering Heights" depicts a series of
tumultuous and passionate relationships which dramatize the power of love. The novel, set in the wild Yorkshire moors, emphasizes the connection between landscape and character, between the physical environment
and the psychological contours of those who inhabit it. It is noteworthy, among other reasons, for its innovative handling of point of view and narrative structure, its resonant but flexible style, and its dramatic psychological realism. Widely read in its own day, "Wuthering Heights" is even more widely read and highly
thought of today.

Her "Complete Poems" has been edited by C. W. Hatfield from the manuscripts (Columbia 1941 $9.00).
Matthew Arnold (*q.v.*) said of her that "for passion, vehemence, and grief she had no equal since Byron"
(*q.v.*).

WUTHERING HEIGHTS. 1847. *Collins* New Class. $3.00 1ea. $5.00; (with Selected Poems) *Dodd* Gt. Ill. Class. $5.50; *Dutton* Everyman's $3.50 pap. $1.75; ed. by Thomas C. Maser *Harcourt* 1962 pap. $3.95 pap. $3.50; *Harper* Class. pap. $.75; ed. by Mark Schorer *Holt* (Rinehart) 1950 pap. $2.25; ed. by V. S. Pritchett *Houghton* Riv. Eds. pap. $1.45; *Macmillan* 1963 $4.95 lib. bdg. $4.24 Collier Bks. pap. $.95; introd. by R. A. Gettmann *Modern Library* $2.95 pap. $1.05; ed. by William Sale *Norton* Critical Eds. 1963 rev. ed. 1972 pap. $1.95; ed. by F. T. Flahiff *Odyssey* 1968 pap. $1.45; *Oxford* World's Class. $2.75; ed. by David Daiches *Penguin* pap. $1.25; *Franklin Watts* $4.50 lg.-type ed. Keith Jennison Bks. $8.95

Other paperback editions are available from Amsco School Pubns., Assoc. Booksellers Airmont Bks., Cambridge Bk. Co., Dell Laurel Eds., New Am. Lib. Signet, Scholastic Bk. Services, Washington Square, $.50–$2.00

GONDAL'S QUEEN: A Novel in Verse. Arranged, with introd. and notes by Fannie E. Ratchford. 1955. *AMS Press* $10.00

GONDAL POEMS. Ed. from the manuscript in the British Museum by H. Brown and J. Mott. 1938. *Folcroft* lib. bdg. $5.00

Books about Emily Brontë

Emily Brontë: A Psychological Portrait. By N. Crandall. 1957 *Kraus* $8.00
An Investigation of Gondal. By William Doremus Paden. *Twayne* 1958 $3.00. This attempts to deduce from Emily's poems and the half-dozen scraps of relevant evidence in prose, the story of the imaginative land of Gondal with which Emily and Anne amused themselves.
The Genesis of Wuthering Heights. By Mark Visick. Introd. by Edmund Blunden. *Oxford* 2nd ed. 1965 pap. $2.25. A study of the apotheosis of the Gondal people of the poems into the immortals of "Wuthering Heights."
Emily Brontë. By John Hewish. *St. Martin's* 1969 $8.95
Emily Brontë. By Winifred Gérin. *Oxford* 1972 $10.95

BRONTË, ANNE ("Acton Bell," pseud.). 1820–1849.

Anne Brontë had talent but not genius. "Agnes Grey" is the story of a governess, and "The Tenant of Wildfell Hall" a tale of the evils of drink and profligacy. Anne's acquaintance with sin and wickedness, as shown in her novels, was so astounding that Charlotte saw fit to explain in a preface that the source of her sister's intimate knowledge of evil was her brother Branwell's dissolute ways. A habitué of drink and drugs, he finally became an addict. Her "Complete Poems" (ed. by Clement K. Shorter, with a biographical introd. by C. W. Hatfield. 1924. *Scholarly Press* 1971 $14.50) are again available.

AGNES GREY. 1847. Ed. by Herbert Van Thal *Dufour* 1966 $4.25 pap. $1.95; *Oxford* World's Class. $2.50

THE TENANT OF WILDFELL HALL. 1848. (and "Agnes Grey") *Collins* New Class. 1959 $3.00 1ea. $5.00; (and "Agnes Grey") pref. by Margaret Lane *Dutton* Everyman's $3.50; *Oxford* World's Class. $3.00

Books about Anne Brontë

Anne Brontë: A Biography. By Ada Harrison and Derek Stanford. 1959. *Shoe String* $8.00. An excellent study.

ELIOT, GEORGE (pseud. of Mary Ann, or Marian Evans, afterwards Cross). 1819–1880.

Born Mary Ann Evans, George Eliot asserted her intellect in her early translations and journalism, her imagination in a series of extraordinary novels, and her independence in her pseudonym and in her personal life. Introduced as a social realist, her first four novels moved from social realism to psychological realism. English rural life became the carefully delineated background for serious dramatizations of human character tested by the interplay between environment and moral choice. Her concern for philosophic and moral issues was illumined by her wide learning and deep compassion for the human situation. Her versatility and learning propelled her into trying the historical novel ("Romola"), the political novel ("Felix Holt"), and a novel about Zionism ("Daniel Deronda"). Like other Victorian novelists, particularly Dickens (q.v.), her style is the triumph of selective realism and psychological perceptiveness given the opportunity of extensive development on a broad canvas of multiple plots. Though Henry James thought "Silas Marner" "nearly a masterpiece," recent opinion holds that her supreme achievement is "Middlemarch."

Gordon Haight's edition of her "Letters" was a major "contribution to literary history, to letter writing and to a deeper interpretation of the novelist that readers once read and loved." It contains 2760 letters and extracts from journals, nearly 2000 of them written by George Eliot herself. "The dominant qualities in the letters are intellectual and moral integrity, with unfaltering courage in saying and doing what she thought right"—(SR).

WRITINGS. With the Life of J. W. Cross. 1907. *AMS Press* 1970 25 vols. each $11.25 set $270.00

ESSAYS. 1897. Ed. by Thomas Pinney. *Columbia* 1963 $12.00

Her best-known novels:

ADAM BEDE. 1859. *Assoc. Booksellers* Airmont Bks. pap. $.95; *Collins* New Class. $3.00; *Dodd* Gt. Ill. Class. $5.95; introd. by R. Speaight *Dutton* Everyman's $3.50 pap. $1.95; ed. by Gordon S. Haight *Holt* (Rinehart) 1949 pap. $2.25; ed. by John Paterson *Houghton* Riv. Eds. 1968 pap. $2.05; *New Am. Lib.* Signet pap. $.95; *Washington Square* 1962 pap. $.60 Reader's Enrich. Ser. pap. $.95

THE MILL ON THE FLOSS. 1860. *Assoc. Booksellers* Airmont Bks. 1964 pap. $.75; *Collins* New Class. $3.00; *Dutton* Everyman's $3.50 pap. $1.95; *Harcourt* 1962 $3.95 ed. by Gordon S. Haight *Houghton* Riv. Eds. pap. $2.25; *Macmillan* Collier Bks. pap. $.95; *New Am. Lib.* Signet pap. $.95; *Oxford* World's Class. $3.00; *Washington Square* 1962 Reader's Enrich. Ser. pap. $.95

SILAS MARNER. 1861. (and Poems and Miscellaneous Writings) *Collins* New Class. $3.00; *Dodd* Gt. Ill. Class. $5.50; introd. by J. Holloway *Dutton* Everyman's $3.50 pap. $1.95; *Harcourt* 1962 $3.95; ed. by J. Thale *Holt* (Rinehart) 1962 pap. $1.25; (and Steinbeck's "The Pearl") ed. by Jay Greene *Noble & Noble* Comparative Class. $3.60; (and "The Lifted Veil" and "Brother Jacob") *Oxford* World's Class. $2.25; *Washington Square* pap. $.45 Reader's Enrich. Ser. pap. $.60 Enriched. Class. pap $.75; *Franklin Watts* lg.-type ed. Keith Jennison Bks. $7.95

Other paperback editions are available from Amsco School Pubns., Assoc. Booksellers Airmont Bks., Dell Laurel Eds., Lancer, New Am. Lib. Signet, Washington Square, Scholastic Bk. Services, $.50–$1.65

ROMOLA. 1863. Introd. by Rudolph Dircks *Dutton* Everyman's $3.50; *Oxford* World's Class. $3.25

FELIX HOLT, RADICAL. 1866. Introd. by Robert Speaight *Dutton* Everyman's $3.50; *Norton* Norton Lib. 1971 pap. $2.45; ed. by Peter Coveney *Penguin* pap. $3.65

MIDDLEMARCH: A Study of Provincial Life. 1871. Introd. by Gerald Bullett *Dutton* Everyman's 2 vols. each $3.50; ed. by Gordon Haight *Houghton* Riv. Eds. pap. $1.85; *Macmillan* Collier Bks. pap. $1.50; *New Am. Lib.* Signet pap. $1.50; ed. by R. M. Hewitt *Oxford* World's Class. $3.00; ed. by William J. Harvey *Penguin* pap. $1.65

DANIEL DERONDA. 1876. Ed. by Barbara Hardy *Penguin* pap. $1.95

THE GEORGE ELIOT LETTERS. Ed. by Gordon S. Haight. Vol. 1 (1836–1851) Vol. 2 (1852–1858) Vol. 3 (1859–1861) Vol. 4 (1862–1868) Vol. 5 (1869–1873) Vol. 6

(1874–1877) Vol. 7 (1878–1880) (*See comment above*). *Yale Univ. Press* 1952–1956 7 vols. each $12.50 set $75.00

Books about Eliot

The Ethics of George Eliot's Works. By John C. Brown. 1879. *Kennikat* 1969 $6.00

George Eliot's Life as Related in Her Letters and Journal. Ed. by John Walter Cross. 1885. *AMS Press* $18.50 *Scholarly Press* 3 vols. 1969 $39.50

A George Eliot Dictionary. By Isadore G. Mudge and Minnie E. Sears. 1924. *Folcroft* lib. bdg. $7.50

The Life of George Eliot. By Simon Dewes. 1939 *Folcroft* lib. bdg. $15.00

George Eliot: Her Mind and Her Art. By Mrs. Joan Bennett. *Cambridge* 1948 $6.95 pap. $1.95

The Novels of George Eliot. By Jerome Thale. *Columbia* 1959 $6.00
  "The author traces her development as a novelist and indicates the quality of her 'vision' and the ways in which it determines her technique"—(*LJ*).

George Eliot. By Lettice Cooper. *British Bk. Centre* $2.38 pap. $1.20

Movement and Vision in George Eliot's Novels. By Reva Stump. 1959 *Russell & Russell* 1973 $16.00

The Novels of George Eliot: A Study in Form. By Barbara Hardy. *Oxford* 1959 pap. $2.25. A solid and well-written analysis which approaches form through the naturalism in all of the works.

Discussions of George Eliot. Ed. by Richard Stang. *Heath* 1960 pap. $2.25

George Eliot. By Walter Allen. *Macmillan* 1964 Collier Bks. pap. $1.95
  "It is hard to imagine a better introduction to George Eliot's novels, or a more companionable commentary for those who need no introduction"—(*TLS*, London).

A Century of George Eliot Criticism. By Gordon S. Haight. *Houghton* 1965 pap. $4.95

Experiments in Life: George Eliot's Quest for Values. By Bernard J. Paris. *Wayne State Univ. Press* 1965 $9.50

George Eliot: A Biography. By Gordon S. Haight. *Oxford* 1968 $12.50. A judicious, carefully written, and definitive biography which is the first to draw fully on the author's edition of the letters.

George Eliot's Early Novels: The Limits of Realism. By U. C. Knoepflmacher. *Univ. of California Press* 1968 $8.00

George Eliot: A Collection of Critical Essays. Ed. by George R. Creeger. *Prentice-Hall* 1970 $5.95 Spectrum Bks. pap. $1.95

Critical Essays on George Eliot. Ed. by Barbara Hardy. *Barnes & Noble* 1970 $6.50. Eleven essays, two of which discuss the novels as a whole, while the rest each treat the tales and novels.

Local Habitations: Regionalism in the Early Novels of George Eliot. By Henry Auster. *Harvard Univ. Press* 1970 $10.00

George Eliot. By R. T. Jones. *Cambridge* 1971 $7.95 pap. $1.95. Discusses the novels in chronological order.

KINGSLEY, CHARLES. 1819–1875.

Charles Kingsley was a clergyman of the Church of England, and late in his life held the chair of history at Cambridge for nine years. His novels are mostly didactic historical romances. He put the historical novel to new uses, not to teach history but to illustrate some religious truth. "Westward Ho!" his best known, is a tale of the Spanish main in the days of Queen Elizabeth I. "Hypatia, or New Foes with Old Faces" is the story of a pagan girl-philosopher who was torn to pieces by a Christian mob. The story is strongly anti-Roman Catholic, reflecting Kingsley's controversy with Cardinal Newman (*q.v.*) at the time of the Oxford Movement. "Hereward the Wake" is a tale of a Saxon outlaw. "The Water-Babies," written for Kingsley's youngest child, "would be a tale for children were it not for the satire directed at the parents of the period," said Andrew Lang. "Alton Locke" and "Yeast" (1851, o.p.) reflect Kingsley's leadership in "muscular Christianity" and his dramatization of social issues.

Kingsley used the pseudonym "Parson Lot" on papers he wrote for magazines. Of his "Poems" (1927. *Scholarly Press* 1970 $14.50) the most characteristic is the ballad-song "Sands of Dee."

LIFE AND WORKS OF CHARLES KINGSLEY. 28 vols. 1880–85. *Adler's* $570.000

ALTON LOCKE. 1850. Ed. by Herbert Van Thal *Dufour* $5.95 pap. $3.95; *Dutton* Everyman's $3.50; *Scholarly Press* repr. of 1928 ed. $19.50

HYPATIA, or New Foes with Old Faces. 1853. *Dutton* Everyman's $3.50

WESTWARD HO! 1855. *Assoc. Booksellers* Airmont Bks. pap. $1.25; *Dutton* Everyman's $3.50; ill. by N. C. Wyeth *Scribner* $6.00

THE HEROES, or Greek Fairy Tales for My Children. 1856. *Children's Press* 1968 $4.50; ill. by Joan Kiddell-Monroe *Dutton* Chil. Ill. Class. 1963 $4.50; ill. by Vera

Bock *Macmillan* New Chil. Class. $4.50; ill. by H. M. Brock *St. Martin's* children's ed. $4.00; *Schocken* 1970 $4.50 pap $1.95

THE WATER-BABIES. 1863. Ill. by Rosalie K. Fry *Dutton* Chil. Ill. Class. $4.50

HEREWARD THE WAKE, or The Watchful. 1866. *Collins* New Class. $3.00; *Dutton* Everyman's 1909 $3.50

CHARLES KINGSLEY: HIS LETTERS AND MEMORIES OF HIS LIFE. Ed. by his wife. 2 vols. 1877. *AMS Press* each $13.00 set $25.00

Books about Kingsley

Charles Kingsley and the Christian Social Movement. By Charles W. Stubbs. 1899. AMS Press $10.00
Canon Charles Kingsley: A Biography. By Una Pope-Hennessy. 1948. *Kraus* 1973 $15.00
The Dust of Combat: A Life of Charles Kingsley. By Robert Bernard Martin. *Hillary House* 1959 $5.00.
    This is a readable biography written with great skill and understanding.

COLLINS, WILKIE. 1824–1889

Wilkie Collins evolved a new type of fiction, the crime novel of intricate plot and baffling mystery. "The Woman in White" was his first sensational success, followed later by his masterpiece, "The Moonstone." Collins was a close friend of Charles Dickens (*q.v.*) and collaborated with him. His mastery of plot influenced Dickens, and he was influenced by Dickens' mastery of character. T. S. Eliot remarked, "To anyone who knows the bare facts of Dickens' acquaintance with Collins, and who has studied the work of the two men, their relationship and their influence upon one another is an important subject of study."

WORKS. 1900. *AMS Press* 30 vols. each $20.00 set $595.00

SHORT STORIES. Sel. by J. I. Rodale with wood engravings by Fritz Eichenberg. 1950. *A. S. Barnes* Perpetua Bks. pap. $1.65. Includes "A Terribly Strange Bed"; "The Caldron of Oil"; "The Fatal Cradle"; "Mr. Captain and the Nymph"; "Blow Up with the Brig"; and About the Author and the Book, by E. J. Fluck.

THE BEST OF WILKIE COLLINS. Ed. by George Bisserov. *Juniper Press* 1959 $5.50

TALES OF TERROR AND THE SUPERNATURAL. Ed. by Herbert van Thal. *Dover* 1972 pap. $3.00. A new collection from magazine pieces.

THE WOMAN IN WHITE. 1860. *Collins* New Class. $3.00; introd. by Maurice Richardson *Dutton* Everyman's $3.50; ed. by Kathleen Tillotson *Houghton* Riv. Eds. pap. $1.95

THE MOONSTONE. 1863. *Assoc. Booksellers* Airmont Bks. pap. $.75; *Collins* New Class. $3.00; *Dutton* Everyman's $3.50; *Harper* abr. ed. $5.95; *Oxford* World's Class. $2.50; ed. by John I. Stewart *Penguin* pap. $1.45; *Franklin Watts* lg.-type ed. Keith Jennison Bks. $9.95

ARMADALE. 1866. *Scholarly Press* 2 vols. 1972 $34.50

POOR MISS FINCH. 1872 *Scholarly Press* 1972 $19.00

AFTER DARK AND OTHER STORIES. 1873. *Bks. for Libraries* $17.75

I SAY NO, or The Loveletter Answered and Other Stories. 1886. *Bks. for Libraries* $15.00

Books about Collins

Dickens, Reade and Collins: Sensational Novelists. By Walter C. Phillips. 1919. *Russell & Russell* 1962 $7.50

Wilkie Collins: A Biography. By Kenneth Robinson. 1952. *Greenwood* 1973 $14.50. The first full-length biography, and a good one.

Wilkie Collins. By William H. Marshall. English Authors Ser. *Twayne* 1970 $4.95

MEREDITH, GEORGE. 1828–1909.

Meredith was an "intellectual" novelist. His style was leisurely, epigrammatic and involved at a time when the public admired the swift narrative flow of Dickens (*q. v.*) and Thackeray (*q. v.*). Meredith's novels were always "the vehicle of some philosophy," "designed to penetrate to the hidden motivations of character by pithy thrusts and subtle implications." His reputation grew slowly. His first important novel, "The Ordeal of Richard Feverel," a fine study of the emotional growth of a young man, is his most epigrammatic work and had little popular success. "The Egoist," a comedy in narrative, regarded by most critics as his masterpiece, was the first to receive popular attention. "Diana of the Crossways" was his most nearly "popular" book.

"The Essay on Comedy, and the Uses of the Comic Spirit" ([and "Bergson's Laughter"] *Doubleday* Anchor Bks. 1956 pap. $1.95; *Peter Smith* $3.75) is the key to his novels. He gave to fiction a new and particularly well-drawn heroine, the woman of fine brain and strong body. He boasted that he never wrote a word to please the public, and counted as the greatest compliment ever paid him the statement that he had brought about a change in public taste.

Meredith, like Hardy (*q. v.*), thought more of his poems than of his novels and preferred to be remembered as a poet. In notes for "The Selected Poetical Works of George Meredith" (1955, o.p.), G. M. Trevelyan says: "His poems are more especially concerned with his philosophy, and the novels with his application of it to ethical problems." Meredith's philosophy was one of optimism, but it was "the optimism of temperament and not of creed."

Works. Ed. by William M. Meredith. 29 vols. *Russell & Russell* 1965 set $325.00

The Ordeal of Richard Feveral. 1859. *Dutton* Everyman's $3.50 pap. $2.25; ed. by J. C. Hill *Holt* (Rinehart) 1964 pap. $1.25; ed. by C. L. Cline *Houghton* Riv. Eds. pap. $3.95; *Modern Library* pap. $1.15; *New Am. Lib.* Signet pap. $.95; introd. by W. A. Marshall *Washington Square* 1963 $.60 Collateral Class. pap. $.75

The Adventures of Harry Richmond. 1871. Ed. by L. T. Hergenhan. *Univ. of Nebraska Press* 1970 $7.95

The Egoist. 1879. Ed. by Lionel Stevenson *Houghton* Riv. Eds. pap. $1.35; *New Am. Lib.* Signet 1964 pap. $.75; *Oxford* World's Class. $2.50

Diana of the Crossways. 1885. *Norton* pap. $2.95; *Scholarly Press* repr. of 1931 ed. $19.50

Short Stories. 1898. *Bks. for Libraries* $11.50

Letters. Ed. by C. L. Cline. *Oxford* 3 vols. 1970 $64.00. The definitive scholarly edition.

Letters of George Meredith to Alice Meynell, 1896–1907. Ed. with annotations by E. Meynell. 1923. *Folcroft* $15.00

Books about Meredith

The Poetry and Philosophy of George Meredith. By George M. Trevelyan. 1906. *Russell & Russell* 1966 $8.00

The Comic Spirit in George Meredith. By Joseph Warren Beach. 1911. *Russell & Russell* 1963 $7.00

The Ordeal of George Meredith. By Lionel Stevenson. 1953. *Russell & Russell* $12.50

Art and Substance in George Meredith. By Walter F. Wright. 1953. *Univ. of Nebraska Press* Bison Bks. pap. $1.50

A Troubled Eden: Nature and Society in the Works of George Meredith. By Norman Kelvin. *Stanford Univ. Press* 1961 $7.50

George Meredith and English Comedy. By Victor S. Pritchett. *Random* 1970 $5.00

Meredith: The Critical Heritage. Ed. by Ioan Williams *Barnes & Noble* 1971 $17.50. Contemporary criticisms of both novels and poetry, arranged chronologically.

Novelists in a Changing World: Meredith, James and the Transformation of English Fiction in the 1880's. By Donald Stone. *Harvard Univ. Press* 1972 $13.50. A broad comparative study that gives a detailed survey of Meredith's novels and the cultural–historical background out of which they come.

CARROLL, LEWIS (pseud. of the Rev. Charles Lutwidge Dodgson). 1832–1898.

"Lewis Carroll" was a minister of the Church of England and a professor of mathematics at Christ Church College, Oxford, where he was considered "conscientious, precise, sometimes inspired, but usually dull." His "Diaries" have been edited by Roger Lancelyn Green (1954, o.p.). "The Mathematical Recreations of Lewis Carroll" contains mathematical studies and diversions originally published under his own name: (*Dover* 2 vols. Vol. I Symbolic Logic and The Game of Logic $2.75 Vol. 2 Pillow Problems and A Tangled Tale $2.50).

In his diary of July 4, 1862, Carroll described "an expedition *up* the river to Godstowe with the three Liddells" the daughters of the dean of Christ Church College, "on which occasion I told them the fairy tale of 'Alice's Adventures under Ground,' which I undertook to write out for Alice." The original manuscript is on display in the British Museum and has been published in facsimile in the United States (*see note below*).

Carroll's particular talent for mathematical puzzles and paradox, for charming and significant nonsense verse, for verbal ingenuity, and for identification with the distortions and dilemmas of a child's view of the world have made "Alice's Adventures in Wonderland" and "Through the Looking Glass" perennial favorites with children. But in recent years there has been a growing tendency to take Carroll quite seriously as a major literary artist for adults as well. Carroll's major works have come under the scrutiny of critics who have explained his permanent attractiveness in terms of existential and symbolic drama: the Alice books dramatize psychological realities in symbolic terms, being commentary on the nature of the human predicament rather than escape from it.

THE COMPLETE WORKS OF LEWIS CARROLL. 1937. *Modern Library* Giants $4.95

THE HUMOROUS VERSE OF LEWIS CARROLL. (Original title "The Collected Verse of Lewis Carroll"). Ill. by the author, John Tenniel and others. 1933. *Dover* pap. $3.00; *Peter Smith* $5.00

THE UNKNOWN LEWIS CARROLL. (Original title "The Lewis Carroll Picture Book"). Ed. by Stuart Dodgson Collingwood. 1899. *Dover* 1961 pap. $3.00. Selections from unpublished works with photos and drawings by Lewis Carroll.

THE WALRUS AND THE CARPENTER AND OTHER POEMS. *Dutton* $3.95

ALICE'S ADVENTURES IN WONDERLAND. 1865. Ill. by Tenniel *Branden* pap. $.95; *Collins* New Class. $3.00; *Dutton* pap. $1.95; ed. by Donald J. Gray *Norton* Critical Eds. 1971 $10.00 pap. $1.95; *Clarkson N. Potter* 1972 $7.95 pap. $3.95; *Rand McNally* Windermere Class. pap. $1.50; *Random* 1957 $1.95 lib. bdg. $3.39; ill. by Tenniel *Scholastic Bk. Services* pap. $.75; (and Other Favorites) ill. by Tenniel *Washington Square* pap. $.60; *Franklin Watts* lg.-type ed. Keith Jennison Bks. $7.95

ALICE'S ADVENTURES UNDER GROUND. 1886. *Dover* facsimile ed. pap. $1.25; *Peter Smith* facsimile ed. $3.75

This is Carroll's own neat hand-lettered early version of "Alice's Adventures in Wonderland," written out for the real Alice Liddell and sent to her in 1864, illustrated with charming drawings by Carroll himself. The first of these recent editions (all are from the same British Museum manuscript) was that of *University Microfilms*, which contains a brief introduction by Luther H. Evans about the genesis of the present publication venture. Very soon afterward, *Dover* brought out the paperback facsimile containing a fascinating introduction by Martin Gardner and material added from the Macmillan facsimile edition of 1886: a poem of "Christmas Greetings" by Carroll, and Carroll's "Easter Greeting"—a sentimental preface in prose—as well as the original Macmillan Table of Contents. *McGraw-Hill* in 1966 brought out the *Dover* version in hardback. All contain an engaging photograph of the original "Alice." The *Peter Smith* edition has the Gardner introduction and the added material. In this less sophisticated version of the story there are many differences from the later Tenniel-illustrated "Alice": the Cheshire Cat, the Mad Tea Party and the Duchess have not yet, for example, been conceived. The manuscript is inscribed, "A Christmas Gift to a Dear Child in Memory of a Summer Day." "The later Alice is a work of literature," said *Time*; "the earlier is a work of love."

THROUGH THE LOOKING GLASS AND WHAT ALICE FOUND THERE. 1871. *St. Martin's* 1953 $5.50. A sequel to, and usually published with "Alice in Wonderland" (*see below*).

ALICE IN WONDERLAND and THROUGH THE LOOKING GLASS. Ill. by Tenniel *Assoc. Booksellers* Airmont Bks. pap. $.60; *Branden* pap. $.85; *Children's Press* 1964 $4.50; *Dutton* Chil. Ill. Class. $3.95 Everyman's $3.50 pap. $1.50; *Grosset* 1957 Companion Lib. $1.25 Ill. Jr. Lib. popular ed. $2.95 special ed. $3.95 deluxe ed. $4.95; ill. by Tenniel *Macmillan* 1963 $4.95 Collier Bks. pap. $.95; *New Am. Lib.* Signet pap. $.60; ed. by Roger Lancelyn Green with ills. by Tenniel *Oxford* repr. of 1897 ed., with all the important variations of earlier eds. 1971. $11.25; *Penguin* Puffin Bks. pap. $1.25

ALICE IN WONDERLAND. French ed. *French & European* $3.50

THE ANNOTATED ALICE: Alice's Adventures in Wonderland and Through the Looking Glass. Introd. and notes by Martin Gardner; ill. by John Tenniel *Clarkson N. Potter* 1960 $10.00; *World Pub.* Meridian Bks. pap. $3.95. Explains, for adults, many now-unfamiliar allusions.

THE HUNTING OF THE SNARK. 1876. *Pantheon* 1966 lib. bdg. $4.39; (and Other Nonsense Verse from Alice in Wonderland, Through the Looking Glass, and Sylvie and Bruno) ill. by Aldren Watson. *Peter Pauper* $2.95; *Franklin Watts* $4.95

THE ANNOTATED SNARK: Full Text of Lewis Carroll's Great Nonsense Epic *The Hunting of the Snark* and the Original Illustrations by Henry Holiday; introd. and notes by Martin Gardner *Simon & Schuster* 1962 $3.95. *See Annotated Alice, above.* Includes bibliography and interesting appendix.

THE NURSERY ALICE. 1889. Introd. by Martin Gardner *Dover* pap. $2.50; *Peter Smith* $3.50; *McGraw-Hill* 1966 $3.25 lib. bdg. $3.22

THE RECTORY UMBRELLA and MISCHMASCH (1882). Fwd. by Florence Milner, with numerous ills. by Lewis Carroll. 1932. *Dover* pap. $2.50. "The Rectory Umbrella" was never published separately.

THE MAD GARDENER'S SONG. Ill. by Sean Morrison. *Bobbs* 1967 $2.95. Nonsense verses of the gardener "who wanders through Lewis Carroll's late books, 'Sylvie and Bruno' and 'Sylvie and Bruno Concluded.' " For Alice fans from six up.

Books about Carroll

Lewis Carroll. By Derek Hudson. 1954. *Greenwood* $15.00
Lewis Carroll. By Derek Hudson. 1955. Writers and Their Work Ser. *British Bk. Centre* $2.38 pap. $1.20
The Lewis Carroll Handbook. By Sidney Williams and Falconer Madan. 1931 rev. ed. 1962 by Roger L. Green *Barnes & Noble* 1970 $17.50. A new version of "A Handbook of the Literature of the Rev. C. L. Dodgson" revised, augmented and brought up to 1960.
The Life of Lewis Carroll. (Original title "Victoria through the Looking Glass"). By Florence Becker Lennon. 1945. *Dover* pap. $3.50
Alice in Many Tongues: The Translations of Alice in Wonderland. By Warren Weaver. *Univ. of Wisconsin Press* 1964 $4.75
"This engaging little book . . . takes us on a delightful excursion into the wonderland of translation . . . it will provide an enjoyable evening to anyone who ever pondered how its puns, parodied nursery rhymes, nonsense words, etc. could be translated without losing their reason for being"—(*Library Quarterly*).

DU MAURIER, GEORGE. 1834–1896.

Du Maurier was first famous as an artist. He contributed incomparable satirical drawings of society to *Punch* and he illustrated novels by authors such as Mrs. Gaskell, Thackeray and Meredith. "Peter Ibbetson," his own first novel, is a fanciful romance of dream life, a work of rare imagination and charm of style. "Trilby" created a literary sensation and brought the name of the character "Svengali"—an evil person who bends others to his will—into the English language. The story is set in the Latin Quarter in Paris and is thoroughly French in atmosphere. Du Maurier was born in Paris, studied art there and illustrated his own novels. "Trilby" contained a portrait of Whistler in caricature, which Du Maurier was forced by law to change.

Peter Ibbetson. 1892. *Scholarly Press* repr. of 1932 ed. 1971 $19.00

Peter Ibbetson (play). Dramatized by Raphael and Collier. *French* 1934 $1.75

Trilby. 1894. *Dutton* Everyman's $3.50 pap. $1.95; *Popular Lib.* pap. $.50

The Martian. 1897. *Scholarly Press* 1971 $29.50

Young George Du Maurier: A Selection of His Letters. Ed. by Daphne Du Maurier, his granddaughter, with ills. from contemporary drawings by Du Maurier. 1952. *Greenwood* $12.00

Books about George Du Maurier

The Du Mauriers. By Daphne Du Maurier. 1937. *Pocket Bks.* pap. $.95
George Du Maurier. By Leonée Ormond. *Univ. of Pittsburgh* 1969 $14.95. A critical biography.

BUTLER, SAMUEL. 1835–1902.

Samuel Butler was a versatile genius. He was an artist who exhibited in the Royal Academy, a musician who composed a cantata and an oratorio of distinction, a man of science who contributed several books to the study of evolution (not taken very seriously by scientists), a translator of Homer (*q. v.*), the author of various books of travel and of at least one immortal novel. "The Way of All Flesh" is a "biographical" novel depicting three generations of the same family. It satirizes the hypocrisy of the ecclesiastical and educational systems in a tone surprisingly modern. "Erewhon" (an anagram for "Nowhere") and its sequel are Utopias. "The Notebooks," edited by Geoffrey Keynes and Brian Hill, contains some of Butler's best work.

"The Family Letters," edited by Arnold Silver, is a selection from the correspondence of Butler and his father, with several letters to and from his mother and sisters and one or two other relatives. Two-thirds of these letters have never before been printed. Those between Butler and his father show how close the early part of the "The Way of All Flesh" was to the events in the son's life. The great bulk of his revealing "Correspondence With His Sister May" (1962, o.p.) remained mostly untouched in the British Museum for over a quarter of a century.

Works. Ed. by A. T. Bartholomew. 20 vols 1923–26. *AMS Press* each $12.50 set $250.00

Erewhon. 1872. Introd. by M. M. Threapleton *Assoc. Booksellers* Airmont Bks. pap. $.60; (and "Erewhon Revisited") *Dutton* Everyman's $3.50; *Fernhill* 1965 $4.75; *New Am. Lib.* Signet pap. $.95; ed. by Peter Mudford *Penguin* pap. $1.25

Erewhon Revisited (Twenty Years Later). 1901. (and "Erewhon") *Dutton* Everyman's $3.50; *Fernhill* 1964 $3.50

The Way of All Flesh. 1903. *Assoc. Booksellers* Airmont Bks. pap. $.75; ill. by Donia Nachsen *Dufour* 1961 $10.50; introd. and notes by G. M. Oklom *Dutton* Everyman's $3.50 pap. $1.95; ed. by R. A. Gettmann *Holt* (Rinehart) 1948 pap. $2.00; *Lancer* pap. $.75; *Modern Library* pap. $1.15; *New Am. Lib.* Signet pap. $.95; *Oxford* World's Class. $2.25; ed. by Richard Hoggart *Penguin* pap. $1.25; *Washington Square* pap. $.50 Collateral Class. pap. $.50; *Franklin Watts* ultratype ed. $5.50

The Notebooks: Selections. Ed. by Geoffrey Keynes and Brian Hill. 1951. Fernhill $4.00

FURTHER EXTRACTS FROM THE NOTEBOOKS. Ed. by A. T. Bartholomew. 1934. *Greenwood* $17.50

THE FAMILY LETTERS OF SAMUEL BUTLER, 1841–1846. Ed. by Arnold Silver. 1962 *Fernhill* $5.00

Other nonfiction titles available are:

EVOLUTION, OLD AND NEW, or The Theories of Buffon, Dr. Erasmus Darwin and Lamarck as compared with Mr. Charles Darwin. 1879. *Gordon Press* $9.95

THE AUTHORESS OF THE ODYSSEY. 1897. Introd. by David Grene. *Univ. of Chicago Press* 1967 $7.50 Phoenix Bks. pap. $2.45. Butler's discussion of why he believed "The Odyssey" to have been written two centuries after "The Iliad" by a Sicilian noblewoman.

ESSAYS ON LIFE, ART AND SCIENCE. Ed. by Richard A. Streatfeild. 1904. *Kennikat* repr. of reissue of 1908 1970 $12.00

THE HUMOUR OF HOMER AND OTHER ESSAYS. Ed. by Richard A. Streatfeild. 1913. *Bks. for Libraries* $9.75

Books about Butler

Samuel Butler: A Memoir. By Henry Festing Jones. 1919. *Folcroft* 1973 2 vols. $24.50; *Octagon* 1968 2 vols. $25.00

Ernest Atheist: A Study of Samuel Butler. By Malcolm Muggeridge. 1936. *Haskell* 1971 $11.95; *Richard West* $10.75. The author, critic and editor of *Punch* maintains that Butler was the epitome of a Victorian writer, rather than a rebel against his times.

The Career of Samuel Butler, 1835–1902: A Bibliography. By Stanley Harkness. 1955. *Burt Franklin* $14.50

An Historical and Critical review of Samuel Butler's Literary Works. By W. G. Bekker. 1925. *Haskell* $7.95; *Russell & Russell* 1964 $8.00

The Cradle of Erewhon: Samuel Butler in New Zealand. By Joseph Jones. *Univ. of Texas Press* 1959 $6.00. A tracing of the effect upon Samuel Butler of his five-year sojourn in New Zealand, 1859–64, in particular the effect of these years upon his satirical work "Erewhon."

Samuel Butler. By Lee E. Holt. English Authors Ser. *Twayne* 1964 $5.50. With a chronology of his life and a selected bibliography.

Samuel Butler. By G. D. H. Cole. *British Bk. Centre.* $2.38 pap. $1.20

The Quest for the Father: A Study of the Darwin-Butler Controversy, as a Contribution to the Understanding of the Creative Individual. By Phyllis Greenacre. New York Psychoanalytic Institute Freud Anniversary Lecture Ser. *Int. Univs. Press* 1963 $6.00

HARDY, THOMAS. 1840–1928.

Hardy had great influence on the writers who followed him. He is known as "the novelist of Wessex" because the scene of nearly all his books is the area of the ancient kingdom of Wessex (used as a fictitious county name by Hardy), that part of England which includes Dorsetshire. His first novel, "The Poor Man and the Lady" (1867), was never published: when George Meredith, then reader for Chapman and Hall, turned it down because it "had not enough plot," Hardy destroyed the manuscript. "The Return of the Native," "Tess of the D'Urbervilles" and "Jude the Obscure" are generally considered his greatest works. He delights to portray the grim irony of life but always with sympathy. In 1895, when he published his last novel, "Jude the Obscure," the storm of blind and perverse criticism which the book aroused led him to give up fiction writing for poetry. He always preferred his poetry to his novels, and wanted to be remembered as a poet. Carl J. Weber, the American authority on Hardy who died in 1966, has written the standard critical biography (*see below*). He also edited "Dearest Emmie" (1963, o.p.), a collection of some 74 letters (1885–1911) from Hardy to his first wife. The "Notebooks of Thomas Hardy" edited by Evelyn Hardy (1956) is now o.p.

GREAT SHORT STORIES. *Harper* Class. pap. $1.25. Basically "Wessex Tales" (*see below*).

DESPERATE REMEDIES. 1871. *St. Martin's* $7.50

UNDER THE GREENWOOD TREE, or The Mellstock Quire. 1872. *Collins* New Class. 1959 $3.00

A PAIR OF BLUE EYES. 1873. *St. Martin's* $10.00 pocket ed. $3.00; *Popular Lib.* pap. $.75

FAR FROM THE MADDING CROWD. 1874. *Dodd* Gt. Ill. Class. 1968 $5.50; *Harper* 1895 $6.95 Mod. Class. $2.52; ed. by Carl Weber *Holt* (Rinehart) 1959 pap. $1.25; ed. by Richard Purdy *Houghton* Riv. Eds. pap. $1.25; *St. Martin's* $7.50 pap. $1.50 Scholar's Lib. $2.95; *Scribner* $3.20

Other paperback editions are available from Assoc. Booksellers Airmont Bks., Bantam, Fawcett Premier Bks., New Am. Lib. Signet, Washington Square, $.60–$1.95

THE HAND OF ETHELBERTA. 1876. *St. Martin's* $7.50

THE RETURN OF THE NATIVE. 1878. *Dodd* Gt. Ill. Class. $5.50; *Harper* $6.95 ed. by J. Paterson pap. $.75; ed. by A. J. Guérard *Holt* (Rinehart) pap. $1.95; ed. by A. Walton Litz *Houghton* Riv. Eds. 1967 pap. $1.50; *Macmillan* Collier Bks. pap. $.65; ed. by James Gindin *Norton* Critical Eds. 1968 $7.00 pap. $1.95; *St. Martin's* $7.50 Scholar's Lib. pap. $2.95; *Scribner* $3.20; *Franklin Watts* lg.-type ed. Keith Jennison Bks. $8.95 ultratype ed. $4.50

Other paperback editions are available from Amsco School Pubns., Assoc. Booksellers Airmont Bks., Cambridge Bk. Co., Dell, Lancer, New Am. Lib. Signet, Scholastic Bk. Services, Washington Square, $.60–$1.80

A LAODICEAN: STORY OF TO-DAY. 1881. *St. Martin's* $7.50

TWO ON A TOWER. 1882. *St. Martin's* $7.50

WESSEX TALES. Short Stories. 1883. *St. Martin's* $7.50

TWO WESSEX TALES: The Withered Arms, and Three Strangers. *Branden* pap. $.85

THE MAYOR OF CASTERBRIDGE. 1886. Ed. by Robert Heilman *Houghton* Riv. Eds. pap. $1.60; introd. by S. L. Chew *Modern Library* pap. $.95; *St. Martin's* $7.50 pap. $1.50

Other paperback editions are available from Amsco School Pubns., Assoc. Booksellers Airmont Bks., Cambridge Bks. Co., Dell, New Am. Lib. Signet, Washington Square, $.60–$1.25

THE WOODLANDERS. 1887. *St. Martin's* $7.50 ed. by C. Aldred Scholar's Lib. $1.75

TESS OF THE D'URBERVILLES: Pure Woman. 1891. *Collins* New Class. $3.00; ed. by Arnold Kettle *Harper* Class. pap. $.85; ed. by William E. Buckler *Houghton* Riv. Eds. pap. $1.40; ed. by S. Elledge *Norton* Critical Eds. $6.00 pap. $1.95; ed. by M. W. Steinberg *Odyssey* pap. $1.65; *St. Martin's* $8.50 pap. $2.25

Other paperback editions are available from Amsco School Pubns., Assoc. Booksellers Airmont Bks., Dell, Modern Library, New Am. Lib. Signet, Washington Square, $.50–$1.95

A GROUP OF NOBLE DAMES. 1891. *St. Martin's* $7.50 pocket ed. $2.50. Short Stories.

THE WELL-BELOVED: Sketch of a Temperament. 1892. *St. Martin's* $7.50

OUR EXPLOITS AT WEST POLEY. 1893. *Folcroft* repr. of 1952 ed. $15.00

LIFE'S LITTLE IRONIES and A FEW CRUSTED CHARACTERS. 1894. *St. Martin's* $7.50. Short Stories.

JUDE THE OBSCURE. 1895. Introd. by N. R. Teitel *Assoc. Booksellers* Airmont Bks. pap. $.75; ed. by F. R. Southerington *Bobbs* 1972 $8.50 pap. $2.25; introd. by W. E. Buckler *Dell* Laurel Leaf Lib. pap. $.75; ed. by R. Heilman *Harper* pap. $.95; ed. by I. Howe *Houghton* Riv. Eds. pap. $1.95; *Lancer* pap. $.75; ed. by Robert C. Slack *Modern Library* $2.95; *New Am. Lib.* Signet pap. $.95; *St. Martin's* $8.25 pap. $1.95

A CHANGED MAN, THE WAITING SUPPER AND OTHER TALES. 1913. *St. Martin's* $7.50

THOMAS HARDY'S PERSONAL WRITINGS: Prefaces, Literary Opinions, Reminiscences. Ed. with pref. by Harold Orel. *Univ. of Kansas Press* 1966 $6.75 pap. $2.95

"Illustrates [Hardy's] sensitivity and defensiveness . . . and makes the reader aware once again of the unity and force of other Hardy attitudes"—(*LJ*).

LIFE AND ART: Essays, Notes and Letters. Ed. by E. Brennecke. 1925. *Bks. for Libraries* $7.75; *Haskell* $8.95

LETTERS. Ed. by Carl J. Weber. 1954. *Kraus* $8.00

Books about Hardy

Thomas Hardy. By Edmund C. Blunden. 1942. *St. Martin's* pap. $2.25 Pock. Lib. $2.00

Hardy in America: A Study of Thomas Hardy and His American Readers. By Carl J. Weber. 1946. *Russell & Russell* rev. ed. 1966 $10.00

On a Darkling Plain: The Art and Thought of Thomas Hardy. By Harvey C. Webster. 1947. *Shoe String* $6.50

Hardy and the Lady from Madison Square. By Carl J. Weber. 1952. *Kennikat* 1973 $12.00. The lady of the title is Rebekah Owen, an admirer of Hardy and his work. The book contains a discussion of Miss Owen's annotated collection of Hardy's works, now in the Colby College Collection.

Thomas Hardy: A Study of His Writings and Their Backgrounds. By William Rutland. *Russell & Russell* 1962 $12.50

Hardy: A Collection of Critical Essays. Ed. by Albert Guérard. *Prentice-Hall* 1963 $5.95 Spectrum Bks. pap. $1.95. Articles by D. H. Lawrence, Delmore Schwartz, W. H. Auden and others.

Thomas Hardy. By Richard C. Carpenter. English Authors Ser. *Twayne* 1964 $5.50

"An intelligent and perceptive analysis of Hardy's work that is cognizant of the traditional viewpoint . . . as well as the more recent attitude toward his work"—(*Choice*).

Thomas Hardy: A Critical Study. By Albert J. Guérard. *New Directions* 1964 pap. $1.95

Thomas Hardy. By Irving Howe. Vol. 7 in the Masters of World Literature ser. *Macmillan* 1967 $5.95 Collier Bks. pap. $2.95

A Thomas Hardy Dictionary. By F. Outwin Saxelby. 1911 1962. *Humanities Press* $10.00. The characters and scenes of the novels and poems alphabetically arranged and described.

Thomas Hardy: A Critical Study. By Lascelles Abercrombie. 1912. *Russell & Russell* $8.00

The Technique of Thomas Hardy. By Joseph Warren Beach. 1922. *Russell & Russell* $8.50

The Life of Thomas Hardy. By E. Brennecke. 1925. *Haskell* 1973 lib. bdg. $12.95

The Life of Thomas Hardy, 1840–1928. Comp. by Florence Emily Dugdale Hardy. 1928. *Shoe String* 1970 $12.00; *Scholarly Press* $19.50. The second Mrs. Hardy, who died in 1937, compiled this life of her husband largely from contemporary notes, letters, diaries, and biographical memoranda, as well as from oral information in conversations extending over many years. The general understanding is that Hardy himself wrote a good deal of the material and that the biography is autobiographical.

Hardy of Wessex. By Carl J. Weber. 1940. *Columbia* 2nd ed. 1965 $10.00. The outstanding critical biography, notable for its scholarly accuracy and balanced appraisal.

The First Hundred Years of Thomas Hardy, 1840–1940. A Centennial Biography. By Carl J. Weber. 1942. *Russell & Russell* 1965 $12.00

The Shaping of the Dynasts: A Study in Thomas Hardy. By Walter F. Wright. *Univ. of Nebraska Press* 1967 $7.95

Thomas Hardy: The Critical Heritage. Ed. by R. G. Cox. *Barnes & Noble* 1970 $13.50. A collection of contemporary reviews and discussions by various critics including Henry James, Coventry Patmore, Havelock Ellis, J. M. Barrie, and Edmund Gosse.

Thomas Hardy: Distance and Desire. By J. Hillis Miller. *Harvard Univ. Press* 1970 $7.75

The Metaphor of Chance: Vision and Technique in the Works of Thomas Hardy. By Bert G. Hornback. *Ohio Univ. Press* 1971 $7.00. Traces the development of Hardy's art as a novelist from the early prose until he turned to the writing of poetry.

Thomas Hardy: A Critical Biography. By J. I. Stewart. *Dodd* 1971 $6.95

Thomas Hardy: The Return of the Repressed, a Study of the Major Fiction. By Perry Meisel. *Yale Univ. Press* 1972 $6.95

Thomas Hardy and Rural England. By Merryn Williams. *Columbia Univ. Press* 1972 $10.00

See also Chapter 6, British Poetry: Middle Period.

HUDSON, WILLIAM HENRY. 1841–1922.

W. H. Hudson, born in South America of American parents, was both a naturalist and a novelist. He chose to serve two masters and reached distinction under both. "The Purple Land" is a story of Uruguay, "the land that England lost." "A Crystal Age" is a Utopia, a picture of a paragon world. "Green Mansions" is an idyllic romance of South America, an allegory. His autobiography, "Far Away and Long Ago," has a matchless charm. Hudson is a stylist whose books are rich in beautiful lyric prose. He combined a gift for storytelling with a deep feeling for nature. "W. H. Hudson's Diary, 1874: Voyages from Buenos Aires to Southampton" (1958, o.p.) contains descriptions of great force and beauty. "W. H. Hudson, A Portrait," (1924, o.p.) by Morley Roberts, the authorized life, is usually considered defamatory.

Collected Works. 24 vols. 1922–23. *AMS Press* each $15.00 set $360.00. The volumes of fiction in this set are listed separately in the bibliography below. Under the subheading Works on Natural History is a selection of titles which should be of interest. For other titles, mostly ornithological, consult the *AMS Press* catalog.

Tales of the Gauchos. Stories. Comp. and ed. by Elizabeth Coatsworth; ill. by Henry C. Pitz. Selections from "Green Mansions," "Tales of the Pampas," "A Little Boy Lost" and others. *Knopf* 1946 $3.50

The Purple Land: Being the Narrative of One Richard Lamb's Adventures in the Banda Oriental in South America as Told by Himself. 1922. *AMS Press* $15.00

Fan, the Story of a Young Girl's Life. 1892 1923 *AMS Press* 1968 $15.00

El Ombú and Other South American Stories. 1902 1923 *AMS Press* 1968 $15.00

Green Mansions: A Romance of the Tropical Forest. 1904 1923. With a note on Hudson's romances by Edward Garnett *AMS Press* 1968 $15.00; *Dodd* Gt. Ill. Class. $5.50; *Grosset* Univ. Lib. pap. $1.50; *Harper* Mod. Class. 1963 $2.00; *Knopf* 1959 $12.50; *Franklin Watts* lg.-type ed. Keith Jennison Bks. $7.95

Other paperback editions are available from Amsco School Pubns., Assoc. Booksellers Airmont Bks., Bantam, Lancer, Scholastic Bk. Services, $.60–$1.10

A Crystal Age. 1906 1922 *AMS Press* $15.00; *Folcroft* $14.50

A Little Boy Lost. Together with the poems. 1905 1918 1922. *AMS Press* $15.00

Works on Natural History, reprinted from the standard uniform edition of 1922–23. AMS Press each $15.00

Idle Days in Patagonia. 1893

Hampshire Days. 1903

The Land's End: A Naturalist's Impressions in West Cornwall. 1908

A Shepherd's Life: Impressions of the South Wiltshire Downs. 1910

Dead Man's Plack, An Old Thorn, and Miscellanea. With an appreciation by Viscount Grey of Fallodon. 1920

A Traveller in Little Things. 1921. With a note by Edward Garnett

A Hind in Richmond Park. 1922. With a prefatory note by Morley Roberts

Books about Hudson

A Bibliography of the Writings of W. H. Hudson. By G. F. Wilson. 1922. *Haskell* 1972 lib. bdg. $7.95;
Kennikat 1968 $5.00. A comprehensive listing.
W. H. Hudson. By Ruth Tomalin. 1954. *Dufour* $3.95; *Greenwood* $8.00
William Henry Hudson. By John T. Frederick. English Authors Ser. *Twayne* 1972 $5.50

STEVENSON, ROBERT LOUIS. 1850–1894.

Stevenson revived Defoe's (*q.v.*) novel of romantic adventure, adding to it psychological analysis. "Kidnapped," with its sequel "David Balfour," and "The Master of Ballantrae" are stories of adventure and at
the same time studies of character. Stevenson died before having finished "St. Ives" (completed by Sir Arthur
Quiller-Couch) and "The Weir of Hermiston" (issued in its incomplete form), by many considered his masterpiece. "He produced not only the best boy's book in English ("Treasure Island") and several masterpieces
of Scottish characterization," but his short stories are vivid, memorable and show a complete mastery of "the
macabre, the eerie, the weird"—("British Authors of the Nineteenth Century"). "Our Samoan Adventure"
(1955, o.p.) by his American wife, Fanny, tells the story of their last years together, throwing light on an obscure period and on personal relationships.

Works. Ed. by L. Osbourne and F. Van de G. Stevenson. The Vailima ed. 26 vols.
1921–23. *AMS Press* each $25.00 set $650.00

Selected Writings. Ed. with an introd. by Saxe Commins. 1947. *Bks. for Libraries*
$34.50. Three novels, ten short stories, three books of travel, a selection of verse.

Seven Works. *Collins* New Class. 7 vols. $21.00. These seven volumes are also avail-
able separately (*see listings below*). They are: Treasure Island; Kidnapped, and Catriona; The Black Arrow, and Prince Otto; The Master of Ballantrae; Dr. Jekyll and
Mr. Hyde; A Child's Garden of Verses; and Familiar Studies.

The Complete Short Stories. With a selection of the best short novels. Ed. with introd. by Charles Neider *Doubleday* 1969 $10.00

Selected Poetry and Prose. Ed. by Bradford A. Booth *Houghton* Riv. Eds. 1965
pap. $1.95. Other collections of poetry are listed under the subdivision Poetry, below.

Prose:

The New Arabian Nights. 1882. Ed. by Herbert Van Thal with fwd. by David Holloway. 1968. *Dufour* $4.50 pap. $2.50; (and "Treasure Island") *Dutton* Everyman's
$3.50 pap. $1.95

Treasure Island. 1883. *Collins* New Class. $3.00 lea. $5.00; Dodd Gt. Ill. Class.
$5.50; ill. by S. Van Abbe *Dutton* 1948 $3.95 (and "New Arabian Nights") Everyman's $3.50 pap. $1.95; *Grosset* Companion Lib. $1.25 special ed. $3.95 lib bdg.
$3.79 deluxe ed. $4.95; *Harper* Class. pap. $.75; *Macmillan* 1963 $4.95 Collier Bks.
pap. $.65; ed. by Frank L. Beals *Naylor* $3.95; ill. with historically accurate representations of ships and seamen of the time by Eleanore Schmidt *N. Y. Graphic Soc.*
1972 $7.95; *Oxford* World's Class. $2.25; *Penguin* Puffin Bks. pap. $.75; ill. by
N. C. Wyeth *Scribner* Ill. Class. $7.50; *Franklin Watts* 1964 lg.-type ed. Keith Jen-
nison Bks. $7.95; ill. by C. B. Falls with introd. by May Lamberton Becker *World
Pub.* Rainbow Class. $2.50 lib. bdg. $3.21

*Other paperback editions are available from Amsco School Pubns., Assoc. Booksellers
Airmont Bks., Bantam, Books, Inc., Cambridge Bk. Co., Dell, Fearon, Lancer, New
Am. Lib., Random, Scholastic Bk. Services, Washington Square, $.50–$1.95*

(with Fannie Van de G. Stevenson) THE DYNAMITERS. 1885. *Bks. for Libraries* repr. of 1898 ed. $10.75

DR. JEKYLL AND MR. HYDE. 1886. Dramatized by Henry Thomas *Baker* $1.25; (and "Island Nights' Entertainments" and "The Merry Men and Other Stories") *Collins* New Class. $3.00 lea. $5.00 (and Other Famous Tales) *Dodd* Gt. Ill. Class. $5.50; (and "The Merry Men and Other Stories") *Dutton* Everyman's $3.50 pap. $1.55; dramatized by Richard Abbott *French* $1.50; (and Other Stories) *Putnam* $5.00; *Franklin Watts* $3.75 lg.-type ed. Keith Jennison Bks. $7.95

Other paperback editions are available from Assoc. Booksellers Airmont Bks., Bantam, Scholastic Bk. Services, Washington Square, $.50–$.75

THE BLACK ARROW. 1889. *Assoc. Booksellers* Airmont Bks. pap. $.60; (and "Prince Otto") *Collins* New Class. $3.00; *Dodd* Gt. Ill. Class. $5.50; ill. by Lionel Edwards *Dutton* Chil. Ill. Class. $3.95; *Lancer* pap. $.60; *Macmillan* Collier Bks. pap. $.95; *Scholastic Bk. Services* pap. $.75; ill. by N. C. Wyeth *Scribner* Ill. Class. $6.00

KIDNAPPED. 1889. (and "Catriona") *Collins* New Class. $3.00 lea. $5.00; *Dodd* Gt. Ill. Class. $5.50; *Dutton* Chil. Ill. Class. 1959 $3.95 Everyman's $3.50; ill. by Lynd Ward *Grosset* Ill. Jr. Lib. special ed. $3.95 lib bdg. $3.79 deluxe ed. $4.95 Companion Lib. $1.25; *Harper* Class. pap. $.75; *Oxford* World's Class. $2.00; ill. by N. C. Wyeth *Scribner* Ill. Class. $10.00; *Franklin Watts* 1966 lg.-type ed. Keith Jennison Bks. $7.95; introd. by May Lamberton Becker *World Pub.* Rainbow Class. $3.95 lib. bdg. $3.91

Other paperback editions are available from Assoc. Booksellers Airmont Bks., Cambridge Bk. Co., Dell Laurel Leaf Lib., Lancer, Macmillan Collier Bks., New Am. Lib., Scholastic Bk. Services, Washington Square, $.60–$1.00

THE MASTER OF BALLANTRAE: A Winter's Tale. 1889. *Assoc. Booksellers* Airmont Bks. 1964 pap. $.60; *Collins* New Class 1959 $3.00; (and "The Weir of Hermiston") *Dutton* Everyman's $3.50; *Lancer* $.60; *Oxford* World's Class. $2.50; *Popular Lib.* pap. $.50

ISLAND NIGHTS' ENTERTAINMENTS: The Beach of Falesá, The Bottle Imp, and The Isle of Voices. 1893. (and "Dr. Jekyll and Mr. Hyde" and "The Merry Men and Other Stories") *Collins* New Class. $3.00; *Scholarly Press* $14.50

(with Lloyd Osbourne). THE WRONG BOX. 1889. *Oxford* World's Class. $2.50

(with Lloyd Osbourne). THE WRECKER. 1892. *Oxford* World's Class. $2.25

DAVID BALFOUR. Sequel to "Kidnapped." 1893. Ill. by N. C. Wyeth *Scribner* Ill. Class. $10.00

CATRIONA. 1893. A Sequel to "Kidnapped," Being Memoirs of the Further Adventures of David Balfour at Home and Abroad. (and "Kidnapped") *Collins* New Class. $3.00 lea. $5.00; *Dutton* Everyman's $3.50

ST. IVES. 1894 *Dutton* Everyman's $3.50

THE WEIR OF HERMISTON: An Unfinished Romance. 1896 *Bks. for Libraries.* $9.50; (and "The Master of Ballantrae") introd. by M. R. Ridley *Dutton* Everyman's $3.50

LETTERS. Ed. by Sidney Colvin. 1911 *Greenwood* 4 vols. $59.25

Poetry:

COLLECTED POEMS. Introd. and notes by Janet Adam Smith. 1954 *Dufour* $12.50; *Viking* 1971 $10.00

POEMS. Ed. by Helen Plotz. *T. Y. Crowell* 1973 $4.50; ed. by George S. Hellman. 1916. *Folcroft* 2 vols. lib. bdg. $50.00

A CHILD'S GARDEN OF VERSES. 1885. *Assoc. Booksellers* Airmont Bks. pap. $.60; *Collins* New Class. $3.00 lea. $5.00; *Dutton* Chil. Ill. Class. $3.95; *Grosset* 1957 $3.95 lib. bdg. $3.99; *Penguin* Puffin Bks. pap. $1.00; ill. by Jessie Wilcox Smith *Scribner* Ill. Class. 1905 $6.00; *Walck* 1947 $4.75; *Franklin Watts* 1966 lib. bdg. $6.95; *Western Publishing* Golden Bks. 1951 $2.95 lib. bdg. $3.95

Books about Stevenson

The Life of Robert Louis Stevenson. By Sir Graham Balfour. 2 vols. 1901. *Scholarly Press* $19.00. Written by his cousin, it reveals a great family pride and maintains loyal silences on many passages in Stevenson's career. The authorized "Life".

Robert Louis Stevenson: A Critical Study. By Frank Swinnerton. 1915. *Kennikat* $7.50

Robert Louis Stevenson. By David Daiches. *New Directions* 1947 $3.00

Voyage to Windward: The Life of Robert Louis Stevenson. By Joseph Chamberlain Furnas. 1951. *Apollo* 1962 pap. $2.50

Robert Louis Stevenson. By G. B. Stern. 1954. *British Bk. Centre* $2.38 pap. $1.20

Robert Louis Stevenson and the Fiction of Adventure. By R. Kiely. *Harvard Univ. Press* 1964 $7.50 "A refreshing reassessment of Stevenson's art and outlook on life arrived at through analysis of text, theme, and pertinent biographical data . . . as much a study of personality as a literary study"—(*Booklist*).

R. L. Stevenson. By Dennis Butts. *Walck* 1966 $2.75

Robert Louis Stevenson and Romantic Tradition. By E. M. Eigner. *Princeton Univ. Press* 1966 $9.00

See also Chapter 5, Essays and Criticism.

MOORE, GEORGE. 1852–1933.

George Moore, "the master of the most subtle rhythm in modern prose"—(Austin Clarke in the *N.Y. Times*, Nov. 20, 1966) was an exponent of the "experimental" novel of Emile Zola (*q.v.*), the novel of realism, written with a polished and careful artistry. Many regard "Sister Theresa" (1901) as his masterpiece, although "Esther Waters," his objective story of a servant girl's seduction and struggle, continues to be read as typical of his "realistic" period.

As an autobiographer Moore was very prolific. His "Confessions of a Young Man," "Memoirs of My Dead Life" and the trilogy "Hail and Farewell!" are all books about himself and his friends. In the latter, says Austin Clarke, "he had mocked at his fellow writers, invented ludicrous conversations for them and succeeded in turning literary Dublin into delightful, irresistible legend. He . . . made many enemies by his candor." "Conversations in Ebury Street" (1924, o.p.) is a volume of actual talks between Moore and his friends in his London home.

A MUMMER'S WIFE. 1884. *Liveright* Black and Gold Lib. $7.95

IMPRESSIONS AND OPINIONS. 1891. *Blom* $12.75

ESTHER WATERS. 1894. *Dutton* Everyman's $3.50; *Liveright* Black and Gold Lib. $7.95; *Oxford* World's Class. $2.50

THE UNTILLED FIELD. 1903. *Bks. for Libraries* $9.50. A group of excellent short stories.

THE BROOK KERITH. 1916. *Liveright* Black and Gold Lib. $7.95

A STORY-TELLER'S HOLIDAY. 1918. *Liveright* Black and Gold Lib. $7.95

HÉLOISE AND ABÉLARD. 1921. *Liveright* Black and Gold Lib. 2 vols. in 1 $7.95

IN SINGLE STRICTNESS. 1922 *Bks. for Libraries* $11.50

Confessions of a Young Man. 1886. *Scholarly Press* repr. of 1926 ed. $16.00

A Communication to My Friends. 1933 *Folcroft* lib. bdg. $5.00. This essay was used as the preface to the Uniform and later editions of "A Mummer's Wife."

George Moore in Transition: Letters to T. Fisher Unwin and Lena Milman, 1894–1910. Ed. by Helmut Gerber. *Wayne State Univ. Press* 1968 $13.95

"This book contains about 300 items from the correspondence of the Irish novelist to his 'publisher' and to Lena Milman, who first introduced him to Russian literature"—(*Choice*)

Books about Moore

George Moore. By Susan L. Mitchell. 1916. *Kennikat* 1970 $6.50
Portrait of George Moore in a Study of His Work. By John Freeman. 1922 *Scholarly Press* 1971 $14.50
George Moore: A Disciple of Walter Pater. By Robert P. Sechler. 1931. *Folcroft* lib. bdg. $10.00
George Moore. By Humbert Wolfe. 1931. *Bks. for Libraries* $9.50
The Life of George Moore. By Joseph M. Hone. 1936. *Greenwood* 1973 $19.25
George Moore: A Reconsideration. By Malcolm Johnston Brown. *Univ. of Washington Press* 1955 $5.00
George Moore. By A. N. Jeffares. *British Bk. Centre* 1965 $2.38 pap. $1.20
George Moore's Mind and Art. Ed. by Graham Owens. *Barnes & Noble* 1970 $6.50. Essays by A. Norman Jeffares and others.
Bibliography of George Moore. By Edwin Gilcher. *Northern Illinois Univ. Press* 1970 $15.00
George Moore. By Janet Egleson. Ed. by James F. Carens. *Bucknell Univ. Press* $4.50 pap. $1.95
Man of Wax: Critical Essays on George Moore. Ed. by Douglas A. Hughes. *New York Univ. Press* $10.00 pap. $3.50. Three reminiscences by W. B. Yeats, John Eglinton, and Austin Clarke. Enid Starke, Granville Hicks, and Brian Nicholas have separate essays on "Esther Waters."

CONRAD, JOSEPH. 1857–1924.

Born a Pole (Josef Konrad Korzeniowski), Joseph Conrad is one of the select few who learned the language of his literary career as an adult and produced an important body of distinguished fiction (another is Vladimir Nabokov [*q.v.*]). A master of the novella as well as the novel, Conrad takes much of the setting for his fiction from his youth as a merchant sailor. Some of his basic fictional situations develop out of the Victorian traditions of the sea adventure tale, the spy and detective novels, and the novels of voyages to unknown countries. Beginning with "Almayer's Folly" in 1895, he produced a series of outstanding fictions, a number of which are considered major modern literary landmarks, particularly "Heart of Darkness," "Lord Jim," "Nostromo," "Victory," "The Secret Agent," and "Under Western Eyes." Conrad's ability to transform metaphor, imagery, and fictional situation into symbols of the moral and psychological condition of modern man and his civilization establish his fiction as a force in modernism rather than in Victorianism. If he is a bridge between two centuries, most of the bridge is in the twentieth. For Conrad's use of indirect narrative and his psychological perceptiveness create a sense of inwardness and existential dimensions of self within his main characters; his symbols directly foreshadow modernism's evocation of alienated and dehumanized man in a corrupt society; and his frequent use of indirect narrative and complicated points of view developed by fictional narrators is in the mainstream of such experiments in modern fiction.

Morton Dauwen Zabel has said: "For Conrad is at basis a tragic novelist, as he is also essentially a moral and psychological realist whose profounder themes are concerned with problems of guilt and honor, with the tests of conscience and moral justice, and with the secret recriminatory and retributive processes of the human personality. . . . And while some of the richest writing comes in his descriptive and atmospheric art, his greatest powers appear when he makes the form and structure of his tales, as well as their stylistic detail and analysis, convey the processes of character, of conscience, and of moral justice."

The Portable Conrad. Includes: The Nigger of the Narcissus, The Heart of Darkness, Typhoon, Shorter Stories, Letters, Autobiographical Writings. Ed. by Morton Dauwen Zabel. *Viking* 1947 lib. ed. $6.50 pap. $3.25

Three Short Novels. The Heart of Darkness, Youth, Typhoon. *Bantam Bks.* pap. $.75

The Great Short Works of Joseph Conrad. The Nigger of the Narcissus, Youth, The Heart of Darkness, Typhoon, The Lagoon and the Secret Sharer. Introd. by Jerry Allen *Harper* Perenn. Class. pap. $.95; *Peter Smith* $4.00

Shorter Tales. 1924. *Bks. for Libraries* $14.50

STORIES AND TALES OF JOSEPH CONRAD. *Funk & Wagnalls* pap. $2.50

THREE GREAT TALES. The Nigger of the Narcissus, The Heart of Darkness and Youth. *Random* Vintage Bks. pap. $1.95

ALMAYER'S FOLLY. 1895. *Bentley* 1971 lib. bdg. $8.50; (and "An Outcast of the Islands") *Collins* New Class. $3.00; (and "The Heart of Darkness" and "The Lagoon") *Dell* pap. $.60; (and Other Stories) *New Am. Lib.* Signet pap. $.60

AN OUTCAST OF THE ISLANDS. 1896. *Assoc. Booksellers* Airmont Bks. pap. $.60; (and "Almayer's Folly") *Collins* New Class. $3.00; *Dell* pap. $.50; *New Am. Lib.* Signet 1964 pap. $.50

THE NIGGER OF THE NARCISSUS. 1897. (and "The End of the Tether") *Dell* pap. $.60; *Doubleday* $3.95; *Harper* $2.00; *Macmillan* Collier Bks. pap. $.65; (and "Typhoon" and Other Stories) *Penguin* 1964 pap. $1.35

THE LAGOON. 1898. (and "The Heart of Darkness" and "Almayer's Folly") *Dell* pap. $.60

TALES OF UNREST. 1898. *Gordon Press* $13.95

LORD JIM. 1900. *Bentley* $8.50; *Dodd* Gt. Ill. Class. 1961 $5.50; *Doubleday* 1927 $5.95; *Harper* Class. pap. $.75; ed. by R. B. Heilman *Holt* (Rinehart) 1957 $2.00; ed. by Morton D. Zabel *Houghton* Riv. Eds. 1959 pap. $1.40; *Modern Library* 1931 $2.95; ed. by Thomas Moser *Norton* Critical Eds. 1967 $6.00 pap. $1.95; *Franklin Watts* 1966 lg.-type ed. Keith Jennison Bks. $8.95

Other paperback editions are available from Amsco School Pubns., Assoc. Booksellers Airmont Bks., Bantam, Cambridge Bk. Co., Dell Laurel Leaf Lib., Lancer, Macmillan Collier Bks., New Am. Lib. Signet, Penguin, Scholastic Bk. Services, Washington Square, $.50–$1.25

YOUTH AND OTHER TALES. 1902. *Amsco School Pubns.* pap. $1.35

TYPHOON. 1902. (and Other Tales) *Dodd* Gt. Ill. Class. 1963 $5.50; (and Other Tales) *New Am. Lib.* Signet pap. $.95; (and "Nigger of the Narcissus" and Other Stories) *Penguin* pap. $1.25

THE HEART OF DARKNESS. 1902. Ed. by Robert Kimbrough *Norton* Critical Eds. 1963. $7.50 pap. $1.75; ed. by Leonard Dean, with backgrounds and criticisms *Prentice-Hall* 1960 pap. $3.95

THE HEART OF DARKNESS. (and "The End of the Tether") *Assoc. Booksellers* Airmont Bks. pap. $.60; ed. by Franklin Walker *Bantam* $.95; (and "Almayer's Folly" and "The Lagoon") *Dell* Laurel Leaf Lib. pap. $.60; (and "The End of the Tether") *Lancer* pap. $.60; (and "The Secret Sharer") *New Am. Lib.* Signet pap. $.60; (and "The Nigger of the Narcissus" and "The Secret Sharer") *Washington Square* pap. $.75 Enrich. Class. pap. $.75

THE END OF THE TETHER. 1902. (and "The Heart of Darkness") *Assoc. Booksellers* Airmont Bks. pap. $.60; (and "The Heart of Darkness") *Lancer* pap. $.60

(with Ford Madox Ford) ROMANCE. 1903. *New Am. Lib.* Signet pap. $.95

NOSTROMO. 1904. Dell pap. $.75; ed. by Robert B. Heilman *Holt* (Rinehart) pap. $2.00; introd. by Robert Penn Warren *Modern Library* 1951 pap. $1.35; *New Am. Lib.* Signet pap. $.95; *Penguin* 1964 pap. $1.95

THE SECRET AGENT. 1907. *Doubleday* Anchor Bks. pap. $1.95

UNDER WESTERN EYES. 1911. *Doubleday* Anchor Bks. pap. $1.95; *Dutton* Everyman's pap. $2.25

CHANCE. 1914. *Norton* Norton Lib. 1968 pap. $1.95

VICTORY. 1915. *Doubleday* Anchor Bks. 1959 pap. $2.50

THE SHADOW LINE. 1917. (and "Typhoon" and "The Secret Sharer") *Doubleday* Anchor Bks. pap. $1.45; *Dutton* Everyman's pap. $2.25

ARROW OF GOLD: A Story between Two Notes. 1919. *Dutton* pap. $4.65; *Norton* Norton Lib. pap. $1.95

THE RESCUE. 1920. *Norton* Norton Lib. 1968 pap. $1.95

LAST ESSAYS. 1926. *Bks. for Libraries* $9.25

CONRAD'S PREFACES TO HIS WORKS. Introd. by Edward Garnett. 1937. *Bks. for Libraries* $10.50; *Haskell* 1970 $11.95

JOSEPH CONRAD ON FICTION. Ed. by Walter F. Wright. *Univ. of Nebraska Press* 1964 $5.95 pap. $2.25

CONRAD TO A FRIEND. 150 Selected Letters to Richard Curle. Ed. by Richard Curle. 1928. *Russell & Russell* 1968 $9.00

Books about Conrad

Joseph Conrad. By Ford Madox Ford. 1924. *Octagon* 1965 $8.50. Ford was his friend and collaborator.

Joseph Conrad the Man. By Elbridge L. Adams. With "A Burial in Kent" by John S. Zelie. 1925. *Folcroft* lib. bdg. $5.00; *Haskell* 1972 lib. bdg. $7.95. "A Burial in Kent" is a description of Conrad's funeral at Canterbury.

Joseph Conrad: Achievement and Decline. By Thomas Moser. 1937. *Shoe String* 1966 $6.00 "Intelligent, thoughtful and sometimes perceptive"—(*N.Y. Times*).

The Great Tradition: A Critical Study of George Eliot, Henry James and Joseph Conrad. By F. R. Leavis. 1948 2nd ed. 1950. *New York Univ. Press* Gotham Lib. 1963 $8.95 pap. $2.45

Sea-Dreamer: A Definitive Biography of Joseph Conrad. By Georges Jean-Aubrey. Trans. by H. Sebba. 1957. *Shoe String* $9.00

Joseph Conrad at Mid-Century. By K. A. Lohf and E. P. Sheehy. *Kraus* 1957 $8.00

Conrad the Novelist. By Albert Joseph Guerard. *Harvard Univ. Press* 1958 $9.00; *Atheneum* 1967 pap. $3.95 "The best critical book on Conrad yet written"—(*N.Y. Times*).

A Reader's Guide to Joseph Conrad. By Frederick R. Karl. *Farrar, Straus* 1960 $6.50 Noonday pap. $2.25

The Art of Joseph Conrad. By Robert W. Stallman *Michigan State Univ. Press* 1960 $7.50

The Political Novels of Joseph Conrad: A Critical Study. By Eloise Knapp Hay. *Univ. of Chicago Press* 1963 $8.50

Eternal Solitary: A Study of Joseph Conrad. By Adam Gillon. *Twayne* $5.00

The Sea Years of Joseph Conrad. By Jerry Allen. *Doubleday* 1965 $1.99

Two Lives of Joseph Conrad. By Leo Gurko. *T. Y. Crowell* 1965 $3.75

Conrad: A Collection of Critical Essays. Ed. by Marvin Mudrick. Twentieth Century Views Ser. *Prentice-Hall* 1966 $5.95 pap. $1.95 "The collection is . . . an excellent one designed to acquaint the reader with some of the more basic 20th-century criticism of Conrad"—(*Choice*).

Conrad's Eastern World. By Norman Sherry. *Cambridge* 1966 $12.00

Joseph Conrad and the Fiction of Autobiography. By Edward Said. *Harvard Univ. Press* 1966 $6.00. Based on the relationship between Conrad's letters and his shorter fiction.

Joseph Conrad: A Psychoanalytic Biography. By Bernard C. Meyer, M.D. *Princeton Univ. Press* 1967 $14.50 pap. $2.95 "Dr. Meyer's book should be the standard work in this phase of Conrad scholarship"—(*LJ*).

Joseph Conrad: A Critical Biography. By J. Baines. *McGraw-Hill* 1967 pap. $2.95

Conrad's Politics: Community and Anarchy in the Fiction of Joseph Conrad. By Avrom Fleishman. *Johns Hopkins Univ. Press* 1967 $9.00

Paradise of Snakes: An Archetypal Analysis of Conrad's Political Novels. *Univ. of Chicago Press* 1967
   $6.50. An analysis of "Nostromo," "The Secret Agent" and "Under Western Eyes."
Conrad's Short Fiction. By Lawrence Graver. *Univ. of California Press* 1968 $8.50
Joseph Conrad's Fiction: A Study in Literary Growth. By John A. Palmer. *Cornell Univ. Press* 1968
   $10.00
Joseph Conrad: The Imaged Style. By Wilfred S. Dowden. *Vanderbilt Univ. Press* 1970 $6.50. Traces
   Conrad's use of imagery in the major works as well as some of the shorter fiction.
The Vision of Melville and Conrad: A Comparative Study. By Leon F. Seltzer. *Ohio Univ. Press* 1970
   $6.50
Conrad's Models of Mind. By Bruce Johnson. *Univ. of Minnesota Press* 1971 $9.00. "The author ana-
   lyzes a number of Conrad's works, explaining Conrad's changing conceptions or models of mind, the
   psychological assumptions which lie behind the creation of fiction"—(Publisher's catalog).
Metaphysics of Darkness: A Study in the Unity and Development of Conrad's Fiction. By Royal Roussel.
   Johns Hopkins Univ. Press 1971 $8.00
Joseph Conrad: An Annotated Bibliography of Writings about Him. Ed. by Bruce E. Teets and Helmut
   E. Gerber. *Northern Illinois Univ. Press* 1971 $20.00
Conrad: The Critical Heritage. Ed. by Norman Sherry. *Routledge & Kegan Paul* 1973 $19.95

GISSING, GEORGE (ROBERT). 1857–1903.

   Recent years have seen a renewed interest in Gissing, almost all of whose novels are now available in reprints. A bridge between late Victorianism and early modernism, Gissing's novels combine two essential
themes of the period, the isolation and struggle of the artist and the economic bondage of the proletariat.
"New Grub Street" and his own indirect autobiography, "The Private Papers of Henry Ryecroft," reveal the
close connections in Gissing between fiction and autobiography, and "Workers in the Dawn" and "Demos:
A Story of English Socialism" dramatize Gissing's conviction that economic and class divisions are central to
human character and individual destiny.

WORKERS IN THE DAWN. 1880. *AMS Press* 3 vols. in 1 $30.00

THYRZA: A Tale. 1887. *AMS Press* 3 vols in 1 $30.00

LIFE'S MORNING. 1888. *AMS Press* 3 vols in 1 $30.00

THE EMANCIPATED. 1890. *AMS Press* 3 vols. in 1 $30.00

NEW GRUB STREET. 1891. Ed. by Irving Howe *Houghton* Riv. Eds. pap. $1.45; ed. by
   Bernard Bergonzi *Penguin* 1968 pap. $1.25; ed. by Bergonzi *Peter Smith* $3.50

DEMOS: A Story of English Socialism. 1892. With a new introd. by Jacob Korg *AMS
   Press* $10.00

BORN IN EXILE. 1892. *AMS Press* 3 vols. in 1 $30.00

THE ODD WOMEN. 1893. *AMS Press* 3 vols. in 1 $30.00; *Norton* Norton Lib. 1970
   pap. $1.95

IN THE YEAR OF JUBILEE. 1894. *AMS Press* $12.50

EVE'S RANSOM. 1895. *AMS Press* $10.00

THE PAYING GUEST. 1895. *AMS Press* $8.00

THE UNCLASSED. 1896. *AMS Press* $8.00; *Somerset Pub.* $7.50

THE TOWN TRAVELLER. 1898. *AMS Press* $10.00

CHARLES DICKENS: A CRITICAL STUDY. 1898. (With title "Critical Studies of Charles
   Dickens") ed. by Temple Scott. 1924. *Haskell* $7.95; *Scholarly Press* repr. of 1898
   ed. 1972 $19.50

THE CROWN OF LIFE. 1899. *AMS Press* $10.00

OUR FRIEND THE CHARLATAN. 1901. *AMS Press* $10.00

By the Ionian Sea. 1901. *Dufour* 1956 $3.00. His impressions and experiences in Italy.

The Private Papers of Henry Ryecroft. 1903. *Dutton* Everyman's 1964 $3.50

Veranilda: A Romance. 1904. *AMS Press* $12.50

Will Warburton: A Romance of Real Life. 1905. *AMS Press* $10.00

The House of Cobwebs and Other Stories. To which is prefixed "The Work of George Gissing, an Introductory Survey" by Thomas Seccombe. 1906. *AMS Press* $12.00; *Bks. for Libraries* $11.50

A Victim of Circumstances and Other Stories. 1927. *Bks. for Libraries* $10.50

Autobiographical Notes. With Comments on Tennyson and Huxley. 1930. *Gordon Press* $10.00

George Gissing's Commonplace Book. Ed. by Jacob Korg. A manuscript in the Berg Collection of the New York Public Library. *N.Y. Public Lib.* 1962 $3.00

Letters of George Gissing to Members of His Family. Collected and arranged by Algernon and Ellen Gissing. 1927. *Haskell* 1970 lib. bdg. $14.95; *Scholarly Press* $19.95

George Gissing and H. G. Wells: A Record of Their Friendship and Correspondence. Ed. by Royal A. Gettmann. *Univ. of Illinois Press* 1961 $4.95

The Letters of George Gissing to Eduard Bertz, 1887–1903. Ed. by Arthur C. Young. *Rutgers Univ. Press* 1961 $6.00

The Letters of George Gissing to Gabrielle Fleury. 1898–1902. Ed. by Pierre Coustillas. *N.Y. Public Lib.* 1965 $6.50 pap. $5.00

"The letters, now in the Berg Collection of the New York Public Library, cover the period from June 23, 1898 (Gissing's first mention of Gabrielle Fleury, the only woman with whom he found both emotional and intellectual fulfillment—and domestic peace) to May 12, 1902."—(*Choice*).

Books about Gissing

George Gissing. By Frank Swinnerton. 1923. *Kennikat* rev. ed. 1966 $7.50
George Gissing. A Critical Biography. By Jacob Korg. *Univ. of Washington Press* 1963 $6.75
Collected Articles on George Gissing. Ed. by Pierre Coustillas. *Barnes & Noble* 1968 $7.50
Gissing East and West. By Shigeru Koike, Glichi Kamo, C. C. Kohler, and Pierre Coustillas. *Enitharmon Press* 1970 $5.00
Gissing: The Critical Heritage. Ed. by Pierre Coustillas and Colin Partridge. *Routledge & Kegan Paul* 1972 $25.00. Contemporary and near-contemporary criticisms and comments.

DOYLE, SIR ARTHUR CONAN. 1859–1930.

In Sherlock Holmes, Conan Doyle created one of the most famous characters in popular fiction. The well-known detective appears in four novels ("A Study in Scarlet," "The Sign of Four," "The Hound of the Baskervilles" and "His Last Bow"), and 56 short stories (contained in "The Adventures of Sherlock Holmes," "The Memoirs of Sherlock Holmes," "The Return of Sherlock Holmes" and "The Case-Book of Sherlock Holmes"). Holmes fans might continue their research in two volumes, both by Vincent Starrett: "The Private Life of Sherlock Holmes" (1933. *AMS Press* $10.00; *Haskell* $10.95) and "221B: Studies in Sherlock Holmes" (1940. *Biblo & Tannen* $10.00). Sir Arthur's son, Adrian, and John Dickson Carr have written "The Exploits of Sherlock Holmes" (1954. *Bks. for Libraries* $11.75). Doyle also won great success with his historical novels. "The White Company," a tale of the War of the Roses, is his masterpiece. In his last years Sir Arthur wrote several books on spiritualism.

The Sherlock Holmes books:

The Complete Sherlock Holmes. *Doubleday* 1952 $8.95 1953 2 vols. $12.50

THE ANNOTATED SHERLOCK HOLMES. Ed. with introd., notes and bibliography by William S. Baring-Gould. *Clarkson Potter* 1967 2 vols. boxed $25.00. The 4 novels and 56 stories complete.

A TREASURY OF SHERLOCK HOLMES. Ed. by Adrian Conan Doyle. *Doubleday* 1955 $4.95

THE ADVENTURES AND MEMOIRS OF SHERLOCK HOLMES. *Modern Library* $2.95

SHERLOCK HOLMES: Selected Stories. Ed. by Charles Verral *Golden Press* $1.00; introd. by S. C. Roberts *Oxford* World's Class. $2.75

THE BEST OF SHERLOCK HOLMES. *Grosset* $2.95

COMPLETE PROFESSOR CHALLENGER STORIES. *Transatlantic* $9.50

THE CONAN DOYLE STORIES. *Transatlantic* $9.50

GREAT STORIES. Ed. by John D. Carr. *British Bk. Centre* 1959 $4.50; *Dell* pap. $.50

FAMOUS TALES OF SHERLOCK HOLMES. *Dodd* Gt. Ill. Class. $5.50

TALES OF SHERLOCK HOLMES. *Macmillan* 1963 $5.95

THE ADVENTURES OF SHERLOCK HOLMES. 1891. *Assoc. Booksellers* Airmont Bks. pap. $.60; *Berkley* pap. $.75; *Harper* 1891 $4.95 lib. bdg. $4.79; *Macmillan* Collier Bks. pap. $.65

THE MEMOIRS OF SHERLOCK HOLMES. 1894. *Berkley* pap. $.75; *Penguin* pap. $1.25

THE HOUND OF THE BASKERVILLES. 1902. *Assoc. Booksellers* Airmont Bks. pap. $.50; *Berkley* pap. $.60; *Dell* pap. $.50; *Dodd* Gt. Ill. Class. $5.50; *Macmillan* Collier Bks. pap. $.65; *Regnery* Gateway Eds. 1959 pap. $.95; *Scholastic Bk. Services* pap. $.75

THE RETURN OF SHERLOCK HOLMES. 1905. *Berkley* pap. $.60

HIS LAST BOW. 1917. *Berkley* pap. $.60

THE CASE BOOK OF SHERLOCK HOLMES. 1927. *Berkley* pap. $.60

Historical novels:

HISTORICAL ROMANCES. 1931. *Transatlantic* $9.50

MICAH CLARK. 1888. *Transatlantic* 1960 $5.25

THE REFUGEES: A Tale of Two Continents. 1891. *Transatlantic* 1960 $5.25

THE WHITE COMPANY. 1891. *Transatlantic* $5.25. The best of his historical novels.

RODNEY STONE. 1896. *Transatlantic* 1960 $5.25

Books about Conan Doyle

The Life of Sir Arthur Conan Doyle. By John Dickson Carr. 1949. *Harper* 1949 $7.95

Sherlock Holmes, Esq. and John H. Watson, M.D.: An Encyclopaedia of Their Affairs. By Orlando Park. *Northwestern Univ. Press* 1962 $10.00

Sherlock Holmes in Portrait and Profile. By Walter Klinefelter. *Syracuse Univ. Press* 1963 $5.50

The Man Who Was Sherlock Holmes. By Michael and Mollie Hardwick. *Doubleday* 1964 $3.50
"Michael and Mollie Hardwick have performed the detective game of tracing various facets of the character and skill of the greatest detective back to the source in the life and interests of his creator"—(*LJ*).

The Real Sherlock Holmes: Arthur Conan Doyle. By Mary Hoehling. *Messner* 1965 $3.50 lib. bdg. $3.34

"An excitingly 'whole' portrait of Conan Doyle as man and writer. . . . She brings her subject to life as a charming, understandable person"—(*LJ*).
Conan Doyle. By P. Nordon. *Holt* 1967 $7.95
"No work about him has been more readable and thoughtful and as generally satisfying"—(*LJ*).
The Late Mr. Sherlock Holmes and Other Literary Studies. By Trevor H. Hall. *St. Martin's* 1972 $7.50

BARRIE, SIR J(AMES) M(ATTHEW). 1860–1937.

Barrie achieved success with both plays and fiction. His novels of homely Scottish life, with their blended pathos and humor, made Scots dialect stories popular. The publication of "The Little Minister" established him as a successful novelist, and its dramatization started his career as a successful playwright.

In "The Little White Bird," a collection of fanciful reveries over "dream children," was a half-elfin child called Peter Pan. From this character came Barrie's most popular success in 1904. "Peter Pan," a play for children. Children's editions of the story are published by *Grosset, Hale, Random* and *Scribner*. "Margaret Ogilvy" (1896. *Scholarly Press* $8.50) is the story-life of Barrie's mother, a bit of true fiction. His autobiography, "The Greenwood Hat" (1938) and his "Letters" (ed. by Viola Meynell 1947) are o.p.

WORKS. 19 vols. Peter Pan ed. 1929–31. *AMS Press* each $19.50 set $350.00

AULD LICHT IDYLLS. (1886) and BETTER DEAD (1896). *Bks. for Libraries* $8.50 (and Other Sketches) $8.00

A WINDOW IN THRUMS. 1889. *Scholarly Press* repr. of 1896 ed. $12.50

THE LITTLE MINISTER. 1891. *Assoc. Booksellers* Airmont Bks. pap. $.75; *Grosset* $2.95; dramatized by Roland Fernand *Dramatic* 1945 $1.00

THE TILLYLOSS SCANDAL. 1893. *Bks. for Libraries* $8.00

SENTIMENTAL TOMMY. 1896 *Scribner* 1918 $5.95

PETER PAN. 1904. *Grosset* $2.95 lib. bdg. $2.18 Thrushwood Bks. $2.95 Silver Dollar Lib. $1.00 Tempo Bks. pap. $.60; ill. by Richard Kennedy *Penguin* Puffin Bks. pap. $1.25; abr. and adapted by Josette Frank *Random* $1.95; ed. by Eleanor Graham with ills. by Nora Unwin *Scribner* 1950 $3.95 lib. bdg. $3.63 pap. $1.95

PETER PAN (dramatization). *Baker* $1.25; *French* $1.75; with an essay by the author *Scribner* $3.50

PETER PAN IN KENSINGTON GARDENS. 1906. Retold by May Byron with the approval of the author; ill. by Arthur Rackham. *Scribner* 1930 $3.50

PETER PAN AND WENDY. 1911. *Scribner* $10.00

Books about Barrie

Barrie: The Story of J. M. B. By Denis G. Mackail. 1941. *Bks. for Libraries* $23.75; *Richard West* $23.00
Sir James M. Barrie: A Bibliography with Full Collations of the American Unauthorized Editions. By Bradley D. Cutler. 1931. *Burt Franklin* $18.50
J. M. Barrie. By Roger Lancelyn Green. *Walck* 1961 $2.75. A critical account in monograph form of the life and works of this author and playwright.
James Barrie. By Harry M. Geduld. English Authors Sers. *Twayne* $5.50
J. M. Barrie: The man behind the Image. By Janet Dunbar. *Houghton* 1970 $8.95

KIPLING, RUDYARD. 1865–1936. (Nobel Prize 1907)

Born of English parents in Bombay, Kipling as a child knew Hindustani better than English. He lived there until he was six and then spent an unhappy period of exile from his parents (and the Indian heat) with a harsh aunt in England. This was followed by the "public" schooling which inspired his "Stalky" stories. He returned to India at 18 to work for a while on the staff of the Lahore *Civil and Military Gazette* and rapidly became a prolific writer.

Short stories form the greater portion of Kipling's work and are of several distinct types. Some of his best are stories of the supernatural, the eerie and unearthly, such as "The Phantom Rickshaw," "The Brushwood

Boy," "They." His tales of gruesome horror include "The Mark of the Beast" and "The Return of Imray." "William the Conqueror," and "The Head of the District" are among his political tales of English rule in India. The "Soldiers Three" group deal with Kipling's Three Musketeers—an Irishman, a Cockney and a Yorkshireman. The Anglo-Indian Tales, of social life in Simla, make up the larger part of his first four books.

Kipling wrote equally well for children ("Just So Stories," "The Jungle Books," "Mowgli," "Kim") and adults. Some critics, like George Orwell and Lionel Trilling, have dismissed him from serious consideration; others, such as T. S. Eliot and Bonamy Dobrée, have affirmed his genius. Edmund Wilson, in "The Wound and the Bow" (q. v.), sees his great failing as an artist in the fact that, though he sometimes appeared to be torn between two cultures, he avoided significant dramatic conflict (which would have brought his work stature) by ending up, predictably, on the side of authority. His short stories—though their understanding of the Indian is often moving—become minor hymns to the glory of Queen Victoria's Empire and the civil servants and soldiers who manned her outposts. "Kim," an Irish boy in India who becomes the companion of a Tibetan lama, at length joins the British Secret Service, without, says Wilson, any sense of the betrayal of his friend this actually meant. Nevertheless, Kipling has left us a vivid panorama of the India of his day.

The chronology of Kipling's books is important in that his earlier works are his best. "Something of Myself," his autobiography (1937), is o.p., as are two volumes of letters, "From Sea to Sea" (1907) and "Letters of Travel: 1892–1913" (1920).

THE COLLECTED WORKS. The Burwash ed. 1941. *AMS Press* 28 vols. $745.00

MAUGHAM'S CHOICE OF KIPLING'S BEST. Ed. by W. Somerset Maugham. *Doubleday* 1953 $5.50

THE BEST SHORT STORIES OF RUDYARD KIPLING. Ed. by Randall Jarrell. *Doubleday* 1961 $7.95

ALL THE MOWGLI STORIES. 1936. Ill. by Kurt Wiese. *Doubleday* 1936 $4.50

KIPLING: A SELECTION OF HIS STORIES AND POEMS. Ed. by John Beecroft. *Doubleday* 1956 2 vols. $10.95

IN THE VERNACULAR: The English in India. Ed. by Randall Jarrell *Peter Smith* $4.75

KIPLING STORIES. *Platt* 1960 $3.50 lib. bdg. $3.79

THE MARK OF THE BEAST AND OTHER STORIES. *New Am. Lib.* Signet 1964 pap. $.50

TWO TALES. The Man Who Would Be King and Without Benefit of Clergy. *Branden* pap. $.85

THE LIGHT THAT FAILED. 1890. A novel. *Assoc. Booksellers* Airmont Bks. pap. $.75; *Doubleday* 1936 $3.95

THE COURTING OF DINAH SHADD AND OTHER STORIES. 1890. *Bks. for Libraries* $8.00

THE JUNGLE BOOK. 1894–95. Ill. by J. L. Kipling, W. H. Drake and P. Frenzeny *Doubleday* $3.50 ill. by Philip Hays $4.95; *Grosset* 1950 Companion Lib. $1.25 Ill. Jr. Lib. pap. $2.95 special ed. $3.95 lib. bdg. $3.79 ill. by Fritz Eichenberg deluxe ed. $4.95 Tempo Bks. pap. $.50

THE SECOND JUNGLE BOOK. 1895. *Doubleday* 1923 $4.50

THE JUNGLE BOOKS. *Assoc. Booksellers* Airmont Bks. pap. $.60; *Bks. for Libraries* repr. of 1895 ed. 2 vols. in 1 $18.75; *Lancer* pap. $.60; *Macmillan* 1964 $3.95; *New Am. Lib.* Signet pap. $.50; *Franklin Watts* lg.-type ed. Keith Jennison Bks. $7.95

MULVANEY STORIES. 1897. *Bks. for Libraries* $9.00

THE SEVEN SEAS. 1897. *Milford House* lib. bdg. $20.00

CAPTAINS COURAGEOUS. 1897. Ill. by William Dempster *Childrens Press* 1969 $4.50; *Doubleday* 1953 $3.95; *Grosset* Thrushwood Bks. 1954 $2.95; *Lothrop* (dist. by Morrow) $4.00; *Franklin Watts* 1966 lg.-type ed. Keith Jennison Bks. $7.95

Other paperback editions are available from Assoc. Booksellers Airmont Bks., Bantam, Lancer, New Am. Lib. Signet, Scholastic Bk. Services, Washington Square

THE DAY'S WORK. 1898. *Bks. for Libraries* $15.00

SOLDIER STORIES. 1899. *Bks. for Libraries* $8.50

STALKY & CO. 1899. *Dell* pap. $.60; *Macmillan* Collier Bks. pap. $.60

KIM. 1901. Introd. by F. R. Gemme *Assoc. Booksellers* Airmont Bks. pap. $.65; *Dell* Laurel Leaf Lib. pap. $.50; *Dodd* Gt. Ill. Class. 1962 $3.95; *Doubleday* $4.50; *Lancer* pap. $.75; introd. by A. L. Rowse *Macmillan* Collier Bks. pap. $.65; *Pyramid Bks.* pap. $.50

JUST SO STORIES. 1902. *Assoc. Booksellers* Airmont Bks. pap. $.60; *Doubleday* 1952 $3.50 1946 $4.50 (with title "New Illustrated Just So Stories") $4.95; *Grosset* 1957 Companion Lib. $1.25; *Lancer* pap. $.75; *Schocken* 1965 $4.50 pap. $1.75; *Franklin Watts* lg.-type ed. Keith Jennison Bks. $7.95

PUCK OF POOK'S HILL 1906. *Dover* 1968 pap. $2.50; *Peter Smith* $4.00

Books about Kipling

Bibliography of the Works of Rudyard Kipling. By Flora V. Livingston. 1927. suppl. 1939. *Johnson Reprint* $25.00; *Burt Franklin* 2 vols. $35.00

The Art of Rudyard Kipling. By J. M. S. Tompkins. 1960. *Barnes & Noble* $4.00; *Peter Smith* $4.00; *Univ. of Nebraska Press* Bison Bks. 1966 pap. $1.90

Kipling's Mind and Art: Selected Critical Essays. Ed. by Andrew Rutherford. *Standord Univ. Press* 1964 $7.50 pap. $2.65

A collection of 11 essays by English and American scholars who agree "that Kipling has been too easily dismissed. . . . These essays do examine Kipling's weaknesses, but they also note his achievements"— (*L J*).

Kipling and the Critics. Ed. by Elliot Gilbert. *New York Univ. Press* 1965 $6.95 pap. $1.95

"Three critical approaches to Kipling—the attack, the defense, and the objective analysis—are represented"—(*Choice*).

Rudyard Kipling. By J. I. M. Stewart *Dodd* 1966 $5.00; *Apollo* pap. $1.95

Rudyard Kipling: Realist and Fabulist. By Bonamy Dobrée. *Oxford* 1967 $8.00. A study of Kipling's work by an eminent critic, who rallies to his defense as a writer "grotesquely misunderstood" and "misrepresented." The first part of the book deals with Kipling's philosophy, milieu and prose writing, the second part with his poetry.

Kipling in India. By Louis L. Cornell. *Macmillan* 1967 $6.95

Rudyard Kipling's India. By K. Bhaskara Rao. *Univ. of Oklahoma Press* 1967 $5.95. A critical view of Kipling's political and racial attitudes (as expressed in his work) which Dr. Rao, an Indian now living in the United States, regards as having strengthened the reactionary forces of British imperialism.

A Kipling Dictionary. By W. Arthur Young and John H. McGivering. 1968. *Burt Franklin* $16.50; *Gordon Press* $11.00

"[Young's outdated *Dictionary*] recoreded some six hundred and thirty titles; Kipling's post-1911 literary output has enabled the present compiler to bring the number up to just under a thousand."—(*L J*).

The Good Kipling. By Elliot L. Gilbert. *Ohio Univ. Press* 1971 $7.50

Kipling: The Critical Heritage. By Roger L. Green. *Barnes & Noble* 1971 $15.00. Contemporary and near-contemporary criticisms, reviews, comments, etc.

—*F.K.*

Chapter 12

Modern British Fiction

"No English novelist is as great as Tolstoy—that is to say has given so complete a picture of man's life, both on its domestic and heroic side. No English novelist has explored man's soul as deeply as Dostoevsky. And no novelist anywhere has analysed the modern consciousness as successfully as Marcel Proust. Before these triumphs we must pause. English poetry fears no one—excels in quality as well as quantity. But English fiction is less triumphant: it does not contain the best stuff yet written, and if we deny this we become guilty of provincialism."
—E. M. FORSTER, *"Aspects of the Novel"*

To E. M. Forster, writing in 1927, a favorable comparison between English novelists and writers like Tolstoy, Dostoevsky, or Proust seemed like provincialism. Certainly the writers he mentions have few equals; but Forster's remarks indicate that he was only partially aware of the greatness of the writers who were his contemporaries.

Forster's modest appraisal of the accomplishments of his compatriots illustrates the difficulty of attempting, even in the most sensible and well-informed manner, to judge the art of one's contemporaries accurately. In dealing with the writers of our own time it is almost impossible to avoid praising mediocrity or ignoring greatness; the objects closest to us are the ones most difficult to focus on. And this perhaps is why Forster, five years after the publication of Joyce's "Ulysses," assumed that no novelist could rival Proust in analyzing the modern consciousness.

Forster's remarks came at the end of an unusually productive period in British fiction. In the 25 or 30 years prior to the publication of his comments, outstanding novels were published by realists like Arnold Bennett and John Galsworthy; by masters of psychological symbolism like Joseph Conrad and D. H. Lawrence; by social observers like Henry James and Ford Madox Ford; and by experimental innovators like James Joyce and Virginia Woolf. And E. M. Forster himself contributed to the lopsided number of masterpieces produced in this era: though he lived until 1970, his last great work, "A Passage to India," had been completed in 1924.

The best British novelists of the next generation, of the 1930s and 1940s, were writers like Evelyn Waugh, Aldous Huxley, George Orwell, and Anthony Powell. All of them are noted for their skill in writing social commentary or satire—and satire, of course, is a form of social commentary. Since they worked in turbulent times, it is natural enough to find these novelists preoccupied with social questions; and the turbulence may explain a decline both in the productivity and variety of English fiction in this period.

After the Second World War enough similarities appeared among the new novelists to make generalizations about the state of fiction possible once again. At one point the phrase "Angry Young Men" was very much in vogue; and when the writers in question protested that they were not really very angry, their protest was taken as a sign that they were. But what many of these newer novelists did seem to have in common—unlike some of their American or French counterparts—was a fictional style that ignored almost entirely the experimental writing of the early decades of the century.

Novelists like Angus Wilson, C. P. Snow, Kingsley Amis, John Braine, Alan Sillitoe, Iris Murdoch, and Doris Lessing have for the most part returned to the traditional naturalism of the Victorian or the Edwardian novel. Few of these writers use devices like symbolism, stream of consciousness, or try to develop new techniques of their own; their main interest is in storytelling.

The British writers who are most interested in experiment, Samuel Beckett, Lawrence Durrell, and Anthony Burgess, have all (for whatever reasons) gone to live abroad. Some interesting novels have been produced in this period, many of them by religious writers like Graham Greene, Muriel Spark, and William Golding. On the whole, however, English fiction today does not seem very exciting. But of course this state of affairs is perhaps an illusion; we may, like Forster in 1927, be guilty of underestimating the quality of the newest writers.

The quality and variety of the fiction of the early part of the century may be a reason why there are so many good studies of individual writers and so few good literary histories of the period as a whole. One of the best books that covers the entire era is William York Tindall's "Forces in Modern British Literature." Tindall avoids the tedium and disorder of a chronological approach; he divides the writers into groups according to their techniques and subject matter. Tindall's book is well-written, comprehensive, and informative.

A good general survey of recent British fiction is to be found in Walter Allen's "The Modern Novel"; Allen is one of the best-known British critics of modern fiction. David Daiches is another prominent British critic; his study, "The Present Age in British Literature," contains valuable essays on the writers of the first half of the century together with individual bibliographies for most of the writers he discusses. Boris Ford's "The Modern Age," a *Penguin* paperback, provides a good low-cost introduction to the period.

James Hall's "The Tragic Comedians" is an interesting study of the writers before World War II; Hall deals mainly with the satirists of the Waugh-Huxley generation. F. R. Karl's "A Reader's Guide to the Contemporary Novel" has chapters on many of the writers of the prewar era as well as on a few prominent writers who came later.

"Postwar British Fiction," by James Ginden, is a sensible study of the most recent British novelists, with chapters on most of the writers who became prominent after the war. Rubin Rabinovitz, in "The Reaction against Experiment," analyzes the return to traditional styles among these novelists, with individual chapters on Snow, Amis, and Angus Wilson. Anthony Burgess, one of the best of the recent novelists, provides a very broad survey of contemporary fiction in "The Novel Now."

One can get a good sense of what's happening at the moment in English fiction from the book pages of the London Sunday papers, like the *Observer* or the *Sunday Times*. The *Times Literary Supplement* is thorough but a bit stodgy when it comes to the most recent writers. Some of the American quarterlies that deal with recent British fiction are *Contemporary Literature*, *Modern Fiction Studies*, and *Critique*. A good bibliographic source for journal articles on recent British fiction is the annual bibliography published by the Modern Language Association.

HISTORY AND CRITICISM

Aldridge, John W., Ed. CRITIQUES AND ESSAYS ON MODERN FICTION, 1920–1951; representing the achievement of modern American and British critics; with a fwd. by Mark Schorer. *Ronald* 1952 $8.50

> TIME TO MURDER AND CREATE: THE CONTEMPORARY NOVEL IN CRISIS. 1960 *Bks. for Libraries* $11.50. *For comment, see Chapter 14, Modern American Fiction: Historical Studies and Critical Works.*

Allen, Walter E. THE ENGLISH NOVEL: A Short Critical History. *Dutton* 1955 $6.95 Everyman's 1957 pap. $1.95. A British author and critic has made a satisfying and useful study extending from the work of the late 17th century through that of Joyce and Lawrence.

THE MODERN NOVEL. *Dutton* 1964 pap. $1.95. An examination of modern British and American fiction.

Baker, Ernest Albert. A HISTORY OF THE ENGLISH NOVEL. Complete in 11 vols. Vol. 9 The Day Before Yesterday (George Moore, Hardy, Henry James, etc.) (1938 1960) Vol. 10 Yesterday (Conrad, Kipling, Bennett, Lawrence, etc.) (1936 1960) Vol. 11 Yesterday and After by Lionel Stevenson (1967). *Barnes & Noble* 1929–39 Vols. 9–10 each $6.50 Vol. 11 $10.00

Beach, Joseph Warren. THE TWENTIETH CENTURY NOVEL: Studies in Technique. *Appleton* 1932 $10.50

Bergonzi, Bernard. HEROES' TWILIGHT: A Study of the Literature of the Great War. *Coward* 1966 $5.00

This "brief study of selected British writers of the First World War [provides] a brilliant analysis of the poetry and prose of the time"—(*LJ*).

THE SITUATION OF THE NOVEL. *Univ. of Pittsburgh Press* 1970 $6.95. Bergonzi's subject is the very recent English novel; he centers on writers like Waugh, Powell, Snow, Amis, and Angus Wilson in his discussion.

Brewster, Dorothy, and John Angus Burrell. MODERN WORLD FICTION. *Littlefield, Adams* 1951 pap. $1.50

Burgess, Anthony. THE NOVEL NOW: A Guide to Contemporary Fiction. *Norton* 1967. $5.95; *Pegasus* pap. $2.25. A survey of modern fiction by an accomplished novelist.

Chew, Samuel C. A LITERARY HISTORY OF ENGLAND, VOL. 4 The Nineteenth Century and After, 1789–1939. *Meredith* (Appleton) 2nd ed. pap. $6.25. *For complete information, see Chapter 3, Reference Books: Histories and Dictionaries of Literature, under Baugh.*

Cross, Wilbur Lucius. FOUR CONTEMPORARY NOVELISTS. 1930. *AMS Press* 1971 $5.50; *Bks. for Libraries* 1966 $9.50. Joseph Conrad, Arnold Bennett, John Galsworthy, H. G. Wells.

Daiches, David. THE NOVEL AND THE MODERN WORLD. *Univ. of Chicago Press* 1939 rev. ed. 1960 $5.95 Phoenix Bks. pap. $1.95. Galsworthy, Conrad, Mansfield, Joyce, Woolf, Huxley.

THE PRESENT AGE IN BRITISH LITERATURE. *Indiana Univ. Press* 1958 $8.50 Midland Bks. pap. $2.25. A good survey of the literature of the first half of the century with bibliographies for important writers.

Dobrée, Bonamy, Gen. Ed. BRITISH WRITERS AND THEIR WORK No. 3: Virginia Woolf, by Bernard Blackstone; E. M. Forster, by Rex Warner; Katherine Mansfield, by Ian Gordon. *Univ. of Nebraska Press* 1964 $1.60

Dutton, Geoffrey, Ed. THE LITERATURE OF AUSTRALIA: History and Criticism. *Peter Smith* $4.50

Edel, Leon J. THE MODERN PSYCHOLOGICAL NOVEL. 1955. *Peter Smith* $5.00. Originally published in 1955 under the title "The Psychological Novel, 1900–1950," this book is a brilliant analysis of the "stream of consciousness" technique in the works of Joyce, Proust, Virginia Woolf, Dorothy Richardson and Faulkner.

Eglington, John. IRISH LITERARY PORTRAITS. 1935. *Bks. for Libraries* $7.50

Ford, Boris, Ed. PELICAN GUIDE TO ENGLISH LITERATURE. Vol. 7 The Modern Age. *Penguin* rev. ed. 1963 pap. $1.65

Forster, E. M. ASPECTS OF THE NOVEL. *Harcourt* 1927 1947 $6.50 Harvest Bks. pap. $1.45. An important study of the aesthetics of fiction, where Forster introduces his idea of "flat" and "round" characters.

Friedman, Alan. TURN OF THE NOVEL. *Oxford* 1966 $6.95 pap. $1.95. An examination of modernism in 20th-century fiction by a critic who is also a highly acclaimed novelist.

Gindin, James. HARVEST OF A QUIET EYE: The Novel of Compassion. *Indiana Univ. Press* 1971 $13.95. Gindin discusses compassion in the works of Bennett, Forster, Woolf, Lawrence, Joyce, Cary, and Angus Wilson; his study also includes a number of Victorian and American writers.

Gogarty, Oliver St. John. AS I WAS GOING DOWN SACKVILLE STREET. 1937 *Harcourt* Harvest Bks. 1967 $2.25. The memoirs of Dr. Gogarty, the Irish poet and playwright, who was Joyce's model for Buck Mulligan in "Ulysses."

Green, H. M. AUSTRALIAN LITERATURE, 1900–1950: History and Criticism. 1964. *Int. Scholarly Bk. Services* (Melbourne Univ. Press) pap. $1.05

Greenblatt, Stephen Jay. THREE MODERN SATIRISTS: Waugh, Orwell, and Huxley. *Yale Univ. Press* 1965 $6.50

"A lively introduction to modern satire"—(*LJ*).

Greene, Graham. THE LOST CHILDHOOD AND OTHER ESSAYS. *Viking* Compass Bks. 1952 pap. $1.25. Excellent critical essays, mostly on contemporaries.

Haines, Helen E. WHAT'S IN A NOVEL. *Columbia* 1942 $10.00. The standard guide from mid-Victorian to modern times; critical evaluations.

Hall, James. THE LUNATIC GIANT IN THE DRAWING ROOM: The British and American Novel since 1930. *Indiana Univ. Press* 1968 $6.95. Among the British authors Hall discusses are Elizabeth Bowen, Graham Greene, and Iris Murdoch.

THE TRAGIC COMEDIANS. Seven Modern British Novelists. *Indiana Univ. Press* 1963 $5.95. Professor Hall has written "a sharp, bright, and thoughtful critique of the modern British comic novel as exemplified in E. M. Forster, Aldous Huxley, Evelyn Waugh, Henry Green, Joyce Cary, L. P. Hartley, and Anthony Powell." In his fine, well-written book, he points out "similarities and differences in content, style, and technique and comments on such other contemporary novelists as Amis, Braine, Wain, and Sillitoe."

Hope, A. D. AUSTRALIAN LITERATURE, 1950–1962. *Int. Scholarly Bk. Services* (Melbourne Univ. Press) pap. $1.05

Howe, Irving. POLITICS AND THE NOVEL. 1957. *Avon* pap. $1.65; *Bks. for Libraries* $11.25. "An intelligent, penetrating, lucid, graceful, persuasive and altogether splendid book."

Humphrey, Robert. STREAM OF CONSCIOUSNESS IN THE MODERN NOVEL. *Univ. of California Press* 1954, 1959, 1962 pap. $1.85. A rewarding discussion of methods and devices as used by Joyce, Faulkner, Virginia Woolf and Dorothy Richardson.

Hyde, Douglas. A LITERARY HISTORY OF IRELAND. *Barnes & Noble* 1967 $11.50

Kain, Richard M. Dublin in the Age of William Butler Yeats and James Joyce. *Univ. of Oklahoma Press* 1962 $3.50

Karl, Frederick R. A Reader's Guide to the Contemporary Novel. *Farrar, Straus* 1963 rev. ed. 1972 $10.00 Noonday pap. $2.95. This comprehensive and valuable study attempts to define and evaluate the main movements in the English novel since Joyce. Dr. Karl devotes separate chapters to each of the following: C. P. Snow, Beckett, Ivy Compton-Burnett, Graham Greene, Lawrence Durrell, Elizabeth Bowen, Evelyn Waugh, Orwell, Henry Green and Joyce Cary. The "Angries" and others are handled in the last three chapters.

(with Marvin Magalaner) A Reader's Guide to Great Twentieth Century English Novels. *Farrar, Straus* 1959 $10.50 Noonday pap. $2.95. An examination of the works of Conrad, Forster, Woolf, Lawrence, Joyce and Huxley.

Kazin, Alfred. Contemporaries. *Little-Atlantic* 1962 $10.00 pap. $2.65. Many of these essays, originally published as book reviews, cover modern British novelists. Written with clarity and originality, the views expressed are intensely personal and penetrating.

Kenner, Hugh. Gnomon: Essays in Contemporary Literature. *Astor-Honor* 1958 $6.95 pap. $1.95

Kermode, Frank. Puzzles and Epiphanies: Essays and Reviews, 1958–1961. *Chilmark Press* $4.95. This collection of 24 book reviews and essays focuses principally on a group of modern critics and novelists. His "brilliance as a reviewer lies in his ability to distill the essence of a work and relate it to the broader currents of its period and to literature as a whole."

Kettle, Arnold. Introduction to the English Novel. Vol. 2 Henry James to the Present. 1953. *Hillary House* (Hutchinson Univ. Lib.) rev. ed. 1968 $5.50. Studies of Butler, Hardy, Joyce, Forster, Huxley, Cary and Greene.

Klinck, Carl, Ed. A Literary History of Canada: Canadian Literature in English. *Univ. of Toronto Press* 1965 $20.00

"This book performs a rare and valuable service: it relates literature to the culture and the history of the land. . . . Never mind the price! it's worth it"—(*LJ*).

Kostelanetz, Richard. On Contemporary Literature: An Anthology of Critical Essays on the Major Movements and Writers of Contemporary Literature. *Avon Bks.* 1964 pap. $1.95; *Bks. for Libraries*, $20.00. Contains sections on British and Canadian writing and on authors Anthony Burgess, Lawrence Durrell, William Golding, Doris Lessing, Malcolm Lowry, Iris Murdoch and Muriel Spark.

Kumar, Shiv K. Bergson and The Stream of Consciousness Novel. *New York Univ. Press* 1963 $6.95 pap. $1.95. Uses Bergson's concepts to analyze the work of Dorothy Richardson, Virginia Woolf and James Joyce.

Kunitz, Stanley J., and Howard Haycraft. Twentieth Century Authors. *Wilson* 1942 $22.00. A Biographical Dictionary of Modern Literature; complete in one volume with 1,850 biographies and 1,700 portraits.

Twentieth Century Authors: First Supplement. Ed. by Stanley J. Kunitz; assistant ed., Vineta Colby. *Wilson* 1955 $18.00. A Biographical Dictionary of Modern Literature.

Lodge, David. THE NOVELIST AT THE CROSSROADS AND OTHER ESSAYS ON FICTION AND CRITICISM. *Cornell Univ. Press* 1971 $8.50. Contains essays on recent trends in fiction, current criticism of the novel, Wells, Greene, Spark, and others.

Longaker, Mark, and E. C. Bolles. CONTEMPORARY ENGLISH LITERATURE. *Appleton* 1953 $5.45. Covers the period from 1890 to 1950 with biographical sketches, a discussion of major works, and a bibliography for every important author.

Mansfield, Katherine. NOVELS AND NOVELISTS. 1930. *Somerset Pub.* $15.50

Mercier, Vivian. THE IRISH COMIC TRADITION. *Oxford.* 1962 Galaxy Bks. pap. $1.95. Deals with wit, satire, and parody, and traces the sophistication of techniques.

Newby, P. H. THE NOVEL, 1945–1950. 1951. *Folcroft* lib. bdg. $5.00

Newquist, Roy, Comp. COUNTERPOINT. 1964. *Simon & Schuster* Clarion Bks. pap. $2.95. Penetrating comments on life and living, writers and writing, by 63 leading authors, critics and playwrights.

O'Connor, Frank. THE MIRROR IN THE ROADWAY: A Study of the Modern Novel. 1956. *Bks. for Libraries* $14.50

O'Connor, William Van. THE NEW UNIVERSITY WITS AND THE END OF MODERNISM. *Southern Illinois Univ. Press* 1963 $4.95. An early study of the writers who came after the Second World War with a discussion of their literary antecedents.

O'Faolain, Sean. THE VANISHING HERO: Critical Essays. 1957. *Bks. for Libraries.* The studies of the novelists of the 1920s include Huxley, Waugh, Graham Greene, Elizabeth Bowen, Virginia Woolf and James Joyce.

Rabinovitz, Rubin. THE REACTION AGAINST EXPERIMENT IN THE ENGLISH NOVEL, 1950–1960. *Columbia* 1967 $9.00. Professor Rabinovitz, of Columbia University, shows how contemporary English novelists have rejected Joycean experimentalism and returned to more traditional novelistic techniques.

Schorer, Mark, Ed. MODERN BRITISH FICTION: Essays in Criticism. *Oxford* Galaxy Bks. 1961 pap. $3.50

Shapiro, Charles, Ed. CONTEMPORARY BRITISH NOVELISTS. *Southern Illinois Univ. Press* 1969 $5.95 pap. $2.25. A series of essays by various hands covering the most important English writers of the post-World War II generation.

Spender, Stephen. THE STRUGGLE OF THE MODERN. 1961. *Univ. of California Press* 1963 pap. $1.75. Spender distinguishes between the Moderns (British writers of the generation of Joyce and Woolf) and the Contemporaries (the generation that came just before or just after them) and points out important differences in their aesthetic thinking.

(And others, Eds.) ENCOUNTERS. *Simon & Schuster* 1965 pap. $2.45 Writings taken from the magazine *Encounter.*

Story, Norah. THE OXFORD COMPANION TO CANADIAN HISTORY AND LITERATURE. *Oxford.* 1967 $18.50

"An invaluable reference work . . . virtually the complete reference work to things Canadian"—(*LJ*).

Thompson, William I. IMAGINATION OF AN INSURRECTION: Dublin, Easter 1916. 1967. *Harper* Colophon Bks. pap. $2.45. Examines the relation between the Irish Literary Renaissance and the birth of Irish nationalism.

Tindall, William York. FORCES IN MODERN BRITISH LITERATURE. 1885–1946. 1956. *Bks. for Libraries* $15.50. Literary criticism of all the major writers, as well as many minor figures, written with wit and understanding.

THE LITERARY SYMBOL. 1955. *Indiana Univ. Press* 1958 Midland Bks. pap. $1.95; *Peter Smith* $4.00. A skillful definition and illuminating history of the symbol, including the emergence of the symbolist novel in Great Britain, America and Europe.

Van Doren, Carl, and Mark Van Doren. AMERICAN AND BRITISH LITERATURE SINCE 1890. *Appleton* 1939 rev. ed. $9.45

Vinson, James, Ed. CONTEMPORARY NOVELISTS. Pref. by Walter Allen. *St. Martin's* 1972 $30.00. An excellent reference work with a short essay and bibliography describing the works of every important contemporary novelist, with an emphasis on English and American writers.

Webster, Harvey Curtis. AFTER THE TRAUMA: Representative English Novelists since 1920. *Univ. Press of Kentucky* 1970 $8.00. Webster includes discussions on Rose Macaulay, Aldous Huxley, Ivy Compton-Burnett, Evelyn Waugh, Graham Greene, L. P. Hartley, C. P. Snow and others.

West, Paul. THE MODERN NOVEL. *Hillary House* Hutchinson Univ. Lib. 2 vols. 1963 2nd ed. 1965 Vol. I England and France $5.00 Vol. 2 The U.S. and Other Countries $5.00 pap. 1967 $2.25. A history of the 20th-century novel; discusses trends in modern fiction as well as representative works of major authors.

West, Rebecca. ENDING IN EARNEST, A LITERARY LOG 1931. *Bks. for Libraries* 1967 $9.75

Williams, Raymond. THE ENGLISH NOVEL FROM DICKENS TO LAWRENCE. *Oxford* 1970 $7.95. Williams is known as a social historian; his book examines the links between the fiction of the late 19th and early 20th centuries and the social changes which occurred during that period.

Wilson, Edmund. O CANADA: An American's Notes on Canadian Culture. *Farrar, Straus* 1965 $4.95 Noonday pap. $1.95

For his many essays on British writers, see his main entry in Chapter 15, Essays and Criticism.

Wittig, Kurt. THE SCOTTISH TRADITION IN LITERATURE. 1961. *Greenwood* $15.25

Woolf, Virginia. *See Chapter 15, Essays and Criticism.*

See also Chapter 3, Reference Books—Literature: Histories and Dictionaries of Literature; Reference Books on Fiction. Also lists in the two preceding chapters, and Chapter 4, Broad Studies and General Anthologies: Discussions of the Novel.

COLLECTIONS

Astor, Stuart L., and Leonard R. N. Ashley. BRITISH SHORT STORIES: Classics and Criticism. *Prentice-Hall* 1968 pap. $5.35. Each of these stories by 22 masters of modern British fiction is followed by excerpts from several critical reviews. Biographical sketches are also included.

Cranfill, Thomas Mabry, Ed. IMAGE OF BRITIAN II: Special Issue of *The Texas Quarterly*. *Univ. of Texas Press* 1961 $6.00. A collection of articles in the fields of foreign relations, education, social change and the intellectual milieu in modern Britain.

Davis, Robert Gorham. TEN MODERN MASTERS: An Anthology of the Short Story. *Harcourt* 2nd ed. 1959 $5.25. Several stories each by Anderson, Chekhov, Conrad, Faulkner, James, Joyce, Lawrence, Mann, Mansfield, O'Connor.

Garrity, Devin A. 44 IRISH SHORT STORIES: From Yeats to Frank O'Connor. *Devin-Adair* $7.50

Gerber, Helmut. THE ENGLISH SHORT STORY IN TRANSITION, 1880–1920. *Pegasus* 1967 $11.95 pap. $3.95

> "An interesting anthology of short stories that covers the transition between the Victorian and modern periods in English literature"—(*LJ*). Contains biographical and critical materials and an annotated bibliography.

Hudson, Derek, Ed. MODERN ENGLISH SHORT STORIES. 2nd series. 1956 *Somerset Pub.* $15.50. A comprehensive anthology with many minor writers as well as familiar names represented.

Marcus, Steven, Ed. THE WORLD OF MODERN FICTION. *Simon & Schuster* 1966 2 vols. boxed set $17.50. The second volume of this work contains selections—mainly short stories—of the writing of a number of British novelists.

Miller, Karl, Ed. WRITING IN ENGLAND TODAY: The Last Fifteen Years. 1968. *Peter Smith* $3.50 An anthology of recent British writing; includes poets and essayists as well as novelists.

Weaver, Robert, Ed. CANADIAN SHORT STORIES. *Oxford* 1960 pap. $2.95. An anthology emphasizing contemporary writing from all parts of Canada.

WELLS, H(ERBERT) G(EORGE). 1866–1946.

> Wells wrote (in a very readable, sometimes journalistic style) scientific and fantastic romances, short stories, realistic novels, sociology, history, science and biography—after 1895 averaging a book or more a year. His sociological works usually take the form of Utopias or of prophecies—"The Shape of Things to Come" (1933, o.p.). His "Science of Life" (1931, o.p.), written with Sir Julian Huxley (*q.v.*), is an outline of biology as comprehensive as his "Outline of History" (*Doubleday* rev. ed. 1956 $9.95). "He insisted on the importance of science during a long epoch when men of letters were heinously ignorant of it. His sense of the continuity and logical development of human destiny is very valuable, and enabled him to make shrewd guesses at future happenings which sometimes have been impressively right"—(Richard Aldington). Wells and Jules Verne (*q.v.*) wrote the first science fiction—and both are still popular in this vein.
>
> It is the opinion of more than one critic that Wells never wrote anything better than his early novels, "Love and Mr. Lewisham" (1900) and "Kipps" (1905). "Mr. Britling Sees It Through" (1916, o.p.) was one of the best novels written during World War I. Later novels, many of them devoted to causes he favored, were less successful as fiction but will still be interesting to the student of English social history. His frank and brilliant "Experiment in Autobiography" (1934, o.p.) describes his rise from humble beginnings to world fame and throws interesting light on the literary, social and political life of his period.

SEVEN SCIENCE FICTION NOVELS: The First Men in the Moon; The Food of the Gods; In the Days of the Comet; The Invisible Man; The Island of Dr. Moreau; The Time Machine; The War of the Worlds. *Dover* 1950 $6.00; *Peter Smith* $5.00

THREE PROPHETIC NOVELS. When the Sleeper Wakes (1899); Story of the Days to Come (orig. publ. in 1933 as "The Shape of Things to Come"); The Time Machine (1895). Introd. by E. F. Bleiler *Dover* pap. $2.25; *Peter Smith* $4.25

TWENTY-EIGHT SCIENCE FICTION STORIES. 1905. *Dover* 1952 $5.95; *Peter Smith* $7.50

BEST SCIENCE FICTION STORIES. *Dover* 1965 $2.25; *Peter Smith* $4.25

THE TIME MACHINE. 1895. *Assoc. Booksellers* Airmont Bks. pap. $.50; *Bentley* lib. bdg. $6.50; *Berkley* pap. $.60; *Dufour* 1966 $5.95; *Dutton* Everyman's 1962 $3.50; *Fawcett* Crest pap. $.95

THE ISLAND OF DR. MOREAU. 1896. *Assoc. Booksellers* Airmont Bks. pap. $.50; *Berkley* pap. $.50

THE WHEELS OF CHANGE. 1896. (and "The Time Machine") *Dutton* Everyman's 1962 $3.50

THIRTY STRANGE STORIES. 1897. *Bks. for Libraries* $14.50

THE INVISIBLE MAN. 1897. *Assoc. Booksellers* Airmont Bks. pap. $.50; *Belmont-Tower* pap. $.75; *Berkley* pap. $.60; *Collins* New Class. 1957 $3.00; *Popular Lib.* pap. $.75; *Scholastic Bk. Services* pap. $.75

THE WAR OF THE WORLDS. 1898. *Assoc. Booksellers* Airmont Bks. pap. $.50; *Berkley* pap. $.60; (and "The Time Machine") *Doubleday* Dolphin Bks. pap. $1.25; (and "The Time Machine" and Selected Short Stories) fwd. by Kingsley Amis *Platt* 1963 $3.50 lib. bdg. $3.97; *Scholastic Bk. Services* pap. $.75; *Washington Square* pap. $.60

WHEN THE SLEEPER WAKES. 1899. *Ace Bks.* pap. $.75; *Collins* New Class. $3.00

LOVE AND MR. LEWISHAM. 1900. *Collins* New Class. $3.00

THE FIRST MEN IN THE MOON. 1901. *Assoc. Booksellers* Airmont Bks. pap. $.60; *Berkley* pap. $.60; *Collins* New Class. $3.00

THE FOOD OF THE GODS. 1904. *Assoc. Booksellers* Airmont Bks. pap. $.60; *Berkley* pap. $.60; *Collins* New Class. $3.00; *Popular Lib.* pap. $.50

KIPPS. 1905. *Collins* New Class. $3.00; *Dell* pap. $.60

IN THE DAYS OF THE COMET. 1906. *Assoc. Booksellers* Airmont Bks. pap. $.60; *Berkley* pap. $.60; *Collins* New Class. $3.00

TONO-BUNGAY. 1909. *Collins* New Class. $3.00; ed. by B. Bergonzi *Houghton* Riv. Eds. pap. $1.85; *New Am. Lib.* pap. $.95

THE HISTORY OF MR. POLLY. 1909 1937. *Collins* New Class $3.00; ed. with introd. by Gordon N. Ray *Houghton* Riv. Eds. 1960 pap. $1.25

THE COUNTRY OF THE BLIND AND OTHER STORIES. 1911. *Bks. for Libraries* $16.50

THE KING WHO WAS A KING. 1929. *Greenwood* 1972 $11.75

THE WEALTH OF MISTER WADDY. Ed. by Harris Wilson. *Southern Illinois Univ. Press* 1969 $5.95

THE ADVENTURES OF TOMMY. Ill. by author. *Knopf* 1967 $3.50 lib. bdg. $4.59

THE FATE OF MAN. 1939. *Bks. for Libraries* $11.25

ARNOLD BENNETT AND H. G. WELLS: The Record of a Personal and Literary Friendship. Ed. by Harris Wilson. *Univ. of Illinois Press* 1960 $4.50. 214 letters written between 1897 and 1931.

Books about Wells

The Outline of H. G. Wells. By Sidney Dark. 1922. *Folcroft* 1973 $15.00

H. G. Wells. By Montgomery Belgion. *British Bk. Centre* $2.38 pap. $1.20

H. G. Wells and His Critics. By I. Raknem. 1962. *Hillary House* $11.00

The Early H. G. Wells: A Study of the Scientific Romances. By Bernard Bergonzi. *Univ. of Toronto Press* 1962 $6.25

H. G. Wells. By Richard Costa. *Twayne* 1966 $5.50

H. G. Wells: His Turbulent Life and Times. By Lovat Dickson. *Atheneum* 1971 $10.00 pap. $3.45

H. G. Wells: A Biography. By Norman and Jean MacKenzie. *Simon & Schuster* 1973 $10.00

BENNETT, ARNOLD. 1867–1931.

"In his time, Arnold Bennett was the shrewdest and most successful tradesman in English letters"—(V. S. Pritchett, in the *New Yorker*). "The Old Wives' Tale" is the masterpiece of this novelist who wrote about the lives of shopkeepers and potters in the North of England—his own boyhood background, though he became immensely successful. "A merchant of words, frankly writing for money," he was able nonetheless to make the dullest characters interesting. In 1968, reviewing "Darling of the Day," a successful musical adaptation of "Buried Alive," Walter Kerr wrote: "I'd forgotten some of the nicer twists of . . . 'Buried Alive' . . . and so was charmed all over again." Kerr reported that on opening night the plot itself was actually applauded— "an odd and gratifying state of affairs." Bennett was the successful historian of the Five Towns; and the two sisters of "The Old Wives' Tale" are "unforgettable, both as individual characters and as representatives of the lower middle class, preoccupied with industry, patriotism and thrift." "A retreat into the will-less accept- ance of circumstance . . . and the fantastic accident, are the continual themes of his stories. Chance, chica- nery—the favorite word—and disillusion, which he called 'detraction,' arouse his sharp inventive powers and animate the irony of his work. He is the aesthete of wry humors and sadnesses"—(Pritchett). Bennett's other important novels are: "The Clayhanger Trilogy" (1910), "Hilda Lessways" (1911), "These Twain" (1916) and "Riceyman Steps." Bennett's voluminous journal (1932–33, o.p.) is of special value for the light it throws on the novelist at work.

GRAND BABYLON HOTEL: A Fantasia on Modern Themes. 1904. *Scholarly Press* $19.50

MATADOR OF THE FIVE TOWNS AND OTHER STORIES. 1905. *Scholarly Press* 1971 $24.50

THE CLAYHANGER FAMILY 1910. *Scholarly Press* repr. of 1925 ed. $59.00

PRETTY LADY. 1918. *Scholarly Press* 1971 $19.50

RICEYMAN STEPS. 1923. *Dufour* 1968 $5.50

ARNOLD BENNETT AND H. G. WELLS: The Record of a Personal and Literary Friend- ship. Ed. by Harris Wilson. *Univ. of Illinois Press* 1960. $4.50. Correspondence ex- tending over more than 30 years.

LETTERS. Ed. by James Hepburn *Oxford* 1966–70 3 vols. Vol. I Letters to J. B. Pinker (1966) $12.75 Vol. 2, 1889–1915 (1968) $14.25 Vol. 3 1916–1931 (1970) $14.25

Books about Bennett

Arnold Bennett. By Walter E. Allen. 1948. *AMS Press* $7.50

Arnold Bennett: Primitivism and Taste. By James Hall. *Univ. of Washington Press* 1959 $5.95

The Art of Arnold Bennett. By James G. Hepburn. 1963. *Haskell* lib. bdg. $10.95

Writer by Trade: A View of Arnold Bennett. By Dudley Barker. *Atheneum* 1966 $6.50

"A peculiarly frank and sympathetic brief biography. . . . It supplements without replacing the published Journals and other sketches"—(*LJ*).

Arnold Bennett. By Frank Swinnerton. Pamphlet. *British Bk. Centre* pap. $2.38 pap. $1.20

Arnold Bennett. By John Wain. Essays on Modern Writers *Columbia* 1967 pap. $1.00. An excellent pamphlet on Bennett's novels and plays.

GALSWORTHY, JOHN. 1867–1933. (Nobel Prize 1932)

Galsworthy wrote novels and plays alternately throughout his life. His master work, "The Forsyte Saga," begun in 1906 and finished in 1928, consisting of six separate novels and two linking interludes, is the famous example of the sequence novel in English literature. It is a study of the property sense, the possessive spirit, in different individuals and generations of English middle-class society. His later years brought him many honors including the presidency of P.E.N. and honorary degrees from Oxford, Cambridge and several other universities. After World War I he was offered a knighthood, which he refused. He did, however, accept the Order of Merit in 1929 and in 1932 he was awarded the Nobel Prize.

Though his posthumous reputation had waned, the centenary of his death in 1967 brought a recreation of "The Forsyte Saga" on British and American television in serial form. All at once interest in him skyrocketed and the Forsyte novels again became best sellers. With new popularity came fresh critical analysis. Pamela Hansford Johnson called "The Forsyte Saga" a work of profound social insight and patchy psychological insight"—(in the *N.Y. Times*). Maurice Richardson wrote in the *Observer* (London): "The fact remains that, even in his best novels, Galsworthy's characters are lacking in that eccentric individuality which is supposed to be so quintessentially English. How he managed and manages to this day to be so phenomenally readable I find rather mysterious. Perhaps the secret is to be found in his sense of theatre. It was no accident that he was successful as a playwright. The characters in his plays all seem to me to be cardboard figures yet his construction and timing are almost faultless."

THE GALSWORTHY READER. Ed. with introd. by Anthony West. *Scribner* 1967 $7.95. Four short stories, two plays, extracts from "The Country House" and "Fraternity" and—from the Forsyte chronicles—most of "Swan Song" and all of "The Man of Property" and "Indian Summer of a Forsyte."

THE APPLE TREE AND OTHER TALES. *Scribner* 1965 pap. $2.45

JOCELYN. 1898. *Greenwood* $11.50; *Scholarly Press* $14.50. Written under the pseudonym of John Sinjohn, along with "Villa Rubein" and "The Man of Devon," both o.p.

THE MAN OF PROPERTY. 1906. *Ace Bks.* pap. $.95; *Ballantine Bks.* pap. $1.50; *Collins* New Class. $3.00; *New Am. Lib.* pap. $.95; *Penguin* pap. $.95; *Scribner* 1906 1960 Contemporary Class. 1970 pap. $2.45; school ed. $3.36

THE FORSYTE SAGA. The Man of Property (1906); In Chancery (1920); To Let (1921) *Scribner* omnibus ed. 1933 $12.50

DARK FLOWER. 1913. *Scholarly Press* 1971 $19.50

FIVE TALES. 1915. *Scholarly Press* 1971 $19.50

CAPTURE. 1923. *Kelley* 1970 $12.50; *Scholarly Press* 1971 $19.50

A MODERN COMEDY. The White Monkey (1924); The Silver Spoon (1926) Swan Song (1928) *Scribner* 1928 omnibus ed. $13.95

A MODERN COMEDY AND THE FORSYTE SAGA. *Scribner* 1970 omnibus vols. boxed $25.00 Contemporary Class. $14.70

IN CHANCERY. 1920. *Scribner* Contemporary Class. 1969 pap. $2.45; *Ballantine Bks.* pap. $1.50

TO LET. 1921. *Ballantine Bks.* pap. $1.50; *Scribner* Contemporary Class. pap. $2.45

ON FORSYTE CHANGE. *Scribner* Contemporary Class. 1970 pap. $2.45. A collection of stories that fill in and round out the Forsytes after the first trilogy.

THE WHITE MONKEY. 1924. *Ballantine Bks.* pap. $1.50; *Scribner* 1928 Contemporary Class. 1969 pap. $2.45

THE SILVER SPOON. 1926. *Ballantine Bks.* 1972 pap. $1.50; *Scribner* Contemporary Class. 1969 pap. $2.45

SWAN SONG. 1928. *Ballantine Bks.* 1972 pap. $1.50; *Scribner* 1928 Contemporary Class. 1970 pap. $2.45

MAID IN WAITING. 1931. *Ballantine Bks.* 1972 pap. $1.50; *Scribner* Contemporary Class. 1970 pap. $2.45

FLOWERING WILDERNESS. 1932. *Ballantine Bks.* 1972 pap. $1.50; *Scribner* Contemporary Class. 1970 pap. $2.45

ONE MORE RIVER. 1933. *Ballantine Bks.* 1972 pap. $1.50; *Scribner* Contemporary Class. pap. $2.45

END OF THE CHAPTER. Maid in Waiting; Flowering Wilderness; One More River (American title. Originally published as "Over the River") *Scribner* 1970 $12.50

LETTERS TO LEON LION. Ed. by Asher B. Wilson. *Humanities* 1968 $12.25

LETTERS FROM GALSWORTHY, 1900–1932. Ed. by Edward Garnett. 1934. *Scholarly Press* 1971. $14.50

Books about Galsworthy

John Galsworthy. By Sheila Kaye-Smith. 1916. *Richard West* $10.00
A Bibliography of the Works of John Galsworthy. By Harold V. Marrot. 1928. *Folcroft* $25.00; *Burt Franklin* $14.50
John Galsworthy. By R. H. Mottram. *British Bk. Centre* $2.38 pap. $1.20
The Man of Principle: A Biography of John Galsworthy. By Dudley Barker. *Stein & Day* 1970 pap. $2.45
John Galsworthy. By David Holloway. *A. S. Barnes* Encore Bks. pap. $1.00

DOUGLAS, NORMAN. 1868–1952.

One of the "liveliest, wittiest, and most original authors of his generation," who exerted a strong influence on modern writers of fantasy, Douglas had tried his "deft hand at music, diplomacy, linguistics and science (zoology, geology, and archeology) before he wrote, and sold in 1917 for a piddling £75, the novel 'South Wind,' a perennially popular satiric classic that made him famous.... The son of a Scottish cottonmill owner, Douglas first journeyed to Capri in 1888, on the trail of a rare species of blue lizard, fell in love with the island and made it his soul's operating base." There he died in penury in a borrowed villa.

The setting of "South Wind," which fascinated many generations after 1917, is an island not unlike Capri called Nepenthe, "inhabited by an extraordinary group of eccentrics who have, in various ways, succumbed to the local atmosphere. By viewing most of the story through the eyes of an English Bishop, Douglas emphasized his theme: the eternal contrast between Northern and Southern Europe." The *Cyclopedia of World Authors*, from which the last quotation is taken, adds that among the cognoscenti of the 1920s and 1930s "not to have read it was a kind of intellectual barbarism." "Experiments" (1925), a book of Douglas's essays on Poe, "A Mad Englishman," "Intellectual Nomadism" and other topics, are all o.p.

SOUTH WIND. 1917. *Int. Pubns. Service* 1965 $3.00; *Scholarly Press* repr. of 1931 ed. $19.50

Books about Douglas

Norman Douglas. By Ian Greenlees. *British Bk. Centre* $2.38 pap. $1.20
Norman Douglas. By Ralph D. Lindeman. English Authors Ser. *Twayne* 1964 $5.50
Norman Douglas. By Lewis Leary. *Columbia* 1968 pap. $1.00

MUNRO, HECTOR HUGH ("SAKI"). 1870–1916.

"Saki's" short stories at their best are extraordinarily compact and cameolike, wicked and witty, with a careless cruelty and a powerful vein of supernatural fantasy. They deal, in general, with the same group of upper-class Britishers, whose frivolous lives are sometimes complicated by animals—the talking cat who reveals their treacheries in love, the pet ferret who is evil incarnate. The *nom de plume* "Saki" was borrowed from the cup-bearer in "The Rubáiyát" of Omar Khayyám (*q.v.*). He used it for political sketches contributed to the *Westminster Gazette* as early as 1896, later collected as "Alice in Westminster" in 1902. The stories and novels were published between that time and the outbreak of World War I when he enlisted as a private, scorning a commission. He died of his wounds in a shell-hole near Beaumont Hamel.

NOVELS AND PLAYS. *Scholarly Press* repr. of 1945 ed. 1971 $22.00; *Viking* repr. of 1933 ed. $3.50

SHORT STORIES. An omnibus volume; introd. by Christopher Morley; biography by E. M. Munro. 1930. *Modern Library* 1951 $2.95; *Viking* $3.50

Books about Munro

H. H. Munro (Saki). By Charles H. Gillen. English Authors. Ser. *Twayne* $5.50

BEERBOHM, MAX (SIR HENRY MAXWELL). 1872–1956. *See Chapter 15, Essays and Criticism.*

FORD, FORD MADOX (originally Ford Madox Hueffer). 1873–1939.

Ford, who changed his German name legally in 1919, was a grandson of the painter Ford Madox Brown, who, together with his cousins the Rossettis (*q. v.*), founded the Pre-Raphaelite Brotherhood. While helping Joseph Conrad (*q. v.*) master English, Ford collaborated with him on "The Inheritors" (1901), "Romance" (1903 reissue 1950) and "The Nature of a Crime (1924), now o. p. in separate volumes. From Conrad he learned the technique of "impressionism," as he explains in his memoir, "Joseph Conrad, A Personal Remembrance" (1924, *Octagon* 1965 $8.50). Ford established the *English Review* in 1908. Among his distinguished contributors were Conrad, Hardy, Galsworthy, Masefield and William James. In his *transatlantic review* (published in Paris, 1924, and devoid of capital letters) he "discovered" James Joyce and Ernest Hemingway. His reminiscences, "Return to Yesterday," are a valuable record of these editorial years; the volume was suppressed in England because it quotes King George V as threatening to abdicate the throne.

Ford's masterpiece is "The Good Soldier," a work which many critics number among the finest British novels of the century. This novel contains an outstanding example of what Ford and Conrad called *progression d'effet*, a technique for the chronological rearrangement of incidents in a story in order to provide the greatest emotional impact on the reader. Ford's "Parade's End," a series of novels set in England during the First World War, is also quite famous. Even more than the war, Ford's concern in these novels is a study of the psychology and interrelationships of a people going through violent change.

Ford's reputation was of slow growth, perhaps because of his association with so many of the great literary figures of his time. His "Portraits from Life" (1960, o.p.) contains memories and criticisms of Henry James, Conrad, Hardy, Wells, D. H. Lawrence, Galsworthy and others. But as shown in some of the recent critical appraisals, Ford is now considered an innovator, a major 20th-century novelist with a "voice patently his own." His literary criticism includes "Critical Writing" (ed. by Frank MacShane *Univ. of Nebraska Press* 1964 $5.95 Bison Bks. pap. $2.75) and "Henry James" (*Octagon* 1964 $7.00).

THE FIFTH QUEEN. 1906–08. Introd. by Graham Greene. Contains The Fifth Queen; Privy Seal; The Fifth Queen Crowned. *Vanguard* 1963 $10.00. A trilogy based on the life of Katherine Howard; first issue in America.

PARADE'S END. *Knopf* 1950 rev. ed. 1961 $10.00; *New Am. Lib.* 4 vols. pap. Vols. 1–2 each $.95 Vols. 3–4 each $.75. The four novels of "The Tietjens Saga."

THE GOOD SOLDIER. 1915. 1951. *Random* Vintage Bks. pap. $1.95. A "Tale of Passion" with an interpretation by Mark Schorer.

MEMORIES AND IMPRESSIONS. 1911. *Scholarly Press* $19.50; *Somerset* Pub. $15.50

THUS TO REVISIT: Some Reminiscences. 1921. *Octagon* 1966 $8.00

RETURN TO YESTERDAY. Reminiscences. 1932. *Octagon* $13.00

IT WAS THE NIGHTINGALE. Reminiscences. 1934. *Octagon* 1972 $12.50

YOUR MIRROR TO MY TIMES: The Selected Autobiographies and Impressions of Ford Madox Ford. Ed. with introd. by Michael Killigrew *Holt* 1971 $10.00

LETTERS. Ed. by Richard M. Ludwig. *Princeton Univ. Press* 1965 $11.00

Books about Ford

Ford Madox Ford: A Study of His Novels. By Richard A. Cassell. *Johns Hopkins Univ. Press* 1961 $9.00
Ford Madox Ford 1873–1939. By D. D. Harvey. 1962. *Gordian* 1971 $22.50
Novelist of Three Worlds: Ford Madox Ford. By Paul L. Wiley. *Syracuse Univ. Press* 1962 $5.50
Ford Madox Ford: The Essence of His Art. By R. W. Lid. *Univ. of California Press* 1964 $5.75
   "The clear and persuasive bent of this study suggests its value to large public and academic libraries"—
   (*LJ*).
Ford Madox Ford: From Apprentice to Craftsman. By Carol B. Ohmann. *Wesleyan Univ. Press* 1964
   $6.00
   "There is nothing here about Ford the man—yet there is everything. Highly recommended"—(*LJ*).
The Invisible Tent: The War Novels of Ford Madox Ford. By Ambrose Gordon, Jr. *Univ. of Texas Press*
   1965 $6.00
   "An interesting, though informal and loosely organized, addition to Ford criticism"—(*Choice*).
The Limited Hero in the Novels of Ford Madox Ford. By Norman Leer. *Michigan State Univ. Press*
   1966 $6.00
Ford Madox Ford. By Charles G. Hoffmann. English Authors Ser. *Twayne* 1967 $4.95 A study including
   bibliography, chronology, index.
The Saddest Story. By Arthur Mizener. *World Pub.* 1970 $20.00. An excellent biography.
The Alien Protagonist of Ford Madox Ford. By H. Robert Huntley. *Univ. of North Carolina Press* 1970
   $7.50
Ford Madox Ford. By Grover Smith. Essays on Modern Writers *Columbia* 1972 pap. $1.00
Ford Madox Ford: The Critical Heritage. By Frank MacShane. *Routledge & Kegan Paul* 1972 $15.00
Ford Madox Ford. By Kenneth Young. *British Bk. Centre* $2.38 pap. $1.20

MAUGHAM, (WILLIAM) SOMERSET. 1874–1965.

In 1959, when Maugham was 85, the *N.Y. Times* reported that he had decided that it was time to stop writing except for himself. "A writer's work must come from inside himself," he said. "He must mingle with life, must be immersed in life—and I am a stranger in the world today." As he once had written: "Invention is a curious faculty, an attribute of youth that with age is lost."

He had retired gracefully from playwriting in 1934. Of his formidable body of work, his novel "Of Human Bondage" has become a modern classic. It reflects his early experiences as a physician in St. Thomas' Hospital, London. It has twice been filmed; the first version, with Leslie Howard and Bette Davis, was the most effective. "The Moon and Sixpence," founded on the life of the artist Paul Gauguin, is still read. Many of his stories were set in far outposts of the British Empire, where he himself had observed the effect of tropical lands on the uprooted European. Maugham said of himself: "I have never pretended to be anything but a storyteller. It has amused me to tell stories and I have told a great many." "The Summing Up," a review of his writing career, which might well be used as a handbook of authorship, largely explains his competent craftsmanship and his thoroughgoing professionalism as a writer. On his death at the age of 92, the *N.Y. Times* wrote: "For decades he cast a clinical eye on human behavior and turned out works that made him a fortune few writers have equaled. . . . His style was neat and simple; his stories were sharply defined, with a clear beginning, middle and end; his characters were a fascinating spectrum of humanity, from dukes to hucksters, from princesses to prostitutes, from governors general to lackeys. His audience was vast."

A multimillionaire, he sold 38 of his art treasures at auction in 1962 for more than $1,400,000, "which along with most of the rest of his estate he . . . earmarked for Britain's Incorporated Society of Authors, Playwrights and Composers to spare 'needy authors from doing hack work.' " "Purely for My Pleasure" (1962, o.p.) is a most enjoyable "summing up" of "his excursions into the visual arts as a collector." His last years were marred by a public dispute with his daughter over the disposition of some of his paintings. Before his death he stipulated that no unpublished work of his should be printed posthumously.

COMPLETE SHORT STORIES. 1952. *Washington Square* 4 vols. pap. each $.75

BEST SHORT STORIES. *Modern Library* 1957 $2.95

THE MAKING OF A SAINT: A Romance of Medieval Italy. 1898. *Popular Lib.* pap. $.75

OF HUMAN BONDAGE. 1915. *Doubleday* 1915 1942 $6.95; (and "A Digression on the Art of Fiction") *Folcroft* repr. of 1946 ed. $4.00; *Modern Library* $2.95; *Pocket Bks.* pap. $1.25; *Random* Vintage Bks. pap. $1.95; *Washington Square* Collateral Class. $.75; (and "A Digression on the Art of Fiction") *Richard West* repr. of 1946 ed. $4.00

THE MOON AND SIXPENCE. 1919. *Pocket Bks.* pap. $1.25; *Washington Square* Collateral Class. pap. $.75

ASHENDEN, or The British Agent. 1928. *Bks. for Libraries* $11.00

CAKES AND ALE, or The Skeleton in the Cupboard. 1930. *Pocket Bks.* pap. $.75

THE NARROW CORNER. 1932. *Pocket Bks.* 1969 pap. $.75

THE RAZOR'S EDGE. *Doubleday* 1944 $5.95; *Pocket Bks.* pap. $.95

WRITER'S NOTEBOOK. 1949. *Greenwood* $14.00. Taken from his journals.

A WRITER'S POINT OF VIEW. 1951. *Bern Porter* 1972. $7.50

POINTS OF VIEW: Five Essays. 1959. *Greenwood* 1969 $12.00

Books about Maugham

Somerset Maugham. By John Brophy. *British Bk. Centre* $2.38 pap. $1.20
Somerset Maugham. By Ivor Brown. *A. S. Barnes* pap. $1.00
Somerset Maugham: A Biographical and Critical Study. By Richard A. Cordell. 1938. *Indiana Univ. Press* rev. and enl. ed. 1961 $7.50. A sympathetic work, the revised edition contains more explicit identification of the originals of characters in novels and plays.
Remembering Mr. Maugham. By Garson Kanin. Fwd. by Noel Coward. *Atheneum* 1966 $5.95. The author, a Broadway director, who with his wife the actress Ruth Gordon was a close friend of Maugham's, here paints an intimate and affectionate picture, showing the kind of loyalty Maugham could inspire in good friends. This one avoids discussing Maugham's less attractive qualities and provides interesting sidelights on his career.
W. Somerset Maugham and the Quest for Freedom. By Robert Calder. *Doubleday* 1972 $7.95

RICHARDSON, DOROTHY (MILLER). 1873?–1957.

The work of Dorothy Richardson is widely acknowledged as significant in the development of the modern English novel. Like Proust, Joyce and Virginia Woolf—though in the test of time her talent has proved less than theirs—she was one of the first to write in the "stream-of-consciousness" manner. She herself hated this term and V. S. Pritchett (in the *New Statesman*) calls her "more a late Jamesian than a streamer, seeing experience through the mind of a chosen character—but this character [Miriam Henderson] was a projection of herself." "Pilgrimage," her autobiographical novel in 12 book-length "chapters" had enjoyed few recent readers until the posthumous discovery and publication of a 13th section, "March Moonlight," aroused new interest and brought fresh evaluations of her work. "The major pleasure 'Pilgrimage' affords now is as a period piece, both in its subject matter and its technique. The years 1890–1915 are richly evoked in all the material detail for which Virginia Woolf took the Edwardian novelists to task in 'Mr. Bennett and Mrs. Brown.' As a chronicler of those years . . . Dorothy Richardson is unsurpassed"—(*Nation*). Though she displayed astonishing self-perceptions, most critics find her writing flawed by its egotistical tone and by her unpoetic, humorless style. The fact that she was treated like a son by her father perhaps explains the strong feminist orientation of her life (and of "Pilgrimage") and her general distrust of men. She gloried in loneliness and independence in a day when these were difficult for women, but tempered these virtues with love affairs both Lesbian and heterosexual. She was briefly a mistress of H. G. Wells (who is portrayed as "Hypo" in "Pilgrimage") and eventually married an artist, Alan Odle. Her book, disdaining "plot," runs to 2,210 pages and some of it is heavy going. "What," says Pritchett, "if time has made the threshing about of Miriam's mind exhausting and monotonous despite her wit? . . . Miriam drifting on, Miriam tying herself into important looking knots, last less well than what Miriam saw." But Leon Edel (in *SR*) writes that "she nevertheless demonstrated that the novel of sensibility could be cast in artistic form and given artistic validity. . . . It is good to know that a new generation . . . can now give Dorothy Richardson that 'second look' which the seriously committed writer always deserves after his life's work is done." Miss Richardson was "hopelessly vague" about her birth date, says Horace Gregory, but on her gravestone (which contains an error in her name) it is given as May 17, 1873.

PILGRIMAGE. 1915–38. Introd. by Walter Allen. *Knopf* 1938 1967 4 vols. each $7.95. boxed $30.00. This edition contains the original 12 volumes published 1915-38 and "March Moonlight," discovered after her death, now published for the first time.

Vol. 1 Pointed Roofs; Backwater; Honeycomb. Vol. 2 The Tunnel; Interim. Vol. 3 Deadlock; Revolving Lights; The Trap. Vol. 4 Oberland; Dawn's Left Hand; Clear Horizon; Dimple Hill; March Moonlight.

Books about Richardson

Dorothy Richardson. By Caesar R. Blake. *Univ. of Michigan Press* 1960 $4.50
Dorothy Richardson: An Adventure in Self-Discovery. By Horace Gregory. *Holt* 1967 $4.95
   "A perceptive biographical-critical essay—a portrait in miniature.... Mr. Gregory's valuable appraisal stems in part from his own interest in the work and personality of Miss Richardson, whom he knew in London in the 1920's and also from the posthumous papers"—(Leon Edel, in *SR*).

CHESTERTON, G. K. 1874–1936. *See Chapter 15, Essays and Criticism.*

MASEFIELD, JOHN. 1878–1967. *See Chapter 7, Modern British Poetry.*

FORSTER, E(DWARD) M(ORGAN). 1879–1970.

E. M. Forster is noted for "the easy grace and lucidity of his style; his humor, his good taste, the wise humanism of his outlook"—(C. J. Rolo, in the *Atlantic*). His "Collected Tales" display wit and irony in the use of fantasy, of which "The Celestial Omnibus" is a most delightful example. His most popular book, "A Passage to India," won both the James Tait Black and the Femina-Vie Heureuse prizes and is his outstanding work. It is a brilliant, discerning study of the British-Indian dilemma, well before the days of Indian independence. "The Hill of Devi" (1953. *Harcourt* Harvest Bks. 1971 pap. $2.65) about his early experiences as private secretary to a maharajah in India, reveals the background against which "A Passage to India" was written. The play "A Passage to India" opened in London in 1960 and on Broadway early in 1962. (It was shown on U.S. television in 1968). Adapted by Santha Rama Rau, it was "thoroughly approved" by Forster. The story, defined by John Sparrow, "deals with the interaction of two types of character, the intersection of two planes of living . . . the conflict of those who live by convention and those who live by instinct."
   "Howards End," another very fine novel, deals with the problems of the changing English class structure. "Maurice," about homosexual love, was suppressed during the author's lifetime and published posthumously in 1972. Forster's last three novels are serious and deal with important social problems. His earlier novels often have similar concerns but are funny and more optimistic. The best of these is "A Room with a View," which contrasts English gravity and Italian lightheartedness; the book is warm, witty, and sensitive.
   One of his most important critical works is "Aspects of the Novel" (1927. *Harcourt* 1947 $6.50 Harvest Bks. pap. $1.45), long a classic on the art of fiction. "Two Cheers for Democracy" (*Harcourt* 1951 Harvest Bks. 1962 pap. $2.25) is divided into two parts, "The Second Darkness" (political reflections) and "What I Believe" (his faith in the arts and personal relationships). His "Alexandria: A History and a Guide" (1922 1961 *Peter Smith* $4.00) is again available. "Marianne Thornton: A Domestic Biography, 1797–1887" (*Harcourt* 1956 Harvest Bks. 1973 pap. $3.45) is the charming life of his great aunt and throws light on his own childhood. "Abinger Harvest" (1936. *Harcourt* Harvest Bks. 1964 pap. $2.45) is "one of the most notable miscellanies of our time"—(John Crowe Ransom, in the *Yale Review*)—a collection of articles, essays, reviews and poems. In 1953 Forster received high recognition for his work from the Queen—the Order of Companion of Honor. Until his death in 1970 he lived quietly in a small apartment in King's College, Cambridge, where he was an Honorary Fellow.

THE ETERNAL MOMENT (1928) AND OTHER STORIES. The Machine Stops; The Point of It; Mr. Andrews; Co-ordination; The Story of the Siren. 1964. *Harcourt* Harvest Bks. 1970 pap. $1.85

THE LIFE TO COME AND OTHER STORIES. *Norton* 1973 $7.95

WHERE ANGELS FEAR TO TREAD. 1905. *Random* Vintage Bks. pap. $1.95

THE LONGEST JOURNEY. 1907. *Knopf* 1922 1953 $5.95; *Random* Vintage Bks. pap. $1.95

A ROOM WITH A VIEW. 1908. *Knopf* 1923 1953 $6.95; *Random* Vintage Bks. pap. $1.95

HOWARDS END. 1910. *Random* Vintage Bks. pap. $1.95

A PASSAGE TO INDIA. 1924. *Harcourt* Harbrace Mod. Class. 1949 $2.95 Harvest Bks. pap. $1.95

MAURICE. *Norton* 1972 $6.95; *New Am. Lib.* 1973 pap. $1.50

Books about Forster

Rhythm in the Novel—with a Special Study of Rhythm in E. M. Forster. By Edward K. Brown. *Univ. of Toronto Press* 1950 pap. $1.75

The Novels of E. M. Forster. By James McConkey. 1957. *Shoe String* 1971 $5.75

E. M. Forster: The Perils of Humanism. By Frederick C. Crews. *Princeton Univ. Press* 1962 pap. $1.95. This valuable book is packed with a "formidable array of data on Forster's heredity, his heritage of Victorian liberalism, his Edwardian resistance to modernity, the influence of his college years at Cambridge, and the Bloomsbury circle of intellectual aristocrats into which he was drawn."

The Achievement of E. M. Forster. By J. B. Beer. *Barnes & Noble* 1962 $5.50. This study shows how "each novel follows naturally from the previous one, in the sense that each time fresh themes are brought into play and the previous ones dealt with more subtly than before."

E. M. Forster: A Tribute. Ed. with introd. by K. Natwar-Singh. *Harcourt* 1964 $4.50

Published on Jan. 1, 1964, his 85th birthday, "this *Festschrift* contains laudatory articles by a group of his Indian friends—Ahmed Ali, Mulk Raj Anand, Narayana Menon, Raja Rao, Santha Rama Rau, and the editor—as well as 12 short excerpts on India and Indians taken from Forster's own works. . . . Not a definitive critique but a pleasant and informative book"—*(LJ)*.

E. M. Forster: A Critical Guidebook. By Lionel Trilling. *New Directions* rev. ed. 1964 pap. $1.50

Art and Order: A Study of E. M. Forster. By Alan Wilde. *New York Univ. Press* 1964 $6.95 pap. $1.95 Professor Wilde of Williams College was in touch with Forster while writing this "sturdy, perceptive, unpretentious, but effective critique"—*(LJ)*.

A Bibliography of E. M. Forster. By B. J. Kirkpatrick. *Oxford* 1965 $13.50

Quest for Certitude in E. M. Forster's Novels. By David Shusterman. 1965. *Haskell* $10.95

E. M. Forster. By Harry T. Moore. Essays on Modern Writers. *Columbia* 1965 pap. $1.00

E. M. Forster. By Rex Warner. Writers and Their Work Ser. *British Bk. Centre.* $2.38 pap. $1.20

The Cave and the Mountain: A Study of E. M. Forster. By Wilfred Stone. *Stanford Univ. Press* 1966 $10.00 pap. $3.85

In two sections, "background and explication, [this book] gives the reader not only a coherent view of Forster's career, but also a careful analysis artistic texture and ideas . . . [a] definitive study"—*(LJ)*.

E. M. Forster: A Collection of Critical Essays. Ed. with introd. by Malcolm Bradbury. *Prentice-Hall* 1966 $5.95

"For people who have been puzzled by Forster's novels, this collection will dispel part of the mystery and bring some valuable insight"—*(LJ)*.

The Fiction of E. M. Forster. By George H. Thomson. *Wayne State Univ. Press* 1967 $9.95. Treats the symbolic aspects of Forster's writings.

E. M. Forster. By Norman Kelvin. Pref. by Harry T. Moore. *Southern Illinois Univ. Press* 1967 $4.95. Forster viewed as novelist, critic and historian.

Perspectives on E. M. Forster's "A Passage to India": A Collection of Critical Essays. Ed. by Vasant A. Shahane. *Wayne State Univ. Press* 1967 $9.95

E. M. Forster. By Frederick P. McDowell. *Twayne* $4.95

WEBB, MARY. 1881–1927.

Mary Webb's principal work, "Precious Bane," had been published 18 months and she was already dead when Stanley Baldwin, Prime Minister of England, in a speech praised her work highly. This was the making of her fame (although the novel had already received the Femina-Vie Heureuse prize for 1924). Her plots are melodramatic and there is almost no real character development, but her lyrical descriptions of the Shropshire countryside, where she was born, provide backgrounds of true magic. Her sympathy is with the sufferer—the fox in "Gone to Earth" (1917, o.p.) and the girl with the hare lip in "Precious Bane."

PRECIOUS BANE. 1924. *New Am. Lib.* Signet 1972 pap. $1.50

GOLDEN ARROW. *Dufour* 1963 $10.95

WODEHOUSE, P(ELHAM) G(RENVILLE). 1881–

Evelyn Waugh once said: "The first thing to remark about Mr. Wodehouse's art is its universality, unique in this century. Few forms of writing are as ephemeral as comedy. Three full generations have delighted in Mr. Wodehouse. He satisfies the most sophisticated taste and the simplest. Belloc, to the consternation of Hugh Walpole, forthrightly declared him to be the best prose writer of the age; Ronald Knox, most fastidious of scholars and stylists, rejoiced in him."

P. G. Wodehouse made his first visit to the U.S. in 1904 and now lives here permanently. Since 1910 he has averaged at least two humorous books a year and created Psmith, the Hon. Bertie Wooster, Jeeves (a gentleman's gentleman) and many others, both British and American. His popularity with Americans can perhaps be explained by the fact that his characters and plots conform to nostalgic images of a Britain that never quite existed, though it once came close. "Author! Author!" is a collection of letters written to his friend, an English short story writer, whose hope it is that their wealth of discussion of literary techniques may help aspiring writers. "It is also an autobiography, packed with Wodehouse's experiences as a librettist in international show business, as a script writer in Hollywood, and as a *bon vivant* on two continents." He has recently (with Scott Meredith) edited "A Carnival of Modern Humor" (*Dell* Delacorte Press 1967 $4.95).

Among his books in print:

MOST OF P. G. WODEHOUSE. *Simon & Schuster* 1969 $7.95 pap. $3.75

THE WORLD OF JEEVES. *Manor Bks.* 1973 2 vols. pap. each $1.25

PLUM PIE. *Simon & Schuster* 1967 $4.95. Nine stories by Wodehouse, who is familiarly known as "Plum."

THE INIMITABLE JEEVES. 1924. *British Bk. Centre* 1949 rev. ed. 1956 $4.95

VERY GOOD, JEEVES. 1930. *British Bk. Centre* 1958 $4.95

HOW RIGHT YOU ARE, JEEVES. *Simon & Schuster* 1960 $3.50

SERVICE WITH A SMILE. *Simon & Schuster* 1960 $3.75

LEAVE IT TO PSMITH. *British Bk. Centre* 1961. $4.95

THE CODE OF THE WOOSTERS. *British Bk. Centre* 1962 $4.95; *Simon & Schuster* $4.95

THE BRINKMANSHIP OF GALAHAD THREEPWOOD. *Simon & Schuster* 1965 $4.50. A Blandings Castle novel.

THE PURLOINED PAPERWEIGHT. *Simon & Schuster* 1967 $4.95

"A thoroughly delightful piece of light whimsy in the true Wodehouse tradition"—(*PW*).

PSMITH, JOURNALIST. *Penguin* 1971 pap. $1.45

AMERICA I LIKE YOU. Ill. by Marc Simont. *Simon & Schuster* 1956 $3.50. "A collection of reminiscent essays, sprinkled with lots of current anecdotes and news items about the U.S.A."

AUTHOR! AUTHOR! *Simon & Schuster* 1962 $4.50. A compilation of letters, 1920–61, written to his friend William Townsend.

Other titles are published by British Bk. Centre, Penguin and Simon & Schuster.

Books about Wodehouse

P.G. Wodehouse. By Richard Voorhees. *Twayne* 1966 $4.95
  "Richard Voorhees, professor of English at Purdue University, weighs (I fear it's the verbe juste) in with an honest, not uninteresting but definitely not-soufflé survey of both the Master and his books"— (Arthur Marshall, in the *New Statesman*).
The World of P. G. Wodehouse. By Herbert Warren Wind. *Praeger* 1972 $5.95

JOYCE, JAMES. 1882–1941.

For many critics, James Joyce is the most important novelist of the century. He perfected the stream of consciousness monologue (which Édouard Dujardin and Dorothy Richardson had used before him); emerged as the most inventive of the experimental novelists; was a polyglot who could pun in a dozen languages; antagonized his friends because of his egoism, yet could write about characters unlike himself with great compassion. Joyce's life was filled with contrasts: he abandoned his home to become an artist and spent his life in exile writing about the city he had abandoned. He was thought of as a great writer by people who had read little of his work, for his books were banned in English-speaking countries. Though "Ulysses" was suppressed for its supposed obscenity, few books have been written that stress the virtues of family life as strongly.

There is always more to Joyce's works than first meets the eye. The stories in "Dubliners" are on the surface straightforward and naturalistic descriptions of city life; but beneath the surface Joyce uses irony and symbolism to show the true sterility of Dublin. One of the stories, "The Dead," seems to be about a festive occasion, the Morkans' annual dance; but the ghostly imagery reveals that the dance is a dance of the dead.

"A Portrait of the Artist as a Young Man" is similarly undercut by irony. The novel tells of Stephen Daedalus—a protagonist seemingly very much like the young Joyce, though ultimately quite different—and his struggle to become a writer. Stephen is certain that he is a great artist, worthy of his classical namesake; but Joyce ironically suggests that he may not be a Daedalus but an Icarus. Daedalus was the great artisan of Greek civilization; Icarus, his son, flew too close to the sun and plunged into the sea. The novel vibrates between the alternatives of greatness and inexperience, triumph and failure, art and sham. And it is filled with subtleties and hidden beauty: intricate imagery; compact prose, filled with significance; and musical, flowing language.

In Joyce's early works the innovative techniques are always subtle, concealed beneath a plain, seemingly conventional story. In his later works this is no longer true. The reader is immediately aware of the experimental techniques; the prose may seem strange or unusual; and very often it is the story which is difficult to discern.

"Ulysses" is such a work, a novel where one is soon aware of many strata of meaning. On one level the book tells of the need Stephen Daedalus has for a father, of Leopold Bloom's yearning for a son, and the story of how the two meet. On another level Stephen is Telemachus, Bloom is Odysseus, and their story is a modern "Odyssey." But here again, irony is important; for it is in the way that Bloom is not Odysseus, in his compassionate refusal to be as brutal as Odysseus, that his greatness and universality are revealed.

Every chapter of "Ulysses" has its own techniques, styles, central symbols, colors: these are ingeniously used to enhance the action. In a chapter where the chief event is the birth of a child, the style delineates the birth of the English language. Joyce accomplishes this by parodying great English writers, moving forward chronologically from the earliest to the most recent. "Ulysses" is a very demanding book; but after the initial difficulties are surmounted it yields many rewards.

"Ulysses" was so inventive that it seemed to exhaust the possibilities for innovation in the English novel. Joyce therefore moved beyond English and wrote "Finnegans Wake" in a new language made up of puns and neologisms. The prose demands a slow reading pace, for the words themselves are as important as the ideas they represent. It cannot be read like most novels, in a few sittings; it must be savored slowly, bit by bit, over months and years. A reader must come to it with a great store of patience, intelligence, and humor; and perhaps also with a good supply of critical commentaries.

Sixty years ago, Joyce's frankness seemed like obscenity, and he encountered difficulty in finding publishers for his works. Typesetters refused to work on his books; "Ulysses" was published in Paris because it was banned in England and the United States; and Americans who were eager to read it had to smuggle it past customs inspectors until 1933 when, in a historic decision, Judge Woolsey declared that it was not obscene.

Today enthusiasm for James Joyce continues to be strong. In 1967 the exciting film versions of "Ulysses" and of passages from "Finnegans Wake" played to eager audiences, as did the play "Stephen D,"—an adaptation of "A Portrait of the Artist as a Young Man" and "Stephen Hero"—and the revival of "The Coach With the Six Insides," Jean Erdman's award-winning dramatic dance interpretation of "Finnegans Wake." 1967 was also notable for the discovery of "Giacomo Joyce," a poetic love story Joyce wrote for a young woman, his pupil in Trieste, with whom he became infatuated. Joyce himself did not publish it, but worked passages from it into "Ulysses" and "Finnegans Wake."

Joyce spent most of his life away from his native Ireland—his last years in Paris. He and his family were visiting in Vichy when France fell in 1940; they finally took refuge in Zurich, practically penniless. His life had been a struggle against increasing blindness and the reluctance of publishers to print him. Stanislaus Joyce's "Dublin Diary" (1952, o. p.), a "little 114 page diary he kept in Dublin between the years 1903 and 1905, possesses a surprising aesthetic worth over and above that of its testimony concerning his celebrated brother"—(N.Y. Times). "Pound/Joyce" (ed. by Forrest Read New Directions 1967. $10.00 pap. $2.75) contains Ezra Pound's (q. v.) critical essays about Joyce and letters to him.

THE PORTABLE JAMES JOYCE. Ed. by Harry Levin *Viking* Portable Lib. 1947 $6.50 pap. $2.85. Includes: A Portrait of the Artist as a Young Man; Collected Poems; Exiles; Dubliners; selections from Ulysses and Finnegan's Wake.

CHAMBER MUSIC. 1907. (and "Pomes Penyeach") *Gordon Press* $12.95; *Grossman* Cape Ed. $3.95 pap. $1.95. 36 poems in "Chamber Music", and 13 in "Pomes Penyeach."

DUBLINERS. Short Stories. 1914. *Modern Library* $2.95; *Viking* 1958 new ed. 1968 by Robert Scholes and Richard Ellmann in the original manuscript style and first ed.

punctuation, new corrections by Joyce $4.50 Compass Bks. pap. $1.45 ed. by R. Scholes and A. Walton Litz Critical Lib. 1969 $5.95 pap. $2.25

A PORTRAIT OF THE ARTIST AS A YOUNG MAN. 1916. Autobiographical novel. Ed. by Richard Ellmann *Viking* 1964 $3.95 Compass Bks. pap. $1.65 ed. by C. G. Anderson Critical Lib. 1968 $6.50 pap. $2.25; *Franklin Watts* lg.-type ed. Keith Jennison Bks. $8.95

EXILES: A play. Introd. by Padraic Colum *Viking* 1951 Compass Bks. pap. $1.45. Includes hitherto unpublished notes by the author, discovered after his death.

ULYSSES. 1922. Introd. and note by the author; fwd. by Morris Ernst and a reprint of the decision by John M. Woolsey *Random* 1934 1946 $10.00 Vintage Bks. pap. $2.95

POMES PENYEACH. 1927. *Bern Porter* 1972 $7.50; *City Lights* pap. $.50. Thirteen poems.

FINNEGAN'S WAKE. *Viking* 1939 1959 $8.95 Compass Bks. pap. $2.95

A SHORTER FINNEGAN'S WAKE. Ed. with introd. by Anthony Burgess *Viking* 1966 $6.00 Compass Bks. pap. $2.25

This abridged version, "with its interspersed commentary and its long introduction, will probably do more than any other work has done to bring to the serious general reader one of the most admired—and most difficult—books of this century. . . . A devoted Joycean, Burgess has reduced the text to somewhat over a third of its original length"—(*LJ*).

PASSAGES FROM FINNEGANS WAKE: A Free Adaptation for the Theatre. Ed by Mary Manning. *Harvard Univ. Press* 1957 $4.00

A FIRST-DRAFT VERSION OF JOYCE'S FINNEGAN'S WAKE. Ed. and annot. by David Hayman. *Univ. of Texas Press* 1962 $10.00. A textual study that gives a unique record of Joyce's quest for form and tone.

STEPHEN HERO. *New Directions* 1963 1969 $5.50 pap. $1.95. In 1955 *New Directions* published a new edition, with a preface by John J. Slocum and Herbert Cahoon, which incorporated newly discovered sections of the manuscript and Theodore Spencer's essay on this early version of "A Portrait of the Artist as a Young Man." This new edition adds five recently discovered manuscript pages.

GIACOMO JOYCE. Introd. by Richard Ellmann *Viking* 1968 $3.95. This edition has four pages of reduced facsimile manuscript.

LETTERS. *Viking* 3 vols. Vol. 1 ed. by Stuart Gilbert (1957) $10.00 Vols. 2 and 3 ed. by Richard Ellmann (1966) $25.00. boxed set $35.00

Volumes 2 and 3 contain "more than thirteen hundred new letters, edited with the most meticulous and informative scholarship, to supplement the volume of letters edited by Stuart Gilbert in 1957. Joyce did not take the epistolary form seriously, as Professor Ellmann's preface admits somewhat ruefully, and these are not masterworks to rival the letters of Keats or Hopkins, but Joyce was sometimes wonderfully funny (mostly in letters to his brother Stanislaus), sometimes wonderfully grovepressy (as in a series of spicy letters to his wife), and at all times the incomparable James Joyce"—(*New Yorker*). Gilbert's Volume 1, which has been corrected by Ellmann, contains about 400 letters written from 1901–40.

Books about Joyce

A Key to the Ulysses of James Joyce. By Paul Jordan-Smith. 1927. *Gordon Press* $3.75; *Folcroft* $4.50, $15.00; *Haskell* $3.95; *City Lights* pap. $1.50

Our Exagmination Round His Factification for Incamination of Work in Progress. By Samuel Becket, W. C. Williams and others. Introd. to reissue by Sylvia Beach. 1929. *New Directions* 1939 1962 reissued 1972 with title "James Joyce—Finnegan's Wake: A Symposium" pap. $2.95. Originally published in Paris (1929) by Sylvia Beach's Shakespeare and Company Bookshop, this "Exagmination" to assist in the reading and comprehension of "Finnegans Wake" came out ten years before Joyce completed his work. The contributors were all friends or acquaintances and Joyce himself is believed to have written here under a pseudonym.

James Joyce's Ulysses: A Study. By Stuart Gilbert. 1931 2nd ed. rev. 1955 *Random* Vintage Bks. pap. $1.95. An early study but still very useful; Joyce explained the Homeric parallels to Gilbert while he was writing this study.

James Joyce. By Harry Levin. *New Directions* 1941 rev. ed. 1960 pap. $1.95. A good introduction.

A Skeleton Key to Finnegan's Wake. By Joseph Campbell and Henry Morton Robinson. 1944. *Viking* Compass Bks. pap. $2.25. An extremely useful book.

James Joyce: Two Decades of Criticism. Ed. by Seon Givens. 1948. *Vanguard* 1963 $10.00. A reissue of this source book that includes essays by Edmund Wilson, T. S. Eliot and 15 other critics.

James Joyce: His Way of Interpreting the Modern World. By William York Tindall. *Scribner* 1950 pap. $2.95. A witty and intelligent discussion of Joyce's work.

Joyce: The Man, The Work, The Reputation. By Marvin Magalener and Richard M. Kain. *New York Univ. Press* 1956 $8.95.

Joyce and Shakespeare: A Study in the Meaning of Ulysses. By William M. Schutte. 1957. *Shoe String* 1971 $6.75

Joyce among the Jesuits. By Kevin Sullivan. *Columbia* 1958 $9.00

My Brother's Keeper: James Joyce's Early Years. By Stanislaus Joyce. Ed. with introd. by Richard Ellmann; pref. by T. S. Eliot. 1958. *Viking* Compass Bks. pap. $1.65

James Joyce. By Richard Ellmann. *Oxford* 1959 $15.00 Galaxy Bks. pap. $3.95. Not only an excellent biography by Joyce, but one of the best literary biographies ever written.

A Reader's Guide to James Joyce. By William York Tindall. *Farrar, Straus* 1959 $6.95. One of the best introductions to Joyce in print. Tindall has essays on Joyce's major works together with annotations that help with difficult passages and allusions.

Sympathetic Alien: James Joyce and Catholicism. By J. Mitchell Morse. *New York Univ. Press* 1959 $6.95

James Joyce and the Making of Ulysses. By Frank Budgen. *Indiana Univ. Press* 1960 Midland Bks. pap. $2.25; *Peter Smith* $4.50

The Art of James Joyce: Method and Design in Ulysses and Finnegan's Wake. By A. Walton Litz. *Oxford* 1960 $5.50 Galaxy Bks. pap. $2.50

Classical Temper: A Study of James Joyce's Ulysses. By S. L. Goldberg. *Barnes & Noble* 1961 $5.50

The Cornell Joyce Collection: A Catalog. Comp. by Robert Scholes. *Cornell Univ. Press* 1961 $8.50

Surface and Symbol: The Consistency of James Joyce's Ulysses. By Robert M. Adams. *Oxford* 1962 $7.95 Galaxy Bks. pap. $2.50. An original and sensible guide; Professor Adams investigates and identifies much of the raw material that went into the novel and often provides information not available elsewhere.

Joyce's Portrait: Criticisms and Critiques. Ed. by Thomas E. Connolly. *Appleton* 1962 pap. $5.45

Structure and Motif in Finnegans Wake. By Clive Hart. *Northwestern Univ. Press* 1962 $8.00

A New Approach to Joyce: The Portrait of the Artist as a Guidebook. By Robert S. Ryf. *Univ. of California Press* 1962 pap. $1.95

Dublin's Joyce. By Hugh Kenner. 1962. *Peter Smith* $5.50

James Joyce's Manuscripts and Letters at the University of Buffalo: A Catalogue Compiled with an Introduction by Peter Spielberg. *State Univ. of N.Y. Press* 1962 $10.00 microfiche $10.00. Invaluable to those using the mss. or borrowing them on microfilm.

A Second Census of Finnegan's Wake: An Index of the Characters and Their Roles. By Adaline Glasheen. *Northwestern Univ. Press* 1963 $7.50. The successor to "A Census of Finnegan's Wake" (1957) by the same author, now o.p.

Joyce's Benefictions. By Helmut Bonheim. *Univ. of California Press* 1964 $5.75. A scholarly work on Joyce's style with emphasis on "Finnegan's Wake."

Exploring James Joyce. By Joseph Prescott. *Southern Illinois Univ. Press* 1964 $4.50

James Joyce in Paris: His Final Years. By Gisele Freund and V. B. Carleton. *Harcourt* 1965 $8.50

The Workshop of Daedalus. By Robert Scholes and Richard Kain. *Northwestern Univ. Press* 1965 $9.00

Twelve and a Tilly: Essays on the Occasion of the 25th Anniversary of Finnegan's Wake. Ed. by Jack P. Dalton and Clive Hart. *Northwestern Univ. Press* 1965 $5.50

Re Joyce. By Anthony Burgess. *Norton* 1965 pap. $2.95; *Peter Smith* $4.00
"An admirable introduction to James Joyce and an aid to those who have already made their own effort but faltered. . . . In fact, this is the best study of Joyce that I have ever read"—(Philip Toynbee, in the *Observer*).

The Argument of Ulysses. By Stanley Sultan. *Ohio State Univ. Press* 1965 $6.95

The Bloomsday Book: A Guide through Joyce's Ulysses. By Harry Blamires. *Barnes & Noble* 1966 $5.75

James Joyce: Common Sense and Beyond. By Robert M. Adams. *Random* 1966 pap. $2.25; *Peter Smith* $4.00

A Concordance to the Collected Poems of James Joyce. By Paul A. Doyle. *Scarecrow Press* 1966 $5.00

James Joyce. By A. Walton Litz. English Authors Ser. *Twayne* 1966 $4.95. Critical analysis relating the works to each other and to the main body of contemporary literature. Annotated bibliography.

James Joyce Today: Essays on the Major Works, Commemorating the Twenty-Fifth Anniversary of His Death. Ed. with pref. by Thomas F. Staley. *Indiana Univ. Press* 1966 $6.50 Midland Bks. pap. $1.95. Seven essays by noted scholars treating each of the major works.

Notes for Joyce: Dubliners and A Portrait of the Artist as a Young Man. By Don Gifford. *Dutton* (orig.) 1967 pap. $1.75. Originally conceived as an aid to students, this set of notes illuminates obscure Joycean references and vocabulary; it is keyed to the *Viking* and *Modern Library* editions to the works.

A Gaelic Lexicon for Finnegans Wake, and Glossary for Joyce's Other Works. By Brendan O Hehir. *University of California Press* 1967 $10.00

The Conscience of James Joyce. By Darcy O'Brien. *Princeton Univ. Press* 1967 $8.50. Joyce seen as "an Irishman in spite of himself."

James Joyce Remembered. By Constantine Curran. *Oxford* 1968 $5.00. A friend of Joyce, the author sheds light on his personal and literary convictions.

James Joyce and His World. By Chester G. Anderson. *Viking* Studio Bks. 1968 $6.95
A pictorial biography. "A grand book. . . . The most human of all the studies I have read"—(Michael MacLiammoir).

Allusions in Ulysses: An Annotated List. By Weldon Thornton. *Univ. of North Carolina Press* 1968 $12.50. Explains many of Joyce's most important allusions; a valuable book.

Joyce's Dubliners: Substance, Vision and Art. By Warren Beck. *Duke Univ. Press* 1969 $8.75

A Reader's Guide to Finnegans Wake. By William York Tindall. *Farrar, Straus* 1969 $6.95 pap. $2.95. A very useful guide and introduction.

Joyce and Aquinas. By William T. Noon. 1957. *Shoe String* 1970 $5.50

James Joyce. By John Gross. *Viking* 1970 $4.95 pap. $1.65. A short introductory work.

The Stream of Consciousness and Beyond in Ulysses. By Erwin R. Steinberg. *Univ. of Pittsburgh Press* 1972 $9.95

James Joyce. By Italo Svevo. *City Lights* pap. $1.25. Svevo, himself a novelist, was a friend of Joyce's in Trieste.

James Joyce. By J. I. M. Stewart. *British Book Centre* $2.38 pap. $1.20

James Joyce. By Fritz Senn. *Bucknell Univ. Press* $4.50 pap. $1.95

Joyce and the Bible. By Virginia Moseley. *Northern Illinois Univ. Press* $6.50

James Joyce. By Herbert Gorman. *Octagon* 1972 $12.00

WOOLF, VIRGINIA. 1882–1941.

Virginia Woolf was a great experimenter. She scorned the traditional narrative form and turned to expressionism as a means of telling her story. Joseph Warren Beach in "The Twentieth Century Novel" points out that her expressionism is the opposite of impressionism and aims "not to give an impression of the look of the object but to express its meaning or essence."

"Mrs. Dalloway" is a "stream-of-consciousness" novel, the action of which takes place in one day. "To the Lighthouse" is of the same type; it covers two days among a group of characters and is entirely without plot. "Orlando" is the chronological life story of a person who begins as an Elizabethan gentleman and ends as a lady of the 20th century; her friend, Victoria Sackville-West (*q. v.*) of the famous Knole Castle, served as the principal model for the multiple personalities. "Flush" is a dog's soliloquy which by indirection recounts the Browning love story and elopement and life in Florence. Her last short novel, "Between the Acts," was left without her final revision. According to Ben Ray Redman, "Here is the imagining, fabricating novelist; the social satirist; the lyric poet and the impressionist; the wilful mystifier; the subtle psychologist; the lover and painter of word pictures, the writer who could miraculously perform the feat of translating music into words."

Fearing a second mental breakdown from which she might not recover, Virginia Woolf drowned herself in 1941. Her husband published a part of her farewell letter to correct the erroneous report that she had taken her life because she could not face the terrible times of war. Leonard Woolf (*q. v.*) has also edited "A Writer's Diary" (1953, o. p.), which provides valuable insights into his wife's private thoughts and literary development. Equally informative are his own autobiographies, particularly "Beginning Again" and "Downhill All the Way," and "The Letters of Virginia Woolf and Lytton Strachey" (ed. by James Strachey and Leonard Woolf 1956, o. p.). There are many sidelights on Mrs. Woolf in the writings, letters and biographies of other members of her "Bloomsbury" circle, such as Roger Fry, John Maynard Keynes, Lytton Strachey. "The Life and Letters of Leslie Stephen," her father, has recently been reprinted by *Gale* (1906, 1967 $7.80). Virginia Woolf's "Granite and Rainbow" (*Harcourt* 1958 $5.75) contains 27 essays on the art of fiction and biography.

JACOB'S ROOM (1923) and THE WAVES (1931). *Harcourt* Harvest Bks. 1960 pap. $2.45

MRS. DALLOWAY. *Harcourt* 1925 Harbrace Mod. Class. 1949 $2.95 text ed. $1.65 Harvest Bks. pap. $1.45

TO THE LIGHTHOUSE. *Harcourt* 1927 Harbrace Mod. Class. 1949 $2.95 Harvest Bks. pap. $1.65

ORLANDO. 1928. Afterword by Elizabeth Bowen. *New Am. Lib.* Signet pap. $.95

FLUSH, A BIOGRAPHY. *Harcourt* 1933 $5.95 pap. $.45. Elizabeth Barrett Browning's cocker spaniel.

THE YEARS. 1937. *Harcourt* Harvest Bks. 1969 pap. $2.85

BETWEEN THE ACTS. *Harcourt* 1941 $5.75 Harvest Bks. pap. $2.45

A HAUNTED HOUSE AND OTHER SHORT STORIES. *Harcourt* 1944 Harvest Bks. pap. $1.65. Includes 12 stories hitherto unpublished in book form.

Books about Woolf

The Moth and the Star: A Biography of Virginia Woolf. By Aileen Pippett. 1955. *Kraus* $15.00
Virginia Woolf. By David Daiches. 1942. *New Directions* rev. ed. 1963 pap. $1.45
Virginia Woolf. By J. Bennett. 1945. *Cambridge* 1958 $4.50 pap. $1.45
Virginia Woolf: A Commentary. By Bernard Blackstone. *Harcourt* 1949 Harvest Bks. pap. 1972 $2.45
Virginia Woolf. By Bernard Blackstone. Writers and Their Work Ser. *British Bk. Centre* $2.38 pap. $1.20
The Glass Roof: Virginia Woolf as a Novelist. 1954. By James Robert Hafley. *Russell & Russell* 1963 $10.00
Virginia Woolf's London. By Dorothy Brewster. *New York Univ. Press* 1960 $5.00
Virginia Woolf. By Dorothy Brewster. *New York Univ. Press* 1962 $6.50 pap. $2.25. A study of the woman, the critic and the artist of great genius.
Virginia Woolf. By C. Woodring. Essays on Modern Writers *Columbia* 1966 pap. $1.00. A good introduction.
Worlds in Consciousness: Mythopoetic Thought in the Novels of Virginia Woolf. By Jean O. Love. *Univ. of California Press* 1970 $7.95
Virginia Woolf's Lighthouse: A Study in Critical Method. By Mitchell A. Leaska. *Columbia* 1970 $7.50
Feminism and Art: A Study of Virginia Woolf. By Herbert Marder. *Univ. of Chicago Press* 1972 pap. $1.95
Virginia Woolf. By Quentin Bell. *Harcourt* 1972 $9.00. A well-written biography.
Virginia Woolf and the Androgynous Vision. By Nancy T. Bazin. *Rutgers Univ. Press* 1972 $9.00

STEPHENS, JAMES. 1882–1951.

An Irish poet and writer of fantasy and romance, Stephens, a product of the Dublin slums, was first employed as a typist for a lawyer in Dublin, where he was discovered by "AE" (George Russell) and encouraged to write. At that time he was contributing sketches to a Dublin paper which later became his masterpiece, "The Crock of Gold," and won the Polignac Prize. This story is characteristic of all Stephens' work in its Celtic and allegorical quality.

An ardent student of Gaelic and an authority on Gaelic art, he hoped to give Ireland "a new mythology" through his books. His prose has been called "nut-flavored, sinewy-supple, antic, high-colored" by Charles A. Brady. Frank Swinnerton wrote: "First it is a tale, and then it is philosophy, and then it is nonsense; but all these qualities are so merged and, for the reader, confounded, that the effect is one of profound laughter." James Joyce once said that if he died before "Finnegans Wake" was finished, the only man capable of finishing it was James Stephens. (*See* "Twentieth Century Authors".) "James, Seumas, and Jacques" is printed from the manuscripts of 42 of Stephens' radio broadcasts for BBC, 1928–50. Their Irish talk is delightful; here he is critic, commentator, poet and recaller of Joyce, Yeats, Synge, Shaw, Moore and the rest. On sales of his poetry to readers in Britain: "The whole forty-two million of them clubbed together and bought nine of my books last year."

MARY, MARY. 1912. *Scholarly Press* 1970 $14.50

THE CROCK OF GOLD. 1912. *Macmillan* 1948 pap. $1.95

IRISH FAIRY TALES. 1920. *Macmillan* $6.95 Collier Bks. pap. $1.95

Deirdre. 1923. *Macmillan* 1970 $5.95

Books about Stephens

> James Stephens. By Hilary Pyle. 1965. *Fernhill* $5.00
> James Stephens. By Birgit Bramsback. *Bucknell Univ. Press* $4.50 pap. $1.95

SWINNERTON, FRANK. 1884–

As the writer of more than 30 novels, Frank Swinnerton has shown himself dependable, compassionate and wise, but he has never been a runaway critical success. In the publishing field from the age of 14, he first came to the eye of the British reading public with the fine and delicate "Nocturne," admired by his friends Arnold Bennett and H. G. Wells. His main fictional interest has been the treatment of English urban life. "Quadrille," tightly constructed and set in present-day London, is the fourth and the only available novel tracing the fortunes of the Grace family. "Sanctuary," says the *New Yorker*, is "a simple and delightful tale of fearsome crisis set in London, in a very unusual home for retired old ladies." It shows that "the octogenarian author has lost none of his vigor of attack on his subject. His opening chapter could serve as a model of how to depict a scene, indicate character and establish a mood"—(*N.Y. Times*). Swinnerton's close association with publishers and authors makes his essays and his autobiography, "Swinnerton" (1936, o. p.), a mine of literary history. His available biographical and critical works include "Arnold Bennett" (*British Bk. Centre* $2.38 pap. $1.20), "George Gissing" (1912. *Kennikat* 1966 $7.00). "Robert Louis Stevenson" (1915. *Kennikat* $7.50) and "A Galaxy of Fathers" (1966. *Bks. for Libraries* $9.50). The latter is an analysis of the adoring relationships of the writers Anna Seward, Fanny Burney, Maria Edgeworth and Mary Russell Mitford with each of their fathers; it is "an acute psychological study that does not read like one, a delightful causerie about writing that is quite profound, and a work that is at once funny and informative"—(*New Yorker*). For many years Mr. Swinnerton contributed occasional letters called "A Word from London," on the British book trade, to the (U.S.) *Publishers' Weekly*.

Nocturne. 1917. *Dufour* 1964 $5.95; *Lancer* pap. $1.25

A Woman in Sunshine. 1944. *Lancer* 1973 pap. $1.25

The Doctor's Wife Comes to Stay. 1949. *Lancer* 1973 pap. $1.25

Tokefield Papers, Old and New. 1949. *Bks. for Libraries* $10.50

Figures in the Foreground, 1917–1940. 1963. *Bks. for Libraries* $11.25

Sanctuary. 1967. *Lancer* pap. $1.50

On the Shady Side. 1970. *Lancer* 1973 pap. $1.25

Nor All Thy Tears. *Doubleday* 1972 $6.95

Books about Swinnerton

> George Gissing and His Critic Frank Swinnerton. By Ruth MacKay. *Folcroft* lib. bdg. $15.00

LEWIS, (PERCY) WYNDHAM. 1884–1957.

Distinguished and highly original, Wyndham Lewis is known for his "darting wit and sardonic insight." A modern master of satire, expert at deflating the pretensions of democracy, he was born off the coast of Maine in his English father's yacht and grew up in England. He was associated with Roger Fry and Ezra Pound on the vorticist magazine *Blast* (1914–15). Lewis served in France in World War I, and his dynamic paintings of war scenes soon gained him wide recognition for his art, now represented in the Tate Gallery and the Victoria and Albert Museum, London, and in the Museum of Modern Art, New York. After the publication of his naturalistic novel "Tarr" (1918), he became prominent as a writer. His dignified view of the artist and the nature and function of art is expressed in "Time and Western Man" (1927, o. p.). "The Demon of Progress in the Arts" (1955, o. p.) is a discussion of esthetics in modern technological society. Lewis "was one of those high-powered, controversial and prophetic figures to whom no one can react with indifference. He was a fellow-traveller with fascism who wrote enthusiastically about Hitler. . . . A toughy, you see: a would-be shocker: a braggart. But his eye for the comic surface of things is marvelous. [His autobiography] remains memorable for a sequence of wonderfully funny set-pieces. . . . A few interpolated passages of fiction serve to remind us of his more formal style—and helps us to forget that Lewis had a very ugly and silly side as well"—(*Observer*, London). So writes Philip Toynbee, reviewing a British reissue of "Blasting and Bombardiering." T. S. Eliot called Wyndham Lewis "the most fascinating personality of our time" and he was described by Yeats as having that rare quality in writers, intellectual passion. His Letters "make fascinating reading"—(*LJ*).

TARR. 1918. *Dufour* 1970 $5.95 pap. $2.95

THE WILD BODY. 1927. *Haskell* $10.95. Short stories: A Soldier of Humour, Beau Jejour, Bestre, The Cornac and His Wife, The Death of the Ankou, Franciscan Adventures, Brotcotnaz, Inferior Religions.

THE CHILDERMASS. 1928. *Scholarly Press* 1972 $19.50

THE HUMAN AGE: The Childermass; Monstre Gai; Malign Fiesta. *Dufour* 1970 each $5.95 pap. each $2.95. These three are volumes of the tetralogy "The Human Age" published together in 1955. The fourth volume, "The Trial of Man," is o. p.

THE SNOOTY BARON. 1932. *Haskell* 1971 lib. bdg. $11.95

SELF-CONDEMNED: A Novel of Exile. *Regnery* Gateway Eds. 1955 1965 pap. $1.95

BLASTING AND BOMBARDIERING: An Autobiography 1914–1926. 1937. *Univ. of California Press* 2nd rev. ed. 1967 $8.50

LETTERS. Ed. with pref. by W. K. Rose. *New Directions* 1963 $8.50. Letters to Pound, Eliot, Joyce, Augustus John and others.

Books about Lewis

A Master of Our Time: A Study of Wyndham Lewis. By Geoffrey Grigson. 1951. *Haskell* 1972 $5.95; *Folcroft* $7.50; *Gordon Press* $5.50
Wyndham Lewis. By Hugh Kenner. *New Directions* 1954. $3.75 pap. $1.75
Wyndham Lewis. By E. W. F. Tomlin. Writers and Their Works Ser. *British Bk. Centre* $2.38 pap. $1.20
Wyndham Lewis. By William H. Pritchard. *Twayne* 1968 $5.50
Wyndham Lewis: Fictions and Satires. By Robert T. Chapman. *Barnes & Noble* 1973 $9.50

LAWRENCE, D(AVID) H(ERBERT). 1885–1930.

One of Lawrence's finest novels, traditional in form and unlike his later work, is "Sons and Lovers," an epic of family life in a colliery district and "unabashed autobiography." Lawrence himself was the son of a miner and was born in the coal region of Nottinghamshire. "The Rainbow," with its forthright treatment of sexual passion, was condemned as obscene in 1915 and the entire edition destroyed. "Lady Chatterley's Lover," which Lawrence considered his greatest work, was written in at least three versions. It was privately printed in Florence, Italy, and banned both in England and the United States until 1959, when *Grove Press* undertook publication of the third manuscript version and issued the first U.S. unexpurgated version. It was immediately banned by the United States Post Office, but in a now-famous opinion, Judge Frederick van Pelt Bryan ruled the ban "unconstitutional" and confirmed it as "illegal and void."

Always in search of warm climates for his tuberculosis, Lawrence spent some time in New Mexico in 1924 on a ranch presented to him by Mabel Dodge Luhan. Here "he found himself as much at harmony as he was ever to be with any place." After Lawrence's death the battle waged by his (often jealous) disciples turned to civil warfare. Abuse, libel, recriminations fill many of the early books about him.

He left behind him "an extraordinarily large body of work for so short a career, nearly all of it strongly marked by his unmistakable literary and philosophical imprint." In his poetry, says Elizabeth Drew, he "makes us feel the intensity of life in the natural world"; his "birds, beasts and flowers have a glowing vigor." The "passion, conflict, turmoil and striving" that marked his brief life are reflected in "Selected Poems (*Viking* Compass Bks. 1959 pap., $1.45); "Complete Poems" (ed. with introd. by Vivian De Sola Pinto and F. Warren Roberts *Viking* 1964 2 vols. boxed $12.50 Compass Bks. pap. $4.50); and "Look! We Have Come Through" (1917, o. p.). "The Complete Plays" (*Viking* 1966 $7.50) contains all eight of his finished plays and two fragments. Three books of travel, no longer available separately, can be found in "D. H. Lawrence and Italy." They are "Sea and Sardinia," (1921) "Twilight in Italy" (1916) and "Etruscan Places" (1932). Of "The Paintings of D. H. Lawrence" (1964, o. p.) *Library Journal* said: "Now, just 35 years after his first and only exhibition at the Warren Gallery in London—an exhibition that ended typically for Lawrence in prosecution—every extant piece has been collected in this handsome volume. . . . These efforts with the brush are interesting and compelling in themselves and they furnish telling insights into the literary achievements of a major writer." He explained his views on love and sex, and their place in literature in "Sex Literature and Censorship," eight essays (ed. with introd. by Harry T. Moore *Twayne* 1953 $4.00; *Viking* Compass Bks. 1959 pap. $1.45). His views on psychology may be found in "Psychoanalysis and the Unconscious and Fantasia of the Unconscious" (1921, 1922, *Viking* Compass Bks. 2 vols. in 1 1960 pap. $1.65). His best critical work, including much material from out-of-print sources, is contained in "Selected Literary Criticism" (ed. by Anthony Beal *Viking* 1956 $5.00 Compass Bks. pap. $2.25). In his collection of essays, "Reflections on the Death of a Porcupine" (1925, *Indiana Univ. Press* Midland Bks. 1963 pap. $1.95), he put down, sometimes in a poetic and allegorical vein, sometimes satirically, his views on life and love, on war and peace and on the writer's craft. "Phoenix: The Posthumous Papers of D. H. Lawrence" (1936, ed. by Edward D. McDonald *Viking* 1967 $12.50 Compass Bks. pap. $4.50) contains essays on art and literature. "Phoenix II" (ed. with introd. by Warren Roberts and Harry T. Moore *Viking* 1967 $12.50 Compass Bks. pap. $3.75) is his prose nonfiction hitherto uncollected, unpublished, or o.p., including the complete essay "Reflections on the Death of a Porcupine," "Assorted Articles" and the discarded prologue to "Women in Love." "The Symbolic Meaning: The Uncollected Versions of 'Studies in Classic American Literature' " (ed. by Armin Arnold, with introd. by Harry T. Moore 1964. *Saifer* $10.00) contains 12 enthusiastic and "perceptive" essays by Lawrence on American literature—conceived as lectures to be incorporated into a book, "The Transcendental Element in American Literature," which was never published. "When Lawrence later came to America, he hated it; his sympathy for its literature turned to contempt, which is expressed with almost hysterical force in 'Studies in Classic American Literature' "—(*LJ*) (1923, *Viking* 1964 $4.50 Compass Bks. pap. $1.75). "Apocalypse" (1931, *Viking* $5.00 Compass Bks. 1931 pap. $1.45) is a reflection on the biblical Book of Revelation. The publication in 1962 of his "Collected Letters" was one of the literary events of the year.

THE PORTABLE D. H. LAWRENCE. Ed. with introd. by Diana Trilling *Viking* 1947 lib. bdg. $6.50 pap. $2.95

THE LATER D. H. LAWRENCE: The Best Novels, Stories, Essays, 1925–1930. Sel. with introds. by William York Tindall. *Knopf* 1952 $7.50

COMPLETE SHORT STORIES. *Viking* Compass Bks. 1955 1961 3 vols. vols. 1–2 each $1.65. Includes the collections originally published as A Modern Lover, The Lovely Lady, Love Among the Haystacks and others.

FOUR SHORT NOVELS. Love Among the Haystacks (1930, really short stories); The Ladybird (1923); The Fox; The Captain's Doll. *Viking* Compass Bks. 1965 pap. $1.65

THE WHITE PEACOCK. 1911. *Southern Illinois Univ. Press* 1966 $6.95

SONS AND LOVERS. 1913. *Modern Library* $2.95; *Viking* $.50 Critical Lib. 1968 $4.75 pap. $2.45

THE PRUSSIAN OFFICER AND OTHER STORIES. 1914. *Bks. for Libraries* $10.50

THE RAINBOW. 1915. *Viking* Compass Bks. pap. $1.95

WOMEN IN LOVE. 1920. *Modern Library* $2.95; *Viking* Compass Bks. 1960 pap. $2.25

THE LOST GIRL. 1920. *Viking* Compass Bks. 1968 pap. $2.45

AARON'S ROD. 1922 *Viking* Compass Bks. pap. $1.85

KANGAROO. 1923. *Viking* 1960 $5.75 Compass Bks. pap. $1.95

(With M. L. Skinner) BOY IN THE BUSH. 1924. *Southern Illinois Univ. Press* 1971 $10.00; *Viking* Compass Bks. 1972 pap. $2.95

ST. MAWR (1925) and THE MAN WHO DIED (1931). *Random* Vintage Bks. 1959 2 vols. in 1 pap. $1.65

THE PLUMED SERPENT, QUETZALCOATL. Introd. by William York Tindall *Knopf* 1926 1951 $8.95; *Random* Vintage Bks. pap. $2.20

Lady Chatterley's Lover. Original unexpurgated version. *Grove* Black Cat Bks. 1962 pap. $.95; *Modern Library* 1960 $2.95; authorized expurgated version *New Am. Lib.* Signet pap. $.95; (with title "John Thomas and Lady Jane") the hitherto unpublished second version. "The longest and most serious." *Viking* 1972 $8.95

Collected Letters. Ed. by Harry T. Moore. *Viking* 1962 2 vols. $17.50. More than 1200 letters with a very useful "Who's Who in the Lawrence Letters" by the editor.

Centaur Letters: Unpublished Letters by D. H. Lawrence. *Univ. of Texas Press* 1970 $9.75

Books about Lawrence

Young Lorenzo: Early Life of D. H. Lawrence. By Ada Lawrence and G. S. Gelder. 1931. *Russell & Russell* 1966 $8.50 Ada Lawrence is his sister.

Lorenzo in Taos. By Mabel Dodge Luhan. 1932. *Kraus* 1969 $15.00

D. H. Lawrence: Pilgrim of the Apocalypse. By Horace Gregory. 1933. *Bks. for Libraries* $8.50; *Grove* 1970 pap. $1.95

D. H. Lawrence and Susan his Cow. By William York Tindall. 1939. *Cooper Square* 1973 $6.50

D. H. Lawrence: Portrait of a Genius But. . . . By Richard Aldington. 1950 *Macmillan* Collier Bks. pap. $1.50

The Life and Works of D. H. Lawrence. By Harry T. Moore. *Twayne* 1951 $6.00

D. H. Lawrence: Novelist. By Frank Raymond Leavis. *Knopf* 1956 $5.95. A study by one of Lawrence's leading advocates in England.

The Love Ethic of D. H. Lawrence. By Mark Spilka; fwd. by Frieda Lawrence Ravagli. *Indiana Univ. Press* Midland Bks. 1955 pap. $1.75; *Peter Smith* $3.75

A D. H. Lawrence Miscellany. Ed. by Harry T. Moore. *Southern Illinois Univ. Press* 1959 $6.50

D. H. Lawrence: A Composite Biography. Ed. by Edward H. Nels. *Univ. of Wisconsin Press* 3 vols. 1957–59 each $7.50 set $20.00

D. H. Lawrence: The Failure and the Triumph of Art. By Eliseo Vivas. *Northwestern Univ. Press* 1960 $4.75; *Indiana Univ. Press* 1964 pap. $2.25

The Priest of Love: A Life of D. H. Lawrence. (Original title "The Intelligent Heart"). By Harry T. Moore. 1962. *Farrar, Straus* 1973 price not set

The Art of Perversity: D. H. Lawrence's Shorter Fictions. By Kingsley Widmer. *Univ. of Washington Press* 1962 $6.95

D. H. Lawrence. By David Daiches. *Folcroft* 1963 $4.00

The Deed of Life: The Novels and Tales of D. H. Lawrence. By Julian Moynahan. *Princeton Univ. Press* 1963 $7.50 pap. $2.95. A chronological analysis of 10 novels and a group of shorter pieces.

Oedipus in Nottingham: D. H. Lawrence. By Daniel A. Weiss. *Univ. of Washington Press* 1963 $5.00

The Utopian Vision of D. H. Lawrence. By Eugene Goodheart. *Univ. of Chicago Press* 1963 $6.50

D. H. Lawrence: A Collection of Critical Essays. Ed. by Mark Spilka. Twentieth Century Views Ser. *Prentice-Hall* Spectrum Bks. 1963 $5.95 pap. $1.95

D. H. Lawrence, Artist and Rebel. By E. W. Tedlock, Jr. *Univ. of New Mexico Press* 1964 $7.00
"A long needed, unpretentious, but very thorough study of Lawrence's development. . . . Perhaps of primary interest to students of literature, the book's good sense and pleasant style will commend it to a wide range of serious readers of 20th-century fiction—(Prof. John R. Willingham, in *LJ*).

Frieda Lawrence: The Memoirs and Correspondence. Ed. by E. W. Tedlock, Jr. *Knopf* 1964 $8.95
By the woman who left her first husband and children to become Mrs. Lawrence. "This book is a mass of styles. Sometimes fiction, sometimes pure narrative, depending on mood or subject. From her youth to directly after D. H. Lawrence's death Frieda Lawrence wrote of her life and of her life with friends and those who were more than friends and the things that were happening. Professor Tedlock has stitched it all together, but the story is not always easy reading. Neither the Memoir nor the Letters add much to the scholar's knowledge of Lawrence, but the book does interpret a woman of *Sturm und Drang* who wanted to know and help in a man's work. . . . The Memoir belongs in Lawrence collections"—(*LJ*).

Double Measure: A Study of the Novels and Stories of D. H. Lawrence. By George H. Ford. *Holt* 1965 $5.95 *Norton* pap. $2.25
"Vigorous, judicious, and readable criticism"—(Prof. Ben W. Fuson, in *LJ*).

Dark Night of the Body: D. H. Lawrence's "The Plumed Serpent." By L. D. Clark. *Univ. of Texas Press* 1964 $6.00
"The Clarks (his wife took the photographs . . .) spent one year assiduously tracing D. H. Lawrence's itinerary and activities in New Mexico and Mexico . . . and interviewing those still alive who had known Lawrence in the 1920's. Their devotion is justified through this book, which effectively illumi-

nates Lawrence's often turgidly incantatory novel, lays bare its structure and interprets its themes and symbols"—(Prof. Ben W. Fuson, in *L J*).

Lawrence and Sons and Lovers: Sources and Criticism. By E. W. Tedlock, Jr. *New York Univ. Press* 1965 $8.95 pap. $2.75

The Forked Flame: A Study of D. H. Lawrence. By Herman M. Daleski. *Northwestern Univ. Press* 1966 $9.00

"Perceptive analysis of Lawrence's dominant theme of male-female duality"—(*Choice*).

D. H. Lawrence and His World. By Harry T. Moore and Warren Roberts. *Viking* Studio Bks. 1966 $6.95 "An elegant book, text and 160 photographs alike, tracing Lawrence's intellectual and moral development more incisively than any I have read"—(Max Lerner, in the *N.Y. Post*).

The Art of D. H. Lawrence. By Keith Sagar. *Cambridge* 1966 $12.50 pap. $2.95

"Dr. Sagar of Manchester University offers a comprehensive view of Lawrence as critic, playwright, novelist, poet, short-story writer, and traveler. . . . A major step towards a solid assessment of D. H. Lawrence"—(*L J*).

The Novels of D. H. Lawrence: A Search for Integration. By John F. Stoll. *Univ. of Missouri Press* 1971 $9.50

D. H. Lawrence and the New World. By David H. Cavitch. *Oxford* 1971 $6.00 pap. $1.95

Toward Women in Love: The Emergence of a Lawrentian Aesthetic. By Stephen Miko. *Yale Univ. Press* 1972 $9.75

D. H. Lawrence: The Phoenix and the Time. By Geoffrey Trease. *Holt* 1973 $4.95

D. H. Lawrence: An Unprofessional Study. By Anais Nin. *Swallow* pap. $2.00

D. H. Lawrence. By Kenneth Young. *British Bk. Centre* $2.38 pap. $1.20

D. H. Lawrence: Novelist, Poet, Prophet. Ed. by Stephen Spender. *Harper* 1973 $12.95. Essays by Diana Trilling, Denis Donoghue, A. Alvarez, and others; the editor is the well-known British poet and critic.

FIRBANK, (ARTHUR ANNESLEY) RONALD. 1886–1926.

Edmund Wilson (*q. v.*) called Firbank "one of the finest English writers of his period." He lived the life of a leisured esthete and died, still a young man, in Rome. His original and subtle novels have appealed to a small but appreciative audience, and in the 1950s and early 1960s he "posthumously acquired a band of devoted disciples." Firbank had a fine disdain for plot and a taste for eccentric characters. "All in all, a felicity, undisturbed by fugues and hints of nonfulfilment, reigns over his novels. There can be no doubt that Firbank has earned his niche of fame. . . . As literature goes, it is a small and creditable world, a true one, looking back at the reader with laughter and sorrow"—(*TLS*, London). From Firbank descend elements in the work of Evelyn Waugh, Ivy Compton-Burnett, Aldous Huxley, Angus Wilson and Iris Murdoch. "The Complete Ronald Firbank," with a preface by Anthony Powell (1961), is unfortunately now o. p.

FIVE NOVELS: Valmouth (1919); The Artificial Princess (1934); The Flower beneath the Foot (1923); The Prancing Nigger (1924); Cardinal Pirelli (1926) 1949. *New Directions* $7.50

THREE MORE NOVELS: Caprice (1916); Inclinations (1916); Vainglory (1915). *New Directions* 1951 $5.00

TWO NOVELS: The Flower beneath the Foot and Prancing Nigger. With a chronology by Miriam Benkovitz. *New Directions* 1962 pap. $1.90

Books about Firbank

Ronald Firbank. By Jocelyn Brooke. *British Bk. Centre* $2.38 pap. $1.20

Ronald Firbank. By Edward M. Potoker. Essays on Modern Writers *Columbia* 1970 pap. $1.00

Ronald Firbank. By James D. Merritt. English Authors Ser. *Twayne* $4.95

The Prancing Novelist: A Defence of Fiction in the Form of a Critical Biography of Ronald Firbank. By Brigid Brophy. *Barnes & Noble* 1973 $20.00

CARY, JOYCE. 1888–1957.

Poet, amateur painter, political scientist and novelist, Cary was born in Ireland of an old Devonshire family. He studied art for several years, but gave it up to enter Oxford. "There I began with history, but changed to law, and took a bad degree. Yet I was not idle. What I worked at was friendship, a vast reading and much talk, especially on ethics and philosophy. I had already then determined to be a writer. And this was one reason why, when I left Oxford, I went straight out to the Balkan War of 1912–13. I wanted the experience of war. I thought there would be no more wars. In short, I was young and eager for adventure." (Cary's recollections of this period, "Memoir of the Bobotes," was published by *Univ. of Texas Press* 1960 $5.00.)

Later, in Africa with the Nigerian colonial service, he was "magistrate, road-builder, a general Pooh-Bah of state." World War I intervened. After serving with the West African Frontier Force through campaigns in the Cameroons, he returned to government service and was finally invalided out. With his wife he settled in Oxford and began to write, but it was ten years before he found an idea of life satisfying to himself. He was a writing invalid, and a courageous one, for a number of years before he died of Parkinson's disease.

"Aissa Saved" (1932, o. p.) was the first of many books which established his reputation as a novelist of great vigor and imagination, a superb craftsman. Some of the early ones about Nigeria show his knowledge of Africa, his perception, compassion and imaginative power. "Mr. Johnson" is the most powerful of these. Among his later works is the marvelous "Horse's Mouth," the portrait of a good artist who is also an outrageous one—perhaps his masterpiece, though the others of that trilogy are also compelling. The Nimmo trilogy (1952–55, o. p.) treats British parliamentary politics with high imagination and merry amorality. All in all, his novels provide "a portrait gallery of some of the most vital, comic, raffish, representative and unforgettable characters in modern fiction"—(Orville Prescott).

His own experiences of novel-writing, together with perceptive comments on fellow novelists, are collected in "Art and Reality: Ways of the Creative Process" (*Doubleday* Anchor Bks. pap. $1.25; *Bks. for Libraries* $7.75). "The Case for African Freedom and Other Writings on Africa" (introd. by Christopher Fyfe *Univ. of Texas Press* 1962 $7.50) is a collection of two pamphlets (1941 and 1946) and three magazine pieces (1951–54). "In view of the enormous changes that have taken place in Africa since Cary expressed his ideas, the background and factual material he cites seem terribly old-fashioned, but his observations, conclusions, and many of his predictions are fresh and accurate, and his involvement with human beings comes through in everything he wrote"—(*LJ*). He expressed his political credo in "Power in Men" (*Univ. of Washington Press* 1963 $5.00).

MISTER JOHNSON. 1939. *Harper* 1969 Perenn. Lib. pap. $2.00

HERSELF SURPRISED. 1941. *Harper* 1948 Mod. Class. $2.00 Perenn. Lib. pap. $1.25. The first novel of the first trilogy.

TO BE A PILGRIM. 1942. *Harper* Perenn. Lib. pap. $1.45. The second novel of the trilogy.

THE HORSE'S MOUTH. 1944. *Harper* 1950 Mod. Class. $2.00 Perenn. Lib. pap. $1.25. The third novel of the trilogy.

A FEARFUL JOY. 1949. *Greenwood* 1973 $13.75

SPRING SONG AND OTHER STORIES. 1960 *Bks. for Libraries* $9.75

Books about Cary

Joyce Cary: A Preface to his Novels. By Andrew Wright. 1958. *Greenwood* 1972 $9.25
Joyce Cary: The Comedy of Freedom. By C. G. Hoffmann. *Univ. of Pittsburgh Press* 1964 pap. $2.25
Joyce Cary. By William Van O'Connor. Essays on Modern Writers *Columbia* 1966 pap. $1.00. A critical pamphlet.
Joyce Cary: A Biography. By Malcolm Foster. *Houghton* 1968 $10.00. Winner of a Houghton Mifflin Fellowship Award.
Joyce Cary: The Developing Style. By Jack Wolkenfeld. *New York Univ. Press* 1968 $7.95 pap. $2.25
Joyce Cary. By Walter Allen. Writers and their Work Ser. *British Bk. Centre* $2.38 pap. $1.20
Joyce Cary. By R. W. Noble. *Barnes & Noble* 1973 $6.00

MANSFIELD, KATHERINE (Katherine Mansfield Beauchamp). 1888–1923.

Katherine Mansfield was born in New Zealand and her native country colors her short stories. She died at the early age of 35. She was chiefly responsible for the renaissance of the short story in England that took place in her lifetime and after. The Femina-Vie Heureuse prize was awarded to "Bliss" in 1921. One of her best, and best-known stories is "The Garden Party" based on memories of her New Zealand childhood.

The wife of the late John Middleton Murry, editor of *The Nation* and *Athenaeum*, she wrote reviews of fiction which appeared over the signature of "K.M." in her husband's paper and attracted wide attention. They are published as "Novels and Novelists" (ed. by J. Middleton Murray 1930, *Somerset Pub.* $15.50). Her "Journal" and "Letters" are remarkable records of her constant search for truth in fiction, undistorted by artificiality or sophistication. Among her books now o. p. are "The Garden Party and Other Stories" (1922), "Poems" (1924) and "The Scrapbook of Katherine Mansfield" (1940).

SHORT STORIES. Complete Collection. *Knopf* 1937 $7.95 Vintage Bks. pap. $1.95

STORIES. Ed. by Elizabeth Bowen. 1956. *Random* Vintage Bks. 1956 pap. $1.65

BLISS AND OTHER STORIES. 1920. *Bks. for Libraries* 1973 $12.25

Books about Mansfield

> A Critical Biography of Katherine Mansfield. By Ruth Elvish Mantz. 1931. *Folcroft* $25.00; *Burt Frank-lin* $16.50
> The Life of Katherine Mansfield. By Ruth E. Mantz and John Middleton Murry. 1933. *Folcroft* $17.50; *Scholarly Press* $18.50
> Katherine Mansfield: A Biography. By Isabel C. Clarke. 1944. *Folcroft* $5.00
> Mansfieldiana: A Brief Katherine Mansfield Bibliography. By G. N. Morris. 1948. *Folcroft* $5.50
> Katherine Mansfield: A Critical Study. By Sylvia L. Berkman. 1951. *Folcroft* 1971. $8.00
> Katherine Mansfield. By Ian Gordon. Writers and Their Work Ser. *British Bk. Centre* $2.38 pap. $1.20
> Katherine Mansfield. By Saralyn Daly. English Authors Ser. *Twayne* 1965 $5.50
> The Fiction of Katherine Mansfield. By Marvin Magalaner. *Southern Illinois Univ. Press* 1971 $5.45

WEST, DAME REBECCA (pseud. of Cicily Isabel Fairfield). 1892–

The work of a brilliant and versatile novelist, critic, essayist and political commentator, one of Rebecca West's greatest literary achievements is undoubtedly her travel diary, "Black Lamb and Grey Falcon: A Journey Through Yugoslavia" (*Viking* 1941 2 vols. in 1 1943 $12.50; Compass Bks. 2 vols. pap. each $2.95). Five years in the writing, it is the story of an Easter trip that she and her husband made through Yugoslavia in 1937. It is an historical narrative with excellent reporting, but is essentially an analysis of our Western culture, "a fully detailed exposition of her views on history, society, and art." During World War II, she superintended British broadcast talks to Yugoslavia. Her remarkable reports of the treason trials of Lord Haw and John Amery appeared first in the *New Yorker* and are included with other stories about traitors in "The Meaning of Treason" (1947, o. p.) which has been "expanded to deal with traitors and defectors since World War II" (*LJ*) as "The New Meaning of Treason" (*Viking* 1964 $6.95 Compass Bks. pap. $1.85). "The Birds Fall Down," which was a best seller, is the story of a young Englishwoman caught in the grip of Russian terrorists. From a true story told to her half a century ago by the sister of Ford Madox Ford (who had heard it from her Russian husband), Miss West "has created a rich and instructive spy thriller, which contains an immense amount of brilliantly distributed information about the ideologies of the time, the rituals of the Russian Orthodox Church, the conflicts of custom, belief, and temperament between Russians and Western Europeans, the techniques of espionage and counter-espionage, and the life of exiles in Paris"— (*New Yorker*).

Two of her critical works are again available: "Strange Necessity: Essays and Reviews" (1938. *Somerset Pub.* $15.00) and "The Court and the Castle" (1958. *Kraus* $12.00), a study of political and religious ideas in imaginative literature. In 1949 she was made a Dame Commander of the Order of the British Empire.

THE THINKING REED. 1936. *Viking* Compass Bks. 1961 pap. $1.65

THE FOUNTAIN OVERFLOWS. *Viking* 1956 $5.95

THE BIRDS FALL DOWN. *Viking* 1966 $5.95

Books about West

> Rebecca West: Artist and Thinker. Ed. by Harry T. Moore. *Southern Illinois Univ. Press* 1971 $5.95

COMPTON-BURNETT, DAME IVY. 1892–1969.

All her many novels, which have been called "morality plays for the tough-minded," are satires of the "least attractive aspects of human nature as found among the nobility and landed gentry" of the late-Victorian world. She writes with subtle, incontestable brilliance. Her melodramatic plots are developed almost exclusively in dialogue. "All the characters in an Ivy Compton-Burnett novel—masters, servants and children alike—talk with a polysyllabic majesty of Samuel Johnson, with a passion for precise meanings of Henry James and with an uninhibited enthusiasm for self-expression."—(Orville Prescott, "In My Opinion"). "The Mighty and Their Fall," centering on a late Victorian family of three generations living in a country house attended by four servants, "holds the reader fascinated by the analysis of character and suspense and—always—detection." "Here is a writer in whom intelligence is paramount; a moralist without a trace of sensationalsim; a novelist difficult at first to read, who repays a hundredfold the effort she exacts." "A God and His Gifts" describes the adventures of an aristocrat who fancies himself as godlike. "Her complete control of her technique, her insights, her wit, her freedom from illusions, her ability to make one believe in a world that one knows is not real—these are virtues not to be underestimated," wrote Granville Hicks, reviewing the book (in *SR*). In 1956 she won the James Tait Black Memorial Award for Fiction for "Mother and Son" (1955, *Int. Pubns. Service* $5.25). In 1967 she was made a Dame Commander of the Order of the British Empire.

PASTORS AND MASTERS. 1925. *Int. Pubns. Service* $5.25

BROTHERS AND SISTERS. 1930 *Int. Pubns. Service* $8.00

MEN AND WIVES. 1931. *Int. Pubns. Service* $6.25

MORE WOMEN THAN MEN. 1933. *Int. Pubns. Service* $8.00

A FAMILY AND A FORTUNE (1939) and MORE WOMEN THAN MEN. *Simon & Schuster* 1965 pap. $2.45

PARENTS AND CHILDREN. 1941. *Int. Pubns. Service* $5.25

ELDERS AND BETTERS 1944. *Int. Pubns. Service* $7.00

MANSERVANT AND MAIDSERVANT. 1947. *Int. Pubns. Service* $6.25

TWO WORLDS AND THEIR WAYS. 1949. *Int. Pubns. Service* $7.50

DARKNESS AND DAY. 1951. *Int. Pubns. Service* $6.25

THE PRESENT AND THE PAST. 1954. *Int. Pubns. Service.* $7.00

A FATHER AND HIS FATE. 1958. *Int. Pubns. Service* $6.25

THE MIGHTY AND THEIR FALL: A Novel. *Simon & Schuster* 1962 $4.50

A GOD AND HIS GIFTS. *Simon & Schuster* 1964 $4.50

Books about Compton-Burnett

Ivy Compton-Burnett. By Frank Baldanza. English Authors Ser. *Twayne* 1964 $4.95
I. Compton-Burnett. By Charles Burkhart. *Int. Pubns. Service* 1965 $7.50
I. Compton-Burnett. By Pamela Hansford Johnson. *British Bk. Centre* $2.38 pap. $1.20
Ivy Compton-Burnett. By Blake Nevius. Essays on Modern Authors *Columbia* 1970 pap. $1.00
Ivy and Stevie: Ivy Compton-Burnett and Stevie Smith Conversation and Reflections. By Kay Dick. 1971 *Int. Pubns. Service* $7.50
The Life of Ivy Comtpon-Burnett. By Elizabeth Sprigge. *Braziller* 1973 $7.95

TOLKIEN, J(OHN) R(ONALD) R(EUEL). 1892–

This English writer of fantasies "is an author whose imagination is kindled by his philology. Language has always been the chief love and concern of this Oxford scholar of the early forms of English." In his greatest book, the trilogy "The Lord of the Rings," Tolkien has invented a language with vocabulary, grammar, syntax, even poetry of its own. "The Middle-Earth of this strange work contains not only men, but other rational beings, elves, dwarfs, and wizards." The book is "the history of an evil power that attempts to become a supreme power, the history of a grand struggle between good and evil, in which the responsibility of saving the sum of things falls on the most trivial, the laziest, the least ambitious, the smallest of the two-legged rational beings, the Hobbit"—("Modern World Literature"). Though readers have imagined various possible allegorical interpretations, Tolkien has said: "It is not about anything but itself. (Certainly it has *no* allegorical intentions, general, particular or topical, moral, religious or political.)" In "The Adventures of Tom Bombadil," J. R. R. Tolkien tells the story of the "master of wood, water, and hill," a jolly teller of tales and singer of songs, one of the multitude of characters in Tolkien's romance, saga, epic or fairy tales about his country of the "Hobbits."

The Tolkien cult is still popular, especially among U.S. college youth; there is now a 1,000-member Tolkien Society and a *Tolkien Journal*. Even the South Vietnamese soldiers have read Tolkien in a translation (by an American officer) of "The Lord of the Rings"; one Vietnamese unit used the lidless eye of the villain Sauron as its battle emblem. "The Road Goes Ever On: A Song Cycle" (*Houghton* 1967 $3.95) contains poems from "The Lord of the Rings" and "The Adventures of Tom Bombadil" set to music by Donald Swann.

THE TOLKIEN READER. *Ballantine Bks.* 1966 pap. $.95. Contains: "Farmer Giles of Ham," "The Adventures of Tom Bombadil," "Tree and Leaf," "The Homecoming of Beorthnoth Beorthholm's Son."

THE TOLKIEN TRILOGY: The Fellowship of the Ring; The Two Towers; The Return of the King. The text, except for minor changes, is the same as that of the *Ballantine Bks.* "Lord of the Rings." New fwd., new appendixes and index. *Houghton* 1967 3 vols. each $7.50 set $22.50

TREE AND LEAF. An essay, "On Fairy Stories," (1938) and an allegory, "Leaf by Niggle." *Houghton* 1965 $4.00

THE HOBBIT. *Houghton* 1938 $4.95; *Ballantine Bks.* pap. $.95

THE FELLOWSHIP OF THE RING. *Houghton* 1954 $7.50; *Ballantine Bks.* pap. $.95

THE TWO TOWERS. *Houghton* 1955 $7.50; *Ballantine Bks.* pap. $.95

THE RETURN OF THE KING. *Houghton* 1956 $7.50; *Ace Bks.* pap. $.75; *Ballantine Bks.* pap. $.95

THE ADVENTURES OF TOM BOMBADIL. *Houghton* 1963 $3.75

FARMER GILES OF HAM. A short story. *Houghton* $3.00

SMITH OF WOOTTON MAJOR. A fairy story. Ill. by Pauline Baynes. *Houghton* 1967 pap. $1.95; *Ballantine* pap. $.95

Books about Tolkien

The Tolkien Relation: A Personal Inquiry by William Ready. *Regnery* 1968 $6.95; (with title "Understanding Tolkien and The Lord of the Rings") *Paperback Lib.* pap. $.75
J.R.R. Tolkien. By Catherine Stimpson. *Columbia* 1969 $1.00
Master of Middle Earth: The Fiction of J. R. R. Tolkien. By Paul H. Kocher. *Houghton* 1972 $5.95

SACKVILLE-WEST, VICTORIA (MARY). 1892–1962.

Born at Knole Castle, scene of Virginia Woolf's novel "Orlando," she was educated in that 365-room dwelling. In 1913 she married the Hon. Harold Nicolson (*q. v.*), journalist, diplomat and biographer. "Poems of East and West," her first writing, was published in 1917. She remained unknown except by a small group of literary connoisseurs until 1927 when she received the Hawthornden Prize for a second volume of poetry. At this time she lived in London and was part of the "Bloomsbury group," which included Lytton Strachey, E. M. Forster, John Maynard Keynes and Virginia Woolf.

Miss Sackville-West has published many novels and volumes of poems, biography, family history and several books on gardening, as well as book reviews and criticism. All her writings reflect the same unhurried approach, deep reflection and brilliantly polished style. Her influence on other writers, especially Virginia Woolf, has been perhaps greater than her own individual achivement. "The Edwardians" and "All Passion Spent" (1931) are her best-known novels. Interesting light on her domestic, and social life is to be found in her late husband's "Diaries and Letters," (*Atheneum* 3 vols. Vol. I $10.00 Vols. 2–3 each $8.50), and in her son's "Portrait of a Marriage" (*see below*).

THE HEIR. 1922. *Bks. for Libraries* $5.50

THE EASTER PARTY. 1953. *Greenwood* $10.75

Books about Sackville-West

V. Sackville-West. By S. R. Watson. English Authors Ser. *Twayne* $4.95
Portrait of a Marriage. By Nigel Nicolson. *Atheneum* 1973 $10.00. Nigel Nicolson is the son of Harold Nicolson and Victoria Sackville-West; his book is based on his parents' journals and letters. It is the story of a marriage tested by emotional upheavals and homosexual encounters which seems not only to have survived but even to have been a success.

WARNER, SYLVIA TOWNSEND. 1893–

Besides writing novels, short stories, poetry and biography, Sylvia Townsend Warner is an expert cook and an authority on music (she spent ten years as one of four editors of a ten-volume "Tudor Church Music"), mysticism and the black arts. Her fiction, precise, delicate, ironically compelling, is touched with the fantastic. Those she writes of—whether "witches" or real people—are unmistakably her own creation.

"Lolly Willowes" concerns a spinster, sympathetically drawn, who makes a compact with the Devil; it was the first selection of the Book-of-the-Month Club and caused Christopher Morley to write: "Here is a new talent, extraordinary in charm and wisdom." "Mr. Fortune's Maggot," about a missionary to the South Seas and his one native convert, brought this comment from Clifton Fadiman: "Her satire, so humorous, so warm, so finely feminine, has the depth and reach that brutally naturalistic rendition of a life-surface can never attain; and the fairy-like locale of her story, her impossible islanders, and her slightly mad, quixotic hero admit the entrance of beauty and wit—two qualities which American satire . . . does not largely possess." Of "The Corner that Held Them," about life in a medieval abbey, Robert Gorham Davis said in the *N.Y. Times:* "Miss Warner is not exploiting the past for romance or quaintness, to escape something or find something or sell us medievalism, but rather to deepen our sense of the common human lot, its limits and possibilities." The stories in "Swans on an Autumn River" "promise to be light accounts of people living simple lives but the author's perception, compassion and command build them into subtly powerful presentations"—(*LJ*). In her best-selling biography, "T. H. White," (*Viking* 1968 $6.50). Miss Warner draws a lively and sympathetic picture of the ill-starred author of "The Once and Future King."

LOLLY WILLOWES (1926) and MR. FORTUNE'S MAGGOT (1927). *Viking* 1966 $6.00; *Popular Lib.* $.60

GARLAND OF STRAW: Twenty-eight Stories. 1943. *Bks. for Libraries* $9.50

THE CORNER THAT HELD THEM. 1948. *Popular Lib.* 1967 pap. $.75

BOXWOOD. *Dufour* 1960 $4.50

THE INNOCENT AND THE GUILTY: Nine Short Stories. *Viking* 1971 $5.95

BENTLEY, PHYLLIS (ELEANOR). 1894–

This Yorkshire novelist, "a true novelist, an alert storyteller, and a born writer"—(*New Yorker*), is a native of the West Riding, where she still lives and which she frequently uses as the background of her stories. Miss Bentley regards the trilogy—"Inheritance" (1932, o. p.), "The Rise of Henry Morcar" (1946, o. p.) and "A Man of His Time"—"as the most important and significant part of my work. It carries the story of the people in the textile industry of the West Riding from 1812 down to 1965. . . . It is human relationships and the effect of life upon character which I am always trying to investigate. I simply take the West Riding as an illustration of basic human themes, at the same time enjoying the depiction of my native land." Of the final novel of the trilogy, the *Saturday Review* wrote: "Phyllis Bentley must be spoken of now as a peer of such novelists of Britain as Trollope, Galsworthy, and Enoch Arnold Bennett. Her new book 'A Man of His Time,' is the latest confirmation of the astonishing breadth and sustained nature of her gifts."

She has written several books on the Brontes, including "The Brontes and Their World" (*Viking* Studio Bks. 1969 $8.95), "The English Regional Novel" (1941. *Haskell* pap. $2.95) and several children's books. "The House of Moreys" recalls "Wuthering Heights," with its Yorkshire setting for an eccentric household. Her well-written autobiography "O Dreams, O Destinations" (1962, o. p.) makes it clear that her novels have been based to a considerable extent on her own life and that of her family in a changing Yorkshire.

THE HOUSE OF MOREYS. 1953. *Ace Bks.* pap. $.75

BRYHER (pseud. of Annie Winifred Ellerman Macpherson). 1894–

Writing reviews and articles for the English *Saturday Review* and the *Sphere* was Bryher's first training as a writer. Her first novel, "Development," was published in 1919 (o. p.). She married Robert McAlmon, the American writer and publisher of "avant-garde" literature at the *Contact Press.* Later, with her second husband, Kenneth MacPherson, she helped to establish *Close Up*, perhaps the finest magazine devoted to the art of the silent film. "Bryher's novels have been praised by critics like Marianne Moore for her 'undeceived eye for beauty and her passion for moral beauty,' and for her ability to recreate the mood of the past without the obstruction of unassimilated historical data. As a stylist she is recognized as being in the first rank of modern writers of prose, and as the creator of a new genre of the historical novel"—("Twentieth Century Authors"). Her autobiography "The Heart to Artemis" (1962, o. p.) is not only a revealing personal record but an important literary and social history of the time. "Primarily it shows 'how external events and unconscious drives help or hinder [the] development of a writer—herself. It is the story of rebellion against 'the narrow

existence [of] the Edwardian woman.' " It records an unusual childhood of travel with parents and govern-
esses, the "shattering" impact of her teen-age schooling, the effects of two World Wars. "Because of her close
association with such men as Havelock Ellis, Freud (she speaks gratefully of psychoanalysis) and Norman
Douglas, she writes with authority—and sympathy—on their idiosyncrasies. As a young woman in the Paris
of exiles, she was familiar with Joyce, Gide, Gertrude Stein, Hemingway, and others"—(*LJ*).

BEOWULF. 1948. *Pantheon* 1956 $5.95. A novel about London during the World War
II blitz.

THE FOURTEENTH OF OCTOBER. *Pantheon* 1951 $5.95. A story of the Saxon resistance
to the Norman invasion of Britain.

THE PLAYER'S BOY. *Pantheon* 1953 $4.95. Set in the years of Elizabethan glory and
Jacobean violence.

ROMAN WALL. *Pantheon* 1954 $4.95. Barbarian encroachment on a Roman outpost in
Switzerland in the 3rd century.

GATE TO THE SEA: *Pantheon* 1958 $4.95. A historical novel of the 4th century. B.C.

RUAN. *Pantheon* 1960 $6.95. Set in 6th-century Britain, this is the story of a young boy,
unhappily preparing for Druid priesthood, who breaks the ties to family and tradition.

THE COIN OF CARTHAGE. *Harcourt* 1963 $4.95 Harvest Bks. pap. $1.35. A story of
Greek traders and Roman soldiers.

VISA FOR AVALON. *Harcourt* 1965 $4.50. An allegory revolving around retired people
in search of a new home.

THIS JANUARY TALE. *Harcourt* 1966 $4.95 The story of the effects of the Battle of
Hastings on a Saxon family.

HUXLEY, ALDOUS. 1894–1963.

Aldous Huxley was a grandson of the great Darwinian apostle, Thomas Huxley. He was a graduate of
Eton and of Oxford and had a reputation for the wit and the wide, curious learning which he packed into his
books. Vincent Spalding thought him enormously cultured but not a great novelist because not a storyteller;
indeed he produced fewer novels than books of nonfiction. While he is always interesting and engages our intelligence, he seldom touches our emotions. Differentiating his characters by their views and opinions, he
wrote novels of ideas, abounding in passages of moralizing and of nonnarrative matter. Huxley was a very
influential writer, at once the satirist and the fascinated chronicler of the hedonism of the 1920s. "Brave
New World," his avid, but entertaining—and in some respects prophetic—vision of the mechanized near
future, became the classic satire on technology carried to extremes.
    Many of his unusual and unorthodox interests, his wide-ranging mind and out-of-the-way learning are dis-
played in his collection "Tomorrow and Tomorrow and Tomorrow and Other Essays" (*Harper* Perenn. Lib.
pap. $1.25; *New Am. Lib.* Signet pap. $.60). "Collected Essays" (*Harper* 1959 Colophon Bks. pap. $2.95) is
"a superlative collection of what William James called 'gossip of the universe' "—(Charles Rolo). In "Literature and Science" (*Harper* 1963 $5.00), his 45th and last book, he "is more concerned with the use that Lit-
erature can make of Science, and the proper attitude of a man of letters toward Science, than with what a scientist might derive from Literature or how Science might recognize, assimilate, and employ the realities
proper to Literature." He believed that we should continue to search for ways to relate science to the worlds
of art.
    After emigrating to California in 1937, "he largely occupied himself with the techniques of mysticism,
since he had concluded by this time that the only hope for mankind lay in an extension of awareness of, and
harmony with, Ultimate Reality." The possibilities of reaching Reality through the drug mescalin were explored in "The Doors of Perception" and "Heaven and Hell" (1954 and 1956, *Harper* 2 vols. in I $4.95 Per-
enn. Lib. 2 vols. pap. each $.95).
    "But Huxley's cleverness developed into concern for the human condition. His concern is strong enough to
keep his readers faithful . . . and is always intellectually barbed enough to keep them awake, and conscious of
human problems and human dangers, individually and collectively"—("Modern World Literature"). Huxley received the Award of Merit Medal (1959) from the American Academy of Arts and Letters. In 1962 he

was elected a Companion of Literature of the British Royal Society of Literature, one of the highest literary awards in Britain (restricted to 10). He died of cancer at the home of friends in Los Angeles, where he and his second wife had been living since 1962, when their own home was destroyed by fire. He had been ill for three years but continued to write until the day before his death. "An old codger, rampant, but still learning," he once said of a Goya drawing—and friends felt it might well be his epitaph.

THE WORLD OF ALDOUS HUXLEY. Ed. with introd. by Charles J. Rolo. 1947. *Peter Smith* $7.50. An omnibus collection of fiction and nonfiction covering three decades.

COLLECTED SHORT STORIES. *Bantam* 1960 pap. $1.95. Twenty-one short stories bringing together most of the contents (except for longer works) of "Limbo," "Mortal Coils," "Little Mexican," "Two or Three Graces" and "Brief Candles," with one excerpt from "Crome Yellow."

GREAT SHORT WORKS. Ed. by Bernard Bergonzi. *Harper* 1969 Perenn. Lib. pap. $1.95

CROME YELLOW. 1922. *Bantam* pap. $.95

ANTIC HAY. *Harper* 1923 pap. $.95 (and "The Gioconda Smile") Mod. Class. $2.00

POINT COUNTER POINT. *Harper* 1928 1939 $6.95 Perenn. Lib. pap. $1.25

BRAVE NEW WORLD. *Harper* 1932 1939 rev. with new fwd. 1946 $5.95 lib. bdg. $4.43 Perenn. Lib. pap. $.95 (and "Brave New World Revisited") Colophon Bks. pap. $2.75

AFTER MANY A SUMMER DIES THE SWAN. 1939. *Harper* Perenn. Lib. pap. $.95

TIME MUST HAVE A STOP. *Harper* 1944 Perenn. Lib. pap. $.95

THE GENIUS AND THE GODDESS. 1955. *Harper* Perenn. Lib. 1973 pap. $.95

BRAVE NEW WORLD REVISITED. *Harper* 1958 $5.95 Perenn. Lib. pap. $.65

ISLAND. A Utopian Novel. *Harper* 1962 $7.95 Perenn. Lib. pap. $1.25

Books about Huxley

Aldous Huxley. By Alexander Henderson. 1936. *Russell & Russell* 1964 $8.00
Aldous Huxley. By Sisirkumar Ghose. *Asia Pub. House* 1962 $6.95
Aldous Huxley. By Jocelyn Brooke. Authors and Their Work Ser. *British Bk. Centre* $2.38 pap. $1.20
Aldous Huxley: A Literary Study. By John Atkins. *Grossman* (Orion Press) 1968 $5.95. Rev. ed. with a new introd. of a valuable earlier work.
This Timeless Moment: A Personal View of Aldous Huxley. By Laura Huxley. *Farrar, Straus* 1968 $6.95. Mrs. Huxley's memoir of his last years.
Aldous Huxley. By Harold H. Watts. English Authors Ser. *Twayne* 1969 $5.50
Aldous Huxley: Satire and Structure. By Jerome Meckier. *Barnes & Noble* 1969 $6.50
Aldous Huxley and the Way to Reality. By Charles M. Holmes. *Indiana Univ. Press* 1970 $7.95
Aldous Huxley and the Way to Reality. By Keith May. *Barnes & Noble* 1973 $12.75

GRAVES, ROBERT. 1895–

Poet, historical novelist, critic, translator, essayist, biblical scholar, historian, lecturer and librettist, Robert Graves has written a prodigious number of books. He has often visited the United States and in 1963 was Poet in Residence at M.I.T. "Happy is the man," he has said, "who has had two separate families, as I have—four in each—it keeps him in touch with contemporary life. There are 34 years between my eldest child and my youngest, who is just beginning his real education." He, his wife and youngest children live in Deya, Majorca. Many of his books were written on the island, which he first visited in 1929 upon Gertrude Stein's (*q. v.*) suggestion. "Majorca Observed" (ill. by Paul Hogarth *Doubleday* 1965 $10.00) is an "outstanding" collection of essays and sketches about the island and its people written in his "perceptive, witty and graceful prose, which has enough salty humor to add tanginess"—(*LJ*). "Mammon and the Black Goddess" (*Doubleday* 1965 $3.95) is another recent collection of essays. His two novels of Roman life are "I,

Claudius," which won both the Hawthornden and the James Tait Black prizes for 1934 and its sequel, "Claudius the God." They are unusual because of their psychological approach to their subject.

"The Transformations of Lucius, Otherwise Known as The Golden Ass" (*Farrar, Straus* 1967 $5.95 Noonday pap. $2.25), his translation from Apuleius, is done in "a dry, sharp, plain style—which is itself a small masterpiece of twentieth-century prose"—(*SR*). He was a friend of T. E. Lawrence and in 1928 published "Lawrence and the Arabian Adventure"; with Liddell Hart he edited "T. E. Lawrence to His Biographers" (1938, o. p.). He writes prose, he says, to support his poetry. By 1965 he had produced 17 volumes of poetry, 15 of fiction and 19 of nonfiction, as well as several translations.

OCCUPATION WRITER. 1950. *Grosset* Univ. Lib. pap. $1.95. Short stories and plays.

I, CLAUDIUS. 1934. *Random* Vintage Bks. pap. $1.95

CLAUDIUS THE GOD. 1935. *Random* Vintage Bks. pap. $1.95

GOODBYE TO ALL THAT. 1929. *Doubleday* Anchor Bks. rev. ed. 1957 pap. $1.95. Autobiography.

See also Chapter 7, Modern British Poetry, for other works by Graves and a bibliography of works about him. A representative selection of his books on Classical mythology will be found in Chapter 3, Reference Books on Literature, section on Classical Dictionaries and Mythology.

HARTLEY, L(ESLIE) P(OLES). 1895–

English novelist, short story writer and literary critic, L. P. Hartley won the James Tait Black Memorial Prize in 1947 for "Eustace and Hilda." Part of a trilogy, the three books were described by the *Times* (London) as " 'unique in modern writing . . . diverting and disturbing.' Beneath a surface 'almost overcivilized' the reviewer found 'a hollow of horror.' " One of this author's special interests is Henry James, to whom he has been compared: "For all the wit and delicacy of his method, he is concerned with such depths of experience as guilt and loneliness and evil. His devotion to the craft of fiction, his respect for form, as well as his fundamentally serious approach to moral problems, are Jamesian."

In "The Tragic Comedians," James Hall devotes a chapter to L. P. Hartley, respected but not popular in England, read by few in America, and praised by discerning critics in both countries: "Along with Green and Powell, Hartley has changed the direction of the comic novel, raising even more seriously than they the question of whether it remains comic at all. . . . His freshness consists at first in simply changing the patterns of the naturalistic novel from social insights to emotional ones; yet in doing so he departs from both the older solid way of conceiving character and the more recent fluid way of conceiving consciousness." Lord David Cecil called "The Go-Between" "impressive," and wrote: "Mr. Hartley is for me the first of living novelists in certain important respects; beauty of style, lyrical quality of feeling and, above all, the power and originality of his imagination, which wonderfully mingles ironic comedy, whimsical fancy and a mysterious Hawthornelike poetry."

THE GO-BETWEEN. 1954 *Dufour* $6.95; *Stein & Day* 1967 $5.95

THE HIRELING. 1957 *Dufour* $6.95

FACIAL JUSTICE. 1960. *Dufour* $5.95

THE BETRAYAL. 1966. *Dufour* $6.25

POOR CLARE. 1968. *Dufour* $6.25

THE LOVE ADEPT. 1969. *Dufour* $6.25

MY SISTER'S KEEPER. 1970 *Dufour* $5.95

THE NOVELIST'S RESPONSIBILITY. 1967. *Hillary House* $4.50. Essays and lectures.

Books about Hartley

L. P. Hartley. By Paul Bloomfield and B. Bergonzi's "Anthony Powell. Writers and Their Work Ser. *British Bk. Centre* 1962 $2.38 pap. $1.20

L. P. Hartley. By Peter Bien. *Pennsylvania State Univ. Press* 1963 $8.50 "A cautious, balanced critical study"—(*LJ*).

CRONIN, A(RCHIBALD) J(OSEPH). 1896–

Dr. A. J. Cronin is a Scottish physician who has drawn on his experience as a ship's doctor and as medical inspector of mines in England for the themes of many of his novels. When his health broke down in 1930 and he was convalescing in a tiny village in the Highlands, he remembered that he had always felt that all he needed was "time" to write a novel. "Hatter's Castle" was written in three months and was the first choice of the English Book Society. "The Citadel" aroused a storm of protest from the medical profession in England for its exposure of dishonest practices largely due to the intense competition among doctors. The autobiographical "Adventures in Two Worlds," his first book of nonfiction, reads like one of his novels, and consists of a collection of anecdotes drawn from his early life as a physician. "A Song of Sixpence," about a sensitive Catholic child growing up in a Protestant Scottish village, draws on his own boyhood memories. Cronin has said: "Of all my novels, and I have laboured over many, 'A Song of Sixpence' is to me, beyond any of the others, the real thing . . . the novel A. J. Cronin should be writing." Dr. Cronin and his family have been making their home in New England for some time. Throughout the years he has been close to people and their problems, and his books reflect a deeply human approach to life. As Orville Prescott wrote in a review of "The Green Years" in the *N.Y. Times:* "Every page Dr. Cronin writes bears the stamp of an honest and simple man, without pretense, affectation or false sophistication."

HATTER'S CASTLE. 1931. *Pyramid Bks.* pap. $.95

THREE LOVES. 1932 1957. *Pyramid Bks.* pap. $1.50

THE CITADEL. *Little* 1937 $6.95; *Bantam* pap. $1.25

THE KEYS OF THE KINGDOM. *Little* 1941 $6.95; *Bantam* pap. $.95

THE GREEN YEARS. *Little* 1944 $6.95; *Bantam* pap. $.75

SHANNON'S WAY. *Little* 1948 $6.95

THE SPANISH GARDNER. 1950. *Pyramid Bks.* pap. $1.25

A THING OF BEAUTY. *Little* 1956 $6.95

THE JUDAS TREE. *Little* 1961 $6.95; *Bantam* pap. $1.25

A SONG OF SIXPENCE. *Little* 1964 $6.95; *Pyramid Bks.* pap. $.95

A POCKET FULL OF RYE. *Little* 1969 $5.95; *Pyramid* pap. $.95

ADVENTURES IN TWO WORLDS. 1952. *Little* 1956 $6.95. Autobiography.

WAUGH, ALEC (pseud. of Alexander Raban Waugh). 1898–

Alec Waugh, the older brother of Evelyn Waugh (*q. v.*) is an "expert if somewhat conventional novelist, a facile raconteur, and, in his travel writings and biography, a keen reporter." The greater part of his large output (more than 40 works) has been fiction, though some of his books may be considered partly autobiographical. "Island in the Sun" provided the story for one of the first American films concerned with an interracial love affair. "Love and the Caribbean: Tales, Characters and Scenes of the West Indies" (*Bantam* pap. $.75) contains selections published previously in his travel books and in magazines. In "A Family of Islands: A History of the West Indies from 1492 to 1898, with an Epilogue Sketching Events from the Spanish-American War to the 1960's" (*Doubleday* 1964 $6.50), "the source of material both ancient and modern is distilled and blended in such a way as to make of the whole a story rather than the usual historical travelogue"— (*N.Y. Times*). "The Mule on the Minaret," a novel set in the Middle East, is entertaining reading.

The *Saturday Review,* commenting on his recent and fascinating "My Brother Evelyn and Other Portraits," (*Farrar, Straus* 1967 $6.95) wrote: "Alec Waugh remains no great shakes as a novelist, a role in which comparisons with Evelyn are inevitable; but he has clearly found his métier as a diarist, a chronicler, and an observer of contemporary literary life." In "My Brother Evelyn" he "chattily," "engagingly," "cheerfully" and most perceptively sketches a gallery of minor writers and some of Britain's brightest literary stars: his brother; Robert Graves; Siegfried Sassoon; Sir Edmund Gosse; Somerset Maugham. "In Praise of Wine and Certain Noble Spirits" (*Morrow* 1959 pap. $2.95) is a guide to their appreciation.

ISLAND IN THE SUN. 1956. *New Am. Lib.* 1971 pap. $1.50

MY PLACE IN THE BAZAAR. *Farrar, Straus* 1961 $3.95

THE MULE ON THE MINARET. *Farrar, Straus* 1965 $6.95

THE EARLY YEARS OF ALEC WAUGH. *Farrar, Straus* 1962 $6.00

A SPY IN THE FAMILY. *Farrar, Straus* 1970 $5.95

BANGKOK. *Little* 1971. $7.95

THE FATAL GIFT. *Farrar, Straus* 1973 $6.95

LEWIS, C(LIVE) S(TAPLES) (Clive Hamilton, pseud.) 1898–1963.

C. S. Lewis, Professor of Medieval and Renaissance English at Cambridge 1954–63 and Fellow at Oxford was a writer of so many varied and exceptional gifts that he fits into no stereotyped classification. His great versatility included novels of fantasy, scholarly literary essays and expositors of Christan doctrine. He became known in this country for the demoniacal "The Screwtape Letters," letters of instruction and encouragement from a shrewd old devil to an undergraduate imp on Earth, a revelation of Hell's best official secrets. "Out of the Silent Planet," "Perelandra" and "That Hideous Strength" form a trilogy of strange and exciting but philosophical fantasies of life on other planets and at last in the earthly setting of a college community. "The Great Divorce" describes a day's excursion by omnibus from Hell to the borders of Heaven. "Four Loves" (*Harcourt* 1960 $5.75 Harvest Bks. pap. $1.75) is a study of the nature of love; "Studies in Words" (*Cambridge* 1960 $12.50 pap. $2.75) links semantics, literary criticism and the history of thought. "Christian Reflections" (*Eerdmans* 1967 pap. $2.25) is a collection of essays. Among his scholarly works on literature at least one has become a classic: "The Allegory of Love: A Study in Medieval Tradition" (*Oxford* 1936 pap. $2.95). Another is "The Discarded Image: An Introduction to Medieval and Renaissance Literature" (1966, o. p.).

OUT OF THE SILENT PLANET. *Macmillan* 1938 1943 $6.95 Collier Bks. pap. $1.25

THE SCREWTAPE LETTERS. 1943. (and "Screwtape Proposes a Toast") *Macmillan* 1943 $4.95 lg.-type ed. $6.95 pap. $.95

PERELANDRA. 1944. *Macmillan* 1968 $4.95 pap. $.95

THE GREAT DIVORCE. *Macmillan* 1946 $4.95 pap. $.95

THAT HIDEOUS STRENGTH: A Modern Fairy Tale for Grown-ups. 1946 *Macmillan* $4.95 Collier Bks. pap. $1.50

TILL WE HAVE FACES. *Harcourt*. 1957 $5.75; *Eerdmans* 1964 pap. $2.45

LETTERS TO MALCOLM: Chiefly on Prayer. *Harcourt* 1964 $3.95. The person to whom these letters are addressed is probably fictitious.

LETTERS TO AN AMERICAN LADY. Ed. with a pref. by Clyde S. Kilby. *Eerdmans* 1967 pap. $1.95. Over 100 letters, Christian in theme, to an American (her identity is withheld) whom Lewis had never met.

SURPRISED BY JOY: The Shape of My Early Life. *Harcourt* 1956 $5.95 Harvest Bks. pap. $1.95

Books about Lewis

The Christian World of C. S. Lewis. By Clyde S. Kilby *Eerdmans* 1964 $4.50
"This book summarizes admirably not only Lewis's Christian writings, but also the shaping influences in his life"—(*LJ*).
Light on C. S. Lewis. Ed. with pref. by Jocelyn Gibb. *Harcourt* 1966 $3.95.
A collection of seven essays that "supplies more sound thinking about Lewis and his career than is available elsewhere in convenient form"—(*LJ*).

FORESTER, C(ECIL) S(COTT). 1899–1966.

Like Somerset Maugham and A. J. Cronin, Forester studied medicine but forsook it for a career as a writer. He was born in Cairo, Egypt, where his father was in government service. With "Payment Deferred"

(1926), a gripping study of the disintegration of the mind of a murderer, he made his entry into his chosen field. In 1937, "The Happy Return," soon followed by "Flying Colours" and "A Ship of the Line" inaugurated the appearance of Captain Horatio Hornblower in the gallery of British heroes of fiction. Selected by both the Book Society of England and the Book-of-the-Month Club, this trilogy also won for its author the James Tait Black Memorial prize for literature. The story of the courageous British naval officer was rounded out in the volume containing "Hornblower During the Crisis," part of a novel on which Forester had been working before his death; he left notes on its further plotting.

Forester fought in World War I and, at the beginning of World War II, he was informed by the British Ministry of Information that he was one of the writers earmarked for work at the Ministry. The next years were ones of great activity, including a voyage in the Atlantic with the Royal Navy to gather material for "The Ship," a spell of duty in the Office of the British Information Services and a cruise with the U.S. Navy. This finally culminated in illness and forced him to a less active life. Following the motion picture successes of the perennial Hornblower and "The African Queen," a grand spoof on adventure stories, he made a place for himself in Hollywood and spent his last years in California.

C. Northcote Parkinson (*q. v.*) has written an excellent "biography" of Forester's famous character Horatio Hornblower, "The Life and Times of Horatio Hornblower" (*Little* 1971 $6.95).

Among his books in print:

THE AFRICAN QUEEN. 1935. *Modern Library* $2.95; *Bantam* pap. $.75

CAPTAIN HORATIO HORNBLOWER: Beat to Quarters; Ship of the Line; Flying Colours. 1939. 1 vol. ed. *Little* $6.95

THE SHIP. *Little* 1943 $6.50. The tale of a British light cruiser in World War II.

LIEUTENANT HORNBLOWER. *Little* 1952 $6.50

THE GOOD SHEPHERD. *Little* 1955 $6.50; *New Am. Lib.* Signet pap. $.75

ADMIRAL HORNBLOWER IN THE WEST INDIES. *Little* 1958 $6.50

HORNBLOWER DURING THE CRISIS AND TWO STORIES: Hornblower's Temptation and The Last Encounter. *Little* 1967 $5.75

The first, a fragment of a novel, was published posthumously in the *Saturday Evening Post.* "These are good yarns"—(*L J*).

HORNBLOWER AND THE "HOTSPUR." *Little* 1962 $6.50; *Bantam* $1.25

LONG BEFORE FORTY. Autobiography. *Little* 1968 $5.95

BOWEN, ELIZABETH. 1899–

Elizabeth Bowen, distinguished Anglo-Irish novelist, was born in Dublin, has traveled extensively, lived in London, and inherited the family estate—"Bowen's Court," in County Cork. Her account of the house, ("Bowen's Court," 1942, o.p.) with a detailed history of the family in Ireland through its three centuries, has "sober charm" and "a warmth and insight that suggest extraordinary imaginative virtuosity." The new edition has an afterword on its recent history. "Seven Winters" is a fragment of autobiography published in England in 1943. "The reminiscences of her Dublin childhood are delightful for their color of the city, their record of a child's perceptions, their characteristic beauty of language and style—just what one expects [and gets] from Miss Bowen's rare sensitivity to places and people"—(*Chicago Sunday Tribune*). The "Afterthoughts" of this volume are critical essays, "indispensable documents," in which she discusses and analyzes, among others, such literary figures as Virginia Woolf, E. M. Forster, Katherine Mansfield, Anthony Trollope and Eudora Welty. Her stories, mostly about people of the British upper middle class, portray simple human relationships which her analysis shows are never simple—except, perhaps, on the surface. Her concern with time and memory is a major theme. Beautifully and delicately written, her stories are symbolic, subtle and terrifying with their oblique psychological revelations. Charles Poore of the *N.Y. Times* considers "The Little Girls" her "most brilliantly accomplished novel." The three girls "first knew each other at St. Agatha's, a school perhaps not far from her own Downe House, in Kent." Nearly 50 years later, they are brought together again, to dig up a mysterious box they had buried at St. Agatha's. "They dug. But it was more into one another's characters, in the event, than into the symbolic coffer. . . . Half a century of chaotically crowded life passes in review" in "this tightly coiled story." "A Time in Rome" (*Knopf* 1960 $5.95) is her brilliant evocation of that city and its layered past.

In the Birthday Honours List of 1948 she was made a Commander of the British Empire. She has spent many summers at Bowen's Court, but lives now in Old Headington, Oxford, the scene of the beginning and end of "The Little Girls." She originally went there to live (1925–35) when her husband, Alan Cameron, was appointed to a teaching position in Oxford.

ANN LEE'S AND OTHER STORIES. 1926. *Bks. for Libraries* $9.00

THE HOTEL. 1927. *Greenwood* $12.50 *Popular Lib.* pap. $.60

JOINING CHARLES AND OTHER STORIES. 1929. *Scholarly Press* 1971 $19.50

THE LAST SEPTEMBER. 1929. With new pref. by the author. *Knopf* 1952 $5.95. A novel of the Irish "troubles" of the 1920 period.

THE HOUSE IN PARIS. *Knopf* 1936 $6.95 *Random* 1957 Vintage Bks. pap. $1.95

THE DEATH OF THE HEART. *Knopf* 1939 $5.95; *Random* Vintage Bks. pap. $1.95

THE HEAT OF THE DAY. *Knopf* 1949 $5.95

THE LITTLE GIRLS. *Knopf* 1963 $5.95

EVA TROUT. *Knopf* 1968 $6.95

SEVEN WINTERS AND AFTERTHOUGHTS: Memories of a Dublin Childhood and Pieces on Writing. *Cuala Press* (dist. by Irish Univ. Press) 1971 $19.50. Her only autobiographical work.

Books about Bowen

Elizabeth Bowen. By Jocelyn Brooke. Writers and Their Works Ser. *British Bk. Centre* $2.38 pap. $1.20
Elizabeth Bowen. By Edwin J. Kennedy. *Bucknell Univ. Press* $4.50 pap. $1.95
Elizabeth Bowen. By Allan E. Austin. English Authors Ser. *Twayne* $5.50

O'FAOLAIN, SEAN. 1900–

"There is an element in Irish fiction that someone has aptly described as malicious affection," writes the *Library Journal*. "Sean O'Faolain has it to the greatest degree. All the 11 stories in ["I Remember! I Remember!"] bare the faults and failings of the characters without losing the reader's sympathy and understanding for those same characters. There is a melancholy strain along with the quiet chuckle, the nostalgic findings of a man who has lived and learned well. He is indeed a past master of the short story." "The Heat of the Sun," a collection of stories "widely hailed as placing him within the half dozen contemporary masters of that form"—(*New Republic*), deals again with the Irish folk—"most attractive when they are being victimized"—(*SR*). "All the pleasures in this book—and there are many—are quiet ones: the quiet tone to the stories, the quiet resolution with which they end, the quietly expert way the author goes about his work"—(*N.Y. Times*). In his autobiography, "Vive Moi!," which contains lovely passages descriptive of the Irish countryside, he tells about his six years in the rebel Irish Republican Army, about Irish Catholicism and about the position of the Irish writer who at one time or another usually finds himself in voluntary exile. The first literary work of "Ireland's leading prose writer" was in Gaelic, though this was acquired and not his native tongue. He first attracted wide attention with "A Nest of Simple Folk" (1933). Two books expounding his art are "Short Stories: A Study in Pleasure" (*Little* 1961 $4.95) and "The Short Story" (1948 *Devin-Adair* $3.50). "The Vanishing Hero" (1957 *Bks. for Libraries* $9.75) is a collection of essays. Among the essays and travelogues published by *Devin-Adair* are "The Irish: A Character Study" (1949 $4.50), "A Summer in Italy" (1950 $5.00) and "Newman's Way" (1952 $5.00), a study in religious thought.

After his I.R.A. experiences Mr. O'Faolain did graduate work at Harvard and married here a girl he imported from home, but he found he could not write away from Ireland and together they returned there. He still frequently lectures, teaches and travels in the U.S., however, and was a visiting professor at Princeton for two years in the early 1960s.

COME BACK TO ERIN. 1940. *Greenwood* $15.25

BIRD ALONE. *Phaedra* pap. $2.95; *William Gannon* lib. bdg. $5.95

Books about O'Faolain

Sean O'Faolain: A Critical Introduction. By Maurice Harmon. *Univ. of Notre Dame Press* 1967 $6.95.
The first full-length study of O'Faolain analyses his development, philosophy and technique.

Sean O'Faolain. By Joseph Browne. *Bucknell Univ. Press* $4.50 pap. $1.95
Sean O'Faolain. By Paul A. Doyle. English Authors Ser. *Twayne* $5.50

HUGHES, RICHARD (ARTHUR WARREN). 1900–

Welsh by birth and descent, Richard Hughes had a varied university life at Oxford—on vacations he tramped, begged, acted as a pavement artist and once led an expedition through Central Europe on some obscure mission which involved political intrigue. As an undergraduate he wrote "The Sisters' Tragedy" (in "Plays: The Sisters' Tragedy; A Comedy of Good and Evil; The Man Born to be Hanged; Danger" 1924, *Harper* 1966 $5.00). George Bernard Shaw called it "the finest one-act play ever written," and it had a West End production while Mr. Hughes was still at Oxford, as did several of his others. Drama was his first effort—which he then abandoned for fiction.

"A High Wind in Jamaica," a modern classic, is an extraordinary tale about the casual cruelty in children—captured, in this case, by soft-hearted pirates. "In Hazard," the vivid description of sailors battling a crippling storm, while "ostensibly a sea story, is in reality a terrifying allegory of the British Empire at this crisis of its existence." The story of a young Englishman's visit at his cousin's home near Munich, Germany, in 1923, the year of Hitler's aborted beer-hall "putsch," "The Fox in the Attic" is a novel of extraordinary brilliance. The London *Times Literary Supplement* wrote: "Magnificent, authoritative, compassionate, ironic, funny and tragic . . . it has that universal authenticity that is the hall-mark of great writing." It is the first volume of a projected series, "The Human Predicament," which the author describes as a long historical novel of his own times, culminating in the Second World War. Mr. Hughes worked as a civilian for the Admiralty during World War II and later collaborated on its official history. He is an unpredictable writer who "preserves the devastating innocence of the child reflected through a highly sophisticated mature intellect." "Hughes is inspired as Tolstoy was by the compulsion to create. Everything that he touches comes to life in a gusty, laughing, tender, tragic interpretation of the weird contradictions that jostle each other so pitifully in the human heart"—(*SR*).

A HIGH WIND IN JAMAICA. 1929. *Harper* 1957 $6.95 Perenn. Lib. pap. $.95 (with title "The Innocent Voyage") Mod. Class. pap. $2.00; *New Am. Lib.* Signet pap. $.95; *Franklin Watts* lg-type ed. $7.95

IN HAZARD. 1938. *Peter Smith* $4.00

THE FOX IN THE ATTIC. *Harper* 1961 $6.50. The first volume of the series "The Human Predicament."

THE WOODEN SHEPHERDESS. *Harper* 1973 $6.95. The second volume of the series "The Human Predicament."

FOREIGN DEVIL: Thirty Years of Reporting from the Far East. *Transatlantic* 1973 $9.50

HONG KONG: Borrowed Place, Borrowed Time. *Praeger* 1968 $6.00

PRITCHETT, V(ICTOR) S(AWDEN). 1900–

V. S. Pritchett attended a number of schools, worked in the leather trade and later as a commercial traveler and shop assistant. After World War II, he was literary editor of the *New Statesman and Nation* and is now a regular contributor to American periodicals and, especially, the *N.Y. Times Book Review*. He is a distinguished short story writer who has often appeared in the *New Yorker*. "His stories are nearly all cameos of the peccadillos of human behavior. He writes of the bore and the narcissist, the over-ambitious and the frustrated, the deceiver and deceived. But it is done with a kindly, humorous pen, not with acid"—(*LJ*). He has collaborated with the photographer Evelyn Hofer on three charming and excellent portraits of cities—"London Perceived" (*Harcourt* 1962 Harvest Bks. pap. $1.65), "New York Proclaimed" (1965, o. p.) and "Dublin: A Portrait" (*Harper* 1967 $15.00)—alive with reminiscences, historical snatches, quotations and intelligent insight. Other books of travel, such as "The Spanish Temper" (*Knopf* 1954 $5.95) and "The Offensive Traveler" (1964, o. p.)—his impressions of Czechoslovakia, Rumania, Spain, Poland, Hungary, Bulgaria, Turkey and Iran—capture the essence of the people as well as of the geographical region involved.

Mr. Prichett has been called "one of the best critics writing in English. [His] pages are full of delightful surprises—of insight, judgment, and real wisdom." In subject matter he ranges widely. "The Living Novel" (1947), a classic of literary criticism, was expanded by 27 new essays as "The Living Novel and Later Appreciations" (*Random* 1964 $8.95). His latest critical work is "Balzac: A Biography of the French Novelist" (*Knopf* 1973 $15.00).

Describing him, the *N.Y. Times* notes: "He is composed primarily of smile, pipe, wispy hair and glasses, and he has the laugh of a man who will seek out a good joke." His venture into autobiography, "A Cab at the Door," drew wide praise for its vivid picture of the embryo intellectual who, by his own efforts, grew beyond his philistine origins. "Now he has given us . . . a supremely good memoir, enchantingly readable in style and . . . almost unique in content. For it is one of the few records from that time—the early years of the century—which brings us news of the world Dickens and Wells wrote about, the lower middle class"—(Elizabeth Janeway, in the *N.Y. Times*).

THE KEY TO MY HEART: A Comedy in Three Parts, Ill. by Paul Hogarth. *Random* 1964 $5.95 Vintage Bks. pap. $1.95

This novel is a "brief but wonderful bit of purely English fun. Highly recommended"—(*LJ*).

A CAB AT THE DOOR: A Memoir. *Random* 1968 $7.95 Vintage Bks. pap. $1.95

STEAD, CHRISTINA (ELLEN). 1902–

Christina Stead was born in Sydney, Australia. Her father was a biologist concerned with government fisheries—an "early twentieth-century Rationalist" and Fabian Socialist. Miss Stead's mother died soon after her daughter's birth and Christina started her storytelling career entertaining her many young stepbrothers and stepsisters. She trained for teaching but became instead a business woman in banking and financial houses—and in time, of course, a writer. In early youth she spent a period working in Paris and since then has traveled widely, eventually making her home in the United States. Among her masters, she says, are Maupassant and other French writers including Hugo and Zola, as well as the Americans Thoreau, Melville and Poe (among others). In 1930 she spent some weeks at the Mozart Festival in Salzburg, Austria, out of which grew many of the stories in "The Salzburg Tales" (1934, o. p.), which first made her reputation.

She continued to write, embarking on novels, such as "House of All Nations" (1938, o.p.) and "The Man Who Loved Children," and achieved critical success and public following for what *Time* called for "Hogarthian humor, brilliant vocabulary, high-keyed imagination, and savage satire." Clifton Fadiman and Rebecca West were among her admirers. Others, such as Mary McCarthy, were cooler in their appraisal; some found her "prolix, aimless and showy"—(*Nation*). She suffered a decline in popularity by the 1950s and published nothing for 14 years.

Now she appears to be achieving new recognition. Randall Jarrell extolled her virtues, and other critics have followed. The *Nation* found "Dark Places of the Heart,"—about Nellie Colter, a lesbian, hater of men and incessant talker—a "great novel," a work in which "the narrative flow, characterizations and the supplest language achieve a classic unity. . . . Miss Stead's ear . . . and psychological wisdom . . . turn her major characters . . . into living presences, full of color, charm and fascination. . . . Miss Stead has one cementing, indispensable attribute: a sensual, deeply joyous appreciation of how life is lived." "The Man Who Loved Children" concerns "a generally pitiable creature with a compulsion to mask his weakness under a cloud of verbiage"—(*LJ*). Its reissue in 1966 brought encomiums from the *Saturday Review* and *Atlantic*, and Hortense Calisher wrote: "Christina Stead's nine books constitute an extraordinary body of work. 'The Man Who Loved Children' is perhaps the one in which her magnificently diverse powers fuse most perfectly. It is a wonderful book." In the four novellas of "The Puzzleheaded Girl" Charles Poore (*N.Y. Times*) found examples of "antic expatriates," people "alienated at home or lost abroad. Their favorite métier is flight. Flight from what? Essentially, I would say, flight from themselves." "Girl from the Beach," of this quartet, appeared in the *Paris Review* and won the Aga Khan prize for 1967.

THE MAN WHO LOVED CHILDREN. 1940. *Holt* 1965 $5.95; with afterword by Randall Jarrell *Avon* 1966 pap. $1.25. Novel.

DARK PLACES OF THE HEART. *Holt* 1966 $6.95. Novel.

THE PUZZLEHEADED GIRL: Four Novellas. The Puzzleheaded Girl; Two Dianas; The Rightangled Creek; Girl from the Beach. *Holt* 1967 $6.95

HOUSE OF ALL NATIONS. *Holt* 1972 $10.00

Books about Stead

Christina Stead. By R. G. Geering. World Authors Ser. *Twayne* $5.50

LEHMANN, ROSAMOND. 1903–

Born in London, Rosamond Lehmann "was never a 'promising' novelist, her first work ('Dusty Answer'), being a full-fledged achievement." Her father, Rudolph Lehmann, was a well-known humorist on the staff of *Punch*; her brother, John, is a poet; her sister, Beatrix, an actress. She has written since childhood, her first published work being a poem in the *Cornhill Magazine* when she was 16. Her prose has a delicate lyrical strain. The novels are written from a distinctly feminine viewpoint with a nostalgic backward glance to the irrecoverable beauties and happiness of youth. Her stories are often records of people and events seen through the eyes of children. "The Ballad and the Source" is original and unconventional in technique, revealing through overtones and undertones the past of a fascinating though sinister grandmother. Distraught over the death of Sally, a beloved daughter, Miss Lehmann tried desperately to get in touch with Sally by psychic means, an effort she describes in "The Swan in the Evening." Eventually, Miss Lehmann believes, she proved to herself the existence of a "world beyond the grave" that "offers modes of expanded consciousness, activities and services which language (as we know it) is inadequate to describe."

INVITATION TO THE WALTZ. 1932. *Harcourt* new ed. 1947 $3.50

THE BALLAD AND THE SOURCE. *Harcourt* 1945 $4.50

THE ECHOING GROVE. *Harcourt* 1953 $4.50

Books about Lehmann

Rosamond Lehmann. By Diana E. LeStourgeon. English Authors Ser. *Twayne* 1964 $5.50

O'CONNOR, FRANK (pseud. of Michael O'Donovan). 1903–1966.

An Irish master of the short story, Frank O'Connor was born Michael O'Donovan in Cork. It is not surprising to learn in the first part of his autobiography, "An Only Child," that he took his adored mother's name. "He recaptures his childhood in vivid word pictures (almost painfully truthful at times) depicting his loneliness, his naïveté, his intense desire to learn, his passion for languages and his brilliant self-development." O'Connor's absorbing interest was the literary treasury of Ireland. He labored tirelessly over translations of ancient Gaelic works, showing himself in these renditions "as poet, master of the trickiest rhythms, the most dissonant rhymes, and noble, common speech." "A Short History of Irish Literature: A Backward Look" (*Putnam* 1967 $6.95 Capricorn Bks. pap. $1.85), "based on a series of lectures delivered at Trinity College, Dublin . . . is an important book because of Mr. O'Connor's profound knowledge of the subject, his first translation from the Gaelic of many new pieces covering traditions, poetry, folklore, song, and superstitions, and because it is his last piece of writing"—(*LJ*). Kevin Sullivan (in the *Nation*) faults it as straight history but admires it enormously as literary introspection—an opinionated "love story." Mr. O'Connor edited an anthology of prose and poetry, "A Book of Ireland" (1959, o. p.) containing some of his own translations from the Gaelic. His "Shakespeare's Progress" (o. p.) is an "audacious appraisal of the Great Bard." In "The Lonely Voice: A Study of the Short Story" (1963, o. p.) he examines the work of those he considers the great short story writers of the past. His interesting thesis is that the true short story must encompass the lonely of this world, the outcasts. But "he was first and foremost a storyteller. His stories will continue to be read for the truth they tell about what it was like to be alive in a country . . . during the first half-century of its political independence"—(*N.Y. Times*). In 1966 "Three Hand Reel," a dramatic adaptation of three of his stories, was presented off-Broadway.

In his last years Frank O'Connor lived mostly in the United States, and taught at Harvard and Northwestern Universities. At the former he first met his wife of 15 years among his students. She wrote a charming brief memoir of him for the *Nation* of Aug. 28, 1967—of how she enjoyed his talk, how seriously he burrowed in Irish history and literature, and of how he translated certain Americans they knew into Irish characters for his stories (many of which appeared in the *New Yorker*). "People are all that matters," he told her. But "people," she writes, "have ultimately to be 'somebody in particular,' [and for that the writer has] to know who you are and all he can about the tradition that has shaped you. . . . He wanted to find the pattern. . . . I believe the search enriched every word he ever wrote."

THE BIG FELLOW. 1937 *Templegate* $3.95

THREE TALES. 1942. *Cuala Press* (dist. by Irish Univ. Press) 1971. $10.50

A PICTURE BOOK. 1943. *Cuala Press* (dist. by Irish Univ. Press) 1971 $11.75

STORIES. *Knopf* 1952 $6.95; *Random* Vintage Bks. pap. $1.95

MORE STORIES. *Knopf* 1954 $5.95

MIRROR IN THE ROADWAY. 1956. *Bks. for Libraries* $12.50

A SET OF VARIATIONS. *Knopf* 1969 $6.95

AN ONLY CHILD. *Knopf* 1961 $6.95. Autobiography.

MY FATHER'S SON. Ed. by Maurice Sheehy. *Knopf* 1969 $6.95

Books about O'Connor

Frank O'Connor. By James Matthews. *Bucknell Univ. Press* pap. $4.50
Michael Frank: Studies on Frank O'Connor. Ed. by Maurice Sheehy. *Knopf* 1969 $6.95

ORWELL, GEORGE (pseud. of Eric Blair). 1903–1950.

A Bengal-born novelist, critic and political satirist, a product of Eton, an anti-Communist wounded while fighting for the Republicans in Spain, Orwell was an independent radical who battled courageously all forms of dictatorships. V. S. Pritchett called him "the conscience of his generation." He first gained recognition in America with "Animal Farm," his satiric fable on Stalin's Russia. His best-selling "Nineteen Eighty-Four" depicts the horrors of a well-established totalitarian regime, and "Big Brother," the government spy, has become common American parlance for the official snooper. "Homage to Catalonia" (1939, *Harcourt* 1952 pap. 1969 $1.95) is a nonfiction account of the Spanish Civil War. His posthumous volumes of essays are "Shooting an Elephant" (*Harcourt* 1950 $5.95) and "Collection of Essays" (*Harcourt* pap. $1.65). His political and literary ideas may be found in "Dickens, Dali and Others" (1946 *Harcourt* $5.95 Harvest Bks. pap. $1.75). "The Road to Wigan Pier" (1937 *Harcourt* 1958 Harvest Bks. pap. $2.25) consists of an account of Orwell's sojourn among the coal miners of northern England as well as his analysis of socialism, which he considered ineffective among working people.

THE ORWELL READER. Introd. by Richard R. Rovere. *Harcourt* 1956 1961 Harvest Bks. pap. $3.25. Contains fiction, essays and reportage.

ANIMAL FARM. *Harcourt* 1946 ill. by J. Batchelor and J. Halas 1954 $4.50; *New Am. Lib* Signet 1954 $.95

NINETEEN EIGHTY-FOUR. *Harcourt* 1949 $7.50; *New Am. Lib*. Signet pap. $.95

NINETEEN EIGHTY-FOUR: Text, Sources, Criticism. Ed. by Irving Howe. *Harcourt* 1963 pap. $3.75

COMING UP FOR AIR. *Harcourt* 1950 $6.50 pap. 1969 $1.65

KEEP THE ASPIDISTRA FLYING. *Harcourt* 1956 pap. 1969 $1.25

DOWN AND OUT IN PARIS AND LONDON. 1933. *Harcourt* pap. $1.75 *Berkley* pap. 1959 $.75. Autobiographical.

BURMESE DAYS. 1934. *Harcourt* new ed. 1950 $5.95; *New Am. Lib*. Signet 1964 pap. $.95. Autobiographical.

COLLECTED ESSAYS, JOURNALISM AND LETTERS OF GEORGE ORWELL. Ed. by Sonia Orwell and Ian Angus. *Harcourt* 4 vols. 1968 Vol. I An Age like This, 1920–1940 Vol. 2 My Country Right or Left, 1940–1943 Vol. 3 As I Please, 1943–1945 Vol. 4 In Front of Your Nose, 1945–1950 each $10.00 boxed set $40.00 Harvest Bks. pap. each $3.95 boxed set $15.80.

Books about Orwell

George Orwell. By Tom Hopkinson. Writers and Their Work Ser. *British Bk. Centre* $2.38 pap. $1.20
Crystal Spirit: A Study of George Orwell. By George Woodcock. *Little* 1966 $7.95; *Funk & Wagnalls* Minerva Press pap. $2.25
  This book "blends literary criticism and biography to yield a sound, sharply analytical picture of both Orwell and his work"—(*LJ*).
The Paradox of George Orwell. By Richard J. Voorhees. *Purdue Univ. Press* 1969 pap. $1.95
The Making of George Orwell: An Essay in English Literary History. By Keith Aldritt. *St. Martin's* 1970 $7.50
George Orwell. By Raymond Williams. *Viking* 1971 $.95 pap. $1.65
Orwell's Fiction. By Robert A. Lee. *Univ. of Notre Dame Press* 1972 $8.50 pap. $2.95
The Unknown Orwell. By William Abrahams and Peter Stansky. *Knopf* 1972 $8.95

WAUGH, EVELYN. 1903–1966.

Evelyn Waugh came from a literary family. His elder brother, Alec (*q. v.*), is a novelist and traveler. Their father, Arthur Waugh, was the influential head of the London publishing house, *Chapman & Hall*. Evelyn Waugh's deeply religious temperament (he later became an ardent Catholic) and literary abilities were evident during his school days. He joined the Royal Marines at the beginning of World War II and was among the first to volunteer for Commando service. In 1944 he was one of three survivors of a plane crash in Yugoslavia and, while hiding in a cave, corrected the proofs of "Brideshead Revisited." Through very conservative eyes looking coldly on modern technology and encroaching democracy as the ancient British class system began to atrophy, Waugh saw his disenchanted world clearly and expressed his cynicism with savage fantasy and satire. His early novels, "Decline and Fall," "Vile Bodies," "A Handful of Dust" and "The Loved One" (his later ironic tale of the extravagant and sentimental Forest Lawn cemetery in California) are brilliantly funny; "Decline and Fall" took the British public by storm and made his youthful reputation. In the later, "serious" novels he became petulant at the disintegration of the staid, stable, indeed snobbish values of the England he imagined to be his, and verged on fascism in his novel "Scoop" (1938 o. p.) and in the "Waugh in Abyssinia" journalistic writings of 1936. Philip Toynbee wrote in the *Observer* (London): "I am not an admirer of his serious books: his values seemed to me to be vulgar and absurd; his conspicuous qualities were not, for the most part, of the kind that I most respect." But [in Mrs. Donaldson's book, *see below*] "what does emerge with great freshness is that Waugh was a man who could charm the birds off a tree; that he could be the best possible company—witty, extravagant, ebullient; that his aggressiveness, exclusiveness, fear of boredom and fierce love of privacy were all far stronger emotions than his "soft-centered' (Mrs. Donaldson's good phrase) regard for the upper classes. What emerges, too, is that he was exceptionally kind and considerate to unknown writers—a great and rare quality in a successful author—and that he was capable of the most notable self-sacrifice."

Evelyn Waugh's novels of the 1920s and 1930s, together with "The Loved One," attack real follies, which can be seen as such from any political or social vantage point. The satire is sharp, unencumbered and to the point; the stories are furiously witty and inventive. On these he may be judged the outstanding satirist of his day. (His son AUBERON WAUGH is also a novelist.)

Two of his biographies are in print: "Rossetti: His Life and Works" (1928. *Folcroft* lib. bdg. $15.00) and "Monsignor Ronald Knox" (*Little* 1960 $5.95). "A Little Learning" (1964, o. p.), the first volume of, his uncompleted autobiography, is "an amusing and thoughtful chronicle of the early years of a man who [had] such a profound influence on the literature and thought of his own day. The prose, as is usual with Mr. Waugh, is elegant and at all times lucid"—(*LJ*).

Among his books in print:

TACTICAL EXERCISE. 1954. *Bks. for Libraries* $10.50. A collection of shorter satiric works including "Work Suspended" and "Love among the Ruins."

DECLINE AND FALL. 1929. (and "A Handful of Dust") *Dell* pap. $.95

A HANDFUL OF DUST. 1934. *Dell* pap. $1.45 (and Decline and Fall") pap. $.95

BRIDESHEAD REVISITED: The Sacred and Profane Memories of Charles Ryder. 1945. *Dell* 1956 pap. $.95

THE LOVED ONE. *Little* 1948 $4.95; *Dell* pap. $.75

MEN AT ARMS. The first novel of the Men at Arms trilogy. *Little* 1952 $5.95; (and "Officers and Gentlemen") *Dell* pap. $.75.

OFFICERS AND GENTLEMEN. *Little* 1955 $4.95; (and "Men at Arms") *Dell* pap. $.75. Continues the Men at Arms trilogy.

THE ORDEAL OF GILBERT PINFOLD. *Little* 1957 $4.95

THE END OF THE BATTLE. *Little* 1961 $4.95. The last novel of the Men at Arms trilogy.

SWORD OF HONOR. *Little* 1966 $8.95. Final text—revised by Waugh to be read as a single story—of the Men at Arms trilogy (Men at Arms; Officers and Gentlemen; The End of the Battle).

BASIL SEAL RIDES AGAIN. *Little* 1963 limited ed. $15.00

Books about Waugh

Evelyn Waugh. By Christopher Hollis. *British Bk. Centre* $2.38 pap. $1.20

The Satiric Art of Evelyn Waugh. By James F. Carens. *Univ. of Washington Press* 1966 $5.95 pap. $2.95
"The material has been studied and condensed into a good prose that is easy to read as it enlightens"—
(*LJ*).

My Brother Evelyn and Other Portraits. By Alec Waugh. *Farrar, Straus* 1968 $6.95
Alec Waugh once wrote: "I lack the key to Evelyn. I cannot enter imaginatively into the mind of a person for whom religion is the dominant force." "But when I wrote that," he recently said, "I could not have forseen that Evelyn would never finish his own autobiography; and though . . . I do not feel myself competent to draw a full-length portrait of him, I do feel that I owe it to his memory to sketch, for the benefit of his readers, a picture of his early days, up till his conversion." In the resulting memoir—which deals with most of 20th-century literary England as well—"Evelyn's early years, his Oxford days and the brief span of his first marriage . . . are conveyed only as a member of the family could convey them"—(*Atlantic*).

Evelyn Waugh. By David Lodge. Essays on Modern Authors Ser. *Columbia* 1971 $1.00

MITFORD, NANCY. 1904–

Nancy is one of six Mitford sisters who rebelled against their uppercrust English family in varying directions: Nancy became a writer and remained a conservative; Unity went to Germany and admired Hitler; Jessica embraced Marxism and later wrote "The American Way of Death," "A Just and Kind Punishment: The Prison Business" and "The Trial of Dr. Spock." Diana married the British fascist Oswald Mosley; and the two younger daughters were pro-Nazi. Their story was brilliantly told as that of the "Radlett" family in Nancy's novel, "The Pursuit of Love," which won her a broad American readership. Since then her elegant and satirical novels and biographies have delighted American as well as British readers. "Voltaire in Love" (1958. *Greenwood* $15.00) is a "wonderfully gay and gossipy book" which tells of Voltaire's association with the Marquise dú Châtelet. "Noblesse Oblige" (1956, o. p.) is concerned with the distinguishable characteristics of the English aristocracy (*see Chapter 3, Reference Books—Literature: Books About Words*). All her work is witty, lively—and barbed. "When I take up my pen," she says, "my thoughts are wicked."

Other sparkling biographies are "Madame de Pompadour" (1953 *Harper* $15.00) "Frederick the Great" (*Harper* 1970 $15.00) and "The Sun King: Louis XIV at Versailles" (*Harper* 1966 $15.00). The latter is "a highly entertaining narrative, written with her accustomed dash and gaiety, in a manner that frequently suggests one of her own delightful novels"—(Peter Quennell). The *New Yorker* said of this Book-of-the-Month Club choice: "What might have been an entertaining picture book with some printed matter is, instead, dominated by the literary distinction and interest of the text . . . The broad outline is sustained, and the most important courtiers, the Children of France, the Princes of the Blood and the royal bastards all come through like characters in a novel." "Madame de Pompadour" is now reissued in a revised and enlarged version (*Harper* 1968 $15.00). Miss Mitford has made her home in France for the past 20 years.

The Pursuit of Love. 1945. *Random* Vintage Bks. pap. $1.45

ISHERWOOD, CHRISTOPHER. 1904–

Isherwood met W. H. Auden (*q. v.*) at an English boarding school. They collaborated on three verse-plays—fantasies—of which two are available in "Two Plays: The Dog beneath the Skin and The Ascent of F-6" (1935 1936. *Random* Vintage Bks. pap. $1.65). In 1938 the two went to China together, financed by their publishers. "Journey to a War" (1939, o. p.) is their diary, kept alternately. In 1939 they came to America intending to become permanent residents. In 1946 Isherwood became a U.S. citizen and in 1949 he was elected a member of the National Institute of Arts and Letters.

His excellent brief novels, largely autobiographical, are written with precision. He is still best known for the brilliance of his Berlin stories, written before World War II. He spent about four years in Germany; the eccentrics of "The Berlin Stories" symbolize the decadence of pre-Nazi Berlin. John Van Druten (*q. v.*) adapted his successful play, "I Am a Camera" from these stories. It won the N.Y. Drama Critics Circle Award. (Its 1966 musical version, "Cabaret," won the N.Y. Drama Circle Award and a "Tony.") The play was the basis of a very popular film starring Liza Minelli and Joel Grey.

"Hinduism and homosexuality have long been favorite themes of Christopher Isherwood. ["A Meeting by the River"] combines them in a short novel, composed entirely of letters and diaries, that is rather old-fashioned in form but distinctly up-to-date in its descriptions of post-British India and post-Genet California"—(*N.Y. Times*). The book, says Stanley Kauffmann (in the *New Republic*), "is credible, moving, and ultimately ironic. [Its] considerable work is accomplished with beautifully spare means, seemingly easy but possible only to an artist who has always been good and who has lost no refinement." "A Single Man," concentrating solely on the homosexual theme, portrays a college professor distraught over the death of his male lover.

Isherwood now lives in California, where he originally wrote movie scripts and, with Aldous Huxley (*q. v.*), became interested in the ancient Indian philosophy of the Vedas. With Swami Prabhavanda, he has made a new translation from the Sanskrit in prose and poetry of the Mahabharata Bhagavadgita (*q. v.*), "The Song of God," with an introduction by Aldous Huxley (1951. *New Am. Lib.* Mentor Bks. pap. $.75). Other books on Vedanta and Yoga which he edited are: "Vedanta for Modern Man" (1951, *New Am. Lib.* Signet pap. $1.50), "Vedanta for the Western World" (*Vedanta Press* 1946 3rd ed. 1951 $4.95; *Viking* Compass Bks. pap. $2.95). He has written "Approach to Vedanta" (*Vedanta Press* 1963 pap. $1.00) and "Ramakrishna and His Disciples" (*Simon & Schuster* 1965 $7.50 Clarion Bks. pap. $3.95; *Viking Press* $5.00), a biography which treats this Hindu mystic in his historical context. "Exhumations" contains poems, articles, essays and stories. Sybille Bedford (in the *N.Y. Times*) called it "a collection that does the writer proud; it is also a portrait of the writer as a man . . . warm, gay, responsible, compassionate, generous. How pleasant to have met Mr. Isherwood."

THE BERLIN STORIES. 1946. *New Directions* new ed. with new pref. by the author 1954 1963 pap. $2.75

THE MEMORIAL. 1946. *Greenwood* $11.50

ALL THE CONSPIRATORS. 1928. *New Directions* 1958 $4.50

THE LAST OF MR. NORRIS. 1935. Published in England as "Mr. Norris Changes Trains." *Berkley* pap. $.60

LIONS AND SHADOWS. *New Directions* 1947 $4.50; Bobbs pap. $1.95. Fictional autobiography.

EXHUMATIONS. *Simon & Schuster* 1966 $5.00

A MEETING BY THE RIVER. *Simon & Schuster* 1967 $4.50

Books about Isherwood

Christopher Isherwood. By Carolyn Heilbrun. Essays on Modern Writers *Columbia* 1970 pap. $1.00
Christopher Isherwood. By Alan Wilde. English Authors Ser. *Twayne* $5.50

GREENE, (HENRY) GRAHAM. 1904–

Graham Greene is "primarily and passionately concerned with Good & Evil." "He writes about sin and God, about the presence of evil and the absence of good"—(*Time*). "By conversion a Catholic, he is by temperament a romantic anarchist." "Theoretically, Greene may recognize original sin, but in his writing the evil in man is always less than the evil without, arising from the collective activities of society. His observations of humanity force him into a revolutionary attitude"—(George Woodcock).

He has spent periods on the staff of the London *Times* and the *Spectator*. In World War II he served at the Foreign Office, with special duties in West Africa. "The Man Within," (1939, o. p.) his first published novel, was not a success here. He wrote several thrillers, which he calls "entertainments," but "The Power and the Glory" and "The Heart of the Matter," considered his two finest novels, convinced critics of his serious intent, subtle characterization and accomplished craftsmanship.

It is significant that Greene names as two great influences on his writing the late John Buchan, a master of the spy thriller, and the Catholic novelist François Mauriac. Greene's work follows this split character, from those sinister spy-chase tales to the works of serious moral and religious reflection. A number of his novels and short stories have been made into successful films, and two of his plays, "The Living Room" (1954 o. p.) and "The Potting Shed" (1957 o. p.), were produced on Broadway. "Carving a Statue," which played off-Broadway in 1968, had its première in London in 1964. It concerns a sculptor's neglect of his son for the 15 years during which he worked on a statue representing God. His 1967 film adaptation of "The Comedians," a best-selling novel set in contemporary Haiti under the terror-ridden dictatorship of President François Duvalier, drew protests from the Haitian government upon its release here. In 1952 Graham Greene was given the Catholic Literary Award for "The End of the Affair."

TWENTY-ONE STORIES. *Viking*. 1962 $4.00 Compass Bks. 1962 $1.45; *Bantam* pap. $.95. Three stories added to "Nineteen Stories" (1949, o. p.) and one withdrawn from this collection.

TRIPLE PURSUIT: A Graham Greene Omnibus. *Viking* 1971 $6.95. Includes "This Gun for Hire," "The Third Man" and "Our Man in Havana."

THE PORTABLE GRAHAM GREENE. Ed. by Philip Stratford. *Viking* 1972 $6.95 Compass Bks. pap. $3.25. A cross section, chosen with the collaboration of the author.

COLLECTED STORIES. *Viking* 1973 $10.00

IT'S A BATTLEFIELD. 1934 1948 *Viking* rev. ed. 1962 $3.95

THE BEAR FELL FREE. 1935. *Folcroft* $8.50

BRIGHTON ROCK: An Entertainment. *Viking* 1938 $5.00 Compass Bks. pap. $2.25; *Bantam* pap. $.95

THE POWER AND THE GLORY (Original U.S. title "The Labyrinthine Ways"). *Viking* 1946 ed. by R. W. Lewis and Peter J. Conn Critical Lib. 1970 $5.95 pap. $2.25 lg. type ed. $8.50; Compass Bks. pap. $2.25; *Bantam* pap. $1.25

Compass Bks. pap. $2.25; *Bantam* pap. $1.25

THE HEART OF THE MATTER. *Viking* 1948 $3.95 Compass Bks. 1960 pap. $1.65; *Bantam* pap. $1.25

THE END OF THE AFFAIR. *Viking* 1951 $5.95 Compass Bks. 1961 pap. $1.65

THE QUIET AMERICAN. *Viking* 1956 Compass Bks. 1957 pap. $1.75; *Bantam* pap. $.95

OUR MAN IN HAVANA: An Entertainment. *Viking* 1958 Compass Bks. pap. $2.45

THE COMPLAISANT LOVER. *Viking* 1961 $3.00

JOURNEY WITHOUT MAPS. *Viking* 1961 Compass Bks. pap. $1.65

THE COMEDIANS. *Viking* 1966 lg.-type ed. $8.95 Compass Bks. pap. $2.25; *Bantam* pap. $1.25. A novel of Haiti.

TRAVELS WITH MY AUNT. *Viking* 1970 $5.95

A SORT OF LIFE. *Simon & Schuster* 1971 $6.95; *Pocket Bks.* pap. $1.25

COLLECTED ESSAYS. *Viking* 1969 $7.95

THE LOST CHILDHOOD, AND OTHER ESSAYS. *Viking* Compass Bks. 1952 pap. $1.25. Personal reminiscences and analyses of contemporaries.

IN SEARCH OF A CHARACTER: Two African Journals. *Viking* 1961 $3.50. After he had conceived the theme of "A Burnt-Out Case" (1961, o. p.) he traveled in the Belgian Congo in February 1959, to gather "an authentic medical background." Although the journals were not kept for publication, they are interesting "as an indication of the kind of raw material a novelist accumulates." The brief notes and his footnotes showing what Mr. Greene did or did not retain for his novel, are especially interesting.

Books about Greene

The Art of Graham Greene. By Kenneth Allott and Miriam Farris. 1951. *Russell & Russell* 1963 $11.00
Graham Greene and The Heart of the Matter. By Marie B. Mesnet. 1954. *Greenwood* 1972 $8.00
Graham Greene. By John Atkins. 1957. *Humanities Press* rev. ed. 1966 $6.00
  Readable, "accurate, scrupulous and just"—(*Spectator*).
Faith and Fiction: Creative Process in Greene and Mauriac. By Philip Stratford. *Univ. of Notre Dame Press* 1964 $2.95
  This thorough examination of the works of Graham Greene and François Mauriac deals comprehensively with all their novels, emphasizing aspects which are mutually illuminating and illustrative of their outstanding differences.

Graham Greene. By A. A. DeVitis. English Authors Ser. *Twayne* 1964 $4.95. A critical study tracing Greene's artistic development and placing him in the framework of English literature.

Graham Greene. By Francis Wyndham. *British Bk. Centre* $2.38 pap. $1.20

Graham Greene. By D. Lodge. Essays on Modern Writers *Columbia* 1966 $1.00. A critical pamphlet.

Graham Greene: A Critical Essay. By Martin Turnell. Contemporary Writers in Christian Perspective Ser. *Eerdmans* 1967 pap. $.85

Graham Greene. By David Pryce-Jones. *Barnes & Noble* 1967 $2.25

Graham Greene: A Checklist of Criticism. By Don J. Vann. *Kent State Univ. Press* 1970 $3.75

RENAULT, MARY (pseud. of Mary Challons). 1905–

Mary Renault was born in London and educated at Oxford. Deciding upon a writing career, she trained for three years as a nurse in order to educate herself in human life. She wrote her first novel, "Promise of Love," but returned to nursing when the war broke out and wrote her next three novels in off-duty time. One of these, "Return to Night" (1947, *Pyramid Bks.* pap. $1.25) was awarded the $150,000 MGM prize. After her release from service she settled in Natal, South Africa. Wanting to write about Greece, she traveled extensively in and around Greece and the Aegean Islands for three months.

"The Last of the Wine" is an historical novel of the third Peloponnesian War in which the real figures Socrates, Alcibiades, and Phaedo appear. This was called by the *Times Literary Supplement* (London) "a superb historical novel. The writing is Attic in quality, unforced, clear, delicate. The characterization is uniformly successful, and, most difficult of all, the atmosphere of Athens is realized in masterly fashion." When visiting Crete, Miss Renault became interested in the legendary figure Theseus, who became the hero of "The King Must Die." Clifton Fadiman called this book about the youth of Theseus "quite literally a wonderful novel—that is, a novel full of wonders." "The Bull from the Sea" continues the story. Her best seller "The Mask of Apollo" concerns the conflict between Dionysios of Syracuse and Dion, a soldier-philosopher, as narrated by a young Athenian actor. The *N.Y. Times* said of it: "She has few peers in the art of reconstructing and making utterly convincing the people and places of classical times."

"Miss Renault is artist enough to let the ancient myth carry the story and to allow the actors to play out their destined parts. Her plain but strong style does not require the addition of apocryphal episodes of sex and adventure to hold the modern reader's interest."

KIND ARE HER ANSWERS. 1940. *Pyramid Bks.* pap. $1.25

RETURN TO NIGHT. 1947. *Pyramid Bks.* pap. $1.25

THE LAST OF THE WINE. *Pantheon* 1956 $6.95; *Pocket Bks.* pap. $1.25

THE KING MUST DIE. *Pantheon* 1958 $6.95; *Pocket Bks.* pap. $1.25

THE CHARIOTEER. *Pantheon* 1959 $7.95. A novel on homosexuality, set in England.

THE BULL FROM THE SEA. *Pantheon* 1962 $7.95; *Pocket Bks.* pap. $1.25

THE LION IN THE GATEWAY. 1964. *Harper* $3.95 lib. bdg. $4.09

THE MASK OF APOLLO. *Pantheon* 1966 $6.95 *Pocket Bks.* pap. $.95

FIRE FROM HEAVEN. *Pantheon* 1969 $7.95; *Popular Lib.* pap. $1.25

THE PERSIAN BOY. *Pantheon* 1972 $7.95; *Bantam* pap. $1.95

Books about Renault

The Hellenism of Mary Renault. By Bernard F. Dick. *Southern Illinois Univ. Press* 1972 $5.95

Mary Renault. By Peter Wolfe. English Authors Ser. *Twayne* $5.50

SHARP, MARGERY. 1905–

Margery Sharp has a gift for light comedy, a barbed wit and a shrewd psychological insight in portraying her leading characters. Social contrast is inherent in her novels of seeming frivolity and gay nonsense. Brock Pemberton, who produced "Lady in Waiting" (1941, o. p.), wrote in the *Book-of-the-Month Club News* of meeting her: "She seemed something out of Dickens by Dali. One of the first things that struck me about Margery Sharp was her naturalness and utter lack of affectation of any kind. Her delicious sense of humor and infectious laugh, her enthusiasms and lack of the sort of inhibitions you come upon in so many writers." Her ingenious, "frequently zany, but always entertaining brand of fiction has won her" tremendous popularity. In this light vein is "In Pious Memory," about a "nice but witless" widow uncertain if her husband is really dead. "The Sun in Scorpio," (1965, o. p.) "a bitter sweet bon-bon from a master confectioner," is the moving story of a girl who must adjust to the ways of England after life on a Mediterranean island. With "pure imagination, wit and style," she has written rare fantasies for grown-ups, illustrated with Garth Williams's enchanting drawings—"The Rescuers" and the "Miss Bianca" books. They are about the clever and the beautiful white mouse, Miss Bianca, and her loving Bernard of the Mouse Prisoner's Aid Society. "The Turret" continues the story of the tender-hearted Miss Bianca on her third rescue mission. In "Miss Bianca in the Salt Mines," four mice save a trapped boy.

BRITANNIA MEWS. 1946. *Popular Lib.* pap. $.95

THE FOOLISH GENTLEWOMAN. 1948. *Popular Lib.* pap. $.60

THE GYPSY IN THE PARLOUR. 1954. *Popular Lib.* pap. $.60

THE RESCUERS. *Little* 1959 $4.95; *Berkley* pap. $.75

MISS BIANCA. Ill. by Garth Williams. *Little* 1962 $4.95; *Berkley* pap. $.75

THE TURRET. Ill. by Garth Williams. *Little* 1963 $4.95; *Berkley* pap. $.75

MISS BIANCA IN THE SALT MINES. Ill. by Garth Williams. *Little* 1966 $4.50

MISS BIANCA IN THE ORIENT. Ill. by Erik Blegvad. *Little* 1970 $4.95

MISS BIANCA IN THE ANTARCTIC. Ill. by Erik Blegvad. *Little* 1971 $4.95

MISS BIANCA AND THE BRIDESMAID. Ill. by Erik Blegvad. *Little* 1972 $4.95

THE INNOCENTS. *Little* 1972 $5.95

THE LOST CHAPEL PICNIC. *Little* 1973 $6.95

GREEN, HENRY (pseud. of Henry Vincent Yorke). 1905–

Henry Green was called by Elizabeth Bowen "one of the novelists most to be reckoned with today" and by W. H. Auden "the best English novelist alive." His "subtly designed" novels, with their one-word titles, are what he calls "an advanced attempt to break up the old-fashioned type of novel." He does not describe his characters, but "has made pioneer explorations of all the ways in which they can describe themselves." "Anything which has a voice is invited to use it," he explains, "but, the reader is left to supply the shapes and colors out of his own head." This oblique method and a fondness for symbols make his novels difficult for the readers who expect straight plot and action, but fascinating to others. He has described his background in the autobiographical "Pack My Bag," his only book of nonfiction.

Two of his best-known novels are "Loving" and "Back" (1950, o. p.). The first is the story of an Irish country house during wartime; even in a neutral country, far from the front, the war has the power to change lives. In the process, Green's characters reveal themselves, weakness and nobility appear where they might be least expected, and the people of a disintegrating society—the microcosm of a larger society—survive by virtue of their hidden strength. "Back" is the story of a soldier returning home from the war; the war is again World War II, but the situation is universal. The novel is filled with surprises: in Green's world people are rarely what they seem to be. In the end, however, it becomes clear that Green's subject is not war, but love; love is the source of anguish, humiliation, despair; it makes puppets of its victims; and yet it is the only thing that can give meaning to life.

LIVING. 1929. *Scholarly Press* 1971 $14.50

LOVING. 1949. *Dufour* $5.25; *Popular Lib.* pap. $.75

NOTHING. 1950. *Kelley* 1970 $10.00

CONCLUDING. 1950. *Kelley* 1970 $10.00

PARTY GOING. 1951. *Kelley* 1970 $10.00

CAUGHT. 1952. *Kelley* 1970 $10.00

DOTING. 1952. *Kelley* 1970 $10.00

Books about Green

> Henry Green: Nine Novels and an Unpacked Bag. By John Russell. *Rutgers Univ. Press* 1960 $5.00
> A Reading of Henry Green. By Kinglsey A. Weatherhead. *Univ. of Washington Press* 1961 $5.00
> Henry Green. By Robert S. Ryf. Essays on Modern Writers *Columbia* 1967 pap. $1.00

SNOW, SIR C(HARLES) P(ERCY). 1905–

Trained as a physicist and at one time a Fellow in physics at Cambridge, C. P. Snow has written a number of papers on the problems of molecular structure. He was knighted in 1957 for his important work in organizing scientific personnel for the Ministry of Labour during World War II and for his services as a Civil Service Commissioner. In "Variety of Men" (*Scribner* 1967 pap. $2.95), "highly polished" biographical essays on nine men—including Einstein, Frost and Stalin—who have influenced the destiny of the 20th century, his "professional experience in the worlds of science, literature, and public affairs . . . enables him to examine these unusual men with a force of objectivity, insight, and political sophistication that is most impressive"— (*New Yorker*). Sir Charles is an influential literary critic, is concerned with the problems of education and has lectured at colleges and universities in this country. He has been at work on his sequence of novels, "Strangers and Brothers," for more than 20 years. "Strangers and Brothers," the first to be written in the series that bears its name, was published in England in 1940 and released here in 1960. The cycle relates the life story of a young English lawyer named Lewis Eliot who is very much like Snow himself. "Like all the novels in the series, 'Strangers and Brothers' is distinguished by virtue of its analysis of motive and character and its anatomization of a world in which a smooth mediocrity is the greatest virtue."

Sir Charles, who has made several long visits to the U.S., drew on his wide experience for his Godkin Lectures at Harvard. These have been published as "Science and Government" (*Harvard Univ. Press* 1961 $3.00; *New Am. Lib.* Mentor Bks. pap. $.75). This book "tells the story of the bitter wartime clash between two eminent British scientist-advisers to government. On the left, Sir Henry Tizard, the loser but Snow's man for a' that—the man who saw that Britain had radar when it was needed. On the right, F. A. Lindemann (later Lord Cherwell), bosom pal of Winston Churchill, and the villain of this piece. The story has a moral and a purpose. We need more scientists and scientific foresight in government." Snow's view that society is split into two antagonistic groups, humanists and scientists, is discussed in "The Two Cultures and the Scientific Revolution" (1959, o. p.). A violent transatlantic debate resulted when F. R. Leavis (*q. v.*) wrote a diatribe against Snow as a novelist and thinker for the *Spectator*. (One of his sharper comments was: "As a novelist [Snow] doesn't exist; he doesn't even begin to exist.") This has been published in "Two Cultures? The Significance of C. P. Snow by F. R. Leavis, and An Essay on Sir Charles Snow's Rede Lecture by Michael Yudkin" (*Pantheon* 1963 $2.95).

Lady Snow is the novelist PAMELA HANSFORD JOHNSON, whose recent "On Iniquity: Some Personal Reflections Arising Out of the Moors Murder Trial" (*Scribner* 1967 pap. $2.45) drew praise from George Steiner and other critics.

THE SEARCH. *Scribner* 1935 2nd ed. rev. 1958 $6.95 pap. $2.95

STRANGERS AND BROTHERS. The omnibus ed. Rev. by the author. *Scribner* 3 vols. 1972 Vol. I The Time of Hope, George Passant (originally titled "Strangers and Brothers"), The Conscience of the Rich, The Dark and the Light Vol. 2 The Masters, The New Men, Homecoming, The Affair Vol. 3 Corridors of Power, The Sleep of Reason, Last Things. Vols. I–2 each $15.00 Vol. 3 $12.50 set $37.50

The same novels available in separate editions:

STRANGERS AND BROTHERS.1940. *Scribner* 1960 $7.95 pap. $2.65

THE LIGHT AND THE DARK. 1948. *Scribner* 1961 $6.95 pap. $2.95

THE TIME OF HOPE. 1949. *Scribner* 1961 $6.95 pap. $1.65

THE MASTERS. 1951. *Scribner* $6.95 pap. $2.95

THE NEW MEN. *Scribner* 1954 $6.95 pap. $1.65

HOMECOMING. *Scribner* 1956 $6.95 pap. $1.65

THE CONSCIENCE OF THE RICH. *Scribner* 1958 $6.95 pap. $2.95

THE AFFAIR. *Scribner* 1960 $6.95 pap. $2.95

THE CORRIDORS OF POWER. *Scribner* 1964 $7.95

Books about Snow

C. P. Snow. By William Cooper. *British Bk. Centre* 1962 pap. $2.38 pap. $1.20
C. P. Snow: The Politics of Conscience. By Frederick R. Karl. *Southern Illinois Univ. Press* 1963 $4.50 pap. $1.65
   "[Mr. Karl's] statement to the effect that Snow is becoming a major writer will be challenged by some readers; certainly it is in contradiction of F. R. Leavis's attack on Snow in 1961. Leavis, in his farewell lecture at one of the Cambridge colleges, allowed the author of 'The Masters' no talent whatsoever. Mr. Karl, characterizing this attack as 'intemperate,' deals with it very sensibly and gives it no more space than it deserves; but he finds some grains of truth in parts of Leavis's lecture"—(From the Preface by Harry T. Moore).
The World of C. P. Snow. By Robert Greacen. Bibliog. by Bernard Stone. *British Bk. Centre* 1963 $2.95
   This "uninspired analysis of C. P. Snow's literary life and contributions . . . presents little more than a summary of the plots of Snow's novels liberally interlarded with quotations extracted from Snow and his critics. . . . Recommended, with reservations, to the large library"—(*LJ*).
C. P. Snow. By Robert Gorham Davis. Essays on Modern Writers *Columbia* 1965 pap. $1.00

POWELL, ANTHONY (DYMOKE). 1905–

Evelyn Waugh once said: "Each succeeding volume of Mr. Powell's 'Music of Time' series enhances its importance. The work is dry, cool, humorous, elaborately and accurately constructed and quintessentially English. It is more realistic than '*A La Recherche du Temps Perdu,*' to which it is often compared, and much funnier." It has been Powell's fate, according to some critics, to be praised as like someone else, and in the 1930s it was Waugh. He was of Waugh's world and the conflicts in his book develop out of the rebellions of the first quarter of the century. It "takes its importance now—and even its length—from its research into a tentative reconstruction of values"—(James Hall). With "The Kindly Ones" he reaches the halfway mark in his chronicle, the end of the uneasy decades between two World Wars. "The Valley of Bones" is the first book of the proposed trilogy devoted to World War II (which will complete "The Music of Time" series). " 'The Soldier's Art' [the second] adds one more section to a complex structure that block by block, layer by layer, continues to grow into a great fictional history and to intensify and reaffirm the art of Anthony Powell"—(*Nation*). According to a *N.Y. Times* interview the author thinks of his work as one long novel appearing a volume at a time, and not like, say C. P. Snow's (*q. v.*) "Strangers and Brothers," a series of connected novels. "What makes Powell's work so exciting is his ability to create truth, emotional, evocative, out of a congeries of mere fact, so that reading Powell is like living someone else's life for an hour or two, inextricably entangled with one's own"—(Elizabeth Janeway, in the *N.Y. Times*).

Born in London, educated at Eton and Oxford, Anthony Powell now lives in Somerset. In 1961 he came to the U.S. and was artist in (brief) residence at Dartmouth, Cornell and Amherst. "John Aubrey and His Friends" (1948, o. p.) is an excellent "witty and scholarly biography"—(*LJ*).

AFTERNOON MEN. 1931. *Little* 1963 $5.95. His first novel.

FROM A VIEW TO A DEATH. 1933. *Little* $4.95

The first American edition of a book that "easily holds its own across the years"—(*N.Y. Times*).

WHAT'S BECOME OF WARING? 1939. *Little* 1963 $4.95

A DANCE TO THE MUSIC OF TIME: FIRST MOVEMENT. A Question of Upbringing (1951) A Buyer's Market (1952) The Acceptance World (1955) *Little* 1963 $7.50

A DANCE TO THE MUSIC OF TIME: SECOND MOVEMENT. Other titles of a trilogy: Casanova's Chinese Restaurant (1960) At Lady Molly's (1958) The Kindly Ones *Little* 1964 $8.50

THE KINDLY ONES. *Little* 1962 $4.95

A DANCE TO THE MUSIC OF TIME: THIRD MOVEMENT. The Valley of Bones (1964) The Soldier's Art (1967) The Military Philosophers (1969) *Little* 1971 $8.95

THE MILITARY PHILOSOPHERS. *Little* 1969 $5.95

TEMPORARY KINGS. *Little* 1973 $6.95. The 11th and penultimate novel in his "Dance to the Music of Time" series.

Books about Powell

Anthony Powell. By Bernard Bergonzi. Writers and Their Work Ser. *British Bk. Centre* $2.38 pap. $1.20
The Novels of Anthony Powell. By Robert K. Morris. *Univ. of Pittsburgh Press* 1968 pap. $2.95
Anthony Powell: A Quintet, Sextet and War. By John Russell. *Indiana Univ. Press* 1970 $7.50

WHITE, T(ERENCE) H(ANBURY). 1906–1964.

T. H. White began his excursions into Malory's medieval England with "The Sword in the Stone," a fantasy about the education of the young King Arthur, "a rare concoction of wisdom and humor, fact and fancy, legend and history, wit and sarcasm." It was his eighth book and made his fame in England and America. "The Witch in the Wood," "The Ill-Made Knight" and "The Candle in the Wind" comprise his modernized Arthurian cycle. In the fall of 1960 "The Once and Future King" was very successfully produced on Broadway by Lerner and Loewe in musical form under the title of "Camelot," the late President Kennedy's favorite musical. White died aboard the U.S. liner *Exeter* in the harbor at Piraeus, Greece. During a 1963 U.S. lecture tour just before his death, he recorded his candid impressions in a journal. "American At Last" "is unique in its easy, graceful, often humorous style, and in the way it reveals as much of its writer as it does of America"—(*LJ*).
White made an authoritative and quietly amusing translation, "The Book of Beasts: Being a Translation from a Latin Bestiary of the Twelfth Century" (*Putnam* Capricorn Bks. 1953 1960 pap. $2.25; *Fernhill* $15.00). This medieval work brought together what was known or believed about animals, their habits and symbolism at that time. "Mistress Masham's Repose," about a young lady and her tiny friends (in size not unlike the friends of Gulliver), can be read by children, but is a delight for their elders as well.

THE ONCE AND FUTURE KING. *Putnam* 1958 $7.95; *Berkley* pap. $1.25

An omnibus volume of the complete Arthurian series, containing "The Sword in the Stone" (1938, *Putnam* 1939 $4.95; *Dell* pap. $.50); "The Witch in the Wood," now entitled "The Queen of Air and Darkness" (1939, o. p.); "The Ill-Made Knight" (1940, o. p.) and "The Candle in the Wind" (now first published in this volume).

THE SWORD IN THE STONE. 1938. *Putnam* 1939 $6.95; *Dell* pap $.60

MISTRESS MASHAM'S REPOSE. 1946. *Putnam* Capricorn Bks. 1960 pap. $2.15

GOSHAWK. 1951. *Viking* Compass Bks. 1970 pap. $2.25

AMERICA AT LAST: The American Journal of T. H. White. *Putnam* 1965 $4.95

Books about White

T. H. White: A Biography. By Sylvia Townsend Warner. *Viking* 1968 $6.50
The "dimension of the near-tragic in which Tim White passed his life . . . makes it impossible to see him merely as another English eccentric. He was a man of quite terrifying self-knowledge. . . . He made at least two attempts to marry, but they got him nowhere. He was, and knew it, a homosexual and a sado-masochist. He came to believe that the condition deprived him of the right to a full relationship with any human being. Almost deliberately, it seems, he settled for the life of an odd-man-out. . . . And if he was unlucky in his life, he has been hugely lucky in his biographer, who never knew him but whom he had admired beyond almost all contemporary novelists. At once sympathetic and detached, brilliantly written, constantly witty and perceptive, and without a superfluous word, this book seems to me a small masterpiece which may well be read long after the writings of its subject have been forgotten"—(Walter Allen, in the *N.Y. Times*).

LLEWELLYN, RICHARD (Richard David Vivian Llewellyn Lloyd). 1907?–

This Welsh novelist and playwright, who has also had a varied career in the movie studios, claims two birth dates and two birthplaces—London and St. David's in Pembrokeshire. He started to write for pleasure when he became a reporter on a film paper in 1931. His first two novels, both of which were made into successful films, are widely contrasted in theme and handling. "How Green Was My Valley" is a lovely nostalgic tale of a Welsh coal-mining community in the days of Victoria, written in a simple and vigorous prose. "None But the Lonely Heart" is a tough, hard-boiled story of the London underworld, told in Limehouse cockney jargon. "How Green Was My Valley" formed the first part of a Welsh trilogy, the story of Huw Morgan. It was followed by "Up, Into the Singing Mountain" (1960, o. p.) and completed with "Down Where the Moon Is Small," (1966, o. p.) "a well written, almost old-fashioned novel which just misses recapturing the lyricism, passion and feeling for the Welsh people so movingly achieved in the first book"—(*LJ*). In 1952 Llewellyn went to Kenya and lived on the Masai Reserve, an experience that provided the background for "A Man in a Mirror" (1961, o. p.). The novelist is "most successful in giving the reader a sense of the tragic impact of the problems that entry into the modern world will make on these people." Of "The End of the Rug," a story of espionage concerning an Englishman and a group of ex-Nazis, *Publishers' Weekly* said: "Dramatic and gripping, [it] will appeal to readers who do not usually go in for ordinary spy fiction."

HOW GREEN WAS MY VALLEY. *Macmillan* 1940 $6.95 pap. $2.75; *Dell* pap. $.95

THE END OF THE RUG. 1968. *Popular Lib.* pap. $.75. A spy story.

A WHITE HORSE TO BANBURY CROSS. 1972. *Pyramid Bks.* pap. $1.25

NIGHT IS A CHILD. *Doubleday* 1972 $5.95; *Pyramid Bks.* pap. $1.25

BRIDE OF ISRAEL, MY LOVE. *Doubleday* 1973 $6.95

GODDEN, RUMER. 1907–

Rumer Godden has alternated her life and writing between England and India. She was born in England, but lived in India until she was 12. Her first husband, a stockbroker in Calcutta, served as a captain in the II Sikhs on the Burma Front during World War II. She traveled to hundreds of canteens and hospitals for the Women's Voluntary Service in India and returned to England in 1945. "Thus Far and No Further" (1946, o. p.) is her episodic story of the few months during World War II that she and her two daughters spent far up in the rarefied atmosphere of the Himalayas. Her novels have the same curiously bewitched quality. Hers is an original and exotic talent. She creates atmosphere with an intense, yet delicate, skill. Her first novel published in this country, "Black Narcissus" (1939, o. p.), deals with Anglican nuns in India. "Breakfast With the Nikolides" and "The River," laid in India (and later authentically filmed there), are beautifully written studies of children and adolescent girls. In reviewing the latter for the *Yale Review*, Orville Prescott wrote "with each book she writes Miss Godden's position as one of the finest of living English novelists becomes more secure. The translucent purity and limpid grace of her prose and the compassionate wisdom and serene understanding of her mind stamp all [her] books with the imprint of her own personality, with her own vision of life." In 1956, Miss Godden's "An Episode of Sparrows," was given the Christopher Award. Based on a medieval Book of Hours which plays a part in the plot, "China Court" is a rare and delightful novel of five generations in an English country house. "The Battle of the Villa Fiorita," set in the English countryside and an Italian villa on Lake Garda and dealing with the theme of adulterous love and divorce, is a moving and skillful work. "The Kitchen Madonna" is the story of a nine-year-old boy and his efforts to acquire a shrine for a family servant. "In this House of Brede" is a story of an English career woman who enters an order of Benedictine nuns. She has written several appealing books for children, published by *Viking*. Rumer Godden's sister, JON GODDEN (1908–), has written several unusual novels published by *Knopf* including "A Winter's Tale" (1961 $4.50), "In the Sun" (1965 $5.95) and "Mrs. Starr Lives Alone" (1972 $5.95; *Bantam* pap. $1.50). In "Shiva's Pigeons: An Experience of India" the sisters have collaborated to write about India and Indian life, and in "Two Under the Indian Sun" to write a memoir of their childhood there.

BREAKFAST WITH THE NIKOLIDES. 1942. *Viking* 1964 $4.50 Compass Bks. pap. $1.65

A CANDLE FOR ST. JUDE. *Viking* 1948 $5.00 Compass Bks. 1956 pap. $1.85

AN EPISODE OF SPARROWS. *Viking* 1955 lg-type ed. $7.95 Compass Bks. 1957 pap. $1.85

THE GREENGAGE SUMMER. *Viking* 1958 $5.75

THE RIVER. *Viking* 1959 $4.75 Compass Bks. pap. $1.65

CHINA COURT: The Hours of a Country House. *Viking* 1961 $5.00

THE BATTLE OF THE VILLA FIORITA. *Viking* 1963 $5.00

THE KITCHEN MADONNA. Ill. by Carol Barker. *Viking* 1967 $3.75 lib. bdg. $3.56

IN THIS HOUSE OF BREDE. *Viking* 1969 $6.95; *Fawcett* Crest pap. $1.25

THE DIDDAKOI. *Viking* 1972 $5.95

(with Jon Godden) TWO UNDER THE INDIAN SUN. *Viking* 1966 $5.50. A memoir of their childhood.

(with Jon Godden) SHIVA'S PIGEONS: An Experience of India. With 150 black and white photographs by Stella Snead. *Viking* Studio Bks. 1972 $16.95

DU MAURIER, DAPHNE. 1907–

Daphne du Maurier's father was Gerald du Maurier, a famous actor-manager, whose life she wrote in "Gerald: A Portrait" (1935, o. p.). Her grandfather was George du Maurier, the artist and novelist (*q. v.*). An earlier ancestor was Robert Busson du Maurier, who trained in the Busson family glass business, and who fled to London at the start of the French Revolution. "The Glass-Blowers" is based on letters written by his sister, Madame Sophie Duval, and is a long, historically colorful novel set before, during and after the French Revolution.

Her books have now sold over a million copies in hardcover editions alone. "Rebecca," her best-known work, "proceeds rapidly on its way toward becoming a minor classic among popular novels." She is a gifted craftsman and a skilful spinner of yarns. Her novels make excellent movies because of their "expert blend of suspense, shrewd realism, and romantic hokum"—(*Time*).

It has been noted that some of her characters, especially in "Rebecca," might have appeared in such Brontë (*q. v.*) novels as "Wuthering Heights." She has written with discernment of the dissolute Brontë brother in "The Infernal World of Branwell Brontë" (o. p.). Besides thoroughly researching her subject "she has woven her own special brand of sorcery around it." "Vanishing Cornwall" (1967, o. p.), with photographs by her son, Christian du Maurier, is a sensitive evocation of the county in which she has lived for some 40 years, scene of several of her novels.

Among her books in print:

JAMAICA INN. 1936. *Doubleday* $5.95

REBECCA. *Doubleday* 1938 $5.95; *Avon* pap. $1.25

FRENCHMAN'S CREEK. 1942. *Avon* pap. $1.25; *Bentley* lib. bdg. $8.50

HUNGRY HILL. 1943 *Avon* pap. $1.25; *Bentley* lib. bdg. $8.50

THE KING'S GENERAL. *Doubleday* 1946 $5.95 *Avon* pap. $1.25; *Pocket Bks.* pap. $.75

MY COUSIN RACHEL. 1951. *Avon* pap. $1.25; *Bentley* lib bdg. $8.50

THE SCAPEGOAT. 1957. *Avon* pap. $1.50

THE BREAKING POINT. 1959. *Pocket Bks.* pap. $1.25. Eight short stories.

(with Arthur Quiller-Couch). CASTLE DOR. 1962 Dell pap. $.60. Sir Arthur's 19th-century version of the Tristan and Iseult legend, completed by Daphne du Maurier

THE GLASS-BLOWERS. *Doubleday* 1963 $6.95; *Avon* pap. $1.25

THE FLIGHT OF THE FALCON. *Doubleday* 1965 $6.95; *Avon* pap. $1.25

HOUSE ON THE STRAND. *Doubleday* 1969 $5.95; *Avon* pap. $1.25

RULE BRITANNIA. *Doubleday* 1972 $6.95; *Hall* lg.-type ed. $11.95

Other titles are published by Avon, Bentley (lib. eds.), and Pocket Bks.

FRAME, JANET.

Janet Frame has been praised as "the most talented writer to come out of New Zealand since Katherine Mansfield." Her first novel, "Owls Do Cry," a study of the disintegration of a poor New Zealand family, was considered "a superior performance." "Faces in the Water," a novel "presented as the memoir of a cured mental patient," was presumably based on her own experience. *Time* said of it: "Her writing is sensitive and her evocation of madness unforgettable." "The Edge of the Alphabet" is a "strange book about three wasted lives in a dim world." "Scented Gardens for the Blind," a bizarre, "perfervid, stream-of-consciousness novel with a limited audience, albeit haunting appeal," tells the bleak story of a family who alienate one another and "shut themselves in separate graves"—(*LJ*). "The Adaptable Man" concerns murder and incest in a contemporary English setting. "A State of Siege," with all the elements of a psychological thriller, provides a fine portrait of an aging teacher. Charles Rolo of the *Atlantic* has said that she is "endowed with a poet's imagination, and her prose has beauty, precision, a surging momentum, and the quality of constant surprise." Her talent, particularly this poetic power with words, is considered brilliant, but far too often "she has used it only to express her own emotions—her melancholy, disillusion and despair."

"Yellow Flowers in the Antipodean Room" is the story of a young man who was mistakenly pronounced dead after an accident; when he roused from deep coma, his world, which had accepted his "death," resented his "resurrection" and his life became a downhill slide. "Intensive Care" relates the story of three generations of Livingstones, then jumps to a generation in the distant future with the characters being led off to execution because a computer has classified them Animal, not Human. Her book of poems, "The Pocket Mirror" (*Braziller* 1967 $4.95), is "a rich mixture of narrative and lyric modes [looking] backward to childhood and forward to death"—(*LJ*). (The author does not supply her date of birth.)

STORIES AND FABLES. Includes "The Reservoir" and "Snowman, Snowman." *Braziller* 1963 2 vols. set $7.00

OWLS DO CRY. *Braziller* 1960 $4.50. First novel.

FACES IN THE WATER. *Braziller* 1961 $4.95; *Avon* pap. $.95

THE EDGE OF THE ALPHABET. *Braziller* 1962 $4.95

SCENTED GARDENS FOR THE BLIND. *Braziller* 1964 $4.50

THE ADAPTABLE MAN. *Braziller* 1965 $4.95

A STATE OF SIEGE. *Braziller* 1966 $5.00

YELLOW FLOWERS IN THE ANTIPODEAN ROOM (English title: "The Rainbirds"). *Braziller* 1969 $5.95

INTENSIVE CARE. *Braziller* 1970 $6.95

DAUGHTER BUFFALO. *Braziller* 1972 $4.95

MacLENNAN, HUGH. 1907–

This Canadian writer, born in Nova Scotia, was a Rhodes Scholar at Oriel College, Oxford, and did research in Roman history at the Graduate School of Princeton. He taught school for several years and has also taught at the university level (McGill). His novel "The Watch that Ends the Night" is skillfully written against a background of Canadian Montreal from the early 1930s up to the present, and catches not only a specific moment of history but also the physical and cultural atmosphere of the times. "Two Solitudes" is a novel of the disparate French and English cultures of Canada, covering the years 1917–1939. "As in much of MacLennan's earlier fiction, the major preoccupation of 'Return of the Sphinx' (1967, o. p.) is with the seemingly insoluble problem of Canada's French-speaking population. [MacLennan's] theme is no less than the survival of Canada as a nation. Hence the importance of MacLennan the writer" said *Library Journal*. Of the same book the *Saturday Review* wrote: "Despite the tendency of his prose to go limp or speechy when he is analyzing motives, his sense of history and his faith in the healing quality of time are traits his country undoubtedly needs now."

Edmund Wilson has written: "Mr. MacLennan seems to aim . . . to qualify, like Balzac, as the 'secretary of society,' and one feels that in his earnest and ambitious attempt to cover his large self-assignment he sometimes embarks upon themes which he believes to be socially important but which do not really much excite his imagination. [But] if he is dull when he is merely being conscientious, he is capable, when an emotional force lays hold of him and charges his material, of enveloping the reader in a spell that makes it hard to separate oneself from the story"—(in "O Canada"). He has published three books of essays invaluable for understanding how he "arrived at the Canadian point of view that he has brought to so sharp a focus"—(Wilson). Mr. MacLennan has five times received the Governor General's award—Canada's equivalent of the Pulitzer Prize. He has been a frequent contributor to Canadian and American periodicals.

TWO SOLITUDES. 1945. *Popular Lib.* pap. $.95

THE PRECIPICE. 1948. *Popular Lib.* pap. $.75

THE WATCH THAT ENDS THE NIGHT. 1959. *New Am. Lib.* Signet pap. $1.25

THE COLOUR OF CANADA. *Little* 1968 $4.95

STOREY, DAVID MALCOLM. 1908–

David Storey, the son of a miner, grew up in Yorkshire. He decided to become a painter and travelled to London to study at the Slade School of Fine Art. The train ride between London and his home began to symbolize for him the distance between various contending elements in his life. In London hé encountered art, culture, and a freer sort of life; at home he heard people tell him that his desire to be an artist was a sign of effeminacy. This must have seemed ironic to a man who for a while became a professional rugby player in order to support himself.

Much of Storey's writing reflects these conflicting elements in his background. He contrasts physicality with sensitivity; the vices of the cultured classes with the ignorance of the working classes; and he is particularly adept in contriving situations in which these contrasts are revealed in an inobtrusive but compelling manner. In "This Sporting Life" class conflict emerges when the hero, a rugby player, begins to meet socially prominent people as a result of his athletic skill; emotional conflict grows out of his relationship with a woman whose maturity is contrasted with his naiveté. "Flight into Camden" (no longer in print in this country) is the story of a miner's daughter who, despite the wishes of her family, goes off to live in London. Here again, the conflict of values that marks Storey's writing is used together with autobiographical elements. "Radcliffe," his third novel, describes the ambivalent relationship of two men, one with an upper-class background, the other from the working classes.

Recently Storey achieved a good deal of success writing for the theater; his plays have found congenial audiences both in London and New York. In his drama Storey often uses locales which are the antechambers for important public events: the central event itself may not be shown, but it becomes the catalyst Storey uses to precipitate the emotions of his character. In "The Changing Room" the catalyst is the rugby game being played outside; in the locker room the players remove their masks as well as their uniforms. "The Contractor" shows workmen setting up and later dismantling a tent—between these events a wedding has taken place in the tent. Lower- and upper-class attitudes are contrasted in the speeches of the workmen and the members of the bride's family who visit the tent; tensions between various members of the family are also revealed. Interwoven with these speeches is the business of erecting the tent and taking it down, a wonderful metaphor for the anticipation and letdown that accompany ceremonial events.

RADCLIFFE. 1963. *Avon* pap. $1.25

THIS SPORTING LIFE. 1960. *Popular Lib.* pap. $.50. Received the Macmillan Fiction Award.

THE CONTRACTOR. 1969 *Random* 1971 $4.95

PASMORE. 1970. *Dutton* 1974 $6.50

THE CHANGING ROOM. 1971. *Random* 1973 $4.95. Drama.

HOME. 1970. *Random* 1971 $4.95. Drama; won an Evening Standard Award.

LOWRY, MALCOLM. 1909–1957.

"Perhaps all artists are born a little askant to life, but Lowry's angle of vision was no one else's," wrote Elizabeth Janeway in the *N.Y. Times.* "There are surely those who will find him eccentric. There are surely others for whom this fresh, askant, individual view of life will come as refreshment and revelation, large, living, vibrant with humor, sympathy and perception, where nothing is skimped." Lowry was one of those "violently headstrong artists" whose early death, in which, as in Dylan Thomas's, alcohol played a part, was likewise explicable: "The tameless engines of both men's creativity were driven by the same wild, wondrous (and finally suicidal) pistons. Both also suggested incredible dolphins leaping or frolicking about in a teeming sea of words"—(Ernest Buckler).

Lowry, the son of a wealthy cotton broker, had always intended to be a writer and he wrote continuously from his early youth. His great love of the sea, he said, came from a Norwegian sea-faring grandfather, via Melville, O'Neill and Joseph Conrad. Although nearly blinded in his youth by an eye disease, Lowry was a brilliant scholar. Before taking his degree at Cambridge he sailed on a tramp steamer to Asia. The journal he kept became his B.A. thesis and the novel "Ultramarine." After acceptance by a publisher, the manuscript was lost and had to be rewritten. There followed a series of calamities in 1944. "In Ballast to the White Sea," a novel, was destroyed in a fire and the manuscript of "Under the Volcano" was lost and later recovered. Mark Shorer spoke of this novel as "a work of genius" and Philip Toynbee in the *Observer* (London) said it was one of the great English novels of this century: "It is a tragic but also a funny book; it is beautifully written; it is a work full of subtle harmonies and internal echoes," the story of the last, poignant, drink-sodden day of his antihero, a British consul in Mexico. In his "Letters," says Mr. Toynbee, he reveals himself "not only as an extremely interesting man, but also as a lovable one. He was courteous, kind and affectionate. He was a creative artist in every aspect of his life and personality."

The new edition of "Ultramarine" has a valuable introductory note by Lowry's widow and the revisions which Lowry had made over the years in the copy of the 1933 edition. He came to see the book as the first in a series of six or seven novels, to be called "The Voyage That Never Ends," and some of the revisions made in "Ultramarine" conform to data in "Under the Volcano." When reviewing the new edition, Ernest Buckler said: "A single year often wilts the ordinary novel. 'Ultramarine,' after 30, is still as green and vivid as the sea itself." Lowry's "Selected Poems" is available (*City Lights* Orig. 1962 pap. $1.50). The reader is referred to the excellent article "Malcolm Lowry in England" by the late Conrad Knickerbocker in the Summer 1966 issue of the *Paris Review. See also Conrad Aiken, in Chapter 9, Modern American Poetry.*

ULTRAMARINE. 1933. *Lippincott* 1962 $4.95

UNDER THE VOLCANO. 1947. *Lippincott* 1964 $6.50; *New Am. Lib.* pap. $.95

HEAR US O LORD FROM HEAVEN THY DWELLING PLACE. *Lippincott* 1961 $4.95; *Putnam* Capricorn Bks. pap. $2.25. Posthumous collection of short stories and novellas.

DARK AS THE GRAVE WHEREIN MY FRIEND IS LAID. *New Am. Lib.* 1968. $5.95. Posthumous novel edited and reconstructed from five drafts by Lowry's widow, Margerie Bonner Lowry, and Douglas Day.

OCTOBER FERRY TO GABRIOLA. *New Am. Lib.* pap. $3.50

LUNAR CAUSTIC. Ed. by Conrad Knickerbocker. *Grossman* Cape Eds. 1963 $3.50

SELECTED LETTERS. Ed. by Margerie Lowry and Harvey Breit. *Lippincott* 1965 $10.00. These Letters, 1928–57, many to people in the literary world, include one that contains a chapter-by-chapter analysis of "Under the Volcano."

Books about Lowry

The Private Labyrinth of Malcolm Lowry. By Pearl Epstein. *Holt* 1969 $6.95
Malcolm Lowry. By Daniel Dodson. Essays on Modern Writers *Columbia* 1970 pap. $1.00
Malcolm Lowry. By Richard H. Costa. World Authors Ser. *Twayne* $5.95
Malcolm Lowry. By Douglas Day. *Oxford* 1973 $10.00. An excellent biography; comprehensive, well-written and judicious.

O'BRIEN, FLANN (pseud. of Brian Nolan). 1910?–1966.

This gifted Irish writer had no less than three identities: Brian Nolan, an Irish civil servant and administrator; Myles na gCopaleen, columnist for the *Irish Times*, poet and author of *"An Beal Bocht"* ("The Poor Mouth"), a satire in Gaelic on the Gaelic revival; and Flann O'Brien, playwright and avant-garde comic novelist praised by James Joyce, Graham Greene, Dylan Thomas and William Saroyan. Though these, as well as a few intellectuals on both sides of the Atlantic were quick to grasp O'Brien's genius, his masterpiece, "At Swim-Two-Birds" went almost unrecognized in its time. This novel, which plays havoc with the conventional novel form, is about a man writing a book about characters in turn writing about him. O'Brien starts off with three separate openings: "One beginning and one ending for a book was a thing I did not agree with." Anthony Burgess has called it "one of the five outrageous fictional experiments of all time that come completely and triumphantly off. What a fuss the French anti-novelists make about their tedious exercises in *chosisme*; how little fuss has been made about Flann O'Brien's humour, humanity, metaphysics, theology, bawdry, mythopoeia, word-play and six-part counterpoint." "The Third Policeman," funny but grim, plunges into the world of the dead, though one is not immediately aware that the protagonist is no longer living. This book, says the *Nation*, "secures his place, already indicated by 'At Swim-Two-Birds,' as the most original comic artist, after Joyce, to come out of Ireland in this century."

THE BEST OF MYLES. *Walker & Co. 1968 $7.50*

AT SWIM-TWO-BIRDS. *Viking* 1939 Compass Bks. pap. $1.85; *Walker & Co.* 1966 $5.95

GOLDING, WILLIAM (GERALD). 1911–

Born in Cornwall and brought up as a scientist, Golding changed to English literature after two years at Oxford. Interested in classical Greek and archeology, he says his literary influences have been Euripedes and the anonymous Anglo-Saxon author of "The Battle of Maldon." He exercises "a consummate control of the novel form, and a superb all-encompassing vision of reality which communicates itself with a power reminiscent of Conrad." E. M. Forster called "Lord of the Flies," "the outstanding novel of the year" (1954). In the United States it got off to a slow start, however, until the paperback edition of 1959 enabled it to become an underground success among college students, who saw in the return to brute force of a group of boys marooned on an ocean island the parallel with modern adult societies intended by its author. Golding himself describes its theme as "an attempt to trace the defects of human nature. The moral is that the shape of a society must depend on the ethical nature of the individual and not on any political system however apparently logical or respectable" (*see* introd. to "Lord of the Flies"). It became a runaway best seller and was made into a film.

"The Inheritors" tells the story of innocent Neanderthal man's defeat and supersession by Homo Sapiens; the first true men are the first evil men, and only a trace of the original innocence is carried forward into human history. "Free Fall" is an artist's autobiographical reminiscent search for the pattern of his life in peace and war, and especially for the mechanism of transition from the guiltless sins of his free childhood to the real sins of his unfree adult life (*see* "Modern World Literature").

In "The Spire," Golding re-creates, through his strange and powerful evocation of human striving in the lifetime of one man, the story behind the building of a great English cathedral—which might have been Salisbury. "The Pyramid" is "a comparatively lighthearted comedy of manners. The novel is not without its serious implications, but it is amusing, even at times hilarious, and the dexterity with which Golding gets his comic effects is a joy"—(*SR*). It is composed of three episodes in the life of a young man in an English village—appropriately called Stilbourne. "The Scorpion God" consists of three short ironic novels set in ancient societies with unconventional social structures. His story "The Brass Butterfly" is available in the collection "Sometime, Never" (*Ballantine Bks.* 1971 pap. $.95). "The Hot Gates and Other Occasional Pieces" (*Harcourt* 1966 $4.50 Harvest Bks. pap. $1.35; *Pocket Bks.* pap. $.75) consists of 20 brief essays (two are autobiographical) from the past decade; here "Golding's taste for the unusual, his ability to sustain a mood, and his striking originality rank him with the masters of this genre"—(*LJ*).

In 1940, Mr. Golding joined the Royal Navy and spent five years in command of a rocket ship. In 1961–62 he was a Visiting Professor at Hollins College in Virginia and lectured at American colleges and universities.

LORD OF THE FLIES. 1954. *Coward* 1962 $5.95; *Putnam* Capricorn Bks. 1959 pap. $1.25 casebook edition ed. by James Baker and Arthur Ziegler, Jr. 1964 pap. $1.45

THE INHERITORS. 1955. *Harcourt* 1962 $4.95 Harvest Bks. pap. $2.25; *Pocket Bks.* pap. $.95

PINCHER MARTIN (original title "The Two Deaths of Christopher Martin"). *Harcourt* pap. 1968 $.85

FREE FALL. 1959. *Harcourt* Harbinger Bks. pap. $2.25

THE SPIRE. *Harcourt* 1964 $4.50 Harvest Bks. pap. $1.85

THE PYRAMID. *Harcourt* 1967 Harvest Bks. 1968 pap. $1.75; *Pocket Bks.* pap. $.95

THE SCORPION GOD. *Harcourt* 1971 $5.95. Includes "The Scorpion God," "Clonk, Clonk" and "Envoy Extraordinary."

Books about Golding

William Golding's Lord of the Flies: A Source Book. Ed. by William Nelson. *Odyssey* 1963 pap. $2.45. Many valuable essays.
William Golding. By Samuel Hynes. Essays on Modern Writers. *Columbia* 1964 pap. $1.00. An intelligent short study.
William Golding: A Critical Study. By James R. Baker. *St. Martin's* 1965 $3.95
The Art of William Golding. By Bernard Oldsey and Stanley Weintraub. *Harcourt* 1965 $5.95; *Indiana Univ. Press* Midland Bks. 1968 pap. $1.95
William Golding: A Critical Essay. By Paul Elman. Contemporary Writers in Christian Perspective Ser. *Eerdmans* 1967 pap. $.85
William Golding. By Bernard F. Dick. English Authors Ser. *Twayne* 1968 $4.95
William Golding: A Critical Study. By M. Kinkead-Weekes and I. Gregor. *Harcourt* 1968 $5.50
The Novels of William Golding. By Howard S. Babb. *Ohio State Univ. Press* 1970 $6.50
Golding. By Leighton Hodson. *Putnam* 1971 pap. $1.25
William Golding. By Clive Pemberton. Writers and Their Work Ser. *British Bk. Centre* $2.38 pap. $1.20

BEDFORD, SYBILLE. 1911–

Sybille Bedford has been called a splendid storyteller and "mistress of a naturally elegant style." Her first novel, "A Legacy," was, "all that the British critics say it is—brilliant, witty, fascinating, astonishing, unconventional, unclassifiable, elegant, radiant, enchanting—but even the impressive sum of these adjectives fails to describe and define the book's character. Perhaps one should content oneself with saying that it is very, very clever. But it makes one wish to say more"—(Ben Ray Redman, in *SR*). V. S. Pritchett called it "a small steely masterpiece." "A Favourite of the Gods," another brilliant portrait of a family and a period, is "a good, exciting and interesting book. If the author fails to bring off her intentions, it is an honorable failure, for she has aimed very high"—(Elizabeth Janeway, in the *N.Y. Times*).

Privately educated in England and France, Sybille Bedford has traveled extensively. She has lived for periods in Provence, New York and Rome. Of her first published work, "The Sudden View: A Traveler's Tale from Mexico" (1954, *Atheneum* 1963 pap. $1.45), the *New Yorker* said: "A travel book about Mexico that is unlike any other. Mrs. Bedford, an Englishwoman with almost feverishly acute perception and strong-willed prejudices, can be witty and funny without seeming to try.... A delightful, unclassifiable, and shimmering book." Aldous Huxley called it "remarkably acute, delicate and vivid." Her interest in the law and unusual court cases has led to the writing of nonfiction on the subject, of which "The Faces of Justice" (*Simon & Schuster* 1961 $4.50 Clarion Bks. pap. $1.75), is a title available here.

A FAVOURITE OF THE GODS. *Simon & Schuster* 1963 $4.50

A COMPASS ERROR. *Knopf* 1969 $5.95

DURRELL, LAWRENCE. 1912–

"Durrell is one of the very best novelists of our time," Gerald Sykes has said in the *N.Y. Times*, and Clifton Fadiman has called him "the first English novelist of his generation." With "Clea," Durrell "completed the last movement of his astonishingly lyric 'Alexandria Quartet' and with it the initiation rites of Irish poet-narrator, Darley.... In the end, ... we find that Mr. Durrell's tetralogy, which some readers have called 'shocking' or 'decadent,' amounts in reality to a massive, marvelously concrete, deeply felt statement of faith"—(Sykes). "What Durrell has here explored is less the realm of knowledge than the realm of doubt, less the hemisphere of light than that of shadow, less the fixed than the uncertain, less the factual than the fancied. In this resides the quartet's true modernity"—(Curtis Cate, in the *Atlantic*).

"Justine," the first of the series, is set in "glitteringly sophisticated" Alexandria. "Balthazar" is the second, written in the same hauntingly sensual mood. Gilbert Highet called "Mountolive," the third, "one of the most interesting and memorable novels of his generation." Mountolive is an English diplomat who becomes tied to Egypt by the love affair of his youth, and who returns as British Ambassador. It is a story of political intrigue, only hinted at in "Justine" and "Balthazar."

"The Black Book," an early work, was first issued in the U.S. in 1960. When it was published in Paris in 1938, T. S. Eliot called it "the first piece of work by a new English writer to give me any hope for the future of prose fiction." The lighter side of Durrell (he also writes thrillers) is represented by books Like "Sauve Qui Peut," the latest and funniest of three short novels about British diplomats. "An Irish Faustus" (*Dutton* 1964 $3.95) is a play, a highly imaginative variation of the Faust legend. Its very successful world première was held in Hamburg, Germany, Dec. 18, 1963. The appearance of "Tunc" (Latin word for "Then," followed by a sequel, "Nunquam." [*Dutton* 1970 $7.95; *Pocket Bks.*] meaning "Never") his first "serious" novel since "Clea," received a mixed welcome in the U.S. in 1968. The theme is a young man's somewhat confusing adventures with a computer, Abel, which he has invented, and with a variety of more human (female) delights; part of the locale is Turkey. To Edward Weeks (*Atlantic*), "This novel from its leering title to the close is too often the work of a lazy satyr." Gerald Sykes (in the *N.Y. Times*) wrote: " 'Tunc' seems as unreal as any of a hundred movie thrillers. The fantasy apparatus is still working, but without lyric passion. The question is, why did Durrell write it? ... The answer is, I think, that a born romantic, warmed for over 30 years by a Mediterranean sun, seems to be trying to come to grips, at least in concept, with 'the real world,' the cold, indifferent world which appears daily in newspapers and daily frustrates the mythmaking desires of realistic minds. [But] in 'Tunc' Durrell has not yet proved equal to the new task he has imposed upon himself.... In time he will produce a sequel to 'Tunc' in which his fantasy, his comic ribaldry, his lyric charm and a new desire for truth, however grim, may unite on a new level that is stronger still than that of the 'Quartet.' "

Lawrence Durrell was born in India of Irish parentage and educated in England. He has worked as a Press Attaché in Athens, Cairo, Alexandria, Rhodes, and Belgrade and been a British Council lecturer in Argentina. He has published several volumes of poetry.

One of the "most important, and certainly one of the most interesting volumes of literary letters in many a year" is "Lawrence Durrell and Henry Miller: A Private Correspondence," a large selection (1933–59). Gerald Sykes wrote in the *N.Y. Times*: "These letters are so lively that they read like fiction. In a sense they are fiction, the conscious effort of two ebulliently gifted writers of romantic temperament to blot out all in a hostile world that might mar the delightful private mythology they symbiotically construct together, even when separated by wars and oceans.... Durrell was 23, Miller 44. Durrell feared 'the English death,' by which he meant specifically the blighting effect of British propriety upon his own ardent muse. . . . Miller in turn welcomed an alliance with a disciple who was brilliant, prolific and vehemently outraged by the very stuffiness that had originally provoked his own scurrility." Mr. Durrell visited the United States (and Henry Miller along the way) for the first time in 1968.

THE BLACK BOOK. 1938. Introd. by Gerald Sykes; pref. by the author. *Dutton* 1960 pap. $1.75`

THE DARK LABYRINTH. First published with the title "Cefalu" in London 1947. *Dutton* 1962 pap. $1.75

STIFF UPPER LIP. *Dutton* 1959 $3.50 (and "Esprit de Corps") pap. $1.45

THE ALEXANDRIA QUARTET: Justine; Balthazer; Mountolive; Clea *Dutton* 1962 4 vols. set $12.50 pap. each $1.75 boxed set $6.95; *Pocket Bks.* 4 vols pap. set $3.80

JUSTINE. *Dutton* 1957 $5.95 pap. $1.75; *Pocket Bks.* pap. $.95

BALTHAZER. *Dutton* 1958 pap. $1.75; *Pocket Bks.* pap. $.95

MOUNTOLIVE. *Dutton* 1959 pap. $1.75; *Pocket Bks.* pap. $.95

CLEA. *Dutton* 1960 pap. $1.75; *Pocket Bks.* pap. $.95

SAUVE QUI PEUT. *Dutton* 1966 $3.95

TUNC. *Dutton* 1968 $6.95; *Pocket Bks.* pap. $1.25

PROSPERO'S CELL and REFLECTIONS ON A MARINE VENUS. *Dutton* $5.95 pap. $2.25. "Prospero's Cell" is a memoir of the boyhood years he and his brother Gerald spent on the island of Corfu.

BITTER LEMONS. *Dutton* 1957 pap. $1.65. The personal narrative of his life in a small village on Cyprus.

(with Alfred Perles). ART AND OUTRAGE: A Correspondence about Henry Miller between Lawrence Durrell and Alfred Perles. *Dutton* 1960 $3.50

LAWRENCE DURRELL AND HENRY MILLER: A Private Correspondence. Ed. with introd. by George Wickes. *Dutton* 1963 pap. $2.25

SPIRIT OF PLACE. Ed. by Alan G. Thomas. 8 repros. in black and white of paintings by the author. *Dutton* 1971 $10.00 pap. $3.45

Books about Durrell

My Family and Other Animals. By Gerald Durrell. *Viking* 1957 $4.95 lg-type ed. $7.95 Compass Bks. 1963 pap. $1.45. This delightful, sun-soaked account of the gifted and happily eccentric Durrell family's Mediterranean island sojourn is by Lawrence Durrell's brilliant naturalist brother. Entrancingly written, it provides amusing sidelights on Lawrence as he appeared to his family in younger days, as well as on Gerald's pets and other wildlife passions—and an assortment of human beings.
The World of Lawrence Durrell. By Harry T. Moore. 1962. *Dutton* pap. $1.75
Lawrence Durrell. By John Unterecker. Essays on Modern Authors *Columbia* 1964 pap. $1.00
Lawrence Durrell. By John A. Weigel. English Authors Ser. *Twayne* 1965 $5.50
Lawrence Durrell: A Critical Study. By G. S. Fraser. *Dutton* 1968 $5.95
Lawrence Durrell and the Alexandria Quartet: Art for Love's Sake. By Alan W. Friedman. *Univ. of Oklahoma Press* 1970 $6.95

See also Chapter 7, Modern British Poetry.

TAYLOR, ELIZABETH (COLES). 1912–

With her first novel, "At Mrs. Lippincote's" (1946, o. p.), Mrs. Taylor showed that she was a "writer of many gifts." She is clever and original and views life with a sharp eye for the violence, frustration and agony lurking under the careful conventions of the world of the English garden and polished mahogany. "Her prose is one of the most beautiful and exact instruments in use today"—(*N.Y. Times*). "She's a stunningly upsetting writer, who mingles horrors and delights that are valid for any period, as long as the two sexes continue to capsize each other"—(Nora Sayre). "The Soul of Kindness" and "The Wedding Group" each deal with a woman of apparent "good intentions" whose selfishness is aimed at wrecking the lives of those around her. Many of Mrs. Taylor's short stories have appeared in the *New Yorker*.

HESTER LILLY AND TWELVE SHORT STORIES. 1954. *Bks. for Libraries* $8.75

THE SOUL OF KINDNESS. *Viking* 1964 $4.50. A novel.

A DEDICATED MAN AND OTHER STORIES. *Viking* 1965 $4.95

MRS. PALFREY AT THE CLAREMONT. *Viking* 1971 $5.95. A novel about old age.

THE DEVASTATING BOYS. *Viking* 1972 $5.95. Short stories set in England.

SANSOM, WILLIAM. 1912–

William Sansom started writing seriously at the age of 30, and four years following (in 1946 and 1947) was awarded literary prizes by the Society of Authors; in 1951 he was elected a Fellow of the Royal Society of Literature. He is one of England's most versatile storytellers, a uniquely accomplished writer of "forceful, at times all but hallucinated imagination"—*N.Y. Times*). Reviewing "The Cautious Heart" (1958, o. p.) *Time* said: "[The novel] is sage, funny, benign and stamped with Sansom's special mastery of situations in which sex, humor, and sympathy fight for supremacy in a human battle that never ends." "Goodbye," (1967, o. p.) about a couple on the verge of separation, again reveals his skill at blending comedy and tragedy. "The Wild Affair," originally published as "The Last Hours of Sandra Lee"—the story of a frenzied British office Christmas party—is a "witty and entertaining departure from the author's more melancholy stories. "Away to it All" (1966, o. p.) is one of his many books of travel sketches. Mr. Sansom frequently contributes to *Harper's*, the *Atlantic, Vogue, Harper's Bazaar* and other American magazines; he has written plays and documentaries for British television.

STORIES. Introd. by Elizabeth Bowen. 1963. *Bks. for Libraries* $14.50. 30 stories.

THE WILD AFFAIR: The Last Hours of Sandra Lee. 1962. *Popular Lib.* pap. $.60

LAVIN, MARY. 1912–

Mary Lavin was born in East Walpole, Mass., but moved to Ireland when still a young child. She received her M.A. from the National University of Ireland, winning first-class honors for her thesis on Jane Austen. She is a member of the Irish Academy of Letters and a recent winner of the Katherine Mansfield Award, as well as president of the Irish P.E.N. She and her husband, William Walsh, a Dublin lawyer, lived on a farm which she describes as "one of the loveliest places in Ireland." Now a widow with three daughters, she still lives there. She has published many novels and short stories; she continues to contribute the latter to American magazines.

Her first collection of stories, "Tales from Bective Bridge" (1942, o. p.) received the James Tait Black Memorial Prize. Reviewing "The Great Wave and Other Stories (1961, o. p.) Padraic Colum (*q. v.*) said in the *N.Y. Times*: "Mary Lavin has distinguishable and distinguished qualities: invention that does not draw attention to itself but is absorbed into a sort of casualness, a penetrating evaluation of a situation, a vocabulary that can point up every nuance. . . . She has something too, that probably belongs to her femininity—a subtlety of discernment, with regard to relationships. . . . To my mind, [her] great distinction is in the fact that she reverses the turn that the usual short-storyteller gives the narrative—the turn to disenchantment." "A Likely Story" is set in the Irish countryside.

COLLECTED STORIES. *Houghton* 1971 $4.95

THE BECKER WIVES. New Am. Lib. pap. $3.50

HAPPINESS. *Houghton* 1970 $4.95

IN THE MIDDLE OF THE FIELDS. *Macmillan* 1972 $4.95

A MEMORY AND OTHER STORIES. *Houghton* 1973 $5.95

Books about Lavin

Mary Lavin. By Zach Bowen. *Bucknell Univ. Press* $4.50 pap. $1.95

DENNIS, NIGEL (FORBES). 1912–

With his first novel, "Boys and Girls Come Out To Play," Nigel Dennis won the Anglo-American Novel Contest in 1949. "Cards of Identity," his second novel, is a "long, rambling, loosely constructed tale which has as its central premise that modern man lacks a strong hold on his own identity." W. H. Auden said of it: "I have read no novel published during the last 15 years with greater pleasure and admiration." He adapted "Cards of Identity" for the theater, and as a play it was published in "Two Plays and A Preface" (1958). "Original, brilliant, witty. . . . If you can imagine a Pirandello plot narrated by Chesterton with dialogue by Evelyn Waugh and Ivy Compton-Burnett, you will have some idea of this exasperating and amusing fantasy" says Gilbert Highet. The author, born in England, educated in Africa and Europe, has been on the staff of *Time* since 1942, transferring to the London bureau in 1949. The "House in Order" is a greenhouse. Trapped within it the "hero" is at once shielded, alienated, exposed. And the world outside is not in order. Granville Hicks calls this book "a remarkable tour de force, saying so much in very little space and saying it with such humor and grace." Mr. Dennis won a Royal Society of Literature Award in 1965 for a new biography of Jonathan Swift. "Jonathan Swift" (*Macmillan* $3.95 Collier Bks. pap. $1.95). He is the author of a delightful and witty history of Malta, "Malta" (ill. by Osbert Lancaster. *Vanguard* 1973 $4.95) and a volume of poems, "Exotics: Poems of the Mediterranean and Middle East" (*Vanguard* 1970 $4.50).

CARDS OF IDENTITY. *Vanguard* 1955 $4.95

TWO PLAYS AND A PREFACE. Includes Cards of Identity and The Making of Moo. *Vanguard* 1958 $3.95

A HOUSE IN ORDER. *Vanguard* 1966 $4.95

WHITE, PATRICK. 1912– (Nobel Prize, 1973)

Born in Britain of Australian parents, Patrick White has spent time in both places. But his heart and his genius are Australian: "Whatever has come since, I feel that the influences and impressions of this strange, dead landscape of Australia predominate." Following a schooling in England which he heartily disliked (though he later returned to Cambridge), White left for Australia and worked in a sheep station, intermittently writing fiction—in the "stream-of-consciousness" mode—and drama. His first successful novel "Happy Valley" (1939), an ironic tale of life in an Australian mining town, won the Australian Literature Society's Gold Medal. His next novel was "The Living and the Dead" (1941), about a young man in England and Europe in the early years of this century. The "dead" represent those caught in the stultifying traditions bequeathed them by a dead past. "The Aunt's Story" chronicles the "lives" of an odd, ugly woman, "whose instincts are greater than her adaptability to life" and her journeyings from Australia to Europe and America.

Of "Voss," which concerns a German explorer in 19th-century Australia, Walter Allen wrote in the *New Statesman*: "I am happy to join in the chorus of praise for Mr. White. It is very fine indeed, by far the most impressive new novel I have read this year. At the least, it is a work of brilliant virtuosity, and I suggest that it is much more than that: I suppose it would need an Australian to gauge its full significance for, as it seems to me, Mr. White is attempting to create an Australian myth." The *New Yorker* said of "Voss": "His prose, which floats heavily off either into semi-poetic passages full of Bunyan-size images like 'the reeling earth,' or into needlessly cramped, studied dialogue, tends to set up an obstinate and exasperating barrier between his subject matter and the reader. Nonetheless, this is a heroic and sometimes brilliant novel." In "The Solid Mandala" Mr. White "further explores the Australian dilemma, the human condition, of life down under. He is a writer of genius, the finest novelist in the world of the Commonwealth [and] this book is one of the finest novels of this decade or of any other"—(*LJ*). "Four Plays" (1966, o. p.) contains "The Ham Funeral," written in 1947 but not produced until 1961, "The Season at Sarsparilla" (1961), "A Cherry Soul" (1962) and "Night on Bald Mountain."

THE BURNT ONES. *Viking* 1964 $4.95

Stories, somewhat "halting and uneven," yet compelling. The title "is a literal translation from a Greek expression meaning 'the poor unfortunates' "—(*LJ*).

RIDERS IN THE CHARIOT. 1961. *Viking* $5.95

THE SOLID MANDALA. *Viking* 1966 $5.00

THE VIVISECTOR. *Viking* 1970 $8.95. A novel of an artist's search for truth.

THE EYE OF THE STORM: A Novel. *Viking* 1974 (in prep.)

Books about White

> Patrick White. By R. F. Brissenden. Writers and Their Work Ser. *British Bk. Centre* 1966 $2.38 pap.
> $1.20
> Commentary on Patrick White's Riders in the Chariot. By Frederick W. Dillistone. *Seabury* 1967 pap.
> $.85

WILSON, ANGUS (Angus Frank Johnstone-Wilson). 1913–

Angus Wilson was born in Sussex, the youngest of six sons, and spent several of his childhood years in South Africa. A series of odd jobs was followed by a position in the Department of Printed Books in the British Museum, where he "worked on replacing as many as possible of the three hundred thousand books destroyed here during the bombing, and subsequently as deputy superintendent of the Reading Room." Writing short stories on weekends, he was immediately successful with them. In 1955 he left the Museum to become a full-time writer.

"Angus Wilson is the best contemporary English novelist. . . . No other contemporary has treated so vast a range of social and intellectual problems or controlled so diverse material from an intelligent and coherent perspective. . . . No other contemporary has used so various and effective techniques . . . to represent the many sides of the human creature"—(James Gindin). "Anglo-Saxon Attitudes" is a long, intricate and witty novel that satirizes, none too gently, such sacred British institutions as the Church, the Universities and Her Majesty's Government. "The Middle Age of Mrs. Eliot" won the James Tait Black Memorial Award for fiction in 1959. "The Old Men at the Zoo" tells crisply, wittily and intelligently a story of conflict and conscience in a microcosm, the London Zoo in the 1970's. . . . The characters are zany, but believably human. The plot reveals the tensions of modern society." In "Late Call" a retired couple face problems of readjustment when they go to live with their widowed son. "No Laughing Matter" traces the fortunes of a British family throughout half a century beginning in 1912. "A large, cozy, comfortable work of fiction, [it] handles a varied cast with ease, and diversified events with sureness of tone and detail"—(*N.Y. Times*).

In addition to short stories and novels, he has written "Emile Zola: An Introductory Study of His Novels" (1952. *Apollo* pap. $1.50; *Peter Smith* $3.75), and "Tempo: The Impact of Television on the Arts" (1966, o. p.). In "Seven Deadly Sins" (1962. *Apollo* pap. $1.50), Wilson and six other outstanding moderns have written on Envy, Pride, Covetousness, Gluttony, Sloth, Lust and Anger. "The Wild Garden, or Speaking of Writing" (*Univ. of California Press* 1963 $4.95 pap. $1.25) discusses his attitude toward the novel and the creative process.

FOR WHOM THE CLOCHE TOLLS: A Scrapbook of the Twenties. 1953. *Curtis* Bks. pap. $.95; *Viking* 1973 $6.95

ANGLO-SAXON ATTITUDES. *Viking* Compass Bks. 1956 pap. $1.85

A BIT OFF THE MAP: 8 New Stories. *Viking* 1957 $3.50

THE MIDDLE AGE OF MRS. ELIOT. *Viking* 1959 $4.95

THE OLD MEN AT THE ZOO. *Viking* 1961 $4.50

LATE CALL. *Viking* 1965 $4.95

NO LAUGHING MATTER. *Viking* 1967 $6.95

DEATH DANCE: Twenty-five Stories. *Viking* 1969 Compass Bks. pap. $2.45

AS IF BY MAGIC. *Viking* 1973 $8.95

Books about Wilson

> Angus Wilson. By K. W. Gransden. Writers and Their Work Ser. *British Bk. Centre* $2.38 pap. $1.20

MacINNES, COLIN. 1914–

Colin MacInnes, the son of the novelist Angela Thirkell, was born in England but grew up in Australia. He published his first novel when he was 36: this was "To the Victor the Spoils" (not in print in this country), a book based on his experiences during the Second World War. His next novel, "June in Her Spring" is also autobiographical; the setting is a sheep ranch in Australia.

MacInnes is best known for his "London Novels," the first of which, "City of Spades," was published in 1957. The book is about a young Nigerian who comes to London. With insight and sympathy MacInnes shows how city life begins to wear away the strength of the protagonist; color prejudice, materialism, and friends who have already succumbed to corruption all collaborate to defeat him. A white welfare officer tries to help the protagonist, but though he is well-meaning he proves ineffectual. At the conclusion of the novel the hero wisely decides that England is not for him and he returns to Nigeria. The success of the book is not in its theme—a theme American readers will certainly find familiar—but in its successful blend of diverse elements: a compassionate understanding of the protagonist; a refusal to sentimentalize or to become didactic; a knowledge of black culture both in Africa and in London; and a sense of tragic inevitability as the hero contends with the social forces that threaten to overwhelm him.

The other "London Novels" also deal with protagonists who introduce the reader to a troubled subculture. "Absolute Beginners" is about a teenager who, though he is at times on the wrong side of the law, perceives moral issues with a clarity respectable society often lacks. In this respect he resembles the protagonists of novels like Sillitoe's "Saturday Night and Sunday Morning" or Burgess's "A Clockwork Orange." The principal characters in "Mr. Love and Justice" are a pimp and a policeman; here again the adventures of the central characters lead easily into the social problems which are MacInnes's concern.

In "Westward to Laughter" MacInnes turns to a different mode, fiction in the tradition of the 18th-century episodic novel. The hero is a young man who runs away to sea and at various stages in his life is a convict, slave, and pirate. Another novel, "Three Years to Play" (not in print in this country) is also historical: it describes the life of an actor in Elizabethan times. Like his earlier books, the historical novels explore social questions, often with an emphasis on the picaresque.

THE LONDON NOVELS. *Farrar, Straus* 1969 pap. $3.95

CITY OF SPADES. 1957. *Ballantine Bks.* pap. $.95

ABSOLUTE BEGINNERS. 1959. *Ballantine Bks.* pap. $.95

MR. LOVE AND JUSTICE. 1960. *Ballantine Bks.* pap. $.95

SWEET SATURDAY NIGHT. 1967. *Int. Pubns. Service* $7.50

WESTWARD TO LAUGHTER. 1969. *Farrar, Straus* 1970 $5.95; *Fawcett* Crest Bks. pap. $.95

AUSTRALIA AND NEW ZEALAND. 1969. *Silver Burdett* (Time-Life) lib. bdg. $5.70

TRACY, HONOR (Lilbush Wingfield). 1915–

Honor Tracy "is a brilliant, tough and witty English woman who writes funny novels. Her humor is both sardonic and absurd. Her inventive imagination is both exuberant and ludicrous. Her prose is deft, supple and smooth. And her contempt for human folly is savage. She finds contemptible folly everywhere, but most successfully for fictional purposes in Ireland"—(Orville Prescott, in the *N.Y. Times*). Her reputation as a leading satirical humorist was established with her first novel, "The Straight and Narrow Path," which the *New Yorker* called "the funniest novel of the year. . . . Her high spirits and abounding invention make every page a delight." In "The First Day of Friday," she returned to that tragic country, Ireland, that offers inexhaustible material for comedy and demonstrated, again, her ability to create characters "sired by Joyce Cary out of Alice in Wonderland." "Men at Work," about a successful novelist who suffers a writing block, "displays her entire surgical kit: A pen for characterization; a thin brush for delicate scenery; several scalpels; and a sledge, which she uses only when patients become unruly. Add to this an ability to keep the whole mad operation in transit . . . and you have a delightful novel"—(*National Observer*). "Settled in Chambers" follows the fortunes of a judge who goes astray. "Sharp, satirical as it is, Miss Tracy's wit is never black humor. . . . She is not lampooning morality but the shallow concern with appearances that has no real moral values behind it"—(*Christian Science Monitor*). She has also written two nonfiction works on Spain, one of which is "Spanish Leaves" (1964, o. p.).

Born in Bury St. Edmunds, Suffolk, England, she was educated in England, and in Dresden, Germany, and later studied for two years at the Sorbonne in Paris. From 1946 to 1953 she was a correspondent in Europe and the Far East for the *Observer*, then Dublin correspondent to the *Sunday Times* and a foreign correspondent for the BBC's "Third Programme." At the same time she was associated with an Irish literary review edited by Sean O'Faolain (*q. v.*). She is a frequent book reviewer for the American *New Republic*. When not traveling she lives in Achill Island, County Mayo.

THE STRAIGHT AND NARROW PATH. 1956. *White Lion Pubns.* 1973 lib. bdg. $5.95.
   First novel.

THE FIRST DAY OF FRIDAY. *Random* 1963 $6.95

SETTLED IN CHAMBERS. *Random* 1968 $6.95

BUTTERFLIES OF THE PROVINCE. *Random* 1970 $5.95

THE QUIET END OF EVENING. *Random* 1972 $6.95

FIELDING, GABRIEL (pseud. of Alan Gabriel Barnsley). 1916–

Orville Prescott of the *N.Y. Times* said of "In the Time of Greenbloom": "This brilliant book is one of the fine English novels of recent years . . . written with such narrative power and psychological insight that it leaves one bedazzled with admiration." Mr. Fielding, who has been called "an unlikely mixture of Galsworthy and Joyce"—(R. J. Thompson), has written three novels about the Blaydons—that "odd, intense, neurotic, ecclesiastical family"—"Eight Days," "Through Streets Broad and Narrow" and "Brotherly Love." The third was the first to be published in England. *Commonweal* said of it: "Manifestly, 'Brotherly Love' is a pertinent study of Anglo-Catholic attitudes. It consolidates Fielding's reputation as an incisive, controlled novelist with a gift for evolving personality in secular as well as religious contexts. And it promises, with its companion novels, to put him in a class with other workers in the *roman fleuve*, that is, with men like Anthony Powell and C. P. Snow." Dorothy Parker wrote of him: "It is a matter of grave doubt that Mr. Fielding could write anything, from a post card to a lexicon, without perception and pace and brilliance . . . so stunning a teller of tales [is he] and so inspired a creator of character."

"The Birthday King" has quite a different theme: "This is a haunting and terrible book. Gabriel Fielding has turned his brilliant and precise genius to a ruthless examination of 'Hitler-Time' in Germany, skillfully interweaving fiction with historical fact. . . . Hitler, Himmler, Goebbels and the rest of the Nazi monsters do not appear but are only voices offstage, echoed by the fictional Fielding characters. . . . It is all so abominable, but Fielding, with maddening precision, makes it all so reasonable"—(*N.Y. Times*). "Gentlemen in Their Season" is a sharply humorous, probing treatment of adultery and marriage. *Library Journal* said of it: "In this novel that is profoundly witty and significant . . . some of the acid of Angus Wilson has dripped into Gabriel Fielding's pen when he describes the fearful pretensions of his nice intellectuals who hate the poor with the same fear with which they deny God." This author is a Catholic convert.

Formerly a practising physician, Mr. Fielding now devotes all his time to writing. He spent the academic year 1966–67 as Author in Residence at Washington State University.

IN THE TIME OF GREENBLOOM. 1957. *Apollo* pap. $1.95

THE BIRTHDAY KING. *Morrow* 1963 $5.95; *Popular Lib.* pap. $.95

NEW QUEENS FOR OLD: A Novella and Nine Stories. *Morrow* 1972 $6.95

DAHL, ROALD. 1916–

Roald Dahl is probably the only major short-story writer who speaks both Swahili and Norwegian. He was born in South Wales of Norwegian parents. At 18 he joined the Shell Oil Company in London and after four years' training was sent to Tanganyika. He enlisted in the RAF when World War II broke out. Invalided home because of injuries, he was sent to Washington, D.C. as Assistant Air Attaché to the British Embassy, and later was in the more exciting field of Intelligence. Since the end of the war he has lived alternately in England and America. He has been described as a "sophisticated teller of tales," a "cunning master of suspense," "clever caricaturist" and "modern purveyor of the macabre, the fantastic, and the bizarre . . . the magician of the short story."

Mr. Dahl's wife is Patricia Neal, the actress, and together they have known more family disaster and near-tragedy than should be any family's lot. Miss Neal has recently made a gallant recovery from a stroke of several years ago that nearly disabled her permanently. She has won her battle, learned to speak again and resumed her stage and screen career.

SELECTED SHORT STORIES. *Modern Library* $2.95

SOMEONE LIKE YOU. Short Stories. *Knopf* 1953 $5.95; *Pocket Bks.* pap. $.95

KISS KISS. Short Stories. *Knopf* $5.95; *Pocket Bks.* pap. $.95

BURGESS, ANTHONY (John Anthony Burgess Wilson). 1917–

Anthony Burgess wrote his first novel while he was a teacher of linguistics and composer of music; "A Vision of Battlements" resulted from his being "empty of music but itching to create." Later he became a British colonial officer in Southeast Asia, and in that capacity produced the trilogy "The Long Day Wanes." He has since scored an impressive record—some 15 works of fiction published within the past decade. "Although there are suggestions of what has come to be called 'black humor' in both 'A Vision of Battlements' and 'The Long Day Wanes,' it was only when he turned to the English scene, as he did in 1960 with 'The Doctor is Sick' and 'The Right to an Answer,' that Burgess showed how wry and bitter he could be"—(*SR*). These two successful satires on present-day England paved the way for two more on the England of the future: "The Wanting Seed" shows a society where people are governed by rigorous laws and homosexuality is encouraged to control a mounting population, while "A Clockwork Orange" paints the bleak picture of a nation over-ridden by teen-age gangs. These two exhibit Burgess's fascination (like that of Joyce and Nabokov) with odd-ities of language; Stanley Edgar Hyman "could not read the book ['A Clockwork Orange'] without com-piling a glossary."

"Honey for the Bears" "is one of [Burgess's] funnier books, but only a small part of the humor is aimed at Russia"—(Granville Hicks, in *SR*), though the implication is that the U.S.S.R. and the U.S.A. are both over-conformist societies. "Nothing Like the Sun" is the story of Shakespeare, "told" by the Bard in the first per-son. The plot of "Devil of a State," set in a new, uranium-rich African nation, "is part black humor, part sat-ire and part English music-hall, and the author takes every opportunity to bite large holes in his characters with his wicked, witty teeth"—(*PW*). In "Tremor of Intent" "using the spy as missile-era folk hero, he creates a gleaming novel of ideas—troubling ideas about the survival value of ideology, the disease of our ap-petites, our malevolent innocence as we perpetrate incredible atrocities and feel no guilt. Brazenly clever, Burgess is Britain's answer to Vladimir Nabokov. . . . He is guided by a foolproof intellectual homing device and possessed by a black sense of humor that barely hold his hostility in check. Outraged by blasphemies against life, he attacks unreason with satire so swift we hardly know we've been hit before we're pronounced morally dead"—(*N.Y. Times*). "Enderby" is about an antisocial poet confined to the bathroom of a small apartment and then pitched into the world again. Burgess is also the author of "Language Made Plain" (1965 *Apollo* pap. $1.95); "In Re Joyce" (*Norton* 1965 pap. $2.95; *Peter Smith* $4.00), a fine scholarly but readable treatment of his master, James Joyce; "Shakespeare" (*Knopf* 1970 $17.50) and "The Novel Now: A Student's Guide to Contemporary Fiction" (*Norton* 1967 $5.95; *Pegasus* pap. $2.25). He edited "A Shorter Finnegans Wake" (*Viking* 1966 $6.00 Compass Bks. pap. $2.25) and wrote the text for "Coaching Days of England" (1966, o. p.).

THE LONG DAY WANES. The Malayan trilogy: Time for a Tiger; The Enemy in the Blanket; Beds in the East. First published in England 1956–59. *Norton* 1965 $6.95; *Ballantine Bks.* 1966 pap. $.95

THE DOCTOR IS SICK. 1960. *Norton* 1966 $4.50; *Ballantine Bks.* pap. $1.25

THE RIGHT TO AN ANSWER. 1960. *Norton* 1961 $4.50

THE WANTING SEED. 1962. *Ballantine Bks.* pap. $1.25

A CLOCKWORK ORANGE. 1962. *Norton* 1963 pap. $1.45; *Ballantine Bks.* pap. $1.25. According to Stanley Edgar Hyman, who has compiled a glossary for the Ballantine edition, the title signifies something mechanical that appears organic.

ENDERBY. 1963. *Norton* 1968 $5.95; *Ballantine Bks.* pap. $1.50

A VISION OF BATTLEMENTS. 1965. *Ballantine Bks.* pap. $1.25. His first novel, written in 1949, not published until 1965.

TREMOR OF INTENT: An Eschatological Spy Novel. 1966. *Norton* 1967 $4.95; *Ballan-tine Bks.* pap. $1.25

URGENT COPY. *Norton* 1969 $6.95

THE EVE OF ST. VENUS. *Norton* 1970 $4.95; *Ballantine Bks.* pap. $.95

MF. *Knopf* 1971 $5.95; *Ballantine Bks.* pap. $.95

ONE HAND CLAPPING. *Knopf* 1972 $5.95; *Ballantine Bks.* pap. $1.25

Books about Burgess

Anthony Burgess. By Carol M. Dix. Writers and Their Work Ser. *British Bk. Centre* $2.38 pap. $1.20
The Consolation of Ambiguity: An Essay on the Novels of Anthony Burgess. By Robert K. Morris. *Univ. of Missouri Press* 1971 $3.00

SPARK, MURIEL. 1918–

Mrs. Spark has been called "our most chillingly comic writer since Evelyn Waugh" by the London *Spectator*, and the *New Yorker* praised her novel "Memento Mori" as "flawless." Her fiction is marked by its remarkable diversity, wit and craftsmanship. "She happens to be, by some rare concatenation of grace and talent, an artist, a serious—and a most accomplished—writer, a moralist engaged with the human predicament, wildly entertaining, and a joy to read. . . . She simply and quite literally has added, whenever convenient, the fourth dimension to otherwise sober and realistically tethered fiction. . . . The fact is that Mrs. Spark has got about everything."—(*SR*). She became more widely known in this country when the *New Yorker* devoted almost an entire issue to "The Prime of Miss Jean Brodie." Set in Edinburgh in the 1930s, this is the story of a schoolteacher, her unorthodox approach to life and its effect on her select group of adolescent girls. Though their idol turns out to have feet of clay, she has left an indelible mark on their lives. A dramatization by Jay Allen, successfully produced on Broadway in 1968, brought Zoë Caldwell a Tony for her portrayal of the title role. "The Girls of Slender Means," also warmly praised, is "an ironic comedy about the exuberance and transcience of youth and the tensions of being young and female and not married." Reviewing "The Mandelbaum Gate" for the *New Republic*, Honor Tracy wrote: "There is an abundance here of invention, humor, poetry, wit, perception, that all but takes the breath away. . . . The story, in fact, is pure adventure, with the suspense as artfully maintained as anywhere by Graham Greene, but this is only one ingredient. There are memorable descriptions of the Holy Land, fascinating insights into the jumble of intrigue and piety surrounding the Holy Places, and penetrating studies of Arabs. . . . In each of [Miss Spark's] novels heretofore one of her qualities has tended to predominate over the others. Here for the first time they are all impressively marshaled side by side, resulting in her best work so far."

Muriel Spark was born and educated in Edinburgh and lived for some years in Central Africa. During World War II, she returned to England, where she worked in the Political Intelligence Department of the Foreign Office. She has been a magazine editor and writes poetry and literary criticism. "Emily Brontë: Her Life and Work" (o. p.) was written with Derek Stanford. "Doctors of Philosophy" (*Knopf* 1966 $4.50) is a recent play. Mrs. Spark has lived in London's Camberwell section, the setting of "The Ballad of Peckham Rye," but now makes her home in New York. Her novels reflect her conversion to Catholicism.

COLLECTED STORIES, I. *Knopf* 1968 $6.95

ROBINSON. 1958. *Avon* 1964 pap. $1.25

MEMENTO MORI. 1959. *Avon* pap. $1.65; (and "The Ballad of Peckham Rye")

THE GO-AWAY BIRD AND OTHER STORIES. *Lippincott* 1962 $3.75 pap. $1.85

VOICES AT PLAY. *Lippincott* 1962 $4.00. Four radio plays and six short stories.

THE PRIME OF MISS JEAN BRODIE. *Lippincott* 1962 $3.95; *Dell* pap. $.75

THE GIRLS OF SLENDER MEANS. *Knopf*. 1963 $4.95

NOT TO DISTURB. *Viking* 1966 $5.00

THE DRIVER'S SEAT. *Knopf* 1970 $4.95

THE PUBLIC IMAGE. *Knopf* 1968 $4.95; *Ballantine Bks.* pap. $.95

THE HOTHOUSE BY THE EAST RIVER. *Viking* 1973 $5.95

Books about Spark

Muriel Spark. By Karl Malkoff. Essays on Modern Writers *Columbia* 1968 pap. $1.00

NEWBY, P(ERCY) H(OWARD). 1918–

"Newby, a Briton who taught English literature at Cairo University from 1942 to 1946, shows us once again in 'A Guest and His Going' how perceptively he understands the foibles of both Britons and Egyptians when they are brought together—and with what elegant skill he can write about them. His touch is light yet sure. His sense of humor is civilized and sophisticated, mischievous but never malicious. Altogehter 'A Guest and His Going' is a delightfully funny novel"—(*Christian Science Monitor*). The story concerns an Egyptian student in London during the Suez crisis. In "One of the Founders" a man with marital and civic preoccupations founds a university on the side. Aileen Pippett wrote of it (in the *N.Y. Times*): "P. H. Newby is not only a witty novelist but Chief of the B.B.C.'s intellectually distinguished Third Program, an observation post which enables him to know what happens when a publicity campaign really gets going. He makes the most of every solemn-ridiculous situation which occurs when local patriotism inflames the imagination, turning apathy into activity, a dream into a realizable fact. . . . He is always in control of his complicated plot." Anthony West of the *New Yorker* has called Mr. Newby "the only English writer with anything approaching genius to be produced by his generation so far."

SPIRIT OF JEM. 1947. *Delacorte* 1967 $3.95 lib. bdg. $3.69

ASHTON-WARNER, SYLVIA.

"Miss Ashton-Warner proves with her first book "Spinster," to be quite as much the mistress of language, image and skinless sensibility as was her famous compatriot, Katherine Mansfield, and larger in vision and scope"—(*SR*). "Incense to Idols" (1960, o. p.) is the portrait of a lost lady, a French pianist who falls in love with a New Zealand clergyman. Virginia Kirkus said of it: "The same volatile, even febrile, nervous, expansive, self-revelatory technique which was so effective in 'Spinster' has again been applied with an equal virtuosity in this novel."

A teacher for some 25 years, Sylvia Ashton-Warner has rarely left New Zealand. Her experiences as an infant-room mistress of a Maori school are the subject of her autobiographical "Teacher." Her new and different teaching methods were designed to prepare her pupils for the difficult transition from a simple, rather primitive culture to that of the complex modern world. With the stories of the daily life of the Maori children, these gave her the background for that rarely perceptive novel, "Spinster." "Bell Call" recounts the persistent efforts of a strong-willed New Zealand woman to keep her son out of school until he declares himself ready to go. In "Greenstone," a tale touched with "magic"—(*PW*), the central figure is a half-white, half-Maori child in conflict between these two ways of life. "Myself" is the diary of a three-year period in the 1940s when she was teaching in a Maori settlement and trying to work out her complex roles as mother, wife, teacher and creative artist.

This unorthodox guider of the young has written: "Teaching is a dangerous activity really; all this plastering on of foreign stuff. . . . Why plaster on when there's so much inside already? . . . I see the infant-room one widening crater, loud with the roar of erupting creativity. . . . The organic design; the growing, changing living design; the normal and healthy design: unsentimental and merciless and shockingly beautiful." Her most recent book on teaching is "Spearpoint: The Teacher in America" (*Knopf* 1972 $5.95).

SPINSTER. 1959. *Simon & Schuster* Clarion Bks. pap. $2.95

BELL CALL. *Simon & Schuster* 1965 $5.00

GREENSTONE. *Simon & Schuster* 1966 $4.50

THREE. *Knopf* 1970 $5.95; *Paperback Lib.* pap. $.95

TEACHER. *Simon & Schuster* 1963 $7.95 pap. $2.45 Clarion Bks. pap. $2.95. Excerpts from her diary and a summary of her observations on the art of teaching.

SPEARPOINT: The Teacher in America. *Knopf* 1972 $5.95

MYSELF. *Simon & Schuster* 1967 $4.95. A short self-appraising diary.

LESSING, DORIS (MAY). 1919–

Professor R. J. Thompson wrote in *Choice* (October, 1967): "Probably the biggest 'sleeper' now at work in England is Doris Lessing . . . author of over a dozen books on domestic relationships constantly receiving more and more favorable recognition." In a shrewd and unsentimental book, half novel, half subjective documentary, called "In Pursuit of the English," Mrs. Lessing tells "how she came to England from Southern Rhodesia, where she grew up, and what a strange experience it was, learning all the 'whys' and 'what's' of the English people and their native land. [She] was born of British parents in Persia, . . . but never had been in the land of her ancestors until going there in 1949." Her two great themes are the problems between the races in Africa and those of the intelligent, liberated woman in a man's world. The "African Stories" volume "contains a wide variety of beautifully-wrought stories by a sensitive and thoughtful but fiercely honest writer whose humanity soon becomes as patent as her love of the sun-washed land where she spent her formative years. These stories are to be savored"—(*SR*). "The Grass is Singing," her first published novel, is about a girl married to a white farmer in South Africa, and her relationship with a black servant. In "Children of Violence," a five-novel series of which four have appeared, she combines her two main themes in the story of Martha Quest, the Marxist, feminist daughter of English settlers in "Zambesia," before and during World War II. Critics have found the going here heavy. Eliot Fremont-Smith noted in the *N.Y. Times*: "As Martha moves in and out of radical South African politics, and into and away from a bad marriage, she becomes, and it would shock her to realize how much, increasingly tiresome; for all her powers of observation, insight and will, her mind is uninformed with humor—and hence, uninformed."

The English *Sunday Times* has called her "not only the best *woman* novelist we have, but one of the most serious, intelligent, and honest writers of the whole post-war generation." The *Saturday Review* wrote of her strongest work to date, "The Golden Notebook": "One can say that Mrs. Lessing is extending the boundaries of the novel or one can say that she is really giving us the raw materials for a novel rather than the novel itself. Both statements are true. That is, she is trying to make the novel do more than it has ever done before, and in the process she does away with even the most rudimentary conceptions of form and structure. The book is chaotic, difficult to read, sometimes puzzling. . . . If she has not wholly succeeded in doing what she wanted to do, she has made an impressive try . . . but this is the kind of thing that somebody has to attempt. And few persons could bring to the job greater resources than Mrs. Lessing: a really imposing intelligence, a fine sensibility, and literary skill of high order."

Mrs. Lessing is an unabashed cat lover; "Particularly Cats" (1966. *Simon & Schuster* 1967 $3.50; *New Am. Lib.* 1971 pap. $.95) is a delightful discussion of some of the felines she has known. "Going Home" (1957, o. p.) is the account of a trip back to Rhodesia after seven years in London. "It's a depressing situation that Miss Lessing surveys, but her material is fascinating reading, a blend of the warm and human (nostalgia and patriotism) mixed with the tart and cynical (an intelligent Marxist puncturing the cliches of a smug Establishment)"—(*PW*).

AFRICAN STORIES. 1964. *Simon & Schuster* 1965 $7.95; *Ballantine Bks.* pap. $1.25

THE GRASS IS SINGING. 1950. *Ballantine Bks.* pap. $.60; *Popular Lib.* pap. $.95

MARTHA QUEST. 1952. *New Am. Lib.* pap. $2.95. In the "Children of Violence" sequence.

A PROPER MARRIAGE. 1954. *New Am. Lib.* pap. $3.50. In the "Children of Violence" sequence.

THE HABIT OF LOVING. 1957. *Popular Lib.* pap. $.95. Short stories.

A RIPPLE FROM THE STORM. 1958 *New Am. Lib.* pap. $2.95. In the "Children of Violence" sequence.

LANDLOCKED. *New Am. Lib.* pap. $2.95. In the "Children of Violence" sequence.

THE GOLDEN NOTEBOOK. 1962. *Simon & Schuster* $5.95; *Ballantine Bks.* pap. $1.50

A MAN AND TWO WOMEN AND OTHER STORIES. 1963. *Simon & Schuster* $5.00. Sixteen sketches and three longer stories.

CHILDREN OF VIOLENCE. *Simon & Schuster* 1965–66. 2 vols. Vol. I Martha Quest and A Proper Marriage $7.50 Vol. 2 A Ripple from the Storm and Landlocked $6.95

THE FOUR-GATED CITY. *Knopf* 1969 $7.50; *Bantam* pap. $1.25

BRIEFING FOR A DESCENT INTO HELL. *Knopf* 1971 $6.95; *Bantam* pap. $1.50

THE TEMPTATION OF JACK ORKNEY AND OTHER STORIES. 1972 $6.95

THE SUMMER BEFORE THE DARK. *Knopf* 1973 $6.95

Books about Lessing

Doris Lessing. By Dorothy Brewster. English Authors Ser. *Twayne* 1965 $5.50

MURDOCH, IRIS. 1919–

Wit, variety and unpredictability characterize the work of this English philosopher-novelist. She was born in Dublin and educated in England, where she took her B.A. degree with first class honors in classical "Greats" at Somerville College, Oxford. She then worked as an assistant principal in the British Treasury and was an administive officer with UNRRA in London, Belgium and Austria. After her return to academic life she studied philosophy for a period at Newnham College, Cambridge, and since 1948 has been at Oxford as a Fellow and Tutor at St. Anne's College. She came to America in 1959 to lecture at Yale. Her husband, John Bayley, is a novelist, poet and critic.

Elizabeth Bowen has said: "Everything that she has written has been remarkable—stamped by the unmistakable authority of mind and vision." Her first novel, "Under the Net" already showed "a deft touch, a delight in strange, intricate and puzzling plots, a wild intelligence and a defiance of the pigeon-hole"—(*PW*). The world of "A Severed Head" is a London society devoid of passion or conviction; a modern world, which the author explores to contrast the artificial and the real in her characters' emotions. Her subtle irony, her wit, her sense of the comic combine in this astonishing novel. "An Unofficial Rose" is a bright existential novel about love. "The Unicorn" is the story of a woman imprisoned in a castle by a curse. Robert Scholes has a fascinating analysis of the book in "The Fabulators." "The contemporary allegorist," he says, "is likely to be both arbitrary and tentative. His world will be idealized but unsystematic, full of meanings but devoid of meaning. The world of 'The Unicorn' is this kind of world." And he proceeds from there. "The Italian Girl" is "another of [Miss Murdoch's] incredible sexual, psychological and philosophical menageries, skillfully presented, and viewed with a classical tolerance and freedom which she dares us to equal"—(*LJ*). "The Red and the Green," more conventional in tone, is set in Ireland in 1916 just before the Easter Rising and concerns a family in conflict. "The Time of the Angels"—of her "excellent melodramas" the "newest and best," said Charles Poore—returns to complexity of symbol and setting; it is a tale of three women caught in the grip of a crazed rector who, having accepted the death of his God, allows himself philosophical and sexual license. Of "The Nice and the Good," which treats the multiple facets of love, Elizabeth Janeway said in the *N.Y. Times:* "Sparkling, daring, great fun, the book sweeps up black magic, science fiction, thriller, and half-a-dozen kinds of novel into the wittiest sort of concoction. It is hard to imagine anyone not enjoying it."

Miss Murdoch's first book, "Sartre, Romantic Rationalist" (1953. *Yale Univ. Press* 1953, 1959 pap. $1.25), has been called "a remarkably intelligent and penetrating introduction to and commentary upon Sartre."

UNDER THE NET. 1954. *Viking* Compass Bks. pap. $2.25; *Avon* pap. $1.25. First novel.

THE FLIGHT FROM THE ENCHANTER. 1955. *Paperback Lib.* pap. $1.25

THE SAND CASTLE. 1957. *Paperback Lib.* pap. $1.25

THE BELL. 1958. *Avon Bks.* 1966 pap. $1.25

A SEVERED HEAD. 1961. *Avon Bks.* pap. $1.25; *Viking* Compass Bks. 1963 pap. $1.85

AN UNOFFICIAL ROSE. 1962. *Paperback Lib.* 1973 pap. $1.25

THE UNICORN. *Viking* 1963 $5.00; *Avon Bks.* 1964 pap. $.95

THE ITALIAN GIRL. 1964. *Viking* 1964 $4.50; *Avon Bks.* pap. $1.25

THE RED AND THE GREEN. 1965. *Viking* 1965 $5.00; *Avon Bks.* 1966 pap. $1.25

THE TIME OF THE ANGLES. 1966. *Viking* 1966 $5.00; *Avon Bks.* 1967 pap. $1.25

THE NICE AND THE GOOD. 1967. *Viking* 1967 Compass Bks. pap. $2.45

BRUNO'S DREAM. *Viking* 1969 $5.75

A FAIRLY HONORABLE DEFEAT. *Viking* 1970 $6.95; *Fawcett* Crest Bks. pap. $1.25

THE BLACK PRINCE. *Viking* 1973 $8.95

THE SOVEREIGNTY OF GOOD. *Schocken* 1971 $5.00 pap. $1.95. A philosophical essay in which Miss Murdoch sets forth her ideas on ethics.

Books about Murdoch

The Disciplined Heart: Iris Murdoch and her Novels. By Peter Wolfe. *Univ. of Missouri Press* 1966 $5.95
"Not for the casual reader and often more complex language than it need be, the book contributes valuable insights into the moral and philosophical content of Iris Murdoch's novels."—(*LJ*)

Iris Murdoch. By Rubin Rabinovitz. Essays on Modern Writers *Columbia* 1968 pap. $1.00
Iris Murdoch. By Donna Gerstenberger. *Bucknell Univ. Press* $4.50 pap. $1.95

MOORE, BRIAN. 1921–

Brian Moore came to prominence with a notable first novel, "The Lonely Passion of Judith Hearne," about a solitary old maid in a Belfast boarding house. Moore "handled [Judith] remarkably: just this side of caricature, she moves through the solid world wrapt away in an interior monologue that borders, at times, on Joyce. The utter emptiness of the world when people fail, when pride fails, and last, when belief falls down before misfortune, is eerily suggested, with Miss Hearne's descent like the everlasting leap of nightmare, through a vacuum. Dry on a tearful subject, this book is at once so astringent and so compassionate that it manages (that rare feat) to be sad without being depressing"—(*Spectator*). "The Luck of Ginger Coffey," which Moore later adapted for the screen, placed an Irishman—a boisterous braggart, an unemployed man whose wife had left him—in a Canadian setting. This is "a breathlessly fast novel, jerky and nervous of style, always on the edge of noisy laughter or sudden tears. Ginger is that rare bird in fiction, the fully realized character"—(*TLS*, London). The one Moore novel that is to some extent autobiographical is "The Emperor of Ice-Cream" (the title is from the Wallace Stevens poem). An Irish lad of 17, feeling depressed and misunderstood at home, at the onset of World War II joins the ARP (Air Raid Precautions), in which he performs heroically and gains maturity. *Library Journal* praised the book highly but warned that its language might offend. "I Am Mary Dunne," chosen by the Literary Guild as part of a dual selection, penetrates, during a period of particular tension, the psyche of a beautiful American woman. "With the publication of 'I Am Mary Dunne,' Mr. Moore transcends his creation of Judith Hearne and firmly establishes his rare gift and unusual status as a writer who so thoroughly understands women that he can write the psychological autobiography of one of the most complex among them. . . . A sophisticated novel rife with revelation and stringent contemporary comment"—(Judith Crist, in the *Literary Guild Magazine*).

Born in Ireland, Brian Moore lived in Canada for ten years, there winning the Governor General's Award in 1960. He now resides in the U.S. and has applied for American citizenship. "The way I write novels," he says, "is by trying to create a voice, to hear that voice and build up a person from it. I try to do it as if I were taking down dictation." He wrote "Canada" (*Time-Life* 1963 $4.95 [dist. by Silver] lib. bdg. $5.70) while he was still living there, and an article for *Life* magazine recommending political unity between the U.S. and Canada. "I nearly got myself killed for it," he says. He has recently written the screenplay for Isaac Bashevis Singer's (*q. v.*) "The Slave."

THE LONELY PASSION OF JUDITH HEARNE. *Little* 1956 $5.95 pap. $2.25

THE LUCK OF GINGER COFFEY. *Little-Atlantic* 1960 $4.95

THE EMPEROR OF ICE-CREAM. *Viking* 1965 $4.95

I AM MARY DUNNE. *Viking* 1968 $4.95

FERGUS. *Holt* 1970 $5.95

Books about Moore

Brian Moore. By Jeanne Flood. *Bucknell Univ. Press* $4.50 pap. $1.95

AMIS, KINGSLEY. 1922–

Kingsley Amis was born "of Baptist stock originating in southeast London" and had, he writes, "an average lower-middle-class childhood of that area." He attended the City of London School, served in the army, then entered St. John's College, Oxford, from which he received his degree, first class, in English language and literature in 1947. He has written poems, stories and criticism for various periodicals. Until 1961, Amis lectured in English at University College, Swansea, and was a Fellow of Peterhouse (Cambridge) until 1963, when he decided to devote all his time to writing.

"Lucky Jim" (1954, o. p.), an entertaining satire on the fortunes of a brash and frivolous young scholar at an English university, won the Somerset Maugham Award in 1955; and it made Amis's reputation. Ironically it was Maugham (*q. v.*) who first attacked that group of English writers called the "Angry Young Men," of whom Amis is one of the best known.

The *Times Literary Supplement* (London) praised "That Uncertain Feeling": "His dialogue is brilliant, his timing of comic situations could hardly be bettered . . . yet by intention he is a serious comic writer, one who apparently means to say something about society." There was a great diversity of critical opinion about "Take a Girl Like You," but the *New Yorker* considered it his best work since the "miraculous 'Lucky Jim' ": "Mr. Amis treats his subject . . . with wit, shrewdness, and humanity, and he shows an uncommon understanding of a kind of girl who exists by the million and who has not been taken seriously in literature for quite some time." "Amis seems to erect a whole comic world through the fabric of his writing. . . . The novels are full of word play and verbal jokes. Any chance observation is likely to bring forth a list of vaguely associated comic improbabilities"—(James Gindin). The "fat Englishman" of the novel of that title is a thoroughly unpleasant British publisher who goes to the United States; his trip is the excuse for some sharp Amis satire on the New World. In "The Anti-Death League," at once a comedy and a spy thriller with serious undertones, "what Mr. Amis has done, with some of his best writing, is to expound his philosophies through a vivid, exciting story and a superior character analysis that challenges your imagination and absorbs your interest—(*Baltimore Sunday Sun*). With Robert Conquest, he has edited "Spectrum" (*Harcourt* 1962–65 Vols. 4–5 each $5.75; *Berkley* Vols. 2–4 pap. each $.60), science-fiction anthologies of short stories by masters who write with imagination and style. A longtime James Bond devotee—who had proved his interest with a study of the superhero, "The James Bond Dossier" (*New Am. Lib.* 1965 $3.95 pap. $.60)—Amis was delegated to produce more Bond books in the manner of the late Ian Fleming, Bond's creator. "The critics," said the *N.Y. Times*, "were outraged, but the public seems to be delighted." "Colonel Sun," his first Bond adventure—written under pseudonym Robert Markham—was published in the U.S. in April, 1968 (*Bantam* pap. $.95). "It was fun," said Mr. Amis—"a kind of holiday."

THAT UNCERTAIN FEELING. 1956 *Ballantine Bks.* pap. $.95

I LIKE IT HERE. 1958. *Harcourt* $4.50; *Ballantine Bks.* pap. $.95

TAKE A GIRL LIKE YOU. 1960. *New Am. Lib.* Signet pap. $.95

MY ENEMY'S ENEMY. *Harcourt* 1963 $4.50. Short stories

ONE FAT ENGLISHMAN. *Harcourt* 1964 $4.50

THE ANTI-DEATH LEAGUE. 1966. *Ballantine Bks.* pap. $1.25

(with Robert Conquest) THE EGYPTOLOGISTS. *Random* 1966 $4.95. A novel about a scholarly society used as a cover for extramarital adventures.

I WANT IT NOW. *Harcourt* 1969 $5.75; *Ballantine Bks.* pap. $1.25

THE GREEN MAN. *Harcourt* 1970 $5.95; *Ballantine Bks.* pap. $1.25

GIRL, TWENTY. *Harcourt* 1972 $5.95; *Ballantine Bks.* pap. $1.25

THE RIVERSIDE VILLAS MURDER: A Mystery Novel. *Harcourt* 1973 $6.95

BRAINE, JOHN. 1922–

John Braine, a Yorkshireman by birth and inclination, started to write "Room at the Top" while hospitalized and recovering from tuberculosis. It is the story of a man obsessed by the need for success who believed he could become an "insider" by donning the proper mask, The film version of "Room at the Top" won the British Oscar and was widely acclaimed in the United States. "From the Hand of the Hunter" deals with the fight against failure by a tubercular. "Life at the Top" is concerned with the hero of "Room at the Top" after he marries the boss's daughter. "He finds he has traded more than the rigors of poverty for his present money-eyed comfort: his personal freedom has been exchanged for a form of elegant slavery. Still angry, still unhappy, he now lacks the will power to break loose." In "The Jealous God," "an author whose earlier concerns have been mainly fiscal and physical now turns his attention to the soul" in what is "perhaps his best novel since 'Room at the Top' "—(Eric Moon, in *LJ*). It is the story of a love affair between a young man, Catholic by upbringing (like Braine) and a charming and lively female librarian (Mr. Braine himself was once a librarian).

John Braine has said: "A novelist's task is to present human beings as they are—*why* they are is not his concern. . . . A writer must have roots, must belong to his own part of the country. He must write only about what he knows—but he mustn't write autobiography, which is one of the curses of the modern novel. And he must love people and things. All people, all things."

ROOM AT THE TOP. 1957. *New Am. Lib.* Signet pap. $.95; *Popular Lib.* pap. $.95

THE JEALOUS GOD. *Houghton* 1965 $4.95

THE CRYING GAME. *Houghton* 1968 $5.95; *Popular Lib.* pap. $1.75

THE VIEW FROM TOWER HILL. *Coward* 1971 $6.95; *Popular Lib.* pap. $.95

Queen of a Distant Country. *Coward* 1973 $6.95

Books about Braine

John Braine. By James W. Lee. English Authors Ser. *Twayne* 1968 $5.50

GRIFFIN, GWYN. 1925–1967.

Orville Prescott once wrote in the *N.Y. Times*: "Have you ever read a novel by Gwyn Griffin? If not you have missed an unusual reading experience unlike any to be encountered in the works of other contemporary writers. The special quality of a Griffin novel is its combination of three factors, each of them magnified to a superlative degree. The first is old-fashioned narrative power, a gift for storytelling which defies one not to be engrossed, defies one with almost insolent assurance. The second is a satirical distaste for most human beings and their institutions, which makes Mr. Griffin's novels seem harsh and even cruel, but which also imparts a theatrical, flamboyant, swaggering life to his unusually hateful characters. The third is Mr. Griffin's Kipling-esque ability to soak himself in the local atmosphere of particular places and in the technical lore of particular occupations. A Griffin novel is never subtle, refined, ambiguous or symbolical. It always packs a wallop and, like a punch in the nose, holds one's complete attention."

Of Welsh ancestry, Mr. Griffin lived a life as exciting as his novels. Born in Egypt, son of a British civil servant stationed there, he was successively a cotton planter in Ethiopia, a cipher officer for Major Ord Wingate, adjutant to a son of Emperor Haile Selassie of Ethiopia, assistant superintendent of the Eritrea police force and a port pilot. His first novel was published in 1956 and he was able in time to devote himself to writing, eventually settling with his wife in Italy, where he died at 42.

"Freedom Observed" is a melodramatic story set in a former French African colony, newly independent. "Mr. Griffin has a tremendous story to tell, and he tells it thrillingly. [He] has made conscientious research into French imperial history and a sympathetic study of the African scene. The result is a moving narrative of no little distinction"—(*TLS*, London). Though Honor Tracy (in the *New Republic*) has pointed out that the events in "A Significant Experience" "technically could" but "actually would not take place," accusing Griffin of "grievous libel" against "a body of men traditionally debarred from making a reply," she finds that he "describes with great brilliance and a tension marvelously sustained an act of sickening brutality against a cadet in a British officers' training camp." "A Last Lamp Burning," the Putnam Award novel set in Naples, "is uncommonly readable, but Griffin is a thoughtful man as well as a first-rate storyteller"—(Granville Hicks, in *SR*). The *Saturday Review*, discussing "A Scorpion on a Stone," found that "one has to dig fairly deep, and through some surprising poorly realized stories, before striking what gold there is in this collection."

Griffin's next-to-last novel, "An Operational Necessity," was a tremendous success. Of this best-selling Book-of-the-Month Club selection, Thomas Lask said in the *N.Y. Times*: "Out of familiar and much-used material, a murderous piece of brutality at sea during the last war and the subsequent court-martial of those responsible for it, Gwyn Griffin has fashioned a novel that will be remembered for its story-telling power and for its probing of the question of individual guilt and responsibility in a time of wholesale destruction and war." *Publishers Weekly* called "The Occupying Power" "highly entertaining . . . satiric commentary on the human condition."

A Last Lamp Burning. *Putnam* 1965 $6.95; *Pocket Bks.* pap. $.95

The Occupying Power. *Putnam* 1968 $6.95. A posthumous novel of an imaginary island off Africa, occupied in World War II by British soldiers.

WAIN, JOHN. 1925–

John Wain grew up in Staffordshire, attended Oxford, became a university lecturer, and since 1955 has been a full-time writer. His early life is described in his autobiography, "Sprightly Running," which gives an interesting picture of a bright boy growing up in an English industrial town. Wain is a very prolific writer: he has published six books of poetry; written studies of Hopkins, Bennett, and Shakespeare; edited a number of anthologies; and reviewed books for *Encounter*, *The Observer*, *The Spectator* and other periodicals.

With the exception of his most recent work, Wain's novels are out of print in this country; among these the most notable is his first novel, "Hurry on Down." The hero of this book is a young man with an excellent education which, he finds, has in no way prepared him for life outside the university. He tries job after job, meets people from various strata of English life, and observes everything with a sardonic eye; in using this episodic sort of plot, Wain gives a comprehensive view of life in postwar England. "The Contenders" is a novel set in the North of England, in a town much like the one in which Wain grew up; the book is about the competitive friendship of an artist and a businessman. "Strike the Father Dead" tells of the struggle of a young jazz musician to free himself from parental influence. "A Winter in the Hills" is Wain's most recent novel. The setting is Wales and the hero is a philologist on leave from his university; it is funny, entertaining, and the best of Wain's more recent novels.

WINTER IN THE HILLS. *Viking* 1970 $6.95

THE LIFE GUARD AND OTHER STORIES. 1971. *Viking.* 1972 $5.95

SPRIGHTLY RUNNING: Part of an Autobiography. *St. Martin's* 1962 pap. $3.50

KOPS, BERNARD. 1926–

Bernard Kops, novelist and playwright, was born in London of Dutch Jewish parents, his father a shoe-maker. He is understandably preoccupied with the adaptation of Jews to the mainstream of English life, but the peripheral problems he touches on are universal. "Yes from No-Man's Land" is "a depressing but moving novel dealing with spiritual courage in the face of physical death," says *Library Journal*, which has called Kops "one of England's most interesting writers." "The central character is a crusty 70-year old Jew who is dying of cancer in a Catholic hospital in London's East End. . . . Each time the old man drifts away his past is illuminated." Dominick Shapiro is a troubled adolescent (recalling Holden Caulfield) who rejcts his middle-class Jewish family and sets out on a series of adventures that result in his being hailed as a sort of British an-tihero. The book is a "cheerful, knowledgeable, and well-written London story [and] Dominick Shapiro—alone and dreaming, or with his family, or trying his strength in the wilds outside his home—is a person worth learning about"—(*New Yorker*). "Enter Solly Gold," about a con man in London's East End (in Robert Corrigan's "Masterpieces of Modern English Drama" *Macmillan* 1967 Collier Bks. pap. $1.50) and "The Hamlet of Stepney Green," about a young Jewish dreamer who yearns to become a crooner (in "Penguin Plays" *Penguin* o. p.), are two of some ten plays Kops has written; he made his early reputation as a dramatist. His autobiography, "The World is a Wedding," (1963, o. p.) received favorable critical notice.

YES FROM NO-MAN'S LAND. *Coward* 1965 $4.50

BY THE WATERS OF WHITECHAPEL. *Norton* 1970 $5.95

THE PASSIONATE PAST OF GLORIA GAYE. *Norton* 1972 $6.95

FOWLES, JOHN. 1926–

John Fowles' first novel, "The Collector," is about a lower-class young man who wins a lottery and thus is able to afford the expenses of acting out a fantasy: he abducts a pretty, talented girl he has admired from afar. Fowles is good at maintaining suspense and in providing realistic details of the kidnapping; but his distaste for the demented protagonist limits the psychological depth of his characterizations. "The Magus" tells of an Englishman who works as a teacher on a Greek island; there he meets a "sorcerer" whom he finds literally enchanting. In this book, as in "The Collector," Fowles is concerned with the issues of enslavement, moral responsibility, and psychological aberration.

"The French Lieutenant's Woman," perhaps Fowles' best-known book, takes place in the small sea-coast village where he makes his home. The time setting and plot of the novel are old-fashioned: a story about a be-trayed woman who lived one hundred years ago. But this is much more than the remake of a Victorian novel; Fowles is quite willing to remind the reader that he lives in the 20th century—anachronisms, philosophical speculations, parodies, and literary allusions are all used to provide a very modern effect. The novel is that rare beast, a work which utilizes unconventional techniques and still manages to get onto the best-seller lists. "The Aristos" is an essay in which Fowles sets forth the ideas which concern him most: prominent among these is his elevation of an ideal of excellence, which, he says, should always be at the core of an artist's motivating instinct. Those who can achieve only mediocrity despise excellence: it intimidates them. The art-ist's struggle therefore is not only to achieve excellence in his own works, but to resist damaging or envious criticism from his inferiors. Fowles' most recent work is a collection of poems he has written over the last 20 years, "Poems" (*Ecco Press* 1973 $7.50). Fowles has said that he considers poetry a relief after the rigors of writing fiction, and this volume indicates that fiction evokes his greatest efforts and his most polished works.

THE COLLECTOR *Little* 1963 $6.95; *Dell* pap. $.95

THE ARISTOS. *Little* 1964 rev. ed. 1970 $5.95; *New Am. Lib.* Signet pap. $.95

THE MAGUS. *Little* 1966 $8.50; *Dell* 1973 pap. $1.25

THE FRENCH LIEUTENANT'S WOMAN. *Little* 1969 $7.95; *New Am. Lib.* Signet pap. $.95

SILLITOE, ALAN. 1928–

Alan Sillitoe grew up in the slums of the industrial city of Nottingham. He began to write while in the RAF, stationed in Malaya. After the war he went to Majorca, where he became a friend of Robert Graves (*q.v.*), who encouraged him to write "Saturday Night and Sunday Morning." The *N.Y. Herald Tribune* said: "Alan Sillitoe has given us one of the better pictures of English working-class life since Arnold Bennett dealt with the Five Towns or D. H. Lawrence with Nottingham colleries." His authors' fee for the manuscript rescued him and his wife from direct poverty and enabled him to afford the balanced diet to which he attributes his recovery from tuberculosis. "Saturday Night" won the Author's Club Prize for the best English novel of 1958 and was made into a movie in 1960. His second book, "The Loneliness of the Long-Distance Runner," was awarded England's Hawthornden Prize for 1960 and was made into a most moving film in 1962.

"William Posters" is Sillitoe's play on the words of the British "Bill Posters Will Be Prosecuted" (U.S. version—"Post No Bills"), a sentence that has haunted him. "The Death of William Posters" (1965, o. p.) is about yet another young man who must escape from the philistinism of the social milieu to which he has been born. Eric Moon wrote of it (in *SR*): "A number of talented young writers of English fiction are mining the newly rich field of the working class. . . . None, however, is as geniune and authentic as Sillitoe. He captures not only the language but the attitudes of the intelligent man buried in the poverty of inertia and routine of the working-class life. . . . After some half-dozen works of fiction, one must conclude that Sillitoe is not a very profound novelist nor yet a 'fine' writer in a stylistic sense. But this is not to say that he is not an important writer. His honesty, his authenticity, his identification make him a unique voice in British fiction. . . . With all his agonizing, I like him fine the way he is." "Tree on Fire," (1968, o. p.) a novel with autobiographical elements, was published in Britain in 1968. "Travels in Nihilon" is a satirical novel about a country controlled by Nihilism. "Raw Material" is a fictionalized memoir of his childhood and an exploration of the making of a writer.

SATURDAY NIGHT AND SUNDAY MORNING. *Knopf* 1959 $4.95; *New Am Lib.* Signet 1960 pap. $.75

THE LONELINESS OF THE LONG-DISTANCE RUNNER. *Knopf* 1960 $4.95; *New Am. Lib.* pap. $.75. Short stories.

A START IN LIFE. *Scribner* 1971 $6.95

TRAVELS IN NIHILON. *Scribner* 1972 $6.95

RAW MATERIAL. *Scribner* 1973 $6.95

Books about Sillitoe

Alan Sillitoe. By Allen R. Penner. English Authors Ser. *Twayne* $5.50

WILSON, COLIN. 1932–

Colin Wilson made his reputation in England and the United States on the publication of his first book, "The Outsider" (*Houghton* 1956 $6.00; *Dell* 1967 pap. $1.95). Sometimes known as the *enfant terrible* of English letters, whose soberer practitioners still do not take him entirely seriously, he has been prolific in many literary fields without ever quite reaching first rank as a novelist. He has written a number of competent thrillers. The Jack-the-Ripper story was the basis of his first novel, "Ritual in the Dark." "The Sex Diary of Gerard Sorme" is not as sensational as its title and clearly grew out of the author's research for "The Origins of the Sexual Impulse" (*Putnam* 1963 $4.95). "The Violent World of Hugh Greene" is a "good, solid, rather old-fashioned novel of a young man making his way"—(*Harper*). In "Necessary Doubt" a German philosopher is plagued by suspicions that a former student is a killer. Wilson has narrative skill and James Gindin writes that his "heroes are innocents, seeking to understand all the violence and irrationality they find around them. . . . Yet, for all their naïveté, his heroes do reflect something about contemporary Britain: the interest in violence and perversion; . . . the search for order and stability; the feeling that organized society is shallow and hypocritical."

Son of a Leicester shoe factory worker, Colin Wilson left school at the age of 16. After a six-month period in the RAF, he held a succession of factory, office, hospital and dishwashing jobs in both London and Paris, worked on the *Paris Review*, and began to write plays, short stories, essays and poetry. Mr. Wilson spent several years in the 1960s as a Writer in Residence at Hollins College, Virginia.

THE GLASS CAGE. 1967 *Bantam* pap. $1.25. A mystery story in which the murderer leaves quotations from William Blake near his victims. Solved by a Blake expert.

THE MIND PARASITES. 1967. *Arkham* $4.00; *Oneiric Press* pap. $2.25

LINGARD. *Pocket Bks.* pap. $.95

THE HEDONISTS. *New Am. Lib.* Signet pap. $.95

See also Chapter 16, on Essays and Criticism.

NAIPAUL, V(IDIADHAR) S(URAJPRASAD). 1932–

Born in Trinidad of Hindu parents, V. S. Naipaul was educated at Oxford and lives in Britain. His talent was established with distinction in the beguiling, warmly humorous "Mystic Masseur," of which the *N.Y. Herald Tribune* wrote: "The characterizations are vivid and witty. Human truths are revealed, and we are entertained." "Miguel Street" describes the aberrant lives of a mean street in Port-of-Spain, Trinidad. "A particular delight of Mr. Naipaul's writing is the dialogue. The West Indian idiom in his hands is full of color and a rich Elizabethan disregard for conventional correctness"—(*TLS*, London). "The Mimic Men" is "a serious, urbane and beautifully written book," wrote the *Nation*, which found it not quite convincing. It is the story of a West Indian, R. R. K. Singh, who becomes a powerful statesman in his newly independent country only to suffer political downfall. Thomas Lask said of it (in the *N.Y. Times*): "It isn't the events that make the novel so impressive, however. It is the author's demonstration that in fair times and foul Singh never fully lives up to his responsibilities as a man and as an individual. He is supine before events, passive before people. His marriage, his wealth, his rise in politics are due more to chance and the will of others than to his own exertions. Singh, like others in the book, is only the shadow of a man. His is not an attractive figure. He does not even have the fascination of a great villain. Yet we read on with interest to the very end. For in anatomizing Singh, Mr. Naipaul has anatomized an entire society." "A Flag on the Island" is a group of short stories about Trinidad.

"The Middle Passage" (1963, o. p.) is a survey of the social orders in Trinidad, British Guiana, Surinam, Martinique and Jamaica. After traveling through the Caribbean regions where many of the slave-carrying ships interrupted their passage from Africa, he feels that "the present character of the regions he visited express their history as colonial territories built on slave labor." In "An Area of Darkness' (1965, o. p.) Mr. Naipaul presents with sympathy and insight his observations on a trip to India, where he saw the meanest physical suffering contrasted with the loftiest human values. Malcolm Muggeridge called it "quite the best book on the subject that has come into my hands." Mr. Naipaul has won a number of British awards, among them the Somerset Maugham Award (1961) and the Hawthornden Prize (1963).

A FLAG ON THE ISLAND. *Macmillan* 1968 $5.95. Short stories.

THE LOSS OF EL DORADO. *Knopf* 1970 $7.50

IN A FREE STATE. *Knopf* 1971 $5.95

Books about Naipul

V. S. Naipul. By William Walsh. *Barnes & Noble* 1973 $5.50

SINCLAIR, ANDREW ANNANDALE. 1935–

Not long after he graduated from Cambridge, Andrew Sinclair published "My Friend Judas," a novel about the experiences of a Cambridge student. The book is well-written and entertaining; it is also an interesting indicator of the changes in English university life since the days of writers like Evelyn Waugh. Sinclair's protagonist is iconoclastic; funny rather than witty; and at times seems actually to believe that learning things is as important an activity as meeting people. A similarly independent hero is introduced in "The Breaking of Bumbo," which is about an army officer (Sinclair served in the Coldstream Guards before he attended Cambridge).

As an undergraduate Sinclair studied American history, and his interest in history and politics is reflected in his nonfiction works: a book on Prohibition; a history of the United States; a study of the womens' emancipation movement; and works on Warren G. Harding and Che Guevara. Sinclair has also written a number of screenplays, among them a film version of "The Breaking of Bumbo"; "My Friend Judas," which he adapted for the stage, was produced in London in 1959.

In his most recent novels, "Gog" and "Magog," he explores various aspects of English society and politics using the myth of the giants Gog and Magog. Sinclair's characters are juxtaposed in a Manichean dichotomy: Gog is gentle, naive, and good; Magog is brutal, wily, corrupt; together they epitomize the best and worst in English society. In the first novel Gog is washed ashore in Scotland after World War II; he has no memory of the past. As he travels to London to discover his identity he meets many unusual characters, both historical and imaginary. Sinclair uses many novel fictional techniques to reveal the historical roots of contemporary social problems. Magog, who is at the center of the second novel, symbolizes the corruption of those who wield power in contemporary Britain: industrialists, politicians, and bureaucrats. The bitterness Sinclair feels about the triumphs of Magog emerges as satirical humor in this novel, where the author's interests in experimental fiction, politics, and myth are combined in a very original fashion.

THE BREAKING OF BUMBO. 1958. *Simon & Schuster* 1959 $3.50

My Friend Judas. 1959. *Simon & Schuster* 1961 $3.95

The Project. *Simon & Schuster* 1960 $3.50

Gog. 1967 *Avon* 1969 pap. $.95

Adventures in the Skin Trade. *New Directions* 1968 $4.50. A play based on Dylan Thomas's novel.

The Last of the Best. *Macmillan* 1969 $7.95

Magog. *Harper* 1972 $6.95

DRABBLE, MARGARET (Mrs. Clive Walter Swift). 1939–

Margaret Drabble graduated from Cambridge, worked for a while as an actress, and then married and began to have children (her husband is the actor Clive Swift). The plots of a number of her novels reflect situations in her own life. "A Summer Bird-Cage" tells of two sisters: one, very bright has recently graduated from Oxford; the other, very pretty, is about to marry (though Miss Drabble's own sister can hardly be considered unintellectual: she is the novelist A. S. Byatt). "The Garrick Year," Miss Drabble's next book, is based on her experiences in the theatrical world. "The Millstone" (not in print in this country) describes the difficulties of a heroine who attempts to raise three children and complete a doctoral thesis in literature. The heroine of "The Needle's Eye" is a divorced woman, again with three children; her involvement with a lawyer leads to Jamesian subtleties as the moral and spiritual dilemmas of her characters are set forth.

Miss Drabble herself has three children, and the central problem in a number of her books is one which has received a good deal of attention recently: the divided loyalties of a mother who seeks more than the simple joys of family life. Like those of a number of her contemporaries, Margaret Drabble's books are written in a traditional novelistic style, with an emphasis on the social and moral issues raised by the predicaments of her characters.

A Summer Bird-Cage. 1963. *Belmont-Tower* 1971 pap. $.95

The Garrick Year. 1964. *Belmont-Tower* 1971 pap. $.95

Jerusalem the Golden. 1967. *Belmont-Tower* 1971 pap. $.95

The Waterfall. *Knopf* 1969 $5.95

The Needle's Eye. *Knopf* 1972 $6.95; *Popular Lib.* pap. 1973 $1.25

Thank You All Very Much. *New Am. Lib.* 1973 pap. $.75

—R.R.

Chapter 13

American Fiction: Early Period

"Judging by our greatest novels, the American imagination, even when it wishes to assuage and reconcile the contradictions of life, has not been stirred by the possibilities of catharsis or incarnation, by the tragic or Christian possibility. It has been stirred, rather, by the aesthetic possibilities of radical forms of alienation, contradiction, and disorder."
— RICHARD CHASE

The earliest American literature consisted chiefly of travel books, diaries, sermons, political writings. Imaginative literature was late in developing. This was, in part, because the early Puritan settlers were suspicious of the merely literary, but also because this continent was a wilderness to be explored, cleared, settled, and governed—all of which meant emphasis on the practical and utilitarian. Urban centers having printing houses and sufficient population with wealth and leisure enough to support the development of non-utilitarian literature were long in coming, and when they did, American printers found it much more profitable to pirate the works of English authors than to pay royalties to lesser-known native authors.

Our earliest writers of fiction were, of course, recently transplanted Britishers who imitated the writers that were popular back home; most of them are unread today and largely forgotten except by specialists working in the period. Although many of them, from the standpoint of literary merit, deserve neglect, there are some who can still be read with interest. Ann Eliza Bleeker, for instance, who wrote the earliest fictional account of Indians in America, "History of Maria Kittle" (1781), anticipated later more skillfully written accounts of Indian and white encounters; and Hugh Henry Brackenridge's "Modern Chivalry" (1792–1805), inspired in part by 18th-century English satirists and by "Don Quixote," was, for its time, a telling satire on certain aspects of American life. Despite obvious unoriginality of style and form, these and other writers of the early years managed to break ground for the growth and development of later novelists, partly by demonstrating that, popular prejudice to the contrary, the realities of American life could be converted into interesting and significant fiction, and also by discovering subjects and ways of feeling that would in time seem genuinely American.

The most important of these early writers was Charles Brockden Brown, a native of Philadelphia, whose novel "Wieland" (1798) appeared more than 20 years before Irving's "Sketch Book." Although Brown never achieved Irving's popularity, his four Gothic novels were solid achievements in the art of fiction and marked the beginning of the kind of psychological–moral fiction later to be written by Poe, Hawthorne, James, and Faulkner. A somewhat later innovator was Washington Irving, who domesticated the German fairy tale by grounding it in the realities of life along the Hudson River. Irving also helped make the profession of authorship respectable in a country that still tended to wonder whether story telling wasn't a waste of time, if not actually sinful. He also convinced the English that America was able to produce a writer who could write English almost as well as an Englishman. Cooper's novels lacked the grace of Irving's—indeed his "Leather-stocking Tales" strike modern readers as heavy-handed and tedious—but in his rambling, melodramatic books about Natty Bumpo and his Indian friends and enemies, Cooper created a myth about pioneer America that has been heavily exploited by popular and serious writers ever since and has put a number of more recent novelists in his debt, including Ernest Hemingway. In Poe's and Hawthorne's tales and sketches one sees the beginning of the American short story and the development of an aesthetic that has influenced succeeding generations of short story writers in Europe as well as in America. And in the romances of Hawthorne and the great symbolic work, "Moby Dick" by Herman Melville, one catches the American romance–novel (to use Richard Chase's phrase) at the point of its most exciting development.

The local color impulses discernable in some of the earliest fiction about life in the New World were carried on and developed in the 19th century by lesser writers, each with his own motive and particular bent. Harriet Beecher Stowe, Joel Chandler Harris, Bret Harte, even, to some extent, Mark Twain, belong to this artistically less exacting fictional tradition.

Historically the most important movement in the later period of American fiction was the "realistic" movement, exemplified by W. D. Howells, who was not only a self-appointed apostle for the movement but one of its chief exemplars as well. Between 1872 and 1920, the year of his death, he published almost 100 novels and travel books. Critics differ, sometimes violently, in their responses to the fiction of Henry James—V. L. Parrington, for one, found James entirely too mental and lacking in social awareness—but hardly anyone denies James's importance in the history of American fiction, for not only did he create an impressively large body of fictional work but he was an astute critic and scholar of the art of fiction as well. It was James, with his knowledge of French and Italian, and his long residence abroad, who brought the American novel, artistically, into the mainstream of international fiction. Every American fiction writer of any stature who came after him has, to some extent, profited from James's discoveries.

As the following selective list of scholarly and critical works will suggest, there has been a great deal written on the subject of early American fiction, in large part because prose fiction has been the most popular of the literary forms in the United States and also because it has seemed most central to the nature of American experience, at least during the past 175 years. Among the histories that might be singled out for special mention are Alexander Cowie's "The Rise of the American Novel" and Arthur Hobson Quinn's "American Fiction: An Historical and Critical Survey," both of considerable use to those who want an overview of this period. Darrel Abel's three-volume history "American Literature" also contains detailed estimates of the major and minor fiction writers of these early years. Among the many theoretical works, two radically different approaches are exemplified in the work of V. L. Parrington and Richard Chase. Parrington's three-volume "Main Currents in American Thought" strains all of American literature through the author's liberal political sieve. Chase's controversial study, "The American Novel and Its Tradition," limits his perspective to what he calls the romance–novel and produces a perceptive, if somewhat restricted, history of the American novel from Brown to Faulkner.

Two basic but very different bibliographic works are Jacob Blanck's "Bibliography of American Literature" and Robert E. Spiller and others' "Literary History of the United States," Vol. 3 with a Second Supplement. Blanck's "Bibliography" describes the various editions of works published by American authors, includes a brief selection of secondary works, and when completed will cover 300 authors from the beginning of the Federal period up to and including writers who died before the end of 1930. Five volumes have so far been published by *Yale University Press* (Vols. 1–4 $20.00, Vol. 5 $25.00): Vol. 1 Henry Adams to Donn Byrne (1955); Vol. 2 George Washington Cable to Timothy Dwight (1957); Vol. 3 Edward Eggleston to Bret Harte (1959); Vol. 4 Nathaniel Hawthorne to Joseph Holt Ingram (1963); and Vol. 5 Washington Irving to Henry Wadsworth Longfellow (1968). (*See Chapter 2, Bibliography, for further comment.*) The Spiller bibliography lists the titles of individual authors but is mainly concerned with secondary materials on those works. (*For further information see below.*)

Three excellent books dealing with the social and historical perspective of the literary period between the Civil War and World War I are "Harvests of Change: American Literature 1865–1914" by Jay Martin, "Realism and Naturalism in Nineteenth-Century Literature" by Donald Pizer, and "The American 1890's: Life and Times of a Lost Generation" by Lazer Ziff.

Critical appraisals and bibliographic and biographical information are included in two series on American writers: *Twayne's* United States Authors Series and *University of Minnesota* Pamphlets on American Writers, individual titles of which are listed below in appropriate bibliographies.

A useful tool for the more scholarly reader will be the carefully edited texts of important American authors (including Howells, Twain, Melville, Crane, Irving) being sponsored by the Modern Language Association (MLA) and its Center for Editions of American Authors. Titles that have so far appeared are listed under appropriate subheadings of individual authors.

NOTE: *In general, only volumes applying to American Fiction: Early Period, or closely related subjects are listed here. For complete histories of American literature, etc., see Chapter 3, Reference Books—Literature. See also Chapter 4, Broad Studies and General Anthologies.*

Abel, Darrel. AMERICAN LITERATURE. *Barron's* 3 vols. 1963 Vol. I Colonial and Early National Writing Vol. 2 Literature of the Atlantic Culture Vol. 3 Masterworks of American Realism each $2.50 1-vol. ed. $14.00. An account of American literature that describes and interprets American writing "in relation to the characters and personal circumstances of the men who wrote it and to the social and political tendencies which conditioned that writing."

AMERICANS IN FICTION. *Gregg* $490.00. (*Complete information available from the publisher.*) "A Noteworthy Series of 75 American Novels" of the 19th century, of which 70 are available. Facsimile editions.

Anderson, Charles R., and others, Eds. AMERICAN LITERARY MASTERS. An anthology. Vol. I Selections from Poe, Hawthorne, Melville, Emerson, Thoreau, Whitman, Dickinson, Twain. Critical introductions, reading suggestions, biographies; index. *Holt* 1965 2 vols. each $12.00

Bartlett, Irving H. THE AMERICAN MIND IN THE MID-NINETEENTH CENTURY. *Crowell* 1967 pap. $1.95

Bewley, Marius. THE ECCENTRIC DESIGN: Form in the Classic American Novel. *Columbia* 1959 1963 pap. $2.45. Able criticism of James, Hawthorne, Cooper, Melville and Scott Fitzgerald, writers who endeavored to understand their emotional and spiritual needs as Americans.

Brooks, Van Wyck. MAKERS AND FINDERS: A History of the Writer in America, 1800–1915. *Dutton* 5 vols. Vol. I The World of Washington Irving, 1800–1840 Everyman's $3.50 Vol. 2 The Flowering of New England, 1815–1865 pap. $2.45 Vol. 3 The Times of Melville and Whitman, 1840–1890 Everyman's $3.50 Vol. 4 New England: Indian Summer, 1865–1915 pap. $2.25 Vol. 5 The Confident Years, 1885–1915 Everyman's $3.50 *See Chapter 14 on Essays for comment on this critical series.*

Brownell, W. C. AMERICAN PROSE MASTERS: Cooper, Hawthorne, Emerson, Poe, Lowell, Henry James. Ed. by Howard Mumford Jones. *Harvard Univ. Press* 1963 $8.00

John Harvard Lib. pap. $2.25. Originally published in 1909. Brownell was unusual for his time in taking American writers seriously. He examines the complete works of each to establish the author's philosophy and the meaning of his style.

Cady, Edwin H. THE LIGHT OF COMMON DAY: Realism in American Fiction. *Indiana Univ. Press* 1971 $7.50. A scholarly discussion of the problem of realism and naturalism in writers from Hawthorne to James. Interesting, readable.

(Ed.) LITERATURE OF THE EARLY REPUBLIC. An anthology. *Holt* (Rinehart) 1950 pap. $3.00; *Peter Smith* $5.00

Canby, Henry Seidel. CLASSIC AMERICANS. 1931. *Russell & Russell* 1959 $13.00. A study of eminent writers from Irving to Whitman, with an introductory survey of the colonial background.

Chase, Richard. THE AMERICAN NOVEL AND ITS TRADITION. *Doubleday* 1957 Anchor Bks. pap. $1.95. A discussion of major American novels in light of Chase's carefully worked out thesis that our best novelists have written novel–romances that express the contradictions in American life rather than the unities.

Cowie, Alexander. THE RISE OF THE AMERICAN NOVEL. 1948. *Van Nostrand-Reinhold* 1951 $10.95. A "solid, informative and very readable" critical history.

Davis, David Brion. HOMICIDE IN AMERICAN FICTION, 1798–1860: A Study in Social Values. *Cornell Univ. Press* 1957 pap. $2.45. Primarily a study of the early 19th century, but touches upon modern fiction. Bibliography and analytical index.

Dick, Everett. TALES OF THE FRONTIER: From Lewis and Clark to the Last Roundup. *Univ. of Nebraska Press* 1963 $6.00 Bison Bk. pap. $2.25

Eichelberger, Clayton L. A GUIDE TO CRITICAL REVIEWS OF UNITED STATES FICTION, 1870–1910. *Scarecrow Press* 1971 $10.00. An index to critical comment on major and minor fiction taken from 30 selected periodicals of the 19th century.

Foerster, Norman, Norman S. Grabo, Russel B. Nye, E. Fred Carlisle and Robert Falk, Eds. AMERICAN POETRY AND PROSE. 5th ed. Houghton 1970 2 pts. each $9.50 set $13.50 pap. 3 vols. each $7.95

(With others) EIGHT AMERICAN WRITERS. *Norton* 1963 $10.50

Fogle, Richard H. THE ROMANTIC MOVEMENT IN AMERICAN WRITING. *Odyssey* 1966 $5.00 pap. $3.75

Foster, Richard, Ed. SIX AMERICAN NOVELISTS OF THE NINETEENTH CENTURY: An Introduction. *Univ. of Minnesota Press* 1967 $8.50. Cooper, Hawthorne, Melville, Twain, Howells and James; reprinted from the *Minnesota* Pamphlets on American Writers Series.

Gaston, Edwin W., Jr. THE EARLY NOVEL OF THE SOUTHWEST 1819–1918. *Univ. of New Mexico Press* 1961 $5.95. A valuable critical study of Southwestern fiction 1819–1918 with synopses of the 40 novels discussed, and biographical sketches of the authors.

Gibson, W.M., and G.W. Arms, Eds. TWELVE AMERICAN WRITERS. *Macmillan* 1962 $9.95. Includes Hawthorne, Poe, Mark Twain and Henry James.

Holman, C. Hugh, Comp. THE AMERICAN NOVEL THROUGH JAMES. 1966 *AHM Pub. Corp.* Goldentree Bibliographies pap. $2.95. Texts, bibliographies, biographies and criticism of 42 novelists.

Howard, Leon. LITERATURE AND THE AMERICAN TRADITION. 1960. *Gordian* 1972 $10.00. An entertaining examination of the formation of our literary individuality.

Jones, Howard Mumford. HISTORY AND THE CONTEMPORARY: Essays in Nineteenth-Century Literature. *Univ. of Wisconsin Press* 1964 $6.00

O STRANGE NEW WORLD: American Culture; the Formative Years. *Viking* 1964 $8.50 Compass Bks. pap. $3.25

This "major work in the field of American studies . . . explores the ideas, the language, the art, the laws, the education, the behavior and the institutions imported by the colonial into our strange new world"—(*LJ*).

Kunitz, Stanley J., and Howard Haycraft, Eds. AMERICAN AUTHORS, 1600–1900. 1,320 biographies. *Wilson* 1938 $12.00

Lawrence, D. H. STUDIES IN CLASSIC AMERICAN LITERATURE. 1923. *Viking* 1964 $4.50 Compass Bks. pap. $1.75. Discussions of Whitman, Melville, Benjamin Franklin, Cooper, Poe, Hawthorne and Dana.

Levin, Harry. THE POWER OF BLACKNESS: Hawthorne, Poe, Melville. *Knopf* 1958 $5.95; *Random* Vintage Bks. 1960 pap. $1.45

"A remarkably provocative, astute study attempts to demonstrate that the introspection, tragic awareness, and sense of alienation inherent in the works . . . give a [true] picture of the American mind and milieu"—(*Booklist*)

Martin, Jay. HARVESTS OF CHANGE: American Literature, 1865–1914. *Prentice-Hall* 1967 $8.95 Spectrum Bks. pap. $2.95

"An excellent study"—(*LJ*).

Matthiessen, F. O. AMERICAN RENAISSANCE: Art and Expression in the Age of Emerson and Whitman. 4 bks. Bk. I From Emerson to Thoreau Bk. 2 Hawthorne Bk 3 Melville Bk. 4 Whitman. *Oxford* 1941 $12.50 Galaxy Bks. pap. $3.95

Maxwell, D.E.S. AMERICAN FICTION: The Intellectual Background. Chapters on Poe, Cooper, Melville, Hawthorne, Mark Twain, Edith Wharton and others. *Columbia* 1963 $10.00

Miller, Perry. THE RAVEN AND THE WHALE: The War of Wits in the Era of Poe and Melville. 1956. *Greenwood* $12.75. A lively chronicle of the literary scene in New York in the 1840s and 1850s and the conflict between "American-" and "foreign-" oriented writers.

Morison, Samuel Eliot. THE INTELLECTUAL LIFE OF COLONIAL NEW ENGLAND. *New York Univ. Press* 1956 $8.50; *Cornell Univ. Press* 1960 pap. $2.45

Mott, Frank Luther. A HISTORY OF AMERICAN MAGAZINES. *Harvard Univ. Press* 5 vols. Vol. I 1741–1850 Vol. 2 1850–1865 Vol. 3 1865–1885 Vol. 4 1885–1905 Vol. 5 Sketches of Magazines, 1905–1930 each $15.00

Parrington, Vernon L., Jr. AMERICAN DREAMS: A Study of American Utopias. 1947. *Russell & Russell* 2nd ed. enlarged with postscript 1964 $10.00

Pattee, Frederick L. THE DEVELOPMENT OF THE AMERICAN SHORT STORY: An Historical Survey. 1923. *Biblo & Tannen* 1967 $10.00. A classic study of the form as used by writers from Irving through O. Henry.

THE FIRST CENTURY OF AMERICAN LITERATURE, 1770–1870. 1935. *Cooper* 1966 $10.00

Quinn, Arthur Hobson. AMERICAN FICTION: An Historical and Critical Survey. *Appleton* 1936 1947 1964 $11.55. A useful, if necessarily general account of American fiction from the beginning to Willa Cather with a final chapter "Retrospect and Prospect" and bibliography.

(Ed.) THE LITERATURE OF THE AMERICAN PEOPLE: An Historical and Critical Survey. *Appleton* 1951 $13.65 Pt. I The Colonial and Revolutionary Period by K. B. Murdock Pt. 2 The Establishment of National Literature by A. H. Quinn Pt. 3 The Later Nineteenth Century by C. Gohdes Pt. 4 The Twentieth Century by G. F. Whicher

Short, Raymond W., Ed. FOUR GREAT AMERICAN NOVELS. The Scarlet Letter; Huckleberry Finn; Billy Budd; Daisy Miller. *Holt* 1946 $7.25

Snell, George. SHAPERS OF AMERICAN FICTION. *Cooper* 1961 $6.00

Spiller, Robert E. AMERICAN LITERARY REVOLUTION 1783–1837. With preface and notes. *New York Univ. Press* $10.00

LITERARY HISTORY OF THE UNITED STATES. *Macmillan* 1948 1953 3rd ed. 1964 Vols. I and 2 in 1 vol. $17.50. Vol. 3 Bibliography $16.50 2nd suppl. $14.95. This is the standard modern history of American literature and is particularly useful because Vol. 3 with the 2nd supplement (the 1st suppl., 1959, was incorporated into the 3rd ed.) is a bibliography which not only lists such useful information as where the chief research centers are in the United States, and describes special catalogs, directories, dictionaries and digests of interest to the student of American literature, but also includes detailed bibliographic entries on all significant American writers from the beginning up to 1970. It includes articles in journals and magazines as well as books and lists reprints of authors' works which have now gone out of print.

Steckmesser, Kent L. THE WESTERN HERO IN HISTORY AND LEGEND. *Univ. of Oklahoma Press* 1965 $6.95

   "Pursuing the thesis that 'the Western hero is typically a product of legend as well as history,' Professor Steckmesser analyzes historical sources and popular literature [and] finds a common pattern"—(*LJ*).

Tebbel, John. FROM RAGS TO RICHES: Horatio Alger, Jr. and the American Dream. *Macmillan* 1963 $4.95. The stories of Horatio Alger (1834–1899) pointed a moral and their heroes always triumphed over adversity. This informative biography includes an interesting bibliography.

Tyler, Moses Coit. A HISTORY OF AMERICAN LITERATURE, 1607–1765. 1878. Fwd. by Howard Mumford Jones. *Cornell Univ. Press* 1949 1966 $15.00; *Peter Smith* $3.75

THE LITERARY HISTORY OF THE AMERICAN REVOLUTION. 1897. Ungar 2 vols. Vol. I 1763–1776 Vol. 2 1776–1783 *Am. Class* set $20.00; *Burt Franklin* set $15.00

THE HISTORY OF AMERICAN LITERATURE, 1607–1783. abr. ed. by Archie H. Jones. *Univ. of Chicago Press* 1967 $8.50 Phoenix Bks. pap. $3.45. Contains selections from the 1878 ed. and "The Literary History of the American Revolution" (1897).

Wegelin, Oscar. BIBLIOGRAPHY OF EARLY AMERICAN FICTION, 1774–1830. Covers books printed prior to 1831. *Peter Smith* 1929 $5.00

Wright, Lyle H. AMERICAN FICTION. 3 vols., each with the subtitle "A Contribution toward a Bibliography." *Huntington Library* Vol. I 1774–1850 (1948 2nd ed. 1969) $10.00 Vol. 2 1851–1875 (1957) with additions and corrections appended 1965) $7.50 Vol. 3 1876–1900 (1966) $15.00. These bibliographies list American editions of prose written by Americans for adults and printed between 1774 and 1900. *Research Publications, Inc.*, 12 Lunar Drive, New Haven, Conn. 06525 is reprinting on microfilm all of the volumes of prose fiction listed by Wright. As of May 1, 1973, items through no. 1275, Vol. 3, had been issued in microfilm.

Wright, Nathalia. AMERICAN NOVELISTS IN ITALY: The Discoverers: Allston to James. *Univ. of Pennsylvania Press* 1965 $9.50

"The effect of their travels in Italy on 13 American writers," including Cooper, Stowe, Hawthorne, Howells and James. "This interesting, well-written study . . . should be of great interest to students of American literature"—(*LJ*).

See also Chapters 4, Broad Studies and General Anthologies, Chapter 2, Bibliography, and Chapter 3, Reference Books—Literature.

BROWN, CHARLES BROCKDEN. 1771–1810.

Charles Brockden Brown, our first full-time man of letters, happens also to be our first important novelist. He is noted chiefly for having written four Gothic novels which were not only comparatively well written but were forerunners of what later developed into one of our most significant traditions, the kind of psychological–moral fiction written by Hawthorne, Poe, Henry James, Faulkner, and Flannery O'Connor. Brown was also admired and imitated by English writers such as Mary and Percy Shelley and Thomas Love Peacock. Brown had his faults, some of which were indigenous to the Gothic tradition which he inherited, but he had a considerable talent for invention and novelistic construction and also for realistic observation and what he called "moral painting." Within the space of four years he published six novels: "Wieland" (1798), his best known and most frequently studied book, was based on an actual murder case in New York, but Brown was less interested in the sensational aspects than in the moral and psychological implications of the case. "Ormond" (1798) deals with an attempted seduction but is ultimately about the struggle of conflicting values. "Arthur Mervyn" (1799), the longest of Brown's books, is flawed by its didacticism and humorlessness but is of interest because of its realistic account of the yellow fever plague that occurred in Philadelphia in 1773. "Edgar Huntly" (1801), though in part incredible, is otherwise skillfully constructed and of significant moral complexity. Before he abandoned novel writing for a career in journalism in 1804, Brown published two more novels, both in 1801: "Clara Howard" (o. p.) and "Jane Talbot," two minor productions.

Although Brown's work has received nothing like the kind of popular or critical attention accorded other writers of no more talent, scholarly interest has quickened somewhat over the past 20 years. All of his fiction is back in print and even his early "dialogue" on women's rights, "Alcuin" (1798), which had not been published in its entirety during Brown's lifetime, has been edited and published. Also, two fragments of unfinished fictional works are now edited and in print ("Sketches of a History of Carsol" and "The Memoirs of Carvin the Biloquist") and there has been in addition to the books devoted exclusively to Brown, rather lengthy considerations of his work in critical histories of American fiction.

THE NOVELS OF CHARLES BROCKDEN BROWN. 6 vols. 1887. *Burt Franklin* 1968 set $75.00

WIELAND, or The Transformation. c. 1798. *Doubleday* Anchor Bks. 1969 pap. $1.95; (with "The Memoirs of Carwin the Biloquist") ed. by Fred Lewis Pattee *Harcourt* 1926 Harbinger Bks. pap. $2.45

ALCUIN: A Dialogue. 1798. Ed. with introd. by Lee R. Edwards. A Gehenna Press facsimile *Grossman* 1971 $7.95 pap. $2.75

ARTHUR MERVYN. 1799. Ed. with introd. by Warner Berthoff *Holt* 1962 Rinehart Eds. 1966 $4.50 pap. $3.00; *Peter Smith* $5.00

ORMOND. 1799. Ed. by Ernest Marchand. Hafner Library of Classics Ser. *Hafner* 1962
pap. $3.35

EDGAR HUNTLEY, or Memoirs of a Sleepwalker. 3 vols. 1799. *AMS Press* $21.50; ed.
by David Stineback *College & Univ. Press* 1973 $6.50 pap. $2.95

JANE TALBOT. 1801. *Saifer* $6.00

SKETCHES OF A HISTORY OF CARSOL. 1815. Utopian Fiction Ser. *McGrath Pub. Co.*
1972 $16.00

Books about Brown

The Life of Charles Brockden Brown. By William Dunlap 1815. *Somerset Pub.* $29.50; *Richard West*
1973 $29.45. The original subtitle to this work was: "together with Selections from the Rarest of His
Printed Works, from His Original Letters and from His Manuscripts Before Unpublished." The work
was begun by a friend of Brown, Paul Allen, and completed by Dunlap. There are inaccuracies but it is
the chief source for information about Brown, printing letters and fragments of his works otherwise not
available.
Brockden Brown and the Rights of Women. Ed. by David L. Clark. 1912. *Folcroft* $6.50. Concerned with
Brown as a proponent of radical ideas about the rights of women.
Charles Brockden Brown: A Study of Early American Fiction. By Martin S. Vilas. 1904. *Folcroft* $8.50.
This is one of the first studies that attempts historical criticism of Brown's work.
Charles Brockden Brown, American Gothic Novelist. By Harry R. Warfel. 1949. *Octagon* 1973 $11.00.
A reliable and useful biography with criticism of the novels.
Charles Brockden Brown. By Donald A. Ringe. U.S. Authors Ser. *Twayne* 1966 $5.50; *College & Univ.
Press* pap. $2.45. A very useful study.

IRVING, WASHINGTON. 1783–1859.

Irving is the earliest American man of letters whose works are still popularly read. He was "the first native
writer to receive critical and popular approval in this country and in Europe." His works are diverse: essays,
biographies, histories, short stories and sketches. His imaginative works are the short stories. Irving may be
said to have assisted in the development of the short story. The short stories consist of three volumes: "The
Sketch Book of Geoffrey Crayon" containing his best works; "Rip Van Winkle" and "The Legend of Sleepy
Hollow"; "Bracebridge Hall, or The Humorist: A Medley"; and "Tales of a Traveler," containing stories of
action and adventure.

For two years Irving was attaché of our legation in Spain, and later served as our Minister to Spain. His
interest in Spanish history inspired four works: "The Life and Voyages of Columbus" and its sequel "The
Voyages and Discoveries of the Companions of Columbus" (1831, o.p.), "A Chronicle of the Conquest of
Grenada" (1829. *AMS Press* 2 vols. $18.50; *Scholarly Press* 2 vols. $18.50); and "The Alhambra."

During a brief stay in the U.S., Irving, as a member of a government commission, made a long trip into the
West. In 1832, after a three-month tour of the Southwest, he wrote "The Western Journals" (o.p.). "A Tour
on the Prairies" was published in 1835. "Astoria" (1836 rev. ed. 1849) was written from records furnished
by John Jacob Astor and was done on commission from the Astor family. The sequel to "Astoria" was "The
Adventures of Captain Bonneville U.S.A. in the Rocky Mountains and the Far West" (1837 *Binfords* 1954
$8.00; ed. with an introd. by E. W. Todd *Univ. of Oklahoma Press* 1961 $9.95).

As a biographer Irving won but little distinction. He wrote lives of Goldsmith, of Mahomet and his successors, and of George Washington, for whom he had been named.

There was a three-day celebration in Madrid in November 1959, commemorating the centenary of his
death. The Mayor of Granada unveiled a plaque to the American whose "Tales of the Alhambra" have frequently been reprinted in both Spanish and English editions and who had devoted "more than 1,000,000
words to Spain, her people and her culture."

THE COMPLETE WORKS OF WASHINGTON IRVING. Under the general editorship of
Henry A. Pochmann. *Univ. of Wisconsin Press.* A projected 5-vol. work, of which 3
are available. Vol. I Journals and Notebooks, 1803–1806. ed. by Nathalia Wright
(1969) $20.00 Vol. 3 Journals and Notebooks, 1819–1827 ed. by Walter A. Reichert
(1970) $20.00 (vol. unnumbered) Mahomet and His Successors ed. by Henry A.
Pochmann and E. N. Feltskog (1970) $20.00

WORKS. The Hudson ed. 27 vols. 1857–1890. *AMS Press* each $20.00 set $495.00; 14
vols. 1850–1851 *Scholarly Press* each $21.50 set $290.00

REPRESENTATIVE SELECTIONS. Ed. by Henry A. Pochmann. 1934. *Scholarly Press* 1971 $19.50

SELECTED PROSE. Ed. by Stanley T. Williams. *Holt* (Rinehart) $9.50 pap. $2.00

THE BOLD DRAGOON AND OTHER GHOSTLY TALES. Ed. by Anne Carroll Moore; ill. by James Daugherty. *Knopf* 1930 lib. bdg. $5.39

THE SKETCH BOOK OF GEOFFREY CRAYON. 1819–1820. *Dutton* Everyman's $3.50; *New Am. Lib.* 1961 pap. $.95

THE LEGEND OF SLEEPY HOLLOW AND OTHER SELECTIONS FROM WASHINGTON IRVING. Ed. and introd. by Austin McC. Fox. *Washington Square* (orig.) 1962 pap. $.60

RIP VAN WINKLE, THE LEGEND OF SLEEPY HOLLOW AND OTHER TALES. *Grosset* $1.25

RIP VAN WINKLE. *Lippincott* 1967 $5.50; *Franklin Watts* 1967 $3.95

RIP VAN WINKLE AND THE LEGEND OF SLEEPY HOLLOW. *McKay* $1.50; *Macmillan* 1963 $3.95; *Franklin Watts* lg.-type ed. $7.95

THE LEGEND OF SLEEPY HOLLOW. *Assoc. Booksellers* Airmont Bks. 1964 pap. $.60; *Franklin Watts* 1966 $3.75

BRACEBRIDGE HALL, or The Humorists. 1822 1902 *AMS Press* $18.00; *Scholarly Press* $24.50

CHRISTMAS AT BRACEBRIDGE HALL. *McKay* $2.50

TALES OF A TRAVELLER. By Geoffrey Crayon. 1824. *Bks. for Libraries* $11.00

THE ALHAMBRA. 1832 *Avon Bks.* 1965 pap. $.60; *Macmillan* lib. bdg. $3.94

A TOUR ON THE PRAIRIES. Ed. by John Francis McDermott. *Univ. of Oklahoma Press* Western Frontier Lib. 1956 $2.95; fwd. by James Playstead Wood *Pantheon* 1967 $4.95

JOURNALS. 1919. *Haskell* 1970 3 vols. $39.95

THE JOURNAL OF WASHINGTON IRVING. Ed. by Stanley T. Williams. 1931. *Shoe String* 1968 $7.50

MR. IRVING'S NOTES AND JOURNAL OF TRAVEL IN EUROPE, 1804–1805. 1921. *Scholarly Press* 3 vols. 1972 $59.95

Books about Irving

The Life and Letters of Washington Irving. By Pierre Monroe Irving. 1894. By Irving's nephew and literary assistant. *Gale Research Co.* 1968 4 vols. set $31.20.

The World of Washington Irving. By Van Wyck Brooks. Written "with warmth and lavishness of detail." Vol. I of Brooks' "Makers and Finders." *Dutton* 1944 Everyman's 1950 $3.50

Washington Irving: Moderation Displayed. By Edward Wagenknecht. *Oxford* 1962 $6.50.
The author draws on manuscript materials and from unpublished dissertations as well as recent literature on Irving. He captures something of Irving's own urbanity in delineating his mastery of "a middle region which he surveyed and described with a winning, companionable charm."

Washington Irving. By Lewis Leary. *Univ. of Minnesota Press* Pamphlets on American Writers 1963 pap. $.95

Washington Irving: An American Study, 1802–1832. By W. L. Hedges. *Johns Hopkins Univ. Press* 1965 $9.00

Shows Irving as "a strange but appealing blend—romantically antiquarian, both genteel and rambunctious, garnering in Germanic and Gothic elements with the conventions of the Spectator. Irving deals with habits and customs in an unsure, not-quite-jelled culture"—(*LJ*).

COOPER, JAMES FENIMORE. 1789–1851.

Cooper is best known for his novels of the American Indian and backwoodsman and of the sea. "The Spy," a story of the American Revolution, was the first American novel to win popularity in foreign countries. Cooper was obliged to publish it first at his own expense, as no American publisher would accept it. Its unexpected success turned him decisively to authorship. The Leatherstocking Tales are a series of five stories which Cooper wrote backwards, as it were, beginning with the old age and death of his hero, and later returning to Leatherstocking's earlier life. Natty Bumpo, known variously as Leatherstocking, Deerslayer, Pathfinder, Hawkeye and *la longue Carabine*, is the noble, fearless frontier scout. The Leatherstocking Tales, when measured against the more skillfully written and the psychologically more subtle novels of later American writers, are crude and melodramatic, but historically they are of great importance. In these tales Cooper managed to create an authentic American myth about pioneer life, including themes and character types still to be found in writers like Ernest Hemingway.

Cooper originated the tale of ships and the sea. Although Smollet's (*q. v.*) "Roderick Random" and "Peregrine Pickle" are known as the first sea tales, they are really stories of sailors. Cooper had served for four years as a midshipman in the United States Navy, and had the knowledge of a professional seaman. "The Pilot" was inspired by "The Pirate" of Sir Walter Scott (*q. v.*). Cooper regarded Scott's novel as inaccurate in seamanship, and he wrote "The Pilot" as a challenge to Scott.

Cooper's public controversies and libel suits were lifelong. "Homeward Bound" and "Home as Found" were both violent attacks on his country and countrymen. "The American Democrat, or Hints on Social and Civic Relations of the United States of America" (1838, *Funk & Wagnalls* $5.95 Minerva Bks. pap. $2.50; *Peter Smith* $3.50) was one of Cooper's political efforts to "bring Americans to self-knowledge and to correct the excesses of the Jacksonian era."

His great productivity included 33 substantial fictional works, "three books of explicit social and political commentary, five travel works, a monumental history of the United States Navy (1839), a book of naval biographies, and an impressive quantity of miscellaneous writings, much of it anonymous and some of it still unknown to scholars." There was no complete edition of his works and no definitive biography. His grandson and namesake edited the miscellaneous selections from the family papers, "The Correspondence of James Fenimore Cooper," which has been reprinted; many titles long out of print are again available in single volumes. A 10-volume edition of his works has also been reprinted.

Works. 10 vols. 1891–93. *Greenwood* $265.00

Precaution. 1820. *AMS Press* 2 vols. $12.50; *Scholarly Press* $14.50

The Spy. 1821. *Dodd* Gt. Ill. Class. 1949 $5.50; *Hafner* Lib. of Class. $3.95; *Oxford* pap. 1968 $5.00; *Popular Lib.* pap. $.95

Leatherstocking Tales:

The Pioneers. 1823. *Assoc. Booksellers* Airmont Bks. 1964 pap. $.75; ed. by Leon Howard *Holt* (Rinehart) pap. $2.25; *Lancer Bks.* pap. $.75; *New Am. Lib.* Signet pap. $.75

The Last of the Mohicans. 1826. *Assoc. Booksellers* Airmont Bks. pap. $.60; *Collins* New Class. $3.00 lea. $5.00; *Dodd* Gt. Ill. Class. 1951 $5.50; *Dutton* Everyman's $3.50 pap. $2.00; *Houghton* Riv. Eds. pap. $1.95; *Lancer Bks.* pap. $.75; *Nelson* Class. pap. $1.75; *New Am. Lib.* Signet pap. $.75; ill. by Wyeth *Scribner* Ill. Class. 1919 $6.00 new ed. $3.00; *Washington Square* pap. $.60 Reader's Enrichment Ser. pap. $.75; *Franklin Watts* lg.-type ed. Keith Jennison Bks. $7.95; ill. by James Daugherty *World Pub.* Rainbow Class. 1957 $3.95

The Prairie. 1827. *Assoc. Booksellers* Airmont Bks. 1964. pap. $.60; *Dodd* Gt. Ill. Class. $5.50; ed. by H. N. Smith *Holt* (Rinehart) 1950 pap. $2.25; *Lancer Bks.* pap. $.75; *New Am. Lib.* 1964 Signet pap. $.95

The Pathfinder, or The Inland Sea. 1840. Introd. by N. H. Pearson *Assoc. Booksellers* Airmont Bks. 1964 pap. $.75; *Dutton* Everyman's $3.50; *Dodd* Gt. Ill. Class. 1954 $5.95; *New Am. Lib.* Signet pap. $.75

THE DEERSLAYER. 1841. *Assoc. Booksellers* Airmont Bks. pap. 1964 $.75; *Dodd* Gt. Ill. Class. $5.50; ed. by Frank L. Beals *Naylor* $3.95; *New Am. Lib.* Signet pap. $.75; *Scribner* Ill. Class. 1925 $6.00; *Washington Square* 1961 pap. $.60 Reader's Enrichment Ser. pap. $.95

NOTIONS OF THE AMERICANS PICKED UP BY A TRAVELLING BACHELOR. 1828. Am. Class. Ser. *Ungar* 2 vols. $12.50

RED ROVER. 1828. Ed. by W. S. Walker. 1963. *Peter Smith* $4.25

WEPT OF WISH-TON-WISH. 1829. *AMS Press* 2 vols. in 1. $18.00; *Scholarly Press* $19.50; (with title "The Borderers, or Wept of Wish-Ton-Wish") rev., corrected, with new pref., notes, etc., by the author. 1833. *AMS Press* $15.50

THE BRAVO. 1831. Ed. by D. A. Ringe. *College & Univ. Press* 1963 $8.50 pap. $3.95

THE WATER WITCH. 1831 1896 *AMS Press* $14.50; *Scholarly Press* $14.50

HOME AS FOUND. 1838. *Putnam* Capricorn Bks. 1961 pap. $2.45

AFLOAT AND ASHORE. 1844. *Dodd* Gt. Ill. Class. 1956 $5.95

SATANSTOE, or The Littlepage Manuscripts. 1845. *Univ. of Nebraska Press* 1962 Bison Bks. pap. $2.45; *Peter Smith* $4.00

THE CHAINBEARER, or The Littlepage Manuscripts. 1845. A sequel to "Satanstoe." *AMS Press* 2 vols. $12.50; *Scholarly Press* $24.50

THE CRATER, or Vulcan's Peak. 1847. Facsimile ed. by Thomas Philbrick *Harvard Univ. Press* 1962 $10.00

SEA LIONS. 1849. Ed. by W. S. Walker *Univ. of Nebraska Press* 1965 pap. $2.45; *Peter Smith* $4.00

WAYS OF THE HOUR. 1850. *Gregg* 1969 $13.50

THE LETTERS AND JOURNALS OF JAMES FENIMORE COOPER. Ed. by James F. Beard. *Harvard Univ. Press* Belknap Press Vols. I and 2 (1960) 2 vols. set $25.00 Vols. 3 and 4 (1965) 2 vols. set $25.00 Vols. 5 and 6 (1968) 2 vols. set $27.50

Journals for the years 1800–51; Vol. 6 includes index and some earlier letters recently discovered. The many letters—some 60 percent of which have not been previously published—reflect the editor's impressive research. "A vivid insight into the . . . dilemma of the artist in relation to his society"—(*N.Y. Herald Tribune*).

CORRESPONDENCE. 1922. *Bks. for Libraries* 2 vols. $32.50; *Haskell* 2 vols. $29.95. Among his titles now o.p. in separate volumes: Lionel Lincoln, 1825; The Heidenmauer, 1832; The Headsman, 1833; The Monikins, 1835; Homeward Bound, 1838; Mercedes of Castille, 1840; The Two Admirals, 1842; Wing and Wing, 1842; Wyandote, 1843; Miles Wallingford, 1844; The Redskins, 1846; Jack Tier, 1848; The Oak Openings, 1848.

Books about Cooper

James Fenimore Cooper and the Development of American Sea Fiction. By Thomas L. Philbrick. *Harvard Univ. Press* 1962 $8.50. A specialized historical and critical work with Cooper its main interest; Freneau, Smollett and Poe are among others discussed.
James Fenimore Cooper. By Donald A. Ringe. *College & Univ. Press* 1962 pap. $2.45; U.S. Author Ser. *Twayne* 1962 $4.95
Fenimore Cooper: Critic of His Times. By Robert E. Spiller. *Russell & Russell* 1963 $9.00
James Fenimore Cooper. By Robert E. Spiller *Univ. of Minnesota Press* 1965 pap. $1.25.
Traces the evolution of Cooper from social observer to social critic, and his steadily growing maturity

as a novelist. The main events of his life and brief summaries of his major works are included. A readable pamphlet in the useful American Writers series. Bibliography.

Cooper's Americans. By Kay Seymour House. *Ohio State Univ. Press* 1965 $6.25

"Though a special study [of two main types from over 400 American characters in Cooper's fiction], it covers in detail the body of Cooper's work and so is a book for many students and most libraries"—(*Choice*).

Leatherstocking and the Critics. By Warren S. Walker. *Scott, Foresman* 1965 $3.75. A useful collection of essays on the Leatherstocking series.

HAWTHORNE, NATHANIEL. 1804–1864.

Compared with a more prolific writer like Cooper, Hawthorne's fictional output seems relatively small (four novels or, as he preferred to call them, "romances," three collections of short fiction for mature readers as well as several children's books), but in quality Hawthorne has no rival in the 19th century except Melville. His stories, such as "Young Goodman Brown," "Rappaccini's Daughter," "My Kinsman, Major Molineaux," were remarkable achievements and Hawthorne has been credited with making a major contribution to the developing art of the American short story. His greatest novel doubtless is "The Scarlet Letter," a symbolic work of subtle moral and psychological complexity. "The House of the Seven Gables" deals mainly with the destructive effects of the past. "The Blithedale Romance" is a skeptical study of various projects of social reform, including "equal rights for women" and socialism. "The Marble Faun" is a modern retelling of the fall of man, dealing with the ambiguous effects of sin. Hawthorne was well acquainted with other New England writers, notably Emerson and Thoreau, and was a friend and mentor of the younger Herman Melville (*q. v.*) on whose great work "Moby Dick" Hawthorne exerted an important influence. At his death Hawthorne left three unfinished romances and voluminous private journals which have since been edited and published. The definitive edition of Hawthorne's works began to appear in 1964 and by 1972 all eight novels had appeared, including his apprentice work "Fanshawe," his collection of essays about England, "Our Old Home," and his children's books, "A Wonder Book" and "Tanglewood Tales," as well as "True Stories from History and Biography," and his "American Notebooks."

THE CENTENARY EDITION OF THE WORKS OF NATHANIEL HAWTHORNE. Ed. by William Charvat, Roy Harvey Pearce and Claude M. Simpson; Fredson Bowers, textual ed. The definitive edition. *Ohio State Univ. Press* 1964 8 vols. Vol. I The Scarlet Letter (1962) $8.00 Vol. 2 The House of the Seven Gables (1963) $10.00 Vol. 3 The Blithedale Romance and Fanshawe (1963) $10.00 Vol. 4 The Marble Faun (1967) $12.00 Vol. 5 Our Old Home (1970) $12.50 Vol. 6 True Stories from History and Biography (1972) $12.50 Vol. 7 A Wonder Book and Tanglewood Tales (1970) $16.00 Vol. 8 ed. by Claude M. Simpson The American Notebooks (1972) $17.50 pap. $8.50

THE COMPLETE NOVELS AND SELECTED TALES. *Modern Library* Giants 1937 $4.95

THE COMPLETE SHORT STORIES OF NATHANIEL HAWTHORNE. *Doubleday* 1959 $5.95

THE COMPLETE GREEK STORIES OF NATHANIEL HAWTHORNE. *Franklin Watts* 1963 $5.95

THE DOLLIVER ROMANCE, FANSHAWE, AND SEPTIMIUS FELTON. With an appendix containing "The Ancestral Footstep." 1883 *Bks. for Libraries* $14.50. Hawthorne's first novel reprinted with his unfinished romances.

TALES, SKETCHES AND OTHER PAPERS. 1883. *Bks. for Libraries* $17.50

REPRESENTATIVE SELECTIONS. 1934. *Scholarly Press* 1971 $19.50

THE BEST KNOWN WORKS: The Scarlet Letter; The House of the Seven Gables; The Best of Twice-Told Tales. 1941. *Bks. for Libraries* $13.75

HAWTHORNE AS EDITOR: Selections from his Writings in the American Magazine of Useful and Entertaining Knowledge. Comp. by Arlin Turner. 1941. *Folcroft* lib. bdg. $20.00; *Kennikat* $11.00

GREAT SHORT WORKS. *Harper* Perenn. Lib. pap. $.95

SHORT STORIES. Ed. with introd. by Newton Arvin *Knopf* 1946 1955 $5.95; ed. by N. Arvin *Random* Vintage Bks. pap. $1.95

THE PORTABLE HAWTHORNE: The Scarlet Letter, selections from other novels, stories, notebooks, letters. Ed. by Malcolm Cowley. *Viking* 1948 $6.50 pap. $2.95

SELECTED TALES AND SKETCHES. Ed. by Hyatt H. Waggoner. *Holt* (Rinehart) 1950 pap. $2.25

THE BEST OF HAWTHORNE. Ed. with introd. by Mark Van Doren. *Ronald* 1951 $4.75. An excellent anthology.

THE GREAT STONE FACE AND OTHER TALES OF THE WHITE MOUNTAINS. *Houghton* $4.95

THE SCARLET LETTER AND OTHER TALES OF THE PURITANS. Ed. by Harry Levin. *Houghton* Riv. Eds. 1962 pap. $1.65

TALES OF HIS NATIVE LAND. Ed. by Neal F. Doubleday. *Heath* 1962 pap. $1.95

THE CELESTIAL RAILROAD AND OTHER STORIES. *New Am. Lib.* Signet 1963 pap. $.75.Afterword by R. P. Blackmur. 19 short stories which explore "the daydreams which edge toward nightmare."

THE GREAT STONE FACE AND OTHER STORIES. *Franklin Watts* 1967 $3.75

SELECTED SHORT STORIES. Ed. by Alfred Kazin. *Fawcett* Premier Bks. pap. $.95

THE SCARLET LETTER AND SELECTED TALES. Ed. by Thomas E. Connolly. *Penguin* pap. 1970 $1.95

THE SCARLET LETTER AND RELATED WRITINGS. Ed. by H. Bruce Franklin. *Lippincott* pap. 1972 $2.50

TWICE-TOLD TALES AND OTHER SHORT STORIES. Introd. by Q. Anderson. *Washington Square Press* 1960 pap. $.95

TWICE-TOLD TALES. 1837. 2nd ed. 1842; 3rd ed. 1851. *Assoc. Booksellers* Airmont Bks. pap. $.60; *Dutton* Everyman's $3.50

THE SCARLET LETTER. 1850. Ed. by Sculley Bradley and others. *Norton* Critical Eds. lib. bdg. $5.50 pap. $1.95. Follows text of first (1850) ed. Includes Hawthorne's "The Custom House," excerpts from his notebooks and journals, and 19 major criticisms by others.

THE SCARLET LETTER. 1850. (with Henry James' "Life of Hawthorne") ed. by B. Rajan and A. G. George *Asia Pub. House* $5.00; ed. by L. Ziff *Bobbs* Liberal Arts pap. $1.25; ed. by H. Waggoner and G. Monteiro *Chandler Pub.* pap. $1.95; *Dodd* Gt. Ill. Class. 1948 $5.00; (and "Young Goodman Brown") *Doubleday* Anchor Bks. pap. $1.45; *Peter Smith* $3.50; *Dutton* Everyman's $3.50; ed. by Van A. Bradley *Fleet* $6.50; ed. by Kenneth S. Lynn *Harcourt* pap. $2.95; introd. by Newton Arvin *Harper* Mod. Class. $2.00 Harper Class. pap. $.75; ed. by Gordon Roper *Hendricks House* 1949 $3.00; (in "Four Great American Novels" ed. by R. W. Short) *Holt* 1946 $7.25 ed. by Austin Warren (Rinehart) 1947 pap. $2.00; ed. by Harry Levin *Houghton* Riv. Lib. $4.95 Riv. Eds. pap. $1.60; *Macmillan* Collier Bks. pap. $.65;

ed. by Edwin Cady *Charles E. Merrill* pap. $.95; introd. by Douglas Grant *Oxford* 1956 pap. $5.00; *Franklin Watts* lg.-type ed. Keith Jennison Bks. $7.95 ultratype ed. $4.50

Other paperback editions are available from Assoc. Booksellers Airmont Bks., Amsco School Publications, Bantam, Coshad Apollo Bks. Dell, Lancer, Modern Lib., New Am. Lib., Scholastic Bk. Services, Washington Square, $.60–$1.80.

THE HOUSE OF THE SEVEN GABLES. 1851. *Dodd* Gt. Ill. Class. 1950 $5.50; ed. by P. Young *Holt* (Rinehart) 1957 1971 pap. $2.00; ed. by Hyatt H. Waggoner *Houghton* 1952 Riv. Bkshelf $4.25 Riv Eds. pap. $1.50; *Macmillan* Collier Bks. pap. 1962 $.65; ed. by Harry Levin *Charles E. Merrill* pap. $1.25; ed. by Seymour L. Gross *Norton* Critical Eds. 1967 $6.00 pap. $2.45; *Franklin Watts* $4.50 lg.-type ed. Keith Jennison Bks. $8.95

Other paperback editions are available from Assoc. Booksellers Airmont Bks., Amsco School Publications, Cambridge Bk. Company, Dell, New Am. Lib., Scholastic Bk. Services, Washington Square, $.60–$1.15.

A WONDER BOOK FOR BOYS AND GIRLS. 1851. *Assoc. Booksellers* Airmont Bks. 1964 pap. $.60; (and "Tanglewood Tales") ill. by Maxwell Parrish *Dodd* 1934 1949 $4.95; ills. by S. Van Abbé *Dutton* Children's Ill. Class. $4.50; *Grosset* $1.25; (and "Tanglewood Tales") *Houghton* Riv. Bkshelf. 1923 $4.95; *Lancer Bks.* pap. $.60

THE BLITHEDALE ROMANCE. 1852. *Dell* pap. $.60; introd. by Arlin Turner *Norton* 1958 pap. $1.65

TANGLEWOOD TALES. 1853. *Assoc. Booksellers* Airmont Bks. pap. $.60; *Collins* $1.95; ill. by S. Van Abbé *Dutton* Children's Ill. Class. new ed. 1952 $4.50; *Grosset* $1.25 lib. bdg. $2.69; (and "A Wonder Book," *see above* under that title for *Dodd* and *Houghton* eds.)

MOSSES FROM AN OLD MANSE. 1854. *Bks. for Libraries* $14.50

THE MARBLE FAUN. 1860. *Assoc. Booksellers* Airmont Bks. pap. $.75; *Dell* pap. $.50; *New Am. Lib.* Signet pap. $.75; *Washington Square* pap. $.45

THE ENGLISH NOTEBOOKS OF NATHANIEL HAWTHORNE. Ed. by Randall Stewart. 1941. *Russell & Russell* 1962 $20.00

HAWTHORNE IN ENGLAND. Ed. by C. Strout. *Cornell Univ. Press* 1965 $6.50 pap. $1.95. Selections from Our Old Home (1863) and The English Note-Books.

THE HEART OF HAWTHORNE'S JOURNALS. Ed. by Newton Arvin. 1929. *Barnes & Noble* 1967 $7.50

Books about Hawthorne

Hawthorne. By Henry James. 1879. Ed. by John Morley. 1887. *AMS Press* $12.50; *Cornell Univ. Press* 1956 1967 pap. $1.45; *Folcroft* repr. of 1879 ed. $4.50; *Gordon Press* $12.95; *St. Martin's* pap. 1968 $1.75. A perceptive estimate of some of Hawthorne's limitations as a writer.

Nathaniel Hawthorne. By Newton Arvin. 1929. *Russell & Russell* 1960 $12.00

Nathaniel Hawthorne. By Mark Van Doren. 1949. *Greenwood* 1973 $12.50

Hawthorne's Fiction: The Light and the Dark. By Richard Harter Fogle. *Univ. of Oklahoma Press* 1952 rev. ed. 1964 $5.50

Hawthorne: A Critical Study. By Hyatt H. Waggoner. *Harvard Univ. Press* Belknap Press 1955 rev. ed. 1963 $8.95

Nathaniel Hawthorne. By Hyatt H. Waggoner. Pamphlets on American Writers. *Univ. of Minnesota Press* 1962 pap. $1.25

A "Scarlet Letter" Handbook. By Seymour L. Gross. *Wadsworth* 1960 pap. $2.95

Nathaniel Hawthorne. By Arlin Turner. American Authors and Critics Ser. 1961. *Holt* 1966 pap. $2.10

Hawthorne's View of the Artist. By Millicent Bell. *State Univ. of New York Press* $6.00 microfiche $6.00

The Sins of the Fathers: Hawthorne's Psychological Themes. By F. Crews. *Oxford* 1966 $7.50 Galaxy Bks. pap. $1.75. A controversial attempt to show Hawthorne's writings as a direct outgrowth of sexual maladjustments.

Hawthorne and Melville in the Berkshires. Melville Annual for 1966. Ed. by Howard P. Vincent. *Kent State Univ. Press* 1967 $8.50. Essays from the Williamstown-Pittsfield Conference, September, 1966, by various hands.

The Pursuit of Form: A Study of Hawthorne and the Romance. By John Caldwell Stubbs. *Univ. of Illinois Press* 1970 $6.95. A study of Hawthorne's possible sources in New England history, theology and earlier romances.

Critics on Hawthorne. Ed. by Thomas J. Rountree. *Univ. of Miami Press* 1971 $3.95. A small collection of early reviews, several "perspectives" on Hawthorne, and several critical essays.

Hawthorne's Early Tales: A Critical Study. By Neal Frank Doubleday. *Duke Univ. Press* 1972 $7.75

HOLMES, OLIVER WENDELL. 1809–1894. *See Chapter 16, Essays and Criticism.*

POE, EDGAR ALLAN. 1809–1849.

Poe was one of the few American writers to achieve international fame: his poetry influenced the French symbolists; his literary criticism, in which he disparaged sentimentality and insisted on the need for objective criteria, anticipated the modern formalist movement. His theory of the short story, as well as his own achievements in that genre, contributed very substantially to the development of the modern short story, in Europe as well as in this country. Poe himself seems to have regarded his talent for fiction writing as of less importance than his poetry and criticism; and though his public preferred his detective stories ("Murders in the Rue Morgue," "Marie Roget," "The Gold Bug"), and other of his analytic tales ("A Descent into the Maelstrom," "The Black Cat" and "The Premature Burial"), his own preference was for works of the imagination ("Ligeia," "The Fall of the House of Usher," "The Masque of the Red Death") which are tales of horror beyond that of the plausible kind found in the analytic stories. The *University of Nebraska Press* has recently published Poe's "Literary Criticism" (ed. by Robert L. Hough 1965 $2.25). His "Letters" (ed. by J. W. Ostrom 1948 *Gordian* 1966 2 vols. $20.00) is a "virtually complete one-volume collection of 333 letters written . . . from 1824, when he was a 15-year-old cadet, to the year of his death in 1849; some proud and high-spirited, some acrimonious, and many more that are deeply pathetic"—(*LJ*). Most of the best criticism on Poe's fiction also deals with his poetry and criticism. However, two very recent works that deal exclusively with his fiction may be cited:

WORKS. Ed. by Edmund C. Stedman and George E. Woodberry. 1895. *Bks. for Libraries* 10 vols. $165.00

COMPLETE WORKS. Ed. by J. A. Harrison. 1902. *AMS Press* 17 vols. each $12.50 set $200.00

THE COMPLETE POEMS AND STORIES, With Selections from His Critical Writings. Introd. and notes by Arthur Hobson Quinn; texts established, with biographical notes, by Edward H. O'Neill; ill. by E. McKnight Kauffer. *Knopf* 1946 2 vols. boxed $17.50

THE COMPLETE TALES AND POEMS. *Modern Library* Giants 1938 $4.95

COMPLETE STORIES AND POEMS. *Doubleday* 1966 $6.95

GREAT SHORT WORKS. Ed. by J. R. Thompson Harper. *Perenn. Lib.* pap. $1.50

THE PORTABLE POE. Stories, poems, articles, letters, opinions. Sel. and ed. with introd. and notes by Philip Van Doren Stern. *Viking* 1945 $5.50 pap. $3.25

POE'S TALES. *Dodd* Gt. Ill. Class. 1952 $5.95

TALES, POEMS AND ESSAYS. *Collins* New Class. 1955 $3.00 lea. $5.00

SELECTED PROSE AND POETRY. Ed. with introd. by W. H. Auden *Holt* (Rinehart) 1950 rev. ed. 1956 pap. $2.50; ed. by T. O. Mabbott *Modern Library* $2.95 pap. $1.25

GREAT TALES AND POEMS. *Washington Square* pap. $.60

SELECTIONS. Ed. with introd. by E. H. Davidson. *Houghton* Riv. Eds. 1956 pap. $2.50

REPRESENTATIVE SELECTIONS. Rev. ed. by Margaret Alterton and Hardin Craig *Hill & Wang* 1962 Am. Century pap. $2.25; *Peter Smith* $5.00

THE GOLD BUG AND OTHER STORIES: The Black Cat, The Pit and the Pendulum. *Branden* 1962 pap. $.85

TALES AND POEMS. *Macmillan* 1963 $4.95

SELECTED STORIES AND POEMS. *Assoc. Booksellers* Airmont Bks. pap. $.60

SHORT STORIES. *Franklin Watts.* 1966 lg.-type ed. Keith Jennison Bks. $7.95

SELECTED TALES. *Oxford* 1967 pap. $5.00

TALES OF MYSTERY AND IMAGINATION. *Dutton* Everyman's $3.50 pap. $1.95; *Oxford* World's Class. $3.00

THE PIT AND THE PENDULUM AND FIVE OTHER TALES. *Franklin Watts* 1967 $3.75

TALES OF TERROR AND FANTASY. *Dutton* Children's Ill. Class. 1972 $4.50

THE NARRATIVE OF ARTHUR GORDON PYM. Novella. 1838. *Godine* (dist. by Book Organization) 1973 $15.00 deluxe ed. $35.00; ed. by Sidney Kaplan *Hill & Wang* Am. Century 1960 pap. $2.25; *Peter Smith* $4.00

THE FALL OF THE HOUSE OF USHER (1839) (AND OTHER TALES.) *New Am. Lib.* Signet pap. $.60; (and Four Other Tales) *Franklin Watts* 1967 $3.75

TALES OF THE GROTESQUE AND ARABESQUE. 1840. *Peter Smith* $4.25

THE PURLOINED LETTER (1844) and THE MURDERS IN THE RUE MORGUE (1843). *Franklin Watts* 1966 $3.75

Books about Poe

"Twentieth Century Interpretations of Poe's Tales: A Collection of Critical Essays" (ed. by William L. Howarth *Prentice-Hall* 1971 $1.45), a useful collection of essays by various critics.
"Poe's Fiction: Romantic Irony in the Gothic Tales" by J. R. Thompson (*Univ. of Wisconsin Press* 1973 $12.50), a perceptive analysis of the tales.

For Poe's poetry, and for biographical and critical works, see Chapter 8, American Poetry: Early Period.

STOWE, HARRIET BEECHER. 1811–1896.

Harriet Beecher was born in Litchfield, Conn., one of nine children of the distinguished Congregational clergyman and stern Calvinist, Lyman Beecher. Of her six brothers, five became clergymen, the most sympathetic perhaps being Henry Ward Beecher. In 1832 she went with her family to Cincinnati. There she taught in her sister's school and began publishing sketches and stories. She married in 1836 the Rev. Calvin E. Stowe, one of her father's assistants at the Lane Theological Seminary, and a strong antislavery advocate. They lived in Cincinnati for 18 years and six of her seven children were born there. The Stowes moved to Brunswick, Me., in 1850, when her husband became a professor at Bowdoin.

The description of the death of Uncle Tom was written first, in one sitting, on scraps of grocer's brown paper after her own supply of paper gave out. She then wrote the earlier chapters. "Uncle Tom's Cabin" was published first (1851–52) in *The National Era*, which paid $300 for the serial rights, and in book form in two volumes by John P. Jewett of Boston. It was an immediate best seller; 10,000 copies sold in less than a week, 300,000 within a year. It was translated into 37 languages. The first American to use a Negro as the hero of a novel, in the South she was hated and her accuracy questioned. Her reply was "A Key to Uncle Tom's Cabin."

Always an industrious writer, she produced almost a novel a year. "Dred, A Tale of Great Dismal Swamp," another tale of the South, sold well. "The Minister's Wooing," "The Pearl of Orr's Island," "Oldtown Folks," "Betty's Bright Idea," and "Agnes of Sorrento" have recently been reprinted. Among her English friends were George Eliot (*q.v.*), the Ruskins and Lady Byron, whom she defended in a controversial article, "The True Story of Lady Byron's Life" (*Atlantic Monthly* 1869). Mrs. Stowe and her husband were both impractical and never free from money worries. She was unspoiled by her literary success and remained "earnest, whimsical, devoted," always somewhat preoccupied and absentminded.

THE WRITINGS OF HARRIET BEECHER STOWE. 1896. *AMS Press* 1967 16 vols. set $350.00

REGIONAL SKETCHES. Ed. by John R. Adams. *College and Univ. Press* 1972 pap. $2.95

UNCLE TOM'S CABIN, or Life among the Lowly. 1852. Ed. by A. T. White *Braziller* 1966 $5.95; *Coward* 1929 lib. bdg. $4.83; *Dodd* Gt. Ill. Class. 1972 $5.50; *Doubleday* Dolphin Bks. pap. $1.45; *Dutton* Everyman's $3.50 pap. $2.25; introd. by J. Larner *Harper* Harper Class. pap. $.85; ed. by Kenneth S. Lynn *Harvard Univ. Press* 1962 $10.00; *Houghton* Riv. Lib. 1929 $6.95; introd. by D. L. Drumond *Macmillan* Collier Bks. pap. $1.50; ed. by Howard Mumford Jones *Charles E. Merrill* pap. $1.15; ed. by John A. Woods *Oxford* 1965 pap. $7.00

Other paperback editions are available from Assoc. Booksellers, New Am. Lib., Washington Square, $.75–$.95

A KEY TO UNCLE TOM'S CABIN. 1853. *Arno Press* pap. $3.95; *Kennikat* 1968 $12.50; *Scholarly Press* $9.50

UNCLE SAM'S EMANCIPATION, EARTHLY CARE A HEAVENLY DISCIPLINE AND OTHER SKETCHES. 1853. *Bks. for Libraries* $8.00; *Scholarly Press* $8.00

DRED, A TALE OF THE GREAT DISMAL SWAMP. 1856. *AMS Press* 2 vols. $18.50; *Scholarly Press* 2 vols. $26.50

THE MINISTER'S WOOING. 1859. *Gregg* 1968 $8.50

THE PEARL OF ORR'S ISLAND. 1862. *Gregg* 1967 $8.50

OLDTOWN FOLKS. 1869. Ed. by H. May with introd. by H. Holyoke. *Harvard Univ. Press* 1966 $15.00; *Scholarly Press* $9.50

"If not a good novel, this is an invaluable and sympathetic rendering of a moral climate, a living evidence of a past life . . . A worthwhile reprint—(*LJ*).

SAM LAWSON'S OLDTOWN FIRESIDE STORIES. 1872. *Gregg* 1967 $8.50

PALMETTO LEAVES. 1873. *Univ. of Florida Press* facsimile ed. 1967 $9.00

BETTY'S BRIGHT IDEA. 1875. *Bks. for Libraries* $7.50

AGNES OF SORRENTO. 1890. *AMS Press* $10.00

Books about Stowe

Harriet Beecher Stowe. By Charles Edward and Lyman Beecher Stowe. 1911. *Gale Research Co.* 1967 $7.80. The authors were Mrs. Stowe's son and grandson.

Crusader in Crinoline: The Life of Harriet Beecher Stowe. By Robert Forrest Wilson. 1941. *Greenwood* $27.25

Harriet: A play. By F. Ryerson and C. C. Clements. 1943. *Baker* $1.25; *French* 1945 $1.25

The Rungless Ladder: Harriet Beecher Stowe and New England Puritanism. By Charles H. Foster. 1954 *Cooper Square* 1970 $7.50. A most useful critical analysis of her novels that is also a study of the decay of Puritanism.

Goodbye to Uncle Tom. By J. C. Furnas. 1956. *Apollo* 1964 pap. $2.95. An absorbing condemnation of "Uncle Tom's Cabin" for its "cheap sagacity about racial traits" which has fostered only stereotypes of the Negro.

Harriet Beecher Stowe: The Known and the Unknown. By Edward Wagenknecht. *Oxford* 1965 $6.50 "discusses the evolution of her novels—on the basis of new source material—paints a vivid picture of his subject . . . and shows how family came first with [her], then her art, and finally her position as a public servant and reformer. Her religious beliefs . . . are outlined briefly"—(*LJ*).

MELVILLE, HERMAN. 1819–1891.

Melville's best known work, "Moby Dick," is "one of the masterpieces not only of American literature but of world literature, yet for a long time it was a book scarcely known by Americans, let alone by the world"—(Lionel Trilling). It is dedicated to Hawthore (*q.v.*), Melville's friend and neighbor in the Berkshires. Its publication lost Melville his literary following established as the writer of the earlier travel books, "for the book was extravagantly disliked, apparently for the very qualities of eloquence and high, free imagination which make it now so greatly admired." It is a story of adventure, a first-rate account of the habits of whales and a superb description of the whaling industry. Melville evidently intended at first to write a realistic narrative, but as the pursuit of the whale continued, the plot took on ever new meanings and the author reconceived it as an epic romance.

The symbolism of "Moby Dick" has been variously interpreted and is too complicated to sum up in brief, but as Darrel Abel has said, "Moby Dick" is "the story of an attempt to search the unsearchable ways of God."

Melville's earlier books, all set in the South Seas, won him a solid reputation with his contemporaries. Descended from prominent Dutch and English families long established in New York, he had gone to sea after the financial failure and death of his father, a prosperous merchant. Melville's first book, "Typee," part memoir and part romance, was a popular success. It told of his hero's adventures after he deserted the whaling ship *Acushnet* (the model for "Moby Dick") when it reached the Marquesas Islands. There he was captured by cannibals, with whom he lived for some weeks in friendship. "Billy Budd," published posthumously, is a brilliant short novel about a young sailor in the Royal Navy at the time of the Nore mutiny of 1797. It was made into an opera by Benjamin Britten in 1950, into a play, and into a memorable film (1962) by Peter Ustinov (*q.v.*). "Benito Cereno," a short novel which Melville included in his "Piazza Tales," was adapted by Robert Lowell as the first play of the trilogy which makes up "The Old Glory" (*Farrar, Straus* 1965 $6.50 Noonday pap. $2.25)

Melville tried at intervals through the years to publish volumes of poetry, and some were printed at his own expense. Much of the poetry is "in some sense autobiographical: reminiscences of people and places; meditations on his reading; even partially concealed details of his personal life—his relation with his mother, for example, and his friendship with Hawthorne." Willard Thorp has said: "Only a few of the poems achieve the artistic unit of rhythmical exactness, propriety of image and melodic beauty which the best poetry possesses." "Collected Poems" (ed. by H. P. Vincent *Hendricks House* 1946 $7.50) and "Selected Poems" (ed. by Robert Penn Warren *Random* 1971 $8.95; *Southern Illinois Univ. Press* 1968 $7.00 pap. $2.45) give the reader a chance to decide for himself.

WRITINGS. Complete, definitive edition of texts as Melville wrote them, each with historical afterword, related documents and editorial notes. *Northwestern Univ. Press* and *Newberry Library* 1967– (See "Typee," "Omoo," "Redburn," "White Jacket," "Pierre" below.)

WORKS. 1924. *Russell & Russell* 16 vols. set $135.00

GREAT SHORT WORKS. Ed. by Warner Berthoff *Harper* Perenn. Class. pap. $.95; *Peter Smith* $3.50

APPLE-TREE TABLE AND OTHER SKETCHES. 1922. *Greenwood* $11.50. Ten prose pieces originally published in periodicals, 1850–1856, collected and published by Princeton Univ. Press.

THE SHORTER NOVELS: Benito Cereno, Billy Budd, Bartleby the Scrivener, and The Encantadas, or Enchanted Isles. Ed. by Raymond Weaver *Fawcett* Premier Bks. 1964 pap. $.60; *Grosset* Univ. Lib. pap. $1.45; *Liveright* Black and Gold Lib. $7.95

SELECTED TALES AND POEMS. Ed. by Richard Chase *Holt* (Rinehart) 1950 pap. $2.50

SELECTED WRITINGS. Complete Short Stories; Typee; Billy Budd, Foretopman. Ed. by Jay Leyda. 1949. *Modern Library* Giants 1951 $4.95

THE PORTABLE MELVILLE. Ed. with introd. by Jay Leyda. Selections of letters linked by biographical comments; "Typee" and "Billy Budd" in full; portions of four other novels; and other writings. *Viking* 1952 $5.50 pap. $3.45

FOUR SHORT NOVELS. *Bantam* pap. $.95

THREE SHORTER NOVELS. *Harper* Mod. Class. 1962 $2.00

FIVE TALES. Ed. with introd. by James H. Pickering. Bartleby the Scrivener; Benito Cereno; I and My Chimney; The Lightning-Rod Man; Billy Budd, Foretopman *Dodd* Gt. Ill. Class. 1967 $5.50

TYPEE: A Peep at Polynesian Life. 1846. *Assoc. Booksellers* Airmont Bks. pap. $.60; ed. by Charles R. Anderson *Bobbs* $7.50 pap. $2.45; ill. by Mead Schaeffer *Dodd* $5.00; (and "Billy Budd") ed. by Milton R. Stern *Dutton* pap. $1.95; *Lancer* pap. $.75; *New Am. Lib.* Signet pap. $.75; *Northwestern Univ. Press* 1967 $13.00 pap. $2.95; ed. by George Woodcock *Penguin* pap. $1.65

OMOO: A Narrative of Adventures in the South Seas. 1847. Sequel to "Typee." Ed. by H. Hayford and W. Blair *Hendricks House* 1966 $7.50; *Northwestern Univ. Press* 1967 $13.00 pap. $2.95

MARDI AND A VOYAGE THITHER. 1849. Ed. by Nathalia Wright *Bobbs* (in prep.); ed. by Tyrus Hillway *College & Univ. Press* $11.00 pap. $4.95; *New Am. Lib.* Signet pap. $.75. A novel in the tradition of "Gulliver's Travels."

REDBURN: His First Voyage. 1849. *Doubleday* Anchor Bks. 1957 pap. $1.95; *Northwestern Univ. Press* 1969 $13.00 pap. $2.95

WHITE-JACKET, or The World in a Man-of-War. 1850. *Holt* (Rinehart) pap. $2.00; *Northwestern Univ. Press* 1970 $15.00 pap. $3.95

MOBY DICK, or The White Whale. 1851. Ed. by Harrison Hayford and Hershel Parker *Norton* Critical Eds. 1967 $8.50 pap. $2.45. A definitive edition, with background and source materials, glossary of nautical and whaling terms and selected critical essays.

MOBY DICK, or The White Whale. 1851. Ed. by Charles Feidelson Jr. *Bobbs* $8.50 Liberal Arts pap. $2.25; *Collins* New Class. $3.00 lea. $5.00; ill. by Mead Schaeffer *Dodd* $5.50; *Dutton* Everyman's $3.50; *Harper* Harper Class. pap. $.95; ed. by Luther Mansfield and Howard P. Vincent *Hendricks House* 1962 $7.50; ed. by Newton Arvin *Holt* (Rinehart) pap. $2.50; ed. by Alfred Kazin *Houghton* Riv. Eds. $2.50; *Macmillan* 1962 $4.95 Collier Bks. pap. $.95; *Modern Library* $2.95 pap. $1.15; *New Am. Lib.* durabind $1.75 Signet pap. $.75; *Oxford* World's Class. $2.50; ed. by Harold Beaver *Penguin* pap. $3.50; *Franklin Watts* lg.-type ed. Keith Jennison Bks. $9.95 ultratype ed. $4.50 Giant ed. $5.50

Other paperback editions are available from Assoc. Bksellers, Amsco School Publications, Bantam, (abridged) Washington Square, $.75–$2.20.

PIERRE, or the Ambiguities. 1852. *Grove* 1957 Evergreen Bks. pap. $2.95; ed. by H. A. Murray *Hendricks House* 1962 $7.50; *New Am. Lib.* pap. $.95; *Northwestern Univ. Press* 1971 $15.00 pap. $3.50

BENITO CERENO (1855): A Text for Guided Research. Ed. with introd. by John R. Runden. *Heath* pap. $2.95. Authoritative text of what the *Reader's Encyclopedia* describes as a "superb" story (included in "The Piazza Tales") with text of its sources and critical and interpretive essays by Yvor Winters, Newton Arvin, Richard Chase and others. Bibliography.

PIAZZA TALES. 1856. Ed. by E. S. Oliver *Hendricks House* 1962 $5.00. Includes "The Piazza," "Bartleby," "Benito Cereno," "The Lightning Rod Man," "The Encantadas" and "The Bell Tower."

THE CONFIDENCE MAN: His Masquerade. 1857. *Assoc. Booksellers* Airmont Bks. pap. $.60; ed. by H. B. Franklin *Bobbs* 1966 $6.50 pap. $2.75; introd. by J. Seelye *Chandler Pub.* facsimile ed. pap. $2.25; ed. by E. S. Foster *Hendricks House* 1954 $7.50; ed. by H. Cohen *Holt* (Rinehart) 1964 pap. $2.00; *Peter Smith* $3.75; *Lancer* pap. $.60; *New Am. Lib.* pap. $.75; ed. by Hershel Parker *Norton* Critical Eds. 1971 $8.50 pap. $2.25

CLAREL: A Poem and Pilgrimage in the Holy Land. 1876. Ed. by W. E. Bezanson *Hendricks House* 1959 $9.50; *Gordon Press* 2 vols. $20.00

BILLY BUDD, SAILOR: An Inside Narrative. Published posthumously, 1924. Ed. by Harrison Hayford and Merton M. Sealts, Jr. *Univ. of Chicago Press* 1962 $8.95 Phoenix Bks. pap. $1.85. The definitive reading text, with extensive notes and commentary, together with a "Genetic Text" enabling the reader to follow the genesis and growth of the story; scholarship of the highest order.

BILLY BUDD. (and "The Encantadas") *Assoc. Booksellers* Airmont Bks. pap. $.50; (with title "Billy Budd, Foretopman") ed. by Hart D. Leavitt *Bantam* pap. $.60; ed. by Milton Stern *Bobbs* 1973 $6.50 pap. $1.95; (and the "Piazza Tales") *Doubleday* Anchor Bks. pap. $1.95; (in "Four Great American Novels") ed. by R. W. Short *Holt* 1946 $6.95; (and Other Stories) ed. by Harold Beaver; includes Bartleby, Cock-a-Coocle Doo, The Encantadas, The Bell Tower, Benito Cereno, John Marr and Daniel Orme *Penguin* 1968 pap. $1.65; (and Other Tales) *New Am. Lib.* Signet pap. $.75; (and "Typee") *Washington Square* pap. $.60 Reader's Enrichment Ser. pap. $.75 (with title "Billy Budd, Foretopman") *Franklin Watts* 1968 $3.75 lg.-type ed. Keith Jennison Bks. $7.95

JOURNAL UP THE STRAITS. Ed. by Raymond Weaver. 1935. *Cooper* $6.00. This is not very accurately edited, but it is the only transcription of Melville's "Journal Up the Straits, Oct. 11, 1856–May 5, 1857."

Books about Melville

Moby-Dick Centennial Essays. Ed. by Tyrus Hillway and Luther S. Mansfield for The Melville Society. *Southern Methodist Univ. Press* 1953 $5.95

Ishmael: The Art of Melville in the Contexts of International Primitivism. By James Baird. *Johns Hopkins Univ. Press* 1956 $14.00

Melville as Lecturer. By Merton M. Sealts, Jr. 1957 *Folcroft* $15.00. For three seasons Melville lectured extensively throughout the eastern United States. This book gives the texts of these lectures, recon-

structed from newspaper accounts, and describes him as a lecturer, his itineraries, fees and critical receptions.

The Long Encounter: Self and Experience in the Writings of Herman Melville. By Merlin Bowen. *Univ.
of Chicago Press* 1960 Phoenix Bks. 1960 pap. $1.95. A reexamination from the viewpoint of his life-
long preoccupation with the riddle of self and its relation to the world of experience; index.

Discussions of Moby-Dick. By Milton R. Stern. *Heath* 1960 pap. $2.25

Herman Melville: A Biography. By Leon Howard. Pamphlets on American Writers *Univ. of Minnesota
Press* 1961 pap. $1.25

Melville's Billy Budd and the Critics. Ed. by William Stafford *Wadsworth* 1961 pap. $2.95

The Example of Melville. By Warner Berthoff. 1963 *Norton* Norton Lib. 1972 pap. $2.25. This is an
overall survey of the writer as a literary craftsman, his use of land and sea-scapes, the vitality of his
imagination.

Melville: A Collection of Critical Essays. Ed. by Richard V. Chase. *Prentice-Hall* 1962 $5.95 pap. $1.95

A Reader's Guide to Herman Melville. By James E. Miller, Jr. *Farrar, Straus* 1962 $6.95 Noonday pap.
$2.45
In this fresh and searching critical study of the fiction and poetry, the author "ranges through all of
Melville's works to reveal his Calvinist bent, his richness and variety of form, and his astonishing com-
plexity"—(*LJ*).

Herman Melville. By A. R. Humphreys. 1962.

The Wake of the Gods: Melville's Mythology. By H. Bruce Franklin. *Stanford Univ. Press* 1963 $7.50
pap. $2.95. A reinterpretation of the major works, demonstrating how mythology determines and de-
fines large parts of their structure and meaning.

Hawthorne and Melville in the Berkshires: Melville Annual for 1966. Ed. by Howard P. Vincent. *Kent
State Univ. Press* 1967 $8.50. Essays from a 1966 conference, by various hands.

The Recognition of Herman Melville. Ed. by Hershel Parker. *Univ. of Michigan Press* 1967 $7.50 Ann
Arbor Bks. 1970 pap. $2.95. A collection of critical essays from 1846 on, in chronological order.

Herman Melville, Mariner and Mystic. By Raymond Weaver. Introd. by Mark Van Doren. 1921. 1960.
Cooper 1961 $6.00. Follows him through his cruises to the South Seas and back again to America for a
background study of his works.

The Meaning of Moby-Dick. By William Gleim. 1938. *Russell & Russell* 1962 $8.00

Herman Melville, The Tragedy of Mind. By William E. Sedgwick. 1944. *Russell & Russell* 1962 $9.00

Herman Melville: A Critical Biography. By Newton Arvin. 1950. *Greenwood* 1973 $13.50. One of the
best and winner of a National Book Award.

Melville: The Ironic Diagram. By John Seelye. *Northwestern Univ. Press* 1970 $7.00. A persuasive argu-
ment that for Melville truth "is a question not an answer, and by abandoning the answers imposed on
existence by his questers, he only the more emphasized the final question. . . ."

Melville and His World. By Gay Wilson Allen. *Viking* 1971 $10.00. A compressed account of Melville's
career with a useful bibliography and chronology and many illustrations of "Melville and his World."

A Critical Guide to Herman Melville: Abstracts of Forty Years of Criticism. By James K. Bowen and
Richard Vanderbeets. *Scott, Foresman* 1971 pap. $1.95. A useful scholarly work.

Twentieth Century Interpretations of "Billy Budd." Ed. by Howard Vincent. *Prentice-Hall* 1971 $4.95
Spectrum Bks. pap. $1.45. A useful collection of essays by various critics.

Clarel: Herman Melville's Spiritual Autobiography. By Vincent Kenny. *Shoe String* 1973 (in prep.)

WALLACE LEWIS (LEW). 1827–1905.

General Wallace was a soldier in the Mexican War and in the Civil War. He began his first novel, "The
Fair God," a tale of Cortez and the conquest of Mexico, at 18 years of age. "Ben Hur, a Tale of the Christ,"
an outstanding best seller, has been called "the only American novel which can be compared with 'Uncle
Tom's Cabin' as a true folk possession." Although sentimentalized in action and language, it is "vivid and
memorable in its authentic detail." "My God! Did I set all this in motion?" the author is said to have remarked when he saw the sets for the Broadway version in 1900. The chariot race, famous on the stage, was
also the high point of the movies of 1927 and 1959—the latter costing $15,000,000. "Ben Hur" was pub-
lished while Wallace was Governor of the Territory of New Mexico. It sold 500,000 copies within eight years
and later over 5,000,000. While Ambassador to Turkey, Wallace wrote his last novel, "The Prince of India"
(1893, o. p.). "Lew Wallace: An Autobiography" is his own account of his life up to 1864 and his wife's
account thereafter.

THE FAIR GOD: A Tale about the Conquest of Mexico. 1873. *Popular Lib.* pap. $.75

BEN HUR. 1880. *Assoc. Booksellers* pap. $.60; *Collins* New Class. $3.00 lea. $5.00;
Dodd Gt. Ill. Class. 1953 $5.50; *Harper* lib. bdg. 1959 $6.99; *Macmillan* Collier
Bks. pap. $.65; *New Am. Lib.* Signet pap. $.95; ed. by Robin Wright *N.Y. Graphic
Soc.* Gerard Art Bks. 1972 $7.95

Lew Wallace: An Autobiography. 1906 *Somerset Pub.* 2 vols. $37.50

STOCKTON, FRANK R. 1834–1902.

Most of Frank Stockton's early stories were for children. His first book for adults, "Rudder Grange" (1879, o. p.), was so popular that he produced two sequels. "The Lady or The Tiger?"—initiating what have been called his "grown-up juveniles"—won instant favor and freed Stockton to write for adults full time. His impossible, whimsical tales take place in an unreal and paradoxical world. One of the most admired fiction writers of his time, he regarded himself primarily as an entertainer. He was a forerunner of O. Henry (*q.v.*) in his use of the trick ending. Many stories long out of print are again available. Little has been written about Stockton but an excellent critical biography, "Frank R. Stockton" by Martin I. J. Griffin (1939) has been reprinted by *Kennikat* for $7.00.

The Novels and Stories of Frank Richard Stockton. 1899–1904. *AMS Press* 23 vols. each $15.00 set $345.00

The Magic Egg and Other Stories. 1908. *Bks. for Libraries* $9.75

Stories of New Jersey. *Rutgers Univ. Press* 1961 $6.00 pap. $2.75

Storyteller's Pack. *Scribner* 1968 $6.95

Ting-a-Ling Tales. 1870. *Scribner* 1955 pap. $3.95. Stories for children.

The Lady or the Tiger? and Other Stories. 1884. *Assoc. Booksellers* Airmont Bks. 1968 pap. $.60

Stockton's Stories. 2 series. 1886. *Bks. for Libraries* 1st ser. $7.00 2nd ser. $8.50

The Casting Away of Mrs. Lecks and Mrs. Aleshine. 1886. (and its sequel, "The Dusantes") ill. by George Richards. 1933. *Hawthorn* $4.95

The Griffin and the Minor Canon. Ill. by Maurice Sendak. *Holt* 1963 lib. bdg. $3.27 pap. $1.65

The Bee-Man of Orn. 1887. For children. *Holt* 1964 $3.50; pap. $1.65

Rudder Grangers Abroad and Other Stories. 1891. *Bks. for Libraries* $7.00

Chosen Few. 1895. *Bks. for Libraries* $7.75

John Gayther's Garden and the Stories Told Therein. 1902 *Bks. for Libraries* $14.50

TWAIN, MARK (pseud. of Samuel Langhorne Clemens). 1835–1910.

Samuel L. Clemens, newspaper reporter, steamboat pilot, prospector, adopted the pen name "Mark Twain" when he began his career as a literary humorist. His pen name is a river term meaning "two fathoms deep." Clifton Fadiman has said of him: "In his own hatred of sham, his special frontier dead-pan humor, his intellectual limitations, his prudery, his independence of judgment, his egalitarianism, his energy, his combination of apparent optimism and underlying uneasiness, Mark Twain was also about as typical a great American as his century produced."

His greatest creative contributions to literature are the characters of Tom Sawyer, Huckleberry Finn and Pudd'nhead Wilson. "Tom Sawyer" (with its deteriorating sequels "Tom Sawyer Abroad" and "Tom Sawyer, Detective") has not the artistic merit of "Huckleberry Finn," his masterpiece. "The Tragedy of Pudd'nhead Wilson" takes third place. "Tom Sawyer" and "Huck Finn" have long passed the million mark in sales; as both are out of copyright, they are published in an increasing number of editions.

William Dean Howells (*q.v.*), a friend of Twain's, encouraged him to write for the *Atlantic Monthly* and later wrote an affectionate memoir, "My Mark Twain" (1910. *Folcroft* $20.00; ed. by Marilyn Baldwin *Louisiana State Univ. Press* 1967 $7.50 pap. $2.25). In 1884 Clemens invested in the Charles L. Webster Company, a publishing house which made enormous profits from its sales of Ulysses S. Grant's (*q.v.*) "Memoirs." In 1894, it went bankrupt. This was only one of the fortunes Clemens made and lost through money-making schemes. His personal life was blighted with the deaths of an infant son and two grown daughters, and the long illness and death of his wife. These contrasts of success, failure and sorrow may account for the contrast in his writings of humor and bitterness. Estimates of his work have shown parallel variations between praise and denigration.

Ever a reformer and protestor, Mark Twain was a "relentless cataloguer of injustice on both the historical and contemporary scene." Later in life he became a bitter satirist. The last writing he did, in 1909, was "such a lugubrious assault on man and God" that his surviving daughter, Clara Clemens Samossoud (d. 1962), refused to let it be published until recently—"Letters from the Earth" (ed. by Bernard De Voto with pref. by Henry Nash Smith *Harper* 1962 $7.95; *Fawcett* Crest pap. $.95). Howard Mumford Jones (*q.v.*) said in his excellent *N.Y. Times* review (Sept. 23, 1962) that "Twain is fascinated by cosmic grandeur, the long lapse of time, and the littleness of the human race. He revels in gigantic concepts. Letters from Earth are from Satan to two archangelic correspondents, and Satan's cosmic assumptions emphasize the pettiness of man and the inconsistencies of God." Jones feels that "the space age is far more moved by the sardonic and disillusioned Mark Twain than it is by Twain the comic lecturer and writer of genial buffoonery." A traveler of many moods, Twain first won fame with "The Innocents Abroad," which combined keen observation with mirth. "Roughing It" is a volume of travel reminiscences. "Life on the Mississippi" records fresh impressions of old scenes. The *N.Y. Times* reported early in 1967 that "A Connecticut Yankee" had been adapted with an anti-Vietnam War twist—the "Yankee" is an American soldier—by an East German playwright, Claus Hammel, and produced successfully in Erfurt, Germany.

Albert Bigelow Paine (1861–1937) was Mark Twain's literary executor and appointed biographer. He began to collect material during Clemens' lifetime, as he knew the humorist intimately and had the advantage of his help and approval. His "Mark Twain, A Biography" (3 vols. 1912 new ed. 1928 2 vols. 1935 Centenary ed.) and the "Short Life of Mark Twain" (1920) are both o.p., but the "Boy's Life of Mark Twain" is still available (*Harper* 1916 $4.95). Paine edited several volumes of Clemens' letters and speeches, now all o.p. In 1947, the trustees of the Mark Twain estate appointed the late Dixon Wecter, literary editor, to succeed Bernard De Voto, who retired after eight years as editor. Mark Twain's daughter Clara released more than a hundred letters written by her father to her mother. These were excellently edited with a biographical commentary by Dixon Wecter as "The Love Letters of Mark Twain" (1949 o.p.). His "Sam Clemens of Hannibal" (*Houghton* 1952 $5.50 Sentry Eds. pap. $1.85) was the first volume of what promised to be the definitive biography. Written with "sympathy, accuracy, and imaginative insight," it ends with Clemens' departure from Hannibal in 1853. Wecter was working on a second volume at the time of his death. In 1953 Henry Nash Smith succeeded him as literary executor.

Among other volumes of Clemens' critical writings are: "Life As I Find It: Sketches and Articles" (ed. by Charles Neider *Doubleday* 1961 $4.95); "1601; or, Conversation at the Social Fireside" (*Wehman* $1.95), which reveals him as "the gusty Rabelaisian" and contains an annotated bibliography of 44 known printings; "Mark Twain on the Damned Human Race" (ed. by Janet Smith, pref. by Maxwell Geismar *Hill & Wang* 1962 $4.95 Am. Century pap. $2.25), a useful anthology of 40 selections, which raises rather than lowers one's estimation of the human race; and, "The Complete Essays of Mark Twain" (ed. with introd. by Charles Neider *Doubleday* 1963 $7.50), which contains 68 essays arranged by date of publication—which is not necessarily the date of composition. (The word "Complete" in the last title is somewhat misleading, as some of the essays have been included in Mr. Neider's previous collections of humorous sketches and short stories.)

Mark Twain is the first of a number of American writers whose complete works are being edited and published in definitive scholarly editions, including discarded chapters and scenes from earlier works as well as items left unfinished (and sometimes in multiple versions) at Twain's death and later found among his papers. So far four volumes have appeared: "Fables of Man," "Correspondence with Henry Huttleston Rogers," "Mark Twain's Hannibal, Huck and Tom," "What is Man? and Other Philosophical Writings." Also, many very minor works long out of print are now being reissued by reprint presses, as, for instance, "The Stolen White Elephant and Others," first published in 1882, and "King Leopold's Soliloquy" (1905), "Following the Equator" (1897), and "The American Claimant" (1897).

WRITINGS. 1869–1909. *Scholarly Press* 25 vols. each $15.00–$23.00 set $245.00

WORKS. Harper 12 vols. $3.95–$6.95; pap. ed. available for some titles, $.60–$.95

See publisher's catalog for individual titles of uniform trade editions.

MARK TWAIN'S LIBRARY OF HUMOR. Ed. by William Dean Howells. 1888. *Somerset Pub.* $19.50. A volume of Twain's short humorous pieces selected by his friend.

THE CURIOUS REPUBLIC OF GONDOUR AND OTHER WHIMSICAL SKETCHES. 1919. *Folcroft* $15.00. Sketches Twain wrote for the *Galaxy*, 1870–71, and the *Buffalo Express*.

THE ADVENTURES OF THOMAS JEFFERSON SNODGRASS. 1928. *Folcroft* lib. bdg. $15.00. Ten humorous letters first published in 1861 in the New Orleans *Daily Crescent.*

THE FAMILY MARK TWAIN. 1935. *Harper* 1972 $12.50. Contains many of Twain's most popular writings, including "Life on the Mississippi," "The Adventures of Tom Sawyer," "The Adventures of Huckleberry Finn."

THE COMPLETE SHORT STORIES. *Bantam* pap. $1.25; ed. by Charles Neider *Doubleday* 1957 $6.50

SELECTED SHORTER WRITINGS. Ed. by Walter Blair. *Houghton* Riv. Eds. pap. $1.55

THE ART, HUMOR AND HUMANITY OF MARK TWAIN. Ed. by Minnie Brashear and Robert M. Rodney. *Univ. of Oklahoma Press* 1959 $7.95. An anthology with commentary and notes.

THE COMPLETE HUMOROUS SKETCHES AND TALES. Ed. by Charles Neider. *Doubleday* 1961 $6.95. Over 100 pieces arranged chronologically from 1863.

THE PORTABLE MARK TWAIN: Huckleberry Finn, The Mysterious Stranger, essays, stories, letters. Ed. by Bernard De Voto. *Viking* 1964 $5.50 pap. $3.50

SATIRES AND BURLESQUES. Ed. with introd. by F. R. Rogers. *Univ. of California Press* 1966 $12.50. MLA-approved text of some minor works.

WHICH WAS THE DREAM? AND OTHER SYMBOLIC WRITINGS OF THE LATER YEARS. Ed. with introd. by J. S. Tuckey. *Univ. of California Press* 1966 $12.50. MLA-approved text of forgotten fiction from Mark Twain's darkest period.

GREAT SHORT WORKS. Introd. by Justin Kaplan. *Harper* Perenn. Class. 1967 pap. $.95

SHORT STORIES. *Assoc. Booksellers* Airmont Bks. pap. $.75; *Funk & Wagnalls* 1967 pap. $1.50

CLEMENS OF THE CALL: Mark Twain in San Francisco. Ed. by Edgar M. Branch. *Univ. of California Press* 1969 $10.00. Examines the relationship between the reporter, Twain, and his newspaper, the San Francisco *Daily Morning Call*, and reprints 200 pieces attributed by Branch to Twain.

MARK TWAIN'S HANNIBAL, HUCK AND TOM. Ed. by Walter Blair. *Univ. of California Press* The Mark Twain Papers 1969 $12.50. Discarded material from early novels about Huck Finn and Tom Sawyer.

FABLES OF MAN. Ed. by John S. Tuckey. *Univ. of California Press* The Mark Twain Papers 1972 $16.50

A PEN WARMED UP IN HELL: Mark Twain in Protest. Ed. by Frederick Anderson. *Harper* 1972 $6.95 Perenn. Lib. pap. $1.50

WHAT IS MAN? AND OTHER PHILOSOPHICAL WRITINGS. Ed. by Paul Baender. *Univ. of California Press* The Iowa-California ed. 1973 $16.50. The title essay is Twain's pessimistic view of man first published in 1917.

EVERYONE'S MARK TWAIN. Ed. by Caroline Thomas Harnberger. *A. S. Barnes* 1972 $15.00. Selections arranged alphabetically by subject.

The Celebrated Jumping Frog of Calaveras County. 1867. Ill. by F. Stroth-
mann. 1903. *Dover* pap. $1.25; *Peter Smith* $3.75; *Filter Press* $3.50 pap. $1.50; ed.
by John Paul *Gregg* $9.00

Autobiography (Burlesque) and First Romance 1871. *Haskell* 1970 $5.95; *Folcroft*
$10.00

(With Charles Dudley Warner) The Gilded Age. 1873. Ed. by Bryant M. French
Bobbs 1973 $10.00 pap. $2.50; ed. by Herbert Van Thal *Dufour* pap. $2.95; *New
Am. Lib.* Signet pap. $1.50; *Trident* 1964 $5.95; ed. by J. D. Kaplan *Univ. of
Washington Press* pap. $2.95

A novel with autobiographical overtones. A "gaudy . . . tale of swindles, political chicanery and sudden
murder"—(*LJ*).

The Adventures of Tom Sawyer. 1876. *Dodd* Gt. Ill. Class. 1958 $5.50; *Dutton*
Children's Ill. Class. $3.95; *Grosset* Ill. Jr. Lib. $3.95 deluxe ed. $4.95; *Harcourt*
$3.95; *Harper* uniform trade ed. $4.50 pap. $.75 Holiday Ed. $3.95 lib. bdg. $4.11;
Macmillan 1962 $3.95 Collier Bks. pap. $.65; *New Am. Lib.* Signet pap. $.50;
Franklin Watts 1g.-type ed. Keith Jennison Bks. $7.95 ultratype ed. $4.50; *World
Pub.* Rainbow Class. $2.50 lib. bdg. $2.91

*Other editions in paperback are available from Assoc. Booksellers, Amsco School Pubns.,
Bantam, Dell, Lancer, Scholastic Bk. Services, Washington Square*

Tom Sawyer and Huckleberry Finn. *Collins* New Class. $3.00 lea. $5.00; *Dutton*
Everyman's 1944 $3.50; pref. by Clara Clemens: "Tom, Huck and My Father"
Platt 1960 $3.95

The Prince and the Pauper. 1882. *Assoc. Booksellers* Airmont Bks. 1964 pap. $.60;
Dodd Gt. Ill. Class. $5.50; *Dutton* Children's Ill. Class. $4.50; *Grosset* Companion
Lib. $1.25; *Harper* 1882 $3.95 Holiday Ed. $4.50 lib. bdg. $4.43; *Lancer* pap. $.60;
Macmillan Collier Bks. pap. $.95; *New Am. Lib.* Signet pap. $.75; *Scholastic Bk.
Services* pap. $.75; *World Pub.* Rainbow Class. lib. bdg. $3.91

The Stolen White Elephant and Others. 1882. *Bks. for Libraries* $9.50. The title
story is also in the Neider collection (*see above*).

The Adventures of Huckleberry Finn. 1885. Ed. by Leo Marx. *Bobbs* Liberal
Arts 1967 $6.50 pap. $1.50; *Dodd* Gt. Ill. Class. 1953 $5.50; *Dutton* Children's Ill.
Class. 1955 $3.95; *Grosset* Companion Lib. $1.25 Ill. Jr. Lib. $2.95 deluxe ed.
$4.95 lib. bdg. $3.79; ed. by Kenneth S. Lynn *Harcourt* $2.95; *Harper* uniform
trade ed. $5.95 pap. $.75 Holiday Ed. $3.95 lib. bdg. $3.79; ed. by Lionel Trilling
Holt (Rinehart) 1948 pap. $2.25; ed. by H. N. Smith *Houghton* Riv. Eds. pap.
$1.90; ed. by Newton Arvin *Macmillan* 1962 $4.95 Collier Bks. pap. $.95; ed. by
Sculley Bradley, R. C. Beatty and Hudson Long *Norton* Critical Eds. 1969 $7.95
pap. $1.95; *Franklin Watts* lg-type ed. Keith Jennison Bks. $7.95 ultratype ed.
$4.95; *World Pub.* Rainbow Class. lib. bdg. $3.91

*Other paperback editions are available from Amsco School Pubns., Assoc. Booksellers
Airmont Bks., Bantam, Chandler Pub., Coshad (Apollo Bks.) Dell, Lancer, New Am.
Lib. Signet, Scholastic Bk. Services, Washington Square, Reader's Enrichment Ser.,
$.50–$1.00.*

A Connecticut Yankee in King Arthur's Court. 1889. *Amsco School Pubns.* pap.
$1.25; *Assoc. Booksellers* Airmont Bks. pap. $.60; ed. by Ralph B. Church *Cambridge Bk. Co.* pap. $1.00; *Chandler Pub.* facsimile ed. pap. $2.75; *Dodd* Gt. Ill.
Class. 1960 $5.50; *Harcourt* 1962 $3.95; *Harper* 1889 uniform trade ed. $4.50
Mod. Class $2.52 Holiday Ed. $3.95 lib. bdg. $4.43; *Hill & Wang* Am. Century
1960 pap. $1.95; *New Am. Lib.* Signet pap. $.60; ed. by Justin Kaplan *Penguin*
pap. $2.75

A Cure for the Blues. 1893. *Tuttle* 1963 $3.25. Twain's somewhat "esoteric" (*LJ*)
introduction to S. W. Royce's no-longer-funny "The Enemy Conquered, or Love
Triumphant by G. R. McClintock," text of which is included. Introd. by C. V. S.
Borst.

£1,000,000 Bank Note and Other New Stories. 1893. *Bks. for Libraries* $8.50

The Tragedy of Pudd'nhead Wilson. 1894. *Assoc. Booksellers* Airmont Bks. pap.
$.60; *Bantam* pap. $.50; *Harper* $5.00; *New Am. Lib.* Signet pap. $.50; ed. by Malcolm Bradbury *Penguin* 1969 pap. $1.45

Tom Sawyer Abroad. 1894. *Grosset* Companion Lib. $1.25 lib. bdg. $2.69

Tom Sawyer, Detective. 1896 *Grosset* Companion Lib. $1.25 lib. bdg. $2.79

Tom Sawyer Abroad and Tom Sawyer, Detective. *Assoc. Booksellers* Airmont
Bks. pap. $.60; *Macmillan* Collier Bks. pap. $.65

The Personal Recollections of Joan of Arc. 1896. *Harper* 1926 2 vols. in 1 $6.95

The American Claimant. 1897. *AMS Press* 1971 $15.00

Diaries of Adam and Eve. *McGraw-Hill* 1971 $2.95. Published originally in 1904 as
"Extracts from Adam's Diary."

Editorial Wild Oats. 1905. *Arno Press* 1970 $7.00; *Bks. for Libraries* $5.00

King Leopold's Soliloquy. Ed. by Stefan Heym. 1905. *Int. Pubns. Co.* 1970 pap.
$1.25. A satiric sketch.

Mark Twain's Mysterious Stranger Manuscripts. Ed. by William M. Gibson.
Univ. of California Press 1969 $16.00 pap. $2.95. Text is based on three holograph
manuscripts at the University of California, Berkeley, of the vol. published posthumously in 1916, reconstructed by Albert Bigelow Paine, who is now known to
have taken liberties with his manuscripts.

The Mysterious Stranger and Other Stories. *Harper* 1916 $5.95; *New Am. Lib.*
Signet 1962 pap. $.95. Two editions of the 1916 version.

Simon Wheeler, Detective. First published in 1963. Ed. with introd. by Franklin R.
Rogers. *N.Y. Public Lib.* 1963 $5.00. An uncompleted novel which *Library Journal*
finds a good one, with an "illuminating" introduction.

The War Prayer. First published in 1923. Ill. by John Groth. *Harper* 1968 $5.95
Perenn. Lib. pap. $.50 Colophon Bks. pap. $.75. An antiwar parable which Twain
allowed to be published only after his death.

Traveling with the Innocents Abroad: Mark Twain's Original Reports from Europe and the Holy Land. Ed. by Daniel Morley McKeithan. *Univ. of Oklahoma*

Press 1958. $7.50. A collection of the 58 lively letters sent to American newspapers, describing his experiences on a pleasure excursion to Europe, the Holy Land and Egypt. Revised by Twain, they became the basis of "The Innocents Abroad."

THE INNOCENTS ABROAD, or The New Pilgrim's Progress. 1869. *Assoc. Booksellers* Airmont Bks. pap. $.75; *Collins* $1.95; *Harper* $6.95; *New Am. Lib.* $.95

ROUGHING IT. 1872. *Assoc. Booksellers* Airmont Bks. pap. $.75; *Harper* $5.95; ed. by R. W. Paul *Holt* (Rinehart) 1953 pap. $2.00; *New Am. Lib.* Signet pap. $1.25; ed. by Franklin R. Rogers. The Iowa-California ed. of the Works of Mark Twain. *Univ. of California Press* 1972 $14.95 pap. $3.95

LIFE ON THE MISSISSIPPI. 1883. *Assoc. Booksellers* Airmont Bks. pap. $.60; *Bantam* pap. $.60; *Dodd* Gt. Ill. Class. $5.50; *Harper* uniform trade ed. $5.50 Holiday Ed. $4.95 lib. bdg. $4.79 text ed. pap. $2.88; *Hill & Wang* Am. Century 1957 pap. $1.45; *New Am. Lib.* Signet pap. $.75; *Oxford* World's Class. $2.50; *Washington Square* Collateral Class. pap. $.50

FOLLOWING THE EQUATOR. 1897. *AMS Press* 1971 $15.00

THE COMPLETE TRAVEL BOOKS OF MARK TWAIN: The Early Works, The Innocents Abroad and Roughing It. Ed. with introd. by Charles Neider. *Doubleday* $7.50

MARK TWAIN'S TRAVELS WITH MR. BROWN. Ed. by Franklin Walker and G. Ezra Dane. 1940 *Russell & Russell* 1971 $14.00. A collection of sketches that Twain wrote for the San Francisco *Alta California*, 1866–67.

MARK TWAIN'S NOTEBOOK. Ed. by Albert B. Paine. 1935. *Scholarly Press* $23.50 *Cooper* $12.00

MARK TWAIN TO MRS. FAIRBANKS. Ed. by Dixon Wecter. *Huntington Lib.* 1949 $5.00. "Mother" Fairbanks was one of Twain's early literary mentors.

THE CORRESPONDENCE OF SAMUEL L. CLEMENS AND WILLIAM D. HOWELLS, 1869–1910. Ed. by Henry Nash Smith and William M. Gibson. *Harvard Univ. Press* Belknap Press 1960 2 vols. boxed $25.00

The letters document publishing practices and critical attitudes, and the formation during the Gilded Age of a characteristic vernacular tradition in American writing. "A model of editorial skill and discretion"— (*LJ*).

SELECTED MARK TWAIN–HOWELLS LETTERS, 1872–1910. Ed. by Frederick Anderson and others. *Atheneum* 1968 pap. $3.95; *Harvard Univ. Press* Belknap Press 1967 $25.00

The edition above with unimportant matter and canceled words deleted to reduce it to one volume. Contains two new letters; otherwise "substantially the same," with editorial aids virtually unchanged—(*LJ*).

MARK TWAIN'S LETTERS TO HIS PUBLISHERS, 1876–1894. Ed. with introd. by Hamlin Hill. *Univ. of California Press* 1966 $11.50. 290 letters, most of them previously unpublished; the MLA-approved text.

MARK TWAIN'S LETTERS TO MARY. Ed. with commentary by Lewis Leary. *Columbia* 1961 $4.00 pap. $1.65. These 30-odd letters and notes, characterized by "cheerful affection and prankish good humor," were addressed during the last four years of his life to the young daughter-in-law of Henry H. Rogers, the Standard Oil executive who had become Mark Twain's business adviser and close friend.

Letters from the Sandwich Islands. 1938. *Folcroft* $10.75; *Haskell* 1972 $10.95. A collection of Twain's contributions to the Sacramento *Union* edited originally by Ezra Dane.

Letters to Will Bowen. 1941. *Folcroft* $7.50. Letters to Twain's "first oldest and dearest friend" first published in a collection edited by Theodore Hornberger.

Correspondence with Henry Huttleston Rogers, 1893–1909. Ed. by Lewis Leary. The Mark Twain Papers *Univ. of California Press* 1969 $17.50

Autobiography. Arr. and ed. by Charles Neider. *Harper* 1959 $10.00.

"Arranged for the first time in chronological order and supplemented . . . many paragraphs and pages have been restored"—(*LJ*). Some remarks about Christianity were omitted, as in previous editions, at the request of Clemens' daughter Clara.

Books about Twain

The Ordeal of Mark Twain. By Van Wyck Brooks. 1920 *Dutton* pap. 1970 $2.25
   The celebrated "attack on Twain." Robert Gorham Davis in the *N.Y. Times* says Brooks's (*q.v.*) "uncertainty and guilt over stressing so strongly the negative" in this book was a contributing cause to the latter's mental breakdown in the 1920s.
Mark Twain's America and Mark Twain at Work. By Bernard De Voto. *Houghton* Sentry Eds. pap. $2.45. "Mark Twain's America" (1932) contains De Voto's defense of Twain'
Mark Twain: The Man and His Work. By Edward Wagenknecht. 1935. *Univ. of Oklahoma Press* rev. ed. 1961 $4.50 3rd ed. 1967 $6.95
The Literary Apprenticeship of Mark Twain, With Selections from His Apprentice Writing. By Edgar M. Branch. 1950. *Russell & Russell* 1966 $15.00
Nook Farm: Mark Twain's Hartford Circle. By Kenneth R. Andrews. 1950. *Shoe String* 1967 $9.00; *Univ. of Washington Press* 1960 pap. $2.95
Turn West, Turn East: Mark Twain and Henry James. By Henry Seidel Canby. 1951. *Biblo and Tannen* 1965 $8.50. A comparative biography of contrasting contemporaries.
Sam Clemens of Hannibal. By Dixon Wecter. *(See biographical notes above.)* *Houghton* 1952 $5.50 Sentry Eds. 1961 pap. $1.85
Mark Twain: Selected Criticism. Ed. by Arthur L. Scott. *Southern Methodist Univ. Press* 1955 $5.95 pap. $2.45
Mark Twain: Social Critic. By Philip S. Foner. *International Pubs.* 1958 1962 pap. $1.95. His thinking on major social, political and economic issues of his day, based largely on previously unpublished material.
Mark Twain Tonight! An Actor's Portrait. By Hal Holbrook. 1959. *Pyramid Bks.* 1967 pap. $.75
   By the actor who depicted Mark Twain at 70 in a one-man show and won a Tony for it. The volume includes the selections used for performance, beautifully edited for the stage, and the history of the growth of this entertainment with observations on the teaching of American literature. (Mr. Holbrook "triumphed" [*N.Y. Times*] in a television version of his monologue in March, 1967.)
Mark Twain: An Introduction and Interpretation. By Frank Baldanza. American Authors and Critics Ser. With chronology, bibliography, index. 1961. *Holt* pap. 1966 $2.50
Mark Twain's Humor: The Image of a World. By Pascal Covici. *Southern Methodist Univ. Press* 1962 $5.95. A useful essay on Mark Twain's use of such devices as parodies, burlesques, hoaxes and bluffs.
Mark Twain, Social Philosopher. By Louis Budd. 1962. *Kennikat* 1973 $10.00. Based predominantly on contemporary speeches, newspaper interviews and unpublished letters and manuscripts.
Mark Twain: The Development of a Writer. By Henry Nash Smith. *Harvard Univ. Press* Belknap Press 1962 $6.50; *Atheneum* pap. $3.45
The Art of Huckleberry Finn: Text, Sources, Criticisms. By Hamlin Hill and Walter Blair. *Chandler Pub.* 1962 pap. $3.95
Huck Finn and His Critics. By Richard Lettis and others. *Macmillan* (orig.) 1962 pap. $2.75
Mark Twain: A Collection of Critical Essays. Ed. by Henry Nash Smith. *Prentice-Hall* 1963 $5.95 Spectrum Bks. pap. $1.95
Mark Twain and Elisha Bliss. By Hamlin Hill. *Univ. of Missouri Press* 1964 $5.95. On the relationship of Twain and the publisher of his first success, "The Innocents Abroad."
Mark Twain in Virginia City. By Paul Fatout. 1964. *Kennikat* $11.00
   A look at the "colorful free-for-all" journalism of the 1860s and its influence on Twain's style. Bibliography. "A significant contribution to the Twain canon"—(*LJ*).
Susy and Mark Twain: Family Dialogues. Arr. and ed. by Edith Salisbury; introd. by F. Anderson. *Harper* 1965 $7.95. Twain's domestic life (1872–96) unfolds as friends and relatives speak for themselves

through letters, books, journals—particularly those of his favorite daughter, Susy, whose own life extended from 1872 to 1896 and whose premature death was one of Twain's heavy afflictions.

Mark Twain: The Fate of Humor. By James M. Cox. *Princeton Univ. Press* 1966 $9.75
  "An admirable study of [his] career and writings"—(*LJ*). Index.

Mr. Clemens and Mark Twain: A Biography. By Justin Kaplan. *Simon & Schuster* 1966 $7.95 Clarion Bks. pap. $2.95; *Pocket Bks.* pap. $1.25
  The definitive life, with notes and index. It won a 1967 National Book Award, the citation reading, in part: "With rare sensitivity Kaplan assimilates the best work of his predecessors in Twain scholarship and transcends it. . . . He gives us a totally realized portrait." Winner of the 1967 Pulitzer Prize, as well.

On the Poetry of Mark Twain, with Selections from His Verse. By Arthur L. Scott. *Univ. of Illinois Press* 1966 $4.50
  "A most original investigation . . . has culminated in a rich little volume"—(*SR*). Professor Scott, in the course of doing other research (*see above*), began recording bits of verse by Twain and references to the poetry of others in Twain's work. "He soon found himself [says *SR*] with a sampler of poems . . . here brought to light. The accompanying essay on Twain's interest in poetry shows how keen that involvement became."

Mark Twain: A Profile. Ed. by Justin Kaplan. *Hill & Wang* 1967 Am. Century pap. $1.75

Mark Twain as Critic. By Sidney J. Krause *Johns Hopkins Univ. Press* 1967 $9.00

HARTE, (FRANCIS) BRET(T). 1836?–1902.

Bret Harte's birth year is variously given as 1836 and 1839 and his tombstone bears the date 1837. He is remembered especially for his two short stories, "The Luck of Roaring Camp" and "The Outcasts of Poker Flat," both achievements in local color. The former is the story of an orphaned baby adopted by the men in a gold-rush-era mining camp; it was dramatized by Dion Boucicault in 1894. The latter is a tale of four undesirables expelled from a mining camp, and their losing battle against a blizzard. Although he was born in the East and lived there and in Europe most of his life, Harte's 17 years of residence in California have associated him most closely with that state, and the scenes of all his successful stories are laid in the West. His contemporary "sketches" of life in San Francisco in the 1860s, written with Mark Twain, were first collected in book form as "Sketches of the Sixties" (1927. *AMS Press* 1969 $8.00; *Scholarly Press* $14.50). When he went east again to settle in Boston in 1871, his talent seems to have deserted him. Much of his later life was spent in England.

COMPLETE WORKS. 1896–1903. *AMS Press* 1967 20 vols. each $17.50 set $350.00

THE BEST OF BRET HARTE. Ed. by Wilhelmina Harper and Aimee Peters. *Houghton* $7.95

CONDENSED NOVELS. 1867. *Bks. for Libraries* repr. of 1871 ed. $7.75 (and Stories) repr. of 1882 ed. $13.50 Second ser. (with "New Burlesques") repr. of 1902 ed. $8.50; *Gregg* repr. of 1871 ed. 1902 $14.00

THE LUCK OF ROARING CAMP. 1868. (and Other Stories) *Lancer* pap. $.60; (and 30 Other Stories) *Franklin Watts* 1968 $3.95

THE OUTCASTS OF POKER FLAT. 1869. (and Other Tales) introd. by Wallace Stegner *New Am. Lib.* Signet 1961 pap. $.95

THE OUTCASTS OF POKER FLAT, THE LUCK OF ROARING CAMP AND OTHER STORIES. *Assoc. Booksellers* 1964 pap. $.60

MRS. SCAGG'S HUSBAND AND OTHER SKETCHES. 1873. *Somerset Pub.* $9.50

TALES OF THE ARGONAUTS AND OTHER SKETCHES. 1875. *Bks. for Libraries* $10.50

GABRIEL CONROY. 1876. *Gregg* $15.00

DRIFT FROM TWO SHORES. 1878. *Bks. for Libraries* $9.75

FLIP, AND OTHER STORIES. 1882. *Bks. for Libraries* $9.50

THE QUEEN OF THE PIRATE ISLE. 1866. *Warne* $3.95

THE HERITAGE OF DEADLOW MARSH AND OTHER TALES. 1889. *Bks. for Libraries* $9.75

ON THE FRONTIER. 1884. *Bks. for Libraries* $11.25

COLONEL STARBOTTLE'S CLIENT AND SOME OTHER PEOPLE. 1892. *Bks. for Libraries* $9.00

SALLY DOWS AND OTHER STORIES. 1893. *Bks. for Libraries* $11.25

IN A HOLLOW OF THE HILLS. 1895. *Gregg* $9.50

MARUJA AND OTHER TALES. 1896. *Bks. for Libraries* $14.50

THANKFUL BLOSSOM AND OTHER EASTERN TALES AND SKETCHES. 1896. *Bks. for Libraries* $15.75

STORIES IN LIGHT AND SHADOW. 1898. *Bks. for Libraries* $11.00

TALES OF TRAIL AND TOWN. 1898. *Bks. for Libraries* $12.25

MR. JACK HAMLIN'S MEDITATION. 1899. *Bks. for Libraries* 1973 $12.50

FROM SANDHILL TO PINE. 1900. *Bks. for Libraries* $11.50

THREE PARTNERS AND OTHER TALES. 1900. *Bks. for Libraries* $13.50

UNDER THE REDWOODS. 1901. *Bks. for Libraries* $12.50

OPENINGS IN THE OLD TRAIL. 1902. *Bks. for Libraries* $12.50

Books about Harte

The Life of Bret Harte. By Thomas E. Pemberton. 1903. *Bks. for Libraries* $12.50
Bret Harte. By Henry W. Boynton. 1903. *Bks. for Libraries* $6.50
The Life of Bret Harte, with Some Account of the California Pioneers. 1911. *Gale Research Co.* 1967 $7.80
Bibliography of the Writings of Bret Harte. By George R. Stewart, Jr. 1933. *Folcroft* $15.00
Bret Harte: Bibliography and Biographical Data. By Joseph Gaer. 1935. *Burt Franklin* 1967 $17.50
Mark Twain and Bret Harte. By Margaret Duckett. *Univ. of Oklahoma Press* 1964 $7.95
    An attempt to offset the damage done to Harte's reputation by the derogatory comments of Mark Twain. "A useful study of two men whose careers began in the same place and ended worlds apart"—(*Choice*).
Bret Harte: A Biography. By Richard O'Connor. *Little* 1966 $7.50
    "An understanding but critical biography of Harte as a foppish man, buffeted by success so suddenly and intensely that he lost his way in the world. It is not a book of literary criticism"—(*LJ*).
Bret Harte. By Patrick Morrow; ed. by Wayne Chatterton and James H. Maguire. Western Writers Ser. 5 *Boise State College Press* 1972 pap. $1.00

HOWELLS, WILLIAM DEAN. 1837–1920.

An editor of the *Atlantic Monthly* and later *Harper's Magazine*, W. D. Howells exercised a considerable influence on American letters during the latter third of the 19th century. He encouraged and helped publish writers such as Twain, Crane, and Henry James, and for many years carried on a battle with the defenders of sentimental fiction and argued for the superiority of the new realistic mode. Howells was also a prolific writer, having published over 100 works of fiction, travel, memoirs, poetry, and drama. Among his early works were "Their Wedding Journey," "A Chance Acquaintance," "The Lady of the Aroostook," and "A Modern Instance"—all forerunners of the book for which he is best remembers, "The Rise of Silas Lapham," a novel about the moral rise of a self-made man who gives up his riches rather than profit from dishonesty. "A Hazard of New Fortunes" reflects Howells' later concern with social issues. Howells's "Criticism and Fiction and Other Essays" (ed. by Clara M. Kirk and Rudolf Kirk *New York Univ. Press* 1959 $10.00) contains in the long title essay his reflections from his monthly department in *Harper's Magazine* (1869–92). Other nonfiction titles include: a facsimile edition of his campaign biography of the "Life of Abraham Lincoln," annotated in Lincoln's handwriting (1960, o.p.), the "Life and Character of

Rutherford B. Hayes" (*Somerset Pub.* $14.50), another campaign biography; "The Complete Plays of W. D. Howells," (ed. by W. J. Meserve *New York Univ. Press* 1960 $15.00); two autobiographical works, once more in print, both dealing with Howells's early life: "A Boy's Town" and "Years of My Youth," as well as three literary reminiscences: "My Literary Passions" (*Greenwood* $9.00), "Literary Friends and Acquaintances" (*Greenwood* $15.00), and "My Mark Twain" (ed. by Marilyn Baldwin *Louisiana State Univ. Press* 1967 $7.50). The two-volume edition of "Life in Letters of W. D. Howells" (ed. by Mildred Howells *Russell & Russell* 1968 $27.50) is again available.

A SELECTED EDITION OF W. D. HOWELLS. *Indiana Univ. Press.* 12 vols. available: Vol. 3 Years of My Youth and Three Essays introd. and notes by David J. Nordloh, text established by Nordloh (1973) $12.50 Vol. 5 Their Wedding Journey ed. by John K. Reeves (1970) $10.00 Vol. 6 A Chance Acquaintance introd. and notes by Jonathan Thomas and D. Nordloh, text established by Thomas, Nordloh and Ronald Gottesman Vol. 11 Indian Summer introd. and notes by Scott Bennett, text established by Bennett and Nordloh (1972) $10.50 Vol. 12 The Rise of Silas Lapham introd. and notes by Walter J. Meserve, text established by Meserve, Nordloh and Gottesman (1971) $12.50 Vol. 14 April Hopes introd. and notes by Kermit Vanderbilt, text established by Don L. Cook, James P. Elliott and D. J. Nordloh (1973) $15.00 Vol. 17 The Shadow of a Dream and An Imperative Duty introd. and notes by Martha Banta, text established by Banta, Gottesman and Nordloh (1970) $10.00 Vol. 20 The Altrurian Romances introd. and notes by Clara and Rudolf Kirk, text established by Scott Bennett (1968) $15.00 Vol. 25 The Kentons introd. and notes by George C. Carrington, Jr., text established by Carrington and Gottesman (1972) $10.00 Vol. 26 The Son of Royal Langbrith introd. and notes by David Burrows, text established by Burrows, Gottesman and Nordloh (1970) $10.50 Vol. 27 The Leatherwood God introd. and notes by Eugene Pattison, text established by Elliott and Nordloh (1972) $12.50 Vol. 32 Literary Friends and Acquaintances ed. by David Hiatt and Edwin H. Cady (1968) $12.50 pap. $3.95

WILLIAM DEAN HOWELLS: Representative Selections. By Clara M. and Rudolf Kirk. 1962. *Peter Smith* $.25

A DOORSTEP ACQUAINTANCE AND OTHER SKETCHES. 1867. *Folcroft* $5.50

A CHANCE ACQUAINTANCE. 1873. *Greenwood* $11.25; *Gregg* 1970 $11.00; *Scholarly Press* 1970 $14.50

A FOREGONE CONCLUSION. 1875. *Folcroft* $10.50; *Gregg* repr. of 1875 ed. $10.50; *Scholarly Press* repr. of 1902 ed. $14.50

THE LADY OF AROOSTOOK. 1879. *Greenwood* repr. of 1907 ed. $11.50; *Scholarly Press* repr. of 1879 ed. $19.50

THE UNDISCOVERED COUNTRY. 1880. *Greenwood* $11.50; *Scholarly Press* $14.50

DOCTOR BREEN'S PRACTICE. 1881. *Folcroft* $10.00; *Greenwood* $10.50; *Scholarly Press* $14.50

A FEARFUL RESPONSIBILITY AND OTHER STORIES. 1881. *Greenwood* $10.00; *Gregg* $10.00; *Scholarly Press* $14.50

A MODERN INSTANCE. 1882. *Houghton* Riv. Eds. pap. $1.40

THE RISE OF SILAS LAPHAM. 1885. *Assoc. Booksellers* Airmont Bks. pap. $.75; *Dodd* Gt. Ill. Class. 1964 $5.50; *Harper* pap. $.75; ed. by George Arms *Holt* (Rinehart) 1949 pap. $2.50; ed. by E. H. Cady *Houghton* pap. $1.80; *Macmillan* 1962 Collier

Bks. pap. $.65; *Modern Library* pap. $.95; *New Am. Lib.* Signet pap. $.75; *Washington Square* Collateral Class. pap. $.75

THE MINISTER'S CHARGE, or The Apprenticeship of Lemuel Barker. 1887. *Folcroft* $19.00; *Scholarly Press* $19.50

ANNIE KILBURN. 1888. *Folcroft* 1973 $11.00; *Gregg* 1970 $12.00; *Scholarly Press* repr. of 1891 ed. $19.50

A HAZARD OF NEW FORTUNES. 1890. *Folcroft* 1973 $10.00; *New Am. Lib.* Signet pap. $1.25. A novel of New York City life, with implicit social criticism.

THE QUALITY OF MERCY. 1892. *Folcroft* $20.00; *Scholarly Press* $24.50

THE SHADOW OF A DREAM and AN IMPERATIVE DUTY. 1892. Ed. by Edwin H. Cady. *College & Univ. Press* 1962 $6.50 pap. $2.95

A TRAVELER FROM ALTRURIA. 1894. Introd. by Howard Mumford Jones *Hill & Wang* Am. Century 1957 pap. $1.95; *Peter Smith* 1959 $3.75. A utopian novel, pointing up what Howells found wrong with America.

SUBURBAN SKETCHES. 1898. *Bks. for Libraries* $9.75; *Folcroft* lib. bdg. $8.00

A PAIR OF PATIENT LOVERS. 1901. *Bks. for Libraries* $11.50; *Folcroft* lib. bdg. $11.00

THE KENTONS. 1902. *Folcroft* $11.00; *Greenwood* $11.50; *Scholarly Press* $19.50

QUESTIONABLE SHAPES. 1903. *Bks. for Libraries* $8.75; *Folcroft* lib. bdg. $7.00

THE LEATHERWOOD GOD. 1916. *AMS Press* 1970 $9.00; *Folcroft* 1973 lib. bdg. $8.50; *Scholarly Press* 1970 $14.50

Books about Howells

William Dean Howells: A Study. By Oscar Firkins. 1924. *Russell & Russell* 1963 $8.50
William Dean Howells, Dean of American Letters. By Edwin H. Cady. *Syracuse Univ. Press* 2 vols. Vol. I The Road to Realism: Early Years, 1837–1885 (1956) $4.00 Vol. 2 The Realist at War: Mature Years, 1885–1920 (1958) $5.00. The definitive biography.
Howells: His Life and World. By Van Wyck Brooks. *Dutton* 1959 $5.50. Howells's experiences are analyzed for the sources of characters, situations, plots and social philosophy.
Howells: A Century of Criticism. Ed. by Kenneth E. Eble. *Southern Methodist Univ. Press* 1962 $5.95. 28 critical articles chronologically arranged to show the development of Howells' fluctuating literary reputation.
William Dean Howells. By Rudolf and Clara Kirk. U.S. Authors Ser. *College & Univ. Press* 1962 pap. $2.45; *Twayne* $4.95.
The Literary Realism of William Dean Howells. By William McMurray; pref. by Harry T. Moore. *Southern Illinois Univ. Press* 1967 $4.95. A chapter is devoted to each of 12 of Howells' novels, discussed in the light of his literary realism and philosophic pragmatism—the latter influenced by William James.
William D. Howells. By William M. Gibson. *Univ. of Minnesota Press* Pamphlets on American Writers 1967 $1.25.
William Dean Howells: A Bibliography. By Vito Joseph Brenni. *Scarecrow Press* 1973 $6.00. A useful scholarly work.

BIERCE, AMBROSE (GWINNETT). 1842–1914?

Bierce has been called "bitter, "wicked" and "mysterious," the latter because of his dramatic disappearance into Mexico in 1913 and his probable death there the following year. He served with distinction through the Civil War, then went to San Francisco, where he contributed to periodicals. He was early known for the vitriolic wit of his journalistic sketches. His short stories, grim horror tales recalling those of Poe (*q. v.*), are his best work. "Can Such Things Be?", a collection of supernatural tales, appeared in 1893. His poetry is epigrammatic but conventional. His "Fantastic Fables" and "The Devil's Dictionary" display his cynical aversion to "labor unions, democracy and socialism." Typical of his "Dictionary" definitions are: "Happiness, *n*. An agreeable sensation arising from contemplation of the misery of another. "Prejudice, *n*. A vagrant opinion without visible means of support."

COLLECTED WORKS. 1909–12. *Gordian* 12 vols. set $125.00; *Gordon Press* 12 vols. set $225.00

COLLECTED WRITINGS. Introd. by Clifton Fadiman. 1946. *Bks. for Libraries* $31.50; *Citadel* 1960 pap. $4.95

IN THE MIDST OF LIFE AND OTHER STORIES. (Original title "Tales of Soldiers and Civilians" *see below*) *Dufour* $3.95; *New Am. Lib.* Signet pap. $.95. Includes "An Occurrence at Owl Creek Bridge."

GHOST AND HORROR STORIES. Ed. by E. F. Bleiler *Dover* 1964 pap. $1.50; *William Gannon* $3.75; *Peter Smith* $3.75

FIEND'S DELIGHT. 1873. *Gregg* 1971 $9.00

FANTASTIC FABLES. 1890. *Dover* 1970 pap. $1.50; *William Gannon* $3.75

TALES OF SOLDIERS AND CIVILIANS. 1892. *Bks for Libraries* $11.00

BLACK BEETLES IN AMBER. 1892. *Gregg* 1970 $11.00

CAN SUCH THINGS BE? 1893. *Bks. for Libraries* $13.00

THE DEVIL'S DICTIONARY. 1911. (First published as "The Cynic's Word Book" 1906) *Dover* 1959 pap. $1.50; *William Gannon* $3.50; *Hill & Wang* Am. Century 1957 pap. $1.95; *Peter Smith* $3.00

LETTERS. Ed. by B. C. Pope. 1921. *Gordian* 1967 $7.50

Books about Bierce

Ambrose Gwinnett Bierce: Bibliography and Biographical Data. By Joseph Gaer. 1935. *Folcroft* $12.00; *Burt Franklin* 1968 $12.50. A useful scholarly work.
Ambrose Bierce. By Robert A. Wiggins. Pamphlets on American Writers. *Univ. of Minnesota Press* 1964 pap. $1.25. According to Wiggins, "[Bierce's] role grows larger as the tradition of the grotesque develops in the twentieth century."
Ambrose Bierce: A Biography. By Richard O'Connor. *Little* 1967 $7.50
Presents Bierce as "perhaps the earliest American exponent of black humor. . . . O'Connor assiduously seeks to illuminate the man's work through his life and . . . has succeeded very well. [His] attitude is appreciative, his style zestful, and his research thorough"—(*PW*).
Ambrose Bierce: A Biography. By Carey McWilliams. With new introd. by the author. *Shoe String* 2nd rev. ed. 1967 $10.00
Ambrose Bierce. By M. E. Grenander. U.S. Authors Ser. *Twayne* 1971 $5.50. A well-researched account of Bierce's life and work.

JAMES, HENRY. 1843–1916.

James is one of a number of American writers who chose to live in Europe, not out of disdain for his native land, but because Europe offered a much richer texture of manners and morals. In most of his best fiction James' subject is the contrast between the simplicity (and sometimes the simple-mindedness) and naturalness (and sometimes the vulgarity) of Americans and the sophistication and decadence of Europeans. From "Daisy Miller" to the later novels like "The Ambassadors" and "The Golden Bowl," James' ultimate concern is with drawing out of this contrast moral distinctions that have seemed too refined for many readers, including H. G. Wells who found James tediously complicated. James' reputation has not only survived such criticism, it has continued to grow; today even his detractors acknowledge his importance and influence. He is commonly regarded as our most technically gifted writer. Caroline Gordon has referred to him as "the scholar of the novel," for in addition to writing over 20 novels and numerous short works of fiction (as well as sketches, plays, memoirs) James wrote copiously on the art of fiction, on the fiction of other writers, and, most interesting of all, on his own fiction. The prefaces he did for the famous New York Edition (recently reprinted) of his own work were later edited by R. P. Blackmur and published as "The Art of the Novel" (*Scribner* 1934 $7.50); these prefaces, along with "The Notebooks of Henry James" provide a fascinating and instructive study of the development of James's art. His single most important contribution to the art of fiction was the development of the device of the "central intelligence" which paved the way for the "stream of consciousness" technique developed in the 20th century by Joyce and others. James' three autobiographical volumes, "A Small Boy and Others" (1913), "Notes of a Son and Brother" (1914) and "The Middle Years" (1917) are all o.p. His bio-critical work "Hawthorne" published in 1879 (ed. by John Morley 1887. *AMS Press* $12.50; *Cornell Univ. Press* 1956 $5.00 pap. $1.45; *Folcroft* repr. of 1879 ed. $6.00) is perceptive, particularly about Hawthorne's limitations, but it tells a good deal about James as well. James' "Letters" are once again in print, as well as James' "Letters to A. C. Benson and Auguste Monod." Seven volumes of James' short stories have also been reprinted recently, including three volumes that were first published after his death: "Travelling Companions" (1919), "The Landscape Painter" (1919), and "Master Eustace" (1920)—all edited by Albert Mordell. The other four collections are: "Terminations" (1895), "The Better Sort" (1903), "Embarrassments" (1896) and "The Soft Side" (1900). Altogether, these seven volumes reprint 49 stories, many of them not available in standard collections. James' early novel "Watch and Ward" (1878) is also in print again as are a late one, "The Sacred Fount" (1901), and his last novel, "The Sense of the Past" (1917), which was published the year after his death. With the republication of the great New York Edition, "The Awkward Age" (1899) is also back in print.

THE NOVELS AND TALES OF HENRY JAMES. The New York Ed. 1907–1917 *Kelley* 26 vols. set $300.00. Titles and prices of the novels are listed below. For information on volumes containing numerous shorter pieces, the reader should consult the publisher's catalog.

GREAT SHORT WORKS. 1909. *Harper* Perenn. Lib. pap. $.95

THE AMERICAN NOVELS AND STORIES. Ed. with introd. by F. O. Matthiessen. *Knopf* 1947 $10.00. Ten stories and three complete novels including "The Ivory Tower," "The Bostonians," "Washington Square" and "The Europeans"—all with an American setting.

EIGHT UNCOLLECTED TALES. Ed. by Edna Kenton. 1950. *Bks. for Libraries* $11.50

THE PORTABLE HENRY JAMES. Ed. with introd. by Morton Dauwen Zabel. *Viking* 1951 $5.50 pap. $3.35. Five of the shorter tales, three "nouvelles," criticism, essays, notebooks, memoirs, letters. Annotated bibliography

SELECTED FICTION. Ed. by Leon Edel. *Dutton* Everyman's Am. ed. 1953 1964 pap. $2.45

SELECTED TALES. *Dufour* 1956 $6.95

FOUR SELECTED NOVELS: The Americans, The Europeans, Daisy Miller, An International Episode. *Grosset* Univ. Lib. 1958 pap. $2.45

THE SHORT NOVELS. *Dodd* Gt. Ill. Class. 1961 $5.95

THE COMPLETE TALES. Ed. with introd. by Leon Edel. *Lippincott* 12 vols. 1962–1965 Vol. I o.p. Vols 2–12 each $6.95

AMERICANS AND EUROPE: Selected Tales. Ed. by N. Wilt and J. Lucas. *Houghton* Riv. Eds. pap. $1.65

SEVEN STORIES AND STUDIES. Ed. by E. Stone. *Meredith* (Appleton) pap. $2.95

GHOSTLY TALES. Ed. by Leon Edel. *Grosset* Univ. Lib. 1963 pap. $2.50

SELECTED SHORT STORIES. Ed. with introd. by Quentin Anderson. *Holt* (Rinehart) 1950 rev. ed. 1957 pap. $3.00; *Penguin* 1963 pap. $.75

STORIES OF THE SUPERNATURAL. Ed. by Leon Edel. *Taplinger* 1970 $7.95

RODERICK HUDSON. 1876. His first novel. *Kelley* New York ed. $15.00; *Penguin* 1969 pap. $1.45

THE AMERICAN. 1877. *Assoc. Booksellers* Airmont Bks. pap. $.75; *Dell* Laurel Eds. 1960 pap. $.60; ed. by J. W. Beach *Holt* (Rinehart) 1949 pap. $2.50; ed. by M. J. Bruccoli and R. H. Pearce *Houghton* $2.50 Riv. Eds. pap. $1.85; *Kelley* New York ed. $15.00; *New Am. Lib.* Signet pap. $.95; *Franklin Watts* ultratype ed. $5.50

WATCH AND WARD. 1878. *Dufour* 1960 $6.50. James' first novel.

THE EUROPEANS. 1878. *Houghton* $2.50

DAISY MILLER. 1878. (and Other Stories) *Assoc. Booksellers* Airmont Bks. pap. $.50; (with "An International Episode" (1878) in "Four Great American Novels") ed. by Raymond W. Short *Holt* 1946 $7.25

CONFIDENCE. 1880. *Grosset* Univ. Lib. pap. $1.95

A BUNDLE OF LETTERS. Written in 1879 for the *Parisian*. *Folcroft* repr. of 1897 ed. $6.00. Unauthorized edition published in 1880.

THE PORTRAIT OF A LADY. 1881. *Assoc. Booksellers* Airmont Bks. pap. $.95; ed. by Leon Edel *Houghton* Riv. Eds. pap. $2.10; *Kelley* New York ed. 2 vols. each $13.50; *Modern Library* $2.95 pap. $1.15; *New Am. Lib.* Signet pap. $.95; introd. by Graham Greene *Oxford* World's Class. 1947 $3.00; *Washington Square* pap. $.95 Collateral Class. pap. $.95

WASHINGTON SQUARE. 1881. *Amsco School Pubns* pap. $.95; *Assoc. Booksellers* Airmont Bks. pap. $.60; *T. Y. Crowell* pap. $3.95; (and "The Europeans") *Dell* pap. $.50; introd. by Clifton Fadiman *Modern Library* 1950 $1.95; *New Am. Lib.* Signet 1964 pap. $.60; *Penguin* 1963 pap. $.85

LADY BARBERINA (1884) AND OTHER TALES. Ed by Herbert Ruhm *Grosset* Univ. Lib. pap. $2.25; ed. by H. Ruhm *Vanguard* $4.50

THE BOSTONIANS. 1886. Introd. by Philip Rahv *Dial* 1945 $4.00; *Modern Library* pap. $1.35

THE PRINCESS CASAMASSIMA. 1886. *Harper* 1959 pap. $1.75; *Kelley* New York ed. 2 vols. each $13.50; *Peter Smith* $4.50

THE ASPERN PAPERS. 1888. (and "The Spoils of Poynton") *Dell* pap. $.60; (and "The Turn of the Screw") *Dutton* Everyman's $3.25

THE TRAGIC MUSE. 1889. *Kelley* New York ed. 2 vols. each $13.50

THE LESSON OF THE MASTER. 1892. Available only from *Kelley* (with "The Death of the Lion," "The Next Time," "The Figure in the Carpet" and "The Coxon Fund") New York ed. $13.50

THE SEIGE OF LONDON. 1893. *Gordon Press* $11.00

THE REAL THING AND OTHER TALES. 1893. *Bks. for Libraries* $10.00; *Folcroft* lib. bdg. $9.50

TERMINATIONS. 1895. *Bks. for Libraries* $8.00. Includes the title story and "The Death of the Lion," "The Coxon Fund," "The Middle Years," "The Altar of the Dead."

THE SPOILS OF POYNTON. Printed as "The Old Thing," 1896; present title, 1897. (and "The Aspern Papers") *Dell* pap. $.60; (and Other Stories) *Doubleday* $6.95; (and "A London Life" and "The Chaperon") *Kelley* New York ed. $15.00

EMBARRASSMENTS. 1896. *Bks. for Libraries* $9.50. Contains title story and "The Figure in the Carpet," "Glasses," "The Next Time," "The Way It Came."

WHAT MAISIE KNEW. 1897. *Doubleday* Anchor Bks. pap. $1.95; (and "In the Cage" and "The Pupil") *Kelley* New York ed. $15.00

THE TURN OF THE SCREW. 1898. *Assoc. Booksellers* Airmont Bks. pap. $.50; (and "The Aspern Papers" and Seven Other Stories) introd. by Michael Swan *Collins* New Class. 1959 $3.00; (and "The Aspern Papers") *Dutton* Everyman's $3.50 pap. $1.75; (and Other Short Novels) *New Am. Lib.* Signet pap. $.95; ed. by Robert Kimbrough *Norton* Critical Eds. $5.00 pap. $1.85; (and Other Stories) *Penguin* pap. $.95; (and Other Stories) *Scholastic Bk. Services* pap. $.75; *Franklin Watts* lg.-typed ed. Keith Jennison Bks. $6.95

THE AWKWARD AGE. 1899. *Kelley* New York ed. $15.00; *Norton* 1969 pap. $2.45

THE SOFT SIDE. 1900. *Bks. for Libraries* $9.75. Contains 12 stories, including "Europe" and "The Real Right Thing."

THE SACRED FOUNT. 1901. *Dufour* 1959 $6.50

THE WINGS OF THE DOVE. 1902. *Kelley* New York ed. 2 vols. Vol. I $12.50 Vol. 2 $13.50; ed. by Reynolds Price *Charles E. Merrill* pap. $1.25.

THE AMBASSADORS. 1903. *Assoc. Booksellers* Airmont Bks. pap. $.75; *Dell* pap. $.60; *Dutton* Everyman's $3.25 pap. $2.50; *Harper* $4.95; ed. by Frederick W. Dupee *Holt* (Rinehart) 1960 pap. $2.00; ed. by Leon Edel *Houghton* Riv. Eds. pap. $1.50; *Kelley* New York ed. 2 vols. each $12.50; *New Am. Lib.* Signet pap. $.75; ed. by S. P. Rosenbaum *Norton* Critical Eds. 1964 pap. $2.25; *Washington Square* pap. $.60

THE GOLDEN BOWL. 1904. *Kelley* New York ed. 2 vols. each $13.50; *Penguin* pap. $2.95; *Popular Lib.* pap. $1.50; ed. by J. Halperin *World Pub.* Meridian Bks. pap. $4.95

THE AMERICAN SCENE. 1907. Ed. by Leon Edel. *Indiana Univ. Press* 1968 $10.00 Midland Bks. pap. $3.95

THE MARRIAGES (1909) AND OTHER STORIES. *New. Am. Lib.* Signet pap. $.50

A SENSE OF THE PAST. 1917. *Kelley* New York ed. $12.50

TRAVELLING COMPANIONS. Ed. with fwd. by Albert Mordell. 1919. *Bks. for Libraries* $11.00; *Liveright* 1970 pap. $2.45. A collection of seven stories written between 1868 and 1874.

THE LANDSCAPE PAINTER. Pref. by Albert Mordell. 1920. *Bks. for Libraries* $9.75. Contains four early uncollected stories: the title story, "Poor Richard," "A Day of Days," "A Most Extraordinary Case."

MASTER EUSTACE. 1920. *Bks. for Libraries* $9.75. Besides the title story, there are four others: "Longstaff's Marriage," "Theodolinde," "A Light Man," "Benvolio."

Books about James

The Method of Henry James. By Joseph Warren Beach. 1918. *Saifer* rev. ed. 1957 $6.00 pap. $3.00. An old study of James' development as a fictional artist, slightly revised, but one of the best things ever written on the subject.

The Three Jameses. By C. Hartley Grattan. A comparison of the lives and achievements of Henry James, Sr., William James and Henry James. *New York Univ. Press* 1932 reissue 1962 $10.00 pap. $2.75

Henry James: The Major Phase. By F. O. Matthiessen. *Oxford* 1944 $6.00 Galaxy Bks. pap. $1.75

The Question of Henry James. Ed. by F. W. Dupee. 1945 *Octagon* $13.00. A useful collection of essays dealing more or less with the controversial aspects of James' art.

The James Family: Including selections from the writings of Henry James, Sr., William, Henry and Alice James. By F. O. Matthiessen. *Knopf* 1947 $10.00

The Great Tradition: A Critical Study of George Eliot, Henry James and Joseph Conrad. By F. R. Leavis. 1948 2nd ed. 1950. *New York Univ. Press* Gotham Lib. 1963 $8.95 pap. $2.45

Turn West, Turn East: Mark Twain and Henry James. By Henry Seidel Canby. 1951. A comparative biography showing two sharply different strains in American culture. *Biblo & Tannen* 1965 $8.50

The Life of Henry James. By Leon Edel. *Lippincott* 1953-1972 5 vols. Vol. I The Untried Years: 1843-1870 (1953) Vol. 2 The Conquest of London: 1870-1881 (1962) Vol. 3 The Middle Years: 1882-1895 (1962) Vol. 4 The Treacherous Years: 1895-1901 (1969) each $10.00 Vol. 5 The Master: 1901-1916 (1972) $12.95 set $49.95

Henry James. By Leon Edel. Pamphlets on American Writers. *Univ. of Minnesota Press* 1960 pap. $.95. A short biography, a longer critical analysis and evaluation of his work with selective bibliographies.

A Casebook on Henry James's "The Turn of the Screw." Ed. by Gerald Willen. *T. Y. Crowell* 1960 2nd ed. 1969 pap. $3.95 Essays by Edmund Wilson, Edna Kenton, Harold C. Goddard, Robert Heilman and others; a radio symposium by Katharine Anne Porter. Alan Tate and Mark Van Doren; James' preface to "The Aspern Papers; the text of "The Turn of the Screw."

The Comic Sense of Henry James: A Study of the Early Novels. By William Richard Poirier. *Oxford* 1960 Galaxy Bks. 1967 pap. $1.75. A "scholarly but unpedantic approach" to James' first six full-length novels.

Reflections of a Jacobite. By Louis Auchincloss. 1961. *Kelley* $10.00. Examines various 19th- and early 20th-century novels concerning social relations. For this critic, the "two peaks of achievement were reached in Henry James . . . and in Marcel Proust."

Henry James. By D. W. Jefferson. 1961. *Putnam* 1965 Capricorn Bks. 1971 pap. $1.25. A good introductory volume in the Writers and Critics Series; its last chapter is a very helpful discussion of some of the basic critical works on James. Bibliography, no index.

Discovery of a Genius: William Dean Howells and Henry James. Ed. by Albert Mordell. Howells' articles on, and reviews of, James' works demonstrate his perception and encouragement of the young James' genius. *Twayne* 1961 $4.00

Henry James and the Jacobites. By Maxwell Geismar. *Houghton* 1963 $7.95; *Hill & Wang* Am. Century 1965 pap. $2.95. In this complete analysis of the stories, novels, and prefaces, Geismar strikes out against the "New Criticism" veneration for James, who, he has said, was "self-enclosed, all-sufficient, isolated and ignorant about the true basis of life and experience." A controversial book.

Henry James: A Collection of Critical Essays. Ed. by Leon Edel. *Prentice-Hall* 1963 $5.95 Spectrum Bks. pap. $1.95

Edith Wharton and Henry James: The Story of Their Friendship. By Millicent Bell. *Braziller* 1965 $6.50 "Based on a scholarly and detailed study of . . . particularly James's side of the correspondence. . . . The very close and affectionate relationship between them is thoroughly explored"—(*LJ*).

Henry James. By Bruce R. McElderry, Jr. *Twayne* 1965 $4.95, *College & Univ. Press* 1965 pap. $2.45 Here the generally reliable *Twayne* United States Authors Series lets us down. Very useful for James chronology, plot outlines, titles and dates of *all* his work, but as artistic interpretation it is "misleading"—(*Choice*).

Henry James: A Reader's Guide. By S. Gorley Putt. Introd. by Arthur Mizener. *Cornell Univ. Press* 1966 $9.50 pap. $2.95
"This is an excellent introductory work that contains at least one reference to each of James's 22 novels and 112 tales. . . . The book is unpretentious, contains few footnotes, and is admirably readable"—(*LJ*).

Perspectives on James's *The Portrait of a Lady:* A Collection of Critical Essays. Ed. with introd. by William T. Stafford. *New York Univ. Press* 1967 $8.95 pap. $2.25. The editor is a well-known James critic and the essays by such writers as Joseph Warren Beach, F. O. Matthiessen, R. P. Blackmur and Walter Allen provide a good cross section of modern criticism.

See also Chapter 15, Essays and Criticism.

CABLE, GEORGE WASHINGTON. 1844-1925.

Cable is the short-story historian of the 19th-century Creole in New Orleans. His first book, "Old Creole Days," a collection of seven short stories for which he is now best remembered, has "preserved an exotic segment of American life which is fast losing its identity." "The Grandissimes," his one long romance, is a strong story but poor in construction. His Puritan inheritance from his New England mother led to his speeches, letters to the editor and other writings now collected in "The Negro Question: A Selection of Writings on Civil Rights in the South" (ed. by Arlin Turner 1958 *Norton* pap. $1.95). As these were being published in the 1860s, he became the subject of vilification by enraged Southerners. Cable was born in the South and fought in the Confederate Army, but in 1884 he moved to Northampton, Mass., and became a Northerner in all his interests and sympathies. The number of Cable's works in print has been increased tremendously with the reprinting of the 19-volume "Collected Works," along with the reprinting of other single titles such as "Doctor Sevier" and "Madame Delphine."

COLLECTED WORKS. *Somerset Pub.* 19 vols. Single vols. $5.50–$20.00 set $245.00. Reprints of original publications from 1879–1918. For full information consult the publisher's catalog.

CREOLES AND CAJUNS: Stories of Old Louisiana. *Peter Smith* 1959 $4.50.

OLD CREOLE DAYS. 1879. *Bks. for Libraries* repr. of 1883 ed. 2 vols. in 1 $7.50; *New Am. Lib.* Signet pap. $.60

THE GRANDISSIMES. 1880. *Hill & Wang* Am. Century 1957 pap. $2.95

DOCTOR SEVIER. 1884. *Gregg* $14.50

BONAVENTURE. 1888. *Gregg* $12.50

STRANGE TRUE STORIES OF LOUISIANA. 1889. *Bks. for Libraries* $14.50

JOHN MARCH, SOUTHERNER. 1894. *Bks. for Libraries* $18.50

MADAME DELPHINE. 1896. *AMS Press* 1969 $5.00; *Scholarly Press* $9.50

STRONG HEARTS. 1899. *Bks. for Libraries* $8.75

BYLOW HILL. 1902. *AMS Press* 1969 $5.50; *Scholarly Press* $12.50

Books about Cable

George W. Cable, His Life and Letters. By Lucy L. Biklé. 1928. *Russell & Russell* 1967 $8.50. Written by his daughter.
George Washington Cable: A Study of His Early Life and Works. By Kjell Ekstrom. 1950 *Haskell* 1969 $10.95
George W. Cable: A Biography. By Philip Butcher. U.S. Authors Ser. *Twayne* 1962 $5.50; *College & Univ. Press* 1963 pap. $2.45
George W. Cable: The Life and Times of a Southern Heretic. By Louis D. Rubin. *Pegasus* 1969 $6.95

HARRIS, JOEL CHANDLER. 1848–1908.

Harris was a newspaper man whose stories in Negro dialect appeared first in the columns of the Atlanta *Constitution*, with which he was associated for 24 years. The character of Uncle Remus became immensely popular. The stories, ten volumes of which have been published, helped to show the literary value of the folklore of the old plantation and of the Negro songs and ballads. Harris was the first writer to "create out of diverse Negro oral dialect stories in the South, in the nineteenth century, a local color literature of lasting form." With the intensifying of the civil rights movement in recent years, however, dialect stories have become suspect as being patronizing; Harris has not escaped partial eclipse. "On the Plantation" (1892, o. p.) is the autobiography of his early life.

THE COMPLETE TALES OF UNCLE REMUS. Ed. by Richard Chase; ill. by Arthur B. Frost and others. *Houghton* 1955 $12.50

THE FAVORITE UNCLE REMUS. Ed. by Richard Chase; ill. by A. B. Frost. *Houghton* 1948 $5.95

UNCLE REMUS: His Songs and His Sayings. 1880. Ed. by M. Aline Bright *Hawthorn* 1921 $4.95; *Grosset* 1947 $2.95 *Schocken* 1965 $3.95 pap. $1.75

NIGHTS WITH UNCLE REMUS: Myths and Legends of the Old Plantation. 1883. *Gale Research Co.* 1971 $15.00.

This collection is the second of Harris's Uncle Remus series, valuable because of the introduction in which he gives details of his methods of collection, and a comparison of the stories included here with a volume of South African Negro stories"—(Publisher's catalog).

MINGO AND OTHER SKETCHES IN BLACK AND WHITE. 1884. *Bks. for Libraries* $9.50; *Gregg* 1970 $11.00

DADDY JAKE THE RUNAWAY AND SHORT STORIES TOLD AFTER DARK BY UNCLE REMUS. 1889. *Bks. for Libraries* $9.75

BALAAM AND HIS MASTER AND OTHER SKETCHES AND STORIES. 1891. *Bks. for Libraries* $10.00

STORIES OF GEORGIA. 1896. *Cherokee Pub. Co.* (Box 1081, Covington, Ga., 30209) $5.95; *Finch Press* $14.00; *Reprint Hse. Intl.* $15.00

TALES OF THE HOME FOLKS IN PEACE AND WAR. 1898. *Bks. for Libraries* $14.50

PLANTATION PAGEANTS. 1899. *Bks. for Libraries* $11.50

ON THE WINGS OF OCCASIONS; Being the authorized version of certain curious episodes of the late Civil War, including the hitherto suppressed narrative of the kidnapping of President Lincoln. 1900. *Bks. for Libraries* $11.50; *Gregg* repr. of 1899 ed. $9.25

THE CHRONICLES OF AUNT MINERVY ANN. 1899. *Somerset Pub.* $9.50

GABRIEL TOLLIVER: A Story of Reconstruction. 1902. *Gregg* $11.50

THE MAKING OF A STATESMAN AND OTHER STORIES. 1902. *Bks. for Libraries* $10.00

TOLD BY UNCLE REMUS. 1905. *Bks. for Libraries* $17.00

Books about Harris

Joel Chandler Harris. By Paul M. Cousins. *Louisiana State Univ. Press* 1968 $7.50 Based on the manuscript material at Emory University. "This highly competent biography is valuable for showing not only the roots of Harris's genius but also the humus of post-bellum Southern culture"—(Gay Wilson Allen, in SR).

JEWETT, SARAH ORNE. 1849–1909.

Sarah Orne Jewett was one of the earliest in American literature to write stories of place. Geography is very pronounced in her work. "Deephaven" (1877) was her native town of South Berwick, Maine, and Maine, "the country of the pointed firs," is always the background of her books. Her stories are pictures, painted in strong local color, with subtle Yankee humor, of a New England social order that is fast becoming a tradition. Mark Van Doren (*q.v.*) has said: "Her fishermen and farmers, and especially their wives, all have amusing deformities of body or spirit; and all of them without exception are artists in understatement, in the wry, oblique remark whose barb may not be felt until somebody attempts to pull it out; yet sooner or later they reveal themselves as the passionate, kind people their unobtrusive creator knows them to be." "A Country Doctor," a portrait of the author's father, is once more in print. Among other titles recently reprinted are "Old Friends and New," "Country By-Ways," "Native of Winby and Other Tales," "Tales of New England," "Life of Nancy," and "The Queen's Twin and Other Stories."

COLLECTED WORKS. *Somerset Pub.* 14 vols. repr. of titles published in 1877–1901: Deephaven (1877) $10.00 Old Friends and New (1879) $10.95 Country By-Ways (1881) $10.00 The Mate of the Daylight and Friends Ashore (1884) $10.00 A Country Doctor (1884) $14.50 A Marsh Island (1885) $12.00 A White Heron and Other Stories (1886) $10.00 The King of Folly Island and Other People (1888) $13.50

Strangers and Wayfarers (1890)$9.95 A Native of Winby and Other Tales (1893) $12.50 The Life of Nancy (1895) $12.50 The Country of the Pointed Firs (1896) $12.50 The Queen's Twin and Other Stories (1899) $9.95 The Tory Lover (1901) $16.50 set $145.00

THE BEST STORIES. *Peter Smith* 2 vols. in 1 1950 $7.50

THE WORLD OF DUNNET LANDING: A Sarah Orne Jewett Collection. Ed. by David Bonnell Green. 1962. *Peter Smith* $5.50

DEEPHAVEN (1877) AND OTHER STORIES. Ed. by Richard Cary. *College & Univ. Press* 1966 $6.50 pap. $2.95

OLD FRIENDS AND NEW. 1879. *Bks. for Libraries* $8.50

COUNTRY BY-WAYS. 1881. *Bks. for Libraries* $7.75

A COUNTRY DOCTOR. 1884. *Gregg* $12.50

A WHITE HERON. 1886. *T. Y. Crowell* 1963 $4.95 lib. bdg. $5.70

A NATIVE OF WINBY AND OTHER TALES. 1893. *Bks. for Libraries* $9.75

TALES OF NEW ENGLAND. 1894. *Bks. for Libraries* $8.75

THE LIFE OF NANCY. 1895. *Bks. for Libraries* $9.50

THE QUEEN'S TWIN AND OTHER STORIES. 1899. *Bks. for Libraries* $10.75

LETTERS. Ed. by Richard Cary. 1956. *College & Univ. Press* 1967 $6.50 pap. $2.95

Books about Jewett

Sarah Orne Jewett. By Francis O. Matthiessen. 1929. *Peter Smith* $4.50
Sarah Orne Jewett. By Richard Cary. U. S. Authors Ser. *Twayne* $5.50; *College & Univ. Press* 1962 $2.45
Sarah Orne Jewett. By Margaret F. Thorp. Pamphlets on American Writers. *Univ. of Minnesota Press* 1966 pap. $1.25 Brief but useful.

BELLAMY, EDWARD. 1850–1898.

It is as the "humane and romantic Utopian, campaigning for equality and social justice, rather than as a novelist or profound thinker, that Bellamy is remembered and read today." While working as a newspaperman in Springfield, Mass., he began to write novels and later short stories, but did not achieve much success until the publication of "Looking Backward." The hero of this fantasy falls asleep in 1887 and awakens in the year 2000 to find himself in a humane, scientific and socialistic Utopia. After selling fewer than 10,000 copies in its first year, "Looking Backward" became enormously popular. Clubs were formed to promote Bellamy's social ideas and he became a leader of a brief "Nationalist Movement," crusading for "economic equality, human brotherhood, and the progressive nationalization of industry." Americans as diverse as Veblen (*q.v.*) and Dewey (*q.v.*) have been influenced by Bellamy's suggestion that the products of industrial energy, intelligently organized, could be used as a device for obtaining a nobler future. His "Religion of Solidarity" (1940 *Folcroft* $6.50) and "Talks on Nationalism" (1938 *Bks. for Libraries* $11.25) are again available.

DR. HEIDENHOFF'S PROCESS. 1880. *AMS Press* $6.50

MISS LUDINGTON'S SISTER. 1884. *Gregg* $10.50

EQUALITY. 1887. *AMS Press* 1970 $10.00; *Greenwood* $15.25; *Gregg* 1969 $11.50; *Scholarly Press* $14.50

LOOKING BACKWARD: 2000–1887. 1888. *Amsco School Pubns.* pap. $1.10; ed. by John L. Thomas *Harvard Univ. Press* Belknap Press 1967 $7.50; ed. by F. R. White *Hen-*

dricks House 1946 pap. $1.95; ed. by R. C. Elliott *Houghton* Riv. Eds. 1967 $1.30; *Modern Library* 1942 pap. $1.05; *New Am. Lib.* Signet pap. $.95

THE BLINDMAN'S WORLD AND OTHER STORIES. 1898. *Somerset Pub.* $9.50

Books about Bellamy

Edward Bellamy Abroad. By Sylvia Bowman and others. *Twayne* 1962 $7.50
The Philosophy of Edward Bellamy. By Arthur E. Morgan. *Community Service* pap. $2.00

ATHERTON, GERTRUDE. 1857–1948.

Mrs. Atherton's fiction stands, in her own phrase, for "intellectual anarchy." A Californian, she was at once a rebel and a snob. Her most famous novel, "The Conqueror," is based on the life of Alexander Hamilton (*q. v.*) The author called it "a character novel," "a dramatized biography." Parts of it are taken from Hamilton's own writings. It is more useful "as a picture of a time and a career than many equally interesting historical novels, because the author successfully undertook to recount the public events in her hero's life as well as the intimacies and the imagined personal crises." "Black Oxen" (1923, o. p.) shocked the 1920s with its tale of a countess of 58 who became seductive and ravishing after a gland treatment.

LOS CERRITOS. 1890. *Gregg* $8.00

THE DOOMSWOMAN. 1892. *Gregg* $10.50

PATIENCE SPARHAWK. 1897. *Gregg* 1970 $14.50

THE CALIFORNIANS. 1898. *Gregg* 1968 $9.00

SENATOR NORTH. 1900. *Gregg* $9.00

THE ARISTOCRATS. 1901. *Gregg* 1968 $8.00

THE CONQUEROR. 1902. *Lippincott* rev. ed. 1916 new ed. 1939 $6.95

THE SPLENDID IDLE FORTIES. 1902. *Gregg* 1968 $9.50

THE BELL IN THE FOG AND OTHER STORIES. 1905. *Somerset Pub.* $9.50

REZANOV. 1906. *Gregg* 1969 $12.00

THE FOGHORN. 1934. *Bks. for Libraries* $9.25

GARLAND, HAMLIN. 1860–1940.

Garland, the son of a pioneer, was himself a literary pioneer in writing of the West. "Main-Travelled Roads" was his first collection of short stories—harsh and objective pictures of a vanishing pioneer dream. This is an important book "in American literary history, a conscious record of the Midwestern farmer's plight during the rapid growth of industrialization. . . . He follows Whitman in advising the artist to tell the truth of the life he saw about him." In later life he turned to romantic fiction which has little interest today. His autobiography, "A Son of the Middle Border," tells his life story up to his 32nd year and is continued in "A Daughter of the Middle Border," which deals with his mother's life and his own to middle age. This last won the Pulitzer Biography Prize in 1922. His four volumes of reminiscence, written in chronological sequence, are "Roadside Meetings" (1930), "Companions of the Trail: A Literary Chronicle" (o. p.), "My Friendly Contemporaries: A Literary Log" (o. p.), and "Afternoon Neighbors: Further Excerpts from a Literary Log" (o. p.). Forty-five volumes of Garland's collected works have recently been reprinted in addition to several individual volumes of early works such as "Spoil of Office," "Rose of Dutcher's Coolly," the latter one of Garland's best pieces.

COLLECTED WORKS. *Somerset Pub.* 45 vols. repr. of titles published 1890–1939. Individual vols. $3.95–$24.50 set $499.00. For titles and prices of each volume consult the publisher's catalog.

MAIN-TRAVELLED ROADS: Six Mississippi Valley Stories. 1891. *Brown Bk.* $4.00 pap. $1.95; *Harper* 1909 $3.50; *New Am. Lib.* Signet 1962 pap. $.75; ed. by T. A. Bledsoe 1954 *Peter Smith* $4.50

MEMBER OF THE THIRD HOUSE. 1892. *Gregg* 1969 $8.50

A SPOIL OF OFFICE. 1892. *Johnson Reprint* $15.00

WAYSIDE COURTSHIPS. 1897. *Bks. for Libraries* $11.50

BOY LIFE ON THE PRAIRIE. 1899. Ill. by Edward W. Deming *Ungar* 1959 $3.75; *Univ. of Nebraska Press* 1961 Bison Bks. pap. $2.25

PRAIRIE FOLKS. 1899. *AMS Press* $7.50

ROSE OF DUTCHER'S COOLLY. 1899. *AMS Press* 1969 $12.50; *Scholarly Press* $19.50; *Univ. of Nebraska Press* Bison Bks. pap. $3.00; *Peter Smith* $5.00

TRAIL-MAKERS OF THE MIDDLE BORDER. 1927. *Scholarly Press* 1971 $19.00

PRAIRIE SONG AND WESTERN STORY. 1928. *Bks. for Libraries* $13.00

HAMLIN GARLAND'S DIARIES. Ed. by Donald Pizer. *Huntington Lib.* 1968 $7.50

ROADSIDE MEETINGS. 1930. *Scholarly Press* 1971 $24.50; *Somerset Pub.* $19.50

COMPANIONS OF THE TRAIL: A Literary Chronicle. 1931. *Somerset Pub.* $21.95

MY FRIENDLY CONTEMPORARIES: A Literary Log. 1932. *Scholarly Press* $24.50; *Somerset Pub.* $22.50

AFTERNOON NEIGHBORS: Further Excerpts from a Literary Log. 1934. *Somerset Pub.* $24.50

A SON OF THE MIDDLE BORDER. 1917. *Macmillan* 1951 $5.95

A DAUGHTER OF THE MIDDLE BORDER. 1921 *Peter Smith* repr. of 1957 ed. 1960 $4.75

Books about Garland

The Beginnings of Naturalism in American Fiction: A Study of the Works of Hamlin Garland, Stephen Crane and Frank Norris, with Special Reference to Some European Influences, 1891–1903. By Lars Ahnebrink. 1950. *Russell & Russell* 1961 $12.50
Hamlin Garland: A Biography. By Jean Holloway. 1960. *Bks. for Libraries* $15.00. Most useful for critical analyses and summaries of Garland's books and the bibliography of his publications.
Hamlin Garland's Early Work and Career. By Donald Pizer. 1960 *Russell & Russell* 1969 $6.00. A useful book, particularly for Garland specialists, it deals with Garland's earliest work, some of which is of minor interest.
Hamlin Garland and the Critics: An Annotated Bibliography. By Jackson Bryer. *Whitston Pub. Co.* 1974 $12.50

WISTER, OWEN. 1860–1938.

A Philadelphian and a grandson of the actress, Fanny Kemble, Owen Wister was educated in private schools in the United States and abroad and graduated from Harvard with highest honors in music. After suffering a nervous breakdown he traveled to Wyoming to recover his health. He then made frequent trips back to the West. His only well-known novel, "The Virginian," a best seller for years, is a pioneer "western." It was dedicated to his lifelong friend Theodore Roosevelt (*q. v.*), another outdoorsman and lover of the West. Two of Wister's books recently reprinted are "Lin McLean" and "Lady Baltimore." A study that includes a consideration of Wister is Edward G. White, "The Eastern Establishment and the Western Experience: The West of Frederic Remington, Theodore Roosevelt and Owen Wister" (*Yale Univ. Press* 1968 $6.75).

THE WEST OF OWEN WISTER: Selected Short Stories. *Univ. of Nebraska Press* 1972. $4.50 Bison Bks. pap. $1.95

LIN MCLEAN. 1898. *Gregg* $11.00; *Popular Lib.* pap. $.50

THE JIMMYJOHN BOSS AND OTHER STORIES. 1900. *Somerset Pub.* $9.50

THE VIRGINIAN: A Horseman of the Plains. 1902. *Assoc. Booksellers* Airmont Bks. pap. $.60; *Macmillan* 1925 $5.95 lg.-type ed. $7.95; *Pocket Bks.* pap. $.75; *Popular Lib.* pap. $.95; *Scholastic Bk. Services* pap. $.75

LADY BALTIMORE. 1906. *Gregg* 1968 $10.50

HENRY, O. (pseud. of William Sydney Porter). 1862–1910.

O. Henry left 250 short stories, an output of six years which filled 15 volumes. These may be divided into his stories of the Southwest, of Latin America and of New York City. "Cabbages and Kings" (1904), his first book, deals with his South American adventures. "The Four Million" contains stories of New York life, a theme continued in "The Trimmed Lamp" (1907) and "Strictly Business" (1910). The typical O. Henry story is the expanded anecdote, ending in a sudden, humorous surprise, a formula imitated by many writers who followed him. Dale Kramer's sympathetic biography, "The Heart of O. Henry" (1955, o. p.) recounts the previously untold story of the author's early love affair and marriage, his conviction for embezzlement, his imprisonment and the eight remaining years in New York where his writing made him famous. It is said that the most plausible explanation for his pen name is that he found it in the "U.S. Dispensatory" while serving as prison drug clerk. It was the name of a celebrated French pharmacist, Étienne-Ossian Henry, abbreviated. The authorized life is "O. Henry Biography" by C. Alphonso Smith (1916, o. p.). His definitive biography is "Alias O. Henry" by Gerald Langford (1957, o. p.). His two best-known stories, "The Gift of the Magi" and "The Ransom of Red Chief," are the title stories of two recently published collections of his work.

COMPLETE WORKS. *Doubleday* 1953 1-vol. ed. $8.95

MY TUSSLE WITH THE DEVIL AND OTHER STORIES. 1918. *Bks. for Libraries* $7.75

BEST SHORT STORIES. Sel. with an introd. by Bennett A. Cerf and Van H. Cartmell. *Modern Library* 1945 $2.95

THE BEST STORIES. *Doubleday* 1954 $4.95

THE POCKET BOOK OF O. HENRY STORIES. Ed. by Harry Hansen. *Pocket Bks.* pap. $.75

69 SHORT STORIES. *Collins* $3.00 lea. $5.00

58 SHORT STORIES. *Collins* $3.00

SURPRISES. Ed. by R. Corbin and N. E. Hoopes. *Dell* 1966 pap. $.60. 27 stories.

TALES. *Doubleday.* $6.95

THE RANSOM OF RED CHIEF. *Hawthorn* 1970 $3.95

THE GIFT OF THE MAGI. *Hawthorn* 1972 $2.95; (and Five Other Stories) *Franklin Watts* 1967 $3.95

THE FOUR MILLION 1906. (and Other Stories) *Assoc. Booksellers* Airmont Bks. 1964 pap. $.50; *Doubleday* 1908 $3.95

Books about O. Henry

My Friend O. Henry. By Seth Moyle. 1914. *Folcroft* $6.50. This is primary material for any account of O. Henry's life.

O. Henry: The Man and His Work. By E. Hudson Long. 1949. *A. S. Barnes* pap. $1.45; *Peter Smith* $4.00

O. Henry (William Sydney Porter). By Eugene Current-Garcia. U.S. Authors Ser. *Twayne* 1965 $5.50; *College & Univ. Press* 1965 pap. $2.45

"A judicious and intelligent appraisal of O. Henry . . . a first-rate introductory work, making no claims to being exhaustive. Current-Garcia writes with clarity and judges with sense and insight. His research is sound and his conclusions provocative"—(*Choice*). Bibliography and index.

—W.J.S.

Chapter 14

Modern American Fiction

"All modern American literature comes from one book by Mark Twain called Huckleberry Finn. *If you read it you must stop where the Nigger Jim is stolen from the boys. That is the real end. The rest is just cheating. But it's the best book we've had. All American writing comes from that. There was nothing before. There has been nothing as good since."* —Ernest Hemingway

Of the above statement from Hemingway's "The Green Hills of Africa," Huck Finn himself might have said, "he told the truth, mainly. There was things which he stretched, but mainly he told the truth." The characteristic hero of American fiction since the late nineteenth century has been a young man both naively innocent and worldly wise. In what is perhaps the best single critical study of the twentieth-century American novel—the appropriately titled "Radical Innocence" (*Princeton Univ. Press* 1961 $10.00 pap. $2.95)—Ihab Hassan finds that the most characteristic feature of our fiction is "its typical anti-hero. The central and controlling image of recent fiction is that of the rebel-victim. He is an actor but also a sufferer. Almost always, he is an outsider, an initiate never confirmed in his initiation, an anarchist and clown, a Faust and Christ compounded in grotesque or ironic measures. The poles of crime and sainthood define the range of his particular fate, which is his character." It is easy to find examples to illustrate Hassan's thesis. Henry Fleming of Stephen Crane's "The Red Badge of Courage" is an idealistic poor boy not unlike Clyde Griffiths of Theodore Dreiser's "An American Tragedy" or Jay Gatz of F. Scott Fitzgerald's "The Great Gatsby" in that all three ambiguous heroes find a disparity between their own ideals and the sorry compromises which society holds out to them. J. D. Salinger's Holden Caulfield of "The Catcher in the Rye," probably the most representative Huck Finn of the 1950s, is a prep-school dropout who goes about Manhattan trying to wipe out four-letter obscenities chalked on the sidewalks, while the most famous anti-hero of the 1960s, Alexander Portnoy of Philip Roth's "Portnoy's Complaint," covers much the same territory in a desperate effort to commit as many obscenities as possible in order to free himself from the social and moral taboos which have made him sex-obsessed and guilt-ridden. Both Holden and Alexander tell their stories to their psychiatrists, but only the most optimistic of readers would assume that they are to be salvaged in a way that will enable them to conform to the values of the society around them, unless of course they were to undergo prefrontal lobotomies such as that performed on the hero of Ken Kesey's "One Flew Over the Cuckoo's Nest."

Whereas Hassan's "controlling image" of the rebel-saint provides a workable thesis with which to describe American fiction for almost a century, it does not account for several distinct phases within that period. Hemingway went on to praise Henry James in additon to Mark Twain—and he might just as well have acknowledged also the considerable debt which later novelists have owed to William Dean Howells, whose earnest and realistic novels about the social climate in various parts of America helped to establish a tradition of the novel of manners which has flourished for more than a half-century in works by such writers as Edith Wharton, Caroline Gordon, John P. Marquand, John O'Hara, and Louis Auchincloss. Henry James's contribution is more difficult to assess, for although that author is justifiably considered the father of modern fiction because—with Flaubert in France and Turgenev in Russia—he was one of the first to insist and to demonstrate that fiction can be as much an art as poetry or drama, he produced a body of work so distinctly his own that it has proved basically inimitable. One "lesson of the Master," however, can be clearly perceived in many American novels and stories of the early modern period. That is an emphasis on sensibility—a story as told by a sensitive and "aware" but somehow detached and passive observer who looks on a counterpart who is more vital and engaged than himself. It is Nick Carraway trying to understand "The Great Gatsby" or the emasculated Jake Barnes of Hemingway's "The Sun Also Rises" watching the confrontation between romantic Robert Cohn and the heroic bullfighter Romero, or it is the cynical reporter Jack Burden of Robert Penn Warren's "All the King's Men" trying to account for the strange mixture of idealism and pragmatism which explains the rise to political prominence as well as the downfall of Willie Stark. Henry James taught writers of many lands how to fuse a story of dramatic action through the sensibility of a reflecting "center of consciousness." In the United States that lesson became so pervasive during the period between the two world wars that almost every first novel and a good many second and third ones were stories of initiation about the quest for identity by a sensitive person suddenly forced to confront the realities of the world around him. Such archetypes as George Willard of Sherwood Anderson's "Winesburg, Ohio" or the Eugene Gant of Thomas Wolfe's "Look Homeward, Angel" as well as the countless forgotten heroes of stories written to the *New Yorker* formula might never have existed if it had not been for Henry James. The earliest phase of modern American fiction was characterized by its impressionistic techniques and a strong focus on individual sensibilities.

Beginning with the 1930s and continuing through the time of the Second World War, the emphasis in American fiction tended to shift away from the individual toward society in general. Works such as John Dos Passos' "U.S.A.," John Steinbeck's "The Grapes of Wrath," and Hemingway's "For Whom the Bell Tolls" heralded a new awareness that man does not stand alone. Just as Americans en masse rallied round the flag during the worldwide devastation of the early 1940s, the young American writers who survived that war and began their literary careers shortly afterwards may have come away from their shared experience with resentment at the discipline they had undergone and some doubts about the cause for which they fought, but they returned also with a mutual conviction that men must work together if they are to improve the human condition. Writers such as John Hersey, James Jones, Irwin Shaw, Mark Harris, and Norman Mailer have continued to see themselves as participants in the history of their time. The second phase of modern American fiction is marked by group-consciousness and social awareness.

These qualities are especially apparent in the regional and ethnic literatures which have tended to dominate American fiction of recent years. No other region has been depicted so extensively and powerfully as the South. Beginning with Ellen Glasgow and continuing through Thomas Wolfe and William Faulkner to Eudora Welty, Truman Capote, Carson McCullers, and Flannery O'Conner, a disproportionate number of the best American writers have been Southerners. They have shared a strong sense of community within a tradition at once grand and blighted. C. Hugh Holman has said that "boundaries of experience" separate the South from the rest of America: "The only group of Americans who have known military defeat, military occupation, and seemingly unconquerable poverty, they have the sense of failure; the sense of guilt, which comes from having been America's classic symbol of injustice, for the enslavement and then the segregation of the Negro; and the sense of frustration which comes from the consistent inadequacy of the means at hand to wrestle with the problems to be faced." This, projected against the rich image of their past and its dignity, has resulted in a serious and tragic literature.

Similar factors help to explain the rise of ethnic literatures. The 1960s in particular saw the ascendency of Jewish and Black writers. Like the Southern novelists, they wrote with an awareness of a long tradition of deprivation and suffering behind them, but whereas Southern fiction is characterized by scenes of gothic decay and a sense of tragedy, the Jewish and Black writers have reacted in different ways to their heritage. Negro writers from Richard Wright to Ralph Ellison and James Baldwin have produced angry fiction imbued with a sense of injustice, outrage, and the need to fight back. The anti-heroes who dominate their fiction are rebels, outcasts, and exiles. The typical anti-hero in recent Jewish fiction, on the other hand, is a slob or a *schlemiel*, a long-suffering buffoon buffeted by circumstances and his own neuroses, fears, and guilts. There is little humor in Black fiction of this century, but "black humor" is the characteristic mode of the American Jewish novel as produced by such writers as Saul Bellow, Bernard Malamud, Bruce Jay Friedman, and Philip Roth. They share a sense of the absurd which enables them to laugh at themselves, but theirs is the kind of laughter which often hides their tears.

Two other general trends have been apparent in fiction of the past decade—the one a movement toward actual life, the other toward increasing artifice. The much-publicized "nonfiction novel" in which sophisticated literary techniques are used to narrate actual events may well have reached its peak almost at its inception with Truman Capote's "In Cold Blood" in 1966, but though few other "novels" such as Capote's have received much attention in the years since then, the influence of this movement is apparent in the "New Journalism" phenomenon. Investigative reporters willing to look in depth at the events they narrate and to see them from their own frankly personal points of view have become culture-heroes in recent years. Normal Mailer is perhaps the most successful and conspicuous recruit to a movement which increasingly blurs the distinctions between fiction and nonfiction; and the whole history of modern American prose literature may someday be summarized in terms of the progression from Thomas Wolfe to Tom Wolfe, whose "The New Journalism" (*Harper* 1973 $10.95) is both a historical account of the movement and an anthology of representative examples from writers as diverse as Gay Talese, Terry Southern, George Plimpton, and Joan Didion. However, even as the nonfiction novel was being submerged within the broader movement of the New Journalism, a very different tendency was becoming increasingly apparent in writings by serious younger novelists eager to expand the frontiers of fiction not in the direction of historical reporting but toward an increasing insistence that art is art. In the fiction of writers such as John Barth, Donald Barthelme, Robert Coover, William Gass, and Ronald Sukenick—most of them academics and all of them strongly influenced by Joyce and other leaders of the early Modernist period as well as by Jorge Luis Borges and such contemporary European experimental writers as Alain Robbe-Grillet—there is a reflexive, self-conscious tendency which makes them write labyrinthine, ingenious stories which seem to deal ultimately with their own composition.

HISTORICAL AND CRITICAL WORKS

Adelman, Irving, and Rita Dworkin. THE CONTEMPORARY NOVEL: A Checklist of Critical Literature on the British and American Novel Since 1945. *Scarecrow Press* 1972 $15.00

Aldrige, John W. AFTER THE LOST GENERATION: A Critical Study of the Writers of Two Wars. 1951. *Bks. for Libraries* $10.75

"A pioneer study. . . . The first serious and challenging book about the new novelists" (Malcolm Cowley in the *N.Y. Herald Tribune*), this work remains of more than historical interest. Aldridge contrasts the writers of the lost generation, principally Hemingway, Fitzgerald, and Dos Passos, with the then-new writers of the forties. Some of the authors Aldridge hailed as especially promising have since faded into near oblivion, but his comments on such novelists as Norman Mailer, Irwin Shaw, Truman Capote, Gore Vidal, and Paul Bowles are sometimes prophetic as well as perceptive.

THE DEVIL IN THE FIRE: Retrospective Essays on American Literature and Culture, 1951–71. *Harper* 1972 $12.50

(Comp.) CRITIQUES AND ESSAYS ON MODERN FICTION, 1920–1951. Representing the achievement of modern American and British critics. Fwd. by Mark Schorer. *Ronald* 1952 $8.50. A most useful collection for general reader or student.

Auchincloss, Louis. PIONEERS AND CARETAKERS: A Study of Nine American Women Novelists. *Univ. of Minnesota Press* 1965 $5.95.

"These are critical studies with liberal biographical interspersings of nine American women from Sarah Orne Jewett to Mary McCarthy. . . . Intelligent, well written, and interesting"—(*LJ*).

Balakian, Nona, and Charles Simmons, Eds. THE CREATIVE PRESENT: Notes on Contemporary American Fiction. 1963. *Gordian* 1972 $8.50

Leading critics evaluate work of 17 contemporary writers; "a valuable and absorbing book that gives a moderately conservative view of the fiction being produced in America today"—(*N.Y. Times*).

Baumbach, Jonathan. THE LANDSCAPE OF NIGHTMARE: Studies in the Contemporary American Novel. *New York Univ. Press* 1965 $6.95 pap. $1.95. Unusually perceptive analyses and interpretations of individual novels by Saul Bellow, Ralph Ellison, Bernard Malamud, Wright Morris, Flannery O'Connor, J. D. Salinger, William Styron, Edward Lewis Wallant, and Robert Penn Warren.

Blake, Nelson Manfred. NOVELISTS' AMERICA: Fiction as History, 1910–1940. *Syracuse Univ. Press* 1970 $6.95 pap. $2.95. The author, a professional historian rather than a literary critic, turns to fiction as a source in the search for historical truth in this rewarding study of three decades of American life as viewed by eight novelists: Sinclair Lewis, Fitzgerald, Faulkner, Wolfe, Steinbeck, Dos Passos, James T. Farrell, and Richard Wright.

Blotner, Joseph. THE MODERN AMERICAN POLITICAL NOVEL: 1900–1960. *Univ. of Texas Press* 1966 $8.50

Bluefarb, Sam. THE ESCAPE MOTIF IN THE AMERICAN NOVEL: Mark Twain to Richard Wright. *Ohio State Univ. Press* 1972 $8.00

Bradbury, Malcolm, and David Palmer, Eds. THE AMERICAN NOVEL AND THE NINETEEN TWENTIES. *Crane-Russak* 1972 $10.50. Included in this distinguished collection of eleven newly published essays are four general studies on the complex relationship between literature and society during the twenties and reassessments of seven major novelists of the period—Sherwood Anderson, John Dos Passos, William Faulkner, F. Scott Fitzgerald, Ernest Hemingway, Sinclair Lewis, and Nathanael West.

Brown, Deming. SOVIET ATTITUDES TOWARD AMERICAN WRITING. *Princeton Univ. Press* 1962 $10.00. An acute, original work probing the works of all U.S. writers who have been known in Soviet Russia, including some who are actually little known here.

Bryer, Jackson R., Ed. SIXTEEN MODERN AMERICAN WRITERS: A Survey of Research and Criticism. Rev. enl. ed. *Duke Univ. Press* 1973 $10.00; *Norton* 1973 pap. $5.95. Prominent academic authorities describe and evaluate biographical, critical, and bibliographical writings on major writers of this century, including Sherwood Anderson, Willa Cather, Theodore Dreiser, William Faulkner, Ernest Hemingway, John Steinbeck, and Thomas Wolfe.

Coan, Otis W., and Richard G. Lillard. AMERICA IN FICTION: An Annotated List of Novels That Interpret Aspects of Life in the United States. *Pacific Bks.* 5th ed. 1967 $6.75

Coindreau, Maurice Edgar. THE TIME OF WILLIAM FAULKNER: A French View of Modern American Fiction. Ed. and trans. by George McMillan Reeves. *Univ. of South Carolina Press* 1971 $9.95. Coindreau deserves a major share of the credit for making modern American fiction popular in France and elsewhere in Europe. As the title of this book suggests, Coindreau sees Faulkner as the dominant American writer of the modern period. This collection brings together no less than eleven commentaries on that writer as well as translated prefaces to French editions of books by Erskine Caldwell, Truman Capote, William Goyen, Flannery O'Connor, and William Maxwell.

Cooperman, Stanley R. WORLD WAR I AND THE AMERICAN NOVEL. *Johns Hopkins Univ. Press* 1967 $10.00 pap. $2.45

"This well written and thoroughly researched book offers an intensive scrutiny of the causes for American involvement in World War I. It discusses ... the attitudes of disillusionment and disgust with war and justifications for war that permeated the American novel for years ... [The author] has evidently read every novel, newspaper, journal, and piece of criticism produced in this benighted period"—(*LJ*).

Cowley, Malcolm. AFTER THE GENTEEL TRADITION: American Writers, 1910–1930. *Southern Illinois Univ. Press* rev. ed. 1964 $4.50

A SECOND FLOWERING: Works and Days of the Lost Generation. *Viking* 1973 $7.95

Cowley's (*q. v.*) "Exile's Return" seemed to be a kind of manifesto for the lost generation when it appeared in 1934. Now, almost forty years later, Cowley looks back on his friends and contemporaries—including Fitzgerald, Hemingway, Dos Passos, Faulkner, Wolfe, and Thornton Wilder—with mellow detachment and balanced judgments. "No less than in 'Exile's Return,' what ultimately unifies the book is the character of Cowley himself—now an old man writing with the elegant grace of a craftsman convinced of the value of his materials and fully confident that he has all the tools and skills he needs to work with"—(Maurice Beebe in *Am. Lit.*).

Edel, Leon J. THE MODERN PSYCHOLOGICAL NOVEL. 1955. *Grosset* Univ. Lib. 1964 pap. $1.95; *Peter Smith* 1962 $4.00

Eisinger, Chester E. FICTION OF THE FORTIES. *Univ. of Chicago Press* 1963 $8.50 Phoenix Bks. pap. $2.25. An "extensive and penetrating" critical assessment of Mary McCarthy, Mailer, Capote, Welty, Algren, Faulkner, Steinbeck and many others.

French, Warren. THE SOCIAL NOVEL AT THE END OF AN ERA. Pref. by Harry T. Moore. Crosscurrents/Modern Critiques *Southern Illinois Univ. Press* 1966 $4.50. Excellent study of the way in which social and historical events affected the writing of five novels published around 1940—Steinbeck's "The Grapes of Wrath," Hemingway's "For Whom the Bell Tolls," Faulkner's "The Hamlet," Dalton Trumbo's "Johnny Got His Gun," and Pietro di Donato's "Christ in Concrete."

(Ed.) THE THIRTIES: Fiction, Poetry, Drama. *Everett Edwards* 1967 $10.50

THE FORTIES: Fiction, Poetry, Drama. *Everett Edwards* 1969 $12.00

THE FIFTIES: Fiction, Poetry, Drama. *Everett Edwards* 1971 $12.00

These volumes contain an abundance of previously unpublished critical essays on individual writers and works as well as general studies of themes and movements within the three decades of American literature covered.

Frohock, Wilbur Merrill. THE NOVEL OF VIOLENCE IN AMERICA. (Orig. "The Novel of Violence in America, 1920–1950") *Southern Methodist Univ. Press* 1950 5th ed. 1971 $5.95; *Beacon* 1964 pap. $1.75

Galloway, David D. THE ABSURD HERO IN AMERICAN FICTION: Updike, Styron, Bellow, Salinger. *Univ. of Texas Press* 1966 rev. ed. 1970 $7.50

> A perceptive critic "shows how four American novelists . . . have used the novel to portray the absurd man in four aspects: as saint, as tragic hero, as picaro, as seeker for love"—(Publisher's note). "An ambitious, discerning and stimulating book"—(*LJ*).

Geismar, Maxwell, REBELS AND ANCESTORS: The American Novel, 1890–1915. *Houghton* 1953 $7.50

> THE LAST OF THE PROVINCIALS: The American Novel, 1915–1925. *Houghton* 1947 $7.50

> WRITERS IN CRISIS: The American Novel, 1925–1940. *Houghton* 1942 $6.95; *Dutton* 1971 pap. $2.25. These books—written and published in reverse order from the chronological listing above—constitute a readable and authoritative critical history of modern American fiction to the Second World War. Each volume deals with five or six major writers of the period in question followed by an overall summary.

Gelfant, Blanche H. THE AMERICAN CITY NOVEL. 1954. *Univ. of Oklahoma Press* 1970 $4.95

Gerstenberger, Donna, and George Hendrick. THE AMERICAN NOVEL: A Checklist of Twentieth Century Criticism. *Swallow* 2 vols. Vol. 1 1789–1959 1960 $12.50 pap. $2.50 Vol. 2 Criticism Written 1960–1968 1970 $12.50

Gross, Seymour L., and John Edward Hardy, Eds. IMAGES OF THE NEGRO IN AMERICAN LITERATURE. *Univ. of Chicago Press* 1966 $7.50 pap. $2.95

> This is "scholarly historiography of the Negro since the Colonial period and essays on the Negro's place in the work of particular authors ranging from Melville to Twain, Faulkner to Baldwin. The 'critics are a match for their subjects' on what is a new, interior, plane of discussion; a 'major breakthrough for the American imagination' "—(*N.Y. Times*).

Guttmann, Allen: THE JEWISH WRITER IN AMERICA: Assimilation and the Crisis of Identity. *Oxford* 1971 $7.95

Handy, William J. MODERN FICTION: A Formalist Approach. Pref. by Harry T. Moore. Crosscurrents/Modern Critiques *Southern Illinois Univ. Press* 1971 $5.95. Includes excellent analyses-in-depth of Dreiser's "Sister Carrie," Faulkner's "As I Lay Dying," Hemingway's "The Old Man and the Sea," and Malamud's "The Fixer."

Harper, Howard M., Jr. DESPERATE FAITH: A Study of Bellow, Salinger, Mailer, Baldwin, and Updike. *Univ. of North Carolina Press* 1967 $6.00 pap. $1.95

> Professor Harper's "useful and occasionally shrewd observations . . . demonstrate that the direction of the novel . . . is away from social criticism and toward an understanding of self"—(*LJ*).

Hassan, Ihab. RADICAL INNOCENCE: Studies in the Contemporary Novel. *Princeton Univ. Press* 1961 $10.00 pap. $2.95. An exhaustive probing, by a distinguished critic, of the nature of the hero in novels of such contemporaries as Saul Bellow, Carson McCullers, Norman Mailer, J. D. Salinger, and others.

Hicks, Granville. Literary Horizons: A Quarter Century of American Fiction. *New York Univ. Press* 1970 $8.95. One of America's most respected senior critics here collects his reviews of works by fifteen postwar novelists: Louis Auchincloss, James Baldwin, John Barth, Saul Bellow, Herbert Gold, Joseph Heller, Bernard Malamud, Norman Mailer, Wright Morris, Vladimir Nabokov, Flannery O'Connor, Reynolds Price, Philip Roth, John Updike, and Kurt Vonnegut, Jr.

Hoffman, Frederick John. The Modern Novel in American, 1900–1950. *Regnery* rev. ed. 1964 pap. $1.45

The Twenties: American Writing in the Postwar Decade. 1955. *Macmillan* (Free Press) 1965 pap. $3.95; *Viking* 1955 $8.00

The Art of Southern Fiction: A Study of Some Modern Novelists. Pref. by Harry T. Moore. *Southern Illinois Univ. Press* 1967 $4.95. Exploration of many of Faulkner's contemporaries from James Agee to Truman Capote.

Holman, C. H. Three Modes of Modern Southern Fiction: Ellen Glasgow, William Faulkner and Thomas Wolfe. *Univ. of Georgia Press* 1967 $4.00

The Roots of Southern Writing: Essays on the Literature of the American South. *Univ. of Georgia Press* 1972 $10.00

"Running throughout the essays is a strain of resigned but optimistic humanism which sees that only through its profound experience of suffering, defeat, and poverty could the South produce the most distinctively tragic regional literature this country has known. Included are three essays on Thomas Wolfe, two on William Faulkner, single pieces on Ellen Glasgow and Flannery O'Connor, and several general essays"— (*Journal of Mod. Lit.*).

Kazin, Alfred. On Native Grounds: An Interpretation of Modern American Prose Literature. *Harcourt* 1942 $8.50 Harvest Bks. pap. $3.95

Brilliant and penetrating literary history of the "relation between American prose writers and our developing society in the years between 1890 and the present"—(*New Yorker*). Highly recommended.

Contemporaries. *Little-Atlantic* 1962 $10.00. More than 70 essays that make up a critical history of modern writing and thought from the Romantics to the present. An important section deals with the new writers—novelists, poets, essayists—who have made their mark since World War II, including C. P. Snow, Robert Penn Warren, Nelson Algren, James Agee, Lawrence Durrell, Dylan Thomas, Bernard Malamud, Saul Bellow, J. D. Salinger, Brendan Behan, Norman Mailer, Truman Capote, James Baldwin.

Klein, Marcus. After Alienation: American Novels in Mid-Century. 1963. *Bks. for Libraries* $10.50

An analysis of Bellow, Ellison, Baldwin, Morris, and Malamud. "A forceful, ground-breaking book for all shelves of modern criticism"—(*LJ*).

Kostelanetz, Richard, Ed. On Contemporary Literature. *Avon* 1964 pap. $1.95; *Bks. for Libraries* $20.00. An excellent overview of contemporary literature in America and Europe with many essays by contributors such as Hyman, Podhoretz, Fiedler, Eric Bentley on individual American novelists. Perhaps the best value for the student or reader wanting to understand modern American writing in its world setting.

Kunitz, Stanley J., and Howard Haycraft, Eds. Twentieth Century Authors: A Biographical Dictionary of Modern Literature. 1850 biographies and 1700 portraits. *Wilson* 1942 $22.00

Fɪʀsᴛ Sᴜᴘᴘʟᴇᴍᴇɴᴛ ed. by Stanley J. Kunitz *Wilson* 1955 $18.00

Litz, A Walton, Ed. Mᴏᴅᴇʀɴ Aᴍᴇʀɪᴄᴀɴ Fɪᴄᴛɪᴏɴ: Essᴀʏs ɪɴ Cʀɪᴛɪᴄɪsᴍ. *Oxford* Galaxy Bks. 1963 pap. $2.95

Lutwack, Leonard. Hᴇʀᴏɪᴄ Fɪᴄᴛɪᴏɴ: The Epic Tradition and American Novels of the Twentieth Century. Pref. by Harry T. Moore, Crosscurrents/Modern Critiques *Southern Illinois Univ. Press* 1971 $5.95

"Lutwack sees as central to the meaning of the epic hero continued faith in the value of purposeful action. Much modern fiction, he concedes, takes a more despairing or deterministic view of man's fate, but he finds a positive philosophy of hope in such works as Frank Norris' 'The Octopus,' Steinbeck's 'The Grapes of Wrath,' Hemingway's 'For Whom the Bell Tolls,' Ralph Ellison's 'Invisible Man,' and several novels by Saul Bellow"—(*Journal of Mod. Lit.*).

Lynn, Kenneth Schuyler. Dʀᴇᴀᴍ ᴏғ Sᴜᴄᴄᴇss: A Study of the Modern American Imagination. 1955 *Greenwood* $11.50

Lyons, John O. Tʜᴇ Cᴏʟʟᴇɢᴇ Nᴏᴠᴇʟ ɪɴ Aᴍᴇʀɪᴄᴀ. *Southern Illinois Univ. Press* 1962 $4.50. A first major attempt to bring the literature of college life together, this covers more than 200 novels, ranging from the early 19th century to the present.

Madden, David, Ed. Aᴍᴇʀɪᴄᴀɴ Dʀᴇᴀᴍs, Aᴍᴇʀɪᴄᴀɴ Nɪɢʜᴛᴍᴀʀᴇs. Pref. by Harry T. Moore. *Southern Illinois Univ. Press* 1970 $6.95 pap. $2.65. Specially commissioned essays on the theme of the American dream and our awakening therefrom in representative literary texts, including modern novels by Ralph Ellison, William Faulkner, F. Scott Fitzgerald, Norman Mailer, Henry Miller, and Thomas Wolfe.

Magny, Claude-Edmonde. Tʜᴇ Aɢᴇ ᴏғ ᴛʜᴇ Aᴍᴇʀɪᴄᴀɴ Nᴏᴠᴇʟ: The Film Aesthetic of Fiction Between the Two World Wars. Trans. from the French by Eleanor Hochman. *Ungar* 1972 $7.50

"This is the first translation into English of a book, originally published in France in 1968, which probably more than any other single critical text helped to turn postwar French novelists towards the 'sort of raw and savage novel' which during the classic period of modern American fiction had been written by Dos Passos, Hemingway, Steinbeck, and Faulkner"—(*Journal of Mod. Lit.*).

Malin, Irving. Nᴇᴡ Aᴍᴇʀɪᴄᴀɴ Gᴏᴛʜɪᴄ. *Southern Illinois Univ. Press* Crosscurrents/ Modern Critiques 1962 $4.95. This study examines a form of fiction which has become extremely popular. It is described as being marked by extreme intensity of character, fierce struggle between self and anti-self, and an unresolved blur of identity banging against walls of complex and equally unresolved reality. The six writers included are Capote, McCullers, Salinger, Flannery O'Connor, Hawkes, and Purdy.

May, John R. Tᴏᴡᴀʀᴅ ᴀ Nᴇᴡ Eᴀʀᴛʜ: Apocalypse in the American Novel. *Univ. of Notre Dame Press* 1972 $8.75. The author traces variations upon the theme of judgment, catastrophe, and renewal in twelve novels from Hawthorne to Vonnegut, among them works by William Faulkner, Nathanael West, Flannery O'Connor, Ralph Ellison, John Barth, and Thomas Pynchon.

Miller, James E., Jr. Qᴜᴇsᴛs Sᴜʀᴅ ᴀɴᴅ Aʙsᴜʀᴅ: Essᴀʏs ɪɴ Aᴍᴇʀɪᴄᴀɴ Lɪᴛᴇʀᴀᴛᴜʀᴇ. *Univ. of Chicago Press* 1967 $7.50

From Poe to Salinger, Professor Miller "traces the 'quest theme' as it is seen in the new 'existential hero' "—(*LJ*).

Millgate, Michael. Aᴍᴇʀɪᴄᴀɴ Sᴏᴄɪᴀʟ Fɪᴄᴛɪᴏɴ: James to Cozzens. *Barnes & Noble* 1964 $6.00 pap. $1.00

Milne, Gordon. THE AMERICAN POLITICAL NOVEL. *Univ. of Oklahoma Press* 1966 $4.95
   pap. $2.50

Newquist, Roy. COUNTERPOINT. Fwd. by Mark Van Doren. 1964. *Simon & Schuster*
   Clarion Bks. pap. $2.95. Short conversations with 63 writers such as Auchincloss,
   Capote, De Vries, Gold, Jones, and Mark Van Doren.

O'Connor, William Van, Ed. FORMS OF MODERN FICTION. 1948. *Indiana Univ. Press*
   1959 Midland Bks. pap. $1.95

   SEVEN MODERN AMERICAN NOVELISTS: An Introduction. *Univ. of Minnesota Press*
   1964 $8.50. As editor of the Minnesota Pamphlets on American Writers, Mr.
   O'Connor has assembled in book form those on Edith Wharton, Sinclair Lewis, F.
   Scott Fitzgerald, Faulkner, Hemingway, Wolfe, and Nathanael West.

Olderman, Raymond. BEYOND THE WASTE LAND: The American Novel in the Nineteen-
   Sixties. *Yale Univ. Press* 1972 $7.95 pap. $1.95. Still another demonstration that
   American novelists of the past decade have moved toward a more affirmative vision of
   life than that held by their predecessors, this worthwhile critical study is particularly
   rich in his considerations of Ken Kesey, Joseph Heller, John Barth, Thomas Pynchon, John Hawkes, and Kurt Vonnegut, Jr.

Perkins, Maxwell E. EDITOR TO AUTHOR. Sel. and ed. with commentary and an introd.
   by John Hall Wheelock. 1950. *Grosset* Univ. Lib. 1960 pap. $1.95; *Scribner* 1950
   $4.50 pap. $1.45

   The letters of *Scribner's* book editor for 37 years to their authors including Thomas Wolfe, Fitzgerald and
   Hemingway; ". . . of enormous and enduring interest to writers, editors and publishers everywhere"—(Alfred A. Knopf).

Pinsker, Sanford. THE SCHLEMIEL AS METAPHOR: Studies in the Yiddish and American
   Jewish Novel. Pref. by Harry T. Moore. Crosscurrents/Modern Critiques *Southern
   Illinois Univ. Press* 1971 $5.45

Rideout, Walter Bates. THE RADICAL NOVEL IN THE UNITED STATES, 1900–1954: Some
   Interrelations of Literature and Society. *Harvard Univ. Press* 1956 $9.00; *Hill &
   Wang* Am. Century 1966 pap. $1.95. This "remarkably intelligent and readable sur-
   vey" traces the development of those writers influenced by socialism and those influenced by communism.

Rubin, Louis D. THE FARAWAY COUNTRY: Writers of the Modern South. *Univ. of
   Washington Press* 1966 pap. $2.45. Professor Rubin of the University of North
   Carolina discusses Faulkner, Wolfe, Warren, Welty, Ransom, Tate, and William
   Styron.

The Curious Death of the Novel. *Louisiana State Univ. Press* 1968 $6.95

   The title essay of this collection covering various topics is "sharp, funny, rabbit-punching"—(Eliot Fremont-Smith). Professor Rubin finds our day a "fallow period" for American fiction.

   (With Robert D. Jacobs, Eds.) SOUTHERN RENASCENCE: THE LITERATURE OF THE
   MODERN SOUTH. *Johns Hopkins Press* 1965 $12.00 pap. $3.95

Rupp, Richard H. CELEBRATION IN POSTWAR AMERICAN FICTION, 1945–1957. *Univ. of
   Miami Press* 1970 $7.95. A critical study of ten contemporary novelists which sees a
   swing away from the alienation and despair of earlier periods. The subjects are

James Agee, James Baldwin, Saul Bellow, John Cheever, Ralph Ellison, Bernard Malamud, Flannery O'Connor, J. D. Salinger, John Updike, and Eudora Welty.

Schorer, Mark. THE WORLD WE IMAGINE. *Farrar, Straus* 1968 $6.95 Noonday pap. $2.95

By "one of our best critics of fiction. . . . After some lucid comments on Hamlin Garland, Conrad Aiken, Katherine Anne Porter, Carson McCullers, and Truman Capote, Schorer undertakes a longer study of the relationship between life and literature. He groups Gertrude Stein, Sherwood Anderson, Scott Fitzgerald, and Ernest Hemingway, brilliantly defining the essential elements of the writings of each, and describing the curious complex of friendships and quarrels"—(Granville Hicks, in *SR*).

Schulz, Max F. RADICAL SOPHISTICATION: Studies in Contemporary Jewish-American Novelists. *Ohio Univ. Press* 1969 $8.50 pap. $2.95. By "radical sophistication" Schulz means a "capacity for belief in the face of 'uncertainties, mysteries, doubts.' " He finds this affirmative theme in the nine writers he discusses in this perceptive study. They include novelists Saul Bellow, Bruce Jay Friedman, Norman Mailer, Bernard Malamud, J. D. Salinger, Nathanael West, and Edward Lewis Wallant.

BLACK HUMOR FICTION OF THE SIXTIES: A Pluralistic Definition of Man and His World. *Ohio Univ. Press* 1973 $8.50

Spiller, Robert E., and others. LITERARY HISTORY OF THE UNITED STATES. *See Chapter 3, Reference Books—Literature: Histories and Dictionaries of Literature.*

(Ed.) A TIME OF HARVEST: AMERICAN LITERATURE 1910–1960. *Hill & Wang* 1962 $3.50 Am. Century pap. $1.45. 15 short essays by literary historians. "Not a full-fledged literary history but a superior kind of blueprint or road map . . ."

Stegner, Wallace, Ed. THE AMERICAN NOVEL FROM JAMES FENIMORE COOPER TO WILLIAM FAULKNER. *Basic Bks.* 1965 $5.95. This collection of talks by eminent authorities for Voice of America broadcasts abroad provides clear and useful introductions to nineteen major American novels including those by modern writers Stephen Crane, Frank Norris, Theodore Dreiser, Edith Wharton, Jack London, Willa Cather, Sherwood Anderson, Sinclair Lewis, F. Scott Fitzgerald, Ernest Hemingway, Thomas Wolfe, and William Faulkner.

Stuckey, William Joseph. THE PULITZER PRIZE NOVELS. *Univ. of Oklahoma Press* 1966 $5.95

An analysis of the motives behind the Pulitzer novel awards (1917–62)—questioning its standards. "A sound book about a fascinating American cultural phenomenon"—(*LJ*).

Tanner, Tony. CITY OF WORDS: American Fiction, 1950–1970. *Harper* 1971 $7.95. A young British critic provides a fresh-eyed look at contemporary American fiction. Especially perceptive are his discussions of Norman Mailer, James Purdy, John Hawkes, Joseph Heller, Philip Roth, Thomas Pynchon, Kurt Vonnegut, Jr., John Barth, Donald Barthelme, and William Gass.

Thorp, Willard. AMERICAN WRITING IN THE TWENTIETH CENTURY. *Harvard Univ. Press* 1960 $9.00

"Until someone does better—and that should be a long while—this is the authority on twentieth-century American literature"—(Robert E. Spiller in *N.Y. Times*).

Tuttleton, James W. THE NOVEL OF MANNERS IN AMERICA. *Univ. of North Carolina Press* 1972 $10.00

"This solid work of scholarly criticism covers the novel of manners in America from Cooper to Auchincloss. Tuttleton consistently sees this particular form of fiction against the background of a changing sociological matrix, but he does not forget that he is dealing with the novel as a form of art as well as a reflection of social history. The result is an unusually responsible and discerning study of a kind of novel which was doomed to become unfashionable precisely because it was to a large extent concerned with fashions. Among the authors discussed at length are Henry James, Edith Wharton, Sinclair Lewis, F. Scott Fitzgerald, John O'Hara, John P. Marquand, and James Gould Cozzens"—(*Journal of Mod. Lit.*).

Van Doren, Carl. THE AMERICAN NOVEL, 1789–1939. *Macmillan* 1921 rev. enl. ed. 1940 $6.95

Vinson, James, Ed. CONTEMPORARY NOVELISTS. *St. Martin's* 1972 $30.00. Some 600 American and British novelists are represented in this ambitious and useful reference work. In most cases each entry includes a listing of writings, a personal statement by the author, and a signed critical commentary by one of the more than 200 prominent authorities who contributed to this large volume.

Waldmeir, Joseph, Ed. RECENT AMERICAN FICTION: Some Critical Views. *Houghton* 1963 pap. $4.00

Westbrook, Max, Ed. THE MODERN AMERICAN NOVEL: Essays in Criticism. *Random* 1966 pap. $2.95

Whitbread, Thomas B., Ed. SEVEN CONTEMPORARY AUTHORS: Essays on Cozzens, Miller, West, Golding, Heller, Albee, and Powers. *Univ. of Texas Press* 1966 $6.00

Wright, Austin M. THE AMERICAN SHORT STORY IN THE TWENTIES. *Univ. of Chicago Press* 1961 $7.50

Ziff, Larzer. THE AMERICAN 1890's: Life and Times of a Lost Generation. *Viking* 1966 $7.50 Compass Bks. pap. $1.95

A discussion that includes, among others, Stephen Crane, Frank Norris and Theodore Dreiser. "A fine rousing book"—(Charles Poore).

See also lists in Chapter 13, American Fiction—Early Period and Chapters 10, 11 and 12, British Fiction; Chapter 3, Reference Books—Literature: Histories and Dictionaries of Literature.

COLLECTIONS OF MODERN AMERICAN SHORT STORIES

Why do short stories entice the writer? Here is Bernard Malamud's answer: "Within a dozen or more pages, whole lives are implied and even understood. Though events are endless, lives aren't, yet there is a temptation in telling of lives to spin them endlessly. But the short story, though it reconceives lives, must limit itself to the sweeping realization of its meaning, which is to say it quickly runs its course because that's its nature, its fate. And that relates it more fittingly to our short lives." The indispensable reference tool for locating a specific story is "The Short Story Index," which is described in detail in Chapter 3, Reference Books—Literature: Basic Indexes for Literature.

Angus, Douglas and Sylvia. CONTEMPORARY AMERICAN SHORT STORIES. *Fawcett* Premier Bks. 1967 pap. $1.25. Includes Flannery O'Connor, Welty, Ellison, Baldwin, Malamud, Philip Roth, Updike, Mary McCarthy, Cheever, Elliott, Bellow, Powers and Purdy, among others.

Auchincloss, Louis. FABLES OF WIT AND ELEGANCE. *Scribner* 1972 $7.95

Bellow, Saul. GREAT JEWISH SHORT STORIES. From the Apocrypha to Bernard Malamud and Philip Roth. *Dell* 1963 pap. $.60

Burrell, John Angus, and Bennett A. Cerf. ANTHOLOGY OF FAMOUS AMERICAN STORIES. (Orig. "The Bedside Book of Famous American Stories") *Modern Library* Giants 1953 $4.95

Clarke, John Henrik, Ed. AMERICAN NEGRO SHORT STORIES. *Hill & Wang* 1966 $5.95 Am. Century pap. $2.45. The stories and excerpts from novels in this collection range from DuBois to Baldwin.

Corrington, John William, and Miller Williams. SOUTHERN WRITING IN THE SIXTIES: Fiction. *Louisiana State Univ. Press* 1966 $7.50. Short stories by writers from the South, with a penetrating introduction by the editors.

Current-Garcia, Eugene, and Walton R. Patrick. AMERICAN SHORT STORIES. *Scott-Foresman* rev. ed. 1964 pap. $4.95. Generous selection of 19th and 20th century stories.

Davis, Douglas M. THE WORLD OF BLACK HUMOR: An Introductory Anthology of Selections and Criticism. *Dutton* (orig.) 1967 pap. $2.45. Includes Heller, Pynchon, Purdy, Burroughs, De Vries, Friedman, and Bellow.

Day, A. Grove, and W. F. Bauer. GREATEST AMERICAN SHORT STORIES: Twenty Classics of Our Heritage. *McGraw-Hill* 1953 $5.95 text ed. $3.68

Downs, R. B. THE BEAR WENT OVER THE MOUNTAIN. *Macmillan* 1963 $6.95; *Gale* 1971 $9.00. An anthology of tall tales by E. B. White, Ring Lardner, James Thurber, and others.

Elkin, Stanley. STORIES FROM THE SIXTIES: A Short Story Anthology. *Doubleday* 1971 $6.95

Flower, Dean. COUNTERPARTS: Classic and Contemporary American Short Stories. *Fawcett* 1971 pap. $1.25

Foley, Martha. THE BEST AMERICAN SHORT STORIES. *Houghton* 1972 $7.95; *Ballantine Bks.* pap. $1.65

(With David Burnett) THE BEST AMERICAN SHORT STORIES. *Houghton* 1969 $6.95, 1970 $6.95, 1971 $7.50; *Ballantine Bks.* 1971 pap. $1.65

(With David Burnett) THE BEST OF THE BEST AMERICAN SHORT STORIES, 1915–1950. *Houghton* 1952 $5.95

(With David Burnett) FIFTY BEST AMERICAN SHORT STORIES, 1915–1965. *Houghton* $12.00 Sentry Eds. pap. $4.95

Gold, Herbert, and David Stevenson, Eds. STORIES OF MODERN AMERICA. *St. Martin's* 1961 1963 pap. $4.50. An outstanding and varied anthology of 23 short stories including brief biographies and editorial analyses.

Hills, Penney Chapin, and L. Rust Hills. HOW WE LIVE: Contemporary Life in Contemporary Fiction. 1968. *Macmillan* Collier Bks. 2 vols. pap. $3.45 each

Hollander, John. AMERICAN SHORT STORIES SINCE 1945. *Harper* 1968 pap. $1.95

Howard, C. Jeriel, and Richard F. Tracz. THE AGE OF ANXIETY: Modern American Stories. *Allyn & Bacon* 1972 pap. $4.25

James, Charles L. FROM THE ROOTS: Short Stories by Black Americans. *Dodd* 1970 pap. $4.95

Jones, LeRoi. THE MODERNS: An Anthology of New Writing in America. *Corinth Bks.* 1963 $5.95 pap. $3.50. A representative collection of modern experimental prose, repudiating "academic pseudo-traditions." "The tide of protest and revolt is strong in it. Style and content vary greatly," but the reader will find "strength, precious little humor, and artistic integrity and self-reliance."

King, Woodie. BLACK SHORT STORY ANTHOLOGY. *Columbia* 1972 $12.50; *New Am. Lib.* Signet 1972 pap. $1.95

Kostelanetz, Richard. TWELVE FROM THE SIXTIES. *Dell* pap. $.75

BREAKTHROUGH FICTIONEERS: An Anthology. *Something Else Press* 1972 $12.45 pap. $3.95. Imaginative collection of highly experimental fiction.

New Yorker Editors. STORIES FROM THE NEW YORKER 1950–1960. *Simon & Schuster* 1960 $7.50 pap. $2.95, 1965 3 vols. boxed pap. $7.95

Oates, Joyce Carol. SCENES FROM AMERICAN LIFE: Contemporary Short Fiction. *Vanguard* 1972 $6.95; *Random* 1973 pap. $3.95

Perkins, George. REALISTIC AMERICAN SHORT FICTION. *Scott-Foresman* 1972 pap. $4.95

Prescott, Orville, Ed. MID-CENTURY: An Anthology of Distinguished Contemporary American Short Stories. *Washington Square* pap. $.95

PRIZE STORIES: The O. Henry Awards. Fifty Years of the American Short Story, 1919–1970. Ed. by William Abrahams. *Doubleday* 2 vols. slip-cased $14.95

Salzman, Jack. THE SURVIVAL YEARS: A Collection of Writings of the 40's. (Orig. "The Years of Survival") *Pegasus* (dist. by Bobbs) 1969 $8.95 pap. $2.95

(With Barry Wallenstein). YEARS OF PROTEST: A Collection of American Writings of the 1930's. *Pegasus* (dist. by Bobbs) 1967 $7.50 pap. $2.95

Sanchez, Sonia. WE BE WORD SORCERERS: 25 Stories by Black Americans. *Bantam* 1973 pap. $1.25

Stegner, May and Wallace. GREAT AMERICAN SHORT STORIES. *Dell* 1957 pap. $.95

Stern, Philip Van Doren, A POCKET BOOK OF MODERN AMERICAN SHORT STORIES. 1943. *Washington Square* 1961 pap. $.75. 20 stories from the period between the World Wars.

Stevick, Philip. ANTI-STORY: An Anthology of Experimental Fiction. *Macmillan* (Free Press) 1971 pap. $3.95. Excellent selection of unusual stories by various contemporary writers, mostly American.

Swados, Harvey. THE AMERICAN WRITER AND THE GREAT DEPRESSION. Anthology which includes short stories. *Bobbs* $7.50 pap. $2.75

Turner, Arlin. SOUTHERN STORIES. *Holt* (Rinehart) 1960 pap. $1.25. Tales Southern in matter and authorship.

WHARTON, EDITH. 1862–1937.

Many honors came to Mrs. Wharton in recognition of her craftsmanship as a writer. She was the first woman ever to be awarded the Gold Medal of the National Institute of Arts and Letters and was elected to membership in the Institute in 1930. She was also the first woman to receive the honorary degree of Doctor of Letters from Yale University. She was made a member of the American Academy of Arts and Letters in 1934.

"The House of Mirth," the American "Vanity Fair," is one of Mrs. Wharton's strongest works; her theme is the conflict between wealth and sensitive human values. It was adapted for the theater by Clyde Fitch. "Ethan Frome," a tragic novelette of New England, is regarded by many as her masterpiece. Dramatized by Owen and Donald Davis (1936 *Dramatists* ms. only) it was one of the successes of the New York theatrical season. As a memorial volume to Mrs. Wharton it was entirely reset and issued in a new edition in 1938 with an introduction by Bernard De Voto. "The Old Maid" (1924), another miniature novel of surpassing work-manship, was dramatized by Zoë Akins and won the Pulitzer Drama Prize. "The Age of Innocence," a psy-chological novel of manners, was the most widely read of all her books and won the Pulitzer Novel Prize. Katherine Cornell appeared in the stage version. The story "Xingu" has been dramatized by Thomas Seller.

Mrs. Wharton was strongly influenced in her writing by her friend Henry James (*q. v.*). She lived abroad and always wrote as a cosmopolitan of an America of yesterday. Irving Howe notes (in his introduction to the essay collection "Edith Wharton") that Mrs. Wharton saw American society as "profoundly inhospitable to human need and desire. The malaise which troubled so many intelligent people during her lifetime—the feel-ing they were living in an age when energies had run down, meanings collapsed, and the flow of organic life been replaced by the sterile and mechanical—is quite as acute in her novels as in those of Hardy and Gis-sing." Mrs. Wharton's autobiography, "A Backward Glance" (1934, o. p.), is reticent on details of her per-sonal life, but contains charming reminiscences of James and other contemporaries. *See also the chapters on "Edith Wharton and Theodore Dreiser" in Kazin's (q. v.) "On Native Grounds," and in Van Wyck Brooks' (q. v.) "The Confident Years 1855–1915."*

THE EDITH WHARTON READER. Introd. and notes by Louis Auchincloss. Includes Ethan Frome; The Bunner Sisters; selections from The House of Mirth and The Age of Innocence; short stories. *Scribner* 1965 $7.50 pap. $2.95

ROMAN FEVER AND OTHER STORIES. *Scribner* 1964 pap. $2.45

MADAME DE TREYMES AND OTHERS. *Scribner* 1970 1973. pap. $2.65. Four novelettes including The Title Story (1907); The Touchstone (1900); Sanctuary (1903); Bun-ner Sisters (1916).

A BOOK OF GHOST STORIES. *Scribner* 1973. $7.95.

ETHAN FROME. *Scribner* 1911 $6.95 Contemporary Class. pap. $1.65. Ed. by Blake Nevius with commentary and sources. 1968 text ed. $2.48 pap. $1.44; *Franklin Watts* lg.-type ed. Keith Jennison Bks. $7.95

THE REEF. Introd. by Louis Auchincloss. *Scribner* 1913 1965 $5.95 pap. $2.65. A novel about an American family.

SUMMER. A New England Novel. 1917. *Scholarly Press* $14.50; *Scribner* 1920 1964 $3.95 pap. $1.45

THE AGE OF INNOCENCE. 1920. *New Am. Lib.* Signet 1962 pap. $.95 *Scribner* 1968 $5.95 pap. $2.65

OLD NEW YORK. 1924. *Scribner* 1964 $4.95 pap. $1.65. Four recently rediscovered short novels: False Dawn (The 'Forties); The Old Maid (The 'Fifties); The Spark (The 'Sixties); New Year's Day (The 'Seventies).

THE WRITING OF FICTION. 1924. *Octagon* 1967 $7.50. A very brief discussion: on gen-eral precepts, on "Telling a Short Story," "Constructing a Novel," "Character and Situation," and "Marcel Proust."

Books about Wharton

Portrait of Edith Wharton. By Percy Lubbock. 1947. *Kraus* 1969 $10.00. A classic of modern literary bi-
ography by the distinguished English essayist and critic.

Edith Wharton: A Study of Her Fiction. By Blake Nevius. *Univ. of California Press* 1953 pap. $1.50. An
analysis and appreciation; "a model of good taste, discreet scholarship and lucid exposition."

Edith Wharton. By Louis Auchincloss. *Univ. of Minnesota Press* 1961 pap. $1.25

Edith Wharton: A Collection of Critical Essays. Ed. by Irving Howe. *Prentice-Hall* 1963 $5.95 pap.
$1.95

Edith Wharton 1862–1937. By Olivia Coolidge. *Scribner* 1964 1970 $3.63 pap. $2.75. An adequate short
biography aimed at young readers but based on fresh research.

Edith Wharton and Henry James: The Story of Their Friendship. By Millicent Bell. *Braziller* 1965
$6.50
"The close and affectionate relationship between them is thoroughly explored. . . . Recommended"
—(*LJ*).

Edith Wharton: A Woman in Her Time. By Louis Auchincloss. *Viking* Studio Books 1971 $10.00. Gen-
erously illustrated biography by the distinguished novelist (*q. v.*) who writes in the Wharton tradition.

Edith Wharton: A Critical Interpretation. By Geoffrey Walton. *Fairleigh Dickinson Univ. Press* 1971
$8.00

NORRIS, FRANK (Benjamin Franklin Norris). 1870–1902.

Frank Norris, born in Chicago, studied art in Paris, attended the University of California and Harvard
and was a war correspondent in South Africa and Cuba. He was a pioneer in American realism.
"McTeague," his masterpiece, is a powerful study of avarice set in the semislum region of San Francisco,
where his well-to-do family lived for a time. His novels are all huge transcripts of the life of a lusty and developing new century.

His trilogy, "The Epic of the Wheat," consists of "The Octopus," "The Pit," and a projected volume,
"The Wolf," which was never written. "The Octopus" is his most impressive work. In it, wheat is a "symbol
of the life force, from its planting in the Western plains to its export to starving Europeans. . . . Battles between the wheat growers . . . of California and the monopolistic Southern Pacific Railroad [represent the]
struggle between the primitive force of fertile Earth and the non-organic force of the machine" (Robert E.
Spiller, in "The Cycle of American Literature"). "Vandover and the Brute" (1914, o. p.), lost in the California earthquake and then rediscovered, traces the course of insantiy and disease in a good man. (*See the chapter on "Frank Norris and Jack London" in Van Wyck Brooks' "The Confident Years, 1885–1915"*). "The
Literary Criticism of Frank Norris" (ed. by Donald Pizer *Univ. of Texas Press* 1963 $7.50) is a compilation
of all of Norris's significant critical essays.

Frank was the older brother of Charles G. Norris (1881–1945), author of such grim "tractarian" novels
as "Salt" (1918), "Brass" (1921), "Bread" (1923), "Pig Iron" (1930)—now o. p. Charles was married to
the popular novelist Kathleen Norris.

COMPLETE WORKS. 1928. *Kennikat* Argonaut ed. 10 vols. set $125.00

A NOVELIST IN THE MAKING: A Collection of Student Themes, and the Novels "Blix"
and "Vandover and the Brute." Ed. by James D. Hart. *Harvard Univ. Press* 1970
$12.50

McTEAGUE: A Story of San Francisco. 1899. *Bentley* $8.50; Ed. by Carvel Collins
Holt (Rinehart) 1950 pap. $2.00; *Fawcett* Premier Bks. pap. $.95; *New Am. Lib.*
Signet pap. $.95; *Peter Smith* $4.25

THE OCTOPUS. A Story of California. 1901. *Assoc. Booksellers* Airmont Bks. pap. $.75;
Bantam pap. $.95; *Bentley* $8.50; *Doubleday* 1947 $6.50; *New Am. Lib.* Signet
pap. $1.25

THE PIT: A Story of Chicago. 1903. *Bentley* $8.50; *Grove* Evergreen Bks. pap. $2.95;
Ed. by James D. Hart *Charles E. Merrill* pap. $1.25; *Peter Smith* $4.75

Books about Norris

Frank Norris: A Biography. By Franklin Walker. 1932. *Russell* 1963 $12.50

Frank Norris: A Bibliography. Comp. by Kenneth Lohf and Eugene Sheehy. *Kraus* 1959 $8.00

Frank Norris. By Warren French. U.S. Authors Ser. *Twayne* 1962 $5.50; *College & Univ. Press* 1963
pap. $2.45

The Novels of Frank Norris. By Donald Pizer. *Indiana Univ. Press* 1966 $6.75

Frank Norris: Instinct and Art. By William Dillingham. *Univ. of Nebraska Press* 1969 $5.95; *Houghton Mifflin* Riverside Studies in Lit. 1969 pap. $4.00

CRANE, STEPHEN. 1871–1900.

Crane was born in Newark, N. J. He attended Syracuse University and began his career as a journalist and writer in New York City before becoming a widely traveled newspaper correspondent. His first book, "Maggie: A Girl of the Streets," a brutal picture of the New York slums, was originally published under the pseudonym of Johnston Smith; reissued in 1896 under the author's name, it is now considered a landmark of literary naturalism. "The Red Badge of Courage," his most famous work, blends a realistic depiction of the Civil War with an impressionistic style and profound religious symbolism. Dead before he was 30, Crane left behind not only these two classic short novels but such memorable short stories as "The Open Boat," "The Blue Hotel," and "The Bride Comes to Yellow Sky." Like his fiction, his "Complete Poems," ed. by Joseph Katz (*Cornell Univ. Press* 1972 pap. $2.45), reflect an existential view of man as an isolated being in a meaningless universe, yet capable of defiant heroism. Robert W. Stallman and Edward Hagemann have edited two volumes of Crane's journalistic writings. "The War Dispatches of Stephen Crane" (*New York Univ. Press* 1964 $9.50) consists of his reports on the Spanish-American, Greco-Turkish, and Boer Wars; "The New York City Sketches of Stephen Crane and Related Pieces" (*New York Univ. Press*, 1966, $8.95) gathers together the products of his career as a reporter in Manhattan. Another collection is "Stephen Crane in the West and Mexico," ed. by Joseph Katz (*Kent State Univ. Press* 1971 $6.75). Professor Katz of the English Department at the University of South Carolina publishes a *Stephen Crane Newsletter* four times a year ($2.00 individuals, $3.00 libraries).

THE WORKS OF STEPHEN CRANE. 1925. Ed. by Wilson Follett. *Russell & Russell* 1963 12 vols. in 6 $100.00

WORKS. Ed. by Fredson Bowers. *Univ. Press of Virginia* 1969–6 vols. available Vol. I Bowery Tales: Maggie and George's Mother (1969) $10.00 Vol. 4 The O'Ruddy (1971) $15.00 Vol. 5 Tales of Adventure (1970) $15.00 Vol. 6 Tales of War (1970) $22.50 Vol. 7 Tales of Whilomville: The Monster, His New Mittens and Whilomville Stories (1969) $10.00 Vol. 8 Tales, Sketches and Reports (1972) $35.00 Vol. 9 Reports of War (1971) $24.00. Recognized as an approved text by the Center for Editions of American Authors created by the Modern Language Association under the sponsorship of the National Foundation on the Arts and Humanities.

COMPLETE SHORT STORIES AND SKETCHES. Ed. by Thomas A. Gullason. *Doubleday* 1963 $7.95

GREAT SHORT WORKS. *Harper* Perenn. Class. pap. $.95

STEPHEN CRANE: AN OMNIBUS. Ed. with introd. and notes by Robert Wooster Stallman. *Knopf* 1952 $7.95. Three novels: Maggie, George's Mother (1896), The Red Badge of Courage; 10 short stories; 16 poems; 4 articles; 57 letters never before published in addition to other letters "reprinted from periodicals and books in which they first appeared."

THE RED BADGE OF COURAGE and SELECTED PROSE AND POETRY. 1950. Ed. by William Merriam Gibson *Holt* 1950 (Rinehart) 1956 pap. $2.25

THE RED BADGE OF COURAGE AND SELECTED STORIES. Ed. by R. W. Stallman. *New Am. Lib.* Signet 1952 pap. $1.50

THE RED BADGE OF COURAGE AND OTHER STORIES. *Franklin Watts* $3.75

THE RED BADGE OF COURAGE AND OTHER WRITINGS. Ed. by Richard Chase. *Houghton* 1960 Riv. Eds. pap. $2.40

THE RED BADGE OF COURAGE AND FOUR GREAT STORIES. *Dell* pap. $.60

STORIES AND TALES. Ed. by Robert Wooster Stallman. *Random* Vintage Bks. 1955 pap. $1.95

THE RED BADGE OF COURAGE AND RELATED READINGS. Ed. by Jay E. Greene and L. E. Bertrand. *Prentice-Hall* 1965 $4.50 text ed. $3.85

UNCOLLECTED WRITINGS. Ed. by O. W. Fryckstedt. *Humanities Press* 1963 $17.50

THE PORTABLE STEPHEN CRANE. Ed. by Joseph Katz. *Viking* 1969 $6.50 pap. $2.25

MAGGIE: A Girl of the Streets. 1893. *Chandler Pub.* facsimile ed. 1968 pap. $1.95; Ed. by Herbert Van Thal. 1966 *Dufour* $3.95 pap. $1.25; (and "George's Mother") *Fawcett* Premier Bks. pap. $.75 (with title "Maggie: Text and Context") Ed. by Maurice Bassan. *Wadsworth* 1966 pap. $2.95

THE RED BADGE OF COURAGE. 1895. *Bantam* pap. $.60; Ed. by Frederick C. Crews *Bobbs* 1964 pap. $1.24; *Dodd* Gt. Ill. Class. 1957 $5.50; ed. by Richard Chase *Houghton* Riv. Eds. 1960 pap. $1.65; *Lancer* pap. $.60; *Macmillan* 1962 $3.95 Collier Bks. pap. $.65; *Modern Library* 1951 $2.95 pap. $.85; ed. by Fredson Bowers. facsimile of the original ms. *NCR Microcard* 1973 $50.00; Annotated text with critical essays ed. by Sculley Bradley and others *Norton* Critical Ed. 1962 pap. $1.95; *Washington Square* pap. $.45 Enriched Class pap. $.75; *Franklin Watts* lg.-type ed. Keith Jennison Bks. $7.95

SULLIVAN COUNTY TALES AND SKETCHES. Ed. by Robert W. Stallman. *Iowa State Univ. Press* 1968 $5.50

LOVE LETTERS TO NELLIE CROUSE. Ed. by Edwin H. Cady and Lester G. Wells. *Syracuse Univ. Press* 1954 $4.50

LETTERS. Ed. by R. W. Stallman and Lillian Gilkes. *New York Univ. Press* 1960 $6.50. Includes letters to and from William Dean Howells, Hamlin Garland, Joseph Conrad, and others; a valuable collection.

Books about Crane

Stephen Crane. By Thomas Beer. 1923. *Octagon* 1972 $11.00. A brilliant biography which helped launch the revival of interest in Crane.

Stephen Crane. By John Berryman. 1950. *Peter Smith* $5.00. Good critical biography with strong psychological slant.

The Poetry of Stephen Crane. By Daniel Hoffman. *Columbia* 1957 $10.00. A critical study.

Cora Crane. By Lillian Giles. *Indiana Univ. Press* 1960 $10.00. Vivid biography of Crane's common-law wife.

Stephen Crane. By Edwin Cady. *College & Univ. Press* 1963 pap. $2.45; *Twayne* 1962 $5.50

Stephen Crane in England. By Eric Solomon. *Ohio State Univ. Press* 1965 $4.50

Stephen Crane: From Parody to Realism. By Eric Solomon. *Harvard Univ. Press* 1966 $8.95.
This study "offers a joyful bonus to serendipitists. Mr. Solomon finds ties for him with John Barth and Joseph Heller, William Golding and Vladmir Nabokov" (*N.Y. Times*). "Should convince serious students . . . that Crane's stature . . . does have s sound footing"—(*LJ*).

Stephen Crane: A Collection of Critical Essays. Ed. by Maurice Bassan. *Prentice-Hall* 1967 $5.95
"Most, if certainly not all, of the best, most representative, and most influential studies of Crane"—(*LJ*). Among the critics are John Berryman, Willa Cather, Joseph Conrad.

Stephen Crane: A Biography. By Robert W. Stallman. *Braziller* 1968 $12.50.
"A very fine book; a literary event"—(*PW*).

The Fiction of Stephen Crane. By Donald Gibson. *Southern Illinois Univ. Press* 1968 $4.95

Stephen Crane's Career: Perspectives and Evaluations. Ed. by Thomas A. Gullason. *New York Univ. Press* 1971 $12.95 pap. $3.95. Generous collection of critical reviews and essays.

A Reading of Stephen Crane. By Marston LaFrance. *Oxford* 1971 $9.50. Well-received critical interpretation.

Stephen Crane in Transition: Centenary Essays. Ed. by Joseph Katz. *Northern Illinois Univ. Press* 1972 $10.00. Ten critical assessments written especially for this volume.

Stephen Crane: A Critical Bibliography. By Robert W. Stallman. *Iowa State Univ. Press* 1973 $25.00. Definitive annotated listing of writings on Crane.

DREISER, THEODORE. 1871–1945.

Dreiser was born in Indiana. He was on the staff of the *Delineator* from 1906 to 1910 and was then made editor-in-chief of the Butterick publications. The various litigations occasioned by Dreiser's novels brought him a reputation as "the most suppressed and insuppressible writer in America." H. L. Mencken (*q. v.*) in "A Book of Prefaces" (o. p.) wrote a fair and able criticism of Dreiser, and told the exciting history of his novels. With Mencken he waged a long fight against censorship that changed the public attitude toward the novelist who pictures life as he sees it. "Sister Carrie," which was in print in England during the time that it was suppressed here, was considered abroad to be "the best story, on the whole, that has come out of America," and such prominent English authors as Bennett, Wells, and Hugh Walpole joined in a written protest against the treatment accorded Dreiser's works in this country. Dreiser wrote his autobiography in "A Book About Myself," "A Traveler at Forty" (1913, o. p.), and "Dawn." His later years are most vividly and frankly described in his wife Helen's memoir, "My Life with Dreiser" (1951, o. p.).

"An American Tragedy," based on an actual murder trial, carrying an overwhelming indictment of American social and business values, is often said to be his most important work. It was successfully dramatized and filmed as "A Place in the Sun." "The Bulwark" (1946, o. p.), Dreiser's first novel in 20 years, was completed shortly before his death. "The Stoic," published posthumously, was his last novel, the final volume in the trilogy including "The Financier" and "The Titan." His studies of the unscrupulous and successful American business man are devastating records of our industrial-commercial era. His prose was fumbling, ungrammatical, often awkward, "elephantine." Yet Dreiser's novels have a raw narrative force which makes them compelling reading. "The Dreiser Newsletter" has been published twice a year since 1970 under the sponsorship of the English Department at Indiana State University in Terre Haute. The subscription rate is $2.50 for four issues. Robert H. Elias's chapter on Dreiser in "Sixteen Modern American Writers: A Survey of Research and Criticism," edited by Jackson R. Bryer (*Duke Univ. Press* rev. enl. ed. 1973 $10.00 pap. $5.95) is the most complete and up-to-date description of writings about Dreiser.

SISTER CARRIE. 1900. *Bantam.* 1963 pap. $.75; ed. by Jack Salzman $6.50 pap. $1.75; *Dell* 1960 pap. $.75; *Harper* pap. $.85; ed. by Kenneth S. Lynn *Holt* (Rinehart) 1957 pap. $3.00; ed. by C. Simpson *Houghton* pap. $1.35; ed. by Louis Auchincloss *Charles E. Merrill* pap. $1.15; ed. by Donald Pizer *Norton* Critical Eds. $6.00 pap. $2.45

THE FINANCIER. 1912. *New Am. Lib.* Signet pap. $1.50

THE TITAN. 1914. *New Am. Lib.* Signet pap. $.95

THE GENIUS. 1915. *New Am. Lib.* Signet pap. $1.50

TWELVE MEN. 1919. *Scholarly Press* $9.50

AN AMERICAN TRAGEDY. 1925. *New Am. Lib.* Signet pap. $1.50

LETTERS OF THEODORE DREISER: A Selection. Ed. by Robert Elias. *Univ. of Pennsylvania Press* 1959 3 vols. boxed $24.00

LETTERS TO LOUISE: Theodore Dreiser's Letters to Louise Campbell. Ed. by Louise Campbell. *Univ. of Pennsylvania Press* 1959 $6.50

Books about Dreiser

Theodore Dreiser: Apostle of Nature. By Robert H. Elias. 1949. *Cornell Univ. Press* rev. ed. 1970 $12.50 pap. $3.45. Sound interpretive biography.

The Writings of Theodore Dreiser: A Bibliography. By Edward D. McDonald 1928. *Folcroft* $15.00; *Burt Franklin* 1967 $15.00

Theodore Dreiser. By Francis Otto Matthiessen. 1951. *Greenwood* $12.00

The Stature of Theodore Dreiser: A Critical Survey of the Man and His Work. Ed. by Alfred Kazin and Charles Shapiro. *Indiana Univ. Press* 1955 Midland Bks. pap. $2.25; *Peter Smith* $4.50

Theodore Dreiser: Our Bitter Patriot. By Charles Shapiro. Crosscurrents/Modern Critiques *Southern Illinois Univ. Press* 1962 $4.95 pap. $1.45

Dreiser: A Biography. By W. A. Swanberg. *Scribner* 1965 $12.50; *Bantam* pap. $1.25.
"This will unquestionably remain the definitive biography of [a] major novelist. . . . Mr. Swanberg's prodigious research has sent him to the most obscure sources, to thousands of letters, and to scores of men and women who knew Dreiser, and with this massive detail he has constructed a fascinating story"—(*LJ*).

Theodore Dreiser: His Work and His Novels. By Richard Lehan. *Southern Illinois Univ. Press* 1969 $8.95. Good scholarly study of the sources and composition of Dreiser's writings.

Two Dreisers. By Ellen Moers. *Viking* 1969 $10.00. A readable account of Dreiser's life and works in terms of the conflict between his divided selves.

Homage to Theodore Dreiser: On the Centennial of His Birth. By Robert Penn Warren. Appreciation in prose and verse. *Random* 1971 $5.95

Dreiser: A Collection of Critical Essays. Ed. by John Lydenberg. *Prentice-Hall* 1972 $5.95 pap. $1.95

GLASGOW, ELLEN. 1874–1945.

In the Virginia edition of her works (12 vols. 1938, o. p.), Miss Glasgow reclassified her books into (1) Novels of Character and Comedies of Manners (5 vols.) and (2) Social History in the Form of Fiction (7 vols.). The Social History stories consist of the earlier books, 1900–16; the Novels of Character are the later books, 1925–35. The new prefaces which the author wrote for each volume of the Virginia edition form a valuable record of her literary growth and a treatise on novel writing similar to Henry James' (*q. v.*) prefaces to the New York edition of his works. They are collected, with the addition of the introduction to "In This Our Life" and published separately in "A Certain Measure." A volume of her poetry is available: "The Freeman and Other Poems" (1902, *Americanist Press* 1966 pap. $4.85).

Miss Glasgow made her native state the background of all her stories. No other Commonwealth has had its social history written in fiction so completely by a single writer. The powerful new Southern literature (*see introduction to this chapter*) may be said to have begun with her. The novels are comedies of manners of the years 1850–1940 in Virginia. She was awarded the Howells Medal "for eminence in creative literature" by the American Academy of Arts and Letters in 1940; the *Saturday Review of Literature* plaque for outstanding service to American Letters in 1941; the Pulitzer Prize for her rich and powerful novel "In This Our Life" in 1942. "The Woman Within" (1954), her own story of her inner life, is now o. p.

THE COLLECTED STORIES OF ELLEN GLASGOW. Ed. by Richard K. Meeker. *Louisiana State Univ. Press* 1963 pap. $1.95

BARREN GROUND. 1925. *Hill & Wang* Am. Century 1957 pap. $2.95

VEIN OF IRON. *Harcourt* Harbrace Mod. Class. 1935 $2.95 pap. $.95

IN THIS OUR LIFE. 1941. *Avon* 1968 pap. $.75

BEYOND DEFEAT: An Epilogue to an Era. Ed. by L.Y. Gore. *Univ. Press of Virginia* 1966 $6.00. A sequel to "In This Our Life" left in an unfinished state at her death.

A CERTAIN MEASURE: An Interpretation of Prose Fiction. 1943 *Kraus* $12.00

Books about Glasgow

Ellen Glasgow and the Ironic Art of Fiction. By Frederick McDowell. The first full-length critical study. *Univ. of Wisconsin Press* 1960 pap. $3.50

Ellen Glasgow. By Blair Rouse. *College & Univ. Press* 1963 pap. $2.45; *Twayne* 1962 $5.50

Ellen Glasgow: A Bibliography. By William W. Kelly. Ed. by O. Steele. *Univ. Press of Virginia* 1964 $8.50

Ellen Glasgow. By Louis Auchincloss. Pamphlets on American Writers. *Univ. of Minnesota Press* 1964 pap. $.95

Ellen Glasgow's American Dream. By Joan F. Santas. *Univ. Press of Virginia* 1965 $6.00

Without Shelter: The Early Career of Ellen Glasgow. By J. R. Raper. *Louisiana State Univ. Press* 1971 $8.95

Ellen Glasgow's Development as a Novelist. By Marion K. Richards. Studies in Amer. Lit. No. 24. *Humanities Press* 1971 $11.00

STEIN, GERTRUDE. 1874–1946.

Gertrude Stein "left behind her the memory of a personage—not a great writer but a bold experimenter and a great woman"—(Malcolm Cowley). In 1946, shortly before her death, she "gave and bequeathed her correspondence and manuscripts to the Yale University Library." Besides the manuscripts, she left more than 20,000 letters, including "notes from her concierge, who wrote in bad French spelled phonetically, and messages from many of the most distinguished writers and painters in Paris, London and New York." From this multitude, 447 letters from 175 persons and organizations covering the years from 1895 to 1946 can be found in "The Flowers of Friendship: Letters Written to Gertrude Stein" (1953, o. p.), which reveal Miss Stein and her place in literary history.

Gertrude Stein was born in Pennsylvania, but spent most of her childhood and early youth in California. After graduating from Radcliffe, where she was strongly influenced by the philosopher William James, she studied medicine for four years at Johns Hopkins but took no degree. In 1903 she went to Paris with her brother Leo. They were among the first to recognize the genius of Mattise, Picasso, and other modern artists, but disagreements of taste led to estrangement. From 1907 until her death Miss Stein lived in France with her lesbian friend and secretary Alice B. Toklas. Their apartment at 27 rue de Fleuris in Paris became renowned as one of the most celebrated and long-lived cultural salons in our century. They lived a "busy and productive life. . . . There was travel, Miss Stein's triumphant lectures in England and America, the nightly sessions at her writing desk, the vicissitudes and obligations of living in wartime and Occupied France." Miss Toklas, who died in 1967, described in her autobiography, "What is Remembered," (1963, o. p.), her long friendship with Gertrude Stein, and the procession of artists, writers, philosophers, and critics who were their friends. Miss Stein returned to America only once, in 1934, to give a lecture tour and to see her opera "Four Saints in Three Acts," with music by Virgil Thomson. She was a master of words and used them entirely for their tonal and associational qualities. Such sentences as "A rose is a rose is a rose" baffled many of her contemporaries but seem less strange, and often masterly, in the light of today's changed taste, which she helped to mold. Of "The Making of Americans" Edmund Wilson says (in "Axel's Castle"), "I confess that I have not read this book all through, and I do not know whether it is possible to do so. The novel suggests some technique of mesmerism . . . some ruminative self-hypnosis . . . a sort of fatty degeneration of her imagination and style." Ernest Hemingway corrected the original proofs. As a playwright—"In Circles" and "What Happened" have had great success in the New York off-Broadway theater—she is "an absurdist whose perfection lies in the fact that her words have no meaning. 'What Happened' . . . won an Obie award in 1964 and is considered a classic of the Happenings theater"—(Rosalyn Regelson, in the N.Y. Times). With the chief exception of "The Autobiography of Alice B. Toklas," her most widely read work, most of Gertrude Stein's writings are too difficult and experimental for general readers, but she has had considerable influence on other writers from the time of Ernest Hemingway (q. v.) and other members of what she called "the lost generation" to the present Post-Modernist period. Today's avant-garde writers often discover that their most daring innovations of language and style were anticipated by Gertrude Stein.

The Yale Edition of the Unpublished Writings of Gertrude Stein. 1951–58. Bks. for Libraries 8 vols. Vol. I Two: Gertrude Stein and Her Brother and Other Early Portraits (1908–1912) fwd. by Janet Flanner $16.50; Vol. 2 Mrs. Reynolds and Five Earlier Novelettes fwd. by Lloyd Frankenberg. $16.50; Vol. 3 Bee Time Vine and Other Pieces (1913–1927) pref. and notes by Virgil Thomson $14.50; Vol. 4 As Fine as Melanctha (1914–1930) fwd. by Natalie Clifford Barney $17.50; Vol. 5 Painted Lace and Other Pieces with introd. by Daniel-Henry Kahnweiler $15.50; Vol. 6 Stanzas in Meditation and Other Pieces (1929–1933) pref. by Donald Sutherland $15.50; Vol. 7 Alphabets and Birthdays. introd. by Donald Gallup $13.50; Vol. 8 A Novel of Thank You introd. by Carl Van Vechten $14.00 set $100.00

Selected Operas and Plays. Ed. by John M. Brinnin. Univ. Pittsburgh Press 1970 $9.95.

Selected Writings. Ed. by Carl Van Vechten Random Vintage Bks. pap. $2.95

A Primer for the Gradual Understanding of Gertrude Stein. Ed. by Robert B. Haas. Black Sparrow 1971 $10.00 pap. $4.00. A selection of her writings together with an interview, a memoir by a niece, and an essay by Ronald Sutherland on Stein's position in 20th-century cultural history

WRITINGS AND LECTURES. Ed. by Patricia Meyerowitz. *Penguin* 1971 pap. $2.25

FERNHURST, Q.E.D., AND OTHER EARLY WRITINGS. *Liveright* 1971 $8.95

THREE LIVES. 1909. Introd. by Carl Van Vechten. *Random* Vintage Bks. pap. $1:65

TENDER BUTTONS. 1914. Prose poems. *Haskell* pap. $5.95

GEOGRAPHY AND PLAYS. 1922. *Haskell* $13.50; *Something Else Press* $6.95 pap. $2.95

THE MAKING OF AMERICANS: Being a History of a Family's Progress. 1925. *Harcourt* Harvest Bks. pap. $2.95; *Something Else Press* 1966 $10.95

LUCY CHURCH AMIABLY. 1930. *Something Else Press* 1969 $6.95 pap. $2.95

MATISSE, PICASSO AND GERTRUDE STEIN (Original title "GMP") 1933. *Something Else Press* 1972 $10.00 pap. $3.45

IDA: A NOVEL. 1941. *Cooper* 1971 $5.00; *Random* Vintage Bks. pap. $1.65

THE AUTOBIOGRAPHY OF ALICE B. TOKLAS. 1933. *Random* Vintage Bks. pap. $3.75; *Peter Smith* $3.75. Miss Stein's autobiography composed as though written by her secretary.

PICASSO. 1938. *Beacon* 1959 pap. $2.95; (with title "Gertrude Stein on Picasso") Ed. by Edward Burns. *Liveright* 1970 $19.75

PARIS, FRANCE. *Liveright* 1940 1970 pap. $1.95

Books about Stein

Art by Subtraction: A Dissenting Opinion of Gertrude Stein. By B. L. Reid. *Univ. of Oklahoma Press* 1958 $6.95. "The first full-scale attempt to downgrade Gertrude Stein."
Catalogue of the Published and Unpublished Writings of Gertrude Stein. By Robert B. Haas and Donald Gallup. 1941. *Folcroft* $12.50
When This You See Remember Me. By W. G. Rogers. 1948 *Greenwood* $11.25
Gertrude Stein: A Biography of Her work. By Donald Sutherland. 1951. *Greenwood* 1972 $10.00. The first extended scholarly study.
The Third Rose: Gertrude Stein and Her World. By John Malcolm Brinnin. 1959. *Peter Smith* $7.50. Still the best biography.
Gertrude Stein. By Frederick J. Hoffman. Pamphlets on American Writers. *Univ. of Minnesota Press* 1961 pap. $1.25
Gertrude Stein and the Present. By Allegra Stewart. *Harvard Univ. Press* 1967 $6.00. A "carefully done . . . piece of scholarly writing" (*LJ*) tracing her theories of creative writing as she applied them in her work.
Gertrude Stein in Pieces. By Richard Bridgman. *Oxford Univ. Press* 1970 $12.50. Good critical introduction.
Gertrude Stein and the Literature of Modern Consciousness. By Norman Weinstein. *Ungar* 1970 $7.00. On her significance for today's writers.
Four Americans in Paris: The Collections of Gertrude Stein and Her Family. Ed. by Irene Gordon. *N.Y. Graphic Soc.* (Museum of Modern Art) 1970 $12.50. Attractively designed book with many illustrations, essays by various hands, and a catalogue of the remarkable MOMA exhibition of 1970–1971.

CATHER, WILLA (SIBERT). 1875–1947.

Willa Cather was born in Virginia but spent her very impressionable youth on a ranch in Nebraska, where her only neighbors were Bohemians and Scandinavians. From two grandmothers at home she learned to appreciate the English and Latin classics. She worked her way through the University of Nebraska and went on to newspaper work. The publication of her "April Twilights" in 1903 and a volume of short stories in 1905 led to *McClure's Magazine*, where she was managing editor from 1906 to 1912. During this time she traveled a great deal.

"Alexander's Bridge," Miss Cather's first novel, was a story of a civil engineer who, under stress of a dishonorable love affair, builds a faultily constructed bridge. Her work from the first was distinguished for its purity of style, serious craftsmanship, artistic integrity, and imaginative power. Her first group of novels ("O Pioneers!" "The Song of the Lark," "My Antonia"), with Western backgrounds, show the conflict between meanness and grandeur with a final triumphant fulfillment of destiny. "A Lost Lady" and "The Professor's House" commemorate with subtle irony the death of idealism in a modern world; they are studies of failure. Her particular interest in Roman Catholicism produced the beauty and serenity of "Death Comes for the Archbishop" and "Shadows on the Rock." Among her other books in print are "April Twilights and Other Poems" (1903, *Knopf* new ed. 1923 $4.50; ed. by Bernice Slote, *Univ. of Nebraska Press* 1962 $5.50), "Not Under Forty" (*Knopf* 1936 $5.95), "On Writing: Critical Studies on Writing as an Art" (*Knopf* 1949 $4.95) and "Willa Cather in Europe: Her Own Story of the First Journey" (ed. by George N. Kates *Knopf* 1956 $4.95), containing her articles for the *Nebraska State Journal* describing England, Paris, and Southern France as she saw them in the summer of 1902.

"One of Ours," her modern Nebraska-and-World-War-I novel, received the Pulitzer Prize in 1922. She received the Prix Femina Américain in 1933 and the gold medal of the National Institute of Arts and Letters in 1944. She died in her Park Avenue apartment in New York: "Her will contains an unqualified prohibition of the publication 'in any form whatsoever of the whole, or any part of any letter or letters written by me' "— a very great literary loss. The Bruce Rogers edition of her Complete Works (*Houghton* 1928, 13 vols.) has recently gone out of print.

COLLECTED SHORT FICTION, 1892–1912. *Univ. of Nebraska Press* 1965 rev. ed. by Virginia Faulkner 1970 $9.50

EARLY STORIES. Ed. by Mildred R. Bennett. *Apollo* pap. $1.95

FIVE STORIES. *Random* Vintage Bks. 1956 pap. $1.65

UNCLE VALENTINE AND OTHER STORIES: Willa Cather's Uncollected Short Fiction, 1915–1929. Ed. by Bernice Slote. *Univ. of Nebraska Press* 1973 $6.95

THE TROLL GARDEN. 1905. Short stories. *New Am. Lib.* pap. $2.95

O PIONEERS! 1913 *Houghton* new ed. 1932 $5.95 Sentry Eds. pap. $2.25; *Franklin Watts* 1966 lg.-type ed. Keith Jennison Bks. $9.95

THE SONG OF THE LARK. *Houghton* 1915 $5.00 Sentry Eds. 1963 pap. $2.65

MY ANTONIA. 1918. *Houghton* new ed. 1926 $6.95 Sentry Eds. 1961 pap. $2.25; *Franklin Watts* 1966 lg.-type ed. Keith Jennison Bks. $9.95

YOUTH AND THE BRIGHT MEDUSA. Short stories. *Knopf* 1920 $6.95

ONE OF OURS. *Knopf* 1922 $6.95; *Random* Vintage Bks. pap. $1.95

A LOST LADY. *Knopf* 1923 $4.95 *Random* Vintage Bks. pap. $1.95

THE PROFESSOR'S HOUSE *Knopf* 1925 $5.95; *Random* Vintage Bks. pap. $2.45

MY MORTAL ENEMY. *Knopf* 1926 $4.95; *Random* Vintage Bks. pap. $1.65

DEATH COMES FOR THE ARCHBISHOP. *Knopf* 1927 $5.95; *Random* Vintage Bks. pap. $1.95

SHADOWS ON THE ROCK. *Knopf* 1931 $5.95; *Random* Vintage Bks. pap. $1.95

OBSCURE DESTINIES. Short stories. *Knopf* 1932 $4.95

LUCY GAYHEART. *Knopf* 1935 $4.95

SAPPHIRA AND THE SLAVE GIRL. *Knopf* 1940 $5.95

OLD BEAUTY AND OTHERS. Short stories. *Knopf* 1948 $4.95

THE KINGDOM OF ART: WILLA CATHER'S FIRST PRINCIPLES AND CRITICAL STATEMENTS 1893–1896. Sel. and ed. with two essays and a commentary by Bernice Slote. *Univ. of Nebraska Press* 1967 $8.95

"Newly recovered pieces she wrote for the *Nebraska State Journal* during 1895–96 just after university graduation. Most are fugitive weekly literary columns or play reviews, but as a whole they throw light on her own formative artistic ambitions"—(*L J*).

THE WORLD AND THE PARISH: Willa Cather's Articles and Reviews, 1893–1902. Ed. by William D. Curtin. *Univ. of Nebraska Press* 1970 2 vols. set $30.00

Books about Cather

Willa Cather: A Critical Introduction. By David Daiches. 1951. *Greenwood* $9.50. The "most extensive commentary" on the novels.

Willa Cather: A Memoir. By Elizabeth Shepley Sergeant. 1954. *Univ. of Nebraska Press* Bison Bks. 1963 pap. $1.95; *Peter Smith* $3.75

Willa Cather: A Critical Biography. By Edward K. Brown, completed by Leon Edel. *Knopf* 1953 $5.95. The only authorized biography.

The World of Willa Cather. By Mildred R. Bennett. *Univ. of Nebraska Press* rev. ed. Bison Bk. 1961 pap. $1.95. Interesting information on the "Red Cloud" background in Miss Cather's work.

Willa Cather's Gift of Sympathy. By Edward A. and Lillian D. Bloom. Crosscurrents/Modern Critiques *Southern Illinois Univ. Press* 1962 pap. $1.95

Willa Cather and Her Critics. By James Schroeter. *Cornell Univ. Press* 1967 $10.00. Reviews and articles by 13 eminent critics, including Commager, Geismar, Hicks, Jones, Trilling, Wilson.

Willa Cather: Her Life and Art. By James Woodress. *Pegasus* 1970 $6.95. Good introduction based on careful scholarship.

ANDERSON, SHERWOOD. 1876–1941.

In 1921 Sherwood Anderson received the first award of the *Dial's* $2,000 annual prize to further the work of the American author considered by its editors to be the most promising, which served to focus the eyes of literary America on him. "Windy McPherson's Son," "Winesburg, Ohio," and "Poor White" had been published. With "Winesburg, Ohio" and Sinclair Lewis's (*q. v.*) "Main Street" (1920) came a new realism of familiarity and revolt against American small-town life. Anderson was among the first to use the unconscious and the psychology of sex. His style is often involved and obscure. "Dark Laughter" (1925) "the only one of his books to approach the 'best-seller' class," is considered by critics one of the poorest.

He was born in Camden, Ohio, of Scottish parents. He led a varied life; as laborer, soldier, advertising man, and later as novelist and newspaper proprietor. The autobiographical element in his work was pervasive. His father was the model for "Windy" in "Windy McPherson's Son." "Tar" is an autobiography of fact; "A Story Teller's Story", a fictional autobiography, recounts his artistic evolution.

His widow, Eleanor Copenhaver Anderson (his fourth wife), gave his private papers to the Newberry Library in Chicago in 1948. They comprise notebooks, memoranda, and more than 10,000 letters, including those "addressed to no one and thus never mailed." In his introduction to the "Letters," Howard Mumford Jones writes: "One can assert that there is no such thing as a work of fiction by Sherwood Anderson. The novels are autobiographical, the autobiographical books have in them elements of fiction, the letters read like the first draft of a novel." "Return to Winesburg" contains Anderson's Marion, Virginia, newspaper articles on "local issues, descriptions of the joy [he] took in the surrounding countryside, anecdotes about colorful local figures, and discussions of incidents that subsequently figured in the author's creative works" (*PW*). "A kindly melancholy fills the pieces, [and] in this new collection as one might expect, 'characters' proliferate"— (*N.Y. Times*).

THE PORTABLE SHERWOOD ANDERSON: Including Poor White; 7 stories from Winesburg, Ohio; The American Country Fair; 6 Other Stories; 5 Biographical Portraits; Letters. Ed. by Horace Gregory. *Viking* 1949 rev. ed. 1971 $6.00

THE SHORT STORIES OF SHERWOOD ANDERSON. Ed. with an introd. by Maxwell Geismar. *Hill & Wang* 1962 $4.95 Am. Century pap. $2.25

WINDY MCPHERSON'S SON. 1916. Introd. by C. Wright Morris. *Univ. of Chicago Press* 1965 $5.95 Phoenix Bks. pap. $2.45

WINESBURG, OHIO. 1919. *Modern Library* $2.95; *Viking* with introd. by Malcolm Cowley 1958 $5.75 Compass Bks. pap. $1.45 ed. by John H. Ferres Critical Lib. 1967 $5.95 pap. $1.95

POOR WHITE. 1920. *Viking* Compass Bks. 1966 pap. $2.45

DARK LAUGHTER. 1925. *Liveright* 1960 rev. ed. $6.95 pap. $2.45

BEYOND DESIRE. 1933. *Liveright* 1961 $6.95 pap. $2.45

A STORY TELLER'S STORY. 1924. Ed. by Ray L. White. *Press of Case Western* 1968
$8.95; *Viking* Compass Bks. 1969 pap. $2.75

TAR: A Midwest Childhood. 1926. Ed. by Ray L. White. *Press of Case Western* 1969
$7.50

SHERWOOD ANDERSON'S MEMOIRS: A Critical Edition. Ed. by Ray Lewis White.
Newly edited from more than 2,200 pages of mss. *Univ. of North Carolina Press*
1969 $15.00

LETTERS. Ed. by Howard Mumford Jones and Walter B. Rideout. 1953. *Kraus* 1969
$20.00

RETURN TO WINESBURG: Selections from Four Years of Writing for a Country Newspaper. Ed. by Ray Lewis White. *Univ. of North Carolina Press* 1967 $6.95

BUCK FEVER PAPERS. Ed. by Welford D. Taylor. *Univ. Press of Virginia* 1971 $12.50

Books about Anderson

Sherwood Anderson: A Bibliography. By K. A. Lohf and E. P. Sheehy. *Kraus* 1960 $8.00
Sherwood Anderson. By Rex Burbank. U.S. Authors Ser. *Twayne* 1964 $5.50; *College & Univ. Press*
pap. $2.45
Sherwood Anderson. By Brom Weber. Pamphlets on American Writers. *Univ. of Minnesota Press* 1964
pap. $1.25
Sherwood Anderson: A Biographical and Critical Study. By Irving Howe. *Stanford Univ. Press* 1966
$7.50 pap. $2.95
The Achievement of Sherwood Anderson: Essays in Criticism. Ed. with introd. by Ray L. White. *Univ. of
North Carolina Press* 1966 $7.50 pap. $2.95
  The essays are by Trilling, Krutch, Cowley, Howe, Faulkner, and others. "This anthology has the vir-
  tue of putting Anderson in perspective without unduly venerating or condemning him"—(*LJ*).
Sherwood Anderson: An Introduction and an Interpretation. By David Anderson. American Author and
Critics Ser. 1967. *Holt* pap. $2.50
Miss Elizabeth: A Memoir. By Elizabeth Anderson and Gerald R. Kelly. Reminiscences by Anderson's
second wife. *Little* 1969 $6.75
The Road to Winesburg: A Mosaic of the Imaginative Life of Sherwood Anderson. By William A. Sutton.
Scarecrow Press 1972 $15.00. Scholarly study with primary emphasis on his sources.

LONDON, JACK. 1876–1916.

Jack London died in his prime, having accomplished an enormous volume of work. Among his 50 books
his short stories bulk the largest. His first great success and his last were the dog stories—full-length novels.
"The Call of the Wild" is a study in reversion to type, the domesticated dog returns to the wild. "White
Fang" reversed the situation and showed the wild dog tamed by kindness. His novel, "The Iron Heel," anticipates fascism. His autobiography, "John Barleycorn" (1913) has been called his "alcoholic memoirs." His
one travel volume is "The Cruise of the Snark" (1911 1928, o. p.), the story of a voyage which Mrs. London
also recorded in "The Log of the Snark" (1915, o. p.). While his early tales were published in a variety of periodicals, his first volume of short stories, based on his experiences in the Klondike, was "The Son of the
Wolf" (1900, o. p.). "Love of Life" (1906) was probably the best of his collections of short stories. "Tales of
the Fish Patrol" (1967 o. p.), told from a young man's point of view, are partly autobiographical and concern
the San Francisco Bay area.
In "On Native Grounds," Alfred Kazin writes: "The clue to Jack London's work is certainly to be found
in his own turbulent life. . . . The greatest story he ever wrote was the story he lived: the story of the illegitimate son of a Western adventurer and itinerant astrologer, who grew up in Oakland, was an oyster pirate at
fifteen, a sailor at seventeen, a tramp and a 'work-beast,' a trudger after Coxey's Army, a prospector in
Alaska, and who quickly became rich by his stories, made and spent several fortunes, and by the circle of his
own confused ambitions came round to the final despair in which he took his own life." He had become an
ardent socialist when, in his oyster pirate days in San Francisco, he read the "Communist Manifesto." The
radical undertone of his work in part accounts for his continuing popularity in Eastern Europe.

About 100,000 persons a year, from almost every country, make the pilgrimage to California's Jack London State Park, where London is buried, in Sonoma County's "Valley of the Moon." "For years, London tramped and rode horseback over this ground, supervising his 1,500-acre cattle ranch after he had finished his daily 1,000-word stint of writing in a little cabin, down the valley. The 'House of the Happy Walls' is full of memorabilia of his career." He "never actually lived in this hillside abode. It was built by his widow in 1919, three years after his death, as a sort of personal memorial" (*N.Y. Times*). Charmian, his second wife, wrote about him in "The Book of Jack London" (1921, 2 vols., o. p.). The *Golden Press* "Letters" cover the years 1879–1916. "These are important documents in the growth of a writer whose fame in his own country is far eclipsed by his popularity in Soviet Russia and the satellite nations"—(*LJ*). Dr. Hensley C. Woodbridge of the Southern Illinois University Library in Carbondale edits the *Jack London Newsletter* ($2.50 a year).

Among his books in print:

THE BODLEY HEAD EDITION OF THE WRITINGS. Ed. by Arthur Calder-Marshall. Vol. 1 Short Stories; The Call of the Wild. Vol. 2 John Barleycorn; The Cruise of the Dazzler; The Road. Vol. 3 Martin Eden. *Dufour* 1966 3 vols. each $6.95

BEST SHORT STORIES. *Doubleday* 1953 $4.95; *Fawcett* Premier Bks. pap. $.75

SHORT STORIES. *Assoc. Booksellers* Airmont Bks. pap. $.75; *Hill & Wang* Am. Century pap. $1.95; *Funk & Wagnall* 1968 pap. $1.50

THE CALL OF THE WILD. 1903. *Assoc. Booksellers* Airmont Bks. pap. $.60; *Grosset* $2.95 Companion Lib. $1.25 Silver Dollar Lib. $1.00; *Lancer* pap. $.60; *Macmillan* 1963 $3.95; *New Am. Lib.* Signet pap. $.60; *Franklin Watts* lg.-type ed. Keith Jennison Bks. $7.95

THE CALL OF THE WILD AND WHITE FANG. *Bantam* pap. $.60; *Washington Square* pap. $.60

THE CALL OF THE WILD AND OTHER STORIES. *Dodd* Gt. Ill. Class. 1960 $5.50; *Grosset* $2.95 special ed. $3.95 deluxe ed. $4.95

THE SEA WOLF. 1904. *Assoc. Booksellers* Airmont Bks. 1964 pap. $.60; with introd. by Lewis Gannett *Bantam* pap. $.60; *Lancer* pap. $.75; *Macmillan* 1935 $5.95; (and SELECTED STORIES) *New Am. Lib.* Signet 1964 pap. $.60

WHITE FANG. 1906. *Assoc. Booksellers* Airmont Bks. 1964 pap. $.50; *Grosset* $2.95; *Macmillan* 1935 $5.95; *Franklin Watts* lg.-type ed. Keith Jennison Bks. 1967 $7.95

THE IRON HEEL. 1907. Bantam pap. $.95; *Hill & Wang* Am. Century 1957 pap. $1.95

MARTIN EDEN. 1909. *Assoc. Booksellers* Airmont Bks. pap. $.60; Ed. by Sam S. Baskett *Holt* (Rinehart) 1956 pap. $2.50; *Macmillan* 1957 $5.95; *Penguin* 1967 pap. $1.85

THE STAR ROVER. 1915. Macmillan 1963 $4.95

Books about London

Jack London, Sailor on Horseback. By Irving Stone. 1938. *Doubleday* 1947 $6.95; *New Am. Lib. Signet* pap. $.95
Jack London: A Biography. By Richard O'Connor. *Little* 1964 $8.50
Jack London. By Charles Child Walcutt. Pamphlets on American Writers. *Univ. of Minnesota Press* 1966 pap. $1.25
Jack London and the Klondike: The Genesis of an American Writer. By Franklin Walker. *Huntington Library* 1966 $7.50. Good scholarly study.
Jack London and His Times: An Unconventional Biography. By Joan London. *Univ. of Washington Press* 1969 $9.50
The Fiction of Jack London: A Chronological Bibliography. Comp. by Dale L. Walker. *Texas Western Univ. Press* 1972 $10.00

SINCLAIR, UPTON (BEALL). 1878–1968.

Sinclair, a lifelong, vigorous socialist, first came into fame with "the most powerful of muck-raking novels," "The Jungle," in 1906. Refused by five publishers and finally published by Sinclair himself, it became an immediate best seller, led to a government investigation of the Chicago stockyards, and was fruitful of much reform. In 1967, he was invited by President Johnson to "witness the signing of the Wholesome Meat Act, which will gradually plug loopholes left by the first Federal meat inspection law" (*N.Y. Times*), a law Mr. Sinclair had helped to bring about. Newspapers, colleges, schools, churches, industries have each been the subject of a Sinclair attack, exposing their evils. Not really a novelist, but a fearless and indefatigable journalist-crusader, all his early books are propaganda for his social reforms. When regular publishers boycotted his work he published it himself, usually at a financial loss. His 80 or so books have been translated into 47 languages and his sales abroad, especially in Russia, have been enormous.

"Dragon's Teeth," a "Lanny Budd" novel, won the Pulitzer Prize in 1942. With "World's End," his 65th novel and a Literary Guild Selection, Sinclair had started his series of best-selling volumes in the ambitious saga of his "hyperthyroid" hero, Lanny Budd—a fictional history of contemporary world events. "Presidential Mission" (1947) brings Lanny up to the invasion of North Africa and the Casablanca Conference with Roosevelt, Churchill, and others, and the 11th volume, "The Return of Lanny Budd," concerns the growth of the Russian menace from 1946 through 1949. More than a million copies of the Lanny Budd novels have been sold, and they have been translated into more than 20 languages. Bernard Shaw (*q. v.*) suggested that there may be readers of the future who will seek to understand the 20th century not by reading the newspaper files but by reading the Lanny Budd, or, as their author preferred to call them, the World's End series.

"The Cup of Fury" (1956. Hawthorn $3.95) is an account of how alcoholism wrecked the lives of such men as Jack London, Stephen Crane, John Barrymore, Dylan Thomas, and others. He has written a volume on psychic research: "Mental Radio" (with introd. by William McDougall, pref. by Albert Einstein *C. C. Thomas* 2nd ptg. rev. ed. 1962 $8.50; *Macmillan* Collier Bks. pap. $1.95). His wife, who had devoted her life to his myriad causes, died in 1961. She described "Uppie" as "a dual personality—a helpless child in his personal affairs and a brave and skillful fighter in the cause he loved"—(*Time*).

Lanny Budd Series

WORLD'S END. 1940. *Curtis Bks.* 1973 pap. $1.25

BETWEEN TWO WORLDS. 1941. *Curtis Bks.* 1973 pap. $1.25

DRAGON'S TEETH. 1942. *Curtis Bks.* 1973 pap. $1.50

WIDE IS THE GATE. 1943. *Curtis Bks.* 1973 pap. $1.50

PRESIDENTIAL AGENT. 1944. *Curtis Bks.* 1973 pap. $1.50

DRAGON HARVEST. 1945. *Curtis Bks.* 1973 pap. $1.50

A WORLD TO WIN. 1946. *Curtis Bks.* 1973 pap. $1.50

PRESIDENTIAL MISSION. 1947. *Curtis Bks.* 1973 pap. $1.50

ONE CLEAR CALL. 1948. *Curtis Bks.* 1973 pap. $1.50

O SHEPHERD, SPEAK! 1949. *Curtis Bks.* 1973 pap. $1.50

THE RETURN OF LANNY BUDD. 1953. *Curtis Bks.* 1973 pap. $1.50

THE JUNGLE. 1906. *Assoc. Booksellers* Airmont Bks. pap. $.60; *Bentley* $8.50; *New Am. Lib.* Signet pap. $.75

OIL! 1927. *Washington Square* pap. $.75

AUGUST TWENTY-SECOND. 1928. With introd. by Michael Mussmano. *Universal Distributors* Award Bks. 1967 pap. $.95. Originally entitled "Boston," it deals with the Sacco-Vanzetti Case.

THEIRS BE THE GUILT: A Novel of the War between the States. *Twayne* 1959 $3.95

My Lifetime in Letters. *Univ. of Missouri Press* 1960 $6.50. Approximately 300 letters dating from 1905 to 1957. Included are letters from Sinclair Lewis, Jack London, Albert Einstein, Bernard Shaw, and others.

The Autobiography of Upton Sinclair. 1962. *Kennikat* $9.25. The candid memoirs of his personal and public life, it carries a revised version of "American Outpost" (1932) a book of reminiscences. When, with some 84 years and 80 books to his credit, he published this autobiography, it was called "a book full of laughter and tears. . . . It is the record of a personality far more important historically than many Americans realize"—(G. W. Johnson, in the *New Republic*).

Books about Sinclair

Upton Sinclair: A Study in Social Protest. By Floyd Dell. 1927. *AMS Press* 1970 $10.00; Folcroft $15.00
Upton Sinclair: An Annotated Checklist. By Ronald S. Gottesman. Serif Series No. 24. *Kent State Univ. Press* 1972 $10.00

CABELL, JAMES BRANCH. 1879–1958.

One of the most extravagantly praised novelists of the twenties, Cabell continued to be a subject of controversy, although his reputation underwent considerable revision as he grew older. His romances are set in the medieval and imaginary country of Poictesme and are filled with sardonic innuendo, sophisticated literary jesting, mockery of provincialism and of Puritanism. "Jurgen" was at first suppressed, then reissued to a delighted public. During his later years he wrote a series of memoirs and pen portraits of the literary people he had known. His "familiar mixture of bleak disillusion and amused persiflage" is still present in the autobiographical "Quiet, Please." Although Cabell's popularity and critical reputation have declined drastically since the days of his greatest fame, he retains a loyal following of dedicated scholars and lovers of fantasy. Their enthusiasm is reflected in *Kalki: Studies in James Branch Cabell*, a journal co-edited by Professor William Leigh Godshalk of the English Department at the University of Cincinnati and the English science-fiction writer James Blish. The subscription rate is five dollars for four issues.

The Cream of the Jest. Ed. by Joseph M. Flora. 1917. *College & Univ. Press* 1973 $6.50 pap. $2.95

Beyond Life: Dizain des Demiurges. Introd. by William Leigh Godshalk. 1919. *Johnson Reprint Corp.* 1970 $12.00

Quiet, Please. Personal reminiscences. *Univ. of Florida Press* 1952 $4.00

Books about Cabell

James Branch Cabell: Three Essays in Criticism. By H. L. Mencken and others. 1932. *Kennikat* $6.00
James Branch Cabell. By Joe Lee Davis. U.S. Authors Ser. *Twayne* 1962 $5.50; *College & Univ. Press* pap. $2.45
Jesting Moses: A Study in Cabellian Comedy. By Arvin R. Wells. *Univ. of Florida Press* 1962 $5.00
James Branch Cabell. By Desmond Tarrant. *Univ. of Oklahoma Press* 1967 $6.95

LEWIS, SINCLAIR. 1885–1951. (Nobel Prize 1930)

"Sinclair Lewis has been called the Bad Boy of the national letters. In a way the celebrated critic of the national manners who established the new realism of the nineteen-twenties in the American mind . . . whose literary career has been marked by controversy, dispute, and perpetual ferment, deserves his title" (Maxwell Geismar). Geismar has also called the novels "a remarkable diary of the middle class mind in America."

Lewis's first novel, "Our Mr. Wrenn" (o. p.), was published by *Harper* in 1914. Up to that time he had written short stories for magazines. "Main Street," his first important work, is a pitying picture of provincialism in a small Middle Western community. "Babbitt" a portrait of the average American business man, "added a new word to the American dictionary because it created a symbol of the little man caught up in the success-worship, the materialism, of a city world in an industrial society" (Robert E. Spiller). "Arrowsmith" shows "the idealism of the devoted scientist and physician in conflict with the forces that attempt to commercialize and monopolize his discoveries" (Bradley, Beatty, and Long, in "The American Tradition in Literature"). In 1926 this novel was awarded the Pulitzer Prize, which Lewis declined—as one who did not believe in prizes nor think himself deserving of it. "Elmer Gantry" is a portrait of a dissolute but successful evangelist. Burt Lancaster won a 1961 "Oscar" in the movie version. "Dodsworth," the last of his important novels, is the search for selfhood by a man whose material success has failed to give his life significance.

Sinclair Lewis won the Nobel Prize in 1930—the first American to receive it for literature. Between 1920 and 1929 he had published his most important books. With Sherwood Anderson (*q. v.*) he had led the "revolt against small-town life in the Middle West." His leading characters were types, but he gave them reality with the talk and actions common to the middle classes of America. Lewis's novels never failed to stir up the groups that considered themselves attacked. "It Can't Happen Here" forecast an imaginary coming of Fascism to America. "Gideon Planish" (1943, o. p.) exposed corruption in organized philanthropy. "Kingsblood Royal" was an effective tract against racial prejudice, but like all these later books, it failed as a serious work of fiction—Neil Kingsblood with his one-thirty-second part Negro blood does not come to life. Although Lewis's novels became increasingly bitter and satiric, he maintained "a distinct and admirable belief in literature as an instrument of popular education, in the sense that Voltaire and Dickens and H. G. Wells understood it" (Alfred Kazin). "With Love From Gracie, Sinclair Lewis: 1912–1925" by Grace Hegger Lewis (1956, o. p.) is an informal and somewhat acid memoir by his first wife describing the time of his early success with "Main Street," "Babbit," and "Arrowsmith"; it contains many hitherto unpublished letters.

LEWIS AT ZENITH. (Main Street, Babbitt and Arrowsmith.) Pref. by Mark Schorer. *Harcourt* 1961 $5.95

MAIN STREET. *Harcourt* 1920 Harbrace Mod. Class. 1950 $2.95; *New Am. Lib.* Signet pap. $1.25

BABBITT. *Harcourt* 1922 Harbrace Mod. Class. 1949 $2.95 *New Am. Lib.* Signet pap. $.95

ARROWSMITH. *Harcourt* 1925 Harbrace Mod. Class. 1949 $2.95 text ed. $1.75; *New Am. Lib.* Signet pap. $1.25

ELMER GANTRY. 1927. *New Am. Lib.* Signet pap. $1.25

DODSWORTH. 1929. *New Am. Lib.* Signet pap. $1.25

WORK OF ART. 1934. *Popular Lib.* pap. $.75

IT CAN'T HAPPEN HERE. 1935. *New Am. Lib.* Signet pap. $1.25

BETHEL MERRIDAY. 1940. *Popular Lib.* pap. $.75

KINGSBLOOD ROYAL. 1947. *Popular Lib.* 1959 pap. $.75

THE MAN FROM MAIN STREET. Ed. by Harry E. Maule and Melville H. Cane. Letters, articles, criticism, autobiography and more. 1953. *Pocket Bks.* 1963 pap. $.60

Books about Lewis

Sinclair Lewis: An American Life. By Mark Schorer. *McGraw-Hill* 1961 $2.98; *Dell* 1963 pap. $3.75; *Univ. of Minnesota Press* 1963 pap. $1.25. This is the definitive biography "on the scale of Boswell. Schorer concentrates not only on Lewis the writer and controversial social critic, but on the strange, turbulent, often ugly human being beneath them" (William Hogan). Here the bizarre career of an American Nobel Prize winner is set forth in merciless and fascinating detail.

Sinclair Lewis: A Collection of Critical Essays. Ed. by Mark Schorer. *Prentice-Hall* 1962 $5.95

Sinclair Lewis. By Sheldon Grebstein. *Twayne* 1962 $5.50; *College & Univ. Press* 1962 pap. $2.45

Dorothy and Red. By Vincent Sheean. *Houghton* 1963 $6.95. A memoir of two American literary figures whose marriage took place at a time when foreign correspondents were most influential. Vincent Sheean, himself a noted newspaper man and author of many books, tells of the life together of Dorothy Thompson and Sinclair Lewis, from his own friendship with them and from their correspondence and diaries.

The Art of Sinclair Lewis. By D. J. Dooley. *Univ. of Nebraska Press* 1967 $5.50 Bison Bk. pap. $2.25. An examination of Lewis's literary merits as well as his curious weaknesses.

Sinclair Lewis. By Richard O'Connor. American Writers Ser. *McGraw-Hill* 1971 $4.75. Biography for young readers, but a useful introduction for the general reader.

LARDNER, RING. 1885–1933.

Ringgold Wilmer Lardner was for many years a sporting journalist in Chicago and wrote in a sporting jargon which was known as Lardner's Ringlish. In his later works he was under "the spell of the misspelled" and "the lure of the illiterate." The stories are witty and cynical and concern contemporary Americans of his period—athletes, soldiers, and others, whose crudities and foibles he portrayed with merciless humor. His comedy about a songwriter, "June Moon," was written with George Kaufman (*French* 1931 $1.25).

John Lardner (1921–1960), son of Ring Lardner, followed his father and became "one of the freshest and funniest sports writers in the country." After two years of Harvard, he became "a reporter, columnist, war correspondent, weekly commentator for *Newsweek*, and an invaluable contributor to the *New Yorker*." His books include "White Hopes and Other Tigers" (1951, o. p.), "Strong Cigars and Lovely Women" (1951, o. p.), and "The World of John Lardner," edited and with an epilogue by Roger Kahn, preface by Walt Kelly (*Simon & Schuster* 1961 $4.50).

THE RING LARDNER READER. Ed. by Maxwell Geismar. *Scribner* 1963 $12.50 pap. $2.95. A brilliant introduction reveals the man and his achievement in this standard collection of his works.

THE BEST SHORT STORIES OF RING LARDNER. *Scribner* 1938 rev. ed. 1958 $4.50

HAIRCUT AND OTHER STORIES. *Scribner* 1962 pap. $1.95

YOU KNOW ME, AL: A Busher's Letters. Introd. by John Lardner. *Scribner* 1916 1960 pap. $1.25. A new edition of Lardner's tale told in a series of letters, of Jack Keefe, a crass baseball player.

GULLIBLE'S TRAVELS ETC. 1925. Introd. by Josephine Herbst. *Univ. of Chicago Press* 1965 $3.95 Phoenix Bks. pap. $1.95

RING AROUND MAX: The Correspondence between Ring Lardner and Maxwell Perkins. Ed. by C. M. Caruthers. *Northern Illinois Univ. Press* 1973 $8.50 pap. $5.00

Books about Lardner

Ring Lardner. By Walton R. Patrick. U.S. Authors Ser. *Twayne* 1963 $5.50; *College & Univ. Press* 1964 pap. $2.45

Ring Lardner. By Otto Friedrich. Pamphlets on American Writers. *Univ. of Minnesota Press* 1965 pap. $1.25

RICHTER, CONRAD. 1890–1968.

Conrad Richter wrote short novels of early American life. He was born in Pennsylvania of "mixed South German, French, English and Scotch-Irish blood," the son, grandson, nephew, and great-nephew of clergymen. He thinks that in his great interest in the American pioneer existence he is a "throw-back" to his earlier ancestors—"tradesmen, soldiers, country squires, blacksmiths and farmers." "The Sea of Grass" about the old Southwest, "Tacey Cromwell" (1942, o. p.) laid in an Arizona mining town, "The Trees," the engulfing forests of early Ohio and its sequel, "The Fields," are considered his best novels. His people are real, his descriptions vivid, his treatment simple and direct. He is a "tireless research worker, searching out old diaries, account books, and newspapers, and spending hours talking to old-timers who can supply details heard from their forebears." "The Town," the concluding volume of his trilogy which includes "The Trees" and "The Fields," was awarded the Pulitzer Prize for 1950. He also won the National Institute of Arts and Letters award. "The Waters of Kronos," a 1960 National Book Award winner, is the story of a man's return to his home town.

In "The Grandfathers" Richter turns from his usual serious character studies to comedy. Here a young, small-town girl reaches independence and maturity in finding out which local elder is her grandfather. "The real grandfather, an old reprobate, as well as other old people are drawn with humor and understanding"—(*LJ*). "A Country of Strangers," the story of a white child captured and brought up by the Indians, is "absorbing reading in Mr. Richter's impeccable style"—(*LJ*).

THE TREES, THE FIELDS, AND THE TOWN. *Knopf* 1950 3 vols. each $5.95 boxed set $17.85; (with title "The Awakening Land") 3 vols. in 1 $10.00

EARLY AMERICANA AND OTHER STORIES. *Knopf* 1936 $5.95

THE SEA OF GRASS. *Knopf* 1937 $5.95; *Franklin Watts* 1966 lg.-type ed. Keith Jennison Bks. $7.95

THE TREES. *Knopf* 1940 $5.95; *Franklin Watts* lg.-type ed. Keith Jennison Bks. $8.95

THE FREE MAN. *Knopf* 1943 $5.95

THE FIELDS. *Knopf* 1946 $5.95

THE TOWN. *Knopf* 1950 $5.95

THE LIGHT IN THE FOREST. *Knopf* 1953 $4.95; *Bantam* pap. $.75

MOUNTAIN ON THE DESERT. *Knopf* 1955 $4.50

LADY. *Knopf* 1957 $4.50

THE WATERS OF KRONOS. *Knopf* 1960 $4.95

SIMPLE HONORABLE MAN. *Knopf* 1962 $4.95

THE GRANDFATHERS. *Knopf* 1964 $4.95

A COUNTRY OF STRANGERS. *Knopf* 1966 $5.95

THE ARISTOCRAT. *Knopf* 1968 $5.95. The story of a Pennsylvania woman.

Books about Richter

Conrad Richter. By Edwin W. Gaston, Jr. U.S. Authors Ser. *Twayne* 1965 $5.50 *College & Univ. Press* 1965 pap. $2.45
Conrad Richter's Ohio Trilogy: Ideas, Themes and Relationships to Literature Tradition. By Clifford D. Edwards. *Humanities Press* 1970 $11.00

MILLER, HENRY. 1891–

Henry Miller's literary career began with the publication of his autobiographical and sexually outspoken "Tropic of Cancer" in 1931. New York's highest court, the Court of Appeals at Albany, held it obscene under New York law, and it was not published in the United States until 1961. Edmund Wilson called "Tropic of Cancer" 'a good piece of writing. . . . He has treated an ignoble subject with a sure hand at color and rhythm. The theme of 'Tropic of Cancer' is the lives of a group of Americans who have all come to Paris with the intention of occupying themselves with literature but who have actually subsided easily into an existence almost exclusively preoccupied with drinking and fornication"—(in "The Shores of Light"). Maxwell Geismar finds Miller "the heir of D. H. Lawrence in the struggle to reassert the natural in man."

Born in Yorkville and raised in Brooklyn, the young Miller worked at many jobs including those of tailor's apprentice, mail sorter, and Western Union messenger. In the 1930s he went, as a nearly penniless writer, to Paris. Because of the frankness of his treatment and his choice of material, his early picaresque novels were published only in Paris, but pirated editions were handed about in the United States. "The Cosmological Eye" was the first book that an American publisher dared print.

An "ex-expatriate," Henry Miller arrived in the Big Sur region near Carmel, California, in 1943, the proclaimed prophet of a group of neo-Bohemian intellectuals practising what was described by Mildred E. Brady as "The New Cult of Sex and Anarchy" (*Harper's* April, 1947). A somewhat different account was given in an interview with the *Paris Review*. He says of Big Sur: "I was dumped on the road there one day by a friend. He left me saying 'I think you'll like it.' . . . It was a wonderful change, Big Sur. There was nothing there, except nature—I was alone, which was what I wanted." "Big Sur and the Oranges of Hieronymous Bosch" (*New Directions* 1957 1964 pap. $2.45) deals with his 11 years there. In 1967 he married Hoki Tokuda, a young cabaret singer from Tokyo and took her off to Paris for the first important showing of his watercolors, which opened there in September, 1967.

The three books on which his reputation is based ("Tropic of Cancer," 1931, "Tropic of Capricorn," 1938, and "Black Spring," 1939) are "autobiographical fictions, dealing outwardly with Miller's adventures in the Bohemian underworld of cosmopolitan Paris (with occasional flashbacks to earlier days in New York)." When "Tropic of Capricorn" was published here in 1962, Eric Moon of *Library Journal* wrote: "Here we go again—across the equator of literature and censorship, from Cancer to Capricorn. . . . A harsher book than 'Cancer,' with more bitterness, 'Capricorn' is another chapter in the same Miller's tale, the same seething biography of a roaring, greedy imagination, defiantly declaring its faith in 'the indestructible world which man has always carried within him.' " "Black Spring" consists of ten autobiographical pieces covering Miller's life until he went to Paris. "Bits are wonderfully done, with vivid scenes of jazzed-up action, like an early silent movie full of custard pies, female underclothes and slightly zany captions"— (*Time*).

"The Rosy Crucifixion," collective title for the novels "Sexus," "Plexus," and "Nexus," is his second major trilogy. These provide yet more fictional autobiography covering, in his usual ribald fashion, the years of his "crucifixion" in America before he went to France. Eric Moon of *Library Journal* believes that the old reasons for rejecting Miller's works as library acquisitions have now largely vanished, in this case as in that of his other works. Miller's literary style is "plain, though always energetic and vivid, with split-angled Braquelike images rising from the hard texture of American speech"—(Harry T. Moore). "The Air-Conditioned Nightmare" (1948. *New Directions* pap. $2.45) contains his impressions of a tour of the United States, in which he found nothing good. "The Colossus of Maroussi" (*New Directions* 1941 1958 pap. $1.75) is "less a guidebook than an account of Greece as an experience"—he saw it as "the source of all true values in life and art," as an "antithesis of the modern civilization of money and progress." "Books in My Life" (*New Directions* 1952 pap. $2.45) contains more of his shrewd and witty reminiscences. "Henry Miller on Writing" (ed. by Thomas H. Moore *New Directions* 1964 pap. $2.75) includes material from unpublished manuscripts and passages from his books. Watercolors contributed sustenance in lean years and some of these are reproduced in "Watercolors, Drawings, and his Essay The Angel is My Watermark!" (*Abrams* 1962 o. p.). "The Time of the Assassins," a study of Rimbaud (pap. $1.75) is published by *New Directions*. "My Friend Henry Miller" (pref. by Miller 1956, o. p.) by Alfred Perlès, is the first biography, told "with sympathy, even affection." In it "Miller emerges a magnetic, warm-hearted, high-spirited eccentric, with a touch of genius."

THE HENRY MILLER READER. Ed. by Lawrence Durrell. *New Directions* 1959 pap. $2.95; *Bks. for Libraries* $14.00

STAND STILL LIKE THE HUMMINGBIRD. Stories and essays. *New Directions* 1961 $4.50 pap. $1.95

THE HENRY MILLER TRILOGY: Tropic of Cancer, Tropic of Capricorn, and Black Spring. *Grove* 1963 3 vols. boxed set $15.00

TROPIC OF CANCER. 1931. *Grove* 1961 Black Cat Bks. pap. $1.25

TROPIC OF CAPRICORN. 1938. *Grove* 1962 Evergreen Bks. pap. $2.45; Black Cat Bks. pap. $.95

THE COSMOLOGICAL EYE. 1939. *New Directions* 1961 1969 $4.50 pap. $2.45

WISDOM OF THE HEART. *New Directions* 1942 pap. $2.45

SUNDAY AFTER THE WAR. *New Directions* 1961. $4.50

BLACK SPRING. 1939. *Grove* 1963 $5.00 Zebra Bks. 1964 pap. $1.25

SEXUS. *Grove* 1965 Black Cat Bks. pap. $.50

PLEXUS. *Grove* 1965 $7.50 Black Cat Bks. pap. $1.25

NEXUS. *Grove* 1965 $5.00 Black Cat Bks. pap. $1.25

LAWRENCE DURRELL AND HENRY MILLER: A Private Correspondence. Ed. and with an introd. by George Wickes. *Dutton* 1962 1964 pap. $2.25

This volume contains a large selection from a voluminous correspondence, 1935–59, between these two nonconformist writers. These letters, not bowdlerized, are spontaneous and revealing; very well arranged and edited, with perceptive comment (*see further annotation in Chapter 12, Modern British Fiction—under Lawrence Durrell*).

COLLECTOR'S QUEST: The Correspondence of Henry Miller and J. Rives Child. Ed. by Richard C. Wood. *Univ. Press of Virginia* 1968 $6.00

Books about Miller

Art and Outrage: A Correspondence About Henry Miller. By Lawrence Durrell and Alfred Perlès. *Dutton* 1960 $3.50

Henry Miller and the Critics. Ed. by George Wickes. Crosscurrents/Modern Critiques. *Southern Illinois Univ. Press* 1963 $4.50

Henry Miller. By Kingsley Widmer. *Twayne* 1963 $5.50; *College & Univ. Press* 1964 pap. $2.45

Henry Miller. By George Wickes. Pamphlets on American Writers. *Univ. of Minnesota Press* 1966 pap. $1.25

The Mind and Art of Henry Miller. By William A. Gordon. Fwd. by Lawrence Durrell, pref. by Richard Harter Fogle. *Louisiana State Univ. Press* 1967 $5.00 pap. $2.25. "Professor Gordon has shown him to be a serious and important writer, very much in the tradition of the great Romantics"—(*LJ*). "By far the most intelligent thing I have ever read on Miller"—(Kenneth Rexroth).

The Literature of Silence: Henry Miller and Samuel Beckett. By Ihab Hassan. *Knopf* 1967 pap. $1.95; *Random* text ed. $4.50 pap. $2.25; *Peter Smith* $4.25

Tropic of Cancer on Trial. By E. R. Hutchinson. *Grove* Evergreen Bks. pap. $2.45

Form and Image in the Fiction of Henry Miller. By Jane A. Nelson. *Wayne State Univ. Press* 1970 $8.50. A turning-point in Miller criticism, this is the first extended study to find careful artistic structure in his works.

Henry Miller: Three Decades of Criticism. Ed. by Edward B. Mitchell. *New York Univ. Press* 1971 $8.50 pap. $2.95

BARNES, DJUNA. 1892–

Although Djuna Barnes is a New Yorker who has spent much of her long life in Manhattan, she has resided also for extended periods in France and England. Her writings, too, are representative Modernist works in that they seem to transcend all national boundaries and to take place in a land peculiarly her own. Kenneth Rexroth (in "Contemporary Novelists") finds her main significance "as a member of the international bohemia of the first quarter of the century" and says that "she is at least as influential as a legend as she is as a writer." Deeply influenced by the French Symbolists of the late 19th century and by the Surrealists of the thirties, she served also, Rexroth comments, as "the very archetype of the liberated woman," one whose unconventional way of life is reflected in the uncompromising individuality of her literary style. Her dreamlike and haunted writings have never found a wide popular audience, but they have strongly influenced such writers as Nathanael West, Nelson Algren, Edward Dahlberg, Malcolm Lowry, Henry Miller, and especially Anaïs Nin (*q. v.*) in whose works a semifictional character named "Djuna" sometimes appears.

Miss Barnes published "The Book of Repulsive Women" anonymously in 1915. She was a member of the Provincetown Players and had three of her plays produced by that theatrical troupe in 1919. Not long afterwards she moved to Paris and became associated with the colony of writers and artists who made Paris the international center of culture during the twenties and early thirties. Her "Ladies Almanack" (new ed. *Harper* 1972 $5.95) was privately printed there in 1928, the same year that Liveright in America published her first novel. "Ryder" (o. p.) is a satire on masculinity, a big, bawdy novel which she thought of as "the female Tom Jones."

The book on which her fame largely depends is "Nightwood," a surrealistic story set in Paris and America which deals with the complex relationships among a group of strangely obsessed characters, most of them homosexuals and lesbians. In his Introduction to the novel, T. S. Eliot wrote that it is a book which would "appeal primarily to readers of poetry." He found in it "the great achievement of a style, the beauty of phrasing, the brilliance of wit and characterisation, and a quality of horror and doom very nearly related to that of Elizabethan tragedy."

She has written little since "Nightwood." In fact, she professed to Malcolm Lowry in 1952 that she had been so frightened by the experience of writing that searing work that she could not write anything afterwards. Fortunately, her literary talents revived with "The Antiphon" (*Farrar, Straus* 1958 $3.50), a versedrama which Edwin Muir called "one of the greatest things that has been written in our time."

SELECTED WORKS. Includes Spillway; The Antiphon; Nightwood. *Farrar, Straus* 1962 $7.95

NIGHTWOOD. 1936. Intod. by T. S. Eliot. *New Directions* 1946 $5.00 pap. $1.50

SPILLWAY: And Other Stories. 1962. *Harper* 1972 pap. $1.95

MARQUAND, JOHN P(HILLIPS). 1893–1960.

Marquand, whom Clifton Fadiman (*q. v.*) called "the best novelist of social comedy now at work in our country" and likened to Thackeray, was born in Wilmington, Delaware, but spent most of his life in New

England and New York. While working in New York as a reporter and copy writer, he found his first efforts in serials and popular mystery-adventure fiction very successful. The "Mr. Moto" stories, about a Japanese secret agent, were published in the thirties.

"The Late George Apley" —Pulitzer Prize winner in 1938—"Wickford Point," and "H. M. Pulham, Esq." are all written in the first person, and with the diary, letters, and allusions to real persons in them, they read like actuality more than fiction. These novels established his reputation. Beginning with "So Little Time" (1943, o. p.), Marquand left Boston and the North Shore and turned his wit and irony on the American scene, from contemporary New York to Hollywood. His ear for modern dialogue, his probing characterization and structural artistry, punctuated with perfect detail, are used in studies of a "play doctor"—"So Little Time"; a young flyer's war marriage—"Repent in Haste"; and the young married daughter of a wealthy industrialist—"B. F.'s Daughter" (1946, o. p.). "Point of No Return" is a cleverly written novel and a very successful play about a young banker. James Hilton wrote that it "does reinforce his reputation as a first-class satirist—probably the best of [his] generation. No writer can extract a wryer humor from the irritants of daily existence, or can play a wintrier sunlight over the destinies of his characters." "Melville Goodwin, U.S.A." is the story of the career of a popular army officer. "Stopover: Tokyo" (1937, o. p.) marks the reappearance of the Japanese sleuth Mr. Moto, and "Life at Happy Knoll" (1957, o. p.) is the amusing story of country club life. In "American Moderns" Maxwell Geismar (q. v.) calls Marquand "an acute and often brilliant observer of middle class manners" whose work, perhaps, "already shows the falling-off of 'handicraft entertainment' in the age of automation." "Timothy Dexter Revisited" (1960, o. p.), published posthumously, is a revision of the 35-year-old biography of the eccentric 18th-century tanner and parvenu of Newburyport. Skillfully imitating the novelist's own techniques, Philip Hamburger wrote an account and analysis called "J. P. Marquand, Esquire: A Portrait in the Form of a Novel" (1952, o. p.).

THIRTY YEARS. Introd. by Clifton Fadiman. *Little* 1954 $6.95. A Collection of Stories, Articles and Essays, which had not previously appeared in book form.

HAVEN'S END. 1933. *Avon Bks.* pap. $.75; *Bks. for Libraries* $11.50

THE LATE GEORGE APLEY: A Novel in the Form of a Memoir. *Little* 1937 $6.95; *Pocket Bks.* pap. $.95; *Washington Square* pap. $.95

WICKFORD POINT. 1939. *Peter Smith* $4.00

H. M. PULHAM, Esquire. *Little* 1941 $6.95

POINT OF NO RETURN. *Little* 1949 $6.95

MELVILLE GOODWIN, U.S.A. 1951 *Avon* pap. $1.25

SINCERELY, WILLIS WAYDE. *Little* 1955 $6.95; *Avon* pap. $1.25

Books about Marquand

John P. Marquand. By John J. Gross. U.S. Authors Ser. *Twayne* 1962 $5.50; *College & Univ. Press* 1964 $2.45. The first full-length critical, analytical study of Marquand.
John P. Marquand. By Hugh C. Holman. Pamphlets on American Writers. *Univ. of Minnesota Press* 1965 pap. $1.25
The Late John Marquand: A Biography. By Stephen Birmingham. *Lippincott* 1972 $10.00

PARKER, DOROTHY. 1893–1967.

During her years of greatest fame Dorothy Parker was known primarily as a writer of light verse, an essential member of the Algonquin Round Table, and a caustic and witty critic of literature and society. She is remembered now as an almost legendary figure of the twenties and thirties. Her reviews and staff contributions to three of the most sophisticated magazines of this century, *Vanity Fair*, the *New Yorker*, and *Esquire*, were famous for their put-downs; and many of the most famous bright remarks of the time were attributed to her—some of them justly so. For all her highbrow wit, however, Dorothy Parker was very liberal in her political views, and the hard veneer of brittle toughness which she showed to the world was often a shield for frustrated idealism and soft sensibilities. The best of her fiction is marked by a balance of ironic detachment and sympathetic compassion, as in "Big Blonde," which won the O. Henry Award for 1929 and is still her best-remembered and most frequently anthologized story.

The best of Dorothy Parker is readily and compactly accessible in "The Portable Dorothy Parker." Her own selection of stories and verse for the original edition of that compilation, published in 1944, remains intact in the revised edition, but included also are more than 200 pages of later stories, reviews, and articles, including the complete text of her "Constant Reader" (*Viking* 1970 $5.95), a collection of her book reviews for the *New Yorker*. The expanded version only enhanced the validity of what Edmund Wilson wrote about the first edition: "She is not Emily Brontë or Jane Austen, but she has been at some pains to write well, and she has put into what she has written a voice, a state of mind, an era, a few moments of human experience that nobody else has conveyed." Her verse is conveniently available in "Collected Poetry" (*Modern Lib.* $2.95).

THE PORTABLE DOROTHY PARKER. 1944. Rev. ed. Intro. by Brendan Gill. *Viking* 1973 $5.95 pap. $2.95

Books about Parker

You Might as Well Live: The Life and Times of Dorothy Parker. By John Keats. *Simon & Schuster* 1970 $7.95

PORTER, KATHERINE ANNE. 1894–

This distinguished short story writer is known for her subtle and delicate perception, her careful, disciplined technique and her precision of word and phrase. She writes slowly and with restraint but achieves an impression of ease and naturalness that is close to perfection. She was born in Texas, schooled in Louisiana convents, and has lived and traveled in Paris, Majorca, Berlin, Vienna, and Mexico, always "up to my chin in paper," with "a suitcase for personal effects and a steamer trunk filled with manuscripts and notes." She has been a newspaper reporter, book reviewer, ghost writer, free-lance journalist, editor, and critic.

"Ship of Fools," 20 years in the writing, "is the story of a voyage. . . . A novel of character rather than of action, it has as its main purpose a study of the German ethos shortly before Hitler's coming to power in Germany. . . . 'Ship of Fools' is also a human comedy and a moral allegory"—(*New Yorker*). "Miss Porter's image, as she points out, is the simple, universal one of the 'ship of this world on its voyage to eternity'; her theme is human folly—the evil done by innocence, the destructiveness of love; further irony derives from the voyage's time and destination. A rich, complex novel of rare distinction in both aim and execution"—(*LJ*). To some critics the book was a disappointment, but all recognized its importance and it appeared on the bestseller list for 28 weeks in 1962. Miss Porter's source was "The Ship of Fools" (*Das Narrensschiff*) by Sebastian Brant (*q. v.*), a satire first published in 1494.

"Her sensibiity is poetic, feminine, subtle, with a realization of the symbolic value of moments of illumination. This coupled with her sense of social mood and social change is the basis of her distinction." She has stated her creed on the freedom of the creative artist in her introduction to Eudora Welty's "A Curtain of Green" (1941 *Harcourt* new ed. 1947 $5.95). Her discriminating taste and fine artistry are as evident in her critical writings as in her short stories.

In 1943 she was elected a member of the National Institute of Arts and Letters, and in the following year was named Fellow in Regional American Literature of the Library of Congress. She has had many honorary degrees. She received the Emerson-Thoreau Award (American Academy of Arts and Sciences) in 1962 and won both the Pulitzer Prize in Fiction and the National Book Award in 1966 for her "Collected Stories," as well as the Gold Medal for Fiction awarded by the National Institute of Arts and Letters in 1967. She has donated her manuscripts, letters, and book collection to the University of Maryland and has announced the formation of the Katherine Anne Porter Foundation to benefit American writers.

THE OLD ORDER. *Harcourt* 1955 Harvest Bks. pap. $1.35. Stories of the South from Flowering Judas; Pale Horse, Pale Rider; and The Leaning Tower. Brings together all the author's Southern stories.

COLLECTED STORIES. *Harcourt* 1966 $8.95. *New Am. Lib.* pap. $3.50. All her stories and short novels—"a superb collection"—(*LJ*). Includes The Fig Tree; Holiday; Virgin Violeta; The Martyr.

FLOWERING JUDAS AND OTHER STORIES. 1930 *Harcourt* 1935 Harbrace Mod. Class. 1949 $2.95 text ed. $1.75; *New Am. Lib.* Signet pap. $.95

PALE HORSE. PALE RIDER. Three Short Novels: Old Mortality; Noon Wine (1937); Pale Horse, Pale Rider. *Harcourt* 1939 3 vols. in 1 $6.95; *New Am. Lib.* Signet 1962 pap. $.95

THE LEANING TOWER, AND OTHER STORIES. 1944. *New Am. Lib.* Signet pap. $.95

SHIP OF FOOLS. Her only novel. *Little-Atlantic* 1962 $8.50; *New Am. Sib.* Signet pap. $1.50

A CHRISTMAS STORY. Ill. by Ben Shahn. *Delacorte* 1967 $2.95. Miss Porter retells the story of Chirst's birth for her five-year-old niece.

COLLECTED ESSAYS AND OCCASIONAL WRITINGS. *Delacorte* 1970 $12.50

KATHERINE ANNE PORTER READING THE DOWNWARD PATH TO WISDOM. A complete short story; recording. *Caedmon* TC 1006 $5.95

KATHERINE ANNE PORTER READING PALE HORSE, PALE RIDER. Recording. *Caedmon* TC 2007 $11.90

KATHERINE ANNE PORTER READING NOON WINE. Recording. *Caedmon* TC 2010 $11.90

Books about Porter

> The Fiction and Criticism of Katherine Anne Porter. By Harry John Mooney, Jr. *Univ. of Pittsburgh Press* 1957 rev. ed. 1962 pap. $1.85
> Katherine Anne Porter. By Ray B. West, Jr. *Univ. of Minnesota Press* 1963 pap. $1.25
> Katherine Anne Porter and the Art of Rejection. By William L. Nance. *Univ. of North Carolina Press* 1964 pap. $1.95
> "A not entirely admiring study of Miss Porter's "theme of rejection with its sense of oppressive or destructive relationships with other people and the consequent urge to escape. Recommended"—(*LJ*).
> Katherine Anne Porter. By George Hendrick. U.S. Authors Ser. *Twayne* 1965 $5.50; *College & Univ. Press* pap. $2.45. Professor Hendrick, who admires her stories more than her essays, "may not seem to search deeply, but he gets to the heart of the matter. His observations bring out deeper meanings which many readers may have overlooked"—(*LJ*).
> Katherine Anne Porter: A Critical Symposium. Ed. by Lodwick Hartley and George Core. *Univ. of Georgia Press* 1969 $7.50
> A Bibliography of the Works of Katherine Anne Porter, and a Bibliography of the Criticism of the Works of Katherine Anne Porter. By Louise Waldrop and Shirley A. Baur. *Scarecrow Press* 1969 $5.00
> Katherine Anne Porter. By John Edward Hardy. Modern Lit. Monographs. *Ungar* 1973 $5.00. Good critical introduction.

GORDON, CAROLINE. 1895–

Most of Caroline Gordon's fiction is set in her native South and reflects her conservative attitude toward that region. Her first novel, "Penhally," traces the decline of a Kentucky plantation family over three generations, a decline brought about by pride and jealousy as well as the devastation of the Civil War. "None Shall Look Back," which had the misfortune to appear shortly after "Gone with the Wind," is a distinguished but neglected novel with a theme similar to her first. Against the story of the Allard family, which, like the house of Penhally, deteriorates through internal weaknesses as well as because of the Civil War, Miss Gordon sets off the heroic figure of the Confederate General Nathan Bedford Forrest. "The Garden of Adonis" picks up the story of the Allards, this time during the Depression of the 1930s, and shows how social conditions as well as their own incapacities have put the men of the family at the mercy of their spoiled and neurotic women.

"Aleck Maury, Sportsman," like Miss Gordon's most famous short story "Old Red," is remarkable for its vivid hunting scenes. Probably no other woman has written so knowledgeably and sympathetically about the outdoor man's love of the fields and streams of his native region and the almost sacramental view of nature which accompanies such allegiance. "Green Centuries" is a novel about a pioneer couple who settle near the Cumberland Gap during the American Revolution. "The Women on the Porch," "The Strange Children," and "The Malefactors" (1956 o. p.) are novels about modern intellectuals found wanting when tested by nature and their own raw emotions.

Caroline Gordon is also a very capable critic of fiction. With her ex-husband, the poet and critic Allen Tate (*q. v.*), she edited "The House of Fiction" (2nd ed. 1960 pap. $4.95), one of the most widely used and influential textbooks in the field. Her "How To Read a Novel" (*Viking* 1957 pap. $1.45) is an excellent introduction to the art of fiction.

PENHALLY. 1931. *Cooper* 1972 $7.00

ALECK MAURY, SPORTSMAN. 1934. *Cooper* 1972 $7.00

NONE SHALL LOOK BACK. 1937. *Cooper* 1972 $9.00

THE GARDEN OF ADONIS. 1937. *Cooper* 1972 $9.00

GREEN CENTURIES. 1941. *Cooper* 1972 $11.00

THE WOMEN ON THE PORCH. 1944. *Cooper* 1972 $7.50

THE STRANGE CHILDREN. 1951. *Cooper* 1972 $7.50

OLD RED AND OTHER STORIES. 1963. *Cooper* 1972 $6.00

DOS PASSOS, JOHN (RODERIGO). 1896–1970.

Dos Passos was born in Chicago, lived all over the world with his parents, graduated from Harvard, and drove an ambulance in World War I. His first book, "One Man's Initiation—1917" was a highly subjective record of his experiences in the French ambulance service. "Three Soldiers" was one of the first war novels to reveal the sordidness of military life. "Manhattan Transfer" marked the beginning of the Dos Passos style—social consciousness infused with a hatred of "the iron combination of men accustomed to run things." "U.S.A." was considered by many critics a massive achievement. Charles Poore wrote in the *N.Y. Times* (1966): "It lit fireworks. The impressionistic, and cinematic, techniques Mr. Dos Passos used there have by now been so widely imitated that they seem traditional." He has been called a more skillful reporter and historian than novelist; his novels are in general "documentary." In them and elsewhere he has been a strong advocate of social reform. During and following World War II, as a correspondent for *Life* he reported on the various theaters of war, our occupation of Germany, the Nuremberg trials, Socialist England, and the industrial United States. Alfred Kazin has said that, like Emerson, Dos Passos "likes Man, not men." Another critic has commented: "Profoundly attached to liberty as the founders of America conceived it, he hates the mechanistic age that swallows up liberty and the men who are the tools of their own technology." Although somewhat disappointing, his later novels are valued for their social insights. In such works as "Adventures of a Young Man," and "Most Likely to Succeed" he bitterly denounces Communism. In 1947 he received the Gold Medal Award for fiction from the National Institute of Arts and Letters, and in 1967 he was awarded the $32,000 Feltrinelli Prize by Rome's Accademia dei Lincei.

He has written many books about travel and the world abroad, including "Journeys Between Wars" (1938, o. p.), "Tour of Duty" (1946, o. p.), and "Brazil on the Move" (1963, o. p.). Among his collected critical and historical essays are "Men Who Made the Nation" (*Doubleday* 1957 $7.50) and "Occasions and Protests" (*Regnery* 1964 pap. $2.95). "Mr. Wilson's War" (*Doubleday* Mainstream of America Series 1962 $7.50) is a narrative history of the United States Government and its foreign relations from 1900 to just after World War I, informally written in terms of the people who made the headlines. His admiration for Thomas Jefferson is reflected in the biographical study, "The Head and Heart of Thomas Jefferson" (1954, o. p.). "The Shackles of Power: Three Jeffersonian Decades" (*Doubleday* Mainstream of America Series 1966 $7.95) is "entertaining popular history"—(*LJ*). His highly adventurous memoirs, "The Best Times" (1966, o. p.), cover the years 1896–1936 and his friendship with Joyce, Hemingway, Fitzgerald, and others.

U.S.A. TRILOGY: The 42nd Parallel; 1919; The Big Money. 1937. Ill. by Reginald Marsh. *Houghton* 1946 1963 3 vols. $14.00 Sentry Eds. pap. $4.95

THE WORLD IN A GLASS: A View of our Century Selected from Novels of John Dos Passos. With introd. by Kenneth S. Lynn. *Houghton* 1966 $6.95. An admirable selection.

DISTRICT OF COLUMBIA. With introd. by Arthur Mizener. The trilogy: Adventures of a Young Man; Number One; The Grand Design. 3 vols. in 1 *Houghton* 1952 $14.00

ONE MAN'S INITIATION: 1917. 1920. With a new introd. by the author and 6 drawings from his Paris sketchbook. *Cornell Univ. Press* 1969 $5.95 pap. $1.75

THREE SOLDIERS. 1921. *Houghton* 1947 $6.95 Sentry Eds. pap. $2.95

MANHATTAN TRANSFER. *Houghton* 1925 $6.00 Sentry Eds. pap. $2.95

42ND PARALLEL. 1930. *New Am. Lib.* Signet pap. $1.25

1919. 1932. *New Am. Lib.* Signet pap. $1.25; *Washington Square* pap. $.60

THE BIG MONEY. 1936. *New Am. Lib.* Signet pap. $1.25

ADVENTURES OF A YOUNG MAN. 1939. *Houghton* 1966 $6.95

THE GRAND DESIGN. 1949. *Houghton* 1966 $7.95; *Popular Lib.* pap. $.75

CHOSEN COUNTRY. 1951. *Houghton* 1962 $10.00 Sentry Eds. pap. $2.45

MOST LIKELY TO SUCCEED. 1954. *Houghton* 1966 $4.95; *Popular Lib.* pap. $.60

THE GREAT DAYS. 1958. *Houghton* 1967 $6.00; *Popular Lib.* pap. $.75

MIDCENTURY. *Houghton* 1961 $5.95; Pocket Bks. pap. $.75

THE FOURTEENTH CHRONICLE: LETTERS AND DIARIES. Ed. by Townsend Ludington. *Gambit* 1973 $15.00 numbered and slipcased ltd. ed. $35.00

Books about Dos Passos

> John Dos Passos. By John M. Wrenn. U.S. Authors Ser. *Twayne* 1961 $5.50; *College & Univ. Press* 1962 pap. $2.45
> John Dos Passos. By Robert Gorham Davis. Pamphlets on American Writers. *Univ. of Minnesota Press* 1962 pap. $1.25
> The Fiction of John Dos Passos. By John D. Brantley. *Humanities Press* 1968 $8.50
> Dos Passos, the Critics and the Writer's Intention. By Allen Belkind. *Southern Illinois Univ. Press* 1971 $8.95
> Dos Passos Path to U.S.A.: A Political Biography, 1912–1936. By Melvin Landsberg. *Colorado Assoc. Univ. Press* 1973 $10.00

FITZGERALD, F(RANCIS) SCOTT (KEY). 1896–1940.

F. Scott Fitzgerald remains one of the best-known American authors of the 20th century in spite of the fact that only occasionally did he write works of genuine distinction. The uneven quality of his output may be attributed in part to his desiring fame, wealth, and a good time at least as much as he wanted to be a literary artist. Fitzgerald was born in St. Paul, Minn., and spent much of his childhood in upstate New York, then attended private schools in St. Paul and New Jersey before enrolling at Princeton in 1913. He left in 1917 without taking a degree, and while serving as an Army lieutenant at Camp Sheridan near Montgomery, Ala., he met and fell in love with Zelda Sayre, a beautiful and popular Southern belle who had many suitors. When their engagement was broken because it seemed unlikely that Scott could support Zelda in her accustomed style, he wrote in cynical despair "This Side of Paradise." The spectacular success of this first of the lost-generation novels enabled Scott and Zelda to marry not long after its publication. They then embarked on a glamorous and well-publicized way of life that saw them traveling back and forth between the best hotels and speakeasies of America and the most fashionable resorts of Europe. Somehow Fitzgerald managed to write his best novel, "The Great Gatsby," in spite of the many distractions around him, but the wild life-style of the Fitzgeralds took its inevitable toll. Zelda gradually lapsed into incurable mental illness. After 1930 she spent much of her life in mental sanitariums before finally dying in an asylum fire of 1948.

Fitzgerald's writings after "Gatsby" are of uneven quality. "Tender Is the Night," his most ambitious novel, is a moving psychological narrative but one so close to the Fitzgeralds' own experiences that it lacks sufficient detachment for full artistic control. To pay for Zelda's medical expenses and their daughter's education in private schools, not to mention his own indulgences, Fitzgerald turned out numerous stories and articles for popular magazines between the time of the Crash in 1929 and his own fatal heart attack in 1940. Only occasionally did his talent rise to the potential suggested by "The Great Gatsby." His short story "Babylon Revisited" (1930) may convey better than any other work of fiction the atmosphere of Paris before and after the Fall; and some critics feel that his posthumously published "The Last Tycoon" might have been equal to "Gatsby" if Fitzgerald had lived long enough to polish and resolve the story. That short novel was edited by Fitzgerald's friend from Princeton days, Edmund Wilson (*q. v.*), who later collected other late pieces, notebook entries, and letters to and from Fitzgerald in a volume appropriately called "The Crack-up" (1945, o. p.).

The tormented yet glamorous lives of Scott and Zelda Fitzgerald have intrigued readers of several generations—so much so in fact that they themselves have become semifictional characters. Sheilah Graham, the Hollywood columnist, told the touching story of her romance with Fitzgerald in his last years in *Beloved Infidel* (with Gerold Frank, 1959, o. p.), which was later adapted for a film starring Gregory Peck. Budd Schulberg's novel "The Disenchanted" (1950, o. p.) is an account of Fitzgerald's boozy trip to the Dartmouth Winter Carnival in 1939. George Zuckerman's "The Last Flapper" (1969, o. p.) is an unsuccessful attempt to turn the story of the Fitzgeralds into a sentimental romance. A film version of "The Great Gatsby" starring Robert Redford has been made, and a television special about the Fitzgeralds was reputed to be the pilot for a weekly series.

The popular attractiveness of the Fitzgeralds has tended to obscure the fact that Scott was indeed a writer of considerable talent who occasionally flashed into genius. His best works have been mainstays in college classrooms during the past three or four decades and have thus evoked a considerable amount of critical attention. Matthew J. Bruccoli started *The Fitzgerald Newsletter* in 1958 and maintained it for more than a decade before assimilating it in the *Fitzgerald-Hemingway Annual* (*NCR Microcard Editions*, now $15 a year), which since 1969 he has co-edited with C. E. Frazer Clark.

THE FITZGERALD READER. Ed. by Arthur Mizener. *Scribner* 1963 $8.95 pap. $3.95. Selections from the novels, stories, and essays, and "The Great Gatsby" complete, with a penetrating introduction about the artist and his career.

BABYLON REVISITED AND OTHER STORIES. *Scribner* 1960 $5.95 pap. $1.95. Contains The Ice Palace, May Day, The Diamond as Big as the Ritz, Winter Dreams; Absolution, The Rich Boy, The Freshest Boy, Crazy Sunday, The Long Way Out.

THE STORIES OF F. SCOTT FITZGERALD. Ed. by Malcolm Cowley. *Scribner* 1951 $6.95 pap. $3.95

SIX TALES OF THE JAZZ AGE AND OTHER STORIES. *Scribner* 1966 pap. $1.95. 9 stories taken from "Tales of the Jazz Age" (1922) and "All the Sad Young Men" (1926).

FLAPPERS AND PHILOSOPHERS. Short stories. Introd. by Arthur Mizener. *Scribner* 1920 1959 pap. $2.45

THE APPRENTICE FICTION, 1909-1917. Ed. with introd. by John Kuehl. *Rutgers Univ. Press* 1965 $5.00. 15 early short stories, previously unpublished, written while Fitzgerald was in high school and college.

THIS SIDE OF PARADISE. *Scribner* 1920 $5.95 pap. $2.45

THE GREAT GATSBY. *Scribner* 1925 $5.95 pap. $1.65 lg.-type ed. $7.95 text ed. pap. $2.80 school ed. pap. $1.76 Scribner Research Anthologies ed. by Henry Dan Piper. Text of novel with background materials and critical essays 1970 pap. $2.95

THE BEAUTIFUL AND THE DAMNED. *Scribner* 1922 $6.95 pap. $2.65

TENDER IS THE NIGHT. *Scribner* 1934 rev. ed. 1951 1960 $6.95 pap. $2.25

TAPS AT REVEILLE. Short stories. *Scribner* 1935 pap. 1971 $2.95. Contains Babylon Revisited, Crazy Sunday, and eight of the Basil Duke Lee and Josephine stories.

THREE NOVELS: The Great Gatsby, Tender Is the Night, The Last Tycoon. Ed. by Malcolm Cowley and Edmund Wilson. *Scribner* 1953 pap. 1970 $3.95

THE LAST TYCOON. An unfinished novel. Ed. with fwd. by Edmund Wilson. *Scribner* 1941 1958 $5.95 pap. 1970 $2.45

THE PAT HOBBY STORIES. With introd. by Arnold Gingrich. *Scribner* 1962 $4.95 pap. $1.95. A belated but authentic first edition of the 17 stories that deal with an aging Hollywood script writer, a pathetic, courageous, amoral figure. Written during the last two years of his life, the stories ran consecutively in *Esquire* magazine.

THE BASIL AND JOSEPHINE STORIES. Ed. by Jackson R. Bryer and John Kuehl. *Scribner* 1973 $8.95. Brings together for the first time two series of stories with autobiographical significance written for the *Saturday Evening Post* in the late twenties and early thirties.

THE CRACK-UP. Ed. by Edmund Wilson. *New Directions* 1945 pap. $1.95. The story
of that title with other uncollected pieces, notebooks and unpublished letters, forming
his autobiography, together with letters to Fitzgerald from Gertrude Stein and others, and essays and poems by Paul Rosenfeld and others.

AFTERNOON OF AN AUTHOR: A Selection of Uncollected Stories and Essays. Introd. and
note by Arthur Mizener. *Scribner* 1958 $5.95 pap. 1972 $2.45. A companion volume
to "Crack-Up."

THE LETTERS OF F. SCOTT FITZGERALD. Ed. by Andrew Turnbull. 1963 *Bantam* pap.
$1.95

Working with Fitzgerald's daughter, Frances Lanahan, Mr. Turnbull has so arranged the letters that they
form a gallant personal and literary history. They are grouped here around the people to whom they were
written (his daughter, wife, editor, friends, etc.), tracing his "career from the time he and Zelda were the
darlings of the Jazz Age to the bitter 1940s when he had little left but his integrity as an artist and the guts to
fight on"—(*LJ*).

DEAR SCOTT, DEAR MAX: The Fitzgerald-Perkins Correspondence. Ed. by John
Kuehl and Jackson Bryer. *Scribner* 1971 $7.95

As EVER, SCOTT FITZ. Ed. by Matthew Bruccoli and Jennifer M. Atkinson. *Lippincott*
1972 $15.00. Letters between Fitzgerald and his literary agent Harold Ober, 1919–
1946.

F. SCOTT FITZGERALD IN HIS OWN TIME: A Miscellany. Ed. by Matthew J. Bruccoli
and Jackson R. Bryer. Collection of fugitive writings by and about Fitzgerald. *Kent
State Univ. Press* 1971 $12.50.

Books about Fitzgerald

Save Me the Waltz. 1932. By Zelda Fitzgerald. *Southern Illinois Univ. Press* 1967 $6.95; pap. $2.25;
New Am. Lib. 1968 pap. $.95
"Zelda Fitzgerald's vision of the life she and Scott Fitzgerald lived together"—(*N.Y. Times*).
The Far Side of Paradise: Biography of F. Scott Fitzgerald. By Arthur Mizener. *Houghton* 1951 rev. enl.
ed. 1965 Sentry Eds. pap. $2.45. A biography that does full justice to the writer as a man representative
of his times.
F. Scott Fitzgerald: The Man and His Work. Ed. by Alfred Kazin. 1951. *Macmillan* Collier Bks. pap.
$.95
Fitzgerald and the Jazz Age. Ed. by Robert and Malcolm Cowley. *Scribner* 1955 pap. $2.95
The Great Gatsby: A Study. Ed. by Frederick J. Hoffman. *Scribner* 1962 pap. $3.50. Useful casebook of
critical and background materials.
Scott Fitzgerald. By Andrew Turnbull. *Scribner* 1962 pap. $2.45; *Ballantine* pap. $1.75
Turnbull, who knew Fitzgerald, says: "Along the way I interviewed everyone I could find who had
known him, and their testimony is part of the fabric of this book." "Here, unmistakably, is first-rate biography which displaces every work before it, including the earnest and admirable pioneering effort of
Arthur Mizener a decade ago. Mr. Turnbull renders vividly the many people in Fitzgerald's life; and,
most important of all, he re-creates in human and poignant terms Fitzgerald's tragic relationship with
his wife, Zelda"—(*Atlantic*).
F. Scott Fitzgerald. By Kenneth Eble. U.S. Authors Ser. *Twayne* 1963 $5.50; *College & Univ. Press*
1964 $2.45
F. Scott Fitzgerald: A Collection of Critical Essays. Ed. by Arthur Mizener. *Prentice-Hall* 1963 $5.95
Spectrum Bks. pap. $1.95
F. Scott Fitzgerald: His Art and His Technique. By James E. Miller, Jr. *New York Univ. Press* 1964
$7.50 pap.
"Miller studies the novels intensively, suggests influences upon Fitzgerald, and reveals him as a con-
scientious professional. Recommended for scholarly collections of Criticism"—(*LJ*).
The Critical Reputation of F. Scott Fitzgerald: A Bibliographical Study. By Jackson R. Bryer. *Shoe
String* 1967 $15.00

F. Scott Fitzgerald: A Critical Portrait. By Henry Dan Piper. 1965. *Southern Illinois Univ. Press* 1968 pap. $2.85. Probably the best single scholarly study of the genesis and composition of Fitzgerald's works.

Twentieth Century Interpretations of The Great Gatsby. Ed. by Ernest Lockridge. *Prentice-Hall* 1968 $4.95 pap. $1.25

College of One. By Sheilah Graham. *Viking* 1967 $5.95

Miss Graham had ended her schooling in a London orphanage at 14, and two years before his death Fitzgerald devised an education for her, as she here recounts. "A moving and not inappropriate coda to his gay, profligate, and nobly striving life"—(Andrew Turnbull, in *Harper's*).

Tender Is the Night: Essays in Criticism. Ed. by Marvin J. LaHood. *Indiana Univ. Press* 1969 $8.50 pap. $1.95

Zelda: A Biography. By Nancy Milford. *Harper* 1970 $10.00; *Avon* 1972 pap. $1.50. This best-seller is a freshly researched study of the Fitzgeralds with emphasis on the Mrs. as seen by a Ms.

The Golden Moment: The Novels of F. Scott Fitzgerald. By Milton R. Stern. Elaborate and ingenious critical analysis of major works. *Univ. of Illinois Press* 1970 $10.00

Crazy Sundays: F. Scott Fitzgerald in Hollywood. By Aaron Latham. *Viking* 1971 $7.95; *Pocket Bks.* pap. $1.25

F. Scott Fitzgerald: A Descriptive Bibliography. Comp. by Matthew J. Bruccoli. *Kent State Univ. Press* 1972 $19.95

Scott Fitzgerald and His World. By Arthur Mizener. In the Pictorial Biographies Series. *Putnam.* 1972 $4.95

FAULKNER, WILLIAM. 1897–1962. (Nobel Prize 1949, awarded in 1950)

William Faulkner received the Nobel Prize in 1950 "for his powerful and artistically independent contribution to the new American novel." His acceptance speech was a simple and impressive statement about artists in the modern world in which he said: "Our tragedy today is a general and universal physical fear so long sustained by now that we can even bear it. There are no longer problems of the spirit. There is only the question: when will I be blown up? Because of this, the young man or woman writing today has forgotten the problems of the human heart in conflict with itself which alone can make good writing because only that is worth writing about, worth the agony and the sweat."

Faulkner was a Mississippi writer of great power who has drawn to themes of abnormality and decadence. His novels are intense in their character portrayal of disintegrating Southern aristocrats, poor whites, and Negroes. A complex, stream-of-consciousness rhetoric often involves him in lengthy sentences, though of such anguished power that impetus and meaning are seldom lost. Most of the tales are set in a place not found on any map—Yoknapatawpha County, Mississippi—and are characterized by the use of many recurring characters from families of different social levels spanning more than a century.

After a brief stint as a flier in the Royal Canadian Air Force near the end of the First World War, Faulkner returned to his home in Oxford, Miss. Unable at first to make a living from his writing, he worked as night superintendent at a power plant, carpenter, roof-painter, and postmaster at the university until such time as his growing reputation enabled him to place stories in popular magazines such as the *Saturday Evening Post* and brought him opportunities to write lucrative screenplays for Hollywood. "The Sound and the Fury" is considered his first major work. It is a tale of the degradation of a Southern family told from four different points of view beginning with that of an idiot son. Also told from multiple viewpoints is "As I Lay Dying," a grotesquely sad-comic story about a family of poor Southern whites who undergo many hardships on a pilgrimage to town in order to bury their dead mother. Less experimental in technique than these two works and therefore a better introduction to the Yoknapatawpha saga is "Light in August," a novel of sure-handed craftsmanship which successfully blends violence with pathos. With "Absalom, Absalom!," the difficult parts of his famous short novel "The Bear" (as published in "Go Down, Moses"), and the allegorical "A Fable," a non-Yoknapatawpha novel set in France during the First World War, Faulkner returned to an innovative and difficult style which is not likely to appeal to average readers. Yet interspersed with the writing of such works are collections of easily readable stories originally published in popular magazines, and there seems to be a growing sentiment among critics that "The Snopes Trilogy," for the most part an example of Faulkner's "moderate" style, could well be his most important single work.

In addition to the Nobel Prize he received the Howells Medal of the American Academy of Arts and Letters in 1950, and in 1951 the Page One Award and the National Book Award for his "Collected Stories." For his novel "A Fable" he received the National Book Award for the second time and the Pulitzer Prize in 1955. "The Reivers" was awarded the Pulitzer Prize in 1963. In 1956 former President Eisenhower asked Faulkner to organize a committee of writers and to submit a program which would help Americans reveal themselves to the world. He had already traveled widely for the State Department. In 1957 and 1958 he was the University of Virginia's first writer-in-residence, and in January, 1959, accepted an appointment as consultant on contemporary literature to the Alderman Library of the University. "Faulkner in the University" (ed. by Frederick L. Gwynn and Joseph L. Blotner 1959, *Random* Vintage Bks. pap. $1.95) contains his class conferences, 1957–58. "Lion in the Garden" (ed. by James B. Meriwether and Michael Millgate *Random* 1968 $8.95) brings together interviews with Faulkner conducted by various people from 1926 to 1962. "The

Wishing Tree" (*Random* 1967 $4.95), a charming children's story, was written for the eight-year-old daughter of a friend. "One guesses that little girls who have never heard of William Faulkner will enjoy it today" (Eliot Fremont-Smith). Faulkner began his literary career as a poet. His first book, "The Marble Faun" (1924), and a later collection of poetry, "A Green Bough" (1933), have been published in a single volume (*Random* 1965 $6.95).

When reporting his death, the *Boston Globe* quoted Faulkner's having once told an interviewer: "Since man is mortal, the only immortality for him is to leave something behind him that is immortal since it will always move. That is the artist's way of scribbling 'Kilroy Was Here' on the wall of the final and irrevocable oblivion through which he must some day pass."

There are many critics and scholars who think that Faulkner is not only the most important American novelist of the 20th century, but also one whose worldwide stature would put him near the top among major modern writers of all countries and genres. Yet when Malcolm Cowley edited "The Portable Faulkner" in 1946, he found that almost all of Faulkner's books were out of print. By arranging selections from the works with intelligence and ingenuity to form a continuous chronicle, Cowley deserves much of the credit for making readers aware of the way in which Faulkner was creating a fictive world on a scale grander than that of any novelist since Balzac. Since 1946 criticism has proliferated at such a voluminous rate that though the list of books about Faulkner is longer than that for any other writer in this chapter, it nonetheless represents a drastic selection of but a few of the more significant works among the many that have been devoted to him.

THE PORTABLE FAULKNER. Ed. by Malcolm Cowley. *Viking* Portable Lib. 1946 rev. ed. 1967 lib. bdg. $6.50 pap. $2.85

The new edition adds two long stories and a chapter from "Absalom, Absalom!," as well as the Nobel Prize Speech. Mr. Cowley's notes have been updated and expanded.

THE FAULKNER READER. Contains The Sound and the Fury; The Bear; and short pieces. 1954. *Modern Library* Giants 1959 $4.95

COLLECTED STORIES. *Random.* 1950 $5.95

BIG WOODS. *Random* 1955 $5.95. Five brief new narratives unite four previously published hunting stories: The Bear, The Old People, A Bear Hunt, and Race at Morning.

SELECTED SHORT STORIES. *Modern Library* 1962 $2.95

THREE FAMOUS SHORT NOVELS: Spotted Horses, The Old Man, and The Bear. *Random* Vintage pap. $1.95

THE SNOPES TRIOLOGY: The Hamlet (1940); The Town (1957); The Mansion (1959). *Random* 1964 3 vols. boxed $20.00

SOLDIER'S PAY. His first novel: *Liveright* 1926 $5.95 pap. $2.45; *New Am. Lib.* 1952 pap. $.95

MOSQUITOES. *Liveright* 1927 $5.95

SARTORIS. 1929. *New Am. Lib.* 1953 pap. $1.25; *Random* $4.95

THE SOUND AND THE FURY. 1929. *Modern Library* 1946 1967 $2.95 pap. $1.45; *Random* $6.95 Vintage Bks. pap. $1.95

AS I LAY DYING. 1930. *Modern Library* $2.95; *Random* $5.95 Vintage Bks. pap. $1.95

LIGHT IN AUGUST. 1932. *Modern Library* 1950 $2.95 pap. $1.65; *Random* $6.95 Vintage Bks. pap. $1.95

PYLON. 1935. *New Am. Lib.* Signet pap. $.95; *Random* 1965 $6.95

ABSALOM! ABSALOM! 1936 *Modern Library* $2.95 pap. $1.65; *Random* $6.95 Vintage Bks. pap. $1.95

THE UNVANQUISHED. 1938. *Random* 1965 $6.95 Vintage Bks. pap. $1.65. Short stories set during the Civil War.

THE WILD PALMS. Two separate narratives—"Wild Palms" and "Old Man"— printed in alternate chapters. *Random* 1939 $6.95 Vintage Bks. pap. $1.95; introd. by R. V. Cassill *New Am. Lib.* Signet pap. $.95

THE HAMLET. *Random* 1940 $6.95 Vintage Bks. pap. $1.95

GO DOWN MOSES AND OTHER STORIES. *Random* 1942 $6.95 Vintage Bks. pap. $1.65

INTRUDER IN THE DUST. *Random* 1948 $6.95 Vintage Bks. pap. $1.65; *Modern Library* $2.95 pap. $1.45

KNIGHT'S GAMBIT. *Gambit* 1949 $6.95. Detective stories

REQUIEM FOR A NUN. *Random* 1951 $6.95 stage adaptation (with Ruth Ford) 1959 $5.50

A FABLE. *Random* 1954 $6.95; *New Am. Lib.* Signet pap. $1.25

THE TOWN. *Random* 1957 $6.95 Vintage Bks. pap. $1.95

THE MANSION. Last volume of the Snopes trilogy. *Random* 1959 $6.95 Vintage Bks. pap. $1.95

THE REIVERS: A Reminiscence. *Random* 1962 $6.95 Vintage Bks. pap. $1.95; *New Am. Lib.* Signet pap. $.95. Unlike many of Faulkner's tales, this story is compelling in all its narrative threads, and in its hilarious and inventive characterization.

FLAGS IN THE DUST. Ed. by Douglas Day. Early version of what was to become "Sartoris." *Random* 1973 $8.95

ESSAYS, SPEECHES, AND PUBLIC LETTERS. Ed. by James B. Meriwether. *Random* 1965 $8.00

Casts light on "Faulkner's ambiguous attitudes toward civil rights and world problems. . . . This valuable collection includes practically all of Faulkner's nonfiction production dating from 1927"—(*LJ*).

THE FAULKNER-COWLEY FILE: Memories and Letters 1944–1962. Ed. with extensive commentary by Malcolm Cowley. *Viking* 1955 $5.00 Compass Bks. pap. $1.45.

This work of devotion by Faulkner's editor, mentor, and friend contains 26 unpublished letters—"A honey of a book for humanists" that "discusses the spelling of Faulkner's name, his moralism, jobs held and outside interests, the importance of the Symbolist tradition to him, his ambition to put everything into one sentence, and daughter Jill's part in getting her father to go to Stockholm"—(*LJ*).

WILLIAM FAULKNER READING. The Nobel Prize Acceptance Speech, Selections from As I Lay Dying, A Fable, and The Old Man. A recording. *Caedmon* TC 1035 $5.95

Books about Faulkner

William Faulkner: Three Decades of Criticism. Ed. by Frederick J. Hoffman and Olga W. Vickery. Distinguished collection of critical essays. *Michigan State Univ. Press* 1960 $7.50; *Harcourt* 1963 pap. $3.65

William Faulkner: A Critical Study. By Irving Howe. 1952. *Random* Vintage Bks. 2nd ed. revised 1962 pap. $1.95

The Novels of William Faulkner: A Critical Interpretation. By Olga W. Vickery. *Louisiana State Univ. Press* 1959 rev. ed. 1964 $7.50

William Faulkner. By William Van O'Connor. Pamphlets on American Writers. *Univ. of Minnesota Press* 1959 rev. ed. 1964. $.95

William Faulkner: From Jefferson to the World. By Hyatt H. Waggoner. *Univ. of Kentucky Press* 1959 pap. $2.25

The Literary Career of William Faulkner: A Bibliographical Study. By James B. Meriwether. 1961. *Univ. of South Carolina Press* 1971 $14.95. The most thorough textual and descriptive bibliography published to date.

William Faulkner. By Frederick J. Hoffman. *Twayne* 1962 $5.50; *College & Univ. Press* pap. $2.45

William Faulkner. By Lawrance Thompson. 1963. *Holt* pap. 1967 $2.75

William Faulkner: The Yoknapatawpha Country. By Cleanth Brooks. *Yale Univ. Press* 1963 $12.50 pap. $3.45

Who's Who in Faulkner. By Margaret Ford and Suzanne Kincaid. *Louisiana State Univ. Press* 1963 $3.75 pap. $1.75

The Tragic Mask: A Study of Faulkner's Heroes. By John Lewis Longley, Jr. *Univ. of North Carolina Press* 1963 $6.00 pap. $1.95

Crowell's Handbook of Faulkner. By Dorothy Tuck. 1964. (With title "Apollo Handbook of Faulkner") Apollo pap. $2.25

A "remarkable literacy Baedeker" (*LJ*) that is "notable for its complete discussions of the plots of each of the novels and for sane and sound critical comments"—(Choice).

A Reader's Guide to William Faulkner. By Edmond L. Volpe. *Farrar, Straus* 1964 $7.50 *Noonday* pap. $2.95

"Massive and scholarly, yet clear and understandable"—(*LJ*). The first section treats Faulkner biographically and critically; the second studies 19 novels in detail; the third provides a chronology of events of 9 novels, notes, and selective bibliography.

A Faulkner Glossary. By Harry Runyan. *Citadel Press* 1964 pap. $2.25.

Includes biographical and bibliographical material. "Recommended"—(*LJ*).

Faulkner's County: Yoknapatawpha. By Martin J. Dain. *Random* 1964 $15.00.

Photographs reflecting "the sadness and compassion and glory of the human heart"—(*LJ*).

The Achievement of William Faulkner. By Michael Millgate. *Random* 1965 $6.00 Vintage Bks. pap. $1.95.

"A valuable guide not only to the man and his books, but also to the present state of Faulkner criticism"—(*N.Y. Times*).

William Faulkner of Oxford. Ed. by James W. Webb and Wigfall A. Green. *Louisiana State Univ. Press* 1965 $4.95 pap. $2.45.

40 local friends and citizens recall Faulkner. "One of the most intimate pictures . . . that we have"—(*Christian Century*).

Faulkner: The Major Years; a Critical Study. By Melvin Backman. *Indiana Univ. Press* 1966 $6.75 Midland Bks. pap. $1.95

"A sustained simplicity of style and tone and a profound appreciation . . . make Professor Backman's study a valuable work. . . . His analysis of [10] novels are revealing and easily understood, although he adds very little that is new"—(*LJ*).

The Faulkners of Mississippi: A Memoir. By Murry C. Faulkner (the only living brother of William Faulkner). *Louisiana State Univ. Press* 1967 $5.95.

"A fascinating . . . recollection—evocative, amusing and absorbing by turns—of the Falkner family and their milieu"—(*N.Y. Times*).

Faulkner: A Collection of Critical Essays. By Robert Penn Warren. Twentieth Century Views Ser. *Prentice-Hall* 1967 $5.95 Spectrum Bks. pap. $2.45.

Essays by Sartre, Aiken, Cleanth Brooks and others. "Probably the most interesting item . . . is the introductory essay by Warren himself. . . . Warren summarizes the course of Faulkner criticism . . . and makes predictions about [its] future course"—(*LJ*).

Yoknapatawpha: Faulkner's "Little Postage Stamp of Native Soil." By Elizabeth M. Kerr. *Fordham Univ. Press* 1969 $10.00. Excellent scholarly study of his home country sources.

William Faulkner: The Journey to Self-Discovery. By H. Edward Richardson. *Univ. of Missouri Press* 1969 $8.50. A close study of the early work.

The Snopes Dilemma: Faulkner's Trilogy. By James Gray Watson. *Univ. of Miami Press* 1970 $7.95

William Faulkner: An Annotated Checklist of Criticism. By John Bassett. *David Lewis* 1972 $18.50. Best and most complete listing of secondary material.

Faulkner's Narrative. By Joseph W. Reed, Jr. *Yale Univ. Press* 1973 $12.50

William Faulkner: Four Decades of Criticism. Ed. by Linda Welshimer Wagner. *Michigan State Univ. Press* 1973 $10.00. Updates without entirely superseding the Hoffman-Vickery collection of 1960.

Faulkner: A Biography. By Joseph Blotner. *Random* 2 vols. 1974 boxed set $30.00

WILDER, THORNTON. 1897—

"The Bridge of San Luis Rey" won its author fame and the Pulitzer Prize. It set the pattern for the novel that gathers a miscellaneous group of characters in one spot in a crisis. Thornton Wilder chose a bridge in

Peru. He had experimented with the same device in his first novel, "The Cabala," set in a pension in modern Rome. After "The Woman of Andros", Wilder turned his attention to plays, except for "Heaven's My Destination." After 12 years came the novel, "The Ides of March," set in the time of Julius Caesar and told in letters and documents covering a long span of years. "The Eighth Day," perhaps "the most substantial piece of fiction of his career" (*N.Y. Times*), is the story of what follows the killing of an incompetent coal mine director who has possibly been shot by his assistant, John Ashley. The truth about the murder—for which Ashley is sentenced to death—and about Ashley's mysterious rescue and disappearance emerges three years later. "[Ashley] is, I believe, meant to be a kind of saint . . . 'a man of faith' but of no recognizable religion, with his 'inner quiet, at homeness in existence' " wrote Edith Oliver in the *New Yorker*. Edward Weeks said of the novel: "This is a modern *Pilgrim's Progress*, pitting against each other the two leading families in Coaltown to show the growth, through suffering, which men and women of the twentieth century might attain" (in the *Atlantic*). "The Eighth Day" won the National Book Award for fiction in 1968.

Wilder was born in Madison, Wis., but at a very early age he was taken to China, where his father was in the consular service. He went to school in California and later to Yale, taught at Lawrenceville School and lectured at the University of Chicago from 1930 to 1936. During World War II he was an intelligence officer with the Army Air Force. He was awarded the American Academy of Arts and Letters Gold Medal in 1952 and on July 4, 1963 was one of the first 31 persons to receive the Presidential Medal of Freedom (the nation's highest civilian award). He won the National Medal for Literature in 1965.

THE CABALA. His first novel. 1926. (And THE WOMAN OF ANDROS, 1930) *Harper* 1968 $5.95

THE BRIDGE OF SAN LUIS REY. 1927. *Harper* 1967 $4.95 lg.-type ed. $6.95; *Pocket Bks.* pap. $.75; *Washington Square* Reader's Enrichment Ser. pap. $.75

HEAVEN'S MY DESTINATION. 1935. *Popular Lib.* 1959 pap. $.70

THE IDES OF MARCH. *Harper* 1948 $6.95 Perenn. Lib. pap. $.70; *Grosset* Univ Lib. 1956 pap. $2.95; *New Am. Lib.* Signet pap. $.75

THE EIGHTH DAY. *Harper* 1967 $6.95 lg.-type ed. $9.95; *Popular Lib.* pap. $1.25

THEOPHILUS NORTH. *Harper* 1973 $7.95 signed ltd. ed. $25.00

A story of an ex-teacher who worked in Newport in the summer of 1926. "Although Wilder's rendering of the mood and life-style of Newport in the 1920's is successful and his philosophical observations on the horrible problems brought by undeserved wealth are pertinent, I found the novel increasingly annoying largely because Teddie [the hero] is too damn smug, humorless and successful to be believable"—(T. Crowell in *LJ*).

Books about Wilder

Thornton Wilder. By Rex Burbank. U.S. Authors Ser. *Twayne* 1961 $5.50; *College & Univ. Press* 1962 pap. $2.45. Analyzes his novels and plays, which, says Burbank, "affirm the dignity of the individual and the peculiar value of life."

Thornton Wilder. By Bernard Grebanier. Pamphlets on American Writers. *Univ. of Minnesota Press* 1964 pap. $1.25

Thornton Wilder: The Bright and the Dark. By M. C. Kuner. Twentieth Century American Writers Series. *Crowell* 1972 $4.50. Biographical and critical introduction for young readers.

HEMINGWAY, ERNEST (MILLER). 1899–1961. (Nobel Prize 1954)

Alfred Kazin observes in "On Native Grounds": "Technically and even morally Hemingway was to have a profound influence on the writing of the thirties. As a stylist and craftsman his example was magnetic on younger men who came after him; as the progenitor of the new and distinctively American cult of violence, he stands out as the greatest single influence on the hard-boiled novel of the thirties." Hemingway was born in Oak Park, near Chicago, the son of a country doctor who was a fisherman and a hunter. He went to Italy as an ambulance driver in the First World War, joined the Italian infantry and was severely wounded. As a correspondent he covered disturbances in the Near East, and about 1921 settled with other American expatriates in Paris. His first books were published there. "The Torrents of Spring", a satirical burlesque of Sherwood Anderson's style, really acknowledges his debt to Anderson (*q. v.*) who with Gertrude Stein (*q. v.*) was his teacher in the natural rhythms of American speech. His first successful novel "The Sun Also Rises" is made up almost entirely of the conversations of a group of the "lost generation" artists and writers in Paris. "Men Without Women" deals with deadpan gangsters and matadors. He used the Italy of World War I as the background for the love story of an English nurse and an American soldier in "A Farewell to Arms."

In 1927 he returned to America and, in 1930, bought a home in Key West, the scene of "To Have and Have Not" which he considered "not so good." In 1936 he went to Spain at the beginning of the bloody Civil War. His play "The Fifth Column" (produced on television in 1960) and his greatest novel, "For Whom the Bell Tolls," were the "matured results of his Spanish experiences." For his many and varied services in World War II he was decorated with a Bronze Star. On his return to Havana in 1946 he was married for the third time and lived on his 15-acre estate (*"Finca de la Vigia"*) in Cuba. He and his wife had two narrow escapes early in 1954 when two planes on which they were traveling crashed in Africa; he was then doing a series of articles on big-game hunting for *Look* magazine. Seven years later, in declining health, partly as a result of injuries suffered in these crashes, "like a samurai, feeling his body had betrayed him," he shot himself in his home in Ketchum, Idaho. With hindsight it is impossible to avoid the knowledge that Hemingway had always been preoccupied with the theme of self-destruction. From the opening story of his first significant book ("In Our Time," 1925), his father's suicide in 1929, and throughout his writings and his life, he was always close to accident, violence, and death.

Almost all of Hemingway's fugitive journalistic writings from his high school days through two world wars to his last years are now available in three volumes—"Ernest Hemingway's Apprenticeship," "Ernest Hemingway, Cub Reporter," and "By-Line: Ernest Hemingway." "Are such pieces worth reprinting? (Hemingway himself didn't think so: 'No one has any right to dig this stuff up.') The answer must be a modified yes. The quality of Hemingway's journalism tends to run parallel to that of his imaginative writing [and the earlier pieces are generally] much the best"—(*New Yorker*).

Charles Poore has said of Hemingway that "he may be the strongest influence in literature that this age will give to posterity." Hemingway's great tale of man's striving and courage, "The Old Man and the Sea," won his first Pulitzer Prize in 1953. With the award of the Nobel Prize in 1954 the Committee cited him for "his powerful style—forming mastery of the art of modern narration." And Hemingway himself said, "Writing is architecture, not interior decoration, and the baroque is over."

Before Hemingway died he left instructions that "under no circumstances should any of his letters ever be published. Thus the letters can only be paraphrased, even by the scholars who will have access to them"—(*N.Y. Times*). Letters from the last ten years of his life, mainly to the critic Harvey Breit, have recently been given to the Houghton Library at Harvard by Dr. and Mrs. Edmundo Lassalle. The collection includes an unpublished burlesque journal "Ernest Von Hemingstein"—lively satire on critics and writers. He left a gross estate of $1,410,310. Mrs. Hemingway, who lives in New York, said after her husband's death that she had several of his unpublished works in her possession. In 1967 Maury A. Bromsen of Boston bought two unpublished Hemingway short stories for $7,650. One of these, "The Bubble Illusion" is an entertaining fictional account of his own brush with military authorities as a war correspondent. His home at Key West, Fla., a two-story Spanish Colonial dwelling was opened as a museum in February 1964; the Cuban government has similarly kept his home there as it was in his lifetime, to be shown to visitors.

A HEMINGWAY READER. Ed. with introd. by Charles Poore. 2 complete novels: The Torrents of Spring, and The Sun Also Rises; episodes from 7 other novels; 11 short stories. *Scribner* 1953 $10.00; pap $3.95

THREE NOVELS. The Sun Also Rises, with introd. by Malcolm Cowley; A Farewell to Arms, with introd. by Robert Penn Warren; The Old Man and the Sea, with introd. by Carlos Baker. *Scribner* 1962 pap. $3.95

THE SHORT STORIES OF ERNEST HEMINGWAY. 1938. *Scribner* 1954 pap. $3.95

THE SNOWS OF KILIMANJARO AND OTHER STORIES. *Scribner* 1961 $3.95 pap. $1.65

THE FIFTH COLUMN AND FOUR STORIES OF THE SPANISH CIVIL WAR. *Scribner* 1969 $4.95 pap. $2.45; *Bantam* pap. $1.25. Hemingway's only play and related short stories.

THE NICK ADAMS STORIES. *Scribner* 1972 $7.95; *Bantam* pap. $1.75. The stories are rearranged in chronological sequence including eight previously unpublished.

IN OUR TIME. *Scribner* 1925 1955 $5.95 pap. 1962 $1.95. Stories of his youth, of war in Italy, of lumber camps, fishing, and matadors.

THE TORRENTS OF SPRING. 1926. *Scribner* 1972 $5.95 pap. $2.45

THE SUN ALSO RISES. *Scribner* 1926 $6.95 text ed. pap. $1.95

MEN WITHOUT WOMEN. Short stories. *Scribner* 1927 1954 $5.95 pap. $2.45

A FAREWELL TO ARMS. *Scribner* 1929 1948 1953 $6.95 pap. $2.45; text ed. pap. $2.36 lg.-type ed. $7.95

DEATH IN THE AFTERNOON. *Scribner* 1932 $14.95 pap. $2.95

WINNER TAKE NOTHING. Short stories. 1933 *Scribner* 1954 $5.95 pap. $2.45

TO HAVE AND TO HAVE NOT. *Scribner* 1937 1954 $6.95 pap. $2.45

FOR WHOM THE BELL TOLLS. *Scribner* 1940 $5.95 pap. 1960 $2.45

ACROSS THE RIVER AND INTO THE TREES. *Scribner* 1950 $6.95 pap. $2.45

THE OLD MAN AND THE SEA. *Scribner* 1952 Contemporary Class. pap. $1.65 college ed. $2.50 school ed. $2.24 school ed. pap. $1.48

ISLANDS IN THE STREAM. *Scribner* 1970 $10.00; *Bantam* pap. $1.50. Posthumous publication of three novelettes about the same central character.

A MOVEABLE FEAST. *Scribner* 1964 $5.95 pap. $2.95; *Bantam* pap. $1.25. A memoir of his youthful years in the Paris of the 1920s.

BY-LINE: ERNEST HEMINGWAY. Selected articles and dispatches of four decades. Ed. by William White *Scribner* 1967 $8.95

ERNEST HEMINGWAY, CUB REPORTER. Ed. by Matthew J. Bruccoli. *Univ. of Pittsburgh Press* 1969 $4.95. *Kansas City Star* stories.

ERNEST HEMINGWAY'S APPRENTICESHIP. Ed. by Matthew J. Bruccoli. *NCR Microcard Editions* 1972 $6.95 limited ed. $12.50

ERNEST HEMINGWAY READING. A recording. Includes the following, whole or in part: the Nobel Prize Acceptance Speech; Second Poem to Mary in London; In Harry's Bar in Venice: A Parody; The Fifth Column; Work in Progress; Saturday Night at the Whorehouse in Billings, Montana. *Caedmon* TC 1185 $5.95

Books about Hemingway

Hemingway: The Writer as Artist. By Carlos Baker. *Princeton Univ. Press* 1952 4th rev. ed. 1973 $12.50 pap. $2.95

Ernest Hemingway. By Philip Young. 1952. (with title "Ernest Hemingway: A Reconsideration") *Pennsylvania State Univ. Press* 2nd ed. 1966 $9.50. Early critical study with prophetic psychological interpretations.

The Apprenticeship of Ernest Hemingway. By Charles Fenton. 1954 *Viking* Compass Bks. 1958 pap. $1.65

Ernest Hemingway. By Philip Young. Pamphlets on American Writers. *Univ. of Minnesota Press* 1959 rev. ed. 1965 pap. $1.25

Hemingway and the Dead Gods. By John Killinger. *Univ. of Kentucky Press* 1960 $5.95

Hemingway and His Critics: An International Anthology. Ed. by Carlos Baker. *Hill & Wang* 1961 $4.95 pap. $1.95

In his introduction, Prof. Baker remarks, "If by nothing else (Hemingway's) world citizenship would be proved by the very intensity with which his faults and virtues have been critically debated in scores of different languages" (at least 40). This anthology is particularly valuable because of the checklist of criticism.

Portrait of Hemingway. By Lillian B. Ross. *Simon & Schuster* 1961 $2.50

Ernest Hemingway: Critiques of Four Major Novels. Ed. by Carlos Baker. *Scribner* 1962 pap. $2.95

My Brother, Ernest Hemingway. By Leicester Hemingway. 1962. *Fawcett* Premier Bks. pap. $.95. A warm, affectionate, and important biography by the famous author's brother.

At the Hemingways: A Family Portrait. By Marcelline Hemingway Sanford. *Little-Atlantic* 1962 $5.95. This is indeed a family portrait and only incidentally a portrait of the writer. This memoir, written with special knowledge and affection, helps to explain the profound influence his family had on all his life.

Hemingway: A Collection of Critical Essays. Ed. by Robert P. Weeks. *Prentice-Hall* 1962 $5.95 Spectrum Bks. pap. $1.95

Ernest Hemingway. By Earl H. Rovit. U.S. Authors Ser. *Twayne* 1963 $5.50; *College & Univ. Press* 1964 pap. $2.45

Papa Hemingway: A Personal Memoir. By A. E. Hotchner. *Random* 1966 $7.95; *Bantam* pap. $1.25. A Book-of-the-Month Club best seller, this "revealing book of intimate recollections" whose accuracy has not been seriously challenged, was the subject of a court suit (which Mrs. Hemingway lost) as an "invasion of privacy." It is an "affectionate and unashamedly frank account of his 14 post-war years of close friendship with Hemingway" and the first to describe the tormented last months of the writer's life.

Ernest Hemingway: A Comprehensive Bibliography. By Andre Hanneman. *Princeton Univ. Press* 1967 $17.50. His works including library holdings of letters and manuscripts, items about him 1918–65, and excerpts from reviews of his novels.

Ernest Hemingway: An Introduction and Interpretation. By Sheridan Baker. American Authors and Critics Ser. 1967. *Holt* text ed. pap. $2.50

Hemingway's Nonfiction: The Public Voice. By Robert O. Stephens. *Univ. of North Carolina Press* 1968 $8.50 pap. $2.95. Excellent scholarly study.

Ernest Hemingway: A Life Story. By Carlos Baker. *Scribner* 1969 $12.50; *Bantam* 1970 pap. $1.95. The definitive biography.

Hemingway's African Stories: The Stories, Their Sources, Their Critics. Ed. by John M. Howell. Research Anthology Ser. *Scribner* 1969 pap. $2.95. Casebook devoted to "The Short Happy Life of Francis Macomber" and "The Snows of Kilimanjaro."

Ernest Hemingway and the Arts. By Emily Stipes Watts. *Univ. of Illinois Press* 1971 $8.95

Hemingway and *The Sun Set*. By Bertram D. Sarason. *NCR Microcard Editions* 1972 $8.95. Collection of memoirs by real-life counterparts of characters in "The Sun Also Rises" and others who knew Hemingway in Paris prefaced by a long scholarly introduction.

A Reader's Guide to Ernest Hemingway. By Arthur Waldhorn. *Farrar, Straus* 1972 $8.95 Noonday pap. $2.95

Hemingway's Craft. By Sheldon Norman Grebstein. Pref. by Harry T. Moore. Crosscurrents/Modern Critiques. *Southern Illinois Univ. Press* 1973 $8.95

Hadley, The First Mrs. Hemingway. By Alice Hunt Sokoloff. *Dodd* 1973 $6.95

WOLFE, THOMAS. 1900–1938.

Wolfe was born in Asheville, N.C., graduated from the University of North Carolina, studied in Professor Baker's 47 Workshop, received his M.A. from Harvard, took up teaching in New York University, and lived abroad in his free time. The publisher's note in "Of Time and the River" announced that "this novel is the second in a series of six" and gave the six titles. Wolfe lived to complete but four. "You Can't Go Home Again" carries the story down to 1937. The novels are all of great length and largely autobiographical. The same hero serves for the four, his name changed from Eugene Gant to George Webber in the last two. Clifton Fadiman has said: "Thomas Wolfe's novel (it is all one novel) recounts the history of a man trying passionately to find out where he belongs." Wolfe's novels are highly emotional, quivering with feeling; rhapsodies and declamations abound in them. "Driven and tormented, incapable of repose or serenity, guilty of wide swings of emotion, frequently unjust and unfair, Wolfe had nevertheless a sovereign imagination and an exalted vision that tried to encompass the entire American experience" (Thomas Lask, in the *N.Y. Times*). He longed at times to be a great poet. In "A Stone, a Leaf, a Door" (with fwd. by Louis Untermeyer, *Scribner* 1945 $6.95 pap. $2.45), John S. Barnes experimented with arranging certain poetical passages in the form of verse.

In addition to writing lengthy novels and some short stories, Wolfe kept expansive notebooks and was a prolific letter writer. Unfortunately, his "Letters" (ed. by Elizabeth Nowell 1960), "The Correspondence of Thomas Wolfe and Homer Andrew Watt" (ed. by Oscar Cargill and Thomas Clark Pollock 1954), and "The Letters of Thomas Wolfe to His Mother" (ed. by C. Hugh Holman and Sue Fields Ross 1968) are all out of print. However, the recently published two volumes of "Notebooks" will give grist to scholars' mills for years to come. "The Story of a Novel" (*Scribner* 1936 $6.95) describes the background and composition of "Of Time and the River." A later statement of his literary credo may be found in "Thomas Wolfe's Purdue Speech 'Writing and Living' " (ed. by William Braswell and Leslie A. Field 1964 o. p.). In his youth Wolfe wrote several dramas, but the only play currently in print is "Mountains" (ed. by Pat M. Ryan. *Univ of North Carolina Press* 1970 $8.50). Ketti Frings has been more fortunate. Her "Look Homeward, Angel" (*French* 1960 $1.75), a comedy drama in three acts based on Wolfe's novel, won the Pulitzer Prize for Playwriting in 1958 as well as the New York Drama Critics Circle award as the best play of the season.

THE SHORT NOVELS OF THOMAS WOLFE. Ed. with introd. and notes by C. Hugh Holman. *Scribner* 1961 $7.95

THE THOMAS WOLFE READER. Ed. by C. Hugh Holman. *Scribner* 1962 $10.00

An anthology of representative selections, the passages chosen being largely the best known and most famous. They "reveal Wolfe's artistry with words, the energy of his prose, and his power of characterization . . . and illustrate his autobiographic method, his preoccupation with such themes as loneliness, time, death, and the immensity of America, and his superb artistry"—(*LJ*).

FROM DEATH TO MORNING. A collection of short stories issued posthumously. *Scribner* 1932 pap. $2.45

LOOK HOMEWARD, ANGEL. *Scribner* 1929 ill. by Douglas Gorsline 1947 $7.95 pap. 1960 $2.95 gift ed. 1963 $10.00

OF TIME AND THE RIVER. *Scribner* 1935 $10.00 pap. 2 vols. each $3.95

THE WEB AND THE ROCK. *Harper* 1939 $10.00 lib. bdg. $7.92 Mod. Class. text ed. $2.40; *New Am. Lib.* Signet pap. $.95

YOU CAN'T GO HOME AGAIN. *Harper.* 1940 $7.50 lib. bdg. 1963 $6.11; *New Am. Lib.* Signet 1966 pap. $1.50

THE HILLS BEYOND. 1941. *Harper* 1944 $6.95; *New Am. Lib.* Signet pap. $.95

WESTERN JOURNAL. *Univ. of Pittsburgh* 1951 pap. $1.50

THE LETTERS OF THOMAS WOLFE TO HIS MOTHER. Ed. by C. Hugh Holman and Sue Fields Ross. *Univ. of North Carolina Press* 1968 $8.50. Her name was Julia Elizabeth Wolfe. A literal and exact transcript including calendar of letters and chronology. It replaces the 1943 volume edited by John Skally, now o. p.

NOTEBOOKS OF THOMAS WOLFE. Ed. by Richard S. Kennedy and Paschal Reeves. *Univ. of North Carolina Press* 1970 2 vols. boxed set $30.00. Carefully edited generous selection from Wolfe's voluminous notebooks.

Books about Wolfe

Thomas Wolfe: The Weather of His Youth. By Louis D. Rubin Jr. *Louisiana State Univ. Press* 1955 $4.00. "An intelligent, sensitive and closely reasoned technical analysis that will be of real value."

Thomas Wolfe's Characters: Portraits from Life. By Floyd C. Watkins. *Univ. of Oklahoma Press* 1957 $5.95

Thomas Wolfe: A Biography. By Elizabeth Nowell. 1960. *Greenwood* 1973 $18.50. Important biography by one who knew him well

Thomas Wolfe. By C. Hugh Holman. Pamphlets on American Writers. *Univ. of Minnesota Press* 1961 pap. $1.25

Thomas Wolfe. By Richard Walser. *Barnes & Noble* 1961 $4.00; *Holt* 1967 pap. $1.95

The Window of Memory: The Literary Career of Thomas Wolfe. By Richard S. Kennedy. *Univ. of North Carolina Press* 1962 $8.95 pap. $3.45. A penetrating scholarly and critical study of the genesis and composition of Wolfe's fiction.

Thomas Wolfe. By Bruce McElderry, Jr. U.S. Authors Ser. *Twayne* 1963 $5.50; *College & Univ. Press* 1964 pap. $2.45

Thomas Wolfe. By Andrew Turnbull. *Scribner* 1967 $7.95; *Simon & Schuster* Clarion Bks. pap. $1.25; *Pocket Bks.* pap. $1.25

Thomas Wolfe: An Introduction and Interpretation. By Richard Walser. American Authors and Critics Ser. 1967. *Holt* pap. $2.10

Thomas Wolfe: Three Decades of Criticism. Ed. by Leslie A. Field. *New York Univ. Press* 1968 $9.95 pap. $2.45

Thomas Wolfe: A Collection of Critical Essays. Ed. by Louis D. Rubin, Jr. Twentieth Century Views Ser. *Prentice-Hall* 1973 $5.95 pap. $1.95

Thomas Wolfe's Albatross: Race and Nationality in America. By Paschal Reeves. *Univ. of Georgia Press* 1969 $7.00. Sound critical study.

Thomas Wolfe: A Checklist. By Elmer D. Johnson. *Kent State Univ. Press* 1970 $7.50. Full listing of critical responses.

Thomas Wolfe and the Glass of Time. Ed. by Paschal Reeves. *Louisiana State Univ. Press* 1971 $6.50. Five essays by noted Wolfe scholars as well as a memoir by his brother Fred.

Thomas Wolfe: Ulysses and Narcissus. By William U. Snyder. *Ohio Univ. Press* 1971 $8.50. A psychological interpretation.

WESCOTT, GLENWAY. 1901–

Twenty-six years after it was first published, Glenway Wescott's novel "The Pilgrim Hawk" came out in a new edition. A lengthy critical review in the *New Yorker* (quoted in this paragraph) described the book as "marvelous," "tantalizing," and "enigmatic." Set in a French village in the 1920s, all the action occurs in the space of a single afternoon. One of the three couples involved has a pet hawk, "a symbol . . . of love's troubles and delusions." " 'The Pilgrim Hawk' poses the captive against the free, and, finding only an armed truce between them, questions the definitions of both. There are no easy definitions, it turns out; they are endlessly definable. To be free—in humans—means being neither wild nor captured. . . . Yet the major theme is clear: 'When love is at stake, love of liberty is as a rule only fear of captivity.' "

Wescott's novel "The Grandmothers," which won the Harper Prize Novel contest in 1927, is a good example of the qualities attributed to him by Dayton Kohler: "He writes with the simplicity of rhythm that we find in folk-poetry and folk tunes, and his beautifully cadenced prose is an aesthetic medium to bring a sense and smell of the soil like some dark intoxicant to the imagination of the reader." His book of criticism "Images of Truth: Remembrances and Criticism" (1962 o. p.) contains essays about friends or acquaintances whose writing he values: Katherine Anne Porter, Somerset Maugham, Colette, Isak Dinesen, Thomas Mann, and Thorton Wilder. "I can think of no living writer in English who practices this art of remembrance with greater finesse, inspiration, and unexpectedness than Glenway Wescott. The last essay in his book, called 'Talks with Thornton Wilder,' is a masterpiece"—(Robert Phelps, in the *N.Y. Herald Tribune*). Mr. Wescott was born in Kesaskum, Wis., attended the University of Chicago and then lived in Paris and on the Riviera for nine years.

THE GRANDMOTHERS: A Family Portrait. 1927 *Atheneum* 1962 pap. $1.45

GOOD-BYE WISCONSIN. Short stories. 1928. *Bks. for Libraries.* $11.50

THE PILGRIM HAWK. 1940. *Harper* 1966 $4.00

APARTMENT IN ATHENS. 1945. *Greenwood* 1972 $11.50

Books about Wescott

Glenway Wescott. By William H. Rueckert. U.S. Authors Ser. *Twayne* 1965 $5.50; *College & Univ. Press* 1965 pap. $2.45

"Rueckert's thesis, that 'Wescott's career up to the present has been that of an unfulfilled (not wasted) talent,' is demonstrated in this book by everything from the general approach (chronological so that he may illustrate both the growth of Wescott as a writer and the growth of his cohesive body of fiction) down to the chapter headings. . . . The tone of the book, however, remains respectful of a remarkable talent always not quite reaching its potential . . . All in all, about the best and clearest book or article on Wescott in existence with none of the heaviness which so often surrounds books on living authors"— (*Choice*).

Glenway Wescott: The Paradox of Voice. By Ira Johnson. *Kennikat* 1971 $10.95

LYTLE, ANDREW. 1902–

Although only one of Andrew Lytle's four novels is in print as of early 1974, he is a prime candidate for rediscovery. Named Editor of *Sewanee Review* in 1961, he has had a distinguished career as a writer and historian since the 1930s. "The Long Night," his first novel, is a story of antebellum Southern society told from a perspective at once respectful and critical. "At the Moon's End" (1941, o. p.) deals with the Spanish conquest of Eldorado and reflects a new interest of Lytle's in ghosts and the supernatural. His "A Name for Evil" (1947, o. p.) is a story reminiscent of Henry James's "The Turn of the Screw" in its evocation of an unexplained haunting which stands in the way of good intentions. "The Velvet Horn" (1957, o. p.) is a novel set in old and recent Tennessee told both realistically and symbolically in a way which suggests a universal Christian allegory about the Fall of Man. Caroline Gordon called it "a landmark in American fiction."

A three-time recipient of Guggenheim fellowships, Lytle has participated in numerous writing workshops and lectured at many universities. His "A Hero with the Private Parts: Essays" (*Louisiana State Univ. Press* 1966 $6.00) is a collection of critical essays which show that though Lytle's own background and the scenes of his fiction may be provincially Southern, he is an astute follower of Flaubert and James in his literary heritage.

THE LONG NIGHT. 1936. *Avon* 1973 pap. $1.25

STEINBECK, JOHN (ERNST). 1902–1968. (Nobel Prize 1962)

Born in Salinas County, California, Steinbeck was of German-Irish parentage, his mother a teacher, his father a county official. As a young man he came to New York, where he worked as a reporter and as a hod-carrier. Returning to California, he devoted himself to writing, with little success; his first three books sold less than 3,000 copies. "Tortilla Flat," dealing with the happy-go-unlucky paisanos, California Mexicans whose ancestors settled in the country 200 years ago, established his reputation. "In Dubious Battle," a labor novel of a strike and strike-breaking, won the gold medal of the Commonwealth Club of California. "Of Mice and Men," a long short story of a homeless moron, written almost entirely in dialogue, was an experiment "to see how like a play he could write a novel" and was dramatized in the year of its publication, winning the Drama Critics Circle award. It gave him fame.

In 1936 he wrote a series of articles about the transient labor camps in California for the Scripps-Howard San Francisco *News.* Out of this experience came his greatest book, "The Grapes of Wrath," the odyssey of the Joad family, dispossessed of their farm in the Dust Bowl and seeking a new home, only to be driven on from camp to camp. The fiction is interrupted at intervals by nonfiction, explaining this new sociological problem of American nomadism. As the American novel "of the season, probably the year, possibly the decade," it won the Pulitzer Prize and was made into a motion picture in 1940. It roused America and won a broad readership by the unusual simplicity and tenderness with which Steinbeck treated social questions. This quality in his work has more recently been seen as oversimplification. Steinbeck communicates great zest for living, but he is "unequipped to deal with the more sombre reality a man must come up against"— (R.W. B. Lewis, in "Modern American Fiction"). Edmund Wilson notes that the "tendency on Steinbeck's part to animalize humanity is evidently one of the causes of his relative unsuccess at creating individual humans"—(in "Classics & Commercials").

His best and most ambitious novel since "The Grapes of Wrath" is "East of Eden," a saga of two American families in California from about 1860 through the First World War. "Through the exercise of a really rather remarkable freedom of his rights as a novelist, Mr. Steinbeck weaves in, and more particularly around, this story of prostitution a fantasia of history and of myth that results in a strange and original work of art"— (Mark Shorer in the *N.Y. Times*). It has been said that although Steinbeck's compassion "often lapses into sentimentality, his best work is sustained by his flair for vivid and realistic description."

Three outstanding works of nonfiction are "Russian Journal" (with Robert Capa as photographer, 1948, o. p.); "Once There Was a War" (*Viking* 1958 $3.95; *Bantam* pap. $.95), his dispatches from England, Africa and Italy of 1943; and "America and Americans" (1966 *Bantam* 1967 pap. $1.25), which features pictures of the United States by 55 leading photographers and a 70-page essay by Steinbeck. His interest in marine biology led to two books primarily about sea life, but interspersed with observations about men and Nature: "Sea of Cortez" (with Edward R. Ricketts. 1941. *Paul P. Appel* $20.00) and "The Log from the Sea of Cortez" (*Viking* 1951 Compass Bks. pap. $2.25; *Bantam* pap. $1.25). "Travels with Charley" (*Viking* 1962 $4.95 Compass Bks. pap. $1.65; *Bantam* pap. $1.25; *Franklin Watts* 1965 lg. type ed. Keith Jennison Bks. $8.95) is his engaging account of his voyage of rediscovery of America, which took him through almost 40 states. He was accompanied by his distinguished French poodle, Charley, and they traveled in a three-quarter-ton pickup truck (with living quarters) named Rocinante, "which you will remember," he says, "was the name of Don Quixote's horse."

Steinbeck won the 1962 Nobel Prize for Literature, the sixth American to be chosen for this award since its inception in 1900. "Mr. Steinbeck has resumed his position as an independent expounder of the truth with an unbiased instinct for what is genuinely American be it good or bad. . . . He likes to contrast the simple joy of life with the brutal and cynical craving for money, but in him we find the American temperament also expressed in his great feeling for nature, for the tilled soil, the wasteland, the mountains and the ocean coasts, all an inexhaustible source of inspiration to Steinbeck in the midst of and beyond the world of human beings."

After "The Grapes of Wrath," the peak of Steinbeck's career, his literary reputation declined somewhat, but there have been signs of a resurgence since his death in 1968. *Steinbeck Quarterly* founded that year as *Steinbeck Newsletter* has full-scale critical articles and serves as a clearing house of information about Steinbeck. Edited by Tetsumaro Hayashi of Ball State University in Muncie, Ind., it is available for eight dollars a year, including membership in The John Steinbeck Society, one of the more active organizations devoted to individual writers.

THE PORTABLE STEINBECK. Sel. by Pascal Covici. *Viking* 1943 enl. ed. lib. bdg. 1946 $5.95 pap. $3.25. Includes of Mice and Men, The Red Pony, short stories and other selections.

THE SHORT NOVELS OF JOHN STEINBECK: Tortilla Flat, Of Mice and Men, The Red Pony, The Moon Is Down, Cannery Row, The Pearl. *Viking* 1963 $6.50

CUP OF GOLD. 1929. *Bantam* 1967 pap. $.95

THE PASTURES OF HEAVEN. 1932. *Bantam* 1967 pap. $95

TORTILLA FLAT. 1935. *Bantam* 1965 pap. $.95; *Viking* 1963 $4.50 Compass Bks. pap. $1.65

IN DUBIOUS BATTLE. 1936. *Bantam* pap. $.95; *Viking* 1963 $5.00 Compass Bks. pap. $1.65

OF MICE AND MEN. 1937. *Bantam* pap. $.75; *Modern Library* $2.95; *Viking* 1963 $4.00 Compass Bks. pap. $1.75

THE RED PONY. A short novel. 1937. *Bantam* pap. $.60; *Viking* 1959 lib. bdg. $3.37 (and THE PEARL) Compass Bks. 1965 pap. $1.65; *Franklin Watts* lg.-type ed. Keith Jennison Bks. $7.95

THE LONG VALLEY. Short stories. 1938. *Viking* $5.00 Compass Bks. pap. $1.95; *Bantam* 1967 pap. $.95

THE GRAPES OF WRATH. 1939. *Bantam* pap. $1.50; *Viking* 1959 $7.50 Compass bks. pap. $1.95 Ed. by Peter Lisca Critical Lib. 1972 $8.95 pap. $3.50

THE MOON IS DOWN. 1942. *Bantam* pap. $1.50; (and Dickens's "Tale of Two Cities") Ed. by Edgar M. Schuster *Noble & Noble* 1961 $3.60; *Viking* Compass Bks. pap. $1.95

CANNERY ROW. 1945. *Bantam* pap. $.95

THE WAYWARD BUS. 1947. *Bantam* pap. $.95

THE PEARL. 1947. *Bantam* 1948 1960 1962 pap. $.75; (and George Eliot's "Silas Marner") Ed. by Greene *Noble & Noble* $3.60; *Viking* 1947 $4.95 (and The Red Pony) Compass Bks. pap. $1.25

BURNING BRIGHT. A play-novelette. 1950. *Bantam* 1967 pap. $.95

SWEET THURSDAY. 1955. *Bantam* 1961 pap. $.95

THE SHORT REIGN OF PIPPIN FOURTH: A Fabrication. *Bantam* 1957 pap. $.95

THE WINTER OF OUR DISCONTENT. 1961 *Bantam* 1967 pap. $1.25

JOURNAL OF A NOVEL: The "East of Eden" Letters. *Viking* 1969 $6.50 limited ed. $25.00 Compass Bks. pap. $1.95. A journal in the form of a series of letters to his friend and editor Pascal Covici.

Books about Steinbeck

Steinbeck and His Critics: A Record of Twenty-five Years. Ed. by Ernest Warnock Tedlock and Cecil Vivian Wicker. *Univ. of New Mexico Press* 1957 pap. $3.45.
   "In this collection of reviews and essays, the editors, professors in the University of New Mexico, have tried to 'include all important attitudes toward Steinbeck and his writing' "—(*LJ*).
The Wide World of John Steinbeck. By Peter Lisca. *Rutgers Univ. Press* 1958 $9.00
John Steinbeck. By Warren French. *Twayne* 1961 $5.50; *College & Univ. Press* 1962 pap. $2.45
John Steinbeck: An Introduction and Interpretation. Ed. by Joseph Fontenrose. American Authors and Critics Ser. *Holt* 1967 pap. $2.50

John Steinbeck: A Concise Bibliography (1930–65). By Tetsumaro Hayashi. *Scarecrow Press* 1967 $5.00.
"Though 'necessarily tentative' in range and completeness, this volume supersedes all previous Steinbeck bibliographies"—(*Choice*).

A Casebook on "The Grapes of Wrath." Ed. by Agnes M. Donohue. *Crowell* 1969 pap. $3.95

Thematic Design in the Novels of John Steinbeck. By Lester J. Marks. Studies in American Literature Ser. *Humanities* 1969 $9.50

Steinbeck, The Man and His Work: Proceedings of the 1970 Steinbeck Conference Sponsored by Oregon and Ball State Universities. Ed. by Richard Astro and Tetsumaro Hayashi. *Oregon State Univ. Press* 1971 $5.00

John Steinbeck. By James Gray. Pamphlets on American Writers. *Univ. of Minnesota Press* 1971 pap. $.95

Steinbeck: A Collection of Critical Essays. Ed. by Robert Murray Davis. Twentieth Century Views Ser. *Prentice-Hall* 1972 $5.95 Spectrum Bks. pap. $1.95

BOYLE, KAY. 1903–

Kay Boyle's "cold beauty of language" is her special gift. Her feeling for France, her understanding of the French character, and her descriptions of the beauty and mystery of the Swiss mountain villages and glacier regions show a sure and sensitive knowledge. Most of her more than twenty volumes of poems and fiction are o. p. Of "Generation without Farewell" (1959, o. p.), her novel about postwar Germany, Virgilia Peterson said: Always a lyrical, troubling writer, Kay Boyle has never written poignantly, never come closer to absolute pitch than in this new novel" (*N.Y. Times*). The short stories in "The Smoking Mountain" grew out of the author's experience of living in Germany during the late 1940s as the wife of a State Department official and question "the enigma of a nation which condemned to death six million of its inhabitants and yet was unable or unwilling to accept the responsibility for the action" (*LJ*). Her "Collected Poems" (1962, o. p.) is a selection from two earlier volumes, "A Glad Day" and "American Citizen," plus new poems not previously published in book form. "Nothing Ever Breaks Except the Heart" was warmly greeted as a distinguished group of short stories. Harry T. Moore's pamphlet (*Minnesota* Pamphlets on American Writers, 1964) on Miss Boyle is no longer in print. "Being Geniuses Together" (1968. *Serendipity* $6.95), by Robert McAlmon, is his memoir of the 1920s in Paris. Miss Boyle has edited it and alternated his memories with her own. Much of her own intimate autobiography is revealed in these supplementary chapters, which show by implication that her first two novels, "Plagued by the Nightingale" and "Year Before Last," were quite closely based on her own experiences in France.

After living in Europe for more than thirty years, Miss Boyle was appointed Professor of English at San Francisco State University in 1963. Her "The Long Walk at San Francisco State and Other Essays" (*Grove* 1970 pap. $1.25) deals with campus disorders there as well as other subjects.

THIRTY STORIES. 1946. *New Directions* 1957 pap. $2.75

THREE SHORT NOVELS. Crazy Hunter, The Bridegroom's Body, Decision. 1940. *Serendipity* pap. $3.00

PLAGUED BY THE NIGHTINGALE. 1931. Pref. by Harry T. Moore. Crosscurrents/Modern Fiction. *Southern Illinois Univ. Press* 1966 $5.95

THE YEAR BEFORE LAST. 1932. Pref. by Harry T. Moore. Crosscurrents/Modern Fiction. *Southern Illinois Univ. Press* 1969 $6.95

NOTHING EVER BREAKS EXCEPT THE HEART. *Doubleday* 1966 $5.95. 20 short stories of "Peace," "War Years," and "Military Occupation."

CALDWELL, ERSKINE. 1903–

Erskine Caldwell is the son of a Presbyterian country preacher, who as secretary of his denomination covered "the entire South from Virginia to Florida, from the Atlantic to the Mississippi." Caldwell studied at the University of Virginia and worked on farms, and in restaurants, mills, and theaters in the East. He has lived and worked in all sections of this country and been a correspondent in Mexico, Spain, Czechoslovakia, and Russia.

"Tobacco Road," his first novel, was dramatized by John Kirkland and ran for eight years, 3,182 performances, 1933–41, on Broadway. All his books are laid in the South and deal with backwoodsmen, sharecroppers, human creatures in the lowest depths of poverty. "In Search of Bisco" (1965, o. p.) describes Caldwell's recent search for his childhood friend the Black boy Bisco, as well as for answers to problems in the

South today. The *Saturday Review* calls Caldwell "perhaps the only white writer of fiction who is able to describe with such precision the crime done the American Negro." His books have been translated into more than 40 languages and have sold more than 65 million copies around the world, making them among the best-selling novels of all time. En route to tour Warsaw in 1963 (his books are best sellers in the Communist countries), Caldwell stated sadly, "I'm not read very much in the South because they are very touchy about what they regard as unkind criticism, and I'm not thought much of in the North either." But he had no apologies for his popularity abroad. "Russians and Europeans get a less erroneous image of America from my books than they do from American films about a mink-penthouse-Cadillac society."

Caldwell spent six months in Russia during World War II reporting for the radio and the newspapers. "All-Out on the Road to Smolensk" (1942, o. p.), is a personal narrative "the first eyewitness story of the fighting in Russia. . . ." "Say! Is This the U.S.A.?" (1941, o. p.) is a documentary account of America, a book of photographs and running commentary, one of three (the other two being "North of the Danube" and "Russia At War"), done in collaboration with the late Margaret Bourke-White, his divorced wife. "Around About America" (1964, o. p.) contains travel articles about his own country, illustrated with line drawings by his wife, Virginia. His very readable literary autobiography, "Call It Experience" (1951, o. p.) was described in the *Saturday Review*: "It is partly autobiographical, partly hortatory, partly instructive. At times it sounds like a literary pep-talk; at other times its burden will all but crush the youthful aspirant. . . . Caldwell's little acre is peculiarly farmed." Himself the author of more than 45 books (inevitably uneven in quality), Caldwell has provided a broad examination of his art in "Writing in America" (*Phaedra* 1967 pap. $2.50; *William Gannon* $4.75) He and his wife make their home in California. He is a member of the National Institute of Arts and Letters.

THE COMPLETE STORIES OF ERSKINE CALDWELL. All the short stories published up to 1953. *Little* 1953 $8.95

POCKET BOOK OF ERSKINE CALDWELL STORIES. Ed. by Henry Seidel Canby. *Pocket Bks.* 1961 $.35

TOBACCO ROAD. 1932. *New Am. Lib.* Signet pap. $.75

GOD'S LITTLE ACRE. 1933. *New Am. Lib.* Signet pap. $.75

TROUBLE IN JULY. 1940. *New Am. Lib.* pap. $.75

GEORGIA BOY. 1943. *New Am. Lib.* Signet pap. $.75

TRAGIC GROUND. 1944. *New Am. Lib.* Signet pap. $75.

THE SURE HAND OF GOD. 1947. *New Am. Lib.* Signet pap. $.75

THIS VERY EARTH. 1948. *New Am. Lib.* Signet 1971 pap. $.75

A PLACE CALLED ESTHERVILLE. 1949. *Fawcett* 1972 pap. $.75

CLAUDELLE INGLISH. 1959. *Fawcett* 1972 pap. $.60

A LAMP FOR NIGHTFALL. 1952. *Fawcett* 1972 pap. $.75

LOVE AND MONEY. 1954. *New Am. Lib.* Signet pap. $.75

GRETTA. 1955. *New Am. Lib.* Signet 1972 pap. $.75

CERTAIN WOMEN. Short stories. 1957. *New Am. Lib.* Signet 1959 pap. $.75

JENNY BY NATURE. 1961 *New Am. Lib.* Signet pap. 1972 pap. $.75

CLOSE TO HOME. 1962. *New Am. Lib.* Signet 1972 pap. $.75

THE LAST NIGHT OF SUMMER. 1963. *New Am. Lib.* pap. $.75

THE WEATHER SHELTER. *Norton* (New Am. Lib.) 1969 $5.95

THE EARNSHAW NEIGHBORHOOD. 1971. *New Am. Lib.* Signet 1972 pap. $.95

A Swell Looking Girl. 1972. *Fawcett* pap. $.75

Erskine Caldwell. A recording. He reads four short stories: Where the Girls Were Different; A Small Day; The People vs. Abe Latham, Colored; It Happened Like This. *Spoken Arts* 721 (H-C) $5.95

Books about Caldwell

Erskine Caldwell. By James Korges. Pamphlets on American Writers. *Univ. of Minnesota Press* 1969 pap. $1.25

COZZENS, JAMES GOULD. 1903–

"Guard of Honor," a study in the clash of personalities and military organization during three days at an Army Air Force base in Florida in 1943, brought its author the 1949 Pulitzer Prize with general agreement that such recognition of his distinguished writing was long overdue. His first novel, "Confusion," was published in 1924 while he was a sophomore at Harvard. He left college without graduating, produced three more youthful novels and, with "S. S. San Pedro" (1931) a brilliant story of disaster at sea, established his reputation as a clever writer and competent craftsman. Four of his master novels are "devoted to particular occupations in modern American life: 'The Last Adam' to medicine, 'Men and Brethren' to the ministry, 'The Just and the Unjust' to the law, and 'Guard of Honor' to the Army Air Force." "By Loved Possessed," a choice of the Book-of-the-Month Club, established Cozzens as a major 20th-century novelist and itself as his major work. In essence, Cozzens writes "about the individual in society, about the obligations, the hazards, the rebellious and painful accommodations of human beings to the way things not *are*—but *work*: the functioning of the world." He does not see "the world as static and society as fixed and immutable [but] as fragile, constantly challenged, and supporting itself only by almost superhuman efforts." His long-awaited "Morning, Noon and Night" is the story of the life of an elderly businessman; it is his first novel in 11 years.

In 1960 he was awarded the Howells medal of the American Academy of Arts and Letters. This medal, given every five years for the most distinguished work of American fiction published in that period, was for his "By Love Possessed."

S. S. San Pedro. 1931. *Harcourt* $3.50 Harvest Bks. 1968 pap. $1.15

Castaway. 1934. *Harcourt* $3.50 Harvest Bks. 1968 pap. $1.15

The Last Adam. *Harcourt* Harvest Bks. 1933 1956 pap. $1.85

Men and Brethren. *Harcourt* 1936 1958 $4.00; uniform ed. $5.95

Ask Me Tomorrow. *Harcourt* 1940 $6.95 Modern Class. $2.50

The Just and the Unjust. *Harcourt* 1942 1950 Harvest Bks. pap. $3.45 Modern Class $2.95

Guard of Honor. *Harcourt* 1948 $7.50 Harvest Bks. pap. $2.45

By Love Possessed. *Harcourt* 1957 $6.95 Harvest Bks. pap. $2.95; *Fawcett* Crest Bks. pap. $.95

Children and Others. *Harcourt* 1964 $5.95

Morning, Noon and Night. *Harcourt* 1968 $5.95; *New Am Lib.* pap. $1.25

Books about Cozzens

The Novels of James Gould Cozzens. By Frederick Bracher. 1959. *Greenwood* 1972 $13.00
James Gould Cozzens: Novelist of Intellect. By Harry J. Mooney, Jr. *Univ. of Pittsburgh Press* 1963 pap. $2.00
James Gould Cozzens. By Granville Hicks. Pamphlets on American Writers. *Univ. of Minnesota Press* 1966 pap. $1.25
James Gould Cozzens: An Annotated Checklist. By Pierre Michel. *Kent State Univ. Press* 1972 $6.50
James Gould Cozzens: A Checklist. By James B. Meriwether. *Gale Research Co.* 1973 $8.50

NIN, ANAÏS. 1903–

Anaïs Nin was a neglected and almost legendary figure in the history of modern art and letters until selections from her monumental diary—drawn from an original 150 volumes comprising 15,000 pages of typescript—began to appear in 1966. She was born in 1903, the daughter of a well-known Spanish pianist and composer who separated from his wife and daughter when Anaïs was eleven years old. She was brought to the United States, where she attended public schools only briefly before embarking on a remarkable program of self-education that included starting her diary as an unmailed letter to her lost father. She returned to Paris during the early 1930s, supporting herself as an artists' model and Spanish dancer while continuing to write. By 1939 she had published in Paris "D. H. Lawrence: An Unprofessional Study" (1932 *Swallow* 1964 pap. $2.25), a prose-poem called "House of Incest" (1936), and three novelettes gathered under the title "Winter of Artifice" (1939). She had become close friends with many leading figures of the Parisian artistic and social scene, including the then-struggling writer Henry Miller (*q. v.*), the young surrealist poet Antonin Artaud (with whom she had an affair), and the psychiatrist Dr. Otto Rank. She returned to America on the outbreak of World War II in 1939. Because she could not place her writings with commercial publishers, she bought her own printing press, and in 1944 produced a small, hand-set edition of her stories under the collective title "Under a Glass Bell." That slim volume, praised by Edmund Wilson (*q. v.*) in the *New Yorker*, was republished four years later by E. P. Dutton Company, and since then she has published eight additional works of fiction and criticism as well as four volumes of her diary. In recent years her writings have become increasingly popular, especially with the college generation, and she has lectured widely at universities while dividing her time between New York and California.

Her friend Lawrence Durrell has said: "Her books are iridescent, held together by a finely spun web of cross references. Their preoccupation is with poetic truth and the human personality, not in terms of rigid valuations but in terms of symbol. Their subjectivity demands complete surrender in the reader. . . . Those who care for finely wrought musical writing shot through with clear insights into the inner world of human beings will not be disappointed." Her best-known work, "House of Incest," is "a prose poem of delicacy and subtle implications. . . . In it, as in all her works, she explores tangential human relationships with a keenness reminiscent of Durrell, but with a passionate presence beyond anything Durrell has done"—(*Denver, Colo., Post*). Her prose has been described as "brilliantly surrealist when reality is fused with dreams." Of the novel "Collages," Henry Miller said, "This book abounds in magical descriptions of a highly original and sensuous nature. The best of collages fall apart with time; these will not."

Miss Nin's diary is significant not only as the source of nearly all her fiction, but as one of the most vivid literary memoirs of the 20th century. The first published volume deals with the beginnings of her life in Paris during the early thirties and is remarkable for its portraits of Henry Miller and others. The second volume adds new friendships, such as Lawrence Durrell, and a houseboat on the Seine; it takes her through the period of the Spanish Civil War and World War II. Daniel Stern wrote (in the *Nation*): "The conflict is always between reality and the dream—between the ice-clear day and the mists of night. But one of the great charms of reading these Diaries is the discovery that the artist has made another choice than she thinks. While adoring the night and its special magics she has created the clairity of time (from 1931 to 1939), the lyrical but utterly specific poetics of place (Paris, New York, Louveciennes, the French suburb where she made her home, Tangier—The Villa Seurat where she found an apartment for Henry Miller—the Seine houseboat on which she made her home in the late thirties), and best of all she has created one of the most magnificent sets of characters to appear in any contemporary work of art." The third and fourth volumes describe her return to America, her life in a Greenwich Village studio, and travels cross-country. They add to the cast of her personal drama such established writers as Edmund Wilson (*q. v.*) and emerging talents such as Gore Vidal (*q. v.*).

ANAÏS NIN READER. Ed. by Philip K. Jason. Introd. by Anna Balakian. *Swallow* 1973 $8.95 pap. $4.95. Selections from both her fiction and her nonfiction—a good introduction to this not easily classified writer.

THE HOUSE OF INCEST. 1931. *Swallow* 1961 pap. $1.50

WINTER OF ARTIFICE. 1939. Three novelettes: Stella; The Voice; Winter of Artifice. *Swallow* 1961 pap. $2.25

UNDER A GLASS BELL. Short stories. 1944. *Swallow* 1961 pap. $1.50

LADDERS TO FIRE. 1946 *Swallow* 1966 $3.50 pap. $2.25

CHILDREN OF THE ALBATROSS. 1947. *Swallow* 1966 pap. $2.00

THE FOUR-CHAMBERED HEART. 1950. *Swallow* 1966 pap. $2.25

A Spy in the House of Love. 1954. *Swallow* 1966 pap. $2.75; *Bantam* pap. $1.25

The Seduction of the Minotaur. *Swallow* 1961 pap. $2.25

Collages. *Swallow* 1964 pap. $2.25

The Diary of Anaïs Nin. Ed. with introd. by Gunther Stuhlmann. *Swallow-Harcourt* 4 vols. Vol. I 1931–1934 (1966); Vol. 2 1935–1939 (1967); Vol. 3 1939–1944 (1970); Vol. 4 1944–1947 (1971) each $7.50 Harvest Bks. pap. each $2.85

Books about Nin

Letters by Anaïs Nin. By Henry Miller. *Putnam* 1965 $7.50
Anaïs Nin. By Oliver Evans. Introd. by Harry T. Moore. *Southern Illinois Univ. Press* 1968 $4.95
The Mirror and the Garden: Realism and Reality in the Writings of Anais Nin. By Evelyn J. Hinz. 1971. *Harbrace* 1973 pap. $2.45

FARRELL, JAMES T. 1904–

To date James T. Farrell has published 47 books including 23 novels and 14 collections of short stories. All but five of his novels form parts of four series on which his reputation largely rests, but the fact that only "Studs Lonigan: A Trilogy" remains in print would suggest that his place in literature is still to be determined. His second major cycle is the Danny O'Neill pentalogy—"A World I Never Made" (1936), "No Star Is Lost" (1938), "Father and Son" (1940), "My Days of Anger" (1943) all o. p., and "The Face of Time" (1953 *see below*). The Bernard Carr trilogy consists of "Bernard Clare" (1946), "The Road Between" (1949), and "Yet Other Waters" (1952) all o. p. All three series are semiautobiographical works with the first two set in Chicago, where Farrell grew up in the Irish slums of the South Side, and the third showing how the central figure achieves success as a writer in New York City from 1927 to 1936. Since 1958 Farrell has been engaged primarily in writing a new series called "The Universe of Time" which also has a central autobiographical character, Eddie Ryan, but which Farrell envisions as "a relativistic panorama of our times" dealing with "man's creativity and his courageous acceptance of impermanence." Of some thirty projected volumes in the series, seven have thus far appeared: "The Silence of History" (1963), "What Time Collects" (1964, o. p.), "When Time Was Born" (1966), "Lonely for the Future" (1966), "A Brand New Life" (1968, o. p.) "Judith" (1969), and "Invisible Swords" (1970, o. p.). In his review of the first volume Robert Gorham Davis commented: "It is an effort to recapture the sounds and inner rhythms of an American experience now gone forever. Sooner or later Farrell will be given his place as a sort of William Dean Howells of Jackson Park in recognition of the scope and faithfulness with which he recorded the day-to-day, almost hour-to-hour, suffering, sentimentality, dignity, coarseness and despair of an important part of the Nation's population at a time of decisive change in its psyche"—(*N.Y. Times*).

Only "Studs Lonigan," however, has captured a wide audience to date. That series is read largely for its historical interest as a vivid period-piece of "slice-of-life" realism. Farrell's objective method of presenting experience, his reluctance to point a moral, and his naturalistic philosophy have offended some readers and critics, but time may show that it is Farrell's freedom from moralism and transient commitments which make him capable of seeing individual experience in broad and universal terms.

"Farrell was perhaps the most powerful naturalist who ever worked in the American tradition, but the raw intensity of that power suggested that naturalism was really exhausted and could now thrive only on a mechanical energy bent on forcing itself to the uttermost. . . . Scene by scene, character by character, Farrell's books are built by force rather than imagination, and it is the laboriously contrived solidity, the perfect literalness of each representation, that gives his work its density and harsh power" (Alfred Kazin). One of the most interesting of his essays, "How Studs Lonigan Was Written," appears in "The League of Frightened Philistines," but as the *New Yorker* observed in reviewing "Literature and Morality" (1947, o. p.)—"Mr. Farrell is an erratic and often exasperating critic; sometimes he is sharp and intuitive and at other times he lambastes the deadest of dogs and seems to be writing in a foreign language." A variety of intense essays, both literary and critical, is found in "A Note On Literary Criticism" (*Vanguard* 1936 $3.00), "The League of Frightened Philistines" (*Vanguard* 1945 $3.00) and "Reflections at Fifty." He has written poetry; his "Collected Poems" (1967 $4.95) are published by Fleet.

Among his books in print:

The Short Stories of James T. Farrell. Collection of 51 stories. 1937. *Grosset* Univ. Lib. pap. $2.95

An Omnibus of Short Stories. *Vanguard* 1956 $10.00

STUDS LONIGAN: A Trilogy. Young Lonigan (1932); The Young Manhood of Studs Lonigan (1934); Judgment Day (1935). With a new introd. by the author. *Vanguard* 1935 $7.50

THE FACE OF TIME. *Vanguard* 1953 $5.00

FRENCH GIRLS ARE VICIOUS AND OTHER STORIES. *Vanguard* 1955 $3.50

A DANGEROUS WOMAN AND OTHER STORIES 1957. *Vanguard* $3.50

WHEN TIME WAS BORN. *Horizon Press* 1966 $3.50 specially bd. signed ed. $25.00

REFLECTIONS AT FIFTY. Critical Essays and Autobiographical Fragments. *Vanguard* 1954 $4.50

Books about Farrell

James T. Farrell. By Edgar M. Branch. Pamphlets on American Writers. *Univ. of Minnesota Press* 1963 pap. $1.25.
Bibliography of James T. Farrell's Writings, 1921–1957. By Edgar M. Branch. *Univ. of Pennsylvania Press* 1959 $9.00
James T. Farrell. By Edgar M. Branch. U.S. Authors Ser. *Twayne* 1971 $5.50

WEST, NATHANAEL (pseud. of Nathan Wallenstein Weinstein). 1904–1940.

Among the novels which chronicle the bitterness, despair, and pessimism of the thirties, Nathanael West's "Miss Lonelyhearts" and "The Day of the Locust" are remarkable, and have been gathering reputation as the Black Humorist writers of fiction have come to the fore. "Miss Lonelyhearts," about a young man conducting a column of advice to the lovelorn, is certainly one of the earliest examples of this "school." Malcolm Cowley called it "one of the books that had very few readers for the first edition, but simply refuse to be forgotten." West's vision of the terror and emptiness of modern life is established most effectively in these two acknowledged masterpieces.

West was married to Eileen McKenney, the original of the play "My Sister Eileen," written by Ruth McKenny; and West's sister married S. J. Perelman. After the publication of "Miss Lonelyhearts," West and his wife went to Hollywood. They remained there until they died in a car accident in 1940. His savage indictment, "The Day of the Locust," has been called the best novel ever written about Hollywood

COMPLETE WORKS: The Dream Life of Balso Snell (1931); Miss Lonelyhearts (1933); A Cool Million (1936); The Day of the Locust (1939). Introd. by Alan Ross. *Farrar, Straus* 1957 $8.50

MISS LONELYHEARTS AND THE DAY OF THE LOCUST. *New Directions* pap. $1.75

THE DREAM LIFE OF BALSO SNELL AND A COOL MILLION. *Avon Bks.* pap. $1. 65; *Farrar, Straus* Noonday 1963 pap. $1.95

MISS LONELYHEARTS. 1933. *Avon Bks.* 1964 pap. $.50

A COOL MILLION. 1936. *Avon Bks.* pap. $.60

Books about West

Nathanael West: An Interpretive Study. By James F. Light. *Northwestern Univ. Press* 1961 2nd ed. 1971 $8.00. The first full-length study—both biographical and critical.
Nathanael West. By Stanley Edgar Hyman. Pamphlets on American Writers. *Univ. of Minnesota Press* 1962 pap. $1.25
Nathanael West: The Ironic Prophet. By Victor Comerchero. *Syracuse Univ. Press* 1964 $5.95; *Univ. of Washington Press* pap. $2.95
    "West's books refuse to be forgotten. . . . Professor Comerchero . . . believes that West, with all his shortcomings, is among America's top dozen writers. His book attempts to reveal West's full achievement and his relevance to our time."—(*LJ*).
The Fiction of Nathanael West. By Randall Reid. *Univ. of Chicago Press* 1968 $4.50
    "According to Mr. Reid, West 'took familiar themes from both literature and popular culture, fused

them into 'classic' case histories, and revealed the disaster latent in them.' . . . Mr. Reid traces West's specific borrowings from Cabell, Huxley, Huysmans, Baudelaire, Sherwood Anderson, Joyce, and others"—(*PW*).

Nathanael West: The Art of His Life. By Jay Martin. *Farrar, Straus* 1970 $10.00; *Hayden* 1971 pap. $4.95. The standard biography.

Twentieth Century Interpretations of "Miss Lonelyhearts." Ed. by Thomas H. Jackson. *Prentice-Hall* 1971 $4.95 Spectrum Bks. pap. $1.45

Nathanael West: A Collection of Critical Essays. Ed. by Jay Martin. *Prentice-Hall* Spectrum Bks. 1971 pap. $1.95 Twentieth Century Views

Nathanael West's Novels. By Irving Malin with pref. by Harry T. Moore. Crosscurrents/Modern Critiques. *Southern Illinois Univ. Press* 1972 $5.95

Nathanael West: The Cheaters and the Cheated. Ed. by David Madden. Collection of critical essays. *Everett Edwards* 1973 $12.00

O'HARA, JOHN (HENRY). 1905–1970.

Before becoming one of the best-selling writers of the century, John O'Hara was "an engineer, boat steward, call boy, frieght clerk, guard in an amusement park, laborer in a steel mill, Hollywood press agent, secretary to Heywood Broun, and critic and feature writer for many New York newspapers and magazines," particularly the *N.Y. Herald Tribune* and the *New Yorker*. From these experiences he distilled his skillful reports of the habitués of Hollywood, the country club, and the hotel bar. He almost always wrote "not only with accuracy and brilliance, but with a kind of terrible, unmerciful disgust. The clarity of his observation and the easy, practical, implicative power of his work are accompanied by a grim, almost moralistic attitude toward his subjects" (Richard Sullivan, in the *N.Y. Times*). "Appointment in Samarra" won him immediate fame. In 1956 his novel "Ten North Frederick" was given the National Book Award for fiction and was made into a successful Hollywood film. Mr. O'Hara has been controversial from the 30's well into the 60's, some critics finding his subjects—rich or near-rich upper middle class Americans—unappetizing to read about in themselves as he presents them, others marveling at his skill in depicting their dead-end lives. Alfred Kazin, in "Contemporaries," found "From the Terrace" a merciless, "repetitive and meaningless detailed documentary of upper middle class life." *Newsweek* wrote that in "The Lockwood Concern" "the obsessions remain money and power, status and sex." Edmund Wilson, on the other hand, has praised him (in "Classics & Commercials") for his analysis of social surfaces—"with delicacy and usually with remarkable accuracy." Mr. O'Hara's ear for contemporary American speech is impeccable. "The old pro still has it," wrote John Barkham. "*The Instrument* is hypnotically readable. . . . No contemporary novelist writes dialogue like John O'Hara." And Edward Weeks (*Atlantic*) said of it: "The story of a playwright on the make, which only an old pro could make so believable. . . . There is not a dull moment in it."

"Waiting for Winter," his collection of short stories, led Webster Schott (in the *N.Y. Times*) to this analysis: "Intuitively, O'Hara has found the motor every great social-fiction writer runs on—a recognizable set of rules for the conduct of human affairs. . . . Receiving the social signal makes all the difference in what O'Hara's people do. It's an operant system verifiable against the facts of American life. But it cannot account for this author's power. He commands belief even in his lesser stories. . . . We believe because O'Hara hears confessions in his head. He sees gestures that tell histories. He detects preferences—in clothing, food, objects—that predict fates. After some 200 stories and 20 novels, he has perfected his art." His nonfiction includes "Sweet and Sour: Comments on Books and People" (*Random* 1954 $3.00), "Five Plays" (*Random* 1961 $5.00) and "My Turn," newspaper articles originally published in *Newsday*, the Long Island newspaper (*Random* 1966 $6.95).

As often happens with prolific and best-selling storytellers, particularly those who choose to write about fashionable characters during a period of more democratic social concerns, O'Hara's critical reputation is unsettled. It will take a while for critics not only to see the forest for the trees, but to distinguish works of lasting value from those of fading interest. There are encouraging signs, however, that O'Hara may escape the oblivion into which many other popular novelists of this century have fallen. Several doctoral dissertations and a few critical essays by prominent critics have appeared since his death in 1970, and Matthew J. Bruccoli, an eminent bibliophile and one of the leading scholarly experts on 20th-century American literature, has started work on the authorized biography of O'Hara.

SERMONS AND SODA WATER. Short stories. *Random* 3 vols. 1960 set $7.95

GREAT SHORT STORIES. 1973. *Popular Lib.* pap. $1.25

APPOINTMENT IN SAMARRA. 1934. *Bantam* 1967 pap. $1.25

BUTTERFIELD 8. 1935. *Bantam* 1967 pap. $.95

HOPE OF HEAVEN. 1938. *Popular Lib.* pap. $1.25

A Rage to Live. *Random* 1949. $8.95; *Bantam* 1967 pap. $1.25

The Farmer's Hotel. *Random* 1951 $4.00

Ten North Frederick. *Random* 1955 $6.95

From the Terrace. *Random* 1958 $7.95; *Bantam* 1967 pap. $1.25

Ourselves to Know. *Random* 1960 $6.95; *Popular Lib.* pap. $1.25

Assembly. 24 new stories and two novellas. *Random* 1961 $7.95; *Popular Lib.* 1973 pap. $1.25

The Cape Cod Lighter. Short stories. *Random* 1962 $7.95; *Popular Lib.* 1973 pap. $1.25

The Hat on the Bed. Short stories. *Random* 1963 $7.95

The Horse Knows the Way. Short stories. *Random* 1964 $7.95

The Lockwood Concern. *Random* 1965 $7.95; *New Am. Lib.* Signet pap. $1.25

Waiting for Winter. *Random* 1966 $6.95; *Popular Lib.* 1973 pap. $1.50

The Instrument. *Random* 1967 $7.95; *Bantam* pap. $1.25

Lovey Childs: A Philadelphian's Story. *Random* 1969 $5.95

The Ewings. *Random* 1972 $6.95; *Popular Lib.* pap. $1.25

The Time Element and Other Stories. *Random* 1972 $10.00; *Popular Lib.* 1973 pap. $1.25

Books about O'Hara

John O'Hara. By Sheldon N. Grebstein. U.S. Authors Ser. *Twayne* 1966 $5.50; *College & Univ. Press* 1967 pap. $2.45
John O'Hara. By Charles C. Walcutt. Pamphlets on American Writers. *Univ. of Minnesota Press* 1969 pap. $1.25
John O'Hara, a Checklist. By Matthew J. Bruccoli. *Random* 1972 $10.00
O'Hara: A Biography. By Finis Farr. *Little* 1973 $8.50

WARREN, ROBERT PENN. 1905–

Robert Penn Warren is an unusually versatile writer who has tried his hand at almost every kind of litera-ture. He has written novels, short stories, short and long poems, plays, biographies, criticism, textbooks, biog-raphies, juveniles, and social commentary. In all these forms he has achieved recognition and distinction, but it is as a poet, critic, and novelist that he is most widely known. *(See his entry in Chapter 9, Modern Ameri-can Poetry for biographical and other information about his career in general.)*

As for his fiction, Malcolm Cowley has said: "He is, I think, more richly endowed than any other Ameri-can novelist born in the present century." His first novel, "Night Rider," uses his birthplace in Todd County, Kentucky, as a background and describes a tobacco war there in the early 1900s. He uses historical incidents in the South as the themes for all books. "All the King's Men," which won the Pulitzer Prize and the South-ern Author's Award in 1947 and was named the best film of 1949, was based on the political life of Huey Long of Louisiana. Its theme, he says, is "the special disease of our time, the abstract passion for power, a vanity springing from an awareness of the emptiness and unreality of the self which can only become real and human by the oppression of people who manage to retain some shreds of reality and humanity."

Mr. Warren was one of the founders and an editor of the *Southern Review*. He has been professor of Eng-lish at the University of Minnesota, poetry consultant of the Library of Congress, and on the faculty of the Yale Drama School as professor of playwriting. With Cleanth Brooks, he has written several influential text-books on rhetoric and literature; a work of literary criticism is "Selected Essays" (*Random* 1958 Vintage Bks. pap. $1.95). He has often made race relations in America the theme of his novels, and has written an elo-quent commentary, "Segregation: The Inner Conflict of the South" (*Random* 1956 $4.50). In "The Legacy of the Civil War" (*Random* 1961 $4.95 *Vintage Bks.* pap. $1.45) he presents his opinions on how the Civil

War has shaped modern America, and the fuller understanding Americans can gain of themselves through its lessons. A condensation of the book has appeared in *Life*. Warren's perceptive "Who Speaks for the Negro?" (*Random* 1965 $7.95 *Vintage Bks.* pap. $1.95) summarizes his tape-recorded interviews with Black leaders, writers and other participants in the Civil Rights movement.

On "The Cave," (1959, o. p.) Arthur Mizener commented: "*The Cave* is Robert Penn Warren at his best, and they don't come much better than that"—(*N.Y. Times*). "Wilderness" is more than a thoughtful, serious novel about a Bavarian Jew who comes to America in 1863 to join the Union Army and fight for freedom; it is an allegory of a man's spiritual quest, searching for the truth about himself and the world. "Flood," which received mixed reviews, is a novel —of "Southern self-laceration" (*LJ*) about a young man who goes back to his Tennessee home town as it is about to be inundated for a new dam. "Meet Me in the Green Glen," the story of a tragic love affair, marks a return to the tighter structure and complex artistry which characterized Warren's earlier novels. John W. Aldridge wrote that the novel can be read "as a romantic parable existing with perfect rightness on the levels of melodrama and moral philosophy; a love story that, contrary to current fashions, is finally neither sentimental nor narcissistic; a prose poem remarkable for its lyric intensity; a Southern novel in which the characters are both realistically depicted cultural types and personifications of forces so violent and destructive that they seem almost more Elizabethan than contemporary"—(*SR*).

Writing in the *Saturday Evening Post* on "Why Do We Read Fiction?" Warren said: "Reconciliation— that is what we all . . . want. All religion, all philosophy, all psychiatry, all ethics involve this human fact. And so does fiction. If fiction . . . relieves us from the burden of being ourselves, it ends, if it is good fiction and we are good readers, by returning us to the world and to ourselves. It reconciles us with reality."

NIGHT RIDER. 1939. *Random* $8.95

AT HEAVEN'S GATE. *Random* 1943 $7.95

ALL THE KING'S MEN. *Harcourt* 1946 $9.75; *Bantam* 1968 pap. $1.25; *Modern Library* 1953 $2.95; (dramatized version) *Random* 1960 $4.50

WORLD ENOUGH AND TIME. *Random* 1950 $7.95

BAND OF ANGELS. *Random* 1955 $6.95; *New Am. Lib.* Signet pap. $.75

WILDERNESS: A Tale of the Civil War. *Random* 1961 $7.95

FLOOD: A Romance of Our Time. *Random* 1964 $8.95

CIRCUS IN THE ATTIC AND OTHER STORIES. *Harcourt* 1968 pap. $1.25

MEET ME IN THE GREEN GLEN. *Random* 1971 $7.95

Books about Warren

Robert Penn Warren. By Paul West. Pamphlets on American Writers. *Univ. of Minnesota Press* 1964 pap. $1.25

Robert Penn Warren. By Charles Bohner. U.S. Authors Ser. *Twayne* 1964 $5.50; *College & Univ. Press* 1964 pap. $2.45

Robert Penn Warren: A Collection of Critical Essays. Ed. by John L. Longley. *New York Univ. Press* 1965 $7.95 pap. $2.25

Robert Penn Warren's "All the King's Men": A Critical Handbook. Ed. by Maurice Beebe and Leslie A. Field. Guides to Literary Study. *Wadsworth* 1966 1969 pap. $2.95

Robert Penn Warren: A Bibliography. Comp. by Mary Nance Huff. Checklist of writings by and about Warren. *David Lewis* 1968 $10.00

Robert Penn Warren and History: "The Big Myth We Live." By L. Hugh Moore, Jr. *Humanities Press* 1970 $12.00

STUART, JESSE (HILTON). 1907–

Jesse Stuart is a Kentuckian who prefers to live in and write about Kentucky. Descended from families who had cleared the land, tilled fields and settled their disputes with shotguns for three generations, young Jesse was the first of the Stuarts ever to go through high school. In order to get the money he needed for school books, and later for college books, he hunted possum at night and sold the skins, did substitute teaching in the lower grades, and worked in a steel mill. His long books of poems "Man With a Bull-Tongue Plow" (*Dutton* 1934, pap. $1.95) was very well received and was selected by Henry Seidel Canby as one of the "100

Best Books in America." A later collection, "Hold April" (*McGraw-Hill* 1962 $4.95), "might be called the summation of his lifetime of poetic thought"—(Everetta Love Blair).

"Taps for Private Tussie" is a loosely constructed ballad like tale, hardly to be called a novel, about lusty Kentuckians. It was a best seller and Book-of-the Month Club choice. Colloquial, sometimes crude, with humorous characterization bordering on caricature, Stuart's writing is simple, fresh, and sympathetic. The stories in "My Land Has a Voice" reflect "an increased maturity and craftsmanship, a sharpened impact and irony; they are less rambling and determinedly folksy, yet preserve the piquant humor and spirited individuality of the hill people"—(*LJ*). In "Daughter of the Legend," a "moving allegorical novel about Tennessee, he demonstrates the effects of segregation and its unreasonable antisocial attitudes"—(*LJ*). His autobiography is "Beyond Dark Hills." "The Thread That Runs So True" (*Scribner* 1949 rev. ed. 1958 $5.95 text ed. pap. $3.20 Contemporary Class. pap. $2.25), about his teaching experiences in secondary schools, was selected as the best book of 1949 by the National Education Association and is widely used in schools throughout the country. From 1941 to 1943 Superintendent of Schools for Greenup, Ky., he still takes an active interest in education, as shown by his "To Teach, to Love" (World Pub. 1970 $5.95). "God's Oddling" (*McGraw-Hill* 1960 $5.95) tells the story of Mitch Stuart, his father, and provides vivid background to his two volumes of autobiography, "Beyond Dark Hills" and "The Year of My Rebirth."

A Jessie Stuart Reader. *McGraw-Hill* 1963 $5.25 text ed. $5.04; *New Am. Lib.* 1968 Signet pap. $.75

Short Stories. Ed. by Lawrence Swinburne. *McGraw-Hill* 1968 pap. $1.72

Taps for Private Tussie. 1943. *Ballantine Bks.* 1973 pap. $1.25

Hie to the Hunters. *McGraw-Hill* 1950 $5.95

Plowshare in Heaven: Stories by Jesse Stuart. *McGraw-Hill* 1958 $5.50

Save Every Lamb. Short stories. *McGraw-Hill* 1964 $5.95

Daughter of the Legend. *McGraw-Hill* 1965 $5.95

My Land Has a Voice. Short stories. *McGraw-Hill* 1966 $6.95

Mr. Gallion's School. *McGraw-Hill* 1967 $6.95

Come, Gentle Spring. Short stories. *McGraw-Hill* 1969 $5.95

Come Back to the Farm. *McGraw-Hill* 1971 $6.95

Dawn of Remembered Spring. *McGraw-Hill* 1972 $6.95

The Land beyond the River. *McGraw-Hill* 1973 $7.95

Beyond Dark Hills: A Personal Story. His memoirs. 1938. *McGraw-Hill* 1972 $6.95 deluxe ed. $25.00

The Year of my Rebirth. Continuation of his autobiography. *McGraw-Hill* 1956 $5.95

Books about Stuart

Jesse Stuart: His Life and Works. By Everetta Love Blair. *Univ. of South Carolina Press* 1967 $8.95
Jesse Stuart. By Ruel E. Foster. U.S. Authors Ser. *Twayne* 1968 $5.50
Jesse Stuart's Kentucky (Orig. "Jesse Stuart, an Appreciation"). By Mary W. Clarke. *McGraw-Hill* 1968 $6.95
Reflections of Jesse Stuart on a Land of Many Moods. By Dick Perry. *McGraw-Hill* 1971 $7.95

MICHENER, JAMES A(LBERT). 1907–

James Michener's first book, "Tales of the South Pacific," a collection of stories about servicemen and the original inhabitants of the southern islands, won the Pulitzer Prize in 1948. It was the basis for the enormously successful musical play by Rodgers and Hammerstein, "South Pacific," and was later made into a Hollywood film. The author had outlined some of the stories during a slack spell when he was stranded on a small island while serving with the Navy in World War II. "Return to Paradise" is a second collection of stories set in the South Pacific. "The Bridges at Toko-Ri," his personal favorite among his works of fiction, and "Sayonara" are short novels of carefully unified craftsmanship set in the Orient. "Hawaii," which is generally considered the best of his longer novels, is a "brilliant panoramic novel about Hawaii from its volcanic origins to its recent statehood—(*N.Y. Times*).

"His choice of locale is significant. Michener sees the Oriental and Polynesian peoples as embodying certain values which the Western World does not fully understand. Many of his books are attempts to discover these values, and to interpret the urgent problem imposed on these people by American influence since the War"—(David Dempsey). "The Voice of Asia" (*Random* 1951 $6.95), is his first-hand account of present conditions and attitudes in the Far East. "The Floating World" (*Random* 1954 $17.95) is a collection of exquisite Japanese color prints to which Michener has added lively and informative history of the art of Japanese prints. He is the author of "Japanese Prints: from Early Masters to the Modern" (*Tuttle* 1959 1963 $24.75), "Modern Japanese Prints: An Appreciation" (*Tuttle* 1968 $5.50), and the editor of "The Hokusai Sketch-Book" (*Tuttle* 1958 $13.75). With A. G. Day, he has written "Rascals in Paradise" (*Random* 1957 $6.95) a series of sketches about adventures in the South Pacific. He was born in New York City, graduated with highest honors at Swarthmore College and has traveled extensively. "I've always had an itching foot," he has said, "which has taken me to a fair portion of the world. As a kid of fourteen I bummed across the country on nickles and dimes. Before I was twenty I had seen all the states except Washington, Oregon and Florida. I had an insatiable love of hearing people tell stories, and what they didn't tell I made up"— ("American Novelists of Today" by Harry R. Warfel). "Iberia: Spanish Travels and Reflections" (*Random* 1968 $12.50; Fawcett pap. $1.95), "a monumental analysis of Spain" (*PW*) is "unfailingly interesting. . . . It sums up the observations of four decades. Yet it is more than a travelogue; it incorporates the author's continuing search for the mystic or romantic aspects of life"—(Oscar Handlin, in the *Atlantic*). This interest in exotic places and the meanings they could hold forth to Westerners is reflected in his novels "Caravans" and "The Source." The former "as a guided tour to some of the most inaccessible regions of Afghanistan is lots of fun." Mr. Michener makes "dramatic use of strange customs, picturesque characters and gorgeous scenery. . . . But as a novel it is implausible in plot and psychologically baffling"—(*N.Y. Times*). "The Source" is "an imaginative and didactic re-creation of the history of Israel from prehistoric to modern times, held within the framwork of an archeological expedition which is uncovering the successive date-levels of a mound in Galilee"—(*New Statesman*).

When not traveling, Michener lives in Bucks County, Penn., where he has played an active role in local politics, including an unsuccessful run for a congressional seat in 1962. Products of his interest in politics are "Report of the County Chairman" (1961, o. p.) and "Presidential Lottery: The Reckless Gamble in Our Electoral System" (*Random* 1969 $5.95). In recent years he has been especially concerned with the social revolution of our times, especially the radical changes in outlook instituted by a younger generation of committed rebels. As part of his research for a long panoramic novel on that subject, "The Drifters," he personally researched the troubles at Kent State University and wrote "Kent State: What Happened and Why" (*Random* 1971 $10.00 *Fawcett* 1972 $1.25).

SELECTED WRITINGS. *Modern Library* 1957 $2.95

A MICHENER MISCELLANY: 1950–1970. Ed. by Ben Hibbs. *Random* (Reader's Digest) 1973 $8.95

TALES OF THE SOUTH PACIFIC. *Macmillan* 1947 $5.95 lg.-type ed. $7.95; *Fawcett* pap. $1.25

THE FIRES OF SPRING. *Random* 1949 1962 $8.95; *Fawcett* pap. $1.25

RETURN TO PARADISE. *Random* 1951 $8.95

THE BRIDGES AT TOKO-RI. *Random* 1953 $5.95; *Fawcett* pap. $1.25

SAYONARA. *Random* 1954 $5.95; *Bantam* pap. $.95

THE BRIDGE AT ANDAU. 1957. *Fawcett* 1972 pap. $.95. A novelized account of the Hungarian revolt against Communism.

HAWAII. *Random* 1959 $10.00; *Vintage Bks.* pap. $3.45; *Fawcett* pap. $1.95

CARAVANS. *Random* 1963 $6.95

THE SOURCE. *Random* 1965 $10.00; *Fawcett* pap. $1.95

THE DRIFTERS. *Random* 1971 $10.00; *Fawcett* pap. $1.75

Books about Michener

James A. Michener. By A. Grove Day. U.S. Authors Ser. *Twayne* 1964 $5.50; *College & Univ. Press*
1964 pap. $2.45

ROTH, HENRY. 1907–

Henry Roth's "Call It Sleep" is one of the few books—if not the only one—which, despite the double dis-
advantage of being at once a paperback and a reissue, made the front page of the *N.Y. Time Books Review*.
Written when he was 27, it enjoyed only mild success until 1964, when it was brought out in paperback,
widely advertised and triumphantly reviewed. It has been translated into German and Italian. It is the author's only novel, although he has been a recent contributor to *Commentary* and *Midstream*. Mr. Roth's
main occupations have been running a waterfowl farm in Maine (when he had his two sons at home to help
him) and tutoring mathematics.

"Call It Sleep" is an extraordinarily sensitive examination of the experience of a young Jewish immigrant
boy. Between the years of 1911 and 1933 David Schearl is exposed to the brutal shocks of living in a New
York slum—the rat-infested tenements, the gutter talk, the stealing, and the whipping. Genya, David's
warmhearted mother, is admirably drawn and plays a central role. Irving Howe wrote in the *N.Y. Times*:
"One of the few genuinely distinguished novels written by a 20th century American, . . . 'Call it
Sleep' . . . achieves an obbligato of lyricism such as few American novels can match."

CALL IT SLEEP. 1934. *Cooper* $5.95; afterword by Walter Allen *Avon* 1964 pap. $1.25

WRIGHT, RICHARD. 1908–1960.

Richard Wright was "generally accounted the most gifted living American Negro writer," until the rise of
James Baldwin (*q. v.*). "With Wright, the pain of being a Negro is basically economic—its sight is mainly in
the pocket. With Baldwin, the pain suffuses the whole man. . . . If Baldwin's sights are higher than Wright's,
it is in part because Wright helped to raise them"—(*Time*). He was born on a plantation near Natchez,
Miss. His father was a farm and mill worker, his mother a country school teacher. At 15 he started to work in
Memphis, then in Chicago, then "bummed all over the country" supporting himself by various odd jobs. His
early writing was in the smaller magazines—first poetry, then prose. He won *Story's* $500 prize—for the
best story written by a worker on the Writers' Project—with "Uncle Tom's Children" in 1938, his first important publication. He wrote "Native Son" in eight months, and it made his reputation. Based in part on
the actual case of a young Negro murderer of a white woman, it was one of the first of the black protest novels, violent and shocking in its scenes of cruelty, hunger, rape, murder, flight and prison. "Black Boy" is the
simple, vivid and poignant story of his early years in the South. It closes as he "heads North."

In 1941 he collaborated with Paul Green in dramatizing "Native Son," which was produced on Broadway. "Black Power: An American Negro Views the Gold Coast" (1954, o. p.) is an "important, informative
and infuriating first-hand account" about African self-government. "White Man, Listen!" (*Doubleday* Anchor Bks. 1957 pap. $1.45) is an interpretation of Black psychology faced by white oppression. After ten ac-
tive years with the Communist party, he terminated his membership in 1944 and "remained politically in-
active." "The Outsider" is a novel about a Negro's life as a Communist. He tells of his political
disillusionment in a chapter of "The God That Failed" (1950, o. p.). He, his wife, and their daughter moved
to Paris in 1946 and made their home there until his death. His "Lawd Today," written before "Native Son"
and published posthumously, is an appalling document of one day in the "dreadful life of Jake Jackson, a
faceless phantom of insulted life from Chicago's black ghetto." The play Wright wrote with the Frenchman
Louis Sapin, "Daddy Goodness," opened off Broadway in 1968. "It is not easy to think of the late Richard
Wright as a comic author, but in 'Daddy Goodness' he and Louis Sapin have written a wonderfully humorous play about the founding of a new religion"—(Richard Watts, in the *N.Y. Post*).

UNCLE TOM'S CHILDREN. Four Novellas. 1938. *Harper* $5.00 Perenn. Lib. pap. $.75

NATIVE SON. *Harper* 1940 $7.50 Perenn. Lib. pap. $.95

THE OUTSIDER. *Harper* 1953 $7.50 Perenn. Lib. pap. $.95

EIGHT MEN. Short stories. 1961 *Pyramid Bks.* pap. $.95

LAWD TODAY. 1963. *Avon* pap. $.75

BLACK BOY: A Record of Childhood and Youth. 1945. *Harper* $6.00 Perenn. Lib. pap.
$.95

Books about Wright

Richard Wright. By Constance Webb. *Putnam* 1968 $9.95 A biography that "vividly delineates the affronts and indignities and sufferings the man endured as a Negro, but it reads, unfortunately, like an apologia"—*(PW)*

Richard Wright. By Robert Bone. Pamphlets on American Writers.*Univ. of Minnesota Press* 1969 pap. $1.25

Richard Wright: An Introduction to the Man and His Works. By Russell C. Brignano. *Univ. of Pittsburgh Press* 1969 pap. $2.95

Example of Richard Wright. By Dan McCall. *Harcourt* 1969 $5.95 pap. $2.25

The Art of Richard Wright. By Edward Margolies with pref. by Harry T. Moore. Crosscurrents/Modern Critiques. *Southern Illinois Univ. Press* 1969 $4.95

Richard Wright's "Native Son": A Critical Handbook. Ed. by Richard Wright. *Wadsworth* 1970 pap. $2.95

Twentieth Century Interpretations of "Native Son." Ed. by Houston A. Baker, Jr. *Prentice-Hall* 1972 $4.95 Spectrum Bks. pap. $1.45

The Emergence of Richard Wright: A Study in Literature and Society. By Kenneth Kinnamon. *Univ. of Illinois Press* 1972 $7.50

The Unfinished Quest of Richard Wright. By Michel Fabre. *Morrow* 1973 $15.00. Best available biography.

SAROYAN, WILLIAM. 1908–

Mr. Saroyan's first short story was published in 1933 in *Hairenik*, an Armenian magazine, and reprinted in O'Brien's "Best Short Stories" in 1934. His parents were Armenians living in California. *Story* accepted "The Daring Young Man on the Flying Trapeze" in 1934. It appeared the same year as his first book, a collection under that story's title, and its breezy, impertinent, tender style made Saroyan famous. He later became a frequent screen writer and director for Hollywood, where he wrote and directed the film "The Human Comedy." (He wrote the novel of that title later, from the filmscript.) "One Day in the Afternoon of the World" (1964, o. p.) is a "rich-textured, slow-developing confessional of a middle-aged man discovering that he needs his family and vice versa"—*(LJ)*. "Short Drive, Sweet Chariot" (*Phaedra* [dist. by Simon & Schuster] 1966 $4.95; *Pocket Bks.* pap. $.75) is, says Saroyan, about "driving from New York to Fresno in a 1941 Lincoln"—in 1963. It covers many topics in the conversation of Mr. Saroyan, including reflections on his own life. "For its philosophy of life and intermittent charm this is recommended"—*(LJ)*. With Arthur Rothstein, a prizewinning *Look* photographer, he has collaborated on a penetrating look at the United States, writing witty captions for Rothstein's photos, under the title "Look At Us. Let Us See. Here We Are. Look Hard, Speak Soft. I See, You See, We All See. Stop, Look, Listen. Beholder's Eye. Don't Look Now but Isn't That You? (Us? U.S.?)" (*Cowles* 1967 $12.50). In recent years he has lived much abroad, where a number of his plays have been produced. Throughout a long writing career his ebullient, facile, fairly prolific output has never developed beyond the attractive gaiety (on which he may have relied too long) of his early literary production. "Here Comes, There Goes You Know Who" purports to be his autobiography, but is rather an idea here, an incident there, with sequence and fact never quite materializing.

THE WILLIAM SAROYAN READER. *Braziller* 1958 $5.95. A representative collection of his writings.

AFTER THIRTY YEARS: THE DARING YOUNG MAN ON THE FLYING TRAPEZE. 1934. *Harcourt* 1964 $5.95. The short-story collection that brought him fame, reissued with a new introd. by the author.

MY NAME IS ARAM. *Harcourt* 1940 Harbrace Mod. Class. 1950 $2.95; *Dell* 1966 pap. $.60. 14 stories and sketches about an Armenian boy.

THE HUMAN COMEDY. Ill. by Don Freeman. *Harcourt* 1943 $6.75; *Dell* 1966 pap. $.75

THE LAUGHING MATTER. 1953. Short Story. *Popular Lib.* 1967 pap. $.60

BOYS AND GIRLS TOGETHER. *Harcourt* 1963 $3.95

NOT DYING. Autobiography. *Harcourt* 1963 $4.95

PLACES WHERE I'VE DONE TIME. Personal memoirs. *Praeger* 1972 $6.95; *Dell* pap. $2.25

Books about Saroyan

William Saroyan. By Howard R. Floan. U.S. Authors Ser. *Twayne* 1966 $5.50; *College & Univ. Press* 1966 pap. $2.45

CLARK, WALTER VAN TILBURG. 1909–1971.

Although Clark wrote but three novels and published a single collection of short stories—"The Watchful Gods and Other Stories" (1950, o. p.)—he is one of the very few Western American writers of fiction during this century to earn a firm reputation as a serious literary artist. His limited output may be attributed not only to the high standards he set for himself but also to his reluctance to repeat himself. Hence his three novels are distinctly different. "The Ox-Bow Incident," which is still widely used in classrooms, particularly at the high school level, is a taut study of mob violence in the Old West. Tightly structured in spite of its large cast of characters, it is remarkable for its psychological insights and its parablelike use of vividly drawn individuals to suggest universal themes. Clark's second novel, "The City of Trembling Leaves," is like most other novelists' first—a long, sprawling, semiautobiographical "Bildungsroman" about a young man growing up in Reno, Nev., where Clark spent his childhood as the son of the president of the University of Nevada. Considered less successful than his other novels, it has the distinction of breaking through old stereotypes by offering as its protagonist a young man who is both an artist and an athlete. "The Track of the Cat" is a heavily symbolic story about the hunting of a marauding mountain lion by three brothers of contrasting temperaments and values. Making skillful use of the hunter-as-the-hunted theme and powerfully evoking the atmosphere of an isolated farmhouse snowbound in the Sierras, Clark succeeds in writing a story of larger-than-life proportions. Not only in its animal antagonist but in its use of symbol and myth "The Track of the Cat" is a work in the tradition of "Moby Dick" and Faulkner's "The Bear."

THE OX-BOW INCIDENT. 1940. *New Am. Lib.* Signet pap. $.95; *Peter Smith* $4.00

THE CITY OF TREMBLING LEAVES. 1945. *Popular Lib.* 1966 pap. $1.25

THE TRACK OF THE CAT. 1949. *New Am. Lib.* Signet pap. $1.25

WELTY, EUDORA. 1909–

Eudora Welty's first collection of stories, "A Curtain of Green," was published at the same time that her story "A Worn Path" won the O. Henry Memorial Award in 1941. In 1942 "The Robber Bridegroom," a novelette, was published and the title story of "The Wide Net" won the 1942 O. Henry Memorial Award. Miss Welty was born in Jackson, Miss. From the Mississippi State College for Women she went to the University of Wisconsin (B.A. 1929); then to Columbia University. She worked for a while in advertising, then returned to Jackson to take a government publicity job that brought her in contact with many kinds of people. She lives quietly with her family in her home town. Her first stories appeared in *Manuscript*, the *Southern Review*, the *Atlantic Monthly* and *Harper's Bazaar* between 1936 and 1941. Most of them concern "ordinary" people of all walks of life in her home state. The stories are entirely original, sometimes melodramatic, sometimes fantastic, and often concerned with human psychological aberration. Her dialogue is expert. In 1944 she was awarded a $1,000 prize by the American Academy of Arts and Letters, and in 1955, the Howells Medal by the Academy for "The Ponder Heart," which was dramatized successfully in 1956. In 1966 she received the Creative Arts Award in writing from Brandeis University.

Katherine Anne Porter (*q. v.*) in her introduction to "A Curtain of Green" says: "These stories offer an extraordinary range of mood, pace, tone, and variety of material. . . . She has simply an eye and an ear sharp, shrewd and true as a tuning fork." Alun Jones says of her technique, "Her approach is . . . intense and . . . robust, and her style, deceptively lucid, . . . approaches the precision and density of poetry. . . . Because of their compression and the unobtrusiveness of their symbolism her stories often call for an unusual effort of imaginative response on the part of the reader."

Although Miss Welty's critical reputation remains largely dependent upon her excellent short stories, she has also written four full-length novels which have been well received. "Delta Wedding" is a densely plotted novel with many characters that centers around the gathering of an aristocratic Mississippi family for the wedding of the family beauty Dabney Fairchild to the plantation overseer. The story is told from multiple points of view and explores with intelligence and subtlety problems of domestic relationships and the mixing of social classes. "The Ponder Heart," a more simply told story, centers around the murder trial of a man unjustly accused of killing his young wife, a common girl from a farming clan whom he had fallen in love with when she clerked at the local five and ten. With "Losing Battles" Miss Welty deals again with the complexities of a large family gathering, this time a family of lower social class meeting for their annual reunion and the celebration of the ninetieth birthday of Granny as well as the recent birth of her first great-great grandchild. "The Optimist's Daughter" is the story of tangled relationships between a 71-year-old judge undergoing a critical eye operation in a New Orleans hospital, his daughter, a withdrawn widow summoned from Chicago, and the judge's second wife, a woman of coarse breeding younger than his daughter. Gradually, a fourth main figure emerges, the judge's first wife, and this subtle story of father-daughter and husband-wives begins to reverberate with further complications. Howard Moss called the book "a miracle of compression . . . the best book Eudora Welty has ever written"—(*N.Y. Times*).

SELECTED STORIES. *Modern Library* 1954 $2.95

THIRTEEN STORIES. Ed. with introd. by Ruth M. Vande Kieft. *Harcourt* 1965 Harvest Bks. pap. $1.85

A CURTAIN OF GREEN AND OTHER STORIES. Introd. by Katherine Anne Porter *Harcourt* 1941 new ed. 1947 $5.95

THE WIDE NET AND OTHER STORIES. *Harcourt* 1943 $4.95

THE ROBBER BRIDEGROOM. 1942. *Harcourt* 1948 $4.95; *Atheneum* 1963 pap. $1.25

DELTA WEDDING. *Harcourt* 1946 $6.95

THE GOLDEN APPLES. *Harcourt* 1949 Harvest Bks. 1956 pap. $1.85

THE PONDER HEART. *Harcourt* 1954 $4.50 pap. $.60

THE BRIDE OF INNISFALLEN. 7 stories. *Harcourt* 1955 Harvest Bks. pap. $2.45

LOSING BATTLES. *Random* 1970 $7.95; *Fawcett* pap. $1.25

THE OPTIMIST'S DAUGHTER. *Random* 1972 $5.95; *Fawcett* pap. $1.25

Books about Welty

Eudora Welty. By Ruth M. Vande Kieft. U.S. Authors Ser. *Twayne* 1962 $5.50; *College & Univ. Press* 1962 pap. $2.45
Eudora Welty. By Joseph A. Bryant, Jr. Pamphlets on American Writers. *Univ. of Minnesota Press* 1968 pap. $1.25
The Rhetoric of Eudora Welty's Short Stories. By Zelma Turner Howard. *Univ. & College Press of Mississippi* 1973 pap. $2.95

AGEE, JAMES. 1909–1955.

"Although he was working on the manuscript when he died, 'A Death in the Family' reads like a finished work—brilliant, moving and written with an objectivity and a control he had not achieved before"—(*New Yorker*). Agee was posthumously awarded the Pulitzer Prize in 1958 for this work. It was dramatized by Tad Mosel in 1960 as "All the Way Home"; the play also won a Pulitzer Prize, the N.Y. Drama Critics Circle award, and was cited by *Life* as "The Best American Play of the Season."

The 70 letters to Father Flye, his instructor at St. Andrew's School and a close and trusted friend throughout his life, show Agee most often in a reflective, self-condemning mood. The final ones, written from the hospital where he was battling daily heart attacks, are touching, as are his sad reflections on the work he yet wanted to do.

Tennessee-born, Agee was a poet, novelist, and critic. "A Death in the Family" remains his fictional masterpiece. "The Morning Watch" is "a finely drawn study of a single day in the life of an adolescent boy, a student in an Anglo-Catholic School in the Tennessee hills"—("Twentieth Century Authors"). He also wrote for television and for the screen; several of his scripts are collected in "Agee on Film: Five Film Scripts". "Let Us Now Praise Famous Men" (1941 *Houghton* 1960 $8.95; *Ballantine Bks.* pap. $1.65) is a report on sharecropper life written for a series of photographs by Walter Evans. His film criticism may be found in "Agee on Film: Reviews and Comments by James Agee" (*Grosset* Universal Lib. 2 vols. Vol. I 1958, Vol. 2 1960 pap. each $2.95). Also available is "Collected Poems" (ed. by Robert Fitzgerald *Houghton* 1968 $4.95; *Yale Univ. Press* 1969 pap. $1.75).

COLLECTED SHORT PROSE. Ed. by Robert Fitzgerald. *Houghton* 1969 $5.95; *Ballantine Bks.* pap. $1.25. Features a valuable memoir by Fitzgerald as well as a selection of Agee's short stories, satiric pieces, movie scripts, and miscellanea.

THE MORNING WATCH. *Houghton* 1951 $4.95

A DEATH IN THE FAMILY 1957. *Grosset* $4.95; *Bantam* pap. $.95

LETTERS OF JAMES AGEE TO FATHER FLYE. 1962. *Houghton* 1971. $5.95; *Ballantine Bks.* pap. $1.25

Books about Agee

Agee. By Peter H. Ohlin. *Astor-Honor* 1965 $7.95 pap. $2.95
James Agee: Promise and Fulfillment. By Kenneth Seib. *Univ. of Pittsburgh Press* 1969 pap. $2.50
James Agee. By Erling Larsen. Pamphlets on American Writers. *Univ. of Minnesota Press* 1971 pap. $1.25
A Way of Seeing: A Critical Study of James Agee. By Alfred T. Barson. *Univ. of Massachusetts Press* 1972 $9.50

ALGREN, NELSON. 1909–

Hemingway named Algren as one of America's finest writers, and praised especially "A Walk on the Wild Side." Born in Detroit, Algren grew up under the shadow of the "El" in the Polish immigrant community of Chicago's West Side, an origin which has determined most of his fiction. Graduating from the University of Illinois in the middle of the Depression with a degree in journalism, he wandered throughout the Southwest as a migratory laborer and door-to-door salesman. Finding himself stranded in an abandoned filling station outside Rio Hondo, Tex., he wrote his first short story, "So Help Me," and sent it to Whit Burnett, who published it in *Story*.

His first novel, "Somebody in Boots" (1935, o. p.) a stark and bitter documentary of "Depression youth," was "spectacularly unsuccessful." But with his grimly realistic novel of Chicago slum life, "Never Come Morning" (1942, o. p.) Algren was recognized as a novelist of importance. He received the 1949 National Book Award for "The Man With the Golden Arm," later made into a motion picture. The story of a morphine addict, the dealer in a gambling club, this is "a powerful book illuminated by flashes of Algren's grisly, antic, almost horrifying humor, by passages of finely poetic writing, and by his love and understanding"—(*N.Y. Times*). "A Walk on the Wild Side" was called "beautiful, grotesque, violent, tender."

Algren's prose-poem, "Chicago: City on the Make" (1951 *Pacific Coast* 1961 pap. $2.95), divided Chicago into two almost-armed camps: Saroyan called it "an extension of Baudelaire," Budd Schulberg "as unflattering as a Goya portrait of nobility," and Harry Hansen "a wonderful hymn to Chicago." "Who Lost an American?" (1962, o. p.) is an account of a tour that he took off the regular tourist's map—a collection of "memories, notes, burlesques and prejudices in a book that is part fact, part fiction"—sometimes funny, sometimes bitterly serious. "Notes from a Sea Diary: Hemingway All the Way" (1965, o. p.) includes stories told on an ostensible voyage through Eastern seas—and first-person comments on Hemingway, Hawthorne, Mailer, Villon, and Dostoyevsky. "Nelson Algren's Own Book of Lonesome Monsters" (1963 Lancer pap. $1.25) which he edited, is a collection, including some of his own stories, with the common theme that men are strange incomprehensible creatures at heart, and that man is always alone. In his introduction, he "repeats his prejudice that brutality, crime, inadequacy and moral nullity are at least as *human* as their opposite qualities. By the tendency of his selection, he implies that they are considerably more interesting, even perhaps richer in their potential for redeeming a world frozen in the sterile equilibrium of conventionality"—(*N.Y. Times*). "Conversations with Nelson Algren" (*Hill & Wang* 1964 $6.50; *Berkley* pap. $.75) by H. E. F. Donahue provides stimulating discussion between two dissimilar men. Algren discusses the role of the writer in America, his affair with Simone de Beauvoir (*q. v.*) on one of her American trips, some of his frustrations, and his personal philosophy. "Many will be entertained, informed, and electrified by the strength of his voice at a time when artists in this country most need to speak out"—(*L J*)

THE NEON WILDERNESS. 1947. Short stories. *Berkley* pap. $.75; *Hill & Wang* 1960 Am. Century pap. $1.75; *Peter Smith* 1960 $4.00

THE MAN WITH THE GOLDEN ARM. 1948. *Fawcett* Crest Bks. 1964 pap. $.95

A WALK ON THE WILD SIDE. 1956. *Fawcett* Crest Bks. 1963 pap. $.95

THE LAST CAROUSEL. *Putnam* 1973 $7.95

HIMES, CHESTER, 1909–

Although Chester Himes has lived abroad since 1953 and devoted his energies in recent years to writing a series of slick detective stories set in Harlem, he has earned a reputation as a serious and forceful novelist whose works show consistent quality. His first six novels are angry and sometimes polemical exercises in naturalism not unlike the "Native Son" of Richard Wright (*q. v.*). "If He Hollers Let Him Go" deals powerfully with the indignities suffered by a Black man in a wartime industrial plant. Both "The Third Genera-tion" and "The Primitive" show how the insecurity, fears, and despair caused by racial discrimination may affect the quality of life within Black families. "Cast the First Stone," which owes much to the seven years Himes served in prison for armed robbery, has as its protagonist a white convict who learns that love is im-possible among men who have been treated like animals. The first volume of Himes's autobiography, "The Quality of Hurt," recounts his first 45 years with an effective mixture of bitterness and pride.

Himes's detective stories have found a wider audience than his serious fiction. Thanks in part to successful movie adaptations of "Cotton Comes to Harlem" (1965, o. p.) and "Come Back, Charleston Blue" (origi-nally "The Heat's On" *Berkley* pap. $.95), Himes's detective team of Coffin Ed Johnson and Grave Digger Jones have become popular folk heroes for Black and white readers alike; and Himes has been credited with pioneering a new genre of ghetto fiction which is at once "hip" and "cool" as well as tough and violent. With the exception of "Blind Man with a Pistol" (1969, o. p.), the nine novels in the series were originally pub-lished in French and later translated for American paperback distribution. The other titles are "The Crazy Kill" (1959 *Chatham Bksellers* $7.50), "The Real Cool Killers" (1959 *Chatham Bksellers* $7.50), "All Shot Up" (1960 *Chatham Bksellers* $7.50) "The Big Gold Dream" (1960 *Chatham Bksellers* $7.50), "Pinktoes" (1967 *Dell* pap. $.75), and "Run Man Run" (1969 *Dell* pap. $.75).

BLACK ON BLACK: Baby Sister and Selected Writings. *Doubleday* 1973 $6.95

IF HE HOLLERS LET HIM GO. 1945. *Chatham Bksellers* $7.50; *New Am. Lib.* Signet 1971 pap. $.95

LONELY CRUSADE. 1947 *Chatham Bksellers* $8.50

CAST THE FIRST STONE. 1952. *Chatham Bksellers* $7.95; *New Am. Lib.* Signet 1972 pap. $1.25

THE THIRD GENERATION. 1954. *Chatham Bksellers* $7.95; *New Am. Lib.* Signet pap. $1.25

THE PRIMITIVE. 1955. *New Am. Lib.* Signet 1971 pap. $.95

FOR LOVE OF IMA BELLE. 1957. *Chatham Bksellers* $7.50

THE QUALITY OF HURT: The Autobiography of Chester Himes, Vol. I. *Doubleday* 1972 $7.95

STEGNER, WALLACE. 1909–

Wallace Stegner was born in Iowa and has taught at universities as far east as Harvard, but his deepest roots, like the setting of most of his fiction, lie in that part of America which stretches westward from the Rocky Mountains. "Angle of Repose," which won the Pulitzer Prize for Fiction in 1972, has a theme similar to that of Stegner's best-known novel, "Big Rock Candy Mountain," in that it deals with a wandering family on the western frontiers, but the later novel is told from the point of view of an older man confined to a wheel-chair writing a part-fictional, part-historical account of his grandmother's life in the Old West. The method of this novel enables Stegner to contrast the dreams and values of the pioneers with the easy compromises and expedient values of modern-day society.

That contrast is apparent throughout Stegner's career as a writer of fiction. "On a Darkling Plain" (1940, o. p.) deals with a young veteran of the First World War who finds it necessary to detach himself from mod-ern civilization by living in an isolated region of western Canada. "Second Growth," unusual among Steg-ner's novels in that it is set in New England, describes the corruption of an Eden-like community by a sophis-ticated and evil woman. The dreams of justice, equality, and a better world to come depicted vividly in "The Preacher and the Slave" (now "Joe Hill") are scarcely present at all in the two novels set in modern-day Cal-ifornia which followed publication of that story of the idealistic leader of the IWW movement. "A Shooting Star" and "All the Little Live Things" both offer a bitter indictment of the direction modern civilization has taken. How could the hard-working western pioneers have known that the Big Rock Candy Mountain they dreamed of finding would turn out to be a welfare state populated by a generation which seeks happiness through free food stamps, escape through drugs, and spiritual salvation through fad religions? That is the question posed by Stegner's recent fiction, a question most skillfully asked in the workmanlike craftsmanship of "Angle of Repose."

Other fiction by Stegner includes three early novels—"Remembering Laughter" (1937, o. p.), "The Pot-ter's House" (1938, o. p.), "Fire and Ice" (1941, o. p.)—and two well-regarded collections of short stories—"The Women on the Wall" and "The City of the Living" (1956, o. p.). A professor of English at Stanford

University since 1945, he has written some half-dozen works of nonfiction dealing with the history of the American West and has edited more than a score of textbooks, anthologies, and other works. "The Sound of Mountain Water" (*Doubleday* 1969 $5.95) is a collection of personal essays.

THE BIG ROCK CANDY MOUNTAIN. 1943. *Doubleday* $8.95

SECOND GROWTH. 1947. *Popular Lib.* 1969 pap. $.75

THE WOMEN ON THE WALL. Short Stories. 1948. *Viking* Compass pap. $1.45

JOE HILL: A Biographical Novel (Orig. "The Preacher and the Slave" 1950). *Doubleday* 1969 $6.95; *Ballantyne* 1972 pap. $1.50

A SHOOTING STAR. *Viking* 1961 $5.00

ALL THE LITTLE LIVE THINGS. 1967. *New Am. Lib.* Signet 1968 pap. $1.25

ANGLE OF REPOSE. *Doubleday* 1971 $7.95; *Fawcett* Crest 1972 pap. $1.50

Books about Stegner

Wallace Stegner. By Merrill and Lorene Lewis. Western Writers Ser. *Boise State College* 1972 pap. $1.00

BOWLES, PAUL. 1910–

In several ways Paul Bowles has played a pivotal role in modern cultural history. He has earned recognition as both a writer and a composer, and the home which he and his talented wife Jane have maintained in Tangier for more than three decades has served as an oasis for artists, writers, and musicians of many lands. He was born in New York City and spent a year at the University of Virginia before going to Europe in the early 1930s to study music under Aaron Copland in Berlin and with Virgil Thomson in Paris. Bowles has written operas and ballets and has composed incidental music for numerous plays; much of his music has been published or recorded.

Bowles's training and talents as a composer help to explain why his literary reputation is largely based on his ability as a stylist with a sensitive ear for rhythm and melodic flow in both prose and verse. He has published two volumes of poetry—"Scenes" (1968, o. p.) and "The Thicket of Spring" (1971, o. p.) in addition to several travel books and translations of works by his Moroccan friends. "The Sheltering Sky," his first novel, made a strong impact and seemed to herald the emergence of a unique new talent. Gothic in atmosphere and heavily charged with symbolism, it is the story of a young couple who arrive in North Africa and undergo a series of strange adventures which gradually undermine their Western values. With this novel Bowles introduced a basic theme—the conflict between the primitive and the civilized—which reappears frequently in his later fiction. "Let It Come Down" (1952, o. p.) traces the moral corruption of a steady young man who gives up a position as a bank clerk in New York in order to work in a friend's travel agency in Tangier. "Up Above the World" is the story of a couple who wander through the dreamlike landscapes of an unspecified plantation republic before being overtaken by hallucination and death. David Galloway (in "Contemporary Novelists") sums up Bowles's career as a novelist in this way: "The hypnotic atmosphere of 'The Sheltering Sky' has been equalled in later work, but never surpassed, and while 'The Spider's House' (1955, o. p.) and 'Up Above the World' demonstrate a refinement of narrative power, they seem finally like somewhat redundant variations on long-established gothic themes."

Journal of Mod. Lit. found "Without Stopping," Bowles's autobiography, disappointing as a record of his friendships and encounters with other artists, but noted that "anyone who has read Bowles's novels will know that it is a well-written book, a work of art in itself which maintains a strong pace of steady narration." His wife, Jane Auer Bowles, has made a distinguished reputation as a writer of plays and fiction in spite of her modest output, much of it available in "The Collected Works of Jane Bowles" (*Farrar* 1966 $8.50 pap. $2.45).

THE SHELTERING SKY. 1949. *New Directions* 1968 pap. $2.75

THE DELICATE PREY AND OTHER STORIES. 1950. *Ecco Press* 1972 $6.95 pap. $2.95

A HUNDRED CAMELS IN THE COURTYARD. Stories. *City Lights* 1962 pap. $1.25

UP ABOVE THE WORLD. 1966. *Pocket Bks.* 1968 pap. $.75

WITHOUT STOPPING: An Autobiography. *Putnam* 1972 $7.95

MORRIS, WRIGHT. 1910–

Born in Nebraska, Wright Morris has traveled throughout this country in a series of "madcap odysseys that were perilous, foolish, inspired and strangely fashionable. One of these jaunts . . . is honestly recorded in 'My Uncle Dudley' (1942, o. p.)." With the publication of "The Huge Season" (1954, o. p.), Mark Schorer, in the *N.Y. Times*, hailed Morris as "probably the most original young novelist writing in the United States." In 1957 "The Field of Vision," about "innocents abroad in Mexico," won the National Book Award. With "Love Among the Cannibals" (1957, o. p.) he turned his "talent to portray, in utterly captivating comedy, the battle between the sexes." November 22, 1963, the day of John Kennedy's assassination, is the subject of "One Day" (1965, o. p.). The national tragedy is related to a local tragedy involving an abandoned infant, and is handled with "unusual delicacy"—(*PW*). "Laying sure hands on the *daily* is Wright Morris's *forte*. What the rest of us may have accepted too casually he sets upon with his own highly specialized focus. In this novel, more than ever, the texture of the day and hour, the fabric of speech, the pattern of action are used to show forth the humor of objects, places, people, lives; and in their deeper, more mysterious interrelations is disclosed the larger shape of tragedy"—(Eudora Welty).

"In Orbit" (1967, o. p.) describes one day in which a young high school graduate and draft dodger terrorizes a small town. "Mr. Morris is gaining momentum with each novel, and is one of the finest practitioners of the philosophic spoof"—(*LJ*). "Morris's work . . . is one of the major achievements of contemporary American literature. [He] can take a minute fragment of American life, as he did with *In Orbit*, write about it with humor that blends sympathy and exasperation, and illuminate all our experience"—(Granville Hicks, in *SR*). Because these qualities are clearly evident in "Fire Sermon"—the story of a chance meeting on the highway between an old man and a boy and three young hippies—Hicks called that book "simon-pure, dyed-in-the-wool honest-to-God Wright Morris of the very highest grade"—(*N.Y. Times*).

Morris's fine sense for the conjunction of time and place is also evident in his three books of photographs with text. "The Home Place" (1948. *Univ. of Nebraska Press* Bison Bks. 1968 pap. $1.95) and "God's Country and My People" (*Harper* 1968 $10.00) deal with the Midwest he knows so well, while "Love Affair: A Venetian Journal" (*Harper* 1972 $12.50) vividly describes a visit to Venice. Other nonfiction includes a collection of essays on contemporary social and political problems, "A Bill of Rites, A Bill of Wrongs, A Bill of Goods" (1967, o. p.), and a widely praised volume of criticism, "The Territory Ahead: Critical Interpretations in American Literature" (1958 *Atheneum* 1963 pap. $1.45; *Peter Smith* $4.00).

WRIGHT MORRIS: A READER. Ed. by Granville Hicks. *Harper* 1970 $12.95

WORLD IN THE ATTIC. 1949. *Univ. of Nebraska Press* Bison Bks. 1972 pap. $1.95

THE WORKS OF LOVE. 1952. *Univ. of Nebraska Press* Bison Bks. 1972 pap. $1.95

CEREMONY IN LONE TREE. 1960. *Univ. of Nebraska Press* Bison Bks. 1973 pap. $2.25

FIRE SERMON. *Harper* 1971 $5.95

WAR GAMES. *Black Sparrow* 1972 pap. $4.00

A LIFE. *Harper* 1973 $5.95

Books about Morris

Wright Morris. By David Madden. U.S. Authors Ser. *Twayne* 1964 $5.50; *College and Univ. Press* 1964 pap. $2.45
Wright Morris. By Leon Howard. Pamphlets on American Writers. *Univ. of Minnesota Press* 1968 pap. $1.25

CHEEVER, JOHN. 1912–

John Cheever's short stories are notable for their cool precision. Many of them deal with the turbulence and uncertainties of the young as they adjust themselves to modern adult life. He was born in Quincy, Mass., was educated at Thayer Academy in South Braintree and spent four years in the Army. In 1951 he received a Guggenheim Fellowship and in 1956 an award from the National Institute of Arts and Letters. Seven of the eight stories in "The Housekeeper of Shady Hill and Other Stories," first appeared in the *New Yorker*. In 1958 his first novel, "The Wapshot Chronicle," won the National Book Award for fiction.

"Some People, Places and Things That Will Not Appear in My Next Novel" (1961, *Bks. for Libraries* $7.75) is a selection of short stories about which the *San Francisco Chronicle* said, "Cheever is a penetrating observer of mid-century American frustration. . . . As a writer [his] stock in trade is a sharply-honed prose style and a sardonic point of view." The Wapshot family appear again in "The Wapshot Scandal," for which he received the Howells Medal of the American Academy of Arts and Letters in 1965. There is a bit of Cheever's birthplace, Quincy, Mass. in the "Wapshots" St. Botolphs, plus bits of Newburyport, Mass., remembered by his father, and bits of the farmland around Hanover (near Plymouth), Mass." "As for Mr. Cheever," writes Elizabeth Janeway in the *N.Y. Times,* "he is a very good writer indeed. His new novel is rich and tricky and full of surprises. More than anyone except perhaps Nabokov (and he does not suffer from Nabokov's sudden plunges into grotesquerie), he is able to use the objects, the scenes and the attributes of contemporary life for the purposes of art. Ugliness, pain, loneliness and horror are not softened but understood and valued without sentiment, without moralizing and (it seems to me) with profound good sense that approaches wisdom." Again in "The Brigadier and the Golf Widow" (1964, o. p.) he "takes apart the hardware of contemporary urban living and recombines it into a mythic entity"—(*LJ*).

THE ENORMOUS RADIO AND OTHER STORIES. 1953. *Funk & Wagnalls* 1966 $4.50

THE WAPSHOT CHRONICLE. *Harper* 1957 $6.95; Perenn. Lib. 1973 pap. $1.25.

THE HOUSEBREAKER OF SHADY HILL AND OTHER STORIES. 1928 *Manor Bks.* pap. $.60

THE WAPSHOT SCANDAL. *Harper* 1964 Perenn. Lib. 1973 pap. $1.25

BULLET PARK. *Knopf* 1969 $5.95

WORLD OF APPLES. *Knopf* 1973 $5.95

McCARTHY, MARY (THERESE). 1912–

"My life-history is printed on a rather polychrome background" says Mary McCarthy. An orphan at six, she fell into the hands of first a "severe great-aunt" and then later her grandfather, a Seattle lawyer of "legalistic temper." In 1933 she graduated from Vassar, where "the discovery of Latin and the Elizabethans [provided] two of those shocks of self-recognition." She began to write book reviews for the *Nation* and the *New Republic* and later became an editor and theater critic of the *Partisan Review.*

Mary McCarthy is known chiefly as a satirist. "Her novels have generally been praised for their vigorous lampooning of contemporary American intellectualism and for their lucid style." Robert Halsband (in *SR*) wrote of her collection "Cast a Cold Eye": "Her brief incisive pieces are etched with corrosive acid, it is true; but they still have a savage honesty, a bristling sensibility, and at bottom a pitiless humanity." "The Group," which became a best seller almost immediately, tells of eight Vassar girls, class of 1933, and the seven eventful years that follow their commencement. "Birds of America" is the story of 19-year-old Peter Levi and his mother Rosamund, a harpsichordist. The first half of the novel contains a series of episodes on the you-can't-go-home-again theme dealing with the return to Rocky Port of the mother and son after a four-year absence; the second half consists largely of a long reflective letter to his mother from Peter in Europe, where he is spending his junior year. That letter, concerned largely with "balancing off esthetics against morals, aristocracy against democracy," caused Helen Vendler to write that "Mary McCarthy, for all her cold eye and fine prose, is an essayist, not a novelist. But then, if we can have nonfiction novels, why not a new McCarthy genre, the fictional essay? It is not an unworthy form, taken for what it is"—(*N.Y. Times*).

Nonetheless, some readers continue to feel that Miss McCarthy's best writing is her nonfictional essays. An astute critic of literature and society, she has published on a wide variety of topics. Some of her reviews and articles on the theater, 1937–62, are found in "Mary McCarthy's Theatre Chronicles" (*Farrar, Straus* 1963 Noonday pap. $1.95). "On the Contrary" (*Farrar, Straus* 1961 $4.50 Noonday pap. $1.95) is a collection of articles on politics and the social scene, woman, and literature and the arts. "The Writing on the Wall and Other Literary Essays" (*Harcourt* 1970 $6.75) gathers together a baker's dozen of memorable critical appreciations on works of literature from Shakespeare's "Macbeth" to Nabokov's "Pale Fire." Her art-history-travel books, "Venice Observed" (*Reynal* 1956 $15.00; *Harcourt* Harvest Bks. pap. $1.65) and "The Stones of Florence" (*Harcourt* 1959 $17.50 Harvest Bks. 1963 pap. $1.65), are notable for their combining sharp observation with personal intensity. That same conjunction helps to explain the impact of her two volumes on the war in the Far East: "Vietnam" (*Harcourt* 1967 pap. $1.95) and "Hanoi" (*Harcourt* 1968 pap. $1.45). The *N.Y. Times* called the former "the most provocative and disturbing analytical indictment yet published of America's role in Vietnam." Sent to that troubled area by the *N.Y. Review of Books,* she took issue with "the people behind the lines who are blueprinting, publicizing, justifying and confusing the war" and interviewed the "do-gooders" (*PW*). In her view, said Eliot Fremont-Smith, "America has suffered and is suffering a moral catastrophe of the first magnitude. . . . Among the dissenting books [this one] makes most of the others seem like Jello." Miss McCarthy advocated unilateral withdrawal.

THE COMPANY SHE KEEPS. *Harcourt* 1942 1960 $4.95 Harvest Bks. pap. $1.95

CAST A COLD EYE. Short stories. *Harcourt* 1950 $3.95; *New Am. Lib.* 1964 Plume pap. $2.95

THE GROVES OF ACADEME. *Harcourt* 1952 $4.75; *New Am. Lib.* Signet pap. $.75
Plume pap. $2.95

A CHARMED LIFE. *Harcourt* 1955 $5.95; *New Am. Lib.* Signet 1964 pap. $.75

THE GROUP. *Harcourt* 1963 $5.95; *New Am. Lib.* Signet 1964 pap. $1.25

BIRDS OF AMERICA. *Harcourt* 1971 $6.95; *New Am. Lib.* $1.50

MEMORIES OF A CATHOLIC GIRLHOOD. *Harcourt* 1957 $4.75 Harvest Bks. pap. $2.45;
Berkley pap. $.75

Books about McCarthy

Mary McCarthy. By Barbara McKenzie. U.S. Authors Ser. *Twayne* 1966 $3.95; *College & Univ. Press*
pap. $1.95
The Company She Kept. By Doris Grumbach. *Coward* 1967 $5.50
Mrs. Grumbach encountered many obstacles in writing about a living author and apparently survived.
Her thesis is that many of Miss McCarthy's characters were drawn from life and that thus much of the
material in her novels can be regarded as autobiography—which leads to character identification
among her friends, a dangerous and not altogether legitimate game. The book is, however, in other respects, "a serious and well-written attempt to evaluate Mary McCarthy's style and her literary contributions, and to analyze her personality" (*PW*). Intended for the general reader, it lacks scholarly apparatus and, unfortunately, an index.

SHAW, IRWIN. 1913–

"The Young Lions," the story of three soldiers—two Americans and a German—and one of the best novels to come out of World War II, was Irwin Shaw's first novel, and was subsequently filmed. He is a native of
New York City, graduated from Brooklyn College, has written radio serials and screenplays, and served in
the Army Signal Corps during World War II. Several of his plays have been produced including the antiwar
"Bury the Dead" (1936) and "The Gentle People" (1939). Shaw's excellent short stories and provocative
first novel established him as one of the most promising writers of this century. That reputation, however, has
become endangered in recent years as his fiction has appeared to depend more and more upon formula and
slickness often shielded by moral earnestness. "The Troubled Air" (1950, o. p.) deals with witch-hunting in
the broadcast industry during the McCarthy era. "Lucy Crown" chronicles the disastrous effect of a failed
marriage upon the only child of that union. "Rich Man, Poor Man" traces a family through three generations and offers a strong indictment of material values. Yet for all the heaviness of Shaw's moral and social
concerns as well as frequent clumsiness of technique, his longer novels contain memorable and effective individual scenes. Thus James Gindin writes that "the most effective parts of Shaw's novels often reveal the talents of the short-story writer, the capacity to present with intelligence, sensitivity, and a kind of forceful honesty, a single scene, atmosphere, character, or relationship"—("Contemporary Novelists").

SELECTED SHORT STORIES. *Modern Library* $2.95

THE YOUNG LIONS. 1948. *New Am. Lib.* Signet 1950 pap. $1.50

LUCY CROWN. 1956. *Dell* pap. $1.25

TWO WEEKS IN ANOTHER TOWN. 1960. *Dell* pap. $1.25

VOICES OF A SUMMER DAY. *Delacorte* 1965 $4.95

RICH MAN, POOR MAN. *Delacorte* 1970 $7.95; *Dell* pap. $1.50

EVENING IN BYZANTIUM. *Delacorte* 1973 $7.95

HERSEY, JOHN (RICHARD). 1914–

John Hersey's parents were American missionaries. He was born in Tientsin, China, and spoke Chinese
fluently before he knew a word of English. The family returned to the United States when he was ten and he
went to the Hotchkiss School, graduated from Yale in 1936 and did graduate work at Cambridge University.
After a summer (1937) as Sinclair Lewis's (*q. v.*) private secretary, he became a writer for, then editor of,
Time and later of *Life*. He was sent to the Orient as a war correspondent for *Time* in 1939 and gained valu-

able firsthand knowledge of the Japanese character. He was considered an expert on Far Eastern matters even before the war.

"Men On Bataan" (1942, o. p.) is the story of the defense of Bataan with a biography of General MacArthur. "Into the Valley" (*Knopf* 1943 $3.95) was named an "Imperative" by the Council on Books in Wartime (as was the later "A Bell for Adano"), and John Chamberlain heralded him as "a new Hemingway." Although his masterly story of the Italian-American Major Joppolo in "A Bell for Adano" was called top war reporting with a message and not properly a novel, it won the Pulitzer Prize for fiction in 1945 and was successfully dramatized. "The Wall," 1950s most praised novel, "based on the martydom of Polish Jewry during the Nazi occupation . . . is the most complex and brilliant of John Hersey's books so far. . . . It is an urgent and remarkable novel on a grand scale, and one which seizes upon our minds and hearts" (Maxwell Geismar in *SR*). "A Single Pebble," "a short novel of classical simplicity and distinction," is the moving and perceptive story of "the power and majesty and mystery" of the great Yangtze river and the Chinese trackers who tow the junks so slowly and painfully against its dangerous currents.

John Hersey's account of the destruction created by the first atom bomb, "Hiroshima" (*Knopf* 1946 $4.00; *Modern Library* $2.95; *Bantam* 1948 pap. $.75) is a "superb impartial report, a human document that is certainly one of the great classics of the war." His 1959 novel "The War Lover" reveals "a conflict between two attitudes toward war that represent two attitudes toward life as a whole, a conflict between those who are ultimately motivated by love of death, and those who, even when they are driven to kill, are motivated by a love of life" (Arthur Mizener, in the *N.Y. Times*). Hersey states in his preface to "Here to Stay" (*Knopf* 1963 $6.95): "Man is here to stay." In answer to his question "What is it that, by a narrow margin, keeps us going, in the face of our crimes, our follies, our passions, our sorrows, our panics, our hideous drives to kill?" he presents nine previously published episodes that illustrate human tenacity for life, in time of danger and suffering. The book includes, among other things, accounts of President Kennedy's PT boat rescue, a Jew's suffering in Auschwitz and escape from Hungary, and the author's famous "Hiroshima."

"The Child Buyer" is a satirical novel about the educational manipulation of young minds. "White Lotus," about an Arizona girl captured and degraded by the Chinese in some intentionally vague period, is a "blazing, troubling, eloquent book about human bondage" in which we are clearly intended to see American Negro slavery in reverse. In 1965 Mr. Hersey was appointed the master of Pierson College at Yale. By then he had already written "Too Far To Walk," an understanding novel about an American student who suffers the malaise of some members of the recent college generation. Mr. Hersey explores what may lie behind the resort to drugs and easy sex—an undertaking not without risks, and Mr. Hersey fails in some of them, but what brave adult would not? The book is a hard one to forget. He continues to wrestle with current human dilemmas in "Under the Eye of the Storm." Here an unhappy doctor, at sea with his wife and two friends, struggles to understand himself and his life while maneuvering his yawl against turbulent waters and destructive winds from a hurricane. Reviews were mixed, but James F. Fixx wrote (in *SR*): "It keeps an unremitting grip on the imagination long after the reader has put it down. . . . He has . . . a shrewd eye for adventure, and he can spin tales that race along from crisis to throat-catching crisis. . . . But Hersey can also do soemthing else, and he does it here with a sustained control that is little short of astonishing. He can weave into the very fabric of his adventure a meaning that grows directly out of it and yet represents a great deal more." "The Conspiracy," a fictional account of the Pisonian conspiracy against the Emperor Nero in the year 65 A.D., shows Hersey trying his hand at a historical narrative told in the form of letters. Although B. F. Dick (in the *N.Y. Times*) called it "Hersey's finest novel to date," most other reviewers found it disappointing. "The Algiers Motel Incident" (*Knopf* 1968 $6.95; *Bantam* 1968 pap. $1.25) tells about the 1967 Detroit race riots and the three Negroes who were killed. "Mr. Hersey's investigation of the incident, based on months of research, reaches profound conclusions about the nature of law and order in this country and the application of justice to black men as well as white" (*PW*). It was criticized, however, as prejudicial to a trial which had not yet taken place, and caused the trial's postponement in July, 1968. John Hersey's concern for humanity, which never descends to sermonizing, has led him to experiment with a wide variety of human themes—with varying success but unfailing invention, readability, and seriousness. This, perhaps—the refusal to stick to successful formulas, the willingness to experiment and take risks—is in itself a measure of his achievement.

A BELL FOR ADANO. *Amsco School Pub.* pap. $1.50; *Knopf* 1944 $4.95; *Bantam* 1965 pap. $.75; *Franklin Watts* 1966 lg.-type ed. Keith Jennison Bks. $8.95

THE WALL. *Knopf* 1950 $8.95; *Bantam* pap. $1.50

THE MARMOT DRIVE. *Knopf* 1953 $4.95; *Bantam* pap. $1.50

A SINGLE PEBBLE. *Knopf* 1956 $4.95; *Bantam* pap. $.75

THE WAR LOVER. *Knopf* 1959 $5.95

THE CHILD BUYER. *Knopf* 1960 $5.95; *Bantam* pap. $.95

WHITE LOTUS. *Knopf* 1965 $6.95; *Bantam* pap. $1.50

Too Far to Walk. *Knopf* 1966 $5.95

Under the Eye of the Storm. *Knopf* 1967 $4.95

The Conspiracy. *Knopf* 1970 $6.95; Bantam $1.50

Books about Hersey

John Hersey. By David Sanders. U.S. Authors Ser. *Twayne* 1967 $4.95; *College & Univ. Press* 1968 pap. $2.45

MALAMUD, BERNARD. 1914–

Most of Malamud's characters are impoverished American Jews, "because," he says, "I know them. But more important, I write about them because the Jews are absolutely the very *stuff* of drama." His Brooklyn, N.Y. childhood has influenced his work and most of his novels are set there. He began writing while in high school. He was graduated from the College of the City of New York and received his M.A. in English from Columbia. During the Depression he worked in factories, later for the U.S. Government, but since 1949 he has combined writing with teaching. He has been on the faculty of Bennington College, Vermont, since 1961. Herbert Gold (*q. v.*) has called Malamud's writings "lyric marvels . . . the headlong architectural daring of a great novelist. . . . His unrelenting pity for straining souls reminds us of Dostoevsky—if we can imagine Dostoevsky tempered by Chagall's lyric nostalgia for a lost Jewish past."

The idea for "The Fixer" originated in the case of Mendel Beiliss, a worker in a Kiev brickyard who was arrested in 1911 for the ritual murder of a Christian boy. Loosely based on the Beiliss case, the novel compels readers to feel for one man what they can't possibly feel for six million. Jailed unjustly for three years, Yakov Bok and his suffering represent "not only the martyrs of Belson and Auschwitz but all victims of man's inhumanity" (*SR*). Granville Hicks (in *SR*) found the novel "realistic in the most precise sense of that term. But the story is told so purely and with such power that it has the . . . 'universal' meanings of legend." Theodore Solotaroff describes it as "a book that one begins in skepticism and ends in amazement as its sustained power of moral perception and feeling: a vision of the hunger for social justice and personal integrity, written with great narrative force and in the heart's blood." Mr. Malamud eventually for the first time visited Kiev, the place he had written about for three years—and found that he had to change only one paragraph.

In his most recent novels Malamud has been concerned with the relation of art to life and love. Whereas the tone of "Pictures of Fidelman," a loosely constructed gathering of episodes in the life of an unsuccessful painter, is largely comic and satirical, "The Tenants" marks a return to the profound compassion found in works like "The Assistant" and "The Fixer." The story deals with two writers, one a Jew, the other a Black, who have staked out squatters' claims on an abandoned tenement on the east side of Manhattan. Against the hostility of the two writers Malamud juxtaposes their relationships with the principal feminine characters of the novel, showing how gentleness and love can go a long way toward breaking the barriers imposed by pride and isolation.

He received the Harry and Ethel Daroff Memorial Fiction Award for "The Assistant," the National Book Award for Fiction for both "The Magic Barrel" and "The Fixer"—the latter also received the 1967 Pulitzer Prize. He was elected a member of the National Institute of Arts and Letters in 1964.

A Malamud Reader. With introd. by Philip Rahv. *Farrar, Straus* 1967 $6.95 Noonday pap. $3.95. Includes The Assistant; 10 stories from Idiots First and The Magic Barrel; excerpts from The Natural, A New Life, and The Fixer.

The Natural. *Farrar, Straus* Noonday 1952 $5.95 Noonday pap. $1.95; Dell pap. $.75; *Pocket Bks.* pap. $1.25. First novel.

The Assistant. *Farrar, Straus* 1957 $6.95 Noonday pap. $2.25; *Dell* pap. $1.25; *New Am. Lib.* Signet pap. $.75

The Magic Barrel. *Farrar, Straus* 1958 $5.95 Noonday pap. $1.95; *Dell* 1966 pap. $.95; *Pocket Bks.* pap. $1.25. Short stories.

A New Life. *Farrar, Straus* 1961 $7.95; *Dell* pap. $.95

Idiots First. *Farrar, Straus* 1963 $6.95; *Dell* pap. $.75 Delta Bks. pap. $1.45 Short stories.

The Fixer. *Farrar, Straus* 1966 $6.95; *Dell* 1967 pap. $.95

Pictures of Fidelman. *Farrar, Straus* 1969 $5.95; *Dell* pap. $.95

The Tenants. *Farrar, Straus* 1971 $6.95; *Pocket Bks.* pap. $1.50

Rembrandt's Hat. *Farrar, Straus* 1971 $6.95

Books about Malamud

> Bernard Malamud. By Sidney Richman. U.S. Authors Ser. *Twayne* $4.95; *College & Univ. Press* 1967 pap. $2.45
> Bernard Malamud: An Annotated Checklist. By Rita N. Kosofsky. *Kent State Univ. Press* 1969 $4.25
> Bernard Malamud and the Critics. Ed. by Leslie A. and Joyce W. Field. *New York Univ. Press* 1970 $10.00 pap. $3.50

ELLISON, RALPH (WALDO). 1914–

Writer and teacher, Ralph Ellison was born in Oklahoma City, Okla., studied at Tuskegee Institute, and has lectured at New York, Columbia, and Fisk Universities and at Bard College. He received the Prix de Rome from the Academy of Arts and Letters in 1955, and in 1964 he was elected a member of the National Institute of Arts and Letters. He has contributed short stories and essays to various publications. "Invisible Man," his first novel, won the National Book Award for 1952 and is considered an impressive work. "Ellison's sensibility is unique and his novel is original—not because he has created a new form (in that sense he has written a traditional novel), but rather because he holds a view we have not known before, or only half knew, and because he has managed to penetrate to a heart of our society which we have hidden, or half hidden, from ourselves. It is a vision of the underground man who is also the invisible Negro, and its possessor has employed this subterranean view and viewer to so extraordinary an advantage that the impression of the novel is that of a pioneer work. This impression was corroborated by James Baldwin, who in *Notes of a Native Son* wrote, 'Mr. Ellison, by the way, is the first Negro novelist I have ever read to utilize in language, and brilliantly, some of the ambiguity and irony of Negro life' " (Harvey Breit, in "The Creative Present"). In 1964 appeared Mr. Ellison's book of essays, "Shadow and Act" (*Random* $8.95 Vintage Bks. pap. $1.95; *New Am. Lib.* Signet pap. $.95), which discuss the Negro in America and Mr. Ellison's Oklahoma boyhood, among other topics. He has been working on—and re-working—a second novel at intervals for the past ten years.

Invisible Man. *Random* 1952 $7.50 Vintage Bks. $1.95; *Modern Library* 1963 $2.95; *New Am. Lib.* Signet pap. $1.25

Books about Ellison

> Twentieth Century Interpretations of "Invisible Man." Ed. by John M. Reilly. *Prentice-Hall* 1970 $4.95; *Spectrum Bks.* pap. $1.45
> The Merrill Studies in "Invisible Man." Ed. by Ronald Gottesman. *Charles E. Merrill* 1971 pap. $1.75
> A Casebook on Ralph Ellison's "Invisible Man." Ed. by Joseph Trimmer. *T. Y. Crowell* 1972 pap. $3.95

BURROUGHS, WILLIAM S. (William Lee, pseud.). 1914–

"Mary McCarthy and Norman Mailer, representing the U.S. at the 1962 Edinburgh Festival, each told an astounded audience that the outstanding contemporary American writer was a man called William Burroughs. Most of those present had never heard of Mr. Burroughs, understandably, since his 'Naked Lunch' had . . . enjoyed publication only in Paris. . . . This is a unique book by an incredibly talented writer, but I am not sure that the communication of an emotive obscene disgust is worthy use of those talents, and the book communicates little else. . . . I don't share the extravagant opinions of McCarthy and Mailer but this is a book for literature collections"—(Eric Moon, in *LJ*). Under the name "William Lee," Burroughs (who was born in St. Louis, Mo.) wrote "Junkie," an account of his 15 years of experimenting with various kinds of drugs in many parts of the world. "Naked Lunch" explores drug addiction from a different point of view. It is written in a complex prose and consists of "episodes" which describe his hallucinations. He says in his introduction: "I awoke from 'The Sickness' at the age of forty-five calm and sane. . . . Most survivors do not remember the delirium in detail. I apparently took detailed notes on sickness and delirium. I have no precise memory of writing the notes, which have now been published under the title . . . suggested by Jack Kerouac. I did not understand exactly what the words say: NAKED Lunch—a frozen moment when everyone sees what is on the end of every fork. . . ."

Richard Kluger wrote in the *N.Y. Herald Tribune*: "Here is an American novelist writing in an existentialist idiom that proclaims the essential absurdity of life and reduces it to a flash series of cruel and often pointless charades. . . . Time and place and plot and character are all missing; yet none of this matters, by the standards invoked. What matters, as in all abstract art, are the effects created, and Burroughs' effects are stunning. He is a writer of rare power. . . . This paean to nihilism strikes me as more than the caterwaulings of a long-time addict."

"The Naked Lunch" was the first of what are now four books about the Nova crime syndicate. Eliot Fremont-Smith wrote in the *N.Y. Times*: "Of all the apocalyptic visions in recent writing, William Burroughs' have been the most shocking and instantly repellent. They have also been the most original. In four overlapping books—'Naked Lunch', 'Nova Express,' 'The Soft Machine' and 'The Ticket That Exploded'—Mr. Burroughs has brought back a vision of hell that in remorseless detail rivals only that of Hieronymus Bosch. . . . The whole resembles some putrid, pulsating, translucent, self-devouring vegetable of addictive erotic menace, death and evil. . . . Maybe—I can hear the caustic tone—one can get used to anything. But maybe, also, art does mirror reality, and maybe just in the nick of time." The novels have characters (Dr. Benway, the Subliminal Kid, Johnny Yen)—who overlap from one book to the next—and wild plots of sorts, sometimes involving the planet Venus and the other science-fiction elements which are less and less fiction these days.

JUNKIE. 1953. *Ace Bks.* pap. $.75

NAKED LUNCH. 1959. *Grove* 1962 Black Cat Bks. pap. $1.25

THE SOFT MACHINE. 1961. *Grove* 1966 Black Cat Bks. pap. $.95

THE TICKET THAT EXPLODED. 1962. *Grove* 1967 Black Cat Bks. pap. $1.25

NOVA EXPRESS. *Grove* 1964 Black Cat Bks. pap. $.95

THE WILD BOYS. *Grove* 1971 $5.95

(With Allen Ginsberg). THE YAGE LETTERS. Written to Allen Ginsberg from South America in 1953. *City Lights* (orig.) 1963 pap. $1.50

Books about Burroughs

The Job: Interviews with William Burroughs. By Daniel Odier. *Grove* 1970 $5.95

STAFFORD, JEAN. 1915–

Jean Stafford's first novel, "Boston Adventure," attracted the attention of the discriminating, and with her second, "The Mountain Lion," she became known for her "sensitive perception, attention to detail, and ability to understand the anxieties of childhood." "The Catherine Wheel" (1952, o. p.) brought her a much larger reading public. *Commonweal* said of it: "Jean Stafford writes, as ever, with an eye to all the implications and resources of the language; her endowments of style, sensibility and imagination, and her rare ability to invest experience with moral value, diminish even the most distinguished of her contemporaries." Many of her short stories have been published in the *New Yorker*. Her "Bad Characters" are "usually eccentric [but] nevertheless very much alive. Loneliness, frustrated idealism and thwarted love are recurrent themes"—(*LJ*). "A Mother in History" (*Farrar, Straus* 1966 $3.95) is a series of interviews with the mother of Lee Harvey Oswald.

Miss Stafford's father was a writer of Western stories. She was born in Covina, Calif., and the family later moved to Colorado, where she took her M.A. degree at the University of Colorado. Her first husband was the Boston poet Robert Lowell. In 1955 she received first prize for her short story "In the Zoo," published in "Prize Stories: The O. Henry Awards."

COLLECTED STORIES. *Farrar, Straus* 1969 $10.00 pap. $2.95

BOSTON ADVENTURE. 1944. *Harcourt* $4.95 pap. $.95

THE MOUNTAIN LION. *Farrar, Straus* 1947 1972 $6.95

BAD CHARACTERS. Short stories. *Farrar, Straus* 1964 $4.95

BELLOW, SAUL. 1915–

Saul Bellow's world "is distinctively a world of his own—in style, in speculative intelligence, in the anguish of its feeling and the conscious buffoonery of its wit"—(Alfred Kazin, in "Contemporaries"). "Muted or released, his language is never dull or merely expedient, but always moves under tension, toward or away from a kind of rich crazy poetry, a juxtaposition of high and low style, elegance and slang. . . . Implicit in the direction of his style is a desire to encompass a world larger, richer, more disorderly and untrammelled than that of any other writer of his generation"—(Leslie A. Fiedler, in "On Contemporary Literature"). Bellow's characters are in general modern intellectuals struggling for a rationale—sensitive, bewildered, inclined to self-abasement. Herzog is such a one. In a *Paris Review* interview Mr. Bellow said, "To me a significant theme of 'Herzog' is the imprisonment of the individual in a shameful and impotent privacy. He feels humiliated by it, and he comes to realize at last what he considered his intellectual 'privilege' has proved to be another form of bondage." "Herzog" won the 1965 National Book Award and the International Literature Prize—the latter as "the work of fiction that will have the most significant influence on the literature of our time." In 1954 Mr. Bellow had received the National Book Award for his first major novel, "The Adventures of Augie March," the lively tale of a kind of "Chicago Tom Jones" (Albert Guérard). And in 1960 he won the Friends of Literature Award for "Henderson the Rain King," a tragicomic fantasy about a Connecticut Yankee millionaire who is searching for a personal philosophy. Mr. Bellow has written several plays, including "The Last Analysis" in 1964 (*Viking* 1965 $3.50 Compass Bks. pap. 1966 $1.85) but has not yet achieved popular or critical success as a dramatist.

Born in a small town in Quebec, of Russian parents, Saul Bellow moved with his family to Chicago when he was nine, attended the universities of Chicago, Northwestern and Wisconsin. "Augie" changed from "a grim book, in the spirit of the first two" to its author's original "favorite fantasy" while he was in Paris in 1948 on a Guggenheim Fellowship. He has taught and lectured at the University of Minnesota, N.Y.U., Princeton, Bard College and the University of Chicago.

THE DANGLING MAN. 1944. First novel. *New Am. Lib.* Signet pap. $.75; *Vanguard* $5.95

THE VICTIM. 1947. *New Am. Lib.* Signet pap. $.95; *Vanguard* $6.95

THE ADVENTURES OF AUGIE MARCH. *Viking* 1953 $6.00 Compass Bks. 1960 pap. $2.95; *Fawcett* Premier Bks. pap. $1.25

SEIZE THE DAY. A novella, three short stories, and a one-act play. *Viking* 1956 $3.00 Compass Bks. 1961 pap. $1.25; *Fawcett* Crest Bks. pap. $.75

HENDERSON THE RAIN KING. *Viking* 1959 Compass Bks. pap. $1.95; *Fawcett* Crest Bks. pap. $.95

HERZOG. *Viking* 1964 $6.00 Compass Bks. pap. $2.00; *Fawcett* Crest Bks. pap. $1.25

MOSBY'S MEMOIRS AND OTHER STORIES. *Viking* 1968 $5.00; *Fawcett* Premier Bks. pap. $.95

MISTER SAMMLER'S PLANET. *Viking* 1970 $6.95; *Fawcett* Crest Bks. pap. $1.25

Books about Bellow

Saul Bellow: In Defense of Man. By John J. Clayton. *Indiana Univ. Press* 1961 $7.50 pap. $2.95. First extended study.
Saul Bellow. By Earl Rovit. Pamphlets on American Writers. *Univ. of Minnesota Press* 1967 pap. $.95
The Novels of Saul Bellow: An Introduction. By Keith Opdahl. *Pennsylvania State Univ. Press* 1967 $7.50. A discussion of his fiction in terms of its relevance to the doubts and problems of our time.
Saul Bellow and the Critics. Ed. by Irving Malin. Essays by Fiedler, Aldrige, Geismar, and others. *New York Univ. Press* 1967 $7.95 pap. $1.95
Saul Bellow. By R. R. Dutton. U.S. Authors Ser. *Twayne* 1971 $4.95
Saul Bellow: A Comprehensive Bibliography. By B. A. Sokoloff. *Folcroft* 1972 lim. ed. $12.50

PERCY, WALKER. 1916–

Walker Percy's witty, provocative, and perceptive first novel, "The Moviegoer" won the 1962 National Book Award. The professional training of this writer from Birmingham, Ala., was medicine; he holds an M.D. from Columbia. "The Moviegoer," with its New Orleans ambience, is a "static, reflective, strange but beautiful [love] story [that cuts] through layers of soft dreams and crusty realities to discover in one man's soul the core of compassion"—(*Commonweal*). Charles Poore considers "The Last Gentleman" "an even better book." Its protagonist is Williston Bibb Barret—an amnesiac Southerner who has dropped out of life—at least until, through his telescope, he sees a beautiful girl walking in New York's Central Park. His adventures—in search of himself—with her and her family are the substance of the novel. Gradually, through passages of superb writing, Will Barret arrives at his own sense of identity. "Love in the Ruins" marks a sharp change in method and subject from the first two novels. A Doomsday story set "at the end of the Auto Age," it exposes many foibles and abuses in contemporary life through sharp satire and extravagant fantasy.

THE MOVIEGOER. *Knopf* 1961 $6.95; *Farrar, Straus* Noonday 1967 pap. $1.95

THE LAST GENTLEMAN. *Farrar, Straus* 1966 $7.50 Noonday $2.95; *New Am. Lib.* 1968 Signet pap. $.95

LOVE IN THE RUINS. The Adventures of a Bad Catholic at a Time Near the End of the World. *Farrar, Straus* 1971 $7.95; *Dell* pap. $1.50

Books about Percy

The Sovereign Wayfarer: Walker Percy's Diagnosis of the Malaise. By Martin Luschei. *Louisiana State Univ. Press* 1972 $10.00

POWERS, J(AMES) F(ARL). 1917–

"Powers is among the greatest of living storytellers," said Frank O'Connor—and his modest production has been chiefly in the medium of the short story. He has contributed to the *New Yorker* and other magazines. Early in his career he wrote with anger at the plight of the Negro as well as his own humiliation during the Depression at being forced to accept jobs as salesclerk and insurance salesman. Later, although "neither a determined and conscious apologist for the church of Rome, nor blindly revolting against her" (*SR*), he found his subject in the lives of priests and their parishes, which he has treated with gentle irony.

The *New Yorker* called "Prince of Darkness" (1947, o. p.), his first collection, "varied and fresh stories, written in delightfully firm and straightforward prose, in which Mr. Powers proves that he has few rivals at creating characters with more than superficial reality." The *N.Y. Times* said of "Presence of Grace," "J. F. Powers is a largely endowed, careful and important short-story writer, one of the best in America. Some of the nine stories in his new collection are distinguished by a high astringent hilarity, and some are filled with terror and pity." His first novel, "Morte d'Urban," won him the 1963 National Book Award. Father Urban, an activist, is dismayed to find himself transferred to a small Minnesota community, and the story comes on from there through his hopes, aspirations, and disappointments. "The prose is clear, lean, and supple: it is the work of a master who has achieved virtuosity.... The gaiety of his wit ... is pertinent here because *Morte d'Urban* could have been better, even savage, in its ridicule of a certain kind of priest"—(*Commonweal*).

THE PRESENCE OF GRACE. 1956. *Atheneum* 1962 pap. $1.25; *Bks. for Libraries* $7.75

MORTE D'URBAN. 1962. *Popular Lib.* pap. $.60

Books about Powers

J. F. Powers. By John V. Hagopian. U.S. Authors Ser. *Twayne* 1968 $4.95; *College & Univ. Press* pap. $2.45

AUCHINCLOSS, LOUIS (STANTON). (Andrew Lee, pseud.) 1917–

Louis Auchincloss, lawyer and writer, followed in his family's solid tradition, attending Groton, Yale (where he edited the *Yale Lit*), and then the University of Virginia Law School. As a product of the war years, during which he served with the Atlantic and Pacific amphibious forces, he wrote his first published novel, "The Indifferent Children," (1947, o. p.) which was very well received. He continues to write—both short stories and novels—and to practice law. Angus Wilson has called Auchincloss a "clever and subtle student of human social behaviour." "Portrait in Brownstone" tells the story of the Denison family of 53rd Street, New York City, in the period 1901–51, from the points of view of the five major characters. "Powers of Attorney," 12 sharply pointed short stories, all of them set in and around a New York City law firm, takes place in "the 'real world' of the law, of business, of the Social Register, of love, of human character and relations [and is] a very literate and polished kind of entertainment" (*N.Y. Times*). The *New Yorker* calls "The Rector of Justin," about a New England preparatory school, "a model novel; ... poise and taste and intelligence strike one on every page as [does Mr. Auchincloss's] unerring knowledge and literary skill." "The Embezzler" examines the life of a man of high social prestige who misappropriates funds during the Depression and tells his tale in three "overlapping and mutually contradictory versions that create patterns of ambiguity.... The result is a tantalizing psychological and moral mystery of human motivation" (*Newsweek*). The 14 stories that comprise "Tales of Manhattan" all touch "the world of wealth, power, and social distinction that Auchincloss has made peculiarly his" (*SR*). "I Come as a Thief," his most recent novel, is a compelling story about a handsome and popular young New York politician who, like a reverse sort of Faust, insists on sacrificing his family and his career to his need to confess that he has taken a bribe. "Reflections of a Jacobite" (1961. *Kelley* $10.00) is a "most attractive and discerning collection of literary essays," in "nostalgic admiration of the nineteenth and early twentieth-century novel of manners, a kind of fiction . . . having as its essential common denominator 'a clearly defined class feeling.' " Mr. Auchincloss has also written three *University of Minnesota Press* Pamphlets on American Writers, "Edith Wharton" (1961 pap. $.95), "Ellen Glasgow" (1964 pap. $.95), and "Henry Adams" (1971 pap. $.95). Other critical works include "Pioneers and Caretakers: A Study of Nine American Women Novelists" (*Univ. of Minnesota Press* 1965 $5.95), a study of Shakespeare called "Motiveless Malignity" (*Houghton* 1969 $5.00), and "Edith Wharton: A Woman in Her Time" (*Viking* Studio Bks. 1971 $10.00).

THE INJUSTICE COLLECTORS. *Houghton* 1950 $4.50

SYBIL. 1952. *Avon* pap. $.95; *Greenwood* $11.50

A LAW FOR THE LION. *Houghton* 1953 $5.00; *Avon* $.95

THE GREAT WORLD AND TIMOTHY COLT. *Houghton* 1956 $4.95

THE PURSUIT OF THE PRODIGAL. 1959 *Avon* pap. $.95

THE HOUSE OF FIVE TALENTS. *Houghton* 1960 $6.00; *Avon* pap. $1.25

PORTRAIT IN BROWNSTONE. *Houghton* 1962 $4.95

POWERS OF ATTORNEY: Twelve Stories. *Houghton* 1963 $5.95; *Avon* pap. $.95

THE RECTOR OF JUSTIN. *Houghton* 1964 $4.95

THE EMBEZZLER. *Houghton* 1966 $4.95

TALES OF MANHATTAN. *Houghton* 1967 $4.95; *Popular Lib.* 1968 pap. $.95. Short stories.

A WORLD OF PROFIT. 1968. *Lanewood* $7.50; *Popular Lib.* pap. $.75. About the powerful Shallcross family and its financial ups and downs.

SECOND CHANCE: Tales of Two Generations. *Houghton* 1970 $5.95; *Popular Lib.* pap. $.75

I COME AS A THIEF. *Houghton* 1972 $6.95; *Avon* 1973 pap. $1.50; *Hall* lg.-type ed. $8.95

McCULLERS, CARSON (SMITH). 1917–1967.

"The Heart is a Lonely Hunter" was a strange and remarkable first novel by a young Georgia woman—"at times almost miraculous in its concise intensity, at times baffling in its meandering immaturity"—(Lewis Gannett, in *The Boston Transcript*). Richard Wright (*q. v.*) wrote of "the astonishing humanity that enables a white writer, for the first time in Southern fiction, to handle Negro characters with as much ease and justice as those of her own race." Its chief character is a deaf mute. "Reflections in a Golden Eye" is the domestic tragedy of an army officer in a Southern camp in peacetime. "The Member of the Wedding," a "brilliant evocation of childhood longings and sorrow," is a psychological study of a 12-year-old girl. The play of the same title, produced in 1950, won the N.Y. Drama Critics Circle Award for the best American play of the year and the Donaldson Award for the best play of the period. Her second play, "Square Root of Wonderful" (*Houghton* 1958 $3.00) was not as well received. Her novella "The Ballad of the Sad Café" (adapted by Edward Albee *Atheneum-Houghton* 1963 $4.95 pap. $2.65) as produced on Broadway, turned her strange, tender "prose poem into a play flecked with weird, halting poetry. It treats of the nature of love and the burden it lays on the lover in relation to an odd triangle—an ox of a woman, a voluptuary of a dwarf and an ex-convict" (*N.Y. Times*). "Clock Without Hands" (1961, o. p.) is a perceptive and poignant study of the change in Southern mores as seen in the actions and thoughts of two men and two adolescents—one a Negro. She wrote it as a tribute to the 1954 Supreme Court decision declaring public school segregation unconstitutional.

Mrs. McCullers wrote seriously from the age of 16. She was born in Columbus, Ga., and after "finishing high school very early" she waited for two years before going to New York where she studied at intervals at

Columbia and New York University. *Story* bought two of her first short stories. In 1943 she received an award from the American Academy of Arts and Letters. "Though her fiction rarely leaves the bounds of a closed southern world, Mrs. McCullers has steadily acquired an international reputation, with French and English critics ranking her close to Faulkner and Hemingway" ("The Creative Present"). Mrs. McCullers fought gallantly throughout the mature years of her short life against the pain and debility resulting from a series of strokes. On her death Ralph McGill wrote a moving tribute to her in the *Saturday Review* of Oct. 21, 1967, which ends: "I think Carson was one of the two or three best Southern writers. She belongs with Faulkner. Health did not allow her to come near the Mississippian's magnificent output, but in quality she ranks with him, and in sensitivity to and interpretation of the juxtaposition of loneliness and love she excels. Carson would not care for comparisons. She was what she was. If bad luck restricted her work, that was just bad luck. She was a very great artist and human being. Let it go at that."

COLLECTED SHORT STORIES AND THE BALLAD OF THE SAD CAFÉ. *Houghton* 1962 $5.95

BALLAD OF THE SAD CAFÉ AND OTHER STORIES. *Bantam* 1967 pap. $.95

THE MORTGAGED HEART: The Previously Uncollected Writings of Carson McCullers. Ed. by Margarita Smith. *Houghton* 1971 $7.95; *Bantam* $1.95

THE HEART IS A LONELY HUNTER. 1940. *Houghton* $4.95; *Bantam* 1953 1967 pap. $1.25

REFLECTIONS IN A GOLDEN EYE. *Houghton* 1941 $4.50; *Bantam* 1953 1961 pap. $.95

THE MEMBER OF THE WEDDING: A Play. 1946. *Houghton* $4.95; *Bantam* 1962 pap. $.75; *New Directions* 1951 1963 pap. $1.50

Books about McCullers

Carson McCullers. By Lawrence Graver. Pamphlets on American Writers. *Univ. of Minnesota Press* 1969 pap. $.95

ELLIOTT, GEORGE (PAUL). 1918–

George P. Elliott became known for his disturbing and sometimes shocking stories published first in literary quarterlies and in anthologies. *Library Journal* said of "Among the Dangs": "George Elliott's technique is expert, his handling of dialogue sure, he breathes life into situations which range from the ordinary to the bizarre, and his imagination is unfettered.... The book reveals a talent of the first rank." His first novel, "Parktilden Village" (1958, o. p.), reported Irving Howe (in the *New Republic*), "is fluently written and except for some flashy wisecracks, yields pleasure sentence by sentence, insight by insight." The narrator of "David Knudsen" (1962, o. p.) is "the son of one of the physicists who made the atom bomb." "Here is a novel as brilliantly evocative of the mushroom-clouded mid-century as 'The Great Gatsby' was (and is) of the 20's" (Eric Moon, in *LJ*). In "An Hour of Last Things and Other Stories" (1968, o. p.) some of the "last things" are love and dignity and death. "In the World" (1965, o. p.), a novel, is a "whopper of a book which is nothing less than an examination of American society itself, its manners and morals, its values and confusions—with the law as the focus of these.... Not one for the casual reader, but it should certainly be on the library shelves for all who seek something more than light diversion from fiction." So wrote Eric Moon (in *LJ*), who found "In the World" also "a pretty long haul" and a little "flat. Not by any means dull, but flat." With "Muriel," however, it became apparent that much of the flatness of Elliott's recent fiction could be deliberate. The story of a possessive woman, her husband, and two children, it spans four decades and is written in a spare style with cliché-ridden dialogue in order to suggest the deadly mediocrity of life in those families of small-town America which practice a rigid and joyless adherence to the conventional

Elliott was born in Knightstown, Ind. He taught English and writing at a number of colleges and writers' workshops before accepting an appointment as Professor of English at Syracuse University in 1963. He has published two volumes of somewhat audacious personal and critical essays—"A Piece of Lettuce" (1964, o. p.) and "Conversions" (*Dutton* 1971 $7.95; *Dell* Delta Bks. pap. $2.45)—and has edited several textbook anthologies of literature.

AMONG THE DANGS. 1961. *Viking* Compass Bks. 1961 pap. $1.45. A collection of 10 short stories.

MURIEL. *Dutton* 1972 $5.95

SALINGER, J(EROME) D(AVID). 1919–

J. D. Salinger was born in New York City of Jewish and Scotch-Irish extraction. He attended Manhattan public schools, a military academy in Pennsylvania and three colleges (no degrees). "A happy tourist's year in Europe," he wrote in 1955, "when I was eighteen and nineteen. In the Army from '42 to '46, most of the time with the Fourth Division. . . . I've been writing since I was fifteen or so. My short stories have appeared in a number of magazines over the last ten years, mostly—and most happily—in the *New Yorker*. I worked on 'The Catcher in the Rye,' on and off, for ten years"—("Twentieth Century Authors"). "Remarkable and absorbing . . . profoundly moving . . . magic," Harrison Smith called this story of a modern 16-year-old boy's three days of wandering in New York after being dropped from his school—(in *SR*). "The Catcher" has been an extremely popular book among young people ever since its appearance and has brought Salinger an international reputation. Donald Barr has commented on his ability "to correspond peculiarly to the psychological aura of our moment of history." "Franny and Zooey" is composed of two long *New Yorker* stories which appeared in 1955 and 1957, recording a significant weekend in the lives of Franny Glass, a troubled twenty-year-old college student, and her brother Zooey, a television actor. "Raise High the Roof Beam, Carpenters" is another story of the Glass family. There are seven Glass children, "two of whom are now dead and all of whom were child prodigies."

Since 1953 "he has secluded himself in a one-story house in Cornish, N.H., writing his stories and books in an adjoining skylit concrete cell. . . . Soon after the war, as an habitué of Greenwich Village, he discovered Zen. Possibly under the influence of this oriental philosophy, and because he was now completely absorbed in his writing, he began a series of withdrawals. He lived for a time in Tarrytown, then in Westport, Conn., and finally retired to Cornish, where even his closest neighbors do not know him"—("The Creative Present"). Unfortunately, Salinger's withdrawal has not led to increased creativity. As of early 1974 his years of seclusion since 1963 had produced only silence, and his critical reputation, which peaked in the early sixties, has suffered accordingly. Little has been written about Salinger in recent years. "The Catcher in the Rye," however, remains a standard text in high school and college classrooms, and a loyal following of readers continue to hope for a continuation of the Glass family saga. They feel that when and if that work is completed, it will be one of the masterworks of 20th-century fiction.

NINE STORIES. *Little* 1953 $5.95; *Bantam* pap. $1.25

THE CATCHER IN THE RYE. *Little* 1951 $5.95; *Bantam* pap. $1.25; *Franklin Watts* 1967 lg. type ed. Keith Jennison Bks. $8.95

FRANNY AND ZOOEY. *Little* 1961 $5.95; *Bantam* 1964 pap. $1.50

RAISE HIGH THE ROOF BEAM, CARPENTERS AND SEYMOUR, AN INTRODUCTION. Two Novellas. *Little* 1963 $5.95; *Bantam* 1965 pap. $1.50

Books about Salinger

The Fiction of J. D. Salinger. By Frederick L. Gwynn and Joseph L. Blotner. 1958. *Univ. of Pittsburgh Press* 1959 $1.95
J. D. Salinger and the Critics. Ed. by W. F. Belcher and J. W. Lee. *Wadsworth* 1962 pap. $2.95
Salinger: A Critical and Personal Portrait. Ed. by Henry A. Grunwald. *Harper* 1962 $5.95 pap. $2.45. Essays by Kazin, Mizener, Updike, Hicks, Geismar, Fiedler and others.
J. D. Salinger. By Warren French. *Twayne* 1963 $4.95; *College & Univ. Press* 1964 pap. $2.45. A critical study.
Studies in J. D. Salinger. Ed. by Marvin Laser and Norman Fruman. *Odyssey* 1963 pap. $2.45. Reviews, essays, and critiques of The Catcher in the Rye and other fiction.
J. D. Salinger. By James E. Miller. Pamphlets on American Writers. *Univ. of Minnesota Press* 1965 pap. $.95

CASSILL, R(ONALD) V(ERLIN). 1919–

The career of R. V. Cassill might provide a kind of object lesson for aspiring writers. His first novel, "The Eagle on the Coin" (1950, o. p.) is the story of an ill-fated attempt by a group of liberals to get a Negro elected to the school board of a small midwestern city. Unfortunately, this novel on a serious theme made little impact on critics or the public, and Cassill during the next decade found it necessary to follow two distinctly different literary paths. While his right hand, so to speak, was composing artistic short stories for little magazines such as *Accent* and *Western Review*, his left hand was turning out at least ten paperback originals with titles like "Lustful Summer" and "Dormitory Women" for such publishers as *Ace*, *Avon*, and *Fawcett* Gold Medal. His next serious novel did not appear until 1961. Of that work, he has written (in "Contemporary

Novelists"): "In 'Clem Anderson' I took the silhouette of Dylan Thomas's life and within that composed the story of an American poet's self-destructive triumph. It probably is and always will be my most embattled work, simply because in its considerable extent it replaces most of the comfortable or profitable clichés about an artist's life with tougher and more painful diagrams." Beginning with "Pretty Leslie," the story of an amoral girl from Cassill's native state of Iowa, he began to pull together the separate strands of his literary apprenticeship by combining his strong interest in sexual themes with the penetrating psychological insights of his more serious fiction. He almost came untracked with "The President," a competent but not especially distinguished academic novel, and "La Vie Passionée of Rodney Buckthorne" (1968, o. p.), a somewhat uncomfortable attempt at farce and black humor. But with "Doctor Cobb's Game" Cassill produced a work successful on both the artistic and the popular levels. Based on the Profumo scandals in England, this best-selling novel is a carefully and elaborately structured work which interweaves sexual, political, and occult themes to form a work that is both entertaining and philosophically rewarding.

Cassill has taught writing at the University of Iowa, Purdue University, and, since 1967, at Brown University. The recipient of Rockefeller and Guggenheim grants, he served as editor for Bantam's series of "Intro" books of new college writing, and some of his essays are collected in "In An Iron Time: Statements and Reiterations" (*Purdue Univ. Studies* 1969 $4.95).

CLEM ANDERSON. *Simon & Schuster* 1961 $5.95; *Avon* 1970 pap. $1.25

PRETTY LESLIE. *Simon & Schuster* 1963 $4.95

THE PRESIDENT. *Simon & Schuster* 1964 $4.95

THE HAPPY MARRIAGE AND OTHER STORIES. *Purdue Univ. Studies* 1967 $3.50

DOCTOR COBB'S GAME. *Geis* 1970 $7.95

JACKSON, SHIRLEY. 1919–1965.

Orville Prescott called Shirley Jackson "a literary sorceress of uncanny prowess," and said in the *N.Y. Times* that she "has always been an original who walks by herself. There is magic in her books, and baffling magic some of it is too. As a storyteller, she is expert, deft in suggesting emotional atmosphere and adroit in conveying nuances of feeling. Her characters may be bizarre and involved in terrifying circumstances, but they are convincing." John Barkman wrote (in *SR*) of the "verbal word-spinning" with which she beguiles her readers, her "artful use of words and images to create just the right mood of isolation and foreboding. . . . This is atmospheric word-weaving of a high order." Her novels and stories contain a "strong element of the fantastic and terrifying . . . supernatural happenings, or the eerie phenomena of morbid mental states, occur disturbingly against the most ordinary backgrounds, among the most ordinary people." A number of her stories have been anthologized and dramatized for television and radio, among them "The Lottery," a chilling fable not unrelated to tendencies in any village or town, which first appeared in the *New Yorker* in 1948. In it a community holds an annual lottery to determine which resident will be stoned to death.

Miss Jackson was born in San Francisco and spent most of her early life in California. She once wrote: "I was married in 1940 to Stanley Edgar Hyman, critic and numismatist, and we live in Vermont, in a quiet rural community with fine scenery and comfortably far away from city life. Our major supports are books and children, both of which we produce in abundance." She died there before her time. Her two autobiographical books, "Life Among the Savages," which she called "a disrespectful memoir of my children" (1953. *Scholastic Bk. Services* Starline pap. $.75) and "Raising Demons" (1957. *Scholastic Bk. Services* Starline pap. $.75) "offer a humorous chronicle of the life of middle-class intellectual family in a small New England town." (Unattributed quotations are from *The Reader's Encyclopedia of American Literature*.)

THE MAGIC OF SHIRLEY JACKSON. Ed. with introd. by Stanley E. Hyman. *Farrar, Straus* 1966 $12.95 pap. $3.95. Includes the Birds Nest, Life Among the Savages, Raising Demons, and 11 short stories.

THE LOTTERY. 1949. Short story. *Avon Bks.* pap. $.95

THE HAUNTING OF HILL HOUSE. *Viking* 1959 $7.95; *Popular Lib.* pap. $.75

WE HAVE ALWAYS LIVED IN THE CASTLE. *Viking* 1962 Compass Bks. pap. $1.95 lg.-type ed. $6.95; *Popular Lib.* $.75

COME ALONG WITH ME. Ed. by Stanley E. Hyman. 1968. *Popular Lib.* pap. $.75

SPENCER, ELIZABETH. 1921–

One of the best Southern regionalist writers (she was born in Mississippi and has lived much of her life there), Elizabeth Spencer has come to be known for her "fine, finished, beautifully controlled writing." Her short stories have appeared in a number of publications and been anthologized in "A New Southern Harvest," "Stories from the New Yorker 1950–1960," and the "O. Henry Prize Stories 1960." "No two ways about it," Brendan Gill said in the *New Yorker*, " 'The Voice at the Back Door' . . . is a practically perfect novel. Miss Spencer has a thrilling story to tell and she tells it quickly and modestly, never raising her voice and never slurring a syllable." "The Voice at the Back Door" won the Rosenthal Award of the American Academy of Arts and Sciences and the Kenyon Review Fiction Fellowship. "The Light in the Piazza," her novella about Americans in Florence, was first published in shorter form in the *New Yorker*. "The peculiar quality of Florence permeates the book, and the spirit of the city is a force in the story. . . . The subtlety with which Miss Spencer makes the most of her little story reminds one of Henry James, but the spirit of the book is perhaps closer to E. M. Forster. . . . She combines great artistry with what Lionel Trilling calls moral intelligence. And the result is a work that is as strong as it is delicate"—(Granville Hicks, in *Saturday Review*).

"Fire in the Morning," her first novel, now reissued, is a story of father and son in the South, and the family tensions in which they are involved. *Harper's* wrote of it: "Miss Spencer's writing is so sure and compelling, her perceptions so acute, and her sense of construction so dramatic and exciting that the book gains momentum from the very start. It is a real literary achievement, and as a first novel, extraordinary." "This Crooked Way" concerns a farm boy in the Mississippi Delta and his climb to ill-used power. Lewis Gannett wrote of it in the *N.Y. Herald Tribune*: "She casts a spell over the reader as well as over her characters. A rich-textured and rewarding novel." "Knights and Dragons" is a "slight" novella (*LJ*) about Americans in Europe in which the atmosphere of Rome and Venice are admirably conveyed. Carlos Baker (in the *N.Y. Times*), though he found Miss Spencer's "manipulation of time sequences" trying, says of "No Place for an Angel": "Earth is no place for angels, or devils either. It is the habitat of that curious mélange of demonic and angelic that we call the human. This, or something like it, is the burden of Elizabeth Spencer's wise and intricate new novel. It is carried out through the internal history of a pair of American marriages." Granville Hicks wrote of it (in *SR*): "Nothing she has previously done is as good."

In "Ship Island and Other Stories" Miss Spencer "dips her pen variously in acid, mercury, moonlight and 100-proof alcohol. . . . Here is a vanishing South, lovingly but sharply recalled, a 'sort of permanent landscape of the heart' " (*PW*). Miss Spencer has spent much time abroad and now lives with her husband, John Rusher, in Montreal.

FIRE IN THE MORNING. 1948. *McGraw-Hill* 1968 $6.95

THIS CROOKED WAY. 1952. *McGraw-Hill* 1968 $5.95

THE VOICE AT THE BACK DOOR. *McGraw-Hill* 1956 $5.95

THE LIGHT IN THE PIAZZA. *McGraw-Hill* 1960 $4.95 pap. $1.95

KNIGHTS AND DRAGONS. *McGraw-Hill* 1965 $3.95

NO PLACE FOR AN ANGEL. *McGraw-Hill* 1967 $5.95

SHIP ISLAND AND OTHER STORIES. *McGraw-Hill* 1968 $5.95

THE SNARE. *McGraw.* 1972 $7.95

JONES, JAMES. 1921–

Illinois-born James Jones' great accomplishment was the writing of his two books about American Army life—"From Here to Eternity" and "The Thin Red Line"—the first a brutal, almost ugly picture of the peacetime Army in Hawaii, the second "a kind of companion piece which describes the Guadalcanal campaign—a 'victorious' come-back in the Pacific which took a terrible toll of human lives." "From Here to Eternity" aroused a critical storm, "many deploring the lurid language and shocking incidents, others admiring its vitality and force"—(quotations from *The Reader's Encyclopedia of American Literature*). It was an immediate best seller, was selected for the National Book Award, and was made into a successful film in 1953. It was remarkable "precisely because it was so original, personal and deeply experienced; it was altogether new in our literature, and there is no other novel like it in our national letters."

Reviewing "The Thin Red Line" for the front page of the *N.Y. Times Book Review*, Maxwell Geismar wrote: "This new novel is going to be attacked and abused for its blunt language, its physical 'vulgarity,' its unrelenting naturalism, its 'low view' of human behavior. In the end, I think, it will be rated as another epic chronicle of the average American citizen undergoing the inferno of modern warfare. . . . The special magic of Jones as a writer is that, discarding all the clichés and slogans of patriotism, of heroism and of war itself, remaining so absolutely honest about his theme, he yet manages to make these typical American fighting men both universally human, and exceptional. "The Thin Red Line' is an experience. And it also proves that 'From Here to Eternity' was no fluke. James Jones would hardly like to be called an 'artist,' but he is one of great distinction." "Go to the Widow-Maker," about a civilian's effort to prove his masculinity and courage in skindiving and shark shooting, was generally poorly received. Wilfrid Sheed commented in the *Atlantic* on his "wooden and undifferentiated" dialogue and "pulp-fiction prose." *Library Journal* shared the general feeling and called it "tedious," but said that "the book does contain sections of rugged power." Its language is outspoken—tough and frank in the modern manner. Jones, who has lived in Paris during recent years, was on the scene at the time of the Students' Rebellion. His "The Merry Month of May" is a novelized version of those events. His most recent novel, "A Touch of Danger," is a straightforward thriller in the manner of the tough-guy novelists of the thirties.

FROM HERE TO ETERNITY. *Scribner* 1951 $9.95; *New Am. Lib.* Signet 1954 pap. $1.50

SOME CAME RUNNING. 1958. *New Am. Lib.* Signet 1959 abr. ed. pap. $1.75; *Pocket Bks.* pap. $1.75

THE PISTOL. 1959. *Dell* Laurel Eds. pap. $1.25

THE THIN RED LINE. *Scribner* 1962 $8.95; *New Am. Lib.* Signet 1964 pap. $1.25

GO TO THE WIDOW-MAKER. *Delacorte* 1967 $7.50 pap. $1.29; *Dell* Laurel Eds. pap. $1.25

THE ICE-CREAM HEADACHE AND OTHER STORIES. *Delacorte* 1968 $5.00; *Dell* Laurel Eds. pap. $.95. 13 stories and a novella.

THE MERRY MONTH OF MAY. *Delacorte* 1971 $7.95; *Dell* pap. $1.25

A TOUCH OF DANGER. *Doubleday* 1973 $7.95

GADDIS, WILLIAM. 1922–

William Gaddis ranks with Henry Roth and Ralph Ellison as one of the few 20th-century writers to establish a firm reputation on the basis of but a single novel. "The Recognitions" baffled and angered most of its initial reviewers, but in the years since its publication it has slowly, steadily attracted a growing number of enthusiastic readers willing to work their way through its more than 900 dense and demanding pages. Its length and encyclopedic complexity have caused some to hail it as the American "Ulysses," but whereas Joyce's novel is centered in one place within a single 22-hour period, "The Recognitions" ranges widely from New York and New England to France, Spain, and Italy, and it covers a wider expanse of time. Its central figure, Wyatt, is a painter who having been told in youth by a Calvinistic aunt that "Our Lord is the only true creator, and only sinful people try to emulate him" finds his natural talent misdirected away from original creation towards the forging of masterpieces by the Old Masters. Scores of other characters appear and reappear in the immense design of the novel, and almost all of them have in common with Wyatt the fact that they are forgers, imposters, counterfeiters, and plagiarists, for "The Recognitions" is essentially about the nature of reality and creativity. "Perhaps it is the very profundity of Gaddis's achievement that appals," writes Robert Nye (in "Contemporary Novelists"), "for at the heart of this giant book . . . lies a seemingly urgent intuition of the improbable nature of reality, expressing in a dozen different ways the feeling that what we perceive as the 'real' world is itself quite possibly counterfeit, and that we therefore somehow plagiarize ourselves by living. It is a formidable idea, but Gaddis shows he has the technique and seriousness to meet it."

THE RECOGNITIONS. *Harcourt* 1955 $8.50 1970 pap. $4.95

HARRIS, MARK. 1922–

Mark Harris worked as a reporter for several papers and magazines from New York to St. Louis during the mid-1940s before attending college at the University of Denver and going on to the University of Minnesota for a Ph.D. in American Studies. His fiction reflects his knowledge of many regions of America and his interest in diverse aspects of our national culture from sports to politics. He is best known for his baseball trilogy—"The Southpaw" (1953, o. p.), "Bang the Drum Slowly," and "A Ticket for a Seamstitch" (1957, o. p.) These comic and poignant stories are told in Lardneresque dialect as if narrated by Henry A. Wiggin, ace pitcher for the New York Mammoth Baseball Club. The best of the three books is "Bang the Drum Slowly," a bittersweet tale of a dying, inarticulate catcher, which was successfully adapted in a 1973 movie scripted by Harris himself.

He has also written three novels centering around questions of racial identity. His first book, "Trumpet to the World" (1946, o. p.), is the story of the difficult maturing of a Black man in a hostile world. "Something about a Soldier" (1957, o. p.) is a semiserious novel about a young Jewish soldier who rejects the army and the Second World War, works militantly for justice for Blacks, goes AWOL, and achieves maturity through serious meditation in prison. "The Goy" is the story of a midwestern gentile who prospers domestically, romantically, and professionally in a world almost entirely Jewish.

"City of Discontent" (1952, o. p.) is a fictionalized biography of the poet Vachel Lindsay, "Being Also the Story of Springfield, Illinois, U.S.A., and of the Love of the Poet for That City, That State, and That Nation." Harris has taught at San Francisco State, Purdue University, and California Institute of the Arts. His knowledge of some of the more ludicrous aspects of academic life was put to good use in what is probably his funniest novel. "Wake Up, Stupid" (1959, o. p.) is told in the form of letters by a man who is both a college professor and a prizefight manager but who has a fantasy-life even more comic and crisis-smitten than his actual life. In addition, Harris has written a play, "Friedman and Son" (1963, o. p.), much miscellaneous journalism, and two volumes of lively autobiography—"Mark the Glove Boy" and "Twentyone Twice: A Journal" (1966, o. p.).

BANG THE DRUM SLOWLY. 1956. *Dell* 1973

THE GOY. 1970. *Bantam* 1973 pap. $.95

KILLING EVERYBODY. *Dial* 1973 $6.95

MARK THE GLOVE BOY; or, The Last Days of Richard Nixon. Autobiography. 1964. *Curtis Bks.* 1972 $.95

KEROUAC, JACK. 1922–1969.

Spokesman for the Beat Generation, Jack or John Kerouac (he was christened Jean and is of French-Canadian extraction) was born in Lowell, Mass. After a short stay at Columbia College, he did a number of odd jobs, served in the Merchant Marine, returned to Columbia for a short while, and roamed through the United States and Mexico, 1943–50. "On the Road," written in only three weeks, was based on his wanderings; parts of it appeared originally in magazines. It gained immediate notoriety and about 500,000 copies were sold in paperbacks alone. "Desolation Angels" (1965, o. p.) continues the account of his travels through the United States, Tangier, and Europe; in "Vanity of Duluoz" (1968, o. p.) he draws on his experiences as a student at Columbia. "The Dharma Bums" tells of a search for truth through alienation and poverty and contains elements from Zen Buddhism and Japanese poetry. The Japanese word *satori*, meaning "sudden illumination"—or "kick in the eye"—provided the title for his autobiographical work "Satori in Paris." "The happenings take place in a haze of cognac and *non-sequiturs* which are amusing although incomprehensible" (*LJ*). His first book of poetry, "Mexico City Blues" (*Grove* Evergreen Bks. pap. $2.45) includes 242 jazz poems on such subjects as Zen, drug addiction, and childhood. "Scripture of Golden Eternity," with more poems, is available from *Citadel Press* (Corinth Bks. orig. pap. $2.00). It is "not so much as writer, but as high priest of a sect that Kerouac was considered important. In eccentric rebellion against the prevailing tone and mood of the fifties . . . Kerouac, asserting a childlike and overly innocent view into the nature of things by intuitive 'Zen' flashes of illumination, scornful of traditional thought and traditional dress, [has become] spokesman for an unkempt, hobo romanticism"—(David L. Stevenson, in "The Creative Present").

ON THE ROAD. *Viking* 1957 $6.50 Compass Bks. 1959 pap. $1.65; *New Am. Lib.* pap. $.95

THE SUBTERRANEANS. *Grove* 1958 pap. $.95; *Ballantine Bks.* 1973 pap. $1.50

DHARMA BUMS. 1958. *New Am. Lib.* Signet pap. $.75; *Viking* Compass Bks. pap. $1.95

DOCTOR SAX. 1959. *Grove* Evergreen Bks. pap. $2.45

THE BOOK OF DREAMS. *City Lights* (orig.) 1961 pap. $2.50

SATORI IN PARIS. *Grove* 1966 Black Cat Bks. pap. $.75

VISIONS OF CODY. *McGraw* 1972 $8.95

Books about Kerouac

Kerouac: A Biography. By Ann Charters. *Straight Arrow* 1973 $7.95

VONNEGUT, KURT, JR. 1922–

"A ruffled humanism warms the razor edges of all Vonnegut's highly imaginative fables, yet what keeps them from dulling with sentimentality is his refusal to offer false hopes" (*Life*). "Player Piano" describes a future America in the grip of automation—a nightmarish situation in which people count for little. In it Mr. Vonnegut exercises "a lively satirical humor that bubbles up, again and again in fragments of fancy. [The book] is evidence of a probing mind and a discerning eye"—(James Hilton).

"Mother Night" is satire on the Nazi mentality, a fictional memoir of an American writer who broadcasts Nazi propaganda in Germany to cover for his true role as an Allied agent, but whose true allegiance (though not his creator's) is constantly in doubt. A succession of somewhat zany short episodes whose extremely funny black humor is at bottom deadly serious, "it is a wonderful splash of bright, primary colors, an artful, zestful cartoon that lets us see despair without forcing us to surrender to it"—(*Harper's*). "God Bless You, Mr. Rosewater," about the president of the "Rosewater Foundation" who fosters the loving approach to humanity, is "an amalgam of short comic strip-like tales, dada dialogue, [with] no characterization and minimal plot.... The net effect is at once explosively funny and agonizing"—(*Book Week*).

Mr. Vonnegut was born in Indianapolis, Ind., and attended Cornell University. During World War II he joined the Army, which trained him as a mechanical engineer. He was captured in the Battle of the Bulge and imprisoned in Dresden, where he experienced the Allied destruction of that city while working in a meat freezer underground. He received a Purple Heart for what he calls a "ludicrously negligible wound". After the war he studied at the University of Chicago, worked for the Chicago City News Bureau as a police reporter and in public relations for the General Electric Corporation. He has published some 100 short stories, some of which were collected in "Canary in a Cathouse" (1960, o. p.). He settled on Cape Cod in 1955, where he lives with his wife and six children.

In recent years Vonnegut's following has grown considerably, particularly among younger readers. Whereas he was once dismissed as little more than a better-than-average writer of science fiction, his books are now hailed as prophetic works with profound meanings and a compassionate understanding of the human dilemma. His "Slaughterhouse Five" was a successful film, and his first play, "Happy Birthday, Wanda June" (*Delacorte* 1971 $6.50; *Dell* Delta Bks. 1971 pap. $1.95) had a moderately successful run in New York in 1970.

PLAYER PIANO. 1952. *Avon Bks.* pap. $1.25; *Delacorte* 1971; $6.00; *Dell* Delta Bks. pap. $2.25

THE SIRENS OF TITAN. 1961. *Delacorte* $6.00; *Dell* 1967 pap. $.95 Delta Bks. pap. $1.25

MOTHER NIGHT. *Delacorte* 1962 $6.00; *Dell* Delta Bks. pap. $2.95

CATS CRADLE. *Delacorte* 1971 $6.00; *Dell* pap. $.95 Delta Bks. pap. $1.95

GOD BLESS YOU, MR. ROSEWATER, OR PEARLS BEFORE SWINE. 1965. *Delacorte* 1971 $6.00; *Dell* 1966 pap. $.95 Delta Bks. pap. $1.75

WELCOME TO THE MONKEY HOUSE. *Delacorte* 1968 $6.00; *Dell* Delta Bks. pap. $1.95. A collection of fictional pieces written from 1950 to 1968.

SLAUGHTERHOUSE-FIVE, or The Children's Crusade. *Delacorte* 1969 $6.00; *Dell* pap. $.95

BETWEEN TIME AND TIMBUKTU, or Prometheus Five. *Delacorte* 1972 $7.95; *Dell* Delta Bks. 1972 pap. $2.45

BREAKFAST OF CHAMPIONS. *Delacorte* 1973 $7.95

Books about Vonnegut

Kurt Vonnegut, Fantasist of Fire and Ice. By David H. Goldsmith. *Bowling Green Univ. Popular Press* 1972 pap. $1.00
Writers for the Seventies: Kurt Vonnegut, Jr. By Peter Reed. *Paperback Lib.* 1972 pap. $1.50
The Vonnegut Statement. Ed. by Jerome Klinkowitz and John Somer. *Dell* Delta Bks. 1972 pap. $2.65. Original essays on Vonnegut's life and writings.

MAILER, NORMAN. 1923–

A gifted writer, Norman Mailer enjoyed the not uncommon but still amusing combination of a Brooklyn childhood, a Harvard education, and a two-year service in the Army, which culminated in what is now considered the best novel by an American about World War II—"The Naked and the Dead." It became a best seller and was made into a powerful movie. His subject in "The Deer Park" is the spiritual suffocation represented, in his view, by Hollywood. He adapted this novel as a play, rewriting it four times over a ten-year period. It became a 1967 off-Broadway success.

Since 1959, he has "not only deserted the 'naturalism' of his first novel but more and more moved from fiction to non-fiction, and of a polemical sort. And increasingly he has enforced upon the public the myth of the man rather than the work of a writer. . . . In 1959, at the not very advanced age of thirty-six [he] published what amounted to a grand view of his literary lifetime. In a single big volume, *Advertisements for Myself*, he not only reprinted virtually everything he had written except his three novels—and there are even excerpts from these—but also prefaced, or connected, his stories, essays and journalism with an extended commentary in which he reported on his states of mind at various stages of his development as an author and public figure, on the reception given his work in the press and by his publishers, and on his present estimate of his earlier performances. . . . By most of its reviewers, *Advertisements* was received reservedly, or with condescension, or irony. . . . To a greater extent than he perhaps recognizes, Mailer is an anti-artist, deeply distrustful of art because it puts a shield between the perception and the act. His writer's role, as he conceived it, is much more messianic than creative"—(Diana Trilling, in "The Creative Present").

"The White Negro" (*City Lights* 1959 reprint pap. $.75) analyzes the "hipster" or devotee of the Beat Movement. Eliot Fremont-Smith in the *N.Y. Times* heartily praises the controversial "Why Are We in Vietnam?" as "the most original, courageous and provocative novel so far this year. Corruption of the soul is Mr. Mailer's theme. [Mr. Mailer sees the Vietnam] war as a wholly destructive, wholly brutalizing exercise of American violence. The war itself is never specifically at issue in the novel. Rather Mr. Mailer has set out to portray the national, self-image that can be sustained by such an enterprise—to expose, in short, how we got this way." Eric Moon, editor of *Library Journal*, on the other hand, finds Mailer here "in an advanced state of decay" in his "worst novel." "The Armies of the Night," his "extraordinary personal tract on the unprecedented demonstration of Oct. 21–22, 1967, when thousands of the New Left attempted to 'March on the Pentagon,' " received general praise, including a front-page notice by Alfred Kazin in the *N.Y. Times Book Review* on publication. Mr. Kazin wrote: "Only a born novelist *could* have written a piece of history so intelligent, mischievous, penetrating and alive, so vivid with crowds, the great stage that is American democracy, the Washington streets and bridges, the Lincoln Memorial, the women, students, hippies, Negroes and assorted intellectuals for peace, the M.P.'s and United States marshals, the American Nazis chanting 'We want dead Reds.' The book cracks open the hard nut of American authority at the center, the uncertainty of our power—and, above all, the bad conscience that now afflicts so many Americans. 'Armies of the Night' is a peculiarly appropriate and timely contribution to this moment of the national drama."

The misleading title "Why Are We in Vietnam?" for Mailer's last novel to date may have been prophetic of the direction his writing was to take. Beginning with "The Armies of the Night: History as a Novel, The Novel as History" (*New Am. Lib.* 1968 $5.95 pap. 1971 $1.25), a book published the same year he ran unsuccessfully for Mayor of New York City, Mailer has turned his considerable talents to his own particular brand of the New Journalism. Unlike other practitioners of that blend of fiction and reportage, Mailer has not been content to investigate the events of his time from the point of view of a detached observer. Instead, he has placed himself squarely in the center of the history he has traced. "The Armies of the Night," "Miami and the Siege of Chicago" (*New Am. Lib.* 1968 pap. $1.50), and "Of a Fire on the Moon" (*Little* 1970 $7.95) are what Richard Poirier describes as "narrative-journals" dealing with national politics and the space program in the United States. When Kate Millet—in "Sexual Politics" (1970 Avon pap. $2.95)— helped to launch the women's liberation movement by attacking Mailer as one of the most prominent of literary male chauvinists, he threw himself vigorously into the fray with "The Prisoner of Sex" (*Little* 1971 $5.95; *New Am. Lib.* Signet Bks. $1.25). It is not surprising that Mailer's recent experiments in movie-making have starred himself. One script, "Maidstone" (*New Am. Lib.* 1971 pap. $1.50), is available for reading in an edition with illustrations from the film. Of related interest is "Marilyn" (*Grosset* 1973 $19.95), his controversial speculations on the meaning of Marilyn Monroe's life and career.

ADVERTISEMENTS FOR MYSELF. 1959. *Berkley* pap. $1.25. A collection of published and unpublished writings.

EXISTENTIAL ERRANDS: Twenty-six Pieces Selected by the Author from the Body of His Writings. *Little* 1972 $7.50; *New Am. Lib.* pap. $1.75

THE NAKED AND THE DEAD. 1948. *Holt* $7.95 pap. $3.00; *New Am. Lib.* 1954 Signet pap. $1.50

BARBARY SHORE. 1951. Introd. by Norman Podhoretz. *New Am. Lib.* pap. $1.25

THE DEER PARK. 1955. *Berkley* pap. $1.25; (dramatization) *Dial* 1967 $4.50

AN AMERICAN DREAM. *Dial* 1964 $5.95; *Dell* 1966 pap. $.95

WHY ARE WE IN VIETNAM? *Putnam* 1967 $6.95; *Berkley* pap. $.95

Books about Mailer

> Managing Mailer. By Joe Flaherty. *Coward* 1970 $5.95. Account of Mailer's campaign for Mayor of New York City in 1968.
> Norman Mailer. By Richard Foster. Pamphlets on American Writers. *Univ. of Minnesota Press* 1968 pap. $.95
> Normal Mailer: The Countdown. By Donald L. Kaufmann. Pref. by Harry T. Moore. Crosscurrents/ Modern Critiques. *Southern Illinois Univ. Press* 1969 $4.95
> The Structured Vision of Norman Mailer. By Barry H. Leeds. *New York Univ. Press* 1970 $8.95 pap. $2.45
> Norman Mailer: The Man and His Work. By Robert F. Lucid. *Little* 1971 $6.95
> Norman Mailer. By Richard Poirier. Modern Masters Series. *Viking* 1972 $6.95 pap. $2.25
> Norman Mailer: A Collection of Critical Essays. Ed. by Leo Braudy. Twentieth-Century Views. *Prentice-Hall* 1972 $5.95 Spectrum Bks. pap. $1.95

PURDY, JAMES. 1923–

"Color of Darkness," James Purdy's first collection of short stories, was printed privately, then brought out in England before being published in his own country. In her introduction to an American edition, Dame Edith Sitwell wrote: "Purdy does more in a whisper than most novelists do by yelling at the tops of their voices. . . . There is never a sentence too much, never a word too much. . . . He is a superb writer, using all the fires of the heart and the crystallizing powers of the brain." W. T. Scott said in the *N.Y. Herald Tribune*: "Even in stories of real life, horror or terror are not, finally, enough. But the talent in 'Color of Darkness' is so authoritative one expects it to do yet deeper things. It is a rich and passionate talent, already capable of memorable work, an excitement in new American writing." Ihab Hassan reviewed "Children Is All" (in *SR*) and found that "we can rejoice again in the possession of this new work by one of America's best writers." "The Nephew" has as its setting rural Ohio, where the author was born. Cabot Wright of "Cabot Wright Begins" is a convicted rapist. "The fragments of his story are pieced together by a predatory group of writers and publishers who are trying to commercialize it into a bestselling sex novel. If this much of the wild plot gives the impression that *this* is a sexy novel, drop your expectations or fears. It isn't. But it is a wildly funny book, beautifully written, and with a deadly serious underlay"—(Eric Moon, in *LJ*). "Eustace Chisholm and the Works" is set in late-Depression Chicago and concerns a group of Depression victims, each searching for the love that can redeem his life. The "grotesque" and "abnormal" (*Nation*) prevail, and Wilfrid Sheed found that the novel "has over-all interest only if it is viewed as a work of black nihilism." Angus Wilson (in *Life*), however, called it "a remarkable achievement. . . . James Purdy is a master of the mixing of the horrible, the wildly funny and the very sad." "Jeremy's Version" is the first part of a projected trilogy to be called "Sleepers in a Moon-Crowned Valley." Its mellow and optimistic tone may be contrasted with the grotesque and sometimes precious exoticism of "I Am Elijah Thrush," an independent novelette in which Purdy returns to a rather nightmarish vision of man's primal impulses. The stage version of "Malcolm" was not a success on Broadway as adapted by Edward Albee. Mr. Purdy was educated in Mexico and, after receiving an M.A. in Romance Languages from the University of Chicago, he spent some time at the University of Madrid. He now lives in Brooklyn, N.Y.

THE COLOR OF DARKNESS. Short stories. *New Directions* 1957 $4.50

MALCOLM. *Farrar, Straus* 1959 $5.95

THE NEPHEW. *Farrar, Straus* 1960 $5.95 Noonday pap. $1.95; *Avon Bks.* 1966 pap. $.60

CHILDREN IS ALL. 10 short stories and 2 plays. *New Directions* 1962 pap. $2.25

CABOT WRIGHT BEGINS. *Farrar, Straus* 1964 $5.95; *Avon Bks.* pap. $.75

EUSTACE CHISHOLM AND THE WORKS. *Farrar, Straus* 1967 $5.95

JEREMY'S VERSION. *Doubleday* 1970 $5.95; *Bantam* pap. $1.25

I AM ELIJAH THRUSH. *Doubleday* 1972 $4.95; *Bantam* pap. $1.50

Books about Purdy

The Not-Right House: Essays on James Purdy. By Bettina Schwarzchild. *Univ. of Missouri Press* 1968 pap. $1.50

BALDWIN, JAMES. 1924–

James Baldwin was born in Harlem, son of a Baptist preacher and oldest of nine children. Concerning himself he writes: "When I was fourteen I became a preacher, and when I was seventeen I stopped. . . . From 1945 (when I got the Saxton Fellowship from Harper's for a much different version of *Go Tell It on the Mountain*) onwards, I turned my attention more and more to writing—that is to say, I wrote more and more and ate less and less . . . mostly, as it turned out, about the Negro problem, concerning which the color of my skin made me automatically an expert." He received (in addition to several fellowships) the 1962 Brotherhood Award of the National Conference of Christians and Jews for "Nobody Knows My Name," and in 1964 he was elected a member of the National Institute of Arts and Letters.

Mr. Baldwin is "not only one of the best Negro writers that we have ever had in this country, he is one of the best writers that we have. He has mastered a taut and incisive style . . . and in writing about what it means to be a Negro he is writing about what it means to be a man" (Edmund Wilson, in "The Bit Between My Teeth"). His "Go Tell It on the Mountain" is a "beautiful, furious first novel." Seen through the eyes of a 14-year-old boy, it is a probing account of Harlem's physical bleakness, emotional tensions, and psychological and spiritual despair, in the midst of which only a fundamentalist church offers a kind of hope.

In 1948 he left this country for Paris intending never to return. His searching essays written there have been collected in "Notes of a Native Son" and "Nobody Knows My Name." Of the latter, Eric Moon wrote (in *LJ*): "These essays are an account of the impact of the world on Baldwin; the impact of places—Europe, which taught him that he was an American as well as a Negro; a return to the hell of Harlem; a first visit to the South, which he had feared all his life; and the impact of people. . . . This is a deeply searching, beautifully written book, and a wonderful fusion of intellect and human feeling." Finding himself "living in limbo" in Europe, Baldwin returned to New York in 1958. The bitter, pessimistic, shocking novel, "Another Country," was considered more ambitious and less successful than his other fiction, but still powerful writing.

In "searing, brilliant prose," "The Fire Next Time" ("God gave Noah the rainbow sign, No more water, the fire next time!") argues its case in two letters: the longest, "Letter from a Region of My Mind" appeared originally in the *New Yorker*; the other and shorter one, "Letter to My Nephew" was published in *Liberation* magazine. In it Baldwin was able to present "a great deal of hatred and despair in a very elegant, graceful style" (Robert F. Sayre). It warned of the self-destruction white America was heading for if it did not rapidly and with all its strength undertake racial reform; events have since borne out Mr. Baldwin's thesis, had readers failed to take "The Fire Next Time" seriously on its first appearance. The book was published in the centennial year of the Emancipation Proclamation—and was the leading nonfiction best seller for 41 consecutive weeks.

Mr. Baldwin then began to write plays. "Blues for Mister Charlie" (*Dial* 1965 $4.95; *Dell* 1966 pap. $.60), which received mixed reviews on Broadway, is a powerful study of the effects in a Southern town on both the Black and the white communities (the latter treated with understanding if not sympathy) of the shooting of a Black man by a white man. "The Amen Corner" (*Dial* 1967 $4.50) describes a woman minister's desperate struggle to hold her church and her family—husband and son—together in Harlem. The short stories of "Going to Meet the Man" "are beautifully made to frame genuine experience in a lyrical language [and] sing with truth dug out from pain" (*SR*). "Tell Me How Long the Train's Been Gone," about the life of a Negro actor, met with mixed reviews in 1968. With the rise of other Black leaders in the North, James Baldwin has now left political activism to them and returned to full-time writing. He has spent recent years in Paris. His "A Dialogue" with Nikki Giovanni (*Lippincott* 1972 $5.95) testifies, however, to his continuing concern with the problems of his native land. "Perhaps I hope by working," he writes, "to help save that country for which Thomas Jefferson trembled when he remembered that God was just"—(*N.Y. Times*).

Go Tell It on the Mountain. 1953. *Dial* 1963 $5.95; *Dell* Laurel Eds. pap. $.95; *Grosset* Univ. Lib. pap. $1.95; Ed. by Virginia F. Allen and Glenn Munson *Noble & Noble* text ed. pap. $.75

Giovanni's Room. *Dial* 1956 $5.95; *Dell* Laurel Eds. pap. $.75

Another Country. *Dial* 1962 $6.95; *Dell* pap. $1.25

Going to Meet the Man. *Dial* 1965 $5.95; *Dell* Laurel Eds. 1966 pap. $.75. Short stories.

Tell Me How Long the Train's Been Gone. *Dial* 1968 $6.95

NOTES OF A NATIVE SON. 1955. *Dial* 1963 $4.95; *Bantam* pap. $.95; *Beacon* 1957 pap. $2.45. Autobiographical essays.

NOBODY KNOWS MY NAME; MORE NOTES OF A NATIVE SON. *Dial* 1961 $5.95; *Dell* pap. 1966 $.60 Delta Bks. pap. $1.95

THE FIRE NEXT TIME. *Dial* 1963 $3.95; *Dell* pap. $.75 Delta Bks. pap. $1.65; *Franklin Watts* lg.-type ed. Keith Jennison Bks. $7.95. Part autobiographical—part philosophical.

Books about Baldwin

The Furious Passage of James Baldwin. By Fern Marja Eckman. A biography. *Lippincott* 1966 $4.50
James Baldwin: A Critical Study. By Stanley Macebuh. *Third Press* 1973 $6.95

BERGER, THOMAS (Louis). 1924–

Thomas Berger has been gradually building a reputation as a comic and satirical novelist of exceptional gifts. Born in Cincinnati, he served in the army from 1943 to 1946, graduated from the University of Cincinnati in 1948, did graduate work at Columbia, and held several editorial and librarian positions while beginning his writing career. His Reinhart trilogy ("Crazy in Berlin," "Reinhart in Love," and "Vital Parts") follows the central character, big and clumsy Otto Reinhart, from youth to middle age. The first volume deals largely with his army service with the occupation troops in Germany; the second with his attending college on the GI Bill and becoming tricked into marriage with a bourgeois shrew; the third with his life 20 years afterward, which finds him still unhappily married and constantly victimized by his wife and children, his employers, and the conditions of life in 20th-century America. Having failed in every endeavor he has attempted, even suicide, this latter-day Candide agrees to serve as a guinea pig in a cryogenic experiment to freeze and perhaps revive a human being, for he has decided that his death might as well be as absurd as his life.

Like other black humorists, Berger sometimes slips into presenting life as such a horror that any laughter it may evoke is strained and hollow. For example, in "Killing Time," we have the story of a murderer who thinks that he is doing his victims a favor by killing them; and "Regiment of Women" is a repugnant fantasy set in a future time when women roam the world like fierce Amazons raping and abusing men in a not very convincing thesis-novel about what would happen if the Women's Liberation Movement did indeed triumph. A much more successful blend of horror and comedy is "Little Big Man," which won the Rosenthal Award of the National Institute of Arts and Letters in 1965. In this best known of Berger's novels—a fame due in large part to a successful movie adaptation starring Dustin Hoffman—the author makes good use of the tall tale in this big, sprawling novel about life in the Old West during the 19th century. The story goes back into the colorful past of 111-year-old Jack Crabb, the only white survivor of the Battle of Little Big Horn and a man peculiarly capable of seeing that and other confrontations between the whites and the Indians from both points of view, for Crabb has lived both as an Indian and an Indian-fighter. This mock-heroic saga gave Berger ample range and scope for his gifts as a satirist. Few writers since the time of Swift and Pope have made better use of extravagant caricature and wild exaggeration to expose the foibles and evils of what man has done in the name of civilization.

CRAZY IN BERLIN. 1958. *R. W. Baron* 1970 $6.95

REINHART IN LOVE. 1962. *R. W. Baron* 1970 $6.95

LITTLE BIG MAN. *Dial* 1964 $7.95; *Fawcett* Crest Bks. 1969 pap. $1.25; *Simon & Schuster* Clarion Bks. pap. $3.95

KILLING TIME. *Dial* 1967 $5.95

VITAL PARTS. *R. W. Baron* 1970 $6.95

REGIMENT OF WOMEN. *Simon & Schuster* 1973 $8.95

CAPOTE, TRUMAN. 1924–

Truman Capote has made his special province the exploration of the dividing line between dream and reality, fiction and truth. Even before his first novel, "Other Voices, Other Rooms," brought him international recognition, he had written memorable short stories such as "A Tree of Night," "Master Misery," and "Miriam" which combine romantic pathos with nightmarish horror. "Other Voices, Other Rooms" is a brilliant and exotic account of the abnormal maturing of a 13-year-old boy, while the short novel "Breakfast at Tiffany's" introduces the delightfully free-spirited Hollie Golightly, one of the more uninhibited characters of modern fiction. That work also marks the transition in Capote's career from his early preoccupation with Southern locales and themes to a concern with the sometimes campy, sometimes sophisticated, lives of people associated with the arts, the theater, and high society. Long before his "In Cold Blood" helped to make "nonfiction novel" a catch phrase of modern criticism, Capote was experimenting with in-depth reportage in profiles of celebrities such as Marlon Brando or vividly personal descriptions of interesting places from New Orleans to Soviet Russia. His nonfiction is now collected in "The Dogs Bark: Public People and Private Places" (*Random* 1973 $8.95). Although such high-level journalism helped Capote to develop some of the techniques he was to use in "In Cold Blood," his previous choice of subjects and his own well-publicized life with "the beautiful people" could not prepare readers for the startling impact of his nonfiction novel. In order to write "In Cold Blood," the story of a senseless murder of a Kansas family and the background of the two murderers, Capote spent considerable time in the Midwest researching the lives of the victims and becoming close friends with both the police officer credited with solving the crime and the two young men responsible for it. The result is a remarkable and dramatic work. Although *Book Week* was justified in calling it "talented, powerful, and enigmatic" and finding that "the enigma lies in Capote's curious neutrality, in the blank eyes that stare up from the book's pages," it is also true that Capote's seemingly objective detachment only masks a deep compassion for human suffering and weakness. Capote's subsequent campaign against capital punishment testifies to his personal involvement, and Richard Brooks's vivid movie adaptation of "In Cold Blood" was faithful to the novel in emphasizing America's social responsibility for crime as well as the stupidity of this particular killing.

In "A Christmas Memory" Capote returns to his birthplace, the South, and recalls his boyhood friendship with a spinster cousin. The considerable success of a television dramatization of this touching story encouraged Capote to write a play based on another childhood experience: "The Thanksgiving Visitor" (*Random* 1968 $4.95 lim. ed. $10.00) was also successfully produced for television. He has written several off-beat screenplays, including John Huston's "Beat the Devil" (1953). His attempts to write for the Broadway stage have been somewhat less fortunate. Both the original dramatization of his short novel "The Grass Harp" and a later musical version had only moderate success, as did "House of Flowers" (1968 o. p.) written in collaboration with Harold Arlen and originally produced in 1954. "Trilogy: An Experiment of Multimedia" (*Macmillan* 1969 $6.95 *Collier* pap. $2.95) consists of the original texts, the scripts, and material relating to the film adaptations by Frank and Eleanor Perry of three short works by Capote—"Miriam," "Among the Paths to Eden," and "A Christmas Memory."

Mr. Capote, who objects to being called a "Southern" writer, was born in New Orleans into a family of Southerners on both sides. He attended six different schools in five sections of the country and began to write very early. He received the O. Henry Short Story Award for "The House of Flowers" in 1951. In 1959 he received the National Institute of Arts and Letters award, and in 1964 was elected a member of that Institute. "We are perhaps surprised by the range of his volatile gift," Mark Schorer has said, "His is, in fact, a various prose, equally at ease—to name the extremes—in situations of dark and fearful nightmare, and of extravagant comedy. Perhaps the single constant in his prose is style, and the emphasis that he himself places upon the importance of style . . . Capote's style changes, of course, with his changing moods and modes, so that the variety is multiplied."

THE GRASS HARP (1951) and A TREE OF NIGHT AND OTHER STORIES (1949). *New Am. Lib.* Signet 1956 pap. $.95

THE SELECTED WRITINGS OF TRUMAN CAPOTE. Introd. by Mark Schorer. *Modern Lib.* $2.95. A selection of 17 titles representing 20 years of his writing, including Breakfast at Tiffany's; The Muses Are Heard; parts of A Tree At Night and Local Color.

OTHER VOICES, OTHER ROOMS. 1948. *New Am. Lib.* Signet pap. $.75; introd. by the author *Random* 1968 $6.95

BREAKFAST AT TIFFANY'S: A Short Novel and Three Stories. *Random* 1958 $4.95; *New Am. Lib.* 1959 pap. $.75

IN COLD BLOOD. *Random* 1966 $6.95; *New Am. Lib.* Signet 1967 pap. $1.50

A CHRISTMAS MEMORY. *Random* 1966 boxed $6.00

Books about Capote

Truman Capote's In Cold Blood: A Critical Handbook. Ed. by Irving Malin. *Wadsworth* 1968 pap. $2.95
The Worlds of Truman Capote. By William L. Nance. *Stein & Day* 1970 $7.95

CONNELL, EVAN S., JR. 1924–

From one of the stories in "The Anatomy Lesson" Connell developed his best-known novel, "Mrs. Bridge." This story about a midwestern housewife who has lived an exemplary but pallid life helping her lawyer husband in his career and raising three children combines irony with sympathy in a distinctive blend. The companion volume, "Mr. Bridge," traces through more than a hundred episodes the lives of a typical suburban couple during the quarter-century between world wars. The Bridges are so concerned with social propriety, the quiet agonies and the surface values of their particular time and place that they never find time to feel anything very deeply. "The Patriot," Connell's second novel, is a long and loosely structured work about the growing up of a young man with principal emphasis on his military career and his uneasy relationship with his chauvinistic father until he begins to realize his true emotional needs as an art student. "The Diary of a Rapist" (1966, o. p.) is the story of an unhappily married government clerk who takes refuge in fantasy and petty acts of violence before lapsing into insanity.

David Galloway (in "Contemporary Novelists") writes that "Connell has repeatedly chronicled the absurdity, the quiet agonies and the vanities of marginal men and women. Occasionally, out of boredom or despair, such characters are drawn into violence, but more often they are doomed to float along on a sea of tedious detail that slowly drowns them. In the hands of a less skillful or a less humane writer, such lives might appear merely comical, but Connell sees the pathos at the heart of their absurdity, and the meticulous prose in which their experiences are rendered raises them above the inconsequence that seems their birthright."

THE ANATOMY LESSON AND OTHER STORIES. 1957. *Bks. for Libraries* $8.75 *Pacific Coast* 1969 pap. $2.95

MRS. BRIDGE. 1957. *Fawcett* Crest 1973 pap. $1.25

THE PATRIOT. *Viking* 1960 $4.95

AT THE CROSSROADS: Stories. *Simon & Schuster* 1965 $5.50

MR. BRIDGE. *Knopf* 1969 $5.95

POINTS FOR A COMPASS ROSE. *Knopf* 1973 $6.95

GASS, WILLIAM. 1924–

William Gass was born in Fargo, N.D. After attending Kenyon College, he received a doctorate in philosophy at Cornell University in 1954. From 1954 until 1969 he taught at Purdue, and then became a Professor of Philosophy at Washington University in St. Louis. His writing talent was first recognized in 1958, when the editors of *Accent* invited him—an unprecedented honor—to fill an entire issue of that distinguished little magazine with some of his stories and essays, but nine more years passed before he published his first book. "Omensetter's Luck," a novel, was well received by critics, who praised it for its exceptional style and its rich evocation of a particular time and place. *Newsweek* described it as "a dense, provoking, vastly rewarding and very beautiful first novel." The following year his collection of stories, "In the Heart of the Heart of the Country," attracted additional readers to this experimental writer. The title story of that volume and several others, in particular the brilliant "The Pedersen Kid," have evoked considerable critical interest, as has Gass's short novel, "Willie Master's Lonesome Wife," a wildly bawdy and richly allusive interior monologue by a latter-day Molly Bloom. In recent years Gass has become a busy contributor to *New American Review*, *New York Review of Books*, and other periodicals. Some of his reviews of individual writers and essays on the theory of fiction are collected in "Fiction and the Figures of Life" (*Knopf* 1971 $6.95; *Random* 1972 pap. $1.95).

OMENSETTER'S LUCK. *New Am. Lib.* 1966 pap. $1.95

IN THE HEART OF THE HEART OF THE COUNTRY. *Harper* 1968 $4.95 pap. $1.25

WILLIE MASTER'S LONESOME WIFE. *Knopf* 1971 $3.95

GOLD, HERBERT. 1924–

"Herbert Gold is not only an impressive novelist but also a versatile and powerful writer of short stories" (Granville Hicks). "Love and Like" is a collection of stories of which most were originally published in such magazines as *The Hudson Review, The Dial,* the *New Yorker,* and *Playboy.* "The Man Who Was Not with It" deals with carnivals, narcotics, and sexual aberration. "Fathers," a novel written in the form of a memoir, deals with the perennial elements in the relations between fathers and sons. Eliot Fremont-Smith called it a "beautiful new book, the best and most deeply felt that this talented, sensitive and dispassionate author has yet produced"—an opinion seconded by most reviewers. "Wittily critical of the 'beats,' " Mr. Gold edited in

1959 a collection of "nonbeat" short stories, "Fiction of the Fifties" (1959, o. p.). "The Age of Happy Problems" (1962, o. p.) is a collection of critical articles and studies of American manners and mores, the products of intelligent, tough-minded speculation on "some matters of teaching, learning, writing, love, marriage, work, and the prospect of death." In "First Person Singular: Essays for the Sixties" (*Dial* 1963 $5.00) he edits and introduces a symposium of personal, direct opinion by a group of top novelists and playwrights. Mr. Gold has won a National Institute of Arts and Letters award and an O. Henry Prize. He has lived in San Francisco since 1930. That city and Berkeley across the bay provide the setting for "The Great American Jackpot," a satirical novel about the disruptive social changes of the late sixties. "My Last Two Thousand Years" is an engaging and candid autobiography with a sharp focus on the social and domestic challenges encountered by this Jewish writer in various parts of the United States and abroad as well as through two marriages, one with a Jewish wife, the other with a gentile.

LOVE AND LIKE. *Dial* 1960 $4.95. Short stories.

THE PROSPECT BEFORE US. 1954. (Orig. "Room Service") *Universal Distributors* Award Bks. 1964 pap. $.60

THE MAN WHO WAS NOT WITH IT. 1956. *Avon* pap. $.75; *Random* Vintage Bks. pap. $1.95. Novel.

SALT. 1963. *Random* 1968 $6.95; *Avon* 1971 pap. $1.25

FATHERS. *Random* 1967 $4.95; *Fawcett* Crest Bks. pap. $.95

THE GREAT AMERICAN JACKPOT. *Random* 1969 $6.95; *Ace Bks.* pap. $.95

THE MAGIC WILL: Stories and Essays of a Decade. *Random* 1971 $7.95

MY LAST TWO THOUSAND YEARS. Autobiography. *Random* 1972 $6.95

HAWKES, JOHN. 1925–

"Right now there is no one else in the U.S. writing in Hawkes's style or from his point of view. . . . Within the context of 'The Lime Twig' there can be no disbelief, the problem which along with the obstinacy of language has separated Hawkes from his audience so long. . . . The terror Hawkes creates is the terror of the nightmare, but we all know it. The comedy is macabre, but we have all laughed at it. Place 'The Lime Twig' . . . beside the recitations of inhumanity and mad comedy confronting us daily in our press and his work acquires the unassailability of truth . . . In Providence, R.I., teaching English at Brown University, is a quiet American . . . who is writing novels of force and imagination at a pitch with the most terrifying and relevant modern drama and fiction reaching our shores from Europe. Hawkes is a prophet in his own country"—(Webster Schott, in the *Nation*). Worked out with meticulous detail, the tale is, on one level, comparable to the finest thriller; on the other, this remarkable novel is a psychological study of the interrelationships of a group of people. "Original and exciting and almost painfully true . . ."—(Santha Rama Rau).

Because of his first work, he has been called "avant-garde and surrealist, terms suggesting the unfamiliar and the obscure," but the ingenious "The Lime Twig" has all the ingredients of a popular novel. "Second Skin" concerns an American ex-naval man, "a man of love" who must come to terms with the brutal facts of his life as he starts it afresh on a tropical island. "The 20th-century Candide, Hamlet, existentialist unaware, or what the reader will, suggests the answer to horror and tragedy is resignation buttressed by faith in self and life. As in his previous works *The Cannibal* and *The Lime Twig* Hawkes's present concern with plot is negligible; time sequences and reality are a matter of the protagonist's conscious or subconscious fantasy. Frequently compared to Graham Greene or Faulkner, he is more at home with the French New Realists such as Claude Simon and Nathalie Sarraute. *Second Skin* is the work of a major American novelist, and it is highly recommended"—(Bill Katz, in *LJ*). "The Blood Oranges" is the story of an erotic quartet set in contemporary times but against the symbolic backdrop of Illyria, the saturnalian scene of Shakespeare's "Twelfth Night." As in Hawkes's early fiction dark comedy combines with dream landscapes in a way that makes his work peculiarly his own.

Born in Stamford, Conn., Hawkes lived in Old Greenwich, Conn. and New York City until he was ten, then went to Juneau, Alaska. He attended Trinity School, Pawling High School and Harvard College, where after graduation he taught creative writing for three years. Since 1967 he has been Professor of English at Brown University, Providence, R.I. In 1962 he received a Guggenheim grant and a National Institute of Arts and Letters Award. The result of a fellowship from the Ford Foundation for study with a professional theater company 1964–65 was "The Innocent Party" (*New Directions* $5.00 pap. $2.95), four short plays exploring the nature of innocence—"its illusions and mutations—in diverse forms"—(Publisher's note). These are

"The Wax Museum," "The Questions," "The Undertaker" and the title play. Herbert Blau, the director, says in his introduction: "The territory of Hawkes' concern is 'emotional oblivion.' . . . Terror be praised, it's a pleasure to read some plays that sing. It makes them worth imagining in the theater." "The Questions" was presented on the NBC series "Experiment" in 1967.

LUNAR LANDSCAPES. *New Directions* 1969 $5.95 signed limited ed. $25.00 pap. $2.50. Contains Charivari, The Goose on the Grave, The Owl, and short stories.

THE CANNIBAL. *New Directions* 1949 $5.95 pap. 1967 $1.95

THE BEETLE LEG. *New Directions* 1951 $4.50 pap. $1.75

THE GOOSE ON THE GRAVE and THE OWL. *New Directions* 1953 $4.50

THE LIME TWIG. Introd. by Leslie A. Fiedler. *New Directions* 1960 $4.50 pap. $1.75

SECOND SKIN. *New Directions* 1964 pap. $1.75; *New Am. Lib.* Signet pap. $.60

THE BLOOD ORANGES. *New Directions* 1972 $6.95 pap. $1.95

Books about Hawkes

Hawkes: A Guide to His Fictions. By Frederick Busch. *Syracuse Univ. Press* 1973 $8.95. Superb critical introduction by a promising young writer.
Comic Terror: The Novels of John Hawkes. By Donald J. Greiner. *Memphis State Univ. Pres* 1973 $7.50

O'CONNOR, FLANNERY. 1925–1965.

Flannery O'Connor was born in Savannah, Ga. She received a number of grants and fellowships and the O. Henry Award (first prize for her story "Greenleaf") in 1957. Her first novel, "Wise Blood," the story of a religious fanatic, was well received—William Goyen found her "a writer of power." In reviewing "A Good Man is Hard to Find" Caroline Gordon said: "She is, like Maupassant, very much of her time, and her stories, like his, have a certain glitter, as it were, of evil which pervades them and astonishingly contributes to their lifelikeness" (*N.Y. Times*). "The Violent Bear It Away" is a novel about murder involving a Tennessee backwoods preacher and a small boy. Here Miss O'Connor again exhibits her interest in the strange forms religion can take and in aberrant human personality; here too she shows herself a writer concerned with the oppressive mores of the Deep South in the Faulkner tradition. "Everything That Rises Must Converge" is a posthumous collection of stories about the Bible Belt. Five of Miss O'Connor's stories were used by Cecil Dawkins to make a play produced off-Broadway in 1966—"The Displaced Person"—which Walter Kerr found effective portraiture but too fragmentary in adaptation to succeed as drama. Granville Hicks said of her, "If there is a young writer who has given clearer evidence of originality and power than Flannery O'Connor, I cannot think who it is." Miss O'Connor's strong talent was strongly influenced by her views as a somewhat unorthodox Catholic. She promised much, and her premature death from cancer was a tremendous loss to American literature.

THREE: WISE BLOOD; A GOOD MAN IS HARD TO FIND; THE VIOLENT BEAR IT AWAY. *New Am. Lib.* Signet pap. $1.25

COMPLETE STORIES OF FLANNERY O'CONNOR. *Farrar, Straus* 1971 $10.00

WISE BLOOD. 1952. *Farrar, Straus* 1962 $5.95 Noonday pap. $1.95

A GOOD MAN IS HARD TO FIND. Short stories. *Harcourt* 1955 $5.95; *Doubleday* Image Bks. pap. $1.25

THE VIOLENT BEAR IT AWAY. *Farrar, Straus* 1960 Noonday pap. $1.95

EVERYTHING THAT RISES MUST CONVERGE. Short stories. *Farrar, Straus* 1965 $6.95 Noonday pap. $1.95; *New Am. Lib.* Signet 1967 pap. $1.25

MYSTERY AND MANNERS: Occasional Prose. Ed. by Sally and Robert Fitzgerald. *Farrar, Straus* 1960 $6.95 Noonday pap. $2.25

Books about O'Connor

The Added Dimension: The Art and Mind of Flannery O'Connor. Ed. by Melvin J. Friedman and Lewis A Lawson. *Fordham Univ. Press* 1966 $6.95

A collection of 11 original critical pieces on Flannery O'Connor's four published books. . . . A sound scholarly enterprise"—(*LJ*). Also included is "Flannery O'Connor in Her Own Words: A Correspondence with William A. Sessions"; a "Collection of Statements" by Miss O'Connor on her Catholicism, on the South, and on writing; and her lecture, "Some Aspects of the Grotesque in Southern Literature."

Flannery O'Connor. By Stanley E. Hyman. Pamphlets on American Writers. *Univ. of Minnesota Press* 1966 pap. $1.25

True Country: Themes in the Fiction of Flannery O'Connor. By Carter W. Martin. *Vanderbilt Univ. Press* 1969 $7.50

The World of Flannery O'Connor. By Josephine Hendin. *Indiana Univ. Press* 1970 $5.75

Eternal Crossroads: The Art of Flannery O'Connor. By Leon Driskell and Joan T. Brittain. *Univ. Press of Kentucky* 1971 $7.50

The Christian Humanism of Flannery O'Connor. By David Eggenschwiler. *Wayne State Univ. Press* 1972 $8.95

Invisible Parade: The Fiction of Flannery O'Connor. By Miles Orvell. *Temple Univ. Press* 1972 $9.00. The best critical study to date.

The Question of Flannery O'Connor. By Martha Stephens. *Louisiana State Univ. Press* 1973 $8.50

Flannery O'Connor. By Dorothy Walters. U.S. Authors Ser. *Twayne* 1973 $5.50

STYRON, WILLIAM (CLARK, JR.). 1925–

William Styron was born in Newport News, Va. After serving in the U.S. Marine Corps he completed his studies at Duke University. "He has produced a first novel ['Lie Down in Darkness'] containing some of the elements of greatness, one with which the work of no other young writer of 25 can be compared, and . . . he has done justice to the southern tradition from which his talent derives" (J. W. Aldridge, in the *N.Y. Times*). For this initial work he received the Prix de Rome of the American Academy of Arts and Letters. With his second novel "Set This House on Fire," which Granville Hicks called "in the Dostoievskyan sense, a mystery story," he became a major American novelist. Writing on Bellow (*q. v.*) and Styron in "The Creative Present," Robert Gorham Davis says: "Affirmative in tone, exuberant in style, free and ambitious in dramatic invention, these novels are unlike the other American fiction of the decade. And yet they represent a kind of philanthropic fantasy, of moral make-believe, conceivable only in America. . . . There is the American belief in goodness, in good intentions. . . . It may not work out in individual cases—which explains both the anguish and the comedy—but the country created by this faith is still very demonstrably there, still trying, still convinced by its own rhetoric. Though unacknowledged and largely unexamined, America itself remains the hero of these novels."

Styron's best seller and Book-of-the-Month Club choice, "The Confessions of Nat Turner," received almost universal praise. Clifton Fadiman wrote: "It may well be the finest work to date of one of the most intensely gifted of our younger novelists. . . . My. Styron has somehow thought himself inside the skin of one of the most remarkable, appalling and tragic figures in the entire chronicle of the American Negro." Philip Rahv in the *N.Y. Review of Books* found that this re-creation of an actual episode in American history—the Nat Turner slave revolt of 1831—fulfilled Matthew Arnold's dictum, "For the creation of a masterwork of literature two powers must concur, the power of the man and the power of the moment." In the novel, Nat Turner, a Negro slave and preacher, believes he has a command from God and with a small band of slave followers attempts the total annihilation of Virginian whites—of whom they slay 60. In reprisal some 200 Negroes are killed and 17 hanged. It is based on a contemporary 20-page pamphlet published by a lawyer, Thomas Gray. In Part I of the novel Nat dictates his account of the affair to Thomas Gray and in later sections provides his "autobiography." Eliot Fremont-Smith said (in the *N.Y. Times*): "It is one of those rare books that show us our American past, our present—ourselves—in a dazzling shaft of light that cuts through the defenses of commonplace 'knowledge' to compel understanding." Robert Penn Warren called it "A book profoundly for our time, but I am sure it will outlive our time." It won the 1967 Pulitzer Prize.

In July, 1968, however, was published "William Styron's *Nat Turner:* Ten Black Writers Respond." Doris Innis wrote (in *PW*): " 'The Confessions of Nat Turner,' which won the 1967 Pulitzer Prize for fiction, was greeted by almost universal praise by the book reviewing establishment. . . . But black writers, leaders, and scholars were almost as single-voiced in their denunciation of the book. It was generally felt that Nat Turner, a revolutionary figure long revered in the black community, had been dehumanized, and made to act like a bungling, indecisive, super-neurotic eunuch. The book was viewed as a major contribution toward the perpetuation of just about every myth with which the black man has been shackled since slavery. The essays in this book are by ten leading black writers, including Lerone Bennett, John Oliver Killens and John Williams, and they seek to show precisely why blacks find 'The Confessions of Nat Turner' so overwhelmingly objectionable. Historical sources are used to document the common charge of the essays that Styron did not merely take literary license in creating his version of Nat Turner, but that he practically rewrote history. The book [is] highly recommended for anyone seeking a clear presentation of the black case against Styron."

LIE DOWN IN DARKNESS. 1951. *Modern Lib.* pap. $2.95; *New Am. Lib.* pap. $.95; *Viking* Compass Bks. 1957 pap. $2.45

THE LONG MARCH. A novelette. 1953. *Random* $4.95 Vintage Bks. pap. $1.65; *New Am. Lib.* Signet pap. $.75.

SET THIS HOUSE ON FIRE. *Random* 1960 $8.95; *New Am. Lib.* Signet pap. $.95

THE CONFESSIONS OF NAT TURNER. *Random* 1967 $7.95; *Modern Lib.* $2.95; *New Am. Lib.* Signet pap. $1.25

IN THE CLAPP SHACK. *Random* 1973 $5.95

Books about Styron

William Styron's Nat Turner: Ten Black Writers Respond. Ed. by John H. Clarke. *Beacon* 1968 pap. $1.95 (*See comment above.*)

William Styron's "The Confessions of Nat Turner": A Critical Handbook. Ed. by Melvin J. Friedman and Irving Malin. Guides to Literary Study. *Wadsworth* 1970 pap. $2.95

William Styron. By Richard Pearce. Pamphlets on American Writers. *Univ. of Minnesota Press* 1971 pap. $.95

VIDAL, GORE. 1925–

Gore Vidal was born at West Point, the U.S. Military Academy, and spent much of his childhood in Washington, D.C., with his maternal grandfather, a scholarly and witty senator from Oklahoma. The young Vidal came into literary prominence after World War II. His first book, "Williwaw" (1946, o. p.), also published under the title "Dangerous Voyage"), reflected his own experiences on an army freight-supply ship in the Aleutian Islands. "The City and the Pillar" (1948, o. p.) dealt frankly with homosexuality. "Julian" (1964, o. p.) is a fresh, lively treatment of Julian the Apostate, the pagan Emperor of Rome during the fourth century. *Library Journal* called it "a delight." "Washington, D.C." is a novel about corruption in that city (c. 1937–54) in the person of a Senator James Burden Day. Eliot Fremont-Smith found it "possibly his most accomplished [novel] to date . . . a nicely complicated, well-told, engrossing and finally rather chilling tale that never once seems foolish." "Myra Breckinridge" which Mr. Vidal refused to release in advance to reviewers (lest they reveal its plot, he said) follows the life of a transvestite. Mr. Fremont-Smith finds it "a brutally witty book, a parody on Hollywood, pop intellectualism, pornography and just about anything else you could name. . . . A funny novel, but it requires an iron stomach." In the essays of "Rocking the Boat" (1962, o. p.) Vidal "is still a young Voltairean rebel trying to 'rock the boat' of modern complacency and mediocrity"—(*LJ*). He says of himself, "I am at heart a propagandist, a tremendous hater, a tiresome nag, complacently positive that there is no human problem which could not be solved if people would simply do as I advise."

THE JUDGMENT OF PARIS. 1952 *Little* 1965 $4.75

MESSIAH. 1954. *Ballantine Bks.* (orig.) pap. $.75

THIRSTY EVIL: Seven Short Stories. 1956. *Bks. for Libraries* $6.50; *New Am. Lib.* Signet pap. $.75

JULIAN. *Little* 1964 $6.95; *Modern Library* $2.95

SEARCH FOR THE KING. *Pyramid Bks.* 1968 pap. $.95

WASHINGTON, D.C. *New Am. Lib.* Signet pap. $.95

MYRA BRECKINRIDGE. *Little* 1968 $5.95; *Bantam* pap. $1.50

BURR: A Novel. *Random* 1973 $8.95

Books about Vidal

Gore Vidal. By Ray Lewis White. U.S. Authors Ser. *Twayne* 1968 $4.95; *College & Univ. Press* pap. $2.45

WILLIAMS, JOHN A(LFRED). 1925–

John A. Williams' literary career since 1960 is almost a history-in-miniature of what has happened generally in Black literature during that period. His first few novels emphasize the plight of solitary Negroes battling against racism in an effort to establish their own individual artistic integrity. "The Angry Ones" deals with an artist fighting discrimination in the quest for jobs and housing. "Night Song" is a biographical novel based on the life of the musician Charlie Yardbird Parker. "Sissie" (1963, o. p.) deals with a playwright serving in the army who is attacked by a white soldier. He begins to seek revenge, then realizes that his antagonist is frightened of him not as an individual person but as a representative of his whole hated race. This realization seems to have come to Williams as well, for "The Man Who Cried I Am" establishes clear links between its hero, a Black novelist dying of cancer in Paris, with fictional characters based on Richard Wright (*q. v.*) and Malcolm X. Max Reddick comes to realize that if the former symbolizes the Black man's need to rebel, the latter shows the way to do so most effectively through group loyalties. "Sons of Darkness, Sons of Light" deals with the conversion to activism in the fight for racial justice by a middle-class Black, while "Captain Blackman" moves up the social scale in its account of an officer wounded in Vietnam who looks back on the disgraceful history of Black men in American armies from the time of the Revolutionary War. According to Leonard Fleischer (in *Saturday Review*), "The novel is a stinging polemic demonstrating how blacks have been used by a racist military establishment that encouraged them to fight and die for a freedom ultimately denied them."

Williams was born in Jackson, Miss., and graduated from Syracuse University in 1950. He has held positions in publishing and advertising as well as for the American Committee on Africa. His nonfiction includes "Africa: Her History, Lands and People" (*Cooper Sq.* 1962 $4.50 pap. $2.50), "This My Country, Too" (*New Am. Lib.* 1965 pap. $.95), and "Flashbacks: A Twenty-Year Diary of Article Writing" (*Doubleday* 1973 $8.95) as well as biographies of Richard Wright and Martin Luther King—"The Most Native of Sons" (*Doubleday* 1970 $3.95 pap. $1.45) and "The King God Didn't Save" (*Coward* 1970 $5.95).

THE ANGRY ONES. 1960. *Pocket Bks.* 1970 pap. $.95

NIGHT SONG. 1961. *Pocket Bks.* 1970 pap. $.95

THE MAN WHO CRIED I AM. *Little* 1967 $7.50; *New Am. Lib.* Signet 1972 pap. $1.95

SONS OF DARKNESS, SONS OF LIGHT. *Little* 1969 $6.95; *Pocket Bks.* 1970 pap. $.95

CAPTAIN BLACKMAN: A Novel. *Doubleday* 1972 $6.95

DONLEAVY, J(AMES) P(ATRICK). 1926–

"Mr. Donleavy's [writing] is dintinguished by humor, often inelegant, even coarse, but explosive and irresistible. ["The Ginger Man"] is a wild and unpredictable outburst"—(Granville Hicks, in *SR*). With the publication of this first novel, which takes place in Dublin and London, J. P. Donleavy attained a reputation as a young author whose "style is poetic, sometimes elliptical, and often with a flavor of Joyce and Ulysses"—(*N.Y. Times*). Critics called Sebastian Dangerfield, the novel's antihero, "zany," "roguish," "a comic roister," "a man of irrepressible gusto" with "a surprising touch of melancholy"; he is, in fact, "a sensitive man out of control." "Yet Mr. Donleavy is anything but an artless writer. Observe, for instance, the adroitness with which he moves from outside Sebastian's mind to inside it, from writing in the third person to writing in the first, and you realize how much control has created this image of chaos"—(Hicks).

In "A Singular Man," Mr. Donleavy takes on the frustrations of a modern businessman. Like his first novel it is "rollicking, exuberant and inventive, but [it] also has ominous undertones"—(*PW*). Granville Hicks found it a "disappointment," the *New Yorker* a "very fine novel by a stylist." The stories of "Meet My Maker the Mad Molecule" include his well-known "Fairy Tale of New York," about a young man's return to that city with the body of his wife who died at sea, and his irrelevant musings at her funeral. "The stories are swift, imaginative, beautiful and funny, and no contemporary writer is better than J. P. Donleavy at his best"—(*New Yorker*).

Samuel in "The Saddest Summer of Samuel S" is a paunchy man desperately trying to pay his psychiatrist's bills and to shape up so he can marry and have children. In the meantime he cavorts with a wealthy widow and a plump American girl. The *New Yorker* says, "Mr. Donleavy manages to be funny about so much that one would have thought nobody could be funny about again . . . hangovers, American expatriates and tourists, and cross-talk from the psychiatrist's couch." In his recent work Donleavy has turned from the absurd and the funny to a view of life which often seems grotesque and Kafkaesque. For instance, the hero of "The Onion Eaters" is a man blessed or cursed with three testicles. Although Donleavy was born and raised in New York, he received part of his education at Trinity College in Dublin, the principal setting of "The Ginger Man," and he has been residing in Ireland during recent years in spite of the fact that his best-known novel may still be banned in that country. His own dramatization of Sebastian Dangerfield's uninhibited story is included in his "Plays" (*Delacorte* 1972 $10.00; *Dell* Delta Bks. pap. $2.95).

THE GINGER MAN. 1955. *Astor-Honor* $5.95 pap. $2.45; *Berkley* pap. $1.25; *Delacorte* $5.95; *Dell* Delta Bks. pap. $1.95

A SINGULAR MAN. 1963. *Delacorte* $6.95. *Dell* pap. $.95 Delta Bks. pap. $1.95

MEET MY MAKER THE MAD MOLECULE. 1964 *Delacorte* $4.95. A collection of 27 short stories.

THE SADDEST SUMMER OF SAMUEL S. *Delacorte* 1966 $3.95

THE BEASTLY BEATITUDES OF BALTHAZAR B. *Delacorte* 1968 $6.95

THE ONION EATERS. *Delacorte* 1971 $7.95; *Dell* pap. $1.25

KNOWLES, JOHN. 1926–

The short first novel of adolescence and prep school life, "A Separate Peace," won immediate critical acclaim. Aubrey Menen called it "the best-written, best designed and most moving novel I have read in many years." Dealing as it does with friendship and betrayal at a very youthful level with great "cool," subtlety of feeling and superb writing, it became (like Golding's "Lord of the Flies" and the Tolkien sagas) immensely popular with young people of the sixties. "Morning in Antibes" (1962 o. p.) takes place in the south of France during the disorders which preceded General de Gaulle's coming to power in 1958, and is preoccupied with the emergence of evil and violence in a place of particular peace and beauty. In "Indian Summer" Mr. Knowles takes an "interesting fictional risk" (*Book Week*) by creating an attractive young man who is exploited by a rich friend and takes unattractive revenge. The *N.Y. Times* called it "a rich book, written with exuberance and eccentric grace." Although "The Paragon" deals with the college generation of 1953, Knowles intends for us to see parallels with the early seventies. The novel received mixed reviews. Webster Schott (*N.Y. Times*), for instance, found it "a beautiful, funny, moving novel," whereas J. W. Charles (in *LJ*) noted that "the scenes involving black problems and marijuana—and especially a harangue wherein the Korean War is described as an imperialist war against Asia—creak with hindsight, and are ultimately embarrassing."

John Knowles was born in West Virginia and educated at Harvard. After three years as an Associate Editor of *Holiday Magazine* he resigned to devote full time to writing. His stories and articles have appeared in numerous periodicals and he has given a series of talks to writing classes at Yale University.

A SEPARATE PEACE. 1959. *Macmillan* 1960 $4.95 lg.-type ed. $6.95; *Bantam* pap. $.95; *Dell* Delta Bks. 1963 pap. $1.45

INDIAN SUMMER. *Random* 1966 $6.95

PHINEAS: Six Stories. *Random* 1968 $4.95; *Bantam* pap. $.75

PARAGON. *Random* 1971 $5.95; *Bantam* pap. $1.25

GARRETT, GEORGE (PALMER, JR.). 1929–

Southerner Garrett attended Princeton University and after serving in the army from 1953 to 1955 has pursued an academic career as a teacher of literature and writing at Wesleyan, Rice, Virginia, Hollins College, and, since 1971, as Professor of English and Writer-in-Residence at the University of South Carolina. He is a versatile writer who has published novels, short stories, poetry, plays, and criticism in addition to editing several anthologies and seeing three of his screenplays made into movies.

Garrett's willingness to try new forms is shown by his novels, which differ considerably in subject and handling. "The Finished Man" (1959, o. p.) is a story of Florida politics. "Which Ones Are the Enemy?" takes place in Trieste during the American occupation after the Second World War. "Do, Lord, Remember Me" (1965, o. p.) deals with the startling consequences of a visit by an evangelist to a small southern town. "Death of the Fox," Garrett's most ambitious work, is a historical novel about the last days of Sir Walter Raleigh, but its moral, social, and philosophical implications far transcend the historical circumstances depicted in this rich and rewarding novel.

Of Garrett's four published volumes of verse only "For a Bitter Season" (*Univ. of Missour Press* 1967 $3.50) is currently in print. R. H. W. Dillard calls Garrett "one of the most interesting writers of his generation, for he has continued to grow and change in his work, while so many of his contemporaries have faltered or simply repeated themselves book after book. His importance becomes clearer year by year, for his fiction has maintained its freshness and its vitality even as it has developed and matured"—(Contemporary Novelists").

In the Briar Patch: A Book of Stories. *Univ. of Texas Press* 1961 $5.00

Which Ones Are the Enemy? 1961. *Popular Lib.* pap. $.50

Cold Ground Was My Bed Last Night. Stories. *Univ. of Missouri Press* 1964 $5.00

Death of the Fox. *Doubleday* 1971 $10.00; *Dell* pap. $1.95

BARTH, JOHN. 1930–

John Barth was born in Cambridge, Md. Intending to become a jazz musician, he attended Juilliard School of Music, but went on to Johns Hopkins for an M.A. and became addicted to the academic life while working in the classics library. Since 1953 he has taught at Pennsylvania State University, the State University of New York at Buffalo, and Boston University while turning out a series of novels and stories which have steadily enhanced his reputation. At least one responsible critic, Robert Scholes, finds him "the best writer of fiction we have at present, and one of the best we have ever had." In a recent interview Barth has complained about his recent fame. "It was nice being underground," he said, "One wants attention until it's paid, and then one wishes it weren't. When everybody starts understanding and approving of you, you feel terribly uncomfortable." His first novel, "The Floating Opera," is an existentialist tale in which the 50-year-old, bored-to-death bachelor protagonist decides not to commit suicide; it is cynical, readable, funny, relatively brief. The antihero of "The End of the Road" suffers from manic depression, which paralyzes his powers of decision. He falls victim to two would-be healers with opposing theories of cure. "The Sot-Weed Factor" (an archaic term for a tobacco peddler) is written in 17th-century English. "A piece of ingenious linguistic play, a joyous series of raids on half-forgotten resources of language," says Leslie Fiedler of this picaresque novel set in England and colonial Maryland: "The book is a joke-book, an endless series of gags. But the biggest joke of all is that Barth seems finally to have written something closer to the 'Great American Novel' than any other book of the last decades. . . . Barth . . . sees the world he renders primarily in terms of sex, and manages somehow to believe that even in America passion is central to the human enterprise. . . . Barth gives us sex straight, gay or vicious, but never moralized. "The Sot-Weed Factor" is, finally, not only a book about sex and society, but also one about art, a long commentary on the plight of the artist in the United States." Terry Southern (in the *Nation*) thought that readers of Mr. Barth's earlier work might find it "prolix" and "tedious" (it is 806 pages)—"this is, of course, part of its destructive function."

"Giles Goat-Boy" is also picaresque—a 700-page allegorical fantasy set in the present. Its symbolic ambience is a university campus (universe) containing two giant computers WESAC (West) and EASAC (East), and peopled by Informationalists (capitalists) and Student Unionists (communists). George Giles is born, perhaps by computer accident, into a herd of goats. Eventually learning he is a boy and not a goat, he struggles to stand and limps to the university, where he conceives of himself as a Grand Tutor (prophet) like the early prophet Enos Enoch (Christ). According to Robert Scholes (in the *N.Y. Times*) "Giles Goat-Boy" is a great novel. "Its greatness is most readily apparent in its striking originality of structure and language, an originality that depends upon a superb command of literary and linguistic tradition." In his critical book "The Fabulators" Scholes says, "It is a work of genuine epic vision, a fantastic mosaic constructed from the fragments of our life and traditions, calculated to startle us into new perceptions of the epic hero and savior." A. Alvarez of the *Observer* (London) disagrees: "At no point does the book seem motivated by anything more profound than supreme ingenuity." And the *New Yorker:* "The book outfoxes itself. . . . Its characters, all of them parodies of the famous and infamous, of the living and dead, have no breath or spirit of their own."

Barth's most recent fiction is even more experimental than his two long novels. The stories in "Lost in the Funhouse" are reflexive to an extreme, self-consciously concerned as they are with technical problems of storytelling. Yet for all their difficulty, Barth's humor and virtuosity make his stories immediately enjoyable. His interest in classic themes and subjects is utilized in "Chimera," which consists of retellings of the legends of Scheherazade, Perseus, and Bellerophon interlocked in such a way that the artist-as-storyteller begins to take on the stature of a mythic hero. Most reviewers in the commercial press found the book confusing and annoying, but it is filled with the kind of labyrinthian riddles and ingenious tricks which make Barth's writings especially attractive to college audiences.

The Floating Opera. *Doubleday* 1956 rev. ed. 1967 $5.95; *Avon* 1965 pap. $.95; *Bantam* pap. $1.25

The End of the Road. *Doubleday* 1958 rev. ed. 1967 $4.95; *Bantam* pap. $.95; *Grosset* Univ. Lib. pap. $2.45

The Sot-Weed Factor. *Doubleday* 1960 rev. ed. 1967 $10.00; *Bantam* pap. $1.25 *Grosset* Univ. Lib. pap. $2.95

GILES GOAT-BOY, or The Revised New Syllabus. *Doubleday* 1966 $6.95 ltd. ed. boxed $25.00; *Fawcett* Crest Bks. pap. $1.95

LOST IN THE FUNHOUSE: Fiction for Print, Tape, Live Voice. *Doubleday* 1968 $4.95 signed ed. $25.00; *Grosset* Univ. Lib. pap. $2.45

CHIMERA. *Random* 1972 $6.95; *Fawcett* pap. $1.50. Three interlocked novellas.

FRIEDMAN, BRUCE JAY. 1930–

Until the success of "A Mother's Kisses" in 1966, Bruce Jay Friedman was an editor of men's magazines by day and a serious writer only at night and on weekends. He grew up in a three-room apartment in the Bronx, graduated from the University of Missouri and now lives on Long Island with his wife and family. "Stern," a "delightful, moving, and sometimes quite beautiful novel" (Alfred Chester), about a Jewish suburbanite and his encounters with anti-Semitism, became "in" reading for the literary underground. "A Mother's Kisses" made Mr. Friedman's name—and the best-seller lists—enabling him to spend his full time writing. It received mixed reviews; some critics found the Jewish mother who smothers her adolescent son with affection and advice overdrawn. But Joseph Stern (in *SR*) called the book a "hilarious, mordant account" by "a wild poet of the secret life, one of the funniest of writers but with a dark edge to the laughter that gets painfully close to the bone." Eliot Fremont-Smith described the stories in "Black Angels" as "nifty-quickies." "One senses," he goes on to say, "—if far off and dimly—the ache and ugliness of life which Mr. Friedman in his best writing so brilliantly illuminates with shafts of ironic lightning." "Scuba Duba" (*Simon & Schuster* 1967 $3.95; *Pocket Bks.* pap. $.75) is Mr. Friedman's extraordinarily successful off-Broadway comedy about a Jewish intellectual who thinks he is cuckolded by a Negro skindiver. His wife's lover is in fact another man, a Negro poet, and the complications and implications make the farce. Clive Barnes found it "wildly comic [with] a quite bitter aftertaste" as did Harold Clurman: "I left the theater with a slight ache. The play is more depressing in its hilarity than 'Who's Afraid of Virginia Woolf' in its drama, more devastating in its zaniness than Pinter in his constriction." Richard Gilman (in the *New Republic*) thought its humor "an exercise in self-indulgence . . . japes, fashionable wit and the most vulgar kind of mockery." "Steambath" (*Knopf* 1971 $4.95; *Bantam* pap. $1.25) was produced on Broadway in 1970 and, like "Scuba Duba," received a mixed response from theater critics. "The Dick," Friedman's most recent novel, repeats some of his earlier themes in a story about a Jewish public relations man for a homicide bureau who changes his name to LePeters and, like Stern, suffers excessively from visions of his wife being raped by aggressive gentiles. Most reviewers found the book more tiresome than amusing.

STERN and A MOTHER'S KISSES. *Simon & Schuster* 1966 Clarion Bks. pap. $2.25

STERN. *Simon & Schuster* 1962 $3.95

A MOTHER'S KISSES. *Simon & Schuster* 1964 $4.95 Clarion Bks. pap. $.75

BLACK ANGELS. Short stories. *Simon & Schuster* 1966 $4.50

THE DICK. *Knopf* 1970 $6.96

BARTHELME, DONALD. 1931–

According to *Newsweek*, Barthelme is "perhaps the most influential young fiction writer today." Born in Philadelphia, he served in the Army, worked as a museum director in Houston during the mid-1950s, and did editorial work before establishing himself as a writer. Four of the five books he has published to date consist of short stories, most of them originally published in the *New Yorker*. His only novel, "Snow White," also appeared in that magazine, taking up almost an entire issue. Very few works have received such distinction, and Barthelme is the youngest writer to be so honored.

"Snow White" is hardly the typical *New Yorker* story. More surreal than realistic, more cynical than sensitive, it updates the fairy tale in startling ways. Barthelme's Snow White shares an apartment with seven short businessmen who have grown prosperous manufacturing oriental baby foods such as Baby Dim Sum and Baby Dow Shew. The evil stepmother is named Jane Villiers de l'Isle Adam, the prince-hero turns out to be a real frog, and the story ends in a way that will surprise readers of the Brothers Grimm. Whereas much modern fiction is reflexive in the sense that it deals with its own composition, making us conscious of the artist behind the work, Barthelme takes us a step further by pulling the reader into his stories. Thus, for example, "Snow White" is interrupted with a questionnaire in which the author solicits advice from his readers as to how his story should proceed.

Most of Barthelme's shorter works of fiction are at least as experimental as his only novel—so much so in fact it is difficult to label them short stories at all. He likes to pepper his fiction with erudite literary references. He makes use of real people as fictional characters—as in the startling reversal of nonfiction fiction shown in "Robert Kennedy Saved from Drowning" (in "Unspeakable Practices, Unnatural Acts"). He likes to break down barriers of time, as in "The Indian Uprising" (also in "Unspeakable Practices") in which an old-fashioned cowboys-and-Indians formula is used to tell about guerrilla warfare in a modern urban ghetto. Because he has been strongly influenced by the visual arts, including film, it is not surprising that recently he has devoted himself to breaking down the usual distinctions between the verbal and visual genres of art. "At the Tolstoy Museum" (in "City Life") and other late works combine illustrations with text in an unusually effective new way which is beginning to find its imitators.

COME BACK, DR. CALIGARI. 1964. *Little* 1971 pap. $2.25

SNOW WHITE. *Atheneum* 1967 $4.50; *Bantam* 1968 pap. $1.25

UNSPEAKABLE PRACTICES, UNNATURAL ACTS. *Farrar* 1968 $5.95; *Bantam* 1969 pap. $.95

CITY LIFE. *Farrar* 1970 $5.95

SADNESS. *Farrar* 1972 $5.95; *Bantam* 1973 pap. $1.50

COOVER, ROBERT. 1932–

Robert Coover is a midwesterner who has only recently started to earn a reputation as one of the most innovative of contemporary writers of fiction. Coover likes to experiment with an abundance of differing styles, and his stories are marked by clever ingenuity and sometimes dizzying displays of verbal pyrotechnics. "The Origin of the Brunists" (1966, o. p.), his first novel, is a religious parable heavily loaded with symbolism and mythic parallels. It deals with the rise following an Appalachian coal-mine disaster of a sect of worshipers made up of both fundamentalists and theosophists whose leader, Giovanni Bruno, is less a preacher than a silent enigma. The principal analogue is apparently meant to be the founding of the Christian religion, but Coover's extensive irony requires that he reverse many of the traditional features of the Christian legend. Thus, for example, it is not Bruno but his principal enemy, a skeptical editor, who is crucified in the novel's last pages. "The Universal Baseball Association," Coover's most successful novel to date, is also dominated by religious symbolism. Over the years J. Henry Waugh, a middle-aged bachelor and accountant, has developed an elaborately structured game whch he plays with dice. His game is based on the mathematical probabilities of baseball, ideal for his purposes because the great American game "by luck, trial, and error . . . had struck on an almost perfect balance between offense and defense." Every evening Henry plays his game and maintains his extensive record books. "There are box scores to be audited," he explains to a friend, "trial balances of averages along the way, seasonal inventories, rewards and punishments to be meted out, life histories to be overseen." J. Henry Waugh is thus a surrogate for God, and the participants in his imaginary baseball league seem almost to come to life, raising as they do age-old questions about fate and free will, success and failure, games and religions.

Coover's "Pricksongs and Descants" is a collection of twenty short pieces and a theoretical "Prólogo" in which the author states his belief that contemporary fiction should be based on familiar historic or mythic forms not in the way of modernist works like Joyce's "Ulysses" or T. S. Eliot's "The Waste Land" which simply use myths as a means of providing an arbitrary, skeletal framework which has no particular thematic importance, but in order to break through the mythic forms and thus expose them, leading the reader "to the real, away from . . . mystery to revelation." Most of the stories in this volume, which was well received by critics, are based on Biblical episodes or classic fairy tales retold in startling new ways.

Coover has also written a substantial quantity of verse, as yet uncollected, and the several challenging plays available in "A Theological Position" (*Dutton* 1972 $6.50 pap. $2.95).

THE UNIVERSAL BASEBALL ASSOCIATION. J. HENRY WAUGH, PROP. *Random* 1968 $6.95; *New Am. Lib.* Plume pap. $2.95

PRICKSONGS AND DESCANTS. *Dutton* 1969 $6.95; *New Am. Lib.* Plume 1970 pap. $2.45

HELLER, JOSEPH. 1932–

The catch in Joseph Heller's antiwar novel "Catch-22" as propounded by the Assyrian bombadier, Captain Yossarian, is stated in the *N.Y. Times* as the following: "Anyone who is crazy must be grounded; anyone who is willing to fly combat missions must be crazy; ergo, anyone who flies should be grounded. But [you have to] request grounding; no one crazy enough to fly missions would ask; and if one should, there's a catch: anyone who wants to get out of combat duty isn't really crazy." Nelson Algren wrote of the book in the *Na-*

tion: "Below its hilarity, so wild that it hurts, . . . this novel is not merely the best American novel to come out of World War II: it is the best American novel that has come out of anywhere in years." And Robert Brustein has written (in the *New Republic*): "Joseph Heller is one of the most extraordinary talents now among us. He has Mailer's combustible radicalism without his passion for violence and self-glorification . . . and he has Salinger's wit without his coquettish self-consciousness." Some critics found the satirical method repetitive and ultimately tiresome: "Heller uses nonsense, satire, non sequiturs, slapstick, and farce. He wallows in his own laughter, and finally drowns in it"—(*New Yorker*).

Seven years later, after two million copies had been sold in paperback, with total copies sold soon to reach three and a half million, Mr. Heller's book was again reviewed in the *N.Y. Times*. This time Josh Greenberg wrote, "I found the antic humor of Catch-22 . . . robustly fresh [and] sidesplittingly funny. I know of no book written in the last 20 years that continues to make me laugh out loud so much."

Like Yossarian, the Brooklyn-born Mr. Heller was a B-25 bombardier during the Second World War. He began "Catch-22" in 1953 and finished it in 1961 by working after his hours on advertising jobs at *McCall's, Look, Time,* and Remington Rand. He had previously taught English at Pennsylvania State College and published short stories in *Story, The Atlantic,* and *Esquire.* His own education was at New York University, at Columbia (M.A.), and at Oxford on a Fulbright Scholarship.

In 1967–68, while Mr. Heller was giving some courses at Yale, the Yale Drama School produced his play "We Bombed in New Haven" (*Knopf* 1968 $4.95; *Dell* Delta Bks. pap. $1.95) again about the Air Force, but the characters are *actors playing* Air Force officers and men—in search of a new play in which they cannot be killed (*Knopf* 1968 $4.50). Clive Barnes (in the *N.Y. Times*) found much of the play "extremely funny" but with an "aftertaste of pain ... too conscientiously striven for" and a lapse into incongruous "sentimentality" at the end.

CATCH-22. 1961 *Dell* pap. $1.25; *Modern Library* $2.95; *Simon & Schuster* 1961 $7.95 lg.-type ed. $10.95; (dramatization) *Delacorte* 1973 $5.95

UPDIKE, JOHN (HOYER). 1932–

The 16 short stories of "The Same Door" were published in the *New Yorker* between 1954 and 1959. John Updike's first novel, "The Poorhouse Fair," is an "anti-utopian" story about a home for the aged in 1974 whose denizens are being "killed with kindness" by a welfare state. "The Home is a microcosm of society as a whole; only after their exile to the poorhouse do these Americans recognize the void which their formerly busy lives had shielded them from"—(Howard M. Harper, Jr.). The *N.Y. Times* called the book "a work of art." In May, 1960, its author received the year's Rosenthal Award from the National Institute of Arts and Letters. Within the grim, nightmare quality of "Rabbit, Run," the 26-year-old hero—repeatedly "trapped" and on the run—is caught in the potentially tragic clash between instinct and the law. Here Updike presents us "with a vision of what persists beneath the adjustments we have made to necessity"—(*Commonweal*). A second collection of short stories, "Pigeon Feathers," creates "a world seen, described and interpreted by a subtle, poetic, intellectual, wondering consciousness. . . . They are wonderfully written pieces"—(*LJ*).

"The Centaur" is a subtle, complicated allegorical novel about the last three days in the life of a small-town high school teacher, and the unspoken love he and his son have for each other. The book may seem, "like the mythical creature of its title, a half-and-half thing—half-novel, half-trick—but the art and heart of John Updike gives it a forceful unity almost as rare in current fiction as the dazzle of its style"—(*Cue*). *Critic* called this winner of the 1964 National Book Award "an achievement of writing excellence on every page: the interweaving of myth and modern narration; the superbly controlled dual-person point of view; the careful description; and scene after scene of glittering technique." About "Of the Farm," a novel of complicated family relationships, *Time* said: "As a delicate cameo that freezes three people in postures that none of them find comfortable, it is almost faultless." The short stories of "The Music School" were also well received. John Updike has said (in a *N.Y. Times* interview, that "Couples" was conceived "to show a group of couples as an organism, something like a volvox, making demands on and creating behavior in the people in it." The "couples" are married people in the village of "Tarbox," Mass., who combine and recombine as sexual partners in what Updike sees as a sort of desperate religion of Play which has usurped in some segments of our society the togetherness—and other qualities—of Christianity. In the end the religion proves empty and the game is over in a mood of cosmic stoicism. "This kind of stoicism is easy enough to fake. And Updike can be quite the virtuoso. But with each book, his position seems a little less flashy and more solid. In 'Couples' he has written a painful natural history of Man, and it would have been in his interests to make it big with personal tragedy. But this goes against his religion. So instead, it trails off on a note of irony. . . . Existence is tragedy enough for a Calvinist temperament like his own: and nothing that happens to anyone in particular can add very much to that"—(Wilfrid Sheed, in the *N.Y. Times*). Diana Trilling (in the *Atlantic*) was less enthusiastic: "The evidence is sufficiently firm that Mr. Updike intended this as a [serious] novel . . . of morals. . . . The question is whether [he] has succeeded in giving us a serious book or whether, in final substance, the product of his moral effort is distinguishable from fashionable pornography."

"Rabbit Redux" continues the story of Harry Angstrom, the antihero of "Rabbit, Run," depicting him ten years after the ending of the earlier novel in such a way that his personal problems seem to reflect America's at the end of the sixties. "Rabbit" Angstrom, now separated from his wife and on the verge of losing his job as a linotype operator, takes into his home a drug-addicted young girl and a militant Black man. His relationships with these representative products of the changing times as well as with his uncomprehending old parents and his call-girl sister enable Updike to offer a profound social commentary in a story marked by mellow wisdom and compassion. Critical response to the novel tended to go to extremes with few reviewers responding moderately. Some found it trifling, unconvincing, even morally irresponsible; but the *N.Y. Times* hailed it as "a great achievement, by far the most audacious and successful book Updike has written," and William T. Stafford (in *Journal of Modern Literature*) found it "the most compelling demonstration yet that John Updike is our finest contemporary novelist—the one writer who is sufficiently exacting, imaginative, talented, and prolific to continue the American novelistic tradition in its most significant vein, that very exclusive vein best represented by Melville, Henry James, and Faulkner."

Updike is also a talented poet. In 1959 he received a Guggenheim fellowship for poetry. Available volumes are "The Carpentered Hen and Other Tame Creatures" (*Harper* 1958 $4.95), "Telephone Poles and Other Poems" (*Knopf* 1963 $4.50), "Verse"—a selection from the two preceding books (*Fawcett* Premier Bks. 1971 pap. $.95), and "Midpoint and Other Poems" (*Knopf* 1969 $4.50; *Fawcett* Crest Bks. pap. $.95). "Assorted Prose" (*Knopf* 1965 $6.95; *Fawcett* Premier Bks. 1969 pap. $.95) contains miscellaneous items that have appeared in various magazines.

Born and raised in Shillington, Penn., where he attended public schools, Mr. Updike was graduated from Harvard *summa cum laude*. After college he studied for a year at the Ruskin School of Fine Arts in Oxford, then worked on the staff of the *New Yorker* from 1955 to 1957. He now lives in Ipswich, Mass. In 1964 he was elected a member of the National Institute of Arts and Letters.

THE SAME DOOR: Short Stories. *Knopf* 1959 $5.95; *Fawcett* Premier Bks. pap. $.95

THE POORHOUSE FAIR. *Knopf* 1959 $4.95; *Fawcett* Premier Bks. $.95

RABBIT, RUN. *Knopf* 1960 $5.95; *Fawcett* Crest Bks. pap. $.95

PIGEON FEATHERS AND OTHER STORIES. *Knopf* 1962 $4.95; *Fawcett* Premier Bks. pap. $.95

THE CENTAUR. *Knopf* 1963 $5.95; *Fawcett* Crest Bks. 1964 pap. $.95

THE OLINGER STORIES. *Random* Vintage Bks. 1964 pap. $1.95

OF THE FARM. *Knopf* 1965 $4.50; *Fawcett* Premier Bks. pap. $.95

THE MUSIC SCHOOL. *Knopf* 1966 $4.95; *Fawcett* Premier Bks. pap. $.95. Short stories.

COUPLES. *Knopf* 1968 $6.95; *Fawcett* Crest Bks. pap. $1.25

BECH: A Book. *Knopf* 1970 $5.95; *Fawcett* Crest Bks. pap. $.95. Related short stories.

RABBIT REDUX. *Knopf* 1971 $7.95 boxed limited ed. $15.00

MUSEUMS AND WOMEN AND OTHER STORIES. *Knopf* 1972 $6.95 boxed ltd. ed. $15.00

Books about Updike

Elements of John Updike. By Alice and Kenneth Hamilton. *Eerdmans* 1970 $6.95
John Updike: Yea Sayings. By Rachael C. Burchard. Pref. by Harry T. Moore. Crosscurrents/Modern Critiques. *Southern Illinois Univ. Press* 1971 $5.45
Pastoral and Anti-Pastoral Themes in John Updike's Fiction. By Larry E. Taylor. Pref. by Harry T. Moore. Crosscurrents/Modern Critiques. *Southern Illinois Univ. Press* 1971 $5.45
John Updike. By Robert Detweiler. *Twayne's* U.S. Authors Ser. 1972 $5.50
John Updike: A Comprehensive Bibliography. By B. A. Sokoloff. *Folcroft* 1972 lim. ed. $12.50
Fighters and Lovers: Theme in the Novels of John Updike. By Joyce B. Markle. *New York Univ. Press* 1973 $8.95

GARDNER, JOHN. 1933–

An English professor and specialist in medieval literature at Southern Illinois University in Carbondale, John Gardner made his first major impact with "Grendel," a short novel which retells the Old English epic of "Beowulf" from the point of view of the dragon rather than the hero. His first novel, "The Resurrection" (1966, o. p.) is the story of a dying philosophy professor of 41 who returns to his childhood home in upstate

New York with his wife and three young daughters to confront his aging mother, his three spinster sisters, and other reminders of his past—and to face for real some of the fundamental questions about the meaning of existence which he has dealt with abstractly in his college classes. "The Wreckage of Agathon" is an experimental work set in the fifth century B.C. which alternates monologues by an old imprisoned seer with a young disciple-apprentice called Peeker. Following the successful "Grendel," Gardner wrote a long philosophical novel called "The Sunlight Dialogues" which deals, on perhaps the most fundamental of its many levels, with the conflict between an earnest but bumbling police chief in Batavia, New Ork, and a bearded, mysterious prisoner in his jail who calls himself "The Sunlight Man" and epitomizes the spirit of freedom and anarchy as emphatically as the police chief represents law and order. Thomas R. Edwards (in the *N.Y. Times*) compared this novel with its predecessor in this way: "Where 'Grendel' was, within its limits, virtually perfect, like a masterfully practiced stage-turn, 'The Sunlight Dialogues' is ambitious, heroically flawed, contemporary (though with rich mythic resonances), absorbing moment by moment and darkly troubling after it's over."

A vigorous and prolific writer, Gardner has written six substantial books in seven years as well as study guides and other material relating to his professional specialty. "Nickel Mountain" is the story of the developing love between a middle-aged man and a young woman and is set in a pastoral, country setting. "Jason and Medea" (*Knopf* 1973 $7.95) is his verse rendering of the classic myth effectively told in a long epic of more than 350 pages.

THE WRECKAGE OF AGATHON. *Harper* 1970 $6.95; *Ballantine* 1972 pap. $1.25

GRENDEL. *Knopf* 1971 $5.95; *Ballantine* 1972 pap. $.95; *G.K. Hall* Large Print Adult Bks. 1972 $6.95

THE SUNLIGHT DIALOGUES. *Knopf* 1972 $8.95

NICKEL MOUNTAIN. *Knopf* 1973 $6.95

KOSINSKI, JERZY. 1933–

Jerzy Kosinski, whose "Steps" won the National Book Award for fiction in 1968, grew up in Poland but emigrated to the United States in 1957 and became a naturalized citizen in 1965. His first two novels are set in Europe—not merely geographically, but in the wider, universal sense which makes the settings of works by Europeans such as Kafka, Céline, or Robbe-Grillet seem the setting of any American's nightmares. "The Painted Bird" is the story of a young boy wandering through Eastern Europe during the years of the Second World War. Looking on scenes of devastation and violence, the mute young observer somehow conveys a sense of mingled horror and compassion for the human condition. "Steps" presents even more neutralized vignettes of abuse, rape, and mutilation, but it achieves a kind of poetic grandeur in its unstated assumption that it is better to see horror than to see nothing at all. A novel without conventional narration, point-of-view, or dialogue, it harks back to works like Djuna Barnes's "Nightwood" in its surrealistic view of human bestiality, but it offers hope nonetheless if only in its demonstration that destruction must precede creation. The debauched woman who is the principal *object* of the subjectless "Steps" must go on living because she is Kozinski's image of his muse.

THE PAINTED BIRD. 1965. Rev. ed. *Modern Library* 1970 $2.95; *Bantam* 1972 pap. $1.25

STEPS. *Random* 1968 $5.95; *Bantam* 1969 pap. $.95

BEING THERE. *Random* 1971 $4.95; *Bantam* 1972 pap. $1.25

THE DEVIL TREE. *Harcourt* 1973 $6.95

PRICE, REYNOLDS. 1933–

After graduating from Duke University in 1955 and spending three years at Oxford as a Rhodes Scholar, Price returned to his alma mater and has been a member of its English faculty ever since. His three novels and two volumes of stories have earned him a reputation as a steadily growing artist of fiction who bears watching closely. He has stated his own purpose as a writer in the Preface to "Permanent Errors" as "the attempt to isolate in a number of lives the central error of act, will, understanding, which, once made, has been permanent, incurable, but whose diagnosis and palliation are hope of continuance." Thus Rosacoke Mustian, the heroine of "A Long and Happy Life," is a North Carolina country girl who dreams of settling down in the conventional way with a free-spirited young motorcylist who cannot be tamed. It is only after Rosacoke has become pregnant with Wesley Beaver's child that she begins to see herself in the larger terms of universal myth. "A Generous Man" extends Price's interest in myth and Christian values by telling of the Mustian family's attempt to capture an escaped circus python called Death. With "Love and Work" Price moves beyond the rural scenes of his first two novels to tell a quiet and ernest story about what it means to try to be a serious artist in a world all too ready to accept "permanent errors" as ultimate values. His "Things Themselves: Essays and Scenes" (*Atheneum* 1972 $8.95) is a collection of nonfictional pieces, including excellent literary criticism, which suggest that Price himself is still searching for something more important then mere self-expression. Everything Price has written to date testifies to his own respect for his craft, an exemplary example of "love and work."

A LONG AND HAPPY LIFE. *Atheneum* 1962 $4.95; *Avon* 1973 pap. $1.65

THE NAMES AND FACES OF HEROES. Stories. *Atheneum* 1963 $4.95 pap. $2.95

A GENEROUS MAN. *Atheneum* 1966 $4.95; *Avon* 1973 pap. $1.65

LOVE AND WORK. *Atheneum* 1968 $4.50

PERMANENT ERRORS. Stories. *Atheneum* 1970 $6.50

ROTH, PHILIP. 1933–

Philip Roth's first novella and short stories, "Goodbye, Columbus" won the 1960 National Book Award and the Daroff Award of the Jewish Book Council of America; he received a National Institute Grant in Literature in the same year. "What many writers spend a lifetime searching for—a unique voice, a secure rhythm, a distinctive subject—seem to have come to Philip Roth totally and immediately"—(Irving Howe); "Roth creates characters who leap off the page the moment he sets them down"—(*New Yorker*); " 'Goodbye, Columbus' is a first book but it is not the book of a beginner. Unlike those of us who come howling into the world, blind and bare, Mr. Roth appears with nails, hair, and teeth, speaking coherently. At 26 he is skillful, witty, and energetic and performs like a virtuoso"—(Saul Bellow). The short stories, which deal with contemporary Jewish life, had appeared previously in the *New Yorker*, the *Paris Review* and *Commentary*. He continued to "investigate the American Jewish community and cultural areas" in "Letting Go," a novel about young university teachers in the 1950s. The *Atlantic* said that "the sharply observant qualities of his first book have been expanded and enriched; he has become more probing, tentative, complex. . . . Mr. Roth is too lavish with his gifts. His talent for swift and concise characterization is such that he tends to bring minor characters unnecessarily into the foreground of the action. The result is that the book becomes too diffuse." In an article in *Commentary* on "Writing American Fiction" Mr. Roth says, "The American writer . . . of the twentieth century has his hands full in trying to understand, and then make credible much of the American reality. It stupefies, it sickens, it infuriates, and finally it is even a kind of embarrassment to one's own meager imagination. If the world is as crooked and unreal as I think it is becoming, day by day; if one feels less and less power in the face of this unreality; if the inevitable end is destruction, . . .—then why in God's name . . . why is it . . . that so many of our fictional heroes . . . wind up affirming life?" "When She Was Good" does not in any way affirm life. The novel presents "all the flatness and bleakness Mr. Roth professed to find in the Midwest"—(Wilfred Sheed). His non-Jewish feminine protagonist in striving for moral perfection ("and when she was good she was horrid") destroys her family and ultimately herself. Raymond Rosenthal said in the *New Leader:* "With a simplicity and modesty that are in the end lethal, Roth has written the most violently satiric book about American life since Evelyn Waugh's 'The Loved One.' . . . He tells us about the real conditions under which sexual relations in America come to disaster." Eliot Fremont-Smith found it "disappointing" but "better, finer and far more provocative and rewarding than most novels about which one is easily enthusiastic."

The best-selling "Portnoy's Complaint" caused a greater stir than any other recent novel. Told in the form of a confession by Alexander Portnoy to his psychiatrist Dr. Spielvogel, this outrageous novel centers around the character of Alexander's mother, Sarah Portnoy, the archetypal Jewish mother. Domineering and humorless (though humorous), she rules over her henpecked, constipated husband, her pathetically plain daughter, and her guilt-ridden son, whose sexual fantasies and graphic descriptions of his lovemaking with *shiksas* make up the bulk of the novel. Virtually the apotheosis of the American Jewish novel, "Portnoy's Complaint" seems almost to have killed off the form it represents, and even Roth himself has been hard put to match or surpass this blackest of comedies. "Our Gang" is a clever political satire directed at President Nixon and his pre-Watergate associates, but those prominent targets of Roth's venomous scorn seem pale and feeble when compared with the formidable Sophie Portnoy. "The Breast" finds Roth rather pathetically groping for a subject equally spectacular. It deals with an English teacher who awakes one morning to find himself transformed into a giant mammary gland. Most reviewers found the subject repugnant, but admired Roth for his artistic skill and his courage at attempting a work in that sub-genre of fiction represented by works like Gogol's "The Nose" and Kafka's "Metamorphosis." John Gardner (*q. v.*) thought it "Roth's best book so far"—(in *N.Y. Times*), but Bruce Allen (in *LJ*) considered it at best "a tempest in a D-cup."

Mr. Roth attended public schools in Newark, N.J., where he was born, received his B.A. from Bucknell University, where he was elected to Phi Beta Kappa in 1954; a year later he received his M.A. from the University of Chicago. During the academic year 1962–63 he was writer in residence at Princeton University. He has received many grants and fellowships.

GOODBYE, COLUMBUS AND FIVE SHORT STORIES. *Houghton* 1959 $5.95; *Bantam* pap. $1.25; *Modern Library* $2.95

LETTING GO. *Random* 1962 $8.95; *Bantam* 1963 pap. $1.25

WHEN SHE WAS GOOD. *Random* 1967 $7.95; *Bantam* 1968 pap. $1.25

PORTNOY'S COMPLAINT. *Random* 1969 $6.95; *Bantam* pap. $1.50

OUR GANG (Starring Tricky and His Friends). *Random* 1971 $5.95; *Bantam* pap. $1.50

THE BREAST. *Holt* 1972 $4.95; *Bantam* 1973 pap. $1.25

KESEY, KEN. 1935–

It may well be appropriate that both the farthermost region of the United States and the farthest-out generation of Americans appear to have found their laureate in Ken Kesey. Born in Colorado, graduated from the University of Oregon, and since then a sometimes vagabond resident of the West Coast, Kesey has published under his own name only two novels, but they have made a nationwide impact upon the younger generation unparalleled since the heyday of J. D. Salinger. "One Flew Over the Cuckoo's Nest" apparently owes much to Kesey's own experience as a ward attendant in a mental hospital. This exciting first novel is told from the point of view of a half-breed who thinks of himself as the "Big Chief" on the writing tablets of everybody's schooldays looking out at the other inmates in a Disney-like world where the "figures are flat and outlined in black, jerking through some kind of goofy story that might be real funny if it weren't for the cartoon figures being real guys." Big Chief, who pretends to be a deaf crazyman oblivious to all that goes on around him, serves as the detached and passive observer of the impassioned, vital Irishman, MacMurphy, who becomes the rebellious hero of all the other inmates of his ward. MacMurphy's vigorous confrontation of "Big Nurse" and all she represents in the way of Establishment values gives courage and renewed hope to the pitiful mental patients who are Big Chief's companions. The rebellion of the inmates against the iron rule of "Big Nurse" and her cruel orderlies results ultimately in tragedy. In spite of MacMurphy's prefrontal lobotomy, "Big Chief" finds a way for the Irishman as well as himself to transcend the cuckoo's nest.

"Sometimes a Great Notion" is a long, complex novel which troubled many of the readers of Kesey's first novel, for though this story of a lumbering family dynasty in the Northwest exalts the romantic values of nature and emotion over the feeble representatives of the Establishment represented in the story, it also seems to champion strong, arrogant individualism against anything that smacks of conformity or easy concessions to group approval. The Ken Kersey who wrote "Sometimes a Great Notion" would not have been likely to attend the festivities at Woodstock. Yet since publishing that daring and misunderstood novel Kesey has publicly renounced "literature" for "life" and has allowed himself to become a cult hero for the commune-and-candlestick generation. As Tom Wolfe reported in his "Electric Kool-Aid Acid Test" (*Farrar* 1968 $7.95; *Bantam* 1969 pap. $1.25), Kesey organized a band of "Merry Pranksters" who went on the road in the far west attempting to live life as if it were a comic book. Married and the father of four children, he has served as a kind of guru for an Oregon commune during the decade since his second novel was published. Although he has thrown out hints that he may have written fiction under a pseudonym, his only publication of record in recent years is "Ken Kesey's Garage Sale" (*Viking* 1973 $6.95 pap. $3.95), a hodge-podge of survival-kit materials which seem to have derived from his many contributions to the last supplement of "The Whole Earth Catalog."

ONE FLEW OVER THE CUCKOO'S NEST. *Viking* 1962 $6.00 Compass pap. $1.85 Critical Lib. Ed. by John C. Pratt (incl. text and criticism) 1973 $7.95 pap. $2.45

SOMETIMES A GREAT NOTION. *Viking* 1964 1971 pap. $3.50; *Bantam* 1971 pap. $1.25

PYNCHON, THOMAS. 1937–

The reader who would know Thomas Pynchon had best read his two novels and, if he then wishes to explore further, look into two interesting explications—one the review of "The Crying of Lot 49" by Richard Poirier in the *N.Y. Times Book Review* on its publication, the other "The New Novel, U.S.A.: Thomas Pynchon" by Robert Sklar, in the *Nation* of Sept. 25, 1967. Mr. Pynchon's knowledge of physics, electronics, philosophy, and psychology, combined with extraordinary writing skill, have enabled him, "more than any other contemporary novelist, to succeed in absorbing and transforming new scientific and philosophical perspectives within his art"—(Sklar). "Pynchon's remarkable ability includes a vigorous and imaginative style, a robust humor, a tremendous reservoir of information (one suspects he could churn out a passable almanac in a fortnight's time) and, above all, a sense of how to use and balance these talents"—(George Plimpton, in the *N.Y. Times*).

Mr. Pynchon was born in Long Island, N.Y., and received his B.A. degree from Cornell University. Shortly after college he published "Entrophy," which appeared in "The Best American Short Stories of 1961." In 1963 "V" won the Faulkner First Novel Award. In it a Benny Profane becomes obsessed with the discovery of "V," a woman's initial, in the diary of his late father, a British foreign officer, and sets off on a quest to find her. The plot revolves around international politics and spying in Europe and Africa from the 1890s to 1939. Mary McCarthy suggests that the book could rank as "one of the most encyclopedic founts of fact in the history of the novel," with its detailed descriptions of a nose operation, the intricacies of British espionage in the Middle East, the history of Malta, and similar abstruse subjects. Richard Poirier sees the quests for V as "substitutes for the pursuit of love . . . interwoven fantastically." Like "Finnegans Wake," but more comprehensible on the surface, "V" beggars description and should be read—in conjunction with Mr. Pynchon's second novel.

"The Crying of Lot 49" is the story of how Mrs. Oedipa Maas discovers a world within her world, an anti-world, an adversary world—or invents one in her imagination. She has been named co-executor for the estate of a California financier . . . with whom . . . she had had a brief affair"—(Sklar). A worldwide conspiracy in which she becomes involved as a result of this duty concerns the U.S. Post Office; "Lot 49" at auction is the dead financier's stamp collection, which assumes tremendous significance to Oedipa. The novel makes use of information and communications theory à la Norbert Wiener, among other subjects. Here again the symbolism, the commentary on America and on human isolation are intricate and masterly—for those readers who seek new directions in the novel. Others may be baffled and bored, like the reviewer for *Best Sellers*. But to Robert Sklar, "Pynchon surely ranks as the most intelligent, most audacious and most accomplished American novelist writing today." He now lives in California.

V. 1963. *Bantam* $1.25; *Lippincott* 1963 $5.95

THE CRYING OF LOT 49. *Lippincott* 1966 $3.95; *Bantam* $.95

GRAVITY'S RAINBOW. *Viking* 1973 $15.00 Compass Bks. pap. $4.95. Winner of the National Book Award 1974.

OATES, JOYCE CAROL. 1938–

Although still a young woman, Joyce Carol Oates has established a reputation as indubitably one of our most prolific writers and very likely one of our best. Born in Lockport, N.Y., the daughter of a tool and die designer, she graduated from Syracuse University in 1960 and took a master's degree the following year at the University of Wisconsin. She married Raymond J. Smith in 1961, and after several years of teaching at the University of Detroit, joined her husband on the English faculty at the University of Windsor in Canada, where they are now both full professors. By the time she was 35, Miss Oates had published six novels, four collections of short stories, three volumes of poetry, and a book of critical essays as well as several unpublished plays that were produced off-Broadway and numerous fugitive stories, poems, reviews, and essays not yet collected in book form.

Her fiction alone demonstrates considerable variety in that it ranges from direct naturalism to complex experiments in form. However, what chiefly makes her work peculiarly her own is a quality of psychological realism, an uncanny ability to bring to the surface of her narratives an underlying sense of foreboding within her characters or a threat of violence which seems to lurk just around the corner from the everyday domestic lives she depicts so realistically. Reviewing one of her collections of stories, "The Wheel of Love," William Abrahams writes: "There is a sense of tension, of nerves strained to the breaking point, of 'the pitch that is close to madness' in much of what she writes"—(*Saturday Review*). And commenting on her own assertion that "the emotion of love, probably that's the essence of what I'm writing about," the critic Alfred Kazin notes that for Miss Oates love means "an attraction of person to person so violent that it expresses itself as obsession and takes on the quality of fatality"—(*Harper's*).

Her six novels express these qualities in varying ways. "With Shuddering Fall" is the story of the intense and violent relationship between a 17-year-old girl and a 30-year-old racing car driver which ends with his fiery death in an accident. "A Garden of Earthly Delights" charts the story of a woman from her childhood with migrant farm workers through a dreary period as a shopgirl until she becomes the wife of a rich man and slips into madness during her middle years. "Expensive People" makes use of reflexive experimental devices in a story told by an 18-year-old boy, the only child of a wealthy suburban couple. Richard Everett, the narrator, is a genius in intelligence, but so unstable emotionally that the reader never knows for sure whether or not what he tells, including his murder of his beautiful and talented authoress-mother, is true or not. "Them," which won the National Book Award for fiction in 1969, is the story of a lower-class family in Detroit from the time of the Depression through the race riots of 1967. "Wonderland" covers much the same period, but centers around the macabre story of a man who can never overcome the trauma of having watched his father years before slaughter all the other members of the family and try to kill him as well. The cycle comes complete when the protagonist of the novel, a respectable doctor, kills his own daughter when she has run off with a hippie and becomes addicted to drugs. "Do With Me What You Will" is a searing story of domestic love–hate which seems to demonstrate that suffering and violence may lie at the root of the most intense emotional relationships.

Miss Oates's three volumes of poetry, all published by Louisiana State University Press, are "Anonymous Sins and Other Poems" (1969 $4.50), "Love and Its Derangements" (1970 $4.50), and "Angel Fire" (1973 $4.95). In addition to editing a collection of short stories, "Scenes from American Life" (*Vanguard* 1972 $6.95 pap. $3.95), she has published a collection of perceptive critical essays in "The Edge of Impossibility: Tragic Forms in Literature" (*Vanguard* 1972 $8.50).

BY THE NORTH GATE. Stories. *Vanguard* 1963 $6.95; *Fawcett* Crest pap. $.95

WITH SHUDDERING FALL. *Vanguard* 1964 $6.95; *Fawcett* Crest pap. $.95

UPON THE SWEEPING FLOOD AND OTHER STORIES. *Vanguard* 1966 $6.95; *Fawcett* Crest 1972 $.95

A GARDEN OF EARTHLY DELIGHTS. *Vanguard* 1967 $5.95; *Fawcett* Crest pap. $1.25

EXPENSIVE PEOPLE. *Vanguard* 1968 $6.95; *Fawcett* Crest pap. $.95

THEM. *Vanguard* 1969 $6.95; *Fawcett* Crest 1973 $1.50

THE WHEEL OF LOVE AND OTHER STORIES. *Vanguard* 1970 $6.95; *Fawcett* Crest pap. $1.25

WONDERLAND. *Vanguard* 1971 $7.95; *Fawcett* Crest pap. $1.50

MARRIAGES AND INFIDELITIES. Stories. *Vanguard* 1972 $7.95; *Fawcett* Crest 1973 pap. $1.25

DO WITH ME WHAT YOU WILL. *Vanguard* 1973 $8.95

—M.B.

Chapter 15

Essays and Criticism

"We are dealing here with a form, the essay, that is peculiarly personal."
—Alfred Kazin

THE ESSAY

Dr. Johnson, the "great cham" of common sense, thought (predictably) of the essay as "a loose sally of the mind, an irregular, undigested piece, not a regular and orderly perform- ance." Leslie Fiedler, on the other hand, in his illuminating introduction to a collection of essays, "The Art of the Essay" (*T. Y. Crowell* 2nd ed. 1969 pap. $4.95), refers to this lit- erary form as a sort of translation of "the speaking voice and the living self into printed prose" and, again, a "brief piece of discursive prose, whose intimacy of tone and relaxed approach to its theme make it the next step beyond intelligent conversation." Both critics are referring to the sort of essay known as "informal" or "familiar." But essays can be— especially when they engage in criticism, whether social, literary, or other—quite as or- derly as Dr. Johnson might have wished. Such is the "formal essay," whose practitioners pursue a serious theme rigorously, sometimes with a relentless marshalling of argument to prove a point, reform a vice, or change a world.

Whatever the history of other literary genres, the essay's course seems to be somewhat teleological. Montaigne invented it in the 16th century and named it, on the grounds that it was a form in which he could "essay" or try out his ideas by reflecting upon various subjects in writing without claiming to be definitive. In so doing, he became the father of what is called, variously, the "personal," "familiar," or "informal" essay. The intimate relationship between author and form is indicated by his observation, "Everyone recog- nizes me in my book, and everyone recognizes my book in me."

But in the early 17th century, Sir Francis Bacon employed the form for more objective and "serious" purposes. The quality of his 58 essays is not conversational, like that of Montaigne's, but sententious, of an intellectual density, and didactic in the purpose of providing "Counsels Civil and Moral."

Thus the quarrel between the two contrasting possibilities, the personal and the imper- sonal uses of the form, occurred at its very inception. The personal potentiality could not completely blossom until two matters were settled: the arts, particularly literature, of course, had to provide ample room for subjective and personal expression; and literature had to acknowledge the fact that prose was not merely "prosaic" but capable of artistic use. In the 18th century, the latter was achieved, especially with the rising and flourishing of the periodicals. The tenor of the age, however, was objective and rational. Thus the pe- riodical essays of Joseph Addison, Sir Richard Steele, Samuel Johnson and others are eloquent compromises of the two possible natures of the form. But when Romanticism in art dominated the spirit of literature, in the early 19th century, the informal essay blos- somed in the works of Charles Lamb, William Hazlitt, Thomas DeQuincey, and others. Many of their best essays first appeared in a new sort of periodical, the "magazine," so named to indicate its inclination to be a storehouse of verbal odds and ends. *Blackwoods* (1817) and *The London Magazine* (1821) aimed at a wider and less "serious" audience than did the political and literary periodicals of the time, and encouraged writing of a light tone and on popular topics. Throughout the century, and to a significant extent in our own time, English and American essayists have found the magazine to be their most congenial host. Today the familiar form is widely employed, though often under the name of editorial, political column, humorous column, book, play or film review, or even, more modestly, "letters to the editor." Many a "personality" today is known chiefly through one of these forms of the essay. M. J. Arlen comments on this visibility: "The essay writer occupies one of the more exposed of all literary positions. Most other writers, novelists and historians, for example, can go about their business and keep their own personalities safely out of sight . . . not so the essayists. Year in, year out, the essayist is right there with us, bravely talking along, telling us what *he* thinks, ..." Or, to return to the original implication of the name, one may say the essay writer is trying to find out what he thinks, in this best of all forms of self-discovery.

The formal essay, on the other hand, has tended to concern itself rather thoroughly with literary criticism. In Montaigne's time, but on the English side of the Channel, Sir Philip Sidney wrote "The Apologie for Poetrie," subtitled "Defence of Poesie," to defend the art against the attacks of Stephen Gosson. Sidney's essay is methodical, thorough, and objective, and constitutes perhaps the earliest significant single piece of English literary criticism still vital today.

Other purposes dominated the prose writings of the 17th century, but the flourishing periodicals of the 18th century gave ample opportunity to the analytical minds of the Age of Reason, who found much to say about the nature, history, and principles of the arts. Literary criticism of the 19th Century was often impressionistic rather than objective, and the familiar essay was a conducive form. In our time, literary criticism has become one of the dominating concerns of writers. The seriousness of their concern has found expression in book-length treatises, and especially in the formal essay.

Twentieth-century literary criticism, especially American, employs so many critical methods that the nonprofessional reader sometimes feels lost in a maze. It may be helpful, then, to delineate the major paths through so rich a jungle.

The most traditional approach—one that goes all the way back to Sidney's "Defence"—is moral criticism. Writers in this "school" are concerned with literature as a criticism of life, a means in aesthetic form of affecting, however obliquely, human behavior. Thus the emphasis is less upon how a work of literary art makes its statement, and more upon the statement itself. Although this is certainly a simple, perhaps even simplistic description of moral criticism, a sense of the complexities and subtleties possible may be restored by mention of some of the leading practitioners: Irving Babbit, Paul Elmer More, T. E. Hulme, Yvor Winters, T. S. Eliot.

A second approach, one that currently dominates, is the psychological. Fundamentally, this is to take insights from this new field of theory and knowledge, and apply them to literature, in order the better to understand the literary work. Critics may, then, study the characters of fiction; or psychoanalyze the authors; or explore the psychological nature of aesthetics, as reader and writer become entangled in their strange and wonderful relationship. Thus Ernest Jones shows us what motivates Hamlet's often bewildering behavior. Thus Marie Bonaparte puts Edgar Allan Poe metaphorically upon the couch. Thus Kenneth Burke reveals how Shakespeare aesthetically manipulates his readers, just as Antony politically guides and controls the emotions of his "friends, Romans and countrymen" to his own ends.

Still another approach examines the sociological impact of literature. Insofar as the sociological critic is concerned more with the ends of literature than with its means, insofar as he feels the ideological content is of greatest significance, he joins the moral critic, although they may strongly disagree as to which ideas and what sorts of ideas are of chief importance. On the other hand, he may be interested to explore the social beliefs lying beneath the surface and perhaps even unknown to the writer himself, as Orwell does with Kipling. In such cases, the sociological critic assumes kinship with the psychological critic.

For several decades—the forties and the fifties—another sort of criticism dominated the field. Commonly referred to as the "New Criticism," it has been brilliantly practiced by such prominent writers as Allen Tate, Cleanth Brooks, and John Crowe Ransom, and many writers in shorter pieces in the periodical dedicated to this approach, *The Explicator*. In essence, the "new critic"—or better, "formalistic" "textual" critic—eschews all material not explicit or implicit in the work itself (e.g. biographical, historical, moral) and studies out the intricate relationship of the parts, as they cooperate to achieve an aesthetic end. At the extreme, the critic examines the literary work as if it were without author, society, or place, and purely as an object with its own purpose and craft.

The current dissatisfaction with reason as man's surest guide to salvation, the current and growing view of man as a more-than-rational being has revived late 19th-century interest in myth as an obliquely valid expression of human nature. If, as Jung claims, myth is retained in the social memory, critics are often interested to find in literature new forms and expressions of ancient patterns and relationships of human behavior. Fiedler expresses this particular critical endeavor as evolving from the critic's sense that "the deepest meanings, meanings which extend beyond the single work to a whole body of books, are to be sought in the archetypal symbols to which . . . writers compulsively return." The writer is not a brilliant neurotic (as he may seem to the psychological critic) but, in the words of C. Hugh Holman, "a shaman, a mythmaker, speaking out of his unconscious a primordial truth." The aim of the archetypal critic then, is to discover and decode the secret language in literary works of art.

No critic of enduring worth adheres to any one single approach, of course. Otherwise the route becomes a rut. But many of the literary critics of our time do emphasize one or another of these approaches. And since they often wish to follow that approach in pursuit of understanding a particular poem, story, or play, rather than a corpus of works, they have turned to the formal essay as the genre most fitting for such exploration. The critic's foot seems to have found the perfect shoe.

LITERARY CRITICISM

Studies of Literary Criticism

This reading list is well supplemented by several of the listings in Chapter 4, Broad Studies and General Anthologies (*q. v.*).

Abercrombie, Lascelles. PRINCIPLES OF LITERARY CRITICISM. *Barnes & Noble* 1960 pap. $2.50

Atkins, John W. ENGLISH LITERARY CRITICISM. 3 vols. Vol. 1 17th and 18th Centuries *Barnes & Noble* 1966 pap. $2.75 Vol. 2 The Medieval Phase *Peter Smith* $4.25 Vol. 3 The Renascence *Barnes & Noble* 1968 $5.00

LITERARY CRITICISM OF ANTIQUITY. *Peter Smith* 2 vols. Vol. 1 Greek $4.00 Vol. 2 Graeco-Roman $6.00. The five vols. of the two Atkins titles above constitute a thoroughly scholarly history of literary criticism from ancient times through the 18th century.

Chiari, Joseph. REALISM AND IMAGINATION. 1960 *Gordian* text ed. $7.50

Surveys the growth of artistic theories from Plato to the present. A "meaty and well-documented study"— (*LJ*).

Cohen Ralph. THE ART OF DISCRIMINATION: Thomson's "The Seasons" and the Language of Criticism. *Univ. of California Press* 1964 $11.50. Explores the different applications of criticism from 1750 to 1950 of Thomson's poem, and becomes, thus, a history of critical interpretation during those years.

Coleman, Elliot, Ed. LECTURES IN CRITICISM. Introd. by Huntington Cairns. Bollingen Ser. *Princeton Univ. Press* 1949 $10.00. A symposium on great critics by Blackmur, Croce, Peyre, Ransom, Read and Tate

Colum, Mary M. FROM THESE ROOTS: The Ideas That Have Made Modern Literature. 1937. *Kennikat* 1967 $11.00

"An interpretation of modern literature in which is developed the thesis that literature is preceded by and directed by great criticism"—(*BRD*).

Daiches, David. CRITICAL APPROACHES TO LITERATURE. *Prentice-Hall* 1956 $9.95; *Norton* 1965 pap. $3.95. An examination of the values of literature, the ways of evaluating literature, and relationships between literary criticism and other fields of knowledge. Contains generous excerpts from critical writings.

Edel, Leon, Ed. LITERARY HISTORY AND LITERARY CRITICISM: Acta of the Ninth Congress of the International Federation for Modern Languages and Literature. *New York Univ. Press* 1964 $8.95

"A most fortunate survey of the current state of the art of literary criticism"—(*LJ*).

Ellmann, Richard, and Charles Feidelson, Jr., Eds. THE MODERN TRADITION: Backgrounds of Modern Literature. *Oxford* 1965 $17.50 text ed. $10.95

"Designed to represent the various factors that any theory [of literary modernism] will be obliged to take into account. The representation is by direct quotation"—(from the Preface). Main headings are Symbolism, Realism, Nature, Cultural History, Myth, Self-Consciousness, Existence, and Faith.

Embler, Weller. METAPHOR AND MEANING. Fwd. by S. I. Hayakawa. *Everett Edwards* 1966 o. p.

"Examines the pervasiveness of metaphor for all cultures . . . an excellent volume for students or interested laymen beginning serious work in literary criticism"—(*LJ*).

Foerster, Norman. AMERICAN CRITICISM: A Study in Literary Theory from Poe to the Present. 1928. *Russell & Russell* 1962 $12.00. *See comment in Chapter 4, Broad Studies and General Anthologies.*

Foster, Richard, THE NEW ROMANTICS: A Reappraisal of the New Criticism. 1962. *Kennikat* 1973 $10.00. A sympathetic evaluation which argues that this movement is "founded on essentially romantic responses and attitudes."

Frailberg, Louis. PSYCHOANALYSIS AND AMERICAN LITERARY CRITICISM. Ed. by Esther Ellen Jacoby. *Wayne State Univ. Press* 1960. o. p. The critics discussed are Van Wyck Brooks, Krutch, Lewisohn, Edmund Wilson, Kenneth Burke and Lionel Trilling.

Frye, Northrop. ANATOMY OF CRITICISM. *Princeton Univ. Press* 1957 $13.50 pap. $2.95. A synoptic view of the scope, theory, principles, and techniques of literary criticism. Four essays on historical, ethical, archetypal, and rhetorical criticism.

Greene, Theodore M. THE ARTS AND THE ART OF CRITICISM. *Gordian* 1947 $22.50. A study of works of art and also of "those aspects of the art of criticism which lend themselves to philosophical analysis"—(from the Preface). Part 2 is especially concerned with the principles of criticism.

Hall, Vernon, Jr. A SHORT HISTORY OF LITERARY CRITICISM. *New York Univ. Press* 1963 $8.00 pap. $2.45

"Deals lucidly with a well-chosen succession of critical viewpoints"—(*LJ*).

Hollingworth, Gertrude Eleanore. A PRIMER OF LITERARY CRITICISM. 1924. *Folcroft* 1973 lib. bdg. $10.00; *Richard West* 1973 $10.00

Hyman, Stanley Edgar. THE ARMED VISION: A Study in the Methods of Literary Criticism. *Knopf* 1948, o. p. A penetrating study.

O'Connor, William Van. AN AGE OF CRITICISM, 1900–1950. *Regnery* 1966 pap. $1.25. Nine chapters on various traditions and types of American literary criticism.

Pritchard, John Paul. CRITICISM IN AMERICA: An Account of the Development of Critical Techniques from the Early Period of the Republic to the Middle Years of the Twentieth Century. *Univ. of Oklahoma Press* 1956 $7.95

LITERARY WISE MEN OF GOTHAM: Criticism in New York, 1815–1860. *Louisiana State Univ. Press* 1963 $6.00

"Fills an important gap in the history of American literature and criticism"—(*LJ*).

Richards, Ivor Armstrong. THE PRINCIPLES OF LITERARY CRITICISM. International Lib. of Psychology, Philosophy and Scientific Method *Harcourt* 1925 2nd ed. 1926 Harvest Bks. pap. $1.95

PRACTICAL CRITICISM: A Study of Literary Judgment. 1929. *Harcourt* 1950 Harvest Bks. 1956 pap. $2.25

Saintsbury, George E. A HISTORY OF CRITICISM AND LITERARY TASTE IN EUROPE. 1900–04. *Humanities Press* 3 vols. 1950 Vol. 1 Classical and Medieval Criticism Vol. 2 From the Renaissance to the Decline of 18th Century Orthodoxy Vol. 3 Modern Criticism each $6.50 set $17.50

A HISTORY OF ENGLISH CRITICISM. 1911. *British Bk. Centre* 1972 $7.95; *Verry* $6.50

Smith, Bernard. FORCES IN AMERICAN CRITICISM: A Study in the History of American Literary Thought. 1939. *Cooper* 1971 $10.95

Stallman, Robert Wooster, Ed. THE CRITIC'S NOTEBOOK. *Univ. of Minnesota Press* 1950 o. p.

"300 quotations [some brief, some extensive] are organized into 8 chapters dealing systematically with central concepts and problems of modern criticism"—(from the Foreword).

Stauffer, Donald, Ed. THE INTENT OF THE CRITIC. Essays by Edmund Wilson, Norman Foerster, John Crowe Ransom, and W. H. Auden. *Peter Smith* 1963 $3.75

Stovall, Floyd, Ed. THE DEVELOPMENT OF AMERICAN LITERARY CRITICISM. Five essays by scholars of American literature on American literary criticism from 1800. 1955. *College & Univ. Press* pap. $2.95

Sutton, Walter. MODERN AMERICAN CRITICISM. A survey. *Prentice-Hall* 1963 $8.95

Tyack, David B. GEORGE TICKNOR AND THE BOSTON BRAHMINS. *Harvard Univ. Press* 1967 $8.00

> A study of an American 19th-century scholar and critic. Chapter IV "is an indispensible essay for those who would understand the Brahmins collectively and individually"—(*Choice*).

Wellek, Rene. A HISTORY OF MODERN CRITICISM: 1750–1950. *Yale Univ. Press* 4 vols. 1955 Vol. 1 The Later 18th Century $10.00 Vol. 2 The Romantic Age $10.00 Vol. 3 The Age of Transition $12.50 Vol. 4 The Later 19th Century $12.50

> A clearly monumental work by a distinguished literary historian, critic and scholar. Covers the major critical tenets and practicing critics in Great Britain, France and Italy. "Faultless scholarship and impeccable judgment"—(*LJ*).

(With Austin Warren). THEORY OF LITERATURE. *Harcourt* Harvest Bks. rev. ed. pap. $2.45. "This is the most ordered, ranging and purposeful attempt that has been made in some time toward keeping the study of literature at once intelligent and liberal."

CONFRONTATIONS: Studies in the Intellectual and Literary Relations Between Germany, England, and the United States During the Nineteenth Century. *Princeton Univ. Press* 1965 $9.50 pap. $2.95. Six essays describing the spread of German philosophical ideas to England and the United States, with attention to Carlyle, De Quincey, and Emerson and the New England transcendentalists.

Wimsatt, William K., Jr., and Cleanth Brooks. LITERARY CRITICISM: A Short History. *Knopf* 1957 $10.00

See also Section on Essay Collections by a single author, below, and Chapter 4, Broad Studies and General Anthologies: General Works of Criticism.

Literary Criticism: Books, Essays and Collections

For major critics, see separate entries in this section.

Abrams, Meyer H., Ed. LITERATURE AND BELIEF. 1957. English Institute Essays *Columbia* 1958 $8.50

Aldridge, John W., Ed. CRITIQUES AND ESSAYS ON MODERN FICTION, 1920–1951. *Ronald* 1952 $8.50

Allen, Gay Wilson, and Harry Haydon Clark, Eds. LITERARY CRITICISM: Pope to Croce. *Wayne State Univ. Press* 1962 $9.95 pap. $5.95

Bate, Walter Jackson, Ed. CRITICISM: The Major Texts. *Harcourt* 1952 $11.95. A collection by a distinguished Harvard scholar. Aristotle to Edmund Wilson, with introductory remarks on each author.

Becker, George J., Ed. DOCUMENTS OF MODERN LITERARY REALISM. *Princeton Univ. Press* 1963 $15.00 pap. $3.95. Selections from critics and authors all over the world illustrate Realism's rise as a reaction to Romanticism.

Beckson, Karl, Ed. GREAT THEORIES IN LITERARY CRITICISM. *Farrar, Straus* Noonday 1963 o. p.

> "A selection of important critical statements from Plato to Arnold, with the emphasis on English criticism. . . . In most cases, the selection is presented in its entirety"—(from the Foreword). Bibliography.

Brown, C. A. THE ACHIEVEMENT OF AMERICAN CRITICISM: Representative Selections from 300 Years of American Criticism. *Ronald* 1954 o. p.

Camden, Carroll, Ed. LITERARY VIEWS: Critical and Historical Essays. By Northrop Frye, Lionel Trilling, Harry Levin, René Wellek and others. *Univ. of Chicago Press* 1964 $5.00

Crane, Ronald S., and others, Eds. CRITICS AND CRITICISM, ANCIENT AND MODERN. With an introd. *Univ. of Chicago Press* 1952 $10.00 Phoenix Bks. (abr.) 1957 pap. $2.45

Durham, Willard Higley, Ed. CRITICAL ESSAYS OF THE EIGHTEENTH CENTURY 1700–1725. 1915. *Russell & Russell* 1961 $10.00

Gilbert, Allan H., Ed. LITERARY CRITICISM: Plato to Dryden. 1940. *Wayne State Univ. Press* 1962 pap. $5.95

Glicksberg, Charles Irving, Ed. AMERICAN LITERARY CRITICISM, 1900–1950. *Hendricks House* $8.50

Goldberg, Gerald Jay, and Nancy Marmer Goldberg, Eds. THE MODERN CRITICAL SPECTRUM. *Prentice-Hall* 1962 $8.95. Essays on eight major critical trends with illustrative examples of each.

Gross, Laila, Ed. INTRODUCTION TO LITERARY CRITICISM. *Putnam* 1971 $7.95 Capricorn Bks. pap. $2.95

Jones, Edmund David. ENGLISH CRITICAL ESSAYS: 16th–18th Centuries. 1922 *Oxford* World's Class. 1930 $1.95

ENGLISH CRITICIAL ESSAYS: 19th Century. 1922 *Oxford* pap. $1.95

Jones, Phyllis M. ENGLISH CRITICAL ESSAYS: 20th Century. *Oxford* World's Class. $2.25

Langer, Susanne K., Ed. REFLECTIONS ON ART: A Source Book of Writings by Artists, Critics and Philosophers. *Johns Hopkins Univ. Press* 1958 $10.00; *Oxford* Galaxy Bks. 1961 pap. $3.50. These 26 significant essays deal mainly with the plastic arts, music and literature.

Lewis, R. W. B. THE AMERICAN ADAM. *Univ. of Chicago Press* 1955 $6.00 pap. $1.75. Mr. Lewis expresses his stimulating point of view on American life and letters.

TRIALS OF THE WORD: Essays in American Literature and the Humanistic Tradition. *Yale Univ. Press* 1965 $6.50

Nine extended literary essays that "cannot fail to delight anyone remotely or professionally involved with literature"—(*LJ*).

A LIBRARY OF LITERARY CRITICISM:

MOULTON'S LIBRARY OF CRITICISM OF ENGLISH AND AMERICAN AUTHORS THROUGH THE BEGINNING OF THE TWENTIETH CENTURY. *Peter Smith* 8 vols. each $11.00; abr. ed. and with additions by Martin Tucker *Ungar* 1966 $45.00

MODERN AMERICAN LITERATURE. Comp. and ed. by Dorothy Nyren. *Ungar* 1964 3rd ed. enl. $15.00 4th ed. 1969 ed. by Dorothy Nyren Curley, Maurice Kramer and Elaine Fialka Kramer 3 vols. $45.00

MODERN BRITISH LITERATURE. Comp. and ed. by Ruth Z. Temple and Martin Tucker. *Ungar* 3 vols. $45.00

Moulton's original 19th-century work has inspired these modern volumes of compilations from criticism in periodicals, newspapers, books, etc., mostly British and American. Alphabetized by author criticized, each excerpt has been chosen to "describe [the author's] qualities, define his status, and show something of his life and personality." Full citations are given for the criticisms, and there is a selective bibliography of each author's work and an index to critics—who are often among the most distinguished of their profession. Many are themselves noted as creative writers.

Lipking, Laurence I., and A. Walton, Eds. MODERN LITERARY CRITICISM, 1900–1970. *Atheneum* 1972 pap. text ed. $12.95. An interesting arrangement: Four Major Critics; Problems and Methods of Modern Criticism; Continental Critics; and Poet Critics.

Lodge, David, Ed. TWENTIETH CENTURY LITERARY CRITICISM: A Reader. *Longman* 1972 pap. text ed. $9.50

Manheim, Leonard, and Eleanor Manheim, Eds. HIDDEN PATTERNS: Studies in Psychoanalytic Literary Criticism. *Macmillan* 1966 o. p. Three essays by psychiatrists, 13 by literary scholars, on the relationship between psychiatry and literature, and on literary works from the psychological point of view.

ENGLISH CRITICAL ESSAYS. *See under Jones, Edmund D., and Jones, Phyllis M., above.*

Rowse, Alfred L. THE ENGLISH SPIRIT: Essays in Literature and History. *Funk & Wagnalls* 1967 $5.95 pap. $2.95

Scott, Wilbur S., Ed. FIVE APPROACHES TO LITERARY CRITICISM. *Macmillan* 1963 $6.95 Collier Bks. pap. $1.50. A clear arrangement of critical methods according to five general categories with examples of each.

Smith, George Gregory, Ed. ELIZABETHAN CRITICAL ESSAYS. *Oxford* 2 vols. 1904 $17.00

Smith, James H., and E. W. Parks, Eds. THE GREAT CRITICS: An Anthology of Literary Criticism. *Norton* 3rd ed. rev. and enl. 1951 $9.95. A standard work.

Stallman, Robert Wooster, Ed. CRITIQUES AND ESSAYS IN CRITICISM, 1920–1948: Representing the Achievement of Modern British and American Critics. Fwd. by Cleanth Brooks. *Ronald* 1949 $8.50. An impressive anthology presenting "a comprehensive view of the new criticism in the Hulme-Eliot-Tate line of descent"; chiefly on poetry and poetics; valuable biographical notes and a selected bibliography of modern criticism, 1920–1948.

Times Literary Supplement (London). ESSAYS AND REVIEWS FROM THE TIMES LITERARY SUPPLEMENT. *Oxford* 10 vols. Vol. I 1962 $8.50 Vol. 2 1963 (1964) $8.50 Vol. 3 1964 (1965) $8.50 Vol. 4 1965 (1966), o. p. Vol. 5 1966 (1967) $10.25 Vol. 6 1967 (1968) $11.00 Vol. 7 1968 (1969) $11.00 Vol. 8 1969 (1970) $11.00 Vol. 9 1970 (1971) $12.00 Vol. 10 1971 (1972) $12.00

"An excellent record of the literary world"—(*L J*).

THE TIMES LITERARY SUPPLEMENT: Annual Bound Volumes, 1902–1964. Vols. 1923–43 ready 1967; Vols. 1902–22 ready 1968; Vols. 1944–64 ready 1969. *Bowker* 1967–69 each vol. $42.50 21-vol. set $810.00 The complete record, in reprint, of this influential weekly.

Trilling, Lionel, Ed. LITERARY CRITICISM: An Introductory Reader. *Holt* 1970 $8.00. 45 essays by critics ranging from Plato through Susan Sontag.

Tucker, Martin, Ed. THE CRITICAL TEMPER: A Survey of Modern Criticism on English and American Literature from the Beginnings to the 20th Century. *Ungar* 3 vols. 1969 $45.00

Van Nostrand, Albert D., Ed. LITERARY CRITICISM IN AMERICA. *Bobbs* 1957 pap. $2.45; *Bks. for Libraries* $15.00. A selection of essays by representative critics, 1800–1940, illustrating "the American accent in criticism."

Zabel, Morton Dauwen, Ed. LITERARY OPINION IN AMERICA. 3rd ed. rev. 1962. *Peter Smith* 2 vols. $12.00

Studies of the Essay

Law, Marie H. THE ENGLISH FAMILIAR ESSAY IN THE EARLY NINETEENTH CENTURY. 1934. *Russell & Russell* 1965 $7.50. A study of the elements that went into the making of the English familiar essay, as exemplified in the writings of Hunt, Hazlitt and Lamb.

O'Leary, R. D. THE ESSAY. 1928. *Richard West* 1973 $20.00

Walker, Hugh. THE ENGLISH ESSAY AND ESSAYISTS. 1900, 1915. *AMS Press* repr. of 1915 ed. $14.00; *Richard West* repr. of 1900 ed. $13.95

Williams, Orlo. THE ESSAY. *Folcroft* 1973 lib. bdg. $5.00

Collections of Essays

Anderson, Carl L., and George W. Williams, Eds. BRITISH AND AMERICAN ESSAYS 1905–1956. *Holt* 1959 pap. text ed. $5.00

Cody, Sherwin, Ed. A SELECTION FROM THE BEST ENGLISH ESSAYS, ILLUSTRATIVE OF THE HISTORY OF ENGLISH PROSE STYLE. 1903. *Bks. for Libraries* 1960 $13.75

Collins, Vere Henry, Ed. THREE CENTURIES OF ENGLISH ESSAYS: From Francis Bacon to Max Beerbohm. 1931. *Bks. for Libraries* 1967 $7.00

Dolmetsch, Carl R., Ed. THE SMART SET. Introd. by S. N. Behrman. *Heritage Press* 1966 o. p. A history of *Smart Set* as well as an anthology of essays by Pound, Joyce, O'Neill, Mencken, Fitzgerald, and others from the "magazine of cleverness" which survived until 1924.

Evans, Bergen, Ed. FIFTY ESSAYS: Sir Walter Raleigh to 20th Century. 1936 *Bks. for Libraries* 1972 $13.75

Fadiman, Clifton. Ed. PARTY OF TWENTY: Informal Essays from *Holiday Magazine*. *Simon & Schuster* 1963 o. p. Authors include Barzun, Thurber, Graves, Menen, Gary, Weidman and others.

Fiedler, Leslie, Ed. THE ART OF THE ESSAY. *Crowell* 1959 2nd ed. 1969 pap. $4.95. An illuminating, entertaining collection of 60 essays covering the whole field from Montaigne to the present.

Fuller, Edmund, Ed. GREAT ENGLISH AND AMERICAN ESSAYS. *Avon* 1970 pap. $.75

Fuller, Edmund, and O. B. Davis, Eds. INTRODUCTION TO THE ESSAY. *Hayden* 1972 $5.25 pap. $3.75

George, John E., and John A. Goodson, Eds. GREAT ESSAYS FROM THE 16TH CENTURY TO THE PRESENT. *Dell* 1969 Laurel Leaf Lib. pap. $.50. Includes some literary criticism.

Gold, Herbert, Ed. FIRST PERSON SINGULAR: Essays for the Sixties. *Dial* 1963 $5.00. By Baldwin, Bellow, Capote, Mary McCarthy and others.

Hamalian, Leo, and Edmund L. Volpe, Eds. GREAT ESSAYS BY NOBEL PRIZE WINNERS. *Farrar, Straus* Noonday 1960 pap. o. p. About one-third of the essays are in literary criticism.

ESSAYS OF OUR TIME. *McGraw-Hill* 2 vols. 1960 1963 Vol. 1 $4.25 Vol. 2 $4.95

PULITZER PRIZE READER. *Popular Lib.* 1967 pap. $.95

NOBEL PRIZE READER. *Popular Lib.* pap. $1.25

(With F. Karl, Eds.) RADICAL VISION: Essays for the Seventies. *T. Y. Crowell* 1970 pap. $4.95

Jepson, Rowland W., Ed. ESSAYS BY MODERN WRITERS. 1935. *Bks. for Libraries* 1968 $8.50; *Richard West* 1973 $8.45

Johnson, Burges, Ed. ESSAYING THE ESSAY. 1927. *Bks. for Libraries* $12.75

Kazin, Alfred, Ed. THE OPEN FORM: Essays for Our Time. *Harcourt* 1961 3rd ed. 1970 pap. $2.50

Lid, Richard W., Ed. ESSAYS: Classic and Contemporary. *Lippincott* 1962 pap. $3.75

McNamee, Maurice B., Ed. ESSAYS BY THE MASTERS. Composition and Rhetoric Ser. *Bobbs* pap. $1.00

Moynihan, William T., Ed. ESSAYS TODAY 6. *Harcourt* 1968 pap. text ed. $2.95

ESSAYS TODAY 7. *Harcourt* 1972 pap. text ed. $2.95

O'Neill, William L., Ed. ECHOES OF REVOLT: An Anthology of The Masses 1911–17. *Quadrangle Bks.* 1966 $15.00. Introd. by Irving Howe. Articles by Carl Sandburg, Upton Sinclair, Amy Lowell, Max Eastman and others.

Partlow, Robert B., Jr., Ed. A LIBERAL ARTS READER. *Prentice-Hall* 1963 $6.95. Excellent selection of essays ranging from the simple to the difficult, from the physical and social sciences to the humanities.

Podhoretz, Norman, Ed. THE COMMENTARY READER: Two Decades of Articles and Stories. *Atheneum* 1966 $12.50. From the journal on Jewish affairs and contemporary issues.

Priestley, John B., Ed. ESSAYISTS PAST AND PRESENT. *Bks. for Libraries* 1925 $9.75

Prtichard, Francis H., Ed. GREAT ESSAYS OF ALL NATIONS: 229 Essays from All Periods and Countries. 1929. *Richard West* 1973 $12.00

Rhys, Ernest, and Lloyd Vaughan, Eds. A CENTURY OF ENGLISH ESSAYS: An Anthology Ranging from Caxton to R. L. Stevenson and the Writers of Our Own Time. *Dutton* Everyman's 1916 $3.50

MODERN ENGLISH ESSAYS. 1922. *AMS Press* 5 vols. each $12.00 set $60.00

Saturday Evening Post. ADVENTURES OF THE MIND. Ed. by Richard Thruelson and John
Kobler. 1st and 2nd series. 1959 1961. *Random* Vintage Bks. 1st series pap. $1.65.
Essays relating to man, mind and the universe; among the authors: Barzun, Tillich,
Hoyle, Oppenheimer, Copland and Mumford.

Shaw, Charles Bunsen, Ed. AMERICAN ESSAYS. enl. ed. *New Am. Lib.* Mentor 1955 pap.
$.95

Smithberger, Andrew T., Ed. ESSAYS: British and American. 1953. *Greenwood* $16.00

Thompson, Elbert N., Ed. 17TH CENTURY ENGLISH ESSAY. 1926 *Haskell* 1969 $9.95

"The best survey of the essay for this whole period"—(Baugh).

Weintraub, Stanley, Ed. THE SAVOY: Nineties Experiment. *Pennsylvania State Univ.
Press* 1966 $9.50. Articles by Conrad, Ford, Beerbohm, Shaw and others from the
magazine which was a literary landmark of the 1890s.

Winchester, Caleb Thomas, Ed. A BOOK OF ENGLISH ESSAYS. 1914 *Bks. for Libraries*
1970 $14.50

BACON, FRANCIS. 1516–1626.

Bacon's essays in the first edition of 1597 numbered only ten. In later editions in 1612 and 1625 he added
new essays until there were 58 in all. "Few books of the kind have been so widely read, and probably no volume of prose in the English language has furnished so many popular quotations"—(Walker). "Bacon is the
greatest of the serious and stately essayists"—(Montaigne) (*q. v.*). "The greatest of the garrulous and com-
municative . . . Bacon always seems to write with his ermine on. Montaigne was different from all this. His
table of contents reads in comparison like a medley, or a catalogue of an auction"—(Alexander Smith).

FRANCIS BACON. Ed. with introd. and notes by Arthur Johnston. *Schocken* 1965 pap.
$1.95. Includes chronology of Bacon's life and writings; In Praise of Knowledge; Ad-
vancement of Learning; Doctrine of Idols; New Atlantis; On Poetry and Wisdom of
the Ancients; Trial of the Earl of Somerset (Bacon's Speech as Attorney-General);
Henry VII; extracts from letters and other essays.

ESSAYS AND COLOURS OF GOOD AND EVIL. 1842. *Bks. for Libraries* repr. of 1862 ed.
1972 $14.50

BACONIAN ESSAYS. Ed. by E. W. Smithson. 1922 *Kennikat* 1970 $8.25

ESSAYS. Ed. by C. S. Northrup. *Houghton* 1923 $3.75

ESSAYS, ADVANCEMENT OF LEARNING, NEW ATLANTIS, AND OTHER PIECES. Ed. by
R. F. Jones. 1937. *Odyssey* $3.50

ESSAYS, 1597–1626. Ed. by Henry L. Finch. *Dutton* Everyman's $3.50

SELECTED ESSAYS. Ed. by J. Max Patrick. 1948. *AHM Pub. Corp.* Crofts Class. pap.
$.85

SELECTED WRITINGS. With an introd. and notes by Hugh G. Dick. *Modern Library*
1955 $2.45

SELECTION OF HIS WORKS. Ed. by S. Warhaft. 1965 *Odyssey* pap. $1.75

ESSAYS, or Counsels Civil and Moral. 1597. *Oxford* World's Class. $2.25

SIDNEY, SIR PHILIP. 1554–1586.

To his fellow Elizabethans, Sidney was the perfect embodiment of the gentleman—a patron of the arts, a brave soldier, a gallant courtier, a notable scholar, and a fine poet. By later generations, he was remembered chiefly as a poet. But he has an important place in the history of literary criticism, as the author of the earliest major work in English in that field: "The Defense of Poesy" (also entitled "An Apology for Poetry"). Published after his death, it seems to have been a response to a narrow Puritanical attack on poetry called "The School of Abuse" by Stephen Gosson. Sidney follows the classical view that poetry both teaches and delights; and establishes, with rigorous logic, the superiority of the poet to the philosopher (the poet is more concrete) and to the historian (the poet is more universal).

COMPLETE PROSE WORKS. Ed. by A. Feuillerat. *Cambridge* 4 vols. 1912–26 Vol. 1 The Countesse of Pembroke's Arcadia $19.50 Vol. 2 The Last Part of the Countesse of Pembroke's Arcadia Vol. 3 The Defence of Poesie, Political Discourses, Correspondence, Translations $14.50 Vol. 4 The Older Arcadia $16.50

AN APOLOGY FOR POETRY. 1595. Ed. by Geoffrey Shepherd Old and Middle English Texts Ser. *Barnes & Noble* 1965 $5.00; ed. by Forrest Robinson *Bobbs* 1970 $5.75 pap. $1.95; ed. by A. Feuillerat *Cambridge* in vol. 3 of "Complete Prose" above; ed. by Mary R. Mahl The Norwich manuscript. *California State Univ.* Renaissance Eds. 1969 $5.00; (with title "Defense of Poetry") *Oxford* 1966 pap. $2.10

See also Chapter 5, British Poetry: Early Period.

BURTON, ROBERT. 1577–1640.

Although Burton also wrote a Latin comedy *"Philosophaster"* in 1606 which was performed at Christ Church in 1617, his only real claim to fame is "The Anatomy." The edition of 1621 was issued as "The Anatomy of Melancholy . . . by Democritus Junior." It contained a long preface, "Democritus to the Reader" in which the author explains his reasons for writing the treatise, and for assuming the name of that earlier philosopher, whom Hippocrates once found in his garden at Abdera studying the cause and cure of "this *atra bilis* or melancholy."

The text of the *Dutton* Everyman's edition is based on that of the sixth edition of 1651–52, revised and corrected by Burton but published posthumously. The book is in three parts: 1. The Causes and Symptoms of Melancholy; 2. The Cure of Melancholy; 3. Melancholy Inspired by Love and Religion. It is filled with quotations from all languages, which Burton gave in the original but which this edition gives in translation. The "Anatomy," which was started as a plain medical dissertation, became a "huge cento of excerpts from all known and unknown authors of Athens and Rome."

THE ANATOMY OF MELANCHOLY. 1621. Ed. by A. R. Shilleto. 1893. *AMS Press* 3 vols. each $18.50 set $55.00; facsimile ed. of 1621 *Da Capo* $65.00; ed. by Holbrook Jackson *Dutton* Everyman's 3 vols. each $3.50; (selections) ed. by Lawrence Babb *Michigan State Univ. Press* 1964 $10.00

Books about Burton

Bibliographia Burtoniana: A Study of Robert Burton's The Anatomy of Melancholy. By Paul J. Smith. 1931 *Burt Franklin* $13.50
Psychiatry of Robert Burton. By Bergen Evans. 1944 *Somerset Pub.* $7.50
Anatomy of Robert Burton's England. By William R. Mueller. 1952 *Folcroft* $10.00
Sanity in Bedlam: A Study of Robert Burton's Anatomy of Melancholy. By Lawrence Babb. *Michigan State Univ. Press* 1960 $5.00. A study that attempts to define Burton's "aims, methods, beliefs, and accomplishments"; traces some of his sources and examines some of the changes in the five editions.

BROWNE, SIR THOMAS. 1605–1682.

Browne, a busy and learned practicing physician, wrote some of the most beautiful cadenced prose in the English language. His *"Religio Medici"* (Religion of a Medical Man) went through 15 editions in his lifetime and is still being read by many medical practitioners and students. He had a love of outlandish words; he loved learned words merely because they were learned, said Coleridge (*q. v.*). Browne found no contradiction between religion and science. "Religion reveals man's relation to God. Science is our partial knowledge of the

Laws of Nature whereby the Divine purpose is carried out in creation. Being a modest man, he never thought his writings would survive his own time. As it is they have survived the centuries."

The *"Religio Medici"* was printed in 1642, without the author's knowledge, although it was probably written as early as 1635, for the author describes himself as under 30. It was reviewed by Sir Kenelm Digby in "Observations" (1643). The resulting interest aroused Browne to put forth a new edition in 1643 in which letters between Digby and Browne were included. "Christian Morals," published posthumously, ed. by John Jeffery (1716), was intended as a continuation of *"Religio Medici."*

WORKS AND LIFE OF THOMAS BROWNE. Ed. by Simon Wilkin. 1835–36. *AMS Press* 4 vols. each $20.00 set $75.00

WORKS. 1928. *Somerset Pub.* 6 vols. $120.00

SELECTED WRITINGS. Ed. by Geoffrey Keynes. *Univ. of Chicago Press.* 1969 $8.50 Phoenix Bks. pap. $3.25

PROSE. Ed. by Norman Endicott. Includes *"Religio Medici," "Hydrotaphia,"* letters and short texts. *New York Univ. Press* 1967 $12.50; *Norton* pap. $5.95

RELIGIO MEDICI AND DIGBY'S OBSERVATIONS. 1643. 1909 *Somerset Pub.* $6.00

RELIGIO MEDICI AND OTHER WRITINGS. With a new introd. by Frank L. Huntley. 1906. *Dutton* Everyman's 1951 $3.50

RELIGIO MEDICI AND OTHER WORKS. Ed. by Leonard C. Martin *Oxford* 1964 $12.00; ed. by W. A. Greenhill *St. Martin's* $2.00

RELIGIO MEDICI, HYDROTAPHIA AND THE GARDENS OF CYRUS. Ed. by R. H. Robbins. *Oxford* 1972 $4.25

RELIGIO MEDICI. 1642. Ed. by Jean-Jacques Denonain, without notes but with biographical and critical introd. *Cambridge* 1955 $3.75 ed. by James Winny 1963 $2.95

URNE-BURIALL AND THE GARDEN OF CYRUS. 1658. Ed. by John Carter. Cambridge $6.50

HYDROTAPHIA [Urne-Buriall] AND THE GARDEN OF CYRUS. 1658. Ed. by Frank L. Huntley. 1966. *AHM Pub. Corp.* Crofts Class. pap. $.85

CHRISTIAN MORALS. 1716. 2nd ed. with the Life of Browne by Samuel Johnson. Ed. by S. C. Roberts. 1927. *Kraus* $10.00

Books about Browne

Sir Thomas Browne: A Biographical and Critical Study. By Frank Livingstone Huntley. A lucid and readable guide to Browne's profound philosophy and difficult style. *Univ. of Michigan Press* 1962 Ann Arbor Bks. pap. $2.45

Sir Thomas Browne: A Man of Achievement in Literature. By Joan Bennett. *Cambridge* 1962 $9.50 An authoritative study of the man and his work, including skillful analysis of his arguments. Bibliography and index. "Invaluable to anyone coming to Browne for the first time whether for pleasure or for information"—*(Economist)*.

STEELE, SIR RICHARD. 1672–1729.

Steele was born in the same year as Joseph Addison (*q. v.*), whom he came to know at Charterhouse School. After writing several comedies he started in 1709 the first of the series of periodicals which became so characteristic a feature of 18th-century writing. Addison was a frequent contributor, as he was to the periodicals that followed. Steele had perhaps less delicacy of wit than his more famous collaborator, but more knowledge of life and wider sympathies. "The Plays of Richard Steele," edited by Shirley S. Kenny (*Oxford* 1971 $17.00) and his best-known play "The Conscious Lovers," edited by Shirley S. Kenny (*Univ. of Nebraska* 1968 $4.75 Bison Books pap. $1.00) are available.

By Addison and Steele (See also Addison, Joseph, following):

THE SPECTATOR. Ed. by Donald F. Bond. Complete. 1711–14. *Oxford* 1966 5 vols. set $96.00

"A herculean labor which makes clear the most obscure reference, translates every Latin tag and motto, fleshes out for the reader the most colorless remark"—(*N.Y. Times*).

THE SPECTATOR PAPERS. A reprint of the 1897–98 edition by Gregory Smith. *Dutton* Everyman's 4 vols. each $3.50

THE COVERLEY PAPERS FROM THE SPECTATOR. Ed. by O. M. Myers. *Oxford* 1922 $1.80

THE COVERLEY PAPERS FROM THE SPECTATOR. 1943. *Somerset Pub.* $6.00

SELECTIONS FROM THE TATLER AND THE SPECTATOR. Ed. by Robert J. Allen *Holt* (Rinehart) 1957 2nd ed. 1970 pap. $2.50; ed. by Allen *Peter Smith* $4.00

CRITICAL ESSAYS FROM THE SPECTATOR. Ed. by Donald F. Bond. *Oxford* 1970. pap. $2.95. Contains the most important critical essays, grouped by topic.

SELECTED ESSAYS FROM THE TATLER, THE SPECTATOR AND THE GUARDIAN. Ed. by Daniel McDonald. Library of Literature *Bobbs* 1972 $12.00 pap. $3.75

By Sir Richard Steele:

THE TATLER. Ed. by Lewis Gibbs. *Dutton* Everyman's $3.50; *Adler's* repr. of 1898 ed. 4 vols. $88.00

NEW LETTERS TO THE TATLER AND SPECTATOR. Ed. by Richmond P. Bond. *Univ. of Texas Press* $7.50. Perhaps the earliest specimens of "letters to the editor." They did not appear in print, but are valuable as examples of the raw material that the two essayists worked into the best-written daily journal in history.

THE ENGLISHMAN. A political journal, started in 1713, censuring the Tory ministry. Ed. by Rae Blanchard. *Oxford* 1955 $14.50

TRACTS AND PAMPHLETS. Ed. by Rae Blanchard. *Octagon* 1966 $18.50

THE THEATRE, 1720. Ed. by John Loftis. *Oxford* 1962 $5.00. Essays on morals, manners, politics and the like from his final periodical. In part a defense of his role as governor of Drury Lane Theater.

Books about Steele

Sir Richard Steele. By Willard Connely. 1934. *Kennikat* 1967 $12.50; *Richard West* 1973 $12.00
Steele at Drury Lane. By John Loftis. 1952. *Greenwood* 1973 $11.50
Captain Steele: The Early Career of Richard Steele. By Calhoun Winton. *Johns Hopkins Univ. Press* 1964 $9.00
"A highly spirited and informed work of scholarship"—(*LJ*).
Richard Steele, M. P.: The Later Career. By Calhoun Winton. *Johns Hopkins Univ. Press* 1970 $9.00

ADDISON, JOSEPH. 1672–1719.

Addison, son of the Dean of Litchfield, took high honors at Oxford and joined the army. He first came to literary fame by writing a poem, "The Campaign," to celebrate the Battle of Blenheim. When Steele (*q. v.*), whom he had known at school, started *The Tatler* in 1709, he became a contributor. Two years later his contributions to a new venture, *The Spectator*, were of even more importance. This paper lasted until December, 1714, with the exception of a period when *The Guardian* took its place. The *Spectator* series introduced the character of Sir Roger de Coverley, around whom Addison wrote many of his best and most characteristic essays.

Of *The Spectator*, a model of lucid prose, Ben Franklin wrote, "I compared my [paper] with the original, discovered my faults and corrected them." Modern readers will find the age of Queen Anne made vivid in this lighthearted journal covering subjects from fashions, religion and criticism to the economics of almsgiving. (*For Addison and Steele, see Steele, Sir Richard, preceding.*)

CRITICISM OF MILTON'S PARADISE LOST, 1711–1712. 1868. *Saifer* $4.00; ed. by Albert S. Cook 1924 *Phaeton Press* (dist. by Gordian) 1968 $7.50

THE MISCELLANEOUS WORKS OF JOSEPH ADDISON. Ed. by A. C. Guthkelch. 1914. *Scholarly Press* 2 vols. 1971 $29.50

LAMB, CHARLES. 1775–1834.

Lamb is the Prince of English essayists, as Bacon (*q. v.*) is the King. "The Essays of Elia" was first published in 1823, and "The Last Essays of Elia" ten years later. Lamb "had mastered the personal style so completely that his essays seem simply the overflow of talk. For months he polished and rewrote these magazine articles till in the finished work of art he mimicked inconsequence so perfectly that his friends might have been deceived"—(G. H. Mair). "The subject of the earliest of the Essays was a description of the South Sea House, with which Lamb had been connected for a short time in his youth; and he signed this first essay in the *London Magazine* with the pseudonym 'Elia,' which was the name of an obscure foreign clerk who worked there"—("Reader's Guide"). Lamb is an appealing figure, gay and sociable, whose devotion to his periodically insane sister, Mary, was an example of quiet heroism.

THE WORKS OF CHARLES AND MARY LAMB. Ed. by E. V. Lucas. 1903–05. *AMS Press* 5 vols. 1968 each $16.00 set $80.00; ed. by Lucas 1903–05 *Scholarly Press* 7 vols. 1970 set $185.00

THE LIFE, LETTERS AND WRITINGS OF CHARLES LAMB. Ed. by Percy Fitzgerald. 1895. *Bks. for Libraries* 6 vols. $115.00

LAMB'S CRITICISM: A Selection from the Literary Criticism of Charles Lamb. Ed. by E. M. Tillyard. 1923. *Greenwood* $7.50; *Richard West* 1973 $7.45

MISCELLANEOUS ESSAYS. Ed. by Alexander H. Thompson. *Cambridge* 1923 pap. $1.50

THE PORTABLE CHARLES LAMB. Ed. with introd. by John Mason Brown. *Viking* 1949 lib. bdg. $4.95 pap. $1.85. Includes letters, poems, essays, arranged to show various aspects of Lamb's character and interests. A wise and sympathetic arrangement.

ESSAYS, LETTERS AND POEMS. Introd. by J. Lewis May. *Collins* New Class. 1953 $3.00

SELECTED ESSAYS. Ed. by John R. Nabholtz. 1967. *AHM Pub. Corp.* Crofts Class. pap. $.85

THE ESSAYS OF ELIA. 1823. *Dutton* pap. 1972 $1.50

THE LAST ESSAYS OF ELIA. 1833. (And "The Essays of Elia") *Dutton* Everyman's $3.50; (And "The Essays of Elia") *Oxford* World's Class. 1949 $2.50

Books about Lamb

The Life of Charles Lamb. By Edward Verrall Lucas. 5th ed. rev. 1921. *AMS Press* 1968 2 vols. in 1 $22.50
Charles Lamb. By Edmund Blunden. Writers and Their Works Ser. *British Bk.* Centre $2.38 pap. $1.20

LANDOR, WALTER SAVAGE. 1775–1864.

Halfway in his long life Landor abandoned poetry for prose and devoted himself to writing a succession of unique "Imaginary Conversations" (1824–1853), 32 in all. The Conversations amount to essays on great characters. They are sprinkled with the epigrammatic verses which make Landor so quotable. According to Vivian Mercier, Landor has been generally snubbed by modern critics—with the notable exception of Ezra Pound, who pays him homage in "ABC of Reading" (*New Directions* pap. $1.60), "The Sculptured Garland," a selection of his lyrical poems, ed. by Richard Buxton (1948. *Folcroft* $5.00) has been reprinted.

COMPLETE WORKS. Ed. by Thomas Earle Welby and Stephen Wheeler. 1927. *Barnes & Noble* 1969 16 vols. $125.00

IMAGINARY CONVERSATIONS. 1824–53. Ed. with bibliographic and explanatory notes by Charles G. Crump. 1891–93. *AMS Press* 6 vols. $180.00

SELECTED IMAGINARY CONVERSATIONS OF LITERARY MEN AND STATESMEN. Ed. by Charles L. Proudfit. *Univ. of Nebraska Press* 1969 $10.00

LAST FRUIT OFF AN OLD TREE. 1853. *Folcroft* 1973 $30.00. Fresh conversations, critical and controversial essays, epigrams and poems.

Books about Landor

Walter Savage Landor: A Critical Study. By Edward W. Evans, Jr. 1892. *Kennikat* 1970 $7.50; *Folcroft* $7.50

HAZLITT, WILLIAM. 1778–1830.

Hazlitt first studied for the ministry, later took up portrait painting, and finally became a journalist. His political convictions gave him violent prejudices, made him quarrel with Lamb (*q. v.*), Coleridge (*q. v.*), Wordsworth (*q. v.*), and other friends, and marred his essays with many digressions. He was a great admirer of Napoleon and his longest work is a biography of his hero (1828–30, o. p.). "Liber Amoris, or The New Pygmalion" (1823) is the love story of his infatuation for the daughter of a tailor. Hazlitt had an extravagant enjoyment of good literature himself, and he was able to impart it to his readers.

WORKS. Ed. by Percival P. Howe after the ed. of A. R. Waller and A. Glover. 1930–34. *AMS Press* 21 vols. each $20.00 set $390.00. The standard Centenary edition.

HAZLITT ON ENGLISH LITERATURE. Ed. by Jacob Zeitlin. 1913. *AMS Press* 1970 $12.00

SELECTED ESSAYS. Ed. by Geoffrey Keynes 1930. *Random* $10.00; ed. by John R. Nabholtz 1969. *AHM Pub. Corp.* Crofts Class. pap. $.85

THE HAZLITT SAMPLER. Ed. by Hershel M. Sikes. *Peter Smith* $4.75

HAZLITT ON THEATRE. Ed. by William Archer and William Lowe; introd. by William Archer. *Hill & Wang* 1957 Drama Bks. pap. $1.25

THE ROUND TABLE: A Collection of Essays. 1817. (With "Characters of Shakespeare's Plays") *Dutton* Everyman's 1957 $3.50. Mostly by Hazlitt, but with ten contributions by Leigh Hunt (*q. v.*).

CHARACTERS OF SHAKESPEARE'S PLAYS. 1817. *Oxford* World's Class. 1929 $2.50

LECTURES ON THE ENGLISH POETS. 1818. 3rd ed. 1941 *Russell & Russell* 1968 $10.00

LECTURES ON THE ENGLISH COMIC WRITERS. 1819. *Dutton* Everyman's $3.50; *Russell & Russell* 1969 $10.00. Lectures delivered at the Surry Institution.

TABLE TALK. 1821–22. *Dutton* Everyman's $3.50

THE SPIRIT OF THE AGE, or Contemporary Portraits. 1825. *Oxford* World's Class. 1904. $2.75

Books about Hazlitt

Memoirs of William Hazlitt. by W. Carew Hazlitt. 1867. *Richard West* 2 vols. $75.00
Life of William Hazlitt. By Percival P. Howe. 1922 1928 1947. *Greenwood* repr. of 1947 ed. 1973 $17.50
William Hazlitt. By J. B. Priestley. Writers and Their Work Ser. *British Bk. Centre* $2.38 pap. $1.20
Hazlitt. By Ralph Martin Wardle. *Univ. of Nebraska Press* 1971. $15.00. Includes bibliographic references.

HUNT, (JAMES HENRY) LEIGH. 1784–1859.

George Saintsbury (*q. v.*) called Leigh Hunt "an essayist born." He ranges from coffee-houses, playgoing, shops, or maidservants, to "Getting Up on Cold Mornings." Some of the pieces are critical, some contain recollections of many writers he knew. He was a constant contributor to the periodicals of his day and in 1808 became the editor of *The Examiner*, a journal owned by his brother. He published, with William Hazlitt, (*q. v.*) a series of essays called "The Round Table." In 1816 he wrote "The Story of Rimini" (1816) which established his fame as a poet and pioneer of the new romantic school. His short poem, "Abou Ben Adhem," was once immensely popular. As a critic of poetry he recognized early and enthusiastically the work of Keats, Shelley, Tennyson and others and helped to establish their reputations.

PREFACES BY LEIGH HUNT, Mainly to His Periodicals. Ed. by R. B. Johnson. 1927. *Kennikat* 1967 $6.50

SELECTED ESSAYS. Ed. by J. B. Priestley. 1929. *Scholarly Press* $19.50; *Somerset Pub.* $15.50

LITERARY CRITICISM. Ed. by Lawrence H. Houtchens and Carolyn W. Houtchens. 1956. *Octagon* 1972 $22.50

LORD BYRON AND SOME OF HIS CONTEMPORARIES. 1828. *AMS Press* $25.00

IMAGINATION AND FANCY: Selections from the English Poets, Illustrative of those First Requisites of Their Art, with Markings of the Best Passages, Critical Notices, and an Essay in Answer to the Question "What is Poetry?" 1844. *AMS Press* $10.00 *Folcroft* repr. of 1883 ed. $17.50; *Richard West* repr. of 1844 ed. 1973 $9.95

CORRESPONDENCE. Ed. by Thornton Hunt. 1862. Kelley 2 vols. in 1 lib. bdg. $20.00

LETTER ON HOGG'S LIFE OF SHELLEY. Ed. by L. A. Brewer 1927 *Folcroft* $5.00

LEIGH HUNT'S AUTOBIOGRAPHY. 1850. (with "Reminiscences of Friends and Contemporaries") *AMS Press* 2 vols. each $13.00 set $24.50; ed. by J. E. Morpurgo *Dufour* 1948 $4.95; ("The Earliest Sketches") ed. by Stephen F. Fogle *Univ. of Florida Press* 1959 $2.00

Books about Hunt

Leigh Hunt's "Examiner" Examined. By Edmund Blunden. 1928. *Shoe String* 1967 $7.00. Reprint of a standard work by one of the foremost modern authorities on Hunt.
Leigh Hunt, A Biography. 1930. *Shoe String* 1970 $12.50
Leigh Hunt's Relations with Byron, Shelley and Keats. 1910. *Folcroft* $17.50

DE QUINCEY, THOMAS. 1785–1859.

De Quincey wrote on a multiplicity of subjects, but is now best known for his "Confessions of an English Opium Eater," his masterpiece. He started to use laudanum for relief of severe pain when he was about 20, but after using opium for over 20 years he disciplined himself and desisted. He was "a master of the curious and obscure in literature; and he was a creator of a poetic prose that, in its range of diction and display of surprising fancy, is the equal of any writing of his time." Among his friends and associates were Lamb (*q. v.*) and Hazlitt (*q. v.*) and the great Romantics, Coleridge (*q. v.*) and Wordsworth (*q. v.*). His "Reminiscences of the English Lake Poets" reveals a unique view of the great men of his day.

COLLECTED WRITINGS. Ed. by David Masson. 1889–90. *AMS Press* 14 vols. each $17.50 set $230.00; *Adler's* set $390.00; *Johnson Reprint* set $245.00; *Scholarly Press* each $19.50 set $240.00

THOMAS DE QUINCEY: Selections from His Writings. Ed. by Bonamy Dobrée. 1965. *Schocken* pap. $1.95

THOMAS DE QUINCEY. Ed. by Bonamy Dobrée. *Schocken* 1965 pap. $1.95. *Library Journal* points out that these "admirably chosen" selections lack notes and index.

NEW ESSAYS. 1827–28. Ed. by S. M. Tave. *Princeton Univ. Press* 1966 $12.50. These are essays originally contributed to the *Edinburgh Saturday Post* and the *Edinburgh Evening Post.*

SELECTED ESSAYS ON RHETORIC. Ed. by Frederick Burwick. *Southern Illinois Univ. Press* 1967 $7.00

CONFESSIONS OF AN ENGLISH OPIUM EATER. 1822. Ed. by E. Sackville-West. 1950. *Dufour* $4.95; ed. by John E. Jordan *Dutton* Everyman's $3.50 pap. 1961 $1.55; (and Other Writings) ed. by A. Ward *New Am. Lib.* Signet 1966 pap. $.95; *Oxford* World's Class. $2.50; ed. by Alethea Hayter *Penguin* 1971 pap. $1.45

REMINISCENCES OF THE ENGLISH LAKE POETS. 1834. *Dutton* Everyman's $3.50

THE ENGLISH MAILCOACH (1849) AND OTHER ESSAYS. *Dutton* Everyman's 1961 $3.50

Books about De Quincy

De Quincy as a Literary Critic. By. J. H. Fowler. 1922 *Folcroft* $4.50
Thomas De Quincey, Literary Critic: His Method and Achievement. By John E. Jordan. 1952. *Gordian* $9.50
De Quincey to Wordsworth: A Biography of a Relationship. With the letters of Thomas De Quincey to the Wordsworth Family. By John E. Jordan. *Univ. of California Press* 1962 $12.00

CARLYLE, THOMAS. 1795–1881.

Thomas Carlyle, while he was a student at Edinburgh University, prepared to enter the Scottish Church. Though he was an erratic student, the stories of his vast reading are almost unbelievable. He acquired a thorough knowledge of German, and his earliest works were translations of "Wilhelm Meister" and "The Life of Schiller." His style was always vivid, majestic and dramatic, with contrasting pathos, humor, grim satire and denunciation. He often coined a word when he needed one. His philosophical "Sartor Resartus" (1837) and his essays on "Heroes and Hero-Worship" and "Past and Present" are perhaps better known to the general reader than his histories.

Carlyle was rough-hewn and often irascible as a human being. He married the beautiful and brilliant Jane Welsh in 1826 and their domestic life—he could be something of a recluse—was often troubled. But their devotion was real, and at her death in 1866 he was inconsolable. In his essays, deeply influenced by the German Romantics, he revolted against the rationalism of the 18th century, gradually coming to expound the glories of enlightened despotism, in which the "heroes" ruled the less intelligent. His "French Revolution" (1837. *Dutton* Everyman's 2 vols. each $3.50) brought him his greatest contemporary acclaim.

CARLYLE: Selected Works, Reminiscences and Letters. Ed. by Julian Symons. *Harvard Univ. Press* Reynard Lib. 1957 $12.00 pap. $4.95

ESSAYS: English and Other Critical Essays. *Dutton* Everyman's $3.50

ESSAYS: Scottish and Other Miscellanies. *Dutton* Everyman's $3.50

CARLYLE READER: Selections from the Writings. Ed. by G. B. Tennyson. *Modern Library* pap. 1968 $1.75

SELECTED WRITINGS. Ed. by Alan Shelston. *Penguin* 1972 pap. $2.45

LIFE OF FRIEDRICH SCHILLER: Comprehending an Examination of His Work. 1821. 1901. *Finch Press* $16.50; *Richard West* $16.45

SARTOR RESARTUS. 1837. Ed. by C. F. Harrold. *Odyssey $3.25*

    A "philosophy" of clothing. Outstanding for its "amazing humorous energy, the moral force, the resourceful (if eccentric) command over English."—("British Authors of the Nineteenth Century").

SARTOR RESARTUS AND SELECTED PROSE. *Holt* (Rinehart) pap. $2.25

SARTOR RESARTUS and ON HEROES AND HERO-WORSHIP. *Dutton* Everyman's $3.50

ON HEROES AND HERO-WORSHIP AND THE HEROIC IN HISTORY. 1841. *Oxford* World's Class. $2.50; ed. by Carl Niemeyer *Univ. of Nebraska Press* 1966 Bison Bks. pap. $1.95; *Peter Smith* $3.75

    Government by the hero-despot, Carlyle's mature political philosophy, is foreshadowed in this extract, a somewhat subdued example of his exuberant, "prophetic" style. "One comfort is, that Great Men, taken up in any way, are profitable company. We cannot look, however imperfectly, upon a great man, without gaining something by him. He is the living light-fountain, which it is good and pleasant to be near. The light which enlightens, which has enlightened the darkness of the world; and this not as a kindled lamp only, but rather as a natural luminary shining by the gift of Heaven; a flowing light-fountain, as I say, of native original insight, of manhood and heroic nobleness;—in whose radiance all souls feel that it is well with them. On any terms whatsoever, you will not grudge to wander in such neighbourhood for a while. . . ."

PAST AND PRESENT. 1843. *Dutton* Everyman's $3.50; *Oxford* World's Class. $2.50

LETTERS. 1923. *Scholarly Press* 1971. $19.50; *Richard West* 1973 $19.45

NEW LETTERS. Ed. by Alexander Carlyle. 1904. *Scholarly Press* 2 vols. $29.50

LETTERS, 1826–1836. Ed. by Charles E. Norton. 1888. *Bks. for Libraries* $29.50

LETTERS TO HIS BROTHER ALEXANDER with Related Family Letters. Ed. by Edwin W. Marrs, Jr. *Harvard Univ. Press* 1968 $20.00

LETTERS TO JOHN STUART MILL, JOHN STERLING AND ROBERT BROWNING. 1923 *Haskell* 1969 $12.95

LETTERS TO HIS YOUNGEST SISTER. Ed. by C. T. Copeland. 1899. *Adler's* $13.95

TWO NOTEBOOKS, from 23rd Mar., 1822 to 16th May, 1832. Ed. by Charles E. Norton. 1898. *Appel* (dist. by Phaeton) $8.50

Books about Carlyle

    Carlyle's Theory of the Hero. By B. H. Lehman. 1928. *AMS Press* $8.50. A classic study of its sources, history and appearance in Carlyle's writing.
    Sartor Called Resartus. By. G. B. Tennyson. *Princeton* 1965 $11.00
        A scholarly study which "should [become] one of the major works of Carlyle criticism"—(*Choice*).
    The Carlyles at Home. By Thea Holme. *Oxford* 1965 $5.60. A light account of their home life, based largely on the letters of Jane Welsh Carlyle.

MACAULAY, THOMAS BABINGTON, 1st Baron. 1800–1859.

    The Dictionary Catalogue of Everyman's Library explains the grouping of Macaulay's essays according to the classification of Cotter Morison in his monograph of Macaulay (o. p.): English History group, Foreign History group; Literary Criticism group. *Dutton.* Everyman's follows this classification strictly; other collections do so less strictly. It has been hard to live down the strong influence of some of Macaulay's essays. His review of (a new edition of) Boswell's "Johnson" is largely responsible for the contempt in which Boswell (*q. v.*) personally has been held until recently, and the unjust accusations heaped upon Bacon (*q. v.*) can be traced in many instances to Macaulay's misstatements. His strongly biased essays—on Addison, Bacon, Byron, Dryden, Walpole and others—made and unmade reputations.

Macaulay, who was already writing elaborate works of prose and poetry before he was ten, made his first mark with an article on Milton in the *Edinburgh Review* of August, 1825. Trained in law, he became a member of Parliament and was made a peer in 1857. He held a number of important Cabinet posts. His chief work is his "History of England" (1849–61. *Dutton* Everyman's 4 vols. each $3.50).

PROSE AND POETRY. Sel. by George M. Young. *Harvard Univ. Press* 1953 $12.00 pap. $4.50

LAYS OF ANCIENT ROME, MISCELLANEOUS ESSAYS, AND POEMS. *Dutton* Everyman's 1954 $3.50

CRITICAL AND HISTORICAL ESSAYS. 1843. *Dutton* Everyman's 2 vols. each $3.50

MILTON. 1900. *Greenwood* $8.75

LETTERS. Ed. by T. Pinney. *Cambridge* 2 vols. each $28.50

Books about Macaulay

The Life and Letters of Lord Macaulay. By Sir George Otto Trevelyan. The basic biography, by his nephew. 1876. 1932. *Oxford* 1961 2 vols. $3.40
Lord Macaulay, 1800–1859. By David Knowles. *Cambridge* 1960 pap. $.75

EMERSON, RALPH WALDO. 1803–1882.

The American essay may be said to begin with Emerson's "Nature," published in 1836. Because of poor health Emerson had left the ministry in 1832. After a long trip to Europe he began his career as a public lecturer. At first he made much use of source material, only later expressing more of his own original ideas; many of his essays were revisions of these lectures. In the process of transformation, the lectures were condensed to such an extent that they sometimes seem to be made up of separate sentences without continuity. Indeed, enthusiasts like to claim that Emerson's pages have almost as much meaning read from end to beginning as from beginning to end. From 1840–44, Emerson was editor, with Thoreau and Margaret Fuller, of *The Dial*, a transcendentalist magazine concerned with literature, philosophy and religion (introd. by George W. Cooke 1902 *Russell & Russell* 1961 6 vols. $75.00).

The transcendentalist movement in New England (1836–1860) began as a revolt against Unitarianism. Its chief tenets were a mystical belief in the harmony of man and nature, and the idea of God as immanent in nature. See Perry Miller, "The American Transcendentalists: Their Prose and Poetry" (1950. *Doubleday* Anchor Bks. pap. $2.50; *Peter Smith* $4.00) and Myron Simon and Thorton H. Parsons, eds., "Transcendentalism and Its Legacy" (*Univ. of Michigan Press* 1966 $6.95 Ann Arbor Bks. pap. $2.45), ten essays by René Wellek, Kenneth Burke and others.

W. C. Brownell in his volume on American Prose Masters has written of Emerson as follows: "His place is with Epictetus, Marcus Aurelius, Montaigne, Rabelais, Pascal, Sir Thomas Browne—with the wisdom writers of the world. . . . The 'Essays' are the scriptures of thought, the Virgilian Lots of modern literature. To open anywhere any of the volumes (including 'Representative Men,' which very strictly belongs with the 'Essays') is to be at once in the world of thought in a very particular sense. . . . Every statement stimulates thought because it is suggestive as well as expressive. Everything means something additional. To take it in, you must go beyond it. . . . Every thought is potent rather than purely reflective. . . . Dr. Holmes gives the number of citations they contain as 3,393, taken from 868 writers." Annual bibliographies, scholarly articles, interpretations and facsimiles of Emerson's manuscripts appear in the Emerson Society Quarterly, established in 1955. (*See also Thoreau, following.*)

COMPLETE WORKS. Ed. by Edward W. Emerson. 1903–04. *AMS Press* 12 vols. each $15.00 set $175.00

NATURE, ADDRESSES AND LECTURES. 1849. Vol. I of the projected "Collected Works of Ralph Waldo Emerson" ed. by Alfred R. Ferguson and Robert E. Spiller. *Harvard Univ. Press* 1972 $15.00

UNCOLLECTED WRITINGS: Essays, Addresses, Poems, Reviews and Letters. Ed. by Charles C. Bigelow. 1912. *Kennikat* 1971 $9.00

YOUNG EMERSON SPEAKS. Ed. by A. C. McGiffert. 1938. *Kennikat* 1968 $9.50

THE PORTABLE EMERSON. Sel. and arr. with introd. and notes by Mark Van Doren. *Viking* 1946 lib. bdg. $5.95 pap. $3.35. Selected essays regrouped under "Programs" "The Ways of Life" and "People."

SELECTED PROSE AND POETRY. Ed. with introd. by Reginald Cook. *Holt* (Rinehart) 1950 2nd ed. 1969 $2.50

SELECTED ESSAYS, LECTURES AND POEMS. Ed. by Robert E. Spiller. *Washington Square* pap. $.60

EMERSON: The Basic Selections. Ed. by Eduard C. Lindeman. *New Am. Lib.* Mentor Bks. 1954 pap. $1.25

FIVE ESSAYS ON MAN AND NATURE. Ed. by Robert E. Spiller 1954. *AHM Pub. Corp.* Crofts Class. pap. $.85

SELECTED WRITINGS. Ed. by Brooks Atkinson. *Modern Library* $2.95 pap. $1.35; ed. by William H. Gilman *New Am. Lib.* pap. $1.50

SELECTIONS. Ed. by Stephen Whicher. *Houghton* Riv. Eds. 1957 pap. $1.75

THE CONDUCT OF LIFE, NATURE, AND OTHER ESSAYS. *Dutton* Everyman's 1963 $3.50

ENGLISH TRAITS. 1856. Ed. by Howard Mumford Jones. *Harvard Univ. Press* 1966 John Harvard Lib. $7.50

LETTERS AND SOCIAL AIMS. 1876. *Bks. for Libraries* repr. of 1883 ed. $15.75

THE JOURNALS AND MISCELLANEOUS NOTEBOOKS OF RALPH WALDO EMERSON. *Harvard Univ. Press* 9 vols. to date 1960–71. Vol. I 1819–22 ed. by William Henry Gilman and others $12.00 Vol. 2 1822–26 ed. by William H. Gilman and others $11.00 Vol. 3 1826–32 ed. by William H. Gilman and Alfred R. Ferguson $10.00 Vol. 4 1832–34 ed. by A. R. Ferguson $12.50 Vol. 5 1835–38 ed. by Merton Miller Sealts, Jr. $14.00 Vol. 6 1834–38 ed. by Ralph H. Orth $12.00 Vol. 7 1838–42 ed. by A. W. Plumstead and Harrison Hayford $15.00 Vol. 8 1841–43 ed. by W. H. Gilman and J. E. Parsons $18.50 Vol. 9 1843–47 ed. by R. H. Orth and A. R. Ferguson $17.00. Excellently edited; the journals record Emerson's continuing search for a satisfactory philosophy.

THE HEART OF EMERSON'S JOURNALS. Ed. by Bliss Perry. 1926. *Dover* pap. $2.75

LETTERS. Ed. by R. L. Rusk. *Columbia* 1939 6 vols. $87.50. 2313 letters not previously published.

THE CORRESPONDENCE OF RALPH WALDO EMERSON AND THOMAS CARLYLE. Ed. by J. Slater *Columbia* 1964 $15.00

Books about Emerson

Ralph Waldo Emerson. By Oliver Wendell Holmes. 1884. *Gale* 1968 $7.80

The Life of Ralph Waldo Emerson. By Ralph Leslie Rusk. This scholarly biography won the National Book Award in 1950 and is based on unpublished manuscripts, journals and letters. 1949. *Columbia* repr. 1957 $10.00

Emerson's Angle of Vision: Man and Nature in American Experience. By Sherman Paul. An attempt to evaluate the transitions in his speculative outlook. *Harvard Univ. Press* 1952 $7.50

Freedom and Fate: An Inner Life of Ralph Waldo Emerson. By Stephen E. Whicher. A biography of the author's intellectual development, especially from 1833–47. *A. S. Barnes* 1961 pap. $1.65

Emerson. By Henry David Gray. A statement of New England transcendentalism as expressed in the philosophy of its chief exponent. *Ungar* 1958 $4.50

One First Love: The Letters of Ellen Louisa Tucker to Ralph Waldo Emerson. Ed. by Edith Gregg. Love letters of Emerson's charming and courageous young wife, who died of tuberculosis after only 17 months of happy marriage. *Harvard Univ. Press* 1962 $5.50

Emerson on the Soul. By Jonathan Bishop. Exposition of Emerson's philosophy as forged in the crises of his life and expressed in his writings. *Harvard Univ. Press* 1964 $7.75

Emerson and Thoreau: Transcendentalists in Conflict. By Joel Porte. The first major study of their intellectual differences. *Wesleyan Univ. Press* 1966 $8.00

See also Chapter 8, American Poetry: Early Period.

HOLMES, OLIVER WENDELL. 1809–1894.

Oliver Wendell Holmes has a place in American letters as essayist, poet and novelist. The brilliant series of essays which first appeared in the *Atlantic Monthly* as a serial and later in book form in 1858, under the title "The Autocrat of the Breakfast Table," brought him a national and almost worldwide vogue and he has been compared with all the great essayists from Montaigne (*q. v.*) to Lamb (*q. v.*). The following year he brought out "The Professor at the Breakfast Table" and ten years later "The Poet at the Breakfast Table." These three volumes are delightfully egotistical talks, mainly of Boston and New England, in which Holmes was by turn brilliantly witty and extremely serious. His sprightly conversational style set the pattern for the modern humorist-columnist. His great versatility was reflected in his life as well—he was "a practicing physician, a professor of anatomy at Dartmouth, a professor of anatomy at Harvard, Dean of Harvard Medical School, and a lecturer of note both on subjects of science and of literature."

Holmes wrote three novels—"Elsie Venner: A Romance of Destiny" (1861, o. p. in separate edition), "The Guardian Angel" (1867. *Gregg* $14.00) and "A Moral Antipathy" (1885. *Gregg* $11.50). He referred to them as "medicated," because they deal with medical cases, but they are "among the first in American literature to utilize a scientific approach." Dr. Oberndorf, clinical professor of psychiatry at Columbia, has shown how advanced Holmes was in his conception of the causes and progress of neuroses and mental disease. His novels are all studies of that "mysterious borderland which lies between physiology and psychology."

His son, Oliver Wendell Holmes, Jr. (1841–1935) was the famous jurist.

THE COMPLETE WORKS. 1892. *Scholarly Press* 13 vols. 1972 each $19.50 set $250.00

THE PSYCHIATRIC NOVELS OF OLIVER WENDELL HOLMES. Abr. with introd. and psychiatric annotations by Clarence P. Oberndorf. 2nd ed. 1946. *Greenwood* 1970. $12.75

THE AUTOCRAT OF THE BREAKFAST TABLE. 1858. *Assoc. Bksellers* Airmont Bks. pap. $.95; *Dutton* Everyman's $3.50; *Hill & Wang* Am. Century 1957 $1.45

THE AUTOCRAT'S MISCELLANIES. *Twayne* 1959 $6.00

Books about Holmes

Oliver Wendell Holmes, the Autocrat and His Fellow-Boarders. By Samuel M. Crothers. 1909. *Bks. for Libraries* facsimile ed. $5.50

Holmes of the Breakfast Table. By Mark Dewolfe Howe. 1939. *Appel* (dist. by Phaeton) 1972 $7.50

Oliver Wendell Holmes. By Miriam R. Small. United States Authors Ser. *Twayne* 1962 $4.95; *College & Univ. Press* 1963 pap. $2.45 Includes chronology of Holmes' life and selected bibliography.

See also Chapter 8, American Poetry: Early Period.

THOREAU, HENRY DAVID. 1817–1862.

Thoreau was the creator and inspirer of our school of nature writers, but he stands apart from them. His essays are the records, not of facts about nature, but of his ideas and emotions in the presence of nature. In "American Literature Since 1870" (1915. *Cooper* $8.50) by Fred Lewis Pattee an interesting contrast is drawn between Thoreau and John Burroughs (*q. v.*): "Burroughs went into the woods to know and to make others to know, Thoreau went in to think and to feel; Burroughs was a naturalist, Thoreau a *super*-naturalist. Thoreau is inclined to wonder and even laugh because of the many times he speaks of hearing the voice of unknown birds. To Burroughs the forest contained no unknown birds; to Thoreau the forest was valuable only because it *did* contain unknown birds." Roland Wells Robbins of Concord, Mass., believed that he had found the exact location of Thoreau's cabin at Walden and described his search there in "Discovery at Walden" (1947. *Thoreau Foundation* 1970 pap. $3.00). The reissuing of "The Journal of Henry David

Thoreau" (ed. by Bradford Torrey and Francis H. Allen) gave the day-to-day record (1837–1861) from which he was to draw for his published books.

Thoreau was an individualist who believed that each man should live according to his conscience, willing to oppose the majority if need be. An early proponent of nonviolent resistance, he was jailed briefly for refusing to pay his poll tax to a government which had not yet outlawed slavery.

When Thoreau died in 1862, the second year of the Civil War, he was little known beyond a small circle of friends and admirers, and only two volumes of his writings had been published—"A Week on the Concord and Merrimack Rivers" and "Walden." Emerson (*q. v.*) said, "The country knows not yet, or in the least part, how great a son it has lost. It seems an injury that he should leave in the midst his broken task, which none else can finish."

Emerson's estimate of his friend has been borne out in the 20th century. Gandhi read Thoreau's essay on "Civil Disobedience" while in a South African jail, and it became the basis for his campaign to free India. Martin Luther King (*q. v.*) has acknowledged his debt to Thoreau and Gandhi as wellsprings of the Montgomery bus boycott and all that brought to birth the strong civil rights movement (and in its wake the more recent antiwar movement) of the last decade in the United States. Thoreau is the 19th-century New Englander who seems to have most relevance for today.

THE WRITINGS OF HENRY D. THOREAU. *Princeton Univ. Press* 4 vols. 1971–73. Vol. I Walden ed. by J. Lyndon Shanley $10.00 Vol. 2 The Maine Woods ed. by J. J. Moldenhauer $12.50 Vol. 3 Reform Papers ed. by W. Glick $12.50 Vol. 4 The Illustrated Walden with photographs from the Gleason Collection $15.00

SELECTED WORKS. Ed. by Henry Seidel Canby. *Houghton* 1937 1947 Cambridge Eds. $8.75

THE PORTABLE THOREAU. Ed. with introd. by Carl Bode *Viking* 1947 lib. bdg. $6.25 pap. $3.25

WALDEN AND SELECTED ESSAYS. Ed. by G. F. Whicher. 1947. *Henricks House* $5.00 pap. $2.45 (*For other editions of Walden in combination or alone, see below.*)

SELECTED WRITINGS. Ed. by Lewis Leary. 1958. *AHM Pub. Corp.* Crofts Class. pap. $.85

WALDEN AND OTHER WRITINGS. Ed. by Joseph Wood Krutch *Bantam Bks.* 1962 pap. $.85; ed. by Brooks Atkinson *Modern Library.* $2.95 pap. $1.25

WALDEN, and CIVIL DISOBEDIENCE. *Assoc. Booksellers* Airmont Bks. pap. $.60; *Harper* Class. pap. $.75; ed. by Norman H. Pearson *Holt* (Rinehart) 1948 pap. $2.00; ed. by S. Paul *Houghton* Riv. Eds. $1.10; *Macmillan* Collier Bks. pap. $.95; *New Am. Lib.* Signet pap. $.75; ed. by Owen Thomas *Norton* Critical Eds. 1966 pap. $1.95; variorum ed. by Walter Harding *Washington Square* pap. $.75

THE ANNOTATED WALDEN AND CIVIL DISOBEDIENCE. Ed. by Philip Van Doren Stern. *Clarkson N. Potter* 1971. $10.95. Contains many previously unpublished passages, bibliography, and a biography of Thoreau. Illustrated with maps, portraits, photographs and contemporary drawings and decorations.

THOREAU'S VISION: The Major Essays. Ed. by Charles R. Anderson. *Prentice-Hall* 1973 $6.95 Spectrum Bks. pap. $2.45. Includes A Winter Walk, Autumnal Tints, Wild Apples, The Beach, Climbing Mt. Ktaadn, Ascent of Saddleback, The Wild, Where I Lived and What I Lived for, Life without Principle, Civil Disobedience.

CIVIL DISOBEDIENCE. 1849. (Original title "Resistance to Civil Government"). *Godine* lit. ed. 1971 $10.00; *Revell* $1.00; variorum ed. by Walter Harding *Twayne* $5.00

A WEEK ON THE CONCORD AND MERRIMACK RIVERS. 1849. *Apollo* pap. $2.45; *Holt* pap. $1.25; *Houghton* $5.50 Sentry Eds. 1961 pap. $2.95

WALDEN, or Life in the Woods. 1854. *Apollo* pap. $2.25; ed. by Joseph Wood Krutch *Bantam Bks.* pap. $.95; *College and Univ. Press* 1965 pap. $2.95; *Dodd* Gt. Ill. Class. 1955 $5.50; introd. by Basil Willey *Dutton* Everyman's $3.50; ed. by Willard Thorp *Charles E. Merrill* 1969 $6.95 pap. $.85; variorum ed. annotated with introd. by Walter Harding *Twayne* 1962 $5.00; *Franklin Watts* 1966 Keith Jennison Bks. lg.-type ed. $8.95

THOREAU'S WALDEN: A Writer's Edition. Ed. by Larzer Ziff. *Holt* 1961 $5.25

EXCURSION. 1863. *Peter Smith* $4.00

THE MAINE WOODS. 1864. *Apollo* pap. $2.25; ed. by Dudley C. Lunt. 1950 *College & Univ. Press* 1965 pap. $2.95

CAPE COD. 1865 *Apollo* pap. $1.95; ed. by Dudley C. Lunt *College & Univ. Press* pap. $2.95; ed. by Lunt with introd. by Henry Beston and ills. by Henry Bugbee Kane *Norton* 1951 $5.50

THOREAU'S GUIDE TO CAPE COD. Ed. by Alexander B. Adams. *Devin-Adair* 1962 $6.50. A selection of the best from his "Cape Cod" with remarkable photographs.

COLLECTED POEMS. Ed. by Carl Bode. 1943. *Johns Hopkins Univ. Press* 1964. $12.00 pap. $3.45

THE JOURNAL OF HENRY D. THOREAU, 1837–1861. Ed. by Bradford Torrey and Francis H. Allen. 1906. With a new fwd. by Walter Harding *Dover* 1963 14 vols. in 2 each $20.00

THE RIVER. Ed. by Dudley C. Lunt. *College & Univ. Press* 1965 pap. $2.25. Selections from his journal.

THE HEART OF THOREAU'S JOURNALS. Ed. by Odell Shepard. 1927. *Dover* pap. $2.00; *Peter Smith* $4.25

H. D. THOREAU: A Writer's Journal. Ed. by Laurence Stapleton. 1960. *Dover* pap. $2.50

SELECTED JOURNALS OF HENRY DAVID THOREAU. Ed. by Carl Bode. 1961. *New Am. Lib.* 1967 pap. $.75; (with title "The Best of Thoreau's Journals") *Southern Illinois Univ. Press* 1971 $8.95

THOREAU'S WORLD: Miniatures from His Journal. Ed. by Charles R. Anderson. *Prentice-Hall* 1972 $10.00. *Caedmon* (TC2052) has available a recording of excerpts from this book read by Archibald MacLeish.

THOREAU: People, Principles and Politics. Ed. with introd. by Milton Meltzer. *Hill & Wang* 1963 $4.50 Am. Century pap. $1.95

Books about Thoreau

Henry David Thoreau: A Critical Study. By Mark Van Doren. 1916 1943. *Russell & Russell* 1961 $8.00
The Life of Henry David Thoreau, including Many Essays Hitherto Unpublished and Some Account of His Family and Friends. By Benjamin Franklin Sanborn. 1917. *Gale* 1968 $7.80; Folcroft $10.00. The author was a friend of Thoreau.
Thoreau. By Henry Seidel Canby. 1939. *Peter Smith* $6.00. A brilliant character analysis as well as a study of Thoreau's relation to Emerson and other Concord neighbors.

Henry David Thoreau. By Joseph Wood Krutch. 1948. *Greenwood* 1973 $13.00
"A nearly perfect fusing of biography and critical study"—*(New Yorker)*. "Krutch's sagely shaded portrait . . . brings out to the full Thoreau's pungent humor, which liked to juxtapose the homely and the ineffable and was keenly alive to the comic aspect of his eccentricities"—*(Atlantic)*.
A Thoreau Handbook. By Walter Harding. A useful volume which attempts to summarize the known facts about Thoreau's life, his works, sources and fame. *New York Univ. Press* 1959 $8.50 pap. $2.95
Thoreau: A Collection of Critical Essays. Ed. by Sherman Paul. *Prentice-Hall* 1962 $5.95
Concord Rebel: A Life of Henry David Thoreau. By August Derleth. For the general reader. *Chilton* 1962 $4.95
The Days of Henry Thoreau. By Walter Harding. *Knopf* 1965 $10.00
"The definitive biography of Thoreau, and readable too"—*(LJ)*.
Emerson and Thoreau: Transcendentalists in Conflict. By Joel Porte. *Wesleyan Univ. Press* 1966 $8.00
"He has given us a new understanding of both"—*(LJ)*.
Thoreau in Our Season. Ed. with introd. by John H. Hicks. *Univ. of Massachusetts Press* 1966 $7.00
Reprint of the Thoreau centennial issue of the *Massachusetts Review*. Essays by many authors, including Martin Luther King and Martin Buber. The role of Thoreau's ideas in modern civil disobedience is stressed. "First-rate contemporary opinions of various aspects of Thoreau's personality and influence"—*(LJ)*.
Henry David Thoreau. By Leon Edel. Pamphlets on American Writers *Univ. of Minnesota Press* 1970 pap. $1.25
Twentieth Century Interpretations of Walden. By Richard Ruland. *Prentice-Hall* 1968 $4.95 Spectrum Bks. pap. $1.25

LOWELL, JAMES RUSSELL. 1819–1891.

Lowell's essays are nearly all critical essays, bookish rather than reflective. Lowell was in his time well known as a leader of the Cambridge intellectual circle which included Emerson, Longfellow, James, Hawthorne and others. Poet, essayist and satirist, he was the first editor of the *Atlantic Monthly* and co-editor with Charles Eliot Norton of the highly respected *North American Review*.

COMPLETE WRITINGS. Ed. by Charles Eliot Norton. 1904. *AMS Press* 16 vols. each $18.50 set $290.00

THE ANTI-SLAVERY PAPERS OF JAMES RUSSELL LOWELL. Ed. by William B. Parker. 1902. *Negro Univ. Press* 2 vols. $19.00. A group of about 50 essays written between 1845 and 1850.

THE FUNCTION OF THE POET AND OTHER ESSAYS. Ed. by A. K. Mordell. 1920. *Folcroft* lib. bdg. $7.50; *Kennikat* $8.00; *Richard West* $15.00

LITERARY CRITICISM. Ed. by Herbert F. Smith. *Univ. of Nebraska Press* 1969 $5.95 pap. $2.25

AMONG MY BOOKS. 1870. *AMS Press* 1970 $11.50; *Scholarly Press* $19.50; *Richard West* $11.45

MY STUDY WINDOWS. 1871 *AMS Press* 1971 $11.25; *Richard West* 1973 $11.00

ESSAYS ON THE ENGLISH POETS (with Lessing, and Rousseau). 1888. *Kennikat* 1970 $10.00; *Richard West* $10.00

LITERARY ESSAYS. 1890. *Bks. for Libraries* 2 vols. $29.50

LATEST LITERARY ESSAYS. 1891. *Richard West* 1973 $12.50

THE OLD ENGLISH DRAMATISTS. 1892. *Bks. for Libraries* 1972 $9.00; *Richard West* $17.50. Lectures delivered at the Lowell Institute, 1887.

Books about Lowell

James Russell Lowell and His Friends. By Edward Everett Hale. 1899. *AMS Press* $11.50; *Folcroft* $11.00; *Richard West* $11.45

James Russell Lowell. By Claire McGlinchee. United States Authors Ser. *Twayne* $5.50; *College and Univ. Press* pap. $2.45

James Russell Lowell. By Martin Duberman. *Houghton* 1966 $8.00 *Beacon Press* pap. $3.45

"A deeply sympathetic, almost apologetic, but valuable, needed, and corrective biography . . . a sound and balanced portrait of a complex, divided and very human man"—(*N.Y. Times*).

ARNOLD, MATTHEW. 1822–1888.

Son of a famous headmaster at Rugby, Arnold rebelled against his father and against the "Philistinism" of his own upbringing. A poet and literary critic influenced by Goethe and Wordsworth, Arnold gradually became a militant social critic. In his essay "Culture and Anarchy" (1869) he inveighed against the materialistic barbarians (as he saw them) of the upper class and the vulgar Philistines of the middle class, and sought to bring education to the ignorant "populace." His efforts to integrate literature and life and to bring higher cultural standards to all ranks of society had repercussions which extended well beyond his own time.

THE COMPLETE PROSE WORKS OF MATTHEW ARNOLD. Ed. by R. H. Super. 10 vols. projected. *Univ. of Michigan Press* 1960– Vol. I On the Classical Tradition (1960) $6.50 Vol. 2 Democratic Education (1962) $8.50 Vol. 3 Lectures and Essays in Criticism (1962) $9.00 Vol. 4 Schools and Universities on the Continent (1964) $9.00 Vol. 5 Culture and Anarchy (1965) $9.50 Vol. 6 Dissent and Dogma (1968) $11.75 Vol. 7 God and the Bible (1970) $14.00 Vol. 8 Essays Religious and Mixed (1972) $15.00 Vol. 9 English Literature and Irish Politics (1973) $15.00

The *Times (London) Educational Supplement*, reviewing Vol. 3, praised the editor's "care over the text, his invaluable critical, explanatory and textual notes and his excellent index especially planned to help the reader to track Arnold's ideas about particular themes through all his prose works." *Library Journal* says of Vol. 5: "Professor Super has . . . established himself as an outstanding editor . . . in this distinguished series."

WORKS. 15 vols. 1903. *AMS Press* each $12.00 set $180.00; *Scholarly Press* $220.00

POETRY AND CRITICISM. Ed. by A. Dwight Culler. *Houghton* Riv. Eds. pap. $2.65

POETRY AND PROSE. With William Watson's Poem, and Essays by Lionel Johnson and H. W. Garrod. Ed. by Edmund K. Chambers *Oxford* 1939 $2.25

FOUR ESSAYS ON LIFE AND LETTERS. Ed. by E. K. Brown. 1947. *AHM Pub. Corp.* Crofts Class. pap. $.85

THE PORTABLE MATTHEW ARNOLD, including Culture and Anarchy (abr.); Poems, Essays, Letters. Ed. with an introd. by Lionel Trilling. *Viking* 1949 lib. bdg. $5.50 pap. $1.85

"Mr. Trilling begins his capital introduction . . . with the assertion that 'of the literary men of the great English 19th century there are few who have stayed quite so fresh, so immediate, and so relevant as Matthew Arnold.' . . . [Arnold's] predicament is ours—he merely knew it a little earlier"—(*SR*).

POETRY AND PROSE. Ed. by John Bryson. *Harvard Univ. Press* 1954 $12.00 pap. $4.50

PASSAGES FROM THE PROSE WRITINGS OF MATTHEW ARNOLD. Ed. by William E. Buckler. *New York Univ. Press* 1963 $8.50 pap. $3.35. Arnold's own one-volume selection. Essays on politics, religion, education and literature.

SELECTED POETRY AND PROSE. Ed. by F. W. Watt. *Oxford* 1964 $2.25

SELECTED PROSE. Ed. by Peter J. Keating. *Penguin* 1971 pap. $1.95 *Peter Smith* $4.25

SELECTED CRITICISM. Ed. by Christopher Risk. *New Am. Lib.* 1972 pap. $1.95

ON TRANSLATING HOMER. 1862. *AMS Press* repr. of 1905 ed. 1972 $7.00

ESSAYS IN CRITICISM. 1865. *Dutton* Everyman's $3.50 pap. $1.95

ESSAYS IN CRITICISM: Second Series. 1865–68. Ed. by S. R. Littlewood. *St. Martin's* $1.95

A STUDY OF CELTIC LITERATURE. 1867. *Kennikat* repr. of 1905 ed. 1970 $7.00

CULTURE AND ANARCHY. 1869. Ed. by Ian Gregor. *Bobbs* Liberal Arts $6.75 pap. $2.95; Ed. by John Dover Wilson *Cambridge* 1932 $7.50 pap. $2.95

LITERATURE AND DOGMA: An Essay towards a Better Apprehension of the Bible. 1873. *AMS Press* repr. of 1883 ed. 1970 $15.00; ed. by James C. Livingston *Ungar* 1950 $5.75 pap. $2.45

GOD AND THE BIBLE: A Review of Objections to "Literature and Dogma." 1875 *AMS Press* $15.00; *Richard West* $14.75

DISCOURSES IN AMERICA. 1896. *Scholarly Press* 1970 $12.50

ESSAYS IN CRITICISM: Third Series. 1910. *Folcroft* $15.00. An unauthorized collection gathered from periodicals, first published in Boston.

LETTERS, 1848–1888. Ed. by George W. Russell. 1904. *Scholarly Press* 2 vols. 1969 $39.50

LETTERS OF MATTHEW ARNOLD TO ARTHUR HUGH CLOUGH. Ed. by Howard F. Lowry *Oxford* 1932 $8.00; ed. by Lowry *Russell & Russell* 1968 $8.00

Books about Arnold

Matthew Arnold. By Edmund K. Chambers. 1947 *Russell & Russell* 1964 $5.50
Matthew Arnold and American Culture. By John H. Raleigh. *Peter Smith* 1962 $4.50; *Univ. of California Press* 1961 pap. $1.95
Matthew Arnold and the Romantics. By Leon Gottfried. *Univ. of Nebraska Press* 1963 $5.00
Matthew Arnold and the Three Classes. By Patrick J. McCarthy. *Columbia* 1964 $9.00
    "Clear exposition of the many forces intellectual and political, which made their impact upon a complex mind"—(*LJ*).
Matthew Arnold and John Stuart Mill. By Edward Alexander. *Columbia* 1966 $7.50.
    Compares the two as representatives of the Victorian traditions of humanism and liberalism, respectively.

See also Chapter 6, British Poetry—Middle Period.

PATER, WALTER. 1839–1894.

Pater was once considered one of the greatest stylists in English literature, though he is not widely read today. Tradition has it that he sought for the right word as laboriously as Flaubert (*q. v.*) did for "le mot juste." Pater's overpolished periods are not, however, the art that conceals art. Some of his critical essays on esthetic subjects have been called "reconstructions of the past toward which he turned his eyes away from the present." "Marius the Epicurean" (1885. *Dutton* Everyman's $3.50; *New Am. Lib.* Signet pap. $1.25) is the best known of his few romances. He spent most of his life in academic seclusion, but greatly influenced the younger artists and critics of his time, especially Oscar Wilde.

ESSAYS FROM THE GUARDIAN. 1896. *Bks. for Libraries* repr. of 1901 ed. $9.00; *Folcroft.* lib. bdg. $7.50

UNCOLLECTED ESSAYS. 1903 *Folcroft* lib. bdg. $15.00

SKETCHES AND REVIEWS. 1919. *Bks. for Libraries* $9.00; *Folcroft* lib. bdg. $7.50

THE RENAISSANCE. 1873. *New Am. Lib.* Mentor Bks. pap. $.95. The volume that established his reputation, particularly the essay on Leonardo Da Vinci.

LEONARDO DA VINCI. 1873. Color Bks. Ser. *Phaedon* 1971 $5.95. Arnold's most famous essay.

MICHELANGELO. 1873. *Kodansha* 1968 pap. $2.75

APPRECIATIONS. 1889. *Richard West* 1973 $10.00

PLATO AND PLATONISM. 1893. *Folcroft* repr. of 1910 ed. $12.00; *Greenwood* repr. of 1910 ed. $12.50. Lectures on aesthetic appreciation.

LETTERS. Ed. by Lawrence Evans *Oxford* 1970 $10.25

Books about Pater

Victorian Portraits: Hopkins and Pater. By David A. Downes. *Twayne* 1965 $4.50
Walter Pater: Humanist. By Richmond Crinkley. *Univ. Press of Kentucky* 1970 $7.75

JAMES, HENRY. 1843–1916.

Henry James was best known for his novels, but he was also one of "the major Anglo-American critics between the age of Matthew Arnold and that of T. S. Eliot. His fiction and his criticism rest on the same general interests and assumptions. Like Matthew Arnold he was greatly concerned with the state of culture, and he believed that culture included art, ideas and manners, but consisted essentially in 'the perfection of the self' "—(F. W. Dupee).

James wrote a number of essays about his travels in America, England, France and Italy, which were collected in "Transatlantic Sketches" (1875), "Portraits of Places" (1883), "English Hours" (1905) and "The American Scene" (1907). His fine autobiography, edited by F. W. Dupee (1956, o. p.), consists of three books originally published separately: "A Small Boy and Others" (1913) "Notes of a Son and Brother" (1914) and "The Middle Years" (1917).

NOTES AND REVIEWS. 1921. *Bks. for Libraries* 1968 $10.00; *Folcroft* 1973 lib. bdg. $9.50

THE ART OF THE NOVEL. Ed. by R. P. Blackmur *Scribner* 1934 $7.95 pap. $2.95. A collection of the prefaces written for the New York edition of his "Complete Novels and Tales."

LITERARY REVIEWS AND ESSAYS: American, English and French Literature. Ed. by Albert Mordell. 1957. *AMS Press* $17.50; *College & Univ. Press* 1962 pap. $3.95

PARISIAN SKETCHES: Letters to the New York *Tribune*, 1875–1876. Ed. by Leon Edel and Ilse Dusoir Lind *New York Univ. Press* 1957 $7.95

FRENCH POETS AND NOVELISTS. 1878. 1st American ed. 1879 2nd ed. 1893. *Burt Franklin* repr. of 1893 ed. $14.00; *Richard West* repr. of 1893 ed. $13.95

HAWTHORNE. 1879. Ed. by John Morley *AMS Press* repr. of 1887 ed. $12.50; *Cornell Univ. Press* 1956 $5.00 pap. $1.45; *Folcroft* repr. of 1879 ed. $6.00

PARTIAL PORTRAITS. 1888. *Greenwood* repr. of 1888 ed. $13.50; *Haskell* repr. of 1911 ed. 1969 lib. bdg. $12.95. Includes the essays "Turgenieff" and "The Art of Fiction," and reviews of George Eliot, R. L. Stevenson, Trollope.

THE QUESTION OF OUR SPEECH. 1905. (and "The Lesson of Balzac") *Folcroft* lib. bdg. $10.00; *Haskell* lib. bdg. $6.95

VIEWS AND REVIEWS. 1908. *AMS Press* 1969 $6.00; *Bks. for Libraries* facsimile ed. $10.00

NOTES ON NOVELISTS, WITH SOME OTHER NOTES. 1914. *Biblo & Tannen* 1969 $15.00

TRANSATLANTIC SKETCHES. 1875. *Bks. for Libraries* $13.75

PORTRAITS OF PLACES. 1883. *Bks. for Libraries* $13.00

THE AMERICAN SCENE. 1907. Ed. by Leon Edel. *Indiana Univ. Press* 1968 $10.00 Midland Bks. pap. $3.95

ESSAYS IN LONDON AND ELSEWHERE. 1893. *Bks. for Libraries* $11.50

THE NOTEBOOKS OF HENRY JAMES. Ed. by F. O. Matthiessen and Kenneth B. Murdock. *Oxford* 1947 Galaxy Bks. 1961 pap. $2.95

LETTERS. Ed. by Percy Lubbock *Octagon* 1969 2 vols. $37.50

LETTERS TO A. C. BENSON AND AUGUSTE MONOD. 1930. *Folcroft* lib. bdg. $7.75; *Haskell* lib. bdg. $7.75

SELECTED LETTERS OF HENRY JAMES. Ed. by Leon Edel. *Farrar, Straus* 1955 $4.75. Letters to Conrad, Wells, Galsworthy, Henry Adams, Howells, Edith Wharton, Fanny Kemble and others.

SAINTSBURY, GEORGE. 1845–1933.

Saintsbury was called "the leviathan of critics," so vast was the number of his books. A professor of English literature in the University of Edinburgh for 20 years, he wrote monumental works on the history of criticism and on English prosody, which were followed by lighter works including some amusing books on wines. He was also recognized as the most prominent English authority on French literature. The many prefaces and introductions that he wrote to other persons' books were collected posthumously in "Prefaces and Essays" and show why he has been called "a critical historian of literature without a rival in English." Oliver Elton has said: "Probably he has applied his canon to more authors, old and new, ancient and native and foreign, than any critic in the language." His important "A Short History of French Literature" (1882) is regrettably out of print. Apropos of this work it used to be said that an Englishman (Saintsbury) wrote the best history of French literature, and a Frenchman (Hippolyte Taine) the best history of English literature.

MISCELLANEOUS ESSAYS: On English and French Literature. 1892. *Bks. for Libraries* $14.50; (including the second series) *Folcroft* 2 vols. 1973 each $19.00

ESSAYS IN ENGLISH LITERATURE. *Bks. for Libraries* 1972 1st ser. repr. of 1891 ed. $15.75 2nd ser. repr. of 1895 ed. $15.00

CORRECTED IMPRESSIONS: Essays on Victorian Writers. 1895. *Bks. for Libraries* 1974 $10.50; *Folcroft* lib. bdg. $15.00

A SHORT HISTORY OF ENGLISH LITERATURE. 1898. *St. Martin's* $12.95

A HISTORY OF CRITICISM AND LITERARY TASTE IN EUROPE. 1900–04. *British Bk. Centre* $17.50; *Humanities Press* 2nd ed. 1950 3 vols. each $7.25 set $17.50

THE FLOURISHING OF ROMANCE AND THE RISE OF ALLEGORY. 1907. *Folcroft* $25.00

A HISTORY OF ENGLISH PROSODY. From the 12th Century to the Present Day. 1906–21, 1923 *Russell & Russell* 1961 3 vols. set $40.00

A HISTORY OF ENGLISH CRITICISM. 1911. *British Bk. Centre* 1972 $7.95; *Somerset Pub.* $23.50; *Verry* $6.50

A HISTORY OF ENGLISH PROSE RHYTHM. 1912. *Indiana Univ. Press* 1965 $12.50

THE ENGLISH NOVEL. 1913. *AMS Press* $13.50; *Folcroft* lib. bdg. $13.00; *Scholarly Press* $13.00

A HISTORY OF THE FRENCH NOVEL. 1917–19. *Russell & Russell* 2 vols. set $25.00

COLLECTED ESSAYS AND PAPERS. 1924. *Bks. for Libraries* facsimile ed. 4 vols. set $39.50; *Johnson Reprint* 1969 4 vols. set $42.50

PREFACES AND ESSAYS. 1933. *Bks. for Libraries* $16.75; *Greenwood* $16.00

JEFFERIES, RICHARD. 1848–1887.

E. D. H. Johnson, introducing the excerpts from Richard Jefferies in the charming anthology "The Poetry of Earth" (*Atheneum* 1966 $10.00), places him "among the supreme historians of the English countryside." Poetic rather than scientific, a journalist who wrote his essays from the country to the *Pall Mall Gazette*, Jefferies' masterpieces are "The Gamekeeper at Home, or Sketches of Natural History and Rural Life," "Wild Life in a Southern County" (1879, o. p.), "The Amateur Poacher" and "Round About a Great Estate" (1880, o. p.). One feels that he spent many hours in all seasons watching the humblest of beasts and birds in grass, hedgerow and stream in order to describe their habits and appearance in vivid, minute detail. "The Story of My Heart" (1883, o. p.) is a spiritual autobiography, a prose poem, rapturous with a mystical love of nature.

JEFFERIES' ENGLAND: Nature Essays. Ed. by Samuel J. Looker. 1937. *Bks. for Libraries*. 1973. $19.75

OLD HOUSE AT COATE AND OTHER HITHERTO UNPUBLISHED ESSAYS. Ed. by Samuel J. Looker. 1948. *Bks. for Libraries* $10.50

THE GAMEKEEPER AT HOME (1878) and THE AMATEUR POACHER (1879). Introd. by David Ascoli. *Oxford* World's Class. 1948 2 vols. in I $2.25

Books about Jefferies

Richard Jefferies, a Critical Study. By W. J. Keith. *Univ. of Toronto Press* 1965 $7.50

HEARN, LAFCADIO. 1850–1904.

Hearn's father was a British Army surgeon and his mother a Greek. At 19 he came to America and lived in New Orleans doing newspaper work. In 1887 he went to Martinique in the West Indies and stayed until he went to Japan in 1890. There he married a Japanese, became a citizen of Japan and was Professor of English at the University of Tokyo. He was buried there with Buddhist rites, though not a Buddhist.

His works fall into three divisions. The first is his early work in New Orleans, when only the strange, bizarre and somber appealed to him. The second includes his colorful tropical sketches of the West Indies, and the third his many works on Japan. Hearn was a stylist, and his great purpose was to contrast the civilizations of the East and the West. His sensitive literary interpretations of Japanese life and culture were among the first of their kind. Among other works which are now available—stories, oriental tales and legends, Oriental curiosities, etc.—are "Some Chinese Ghosts" (1887. *Somerset Pub.* $9.50), "Chita," a story of a terrible tidal wave that swept Last Island (1889. *AMS Press* 1969 $7.00; *Scholarly Press* 1970 $14.50; with fwd. by Arlin Turner *Univ. of North Carolina Press* 1969 $7.50 pap. $2.95), "Youma," a story of a West Indian slave insurrection (1890. *AMS Press* $6.00), "Kotto: Being Japanese Curios with Sundry Cobwebs" (1902. *Bks. for Libraries* $9.75; *Tuttle* 1972 $2.25), "Japanese Fairy Tales" (*Liveright* $5.95), "Earless Ho-ichi" (*Kodansha* 1965 $6.50), "Japanese Lyrics" (*Folcroft* $15.00), and "Kwaidan: Stories and Studies of Strange Things" (with introd. by Oscar Lewis *Dover* 1968 pap. $1.25; *Tuttle* 1971 pap. $1.95).

COLLECTED WORKS. 1922. *Gordon Press* 16 vols. set $200.00

INTERPRETATIONS OF LITERATURE. Ed. by John Erskine. 1915. *Richard West* 2 vols. $22.45

APPRECIATIONS OF POETRY. Sel. and ed. by John Erskine. 1916. *Bks. for Libraries* $14.25; *Kraus* $17.00. Selected from notes by students of lectures delivered at the University of Tokyo, 1896–1902.

LIFE AND LITERATURE. Sel. and ed. by John Erskine. 1917. *Bks. for Libraries* $14.50; *Folcroft* $5.00. Contains essays on literature, criticism, etc., and studies of individual writers: Meredith, Borrow, Rossetti, Beddoes, Lord De Tabley, Tolstoy.

TALKS TO WRITERS. Sel. and ed. by John Erskine. 1920. *Bks. for Libraries*. 1967 $9.75

BOOKS AND HABITS: From the Lectures of Lafcadio Hearn. Sel. and ed. by John Erskine. 1921. *Bks. for Libraries* $11.50; *Richard West* $11.45

PRE-RAPHAELITE AND OTHER POETS. Lectures sel. and ed. by John Erskine. 1922. *Bks. for Libraries* $11.75

ESSAYS IN EUROPEAN AND ORIENTAL LITERATURE. Ed. by Albert Mordell. 1923. *Bks. for Libraries* $9.75

OCCIDENTAL GLEANINGS: Sketches and Essays. Collected and ed. by Albert Mordell. 1925. *Bks. for Libraries* 2 vols. $18.50

EDITORIALS. Ed. by Charles Woodward Hutson. 1926. *Beekman Pubs.* 1973 $14.00. First published in the New Orleans *Item*, 1878–81, and in the New Orleans *Times-Democrat*, 1882–87.

POETS AND POEMS. Ed. by Ryuji Tanabé. 1926. *Folcroft* lib. bdg. $17.50

SOME STRANGE ENGLISH LITERARY FIGURES OF THE 18TH AND 19TH CENTURIES. Ed. by Ryuji Tanabé. 1927. *Bks. for Libraries* $8.75

LECTURES ON SHAKESPEARE. Ed. by Iwao Inagaki. 1928. *Folcroft* lib. bdg. $15.00. Lectures delivered in 1899 at the Imperial University of Tokyo, first published in a limited edition in 1928.

LECTURES ON PROSODY. Comp. and ed. by Teisaburo Ochiai. 1929. *Folcroft* lib. bdg. $15.00

LECTURES ON TENNYSON. Ed. by Shigetsugu Kishi. 1941. *Folcroft* lib. bdg. $15.00

SELECTED WRITINGS. Ed. by Henry Goodman; introd. by Malcolm Cowley. *Citadel Press* 1971. pap. $3.95

TWO YEARS IN THE FRENCH WEST INDIES. 1890. *Gregg Press* 1970 $15.00

GLIMPSES OF UNFAMILIAR JAPAN. 1894. *AMS Press* 1969 $18.00; *Scholarly Press* 1970 $24.50

OUT OF THE EAST: Reveries and Studies in New Japan. 1895. *Bks. for Libraries* 1972 $12.75; *Tuttle* 1972 pap. $2.95

KOKORO: Hints and Echoes of Japanese Inner Life. 1896. *Greenwood* $14.75; *Tuttle* 1972 pap. $2.75

EXOTICS AND RETROSPECTIVES. 1898 *Gregg* 1969 lib. bdg. $11.50; *Tuttle* 1971 pap. $2.20. Exotics: Fuji-no-Yama, Insect Musicians, A Question in the Zen Texts, The Literature of the Dead, Frogs, Of Moon-desire. Retrospectives: First Impressions, Beauty Is Memory, Sadness in Beauty, Parfum de jeunesse, Azure Psychology, A Serenade, A Red Sunset, Frisson, Vespertino Cognitio, The Eternal Haunter.

IN GHOSTLY JAPAN. 1899. *Tuttle* 1971 pap. $2.20

SHADOWINGS. 1900. *Tuttle* 1971 pap. $2.20

A Japanese Miscellany. 1901. *Tuttle* 1954 pap. $2.20

Gleanings in Buddha-Fields: Studies of Hand and Soul in the Far East. 1904. *Blom* $10.50; *Tuttle* 1971 pap. $2.75

Letters from the Raven: Being the Correspondence of Lafcadio Hearn with Henry Watkin. Ed. with introd. by Milton Bonner. 1907. *Bks. for Libraries* 1972. $9.75

The Japanese Letters. Ed. by Elizabeth Bisland. 1910. *Scholarly Research, Inc.*

Some New Letters of Lafcadio Hearn. Ed. by Sanki Ichikawa. *Folcroft* 1973 lib. bdg. $35.00

Books about Hearn

Lafcadio Hearn. By Vera McWilliams. 1946. *Cooper* 1971 $12.50. The standard biography.
An Ape of Gods: The Art and Thought of Lafcadio Hearn. By Beong-cheon Yu. *Wayne State Univ. Press* 1964 $11.00

STEVENSON, ROBERT LOUIS. 1850–1894.

Professor Hugh Walker has said that since Lamb (*q. v.*) there has been no more accomplished essayist than Stevenson. Many of the essays are based upon events in the writer's life. But the narration of the event is rarely sufficient in itself. "Storyteller as he was, he was still more a moralist," and a delightful one. "*Virginibus Puerisque*" ("Concerning Maidens and Youths") is an essay on love, marriage and the conduct of life. "Travels with a Donkey" describes Stevenson's journeys in southern France, and "An Inland Voyage" is the charming account of a canoe trip through France and Belgium. His travel sketches show "his fine eye for color and vivid impressions, that sort of sensitivity that was to add so much to the popularity of his fiction."

Works. The Vailima ed. 1921–23. *AMS Press* 26 vols. each $25.00 set $650.00

Selected Writings. Ed. by Saxe Commins. 1947. *Bks. for Libraries* $34.50

Selected Essays. Ed. by George Scott-Moncrieff. *Regnery* Gateway Eds. pap. $1.25

Familiar Studies of Men and Books (1882); Virginibus Puerisque; and Selected Poems. *Collins* New Class. $3.00

An Inland Voyage (1878); Travels with a Donkey (1879); The Silverado Squatters (1883). Introd. by M. Roy Ridley *Dutton* Everyman's $3.50

Virginibus Puerisque. 1881. *Bks. for Libraries* 1972 $11.50

Memories and Portraits. 1887. *Scholarly Press* repr. of 1900 ed. 1969 $14.50

Across the Plains: With Other Memories and Essays. 1892. *Bks. for Libraries* $12.00

From Scotland to Silverado. Ed. by James D. Hart. *Harvard Univ. Press* 1966 $6.95

Young Stevenson's account, compiled from his writings, of his trip to California (1879–80) and honeymoon with his American wife. "Modern editorial techniques at their best"—(*LJ*).

Vailima Letters: Being Correspondence Addressed to Sidney Colvin, Nov. 1890 to Oct. 1894. 1895. *Bks. for Libraries* 2 vols. set $18.75

See also Chapter 11, British Fiction: Middle Period, for biographical material.

HUNEKER, JAMES GIBBONS. 1860–1921.

Huneker's many volumes of essays, most of which are now o. p., embrace the arts of music, drama, painting and literature. His daily bread was earned as critic (mainly of music and art) for the New York *Sun*,

Times and *World* and the Philadelphia *Press*. Huneker's literary and historical allusions are so far-reaching and so abundant that his essays must be read with reference books at hand, and he infers such a rich culture in his reader that he scorns to mark as quotations any but the most obscure references. In "A Book of Prefaces," H. L. Mencken (*q. v.*) writes: "Huneker assumes that the elements are already well-grounded, that he is dealing with the initiated, that a pause to explain would be an affront. Sad work for the Philistines—but a joy to the elect!"

ESSAYS. Sel. and with introd. by H. L. Mencken. 1929. *AMS Press* $27.50

THE MELOMANIACS. 1902. *AMS Press* $11.00; *Gordon Press* $11.00; *Greenwood* $13.75

OVERTONES: A Book of Temperaments. 1904. *Bks. for Libraries* $11.25

THE ICONOCLASTS: A Book of Dramatists. 1905. *Bks. for Libraries* $14.50; *Greenwood* $13.50; *Richard West* 1973 $14.45. Ibsen, Strindberg, Becque, Hauptman, Suderman, Hervieu, Gorky, Duse, D'Annunzio, Maeterlinck and Bernard Shaw.

MEZZOTINTS IN MODERN MUSIC. 1905. *AMS Press* $11.50; *Scholarly Press* $19.50. Brahms, Tchaikovsky, Chopin, Richard Strauss, Liszt, Richard Wagner.

FRANZ LISZT. 1905. 1924 *AMS Press* 1971 $12.50

THE EGOISTS: A Book of Supermen. *Gordon Press*. Stendhal, Beaudelaire, Flaubert, Anatole France, Huysmans, Barres, Nietsche, Blake, Ibsen, Stirner, Ernest Hello.

PROMENADES OF AN IMPRESSIONIST. 1910. *Bks. for Libraries*. $14.50

THE PATHOS OF DISTANCE: A Book of a Thousand and one Moments. 1913. *AMS Press* $20.00

IVORY, APES AND PEACOCKS. 1915. *Hill & Wang* Am. Century 1959 pap. $1.25; *Richard West* 1973 $10.00

CHOPIN: The Man and His Music. 1900. Introd. by Herbert Weinstock *Dover* 1966 pap. $2.00; *Peter Smith* $4.50; *Scholarly Press* $24.50

THE BEDOUINS. 1920. *AMS Press* $14.00. Mary Garden, Debussy, Chopin, or The Circus, Botticelli, Poe, Brahmsody, Anatole France, Mirbeau, Caruso on Wheels, and Ambergris, with The Supreme Sin, Grindstones, A Masque of Music, and The Vision Malefic.

PAINTED VEILS. 1920. *Liveright* Black and Gold Lib. $6.95

INTIMATE LETTERS OF JAMES GIBBONS HUNEKER. Ed. by Josephine Huneker. 1924. *Liveright* Black and Gold Lib. $7.95; *Richard West* 1973 $25.00

STEEPLEJACK. 1920. *Gordon Press* 2 vols. set $20.95. Autobiographical.

Books about Huneker

James Gibbons Huneker: Critic of the Seven Arts. By Arnold T. Schwab. *Stanford Univ. Press* 1963 $10.00

CHAPMAN, JOHN JAY. 1862–1933.

"Chapman, whom Edmund Wilson [*q. v.*] has called 'the best writer on literature of his generation who made the Babbitts and the Mores and the Brownells look like provincial schoolmasters,' was a gadfly who persistently prodded and reasoned his generation into looking at the flaws and pretensions in American culture." In addition to an impressionistic portrait of the life and times of William Lloyd Garrison, there are shorter essays on Whitman, Emerson, William James and Julia Ward Howe. "All combine great felicity of expression with that intellectual daring and iconoclasm which anticipated Mencken."

Chapman was born in New York City. A graduate of Harvard, he was admitted to the bar in 1888, but after ten years he abandoned law for literature. Passionate and erratic, he once burned his left hand in remorse at having beaten someone; the hand required amputation. He was a friend of William James (*q. v.*) and other Boston intellectuals, and a "fiery and pertinent observer of his environment" with an understanding of the Negro rare in his day. Edmund Wilson's essay "John Jay Chapman: The Mute and The Open Strings," in his book "The Triple Thinkers," (*q. v.*) is well worth reading for the light it throws on an astonishing and neglected writer.

EMERSON AND OTHER ESSAYS. 1898. *AMS Press* $8.00; *Gordon Press* $10.95

LEARNING AND OTHER ESSAYS. 1910. *Bks. for Libraries* facsimile ed. $9.00

GREEK GENIUS AND OTHER ESSAYS. 1915. *Bks. for Libraries* $10.50

MEMORIES AND MILESTONES. 1915. *Bks. for Libraries* facsimile ed. $10.25

Books about Chapman

John Jay Chapman: An American Mind. By Richard B. Hovey. *Columbia* 1959 $7.50. This careful study presents him as "a man of brilliant intellect, a thinker ahead of his time, and a great prose writer whose analysis of American civilization is of continuing significance."

John Jay Chapman. By Melvin H. Bernstein. *College & Univ. Press* 1964 pap. $2.45; United States Authors Ser. *Twayne* 1964 $4.95

QUILLER-COUCH, SIR ARTHUR (THOMAS). 1863–1944.

Sir Arthur Quiller-Couch ("Q") is particularly well known as editor of the *Oxford* books of "English Verse," "English Prose," "English Ballads" and "Victorian Verse." In his essays he writes always of other days, in an informal but nonetheless academic manner. A delicacy of phrasing and the deftness of a master characterize his 50 books of essays, criticism, fiction and poetry. "Memories and Opinions" (1945, o.p.) is only a fragment of an autobiography, leaving "Q" at 24, when his first book, "Dead Man's Rock" (1887, o.p.,), was published. He left unfinished a "lushly romantic" 19th-century version of the legend of "Tristan and Iseult" (*q. v.*). This has been completed by Daphne Du Maurier (*q. v.*) and published as "Castle Dor" (o. p.). Most of his novels are set in Cornwall.

ADVENTURES IN CRITICISM. 1896. *Gordon Press* $11.00; *Scholarly Press* $14.50

STUDIES IN LITERATURE. 1919. *Richard West* 1973 $15.00; Second Series. 1922. *Greenwood* $11.75; *Richard West* $11.50 Third Series. 1929. o.p.

CHARLES DICKENS AND OTHER VICTORIANS. 1925. *Kraus* 1968 $12.00

THE POET AS CITIZEN AND OTHER PAPERS. 1934. *Richard West.* $12.50

CAMBRIDGE LECTURES. 1943. *Bks for Libraries* 1972 $11.50

Books about Quiller-Couch

Sir Arthur Thomas Quiller-Couch: A Biographical Study of Q. A portrait of him "as poet and novelist, critic and professor, yachtsman and patriot, Cornishman and Mayor of Fowey"; as admirable in insight as in composition. By Fred Brittain. 1948. *Richard West* $10.00

SMITH, LOGAN PEARSALL. 1865–1946.

Smith was an eminent Quaker expatriate living in England. He was very active in the Society for Pure English, for which he wrote a number of tracts. He claimed to have known only interesting people—and he knew many. Bernard Berenson (*q. v.*) and Bertrand Russell (*q. v.*) were his brothers-in-law. "Two weeks before his death, a friend asked him half jokingly if he had discovered any meaning in life. 'Yes,' he replied, 'there is a meaning; at least, for me there is one thing that matters—to set a chime of words tinkling in the minds of a few fastidious people' "—(Cyril Connolly).

The once popular "Trivia" (1917) and its sequels "More Trivia" (1921), "Afterthoughts" (1931), "Last Words" (1933), are now regrettably o.p. "Reperusals and Re-Collections" is the last of this group. They consist of paragraph essays—a "new" prose form, very simple and very subtle. The author himself called them "pieces of moral prose, pensées, reflections, meditations, observations, dealing with the place and habits of men in nature and society." He added that it was "the prose of leisure, bearing no marks of economic necessity." "Milton and His Modern Critics" is a defense of Milton against the attacks of T. S. Eliot and Ezra Pound.

THE ENGLISH LANGUAGE. 1912. *Oxford* 2nd ed. 1952. pap. $1.75. The 3rd ed. of 1966 is no longer in print.

WORDS AND IDIOMS: Studies in the English Language. 1925. *Gale* $14.50

ON READING SHAKESPEARE. 1933. *Somerset Pub.* $11.50

REPERUSALS AND RE-COLLECTIONS. 1937. *Bks for Libraries* 1968 $11.50

MILTON AND HIS MODERN CRITICS. 1940. *Shoe String* 1967. $4.00

LEACOCK, STEPHEN (BUTLER). 1869–1944.

Leacock was head of the department of political science and economics at McGill University in Montreal, but he is chiefly known for other accomplishments. A. P. Herbert called him "the greatest humorist of the age." "To Leacock it was given to have always a cap and gown in his cupboard as well as a cap and bells. He frequently contrived to wear both costumes at once, with original and striking effect"—(London *Times*). Of his many humorous books, "Nonsense Novels" is generally considered the best.

THE LEACOCK ROUNDABOUT: A Treasury of the Best Works of Stephen Leacock. *Dodd* 1946 $6.50

LAUGH WITH LEACOCK: An Anthology of His Best Work. *Apollo* 1961 pap. $2.25

THE LAUGH PARADE. *Apollo* 1962 pap. $2.25

THE PURSUIT OF KNOWLEDGE. *Liveright* 1934 $3.95. Some of his more serious work.

NONSENSE NOVELS. 1912. *Dover* pap. $1.75; *Peter Smith* $4.00

SUNSHINE SKETCHES OF A LITTLE TOWN. 1912. *Bks. for Libraries* $9.00

LITERARY LAPSES. 1917. *Bks. for Libraries* $8.00

FRENZIED FICTION. 1918. *Bks. for Libraries* $9.50

HERE ARE MY LECTURES AND STORIES. 1937. *Bks for Libraries* $12.00

MODEL MEMOIRS AND OTHER SKETCHES FROM SIMPLE TO SERIOUS. 1938. *Bks. for Libraries* $12.50

Books about Leacock

Stephen Leacock. By David M. Legate. *Doubleday* 1971 $8.95
Leacock. By Stephen Franklin. *Grossman* Canadian Jackdaw Bk. 1917 $3.75

BELLOC, (JOSEPH) HILAIRE (PIERRE). 1870–1953.

Belloc was born in France but was naturalized as a British subject in 1902. In "Shandygaff" Christopher Morley (*q. v.*) said: "In Belloc we find the perfect union of the French and English minds. Rabelaisian in fecundity, wit, and irrepressible sparkle, he is also of English blood and sinew. . . . History, politics, economics, military topography, poetry, novels, satires, nonsense rhymes—all [were the] curiosities of an eager mind." With his close friend and fellow Catholic, G. K. Chesterton, Belloc founded the *New Witness*, a weekly newspaper opposing capitalism and free thought, and supporting a philosophy known as distributism. The pair were so close in thought and association that Bernard Shaw nicknamed them "Chesterbelloc." Belloc lived quietly in the country in England until his tragic death in 1953 from burns caused by his dressing gown's catching fire from the hearth.

Some of his famous humorous books for children are still in print: "The Bad Child's Book of Beasts" (1896. *Knopf* $3.25 lib. bdg. $4.19; *Peter Smith* $3.75); "The Bad Child's Book of Beasts, More Beasts for Worse Children and A Moral Alphabet" (*Dover* pap. $1.50; *Grosset* $1.50); and "Cautionary Verses" (*Knopf* 1950 $7.50).

AVRIL. 1904. *Bks. for Libraries* $10.75. Essays on the poetry of the French Renaissance.

On Nothing and Kindred Subjects. 1908. *Bks. for Libraries* facsimile ed. $11.00

On Everything. 1910. *Bks. for Libraries* $11.00

On Anything. 1910. *Bks. for Libraries* $9.75

On Something. 1910. *Bks. for Libraries* facsimile ed. 1968 $9.25

First and Last. 1911. *Bks. for Libraries* 1968 $9.75

This and That and the Other. 1912. *Bks. for Libraries* facsimile ed. 1968 $13.25

At the Sign of the Lion and Other Essays. 1916. *Bks. for Libraries* $7.00

On. 1923. *Bks. for Libraries* $9.00

Short Talks with the Dead and Other Essays. 1926. *Bks. for Libraries* $9.50

Conversations with a Cat and Other Essays. 1929. *Bks. for Libraries* $9.75

Conversation with an Angel and Other Essays. 1929. *Bks. for Libraries* 1968 $11.50

Essays of a Catholic. 1931. *Bks. for Libraries* facsimile ed. $9.75

Characters of the Reformation. 1936. *Bks. for Libraries* $15.50

Silence of the Sea and Other Essays. 1940 *Bks. for Libraries* $10.50

Places. 1941. *Bks. for Libraries* $9.75

Books about Belloc

> Some Thoughts on Hilaire Belloc: Ten Studies. By Patrick Braybrooke. 1923. *Haskell* 1969 lib. bdg. $7.95; *Richard West* $7.75
> Hilaire Belloc: No Alienated Man. By Frederick Wilhelmsen. 1954. *Fernhill* $2.50
> The Life of Hilaire Belloc. By Robert Speaight. 1957. *Haskell* lib. bdg. $7.95
> Hilaire Belloc. By Renée Haynes. *British Bk. Centre.* $2.38 pap. $1.20

BEERBOHM, SIR MAX. 1872–1956.

Beerbohm carried on the high tradition of satire in English letters. He succeeded Bernard Shaw (*q. v.*) as dramatic critic of the *Saturday Review*, Shaw introducing his successor as "the incomparable Max." In the early 1890s Oscar Wilde (*q. v.*) announced that Beerbohm had "mastered the secret of perpetual old age." In commenting on the timeless quality of the pieces in "Mainly on the Air," the *Christian Science Monitor* said: "Sir Max was always looking backward on yesterday with what seemed almost like anticipation. He even had invented ways to project the present into the future so that 'doomed' to live in the contemporary scene, he could pretend he had returned to it from an even more advanced and less satisfactory age . . . ." Sir Max's only novel, "Zuleika Dobson" (1911, *New Am. Lib.* Signet pap. $.75; *Modern Library* $2.45) is a delightful burlesque of his own college days at Oxford. His essays are light, witty and stimulating.

Beerbohm was an accomplished caricaturist. Of the 46 portrait drawings "Max's Nineties: Drawings 1892–1899" (1958, o. p.) only a few have appeared in book form; most of the others were taken from periodicals of the nineties. The first book publication of his light verse, "Max in Verse: Rhymes and Parodies" collected and annotated by J. G. Riewald with a foreword by S. N. Behrman, his friend and biographer (*Stephen Greene Press* 1963 $6.50 pap. $2.95), contains material never before published.

Works (1896) and More (1899) 1930. *Scholarly Press* $8.00

More. 1899. 4th ed. 1921. *Bks. for Libraries* $8.50

And Even Now. 1920. *Bks. for Libraries* 1972 $12.50; (and "A Christmas Garland" [1895]) *Dutton* pap. $1.85

Around Theaters, 1898–1903. 1924. Ed. by Rupert Hart-Davis. 1930. *Greenwood* 1969 $20.75; *Taplinger* $7.95. Essays originally published in the *Saturday Review*.

OBSERVATIONS. 1925. *Haskell* 1971 $18.95; *Richard West* 1973 $18.75

MAINLY ON THE AIR. 1946. enl. ed. 1958. *Bks. for Libraries* $9.50. Broadcasts and essays.

MORE THEATERS, 1898–1903. Ed. by Rupert Hart-Davis *Taplinger* 1969 $15.00

LAST THEATERS, 1904–1910. Ed. by Rupert Hart-Davis *Taplinger* 1970 $15.00

Books about Beerbohm

Max: A Biography. By Lord David Cecil. *Houghton* 1965 $6.95.
    "The definitive biography . . . by an old friend"—(*LJ*).
At Ease in Zion: Max Beerbohm's Parody and Caricature. By John Felstiner. *Knopf* 1972 $8.95

CHESTERTON, G(ILBERT) K(EITH). 1874–1936.

Chesterton did fine work in many fields of literature, but it is as an essayist that his humor and his paradoxical style are most apparent. As a critic he wrote several noteworth literary studies, among them "Robert Browning" (1903. *Richard West* $10.00) and "George Bernard Shaw" (1909. *Hill & Wang* Dramabks. 1957 pap. $1.25). "The Victorian Age in Literature" (1913. *Oxford* Galaxy Bks. pap. $1.50; *Univ. of Notre Dame Press* pap. $1.75) is a standard work. In his Father Brown detective stories he created a character popular with mystery fans. "The Father Brown Omnibus" (*Dodd* 1933 $6.00) and "Father Brown Mystery Stories" (ed. by Raymond T. Bond *Dodd* 1962 $3.50) are still available. Of his other works of fiction only "The Man Who Was Thursday" (1908. Dodd $3.50; Putnam Capricorn Bks. pap. $1.95) is in print.

His ardent Catholicism is reflected in his religious works, such as "Orthodoxy" (1909. *Doubleday* Image Bks. pap. $1.25) and "The Everlasting Man" (1925. *Apollo* pap. $2.25) and in his biographies of "St. Thomas Aquinas" (*Doubleday* Image Bks. pap. $1.25) and "St. Francis of Assisi" (*Doubleday* Image Bks. pap. $1.25). His own "Autobiography" is o.p. (*See also Hilaire Belloc.*)

THE MAN WHO WAS CHESTERTON. Comp. and ed. by Raymond T. Bond. 1937. *Bks. for Libraries* $22.50. The best essays, stories, poems and other writings.

LUNACY AND LETTERS. Ed. by Dorothy Collins (Chesterton's literary executor). 1958. *Bks. for Libraries* $9.00. 38 nonpolitical light essays, some rich in fantasy, from the *Daily News,* 1901–12.

ALL THINGS CONSIDERED. 1908. *Bks. for Libraries* $11.25; *Dufour* $6.25; *Folcroft* 1973 lib. bdg. $14.50

MISCELLANY OF MEN. 1912. *Bks. for Libraries* $10.75; *Dufour* $6.25; *Scholarly Press* 1972 $19.50

UTOPIA OF USURERS AND OTHER ESSAYS. 1917. *Bks. for Libraries* $9.00; *Folcroft* 1973 $8.50

G. K. C. AS M. C.: Being a Collection of Thirty-Seven Introductions. *Bks. for Libraries* $9.50; *Folcroft* 1973 lib. bdg. $7.50; *Richard West* 1973 $9.45

GENERALLY SPEAKING. 1929. *Bks. for Libraries* $10.00; *Folcroft* lib. bdg. $9.00

COME TO THINK OF IT. 1931. *Bks. for Libraries* $9.75; *Folcroft* 1973 $7.50

ALL IS GRIST. 1932. *Bks. for Libraries* $9.00; *Scholarly Press* 1971 $14.50

SIDELIGHTS OF NEW LONDON AND NEWER YORK AND OTHER ESSAYS. *Bks. for Libraries* $9.75; *Folcroft* 1973 lib. bdg. $9.50; *Scholarly Press* 1970 $14.50

AS I WAS SAYING. 1936. *Bks. for Libraries* $9.00; *Folcroft* 1973 lib. bdg. $8.50

Books about Chesterton

G. K. Chesterton. By Maurice Evans. 1939. *Haskell* $8.95

MARQUIS, DON. 1878–1937.

Don Marquis created the epic of "archy the cockroach" and "mehitabel the cat." Striking the typewriter keys with his head and writing in lower case because he cannot work the shift key, Archy pounds out the story of Mehitabel's loose living. In his excellent preface to "The Best of Don Marquis" (o. p.), Christopher Morley (*q. v.*) compared his friend's versatility and brilliance to that of Mark Twain (*q. v.*). He was less successful with other satirical pieces; "Carter and Other People" (1921. *Bks. for Libraries* $10.75); short stories, "Chapters for the Orthodox" (1934. *Bks. for Libraries* $11.00), "When the Turtles Sang and Other Tales" (1928. *Bks. for Libraries* $9.50) "Sun Dial Time" (1936. *Bks. for Libraries* $9.50); drama and nonsatirical works, most of which are now o.p. The "biography" by Edward Anthony is also o.p.

THE LIVES AND TIMES OF ARCHY AND MEHITABEL. Introd. by E. B. White; ill. by George Herriman. *Doubleday* 1940 1943 new ed. 1950 $5.95; *Noble & Noble* pap. $.75. Omnibus volume of the three "archy" books.

ARCHY AND MEHITABEL. *Doubleday* 1927 $4.50 Anchor Bks. pap. $1.45

MENCKEN, H(ENRY) L(OUIS). 1880–1956.

The great Baltimore iconoclast, lexicographer and newspaper man made his *American Mercury* a famous battleground for everything it discussed in the 1920s. From him "flowed a great stream of literally millions of words of reporting, editorials, essays, commentary, articles and books, all of it bearing the unmistakable stamp of individuality possessed by a master craftsman who was also a man of honor, of intellectual curiosity, of humanity and of superb wit. He became famous as an editor, first of *The Smart Set* and then of *The American Mercury* and as author of the 'Prejudices' series [separate volumes now o.p.], . . . the mellow reminiscences of the 'Days' volumes, and the astonishing performance in 'The American Language' and its supplements [*see Chapter 3, Reference Books—Books About Words*]. . . . He was producing brilliant pyrotechnics against stupidity long before the Twenties, and continued to do so long afterward, but as the event seems to have proved this is likely to be the most ephemeral part of his work. His more enduring monuments seem to be promised in the incomparable autobiographical and linguistic volumes"—(*N.Y. Times*). In 1950 Mencken received the National Institute and American Academy of Arts and Letters Gold Medal.

In the December 1958 issue of the *Reader's Digest*, H. Allen Smith concludes his "Most Unforgettable Character" article on Mencken: "I thought of that gay yet poignant epitaph he once composed for himself: 'If, after I depart this vale, you ever remember me and have thought to please my ghost, forgive some sinner and wink your eye at some homely girl'. Any man possessed of the sense and sensibility implicit in those lines . . . well, that man is qualified to be a hero, even though he himself had little use for the word."

A MENCKEN CHRESTOMATHY. Ed. and annot. by the author. *Knopf* 1949 $8.95. A selection from his out-of-print books, magazine articles and newspaper pieces.

THE VINTAGE MENCKEN. Gathered by Alistair Cooke. *Random* Vintage Bks. 1955 pap. $1.95

H. L. MENCKEN PREJUDICES: A Selection. Ed. by James T. Farrell. *Random* Vintage Bks. 1958 pap. $1.65

A CARNIVAL OF BUNCOMBE. Ed. by Malcolm Moos. *Johns Hopkins Univ. Press* 1956 $9.00

THE AMERICAN SCENE: A Reader. Ed. by H. Cairns. *Knopf* 1965 $10.00

"Excellent selection of texts"—(*LJ*).

THE BATHTUB HOAX AND OTHER BLASTS AND BRAVOS FROM THE CHICAGO TRIBUNE. Ed. with introd. and notes by Robert S. McHugh. *Chicago Tribune* columns in book form for the first time. *Knopf* 1958 $4.50

H. L. MENCKEN ON MUSIC: A Selection of his Writings on Music Together with an Account of H. L. Mencken's Musical Life and a History of the Saturday Night Club. Ed. by Louis Cheslock. *Knopf* 1961 $5.95

SMART SET CRITICISM. Ed. by William H. Nolte. *Cornell Univ. Press* 1968 $10.00

THE YOUNG MENCKEN: The Best of His Work. Ed. by Carl Bode. *Dial* 1973 $15.00

BOOKS OF BURLESQUES. 1920 *Scholarly Press* 1971 $19.50

TREATISE ON THE GODS. *Knopf* 1930 2nd ed. corrected and rewritten 1946 $5.95

THE DAYS OF H. L. MENCKEN: Happy Days (1940), Newspaper Days (1941), Heathen Days (1941). 3 vols. *Knopf* 1947 each $6.95 set $20.85

MINORITY REPORT: H. L. Mencken's Notebooks. *Knopf* 1956 $5.95. Selected observations culled during "long years devoted to the pursuit, anatomizing and embalming of ideas."

LETTERS OF H. L. MENCKEN. Ed. and annotated by Guy J. Forgue; personal note by Hamilton Owen. *Knopf* 1961 $10.00

"An astute selection"—(*LJ*) from an enormous correspondence with some of the most prominent literary figures of his time.

Books about Mencken

H. L. Mencken: Disturber of the Peace. By William Manchester; introd. by Gerald W. Johnson. 1950 1951 *Macmillan* Collier bks. 1962 pap. $.95

H. L. Mencken: A Portrait from Memory. By Charles Angoff. *A. S. Barnes* (Yoseloff) 1956 1961 Perpetua Bks. pap. $1.45. Mencken's racy conversation reported by an editor who worked for him on the *American Mercury* 1924–1935.

The Mencken Bibliography. Comp. by Betty Adler and Jane Wilhelm. *Johns Hopkins Univ. Press* 1961 $12.50

H. L. Mencken and the *American Mercury* Adventure. By Marvin K. Singleton. *Duke Univ. Press* 1962 $7.50. Adequate and vigorous documentation.

The Irreverent Mr. Mencken. By Edgar Kemler. *Peter Smith* $5.00. An excellent biography, balanced in its appraisal of the man, his causes and catastrophes.

H. L. Mencken, Literary Critic. By William H. Nolte. *Wesleyan Univ. Press* 1966 $8.50; *Univ. of Washington Press* pap. $2.95

"Reopens half forgotten vistas of Mencken's tirades and tarantellas in all their vivid hurly-burly"— (Charles Poore).

Mencken. By Carl Bode. *Southern Illinois Univ. Press* 2nd ed. 1970 $10.00

See also Chapter 3, on Reference Books—Books of Quotations, Books on Usage.

WOOLF, VIRGINIA. 1882–1941.

Virginia Woolf was the daughter of Sir Leslie Stephen, critic and historian, and the wife of Leonard Woolf, critic and writer on economics with whom she founded *The Hogarth Press* (still thriving in London) in 1917. The venture is charmingly described in Mr. Woolf's autobiography, "Beginning Again" (*Harcourt* $5.95 Harvest Bks. pap. $2.75.).

She was known first for her novels, but she was a discerning and influential critic, with a rare literary sensibility. "Modern Fiction," written in 1919 and reprinted in the first "Common Reader," gives the best description of the "stream of consciousness" which she used in her own novels. "The Captain's Death Bed" contains the well-known "Mr. Bennett and Mrs. Brown," first published in pamphlet form, in which she repudiated the aims of the naturalists, Bennett (*q. v.*), Wells (*q. v.*) and Galsworthy (*q. v.*). In "A Room of One's Own" and "Three Guineas" she champions an independent life for women with an opportunity for creative work. "Granite and Rainbow" contains 27 essays on the art of fiction and the art of biography. The latter, she said, fuses the hard and solid granite of truth with the elusive beauty of the rainbow. According to her husband's note, she only "spasmodically kept copies of essays and reviews written by her for journals and there was often no record of their publication among her papers." Many of her essays appeared anonymously and some were written under her maiden name, Virginia Stephen.

COLLECTED ESSAYS. *Harcourt* 1967 4 vols. Vols 1–2 each $6.50 vols 3–4 each $5.95

THE COMMON READER. 1925. *Harcourt* Harvest Bks. pap. $2.75

THE SECOND COMMON READER. 1932. *Harcourt* Harvest Bks. pap. $2.75

A ROOM OF ONE'S OWN. *Harcourt* 1929 Harbinger Bks. pap. $1.95

THREE GUINEAS. 1938. *Harcourt* 1963 Harbinger Bks. pap. $1.95

THE CAPTAIN'S DEATH BED, AND OTHER ESSAYS. Ed. by Leonard Woolf. *Harcourt* 1950 Harvest Bks. 1973 pap. $2.45

GRANITE AND RAINBOW. With an editorial note by Leonard Woolf. *Harcourt* 1958 $5.75

WRITER'S DIARY. Ed. by Leonard Woolf. *Harcourt* Harvest Bks. 1973 pap. $2.95. Provides insight into her mind and method using abstracts from her diary.

See also Chapter 12, Modern British Fiction.

BROOKS, VAN WYCK. 1886–1963.

Van Wyck Brooks can be said to have brought new dignity to the concept of "American" literature; to the recording of its history he made a tremendous contribution.

Brooks, says Robert Gorham Davis in the *N.Y. Times*, "devoured 2000 volumes to produce one volume"—of each of the five collectively known as "Makers and Finders." "Proud, reserved, reticent . . . easily hurt" (Davis's description), he found himself often the object of literary controversy—particularly in respect to his "attack" on Mark Twain in "The Ordeal of Mark Twain," his later uneasiness about which is said to have been responsible in part for his four-year "breakdown" in the late 1920s. Bernard De Voto (*q. v.*) wrote a reply to the "Ordeal."

The death of his first wife affected him deeply, as did—in another way—the attacks of other critics on certain of his harsher literary judgments on modern writers who have now found their own honored places—such as Joyce, Pound, Proust. But on his own special period of study he was in most respects superb and remarkably readable, and he enjoyed many enduring literary friendships. "Brooks argued that much of American writing was second rate, that U.S. materialism thwarted genius, and that the true fulfillment of America is yet to come"—(*Time*). The American writer, he felt, lacked a sense of tradition; "Makers and Finders" was aimed at establishing what he called "a usable past." "The Flowering of New England" won the Pulitzer History Prize in 1937 and the Limited Editions Club gold medal in 1938, for the book of the preceding three years "considered most likely to attain the stature of a classic." Two of his important works are recently o.p.: "America's Coming of Age" (1915), a revised collection of earlier pieces; and "The Opinions of Oliver Allston" (1941), which presents in the third person his own lively opinions on the current state of literature and criticism, human nature, communism, socialism and the like.

"[Brooks'] literary style reveals a man of wit, briskness and suavity whose books, for all their tranquility of surface, probe to the depths beneath." The *N.Y. Times* obituary (May 5, 1963) spoke of the pictorial quality of his work and its popular appeal: "It was his custom to word-paint periods of American history by means of brilliant, incisive biographies of authors, many of them well known and many long forgotten. . . . In his 'Critic at Large' column of The Times of Sept. 22, 1961, Brooks Atkinson said of the author that he had 'helped more than anyone else to define the cultural climate of the United States. In the last half century . . . he has never wavered in his conviction that humanism and liberalism are the essence of the American spirit. He would rather believe too much than too little.' "

Van Wyck Brooks and Edmund Wilson (*q. v.*) between them—and each in his own way—have produced the most readable, brilliant and voluminous records we possess of the American literary scene from its beginnings. They have shown what it is to be an *American* writer in a fertile native vein.

VAN WYCK BROOKS: The Early Years: A Selection from His Works, 1908–1921. Ed. by Claire Sprague *Harper* Torchbks. pap. $2.95

THE WORLD OF H. G. WELLS. 1915. *Scholarly Press* 1970 $9.50

THE ORDEAL OF MARK TWAIN. 1920 *Dutton* pap. $2.25. The controversial biography (see note above).

THE PILGRIMAGE OF HENRY JAMES. 1925. *Octagon* 1972 lib. bdg. $10.75

THREE ESSAYS ON AMERICA. 1934. Dutton 1970 pap. $1.75

MAKERS AND FINDERS: A History of the Writer in America, 1800–1915. *Dutton* Everyman's 5 vols. each $3.50 set $14.00. Brooks' great regional and critical history of American literature. The narrative style, with its humor and anecdote, has high entertainment value. The separate vols. arranged chronologically by publication date:

THE FLOWERING OF NEW ENGLAND, 1815–1865. Vol. 2 *Dutton* 1936 rev. ed. 1937 pap. $2.45 Everyman's $3.50

NEW ENGLAND INDIAN SUMMER, 1865–1915 Vol. 4 *Dutton* 1940 pap. $2.45 Everyman's $3.50

THE WORLD OF WASHINGTON IRVING. Vol. 1 *Dutton* 1944 Everyman's $3.50

THE TIMES OF MELVILLE AND WHITMAN. Vol. 3 *Dutton* 1947 Everyman's $3.50

THE CONFIDENT YEARS: 1885–1915. Vol. 5 *Dutton* 1952 Everyman's $3.50

A CHILMARK MISCELLANY: Essays Old and New. 1948. *Octagon* 1973 lib. bdg. $12.00

(With Otto L. Bettmann). OUR LITERARY HERITAGE: A Pictorial History of the Writer in America. An abridgment of Van Wyck Brooks' "Makers and Finders" (*see above*) *Dutton* 1956 $9.95

THE VAN WYCK BROOKS–LEWIS MUMFORD LETTERS. Ed. by Robert E. Spiller *Dutton* 1970 $12.95

AN AUTOBIOGRAPHY. Including "Scenes and Portraits" (1954), "Days of the Phoenix" (1957) and "From the Shadow of the Mountain" (1961). Introd. by Malcolm Cowley. Foreword by John Hall Wheelock. *Dutton* 1965 $10.00. *Library Journal* calls this trilogy-in-one-volume "a new contribution to literary history."

ELIOT, T(HOMAS) S(TEARNS). 1888–1965. (Nobel Prize 1948)

T. S. Eliot's influence on esthetic criticism was almost as great as on modern poetry. His importance in both fields derived from his double endowment of a sense of language and a sense of structure and from his most fundamental belief as an artist: the necessary union of intellect and emotion. "The consummate art" of the finest philosophic prose style of our language, he felt, is that "in which acute intellect and passionate feeling preserve a classic balance."

His earlier critical writings were published in the time of disintegration and disillusion, when there were "no publicly acceptable structural principles, no current literary conventions." They embody his own search as a poet for material and principles. He pointed out writers who should have special significance—the Jacobean dramatists, Donne (*q. v.*) and the metaphysical poets, Dante (*q. v.*) and Baudelaire (*q. v.*). He felt that the greatest art is "impersonal, in the sense that personal emotion, personal experience is extended and completed in something impersonal, not in the sense of something divorced from personal experience and passion." The recent publication of Eliot's Harvard doctoral thesis, "Knowledge and Experience in the Philosophy of F. H. Bradley" (1916 *Farrar, Straus* 1964 $4.50), throws interesting light for scholars on the roots of Eliot's poetry and criticism. Works in print which he edited include St. John Perse's "Anabasis" (*Harcourt* rev. ed. French and English 1949 pap. $1.85) and Ezra Pound's "Literary Essays" (*New Directions* 1953 $3.25). Eliot did not confine his criticism to poetry, but considered some of the main cultural, religious and political problems of his day. Louis Untermeyer has said of him: "Although the manner of his criticism is pontifical, the matter is always provocative; there are few critics who surpass Eliot in scholarliness, few who equal him in subtlety, coolness and clarity. Wholly unlike his poetry, sometimes oppressively academic, sometimes marred by fantastic theories, Eliot's criticism is persuasive and backed by authority."

A good single introduction to Eliot's work that provides information about the poems and especially good material on his critical position is F. O. Matthiessen's "The Achievement of T. S. Eliot: An Essay on the Nature of Poetry" (*Oxford* 1939 3rd ed. 1959 $6.50 Galaxy Bks. pap. $2.75). "T. S. Eliot: Aesthetics and History" by Lewis Freed (*Open Court* 1962 $5.95 pap. $1.95) is the "first philosophically oriented exposition of Eliot's theory of poetry, its sources, and the issues it raises. It shows that the theory is derived from F. H.

Bradley's theory of experience, subject to certain scholastic reservations; and it relates the poetic theory to such critics as Johnson, Wordsworth and Arnold."

SELECTED ESSAYS, 1917–1932. The Sacred Wood; For Lancelot Andrews; Dante, and others. *Harcourt* 1932 rev. ed. 1950 $8.50

THE SACRED WOOD: Essays on Poetry and Criticism. 1920. *Barnes & Noble* 6th ed. 1948 7th ed. 1950 $3.75 pap. $2.50

THE USE OF POETRY AND THE USE OF CRITICISM. 1933. *Barnes & Noble* 1955 2nd ed. 1964 $3.75 pap. $2.00

ESSAYS ON ELIZABETHAN DRAMA. 1934. *Harcourt* Harvest Bks. 1956 pap. $1.95

NOTES TOWARDS A DEFINITION OF CULTURE. *Harcourt* 1949 $3.75

CHRISTIANITY AND CULTURE. Two essays (*see above*): "The Idea of a Christian Society" (1940) and "Notes Towards the Definition of Culture" (1949). *Harcourt* Harvest Bks. pap. $2.75

ON POETRY AND POETS. *Farrar, Straus* 1957 $4.50 Noonday pap. $2.65. 16 critical essays including "The Frontiers of Criticism."

TO CRITICIZE THE CRITIC AND OTHER WRITINGS. *Farrar, Straus* 1965 $7.95 Noonday 1967 pap. $2.65. 12 essays not previously published in book form, including "From Poe to Valéry," "Reflections on Vers Libre" and "Ezra Pound: His Metric and Poetry."

(Ed.) THE CRITERION, 1922–1939. *Barnes & Noble* 18 vols. set 1967 $230.00

A reprint of the literary journal edited by Eliot. "The best thought of the 1920's and 1930's [edited by] the most influential literary figure in England and America for almost three decades"—(*LJ*).

See also Chapter 7, Modern British Poetry.

BENCHLEY, ROBERT (CHARLES). 1889–1945.

Benchley could take everyday experiences and make them hilarious. Gluyas Williams' illustrations, which became a part of every book, portrayed Benchley himself typically as the poor human being living his life of continuing humiliations and frustrations. Benchley had a triple and highly successful career as writer, actor on stage and screen and master of ceremonies on radio broadcasts. "As a writer of nonsense for nonsense's sake, he is unsurpassed," said Stephen Leacock (*q. v.*). After his death James Thurber (*q. v.*) wrote: "[One of his friends] said 'They're going to have to stay up late in heaven now.' Yes, they're staying up late, I know, and what is more, they must be having the time of their infinities. Lucky angels." His son NATHANIEL BENCHLEY is a humorous novelist.

THE BENCHLEY ROUNDUP: A Selection by Nathaniel Benchley of His Favorites. Drawings by Gluyas Williams. *Harper* 1954. $5.95

BENCHLEY LOST AND FOUND: 39 Prodigal Pieces. *Dover* 1970 pap. $1.50; *Peter Smith* $3.50

Books about Benchley

Robert Benchley: A Biography. By Nathaniel Benchley; Fwd. by Robert Benchley. *McGraw-Hill* 1955 $6.95
Robert Benchley. By Norris W. Yates. United States Authors Ser. *Twayne* 1968 $4.95

JONES, HOWARD MUMFORD. 1892–

Howard Mumford Jones, Abbott Lawrence Lowell Professor of the Humanities, Emeritus, at Harvard, writes eloquently of the value of the humanities, especially in modern American life. "But I suppose my main line of endeavor has been to fulfill, so far as I can, the function of 'man of letters' exemplified by James Russell Lowell and defined by Archibald MacLeish," he wrote in "Twentieth Century Authors." "This means that in addition to specialized contributions to scholarship, principally concerning English literature in the nineteenth century and American literary scholarship over the whole range of our development, I have tried, consciously or not, to present to that smaller segment of the public which really likes serious reading, the results of scholarly investigation and academic discussion, especially of the national letters." Professor Jones has written much on education: "One Great Society" (1959, o. p.) discusses the meaning, purpose and content of the humanities: "Reflections on Learning" (1958. *Bks. for Libraries* $7.50) is critical of an overemphasis on practical knowledge. "Education and World Tragedy" (1946. *Greenwood* $8.50) prescribes a "major reorganization of educational patterns."

One former Radcliffe student of the 1930s recalls his lucid and brilliant lectures on the English novel. The all-girl classes of those days did not appear to inhibit a Rabelaisian puckishness in the professor which sharpened and lightened a serious, cosmopolitan approach to his subject.

THE THEORY OF AMERICAN LITERATURE. 1948. *Cornell Univ. Press* enl. ed. 1965 $7.50 1966 pap. $1.95

THE PURSUIT OF HAPPINESS. 1953. *Cornell Univ. Press* 1966 pap. $1.95

(with Richard M. Ludwig) GUIDE TO AMERICAN LITERATURE AND ITS BACKGROUNDS SINCE 1890. 1953. *Harvard Univ. Press* 3rd ed. rev. and enlarged 1964 pap. $1.95 $6.00 pap. $2.75 4th ed. 1972 $10.00 pap. $2.95.

"An attempt," according to its authors, "to impose intellectual order upon confusion," in which it brilliantly succeeds. In bibliographic, well-organized form with brief, clear introductions and broad coverage. Invaluable for the student.

O STRANGE NEW WORLD: American Culture: the Formative Years. *Viking* 1964 $8.50 Compass Bks. 1967 pap. $3.25

"A major work"—(*LJ*). Winner of the 1965 Pulitzer Prize for general nonfiction.

HISTORY AND THE CONTEMPORARY: Essays in Nineteenth-Century Literature. *Univ. of Wisconsin Press* 1964 $6.00

BELIEF AND DISBELIEF IN AMERICAN LITERATURE. *Univ. of Chicago Press* 1967 $5.00 Phoenix Bks. pap. $1.95

"In a series of essays, lucidly and gracefully written, which could be a model for all scholarly writing, [he] sums up for us what the works of a handful of representative American writers reveal about their religious faith or lack of it"—(Thomas Lask).

VIOLENCE AND REASON: Essays. *Atheneum* 1969 $6.95

READ, SIR HERBERT (EDWARD). 1893–1968.

Allen Tate says of Sir Herbert: "No other Anglo-American critic of our time has pursued with greater learning and profundity a single theory of the arts." A critic of literature as well, he was also prolific as poet, philosopher and student of esthetics and was an authority on education. He is widely read in the United States: "Books in Print" for 1973 devoted 45 entries to him, of which 36 were separate titles of works entirely his own. He also edited and co-authored many volumes.

Born on a Yorkshire farm, Sir Herbert knew country life as a child and the life of industrial cities as a student in Halifax and Leeds, and later served in World War I—experiences which were deeply to influence his mature broodings on how a man "can live a natural life, attending to what is within," while coping with the modern world. In the *Saturday Review* he wrote that "the pursuit of power, whether by the individual or the state, is the root of all the evil we endure, and against power only a spiritual weapon can prevail." He sees man's only salvation in the return to a few "simplicities" such as the idea of "fidelity" and of "an education that above all takes into account the symbolic needs of the unconscious—therefore education through art." He has been a professor of fine arts as well as of literature, and has been ceaselessly active in British cultural life.

The "Collected Poems" (1946, o. p.) of this lyrical and metaphysical poet are notable, says Francis Berry, for "acuity of observation, purity of style, point and concentration." His one novel, "The Green Child" (1935. *New Directions* $4.50 pap. $1.75), which won the admiration of T. S. Eliot and Graham Greene and has been described by Kenneth Rexroth as of an "unearthy, hypnotic radiance," is the curious story of a man of action who finds Utopia in the land to which he is led in maturity by a woman of strange origin—the "Green Child" of his boyhood. It marks a significant stage in the development of Read's major theme. He was influenced by Jung (whose works he has helped to edit) and interested especially in the English Romantics. His writings on art are universal in scope.

Among his critical works:

REASON AND ROMANTICISM. Essays. 1926. *Russell & Russell* 1963 $7.50

ENGLISH PROSE STYLE. 1928 rev. ed. 1952. On metaphor, imagery, tradition. *Beacon* 1955 pap. $2.45

THE SENSE OF GLORY: Essays in Criticism. 1930. *Bks. for Libraries* $9.50; *Richard West* 1973 $9.00

THE MEANING OF ART. 1931. *Pitman* 4th ed. 1969 $6.75; *Praeger* 1972 pap. $2.95

FORM IN MODERN POETRY. 1932. *Folcroft* lib. bdg. $9.00

ART AND SOCIETY. 1937. *Schocken Bks.* 1966 $7.50; pap. $2.45. Harold Rosenberg in the *N.Y. Times* calls this "again thoroughly timely."

TO HELL WITH CULTURE, AND OTHER ESSAYS ON ART AND SOCIETY. 1940. *Bks. for Libraries* 1972 $9.50; *Schocken Bks.* 1963 pap. $1.95

Dedicated to the late Eric Gill, who once said, "to hell with culture as a thing added like a sauce to an otherwise unpalatable stale fish."

THE PHILOSOPHY OF MODERN ART: Collected Essays. 1952. *Bks. for Libraries* $14.50; Folcroft 1973 $12.00

ICON AND IDEA: The Function of Art in the Development of Human Consciousness. 1955. *Bks. for Libraries* $14.50; *Schocken Bks.* pap. $2.75. The Charles Eliot Norton Lectures delivered at Harvard in 1953.

THE NATURE OF LITERATURE. 1956. *Bks. for Libraries* $14.50. In two parts: on the nature of poetry and criticism; on individual writers.

THE ORIGINS OF FORM IN ART. *Horizon Press* 1965 $7.50

REDEMPTION OF THE ROBOT: My Encounter with Education through Art. *Simon & Schuster* $4.95 Clarion Bks. pap. $2.45

Books about Read

Herbert Read: An Introduction to His Work by Many Hands. Ed. by Henry Treece. 1944. *Kennikat* 1969 $6.50
Herbert Read. By Francis Berry. 1953 rev. ed. 1961 *British Bk. Centre* pap. $2.38 pap. $1.20. A pamphlet in the British Council series, beautifully written, which treats his life, his philosophy and his literary work (rather than his work in the arts) in interesting detail. Select bibliography.

RICHARDS, I(VOR) A(RMSTRONG). 1893–

"Perhaps no one in the last generation has exerted more influence upon literary criticism, both theoretic and applied than has I. A. Richards. His distinction, made in 'The Meaning of Meaning' between the 'referential' aspect of words and the 'emotive,' seemed to split in two, not merely the world of words, but the universe itself, wrenching asunder fact and fiction, science and poetry, thought and emotion. (In some quarters his use of the distinction was hailed as a necessary liberation of science; in others, as a ruthless amputation of poetry)"—(Cleanth Brooks). According to Irving Howe ("Modern Literary Criticism"), Richards' early concern for the relationship between poetry and science was anticipation of the "New Criticism" (*see introduction to this Chapter*).

Professor Richards was born and educated in England, and lectured on literary criticism at Harvard from 1939 until his retirement in 1963. He has done a great deal of work in semantics and is one of the authorities on Basic English, which he believes ("Nations and Peace" [1947 o. p.] and "So Much Nearer: Essays toward a World English" [*Harcourt* 1968 $7.50]) would do much to avoid unnecessary misunderstanding, now so often the result of "somniferous verbiage." In "Tomorrow Morning, Faustus! An Infernal Comedy" (*Harcourt* 1962 $4.50), he has modernized the Faust theme in a verse play. "Why So, Socrates?" (*Cambridge* 1964 pap. $1.45) is a dramatization of the Platonic dialogues. "Internal Colloquies" (*Harcourt* 1971 $12.00) is a collection containing two earlier volumes: "Goodbye Earth and Other Poems," (1958) in which he attempts to follow his own principles of criticism including some reassessments of earlier ideas; "The Screens and Other Poems" (1960) containing 28 poems and the essay "The Future of Poetry"; as well as 30 new poems "Further Poems: 1960–1970" and the complete text of "Tomorrow Morning, Faustus!"

POETRIES AND SCIENCES. A reissue, with commentary, of "Science and Poetry" (1926) *Norton* 1970 $6.00 pap. $2.25

(with C. K. Ogden) THE MEANING OF MEANING: A Study of the Influence of Language upon Thought and of the Science of Symbolism. Introd. by J. P. Postgate. *Harcourt* 1925 Harvest Bks. pap. $2.95

THE PRINCIPLES OF LITERARY CRITICISM. Int'l. Lib. of Psychology, Philosophy and Scientific Method *Harcourt* 1925 2nd ed. 1926 Harvest Bks. pap. $1.95

PRACTICAL CRITICISM: A Study of Literary Judgment. 1929. *Harcourt* 1950 Harvest Bk. 1956 pap. $2.25

COLERIDGE ON IMAGINATION. 1934. 2nd ed. 1950 1959. *Indiana Univ. Press* 1960 pap. $1.95; *Peter Smith* $4.25

THE PHILOSOPHY OF RHETORIC. *Oxofrd* 1936 Galaxy Bks. pap. $1.25

SPECULATIVE INSTRUMENTS. *Harcourt* 1955 Harvest Bks. pap. $1.95

HOW TO READ A PAGE. 1959. *Beacon* pap. $1.45

Books about Richards

I. A. Richards' Theory of Literature. By Jerome P. Schiller. *Yale Univ. Press* 1969 $6.00

THURBER, JAMES. 1894–1961.

Through his friend E. B. White (*q. v.*), Thurber joined the staff of the *New Yorker* in 1927 and, after resigning, continued to contribute his highly individual pieces and those strange, pathological pen-and-ink drawings of "huge, resigned dogs, the determined and sometimes frightening women, the globular men who try so hard to think so unsuccessfully." The turbulent years from 1925 when the *New Yorker* was founded until its creator-editor's death in 1951 were described by Thurber in the completely absorbing and almost unbelievable "The Years with Ross" (1959. *Ballantine Bks.* pap. $1.25). Of his two great talents, Thurber preferred to think of himself primarily as a writer, illustrating his own books. T. S. Eliot (*q. v.*) described his work as "a form of humor which is also a way of saying something serious. . . . His writings and also his illustrations are capable of surviving the immediate environment and time out of which they spring. To some extent they will be a document of the age they belong to."

His "fables" (published by *Harper* and *Simon & Schuster*) are more or less in the style of Aesop (*q. v.*) and LaFontaine (*q. v.*), but usually have a "barbed tip of contemporary significance." Several of his children's books are published by *Harcourt* and *Simon & Schuster*. His play, "The Male Animal" (1940. *Baker* $1.25; *French* 1941 $2.00) which he wrote with Elliott Nugent, was again a hit of the season when it was revived in 1952. In March, 1960, after "A Thurber Carnival" (*Baker* $1.25; *French* $1.75) opened on Broadway and became one of its biggest hits, Thurber announced that he was not going to be hurried into preparing new works: "I'm 65 and I'm not a 600-mile-an-hour jet-propelled writer." In 1963 "The Beast in Me," a musical revue based on his book and adapted by James Costigan, was produced on Broadway.

He has "left us a magnificent legacy of laughter. We can best appreciate how he created it by reading his 'Credos and Curios,' a wonderful collection of random pieces 'hitherto uncollected' that trace the whole course of his career. We should be doing ourselves an injustice if we regarded the book only as a last harvest. For it is far more than that. It is a refutation of Thurber's idea, frequently expressed in his later years, that American humor was bound for the suburbs of oblivion. It was not. It never will be, all soothsaying, including Thurber's, to the contrary. . . . The tragic sense of life will forever be balanced precariously against the comic one, as it is in Thurber's works"—(Charles Poore in the *N.Y. Times*).

Thurber was white-haired except for a black streak in front, weighed 154 lbs. and was six feet one and a half inches tall. He once said: "Everyone thinks I look like the man I draw—bald and 5 foot 1. Actually, I draw the *spirit* of the man I am—and I'm a pussy cat"—(*Life* March 14, 1960). "Thurber & Company" (*Harper* 1966 $6.95), a book of his cartoons, "is not the first posthumous collection of his work, but it is one of the best"—(*N.Y. Times*).

Among his books in print:

THE THURBER CARNIVAL. Selections. *Dell* pap. $1.95; *Harper* 1945 $5.95; *Modern Library* $2.95

(with E. B. White). IS SEX NECESSARY? or Why You Feel the Way You Do. 1929. New introd. by E. B. White *Dell* 1963 pap. $1.45; *Harper* new ed. 1950 $4.95 Colophon Bks. pap. $1.95

MY LIFE AND HARD TIMES. 1933. *Grosset* Univ. Lib. 1960 pap. $1.95

MY WORLD AND WELCOME TO IT. *Harcourt* 1942 $6.95 Perenn. Lib. pap. $1.95

THE BEAST IN ME AND OTHER ANIMALS: A New Collection of Pieces and Drawings about Human Beings and Less Alarming Creatures. *Harcourt* 1948 $5.95 Harvest Bks. 1973 pap. $1.95

THURBER COUNTRY. *Simon & Schuster* 1953 $6.50 lg.-type ed. $7.95

THE THURBER ALBUM: A New Collection of Pieces about People. *Simon & Schuster* 1952 $6.50 pap. $1.95

THURBER'S DOGS: A Collection of the Master's Dogs, Written and Drawn, Real and Imaginary, Living and Long Ago. *Simon & Schuster* 1955 $3.95 pap. $1.95

LANTERNS AND LANCES. *Harper* 1961 $6.95

In his foreword he states that, in addition to throwing "a few lantern beams here and there," he has endeavored to "cast a few lances at the people and ideas which have disturbed me."

CREDOS AND CURIOS. Fwd. by Helen Thurber. The posthumously published collection. Harper 1962 $5.95

Books about Thurber

James Thurber. By Robert E. Morsberger. United States Authors Ser. *Twayne* 1964 $5.50; *College & Univ. Press* pap. $2.45
The Art of James Thurber. By Richard C. Tobias. *Ohio Univ. Press* 1969 $8.50
James Thurber: His Masquerades, A Critical Study. By Stephen A. Black. *Humanities Press* 1970 $10.00
The Clocks of Columbus: A Literary Portrait of James Thurber. By Charles S. Holmes. *Atheneum* 1972 $10.00

VAN DOREN, MARK. 1894–1972.

The "happy critic" was also a poet–philosopher, novelist, short-story writer and editor. He served as literary editor and film critic for *The Nation* in the twenties. He taught in the English Department at Columbia for almost 40 years and retired in 1959. His critical writings are outstanding. His "Collected Stories" (*Hill & Wang* 1962 1965 3 vols. Vols. I and 2 each $5.95 Vol. 3 $7.50) contains his choice of favorites and other stories which appear for the first time in book form. With Maurice Samuels he has written an excellent commentary on the Old Testament, "In the Beginning . . . Love" (Ed. by Edith Samuels *John Day* rev. ed. 1972 $8.95).

Among his critical works:

HENRY DAVID THOREAU: A Critical Study. 1916. *Russell & Russell* $8.00

THE POETRY OF JOHN DRYDEN. 1920. *Haskell* 1969 lib. bdg. $13.95

THOMAS HARDY, POET. 1930. *Richard West* 1973 $20.00

THE NOBLE VOICE. 1936. (Reprinted as MARK VAN DOREN ON TEN GREAT POEMS)
Collier pap. $.95

SHAKESPEARE: A Critical Study. 1939. *Doubleday* 1953 Anchor Bk. pap. $1.95

PRIVATE READER: Selected Articles and Reviews. 1942. *Kraus* 1968 $13.00

LIBERAL EDUCATION. 1943. With new preface. *Beacon* 1959 pap. $2.95

NATHANIEL HAWTHORNE. 1949. *Greenwood* 1973 $12.50

JOHN DRYDEN: A Study of His Poetry. *Indiana Univ. Press* 1960 Midland Bks. pap.
$1.95; *Peter Smith* $4.50

THE HAPPY CRITIC AND OTHER ESSAYS. *Hill & Wang* 1961 Am. Century pap. $1.45.
A collection of essays on poetry, translation and literature.

AUTOBIOGRAPHY. 1958. *Greenwood* 1968 $17.25

See also Chapter 9, Modern American Poetry.

LEAVIS, F(RANK) R(AYMOND). 1895–

This lecturer in English at Downing College, Cambridge University, was editor of the critical journal,
Scrutiny, during its entire span. "Mr. Leavis is tough and querulous because he wants to rouse his opponents
out of a sleepy gentility that accepts everything and demands nothing. . . . Mr. Leavis's critical judgments are
similar to his manners: brusque and direct, concerned mainly with the right and wrong of a thing, and not
bothered by shades, tones, or mere conventions"—(*Nation*).

"Two Cultures?" includes the reprint of Leavis's diatribe against C. P. Snow's "The Two Cultures."
This critical essay, originally published in *The Spectator*, initiated a transatlantic debate on the merits of
Snow (*q. v.*) as a novelist and thinker. The second essay in "Two Cultures?" is a more objective criticism by a
Cambridge biochemist.

Mr. Leavis has many partisans who find his criticism stimulating and valid. "What stamps his work as
being by a critic of the first rank," says Noel Annan in the English *Guardian*, "is the quality of his perception." Vincent Buckley has written of the criticism of Leavis, along with that of Matthew Arnold and
T. S. Eliot, in "Poetry and Morality" (*Humanities Press* 1959 $5.00).

D. H. LAWRENCE: Novelist. 1930. *Folcroft*. lib. bdg. $4.75; *Haskell* $5.95; *Knopf* 1956
$5.95; *Simon & Schuster* Clarion Bks. 1969 pap. $2.45

MASS CIVILIZATION AND MINORITY CULTURE. 1930. *Folcroft* lib. bdg. $7.50

NEW BEARINGS IN ENGLISH POETRY. 1932. *Univ. of Michigan Press* 1960 $4.40 Ann
Arbor Bks. pap. $1.85. An appraisal of significant 20th-century English poets, with
emphasis on Eliot, Pound and Hopkins.

(with Denys Thompson) CULTURE AND ENVIRONMENT. 1933. 1959. *Barnes & Noble*
$3.25

TOWARDS STANDARDS OF CRITICISM: Selections from the Calendar of Modern Letters,
1925–1927. 1933. *Johnson Reprint* 1969 lib. bdg. $9.00; *Folcroft* lib. bdg. $8.50

FOR CONTINUITY. 1933. *Bks. for Libraries* $13.50

THE GREAT TRADITION: Critical Study of George Eliot, Henry James and Joseph
Conrad. 1948. *New York Univ. Press* 1963 $8.95 pap. $2.45

THE COMMON PURSUIT. 1952. *New York Univ. Press* 1964 $8.50

Essays on writers ranging from Bunyan and Shakespeare to Lawrence and Eliot. "Some of Dr. Leavis' most mature criticism"—(*Observer*, London).

RETROSPECT. *Cambridge* 1963 pap. $.75

(with Michael Yudkin) Two CULTURES?: The Significance of C. P. Snow by Leavis and An Essay on Sir Charles Snow's Rede Lecture by Yudkin. *Pantheon* 1963 $2.95

SCRUTINY. A Critical Journal Complete: 1932–1953. *Cambridge* 20 vols. each $12.50 set $195.00

SELECTIONS FROM SCRUTINY. *Cambridge* 2 vols. each $9.50 pap. each $2.95

ANNA KARENINA AND OTHER ESSAYS. *Pantheon* 1968 $7.95; *Simon & Schuster* Clarion Bks. pap. $1.95

(with Q. D. Leavis) LECTURES IN AMERICA. *Pantheon* 1969 $4.95

NOR SHALL MY SWORD: Discourses on Pluralism, Compassion and Social Hope. *Barnes & Noble* 1972 $8.50

WILSON, EDMUND. 1895–1972.

. Reviewing the new "Europe Without Baedeker" in the *N.Y. Times*, V. S. Pritchett said, "In breadth of knowledge and experience, Edmund Wilson is unique in American criticism. A learned and alert eupeptic, he early slipped out of the academic handcuffs, and . . . he is as actively curious about life as he is saturated in many literatures. . . . As a traveling diarist and responsive looker-on, he has no equal in English or American writing." Wilson roamed the world and read vastly in many languages. Eternally productive and endlessly readable, he also made American literature his own, in essay after fascinating essay. If he is idiosyncratic and lacks a rigid mold, it is safe to say that he will be read for generations for the sheer entertainment of his serious insights, as well as for the illumination he shed on native American literary production. His enthusiasm is disarming, but it is a tough kind of enthusiasm, a delight in what is worth delighting in—and only that. He allows himself frivolities for sober ends, such as the "Lamentable Tragedy of the Duke of Palermo" in the *N.Y. Review of Books* for Jan. 12, 1967—a lampoon of the Academe whose jargon has never sullied his own prose. "For Wilson," says Alfred Kazin, ". . . a literary critic is first of all a man and a citizen, a man who would be as ashamed to take the side of power as to write a bad sentence."

Mr. Wilson, who—like so many of his generation—went through a brief Marxist period, has tried various types of writing including novels, poems and plays. He was book reviewer for the *New Yorker*, 1944–48. "Axel's Castle," a penetrating analysis of the symbolist writer, has exerted a great influence in contemporary literary criticism. Its dedication, to Christian Gauss of Princeton, reads: "It was principally from you that I acquired . . . my idea of what literary criticism ought to be—a history of man's ideas and imaginings in the setting of the conditions which have shaped them."

The volume of satiric short stories, "Memoirs of Hecate County" (1946 *Farrar, Straus* 1959 $6.95), with frankly erotic passages, was the subject of court cases in a less tolerant decade than the present one. It was his own favorite among his writings, but he complained that those who like his other work tend to disregard it. Wilson also edited a valuable collection of American literary documents, "The Shock of Recognition: The Development of Literature in the United States Recorded by the Men Who Made It" (1943, o. p.). "The Scrolls from the Dead Sea" (*Oxford* 1955 $6.50) was the first popular account of this great discovery. "Wilson's Night Thoughts" (*Farrar, Straus* 1961 $4.50) is predominantly a selection of his work from the 1920s to the early 1950s. It contains a section of "unforgettable reminiscences" entitled "Prose of the Thirties." "I Thought of Daisy" and "Galahad" are amusing novels about Greenwich Village Bohemia in the 1920s. His "The Duke of Palermo and Other Plays" (*Farrar, Straus* 1969 $6.95) is also available.

Wilson received the 1955 Gold Medal for Essays and Criticism of The American Academy of Arts and Letters and the National Institute of Arts and Letters, and in 1963 he was one of 31 winners of the Presidential Medal of Freedom, the nation's highest civilian award, instituted that year by President Kennedy. He also received the 1966 National Medal for Literature and the 1968 $30,000 Aspen Prize.

AXEL'S CASTLE. A study in the imaginative literature of 1870–1930. *Scribner* 1931 $6.95 1960 pap. $2.95

THE AMERICAN JITTERS: A Year of the Slump. 1932. *Bks. for Libraries* $10.00

THE TRIPLE THINKERS: Twelve Essays on Literary Subjects. 1938. *Oxford* rev. and enl. ed. 1948 $6.50 Galaxy Bks. 1963 pap. $2.50

To the Finland Station: A Study in the Writing and Acting of History. 1940. *Doubleday* Anchor Bks. 1953 pap. $2.95; *Farrar, Straus* 1972 $15.00

The Wound and the Bow. Seven Studies in Literature. 1941. *Oxford* 1947 $7.50

Classics and Commercials: A Literary Chronicle of the Forties. *Farrar, Straus* 1950 $10.00 Noonday 1967 pap. $2.65. A collection of articles and reviews.

The Shores of Light: A Literary Chronicle of the Twenties and Thirties. *Farrar, Straus* 1952 Noonday 1967 pap. $2.95. A collection of articles and reviews.

Red, Black, Blond and Olive: Studies in Four Civilizations: Zuni, Haiti, Soviet Russia, Israel. *Oxford* 1956 $8.50. Essays "distinguished for their delightful style and realistic approach."

The American Earthquake: A Documentary of the Jazz Age, the Great Depression and the New Deal. *Octagon* 1971 $17.50. Essays from periodicals and some reprinted from "The American Jitters" (*see above*) and "Travels in Two Democracies" (1938, o. p.).

Apologies to the Iroquois. (bound with Joseph Mitchell's "The Mohawks in High Steel") *Farrar, Straus* 1960 $7.95; *Random* Vintage Bks. pap. $1.95. Sympathetic articles on these Indians and their present-day troubles.

Patriotic Gore: Studies in the Literature of the American Civil War. *Oxford* 1962 $9.50 Galaxy Bks. pap. $3.95. Excellent discussions of the lives and works of some 30 persons.

The Bit between My Teeth: A Literary Chronicle of 1950–1965. *Farrar, Straus* 1967 $10.00 Noonday pap. $2.85. A collection of articles and reviews.

O Canada: An American's Notes on Canadian Culture. *Farrar, Straus* 1965 $4.95

"A most necessary volume in any American library"—(*LJ*).

Europe Without Baedeker: Sketches among the Ruins of Italy, Greece and England, Together with Notes from a European Diary 1963–1964. Reissue of a 1947 work with recent notes added. *Farrar, Straus* 1966 $8.95 Noonday pap. $2.45

A Prelude: Landscapes, Characters and Conversations from the Earlier Years of My Life. *Farrar, Straus* 1967 $6.50. Journal entries and other autobiographical jottings, some rather slight—but conveying an atmosphere—from Wilson's life through World War I, in which he took part.

The Devils and Canon Barham: Essays on Poets, Novelists and Monsters. Fwd. by Leon Edel *Farrar, Straus* 1973 $7.95

BUSH (JOHN NASH) DOUGLAS. 1896–

Douglas Bush is a distinguished scholar who has produced over a dozen volumes of biography, criticism, essays and literary history. Born in Ontario, he received a Classical education at the University of Toronto and a Ph.D. from Harvard in 1923, as well as countless honorary degrees from other institutions. He taught at Harvard for 33 years, retiring in 1966 as Gurney Professor of English Literature.

Dr. Bush has frequently risen to the defense of the humanities in answer to the challenges of science and of the "[lack of] ethical direction and stability" of the modern literary spirit. He believes that "one great mark of health and maturity in any culture is the capacity for tragic vision" and "truly comic vision"—denied, he says, by most modern psychologists and writers. "Of course we must read contemporary authors just because they are contemporary, and because a few of them are important interpreters. But we can renew and nourish our humanness much more fully by living with writers of finer genius and insight who recognize both the littleness and greatness of man."

MYTHOLOGY AND THE RENAISSANCE TRADITION IN ENGLISH POETRY. 1932. *Norton* rev. ed. 1963 pap. $2.45

MYTHOLOGY AND THE ROMANTIC TRADITION IN ENGLISH POETRY. 1937. *Harvard Univ. Press* rev. ed. 1969 $12.50; *Norton* pap. 1963 $4.45

THE RENAISSANCE AND ENGLISH HUMANISM. 1939. *Univ. of Toronto Press* pap. $1.95. The Alexander Lectures delivered at the University of Toronto in 1939.

ENGLISH LITERATURE IN THE EARLIER SEVENTEENTH CENTURY: 1600–1660. Vol. 5 Oxford History of English Literature. *Oxford* 1945 rev. ed. 1962 $11.50

PARADISE LOST IN OUR TIME. 1945. *Peter Smith* $3.75

SCIENCE AND ENGLISH POETRY: A Historical Sketch, 1590–1950. *Oxford* 1950 $5.50

ENGLISH POETRY: The Main Currents from Chaucer to the Present. 1952. *Oxford* pap. $1.95

JOHN MILTON. 1964. *Macmillan* Collier Bks. pap. $1.95

PREFACES TO RENAISSANCE LITERATURE. 1965. *Harvard Univ. Press* 1965 $4.50; *Norton* Norton Lib. 1965 pap. $1.95

JOHN KEATS: His Life and Writings. *Macmillan* 1966 Collier Bks. pap. $1.95

ENGAGED AND DISENGAGED. *Harvard Univ. Press* 1966 $6.00

A collection of 19 essays (1929–66) on timely subjects "explored with a cool intelligence and an occasional snap of wit"—(*New Yorker*).

PAGAN MYTH AND CHRISTIAN TRADITION IN ENGLISH POETRY. *Amer. Philosophical Society* 1968 $2.50

MATTHEW ARNOLD. *Macmillan* 1971 $6.95

DE VOTO, BERNARD (AUGUSTINE). 1897–1955.

"In an age in which most polemical writing is shoddy journalese, Mr. De Voto had the rare distinction of being a commentator whose artistry and learning were as impressive as his firepower"—(C. J. Rolo in the *Atlantic Monthly*). From 1935 to 1952 De Voto wrote "The Easy Chair" section for *Harper's Magazine*. He often commented on highly controversial issues, ranging from the functions of Congress to an interpretation of the Civil War, from television to ex-Communists. He could be stubborn, blunt, opinionated, but was always stimulating and challenging.

For a time he acted as literary editor for Mark Twain's (*q. v.*) estate, and was throughout his literary life active in that author's behalf, countering Van Wyck Brooks' attack (in Brooks' "Ordeal of Mark Twain") with what James M. Cox calls "spirited defense." He wrote "Mark Twain at Work" (1942) and "Mark Twain's America" (1935) (*Houghton* 2 vols. in 1951 Sentry Eds. pap. $2.45) and edited many volumes of Twain. His research in American history resulted in several notable books in this field. He was "a historian above all, a novelist, prolific journalist, editor, commentator, and confessed maverick, and his special gift lay in interpreting America, especially Western America, to itself and the world."

FORAYS AND REBUTTALS. 1936. *Bks. for Libraries* $16.75

MINORITY REPORT. 1940. *Bks. for Libraries* facsimile ed. $12.50

LITERARY FALLACY. 1944. *Kennikat* 1969 $7.00

THE WORLD OF FICTION. 1950 *Houghton* pap. $3.50; *The Writer* new ed. 1956 $5.95

THE HOUR. 1951. *Greenwood* $7.50; *Houghton* 1951 $3.00. Some barbed witticisms on the cocktail hour.

THE EASY CHAIR. 1955. *Bks. for Libraries* $13.50

Books about De Voto

Four Portraits and One Subject: Bernard De Voto. By Catherine Drinker Bowen, Edith Mirrielees, Arthur M. Schlesinger, Jr., and Wallace Stegner. With a Bibliography of his writings, prepared by Julius P. Barclay with the collaboration of Elaine Helmer Parnie. *Houghton* 1963 $4.00

BURKE, KENNETH. 1897–

Kenneth Burke began as a poet, but has become best known for his criticism of music and literature. A music critic for the *Dial* (1927–29) and for the *Nation* (1934–36), he won the $2,000 *Dial* award for distinguished service to American literature in 1928. He has lectured widely and taught at Bennington (1943–51) and the University of California (1964–65). Notable among his numerous translations from the German are works by Thomas Mann, Arthur Schnitzler and Hugo von Hofmannsthal. Identified with the New Criticism (*see the introduction to this Chapter*), "he belongs to the most 'advanced' school of literary theory, and has tended to become more and more a critical philosopher rather than a mere commentator on contemporary literature"—("Twentieth Century Authors"). Stanley Edgar Hyman said of his work: "After 'Attitudes Toward History' it was never again possible to read literature as though it didn't matter."

In fields outside of literary criticism, his stories have been collected under the title "The Complete White Oxen: Collected Short Fiction" (*Univ. of California Press* 1968 $7.50 pap. $2.45) and his poems in "Collected Poems, 1915–1917" (*Univ. of California Press* 1968 $7.50).

COUNTER-STATEMENT. 1931. *Hermes* rev. ed. 1953 $7.95; *Univ. of California Press* 1968 pap. $2.25

"The most brilliant essay on technical criticism written in this generation"—(*N.Y. World-Telegram*).

PERMANENCE AND CHANGE. 1935. *Bobbs* Lib. Arts. pap. $1.95; *Hermes* rev. ed. 1954 $9.95. His central purpose is to work out a usable attitude towards the present, with a view to deciding what form one's "resignation" must take.

ATTITUDES TOWARD HISTORY. 1937. *Hermes* rev. ed. 1959 $19.95

THE PHILOSOPHY OF LITERARY FORM. 1941. *Univ. of California Press* 1973 pap. $3.50

A GRAMMAR OF MOTIVES. 1945. *Univ. of California Press* 1969 $10.00 pap. $2.95

A RHETORIC OF MOTIVES. 1950. *Univ. of California Press* 1969 $10.00 pap. $2.25

THE RHETORIC OF RELIGION. 1961. *Univ. of California Press* 1970 pap. $2.95

PERSPECTIVES BY INCONGRUITY: Studies in Symbolic Action and Terms for Order: Studies in Evaluation. Ed. by Stanley Edgar Hyman and Barbara Karmiller. *Indiana Univ. Press* 1964 Midland Bks. pap. $2.45; *Peter Smith* $4.50

TOWARDS A BETTER LIFE. *Univ. of California Press* 1966 $6.00

LANGUAGE AS SYMBOLIC ACTION: Essays on Life, Literature, and Method. *Univ. of California Press* 1967 $11.50 pap. $4.95

DRAMATISM AND DEVELOPMENT. *Barre Pub.* 1972 $5.95

Books about Burke

Critical Moments: Kenneth Burke's Categories and Critiques. By George Knox. *Univ. of Washington Press* 1957 $4.50

Kenneth Burke and the Drama of Human Relations. By William H. Rueckert. *Univ. of Minnesota Press* 1963 $6.00. Describes the development and unity of Burke's critical thought in relation to his vision of a moral universe.

Critical Responses to Kenneth Burke, 1924–1966. Ed. by William H. Rueckert. *Univ. of Minnesota Press* 1969 $14.50

COWLEY, MALCOLM. 1898–

Malcolm Cowley, critic, poet, editor and translator, has long been an important figure on the American literary scene. His book "The Faulkner-Cowley File" shows him as an early encourager of Faulkner (q. v.). "The Portable Faulkner" (*Viking* rev. ed. 1967 pap. $2.45) was published at Cowley's instigation and under his editorship in 1946, when all 17 of Faulkner's books were o. p. Its publication proved to be "a critical event in American literary history. . . . [The selection] was so arranged as to give the reader a sense of the unity of Faulkner's work, with a first-rate piece of interpretation and evaluation as introduction, and the Faulkner boom was on"—(*SR*).

The son of a Pittsburgh physician, Mr. Cowley studied at Harvard and the University of Montpellier, "starved" in Greenwich Village ("and that's no figure of speech") and lived in France, where he met the Dada crowd and worked on two expatriate magazines, *Secession* and *Broom*. From 1929 to 1944 he was associate editor of the *New Republic*. Though he is represented in many anthologies, only one of his volumes of poetry, "Blue Juniata," (1929 *Viking* 1968 $5.95) is in print. Among the many books that he has edited are "After the Genteel Tradition: American Writers since 1910" (*Southern Illinois Univ. Press* rev. ed. 1964 $4.50) and the first "Writers at Work: The Paris Review Interviews" (1958 *Viking* $7.95 Compass Bks. pap. $1.65).

EXILE's RETURN: A Literary Odyssey of the 1920's. 1934. *Viking* rev. ed. 1951 Compass Bks. pap. $2.25. Personal memories of the "lost generation."

THE LITERARY SITUATION. 1954. *Viking* 1958 Compass Bks. pap. $1.65; *Peter Smith* $4.00

"A fascinating account of the American writer as a human being"—(*N.Y. Herald Tribune Book Review*).

THE FAULKNER-COWLEY FILE: Letters and Memories, 1944–1962. *Viking* 1966 $5.00 Compass Bks. pap. $1.45

THINK BACK ON US: A Contemporary Chronicle of the 1930's. Ed. with introd. by Henry Dan Piper *Southern Illinois Univ. Press* 1967 2 vols. $10.00 pap. 2 vols. each $2.45

A fine "source book . . . in the intellectual, social and literary history of the 'Thirties' "—(*PW*).

MANY WINDOWED HOUSE: Collected Essays on American Writers and Writing. Ed. by Henry Dan Piper *Southern Illinois Univ. Press* 1970 $10.00 pap. $2.95

A SECOND FLOWERING: Works and Days of the Lost Generation. *Viking* 1973 $8.95. A statement about the author's own generation in terms of Hemingway, Fitzgerald, Dos Passos, Cummings, Wilder, Faulkner, Wolfe and Hart Crane.

WEEKS, EDWARD (AUGUSTUS), JR. 1898–

Witty, urbane, liberal-minded and forward-looking, Edward Weeks was editor-in-chief of the *Atlantic Monthly* 1938–1966. He was educated at Cornell, Harvard and Cambridge Universities and has received 20 honorary degrees. He served as an ambulance driver in France in World War I and received the Volunteers' Medal and the Croix de Guerre. He went to the *Atlantic* in 1924 as associate editor, and during his editorship the policy was broadened and the circulation tripled. One of his greatest services to the book world was his fight against the antiquated censorship laws of Massachusetts. He has published eight books which reflect his philosophy of life as a perceptive and sympathetic editor. With Emily Flint, he edited the volume of prose, fiction and poetry, "Jubilee: One Hundred Years of the Atlantic" (*Little-Atlantic* 1957 $7.50). In what he calls his "second career" he is editing *Atlantic Monthly Press* books and writing on his own. "Fresh Waters" (*Little-Atlantic* 1968 $7.95) is a book about fishing and fishermen.

IN FRIENDLY CANDOR. *Little-Atlantic* 1959 $4.75

BREAKING INTO PRINT: An Editor's Advice on Writing. *The Writer* 1962 $5.00

TATE, ALLEN. 1899–

Tate began his literary career in 1922 as an editor of *The Fugitive*, a magazine of Southern poets and critics, many of them associated with Vanderbilt University (J. C. Ransom, Donald Davidson, Laura Riding Jackson, R. P. Warren, Merrill Moore [*qq. v.*], and Tate himself). As editor, and in his own works, Tate has advocated regionalism (see the symposia "I'll Take My Stand" [1930], "The Critique of Humanism" [1930], and "Who Owns America?" [1936], all o. p.). In 1943 he held the Chair of Poetry in the Library of Congress, and succeeded this as Fellow in American Letters there. At the same time he edited (1944–47) another important journal of literary criticism, *Sewanee Review*. Still another facet of his profession of literature is his activity as a teacher in various universities—Minnesota, Indiana, Princeton. He is both a poet and a critic, and it is hard to say in which his primary contribution is. His poetry is often considered as "modern metaphysical," with a neoclassical polish. He describes his technique thus: "gradually circling round a subject, threatening it and using the ultimate violence upon it." As a critic, he is generally placed with the "New" or Formalist critics, though he adds a strong strain of religious humanism, reflected by his conversion in 1950 to Roman Catholicism. He is also author of a novel, "The Fathers" (1938. *Swallow* pap. $2.95).

REACTIONARY ESSAYS ON POETRY AND IDEAS. 1936. *Bks. for Libraries* 1968 $11.50

REASON IN MADNESS: Critical Essays. 1941. *Bks. for Libraries* 1968 $10.75

RECENT AMERICAN POETRY AND POETIC CRITICISM. 1943. *Folcroft* lib. bdg. $5.00

SIXTY AMERICAN POETS. 1945. *Folcroft* lib. bdg. $15.00

ON THE LIMITS OF POETRY: 1928–1948. 1948. *Bks. for Libraries* $15.50

FORLORN DEMON. 1953. *Bks. for Libraries* $9.75

ESSAYS OF FOUR DECADES. *Swallow* 1969 $10.00; *Apollo* 1970 pap. $4.95

WHITE, E(LWYN) B(ROOKS). 1899–

When "One Man's Meat" was published, Irwin Edman wrote: "Wisdom, poetry and laughter are united—a prose deft, exact; musical and gay: Mr. White is our finest essayist, perhaps our only one." E. B. White, as he prefers to sign himself, began writing early in life. Interrupting his college course at Cornell to serve as a private in the First World War, he returned to graduate. After several years at different jobs, he joined the staff of the *New Yorker*, then in its infancy. For 11 years he wrote most of the "Talk of the Town" department. He retired then to a saltwater farm in Maine, where he wrote essays regularly for *Harper's Magazine* under the title "One Man's Meat." With ten new chapters, this was awarded The Limited Editions Club's Gold Medal as "the book which is considered most nearly to attain the stature of a classic." In 1960 he received the gold medal of the American Academy of Arts and Letters, and in 1963 he was one of 31 persons to receive a Presidential Medal of Freedom, the nation's highest civilian award, instituted that year by President Kennedy, the other two authors so honored being Thornton Wilder (*q. v.*) and Edmund Wilson (*q. v.*).

His verse is original and witty, with serious undertones. His friend, the late James Thurber (*q. v.*), described him as "a poet who loves to live half-hidden from the eye," whose almost indescribable prose is fashioned of "those silver and crystal sentences which have a ring like nobody else's sentences in the world." Two books have become children's classics: "Stuart Little" (*Harper* 1945 $3.95; *Dell* 1967 Laurel Leaf Lib. pap. $.95), about a mouse born into a human family, and "Charlotte's Web" (*Harper* 1952 $3.95 lg.-type ed. $7.95; *Dell* Laurel Leaf Lib. pap. $.95) about a spider.

In "The Points of My Compass," he says, "As a writing man, or secretary, I have always felt charged with the safekeeping of all unexpected items of worldly or unworldly enchantment, as though I might be held personally responsible if even a small one were to be lost." And M. J. Arlen concludes his *N.Y. Times* review: "It is E. B. White's special virtue that he can tell us what he thinks of the United Nations, or of the way a coon comes down a tree, and with what seems an instinctive natural concern for each. One feels that no item of enchantment he safekeeps for us, or any of the other items he has cared to write about, is really likely to be lost."

E. B. WHITE READER. Ed. by W. Watt and R. W. Bradford *Harper* 1966 pap. $5.50

(with James Thurber) IS SEX NECESSARY? or Why You Feel the Way You Do. *Harper* 1929 Colophon Bks. pap. $1.95

QUO VADIMUS? or The Case for the Bicycle. 1939. *Bks. for Libraries* $10.75

ONE MAN'S MEAT. *Harper* 1942 new enl. ed. 1944 $6.95 pap. $.95 introd. by Morris Bishop Mod. Class. $2.00

THE SECOND TREE FROM THE CORNER. *Harper* 1954 $6.50. Pieces written over 20 years which the author thinks stand the test of time.

(with William Strunk, Jr.) THE ELEMENTS OF STYLE. *Macmillan* 1959 1962 $2.95 pap. $.95 2nd ed. 1972 pap. $1.25

THE POINTS OF MY COMPASS: Letters from The East, The West, The North, The South. *Harper* 1962 $4.95. His writings from the *New Yorker*, 1954–62, with new postscripts and one addition.

POTTER, STEPHEN. 1900–1969.

Stephen Potter became known on both sides of the Atlantic with the publication of "The Theory and Practice of Gamesmanship." He is "a witty observer of the foibles of modern man in a competitive society." Untermeyer calls Potter's work "amoral spoofing" and Bob Considine "a shadowy endeavor between sportsmanship and downright crookedness." "Supermanship" (1958)—gamesmanship raised to the n'th power—is now o. p. Potter gives these details about his earlier achievements: "I was at Westminster School and Merton College, Oxford. . . . My early career is somewhat nil, as I did not start really working until I was about 35, but I was a part-time lecturer in Literature at various Universities and the only word I invented before Gamesmanship was quite a valuable one, I think namely 'Eng. Lit.' which means the racket, the flummery, the techniques and gambits of English Literature teaching."

Potter had been associated with the BBC since 1938. With Joyce Grenfell he did a popular radio series on "How to Woo," "How to Blow Your Own Trumpet," etc. He considered his *best* work to be "Coleridge and S. T. C.: A Study of Coleridge's Dual Nature" (1935. *Russell & Russell* 1965 $8.50). He edited a collection of Coleridge's "Selected Poetry and Prose" (*Random* $12.50) as well as Mrs. Coleridge's letters to Thomas Poole, "Minnow among Tritons" (1934. *AMS Press* $14.00; *Folcroft* $20.00).

THE COMPLETE UPMANSHIP: Gamesmanship, Lifemanship, One-Upmanship, Supermanship. *Holt* 1971 $8.95

GAMESMANSHIP, or The Art of Winning Games Without Actually Cheating. *Holt* 1948 $3.95

LIFEMANSHIP, or The Art of Getting Away With It Without Being an Absolute Plonk. Ill. by Frank Wilson. *Holt* 1951 $3.95

ONE-UPMANSHIP: Being Some Account of the Activities and Teaching of the Lifemanship Correspondence College of One-Upness and Gameslifemastery. *Holt* 1952 pap. $1.75

THREE-UPMANSHIP. *Holt* 1962 $4.95

WINTERS, YVOR. 1900–1968.

Yvor Winters retired as Professor of English Literature at Stanford University in 1966 and died early in 1968. He was recognized as a critic of major importance and influence after the publication of "In Defense of Reason." R. P. Blackmur (*q. v.*) called his work "powerful, informed, consistent, and for the most part just." His literary point of view is moralistic, based on absolute truths and values. He has been called "our foremost and perhaps sole representative of Johnsonian criticism."

Two books of poetry are in print: "Collected Poems" (1940. *Swallow* 1952 pap. $1.95) and "The Early Poems of Yvor Winters: 1920–1928" (*Swallow* 1966 $4.00). His verse is characterized by "integrity, clarity of poetic conception and skillful versification." He received the 1945 Oscar Blumenthal Prize for a group of poems; a National Institute Grant in Literature (1952); a Brandeis University Creative Arts Award medal (1959–60); the 1960–61 Harriet Monroe Poetry Award and the 1961 Bollingen Prize in Poetry. His verse is cool, taut and incisive.

PRIMITIVISM AND DECADENCE. 1937. *Haskell* 1969 $8.95. In which he shows the obscurity of modern American poetry as the result of Romanticism qualified by certain aspects of American history.

EDWIN ARLINGTON ROBINSON. 1946. *New Directions* 1971 $7.95 pap. $3.45

IN DEFENSE OF REASON. *Swallow* 1947 pap. $3.95. Contains Primitivism and Decadence: A Study of American Experimental Poetry (1937); Maule's Curse: Seven Studies in the History of American Obscurantism: Hawthorne, Cooper, Melville, Poe, Emerson, Jones Very, Emily Dickinson, Henry James (1938); The Anatomy of Nonsense.

THE FUNCTION OF CRITICISM: PROBLEMS AND EXERCISES. *Swallow* 1957 $4.00 pap. $2.50

FORMS OF DISCOVERY: Critical and Historical Essays on the Form of the Short Poem in English. *Swallow* 1968 $8.95 pap. $3.95

HICKS, GRANVILLE. 1901–

As a young Harvard graduate, Hicks says, he "gave up my somewhat inexplicable plan of entering the ministry" to teach at Smith College, where he came under the influence of Van Wyck Brooks—an influence which survived his Marxist period. His growing interest in Marxism in the 1930s led to an editorial position on the *New Masses*, dismissal from an assistant professorship at Rensselaer Polytechnic Institute, and membership in the Communist party. Disillusioned over the Nazi-Soviet pact, he left the party in 1939 and developed "a set of political attitudes which he calls critical liberalism and agnosticism. He is pragmatic, skeptical, cautiously optimistic"—(*SR*). Since 1935 he has lived on a small farm near Grafton, N.Y., which has furnished the background for his three novels—"Only One Storm" (1942); "Behold Trouble" (1944); "There Was a Man in Our Town" (1952)—and his semiautobiographical study, "Small Town" (1946), all o. p. Mr. Hicks was a contributing editor of the *Saturday Review* from 1958 to 1969 as the author of the "Literary Horizons" column, now available in book form (*see below*).

THE GREAT TRADITION: An Interpretation of American Literature since the Civil War. 1935. *Biblo & Tannen* 1966 $8.50

FIGURES OF TRANSITION: An Interpretation of British Literature at the End of the 19th Century. 1939. *Greenwood* $12.00

WHERE WE CAME OUT. 1954 *Greenwood* 1973 $11.25

JAMES GOULD COZZENS. Pamphlets on American Writers. *Univ. of Minnesota Press* pap. $1.25

LITERARY HORIZONS: A Quarter Century of American Fiction. *New York Univ. Press* 1970 $8.95

GOLDEN, HARRY L. 1902–

Harry Golden grew up in New York's Lower East Side during the time of the great influx of Eastern European Jews prior to 1917. During the 1930s he was a reporter for several New York dailies. He moved to North Carolina in 1939, where he wrote and published (until 1968) a unique paper, *The Carolina Israelite*. The essays in his books, varying from a short paragraph to a page or two, are taken from his newspaper. They might be considered extended epigrams. They are all "the results of his observations and cogitations on Jews, Negroes, politicians and presidents, the old East Side and the new South, and the mores, folkways and foibles of our times and our people"—(*LJ*). Written in a quizzically warm and humorous style, they are reminiscent of Finley Peter Dunne. "Practically no subject is too controversial or delicate for Golden's astringent comments."

ONLY IN AMERICA. Fwd. by Carl Sandburg. 1950. *Greenwood* 1973 $12.50

ESS, ESS, MEIN KINDT. *Putnam* 1966 $5.95

SO LONG AS YOU'RE HEALTHY. *Putnam* 1970 $6.95

THE ISRAELIS. *Putnam* 1971. $6.95

THE GOLDEN BOOK OF JEWISH HUMOR. *Putnam* 1972 $6.95

THE GREATEST JEWISH CITY IN THE WORLD. *Putnam* 1972 $12.95

OUR SOUTHERN LANDSMAN. *Putnam* 1974 $8.95

TRAVELS THROUGH JEWISH AMERICA. *Doubleday* 1973 $7.95

THE RIGHT TIME: An Autobiography. *Putnam* 1969 $6.95; *Pyramid Bks.* pap. $1.25

HOFFER, ERIC 1902–

A San Francisco longshoreman and philosopher, Eric Hoffer views society from a perspective quite different from that of the academic intellectual. Son of a German immigrant and blind most of his youth, he received no formal education. After mysteriously recovering his sight at 15, Hoffer worked at odd jobs around California, reading voraciously in his spare time and carrying library cards from a dozen towns. Now well-known as a successful author and political theorist, he continues his 25 years' labor on the San Francisco docks part time. He also advises young writers one day a week at the University of California (Berkeley). President Johnson invited him to the White House in the fall of 1967 as a "philosopher he likes"—(*N.Y. Times*).

His writing explores the inner conflicts of man in modern society, particularly those caused by the threat of automation, in light of his belief that hard manual labor gives man a sense of individual worth. Mistrusting the intellectual (and today's rebel youth as well), his philosophy is marked by a passionate faith in the common man. "Hoffer is not a professional social thinker and therefore has no need to comply with the guild rule that makes it unethical to generalize . . . he is a born generalizer with a mind that inclines to the wry epigram and the icy aphorism as naturally as did that of the Duc de La Rochefoucauld"—(*New Yorker*). Of "The Temper of Our Time" *Library Journal* said, "Thoughtful, iconoclastic, synthesizing an immense amount of reading, these essays deserve to be pondered by a wide audience." Milton R. Konvitz (in *SR*), however, although he found it "at once deep and shallow, satisfying and frustrating, profoundly wise and merely clever," considers Hoffer grossly unfair—"a hit-and-run thinker"—where the just and serious claims of the American Negro are involved.

THE TRUE BELIEVER: Thoughts on the Nature of Mass Movements. *Harper* 1951 $4.50 Perenn. Lib. pap. $.75

THE PASSIONATE STATE OF MIND, AND OTHER APHORISMS. *Harper* 1955 $4.50 Perenn. Lib. pap. $.75

"Neat, 17th-century style brooding on 20th-century problems"—(*Time*).

THE ORDEAL OF CHANGE. *Harper* 1963 $4.95 Perenn. Lib. pap. $.75. Stimulating essays around his major thesis that the masses provide the greatest impetus for change.

THE TEMPER OF OUR TIME. *Harper* 1967 $4.95 Perenn. Lib. pap. $.75

Six essays on topics ranging "from Montaigne to the fevered quest for leisure, from automation to social justice, from adult delinquency to juvenile creativeness"—(*N.Y. Times*).

WORKING AND THINKING ON THE WATERFRONT. *Harper* 1969 $4.95 Perenn Lib. pap. $.75

FIRST THINGS, LAST THINGS. *Harper* 1971 $4.95 Perenn. Lib. pap. $1.25

REFLECTIONS ON THE HUMAN CONDITION. *Harper* 1973 $4.95

Books about Hoffer

Eric Hoffer: An American Odyssey. By Calvin Tomkins. *Dutton* 1968 $4.95; *Harper* pap. $.95. A biography by the man who wrote the *New Yorker* profile, which is a part of the present work.

CONNOLLY, CYRIL. 1903–

Critic and editor of *Horizon*, the English literary monthly, Connolly was introduced to America first by a novel, "The Rock Pool" (1936 new ed. 1947 *Atheneum* 1968 $3.95), followed by "Enemies of Promise" (1939, o. p.), criticism of such moderns as Virginia Woolf (*q. v.*), Aldous Huxley (*q. v.*), Hemingway (*q. v.*) and Joyce (*q. v.*). "The Unquiet Grave," a stimulating volume of brief observations on life, his own life and literature, established his reputation, and "The Condemned Playground: Essays 1927–1944" (1946 o. p.)

certainly enhanced it. He is not afraid to back his own literary taste, to tilt at established reputations, to make fun of the "pompous and pretentious." According to the *Times Literary Supplement*, he "has not fully used his talent for criticism which at heart he despises in comparison with any sort of artistic creation, because the pleasures of food, drink, conversation, book collecting, and the satisfaction of fifty odd forms of curiosity have taken him away from writing." To this Edmund Wilson replies, in his essay on Connolly in "Classics & Commercials" (*q. v.*), "It is no use being angry with Connolly. Whatever his faults may be . . . he is one of those fortunate Irishmen, like Goldsmith and Sterne and Wilde, who are born with a gift of style, a natural grace and wit, so that their jobs have the freshness of *jeux d'esprit*, and sometimes their *jeux d'esprit* turn out to stick as classics." Two other volumes of essays, reviews, etc., are also out of print: "Ideas and Places" (1953) and "Previous Conviction" (1963).

THE UNQUIET GRAVE: A Word Cycle by Palinurus. 1945. *Harper* Colophon Bks. 1972 pap. $2.45

"It is a book which, no matter how many readers it will have will never have enough"—(Ernest Hemingway).

BLACKMUR, R(ICHARD) P. 1904–1965.

R. P. Blackmur, a native of Massachusetts, was one of America's foremost critics. Though himself lacking a college education, he was on the Princeton faculty from 1940 till his death, and in 1961–62 was Pitt Professor of American History and Institutions at Cambridge University. He contributed criticism to literary journals and "little" magazines, chiefly on the 19th- and 20th-century novelists and poets. In "A Burden for Critics," (1948, o. p.) he called for "modern criticism to enlarge its scope, and to add to analysis, elucidation, and comparison the important function of judgment based on rational standards." The *Times Literary Supplement*, London, said of him: "Here, working with the precision and the trained effortlessness of a great athlete, is a powerful and discriminating intelligence which is brought to bear on the work itself. So thorough is his examination, so high the standards he sets, and so fascinating the mind brought to bear on the work that [his] judgement is always impressive, even where it is at odds with the personal conviction of the reader." He is also the author of esoteric and highly polished poems: "From Jordan's Delight" (1937 *Folcroft* $10.00), "Second World" (1942, o. p.), and "Good Europeans and Other Poems" (1947, o. p.).

DIRTY HANDS, or The True-Born Censor. 1930. *Folcroft* lib. bdg. $6.50

THE DOUBLE AGENT: Essays in Craft and Elucidation. 1935. *Peter Smith* 1962 $5.00

THE EXPENSE OF GREATNESS. 1940. *Peter Smith* $5.00; *Somerset Pub.* $11.50

ANNI MIRABILES 1921–1925: Reason in the Madness of Letters. 1956. *Folcroft* lib. bdg. $6.50

NEW CRITICISM IN THE UNITED STATES. 1959 *Folcroft.* lib. bdg. $15.00

ELEVEN ESSAYS ON THE EUROPEAN NOVEL. *Harcourt* 1964 $5.75 Harbinger Bks. pap. $2.95

FADIMAN, CLIFTON. 1904–

In his witty and charming collection of essays, reviews, comments and prefaces, "Party of One" (1955, o.p.) Clifton Fadiman includes "A Gentle Dirge for the Familiar Essay." He fears that it is being starved by our age of anxiety, although his own writings during the past quarter century have done much to stay its decline. Mr. Fadiman first became known to the general public through radio and television as the affable and urbane host of "Information Please." His place in the book world is assured as translator, editor at *Simon & Schuster*, lecturer and member of the Board of Judges of the Book-of-the Month Club. He has edited with wit and discretion many anthologies for *Simon & Schuster* and other publishers, including "Fifty Years" (*Knopf* 1965 $10.00), a compilation of excerpts from *Knopf* books to celebrate the publisher's half-century mark.

An example of his engaging style is the following from "Any Number Can Play": "The most genuinely cheerful and well-integrated men I know are those whose lives are concerned mainly with ideas. Equations kept Einstein equable. Indeed this very equanimity may be one reason why some of us distrust intellectuals. Our distrust masks unconscious envy."

(Ed.) READING I'VE LIKED. *Simon & Schuster* 1958 pap. $3.50

(Ed.) FANTASIA MATHEMATICA. *Simon & Schuster* 1958 $6.00 pap. $2.95. A set of stories and a group of oddments all taken from the universe of mathematics.

(Ed.) CLIFTON FADIMAN'S FIRESIDE READER. *Simon & Schuster* 1961 $5.95

(Ed.) THE MATHEMATICAL MAGPIE. *Simon & Schuster* 1962. pap. $1.95. More stories, with subsets of essays, rhymes, anecdotes, etc., derived from the domain of mathematics.

PERELMAN, S(IDNEY) J(OSEPH). 1904–

Called a king of the "dementia praecox field" by Robert Benchley (*q. v.*) and "the most proficient surrealist in the United States next to Poe and not excepting Henry Miller" by *Time*, Perelman excels in the unconventional, the concentrated, the sophisticated in humor. Dorothy Parker (*q. v.*) said that he has "a disciplined eye and a wild mind" and "a magnificent disregard" of his reader.

ACRES AND PAINS: The Best of S. J. Perelman. 1947. *Simon & Schuster* Clarion Bks. pap. $1.95

THE MOST OF S. J. PERELMAN. *Simon & Schuster* 1958 $5.95 pap. $2.95

CRAZY LIKE A FOX. 1944. *Random* Vintage Bks. pap. 1973 $1.95. 46 short pieces.

LISTEN TO THE MOCKING BIRD. *Simon & Schuster* 1949 pap. 1970 $2.25

THE SWISS FAMILY PERELMAN. *Simon & Schuster* 1950 pap. 1970 $1.95

PERELMAN'S HOME COMPANION: A Collector's Item (The Collector Being S. J. Perelman) of 36 Otherwise Unavailable Pieces by Himself. *Simon & Schuster* 1955 $3.50

ROAD TO MILTOWN, or Under the Spreading Atrophy. *Simon & Schuster* 1957 $3.50 lg.-type ed. $7.95

RISING GORGE. *Simon & Schuster* 1961 pap. 1969 $1.95

CHICKEN INSPECTOR No. 23. *Simon & Schuster* 1966 $4.95. "Honey-dipped slings and arrows such as 'Are You Decent Memsahib?' . . . and 'A Soft Answer Turneth Away Royalties'."

BABY, IT'S COLD INSIDE. *Simon & Schuster* 1970 $5.95

LIEBLING, A(BBOTT) J(OSEPH). 1904–1963.

A. J. Liebling, a master of pungent and mordant humor, inherited the "Wayward Press" column of the *New Yorker* from Robert Benchley in 1946 and for over 15 years reveled in "lampooning the foibles of the press." He was "a reporter with few peers"—(*Bookweek*) and an expert caricaturist. Martin Levin (in the *N.Y. Times*) has said, "If you are shopping around for a universal man this far away from the Renaissance, you could do worse than pick up 'The Most of A. J. Liebling.' Liebling is the Most." He wrote "The Earl of Louisiana: The Liberal Long" (1961. *Louisiana State Univ. Press* 1970 $5.95 pap. $2.45) about Earl Long, brother of Huey.

THE MOST OF A. J. LIEBLING. *Simon & Schuster* 1963 $5.95 Clarion Bks. pap. $2.45 A delightful potpourri of essays on food, Algeria, sports, the press.

THE WAYWARD PRESSMAN. 1947. *Greenwood* $11.75

MINK AND RED HERRING, the Wayward Pressman's Case Book. 1949. *Greenwood* $10.75

THE PRESS. *Ballantine Bks.* 1961 pap. $1.50

BETWEEN MEALS: An Appetite for Paris. *Simon & Schuster* 1962 $3.95

"Succulent and ineluctably Parisian"—(Edward Weeks).

TRILLING, LIONEL. 1905–

The London *Times Literary Supplement* has called Trilling "perhaps the most outstanding of the general American critics today." His influence has been great both as critic and as a professor of English Literature at Columbia. Clifton Fadiman (*q. v.*) has observed, "Though a professor . . . he does not write as if his cloister were the world. . . . Rather, he seems linked to that gleaming chain of English and American critics that starts in glory with Ben Jonson." Trilling has been associated with the *Partisan Review* and the *Kenyon Review*, and was founder of the Kenyon School of English, now the School of Letters, Indiana University. His first and only novel "The Middle of the Journey" (1947. *Avon Bks.* 1966 pap. $1.25) is intellectually provocative and attained some additional fame because of its parallels with the Alger Hiss-Whittaker Chambers story. In 1964–65 Dr. Trilling was George Eastman visiting professor at Oxford. He has been at Columbia since 1931 where he was Woodberry Professor of Literature and Criticism from 1965–1970. In 1969–70 he was Charles Eliot Norton Visiting Professor of Poetry at Harvard. Since 1970 he has been a University Professor at Columbia.

MATTHEW ARNOLD. 1939. *Columbia* 1949 $3.50

E. M. FORSTER. 1943. *New Directions* rev. ed. 1964 pap. $1.50

THE LIBERAL IMAGINATION: Essays on Literature and Society. 1950. *Peter Smith* $4.50

THE OPPOSING SELF: Nine Essays in Criticism. *Viking* Compass Bks. 1955 1959 pap. $1.95. The Romantic Image of the Self in Keats, Jane Austen, Wordsworth, Tolstoy, Dickens, Flaubert, Howells, Henry James and George Orwell; "distinguished literary essays."

SINCERITY AND AUTHENTICITY: Six Lectures. *Harvard Univ. Press* 1972. $7.95. The Charles Eliot Norton Lectures for 1969–70.

MIND IN THE MODERN WORLD. *Viking* Compass Bks. 1973 pap. $2.50. The text of the First Annual Thomas Jefferson Lecture in the Humanities.

WARREN, ROBERT PENN. 1905–

Warren is an important member of the "New Critics" (*see introduction to this Chapter*). As a literary critic, he has for the most part allowed his essays to remain in the periodicals to which he contributed them. One exception obtains: "Selected Essays" (1958 *Random* $6.95 pap. $1.95). Since he is even more active as a poet and novelist, *see Chapter 9, Modern American Poetry and 14, Modern American Fiction. See also Brooks, Cleanth, joint author and editor, below.*

EMPSON, WILLIAM. 1906–

"Empson is the meteor of modern criticism in English, a living figure of almost legendary brilliance. As a critic he has almost every conceivable virtue. He has wit, imagination, patience and restraint. His learning is not only both large and precise; it is volatile with surprise. If Empson has a fault, it is the Schoolman's tendency to worry his word beyond reason, to overplay a situation"—(*N.Y. Times*). Empson took a B.A. degree in mathematics at Cambridge University and then studied under Professor I. A. Richards, both being brilliant English formulators of the "New Criticism." He went as Lecturer in English Literature to the Peking National University in 1937 and "refugeed with the University for two years during the Japanese invasion." During World War II he served as Chinese Editor for BBC in London and returned to Peking (1947–48). Since 1953 he has held a professorship at Sheffield University, England. His "Collected Poems" (1949) are available in paperback (*Harcourt* Harvest Bks. 1961 pap. $1.15).

SEVEN TYPES OF AMBIGUITY. 1930. *New Directions* 1947 $7.50 pap. $2.75

SOME VERSIONS OF PASTORAL. 1935. *New Directions* new ed. 1950 pap. $2.35

ENGLISH PASTORAL POETRY. 1938. *Bks. for Libraries* facsimile ed. $11.50. This is the American edition of "Some Versions of Pastoral" above.

THE STRUCTURE OF COMPLEX WORDS. 1951. *Univ. of Michigan Press* Ann Arbor Bks. pap. $2.95

MILTON'S GOD. *New Directions* 1961 $10.00. Empson brings together the last 60 years of Miltonic criticism to see what we have learned about "Paradise Lost".

Books about Empson

William Empson. By J. R. Willis. Essays on Modern Writers *Columbia* 1969 pap. $1.00

BROOKS, CLEANTH. 1906–

R. S. Stallman has said: "Of all our critics no one has done more towards revolutionizing our reading of a poem than Cleanth Brooks, and no critic has been of greater practical influence. . . . Brooks and Warren have brought the New Criticism into the universities. . . . Their analytical anthologies have influenced the younger writers tremendously. They were written while teaching at Louisiana State University, where he and Warren edited the famous *Southern Review* (1935–1942). His books of criticism are 'Modern Poetry and the Tradition' and 'The Well Wrought Urn,' a brilliantly careful analysis of ten representative English poems." In 1963 he published "The Hidden God," notable as a fresh perspective on five distinguished literary figures whose Christian commitment has long been regarded as nonexistent or nebulous. He has edited "Tragic Themes in Western Literature" (*Yale Univ. Press* 1955 $6.50). Since 1947 he has held a professorship in English at Yale University.

(with Robert Penn Warren) UNDERSTANDING POETRY: An Anthology for College Students. 1938 *Holt* (Rinehart) 3rd ed. 1960 $10.95 text ed. $7.75

MODERN POETRY AND THE TRADITION. *Univ. of North Carolina Press* 1939 $4.00 pap. $2.25

(with Robert Penn Warren) UNDERSTANDING FICTION. *Appleton* 1943 2nd ed. 1959 $8.40

(with Robert B. Heilman) UNDERSTANDING DRAMA: Twelve Plays. *Holt* 1948 $10.50

THE WELL WROUGHT URN: Studies in the Structure of Poetry. *Harcourt* 1947 Harvest Bks. 1956 pap. $1.85

(with Robert Penn Warren) MODERN RHETORIC: With Readings. *Harcourt* 1949 2nd ed. 1958 shorter ed. pap. $4.75 3rd ed. 1972 $8.95 abr. ed. pap. $5.25

(with Robert Penn Warren) FUNDAMENTALS OF GOOD WRITING: A Handbook of Modern Rhetoric. For general use. *Harcourt* 1950 $10.75

(with William K. Wimsatt, Jr.) LITERARY CRITICISM. 1957. *Random* Vintage Bks. pap. $3.45

(with Robert Penn Warren) THE SCOPE OF FICTION. *Appleton* 1960 $6.80

THE HIDDEN GOD: Hemingway, Faulkner, Yeats, Eliot, and Warren. *Yale Univ. Press* 1963 $5.00 pap. $1.45

WILLIAM FAULKNER: The Yoknapatawpha Country. *Yale Univ. Press* 1963 $13.50 pap. $3.75

A SHAPING JOY: Studies in the Writer's Craft. *Harcourt* 1972 $7.95. Critical essays on Eliot, Joyce, Yeats, Auden, James, Fitzgerald, Faulkner, Poe, Housman, Wordsworth, Milton, Marlowe (*q. v.*), and others.

MACDONALD, DWIGHT. 1906–

Dwight Macdonald believes thoroughly that "a people which loses contact with its past becomes culturally psychotic." A staff writer on the *New Yorker* since 1951, he was born in New York, was graduated from Phillips Exeter Academy in 1924 and from Yale in 1928. A brief interlude on the executive training squad of R. H. Macy convinced him that his talents were literary. He then became, successively, an associate editor of

Fortune, an editor of *Partisan Review*, the editor and publisher of *Politics*, and, in 1956–57, an advisory editor of the English monthly, *Encounter*. In his younger years, he went through the stages of being "a Trotskyist, a pacifist and an anarchist," but his interests of late years have shifted from the political to the literary because "he thinks that he can do more about the latter than about the former." He has edited a compilation of irreverent poetry and prose, "Parodies: An Anthology from Chaucer to Beerbohm and After" (*Random* 1960 $10.00), which the *Atlantic* has described: "As near perfection as any anthology can be. It begins with Chaucer's demolition of conventional medieval romance and rolls on hilariously to the present, skipping few worthy targets and sparing none."

THE ROOT IS MAN. Essays. 1953. *Gordon Press* $7.95

AGAINST THE AMERICAN GRAIN. Essays on the "Effect of Mass Culture." *Random* 1962 $10.00 Vintage Bks. pap. $1.95

"When I came to assemble these essays, written over the last ten years, I was hardly surprised to find they have a common theme: the influence of mass culture on high culture. As an earlier settler in the wilderness of masscult who cleared his first tract thirty years ago . . . I have come to feel like the aging Daniel Boone when the plowed fields began to surround him in Kentucky. The plowing of this particular field has been intense but, except for H. L. Mencken and Edmund Wilson, most writers on the subject have treated it in a sociological rather than a literary way. My interest in mass culture, however, puts the emphasis on 'culture' rather than on 'mass' "—(author's Preface).

DWIGHT MACDONALD ON THE MOVIES. *Prentice-Hall* 1969 $9.95. Collected articles and reviews annotated from the viewpoint of 1969.

POLITICS PAST. *Viking* Compass Bks. 1970 pap. $2.75. Originally published in 1957 with the title "Memoirs of a Revolutionist," it is a collection of essays in political criticism, many of which first appeared in the magazine *Politics*.

HIGHET, GILBERT. 1906–

Emeritus Anthon Professor of Latin at Columbia, a member of the Book-of-the-Month Club's celebrated panel of judges, author, lecturer and radio personality on the radio station WQXR, Gilbert Highet's various contributions to the book world are "flavorsome, scholarly, charming." The radio book talks which he gave for some years were collected in such volumes as "People, Places and Books," "A Clerk of Oxenford" (1954, o. p.) and "Talents and Geniuses" (1957, o. p.). They have been called the "most witty, urbane and perceptive aural essays to be found on the local airwaves." The range is wide—from science fiction to Tennyson (*q. v.*) and Yeats (*q. v.*). For "The Anatomy of Satire" Mr. Highet received the Award of Merit in 1963 from the American Philological Association. His lifelong enthusiasm for Latin poetry resulted in a Guggenheim fellowship for the study of the Roman satiric poet, Juvenal (*q. v.*), in translations of Greek and Latin poetry and his several volumes on the Classics. He is also the translator, from the German, of Werner Jaeger's "Paideia: The Ideals of Greek Culture" (*q. v.*) (*Oxford* 1944 3 vols. $10.00 Galaxy Bks. pap. $3.95). "Man's Unconquerable Mind" is a notable essay in "quiet praise of man's distinctive power and its application to the forces of evil." "Explorations" is a collection of essays on unusual books, odd people, the life of language and the art of writing. Born in Glasgow, Highet became a U.S. citizen in 1951. He is married to the novelist Helen MacInnes.

THE CLASSICIAL TRADITION: Greek and Roman Influences on Western Literature. *Oxford* 1949 $14.50 Galaxy Bks. pap. $3.95

THE ART OF TEACHING. *Knopf* 1950 $6.95; *Random* Vintage Bks. pap. $1.95

PEOPLE, PLACES AND BOOKS. *Oxford* 1953 $6.75

MAN'S UNCONQUERABLE MIND. *Columbia* 1954 $6.00 1960 pap. $1.95

JUVENAL THE SATIRIST: A Study. *Oxford* 1954 Galaxy Bks. pap. $2.95

POETS IN A LANDSCAPE. *Knopf* 1957 $8.95. Delightful studies of Catullus, Virgil, Horace, Propertius, Tibullus, Ovid and Juvenal with translations of their verse.

THE POWERS OF POETRY. *Oxford* 1960 $8.50

THE ANATOMY OF SATIRE. *Princeton Univ. Press* 1962 $9.50 pap. $2.95. A brillant dissection of satirical literature as practised from the time of Homer to the time of Eisenhower.

EXPLORATIONS. *Oxford* 1971 $8.50

BARZUN, JACQUES. 1907–

Jacques, Barzun, critic and historian, who calls himself "a student of cultural history," writes always with a "combination of sound scholarship and fresh, independent interpretation which is the mark of the humanist man-of-letters." His wise and witty books are mainly in the fields of criticism, education and musicology. His "Teacher in America" was called "one of the few volumes on education by which no intelligent reader can be bored." An American citizen of French birth, he writes of his adopted country with humor and perception in "God's Country and Mine." This is frank, friendly and always challenging criticism. "The Modern Researcher," which he wrote with Henry F. Graff (*Harcourt* 1957 $8.50 pap. $3.95) is a very helpful discussion of the purposes, methods and problems of research, especially of historical research. In "The House of Intellect" he attacks the whole intellectual (or pseudo-intellectual) world for its betrayal of true intellect in such areas as public administration, communications, conversation and home life, education, business and scholarship. He became Professor of History at Columbia in 1945 and served as Dean of Faculties and Provost until 1967.

THE FRENCH RACE: Theories of Its Origins and Their Social and Political Implications Prior to the Revolution. 1932. *Kennikat* $9.00

RACE: A Study in Modern Superstition. 1937. *Harper* rev. ed. 1965 $5.95 Torchbks. pap. $2.45. Still very relevant to today's racial conflicts.

TEACHER IN AMERICA. *Little-Atlantic* 1945 $7.50 pap. $2.25

GOD'S COUNTRY AND MINE. 1954. *Greenwood* $13.75. A Declaration of love with a few harsh words.

DARWIN, MARX, WAGNER: Critique of a Heritage. *Doubleday* Anchor Bks. 2nd rev. ed. 1958 $2.50; *Peter Smith* $4.25

THE HOUSE OF INTELLECT. *Harper* 1959 Torchbks. pap. $1.75

MUSIC IN AMERICAN LIFE. *Indiana Univ. Press* Midland Bks. 1962 pap. $1.75; *Peter Smith* $4.00

SCIENCE: The Glorious Entertainment. *Harper* 1964 $6.95. The author distrusts science as a strong cultural force in the modern world.

BERLIOZ AND THE ROMANTIC CENTURY. *Columbia* 3rd ed. 1969 2 vols. $30.00

ON WRITING, EDITING AND PUBLISHING: Essays Explicative and Hortatory. *Univ. of Chicago Press* Phoenix Bks. 1971 pap. $1.50

GEISMAR, MAXWELL (DAVID). 1909–

"Geismar is one of the small band of non-academic reviewers whom one can trust and genuinely respect"—(*New Republic*). He graduated from Columbia in 1931, taught at Sarah Lawrence College 1933–1944 (which was "probably the most valuable part of my early training") and since then has free-lanced as writer and lecturer, contributing to the *N.Y. Times, Nation, Saturday Review* and *Atlantic Monthly*. As a critic, "generally, Mr. Geismar is anti-New Criticism and emphasizes social-political themes, with sometimes a rather heavy emphasis on psychological interpretations"—(*LJ*). The *Saturday Review* has called him "a dedicated, even evangelical, Freudian." His three books on the American novel (*see below*) are part of a projected 5-volume history to be called "The Novel in America," covering the period 1840–1940. He has edited works by Sherwood Anderson, Ring Lardner, Herman Melville and Walt Whitman.

WRITERS IN CRISIS: The American Novel 1925–1940. *Houghton* 1942. $6.95; *Dutton* 1971 pap. $2.25

THE LAST OF THE PROVINCIALS: The American Novel 1915–1925. *Houghton* 1947 $7.50

REBELS AND ANCESTORS: The American Novel 1890–1915. *Houghton* 1953 $5.95

HENRY JAMES AND THE JACOBITES. *Houghton* 1963 $7.95; *Hill & Wang* Am. Century 1965 pap. $2.95

MARK TWAIN: An American Prophet. *Houghton* 1970 $10.00; *McGraw-Hill* 1973 pap. $2.95

RING LARDNER AND THE PORTRAIT OF FOLLEY. *T. Y. Crowell* 1972 $4.50

PARKINSON, C(YRIL) NORTHCOTE. 1909–

Originator of the famous "Parkinson's (first) Law"—that work will increase to fill the available time—this British professor and historian is noted for his humorous satires on British and American institutions. "Parkinson's Law, and Other Studies in Administration" is a hilarious attack on bureaucratic waste and managerial sinecure in big business. It was hailed by the *Saturday Review* as "just plain superb" and by the *N.Y. Times* as "a slender but deadly intercontinental ballistic missive." Parkinson's style is nonchalant, sometimes brutal, and his humor dry; "his mastery of pseudo-academic and quasi-official prose is complete"—(*Atlantic*). He has written two novels: "The Life and Times of Horatio Hornblower" (*Little* 1971 $6.95), a fictional biography of C. S. Forester's (*q. v.*) hero, and "The Devil to Pay" (*Houghton* 1973 $5.95), a novel set in England in 1794. Its hero, Lt. Richard Delancey, "is a worthy successor to Horatio Hornblower"—(*LJ*).

After eight years as Raffles Professor of History at the University of Malaya, Singapore, 1950–58, Parkinson traveled and lectured widely in the United States. His humorous articles have appeared in *Fortune, Punch* and *Harper's*. His more serious works in history and political science are published by *Houghton, Viking, New American Library, Oxford* and *Verry*. He is known as an excellent historian, if a somewhat eccentric theorist.

PARKINSON'S LAW, and Other Studies in Administration. *Houghton* 1957 $3.50 Sentry Eds. 1963 $1.75; *Ballantine Bks.* pap. $.95

THE LAW AND THE PROFITS. *Houghton* 1960 $3.50; *Ballantine Bks.* pap. $.95. Presenting his second law—"expenditure rises to meet income."

IN-LAWS AND OUTLAWS. *Houghton* 1962 $4.00 Twelve humorous essays on how to succeed in business.

PONIES' PLOT. *Houghton* 1965 $3.25. Spoof on horse stories, for children and adults.

LEFT LUGGAGE: A Caustic History of British Socialism from Marx to Wilson. *Houghton* 1967 $4.95

The Labor Party under a microscope; "for right-wing patrons only"—(*LJ*).

MRS. PARKINSON'S LAW. *Houghton* 1968 $4.95; *Avon Bks.* pap. $.95. A third law— "work under pressure produces a heat which expands to fill the mind available from which it will pass only to a mind that is cooler."

THE LAW OF DELAY: Interviews and Outerviews. *Houghton* 1971 $4.95; *Ballantine Bks.* pap. $.95. Fourteen essays on the manners and mores of men and women, and topics ranging from qualities of leadership to beards.

THE FUR-LINED MOUSETRAP. *Leviathan House* 1972 $5.75

LEVIN, HARRY (TUCHMAN). 1912–

This American scholar and critic has taught at Harvard since 1939 and is at present Irving Babbitt Professor of Comparative Literature. "Perhaps because my father was born in Germany and brought to this country as a child, perhaps because my wife was born in Russia and emigrated from the other direction, Europe has always loomed large upon my horizon, and literary study has meant comparative literature. The authors whom I have tried most to follow are those who have done the most to develop the ranges and artistic techniques at their command. . . . My ultimate hope is for a kind of criticism which, while analyzing the formal and esthetic qualities of a work of art, will fit them into the cultural and social pattern to which it belongs"— ("Twentieth Century Authors"). In addition to his own work, he has edited "Perspectives in Criticism" (1950. *Russell & Russell* 1970 $11.00) and "Veins of Humor" (*Harvard Univ. Press* 1972 $11.00).

JAMES JOYCE: A Critical Introduction. 1941. *New Directions* rev. ed. 1960 pap. $3.25

THE OVERREACHER: A Study of Christopher Marlowe. 1952. *Peter Smith* $4.50

CONTEXTS OF CRITICISM. 1957 *Atheneum* 1963 pap. $1.65; *Harvard Univ. Press* 1957 $8.00. Literary essays including revaluations of Joyce, Proust, Balzac, Melville, Cervantes and Hemingway.

THE POWER OF BLACKNESS: A Critical Study of Hawthorne, Poe and Melville. *Knopf* 1958 $5.95; *Random* Vintage Bks. pap. $1.45

THE GATES OF HORN: A Study of Five French Realists. Stendhal, Balzac, Flaubert, Zola and Proust. *Oxford* 1963 $9.50 Galaxy Bks. pap. $3.95

REFRACTIONS: Essays in Comparative Literature. *Oxford* 1966 $8.00 Galaxy Bks. pap. $2.50

"A seedtime of ideas, sending our thinking off in many directions . . . 18 essays, none new, collected to represent a criticism that traces ideas and analyzes cultures as well as books"—(*L J*).

WHY LITERARY CRITICISM IS NOT AN EXACT SCIENCE. *Harvard Univ. Press* 1967 pap. $1.50. A 27-page essay.

GROUNDS FOR COMPARISON: Studies in Comparative Literature. *Harvard Univ. Press* 1972 $13.50

DAICHES, DAVID. 1912–

David Daiches, prolific English critic, has taught at the Universities of Edinburgh, Oxford, Cornell, Indiana and Cambridge. During the war he worked at the British Information Service in New York and was later Second Secretary at the British Embassy in Washington. He has been Professor of English, since 1961, and Dean of the School of English and American Studies, from 1961–68, at the University of Sussex. Of "A Critical History of English Literature" the *N.Y. Times* said: "We are . . . impressed that this comprehensive critical history should be the work of one man. There is nothing equal to it—indeed nothing quite like it—in the field of English literature."

Professor Daiches has also written individual critical studies of D. H. Lawrence, Milton, his countrymen Robert Burns, Sir Walter Scott, and R. L. Stevenson, Virginia Woolf and Willa Cather, which are listed herein under the main entry of each one.

THE NOVEL AND THE MODERN WORLD. *Univ. of Chicago Press* 1939 2nd rev. ed. 1960 $5.95 Phoenix Bks. pap. $1.95

POETRY AND THE MODERN WORLD: A Study of Poetry in England between 1900 and 1939. 1940 *Biblo & Tannen* 1969 $8.50

CRITICAL APPROACHES TO LITERATURE. *Prentice-Hall* 1956 $9.95; *Norton* 1965 pap. $3.95

THE PRESENT AGE IN BRITISH LITERATURE. *Indiana Univ. Press* 1958 $8.50 Midland Bks. pap. $2.65

A CRITICAL HISTORY OF ENGLISH LITERATURE. *Ronald* 1960 2nd ed. 1970 2 vols. $15.00

ENGLISH LITERATURE. *Prentice-Hall* 1965 $7.95

A Study of Literature for Readers and Critics. 1948. *Greenwood* $10.50; *Norton* 1964 pap. $1.95

Literary Essays. *Univ. of Chicago Press* 1968 $6.95

More Literary Essays. *Univ. of Chicago Press* 1968 $8.50

FRYE, NORTHROP. 1912–

Professor of English and Principal of Victoria College at the University of Toronto, Northrop Frye first became known in this country for his intelligent and beautifully written critical interpretation of the poetry and symbolic thought of William Blake, "Fearful Symmetry." He interprets literature in the light of his major thesis that "myth is a structural element in literature because literature as a whole is a 'displaced' mythology." In describing his view of "literature as the working out of a few fundamental mythic archetypes . . . Mr. Frye is admirably lucid, establishing for 'myth' and 'archetype' clear, precise definitions which apply directly to literary tradition"—(*Book Week*).

He has written educational radio and television programs for the Canadian Broadcasting Corporation, contributed to some 30 other books and written numerous articles; he has edited "Blake: A Collection of Critical Essays" (*Prentice-Hall* 1966 Spectrum Bks. pap. $1.95).

Fearful Symmetry: A Study of William Blake. 1947. *Princeton Univ. Press* 1969 $14.50 pap. $3.45

Anatomy of Criticism. *Princeton Univ. Press* 1957 $13.50 pap. $2.95

"Of the classics of modern criticism this is probably the most scintillatingly provocative"—(*TLS*, London).

The Well-Tempered Critic. *Indiana Univ. Press* 1963 Midland Bks. pap. $1.75; *Peter Smith* $3.75. "A little primer of criticism."

Fables of Identity: Studies in Poetic Mythology. *Harcourt* 1963 Harbinger Bks. pap. $3.45. Critical essays on writers from Spenser to Wallace Stevens, previously published separately.

The Educated Imagination. *Indiana Univ. Press* 1964 $4.50 Midland Bks. pap. $1.75. Informal lectures on the social value of literary study.

Return of Eden: Five Essays on Milton's Epics. *Univ. of Toronto Press* 1965 $4.95

Stubborn Structure: Essays on Criticism and Society. Ed. by Max Black. *Cornell Univ. Press* 1970 $8.50 pap. $2.95

Critical Path: An Essay on the Social Context of Literary Criticism. *Indiana Univ. Press*. 1971 $4.95 Midland Bks. pap. $2.50

Books about Frye

Northrop Frye in Modern Criticism: Selected Papers from the English Institute. Ed. by Murray Krieger. *Columbia* 1966 $7.00

For serious students of Frye, "one of the most influential of modern critics"—(*LJ*). These papers by various hands show him as a controversial figure in the critical world. Includes a full bibliography of works by and about him.

KAZIN, ALFRED. 1915–

A "sound, lucid and discriminating" study of American literature, "On Native Grounds" established Kazin's critical reputation in the mid-forties. "He is sensitive, sympathetic and informed," Howard Mumford Jones wrote in the *Saturday Review*. Kazin started work on it at the suggestion of Carl Van Doren in 1939, while he was "half-heartedly doing a master's essay at Columbia on Gibbon and wondering what would ever become of me or of the maddening age." Other critical works have followed. He is a man of catholic interests, has lectured in this country and abroad and has worked with the State Department on cultural missions. "Contemporaries" includes reflective essays on travel, five essays on Freud and some very perceptive essays on literary and political matters. The final section, "The Critic's Task," is especially valuable. It concerns itself with the critic's function within a popular and an academic context and with critical theory and principles.

His poignant memoir of his childhood in Brooklyn, "A Walker in the City," brought him added praise from the critics. "Starting Out in the Thirties" describes his early years with the *New Republic* as book reviewer, and evaluates his contemporaries—Malcolm Cowley, Mary McCarthy, Philip Rahv, Granville Hicks and others—in the period when the Depression and radical political thought, pro and con, deeply affected literary production. He has also edited critical studies of Theodore Dreiser and F. Scott Fitzgerald.

ON NATIVE GROUNDS: An Interpretation of Modern Prose Literature. 1942. *Harcourt* 1956 $8.50 Harvest Bks. pap. $3.95

(Ed.) THE OPEN FORM: Essays for Our Time. *Harcourt* 1961 3rd ed. 1970 pap. $2.50. These essays by modern authors are linked by Kazin's perceptive notes.

CONTEMPORARIES. *Little-Atlantic* 1962 $10.00

BRIGHT BOOK OF LIFE: American Novelists and Storytellers from Hemingway to Mailer. *Little-Atlantic* 1973 $8.95

A WALKER IN THE CITY. 1951. *Harcourt* 1968 $4.95 Harvest Bks. pap. $1.95. Autobiographical memories and reflections.

STARTING OUT IN THE THIRTIES. *Little-Atlantic* 1965 $4.95 pap. 1967 $1.95

Sequel to "A Walker in the City." "Entertaining, perceptive and intellectual"—(*PW*).

FIEDLER, LESLIE A(ARON). 1917–

The critic Leslie Fiedler, says Saul Maloff in the *N.Y. Times*, has "a voice like that of no one else: swashbuckling, hectoring, raucous, calculatedly outrageous—and, at his best, brilliant, wonderfully suggestive, not in the way of most criticism but in the way of imaginative literature." Again: "Mr. Fiedler is a frustrating critic in the sense that he is more adept than most at stirring his readers to ready disagreement. [And] the Freudian limitations of his perspective are a source of annoyance. But he has drawn a steady critical bead upon the body of American literature and I, for one, find his central thesis a valid one"—(Bernard Murchland, *Commonweal*). His major work, "Love and Death in the American Novel," argues that American writing has been shaped by an inability to portray mature sexual relationships and by an underlying fear of death. He has published two novels, both o. p.: "the Second Stone" (1963) and "Back to China" (1965). His short stories have been collected under the title "The Nude Croquet" (*Stein & Day* 1969 $5.95). Reviewers have been lukewarm toward his fiction—Saul Maloff finds that in it "the 'voice' of the critic is so distinctive that it engulfs—or pierces and overcomes—any other sound he might make." Dr. Fiedler has taught at the University of Montana for over 20 years, as well as at Princeton, New York University, Columbia and the Universities of Rome and Bologna. He was an associate editor of *Ramparts*, 1959–65.

COLLECTED ESSAYS. *Stein & Day* 1971 2 vols. each $12.50

AN END TO INNOCENCE. *Beacon* 1955 pap. $1.95; *Stein & Day* pap. $2.95. Essays on culture and politics, some reprinted from *Commentary* and *Partisan Review*.

LOVE AND DEATH IN THE AMERICAN NOVEL. *Stein & Day* 1960 rev. ed. 1966 $12.50

"There is much with which a reader may disagree but not much that he is justified in brushing off"—(Granville Hicks).

NO! IN THUNDER: Essays on Myth and Literature. 1960. *Stein & Day* pap. $2.95

WAITING FOR THE END. *Stein & Day* 1964 $5.95 pap. $2.95

View of current American culture. "A justly bitter book that withholds neither his derisive intelligence nor his superior independence"—(*Book Week*).

THE RETURN OF THE VANISHING AMERICAN. *Stein & Day* $5.95 pap. $1.95. Here Mr. Fiedler explores the American "Western" from its classic form to the cowboy's descendent the hippie, with observations on regional influences on the American novel.

HYMAN, STANLEY EDGAR. 1919-1970.

Stanley Edgar Hyman was a prominent critic who worked as staff writer on the *New Yorker* and book reviewer for the *New Leader*. Eliot Fremont-Smith has said of him, "For slightly more than four years, from May, 1961, to June, 1965, Stanley Edgar Hyman wrote the best regular book-review column in the United States." Over half these *New Leader* reviews have been collected in his recent book, "Standards." In its afterword, Hyman summarized his "few persistent ideas" about art and life: "form, as the ordering of disorder, is a moral act; [and] all true humor is deeply tinged with melancholy." He claimed "a very bleak view of my moment and milieu, and in consequence an insistence that only accounts of inadequacy and alienation can be true or honest."

Hyman wrote studies of individual authors in the Minnesota Pamphlets on American Writers Series—"Nathanael West" (*Univ. of Minnesota Press* 1962 pap. $1.25) and "Flannery O'Connor" (1966, o. p.); and edited several collections of criticism as well as the works of his deceased wife (*q. v.*), "The Magic of Shirley Jackson" (*Farrar, Straus* 1966 $12.95).

THE PROMISED END: Essays and Reviews, 1942-1962. 1963 *Bks. for Libraries* $13.50. Provides a good sampling of his thought.

STANDARDS: A Chronicle of Books for Our Time. *Horizon* 1966 $6.75

IAGO: Some Approaches to the Illusion of His Motivation. *Atheneum* 1970 $5.95

HOWE, IRVING. 1920-

"Without doubt, Professor Howe is one of today's most cogent and caustic proponents of change within the democratic framework. It is not necessary to agree with all of his positions to recognize him as an extremely valuable intellectual and political gadfly"—(*LJ*). A "democratic socialist," editor of the radical journal *Dissent* and a regular contributor to the *New Republic*, Irving Howe is now a professor of English at Hunter College. He has also taught at Brandeis, Stanford and Princeton.

He first achieved notice as a literary critic in 1951, when the *N.Y. Times* said of his "Sherwood Anderson": "[Mr. Howe writes] with a quiet, patient, discerning, instructed power that makes his own book itself a literary event, and indicates the definite arrival upon the scene of a considerable critical talent." The following year he confirmed this impression with "William Faulkner: A Critical Study." Fortunately, his strong political commitments have not put blinders on his literary perception, and "once the reader learns to accept the contradiction between Mr. Howe, the literary critic, and Mr. Howe, the critic of ideas, he finds himself free to enjoy a really first-rate intelligence"—(*N.Y. Times*). Among the several works he has edited are "The Radical Papers: Essays in Democratic Socialism" (1966 *Peter Smith* $4.25), and, with Michael Harrington, "The Seventies: Problems and Proposals" (*Harper* 1972 $12.50 Colophon Bks. pap. $2.75) and "The Idea of the Modern in Literature and the Arts" (*Horizon* 1971 pap. $2.95).

SHERWOOD ANDERSON. 1951. *Stanford Univ. Press* 1966 $7.50 pap. $2.95

WILLIAM FAULKNER: A Critical Study. 1952. *Random* Vintage Bks. rev. ed. 1962 pap. $1.65

POLITICS AND THE NOVEL. 1957. *Bks. for Libraries* $11.25; *Avon Bks.* pap. $1.65. Essays on Stendhal, Dostoyevsky, Conrad, Malraux and others.

A WORLD MORE ATTRACTIVE: A View of Modern Literature and Politics. Essays, 1950-1963 $12.00

STEADY WORK: Essays in the Politics of Democratic Radicalism 1953-1966. *Harcourt* 1966 $6.95 pap. $2.45. On topics from Leon Trotsky to Vietnam and civil rights.

THOMAS HARDY. *Macmillan* 1967 $5.95 Collier Bks. pap. $2.95

THE DECLINE OF THE NEW: A Collection of Essays on Modern Writers and Their Books. *Harcourt* 1970 $7.50; *Horizon* pap. $3.95

THE CRITICAL POINT. *Horizon* 1974 $7.95. A collection of recent essays.

ROSS, LILLIAN. 1926–

During her years on the staff of the *New Yorker* (since 1948) Miss Ross "has handled . . . feature assignments in the tradition of cool, detached reporting perfected by Thurber, White, Maloney, Hellman, Behrman, McKelway, et al."—(*SR*). She has treated journalism as an art and has won a reputation for her ability to make the commonplace fascinating, keeping herself out of sight and capturing the minute details, mannerisms and tones of voice that bring an interview to life. In 1950 she gained fame (or notoriety) when two separate articles aroused uproars of indignation: her profile of Hemingway—which some declared unjust, though he himself called it "funny and good"—and her lengthy piece, published in book form as "Picture" (o. p.), on the production of John Huston's "Red Badge of Courage," which did not please all concerned in Hollywood. Both are included in "Reporting."

For the *New Yorker* Miss Ross writes profiles and contributes to "Reporter at Large" and "Talk of the Town."

PORTRAIT OF HEMINGWAY. *Simon & Schuster* 1961 $2.50

REPORTING. *Simon & Schuster* 1964 $6.50 pap. $3.45

TALK STORIES. *Simon & Schuster* 1966 $5.95. 60 selections from the *New Yorker's* "Talk of the Town"—on people in government and on other timely topics.

REPORTING, 2. *Simon & Schuster* 1969 $5.95 pap. $3.45

STEINER, GEORGE. 1929–

"Literary criticism should arise out of a debt of love. . . . We are not the same when we put down [a] work as we were when we took it up. . . . Great works of art pass through us like storm-winds, flinging open the doors of perception, pressing upon the architecture of our beliefs with their transforming powers." The task of criticism is to persuade others to "lay themselves open" to "the quality and force of our experience." On this exhilarating note begins "Tolstoy or Dostoevsky: Essays in the Old [that is, appreciative, positive] Criticism" by George Steiner, whose learning in many literatures is surpassed only by his ability to make them relate to each other and to their times. Eliot Fremont-Smith wrote in the *N.Y. Times* that " 'Language and Silence' will confirm, if confirmation is necessary, his reputation as one of the most erudite, resourceful and unrelentingly serious critics writing today."

Mr. Steiner belongs to no critical "school"—deliberately not—nor is his writing ever "academic" in the dead sense. He is seeking, he says, a "philosophy of language" which can help rescue us from the cheapening torrent of words with which we are assaulted by Marshall McLuhan's (*q. v.*) "media" and from diminution of intellectual, political and humane values which threaten us with the silence of total ruin. It is a "bestial" age, in which "We know now that a man can read Goethe or Rilke in the evening . . . and go to his work at Auschwitz in the morning. To say that he has read them without understanding or that his ear is gross, is cant." "Mr. Steiner's concerns are not to be brushed off," says Eliot Fremont-Smith, ". . . Cassandra wasn't wrong."

Son of a Jewish father who left Vienna in 1924, Mr. Steiner was brought up in France and came to the United States in 1940. After a period as a Rhodes Scholar at Oxford, he worked for the London *Economist*. At an early age he was a member of the Institute for Advanced Studies at Princeton, where he wrote most of his first two books, both of which have been translated into many languages. He has taught at a number of American universities and in 1967 was Schweitzer Visiting Professor at New York University. He lives in England, where he is Director of English Studies at Churchill College, Cambridge. "Anno Domini" (*Atheneum* 1964 $3.95)—three long stories—is his only venture into fiction. He has contributed to many periodicals here and abroad.

TOLSTOY OR DOSTOEVSKY: An Essay in the Old Criticism. *Knopf* 1959 $8.95; *Dutton* 1971 pap. $2.25

THE DEATH OF TRAGEDY. *Knopf* 1961 $5.95; *Hill & Wang* Dramabks. 1963 pap. $3.25

LANGUAGE AND SILENCE: Essays on Language, Literature, and the Inhuman. *Atheneum* 1967 $8.00 pap. $3.95

IN BLUEBEARD'S CASTLE: Some Notes toward the Redefinition of Culture. *Yale Univ. Press* 1971 $6.50 pap. $1.95

EXTRATERRITORIAL: Papers on Literature and the Language Revolution. *Atheneum* 1971 $7.95

WILSON, COLIN. 1932–

Colin Wilson is the self-educated son of a shoe factory worker. He became well known in England and the United States following the publication of his first book, "The Outsider," which placed him among England's Angry Young Men, although he has strongly denied membership. Wilson's Outsider philosophy begins with the rejection of humanism and rationalism and tries to develop a deeply subjective religious existentialism. The Outsider stands for truth, while the "insider" builds his life upon illusions which keep out the truth. These views are expounded further in "Religion and the Rebel" (1957, o. p.), the "other half" of "The Outsider," which is also partly autobiographical, and in "Stature of Man." In "The Origins of the Sexual Impulse" (1963, o. p.) Wilson presents his views on psychology. "Voyage to a Beginning" (1966, o. p.) is his autobiography.

THE OUTSIDER. 1956. *Dell* Delta Bks. 1967 pap. $1.95

STATURE OF MAN. 1959 *Greenwood* $8.25

THE STRENGTH TO DREAM: Literature and the Imagination. 1962. *Greenwood* 1973 $12.25

RASPUTIN AND THE FALL OF THE ROMANOVS. 1964. *Citadel Press* 1967 pap. $2.45

The mad Russian monk presented as an authentic "outsider." "A beguiling portrait even if it has no relation to historical fact"—(*N.Y. Times*).

BEYOND THE OUTSIDER. *Houghton* 1965 $4.95

BERNARD SHAW: A Reassessment. *Atheneum* 1969 $6.95

See also Chapter 12, Modern British Fiction.

SONTAG, SUSAN. 1933–

Miss Sontag, who has a Harvard Ph.D. in Philosophy, is "the most fluent, and well known, of a small group of liaison critics who travel between the new art world and the intellectual community at large"—(*Commonweal*). Proclaiming a "new sensibility," she supports the cause of pop art and "underground" films. Her reputation as a formidable critic has been established by her numerous reviews, essays and articles (she has also published short stories) appearing in the *N.Y. Review of Books, Book Week*, the *N.Y. Times* and *Harper's*, among others. "Against Interpretation" includes her controversial essay "Notes on Camp," first published in *Partisan Review*. The title of the book introduces her argument against what she sees as the distortion of an original work by the countless critics who bend it to their own interpretations. "The aim of all commentary on art," she writes, "should be to make works of art—and, by analogy, our own experience—more, rather than less, real to us. The function of criticism should be to show *how it is what it is*, even *that it is what it is*, rather than to show *what it means*." Of "Death Kit," whose hero is a businessman called "Diddy" trying to come to terms with death, Granville Hicks said (in *SR*), "What is now clear is that Miss Sontag is a writer of great talent, so gifted that one is compelled to struggle with her obscurities and ambiguities and [mannerisms]. . . . She has her peculiar feeling for life and especially death, and she has created her own way of expressing it." Miss Sontag has lectured extensively around the United States and has taught philosophy at Harvard, Sarah Lawrence and Columbia. She has appeared frequently on television discussion sessions, where her fresh and youthful appearance belies her learning.

THE BENEFACTOR. *Farrar, Straus.* 1963 $4.50; *Avon Bks.* pap. $1.45

"A difficult but interesting first novel"—(*Commonweal*).

AGAINST INTERPRETATION AND OTHER ESSAYS. *Farrar, Straus* 1966 $6.95; *Dell* 1967 pap. $1.95. A selection of critical writings, 1961–65, on modern novels, films and theater. A runner-up for the 1967 National Book Award.

DEATH KIT. *Farrar, Straus* 1967 $5.95; *New Am. Lib.* Plume Bk. pap. $2.95 Signet pap. $.95. A novel.

STYLES OF RADICAL WILL. *Farrar, Straus* 1969 $5.95; *Dell* Delta Bks. pap. $2.45

BROTHER CARL. *Farrar, Straus* 1974 $6.95 pap. $2.95

—W.S.S.

Chapter 16

Literary Biography and
Autobiography

> *"Things have not happened to me: on the contrary it is I who have happened to them; and all my happenings have taken the form of books and plays. Read them, or spectate them; and you have my whole story: the rest is only breakfast, lunch, dinner, sleeping, wakening, and washing, my routine being just the same as everybody's routine."*
> —BERNARD SHAW

The quotation above illustrates the problems inherent in a specialized, yet flourishing, branch of biography: the writing of the lives of men and women who were themselves writers. All the principles and practices of biography and autobiography apply to those who are writers by trade or habit; nevertheless a "life" of a writer must necessarily emphasize that which differentiates the writer from those whose achievement lay in other directions. And the autobiography of a writer in a larger sense is the body of his writing. All his work is confession—least of all, in some cases, his autobiography itself.

Despite the likelihood that the life of writing has left a larger documentary record than other lives, the problems of writing about writers are not any less, and the biographer must have a greater literary sensitivity to apply to his material. His other obligations remain. Even if he is overwhelmed by tons of documents and miles of tape-recorded interviews, he has at best only a small fraction of the facts. He has what his subject wanted to survive him, what the selective memories of his contemporaries revealed, and what accidentally or deliberately survived the wastebasket and the grave. From his material the literary biographer must not only attempt to evoke the truth of a life and suggest the essence of a personality but reveal the creative process, with its impact upon the writer and its impact upon the writer's world.

Biography and autobiography can certainly possess high literary quality without being "literary" biography. Many of the great contributions to biographical—and even autobiographical—literature do not have writers as their subjects. These appear elsewhere in *"The Reader's Adviser"* under "General Biography." For biographical reference works in the field of authorship generally, the reader is referred to Chapter 3, Reference Books—Literature: Histories and Dictionaires of Literature.

GENERAL WORKS ON LITERARY BIOGRAPHY

Altick, Richard D. LIVES AND LETTERS: A History of Literary Biography in England and America. *Knopf* 1965 $10.00.

> "Mr. Altick gives attention to theories of biographical writing and has much to say on general trends, fashions, and the changing attitudes toward 'the limits of biographical candor.' But his interest is in one special field: the writing of biographies of writers.... It will certainly be ... the standard work on the subject"— (*LJ*).

BIOGRAPHY INDEX. *See Chapter 3, Reference Books—Literature: Basic Indexes for Literature.*

Bowen, Catherine Drinker. BIOGRAPHY: The Craft and the Calling. *Little-Atlantic* 1969 $5.95. "Mrs. Bowen draws on her own techniques to provide a handbook of biographical practice."

Edel, Leon. LITERARY BIOGRAPHY. 1957, 1959. *Indiana Univ. Press* repr. of 1959 ed. 1973 $5.95 Midland Books pap. $1.95. Mr. Edel draws on his own experience, particularly in his earlier Henry James biographies, for the Alexander Lectures at the University of Toronto in 1956.

Kendall, Paul Murray. THE ART OF BIOGRAPHY. *Norton* 1965 pap. $1.45

"The book is not a full-scale history, but rather a comparison of the types and eras of biographical writings—the biography of recollection as opposed to that of research, the comprehensive multi-volume work, the interpretive biography, and that of double simulation—the simulation of a life in words and a simulated life-relationship between subject and author"—(*LJ*).

Shaw, Thomas Shuler, Comp. INDEX TO PROFILE SKETCHES IN THE NEW YORKER MAGAZINE, 1925–1970. *Faxon* 1946 2nd rev. ed. 1972 $10.00

Weintraub, Stanley. BIOGRAPHY AND TRUTH. The Bobbs-Merrill Series in Composition and Rhetoric. *Bobbs* 1967 pap. $1.00. Mr. Weintraub extracts both problems and solutions in learning, and writing, the truth about a life from contemporary and classic biographers, with an emphasis on literary biography.

BIOGRAPHIES IN SERIES

All of the series noted provide within a limited space literary appraisals as well as biographical information and bibliographies; thus the biographical data is often sketchy. Each series is uneven in quality, with the *Twayne* series the most unpredictable in quality although at the same time the most biographically informative. *Consult publishers' catalogs for individual titles.*

British Book Council—WRITERS AND THEIR WORK. Dist. by British Bk. Centre. Ed. by Bonamy Dobree and Geoffrey Bullough. 226 monographs on English-language authors. permabound each $2.38 unbound each $1.20. An ongoing series begun in 1950, each monograph has a biocritical essay and bibliography.

Bucknell University Press—IRISH WRITERS SERIES. 1971 to date, with 25 pamphlets projected pap. each $1.95

Columbia—COLUMBIA ESSAYS ON MODERN WRITERS. 64 pamphlets pap. each $1.00

Twayne—TWAYNE'S UNITED STATES AUTHORS SERIES. 216 vols. Vols. 1–200 each $4.95. Vols. 201–216 each $5.50.

TWAYNE'S ENGLISH AUTHORS SERIES. 150 vols. Vols. 1–135 each $4.95. Vols. 136–150 each $5.50.

TWAYNE'S WORLD AUTHORS SERIES. 239 vols. various prices. $5.50–$6.50.

Most of the hardbacks are eventually reprinted in paper by *College & University Press* at $2.45.

Univ. of Minnesota Press—UNIVERSITY OF MINNESOTA PAMPHLETS ON AMERICAN WRITERS. Ed. by William Van O'Connor, Allen Tate, Robert Penn Warren and Leonard Unger. A series of pamphlets which provide critical appraisals, biographical information, and bibliographies. 1959 to date. 103 pamphlets pap. each $1.25.

See also Chapter 3, Reference Books—Literature: Histories and Dictionaires of Literature.

"Classic" and Modern Autobiographers and Journal-Writers

EVELYN, JOHN. 1620–1706.

As the diary of a devout and honorable gentleman of scholarly attainment and exemplary character, Evelyn's diary is in sharp contrast to that of his friend and contemporary Pepys. Evelyn was far more self-righteous and less likable than Pepys. His journals cover the eras of the Civil War, the Commonwealth and the reign of Charles II, a period of 56 years. It has been Evelyn's misfortune always to be thought of with Pepys, writes D. W. Brogan in the *N.Y. Times*, when the real parallel is "not with Pepys but with such French contemporaries as Madame de Sévigné and the Duc de Saint-Simon. . . . Except that they were friends, both Fellows of the Royal Society, contemporary witnesses, Evelyn and Pepys are not really to be linked together. This scholarly country gentleman, so much more a high Anglican than a passionate royalist, is very different from Pepys, the climbing bureaucrat of bourgeois Dissenting origin who had to swim for his life in the turbulent seas of the Restoration. So readers of this magnificent (and highly readable) edition [by E. S. de Beer] must begin by not expecting the same kind of entertainment they get from Pepys."

THE DIARY OF JOHN EVELYN. Now first printed in full from the manuscript belonging to John Evelyn and edited by E. S. de Beer. *Oxford* 1955 6 vols. set $83.00

THE DIARY OF JOHN EVELYN. Ed. by E. S. de Beer. Selections from the 6-volume set (*above*) including his accounts of the social, religious, and cultural events of the 17th century. *Oxford* 1959 $8.50

DIARY. Ed. by William Bray. 1818–19. *Dutton* Everyman's 2 vols. each $3.50

PEPYS, SAMUEL. 1633–1703.

Pepys' candid and endlessly entertaining anecdotal diary was written in cipher and remained unreadable for over a century after his death. Lord Grenville is credited with discovery of the key to the cipher. He gave the key to the Reverend John Smith, then a college undergraduate, who took three years to transcribe the manuscript. The Smith transcription was edited by Lord Braybrooke and first published in 1825. Braybrooke regarded the Diary of value only as a record of public events and expurgated the personal material as much as was possible. The Braybrooke text, therefore, is not complete. A less abridged edition by the Reverend Mynors Bright appeared in 1875–79 (6 vols., o.p.). The first purportedly complete and unabridged edition was that by Henry B. Wheatley, based on Bright's transcription and first published in ten volumes in the Bohn Library, 1893–1905, the ninth volume being Pepysiana. This edition was reissued as a subscription edition in 18 volumes, again on India paper in three volumes by *Harcourt* (o.p.) and was eventually published in two volumes by *Random House* (*see below*), but without the Braybrooke notes.

Pepys was not a man of letters. He served 28 years in the Admiralty Department after the Restoration of the Stuarts in 1660. He was twice Secretary of the Admiralty and the foremost authority on naval matters in his time. He portrays himself candidly in his Diary as a "man of wide interests and varied affairs: an inveterate playgoer and a minor patron of the arts, a conscientious husband and householder, a responsible public official, and a friend (sometimes a self-acknowledged flatterer) of the great and powerful." His personal foibles and amorous adventures (in spite of his "conscientious" status as husband) have lent his journals a fascination that appears to be perennial.

The Diary covers only nine and a half years and was discontinued because of failing eyesight. Pepys' later life has been studied by J. R. Tanner in his edition of "The Private Correspondence of Samuel Pepys, 1697–1703" (1926, o.p.), "Further Correspondence of Samuel Pepys, 1662–1679" (1928, o.p.), and "Mr. Pepys: An Introduction to His Diary with a Sketch of His Later Life" (1924, *Greenwood* $13.00). Pepys' second diary, a journal of a trip to Tangier, 1683–84. is contained in "The Letters and Second Diary of Samuel Pepys" (ed. by R. E. Haworth 1933, o.p.). Two more diaries, dealing with the period of the so-called Popish plot, were discovered in 1935 at Magdalene College, Cambridge, by Arthur Bryant and Francis Turner.

DIARY, 1660–1669. Ed. by Robert Latham and William Matthews. 11 vols. projected. *Univ. of California Press* Vols. 1–3, 1660–1662 (1970) set $28.50 Vols. 4–5, 1663–1664 (1971) set $20.00 Vols. 6–7, 1665–1666 (1973) set $25.00. Vols. 1–8 each represent the unabridged and unexpurgated diary of one year, while Vol. 9 will extend from January 1668 through May 1669. The final volumes will be a companion (commentary) and an index to the previous volumes (each of which has its own index). This is the definitive edition, scrupulous in its textual readings and unexpurgated. Earlier editions include the following, each under the same title of DIARY, 1660–1669. Ed. by Lord Braybrooke 1825 *Dutton* Everyman's 3 vols. each $3.50;

transcribed by Mynors Bright from the shorthand ms. in the Pepysian Library, Magdalene College, Cambridge, and ed. with additions by Henry B. Wheatley complete and unabridged *Random* 1946 2 vols. boxed $15.00; ed. by Wheatley and transcribed by Bright *AMS Press* repr. of the 1893–1899 ed. 10 vols. each $22.75 set $225.00 with the notes of Lord Braybrooke (not in the *Random* ed).

EVERYBODY'S PEPYS. The Wheatley text abridged. Ed. by O. F. Morshead; ill. by E. H. Shepard. 1926. *British Bk. Centre* $6.75

THE DIARY: Selections. Ed. by O. F. Morshead *Peter Smith* 1960 $5.50

THE LETTERS OF SAMUEL PEPYS AND HIS FAMILY CIRCLE. Ed. by H. T. Heath. *Oxford* 1955 $7.75

CHARLES II'S ESCAPE FROM WORCESTER: A Collection of Narratives Assembled by Samuel Pepys. Ed. by William Matthews. *Univ. of California Press* 1966 $5.75. First-hand accounts of King Charles II's flight to France in October, 1651, now collected in a single volume in their entirety, some in print for the first time.

MEMOIRS OF THE ROYAL NAVY. 1906. *Haskell* 1969 $9.95

Books about Pepys

Pepys and Shakespeare. By Sidney Lee. 1906. *Folcroft* $4.50
Pepys on the Restoration Stage. Ed. by Helen McAfee. 1916. *Blom* $10.75
Samuel Pepys and the Royal Navy. By Joseph R. Tanner. 1920. *Haskell* 1971 $7.95
The Soul of Samuel Pepys. By Gamaliel Bradford. 1924. *Kennikat* 1969 $10.00
Samuel Pepys. By Arthur Ponsonby. 1928. *Bks. for Libraries* $9.00; *Kennikat* $7.75
Mister Pepys and Mr. Evelyn. By Clara Marburg. 1935 *Folcroft* $12.50
Samuel Pepys in the Diary. By Percival Hunt. *Univ. of Pittsburgh Press* 1958 pap. $1.95
Samuel Pepys. By Ivan E. Taylor. English Authors Ser. *Twayne* 1967 $5.50
Samuel Pepys, Esq. By Richard Barber. *Univ. of California Press* 1970 $4.95

MONTAGU, LADY MARY WORTLEY. 1689–1762.

Lady Mary, one of the first of independent Western women, was noted in the 18th century as a wit, as a poet and for her sparkling letters. Misunderstood in her own time and later, she quarreled with her friends Pope and Swift and was bitterly attacked by them. She finally left her husband and country to live in Italy (1739–61) and from there wrote letters to her daughter, the Countess of Bute. She continued, however, to write to her husband, and they apparently remained on friendly, if only epistolary, terms. Halsband's scholarly and definitive biography (*see below*) contains a series of hitherto unpublished love letters from her to Count Algarotti, the eminent Italian man of letters and friend of Voltaire. Of "The Complete Letters, Vol. 3" (*see below*), *SR* said: "It is exemplary in every respect: the text has been meticulously prepared, the notes are helpful yet tactfully concise, the index and supplementary apparatus most useful."

THE COMPLETE LETTERS. Ed. by Robert Halsband. 3 vols. *Oxford* 1965–67 Vol. I 1708–20 $17.00 Vol. 2 1721–51 $17.50 Vol. 3 1752–62 $13.45

LETTERS AND WORKS. Ed. by Lord Wharncliffe. 1861. 3rd ed. with additions and a New Memoir by W. M. Thomas. *AMS Press* 2 vols. set $25.00

SELECTED LETTERS. Ed. by Robert Halsband. *St. Martin's* 1971 $15.00

LETTERS FROM THE LEVANT: During the Embassy to Constantinople, 1716–18. 1838. *Arno* 1970 $14.50

Books about Montagu

The Life of Lady Mary Wortley Montagu. By Robert Halsband. *Oxford* 1956 $10.25 Galaxy Bks. pap. $2.95

This is the first completely documented biography, written in a delightful prose, after years of careful and intelligent research. "From it Lady Mary emerges as a credible human being . . . The Algarotti story, and a later imbroglio with another Italian swindler, Count Palazzi, are told here for the first time"—(*N.Y. Times*).

CHESTERFIELD, (PHILIP DORMER STANHOPE) 4th Earl of. 1694–1773.

An English statesman, celebrated wit and conversationalist, Lord Chesterfield achieved lasting fame through his letters to his natural son and to his adopted godson. The brilliant "Letters to His Son," first published by his widow in 1774, were written to acquaint the boy with, and encourage him to acquire, the manners and standards of a man of the world. They are "shrewd and exquisitely phrased observations, witty, elegant, cynical." The similar "Letters to His Godson," of which 236 are extant, were not published until 1890. Chesterfield was an intimate of Pope and Swift and corresponded with Voltaire. As the patron of Samuel Johnson, he provoked Johnson's famous letter of rebuke after his belated praise of Johnson's "Dictionary" (1755), which he had ignored in prospectus since 1747.

LETTERS. Ed. by Bonamy Dobrée. 6 vols. 1932 *AMS Press* each $27.50 set $127.50

LETTERS TO HIS SON. 1774. *Dutton* Everyman's $3.50 pap. $1.75

Books about Chesterfield

Lord Chesterfield and His World. By Samuel Shellabarger. 1941. *Biblo & Tannen* 1971 $13.50

ROUSSEAU, JEAN JACQUES. *See entry under Lester Crocker in A Selected List of "Literary" Biographies, below.*

WALPOLE, HORACE, 4th Earl of Orford. 1717–1797.

Walpole's charming, vivacious and often brilliant letters (7000 extant letters written and received) are "a monument to his writing skill as well as an invaluable picture of Georgian England." He always professed to be an amateur in literary affairs, as he amused himself with printing on his private printing press at his Strawberry Hill estate, where he printed many of the first editions of his own works and Thomas Gray's (*q.v.*) "Odes." "The Castle of Otranto" (1764. *Collier* 1963 pap. $.65; [with Anne Radcliffe's "Mysteries of Udolpho" and Jane Austen's "Northanger Abbey"] ed. by A. Wright *Holt* [Rinehart] 1963 pap. $3.00; ed. by Wilmarth S. Lewis *Oxford* 1964 $4.25 pap. $1.75; [with W. Beckford's "Vathek" and J. Polidori's "Vampyre" in "Three Gothic Novels"] ed. by E. F. Bleiler *Dover* pap. $2.50; *Peter Smith* $4.50) was an important "Gothic" novel and an ancestor of the modern detective story. The Persian and Indian tales (published in Venice in 1557) that inspired this novel are now available in a translation by Augusto and Theresa Borselli entitled "Serendipity and the Three Princes: From the Peregrinaggio of 1557" (ed. by Theodore G. Remer *Univ. of Oklahoma Press* 1965 $6.95). Mr. Remer became interested in them through his interest in Walpole. The first English translation (1722) was incomplete.

Wilmarth Sheldon Lewis, a remarkably dedicated—and independently wealthy—scholar, who has kept the *Yale* Walpole project going since its start in 1933, has told his own story in an autobiography, "One Man's Education" (*Knopf* 1967 $10.00), which is "an engaging book of reminiscences"—(*LJ*). Lewis's "Collector's Progress" (1951 o.p.), is an account of his "lifelong enthusiasm for collecting which finally focused on Horace Walpole and saw its fruition in his justly famous Walpole collection"—(*LJ*).

THE YALE EDITION OF HORACE WALPOLE'S CORRESPONDENCE. Ed. by Wilmarth Sheldon Lewis and others. *Yale Univ. Press* 1937—. 37 vols. (of a projected 50) each $20.00 except vols. 13–14, sold as a set $40.00. Vols. 1–2, Correspondence with The Rev. William Cole (1937) Vol. 3, Correspondence with Madame Du Deffand and Wiart (1939) Vol. 4, Correspondence with Madame Du Deffand (1939) Vol. 5, Correspondence with Madame Du Deffand and Mademoiselle Sanadon (1939) Vol. 6, Correspondence with Madame Du Duffand and Wiart (1939) Vol. 7, Correspondence with Madame Du Duffand and Wiart (1939) Vol. 8, Correspondence with Madame Du Duffand (1939) Vols. 9–10, Correspondence with George Montagu (1941) Vol. 11, Correspondence with Mary and Agnes Berry and Barbara Cecilia Seton (1944) Vol. 12, Correspondence with Mary and Agnes Berry (1944) Vols. 13–14, Correspondence with Thomas Gray, Richard West, and Thomas Ashton (Vol. 13); with Thomas Gray (Vol. 14); Vol. 15, Correspondence with Sir David Dalrymple, Conyers Middleton, Daniel Lysons, William Robertson, William Rosco, William Belou, the Earl of Buchan, Samuel Lysons, Robert Henry, James Edwards and Robert Nares (1951) Vol. 16, Correspondence with Thomas Chatterton, Michael Lort, John Pinkerton, John Fenn and Mrs. Fenn, William Bewley, Nathaniel Hillier and Henry Zouch (1951) Vols. 17–27, Correspondence with Sir Horace Mann (1954–71). The index is in Vol. 26. Vols. 28–29, Correspondence with William Mason (1955) Vol. 30, Correspondence with George Selwyn, Lord Lincoln, Sir Charles Handbury Williams, Henry Fox and Richard Edgcumbe (1961) Vol. 31, Correspondence with Hannah More, Lady Browne, Lady Mary Coke, Lady Hervey, Mary Hamilton (Mrs. John Dickinson), Lady George Lennox, Anne Pitt and Lady Suffolk (1961) Vols. 32–34, Correspondence with the Countess of Upper Ossory (1965) Vol. 35, Correspondence with John Chute, Richard Bentley, the Earl of Stafford, Sir William Hamilton, the Earl and Countess Harcourt, Geroge Hardinge (1973) Vol. 36, Correspondence with the Walpole Family (1973)

"In many ways the Walpole edition has become a model of editing procedure, often imitated, and constantly used as a standard by which to measure the effectiveness of other projects"—(*SR*). "One of the most notable literary projects of all time"—(*N.Y. Times*). "It has become the encyclopedia of the 18th century"— W. S. Lewis).

LETTERS. Ed. by W. Hadley. *Dutton* Eveyman's 1959 $3.50

SELECTED LETTERS. Ed. by Wilmarth Sheldon Lewis. *Yale Univ. Press* 1973 $12.50 pap. $3.95

AN HONEST DIPLOMAT AT THE HAGUE: The Private Letters of Horatio Walpole, 1715–1716. Ed. by John J. Murray. 1955 *Bks. for Libraries* $16.00

MEMOIRS OF THE REIGN OF KING GEORGE THE SECOND. Ed. from the original mss. by Lord Holland. 2nd ed. 1846. *AMS Press* 3 vols. each $22.50; set $65.00

LAST JOURNALS. Ed. by A. Francis Stuart. 1910. *AMS Press* 2 vols. $32.50

MEMOIRS OF THE REIGN OF KING GEORGE THE THIRD. First published by Sir Denis Le Marchant, and now reedited by G. F. Russell Barker. 1894. *AMS Press* 4 vols. each $22.50, set $90.00; *Bks. for Libraries* set $66.50

Books about Walpole

Sir Robert Walpole. By J. H. Plumb. 2 vols. 1956, 1961. *Kelley* $30.00
Horace Walpole's Memoirs. By Gerrit Parmele Judd. 1959. *College & Univ. Press* 1962 pap. $1.25
Horace Walpole. By Wilmarth Sheldon Lewis. Bollingen Ser. *Princeton Univ. Press* 1961 $10.00. The facts of his life plus many anecdotes distilled from 35 years of scholarly enthusiasm by the editor of the famous Yale edition of Walpole's correspondence.
Horace Walpole: A Biography. By R. W. Ketton-Cremer. *Cornell Univ. Press* 3rd ed. 1966 $8.50
  "[The author] has tried to rescue Walpole from a reputation for malice, affectation and triviality, a tone set by Macaulay, and to show [him] as a 'kindlier, wiser, more consistent and straightforward man' "—(*LJ*). A "delightful, admirable biography"—(*South Atlantic Quarterly*).
Horace Walpole, Writer, Politician, and Connoisseur: Essays on the 250th Anniversary of Walpole's Birth. Ed. by Warren Hunting Smith and dedicated to Wilmarth S. Lewis. *Yale Univ. Press* 1967 $15.00. 19 essays by Walpolian scholars throughout the world. Scholarly in its appeal but important for the first-published material it contains.

CASANOVA (or CASANOVA de SEINGALT: Giovanni Jacopo [or Giacomo] Casanova de Seingalt). 1725–1798.

Casanova's "Memoirs," written in French, create an absorbing portrait of an 18th-century Italian—a shallow, amoral and vital man, whose private life, as he records it, was a succession of amorous adventures. His public life, also not without intrigue, was spent in the service of police, kings, and Popes. At his death, Casanova was a 73-year-old librarian for Count Waldstein in Bohemia.

Of the 4000-page *Harcourt* edition of his memoirs, now underway, Robert J. Clements wrote (in the *Saturday Review*—he was its European correspondent and vice-president of the International Association for the Study of Italian Language and Literature): "At the rate of one liaison every score of pages or so, this would promise about 100 to be recorded. What drove Giacomo on? . . . Perhaps the simplest explanation is that Casanova was in love with love. . . . He was fortunate to find women seriatim with whom he believed himself in love and achieving . . . perfect accord. [These darted] like guppies (Dr. Kinsey's metaphor) into Casanova's silken net. Granted his charisma, and even his stamina, Casanova's vaunted seductions strain our belief. Are we reading fiction, a novel for which Giacomo could find no better hero than himself? . . . Our skepticism is reinforced by the coincidence that eighteenth-century fiction so often took the form of first-person picaresque novels. . . . [But] one harbors a grudging admiration for a beloved rogue who created such happiness for so many women. It was all done with taste and a flair. . . . With a touch of envy we share the life of this boudoir sportsman who is welcomed by lofty noblemen and prelates, and in Voltaire's phrase gorges on 'the whipped cream of Europe.' " Casanova published in his lifetime some 24 verifiable works, from pamphlets to a five-volume literary romance, none of which had the enduring quality of his memoirs.

The "Memoirs" have an interesting bibliographical history. The original manuscript is owned by the *Brockhaus Company* in Wiesbaden, who bought it in 1820 from Carlo Angiolini, Casanova's grand-nephew. The first edition in 12 volumes (an expurgated edition) was published in Germany by *Brockhaus* from 1822 to 1828, according to the *N.Y. Times*. "The English translation by Machen (1794, o.p.) first appeared in London in 1894 in 12 volumes. It was based on the Laforgue edition in French of 1826 generally considered the most satisfactory and complete and the one on which most [editions in English until the Trask translation] have been based. The London 1894 edition was reprinted in the U.S. in 1920. It came out again in New York in 1925 under the Aventuros imprint with the addition of [an Arthur] Symons introduction. This reappeared, privately printed, in 1930 with the 12 volumes in six"—(*LJ*). The *Putnam* hardcover edition of Machen's translation (6 vols. 1959–61, o.p.) is reproduced by *Dover* in three volumes. Scholars now agree that the edition prepared by Jean Laforgue (from which Machen translated) is somewhat "truncated, bowdlerized and embellished"—(*LJ*). *Brockhaus*, in collaboration with *Plon* of Paris, therefore published the original, unexpurgated manuscript in Europe, 1960–62, from which Willard Trask has made his translation. *Harcourt* has published the original twelve volumes in six double volumes translated by Trask. For his translation of Volumes 1 and 2, Willard Trask received the 1967 National Book Award, "in recognition of the lucidity, tact and *joie de vivre* with which he has rendered into contemporary English the first two volumes of the 'History of My Life.' While remaining loyal to both the tempo and spirit of the original French, Mr. Trask has written a version in an English fully contemporary yet remarkably Italian in sensibility. With admirable restraint and refinement, he has conveyed the zest and sensuous delight of the original." The complicated story of the first posthumous publication of the work and subsequent editions in German, French, English and other languages is told in Mr. Trask's introduction to Volumes I and 2.

MEMOIRS. Ed. by Leonard L. Levinson. *Macmillan* Collier Bks. pap. $.95

GIACOMO CASANOVA: History of My Life. Trans. with introd. by Willard Trask (*see note above*). *Harcourt* 12 vols. Vols. 1–2 (from the Italian) (1966) 2 vols. in 1 boxed Vols. 3–4 (from the French) (1967) Vols. 5–6 in 1 vol. (1966) Vols. 7–8 in 1 vol. (1969) Vols. 9–10 in 1 vol. (1970) Vols. 11–12 in 1 vol. (with index) (1971) each $10.00

Books about Casanova

Casanova, An Appreciation. By Havelock Ellis. *Branden* $3.00

Classic Literary Autobiographers: A Selection

BOSWELL, JAMES. 1740–1795. *See section on Literary Biography for his "Private Papers."*

ADAMS, HENRY (BROOKS). 1838–1918.

"The Education of Henry Adams" might be called the story of an education and the recovery from it, although the writer felt that he never recovered! The reader should contrast the earlier work, "Mont-Saint-Michel and Chartres" (1904 1913, *Gordon Press* $7.95; with an introd. by R. A. Cram *Houghton* 1936 Sentry Eds. pap. $2.65; *Doubleday* Anchor Bks. 1959 pap. $1.95), a study of 13th-century unity, with the "Education," a study of 20th-century multiplicity. It is the multiplicity of modern life, says Adams, that makes education so destructive. (The reader can only conclude that the material *he* was made of was too good to spoil.) Beautifully written, original in conception, these two books are generally considered his masterpieces.

Two volumes of letters are out of print: "Letters of Henry Adams, 1892–1918," edited by W. C. Ford (1938); and the excellent "Selected Letters" (ed. with introd. by Newton Arvin, 1951).

Henry Adams wrote two novels, "Esther" (1884 o.p.), and the earlier cutting satire on the U.S. government, "Democracy: An American Novel" (1880, *Assoc. Booksellers* Airmont Bks. $.60). In 1905 President Theodore Roosevelt called "Democracy" "that novel which made a great furor among the educated incompetents and the pessimists generally. . . . It had a superficial and rotten cleverness, but it was essentially false, essentially mean and base, and it is amusing to read it now and see how completely events have given it the lie." "Memoirs of Arii Taimai e Marama of Eimeo, Teriirere of Tooarai, Teriinui of Tahiti, Tauraatua i Amo" (1901, *Gregg Press* $20.00) is Adams' account of the native history of Tahiti as related to him by Arii Taimai and her daughter Marau Taaroa during his visit to the South Seas in 1890–91.

THE EDUCATION OF HENRY ADAMS: An Autobiography. Privately printed 1907. *Houghton* 1918 popular ed. 1927 new ed. 1935 $6.95 Sentry Eds. pap. $3.95; ed. by Ernest Samuels 1973 $10.00 Riv. Eds. pap. $4.95; *Modern Library* $2.95; (and Other Selected Writings) ed. by Edward N. Savath *Twayne* 1964 $6.50

LETTERS OF HENRY ADAMS, 1858–1891. Ed. by Worthington C. Ford. 2 vols. 1930, 1938 *Kraus* $49.50

A CYCLE OF ADAMS LETTERS, 1861–1865. Ed. by Worthington Chauncey Ford. 1920. *Kraus* 2 vols. in 1 $25.00. A collection of letters between Henry and his family.

HENRY ADAMS AND HIS FRIENDS: A Collection of His Unpublished Papers. Ed. by Harold D. Cater. 1938. *Octagon* 1967; 1970 $25.00. A collection of 650 unpublished letters to many different people, edited with a biographical and interpretative introduction by Harold Dean Cater.

Books about Adams

Henry Adams. By Ernest Samuels. *Harvard Univ. Press* Vol. 1 Young Henry Adams (1948) $10.00 Vol. 2 The Middle Years (1958) $12.00 Vol. 3 The Major Phase (1964) $15.00
Henry Adams: A Biography. By Elizabeth Stevenson. 1955. *Macmillan* Collier Bks. pap. $1.50
   "The fullest, finest account yet written of one of the fullest finest Americans"—(Paul Engle). It received the Bancroft Prize in 1956.

GIDE, ANDRÉ (PAUL GUILLAUME). 1869–1951. (Nobel Prize 1947)

Gide was awarded the Nobel Prize in 1947 for the "extensive and artistically important authorship in which he exposed the problems and conditions of mankind." In that year, too, the first volume of his "Journals" was published in English. "Always honest, incisive and stimulating, they are nevertheless organically uncomposed variations upon multiple themes: Christianity, literature, Communism, travel, music, sex. . . . Measured against their time, they partially document intellectual interests of Europe throughout half a century"—("Twentieth Century Authors: First Supplement").

JOURNALS. Trans. with introd. and notes by Justin O'Brien. 1947 1948 1949 1951. *Random* Vintage Bks. 1956 2 vols. pap. (abr.) Vol. I 1889–1924 $1.65 Vol. 2 1924–1949 $1.95. Originally published by *Knopf* in 4 vols.

SO BE IT, OR THE CHIPS ARE DOWN. Trans. with introd. and notes by Justin O'Brien. Informal journal of random reflections. *Knopf* 1959 $3.95

THE CORRESPONDENCE OF ANDRÉ GIDE AND EDMUND GOSSE, 1904–1928. Ed. by Linette Fisher Brugmans. Although temperamentally different and separated by age and by language, the English critic Gosse shared with Gide a profound regard for French literature. *New York Univ. Press* 1959 $7.50

SELF-PORTRAITS: The Gide–Valery Letters. Ed. by Robert Mallet; trans. by June Guieharnaud. *Univ. of Chicago Press* 1966 $10.00

WOOLF, LEONARD. 1880–1969.

Editor of liberal journals on political and international affairs, publisher, writer, colonial civil servant, consultant to the British Labor Party on foreign policy and, not least, the supportive husband of the sensitive and unstable Virginia Woolf, Leonard Woolf had an extraordinarily interesting and productive life. The *Hogarth Press*, which he founded in their kitchen as a hobby for Virginia, brought first publication to many of the finest of British writers and was the first British publisher of Freud; it eventually gave the Woolfs financial security. But Mr. Woolf's most visibly lasting accomplishment will surely be the volumes of his autobiography, now numbering four. "Sowing" (o.p.) describes his childhood and his youth at Cambridge, where he encountered many of the not-yet-famous including the embryo "Bloomsbury" group and Virginia Stephen, who later married him. "Growing" (1964, o.p.) is a fascinating account of his years as colonial civil servant in Ceylon. "Beginning Again" treats his return to England, marriage, the setting up of the *Hogarth Press* and the horror of World War I, in which his health prevented his serving. "Downhill All the Way"— its title has to do with Mussolini, Stalin and Hitler and his own sorrows in advancing age—describes Virginia's success and the Press's prosperity, his political activities and Virginia's death: "On March 28 she drowned herself in the Ouse." Mr. Woolf's understatement—he says nothing of his own suffering—his wry humor, his eye for people and instinct for revealing anecdote, his stability, compassion and hardheadedness, his skillful selection of material and breadth of interest come through as conveyed by a mind finely honed and without illusion or particular hope: civilization has "ended" and governments will never learn to do in time what they will do 20 years after, when it is too late. Malcolm Muggeridge has written (in the *Observer*, London) "Woolf has to a nostalgic degree that passion for truth which is perhaps the most admirable of human qualities, and he is ever watchful lest he fall unconsciously into accepting legend as fact, hopes as achievement." Walter Allen found "Sowing" "written with great distinction"; J. M. Edelstein says (in the *New Republic*): "He has a seemingly effortless way with words that is beautiful and spellbinding"; Christopher Sykes (in the *Nation*) called "Beginning Again" "a masterpiece of tragic beauty."

BEGINNING AGAIN: An Autobiography of the Years 1911–1918. *Harcourt* 1964 $6.95 pap. $2.75

DOWNHILL ALL THE WAY: An Autobiography of the Years 1918–1939. *Harcourt* 1967 $5.95

SASSOON, SIEGFRIED (LORRAINE). 1886–1967.

The handsome young Siegfried Sasson, son of Sir Alfred Sassoon of a remarkable and wealthy family of Sephardic Jews, was perhaps of recent years the third most famous of the British World War I poets, after Rupert Brooke, the romantic, and Wilfred Owen, whose disillusioned poems Sassoon collected and published after Owen's death. Sassoon himself, in the course of a brave, brilliant career as an infantry officer—he was often decorated—was of the bitter school ("Does it matter?—losing your legs? . . ./ For people will always be kind/ . . . Does it matter?—losing your sight? . . ./ There's such splendid work for the blind . . .). His most famous, often anthologized, war poem was one on a note of hope—the poignant contrasting of the "horror" of war with natural joy—"Everyone suddenly burst out singing." Mr. Sassoon, known in the trenches as "Mad Jack" for his reckless courage, was wounded and returned to England, where, after a period of reconsideration, he threw his Military Cross into the Mersey River and wrote to his colonel that he could no longer be a party to the "sufferings of the troops" for "ends which I believe to be evil and unjust." He was not allowed a court-martial but confined as "temporarily insane" to a mental institution; he later went back to the trenches. Many of these experiences are described in "Memoirs of an Infantry Officer."

S. N. Behrman has recounted (in the *N.Y. Times*) some episodes of his 40-year friendship with Sassoon: "I recalled a remark of Copey's—Charles Townsend Copeland's—in English 12 at Harvard: that poets wrote the best prose. I nudged him toward trying prose. . . ." The eventual result is an exquisite classic: "The Memoirs of a Fox-Hunting Man." (1928, o.p.). This picture of idyllic country life (Sassoon's own, prewar) in Edwardian England won the Hawthornden and James Tait Black Memorial prizes. It was followed by the two others; the three were eventually published together in England as "The Complete Memoirs of George Sherston." Irwin Edman wrote of it in the *N.Y. Times*: "Where else can one find so precise and yet passionate an evocation of the very texture of the English sky and the English landscape, or where find so much good sense and freshening insight into so many figures, famous and obscure, in English society, politics and literature?"

Other autobiographical works followed, which did not attain the stature of the first three: "The Old Century" (1938); "The World of Youth" (1942); and "Siegfried's Journey" (1945). Sassoon continued to write poetry, in later years religious in tone (he became a Roman Catholic late in life), and to live out his years in the 52-room Heytesbury House in his estate in Wiltshire. His poetry is o.p. in this country except for "Selected Poems" (*British Bk. Centre* pap. $2.25).

MEMOIRS OF AN INFANTRY OFFICER. 1930. *Macmillan* Collier Bks. pap. $1.50

SITWELL, SIR OSBERT. 5th Bart. 1892–1969.

The Sitwell brothers and their sister, Edith, were all literary. Their essays are rich in discussions of archeology, architecture, painting, music and the reverie evoked by names and places. Their culture, charm and urbanity are recorded in Sir Osbert's reminiscences of their patrician family and estate. Begun in "Left Hand, Right Hand," they are continued in "The Scarlet Tree," which won the London *Times* Award in 1948. "Great Morning!" is the third volume of his autobiography. The fourth volume, "Laughter in the Next Room," covers the period from 1918 to the death of Sir George Sitwell, their remarkable and eccentric father, in 1944. It is notable for its portraits of extraordinary people in the arts whom Sir Osbert encountered in his career as a writer. The fifth and final volume, "Noble Essences," contains more brilliant reminiscences of his talented friends. In addition to "Tales My Father Taught Me," which rounds out the character of Sir George in rather a grand manner, Sir Osbert has issued his own selections of his essays under the title "Pound Wise" (1963 *Bks. for Libraries* $12.50).

"Sir Osbert dares to be witty, leisurely and personal. His long, lithe sentences, pirouetting in periods and eddying in parentheses, perfectly hold the drift of his thoughts without ever losing their own living structures. His writing is almost painting, a miracle of evocation, whether the picture presents the gloomy trenches of the first war or a sun-drenched courtyard in Italy. The pages vibrate with color"—(D. A. Stauffer).

AUTOBIOGRAPHY. 5 vols. Vol. 1 Left Hand, Right Hand (1944) *Peter Smith* $5.50 Vol. 2 The Scarlet Tree (1946) o.p. Vol. 3 Great Morning! (1947) *Greenwood* $15.25 Vol. 4 Laughter in the Next Room (1948) *Greenwood* $16.25 Vol. 5 Noble Essences: A Book of Characters (1950)*Greenwood* $15.25

OSBERT SITWELL READING FROM HIS POETRY. *Caedmon* TC 1013 $5.95

Books about Sitwell

Bibliography of Edith, Osbert, and Sacheverell Sitwell. By Richard Fifoot. 1963 *Humanities* 2nd ed. 1971 $15.00; *Shoe String* 1971 $15.00
Osbert Sitwell. By Roger Fulford. *British Bk. Centre* pap. $2.38 pap. $1.20

A Selected List of Recent "Literary" Autobiographies

There are many excellent autobiographies listed throughout *"The Reader's Adviser."* Most listed here do not appear elsewhere. Not all are new, but all have recently been published or republished.

Adams, Henry. *See Section on Classic Literary Autobiographers, above.*

Baldwin, James. NOTES OF A NATIVE SON. *Dial* 1955 $4.95; *Bantam* 1957, 1964 pap. $2.45. A sensitive and powerful autobiography, written at 31, by a black novelist and essayist.

Carrington, Dora. CARRINGTON: Letters and Extracts from Her Diaries. Ed. by David Garnett. *Holt* 1971 $12.50. The self-revealing writings of the child-woman campfollower of the Bloomsbury set, who comitted suicide following Lytton Strachey's death.

Dos Passos, John. THE FOURTEENTH CHRONICLE. Letters and Diaries of John Dos Passos. Ed. by Townsend Ludington. *Gambit* 1973 $15.00. ". . . an indispensable cyclorama of the belle epoque in which Dos Passos memorably flourished"—(Carlos Baker).

Gorky, Maxim [Aleksei Maksimovich Peshkov]. THE AUTOBIOGRAPHY OF MAXIM GORKY. 3 vols. in 1. trans. by Isidore Schneider. Includes: My Childhood (1913), In the World (1915) and My Universities (1923) *Citadel* 1969 pap. $3.45; *Peter Smith* $6.75; *Macmillan* 1962 Collier Bks. pap. $1.50

MY CHILDHOOD. Trans. by Ronald Wilks. *Penguin* $1.45

CHILDHOOD. *Oxford Univ. Press* World's Class. 1961 $2.75

Greene, Graham. A SORT OF LIFE. *Simon & Schuster* 1971 $6.95; *Pocket Bks.* 1973 pap. $1.25.

> "Not a conventional autobiography, but the 'feel' of a life evoked with a haunting vividness undiminished by careful understatement"—(*Phila. Sunday Bulletin*).

Morrell, Ottoline. MEMOIRS OF LADY OTTOLINE MORRELL: A Study in Friendship, 1873–1915. Ed. by Robert Gathorne-Hardy. *Knopf* 1964 $6.95

> "By [1914] she had made her various homes the meeting places of the outstanding young writers and artists of England and the Continent. . . . Lady Ottoline's life is a perfect picture of a pleasant, civilized life in England from the 1890's to World War II"—(*LJ*). She was a friend of Leonard and Virginia Woolf, Bertrand Russell, Lord David Cecil, D. H. Lawrence and many more of the European illustrious.

Muggeridge, Malcolm. CHRONICLES OF WASTED TIME. Vol. I The Green Stick. *Morrow* 1973 $6.95

> The first volume of the autobiography of the British writer, editor and wit. "Of people and their follies, Gods that failed, as they obtruded themselves into the author's life; the melancholy tone with its hint of cynicism reminds of Thackeray but the comedy is Dickensian"—(*New York Times Book Review*).

Nabokov, Vladimir. SPEAK, MEMORY. *Putnam* 1966 $7.95 Capricorn Bks. pap. 1970 $2.95. A revised edition of the cosmopolitan novelist's earlier memoir "Conclusive Evidence" (1951, o.p.), elaborate in symbolism and in visual and aural details.

Nicolson, Harold. DIARIES AND LETTERS. *Atheneum* 3 vols. Vol. 1 Harold Nicolson: Diaries and Letters, 1930–1939 (1960) $10.00 Vol. 2 The War Years, 1939–1945 o.p. Vol. 3 The Later Years, 1945–1962 (1968) $8.50. A brilliant evocation, by a biographer as well as an insider, of the intellectual and cultural atmosphere of London in the last decades of the primacy of the British Empire, but now seen as marred by the editor's reticence, in sexual matters, with respect to Nicolson, his wife and their friends.

Pritchett, Victor Sawdon. CAB AT THE DOOR: A Memoir. *Random* 1968 $7.95 Vintage Bks. pap. $1.95. The British critic and novelist evokes his childhood and early maturity with cinematic recall.

MIDNIGHT OIL. *Random* 1972 $6.95 Vintage Bks. pap. $1.95. A sequel to "Cab at the Door," describing the years 1921–50.

Russell, Bertrand. THE AUTOBIOGRAPHY OF BERTRAND RUSSELL. 3 vols. 1967–68. Vol. 1, 1872–1914 *Little-Atlantic* (1967) $7.95 Vol. 2, 1914–1944 *Little-Atlantic* (1968) $8.95 Vol. 3, 1944–1969 *Simon & Schuster* (1969) $8.95; *Bantam* 1971 3 vols. pap. boxed set $4.95

> "There is a mixture here of narrative text and letters. . . . This method has a certain appropriateness. Russell is enough of a Victorian for his life to be presented in a Victorian way"—(*TLS*, London).

Shaw, Bernard. SHAW: An Autobiography. Sel. from his writings by Stanley Weintraub. *McKay* (Weybright & Talley) 2 vols. Vol 1 Shaw: An Autobiography, 1856–1898 (1969) Vol. 2 Shaw: The Playwright Years, 1898–1950 (1970) each $10.00

> "Weintraub's book at least proves that Shaw was perhaps the greatest autobiographer who never wrote one"—(*Time*).

Sitwell, Sacheverell. FOR WANT OF THE GOLDEN CITY. *John Day* 1973 $12.95

"In this prodigious autobiography, the poet brother of Edith and Osbert Sitwell roams freely, pausing often to develop rich associations between his life and Western culture"—(*PW*).

Woolf, Virginia. A WRITER'S DIARY. Ed. by Leonard Woolf. *New Am. Lib.* Signet 1973 pap. $1.25. An illuminating account of Virginia Woolf's creative life with the then-censorable or censurable material imperceptibly excised by Leonard Woolf. First published in 1954.

Yeats, William Butler. MEMOIRS. *Macmillan* 1973 $7.95

The original draft of Yeats' early memoirs, not published in his lifetime because of its explicitness, but from which the poet drew heavily for his autobiographies. "It is surely no vulgar curiosity that moves us to be acquainted with great authors in their slippers. The unique value of both draft autobiography and journal [the *Memoirs*] is that they bring us nearer to the human, the vulnerable Yeats, a man stripped of pose and gesture, of like weakness with ourselves. And this surely is the Yeats of the greater poems"—(*TLS*, London).

A Selected List of Recent "Literary" Biographies

There are many excellent biographies listed throughout "*The Reader's Adviser.*" Here are some that do not appear elsewhere. Not all are new, but all have recently been published or republished.

Bell, Quentin. VIRGINIA WOOLF. *Harcourt* 1972 $12.50

"However magical was her sensibility and her genius to transmit it into art, what we do learn is that Virginia Woolf was always afraid of Virginia Woolf"—(Stanley Weintraub in *The New Republic*).

Crocker, Lester G. JEAN-JACQUES ROUSSEAU. *Macmillan* 2 vols. Vol. 1 The Quest, 1712–1759 (1968) $9.95 Vol. 2, The Prophetic Voice, 1758–1778 (1973) $10.95. A sensitive, detailed psychoanalytic biography written with narrative skill.

Day, Douglas. MALCOLM LOWRY: A Biography. *Oxford* 1973 $10.00

"It is characteristic of Day's book that he neither whitewashes Lowry nor accuses him of suicidal tendencies. Day . . . is fair-minded and sensible to a degree quite remarkable in an academic biographer of a contemporary figure"—(*N.Y. Times Books Review*).

Flexner, Eleanor. MARY WOLLSTONECRAFT. *Coward* 1972 $8.95

A thoroughly researched but somewhat turgidly written biography "destined to be an important contribution to the literature of women's rights"—(*PW*).

Fruman, Norman. COLERIDGE: The Damaged Archangel. *Braziller* 1971 $12.50

A contentious but compelling biographical inquiry which "lays it down as axiomatic that any biographer who accepts any assertion made by Coleridge regarding his own career and performance does so entirely at his own risk. It is unpleasant to be reminded that a great man can also be a great liar"—(*TLS*, London).

Gérin, Winifred. CHARLOTTE BRONTË: The Evolution of Genius. *Oxford* 1967 $15.00 Galaxy Bk. 1969 pap. $2.95

"She shows us Charlotte's development as an organic growth. Moreover . . . she has not allowed herself to become too much involved emotionally with her subject. . . . We are enabled to trace how Charlotte used her own life, both her interior and her outward life, in all its relationships, as material for her novels and how, directed by her shaping imagination, this gave them their dynamic power"—(*TLS*, London).

Haight, Gordon S. GEORGE ELIOT: A Biography. *Oxford* 1968 $15.00

"His biography leans heavily upon . . . the first memoir, by George Eliot's second (and only legal) husband, John Walter Cross, the very life which in its Victorian textual reticences had spurred Haight on his [biographical] quest. Cross had written in 1885 of his wife's capacity for affection, and of the reassurance and reciprocal affection she required, that she had 'absolute need of some one person who should be all in all to her, and to whom she should be all in all.' Haight chronicles that need, and how Mary Ann Evans [George Eliot] responded to its frustration and to its fulfillment"—(*N.Y. Times Book Review*).

Holroyd, Michael. LYTTON STRACHEY AND THE BLOOMSBURY GROUP, HIS WORK, THEIR INFLUENCE. *Penguin* pap. $2.25

This is a recasting of the 2-vol. biography "Lytton Strachey" (1968, o.p.), of which the *Times Literary Supplement*, London, said: "He has set Strachey before us as his subject would have wished, with no defect, no unpleasantness concealed."

Mackenzie, Norman and Jeanne. H. G. WELLS. *Simon & Schuster* 1973 $10.00

"Their treatment of Wells's life is full, but it is not inflated, and it is never boring; clearly the Mackenzies agree that biography is a narrative art, that it must have clarity and movement and must be kept free of the congestions of unassimilated facts"—(*TLS*, London).

Sartre, Jean-Paul. SAINT GENET: Actor and Martyr. Trans. from the French by Bernard Frechtman. *Braziller* 1963 $8.50, *New Am. Lib.* pap. $3.95. An ingenious biographical exposition that combines narrative of a life with the argument, detailed at great length, that any revulsion we may feel toward Genet and his work results from the reader's guilt regarding his complicity in the intolerance of the society which shaped Genet.

Stallman, R. W. STEPHEN CRANE. *Braziller* 1968 $12.50 pap. $4.95. A long book about a short life, leaving few facts unrecorded—and many of those are retained for the appendix.

Starkie, Enid. FLAUBERT. *Atheneum* 2 vols. Vol. I The Making of the Master (1967) $8.50 Vol. 2 The Master (1971) $10.00

". . . More than a biography. It combines the events of Flaubert's life with an explanation of his aesthetic theories and considers how both formed his work"—(*Atlantic Monthly*).

Symons, A. J. A. THE QUEST FOR CORVO. 1934. *Michigan State Univ. Press* 1955 $5.00; *Penguin* pap. 1967 $1.45. A biography in the form of the biographer's search for the facts about his subject—a model for later writers who used the device, but who never managed it with as much fascination.

BOSWELL, JAMES. 1740–1795.

"The most criticised biography in English is by general consent also the greatest. Partly because of the personality of Dr. Johnson, partly because of Boswell's art and admiration for his subject, his work cannot be superseded and even attracts readers who are antipathetic to both"—(F. Seymour Smith). "The longest biography in the English language is also the best. Boswell's Life of Johnson is indeed reckoned the best specimen of biography that has yet been written in any tongue"—(Sir Sidney Lee).

Boswell has had many editors. The edition by Dr. Birkbeck Hill is usually considered the best because of its exhaustive annotations. The Roger Ingpen Bicentenary edition (3 vols. 1907 2nd ed. 1925, o. p.) contained 112 illustrations and was a particularly beautiful one. The greatest of all editions is The Temple Bar edition by Clement Shorter, published by *Gabriel Wells* in 1923. It contains prefaces by Aleyn Lyell Reade, Gilbert K. Chesterton, A. Edward Newton, John Drinkwater, Chauncey Tinker, R. B. Adam and others.

Frederick A. Pottle, Sterling Professor of English Emeritus at Yale, is the notable editor of the new Yale editions of "The Private Papers of James Boswell," published by *McGraw-Hill* (*see following*). The "Private Papers of James Boswell from Malahide Castle," from the collection of Lt.-Col. Ralph Heywood Isham

(18 vols. Vol. 1–6. by Geoffrey Scott, Vols. 7–18 ed. by Frederick Pottle 1932) is now o. p., but the "Index to the Private Papers" is still available (ed. by F. A. Pottle and Others *Oxford* 1937 $13.25). "The discovery of cache after cache of Boswell's manuscripts, journals and letters at Malahide and Fettercairn between 1925 and 1948 is one of the truly extraordinary events in the history of English letters. It gave us the original journal of the *Tour of the Hebrides*, before the war and now we have a totally new manuscript appearing 180-odd years after it was written. This is the London journal which Boswell wrote in 1762 and 1763 when, twenty-three years old, he came to London to get a commission in the Guards, and, failing in that, met the man who was to be his god, his subject and his insurance of fame. What, we wonder, will be the state of our old editions of the *Life of Johnson* when the manuscripts yet to be seen are published?"—(V. S. Pritchett, in "Books in General"). Chauncey Brewster Tinker, the great Yale teacher and scholar who made the Malahide discovery of these papers (supposed to have been destroyed), died in 1963. Tinker was keeper of Yale's rare book collection, of which the "Private Papers" are now a part.

Second only to Boswell among writers on Dr. Johnson is his vivacious friend, Hester Lynch Piozzi, known usually as Mrs. Thrale (1741–1821). During a 20-year friendship, Dr. Johnson "became more or less domesticated in the home of the Thrales and accompanied them to Wales (1774) and to France (1775)." After the death of Henry Thrale, she married an Italian musician, Gabriel Piozzi, much to Dr. Johnson's displeasure. She wrote verse, as well as "Anecdotes of Dr. Johnson" (1786 1925,). Her important diary is "Thraliana: The Diary of Mrs. Hester Lynch Thrale (later Mrs. Piozzi) 1776–1809" (ed. by Katharine C. Balderston; published in cooperation with the Huntington Library 1942, o. p.). From 1784 to 1787, Mrs. Piozzi and her husband toured Europe. Her impressions of the trip are recorded in "Observations and Reflections Made in the Course of a Journey Through France, Italy, and Germany" (1789, ed. by H. Barrows *Univ. of Michigan Press* 1967 $12.50), at once a travelogue and a sourcebook on 18th-century customs and mores.

Two significant works about Johnson and Boswell, now o. p., are Sir John Hawkins' "Life of Samuel Johnson" (1787) and Hesketh Pearson's "Johnson and Boswell: The Story of Their Lives" (1959).

Life of Johnson together with Boswell's Journal of a Tour to the Hebrides and Johnson's Diary of a Journey into North Wales. Ed. by George Birbeck Hill; rev. and enl. by L. F. Powell. *Oxford* 1934–50 6 vols. Vols. 1–4 $47.50, Vols. 5–6 2nd ed. 1965 $34.00.

The Life of Samuel Johnson. 1791. Ed. by Edmund Fuller (abr.) *Dell* 1960 pap. $.75; *Dutton* Everyman's 2 vols. each $3.50; *Modern Library* 1931 pap. $1.25; ed. by Frank Brady (abr.) *New Am. Lib.* Signet pap. $1.25; ed. by R. W. Chapman and Chauncey B. Tinker *Oxford* Stand. Authors 1922 1953 $9.50 ed. by R. W. Chapman rev. ed. corrected by J. D. Fleeman pap. $5.95; *Scribner* Mod. Student's Lib. Eng. Ser. pap. $1.95; ed. by Irvin and Anne Ehrenpreis (abr.) *Washington Square* pap. $.90

Other Works by James Boswell:

Yale Editions of the Private Papers of James Boswell. Ed. by Frederick A. Pottle and others. *McGraw-Hill* 1950– 10 vols. published; titles and prices as follows:

Boswell's London Journal, 1762–1763. Now first published from the original ms. Prepared for the press with introd. and notes by Frederick A. Pottle; pref. by Christopher Morley. *McGraw-Hill* 1950 pap. $2.45

"The better I get to know James Boswell, the more—despite his glaring faults—I am captivated by his Journals. He was inordinately vain, a fearful snob, and an insufferable prig. But what stands out, most vividly, in the Boswell papers is the young Scotsman's enthusiasm, his exceeding oddity, his almost lunatic candor. And, of course, his genius as a diarist"—(C. J. Rolo, in the *Atlantic*).

Boswell in Holland, 1763–1764, including his Correspondence with Belle de Zuylen (Zélide). Ed. by Frederick A. Pottle. *McGraw-Hill* 1952 $12.45

Boswell on the Grand Tour: Germany and Switzerland, 1764. Ed. by Frederick A. Pottle. *McGraw-Hill* 1953 o.p.

Boswell on the Grand Tour: Italy, Corsica, and France, 1765-1766. Ed. by
Frank Brady and Frederick A. Pottle. *McGraw-Hill* 1955 o.p.

Boswell in Search of a Wife, 1766–1769. Ed. by Frank Brady and Frederick A.
Pottle. *McGraw-Hill* 1956 o.p.

"Most entertaining since the first sensational 'London Journal.' It has every ingredient to make it popular—a succession of amorous adventures, scenes of high comedy in Boswell's most artful manner, long conversations with Samuel Johnson, and even a conventional happy ending"—(*N.Y. Times*).

Boswell for the Defense, 1769–1774. Ed. by William K. Wimsatt and Frederick
A. Pottle. *McGraw-Hill* 1962 $12.50

This volume "records his marital ups and downs, his drinking bouts and occasional wenching, and his unsuccessful defense of John Reid, a sheep- stealer, who, unfortunately for James's peace of mine, was exe-
cuted"—(*LJ*).

Journal of the Tour of the Hebrides with Samuel Johnson. Ed. by Frederick
A. Pottle. *McGraw-Hill* 1962 o.p.

A reprint of the 1936 Viking edition by Professor Pottle and Charles H. Bennett with a new introduction,
new illustrations and a supplement based on the documents recovered since 1936.

The Ominous Years, 1774–1776. Ed. by Charles Ryskamp and Frederick A. Pottle.
McGraw-Hill 1963 $14.11

The eighth volume in this distinguished series covers 20 months of indecisiveness, hypochondria, self-delu-
sions and downright despair with ample Johnsoniana and other records of a busy, frenetic London.

The Correspondence of James Boswell and John Johnston of Grange. Ed.
with introd. by Ralph S. Walker. Covers the years 1759–86. *McGraw-Hill* 1966
$17.50

This work is Volume 1 of the planned 40-volume series of the Private Papers of James Boswell, Research
Edition, "designed chiefly for scholars and libraries." John Johnston was "Boswell's *alter ego*, his 'constant
resort in moments of distress' "—(*LJ*).

Boswell in Extremes: 1776–1778. Ed. by Charles M. Weis and Frederick A.
Pottle. *McGraw-Hill* 1970 $15.00

The Portable Johnson and Boswell. Ed. by Louis Kronenberger. *Viking* Portable
Lib. 1947 $5.50 pap. $2.25. Contains substantial selections from the "Life" and
from "Journal of a Tour to the Hebrides."

Journal of a Tour to Corsica. *Cambridge* 1923 $2.75

Journal of a Tour to the Hebrides. 1773 *Collins* 1959 $3.00; ed. by Lawrence F.
Powell *Dutton* Everyman's $3.50; (and S. Johnson's "Journey to the Western Isles
of Scotland") ed. by A. Wendt *Houghton* Riv. Eds. pap. $1.95; (and S. Johnson's
"Journey to the Western Isles of Scotland") ed. by R. W. Chapman *Oxford* Stand.
Authors $5.00 pap. $2.75

Works by Dr. Samuel Johnson, 1709–1784:

A Dictionary of the English Language: In Which the Words Are Deduced from
Their Originals, and Illustrated in Their Different Significations by Examples from
the Best Writers. To Which Are Prefixed, A History of the Language, and an English Grammar. 1755. *AMS Press* facsimile ed. 1967 2 vols. set $100.00

JOHNSON'S DICTIONARY: A Modern Selection. Ed. by E. L. McAdam, Jr. and George Milne. *Pantheon* 1963 $8.95; *Modern Library* $2.45

"A generous slice of the fruits of Johnson's gargantuan labors"—(*N.Y. Times*).

YALE EDITION OF THE WORKS OF SAMUEL JOHNSON. *Yale Univ. Press* 1958– 7 vols. published; titles and prices as follows:

DIARIES, PRAYERS, AND ANNALS. Ed. by E. L. McAdam, Jr., with Donald and Mary Hyde. *Yale Univ. Press* 1958 $12.50

THE IDLER (1758–60) and THE ADVENTURER. Ed. by W. J. Bate, John M. Bullitt and L. F. Powell. *Yale Univ. Press* $15.00

POEMS. Ed. by E. L. McAdam, Jr., with George Milne. *Yale Univ. Press* 1964 $12.50

JOHNSON ON SHAKESPEARE. Ed. by Arthur Sherbo; introd. by Bertrand Bronson. *Yale Univ. Press* 1967 2 vols. set $25.00

SELECTED ESSAYS FROM THE RAMBLER, ADVENTURER, AND IDLER. Ed. by W. J. Bate. *Yale Univ. Press* 1968 pap. $3.75

THE RAMBLER. Ed. by W. J. Bate and Albrecht B. Strauss. *Yale Univ. Press* 3 vols. 1969 $35.99

A JOURNEY TO THE WESTERN ISLANDS OF SCOTLAND. Ed. by Mary Lascelles. *Yale Univ. Press* 1971 $8.75

THE PORTABLE JOHNSON AND BOSWELL. Ed. by Louis Kronenberger. *Viking* Portable Lib. 1947 $5.50 pap. $2.25. Contains the best poems and letters, prefaces to "Shakespeare" and the "Dictionary," "Lives" of Pope and Savage.

A JOHNSON READER. Ed. by E. L. McAdam, Jr., and George Milne. *Pantheon* 1964 $10.00; *Modern Library* pap. $1.45

SELECTIONS. Ed. by R. W. Chapman. *Oxford* 1955 World's Class. $2.50

SELECTED WRITINGS. Ed. by R. T. Davies. *Northwestern Univ. Press* 1965 $7.95

PROSE AND POETRY. (with Boswell's "Character," Macauley's "Life" and Raleigh's "Essay") ed. by R. W. Chapman *Oxford* 1922 $2.50; ed. by Mona Wilson *Harvard Univ. Press* 1951 $12.00 pap. $4.50

POEMS. Ed. by David Nichol Smith and E. L. McAdam, Jr. *Oxford* English Texts 1942 $9.75. The first complete edition of the poems, with valuable notes.

POEMS. Ed. by J. D. Fleeman. *Penguin* 1971 pap. $2.75

RASSELAS, POEMS AND SELECTED PROSE. Ed. by Bertrand H. Bronson. *Holt* (Rinehart) 1958 $4.95 pap. $2.50

RASSELAS. Ed. by Warren L. Fleischauer. *Barron's* Lib. of Literary Masterpieces 1961 $3.00 pap. $1.50

THE HISTORY OF RASSELAS, PRINCE OF ABYSSINIA. 1759. Ed. by Gwin J. Kolb *AHM Pub. Corp.* Crofts Class. 1962 pap. $.85; ed. by J. P. Hardy *Oxford* 1968 pap. $1.90 ed. by Geoffrey Tillotson and Brian Jenkins 1971 $5.00

THE RAMBLER. 1750–52. Ed. by S. C. Roberts. *Dutton* Everyman's $3.50

JOURNEY TO THE WESTERN ISLANDS OF SCOTLAND. (and Boswell's "Journey of a Tour to the Hebrides with Samuel Johnson") Ed. by R. W. Chapman. *Oxford* Stand. Authors 1930 $5.00 pap. $2.75

DIARY OF A JOURNEY INTO NORTH WALES WITH BOSWELL'S LIFE OF SAMUEL JOHNSON AND JOURNAL OF A TOUR TO THE HEBRIDES. Ed. by G. B. Hill. *Oxford* 1934–1950 6 vols. Vols. 1–4 $20.80, Vols. 5–6 2nd ed. 1965 $34.00

LETTERS. Ed. by George B. Hill. 1892. *Bks. for Libraries* 1973 $38.75

LETTERS: With Mrs. Thrale's Genuine Letters to Him. Coll. and ed. by R. W. Chapman. Vol. 1 1719–1774 Vol. 2 1775–1782 Vol. 3 1783–1784 *Oxford* 1952 3 vols. set $32.25

"The volumes constitute the magnum opus and a considerable part of the life work of the editor who has devoted more than thirty years to the task. . . . They are certain to be almost as nearly indispensable to students as the 'Life' itself"—(J. W. Krutch, in the *N.Y. Herald Tribune*).

DR. JOHNSON: HIS LIFE IN LETTERS. Sel. and ed. with introd. by David Littlejohn. *Prentice-Hall* 1965 $5.95 pap. $2.95

"These carefully edited letters with an interspersed running commentary give a concise, intimate, and revealing portrait of the life and times of this 18th-century literary colossus, and should serve as a useful supplement to Boswell's biography"—(*LJ*).

THE CRITICAL OPINIONS OF SAMUEL JOHNSON. Comp. by Joseph Epes Brown. 1926. *Russell & Russell* 1961 $12.50

Books about Dr. Johnson and Boswell

Johnson's England: An Account of the Life and Manners of His Age. Ed. by Arthur Stanley Turberville. *Oxford* 1933 1953 2 vols. set $18.75

Samuel Johnson. By J. W. Krutch. 1944. *Harcourt* 1963 pap. $2.95

The Achievement of Samuel Johnson. By Walter J. Bate. *Oxford* 1955 $7.50; *Somerset Pub.* $11.50

New Light on Dr. Johnson: Essays on the Occasion of his 250th Birthday. Ed. by Frederick W. Hilles. 1959. *Shoe String* $10.00

Samuel Johnson: A Layman's Religion. By Maurice J. Quinlan. *Univ. of Wisconsin Press* 1964 $7.50
   "The first book since 1850 to treat the aspects of Johnson's religious beliefs. . . . A fascinating examination"—(*LJ*).

Samuel Johnson and Moral Discipline. By Paul Kent Alkon. A study of the moral essays that Johnson wrote in the 1750s. *Northwestern Univ. Press* 1967 $6.95

Passionate Intelligence: Imagination and Reason in the Work of Samuel Johnson. By Arieh Sachs. *Johns Hopkins Press* 1967 $6.00
   "The main contribution of this volume is Professor Sachs's assertion that for Johnson, reason and imagination are the basic sets of concepts that form the context of human endeavor"—(*LJ*).

Dr. Johnson and His World. By F. E. Halliday. A biography with more than 150 portraits, drawings, engravings and photographs relating to Dr. Johnson's life. *Viking* 1968 $6.95

Note: Johnson, Samuel. 1696–1772. American clergyman and educator, first president of King's College, now Columbia University. The 4-vol. biography by H. W. and C. C. Schneider (*Columbia* 1929, o.p.) deals with *this* Samuel Johnson.

LOCKHART, JOHN GIBSON. 1794–1854.

Lockhart's magnum opus, "Memoirs of the Life of Sir Walter Scott" (1837–38 7 vols.), is usually rated next to Boswell's Johnson (*q.v.*) amont the great biographies in English. He was Scott's son-in-law, editor of the *Quarterly Review* from 1825 to 1853 and the author of several novels, of which "Some Passages in the Life of Adam Blair" (1822. *Aldine* $4.95), the story of the sin and atonement of a Scottish clergyman, is the best. The biography of Scott has always been recognized for "proportion, humour, sympathy, sound criticism, a sense of drama, and brilliant, concentrated character-sketches." Yet despite—perhaps because of—its sympathy with its subject and fund of first-hand anecdote, it lacks the warts-and-all approach of a Boswell.

As Lockhart himself declared in his "Scott," "I consider no man justified in journalising what he hears and sees in a domestic circle where he is not thoroughly at home; and I think there are still higher and better reasons why he should not do so where he is."

THE LIFE OF ROBERT BURNS. 1828. Ed. by William S. Douglas. *AMS Press* repr. of 1892 ed. $16.00

THE LIFE OF NAPOLEON BONAPARTE. 1829. *Dutton* Everyman's $3.50

THE LIFE OF SIR WALTER SCOTT. 10 vols. 1837–38. *AMS Press* repr. of 1902 ed. each $15.00; 1 vol. biography abr. by the author. 1848. *Dutton* Everyman's $3.50

Books about Lockhart

The Life and Letters of John Gibson Lockhart. From Abbotsford and Milton Lockhart Mss. and Other Original Sources. By Andrew Lang. 1897. *AMS Press* 2 vols. set $32.50

GASKELL, MRS. ELIZABETH (CLEGHORN). 1810–1865.

Mrs. Gaskell's "Life of Charlotte Brontë" is the most famous biography of a woman written by a woman. She knew the Brontës personally and wrote of the three sisters at first hand. Her biography appeared in 1857, two years after the death of Charlotte. The discovery of the lost letters of Charlotte to Constantin Héger, who was the original of "The Professor" and the husband of the principal of the school in Brussels where Charlotte had taught, has given rise to many new biographies and reinterpretations of Charlotte. Mrs. Gaskell quotes from three of the letters, from Madame Héger to her children, now in the British Museum, showing she had knowledge of them but not betraying their full import. The letters may be read in Clement Shorter's "The Brontës and Their Circle" (1896. *Gale* 1969 $15.00) and in "The Brontë Sisters" by Ernest Dimnet (1928, o.p.)

THE LIFE OF CHARLOTTE BRONTË. 1857. *Dutton* Everyman's $3.50

LETTERS. Ed. by John A. Chapple and Arthur Pollard. *Harvard Univ. Press* 1966 $27.50

Books about Gaskell

Mrs. Gaskell: Novelist and Biographer. By Arthur Pollard. *Harvard Univ. Press* 1965 $7.50
  "Mr. Pollard's critical approach is unpretentious: he is not out to re-interpret his subject in psychological or mythic terms but rather to investigate her art, using the traditional tools of plot, character, setting, and moral purpose. . . . [A] fair and candid treatment"—(*LJ*).
Mrs. Gaskell: The Basis for Reassessment. By Edgar Wright. *Oxford* 1965 $6.75
Elizabeth Gaskell. By Miriam Allott. Pamphlet. *British Bk. Centre* $2.38 pap. $1.20
Charlotte Brontë: The Evolution of Genius. By Winifred Gérin. *Oxford* 1967 $15.00 Galaxy Bks. pap. 1969 $2.95. (*For comment see the Selected List of Recent "Literary" Biographies, above.*)

See also Chapter 11, British Fiction—Middle Period, for the Brontës and for Mrs. Gaskell's novels.

CONTEMPORARY LITERARY BIOGRAPHERS: A SELECTION

In this section *"The Reader's Adviser"* departs from its customary chronological order in favor of an alphabetical sequence. We hope that, since most of the names listed here are familiar ones, such an arrangement will provide greater ease in locating them.

CECIL, LORD DAVID. 1902–

Lord David, a member of one of the oldest and most aristocratic of British families and Goldsmith's Professor of English Literature at Oxford, writes mainly of literary figures of the 18th and 19th centuries. "The Stricken Deer, or The Life of Cowper" won the James Tait Black Prize and the Hawthornden Prize. "The Young Melbourne" (1939, o.p.) was hailed as a masterpiece. Another of his distinguished biographies is "Two Quiet Lives: Dorothy Osborne; Thomas Gray" (1948, o.p.). In "The Fine Art of Reading" (1957, o.p.) he deals with a wide variety of books and authors. He has edited, with Allen Tate (*q.v.*), "Modern Verse in English: 1900–1950" (*Macmillan* 1959 $8.50). "His university lectures, his radio talks, and his written essays are all distinguished by impeccable scholarship and a felicitous style." He possesses, as Professor George F. Whicher has said, "the wide knowledge of the past, the nice judgment of men, and the esthetic appreciation that ideally equip him for the work."

THE STRICKEN DEER, or The Life of Cowper. 1930 1935 repr. of 1947 ed. *Somerset Pub.* $15.50

WILLIAM COWPER. 1932 *Folcroft* $4.50 (*See also* "Stricken Deer," *above*)

SIR WALTER SCOTT. 1933. *Scholarly Press* $7.50

JANE AUSTEN. 1935. *Folcroft* $5.00

HARDY THE NOVELIST. 1946. *Paul P. Appel* (dist. by Gordian) 1972 $8.50

MELBOURNE. 1954 *Greenwood* 1971 $16.75

WALTER PATER: Scholar Artist. 1955. *Folcroft* $4.50

VICTORIAN NOVELISTS. *Univ. of Chicago Press* 1958 $7.00 Phoenix Bks. pap. $2.25

MAX: A Biography. *Houghton* 1965 $6.95

"The definitive biography of the inimitable Max Beerbohm"—(*LJ*).

VISIONARY AND DREAMER: Two Poetic Painters, Samuel Palmer and Edward Burne-Jones. *Princeton Univ. Press* 1969 $17.50

THE CECILS OF HATFIELD HOUSE: An English Ruling Family. *Houghton* 1973 $15.00

"Lord David Cecil . . . writes with an elegant sense of history and the pride of family in this chronological account of his own forbears. He begins with an infectious personal description of one of England's architectural landmarks, Hatfield House, and his own childhood there. The rest is a well-turned impersonal narrative beginning with the story of William Cecil, Lord Burghley, trusted minister of Elizabeth I, whose undeviating loyalty to the throne set the tone for succeeding Cecils from Robert, First Earl of Salisbury up to the present. . . . The book has that heraldic aura which should make it a must for Anglophiles"—(*PW*).

CHUTE, MARCHETTE (GAYLORD). 1909–

Not the least remarkable feature of Miss Chute's biographies is the fact that these books were based almost entirely on research done in the New York Public Library. Her biographies are lively and written with great charm of manner; they contain many fascinating documentary details based on the soundest research. "The Worlds of Shakespeare" (*Dutton* 1963 $3.95 pap. $1.25), written with Ernestine Perrie, offers a script designed for two players presenting a condensed view of the whole range of Shakespeare's plays. "An Introduction to Shakespeare" (*Dutton* 1951 $3.95) is an excellent study of Shakespeare's world and the theater of his day for high school students. *Dutton* also publishes several of Miss Chute's juveniles and religious books.

GEOFFREY CHAUCER OF ENGLAND. *Dutton* 1946 1951 $7.50 pap. $1.75

SHAKESPEARE OF LONDON. *Dutton* 1949 $7.95

BEN JONSON OF WESTMINSTER. *Dutton* 1953 $6.95

TWO GENTLE MEN: The Lives of George Herbert and Robert Herrick. *Dutton* 1959 $6.95

EDEL, (JOSEPH) LEON. 1907–

Edel has been Henry James Professor of English and American Letters at New York University, and is now Citizens Professor of English at the University of Hawaii. John Leonard, in the *N.Y. Times*, has called "Henry James" "the finest biography ever written by and about an American author." Two of the volumes won for the author the National Book Award and the Pulitzer Prize in Biography. A one-volume edition is planned by Edel. He has also edited James's plays and short fiction and is currently preparing an edition of James's letters.

Among his critical works are "The Modern Psychological Novel, 1900–1950" (1955 1959 *Peter Smith* $5.00), "Literary History and Literary Criticism" (*New York Univ. Press* 1964 $8.95) and "Literary Biography" (*see General Bibliography, above*). Among his current projects is the editing of Edmund Wilson's journals and a book on the Bloomsbury circle.

HENRY JAMES. Lippincott 5 vols. 1953–72 Vol. I The Untried Years: 1843–1870 (1953) $10.00 Vol. 2 The Conquest of London: 1870–1881 (1962) $10.00 Vol. 3 The Middle Years: 1882–1895 (1962) $10.00 Vol. 4 The Treacherous Years: 1895–1901 (1969) $10.00 Vol. 5 The Master: 1901–1916 (1972) $12.95 boxed set $42.95

(with Edward K. Brown) WILLA CATHER. *Knopf* 1953 $5.95. A biography completed by Edel after the death of Brown.

HENRY DAVID THOREAU. Pamphlets on American Writers *Univ of Minnesota Press* 1970 pap. $1.25

LITERARY BIOGRAPHY. (*See under General Works on Literary Biography.*)

ELLMANN, RICHARD. 1918–

Richard Ellmann, American teacher and scholar, has been Goldsmith Professor of English at New College, Oxford University since 1968. His research and writing have been primarily identified with turn-of-the-century Irish writers, especially Joyce, Yeats, and Wilde—on whose biography he is currently working. His "James Joyce" received the National Book Award for Biography. "This immensely detailed, massive, completely detached and objective, yet loving biography translates James Joyce's books back into his life"—(Stephen Spender in *N.Y. Times Book Review*). In "Ulysses on the Liffey," a biographical–critical examination of Joyce's masterwork, the novel "is seen to work as the most complex fictional structure of all time, but, through that, it is seen to work also as a great testament to human love"—(Anthony Burgess). Of "Yeats" Sean O'Faolain has said: "This is the first lucid interpretation we have had of Yeats's literary pilgrimage and poetic metabolisms. It is a masterly book, thoroughly documented, sensitive and sure-footed." Because Yeats attained literary eminence early in life and kept it so long, he became a focal center for disciples and rebels. In "Eminent Domain" Ellmann examines the complicated interactions among selected writers who responded literarily to them. "Golden Codgers" is a volume of biographical–critical speculative essays from George Eliot to T. S. Eliot. ". . . We learn simultaneously about the author, his work and the period to which both belong with such a sense of the integrity of these elements that the abrupt and splintered techniques of the New Criticism and the Life and Letters approach seem crude and deservedly out of date in comparison"—(*TLS*, London).

With Ellsworth Mason he edited "The Critical Writings of James Joyce" (*Viking* 1959 $4.50 Compass Bks. pap. $2.25). He has also edited Volume 2 of the "Letters of James Joyce" (*Viking* 1966 $12.50) and Stanislaus Joyce's "My Brother's Keeper: James Joyce's Early Years" (1958. *Viking* Compass Bks. 1969 pap. $1.65). His Wilde editions include "Oscar Wilde: A Collection of Critical Essays" (*Prentice-Hall* 1969 $5.95 Spectrum Bks. pap. $1.95) and "The Artist as Critic: Critical Writings of Oscar Wilde" (*Random* 1969 $10.00 Vintage Bks. pap. $2.45)

YEATS: The Man and the Masks. 1948. *Dutton* pap. $1.95

THE IDENTITY OF YEATS. *Oxford* 1954 2nd ed. 1964 $10.00

JAMES JOYCE. *Oxford* 1959 $17.50 Galaxy Bks. pap. $4.95

EMINENT DOMAIN. Years among Wilde, Joyce, Eliot and Auden. *Oxford* 1967 $5.00 Galaxy Bks. pap. $1.75

ULYSSES ON THE LIFFEY. *Oxford* 1972 $8.95 pap. $2.50

GOLDEN CODGERS: Biographical Speculations. *Oxford* 1973 $7.95

HARRIS, FRANK (JAMES THOMAS). 1856–1931.

Born in Galway, Ireland, a controversial figure in both his private life and writings, Harris became the editor of the *Fortnightly Review* and the (British) *Saturday Review* after a varied early career in the United States as a sandhog, cattle wrangler and law student at the University of Kansas. His autobiography, first published in four volumes, 1925–29 (with a reputedly spurious fifth volume published in Paris in 1958), was banned for 40 years in this country and England. *Library Journal* said of it: "This 'most honest' autobiography, despite the boasting, exaggeration, and occasional inaccuracy, does reveal, with unintentional honesty, one suspects, Harris as the self-centered braggart he must have been. . . . The Gallagher footnotes carefully verify or invalidate the author's recollections, often trying to excuse or explain the old man's sometimes faulty memory. . . . The characters are the great of the period, and for this contribution to literary and social history the book has merit. It is too long, often badly written, may offend some, but there will be a demand for it, and this reviewer feels libraries should help to supply it."

Among Harris's other works of biographical interest in print are "The Man Shakespeare" (1909 *Horizon* 1969 $10.00 pap. $3.95), "Oscar Wilde" (1916, o.p.) and two volumes of his five collections of biographical essays (1815–1927) on figures of his own time: "Contemporary Portraits," 3rd series (1920. *Greenwood* $11.00) and "Latest Contemporary Portraits" (1927. *Johnson Reprint* $11.00). His unreliable memoir "On the Trail, Being My Reminiscences as a Cowboy" (1930) is o.p.

My Life and Loves. Ed. with introd. by John F. Gallagher. 1925. *Grove* Black Cat pap. $2.45

MAUROIS, ANDRÉ, (pseud. of Émile Herzog). 1885–1967.

Justin O'Brien has said (in *SR*): "André Maurois possesses a genius for depicting the life of genius. Early in his long and glorious career he felt drawn chiefly to England, doubtless because he was brought up in Normandy—Elbeuf and Rouen—and because of his assignment as interpreter to a British regiment during World War I [after which] he quite naturally turned to biographies of Shelley, Byron, Disraeli. Then, moving to his native France for subjects, he produced dazzling life-size portraits of Victor Hugo, Marcel Proust, George Sand, the Dumas family, and others." And Sir Harold Nicolson commented: "Maurois is a professional biographer, and to my mind the most gifted biographer in any language today." V. S. Pritchett has spoken of the French author's "intelligence and his powers of vivid summary and portraiture," and wrote in the *New Statesman:* "M. Maurois' accomplishment as a biographer is now immense and his new life of Hugo is rich in detail, intimate, wise, sympathetic and delightful." Of "Prometheus," Maurois' final biography, the *National Observer* said: "Mr. Maurois has reached the heights of critical biography. . . . He is a superb storyteller. Through his engrossing narrative and incisive literary analysis . . . a life story unfolds that is as fascinating and ironic as anything concocted in the fictional microcosm that was Balzac's mind." The charming and perceptive "Ariel: The Life of Shelley" was the first work of literary biography to bring Maurois to the notice of English readers. His "Proust: Portrait of a Genius" (1950) and "Adrienne: The Life of the Marquise de la Fayette" (1961) are now o.p.

In 1938 he was elected to the French Academy. He joined the French army at the outbreak of World War II and, after the fall of France, came to this country, where he lectured and taught. "From My Journal" (1948, o.p.) describes his experiences in the U.S. It became the core about which he wrote his "Memoirs, 1885–1967" (*Harper* 1970 $10.00). His wide culture and intellectual honesty made him a brilliant interpreter of English civilization, as well as the French.

Ariel: The Life of Shelley. 1924. Trans. by Ella D'Arcy. *Ungar* 1958 $7.50 pap. $2.75

Aspects of Biography. 1929. Trans. by Sydney Castle Roberts. *Ungar* $4.50

Byron. 1930. Trans. by Hamish Miles. *Ungar* $10.50 pap. $2.75

Chateaubriand: Poet, Statesman, Lover. Trans. by Vera Fraser. 1938. *Greenwood* $13.00

Voltaire. Trans. by Hamish Miles. 1952. *Dufour* $3.50

Cecil Rhodes. 1953. Makers of History Ser. *Shoe String* 1967 $4.00

Lélia: The Life of George Sand. 1953. Trans. by Gerard Hopkins. *Pyramid Bks.* pap. $1.25

Alexandre Dumas. Trans. by Jack P. White. Great Lives in Brief *Knopf* 1955 $3.95

The Titans: A Three-generation Biography of the Dumas. 1958. Trans. by Gerard Hopkins. *Greenwood* $20.75; *Pyramid Bks.* pap. $1.25

The Life of Alexander Fleming, Discoverer of Penicillin. Trans. by Gerard Hopkins. *Dutton* 1959 $7.95

Napoleon. Trans. by D. J. S. Thomson. *Viking* Studio Bks. 1964 $6.95

Prometheus: The Life of Balzac. Trans. by Norman Denny. *Harper* 1966 $10.00

Dickens. Trans. by Hamish Miles. *Ungar* $4.50 pap. $1.45

Points of View: Essays on British Writers from Kipling to Graham Greene. *Ungar* 1968 $8.50

Books about Maurois

Maurois: The Writer and His Work. By Georges Lemaitre. *Ungar* rev. ed. 1968 $6.50

PEARSON, HESKETH. 1887–1964.

Witty and urbane, Hesketh Pearson chose to write anecdotal biographies of men of wit and talent, several of which are now o.p. Bernard Kale in *SR* called him "a high-speed British biography machine built like a six-foot-two gentleman, [who] has been writing someone or other's life story since he himself was four-teen...." Of his autobiography "Hesketh Pearson by Himself" (1966, o.p.), published posthumously, *Library Journal* said: "Humor, frankness, and wisdom are joined in the account of his early years on the stage, ... his World War I experiences and his career as a writer. Mr. Pearson's writing is warm and intimate.... His philosophy of life, like his style of writing, is clear and direct."

Doctor Darwin. 1930. *Richard West* $20.00. A biography of Erasmus Darwin, early psychologist, physician, poet and grandfather of the evolutionist Charles Darwin.

The Fool of Love: The Life of William Hazlitt. 1934. *Scholarly Press* 1971 $14.50; *Somerset Pub.* 1971 $11.50

The Smith of Smiths, Being the Life, Wit and Humor of Sydney Smith. 1934. *Scholarly Press* 1972 $13.50; *Richard West* $13.45

Gilbert and Sullivan. 1935. *Bks. for Libraries* $12.50; *Scholarly Press* repr. of 1951 ed. $19.50; *Richard West* $19.45

The Last Actor-Managers. 1950. *Bks. for Libraries.* $12.50

George Bernard Shaw: His Life and Personality. (Original title "G. B. S. A Full Length Portrait" [1942] and "A Postscript" [1950]) *Atheneum* 1963 pap. $1.95

Beerbohm Tree: His Life and Laughter. 1956. *Greenwood* 1971 $12.25

Johnson and Boswell: The Story of Their Lives. 1959. *Greenwood* 1972 $15.75

QUENNELL, PETER (COURTNEY). 1905–

Peter Quennell has had a long and distinguished career as a biographer, critic and editor; he is perhaps best known for his works on Byron and Pope. After undergraduate work at Balliol College, Oxford (he did not take a degree) he began to write poetry and then criticism—for the *New Statesman* and other journals. He spent a year in Tokyo teaching English literature at the government university there. From 1944 to 1951 he edited the *Cornhill Magazine*; he has also been editor of *History Today*. Throughout his mature life he has produced a stream of literary biographies—accomplished and urbane, if seldom startling, of impeccable scholarship and grace of style. His books on Byron made him known in the United States; the *New Yorker* called "Byron in Italy" "a superb narrative, charming, subtle and intelligent, with some penetrating reflections on the interplay of talent and personality in the literary process." He is the author of "Caroline of England: An Augustan Portrait" (1940. *Bks. for Libraries* 1973 $6.95), "Hogarth's Progress" (1955. *Bks. for Libraries* 1972 $19.75) and many other titles. But he came into his own with "Alexander Pope: The Education of a Genius," which achieved a front-page critique in the *N.Y. Times Book Review* (December, 1968), in which Horace Gregory wrote: "It has remained for Peter Quennell to place the materials on Pope in the best order, for his 'Alexander Pope' is one of the finest literary biographies of our time. The book is easy in tone, graceful, harmonious, an evenly paced reconstruction of Pope's life as it affected his poetry." (It brings Pope to the age of 40.) Mr. Quennell's autobiography, "The Sign of the Fish" (an allusion to his having been born under Pisces), is the memoir of a "man of letters" who knew George Moore, Virginia Woolf, Colette and André Gide, among others, but cares little in general for his contemporaries in the literary "set." Walter Allen said of the book in the *New Statesman*: "It is in its reticence and single-mindedness an austere book. It seems to me a very distinguished one. At a time when it often seems to have become good form to write gracelessly, it is an uncommon pleasure to read prose as good as Peter Quennell's—elegant, chaste, controlled, sonorous, and capable of eloquence when eloquence is called for."

He is the editor of "The Journals of Thomas Moore" (*Macmillan* 1964 $4.00 pap. $1.95), "Byron: A Self-Portrait" (*Humanities Press* 1967 $15.00) and "Marcel Proust" (*Simon & Schuster* 1971 $12.95).

BAUDELAIRE AND THE SYMBOLISTS. 1929 1954. *Bks. for Libraries* repr. of 1954 ed. $9.75; *Kennikat* repr. of 1929 ed. 1970 $8.50

BYRON: The Years of Fame. 1936. *Shoe String* 1967 $7.00

BYRON IN ITALY. 1941. *Bks. for Libraries* 1973 $14.00

FOUR PORTRAITS: Studies of the Eighteenth Century. (Original title: "The Profane Virtues: Four Studies of the Eighteenth Century") 1945. *Shoe String* 1965 $6.00. Studies of Boswell, Gibbon, Sterne, Wilkes.

JOHN RUSKIN: The Portrait of a Prophet. 1949. *Richard West* 1973 $17.50

SINGULAR PREFERENCE: Portraits and Essays. 1953. *Kennikat* 1971 $9.25

RUSKIN. Writers and Their Works Ser. *British Bk. Centre* $2.38 pap. $1.20

ALEXANDER POPE: The Education of a Genius, 1688–1728. *Stein & Day* 1968 $7.95 pap. $2.95

ROMANTIC ENGLAND. *Macmillan* 1970 $11.95

CASANOVA IN LONDON. *Stein & Day* 1971 $7.95

SAMUEL JOHNSON: His Friends and Enemies. *McGraw-Hill* 1973 $12.95

THE SIGN OF THE FISH. Autobiography. *Viking* 1960 $4.50

THARP, LOUISE HALL. 1898–

Louise Hall Tharp has focused her biographical attentions on New England writers, artists and patrons of the arts in the 19th century. Two additional books in this vein, both now o.p., are "Until Victory: Horace Mann and Mary Peabody" (1953) and "The Baroness and the General" (1962), about the lives and loves of Fredericke von Massow and the Revolutionary War mercenary officer Baron von Riedesel. She has also written biographies for children on such figures as Samuel Champlain and Louis Agassiz. Her work is usually anecdotal, romantic and reliable. Several interesting "literary" biographies are currently o.p.: "Three Saints and a Sinner: Julia Ward Howe, Louisa, Annie and Sam Ward (1959) (Mrs. Howe is author of "The Battle Hymn of the Republic"; "Mrs. Jack: A Biography of Isabella Stewart Gardner" (1965); "Adventurous Alliance: The Story of the Agassiz Family of Boston" (1959) and "Saint-Gaudens and the Gilded Era" (1969).

THE PEABODY SISTERS OF SALEM. *Little* 1950 $6.95; *Pyramid Bks.* pap. $.95. Two sisters in the gifted family married to Nathaniel Hawthorne and Horace Mann.

THE APPLETONS OF BEACON HILL. *Little* 1973 $8.50

WEINTRAUB, STANLEY. 1929–

Stanley Weintraub is a biographer, critic and professor who has edited *The Shaw Review* (*Pennsylvania State Univ. Press*) since 1956. Many of his two dozen books concern Shaw or his contemporaries, and the books he has edited contain large segments of biographical material. His anthologies of the Beardsley-identified "Yellow Book" (1964, o.p.) and "The Savoy" (*Pennsylvania State Univ. Press* 1966 $7.50) have biographical prefaces, as do his "The Literary Criticism of Oscar Wilde" (*Univ. of Nebraska Press* 1968 $5.95), "The Nondramatic Literary Criticism of Bernard Shaw" (*Univ. of Nebraska Press* 1972 $7.95) and his edition of Robert Hichens's scandalous novel of 1894, "The Green Carnation" (*Univ. of Nebraska Press* 1970 pap. $1.95). His biographies emphasize the interaction of both the political and artistic worlds with the English literary world, and range the century which ended with World War II (approximately the life-span of Bernard Shaw). Of his "Private Shaw and Public Shaw" Harry T. Moore (in *SR*) says: "The 'public' Shaw was Bernard, the aging playwright; while 'Private' Shaw was precisely and technically that for a number of years, although he had once been a colonel. . . . These two Shaws met by the thinnest chance early in 1922, when Bernard Shaw at sixty-six, considered himself perhaps finished as a dramatist . . . and when Lawrence-Shaw at thirty-four, had just completed the second version of his war experiences, the subsequently famous 'Seven Pillars of Wisdom.' These contrasting eccentrics magnetized each other; and now Stanley Weintraub has written an animated story of their friendship, which only ended with the violent death of Lawrence in 1935." In the two-volume "autobiography" of Shaw only the introduction is Weintraub. "All the rest is Shaw—Shaw on Shaw, Shaw on everything he saw, smelled, tasted, touched, experienced. . . . In plain words, Weintraub has created an 'autobiography' of George Bernard Shaw by means of assembling his writings (non-dramatic) over this creative span of his life—and the results are scintillating"—(*PW*). "Journey to Heartbreak" portrays Shaw "an an 'embattled intellectual in wartime,' through his effect upon his times and their impact upon him as a creative person. . . . There is so much in this book that shows the courage and magnitude of G. B. S. during the most extraordinary period of his long life . . ."—(Hector Bolitho, in the *Evening Star*, Washington, D.C.).

Although there is a picture of Reginald Turner as an old man in D.H. Lawrence's "Aaron's Rod" (*Viking Compass Bks.* pap. $1.50), and his name appears frequently in memoirs and reminiscences, "Stanley Weintraub's 'Reggie' is the first full-length study of him. . . . It was very well worth doing and Mr. Weintraub has done it well. . . . Mr. Weintraub maintains an attitude of affectionate impartiality toward this curious man. Without being lachrymose, he shows the pathos of his life, and rescues from oblivion a minor figure by no means without significance in the context of his times"—(Malcolm Muggeridge, in *Esquire*). "The Last Great Cause" is "a fine blending of personal sympathy, even nostalgia, with detached observation. Much has been written about Spain in retrospect, but nothing I know of that so successfully combines the struggle itself with those who defined its hopes and lived to lament its failure"—(David Dempsey, in the *N.Y. Times Book Review*). Mr. Weintraub's most recent biography is his study of Whistler. "New material, superb scholarship, human and artistic insights, will probably establish Weintraub's elegant biography . . . as definitive"—(*PW*). His study of Aubrey Beardsley in "Beardsley: A Biography" (1967, o.p.) is also excellent. "As a biography—a life's story, that is to say—Mr. Weintraub's book needs no successor"—(John Russell, in the *N.Y. Times Book Review*).

His one venture into autobiography is "The War in the Wards" (1964, o.p.), the chronicle of a prisoner of war hospital mutiny in the Korean War in 1952. War correspondent Robert S. Elegant wrote of the book in the *Los Angeles Times*, "Although he modestly calls it a mere footnote to history, the story of an incident that did not attain even the transient dignity of becoming 'news,' Weintraub's book is of greater importance." Weintraub is Director of the Institute for the Arts and Humanistic Studies at The Pennsylvania State University.

PRIVATE SHAW AND PUBLIC SHAW: A Dual Portrait of Lawrence of Arabia and G. B. S. *Braziller* 1963 $5.00

REGGIE: A Portrait of Reginald Turner. *Braziller* 1965 $6.00

BIOGRAPHY AND TRUTH. *(See General Works on Literary Biography, above).*

THE LAST GREAT CAUSE: The Intellectuals and the Spanish Civil War. *McKay* (Weybright & Talley) 1968 $8.50

SHAW: An Autobiography. *McKay* (Weybright & Talley) 2 vols. Vol. I Shaw: An Autobiography, 1856–1898 (1969) Vol. 2 Shaw: The Playwright Years, 1898–1950 (1970) each $10.00

JOURNEY TO HEARTBREAK: The Crucible Years of Bernard Shaw. 1914–1918. *McKay* (Weybright & Talley) 1971 $8.95

WHISTLER: A Biography. *McKay* (Weybright & Talley) 1974 $12.50

—S.W.

Author Index

For reasons of space, the names of authors and editors are listed by their last names and initials only or, in some cases, with the initials by which they are best known (thus Leigh Hunt is given as Hunt, L., and not as Hunt, J. H. L.). When the last names and initials of two or more authors are the same, the first names are given in full in the alphabetical sequence in which they would fall if initials only were used. Page numbers for an author's main entry are given in boldface. Translators, illustrators, and writers of forewords are not indexed, and neither are the names of persons quoted in the critical annotations.

Title and Subject Index

Book titles are listed here, and also titles of smaller works such as individual poems, essays, and plays mentioned in the annotations. In general, subtitles are omitted, as well as broad generic titles, as "Complete Works," "Selected Letters," and the like. Wherever identical titles by two or more different authors appear—either because they are in fact identical or seem to be because of the deletion of a subtitle—the last name of the author is given in parentheses following the title. Where the title of a work includes the name of a main-entry author and concerns only that author (for example "Coleridge" by Walter Jackson Bate), it is not listed here. Such a book should be sought at the end of the author's main-entry listing, given in bold face in the author index. Whenever such titles are found here, the reference is to a page that is not part of the author's main entry. Subject headings are shown in italic capital letters, and cover broad subject matter only.